PAPERS IN SPEECH COMMUNICATION:
SPEECH PERCEPTION

PAPERS IN SPEECH COMMUNICATION: SPEECH PERCEPTION

Joanne L. Miller, Raymond D. Kent, Bishnu S. Atal (Eds.)

This volume is part of a three-volume series
published by the Acoustical Society of America
through the American Institute of Physics

Joanne L. Miller, Editor-in-Chief

Papers in Speech Communication: Speech Production
R. D. Kent, B. S. Atal, J. L. Miller, Eds.

Papers in Speech Communication: Speech Perception
J. L. Miller, R. D. Kent, B. S. Atal, Eds.

Papers in Speech Communication: Speech Processing
B. S. Atal, J. L. Miller, R. D. Kent, Eds.

Published by the
Acoustical Society of America
500 Sunnyside Boulevard
Woodbury, New York 11797-2999

Library of Congress Cataloging-in-Publication Data

Papers in speech communication. Speech perception / Joanne L. Miller, Raymond D. Kent,
    Bishnu S. Atal (eds.).
        p.   cm.
    Sponsored by the Acoustical Society of America.
    Includes bibliographical references and index.
    ISBN 0-88318-959-3
    1. Speech perception—Congresses.   I. Miller, Joanne L.   II. Kent, Raymond D.
III. Atal, Bishnu S. IV. Acoustical Society of America.   V. American Institute of Physics.
VI. Title: Speech perception.
    BF463.S64P36   1991
    401'.9–dc20   91-28290
                                                                                                              CIP

This book is part of a three-volume series entitled *Papers in Speech Communication*; the three volumes are *Speech Production, Speech Perception*, and *Speech Processing.*

Papers in Speech Communication: Speech Perception

TABLE OF CONTENTS

THEORETICAL PERSPECTIVES

PERCEPTION OF CONSONANTAL DISTINCTIONS

PERCEPTION OF VOCALIC DISTINCTIONS

PROSODY AND SPEECH INTELLIGIBILITY

DEVELOPMENTAL ISSUES

PREFACE

Over the past few decades there has been great progress in understanding the nature of human speech production and perception, and in applying this knowledge to problems of speech processing (coding, recognition, and synthesis). Given the interdisciplinary nature of the enterprise, important papers in these areas have appeared in a wide range of journals, proceedings, and books from such diverse fields as engineering, linguistics, physics, psychology, and speech and hearing science. The current volume forms part of a three-volume series whose purpose is to bring together a number of these important papers. The series is sponsored by the Acoustical Society of America and, following the classification system of the Society's journal, one volume focuses on speech production, one on speech perception, and one on speech processing.

The idea of the three-volume series originated within the Speech Technical Committee of the Society. The Committee discussed and enthusiastically endorsed the project at the Society's fall 1989 meeting in St. Louis, Missouri, and subsequently chose the editors and editorial boards. A formal proposal for the project was then drafted by the Chair of the Speech Technical Committee and was forwarded to the Executive Council of the Society. The Council gave final approval for the project at the Society's spring 1990 meeting in State College, Pennsylvania.

We have organized each of the three volumes into topical sections, with the papers within each section ordered alphabetically by author. To help guide readers—especially students and nonexperts—we have written editorial commentary for each section. The commentary is intended to provide a brief context for the individual papers, placing them within the history of the discipline. We have also included a topical subject index at the end of each volume, keyed to individual papers. Finally, because the three volumes are so closely interrelated, at the end of each volume we have included the table of contents and the index of each of the other two volumes.

We have worked closely with our editorial boards in selecting the papers that appear in these volumes. The members of the boards were involved in all stages of the selection process, from the initial generation of a list of potential papers to the final decisions on selection. In making the selections, we were guided by the goal of including papers that are important in their own right and, in addition, collectively reflect progress in the field and present a range of viewpoints, approaches, and methodologies. Given the vast literature on speech, and practical constraints on the size of the volumes, the choices were difficult, and many important papers are not included. We can only hope that the volumes, as constituted, will prove useful to the speech community as research on speech communication proceeds.

Joanne L. Miller
Raymond D. Kent
Bishnu S. Atal

DEDICATION

This three-volume series is dedicated to the memory of Dennis Klatt in recognition of the breadth and quality of his research on speech communication.

Dennis Klatt's undergraduate and early graduate studies were in electrical engineering at Purdue University. In 1964 he completed his doctorate with Gordon Peterson in the communication sciences program at the University of Michigan, with a thesis entitled *Theories of Aural Physiology*. He spent most of his professional career at the Massachusetts Institute of Technology (MIT), in the Department of Electrical Engineering and Computer Science, and in the Research Laboratory of Electronics. His activities at MIT and his role as consultant to industry consisted of a balanced combination of fundamental research into the mechanisms of human speech production and perception and applied research leading to practical devices.

Klatt's fundamental contributions to an understanding of speech processes covered a broad range of topics. His detailed experimental studies of speech timing in English led to several important papers on how speakers control the durations of the sounds, words, and phrases that make up sentences. He had a continuing interest in the problem of how speech is processed in the auditory system and central nervous system of human listeners. His speech perception research ranged from detailed experimental studies on how listeners extract information from the rapidly changing events in speech to models of how lexical information is stored and accessed by listeners. The models he suggested for auditory processing and for lexical access were the basis for proposals he made for the design of automatic speech recognition systems. His research on "distance metrics" is a foundation for perceptually based criteria to evaluate the degree of closeness of two different utterances. In his publications, Klatt argued convincingly that the development of appropriate distance metrics is a central problem in determining whether two utterances represent two tokens of the same word or represent two different words. His contributions to the advancement of automatic speech recognition included serving on the advisory committee of a national effort in this area in the 1970s.

Klatt also developed a flexible computer-based synthesizer that can be used to generate sounds in basic studies of human speech perception. The software for this synthesizer has been available to research laboratories, making possible new quantitative research on the processes of auditory and speech perception. With this synthesizer as a base, Klatt developed a complete system for synthesis of speech from English orthography. In one of his last research efforts, he and his daughter Laura examined in a detailed way the characteristics of the glottal source, particularly for female talkers, in an effort to improve further the naturalness of synthesized speech.

Adapted from the encomium for the 1987 Acoustical Society of America Silver Medal in Speech Communication.

ACKNOWLEDGMENTS

We give our sincere thanks to the many people who helped us in creating this three-volume series. We are especially grateful for the cooperation of the authors and publishers of the papers that are reprinted in the volumes, and for the expertise provided by the editorial board members. We are deeply indebted to Elaine Moran, of the Acoustical Society of America—her unwavering enthusiasm for the project and her resourcefulness in guiding the volumes through the production process were major factors in bringing the series to fruition.

Joanne L. Miller
Raymond D. Kent
Bishnu S. Atal

The following organizations and publishers kindly granted permission to reprint their material in this volume:

Ablex Publishing Corporation

Academia, Publishing House of the Czechoslovak Academy of Sciences

Academic Press

Academic Press, Inc. (London) Ltd.

American Association for the Advancement of Science

American Psychological Association

Elsevier Science Publishers, B.V.

Kingston Press Service, Ltd.

Macmillan Magazines, Ltd.

The Psychonomic Society

THEORETICAL PERSPECTIVES

Paper 1. P. D. Eimas and J. D. Corbit (1973), Selective adaptation of linguistic feature detectors. *Cognitive Psychology* 4, 99–109.

Paper 2. C. A. Fowler (1986), An event approach to the study of speech perception from a direct-realist perspective. *Journal of Phonetics* 14, 3–28.

Paper 3. D. H. Klatt (1979), Speech perception: A model of acoustic-phonetic analysis and lexical access. *Journal of Phonetics* 7, 279–312.

Paper 4. A. M. Liberman, F. S. Cooper, D. P. Shankweiler, and M. Studdert-Kennedy (1967), Perception of the speech code. *Psychological Review* 74, 431–461.

Paper 5. A. M. Liberman and I. G. Mattingly (1985), The motor theory of speech perception revised. *Cognition* 21, 1–36.

Paper 6. B. Lindblom (1986), Phonetic universals in vowel systems. In J. J. Ohala and J. J. Jaeger (Eds.), *Experimental Phonology*, pp. 13–44. New York: Academic Press.

Paper 7. J. L. McClelland and J. L. Elman (1986), The TRACE model of speech perception. *Cognitive Psychology* 18, 1–86.

Paper 8. G. C. Oden and D. W. Massaro (1978), Integration of featural information in speech perception. *Psychological Review* 85, 172–191.

Paper 9. K. N. Stevens and S. E. Blumstein (1978), Invariant cues for place of articulation in stop consonants. *Journal of the Acoustical Society of America* 64, 1358–1368.

Paper 10. M. Studdert-Kennedy and D. Shankweiler (1970), Hemispheric specialization for speech perception. *Journal of the Acoustical Society of America* 48, 579–594.

The field of speech perception has a rich history of diverse theoretical approaches to a number of fundamental issues in speech research. These include questions about the mapping between the acoustic signal of speech and the phonetic structure of language, the mechanisms underlying the listener's ability to recover phonetic structure from the signal, the neurobiological underpinnings of speech perception processes, and the nature of the interface between the consequences of speech perception and lexical access. This section of the volume contains theoretical papers reflecting major viewpoints regarding these issues. These viewpoints have provided much of the impetus for the vast number of experimental investigations of speech perception over the past four decades, investigations that are represented in the remaining sections of the volume.

A fundamental issue that has driven much of the research on speech perception is the type of mechanism that analyzes the speech signal and yields the phonetic structure of the utterance. (The precise form of this structure, for example, whether its units are phonetic features, phonetic segments, or syllables, is itself controversial.) One highly influential approach to the issue of perceptual mechanism is the motor theory of speech perception. An early version of motor theory is found in Liberman, Cooper, Shankweiler, and Studdert-Kennedy (1967) and a more recent version is found in Liberman and Mattingly (1985). A core tenet of the theory is that it is only through reference to articulation that the listener can recover phonetic structure despite the context-conditioned variability in the speech signal. On this view, the listener uses tacit knowledge of the acoustic consequences of articulatory gestures to recover the intended articulatory act and, hence, the underlying phonetic representation. In the latter paper, this representation takes the form of abstract phonetic gestures.

An alternative position, proffered by Stevens and Blumstein (1978), is that there is no need to postulate a specialized, articulatorily-based speech processing system for recovering phonetic information because context-conditioned variation only exists at certain levels of analysis. According to this view, if phonetically relevant acoustic properties are characterized appropriately, invariance in the mapping between acoustic and phonetic levels of language (in particular, between acoustic signal and phonetic features) can be found. Fowler (1986), working within an event approach to perception wherein perception is assumed to be a direct reflection of objects and events in the world, also proposes that all the necessary information required for speech perception resides in the acoustic signal, obviating the need for a specialized speech processor. However, her view also shares features with motor theory, in particular, the claim that the objects of perception are articulatorily-based structures. In their information-theoretic view, Oden and Massaro (1978) focus explicitly on how multiple sources of relevant acoustic information combine to yield a phonetic percept, specifically, on how disparate information for individual linguistic features combines to yield segmental (or syllabic) representations. They treat the problem of context-dependency by building it into the stored linguistic representations themselves.

The papers by Eimas and Corbit (1973) and Studdert-Kennedy and Shankweiler (1970) represent attempts to discover the nature of the neurobiological underpinnings of speech perception. Eimas and Corbit (1973), borrowing from paradigms in vision research on channels of analysis, propose the existence of feature detectors tuned to linguistically relevant acoustic information, and offer some initial evidence in support of this view—a view that has since come to be quite controversial. In a different vein, Studdert-Kennedy and Shankweiler (1970) argue that whatever their precise form, the mechanisms underlying phonetic perception are localized in the dominant (usually left) cerebral hemisphere: Just as lateralized, dedicated neural mechanisms underlie the processing of higher levels of language (e.g., syntax), so too do such mechanisms underlie the listener's ability to derive the phonetic structure of the utterance from the acoustic signal.

A complete theory of speech perception must offer not only an explanation of how the listener maps acoustic information onto phonetic structure, but also an explanation of the relation between speech perception and lexical access. Although most of the research on speech perception over the years has not addressed issues of lexical access *per se* (and lexical access research has virtually ignored the tough problems of speech perception), there have been attempts to tie the two domains together. McClelland and Elman (1986) and Klatt (1979) both confront the problem head-on, although they do so in quite different ways. One distinction concerns the architecture of the models they propose. McClelland and Elman's TRACE model involves a highly interactive network with connections both between and within levels, whereas Klatt's LAFS model is noninteractive, with lexical access based directly on acoustic information. Another distinction concerns a long-standing debate in the literature on whether a sublexical level of phonetic representation, whatever the unit (e.g., feature or segment), is involved in lexical access: TRACE includes such a level, whereas LAFS does not.

Finally, Lindblom (1986) considers the way in which properties of speech perception may contribute to the evolution of language itself. Focusing on vowel perception, he develops a model in which universal aspects of auditory processing (such as filtering and masking) and constraints provided by perceptual contrast play a central role in predicting the distributional characteristics of vowel systems across languages.

Reprinted from Cognitive Psychology, Volume 4, Number 1, January 1973
Copyright © 1973 by Academic Press, Inc. *Printed in U. S. A.*

cognitive psychology **4**, 99–109 (1973)

Selective Adaptation of Linguistic Feature Detectors[1]

Peter D. Eimas[2] and John D. Corbit

Brown University

Using a selective adaptation procedure, evidence was obtained for the existence of linguistic feature detectors, analogous to visual feature detectors. These detectors are each sensitive to a restricted range of voice onset times, the physical continuum underlying the perceived phonetic distinctions between voiced and voiceless stop consonants. The sensitivity of a particular detector can be reduced selectively by repetitive presentation of its adequate stimulus. This results in a shift in the locus of the phonetic boundary separating the voiced and voiceless stops.

Coverging evidence from electrophysiological studies of single neurons in animals (e.g., Lettvin *et al.*, 1959; Hubel & Wiesel, 1962) and from psychopyhsical studies of human perception (Blackmore & Campbell, 1969; Blackmore & Sutton, 1969) indicates that there are detector mechanisms in the brain that are uniquely sensitive to particular and relatively restricted patterns of stimulation. In this study of speech perception, we attempted to demonstrate the existence of feature detectors for linguistic information by use of a selective adaptation procedure. The acoustic dimension that was investigated was voice onset time (VOT), variations in which are sufficient for the perceived distinctions between the voiced and voiceless stop consonants of English in initial position[3] (Lisker & Abramson, 1970).

Voice onset time is defined as the time between the release burst and laryngeal pulsing (Lisker & Abramson, 1964). Very short lags in the onset of voicing are perceived in English as voiced stops, [b, d, g], whereas

---

[1] We thank Dr. F. S. Cooper for generously making available the facilities at the Haskins Laboratories and Drs. R. M. Church, D. J. Getty, and A. M. Liberman for their critical comments. We also thank Mrs. Catherine G. Wolf for her assistance in conducting these experiments. Supported by PHS Grants HD 05331 and MH 16608.

[2] Department of Psychology, Brown University, Providence, Rhode Island 02912.

[3] It should be noted that the cues underlying the voicing distinctions discussed in the present paper apply to sound segments in absolute initial position. Although, as Lisker and Abramson (1964) noted, voice onset time does effectively separate stop categories in sentences, there is some effect of embedding the various stops in continuous speech. As a consequence we have limited our research to voicing distinctions in initial positions, where voice onset time is relatively insensitive to contextual effects (Lisker & Abramson, 1967).

99

100   EIMAS AND CORBIT

relatively long lags in the onset of voicing are perceived in English as voiceless stops, [p, t, k]. It is possible to produce synthetic speech with variations in VOT. Figure 1 shows two spectrograms of synthetic speech which illustrate two values along the VOT continuum. The sound pattern shown in the upper spectrogram has a short (10 msec) lag in VOT and is perceived in its acoustic form as a voiced stop, in this instance as [b] plus the vowel [a]. The lower spectrogram depicts a sound with a longer (100 msec) lag in voicing, which is perceived as a voiceless stop, [p] in this case, plus the vowel [a].

The perception of series of synthetic speech varying continuously in

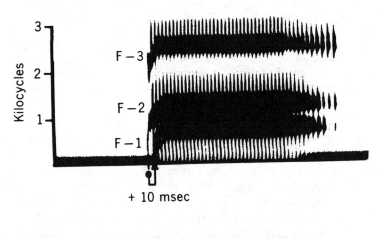

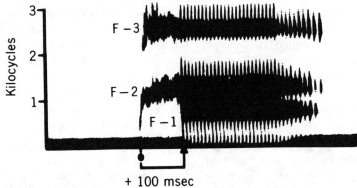

FIG. 1. Spectrograms of synthetic speech showing two values of voice onset time: a slight voicing lag represented by [ba] in the upper figure and a long voicing lag in the lower figure, represented by [pa]. The symbols F-1, F-2, and F-3 represent the first three formants, that is, the relatively intense bands of energy in the speech signal. (Courtesy of L. Lisker & A. S. Abramson.)

VOT alone has been found to be very nearly categorical for English listeners (Abramson & Lisker, 1970; Wolf, 1972). That is, for these series of stimuli the percept exists only in one of two stages: the voiced or voiceless stop. As a consequence, listeners are able to assign stimuli to phonetic categories with great consistency. Moreover, their ability to detect differences between stimuli is limited by their ability to assign differential labels to the stimuli. The latter is evidenced by marked peaks in the discriminability functions at the region of the phonetic boundary; that is, the discrimination of a given difference in VOT is considerably better when two stimuli lie in different phonetic categories than when the two stimuli are from the same phonetic category.

Of particular interest is the fact that the categorical nature of the perception of the VOT continuum appears to be universal. That is, it is characteristic not only of adult speakers of English but also of adult speakers of other languages, e.g., Thai, and more importantly it is present in preverbal human infants as young as 1 month of age (Eimas *et al.*, 1971). The apparent universality of this phenomenon suggests that it is a manifestation of the basic structure of the human brain.

Another line of evidence consistent with this idea comes from the cross-language research of Lisker and Abramson (1964). They found that the manner in which speakers of 11 diverse languages divided the VOT continuum was notably consistent. The phonetic tokens produced by these speakers, although not the same for all languages, nevertheless tended to fall at three modal values of VOT. Two of these values are used for the English voiced and voiceless stops. English does not use the third distinction, long voicing lead, found in Thai, for example.[4] It would seem reasonable that this uniformity in producing voicing distinctions is matched by specialized perceptual structures. These structures might well take the form of detectors that are differentially tuned to the acoustic consequences of the modes of production (see Lieberman, 1970, for an extended discussion of the relation between the processes of speech production and speech perception).

EXPERIMENT 1

Our experimental plan to obtain evidence for these linguistic feature detectors was based on a selective adaptation procedure. We reasoned that if there are linguistic feature detectors mediating the perception of the voiced and voiceless stops, then repeated presentation of the feature (i.e., appropriate VOT value) to which a given detector is sensitive

---

[4] Inasmuch as this distinction, long voicing lead, does not exist in English and in fact may not be detectable by adult English speakers, we have restricted our research to the two voicing distinctions found in English.

should fatigue the detector and reduce its sensitivity. As a consequence, the manner in which stimuli are assigned to phonetic categories would be altered, especially for those stimuli near the phonetic boundary where both detectors may be somewhat sensitive to the same VOT values. In order to test this idea, we first obtained identification functions for two series of stop consonants, the bilabial stops [b, p] and the apical stops [d, t], when listeners were in the normal unadapted state. Next, identification functions were obtained for the same series of stimuli after adaptation by repeated presentations of good exemplars of both modes of voicing.

Method

Stimuli. The stimuli were two series of 14 synthetic speech stimuli prepared by means of a computer-controlled parallel resonance synthesizer by Lisker and Abramson (1970). For greater detail concerning the construction of synthetic speech by a computer-controlled synthesizer the reader is referred to Mattingly (1968). To produce variations in VOT in the context of the English stop consonants, the onset of the first formant relative to the onset of the second and third formants is varied and the second and third formants are excited by a noise source rather than a periodic source when the first formant is absent (see Fig. 1. for two examples of VOT). In the [b, p] series the VOT values ranged from −10 msec (short voicing lead) to +60 msec (relatively long voicing lag) in 5-msec steps except for the final two stimuli which were separated by 10 msec. The [d, t] series had VOT values ranging from 0 msec (voicing and first formant onset coincident with the onset of the second and third formants) to +80 msec. The difference between stimuli was 5 msec except for the final four stimuli in which the difference was 10 msec. The acoustic differences between the two series were in the starting frequency and direction of the second- and third-formant transitions, these differences being sufficient cues for the perceived phonetic differences, that is, for the perceived differences between [b] and [d] and between [p] and [t] (Liberman *et al.*, 1967).

Procedure. To obtain the initial identification functions when the listeners were in an unadapted state, the 14 stimuli from each series were presented binaurally by means of a tape recorder at a comfortable listening level. For both series, which were presented separately, the order of presentation was randomized, and 50 identification responses were obtained for each stimulus. The interval between stimuli was always 3 sec. Next, identification functions were obtained after selective adaptation. For example, if the detector assumed to underlie perception of the voiced stops were to be adapted, listeners were exposed to repetitive presentations of a [b] with a VOT value of −10 msec or to a [d] with a VOT value of 0 msec for 2 min at the beginning of each session, and then for 1 min before each stimulus was to be identified. When adapting the detector for the voiceless stops, either a [p] with a VOT value of +60 msec or a [t] with a VOT value of +80 msec was repeatedly presented before each identification response. There were eight adaptation conditions in all: each of the two series was identified after adaptation with [b], [d], [p], and [t]. In any single adaptation session, listeners heard 2 min (150 presentations) of the adapting sound pattern, with each presentation being 500 msec in duration and separated by 300 msec of silence. Next 70 adaptation trials were administered in which each individual adaptation trial consisted of 1 min of the adapting stimulus (75 presentations), followed by 500 msec of silence and then a single stimulus to be identified. Five seconds elapsed before the next trial occurred, and short breaks were given every 14 trials. For any session, the adapting stimulus and series to be identified were randomly determined as was the order in which the individual stimuli were presented for identification. There was a total of 16 adaptation sessions, with at least 24 hr between sessions, yielding 10 identification responses to each stimulus of both series under each of the four adaptation conditions.

Subjects. The subjects were two undergraduate students and one graduate student at Brown University who were paid for their participation. Two of the subjects had previous experience in listening to synthetic speech.

Results and Discussion

In Fig. 2, the identification functions for a single subject are shown. In each instance, adaptation caused a notable shift in the phonetic boundary and moreover, the direction of the shifts in the locus of the phonetic boundary were uniformly consistent; the boundary moved closer to the adapting stimulus indicating a greater number of identification responses representing the unadapted mode of voicing had occurred. After adaptation with a voiced stop, the listener gave more identification responses belonging to the voiceless category, especially when attempting to identify stimuli near the original phonetic boundary. Conversely, after adaptation with a voiceless stop, a greater number of identification responses belonged to the voiced category. Again the effect was most pronounced for stimuli near the phonetic boundary.

Of particular interest was the finding that the shifts in the locus of the phonetic boundary occurred when the adapting stimulus and identification stimuli were from different series. For example, adaptation with a

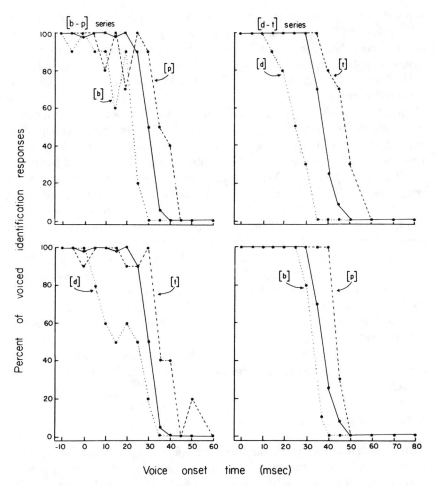

Fig. 2. Percentages of voiced identification responses ([b or d]) obtained with and without adaptation for a single subject. The functions for the [b, p] series are on the left and those for the [d, t] series are on the right. The solid lines indicate the unadapted identification functions and the dotted and dashed lines, the identification functions after adaptation. The phonetic symbols indicate the adapting stimulus.

bilabial stop produced an approximately equivalent effect on the identification of both bilabial and apical stops. These cross-series effects rule out explanations based on adaptation of the sound pattern as a phonetic unit. If this were the case, it is difficult to understand, for example, how alterations in the system underlying perception of [b] would likewise affect perception of the apical stops. In addition, given the acoustic differences between the two series with respect to the second- and third-formant transitions, and the cross-series adaptation effects, it is unlikely that what was, in fact, selectively adapted were detectors for simple acoustic information. Rather the evidence indicates that detectors for those complex aspects of the sound pattern that both series had in common, namely, voice onset time, were selectively adapted.

The identification functions for the remaining two subjects were very similar to those shown in Fig. 2. In all, there were 24 instances of attempted adaptation, eight adapting conditions for each of three subjects. In each instance there was a shift in the phonetic boundary, and furthermore the direction of the shift was always toward the voicing distinction that had been adapted, i.e., more identification responses belonged to the unadapted mode of voicing. The individual data are shown in Table 1. The mean shift in the locus of the phonetic boundary was 8.0 msec. It should be noted that the effects of adaptation were not symmetrical: the mean shift was 6.1 msec after adaptation with voiced stops and 10.0 msec after adaptation with voiceless stops. In addition for all listeners the mean magnitude of the boundary shift was only slightly (less than 2 msec) contingent upon the adapting stimulus and the identification series belonging to the same class of stop consonants (i.e., bilabial or apical).

Although we have not systematically investigated the time-course of recovery from adaptation, some preliminary investigations indicated that recovery is no more than 50% complete at the end of 90 sec and that complete recovery will require 30 min or more.

TABLE 1

Shift in the Locus of the Phonetic Boundary in Milliseconds of VOT for the Identification Experiment

Identification series	Subjects	Adapting stimulus			
		[b]	[p]	[d]	[t]
[b, p]	1 (29.0)[a]	+6.3	−13.8	+ .5	−15.0
	2 (28.8)	+7.5	− 6.8	+ 2.8	−16.3
	3 (30.0)	+7.5	− 7.5	+10.0	− 7.5
	$\bar{X}$ (29.3)	+7.1	− 9.4	+ 4.4	−12.9
[d, t]	1 (42.5)	+3.8	− 8.0	+ 3.5	−10.0
	2 (37.5)	+5.3	− 4.8	+ 8.0	−14.5
	3 (37.5)	+5.5	− 6.0	+12.0	−10.0
	$\bar{X}$ (39.2)	+4.9	− 6.3	+ 7.8	−11.5

[a] The number in parentheses shows the locus of the unadapted phonetic boundary.

EXPERIMENT 2

Given the categorical nature of the perception of the stop consonants as most markedly evidenced by a peak in the discriminability function of adjacent stimuli at the region of the phonetic boundary, we reasoned that the peak would shift after selective adaptation of one of the voicing detectors. That is, inasmuch as the ability to discriminate these stimuli has been found to be closely related to the ability to apply differential phonetic labels, then any shift in the locus of the phonetic boundary should be paralleled by a corresponding shift in the peak of the discriminability functions. To verify this we obtained discriminability functions for the [b, p] series before and after adaptation with the voiceless stop [p].

Method

Stimuli. The stimuli to be discriminated were 11 synthetic speech patterns taken from the [b, p] series of Experiment 1. The VOT values ranged from 0 to +50 msec in 5-msec steps. The adapting stimulus had a VOT value of +60 msec and was perceived uniformly as [p] plus the vowel [a].

Procedure. The psychophysical method of ABX was used to measure discriminability. For any set of three stimuli, the first stimulus A differed from the second stimulus B, and the third stimulus X was identical to the first stimulus or to the second stimulus. The listeners' task was to indicate whether the third stimulus was the same as the first or the second stimulus. Sets of stimuli to be discriminated were arranged by pairing each stimulus with the stimulus two steps (10 msec) removed. That is, the discriminability of VOT values 0 and +10, +5, and +15, and so forth was measured. There are nine such pairs in all and four permutations for each pair (ABA, ABB, BAB, and BAA) for a total 36 possible triads.

To obtain the discriminability function without adaptation the 36 triads were presented to the listeners in random order. The stimuli within each triad were separated by 1.5 sec and each triad was separated by 5 sec. A total of 24 measures were obtained for each stimulus pair.

The procedure used to obtain the discriminablity function when the listeners were adapted was the same as that used during the identification study, except that in place of a single stimulus to be identified a randomly selected ABX triad was presented for discrimination. Twenty-four measures were obtained from each listener for each pair of stimuli.

Subjects. Two of the subjects had served as listeners in the first experiment and together with the third subject had had extensive experience in listening to synthetic speech.

Results

Figure 3 depicts the mean discriminability function for the three subjects. We have used an average function in this instance since the
individual functions were more variable than were the individual identification functions. This variability was most likely a function of the
greater difficulty of the discrimination task. However, the effects evident
in the group function also appear in each of the individual functions.
Exposure to the voiceless stop [p] radically altered the discrimination
function. There was a shift in the peak of the discrimination function
that corresponded to the shift in the locus of the phonetic boundary,
demonstrating in a novel manner that discrimination of the stop consonants is closely related to the ability to differentially identify the
stimuli. The magnitude of the shift was 5 msec for two listeners and 10
msec for the third listener. The discriminability function clearly shows
that after adaptation, when the likelihood is increased that the stimuli

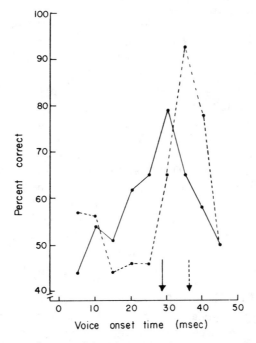

Fig. 3. The group discriminability function. The points are plotted midway between the two values of voice onset time being discriminated. The dashed line
represents the discriminability function after adaptation with [p]. The arrows indicate
the locus of the phonetic boundaries found from identification functions with (dashed
arrow) and without (solid arrow) adaptation with [p].

being discriminated belong to the same phonetic class, discriminability is at or very near chance. Conversely, for those stimuli which after adaptation have a greater probability of being assigned to different phonetic categories, there is a marked increase in the level of discrimination.

GENERAL DISCUSSION

The fact that repeated presentation of a member of one of the voicing categories dramatically reduces the sensitivity of the system to members of that category may be explained by assuming two linguistic feature detectors, each of which is tuned to a restricted range of VOT values and mediates the perception of one of the two voicing distinctions found in the stop consonants.

To explain how these detectors might operate to produce the identification and discrimination functions that are obtained with and without experimentally induced adaptation, the following assumptions are needed: (a) There exist detectors that are differentially sensitive to a range of VOT values with greatest sensitivity (as might be measured, in principle, by the output signal of the detector) occurring at the modal production value for a particular voicing distinction (Lisker & Abramson, 1964). (b) Some VOT values excite both detectors, but, all other things being equal, only the output signal with the greater strength reaches higher centers of processing and integration. (c) The phonetic boundary will lie at the VOT value that excites both detectors equally, all other factors being equal. (d) After adaptation, the sensitivity of a detector is lessened; that is, the output signal is weakened or decreased. Furthermore, for purposes of simplicity, the signal strength is assumed to decrease equally for the entire range of VOT values to which the detector is sensitive. From this it follows that selective adaptation shifts the phonetic boundary by shifting the point of equilibrium along the VOT continuum. If we further assume (e) that no distinction is made by higher-order processing elements between two output signals from the same detector, that is, no distinction is made when the same detector is excited by two different values of VOT, then the peaked discriminability functions are readily accounted for.

The existence of linguistic feature detectors for the voicing distinctions among the stop consonants has a number of important implications. First, it provides a mechanism whereby infants can perceive the VOT continuum in a nearly categorical manner. Second, it adds credence to theoretical descriptions of the basic sound units of language based on distinctive features (Halle, 1962; Jakobson, Fant, & Halle, 1963). And finally it provides an example of a complex analysis of linguistic information in a manner at least analogus to that previously demonstrated in the visual system.

REFERENCES

ABRAMSON, A. S., & LISKER, L. Discriminability along the voicing continuum: cross-language tests. In *Proceedings of the Sixth International Congress of Phonetic Sciences, Prague, 1967*. Prague: Academia, 1970, 569–573.

BLAKEMORE, C., & CAMPBELL, F. W. On the existence of neurons in the human visual system selectively sensitive to the orientation and size of retinal images. *Journal of Physiology*, 1969, **203**, 237–260.

BLAKEMORE, C., & SUTTON, P. Size adaptation: A new aftereffect. *Science*, 1969, **166**, 245–257.

EIMAS, P. D., SIQUELAND, E. R., JUSCZYK, P., & VIGORITO, J. Speech perception in infants. *Science*, 1971, **171**, 303–306.

HALLE, M. Phonology in generative grammar. *Word*, 1962, **18**, 54–72.

HUBEL, D. H., & WIESEL, T. N. Receptive fields, binocular interaction and functional architecture in the cat's visual cortex. *Journal of Physiology*, 1962, **160**, 106–154.

JAKOBSON, R., FANT, C. G. M., & HALLE, M. *Preliminaries to speech analysis*. Cambridge, Massachusetts: M. I. T. Press, 1963.

LETTVIN, J. Y., MATURANA, H. R., McCULLOCH, W. S., & PITTS, W. H. What the frog's eye tells the frog's brain. *Proceedings of the Institute of Radio Engineers*, New York 47, 1959, 1940–1951.

LIBERMAN, A. M., COOPER, F. S., SHANKWEILER, D. P., & STUDDERT-KENNEDY, M. Perception of the speech code. *Psychological Review*, 1967, **74**, 431–461.

LIEBERMAN, P. Towards a unified phonetic theory. *Linguistic Inquiry*, 1970, **1**, 307–322.

LISKER, L., & ABRAMSON, A. S. A cross-language study of voicing in initial stops: acoustical measurements. *Word*, 1964, **20**, 384–422.

LISKER, L., & ABRAMSON, A. S. Some effects of context on voice onset time in English stops. *Language and Speech*, 1967, **10**, 1–28.

LISKER, L., & ABRAMSON, A. S. The voicing dimension: some experiments in comparative phonetics. In *Proceedings of the Sixth International Congress of Phonetic Sciences, Prague, 1967*. Prague: Academia, 1970, 563–567.

MATTINGLY, I. G. Synthesis by rule of General American English. Supplement to *Status report on speech perception*, April 1968. New Haven: Haskins Laboratories.

WOLF, C. G. The perception of step consonants by children. Unpublished Masters Thesis, Brown University, 1972.

(Accepted May 23, 1972)

Journal of Phonetics (1986) **14**, 3–28

An event approach to the study of speech perception from a direct–realist perspective

Carol A. Fowler

Dartmouth College, Hanover, New Hampshire, 03755, U.S.A.
and Haskins Laboratories, New Haven, Connecticut, 06510, U.S.A.

1. Introduction

There is, as yet, no developed event approach to a theory of speech perception and, accordingly, no body of research designed from that theoretical perspective. I will offer my view as to the form that the theory will take, citing relevant research findings where they are available. The theory places constraints on a theory of speech production too. Therefore, I will also have something to say about how talkers must talk for an event approach to be tenable. I will begin by defining the domain of the theory as I will consider it here.

An ecological event is an occurrence in the environment defined with respect to potential participants in it. Like most ecological events (henceforth, events), one in which linguistic communication takes place is highly structured and complex. Accordingly, it can be decomposed for study in many different ways. One way in which it is almost invariably decomposed by psycholinguists and linguists is into the linguistic utterance itself on the one hand, and everything else on the other. In ordinary settings in which communication takes place, this is almost certainly not a natural partitioning because it leaves out several aspects of the setting that contribute interactively with the linguistic utterance itself to the communication. These include the talker's gestures (McNeill, 1985), aspects of the environment that allow the talker to point rather than to refer verbally, and the audience, whose shared experiences with the talker affect his or her speaking style. The consequences of making this cut have not been worked out but, at least for purposes of studying language as communication, they may be substantial (cf. Beattie, 1983). For the present, however, I will preserve the partitioning and one within that as well.

The linguist, Hockett (1960), points out that languages have "duality of patterning": that is, they have words organized grammatically into sentences, and phonetic segments organized phonotactically into words. Both levels are essential to the communicative power of language.

Grammatical organization of words into sentences gives linguistic utterances two kinds of power. First the communicative content of an utterance is superadditive with respect to the contents of the words composing the sentences taken as individuals. Secondly, talkers can produce novel utterances that the audience has not heard before; and yet the utterance can convey the talkers' message to the audience. I will refer to a linguistic utterance at this level of description as a "linguistic event" and, having defined it, I will have little else to say about it until the final section of the paper.

0095 4470/86/010003 + 26 $03.00/0

The second structural tier, in which phonetic segments constitute words, support an indefinitely large lexicon. Were each word to consist of an holistic articulatory gesture rather than a phonotactically organized sequence of phonetic segments, our lexicons would be severely limited in size. Indeed, recent simulations by Lindblom (Lindblom, MacNeilage & Studdert-Kennedy, 1983) show that, as the size of the lexicon is increased (under certain constraints on how new word labels are selected), phonetic structure emerges almost inevitably from a lexicon consisting initially of holistic closing and opening gestures of the vocal tract. These simulations may show how and why phonetic structure emerged in the evolution of spoken language, and how and why it emerges in ontogeny.

I will refer to a talker's phonetically structured articulations as "speech events". It is the perception of these events that constitute the major topic of the paper. A speech event may also be defined as a linguistic utterance having phonetic structure as perceived by a listener. In defining speech event interchangeably from the perspectives of talkers and listeners, I am making the claim, following others (e.g. Shaw, Turvey & Mace, 1982) that a theory of event perception will adopt a "direct realist" stance. According to Shaw *et al.* (p. 159):

> [S]ome form of realism must be captured in any theory that claims to
> be a theory of perception. To do otherwise would render impossible
> an explanation of the practical success of perceptually guided activity.

That is, to explain the success of perceptually guided activity, perception is assumed to recover events in the real world. For this to be possible consistently (see Shaw & Bransford, 1977), perception must be direct and, in particular, unmediated by cognitive processes of inference or hypothesis testing, which introduce the possibility of error.[1]

By focusing largely on speech events, I will be discussing speech at a level at which it consists of phonetically structured syllables but not, necessarily, of grammatical, meaningful utterances. It is ironic, perhaps, that a presentation at a conference on event perception should focus on a linguistic level that does not have transparent ecological significance. However, speech events can be defended as natural partitionings of linguistic events—that is, they can be defended as ecological events—and there is important work to be done by event theorists even here.

The defense is that talkers produce phonetically structured speech, listeners perceive it as such and they use the phonetic structure they perceive to guide their subsequent behavior. Talkers reveal that they produce phonetically structured words when they make speech errors. Most submorphemic errors are misorderings or substitutions of single phonetic segments (e.g. Shattuck-Hufnagel, 1983). For their part, listeners can be shown to extract phonetic structure from a speech communication, at least in certain experimental settings. That they extract it generally, however, is suggested by the observation that they use phonetic variation to mark their identification with a social group, or to adjust their speaking style to the conversational setting. Of course, infant

---

[1]It may be useful to be explicit about the relationships among some concepts I will be referring to. Events are the primitive components of an "ecological" science; that is, of a study of actor/perceivers in contexts that preserve essential properties of their econiches. In the view of many theorists who engage in such studies (see, for example, the quotation from Shaw *et al.* above), the only viable version of a perceptual theory that can be developed within this domain is one that adopts a direct–realist perspective. I will take this as essential to the event (or ecological) approach, although, imaginably, a theory of the perception of natural events might be proposed from a different point of view.

Event approach to the study of speech perception   5

perceivers must recover phonetic structure if they are to become talkers who make segmental speech errors.

This defense is not intended to suggest that perception of speech events is primary or privileged in any sense. It is only to defend it as one of the partitionings of an event involving linguistic communication that is perceived and used by listeners; therefore it is an event in its own right and requires explanation by a theory of perception.

I will discuss an event approach to phonetic perception in the next three major sections of the paper. In Sections 2 and 3 direct perception, first of local, short-term events, and then of longer ones is considered. In Section 4 some affordances of phonetically structured speech are considered.

Although there is a lot of work to be done at this more fine-grained of the dual levels of structure in language, there are also great challenges to an event theory offered by language considered as syntactically structured words that convey a message to a listener. I will discuss just two of these challenges briefly at the end of the paper, and I will suggest a perspective on linguistic events that an event theory might take.

2. Perception of speech events: a local perspective

There is a general paradigm that all instances of perception appear to fit. Perception requires events in the environment ("distal events"), and one or more "informational media"—that is, sources of information about distal events in energy media that can stimulate the sense organs—and a perceiver. As already noted, objects and occurrences in the environment are generally capable of multiple descriptions. Those that are relevant to a perceiver refer to "distal events". They have "affordances"; that is, sets of possibilities for interaction with them by the perceiver. (Affordances are "what [things] furnish, for good or ill" (Gibson, 1971/1982; see also, Gibson, 1979).) An informational medium, including reflected light, acoustic signals and the perceiver's own skin, acquires structure from an environmental event specific to certain properties of the event; because it acquires structure in this way, the medium can provide information about the event properties to a sensitive perceiver. A second crucial characteristic of an informational medium is that it can convey its information to perceivers by stimulating their sense organs and imparting some of its structure to them. By virtue of these two characteristics, informational media enable direct perception of environmental events. The final ingredient in the paradigm is a perceiver who actively seeks out information relevant to his or her current needs or concerns. Perceivers are active in two senses. They move around in the environment to intercept relevant sources of information. In addition, in ways not yet well understood, they "attune" their perceptual systems (e.g. Gibson, 1966/1982) to attend selectively to different aspects of available environmental structure.

In speech perception, the distal event considered locally is the articulating vocal tract. How it is best described to reflect its psychologically significant properties is a problem for investigators of speech perception as well as of speech production. However, I will only characterize articulation in general terms here, leaving its more precise description to Kelso, Saltzman & Tuller in their presentation. One thing we do know is that phonetic segments are realized as coordinated gestures of vocal-tract structures; that is, as coupled relationships among structures that jointly realize the segments (e.g. Kelso, Tuller, Vatikiotis-Bateson & Fowler, 1984). Therefore, studies of the activities of individual muscles or even individual articulators will not in themselves reveal the systems that constitute articulated phonetic segments.

6   *C. A. Fowler*

The acoustic speech signal has the characteristics of an informational medium. It acquires structure from the activities of the vocal tract, and it can impart its structure to an auditory perceptual system thereby conveying its informational to a sensitive perceiver. In this way, it enables direct perception of the environmental source of its structure, the activities of the vocal tract. Having perceived an utterance, a listener has perceived the various "affordances" of the conversational event and can guide his or her subsequent activites accordingly.

This, in outline form, is a theory of the direct perception of speech events. The theory promotes a research program having four parts, three relating to the conditions supporting direct perception of speech events and the last relating to the work that speech events do in the environment. To assess the claim that speech events are directly perceived, the articulatory realizations of phonetic segments must be uncovered and their acoustic consequences identified. Next, the listener's sensitivity to, and use of, the acoustic information must be pinned down. Finally, the listener's use of the structure in guiding his or her activities must be studied. Although, of course, a great deal of research has been done on articulation and perception of speech, very little has been conducted from the theoretical perspective of an event theory, and very little falls within the research program just outlined.

Indeed my impression, based on publishing investigations of speech conducted from this perspective and on presentations of the theoretical perspective to other speech researchers, is that it has substantial face invalidity. There are several things seemingly true of speech production and perception that, in the view of many speech researchers, preclude development of a theory of direct perception of speech events. I will consider four barriers to the theory along with some suggestions concerning ways to surmount or circumvent them.

2.1. *The first barrier: if listeners recover articulation why do they not know it?*

A claim that perceivers see environmental events rather than the optic array that stimulates their visual systems seems far less radical than a claim that they hear phonetically structured articulatory gestures rather than the acoustic speech signal. Indeed, when Repp (1981) makes the argument that phonetic segments are "abstractions" and products of cognitive processes applied to stimulation, he says of them that "*they have no physical properties*—such as duration, spectrum and amplitude—and, therefore, *cannot be measured*" [p. 1463, italics in the original]. That is, he assumes that if phonetic segments were to have physical properties, the properties would be acoustic. Yet no-one thinks that, if the objects of visual perception—that is, trees, tables, people, etc.—do have physical properties, their properties are those of reflected light.

Somewhat compatibly, our phenomenal experience when we hear speech certainly is not of lips closing, jaws raising, velums lowering, and so on, although our visual experience is of the objects and events in the world. Of course, we do not experience surface features of the acoustic signal either; that is, silent gaps followed by stop-bursts, or formant patterns or nasal resonances.

I cannot explain the failure of our intuitions in speech to recognize that perceived phonetic events are articulatory, as compared to our intuitions about vision, which we do recognize that perceived events are environmental, but I can think of a circumstance that exacerbates the failure among researchers. If, in an experimental study, listeners do indeed recover articulatory events in perception, there is likely to be a large mismatch between the level of description of an articulatory event that they recover and a researcher's description of the activities of the individual articulators. That is, speech researchers do not yet know what articulatory events consist of. If a perceiver does not experience "lips closing", for example, that is as it should be, because lip closure *per se* is not an articulatory speech event. Rather (see the contribution by KST), an articulatory event that is a phonetic event, for example, is a coordinated set of movements by vocal-tract structures.

By hypothesis, the percept [b] corresponds to extraction from the acoustic speech signal of information that the appropriate coordinated gestures occurred in the talker's vocal tract, just as the perceptual experience of a zooming baseball corresponds to extraction of information from the optic array that the event of zooming occurred in the environment.

The literature offers evidence from a wide variety of sources that listeners do extract information about articulation from the acoustic speech signal. Much of this evidence has recently been reviewed by Liberman & Mattingly (1985) in support of a motor theory.[2] I will select just a few examples.

2.1.1. *Perceptual equivalence of distinct acoustic "cues" specifying the same articulatory event*

In non-phonetic contexts, silence produces a very different perceptual experience from a set of formant transitions. However, interposed between frication for an [s] and a syllable sound like [lIt] in isolation, they may not (Fitch, Halwes, Erickson & Liberman, 1980). An appropriate interval of silence may foster perception of [p]; so may a lesser amount of silence, insufficient to cue a [p] percept in itself, followed by transitions characteristic of [p] release. Strikingly, a pair of syllables differing both in the duration of silence after the [s] frication, and in presence or absence of [p] transitions following the silence, are either highly discriminable (and more discriminable than a pair of syllables differing along just one of these dimensions) or nearly indiscriminable (and *less* discriminable than a pair differing in just one dimension) depending on whether the silence and transitions "co-operate" or "conflict". They co-operate if, within one syllable, both acoustic segments provide evidence for stop production and, within the other, they do not. They conflict if the syllable having a relatively long interval of silence appropriate to stop closure lacks the formant transitions characteristic of stop release, while the syllable with a short interval of silence has transitions. Depending on the durations of silence, these latter syllables may both sound like "split" or both like "slit".

---

[2] There are fundamental similarities between the view of speech perception from a direct—realist perspective and from the perspective of the motor theory. An important one is that both theories hold that the listener's percept corresponds to the talker's phonetic message, and that the message is best characterized in articulatory terms. There are differences as well. As Liberman & Mattingly (1985) note, one salient difference is that the direct—realist theory holds that the acoustic signal is, in a sense, transparent to the perceived components of speech, while the motor theory does not. According to the motor theory, achievement of a phonetic percept requires special computations on the signal that take into account both the physiological—anatomical and the phonetic constraints on the activities of the articulators. A second difference is more subtle and perhaps will disappear as the theories evolve. Liberman & Mattingly propose that the objects of speech perception (at the level of description under consideration) are the "control structures" for observed articulatory gestures. Due to coarticulatory smearing, these control structures are not entirely redundant with the collection of gestures as they occur. My own view is that the smearing is only apparent and, hence, the control structures are wholly redundant with the collections of articulatory gestures (properly described) constituting speech.

8   *C. A. Fowler*

The important point is that very different acoustic properties sound similar or the same just when the information they convey about articulation is similar or the same. It should follow, and does, that when an articulation causes a variety of acoustic effects (for example, Lisker, 1978, has identified more than a dozen distinctions between voiced and voiceless stops intervocalically), the acoustic consequences individually tend to be sufficient to give rise to the appropriate perception, but none is necessary (see Liberman & Mattingly, 1985, for a review of those findings).

2.1.2. *Different perceptual experiences of the same acoustic segment just when it specifies different distal sources*

By the same token, the same acoustic segment in different contexts, where it specifies different articulations or none at all, sounds quite different to perceivers. In the experiment by Fitch *et al.* just described, a set of transitions characteristic of release of a bilabial stop will only give rise to a stop percept in that context if preceded by sufficient silence. This cannot be because, in the absence of silence, the [s] frication masks the transitions; other research demonstrates that transitions at fricative release themselves do contribute to fricative place perception (e.g. Harris, 1958; Whalen, 1981). Rather, it seems, release can only be perceived in this context given sufficient evidence for prior stop closure.

Similarly, if transitions are presented in isolation where, of course, they do not signal stop release, or even production by a vocal tract at all, they sound more or less the way that they look on a visual display; that is, like frequency rises and falls (e.g. Mattingly, Liberman, Syrdal & Halwes, 1971).

2.1.3. *"P centers"*

Spoken digits (Morton, Marcus & Frankish, 1976) or nonsense monosyllables (Fowler, 1979), aligned so that their onsets of acoustic energy are isochronous, do not sound isochronous to listeners. Asked to adjust the timing of pairs of digits (Marcus, 1981) or monosyllables (Cooper, Whalen & Fowler, 1984) produced repeatedly in alternation so that they sound isochronous, listeners introduce systematic departures from measured isochrony—just those that talkers introduce if they produce the same utterances to a real (Fowler & Tassinary, 1981; Rapp, 1971) or imaginary (Fowler, 1979; Tuller & Fowler, 1980) metronome. Measures of muscular activity supporting the talkers' articulations are isochronous in rhyming monosyllables produced to an imaginary metronome (Tuller & Fowler, 1980). Thus, talkers follow instructions to produce isochronous sequences, but due (in large part) to the different times after articulatory onset that different phonetic segments have their onsets of acoustic energy, acoustic measurements of their productions suggest a failure of isochrony. For their part, listeners appear to hear through the speech signal to the timing of the articulations.

2.1.4. *Lip reading*

Liberman & Mattingly (1985) describe a study in which an acoustic signal for a production of [ba] synchronized to a face mouthing [bɛ], [vɛ] and [ðɛ] may be heard as [ba], [va] and [ða], respectively (cf. McGurk & MacDonald, 1976). Listeners experience hearing syllables with properties that are composites of what is seen and heard, and they have no sense that place information is acquired largely visually, and vowel information auditorily. (This is reminiscent of the quotation from Hornbostel (1927), reprinted in Gibson (1966): "it matters little through which sense I realize that in the dark I have blundered into a pigsty". Likewise, it seems, it matters little through what sense we realize what speech event has occurred.) Within limits anyway, information about articulation gives rise to an experience of hearing speech, whether the information is in the optic array or in the acoustic signal.

2.2. *The second barrier: linguistic units are not literally articulated*

A theory of perception of speech events is disconfirmed if the linguistic constituents of communications between talkers and listeners do not make public appearances. There are two kinds of reason for doubting that they do, both relating to an incommensurability that many theorists and researchers have identified between knowing and doing, between competence and performance, or even between the mental and the physical realizations of language.

One kind of incommensurability is graphically illustrated by Hockett's Easter egg analogy (Hockett, 1955). According to the analogy, articulation, and in particular, the coarticulation that inertial and other physical properties of the vocal tract requires, obliterates the discrete, context-free phonetic segments of the talker's planned linguistic message. Hockett suggests that the articulation of planned phonetic segments is analogous to the effects that a wringer would have on an array of (raw) Easter eggs. If the analogy is apt, and listeners nonetheless can recover the phonetic segments of the talker's plan, then direct detection of articulatory gestures in perception cannot fully explain perception, because the gestures themselves provide a distorted representation of the segments. To explain recovery of phonetic segments from the necessarily impoverished information in the acoustic signal, reconstructive processes or other processes involving cognitive mediation (Hammarberg, 1976, 1982; Hockett, 1955; Neisser, 1967; Repp, (1981) or non-cognitive mediation (Liberman & Mattingly, 1985) must be invoked.

Hockett is not the only theorist to propose that ideal phonetic segments are distorted by the vocal tract. For example, MacNeilage & Ladefoged (1976) describe planned segments as discrete, static, and context-free, whereas uttered segments are overlapped, dynamic, and context-sensitive.

A related view expressed by several researchers is that linguistic units are mental things that, thereby, cannot be identified with any set of articulatory or acoustic characteristics. For example:

> [Phonetic segments] are *abstractions*. They are the end result of complex perceptual and cognitive processes in the listener's brain. (Repp, 1981, p. 1462)

> They [phonetic categories] have no physical properties. (Repp, 1981, p. 1463)

> Segments cannot be objectively observed to exist in the speech signal nor in the flow of articulatory movements . . . [T]he concept of segment is brought to bear *a priori* on the study of physical–physiological aspects of language. (Hammarberg, 1976, p. 355)

> [T]he segment is internally generated, the creature of some kind of perceptual—cognitive process. (Hammarberg, 1976, p. 355)

This point of view, of course, requires a mentalist theory of perception.

For a realist event theory to be possible, what modifications to these views are required? The essential modification is to our conceptualization of the relation between

10   C. A. Fowler

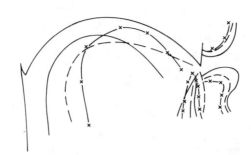

Figure 1. Cinefluorographic tracing of the vocal tract during three phases in production of /husi/ (redrawn from Carney & Moll, 1971). ——, /u/ in /husi/; ----, /s/ in /husi/; × – × – ×, /i/ in /husi/.

knowing and doing. First, phonetic segments as we know them can only have properties that can be realized in articulation. Indeed, from an event perspective, the primary reality of the phonetic segment is its public realization as vocal-tract activity. What we know of the segments, we know from hearing them produced by other talkers or by producing them ourselves. Secondly, the idea that speech production involves a translation from a mental domain into a physical, non-mental domain such as the vocal tract must be discarded.

With respect to the first point, we can avoid the metaphor of Hockett's wringer if we can avoid somehow ascribing properties to phonetic segments that vocal tracts cannot realize. In view of the fact that phonetic segments evolved to be spoken, and indeed, that we have evolved to speak them (Lieberman, 1984), this does not seem to be a radical endeavor.

Vocal tracts cannot produce a string of static shapes, so for an event theory to be possible, phonetic segments cannot be inherently static. Likewise, vocal tracts cannot produce the segments discretely, if discrete means "non-overlapping". However, neither of these properties is crucial to the work that phonetic segments do in a linguistic communication, and therefore can be abandoned without loss.

Phonetic segments do need to be separate from one another and serially ordered, however, and Hockett's Easter egg analogy suggests that they are not. But my own reading of the literature on coarticulation is that the Easter egg analogy is misleading and wrong. Figure 1 is a redrawing of a figure from Carney & Moll (1971): it is an outline drawing of the vocal tract with three tongue shapes superimposed. The shapes were obtained by cinefluorography at three points in time during the production of the disyllable [husi]. The solid line reflects the tongue shape during a central portion of the vowel [u]; the dashed line is the tongue shape during closure for [s]; the line of crosses is the tongue shape during a central portion of [i]. Thus, the figure shows a smooth vowel-to-vowel gesture of the tongue body taking place during closure of [s] (cf. Öhman, 1966). The picture these data reveal is much cleaner than the Easter egg metaphor would suggest. The sets of gestures for different segments overlap, but the separation and ordering of the segments is preserved.[3]

---

[3]This characterization may appear patently incorrect in cases where the same articulator is involved simultaneously in the production of more than one phonetic segment (for example, the tongue body during closure for [kh] in "key" and "coo" and the jaw during closure for [b] in "bee" and "boo"). However, Saltzman and Kelso (Saltzman, in press; Saltzman & Kelso, 1983) have begun to model this as overlapping, but separate demands of different control structures on the same articulator and my own findings on perceived segmentation of speech (Fowler, 1984; see also Fowler & Smith, 1986) suggest that perceivers extract exactly that kind of parsing of the speech signal.

With respect to the second point, Ryle (1949) offers a way of conceptualizing the relation between the mental and the physical that avoids the problems consequent upon identifying the mental with covert processes taking place inside the head:

> When we describe people as exercising qualities of mind, we are not referring to occult episodes of which their overt acts and utterances are effects, we are referring to those overt acts and utterances themselves. (p. 25)

> When a person talks sense aloud, ties knots, feints or sculpts, the actions which we witness are themselves the things which he is intelligently doing . . . He is bodily active and mentally active, but he is not being synchronously active in two different "places", or with two different "engines". There is one activity, but it is susceptible of and requiring more than one kind of explanatory description. (pp. 50–51)

This way of characterizing intelligent action does not eliminate the requirement that linguistic utterances must be planned: rather it eliminates the idea that covert processes are privileged in being mental or psychological, whereas overt actions are not. Instead, we may think of the talker's intended message as it is planned, uttered, specified acoustically, and perceived as being replicated intact across different physical media from the body of the talker to that of the listener.

An event theory of speech *production* must aim to characterize articulation of phonetic segments as overlapping sets of coordinated gestures, where each set of coordinated gestures conforms to a phonetic segment. By hypothesis, the organization of the vocal tract to produce a phonetic segment is invariant over variation in segmental and suprasegmental contexts. The segment may be realized somewhat differently in different contexts (for example, the relative contributions of the jaw and lips may vary over different bilabial closures (Sussman, MacNeilage & Hanson, 1973)), because of competing demands on the articulators made by phonetic segments realized in an overlapping time frame. To the extent that a description of speech production along these lines can be worked out, the possibility remains that phonetic segments are literally uttered and therefore are available to be directly perceived if the acoustic signal is sufficiently informative. Research on a "task dynamic" model of speech production (e.g. Saltzman, in press; Saltzman & Kelso, 1983; KST, this issue) may provide, at the very least, an existence proof that systems capable of realizing overlapping phonetic segments nondestructively can be devised.

2.3. *The third barrier: the acoustic signal does not specify phonetic segments*

Putting aside the question whether phonetic segments are realized non-destructively in articulation, there remains the problem that the acoustic signal does not seem to reflect the phonetic segmental structure of a linguistic communication. It need not, even if phonetic segments are uttered intact. Although gestures of the vocal tract cause disturbances in the air, it need not follow that the disturbance specify their causes. For many researchers, they do not. Figure 2 (from Fant & Lindblom, 1961, and Cutting & Pisoni, 1978) displays the problem.

A spectrographic display of a speech utterance invites segmentation into "acoustic segments" (Fant, 1973). Visibly defined, these are relatively homogeneous intervals in the display. Segmentation lines are drawn where abrupt changes are noticeable. The difficulty with this segmentation is the relation it bears to the component phonetic

12   *C. A. Fowler*

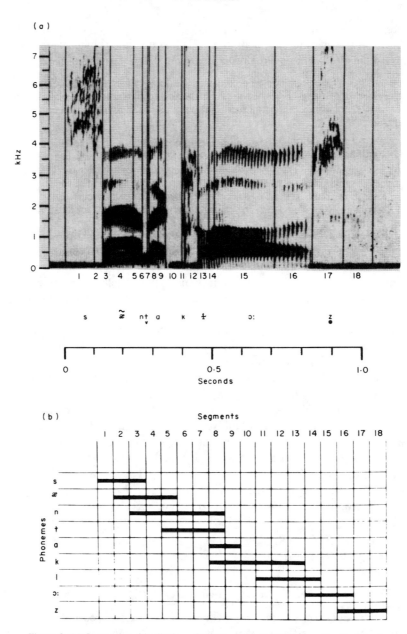

Figure 2. (a) Spectrographic display of "Santa Claus". (b) Schematic display of the relationship between acoustic and phonetic segments (reprinted with permission from Cutting & Pisoni (1978), and Fant & Lindblom (1961)).

segments of the linguistic utterance. In the display, the utterance is the name, "Santa Claus", which is composed of nine phonetic segments, but 18 acoustic segments. The relation of phonetic segments to acoustic segments is not simple, as the bottom of Figure 2 reveals. Phonetic segments may be composed of any number of acoustic segments, from two to six in the figure, and most acoustic segments reflect properties of more than one phonetic segment.

Event approach to the study of speech perception   13

How do listeners recover phonetic structure from such a signal? One thing is clear; the functional parsing of the acoustic signal for the perceiver is not one into acoustic segments. Does it follow that perceivers impose their own parsing on the signal? There must be a "no" answer to this question for an event theory devised from a direct–realist perspective to be viable. The perceived parsing must be in the signal; the special role of the perceptual system is not to create it, but only to select it.

Notably, there is more than one physical description of the acoustic speech signal. A spectrographic display suggest a parsing into acoustic segments, but other displays suggest other parsings of the signal. For example, Kewley-Port (1983) points out that in a spectrographic display the release burst of a syllable-initial stop consonant looks quite distinct from the formant transitions that follow it (for example, see the partitioning of /k/ in "Claus" in Figure 2). Indeed, research using the spectrographic display as a guide has manipulated burst and transition to study their relative salience as information for stop place (Dorman, Studdert-Kennedy & Raphael, 1977). However, Kewley-Port's "running spectra" for stops (overlapping spectra from 20 ms windows taken at successive 5 ms intervals following stop release) reveal continuity between burst and transitions in changes in the location of spectral peaks from burst to transition.

It does not follow, then, from the mismatch between acoustic segment and phonetic segment, that there is a mismatch between the information in the acoustic signal and the phonetic segments in the talker's message. Possibly, in a manner as yet undiscovered by researchers but accessed by perceivers, the signal is transparent to phonetic segments.

If it is, two research strategies should provide converging evidence concerning the psychologically relevant description of the acoustic signal. The first seeks a description of the articulatory event itself—that is, of sequences of phonetic segments as articulated —and then investigates the acoustic consequences of the essential articulatory components of phonetic segments. A second examines the parsing of the acoustic signal that listeners detect.

The research that comes closest to this characterization is that of Stevens & Blumstein (1978, 1981; also Blumstein & Stevens, 1979, 1981). They begin with a characterization of phonetic segments and, based on the acoustic theory of speech production (Fant, 1960), develop hypotheses concerning invariant acoustic consequences of essential articulatory properties of the segments. They then test whether the consequences are, in fact, invariant over talkers and phonetic-segmental contexts. Finally, they ask whether these consequences are used by perceivers.

Unfortunately for the purpose of an event approach, perhaps, they begin with a characterization of phonetic segments as bundles of distinctive features. This characterization differs in significant ways from one that will be developed from a perspective on phonetic segments as coordinated articulatory gestures. One important difference is that the features tend to be static; accordingly, the acoustic consequences first sought in the research program were static also. A related difference is that the characterization deals with coarticulation by presuming that the listener gets around it by focusing his or her attention on the least coarticulated parts of the signal. As I will suggest shortly, that does not conform with the evidence; nor would it be desirable, because acoustic consequences of coarticulated speech are quite informative (cf. Elman & McClelland, 1983).

To date, Stevens and Blumstein have focused most of their attention on invariant information for consonantal place of articulation. Their hypotheses concerning possible invariants are based on predictions derived from the acoustic theory of speech production concerning acoustic correlates of constrictions in various parts of the vocal tract. When articulators adopt a configuration, the vocal tract forms cavities that have natural resonances, the formants. Formants create spectral peaks in an acoustic signal; that is, a range of frequencies higher in intensity than their neighbors. With the exception of posterior places of articulation, e.g. pharynx, a consonantal constriction in the vocal tract lowers F_1 (the lowest formant) relative to its frequency for a corresponding vowel and it affects the frequencies and intensities of higher formants. Stevens & Blumstein (1978) argue that stop consonants with different places of articulation have characteristic burst spectra independent of the vowel following the consonant, and independent of the size of the vocal tract producing the constriction.

Blumstein & Stevens (1979) created "template" spectra for the stop consonants, /b/, /d/, and /g/, and then attempted to use them to classify the stops in 1800 CV and VC syllables in which the consonants were produced by different talkers in the context of various vowels. Overall, they were successful in classifying syllable-initial stops, but less successful with final stops, particularly if the stops were unreleased. Blumstein & Stevens (1981) also showed that listeners could classify stops by place better than chance when they were given only the first 10–46 ms of CV syllables.

However, two investigations have shown that the shape of the spectrum at stop release is not an important source of information for stop place. These studies (Blumstein, Isaacs & Mertus, 1982; Walley & Carrell, 1983) pitted place information contributed by the shape of the spectrum at stop release in CVs, against the (context-dependent) information for place contributed by the formant frequencies themselves. In both studies, the formants overrode the effect of spectral shape in listeners' judgments of place.

Recently, Lahiri, Gewirth & Blumstein (1984) have found in any case that spectral shape does not properly classify labial, dental and alveolar stops produced by speakers of three different languages. In search of new invariants and following the lead of Kewley-Port (1983), they examined the information in running spectra. They found that they could classify stops according to place by examining relative shifts in energy at high and low frequencies from burst to voicing onset. Importantly, pitting the appropriate running spectral patterns against formant frequencies for 10 CV syllables in a perceptual study, Lahiri *et al.* found that the running spectral patterns were overriding. The investigators identify their proposed invariants as "dynamic", because they are revealed over time during stop release, and relational because they are based on relative changes in the distribution of energy at high and low frequencies in the vicinity of stop release.

Lahiri *et al.* are cautious whether their proposed invariants will withstand further test —and properly so, because the invariants are somewhat contrived in their precise specification. I suspect that major advances in the discovery of invariant acoustic information for phonetic segments will follow advances in understanding how phonetic segments are articulated. However, the proposals of Lahiri *et al.* (see also Kewley-Port, 1983) constitute an advance over the concept of spectral shape in beginning to characterize invariant acoustic information for gestures rather than for static configurations.

2.4. *The fourth barrier: perception demonstrably involves "top down" processes and perceivers do make mistakes*

Listeners may "restore" missing phonetic segments in words (Samuel, 1981; Warren, 1970), and talkers shadowing someone else's speech may "fluently restore" mispronounced words to their correct forms (e.g. Marslen-Wilson & Welsh, 1978). Even grosser departures of perceptual experience from stimulation may be observed in some mishearings (for example "popping really slow" heard as "prodigal son" (Browman, 1980) or "mow his own lawn" heard as "blow his own horn" (Garnes & Bond, 1980)).

These kinds of findings are often described as evidence for an interaction of "bottom-up" and "top-down" processes in perception (e.g. Klatt, 1980). Bottom-up processes analyze stimulation as it comes in. Top-down processes draw inferences concerning stimulation based both on the fragmentary results of the continuing bottom-up processes and on stored knowledge of likely inputs. Top-down processes can restore missing phonemes or correct erroneous ones in real words by comparing results of bottom-up processes against lexical entries. As for mishearings, Garnes & Bond (1980) argue that "active hypothesizing on the part of the listener concerning the intended message is certainly part of the speech perception process. No other explanation is possible for misperceptions which quite radically restructure the message . . ." (p. 238).

In my view (but not necessarily in the view of other event theorists), these data do offer a strong challenge to an event theory. It is not that an event theory of speech perception has nothing to say about perceptual learning (for example, Gibson, 1966; Johnston & Pietrewicz, 1985). However, what is said is not yet well enough worked out to specify how, for example, lexical knowledge can be brought to bear on speech input from an direct–realist, event perspective.

With regard to mishearings, there is also a point of view (Shaw, Turvey & Mace, 1982) that when reports of environmental events are in error, the reporter cannot be said to have perceived the events, because the word "perception" is reserved for just those occasions when acquisition of information from stimulation is direct and, therefore, successful. The disagreement with theories of perception as indirect and constructive, then, may reduce to a disagreement concerning how frequently bottom-up processes complete their work in the absence of top-down influence.

I prefer a similar approach to that of Shaw *et al.* that makes a distinction between what perceivers *can do* and what they may do in particular settings. As Shaw *et al.* argue, there is a need for the informational support for activity to *be able to be* directly extracted from an informational medium and for perception to be nothing other than direct extraction of information from proximal stimulation. However, in familiar environments, actors may generally guide their activities based not only on what they perceive, but also on what the environment routinely affords. In his presentation at the first event conference, Jenkins (1985) reviews evidence that the bat's guidance of flying sometimes takes this form. Placed in a room with barriers that must be negotiated to reach a food source, the bat soon learns the route (Griffin, 1958). After some time in which the room layout remains unchanged, a barrier is placed in the bat's usual flight path. Under these novel conditions, the bat is likely to collide with the barrier. Although it could have detected the barrier, it did not. By the same token, as a rule, we humans do not test a sidewalk to ensure that it will bear our weight before entrusting our weight to it. Nor do we walk through (apparent) apertures with our arms outstretched just in the case the aperture does not really afford passage because someone has erected a difficult-to-see plate-glass barrier. In short, although the affordances that guide action *can be* directly perceived, often they are not wholly. We perceive enough to narrow down the possible environments to one likely environment that affords our intended activity, and other remotely likely ones that may not.

16   *C. A. Fowler*

Perceptual restorations and mishearings imply the same perceptual pragmatism among perceivers of speech. It is also implied, I think, by talkers' tendencies to adjust the formality of their speaking style to their audience (e.g. Labov, 1972). Audiences with whom the talker shares substantial past experiences may require less information to get the message than listeners who share less. Knowing that, talkers conserve effort by providing less where possible.

It may be important to emphasize that the foregoing attempt to surmount the fourth barrier is intended to do more than translate a description of top-down and bottom-up processes into a terminology more palatable to event theorists. In addition, I am attempting to allow a role for information not currently in stimulation to guide activity, while preserving the ideas that perception itself must be direct and hence, errorless, and that activity *can be* (but often is not) guided exclusively by perceived affordances.

As to the latter idea, the occurrence of mishearings that depart substantially from the spoken utterance should not deflect our attention from the observation that perceivers *can* hew the talker's articulatory line very closely if encouraged to do so. One example from my own research is provided by investigations of listeners' perceived segmentation of speech. Figure 1 above, already described, displays coarticulation of the primary articulators for vowels and consonants produced in a disyllable. This overlap has two general consequences in the acoustic signal (one generally acknowledged as a consequence, the other not). First, within a time frame that a conventional acoustic description would identify with one phonetic segment (because the segment's acoustic consequences are dominant), the acoustic signal is affected by the segment's preceding and following neighbors. Secondly, because the articulatory trajectories for consonants overlap part of the trajectory of a neighboring vowel (cf. Carney & Moll, 1971; Öhman, 1966), the extent of time in the acoustic signal during which the vowel predominates in its effects—and hence the vowel's measured duration—decreases in the context of many consonants or of long consonants as compared to its extent in the context of few or short consonants (Fowler, 1983; Fowler & Tassinary, 1981; Lindblom & Rapp, 1973).

Listeners can exhibit sensitivity to the information for the overlapping phonetic segments that talkers produce in certain experimental tasks. In these tasks, the listeners use acoustic information for a vowel within a domain identified with a preceding consonant (for example, within a stop burst or within frication for a fricative consonant) as information for the vowel (Fowler, 1984; Whalen, 1984). Moreover, listeners do not integrate the overlapping information for vowel and consonant. Rather, they hear the consonant as if the vowel information had been factored out of it (Fowler, 1984) and they hear the vowel as longer than its measured extent by an amount correlated with the extent to which a preceding consonant should have shortened it by overlapping its leading edge (Fowler & Tassinary, 1981).

These studies indicate that listeners can track the talker's vocal-tract activities very closely and, more specifically, that they extract a segmentation of the signal into the overlapping phonetic segments that talkers produce, not into discrete approximations to phonetic segments and not into acoustic segments. Of course, this is as it must be among young perceivers if they are to learn to talk based on hearing the speech of others. But whether or not a skilled listener will track articulation this closely in any given circumstance may depend on the extent to which listener estimates that he or she needs to in order to recover the talker's linguistic message.

3. Perception of speech events in an expanded time frame: sound change

Two remarkable facts about the bottom tier of dually structured language are that its structure undergoes systematic change over time, and that the sound inventories and phonological processes of language reflect the articulatory dispositions of the vocal tract and perceptual dispositions of the ear (Donegan & Stampe, 1979; Lindblom *et al.*, 1983; Locke, 1983; Ohala, 1981). There are many phonological processes special to individual languages that have analogues in articulatory—phonetic processes general to languages. For example, most languages have shorter vowels before voiceless than voiced stops (e.g. Chen, 1970). However, in addition, among languages with a phonological length distinction, in some (for example, German; see Comrie, 1980), synchronic or diachronic processes allow phonologically long vowels only before voiced consonants. Similarly, I have already described a general articulatory tendency for consonants to overlap vowels in production, so that vowels are measured to shorten before clusters or long consonants more than before singleton consonants or short consonants. Compatibly, in stressed syllables, Swedish short vowels appear only before long consonants or multiple consonants; long vowels appear before a short consonant or no consonant at all. In Yawelmani (see Kenstowiscz & Kisseberth, 1979), a long vowel is made short before a cluster. Stressed vowels also are measured to shorten in the context of following unstressed syllables in many languages (Fowler, 1981; Lehiste, 1972; Lindblom & Rapp, 1973; Nooteboom & Cohen, 1975). Compatibly, in Chimwi꞉ni (Kenstowiscz & Kisseberth, 1979), a long vowel may not generally occur before the antepenultimate syllable of a word.

These are just a few examples involving duration that I have gathered, but similar examples abound, as do examples of other phonological tendencies. We can ask: how do linguistic–phonological processes that resemble articulatory dispositions enter language?

An interesting answer that Ohala (1981) offers to cover some cases is that they enter language via sound changes induced by systematic misperception by listeners. One example he provides is that of tonal development in "tone languages", including Chinese, Thai, and others. Tonal development on vowels may have been triggered by loss of a voicing distinction in preceding consonants. A consequence of consonant voicing is a rising tone on the following vowel (e.g. Hombert, 1979). Following a voiceless consonant, the tone is high and falling. Historical development of tones in Chinese may be explained as the listeners' systematic failure to ascribe the tone to consonant voicing —perhaps because the voicing distinction was weakening—and to hear it instead as an intentionally produced characteristic of the vowel.

This explanation is intriguing because, in relation to the perspective on perceived segmentation just outlined, it implies that listeners may sometimes recover a segmentation of speech that is not identical to the one articulated by the talker. In particular, it suggests that listeners may not always recognize coarticulatory encroachments as such and may instead integrate the coarticulatory influences with a phonetic segment with which they overlap in time. This may be especially likely when information for the occurrence of the coarticulating neighbor (or its relevant properties, as in the case of voicing in Chinese) is weakening. However, Ohala describes some examples where coarticulatory information has been misparsed despite maintenance of the conditioning segment itself. Failures to recover the talker's segmental parsing may lead to sound change when listeners themselves begin producing the phonological segment as they recovered it rather than as the talkers produced it.

18   *C. A. Fowler*

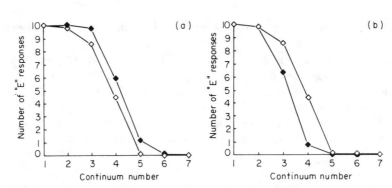

Figure 3. Identification of vowels in the experiment of Krakow, Beddor, Goldstein & Fowler (1985): see text for explanation. (a) ◆, Original [bẽnd]; ◇, original [bɛd]: (b) ◆, original [bẽd]; ◇, original [bɛd].

Recent findings by Krakow, Beddor, Goldstein & Fowler (1985) suggest that something like this may underlie an on-going vowel shift in English. In English, the vowel /æ/ is raising in certain phonetic contexts (e.g. Labov, 1981). One context is before a nasal consonant. Indeed, for many speakers of English, the /æ/ in "can", for example, is a noticeably higher vowel than that in "cad".

One hypothesis to explain the vowel shift in the context of nasal consonants is that listeners fail to parse the signal so that all of the influences of the nasalization on the vowel are identified with the coarticulatory influence of the nasal consonant. As Wright (1980) observes, the nasal formant in a nasalized vowel is lower in frequency than F_1 of /æ/. Integrated with F_1 of /æ/ or mistakenly identified as F_1, the nasal formant is characteristic of a higher vowel (with a lower F_1) than F_1 of /æ/ itself.

Krakow *et al.* examined this idea by synthesizing two kinds of continua using an articulatory synthesizer (Rubin, Baer & Mermelstein, 1979). One continuum was a /bɛd/ to /bæd/ series (henceforth, the bed–bad series) created by gradually lowering and backing the height of the synthesizer's model tongue in seven steps. A second, /bɛnd/ to /bænd/, continuum (henceforth bend–band) was created in similar fashion, but with a lowered velum during the vowel and throughout part of the following alveolar occlusion. (In fact, several bend–band continua were synthesized with different degrees of velar lowering. I will report results on just one representative continuum.) Listeners identified the vowel in each series as spelled with "E" or "A". Figure 3(a) compares the responses to members of the bed–bad continuum with responses to a representative bend–band series. As expected, we found a tendency for subjects to report more "E"s in the bend–band series.

We reasoned that if this were due to a failure of listeners to parse the signal so that all of the acoustic consequences of nasality were ascribed to the nasal consonant, then by removing the nasal consonant itself, we would see as much or even more raising than in the context of a nasal consonant. Accordingly, we altered the original bed–bad series by lowering the model velum throughout the vowel. (I will call the new /bɛd/–/bæd/ continuum the bed(N)–bad(N) series. Again, different degrees of nasality were used over different continua. I will report data from a representative series.) Figure 3(b) shows the results of this manipulation. Rather than experiencing increased raising, as expected, the listeners experienced significant lowering of the vowel in the bed(N)–bad(N) series. Although this outcome can be rationalized in terms of spectral changes to the oral

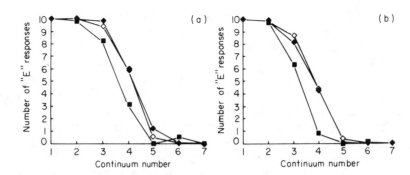

Figure 4. Identification of vowels in continua having vowels matched in measured duration (data from Krakow *et al.*, 1985). (a) Short: ◇, [bɛd]; ■, [bɛ̃d]; ◆, [bɛ̃nd]. (b) Long: ◇, [bɛd]; ■, [bɛ̃d]; ◆, [bɛ̃nd].

formants of the vowel due to the influence of the nasal resonance on them, it does not elucidate the original of the raising observed in the first study.

A difference between our bend–band and bed–bad series was in the measured duration of the vowels. Following measurements of natural productions, we had synthesized syllables with shorter measured vowels in the bend–band series than in the bed–bad series. We next considered the possibility that this explained the raising we had found in the first experiment. /ɛ/ is an "inherently" shorter vowel than /æ/ (e.g. Peterson & Lehiste, 1960). It seemed possible that raising in the bend–band series was not due to misparsing of nasality, but to misparsing of the vowel's articulated extent from that of the overlapping nasal consonant. In particular, the vowels in the bend–band continua might have been perceived as inherently shorter (rather than as more extensively over-lapped by the syllable coda) than vowels in the bed–bad series, and hence as more /ɛ/-like.

To test that idea, we synthesized a new bend–band series with longer measured durations of vowels, matching those in the original bed–bad (and bed(N)–bad(N)) series, and new bed–bad and bed(N)–bad(N) series with vowels shortened to match the measured duration of those in the original bend–band series. Figures 4(a) and (b) show the outcome for the short and long series respectively. Identification functions for bed–bad and bend–band are now identical. Listeners ascribe all of the nasality in the vowel to the consonant, and when vowels are matched in measured duration, there is no raising. Stimuli in the bed(N)–bad(N) series show lowering in both Figures 4(a) and (b).

These results are of interest in several respects. For the present discussion, they are interesting in suggesting limitations in the extent to which these listeners could track articulation. Although listeners do parse speech along its coarticulatory lines in this study, ascribing the nasality during the vowel to the nasal consonant, they are not infinitely sensitive to parts of a vowel overlaid by a consonant. The difficulty they have detecting the trailing edges of a vowel may be particularly severe when the following consonants are nasals as in the present example, because, during a nasal, the oral cavity is sealed off and the acoustic signal mainly reflects passage of air through the nasal cavity. Consequently, information for the vowel is poor. (There is vowel information in nasal consonants, however, as Fujimura (1962) has shown.)

In a study mentioned earlier, Fowler & Tassinary found that in a vowel-duration continuum in which voicing of a final alveolar stop was cued by vowel duration (cf. Raphael, 1972), the "voiceless" percept was resisted more for vowels preceded by consonants that, in natural productions, shorten the measured extents of the vowels substantially than by consonants that shorten them less. In the study, however, the effect on the voicing boundary was less than the shortening effect of the preceding consonant would predict. Together, this study and that by Krakow *et al.* suggest that although listeners do parse the speech signal along coarticulatory lines, they do not always hear the vowels as extending throughout their whole coarticulatory extent.[4]

As Ohala has suggested (1981), these perceptual failures may provoke sound change. Thereby they may promote introduction into the phonologies of languages, processes that resemble articulatory dispositions.

What are the implications of this way of characterizing perception and sound change for the theory of perception of speech events? In the account, perceivers clearly are extracting affordances from the acoustic signal. That is, they are extracting information relevant to the guidance of their own articulatory activities. (See the following section for some other affordances perceived by listeners.) However, just as clearly, the distal event they reported in our experiment and that they reproduce in natural settings is not the one in the environment. The problem here may or may not be the same as that discussed as the "fourth barrier" above. In the present case, the problem concerns the salience of the information provided to the listener in relation to the listener's own sensitivity to it. Information for vowels where consonants overlap them presumably is subtle and therefore difficult (but not impossible, see Fowler, 1984; Whalen, 1984) to detect. One way to handle the outcome of the experiment by Krakow *et al.* within a direct–realist event theory is to suppose that listeners extract less information from the signal than they need to report their percept in an experiment or to reproduce it themselves, and they fill in the rest of the information from experience at the time of report or reproduction. An alternative is that listeners are insensitive to the vowel information in the nasal consonant and use that lack of information as information for the vowel's absence there. Presumably it is just the cases where important articulatory information is difficult to detect that undergo the perceptually driven sound changes in languages (cf. Lindblom, 1972).

4. How perception guides action

4.1. *Some affordances of phonetically-structured speech*

For those of us engaged in research on phonetic perception, it is easy to lose sight of the fact that, outside of the laboratory, the object of perceiving is not the achievement of a percept, but rather the acquisition of information relevant to guidance of activity. I will next consider how perception of phonetically structured vocal activity may guide the listener's behavior. This is not, of course, where most of the action is to be found in speech perception. More salient is the way the perception of the linguistic message guides the listener's behavior. This is a very rich topic, but not one that I can cover here.

Possibly, the most straightforward activity for listeners just having extracted information about how a talker controlled his or her articulators (but not, in general, the most appropriate activity), is to control their own articulators in the same way—that is,

---

[4]Javkin (1976) has provided evidence for the opposite kind of error. In his research, listeners heard vowels as longer before voiced than voiceless consonants, perhaps because of the continuation of voicing during the consonant.

to imitate. Indeed, research suggests that listeners can shadow speech with very short latencies (Chistovich, Klaas & Kuzmin, 1962; Porter, 1977) and that their latencies are shorter to respond with the same syllable or one that shares gestures with it than with one that does not (Meyer & Gordon, 1984).

Although this has been interpreted as relevant to an evaluation of the motor theory of speech perception (Liberman, Cooper, Shankweiler & Studdert-Kennedy, 1967) it may also, or instead, reflect a more general disposition for listeners to mimic talkers (or perhaps to entrain to them). Research shows that individuals engaging in conversation move toward one another in speech rate (defined as the number of syllables per unit time excluding pauses; Webb, 1972) in loudness (Black, 1949) and in average duration of pauses (Jaffe, 1964), although the temporal parameters of speaking also show substantial stability among individual talkers across a variety of conversational settings (Jaffe & Feldstein, 1970). In addition, Condon & Ogston (1971; see also Condon, 1976, for a review), report that listeners (including infants aged 1–4 days; Condon & Sander, 1974) move in synchrony with a talker's speech rhythms.

Although it is possible that this disposition for "interactional synchrony" (Condon, 1976) has a function, for example, in signaling understanding, empathy, or interest on the listener's part (cf. Matarazzo, 1965), the observations that some of the visible synchronies have been observed when the conversational partners cannot see one another, and some have been observed in infants, may suggest a more primitive origin. Condon (1976) suggests that interactional synchrony is a form of entrainment.

The disposition to imitate among adults may be a carry-over from infancy, when presumably it does have an important function (Studdert-Kennedy, 1983). Infants must extract information about phonetically structured articulations from the acoustic speech signals of mature talkers in order to learn to regulate their own articulators to produce speech. Although it seems essential that infants do this, very little research does more than hint that infants have the capacity to imitate vocal productions.

Infants do recognize the correspondence between visible articulation of others and an acoustic speech signal. They will look preferentially to the one of two video displays on which a talker mouths a disyllable matching an accompanying acoustic signal (MacKain, Studdert-Kennedy, Spieker & Stern, 1983). Moreover, infants recognize the equivalence of their own facial gestures to those of someone else. That is, they imitate facial gestures, such as lip or tongue protrusion (Meltzoff & Moore, 1985) even though, as Meltzoff & Moore point out, such imitation is "intermodal", because the infants cannot see their own gestures. Together, these findings suggest that infants should be capable of vocal imitation.

However, relatively few studies have examined infants' imitation of adult vocalizations. Infants are responsive to mothers' vocalizations, and indeed, vocalize simultaneously with them to a greater-than-chance extent (Stern, Jaffe, Beebe & Bennett, 1975). There are a few positive reports of vocal imitation (e.g. Kessen, Levine & Wendrick, 1979; Kuhl & Meltzoff, 1982; Tuaycharoen, 1978; Uzgiris, 1973). However, few of them have been conducted with the controls now recognized as required to distinguish chance correspondences from true imitations.

Of course, imitative responses are not the only activities afforded by speech, even speech considered only as phonetically structured activity of the vocal tract. A very exciting area of research in linguistics is on natural variation in speaking (e.g. Labov, 1966/1982, 1972, 1980). The research examines talkers in something close to the natural environments in which talking generally takes place. It is exciting because it reveals a remarkable sensitivity and responsiveness of language users to linguistically, psychologically and socially relevant aspects of conversational settings. Most of these aspects must be quite outside of the language users' awareness much of the time; yet they guide the talker's speech in quite subtle but observable ways.

Labov and his colleagues find that an individual's speaking style varies with the conversational setting in response, among other things, to characteristics of the conversational partner, including, presumably, the partner's own speaking style. Accordingly, adjustments to speaking style are afforded by the speech of the conversational partner.

An example of research done on dialectal affordances of the speech of other social groups is provided by Labov's early study of the dialects of Martha's Vineyard (1963). Martha's Vineyard is a small island off the coast of New England that is part of the state of Massachusetts. Whereas residents were traditionally farmers and fishermen, in recent decades the island has become a popular summer resort. The addition of some 40 000 summer residents to the year-round population of 5000–6000 has, of course, had profound consequences for the island's economy.

Labov chose to study production of two diphthongs, [ai] and [au], both of which had lowered historically from the forms [əi] and [əu]. These historical changes were not concurrent; [au] had lowered well before the settlement of Martha's Vineyard by English speakers in 1642; [ai] lowered somewhat after its settlement.

Labov found a systematically increasing tendency to *centralize* the first vowel of the diphthongs—that is, to reverse the direction of sound change just described—in younger native residents when he compared speakers ranging in age from 30 years upwards. The tendency to centralize the vowels was strongest amongst people such as farmers, whose livelihoods had been most threatened by the summer residents. (The summer residents have driven up land prices as well as the costs of transporting supplies to the island and products to the mainland.) In addition, the tendency to centralize was correlated with the speaker's tendency to express resistance to the increasing encroachment of summer residents on the island. Among the youngest group studied, 15-year-olds, the tendency to centralize the vowels depended strongly on the individual's future plans. Those intending to stay on the island showed a markedly stronger tendency to centralize the diphthongs than those intending to leave the island to make a living on the mainland. Labov interpreted these trends as a disposition among many native islands to distinguish themselves as a group from the summer residents.

I find these data and others collected by Labov and his colleagues quite remarkable in the evidence they provide for listeners' responsiveness to phonetic variables they detect in conversation. In natural conversational settings, talkers use phonetic variation to psychological and social ends; and, necessarily given that, listeners are sensitive to those uses.

4.2. *What enables phonetically structured vocal-tract activity to do linguistic work and how is that work apprehended?*

Confronted with language perception and use, an event theory faces powerful challenges. Gibson's theory of perception (1966, 1979) depends on a necessary relation between structure in informational media and properties of events. The physical law relating vocal-tract activities to acoustic consequences may satisfy that requirement. But how is the relation between word and referent and, therefore, between acoustic signal and referent, to be handled? These relations are not universal; that is, different languages use different words to convey similar concepts. Accordingly, in one sense, they are not necessary and not, apparently, governed by physical law.

I have very little to offer concerning an event perspective on linguistic events (but see Verbrugge, 1985), and what I do have to say, I consider very tentative indeed. However, I would like to address two issues concerning the relation of speech to language. Stated as a question, the first issue is: What allows phonetically structured vocal-tract activity to serve as a meaningful message? The second asks: Can speech *qua* linguistic message be directly perceived?

As to the first question, Fodor (1974) observes that there are two types of answer that can be provided to questions of the form: "What makes X a Y?". He calls one type of answer the "causal story" and the other the "conceptual story". To use Fodor's example, in answer to the question: "What makes Wheaties the Breakfast of Champions?", one can invoke causal properties of the breakfast cereal, Wheaties, that turn non-champions who eat Wheaties into champions. Alternatively, one can make the observation that disproportionate numbers of champions eat Wheaties. As Fodor points out, these explanations are distinct and not necessarily competing.

In reference to the question, what makes phonetically structured vocal-tract activity phonological (that is, what makes it serve a linguistic function), one can refer to the private linguistic competences of speakers and hearers that allow them to control their vocal tracts so as to produce gestures having linguistic significance. Alternatively, one can refer to properties of the language user's "ecological niche" that support lingusitic communication. Vocal-tract activity can only constitute a linguistic message in a setting in which, historically, appropriately constrained vocal-tract activity has done linguistic work. A listener's ability to extract a linguistic message from vocal-tract activity may be given a "conceptual" (I would say "functional") account along lines such as the following: listeners apprehend the linguistic work that the phonetically structured vocal-tract activity is doing by virtue of their sensitivity to the historical and social context of constraint in which the activity is performed.

According to Fodor (p. 9):

> Psychologists are typically in the business of supplying theories about
> the events that causally mediate the production of behavior . . . and
> cognitive psychologists are typically in the business of supplying
> theories about the events that causally mediate intelligent behavior.

He is correct; yet there is a functional story to be told, and I think that it is an account that event theorists will want to develop.

As to the second question, whether a linguistic message can be said to be perceived in a theory of perception from a direct–realist perspective, (direct) perception depends on a necessary relation between structure in informational media and its distal source. But as previously noted, this does not appear to apply to the relation between sign and significance.

Gibson suggests that linguistic communications, and symbols generally, are perceived (rather than being apprehended by cognitive processes), but indirectly. His use of the qualifier "indirect" requires careful attention (1976/1982, p. 412):

> Now consider perception at second hand, or vicarious perception;
> perception mediated by communications and dependent on the
> "medium" of communication, like speech sound, painting, writing or
> sculpture. The perception is indirect since the information has been

24   *C. A. Fowler*

> presented by the speaker, painter, writer or sculptor, and has been
> *selected* by him from the unlimited realm of available information.
> This kind of apprehension is complicated by the fact that direct
> perception of sounds or surfaces occurs along with the indirect
> perception. The sign is often noticed along with what is signified.
> Nevertheless, however complicated, the outcome is that one man can
> metaphorically see through the eyes of another.

By indirect, then, Gibson does not mean requiring cognitive mediation, but rather, perceiving information about events that have been packaged in a tiered fashion, where the upper tiers are structured by another perceiver/actor.

What is the difference for the perception of events that have a level of indirect as well as of direct specification? I do not see any fundamental difference in the *manner* in which perception occurs, although *what* is perceived is different. (That is, when I look at a table, I see it; when I hear a linguistic communication about a table, I perceive selected *information about tables*, not tables themselves.)

When an event is perceived directly, it is perceived by extraction of information for the event from informational media. When a linguistic communication is indirectly perceived, information for the talker's vocal-tract activities is extracted from an acoustic signal. The vocal-tract activity (by hypothesis) *constitutes* phonetically structured words organized into grammatical sequences, and thereby indirectly specifies whatever the utterance is about.

It is worth emphasizing that the relation between an utterance (uttered in an appropriate setting) and what it signifies *is* necessary in an important sense. The necessity is not due to physical law directly, but to cultural constraints having evolved over generations of language use. These constraints are necessary in that anyone participating in the culture who communicates linguistically with members of the speech community must abide by them to provide information to listeners and must be sensitive to them to understand the speech of others.

Indeed, in view of this necessity, it seems possible that the distinction between direct and indirect perception could be dispensed with in this connection. Both the phonetically structured vocal-tract activity and the linguistic information (i.e. the information that the talker is discussing tables, for example) are directly perceived (by hypothesis) by the extraction of invariant information from the acoustic signal, although the origin of the information is, in a sense, different. That for phonetic structure is provided by coordinated relations among articulators; that for the linguistic message is provided by constraints on those relations reflecting the cultural context of constraint mentioned earlier. What is "indirect" is apprehension of the table itself—which is not directly experienced; rather, the talker's perspective on it is perceived. Therefore, it seems, nothing is indirectly *perceived*.

I have attempted to minimize the differences between direct and "indirect" perception. However, there is a difference in the reliability with which information is conveyed. It seems that this must have to do with another sort of mediation involved in linguistic communications. As already noted, in linguistic communications the information is packaged into its grammatically structured form by a *talker* and not by a lawful relation between an event and an informational medium. And as noted much earlier, talkers make choices concerning what the listener already knows and what he or she needs to be told explicitly. Talkers may guess wrongly. Alternatively, they may not know exactly what they are trying to say and therefore may not provide useful information. For their

Event approach to the study of speech perception   25

part, listeners, knowing that talkers are not entirely to be trusted to tell them what they need to know, may depend relatively more on extraperceptual guesses.

Preparation of this paper was supported by NICHD Grant HD 16591 to Haskins Laboratories. I thank Ignatius Mattingly for his comments on an earlier draft of the manuscript.

References

Beattie, G. (1983). *Talk: an analysis of speech and non-verbal behaviour in conversation*. Milton Keynes, England: Open University Press.

Black, J. W. (1949). *Loudness of speaking, I. The effect of heard stimuli on spoken responses*. Joint Project No 2 Contract N 7 Nmr-411 T. O. I., Project No NM 001 053 US Naval School of Aviation, Medicine and Research. Pensacola, Florida and Kenyon College, Gambier, Ohio (cited in Webb, 1972).

Blumstein, S., Isaacs, E. & Mertus, J. (1982). The role of the gross spectral shape as a perceptual cue to place of articulation in initial stop consonants, *Journal of the Acoustical Society of America*, **72**, 43–50.

Blumstein, S. & Stevens, K. (1979). Acoustic invariance in speech production: Evidence from measurement of the spectral characteristics of stop consonants, *Journal of the Acoustical Society of America*, **66**, 1001–1017.

Blumstein, S. & Stevens, K. (1981). Phonetic features and acoustic invariance in speech, *Cognition*, **10**, 25–32.

Browman, C. (1980). Perceptual processing: evidence from slips of the ear. In: V. Fromkin (ed.), *Errors in linguistic performance: Slips of the tongue, ear, pen, and hand*. New York: Academic Press.

Carney, P. & Moll, K. (1971). A cinefluorographic investigation of fricative-consonant vowel coarticulation, *Phonetica*, **23**, 193–201.

Chen, M. (1970). Vowel length variation as a function of the voicing of the consonant environment, *Phonetica*, **22**, 129–159.

Chistovich, L., Klaas, I. & Kuzmin, I. (1962). The process of speech sound discrimination, [translated from] *Voprosy Psikhologii*, **6**, 26–39.

Comrie, B. (1980). Phonology: a critical review. In: B. Butterworth (ed.), *Language production, I*. London: Academic Press.

Condon, W. (1976). An analysis of behavioral organization, *Sign Language Studies*, **13**, 285–318.

Condon, W. & Ogston, W. (1971). Speech and body motion synchrony of the speaker-hearer. In: D. Horton & J. Jenkins (eds.), *The perception of language*. Columbus, Ohio: Charles C. Merrill.

Condon, W. & Sander, W. (1974). Neonate movement is synchronous with adult speech: interactional participation and language acquisition, *Science*, **183**, 99–101.

Cooper, A., Whalen, D. & Fowler, C. A. (1984). Stress centers are not perceived categorically. Paper presented to the 108th meeting of the Acoustical Society of America, Minneapolis, Minnesota.

Cutting, J. E. & Pisoni, D. B. (1978). An information-processing approach to speech perception. In: J. F. Kavanagh & W. Strange (eds.), *Speech and language in the laboratory school, and clinic*. Cambridge, Mass.: MIT Press.

Donegan, P. & Stampe, D. (1979). The study of natural phonology. In: D. Dinnsen (ed.), *Current approaches to phonological theory*. Bloomington, Indiana: Indiana University Press.

Dorman, M., Studdert-Kennedy, M. & Raphael, L. (1977). Stop-consonant recognition: release bursts and formant transitions as functionally-equivalent context-dependent cues, *Perception and Psychophysics*, **22**, 109–122.

Elman, J. & McClelland, J. (1983). Speech perception as a cognitive process: The interactive activation model. ICS Report No 8302. San Diego: University of California, Institute of Cognitive Science.

Fant, G. (1960). *Acoustic theory of speech production*. The Hague: Mouton.

Fant, G. (1973). *Speech sounds and features*. Cambridge, Mass.: MIT Press.

Fant, G. & Lindblom, B. (1961). Studies of minimal speech and sound units, *Speech Transmission Laboratory: Quarterly Progress Report*, **2/1961**, 1–11.

Fitch, H., Halwes, T., Erickson, D. & Liberman, A. (1980). Perceptual equivalence of two acoustic cues for stop consonant manner, *Perception and Psychophysics*, **27**, 343–350.

Fodor, J. (1974). *The language of thought*. New York: Thomas Y. Crowell.

Fowler, C. A. (1979). "Perceptual centers" in speech production and perception, *Perception and Psychophysics*, **25**, 375–388.

Fowler, C. A. (1981). A relationship between coarticulation and compensatory shortening, *Phonetica*, **38**, 35–50.

Fowler, C. A. (1983). Converging sources of evidence for spoken and perceived rhythms of speech: cyclic production of vowels in sequences of monosyllabic stress feet, *Journal of Experimental Psychology: General*, **112**, 386–412.

Fowler, C. A. (1984). Segmentation of coarticulated speech in perception. *Perception and Psychophysics*, **36**, 359–368.

26   *C. A. Fowler*

Fowler, C. A. & Smith, M. R. (1986). Speech perception as "vector analysis": an approach to the problems of segmentation and invariance. In: J. Perkell & D. Klatt (eds.), *Invariance and variability of speech processes*. Hillsdale, N.J.: Lawrence Erlbaum Associates.

Fowler, C. A. & Tassinary, L. (1981). Natural measurement criteria for speech: the anisochrony illusion. In: J. Long & A. Baddeley (eds.), *Attention and performance IX*. Hillsdale, N.J.: Lawrence Erlbaum Associates.

Fujimura, O. (1962). Analysis of nasal consonants, *Journal of the Acoustical Society of America*, **34**, 1865–1875. Reprinted in I. Lehiste (ed.), *Readings in acoustic phonetics*. Cambridge, Mass.: MIT Press, 1967.

Garnes, S. & Bond, Z. (1980). A slip of the ear: A snip of the ear? A slip of the year? In: V. Fromkin (ed.), *Errors in linguistic performance: slips of the tongue, ear, pen, and hand*. New York: Academic Press.

Gibson, J. J. (1966). The problem of temporal order in stimulation and perception, *Journal of Psychology*, **62**, 141–129. Reprinted in E. Reed & R. Jones (eds.), *Reasons for realism*. Hillsdale, N.J.: Lawrence Erlbaum Associates, 1982.

Gibson, J. J. (1971). A preliminary description and classification of affordances. In: E. Reed & R. Jones (eds.), *Reasons for realism*. Hillsdale, N.J.: Lawrence Erlbaum Associates, 1982.

Gibson, J. J. (1966). *The senses considered as perceptual systems*. Boston, Mass.: Houghton-Mifflin.

Gibson, J. J. (1979). *The ecological approach to visual perception*. Boston, Mass.: Houghton-Mifflin.

Griffin, D. R. (1958). *Listening in the dark: the acoustic orientation of bats and men*. New Haven: Yale University Press.

Hammarberg, R. (1976). The metaphysics of coarticulation, *Journal of Phonetics*, **4**, 353–363.

Hammarberg, R. (1982). On redefining coarticulation, *Journal of Phonetics*, **10**, 123–137.

Harris, K. (1958). Cues for the discrimination of American English fricatives in spoken syllables, *Language and Speech*, **1**, 1–7.

Hockett, C. (1955). *Manual of phonology*. Publications in Anthropology and Linguistics, No 11. Bloomington, Indiana: Indiana University Press.

Hockett, C. (1960). The origin of speech, *Scientific American*, **203**, 89–96.

Hombert, J.-M. (1979). Consonant types, vowel quality and tone. In: V. Fromkin (ed.), *Tone: a linguistic survey*. New York: Academic Press.

Hornbostel, E. M. von (1927). The unity of the senses, *Psyche*, **7**, 83–89.

Jaffe, J. (1964). Computer analyses of verbal behavior in psychiatric interviews. In: D. Rioch (ed.), *Disorders of communication: Proceedings of the Association for Research in Nervous and Mental Diseases*. Vol. 42. Baltimore: Williams and Wilkins.

Jaffe, J. & Feldstein, S. (1970). *Rhythms of dialogue*. New York: Academic Press.

Javkin, H. (1976). The perceptual bases of vowel-duration differences associated with the voiced/voiceless distinction, *Reports of the Phonology Laboratory* (Berkeley), **1**, 78–89.

Jenkins, J. (1985). Acoustic information for objects, places and events. In: W. Warren & R. Shaw (eds.), *Persistence and change*. Hillsdale, N.J.: Lawrence Erlbaum Associates.

Johnston, T. & Pietrewicz, A. (eds.), *Issues in the ecological study of learning*. Hillsdale: N.J.: Lawrence Erlbaum Associates.

Kelso, J. A. S., Tuller, B., Vatikiotis-Bateson, E. & Fowler, C. A. (1984). Functionally specific articulatory cooperation following jaw perturbations during speech: evidence for coordinative structures, *Journal of Experimental Psychology: Human Perception and Performance*, **10**, 812–832.

Kenstowicz, M. & Kisseberth, C. (1979). *Generative phonology: Description and theory*. New York: Academic Press.

Kessen, W., Levine, J. & Wendrick, K. (1979). The imitation of pitch in infants. *Infant Behavior and Development*, **2**, 93–100.

Kewley-Port, D. (1983). Time-varying features as correlates of place of articulation in stop consonants, *Journal of the Acoustical Society of America*, **73**, 322–335.

Klatt, D. (1980). Speech perception: A model of acoustic–phonetic analysis and lexical access. In: R. Cole (ed.), *Perception and production of fluent speech*. Hillsdale, N.J.: Lawrence Erlbaum Associates.

Krakow, R., Beddor, P., Goldstein, L. & Fowler, C. A. (1985). Effects of contextual and noncontextual nasalization on perceived vowel height. Paper presented at the 109th Acoustical Society of America, Austin, Texas.

Kuhl, P. & Meltzoff, A. (1982). The bimodal perception of speech in infancy, *Science*, **218**, 1138–1141.

Labov, W. (1963). The social motivation of a sound change, *Word*, **19**, 273–309.

Labov, W. (1966). *The social stratification of English in New York City*. Washington, D.C.: Center for Applied Linguistics (third printing, 1982).

Labov, W. (1972). *Sociolinguistic patterns*. Philadelphia: University of Pennsylvania.

Labov, W. (ed.) (1980). *Locating language in time and space*. New York: Academic Press.

Labov, W. (1981). Resolving the neogrammarian controversy, *Language*, **57**, 267–308.

Lahiri, A., Gewirth, L. & Blumstein, S. (1984). A reconsideration of acoustic invariance for place of articulation in diffuse stop consonants: evidence from a cross-language study, *Journal of the Acoustical Society of America*, **76**, 391–404.

Event approach to the study of speech perception   27

Lehiste, I. (1972). The timing of utterances and linguistic boundaries, *Journal of the Acoustical Society of America*, **51**, 2018–2024.

Liberman, A. M., Cooper, F. S., Shankweiler, D. & Studdert-Kennedy, M. (1967). Perception of the speech code, *Psychological Review*, **74**, 431–461.

Liberman, A. M. & Mattingly, I. G. (1985). The motor theory of speech perception revised, *Cognition*, **21**, 1–36.

Lieberman, P. (1984). *The biology and evolution of language*. Cambridge, Mass.: Harvard University Press.

Lindblom, B. (1972). Phonetics and the description of language. *Seventh International Congress of Phonetic Sciences*. The Hague: Mouton.

Lindblom, B., MacNeilage, P. & Studdert-Kennedy, M. (1983). Self-organizing processes and the explanation of phonological universals. In: B. Butterworth, B. Comrie & D. Dahl (eds.), *Explanations of linguistic universals*. The Hague: Mouton.

Lindblom, B. & Rapp, K. (1973). Some temporal regularities of spoken Swedish, *Papers in Linguistics from the University of Stockholm*, **21**, 1–59.

Lisker, L. (1978). *Rapid* vs *Rabid*: A catalogue of acoustic features that may cue the distinction, *Haskins Laboratory Status Reports on Speech Research*, **SR-54**, 127–132.

Locke, J. (1983). *Phonological acquisition and change*. New York: Academic Press.

MacKain, K., Studdert-Kennedy, M., Spieker, S. & Stern, D. (1983). Infant intermodal speech perception is a left-hemisphere function, *Science*, **219**, 1347–1349.

MacNeilage, P. & Ladefoged, P. (1976). The production of speech and language. In: E. C. Carterette & M. P. Friedman (eds.), *Handbook of perception: Language and speech*. New York: Academic Press.

Marcus, S. (1981). Acoustic determinants of perceptual center (P-center) location, *Perception and Psychophysics*, **30**, 247–256.

Marslen-Wilson, W. & Welsh, A. (1978). Processing interactions and lexical access during word recognition in continuous speech, *Cognitive Psychology*, **10**, 29–63.

Matarazzo, J. D. (1965). The interview. In: B. B. Wolman (ed.), *Handbook of clinical psychology*. New York: McGraw-Hill.

Mattingly, I., Liberman, A., Syrdal, A. & Halwes, T. (1971). Discrimination in speech and nonspeech modes, *Cognitive Psychology*, **2**, 131–159.

McGurk, H. & MacDonald, J. (1976). Hearing lips and seeing voices, *Nature*, **264**, 746–748.

McNeill, D. (1985). So you think gestures are nonverbal? *Psychological Review*, **92**, 350–371.

Meltzoff, A. & Moore, M. K. (1985). Cognitive foundations and social functions of imitation. In: J. Mehler and R. Fox (eds), *Neonate cognition*. Hillsdale, N.J.: Lawrence Erlbaum Associates.

Meyer, D. & Gordon, P. (1984). Perceptual-motor processing of phonetic features in speech, *Journal of Experimental Psychology: Human Perception and Performance*, **10**, 153–171.

Morton, J., Marcus, S. & Frankish, C. (1976). Perceptual centers (P-centers), *Psychological Review*, **93**, 457–465.

Neisser, U. (1967). *Cognitive psychology*. Englewood Cliffs, N.J.: Prentice-Hall.

Nooteboom, S. G. & Cohen, A. (1975). Anticipation in speech production and its implications for perception. In: A. Cohen & S. G. Nooteboom (eds.), *Structure and process in speech perception*. New York: Springer-Verlag.

Ohala, J. (1981). The listener as a source of sound change. In: C. S. Masek, R. A. Hendrick & M. F. Miller (eds.), *Papers from the parasession on language and behavior*. Chicago: Chicago Linguistics Society.

Öhman, S. (1966). Coarticulation in VCV utterances: spectrographic measurement, *Journal of the Acoustical Society of America*, **39**, 151–168.

Peterson, G. & Lehiste, I. (1960). Duration of syllabic nuclei in English, *Journal of the Acoustical Society of America*, **32**, 693–703.

Porter, R. (1977). Speech production measures of speech perception: systematic replications and extensions. Paper presented to the 93rd meeting of the Acoustical Society of America, Pennsylvania State University.

Raphael, L. (1972). Preceding vowel duration as a cue to the perception of voicing characteristic of word-final consonants in American English, *Journal of the Acoustical Society of America*, **51**, 1296–1303.

Rapp, K. (1971). A study of syllable timing, *Papers in Linguistics from the University of Stockholm*, **19**, 14–19.

Repp, B. (1981). On levels of description in speech research, *Journal of the Acoustical Society of America*, **69**, 1462–1464.

Rubin, P., Baer, T. & Mermelstein, P. (1979). An articulatory synthesizer for perceptual research, *Haskins Laboratories Status Reports on Speech Research*, **SR-57**, 1–15.

Ryle, G. (1949). *The concept of mind*. New York: Barnes and Noble.

Saltzman, E. (in press). Task dynamic coordination of the articulators: A preliminary model, *Experimental Brain Research Supplementum*.

Saltzman, E. & Kelso, J. A. S. (1983). Skilled actions: A task dynamic approach, *Haskins Laboratories Status Reports on Speech Research*, **SR-76**, 3–58.

Samuel, A. (1981). Phonemic restoration: Insights from a new methodology, *Journal of Experimental Psychology: General*, **110**, 474–494.

28   *C. A. Fowler*

Shattuck-Hufnagel, S. (1983). Sublexical units and suprasegmental structure in speech production planning. In: P. MacNeilage (ed.), *The production of speech*. New York: Springer-Verlag.

Shaw, R. & Bransford, J. (1977). Introduction: psychological approaches to the problem of knowledge. In: R. Shaw & J. Bransford (eds.), *Perceiving, acting and knowing: toward an ecological psychology*. Hillsdale, N.J.: Lawrence Erlbaum Associates.

Shaw, R., Turvey, M. T. & Mace, W. (1982). Ecological psychology: The consequences of a commitment to realism. In: W. Weimer (ed.), *Cognition and the symbolic processes, 2*. Hillsdale, N.J.: Lawrence Erlbaum Associates.

Stern, D., Jaffe, J., Beebe, B. & Bennett, S. (1975). Vocalizing in unison and in alternation: two modes of communication within the mother–infant dyad. In: D. Aaronson and R. Reiber (eds.), *Developmental psychology and communication disorders. (Annals of the New York Academy of Sciences, 263, 89–100.)*

Stevens, K. & Blumstein, S. (1978). Invariant cues for place of articulation in stop consonants, *Journal of the Acoustical Society of America, 64*, 1358–1368.

Stevens, K. & Blumstein, S. (1981). The search for invariant correlates of phonetic features. In: P. Eimas & J. Miller (eds.), *Perspectives on the study of speech*. Hillsdale, N.J.: Lawrence Erlbaum Associates.

Studdert-Kennedy, M. (1983). On learning to speak, *Human Neurobiology, 2*, 191–195.

Sussman, H., MacNeilage, P. & Hanson, R. (1973). Labial and mandibular dynamics during the production of bilabial consonants: Preliminary observations, *Journal of Speech and Hearing Research, 16*, 397–420.

Tuaycharoen, P. (1978). The babbling of a Thai baby: echoes and responses to the sounds made by adults. In: N. Waterson & C. Snow (eds.), *The development of communication*. Chichester: John Wiley.

Tuller, B. & Fowler, C. A. (1980). Some articulatory correlates of perceptual isochrony, *Perception and Psychophysics, 27*, 277–283.

Uzgiris, I. (1973). Patterns of vocal and gestural imitation in infants. In: L. J. Stone, H. T. Smith & L. B. Murphy (eds.), *The competent infant*. New York: Basic Books.

Verbrugge, R. (1985). Language and event perception: Steps toward a synthesis. In: W. Warren & R. Shaw (eds.), *Persistence and change*. Hillsdale, N.J.: Lawrence Erlbaum Associates.

Walley, A. & Carrell, T. (1983). Onset spectra and formant transitions in the adult's and child's perception of place of articulation in stop consonants, *Journal of the Acoustical Society of America, 73*, 1011–1022.

Warren, R. (1970). Perceptual restoration of missing speech sounds. *Science, 167*, 392–393.

Warren, W. & Shaw, R. (1985). Events and encounters as units of analysis for ecological psychology. In: W. Warren & R. Shaw (eds.), *Persistence and change*. Hillsdale, N.J.: Lawrence Erlbaum Associates.

Webb, J. (1972). Interview synchrony: an investigation of two speech rate measures. In: A. W. Siegman & B. Pope (eds.), *Studies in dyadic communication*. New York: Pergamon Press.

Whalen, D. (1981). Effects of vocal formant transitions and vowel quality on the English [s]–[š] boundary, *Journal of the Acoustical Society of America, 69*, 275–282.

Whalen, D. (1984). Subcategorical mismatches slow phonetic judgments, *Perception and Psychophysics, 35*, 49–64.

Wright, J. (1980). The behavior of nasalized vowels in the perceptual vowel space, *Report of the Phonology Laboratory* (Berkeley), *5*, 127–163.

Journal of Phonetics (1979) **7**, 279–312

Speech perception: a model of acoustic–phonetic analysis and lexical access

Dennis H. Klatt

Room 36-523, Massachusetts Institute of Technology, Cambridge, MA 02139, U.S.A.

Received 1 *November* 1978

Abstract: Lexical hypothesis formation from acoustic input is an important component of the normal speech perception process. Any model of bottom-up lexical access must address the well-known problems of (1) acoustic-phonetic non-invariance, (2) phonetic segmentation, (3) time normalization, (4) talker normalization, (5) specification of lexical representations for optimal search, (6) phonological recoding of word sequences in sentences, (7) ambiguity caused by errors in the preliminary phonetic representation, and (8) interpretation of prosodic cues to lexical identity. Previous models of speech perception, such as the motor theory, analysis by synthesis, and the Logogen, have not detailed solutions to all eight problems. The LAFS (*Lexical Access From Spectra*) model is proposed here as a response to those issues; it combines expected phonological and acoustic-phonetic properties of English word sequences into a simple spectral-sequence decoding network structure. Phonetic segments and phonological rules play an important role in network compilation, but not in the direct analysis of the speech waveform during lexical search. There is no feature-detector stage in LAFS either. If viewed as a perceptual model, LAFS constitutes a simple "null hypothesis" against which to compare and refine alternative theories of acoustic analysis and lexical search.

Introduction

Recent spectrogram-reading experiments (Cole, Rudnicky, Reddy & Zue, 1978) have shown that the acoustic signal is rich in phonetic information. Without knowing anything about the words that are present, an expert spectrogram reader can produce a broad phonetic transcription that agrees with a panel of phoneticians from 80 to 90% of the time, depending on the scoring method used. Furthermore, perceptual experiments by Liberman & Nakatani (pers. comm.) indicate that listeners can transcribe nonsense names embedded in sentences (and obeying the phonological constraints of English) with better than 90% phonemic accuracy.

These experiments call into question the view that the speech signal is so impoverished of phonetic information that speech perception usually proceeds "top-down" with syntactic and semantic knowledge sources hypothesizing lexical candidates to be compared with aspects of the acoustic signal for verification. Of course there are listening conditions where noise or distortions force the listener to rely more heavily on expectations and higher-level knowledge to hypothesize words, but I believe that a bottom-up method of lexical access is an essential part of the normal speech decoding process. This paper

0095–4470/79/030279+34 $02.00/0

will be concerned with the process of lexical hypothesis formation from acoustic data. Little will be said about how such a bottom-up component of the speech understanding process interfaces with other components of a complete model of sentence perception.

There have been several recent efforts to build computer-based speech understanding systems that accept spoken input sentences within some limited domain, and respond with the correct answer better than 95% of the time (see Klatt, 1977 for a review). Of particular interest are the HARPY system (Lowerre & Reddy, 1978), which represents a large but finite set of sentences by a network of expected spectra, and the HWIM system (Klovstad, 1978; Wolf & Woods, 1978), which takes into account the phonological recoding of words and word sequences in normally spoken sentences. Examination of these systems has changed my views about how speech is normally perceived. Perhaps it is not wise to draw conclusions about the functioning of the human brain from analogies to computer algorithms, but the theoretical advantages of combining some of these strategies into a perceptual model are compelling.

A typical three-step machine method of lexical access is shown in Fig. 1(a). Parameters are extracted from the speech waveform, a phonetic transcription is derived, and then lexical hypotheses are proposed. Parameters might include formant frequencies (Zue & Schwartz, 1978), articulatory configurations (Wakita & Kasuya, 1977) or spectra (Lowerre & Reddy, 1978). The phonetic representation might be a distinctive feature matrix (Medress, 1969) or a lattice of segmental alternatives (Wolf & Woods, 1978). Lexical search might proceed in an analysis-by-synthesis mode at the syllable level (Weeks, 1974) or by precompiling phonological knowledge into a network of expected phonetic sequences for words, using scoring penalties for incorrect, missing, or extra segments in the input (Klovstad, 1978). The relative advantages among these choices are discussed in Klatt (1978a).

This chapter presents an alternative method of lexical access from acoustic input. In the next section, eight problems associated with word identification in running speech are

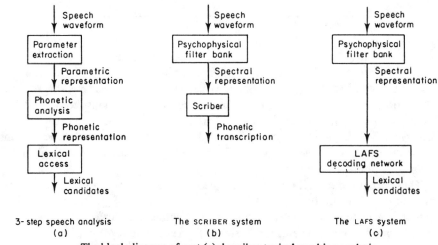

| 3- step speech analysis | The SCRIBER system | The LAFS system |
| (a) | (b) | (c) |

Figure 1   The block diagram of part (a) describes typical machine analysis procedures for bottom-up lexical access. Parts (b) and (c) outline the structure of two models of the early stages of speech perception to be described in the Sections "SCRIBER: a proposed solution to automatic phonetic analysis" and "LAFS: a proposed solution to the problem of lexical access".

identified. In later sections, two new computer systems, SCRIBER and LAFS, are proposed as potential engineering solutions to these problems. The LAFS system is then modified to form the perceptual model described in the section entitled "Implication for models of speech perception".

The SCRIBER phonetic transcription system described in detail later and shown here in Fig. 1(b) is proposed as an alternative to the more traditional methods of phonetic analysis. Knowledge of auditory psychophysics (such as critical bands, loudness, forward and backward masking, etc.) is used to derive an appropriate spectral representation for speech. Phonetic decoding rules then take the form of a network of expected sequences of static spectra for each possible transition between phonetic segments.

The LAFS system shown in Fig. 1(c) is proposed as a method for generating lexical hypotheses directly from a spectral representation of speech without first recognizing phonetic segments. Acoustic-phonetic knowledge and word-boundary phonology are precompiled into a decoding network of expected spectral sequences for all possible word sequences from the lexicon. This system avoids making possibly errorful early phonetic decisions and thus avoids the problems inherent in using an errorful phonetic transcription to search the lexicon.

The section entitled "Implications for models of speech perception" is concerned with modeling how humans generate lexical hypotheses from acoustic information. A new perceptual model of bottom-up lexical access is described that incorporates both SCRIBER and LAFS as components. The model departs from most current views of how speech is perceived in that phonetic segments and phonological rules play a role only in LAFS network compilation, and not in the direct analysis of the speech waveform during lexical search.

In the final section, the perceptual model proposed in the section entitled "Implications for models of speech perception" is compared with other models. One of these models, analysis by synthesis at the lexical level, is described in some detail in order to establish the relative advantages of precompilation of acoustic-phonetic and phonological relations to active synthesis of the same knowledge.

The problem

Before describing SCRIBER and LAFS, eight problem areas are identified that have plagued designers of speech recognition and speech understanding systems for decades. All have to do with the identification of words in spoken sentences, given some representation of the input acoustic waveform. The problems listed in Table I are endemic to speech com-

Table I   Eight problem areas that must be dealt with by any model of bottom-up lexical access

1. Acoustic-phonetic non-invariance.
2. Segmentation of the signal into phonetic units.
3. Time normalization.
4. Talker normalization.
5. Lexical representations for optimal search.
6. Phonological recoding of words in sentences.
7. Dealing with errors in the initial phonetic representation during lexical matching.
9. Interpretation of prosodic cues to lexical items and sentence structure.

munication; they must be overcome by any speech processing system or model of human speech perception.

Acoustic-phonetic non-invariance

The acoustic manifestations of a phonetic segment are known to vary in different phonetic environments (Liberman, Cooper, Shankweiler & Studdert-Kennedy, 1967; Klatt, 1978*b*) While many acoustic cues are largely context independent and thus form invariant properties of a given phonetic segment (Blumstein, Stevens & Nigro, 1977; Cole & Scott, 1974; Fant, 1974; Stevens, 1975) there are also context-dependent cues to the same phonetic distinctions. Listeners seem to be able to process these latter cues when the invariant cues are artificially removed (Delattre, Liberman & Cooper, 1955), and are probably able to make use of context-dependent information under normal listening conditions as well. What decoding strategy permits the listener to interpret cues that depend on phonetic context (so as to make optimum use of all the information contained in the speech waveform), especially when phonetic environment itself is not known with any certainty? More importantly, what are the perceptually relevant acoustic cues to each phonetic contrast, and how are cues combined?

Segmentation into phonetic units

Is segmentation an independent process, preceding phonetic labeling, or is it simply an automatic consequence of the phonetic decision process itself? If the speech waveform could first be segmented reliably into chunks corresponding to phonetic segments, the job of identifying each segment would be much simplified. Unfortunately, segmentation criteria depend on detailed knowledge of articulatory-acoustic relations, the permitted phonetic categories of the language in question, and other phonological constraints (see Klatt, 1978*a*; Cole *et al.*, 1978 for examples). Ambiguities in segment boundary locations are produced when the various articulators move asynchronously, as is often the case. A particular difficulty with feature-detector models of phonetic perception, such as the model described by Pisoni & Sawusch (1975) is the problem of interpreting detector outputs in order to align the columns of the derived feature matrix and see how many segments are present.

No matter how segmentation is accomplished, it appears that errors are inevitable. When a system commits itself to an error in an early stage of the analysis, such as a segmentation error, it is difficult for other components to recover and find the correct analysis. If a way could be found to defer or avoid segmentation decisions, overall system performance might improve.

Time normalization

Segmental durations are influenced by many factors, including speaking rate, locations of syntactic boundaries, syllable stress, and features of adjacent segments (Klatt, 1976*b*; 1979; Lehiste, 1970). A segment can vary in duration by a factor of two or three depending on its environment in the utterance. This kind of temporal variation clearly rules out the use of spectral prototypes of fixed duration in phonetic recognition. Some sort of time warping, time normalization, or method of ignoring the time dimension must be devised.

In addition, there are cases where the duration of an acoustic event can play a decisive role in a phonetic contrast of English (e.g. /ɛ/–/æ/ or /s/–/z/), but the durational dividing line between the two phonetic categories is sensitive to the factors listed above. Thus there are really two parts to the time-normalization problem: (1) how to ignore irrelevant variations in segmental durations, and (2) how to incorporate durational information in selected segmental decision strategies when durational perturbations due to syntax, semantics, and stress are not known at this level. A phonetic transcription system can be designed to solve the first half of the time-normalization problem, but can never be entirely successful at the interpretation of durational cues to segmental contrasts. We are faced with the classical chicken-or-egg problem; phonetic decisions depend in part on lexical and syntactic factors that cannot be resolved until the phonetic decisions have already been made. This appears to be another example where the principle of delayed commitment is applicable: if possible, one should not make phonetic decisions prior to lexical hypothesis formation. The decoding of durational cues to syntactic structure and semantic emphasis is discussed more fully below under problem eight—interpretation of prosodic cues.

Talker normalization

Talkers differ in the length and general shape of their vocal tracts, in the articulatory-acoustic targets they use for each phonetic segment type, in their coarticulatory strategies as a function of stress and speaking rate, and in the dialect they employ (Stevens, 1972c). In addition, speech is heard in many different kinds of noise, reverberation conditions, and telephone channels. The variability created by these various factors does not seem to cause great difficulties for the listener, but little is known about the perceptual strategies used to normalize for different talkers and listening environments.

Lexical representations for optimal search

It is often tacitly assumed that the lexical representations used for matching during speech perception come from the same stored lexicon that is used for speech production (Liberman & Studdert-Kennedy, 1978), and that this single lexicon contains fairly abstract forms for morphemes (forms of the kind discussed by Chomsky & Halle, 1968). However, it seems clear that speech analysis routines cannot be expected to derive these abstract phonemic forms using bottom-up analysis (reasons are suggested by the examples of Table II below). The actual lexical representations used during matching are probably more nearly phonetic or acoustic in nature. These forms are either derived on the fly by generative rules, or (as is more likely given the computational efficiency) precompiled into some optimal form for rapid lexical search. The precise nature of the lexical representations used in bottom-up speech analysis is not known.

Phonological recoding

The expected phonetic realization of a word depends on the sentence context in which it appears (Oshika, Zue, Weeks, Neu & Aurbach, 1975). Consider for example the phonetic string observed for the spoken utterance "Would you hit it to Tom?" shown in Table II. No word boundaries are indicated in the phonetic transcription because acoustic cues to word boundary locations are rarely present within phrases (although the utilization of separate prevocalic and postvocalic allophones of liquids and voiceless plosives helps to constrain the possible locations of some word boundaries). Each of the simplifications listed in Table II can be described by general phonological rules. During speech production, such rules are assumed to operate on an underlying abstract phonemic representation for each word or morpheme. For example, an (optional) word-boundary phonological rule $/d \neq y/ \rightarrow [j]$ transforms the word-final phoneme /d/ and the word-initial /y/ into the phonetic segment [j] in "would you".

284   *Dennis H. Klatt*

Table II   Examples of word-boundary phonology

"Would you hit it to Tom"

[W ʊ ɟ ə h I ʃ I t ə̥ t ɑ m]

1. Palatalization of /d/ before /y/.
2. Reduction of unstressed /u/ to schwa in "you".
3. Flapping of intervocalic [t] in "hit it"
4. Reduction to schwa and devoicing of /u/ in "to".
5. Reduction of geminate [t] in "it to".

In most models of lexical access, such modifications must be viewed as a kind of noise that makes it more difficult to hypothesize lexical candidates given an input phonetic transcription. To see that this must be the case, note that (a) pronunciation variants cannot be stored in the dictionary, since one doesn't want to accept [jə] for "you" in the word sequence "are you", and (b) each phonological rule example of Table II results in irreversible ambiguity—the [j] observed in the sample phonetic transcription of Table II could be the first or last segment of a word like "judge", or it could be the surface manifestation of an underlying /d/≠/y/. The number of phonological phenomena is quite large and their effects on unstressed syllables can be dramatic, as suggested by the examples in Table II. Phonological recoding, both within words and across word boundaries, must be accounted for in a perceptual strategy. The significant amount of ambiguity introduced by cross-word-boundary phonological rules seems to support a "top-down" analysis-by-synthesis model of lexical access unless knowledge of the effects of these rules can be precompiled into an appropriate "bottom-up" decoding structure.

Dealing with phonetic errors

Even an ideal phonetic transcription component will make errors in the presence of environmental noises, talker variability, and other factors. Thus the lexical matching component must be able to find the (hopefully correct) best-scoring word even when no words match the input perfectly. The derivation of scoring algorithms for segmental substitution, omission, and insertion errors is difficult because some phonetic confusions are likely only in particular phonetic and stress environments. Very little is known about perceptually motivated scoring algorithms and decision strategies appropriate for lexical search.

Interpretation of prosodic cues

Prosodic cues (fundamental frequency contour, pattern of segmental durations, and intensity contour) are used by the talker to distinguish between stressed and unstressed syllables, to delimit syntactic units, to indicate contrastive stress or emphasis, and to signal psychological state or attitude toward the utterance (Klatt, 1976*b*; Lea, 1973; Lehiste, 1970; Lieberman, 1967). For purposes of lexical access, cues to the stress pattern can be quite useful. Many lexical alternatives can be ruled out if they do not have the right pattern of stressed, unstressed and reduced syllables.

Unfortunately, perturbations to prosodic contours that depend on syntactic, semantic, and psychological variables confound the situation and make interpretation of the stress pattern difficult. In addition, interpretation of syllable stress from prosodic variables is complicated by segmental factors. Some phonetic segments are inherently more intense, or they are of greater duration, or they perturb the fundamental frequency contour. The listener appears to make stress judgments that are relative to these intrinsic properties of segments. As noted earlier, segmental decisions such as /ɛ/–/æ/ depend on duration cues that can only be interpreted with certainty after the stress pattern is known; it seems that segmental judgments and stress judgments must be computed simultaneously and interactively.

Of the eight problems outlined above and in Table I, the first four are addressed by the SCRIBER phonetic transcription system. The second computer system to be described, the LAFS lexical access algorithm not only takes advantage of the solutions embodied in SCRIBER, but also adds strategies that effectively deal with the final four problems. Sections describing the computational algorithms of SCRIBER and LAFS are followed by a discussion of the relations between these components and models of speech perception.

SCRIBER: a proposed solution to automatic phonetic analysis

This section is concerned with the specification of a new computer algorithm for generating a phonetic transcription of the acoustic waveform corresponding to an unknown English sentence. The system is called SCRIBER, and is presently under development in the Speech Communication Laboratory at M.I.T. This preliminary report is concerned only with the design philosophy of the system since there are no results to report as yet.

A tentative set of about 55 output phonetic categories has been selected. The inventory of phonetic segment types is large enough to preserve distinctions useful in lexical decoding (e.g. postvocalic allophones of the liquids, unstressed and unreleased allophones of the plosives, etc.), but it is by no means intended to represent a narrow phonetic transcription.

Representation of acoustic-phonetic knowledge

As an engineering approximation, it is assumed that transitions between phonetic segments can be represented succinctly and accurately by sequences of a few static spectra. For example, Fig. 2 illustrates a sequence of four spectra used to characterize the transition between [t] and [a] in the phrase "the top of the hill". Such a transition from the middle of one phone to the midpoint of the next is called a diphone. It has been argued that the coarticulatory influences of one phone on its neighbors do not usually extend much further than half-way into the adjacent phones (Peterson, Wang & Sivertsen, 1958; Gay, 1977). To the extent that this approximation is true (see Lehiste & Shockey, 1972 for supporting perceptual evidence), diphone concatenation captures much of the context-dependent acoustic encoding of phonetic segments.

There exist a number of special cases that require attention in a diphone system. For example, a vowel followed by a nasal can be nasalized to a variable degree. The SCRIBER system is designed to produce, as output, the intended non-nasalized vowel. The technique employed is to define two (or more if necessary) alternative spectral sequences that describe the same diphone—one with a nasalized vowel, and one without. Similar solutions are required to decode other optional coarticulatory phenomena and to deal with certain unstressed allophones.

The choice of the diphone as the unit used to relate acoustic and phonetic levels is not central to any of the models to be described. A diphone dictionary is a convenient tabular way of cataloging acoustic-phonetic relations, but the same relations could, in principle, be described by rules (if the appropriate rules were known) or in terms of a dictionary describing the spectral manifestations of larger units such as triphones (Wickelgren, 1969), demisyllables (Fujimura & Lovins, 1978), or syllables (Studdert-Kennedy, 1976).

286   *Dennis H. Klatt*

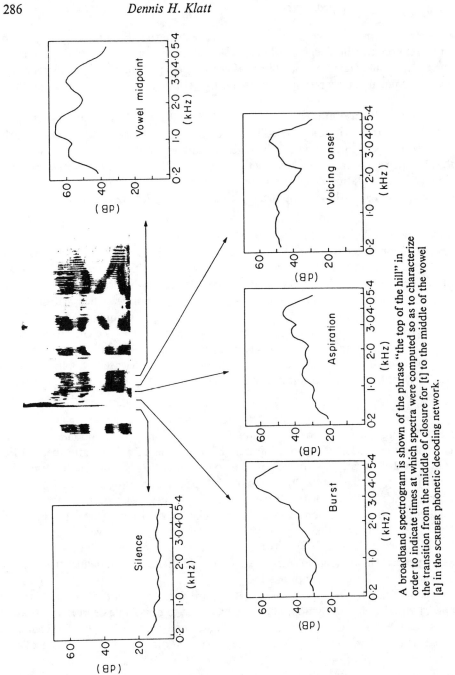

A broadband spectrogram is shown of the phrase "the top of the hill" in order to indicate times at which spectra were computed so as to characterize the transition from the middle of closure for [t] to the middle of the vowel [a] in the SCRIBER phonetic decoding network.

Figure 2.

The spectral representation that has been chosen is based on the psychophysical considerations given in Table III (Klatt, 1978*a*). A short-term spectrum is computed every 10 ms using a set of 30 overlapping critical-band filters. Several examples of these spectra are shown in Fig. 2. It is up to the experimenter to select sufficient sample spectra to characterize each possible phonetic transition of English. There are 55 phonetic segment types in the inventory of SCRIBER, but many of the 55-by-55 possible acoustic transitions do not occur. Only about 2000 *diphones* are phonologically permissible in English. Each of these diphones is thus characterized by a sequence of three or four spectral templates, as in Fig. 2.

Table III   Psychophysical consideration in the design of a spectral representation for speech processing

1. Include frequency components from at least 270 to 5600 Hz since this is the minimum passband for which there is no measurable loss in intelligibility when compared with systems containing wider bandwidths (French & Steinberg, 1947).
2. Include a dynamic range of at least 50 dB so as to adequately represent spectra of both the intense and weak speech sounds.
3. Provide a temporal resolution of about 10 ms since this is the best current guess as to the shortest spectral window employed by the auditory system, and since otherwise certain rapid formant transitions and brief plosive bursts might be missed.
4. Take into account the observation that our ears cannot resolve individual harmonics of a voiced sound if the harmonics are spaced within a critical bandwidth of about a quarter of an octave (Houtgast, 1974; Plomp & Mimpen, 1969; Sharf, 1970).
5. Take account of the fact that the contribution to intelligibility from different portions of the spectrum is not uniform (French & Steinberg, 1947). The relative importance to speech intelligibility of different frequency components is in good agreement with a theory stating that each critical bandwidth contributes about equally to intelligibility, at least over the range from 270 to 5600 Hz.
6. Design the slopes of the critical band filters so as to account for the spread of masking (i.e. low frequencies mask weak higher-frequency components better than vice-versa, so the filters have more gradual low-frequency skirts).
7. Express the output of each filter in dB (because decibels are an approximately equal-interval scale for loudness), and quantize filter outputs to about 1 dB (because the just-noticeable difference for changes to formant amplitudes change is 1 dB or more, depending on the circumstances (Flanagan, 1957)).
8. Process only the *magnitude* of the spectrum because the phase spectrum is too unpredictable to be used in phonetic decoding.
9. Use a number of overlapping critical-bandwidth filters sufficient to discriminate spectral changes caused by formant frequency changes of about 3 to 5 % since this is the just-noticeable difference for a formant frequency shift (Flanagan, 1957).
10. Employ a pre-emphasis filter based on a pure tone threshold curve which indicates that there is an effective emphasis of frequencies in the 2 to 3 kHz range. Use equal-loudness contours to compute the growth in loudness with increases in signal intensity (Zwicker, Terhardt & Paulus, 1979).

288   *Dennis H. Klatt*

There can be template sharing for portions of diphones that are acoustically similar. For example, Fig. 3 indicates expected spectral sequences for the prestressed aspirated consonant [t] followed by any stressed vowel of English. The decoding structure summarizes the obvious fact that the closure (silence) spectrum for [t] is the same before any vowel, and the observation that onset spectra for [t] are virtually identical before all front vowels, identical before all back unrounded vowels, and identical before all rounded vowels (Klatt, 1978*b*; Zue, 1976). As indicated in the figure, spectral characteristics observed during aspiration are dependent on both [t] and the vowel, since formant onset values depend on the vowel (Klatt, 1978*b*). In general, a new spectral template is defined for each distinctive spectrum that is observed in a phonetic transition. If the transition is

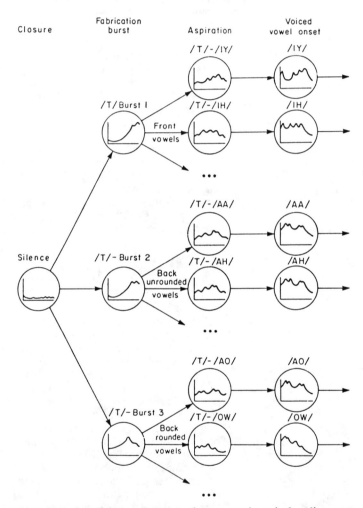

Figure 3.   A small portion of the SCRIBER spectral sequence phonetic decoding network is shown to illustrate the defining characteristics of prestressed prevocalic [t]. Each state of the network (circle) is characterized by a spectral template (dB versus frequency, as shown inside the circle). Not shown are durational constraints in the form of a feedback path to each state indicating the expected number of input 10-ms spectra that can be associated with each state during recognition.

rapid, templates may be defined as often as every 10 or 20 ms, while for gradual spectral changes, few templates are defined per unit time.

A complete spectral sequence phonetic decoding network is compiled automatically from transition definitions of the type shown in Fig. 2. The network is highly interconnected since all possible phonetic transitions must be represented by spectral sequences. However, there exists a relatively simple recognition strategy for utilizing this compact representation of acoustic-phonetic knowledge.

Recognition strategy

Once a network has been created, the input waveform is analyzed by computing a spectrum every 10 ms (using overlapping 25·6 ms chunks of windowed waveform). The recognition strategy consists of comparing this input spectral sequence with spectral templates of the network. The idea is to find the path through the network that best represents the observed input spectra. This path defines the optimal phonetic transcription.

A Euclidean distance metric involving differences in dB in selected frequency bands will be used to compute matching scores for each input spectrum with the spectral templates, in a manner very similar to the strategy employed in the HARPY sentence recognition system (Lowerre & Reddy, 1978). The metric has some perceptual validity for static spectral comparisons (Lindblom, 1978), but it will no doubt have to be modified to take into account changes in average speech spectrum and noise background associated with a new speaker or a new recording environment (Klatt, 1976a). Modifications may also be needed for comparison of template sequences so as to emphasize dynamic over static properties of the speech signal. For example, a long vowel probably should not contribute much more to dynamic distance than a brief plosive burst.

Input spectra are processed one at a time and used to try to extend the most promising "phonetic hypotheses". A hypothesis consists of (a) a pointer to a state in the decoding network, (b) the duration of the input that has been associated with that state, (c) a cumulative spectral matching score, and (d) the last two phones of the implied phonetic transcription. An hypothesis is extended by assigning the new 10-ms input spectrum to the current state in the network or to one of the network states that can be reached from this state. An hypothesis will generate several daughter hypotheses if alternative paths from the current network state score reasonably well.

When the best-scoring hypothesis in the (ordered) list of all current alternatives reaches a place in the network calling for the output of a phonetic symbol, it is assumed that the earlier of the two previous phonetic symbols that have been saved with the hypotheses is correct. The phonetic symbol is outputed and all hypotheses not possessing this symbol are pruned from further consideration. A large number of best-scoring hypotheses are pursued in parallel during a HARPY-like "beam search" of all alternative paths having scores that are within some fixed distance of the best-scoring path to date (Lowerre & Reddy, 1978). Given this strategy, SCRIBER evaluates nearly all reasonable phonetic transcriptions of the input and selects the optimum transcription.

Phonetic non-invariance

How does SCRIBER deal with the first four problems listed in Table I? As a solution to the acoustic-phonetic non-invariance problem, SCRIBER incorporates diphone definitions. Any acoustic cue that is dependent on immediate phonetic context can be represented in a SCRIBER decoding network. Thus, for example, the burst spectrum for [t] is expected to have its most prominent spectral peak at lower frequencies before rounded vowels than

290   *Dennis H. Klatt*

before unrounded vowels (as shown in Fig. 3), and systematic differences in formant motions following [t] release into various vowels are described by individual aspiration templates for each [t]-vowel diphone. To the extent that acoustic invariance is present, states in the network are combined (for example, the [t] burst is represented by the same template before all front vowels in Fig. 3).

Diphone prototypes have been defined in terms of sequences of spectra in order to test the simplest possible hypothesis concerning which acoustic cues are most salient to each phonetic decision. It is hoped that, if the right metric can be devised for comparing spectra, SCRIBER will perform well and there will be no need to postulate a representational level between spectra and phonetic segments. The alternative is to interpose certain kinds of property detectors or phonetic feature detectors that extract particular attributes from the spectra. Such a level will not be included in SCRIBER unless the simpler model fails to account for various natural acoustic-phonetic distinctions (see Stevens, 1972*a* for a partial list). Thus while sequences of spectra are not acoustic cues in the usual sense, they imply a theory in which spectra form a Gestalt or holistic unanalyzed representation rather than the input to a system of feature analyzers.

Segmentation

There is no explicit segmentation step in the SCRIBER decoding strategy. In a sense, all possible segmentations (alternative assignments of input spectra to network states) are evaluated in parallel. Since the input is not segmented before phonetic labeling, there is no need to develop strategies for correcting errors in segmentation. The final transcription provides an implicit segmentation since each 10-ms input spectrum has been associated with a particular state of the best-scoring path through the network. Therefore, durations of acoustic events can be computed if relevant to a phonetic contrast (see next paragraph).

Time normalization

The sequence-of-spectra concept is attractive for a number of reasons. For example, if desired, one could allow acoustic events to have any arbitrary duration without penalty, and irrelevant durational variability would be ignored. However, it is well known that duration is important for a number of phonetic contrasts, and some mechanism for incorporating durational constraints in the network representation is essential. To achieve this goal, the system is augmented in the following way. The expected duration of the input to be associated with each spectral template of a phonetic transition definition can be added to the diphone definitions for those cases where duration is deemed important. The result is that any state in the network of Fig. 3 can be assigned an explicit feedback path specifying the expected number of input spectra that can be associated with that state during recognition. For example, the number of input spectra associated with the burst spectrum plus the number associated with the aspiration spectrum in Fig. 3 should be about 5 (50 ms, i.e. the voice onset time should exceed about 25 ms) for a prestressed [t] to be recognized. In those cases where duration is determined to be important to a phonetic contrast, differences between expected and observed durations of the input assigned to a spectral template contribute to the distance score for a hypothesis. In this way, durations of acoustic events can be measured and compared with an accuracy that seems consistent with the relatively large (25 ms or more) durational just-noticeable differences observed during sentence perception (Klatt & Cooper, 1975).

Rate of spectral change is not represented by this means because it appears that cases where rate seems important [e.g. in distinguishing between /ba/ and /wa/, (Liberman,

Delattre, Gerstman & Cooper, 1956] depend more on the duration of the initial [w]-like spectrum, and thus can be better represented by specifying the expected duration of an initial steady state spectrum, and specifying that a certain spectral sequence be traversed. Rate of formant transitions or rates of other spectral changes are difficult to represent in discrete networks of this sort. One cannot easily constrain the relative duration of each component template of a transition definition—only the overall duration of the transition and/or the duration of any initial or final steady states. If rate turns out to be a perceptually important *independent* acoustic cue, this would constitute evidence against the template-sequence approach outlined here.

As argued earlier, variations in segmental durations due to speaking rate, syntactic factors, stress, and phonetic environment make it very difficult to rely on absolute durational constraints to distinguish among phonetic segments. The SCRIBER system can be set up to ignore irrelevant variations in segmental duration, but higher-level variables that influence segmental durations contribute durational ambiguity that simply cannot be overcome. Duration ratios among adjacent acoustic events may serve as useful speaking-rate-invariant cues for certain phonetic contrasts (Port, 1978), but a minimum-use-of-duration strategy still seems wise in any attempt to build a phonetic recognizer. The inability to make effective use of durational (and FO) cues to segmental contrasts is one of the primary reasons why I feel that a phonetic transcription component is not an appropriate driver for lexical search.

Talker normalization

One criticism of previous template models of speech recognition is that they cannot be modified very easily to handle different talkers. There is considerable variation in the details of spectra characterizing phonetic segments spoken by men, women, and children. On the other hand, acoustic patterns observed for adult talkers are more similar in a critical-band spectral representation than one might expect (Searle, Jacobson & Rayment, 1979). This observation lends support to a talker normalization procedure proposed by Lowerre (1977). He restricted the HARPY sentence recognition network to contain only 98 different spectral template types, and all sentences had to be represented in terms of sequences of spectra drawn from these 98 templates. Templates were modified incrementally toward spectra seen for a new speaker in the following way. If a sentence could be recognized using templates representative of an "average talker" (the sentence error rate was about four times as great as when talker-specific templates are available), then the observed input spectra were used to modify those spectral templates of the network that were matched during recognition.

An added advantage of this approach is that it captures some idiosyncratic aspects of acoustic targets employed by each talker in realizing different phonetic segments. For example, if the speaker habitually uses a fronted /u/, the appropriate template(s) converge toward spectra that reflect this habit. The network is intended to represent the acoustic-phonetic characteristics of a particular dialect of English, while the spectral templates represent acoustic targets that are talker-dependent. The separation of the SCRIBER system into talker-dependent templates and a talker-independent knowledge network has important theoretical implications. Speech processing by man and machine would be considerably simplified if such a separation could be experimentally validated.

In the SCRIBER system, more than 98 spectral templates will be required to make fine phonetic contrasts (about 300 may be sufficient), but the dynamic talker normalization procedure of HARPY can still be applied. In addition, several generalized methods of talker

292   *Dennis H. Klatt*

normalization will be investigated, such as starting with an average female template if the new talker seems female, or modifying all templates on the basis of average spectral properties of a new voice, or estimating vocal tract length, or saving template sets for familiar voices.

When compiled into a decoding network, SCRIBER is not particularly large. A complete 2000-diphone inventory requires an average of about two new states per diphone, resulting in a network of about 4000 states and 6000 paths. (This is substantially smaller than the 15000-state HARPY sentence-decoding network that can recognize ten-to-the-eight different sentences.) Sentence decoding then involves a large number of similar computations that can be performed in real time on a present-day fast digital processor such as the Floating Point Systems AP-120B.

Advantages of SCRIBER

The main advantages of SCRIBER are (1) the possibility of embedding all acoustic-phonetic knowledge concerning English (including phonological constraints on permitted phonetic sequences) into a single uniform network representation, (2) the ability to produce a phonetic transcription by simultaneously evaluating the scores for most of the likely alternative phonetic transcriptions, and (3) no need for explicit phonetic segmentation. Knowledge appears in a transparent form (the dictionary of spectral sequences for each phonetic transition) that makes optimization relatively easy. If it is successful, SCRIBER has possible applications as a limited-performance phonetic typewriter, as a "front end" for a computerized speech understanding system, as an aid for the deaf, and as a part of a model of speech perception (discussed later).

LAFS: a proposed solution to the problem of lexical access

The LAFS (lexical access from spectra) system is a computer algorithm for efficient accurate lexical search. LAFS avoids explicit phonetic transcription by precompiling knowledge of acoustic-phonetic relations into lexical definitions, in a way that is based on SCRIBER. The system deals with ambiguity generated by phonological recoding rules by precompiling knowledge of the rules into a decoding network.

Lexical representations

The first step in the design of LAFS is to construct a tree of expected *phonemic* sequences for all words of the lexicon, as shown in Fig. 4(a). An abstract phonemic lexicon is assumed as a starting point because of the many theoretical advantages of postulating abstract underlying forms for words and morphemes (Chomsky & Halle, 1968), even though the psychological lexicon may not include some of the more abstract, less productive rules (Ohala, 1974). The phonemic lexicon is organized into the form of a tree [Fig. 4(a)], such that words having the same initial phoneme sequence share nodes (phonemes) and branches until the words diverge in phonemic representation. Initial portions of words are shared so as to save storage, increase search speed, and facilitate application of phonological rules. Of course, a pair of words cannot share tree nodes if the words react differently to phonological rules due to stress differences or other factors.

Precompiled phonological rules

Phonological rules are used to derive phonetic forms for each word. Rule application often depends on characteristics of adjacent words, so the lexical tree is first modified in the following way. The end of each word in the tree is attached to all word-beginning

Lexical access   293

Step 1 : lexical tree (phonemic)

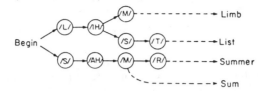

Step 2 : lexical network (phonetic)

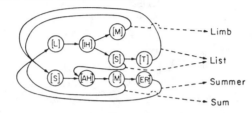

Step 3 : lexical access from spectra (spectral templates)

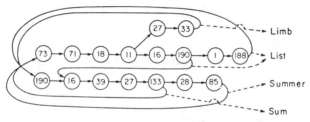

Figure 4.   The LAFS lexical-access-from-spectra decoding network that is shown in part (c) is derived by first constructing a tree of phonemic representations for all words in the lexicon, a portion of which is shown in part (a), and then connecting all word terminations to word beginnings and applying a set of phonological rules in order to form a phonetic sequence lexical decoding network, as shown in part (b). The numbers inside the states in the spectral sequence decoding network of part (c) refer to spectral templates from an inventory of about 300.

states. Then a set of phonological rules are applied to replace each phoneme by an appropriate phonetic allophone, delete or replace some segments, and modify the connectivity pattern (Klovstad, 1978). The result is a phonetic-sequence lexical decoding network of the type shown in Fig. 4(b), representing expected phonetic properties of all possible (grammatical and ungrammatical) word sequences of the lexicon. Cross-word-boundary phonological phenomena that must be described include the possible insertion of a silence or juncture phone such as the glottal stop, normal phonetic coarticulation, and various simplifications such as palatalization, flapping, [t]-deletion, etc. (Oshika *et al.*, 1975).

For example, the effect of the [st # s] → [s] phonological rule in Fig. 4(b) is to create an extra path from near the end of words ending in [st] to the second phonetic segment of words beginning with [s], so that a word pair such as "list some" can be recognized when spoken in the normal way, i.e. without the [t]. Since the rule is optional, the network must represent both alternatives, and the path from the final [t] of "list" to words beginning with [s] is therefore not broken. In the past few years, phonologists have developed formal rules of considerable predictive power (Chomsky & Halle, 1968; Cohen & Mercer, 1975;

Oshika, *et al.* 1975; Woods & Zue, 1976) that should prove useful in the context of lexical access.

If lexical access is attempted from a phonetic transcription, even given this decoding network in which words are represented in terms of phonetic segments, and phonological rule phenomena are represented by the connectivity pattern, one still requires a sophisticated matching strategy to select words corresponding to the derived phonetic string. A metric is needed to determine penalties for mismatches and for segmental intrusions or deletions because the automatic phonetic analyzer will make many errors of these types. Experience with the BBN lexical decoding network has shown that metrics to handle errors are very important in that unexpected transcription errors may result in a fatal rejection of the correct word (Wolf & Woods, 1978).

The ideal way to deal with transcription errors would be to go back to the acoustic data to see if the expected phonetic sequence for a word scores reasonably well. A phonetic transcription intentionally throws away this information, reducing large amounts of acoustic data to a sequence of discrete phonetic elements, and thus, it has been argued, makes the lexical search problem computationally tractable. Why not avoid the problem of recovering from errorful intermediate phonetic decisions by not making phonetic decisions at all? To accomplish this goal within LAFS, each state transition in Fig 4(b) is replaced by a mini-network of spectral templates. Each min-network is obtained from the SCRIBER diphone dictionary.

The result is shown in Fig. 4(c), a lexical-access-from-spectra decoding network that has no intermediate phonetic level of representation. The network is quite large, but only on the order of three times as large as the lexical decoding network made up of phonetic segments that is shown in Fig. 4(b) (i.e. there are, on the average, about three new states required to represent a phonetic transition).

Recognition strategy

The LAFS network of Fig. 4(c) is very similar in structure to SCRIBER, and the decoding strategy of SCRIBER, i.e. find the best path using a simple spectral metric, can be applied. A lexical decision confirming the presence of word X is made when all alternative word sequence hypotheses not containing this word are unlikely to increase in score as more of the input waveform is processed. Hypotheses not containing the identified word are then pruned from further consideration in order to minimize the number of alternative word sequences that need be considered in parallel.

In a system containing a large lexicon, one cannot postpone a lexical decision very long because too many alternative partial phrases would then have to be considered. Hopefully, in most practical applications, decisions can be held in abeyance for up to 0·5 s after the end of the hypothesized word, and the lexical hypothesis buffer need not grow any larger than about 1000.

Interpretation of prosodic cues

Not only is it possible to evaluate all reasonable lexical alternatives simultaneously in LAFS, but one can specify tighter durational, voice-onset-time, and stress-related constraints on acoustic events associated with words in LAFS than in SCRIBER because one knows more about the expected stress pattern and phonetic environment. For example, a shorter vowel duration is expected in "better" than in "bet", although both contain the same stressed vowel; such a constraint is easily applied in LAFS, but cannot be handled by a phonetic decoder.

The LAFS system also offers a mechanism for preliminary hypotheses to be formed concerning the syntactic structure of the sentence and the locations of semantically important words. Since the LAFS network is derived from lexical representations, one can specify not only the expected phonemic string and the expected durational pattern, but also the expected fundamental frequency contour and the intensity envelope that would normally be seen in a stressed (or unstressed) sentence environment. Differences between expected and observed prosodic variables either signal that the lexical candidate is inconsistent with the input, or the differences might be interpretable as cues to syntactic structure. For example, an unusually long final syllable in a word would indicate the presence of a phrase or clause boundary. Other possibilities include identifying the first part of a compound by a shorter-than-usual word duration, or detecting an emphasized word by a higher-than-usual fundamental frequency peak. Assuming that the network contains absolute values of prosodic cues to be expected, some form of normalization will be required to compensate for average speaking level, speaking rate, and fundamental frequency range employed by the current talker before direct comparision of observed and expected data is possible.

While duration and intensity contour ought to be effectively interpreted at a lexical level, there is reason to question whether FO can be processed in this way. A word receives a number of alternative FO contours depending on sentence type (statement/question), syntactic position, and emotional nuances imparted by the speaker. Thus to interpret FO within LAFS, it may be necessary to have some current hypothesis in mind as to the prosodic interpretation of the previous input.

Morphemes versus words

If the lexicon is broken down into morphemes (e.g. books = book + s, baseball = base + ball), there can be considerable savings in both storage and processing time. Allen (1973) has assembled a morpheme dictionary that can represent at least ten times as many English words as there are morphemes. LAFS should probably be organized in terms of the more common morphemes, but for recognition purposes, a lexical decoding network must keep separate representations for morphemes that change pronunciation when bound together (e.g. applicability = apply + able + ity). Even so, an English lexicon containing e.g. 15000 morphemes would result in a phonemic tree of only about 50000 states, and the resulting LAFS decoding network would have less than 150000 states.

Relation to HARPY

The HARPY speech recognition system (Lowerre, 1976; Lowerre & Reddy, 1978) represented a finite set of sentences in terms of a network of words, represented words in terms of phonemic sequences, used a few phonological rules to select allophones and modify the connectivity pattern across word boundaries, and represented each of 98 phonetic segment types in terms of a single spectral template. While LAFS is based on these concepts, it differs from HARPY in several ways. For example, the set of acceptable input sentences is unbounded in LAFS. More importantly, LAFS has augmented abilities to characterize acoustic characteristics of phonetic transitions via diphone and triphone definitions. LAFS incorporates a better motivated spectral representation and distance metric than the HARPY linear prediction spectrum and minimum residual error metric. Finally, complex phonological recodings within words and across word boundaries can be expressed within LAFS, and prosodic cues can be interpreted.

Advantages of LAFS

LAFS has been designed to deal with all eight problems identified in Table I. The first four problems (acoustic-phonetic non-invariance, segmentation, temporal variability, and talker variability) are addressed by using the spectral-sequence diphone definitions and recognition strategy employed by SCRIBER. The fifth problem, how to represent words of the lexicon for optimal search, was solved by converting abstract phonemic forms into spectral sequences. The sixth problem, how to take into account phonological recoding across word boundaries, was solved by applying a set of phonological rules to augment and adjust the connectivity pattern of the lexical network. The seventh problem, how to recover from errorful phonetic decisions, has been nullified by not making intermediate phonetic decisions. Error recovery is still an issue in that background noises or mis-pronunciations can corrupt the input. Recovery from these distortions depends on the ability of the beam-search strategy to find the best path through the lexical network even when no words score very well. The eighth and final problem, interpretation of prosodic cues, has been solved by storing expected prosodic attributes of words in the lexical decoding network and by interpreting deviations from these expectations either (1) as an indication that the lexical hypothesis is not compatible with the input, or (2) as cues to syntactic and semantic structure.

Thus, in theory, a LAFS processor has the capability of representing all of the acoustic-phonetic and phonological knowledge needed to recognize words in spoken sentences. Lexical hypotheses can be generated rapidly and more accurately in a LAFS structure than in any two-step model (phonetic recognition followed by lexical access) containing the same acoustic-phonetic and phonological knowledge. Two-stage models violate the principle of delaying absolute decisions until all of the relevant information is available, and errors thereby introduced cannot always be overcome. LAFS will make fewer errors than SCRIBER for another reason: LAFS does not evaluate all phonologically possible phonetic sequence alternatives—only phonetic sequences that make up English words—and the consideration of fewer alternatives means fewer chances to make an error. The cost of recasting LAFS as a two-stage model would be both a decrement in performance and a need to add strategies for comparing errorful phonetic strings with expected phonetic strings; these strategies are totally unnecessary in a model that does not make phonetic decisions.

Implications for models of speech perception

Do the computational strategies of SCRIBER and LAFS have any relation to plausible models of speech perception? I believe that it is worthwhile to seriously entertain this possibility. A perceptual model based on LAFS may turn out to be too simple-minded to stand the test of time, but it can serve as an excellent framework for asking new kinds of experimental questions.

Figure 5 presents one such model of speech perception in the form of a block diagram. The model consists primarily of a LAFS bottom-up lexical hypothesis component. Tentatively, it is also postulated that the model also include a SCRIBER phonetic transcription component that is used for adding new words to the LAFS decoding network, and perhaps also for early verification of top-down lexical hypotheses.

Normal mode of lexical access

An input speech waveform ([1] in Fig. 5) is transformed into a sequence of spectra [2] by a spectral analysis component analogous to the peripheral auditory system. The LAFS

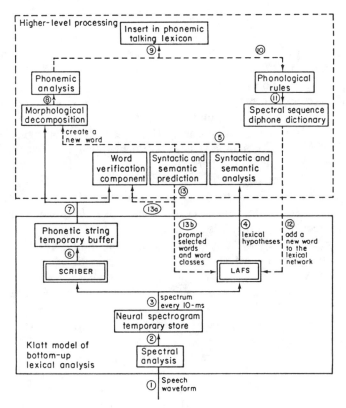

Figure 5.   Block diagram of a proposed perceptual model of lexical access (enclosed in solid lines) and how it interfaces with higher-level components (enclosed in dashed lines). The numbers are included to aid the reader in following the explanation of information flow in the text.

lexical-access-from-spectra component reads information off the resulting "neural spectrogram" temporary store (a name coined by Peter Bailey to draw an analogy with a broadband spectrogram) in a single left-to-right pass by processing the input in 10-ms sequential chunks. The box labelled "LAFS" in Fig. 5 includes the spectral sequence lexical decoding network and the buffer of active lexical hypotheses generated by the recognition strategy. As output, LAFS produces lexical hypotheses [3] that are analyzed by higher-level syntactic and semantic components [4]. The output of LAFS consists not only a sequence of best-scoring words, but also matching scores that are used by the higher-level components to decide whether to accept a bottom-up lexical hypotheses.

There is no reason to suppose that the peripheral auditory system transforms speech into a sequence of discrete spectra sampled every 10 ms, as in LAFS. However, both the spectral representation and the LAFS network could be reformulated as a quasi-continuous model by sampling the spectrum every 1 ms, or even more frequently. It appears that there would be little change in performance if this were done since speech waveforms do not change that rapidly, and spectra sampled using a 10-ms time weighting window cannot change very much when the window is shifted only 1 ms forward in time.

More important issues are the duration and shape of the window over which short-term spectra are computed. The 25.6 ms Kaiser window that is employed in LAFS has an effective duration of about 10 ms. This value was chosen so as to maximize the accuracy of a

298   *Dennis H. Klatt*

spectral estimate while still retaining an ability to track the rapid spectral changes that occur in speech. To model the human, the choice of window (or windows) will ultimately have to be justified on the basis of psychophysical data, physiological data, and LAFS performance data.

A second issue concerning the neural spectrogram is whether the spectrum is computed in the same way no matter what the signal. Physiological and psychophysical evidence suggests that spectral computations depend on signal properties in several ways: the spread of masking is level dependent (Egan & Hake, 1950); the response to stationary signals diminishes over time (Kiang, Watanabe, Thomas & Clark, 1965); and sudden onsets may be represented differently (Leshowitz & Cudahy, 1975). There is also evidence of non-linear processes that have the effect of enhancing peaks in vowel spectra (Houtgast, 1974). Research is needed to improve the simulation of preliminary spectral analysis in the model because it is not possible to evaluate proposed metrics for the comparison of spectral sequences until issues of spectral representation are settled.

Other cues to segmental contrasts   Up to this point, emphasis has been placed the utility of a spectral sequence in characterizing each possible phonetic transition. I believe that spectral sequences are the raw material on which speech perception strategies are based (not formants or the outputs of various kinds of property detectors), but some qualifying remarks are in order. At least two other independent dimensions are known to play a limited role in the perception of certain phonetic contrasts.

One is the fundamental frequency of vocal fold vibrations (FO). For example, FO is usually lower in voiced obstruents than in a following vowel, while following a voiceless obstruent, FO is usually higher at voicing onset than it is later in the vowel (Lea, 1973). This kind of FO cue can influence a voiced-voiceless decision (Haggard, Ambler & Callow, 1970). In addition, a strictly spectral explanation, such as the hypothesis that an FO increase changes the amount of low-frequency energy in the spectrum, cannot account for the perceptual influence of the FO contour (Massaro & Cohen, 1976).

A second acoustic dimension that can influence a phonetic decision, but which is not subsumed by the proposed spectral sequence prototype for a phonetic transition, is the degree to which the spectrum is periodic (as in a vowel), aperiodic (as in a voiceless consonant), or contains both low-frequency periodicity and high-frequency aperiodic noise (as in a voiced fricative or voiced /h/). Differentiating between, e.g. a voiced /h/ and a vowel on the basis of spectral cues alone can be difficult. Perceptual data on the importance of a "degree-of-periodicity" cue are not available. Nevertheless, a measure of the degree of periodicity in the spectrum above about 1 kHz might be a useful acoustic parameter. It appears that the auditory system would have no difficulty in computing such a periodicity measure at high frequencies (Searle *et al.*, 1979).

The role of formant frequencies   No mention has been made of formant frequencies and formant motions as possible cues for phonetic perception. In the acoustic theory of speech production, formant frequencies play a central role, characterizing the natural resonant modes of the vocal tract for a given articulatory configuration (Fant, 1960). However, automatic extraction of formant frequency information from the speech waveform is a difficult engineering task. It is still tacitly assumed by many that formant frequencies are psychologically real dimensions employed in perceptual decoding strategies (Delattre *et al.*, 1955; Carlson, Fant & Granstrom, 1975). We have no perceptual data that would refute this assumption, but there are several reasons to question its plausibility. For example, occasional formant tracking errors should result in dramatic errors in phonetic perception, whereas observed phonetic errors demonstrate a strong tendency to be acoustically similar to the intended vowels and consonants (see, e.g. Miller & Nicely, 1955). As we have argued, absolute decisions at any level below the word (parametric representation, phonetic feature representation, or segmental representation) should be avoided if at all possible for optimal lexical decoding.

Metrics for spectral comparisons

Assuming that a reasonable characterization of the information residing in the neural spectrogram can be established, simple metrics for determining the similarity between phonetic segments can be proposed and evaluated against psychophysical data. The objective is to simulate, e.g. perceptual distance data (Singh, 1971) and also category boundary shifts as acoustic cues are manipulated. For example, one can simultaneously manipulate several acoustic dimensions of synthetic speech-like stimuli (Massaro & Cohen, 1976; Stevens & Klatt, 1974), and try to account for cue tradeoffs. The simplest static metric might consist of summing the squares of the differences in dB across a set of critical-bandwidth filters. The simplest dynamic metric might consist of summing the static distances over time. If these and other kinds of simple metrics are falsified by perceptual studies, we would have evidence in favor of an intermediate level of analysis, perhaps one involving property detectors.

Several alternative talker-normalization procedures were proposed for LAFS. One involved continual modifications to the spectral templates used in the network on the basis of experience with the speech of the current talker. In order to retain this knowledge in long-term memory, a set of templates could also be saved for each familiar talker and for prototypical male and female talkers. Other techniques include computational procedures for modifying templates on the basis of vocal tract length estimates, average speech spectrum estimates, and average background noise spectrum estimates. All of these techniques are theoretically well motivated and thus potentially psychologically valid.

Experiments that examine the limits of listener's abilities to normalize for unusual spectral distortions may help to constrain the nature of the normalization process. For example, it seems that listeners are remarkably insensitive to changes in the relative amplitudes of spectral peaks caused by playing speech through fixed filters, but the limits of this ability have not been quantified when formant amplitude relations are disturbed dynamically.

Learning new words

In the event that the higher-level components determine that an unfamiliar word has been spoken [5], a phonetic representation of this speech interval [6] (produced by SCRIBER or perhaps by an augmented LAFS model) is recovered from a temporary phonetic buffer [7], submitted to morphological analysis [8], converted to a phonemic representation [9], and stored in the primary lexicon along with syntactic, semantic, and morphological properties. The new word is then incorporated into the spectral-sequence decoding network of LAFS through activation of procedures that include processing the abstract phonemic representation by a set of phonological rules [11], and expanding the resulting alternative phonetic forms into expected spectral sequences [12] that are then integrated with the LAFS network.

Addition of a new form to the network includes attaching it to the appropriate bound morphemes. For example, assuming that the talker has learned the pluralization rule of English in the form of a productive rule, she/he would have to look at the final phoneme of a new word, determine the distinctive feature categories to which it belonged, and define a network path from the end of the new word to the appropriate plural morpheme sub-network[1]. The advantage of placing common bound morpheme suffixes, like the regular plural, in a special sub-network is to ensure that they be preceded only by the appropriate words.

Verification of top-down lexical predictions

There exist listening situations where specific words can be anticipated on the basis of situational context and prior dialog. In this case, one need not wait for LAFS to complete its bottom-up analysis, but, instead, the higher level components can scan the input as it arrives so as to make an early lexical decision and prepare for the next word.

The way that this is accomplished is not at all clear. LAFS might be modified to work interactively with syntactic and semantic routines (see Newell, 1978, for an extreme version of this alternative), or there may exist a special mechanism for top-down lexical prediction and verification. Both alternatives are shown in Fig. 5. A top-down lexical hypothesis [13] is sent to a special word verification component [13a] that scans the phonetic transcription produced by SCRIBER to compute a matching score that can be used to disconfirm the presence of an expected word even if the complete phonetic representation has not been received. This alternative has the advantage of preserving the autonomy of LAFS from syntactic/semantic influences (Forster, 1976). The second (non-exclusive) alternative, path [13b], is discussed below. Both are presented in dashed lines because of my limited interest in pursuing here the implications of this part of the model, and because there are other ways in which top-down lexical predictions could be verified.

Lexical ambiguity in noise   As presently conceived, LAFS does not output a word until a certain amount of additional input is scanned. LAFS must wait long enough to resolve lexical ambiguities introduced when sub-words like "see" are contained in words like "cement", or alternative word sequences like "see mental loudmouths" and "cement allowed mountains" cover part of the phonetic input equally well. Unfortunately, the search space increases rapidly with delayed commitment. There is an exponential growth in alternative hypotheses with increased delay in commitment, so an autonomous LAFS probably cannot be allowed to defer decisions until several additional morphemes worth of input is scanned, but rather must try to make commitments with a minimum delay, no matter what the cost in performance.

Thus it is not at all clear how well an autonomous LAFS model (or any autonomous model of bottom-up lexical hypothesis formation) can perform in the context of a morpheme lexicon as large as in unconstrained English, or in the context of commonly encountered

---

[1]Derivation of phonological and morphological facts about new words appears to require a sophisticated network-building "demon". A computationally equivalent more plausible embodiment of precompiled knowledge might be to realize cross-word phonological recoding as a set of subroutines (rather than activate a demon to modify every word pair in the network that satisfies the preconditions for rule applicability). To learn a phonological rule would be equivalent to creating this subroutine. For example, when evaluating the score for a portion of the network corresponding to a postvocalic /st/ cluster for "list", one would scan the list of phonological rules that apply to postvocalic segments, detect the /st≠s/ → [s] rule, and thereby jump to the appropriate nodes of the network. The computational cost of scanning possible rules is offset by the need for a less-powerful demon. This is a standard tradeoff between computational speed and storage requirements that comes up often in computer programming, but we have no idea how the nervous system has solved the trade-off problem.

background noises. Speech can be understood in a moderately high noise background. The performance of an autonomous LAFS is likely to degrade significantly in noise (perhaps to a point where its output is essentially useless for moderate amounts of noise).

Given these observations, my present intuitions favor an interactive LAFS network in which particular lexical items or classes of items can be facilitated by a predictive syntactic/ semantic module (path 13b of Fig. 5). The matching scores for these words are increased in proportion to the confidence of the top-down predictions, analogous to the Logogen model of Morton (1970). If message redundancy is high and these constraints can narrow the lexical search, fewer errors will be made in general, and performance should not degrade as rapidly in the presence of noise and ambiguity. The alternative ways to integrate acoustic and semantic cues to lexical items are discussed in greater detail in Marslen-Wilson & Welsh (1978) and in Morton & Long (1976). However, it is important to emphasize that the present paper is not concerned with this issue since the principles embodied in LAFS, i.e. lexical access from a network of spectral sequences for words, can be incorporated in either an autonomous module or an augmented interactive data structure.

In conclusion, steps have been taken in this section to transform LAFS into a plausible perceptual model. This has required few modifications to the LAFS network representation of knowledge or to the recognition strategy. However, additional components have been postulated for adding new words to LAFS, and it has been argued that a method is needed for applying predictive constraints within LAFS to narrow the search space.

Discussion

Why propose a new model of lexical access? Modeling efforts can serve several purposes: (1) to unify seemingly disparate facts into a cohesive theory, (2) to detect gaps in the knowledge available to support any model, and (3) to define testable alternatives to mechanisms described in previous models. The present model of the early stages of speech perception is far too speculative to qualify as a theoretical synthesis of available data. In the following paragraphs, the model is discussed with reference to the latter two objectives.

Precompiled knowledge

The most important idea to come out of recent efforts to build computerized speech understanding systems is that one can precompile detailed relations between acoustic and lexical events into an efficient high-performance decoding structure for speech analysis. Precompilation is a fundamental computational technique that is clearly potentially applicable in other domains. For example, during the development of speech production strategies, the motor commands to the articulators to realize a particular phonetic segment must be adjusting as a function of the current state of the articulatory apparatus, i.e. as a function of the previous phonetic segment. These adjustments can be learned as rules in a feature-based system, but they might also be precompiled and stored in the form of a network of motor instructions for all phonologically possible phonetic sequences of English.

Phonological rules

It is well known that words have different phonetic realizations depending on the sentence context. Phonological recoding seems to occur so as to simplify the task of the talker. Do these simplifications add a significant burden to the listener by increasing the ambiguity of speech? There is no doubt that ambiguity is generated since it is not possible

302   *Dennis H. Klatt*

to write a unique inverse decoding rule for most phonological rules. How much ambiguity depends on whether the listener must consider all applicable inverse decoding rules at all phonetic positions in an unknown utterance, or whether a psychological equivalent of LAFS rule precompilation occurs.

It may be possible to determine experimentally whether phonological recodings are learned as generalized rules and precompiled into a decoding structure. For example, "list some" is likely to have a deleted [t], while "list one" may not. Reaction time experiments are needed to see if word strings subjected to phonological recoding and simplification require greater processing time. One would predict an insignificant increase in lexical access time if rule effects have been precompiled into a decoding structure like the LAFS spectral sequence decoding network. However, if rules are not precompiled and the effects of phonological recoding make lexical access considerably more difficult by introducing many alternative underlying phonetic strings, reaction time is likely to increase. Careful experimentation may reveal which, if any, phonological phenomena are detrimental to speech decoding.

Phonetic segments

The lexical recognition procedures of LAFS call into question the status of phonetic segments as units to be recognized during the bottom-up lexical hypothesis formation. The psychological reality of phonetic segments has been emphasized in the past on grounds of linguistic parsimony, in order to reduce the size of the knowledge store, in order to minimize the processing burden on the listener, and to serve as an interface between talking and listening. The model that we have proposed demands re-examination of these arguments.

A number of experiments have been devised to determine which units are involved in speech perception. For example, the LAFS model is consistent with reaction time data that indicate quicker reaction times for word processing over phoneme monitoring (Rubin, Turvey & Van Gelder, 1976; Savin & Bever, 1970). It has been suggested that the listener cannot access the phonemes that were used to recognize a word, but a clear alternative possibility is that word recognition does not usually involve phoneme recognition as an intermediate step. The absence of phonetic identification in LAFS is also consistent with the phonetic restoration effect (Warren, 1970) since all that is available from the output of LAFS is the best-scoring word. The LAFS model is also consistent with studies which indicate the perceptual migration of clicks to word boundaries (Ladefoged and Broadbent, 1960), with details of word advantage effects on a voice-onset-time continuum (Ganong, 1978), and with information theoretic arguments to the effect that listeners should not be required to make too many serial decisions per unit time (Miller, 1962).

Of course, we do not propose to discard the phonetic segment entirely in the perceptual model. Phonetic analysis skills are essential for adding words to the lexicon used for talking and for adding morphemes to LAFS. At an earlier developmental stage, phonetic analysis skills are probably essential for learning to talk (see below for a discussion of developmental issues).

Phonetic features

The model is intentionally provocative in its attempt to define a speech analysis system that does not make use of either simple acoustic property detectors or sophisticated phonetic feature detectors in any module (except that features serve as names for sets of phonetic segments that participate in particular phonological rules of higher-level components). Phonetic feature analyzers are included in most current models of speech processing (Blumstein, *et al.*, 1977; Jakobson, Fant & Halle, 1953; Oden & Massaro, 1978; Pisoni & Sawusch, 1975; Pisoni, 1976). Evidence cited in support of feature analyzer concepts includes (1) the structure of perceptual confusion matrices (Miller & Nicely, 1955; Shankweiler & Studdert-Kennedy, 1967), (2) the phenomena of cross-adaptation (Cooper, 1978), (3) data on the perception of competing acoustic cues (Massaro & Cohen, 1976), and (4) categorical perception of consonants. Recent reviews of this literature (Ades, 1978; Ganong, 1979; Parker, 1977; Studdert-Kennedy, 1979) suggest that all of the effects noted are consistent with *acoustic* properties of phonetic segments taken as a whole, and that one is not *required* to conclude that segments are represented in terms of distinctive features at early stages of speech perception. There appear to be no data that would rule out either SCRIBER or LAFS as components of perceptual processing.

Along the same line, recent analyses of speech production error data suggest that segments are manipulated as unanalyzed wholes during the initial stages of speech production (Shattuck-Hufnagel & Klatt, 1979). The authors have shown that exchange errors of the type "*m*itt or *h*iss" involve the movement of whole segments rather than the movement of component distinctive features. Is it possible that distinctive features are nothing more than names for sets of phonetic segment types that participate in phonological rules during both speech production and perception? Distinctive feature theory will always serve as a set of unifying principles for the organization of languages and the definition of natural phonetic contrasts for humans to produce and perceive (Chomsky & Halle, 1968; Jakobson, Fant & Halle, 1953; Stevens, 1972*a*), but it really has not been established that this representation is employed by the language user at acoustic and articulatory levels.

Perhaps the promulgation of LAFS as a creditable psychological model will stimulate the design of new types of experiments that can distinguish between feature-based, segment-based, and word-based accounts of acoustic-phonetic processing and lexical access. While I offer below a few suggestions on this point, note the cautionary words of Licklider (1952) who pointed out that certain classes of feature-analysis systems and template-based systems are functionally equivalent in the restricted mathematical sense that either can compute the same input-output transformation.

The model described here represents speech by sequences of acoustic events. Identification is determined by how well the input matches individual category prototypes. Our approach is thus similar to one advocated by Oden and Massaro (1978), except that our prototypes are defined in terms of sequences of spectral templates, rather than in terms of the outputs of feature detectors. In order to distinguish between a spectral-sequence model and a feature-detector model, two hypotheses must be tested: (1) whether metrics can be developed to predict psychophysical similarity between phones on the basis of general spectral and temporal properties, and (2) whether rate of spectral change is an important *independent* variable in speech perception.

Stevens (1972*a*) and others have argued that certain properties (such as the distinction between a rapid onset versus a gradual onset, or simultaneous versus sequential acoustic onsets) are natural psychophysical dimensions along which languages divide their phonetic inventories. It will be interesting to see whether the spectral representation and distance metrics proposed here can account for these and other natural phonetic contrasts, or whether special property detectors (or prototypes more complex than a sequence of spectral templates) must be postulated.

304   *Dennis H. Klatt*

Relation to other models of speech perception

Analysis by synthesis   An analysis-by-synthesis strategy was first formulated at the level of phonetic segments and features in order to overcome the non-invariance problem (Halle & Stevens, 1962; Stevens & Halle, 1964; Stevens, 1972b). The theoretical advantages of analysis-by-synthesis concepts applied at the lexical level have been hinted at in the section entitled "The problem". Since the literature does not contain a description of how such a lexically-based model might work, the following paragraphs describe one possible realization.

A block diagram of an Analysis-by-synthesis model is shown in Fig. 6. The speech waveform corresponding to an unknown utterance arrives at the left in the diagram and the best-scoring word string leaves at the right. It is assumed that peripheral cochlear spectral analysis and central neural processing result in a spectral representation for the incoming speech. This representation is placed in a temporary "echoic" memory store having characteristics that are not unlike those listed earlier in Table III.

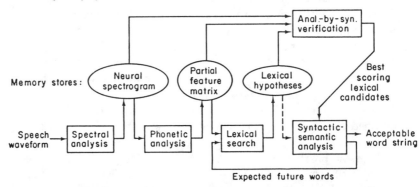

Analysis-by-synthesis model of speech perception

Figure 6.   Simplified block diagram of an analysis-by-synthesis model of speech perception. Memory buffers are represented by ovals, processes by rectangles, and information flow by arrows.

Results of backward recognition masking experiments suggest that only about 200–300 ms of speech can be retained in this memory store at any given time (Massaro, 1975). Certain kinds of transient acoustic information contained in the neural spectrogram may be lost unless they are quickly recoded into phonetic form, although prosodic information such as aspects of the fundamental frequency contour, intensity envelope, segmental durations, and vowel quality are presumably recoded and placed in a short-term memory store to permit relative comparisons across greater time spans of the input.

Phonetic feature analyzers read off information from the neural spectrogram. The phonetic feature detectors are thought to place their outputs in a matrix, where the columns represent a division of the time dimension into phonetic segments and the rows represent different phonetic features. Each entry in the matrix indicates whether or not a particular segment has a given feature, or is left unspecified. The phonetic feature specification for a segment may be incomplete for two reasons. Either sloppy articulation or environmental noise has led to an ambiguity, or some decisions involving complex context-dependent acoustic-phonetic relations are not attempted in the preliminary phonetic transcription. If specified, features are usually thought to be binary, representing the presence or absence of some attribute in the partial feature matrix representation of

Fig. 6. Alternatively, there may be an advantage in using continuous scales to represent the degree of confidence in each feature decision in order to provide more information for lexical hypothesis formation.

Information drawn from the phonetic feature matrix is used to search through the lexicon for possible sentence-initial words (or morphemes). Lexical candidates expected on the basis of the situation and previous dialog may be "facilitated" so that even if the feature match is not perfect, these highly probable words will be included in the lexical hypothesis memory store.

Due to the errorful and incomplete nature of the preliminary phonetic feature representation of the input speech, a rather large number of lexical candidates are likely to be found—perhaps an unreasonably large number (Klatt & Stevens, 1973). Syntactic/semantic routines would be hard-pressed to choose the correct initial word and succeeding words given this amount of ambiguity. Thus the model of Fig. 6 includes an analysis-by-synthesis component that accepts both bottom-up and top-down lexical hypotheses and returns to the acoustic and phonetic data to verify the presence of details to be expected given the whole word (Klatt, 1975). Verification takes into account not only the acoustic manifestations of phonetic expectations, but also perturbations caused by the prosodic cues that are expected given the lexical stress pattern and syntactic category(s).

Once the best-scoring sentence-initial lexical candidate has been accepted by the syntactic/semantic module, the whole process is iterated, starting from the position in the partial feature matrix where the first word ended. [The limited capacity of the partial feature matrix memory store probably means that sentence processing must proceed in near real time.] The words of a candidate sentence must also fit together properly. Given a knowledge of the previous word in an hypothesized sentence fragment, phonological rules contained in the verification component can be used to specify permitted segmental recoding across word boundaries and thus determine whether the word pair is compatible with the acoustic data. Significant cross-word phonological and coarticulatory interactions are common in sentences. Words rarely appear in a canonical form specified by the lexicon, and some means of dealing with word variability is essential.

As the sentence is elaborated, greater reliance is made on predictions given by syntactic/semantic expectations. These expectations might be used to order the lexical candidates in the lexical hypothesis memory store, or to indicate to the verification component that verification need not be as detailed, or to indicate that not all candidates need evaluation if the expected word scores reasonably well. While the process should rarely reach a dead end (signifying an incorrect analysis), when it does, memory stores are searched to try to backtrack to the next-best alternative partial sentence.

The block diagram of Fig. 6 is just a framework or philosophy for speech understanding, not a complete model. None of the components have been fleshed in with very great detail, particularly the partial feature analysis stage and how the lexicon is searched to find lexical candidates bottom up. It is hoped that this paper will stimulate efforts to refine feature-based analysis-by-synthesis theories of speech perception that deal with the eight problem areas of Table II, and that the paper will help to generate critical experiments to determine whether feature-based analysis-by-synthesis theories are more realistic models of human sentence perception than the model of Fig. 5.

Analysis by synthesis is a powerful (though expensive) method of weeding out false word candidates. The power derives from the fact that segment durations, intensity contour and fundamental frequency contour must make sense given the large number of factors that contribute to the expected patterns. Similarly, all of the acoustic cues that contribute to phonetic distinctions make more sense when a lexical hypothesis is under consideration. However, these advantages can be incorporated directly in a LAFS structure. Precompilation of knowledge is an attractive form of analysis by synthesis; the LAFS strategy permits the evaluation of far more lexical possibilities in parallel than if a single analysis-by-synthesis module were to be activated by one top-down lexical hypothesis at a time.

For familiar words, precompilation of acoustic-phonetic and phonological knowledge is a big winner. However, there probably are situations where precompilation is not the best solution, and other strategies (such as analysis-by-synthesis) may be invoked by the listener. For example, when listening to speakers with foreign accents or unfamiliar dialects, understanding improves when one has deduced a theory of the phonetic recoding, but it may not be desirable to compile this special knowledge into LAFS.

The motor theory   Liberman *et al.* (1967) and Studdert-Kennedy, Liberman, Harris & Cooper (1970) have argued that the acoustic encoding of phonetic elements in spoken utterances is so complex that it requires a special decoder. The decoder attempts to determine an articulatory sequence that could have produced the observed acoustic pattern. This motor theory of speech perception postulates an intermediate articulatory representation between the acoustic data and the phonetic interpretation. The need for referral to a motor component in speech perception has been further elaborated by Liberman and Studdert-Kennedy (1978). A model based on this philosophy has never been specified in very great detail. However, no matter what form the model takes, in principle all of the complex acoustic-articulatory-phonetic relations implicit in a motor theory can be precompiled into a network of expected spectra for each phonetic transition. If this were done, the resulting network would hopefully be indistinguishable from SCRIBER. In a sense, SCRIBER can be viewed as a computationally equivalent passive form of an active motor theory.

Is it possible to reformulate SCRIBER or LAFS to include an intermediate articulatory level? An acoustic-to-articulatory transformation can be computed, at least approximately (Atal, 1975), and could form an intermediate step in a modified LAFS model of lexical access in which states become articulatory configurations. Such a system would have no computational advantage over the present LAFS, since both can compute the same decoding transformation with about the same computational cost, but an articulatory LAFS might be more suitable for the interface between speech perception and speech production. A lexical-access-from-articulatory-sequences model seems worthy of investigation for this reason, but it does not appear that a lexical decoding network based on articulation could be used simultaneously for speech production. The representation is not sufficiently abstract—all of the coarticulatory and phonological details that are a consequence of low-level articulatory dynamics are already represented in the decoding network, whereas the lexicon used for talking is almost certainly phonemic (Fromkin, 1971; Shattuck-Hufnagel & Klatt, 1979).

The logogen   Morton (1970) has proposed a model of lexical access in which each word in the lexicon has an associated "logogen" that specifies defining characteristics of the word along various acoustic and semantic dimensions. If enough of these features are satisfied during sentence processing, the word is recognized. A Logogen model can account for many kinds of experimentally determined interactions between acoustic and semantic cues to lexical identity (Morton & Long, 1976) by postulating a threshold mechanism whereby top-down expectations can push a word over threshold before all acoustic cues are seen. There is no description of how acoustic cues are processed in a

Logogen model. The model is clearly compatible with the general acoustic-to-lexical analysis framework outlined here. In fact, LAFS could be considered as a more specific characterization of how the bottom-up part of a Logogen model would function.

A Logogen model has some difficulty in accounting for details of word reaction time data (Marslen-Wilson & Welsh, 1978). However, the autonomous LAFS model is similarly deficient in that there must be a delay before identifying each word (because one has to wait until at least the next word is over to be confident of selecting the best path in the beam search) and this is also inconsistent with reaction time data.

Context-sensitive allophones   Wickelgren (1969, 1976) proposed a theory of speech perception in which a large set of context-dependent allophones are used to derive a phonetic representation for an unknown utterance. For each phoneme X, a set of context-dependent allophones aXb were defined for all possible preceding phonemes, a, and all possible following phonemes, b. While such an approach solves the non-invariance problem, it does not address most of the other problems listed in Table I. The solution to the non-invariance problem proposed by Wickelgren is slightly more powerful than the diphone approach (and considerably more costly in terms of number of basic elements to be recognized). It suggests a way in which SCRIBER and LAFS can be improved in those cases where diphones do not capture all of the context dependency of speech. If, for example, the acoustic characteristics of /I/ in a word like "will" cannot be predicted from diphones obtained from "*wi*th" and "h*ill*" because the /w/ and /l/ collectively velarize the /I/ to a greater extent, then a special context-dependent allophone, or "triphone", can be defined in terms of a sequence of spectral templates and placed in the network in place of the two concatenated diphones.

Sequential word recognition   Cole & Jakimik (1978) have used a mispronunciation detection task to show that sentence perception generally involves the direct left-to-right decoding of words, one after the other. The advantage of such a strategy is that the end of one word defines the beginning of the next word in time, thus reducing the potential ambiguity of looking for words starting at other phonetic positions in the sentence. LAFS incorporates this advantage of direct left-to-right processing of a sentence, and it adds the further advantage of being able to deal with phonological recoding across word boundaries.

The hearsay II blackboard   Hearsay II is one of several computer-based speech understanding systems developed during the ARPA speech understanding project (for a review, see Klatt, 1977). The Hearsay II blackboard model of speech perception is described by Erman (1978). In this model, or framework for speech understanding, a set of knowledge sources work asynchronously toward the decoding of a sentence by taking their input from a common blackboard and placing the results of their analyses back on the blackboard. LAFS could function as a component of such a blackboard model. Alternatively, the theories being considered in parallel by LAFS could be placed on the blackboard for examination by other modules, even before LAFS has made a final decision. The latter possibility forms the basis for a number of attractive alternative models of speech perception, but they all will have to face such inherent problems as how to schedule activity among the modules that interact with the blackboard, and how to deal with the halting problem (Reddy, 1978).

Is speech special?

If our model is correct, one need not postulate the existence of innate feature detectors sensitive only to the phonetic contrasts of spoken language (Eimas & Miller, 1978).

308   *Dennis H. Klatt*

Instead, certain natural discriminations (so natural as to be made by infants) would be the consequence of properties of the spectral sequence representation of auditory signals.

However, speech could be special in several other respects. For example, speech stimuli may be distinguished from non-speech stimuli because they are the only signals that receive high-enough matching scores in the outputs of LAFS and SCRIBER to be processed as language. Also, the steps involved in constructing and augmenting a LAFS decoding network are complex. Is LAFS representative of general cognitive strategies (in which precompiled knowledge networks play a prominent role) or does speech acquisition require the postulation of special innate structures for the development of LAFS and supporting higher-level components?

Developmental issues

The earliest representation of words by an infant is probably in the form of a crude direct encoding of what appears on the (hard-wired?) neural spectrogram. Perhaps only a few of the most prominent spectral details within a word are remembered at first. The actual memory representation for words may thus be quite similar to a LAFS sequence of spectra representation right from the beginning. On the basis of further experience, spectral details are filled in, but only when needed to differentiate between new words.

In order to learn to talk, a phonemic analysis of the input speech must then be discovered by relating the processes of listening (acoustic events) and talking (articulatory commands). The creation of a phonemic talking lexicon is no doubt facilitated by the presence of partial acoustic-phonetic invariance. It seems that many invariant (or nearly invariant) cues must be present if the child is to discover the phonemic structure of his/her native language. However, according to the views expressed here, the acquisition of phonemic analysis capabilities and of a phonemic talking lexicon does not lead to any fundamental changes in bottom-up lexical access of familiar words via LAFS.

Relations between the two representations used for talking and listening are then internalized by associating spectral sequences with each phoneme or phoneme pair so as to create the diphone dictionary required for top-down augmentations of LAFS. The final steps needed to acquire an adult-like LAFS decoding network are the acquisition of morphological decomposition skills and the discovery of how word sequences are modified by phonological rules. The perceptual model thus acknowledges the psychological reality of linguistic units and rules that never appear explicitly in LAFS. Just how sophisticated these processes are, however, is a subject for experimentation (Ohala, 1974).

Elaboration of a concrete model of speech acquisition along these lines would be an important contribution to the general theory of speech perception. Hopefully, many testable alternatives can be isolated by comparing this account of language development with other current theories.

The validation issue   The presence of both LAFS and SCRIBER in the proposed perceptual model makes it much more difficult to determine the psychological validity of either. Depending on the perceptual task (nonsense-syllable identification, repeated listening to the same pair of words, or listening to unpredictable sentences made up of familiar words), the listener may engage either or both mechanisms. Similarly, analysis by synthesis or another form of top-down verification employing generative rules that are computed on the fly may be invoked when listening to some speakers. Nevertheless, I believe that the efficient decoding of normal conversational speech depends critically on mechanisms found in LAFS, whether or not these are the only mechanisms used in speech perception.

Lexical access   309

Conclusions

The perceptual model shown in the bottom half of Fig. 5 has been proposed and compared with a number of alternative models. I have established the theoretical advantages of a spectrally based decoding network approach to speech analysis, and have suggested several kinds of experiments that might settle the issues that have been raised concerning its perceptual reality. The essential features of the model are (a) precompilation of phonological rules that describe phonetic recoding of words in sentences so as to avoid having to consider application of inverse rules indiscriminately, (b) no calculation of a phonetic level of representation during lexical search because calculation of such an intermediate representation must introduce errors (due in part to the greater number of alternatives in a phonetic transcription and in part to an inability to interpret durational and FO cues to segmental contrasts) thus violating the principle of delayed commitment, and (c) representation of acoustic-phonetic knowledge in terms of sequences of spectra for each possible phonetic transition rather than postulating the existence of invariant attributes for phones or the existence of low-level property detectors and phonetic feature detectors until such time as simpler assumptions are proven unworkable. This model, summarized in Fig. 5, is offered as the most complete, most simply structured current theory of the initial stages of acoustic-phonetic analysis and lexical search.

Preparation of this manuscript was supported by an NIH grant. My sincere thanks go to R. Cole, A. Liberman, M. Liberman, D. Pisoni, R. Reddy, B. Repp, and K. Stevens for numerous suggestions for improvements to an earlier draft. I alone take responsibility for the views expressed here.

References

Ades, A. E. (1978). Theoretical notes: vowels, consonants, speech and nonspeech. *Psychological Review* **84**, 524–30.

Allen, J. (1973). Speech synthesis from unrestricted text. In *Speech Synthesis* (J. L. Flanagan & L. R. Rabiner, eds). Stroudsberg, PA: Dowden, Hutchinson & Ross.

Atal, B. S. (1975). Towards determining articulator positions from the speech signal. In *Speech Communication* (G. Fant, ed.), Vol. 1, pp. 1–9. Stockholm: Almqvist & Wiksell.

Blumstein, S. E., Stevens, K. N. & Nigro, G. N. (1977). Property detectors for bursts and transitions in speech perception. *Journal of the Acoustical Society of America* **61**, 1301–13.

Carlson, R., Fant, G. & Granstrom, B. (1975). Two-Formant Models, Pitch, and Vowel Perception. In *Auditory Analysis and Perception of Speech* (G. Fant & M. A. A. Tatham, eds). New York: Academic Press.

Chomsky, N. & Halle, M. (1968). *The Sound Pattern of English.* New York: Harper & Row.

Cohen, P. S. & Mercer, R. L. (1975). The phonological component of an automatic speech recognition system. In *Speech Recognition: Invited Papers Presented at the 1974 IEEE Symposium* (D. R. Roddy, ed.), 275–320. New York: Academic Press.

Cole, R. & Jakimik, J. (1978). A model of speech perception. In *Perception and Production of Fluent Speech* (R. Cole, ed.). Hillsdale, NJ: Erlbaum Assoc.

Cole, R. A. & Scott, B. (1974). Toward a theory of speech perception. *Psychological Review* **81**, 348–74.

Cole, R., Rudnicky, A., Zue, V. and Reddy, D. R. (1978). Speech as patterns on paper. In *Perception and Production of Fluent Speech* (R. Cole, ed.). Hillside, NJ: Erlbaum Assoc.

Cooper, W. E. (1978). *Speech Perception and Production: Selected Studies on Adaptation.* Cambridge, England: Cambridge University Press.

Delattre, P. C., Liberman, A. M. & Cooper, F. S. (1955). Acoustic loci and transitional cues for consonants. *Journal of the Acoustical Society of America* **27**, 769–73.

Egan, J. P. & Hake, H. W. (1950). On the masking pattern of a simple auditory stimulus. *Journal of the Acoustical Society of America* **22**, 622–30.

Eimas, P. D. & Miller, J. L. (1978). Effects of selective adaptation on the perception of speech and visual patterns: evidence for feature detectors. In *Perception and Experience* (R. D. Walk & H. L. Pick, eds). pp. 307–45. New York: Plenum Press.

Erman, L. (1978). The HEARSAY-II speech understanding system. In *Trends in Speech Recognition* (W. A. Lea, ed.). New York: Prentice-Hall.

Fant, G. (1960). *Acoustic Theory of Speech Production.* The Hague: Mouton.

310   *Dennis H. Klatt*

Fant, G. (1974). *Speech Sounds and Features*. Cambridge, MA: MIT Press.

Flanagan, J. L. (1957). Estimates of the maximum precision necessary in quantizing certain dimensions of vowel sounds. *Journal of the Acoustical Society of America* **29**, 533–4.

Forster, K. I. (1976). Accessing the mental lexicon. In *New Approaches to Language Mechanisms*. (R. J. Wales & E. C. T. Walker, eds). Amsterdam: North-Holland.

French, N. R. & Steinberg, J. C. (1947). Factors governing the intelligibility of speech sounds. *Journal of the Acoustical Society of America* **19**, 90–119.

Fromkin, V. (1971). The non-anomalous nature of anomalous utterances. *Language* **47**, 27–52.

Fujimura, O. & Lovins, J. B. (1978). Syllables as concatenative phonetic units. In *Syllables and Segments*. (A. Bell & J. B. Hooper, eds).

Ganong, F. (1978). A word advantage in phoneme boundary experiments. *Journal of the Acoustical Society of America* **63**, Suppl. 1, S20 (A).

Ganong, F. (1979). Dichotic feature recombination errors and distinctive features. Unpubl. manu.

Gay, T. (1977). Articulatory movement in VCV sequences. *Journal of the Acoustical Society of America* **62**, 183–193.

Haggard, M., Ambler, X. & Callow, M. (1970). Pitch as a voicing cue. *Journal of the Acoustical Society of America* **47**, 613–17.

Halle, M. & Stevens, K. N. (1962). Speech recognition: a model and a program for research. *IRE Transactions on Information Theory IT*-8, 155–9.

Houtgast, T. (1974). Auditory analysis of vowel-like sounds. *Acoustics* **31**, 320–4.

Jakobson, R., Fant, G. & Halle, M. (1953). *Preliminaries to Speech Analysis: The Distinctive Features and Their Correlates*. Cambridge, MA: MIT Press.

Kiang, N., Watanabe, T., Thomas, E. & Clark, L. (1965). *Discharge Patterns of Single Fibres in the Cat's Auditory Nerve*. Cambridge, MA: MIT Press.

Klatt, D. H. (1975). Word verification in a speech understanding system. In *Speech Recognition: Invited Papers Presented at the 1974 IEEE Symposium* (D. R. Reddy, ed.), pp. 321–41. New York: Academic Press.

Klatt, D. H. (1976*a*). A digital filter bank for spectral matching. In *Conference Record of the 1976 IEEE International Conference on Acoustics Speech and Signal Processing* (C. Teacher, ed.). Philadelphia, PA. (IEEE Catalog No. 76CH1067-8 ASSP), 537–40.

Klatt, D. H. (1976*b*). Linguistic uses of segmental duration in English: acoustic and perceptual evidence. *Journal of the Acoustical Society of America* **59**, 1208–21.

Klatt, D. H. (1977). Review of the ARPA speech understanding project. *Journal of the Acoustical Society of America* **62**, 1345–66.

Klatt, D. H. (1978*a*). SCRIBER and LAFS: two new approaches to speech analysis. In *Trends in Speech Recognition* (W. A. Lea, ed.). New York: Prentice-Hall.

Klatt, D. H. (1978*b*), Analysis and synthesis of consonant-vowel syllables in English. *Journal of the Acoustical Society of America* **64**, Suppl. 1, S43 (A).

Klatt, D. H. (1979), Synthesis by rule of segmental durations in English sentences. In (B. Lindblom & S. Ohman, eds). *Frontiers of Speech Communication Research* eds. New York: Academic Press.

Klatt, D. H. & Cooper, W. E. (1975). Perception of segment duration in sentence contexts. In *Structure and Process in Speech Perception* (A. Cohen & S. G. Nooteboom, eds), pp. 69–89. New York: Springer-Verlag.

Klatt, D. H. & Stevens, K. N. (1973). On the automatic recognition of continuous speech: implications of a spectrogram-reading experiment. *IEEE Transactions on Audio and Electroacoustics AU*-21, 210–17.

Klovstad, J. W. (1978). Computer-automated speech perception system. Ph.D. Dissertation. MIT, unpubl.

Ladefoged, P. & Broadbent, D. E. (1960). Perception of sequence in auditory events. *Quarterly Journal of Experimental Psychology* **13**, 162–70.

Lea, W. A. (1973). Segmental and suprasegmental influences on fundamental frequency contours. In *Consonant Types and Tone* (L. Hyman, ed.). Southern California Occasional Papers in Linguistics, No. 1.

Lehiste, I. (1970). *Suprasegmentals*. Cambridge, MA: MIT Press.

Lehiste, I. & Shockey, L. (1972). On the perception of coarticulation effects in english VCV syllables. *Journal Speech and Hearing Research* **15**, 500–6.

Leshowitz, B. & Cudahy, E. (1975). Masking patterns for continuous and gated sinusoids. *Journal of the Acoustical Society of America* **58**, 235–42.

Liberman, A. M., Cooper, F. S., Shankweiler, D. S. & Studdert-Kennedy, M. (1967). Perception of the speech code. *Psychological Review* **74**, 431–61.

Liberman, A. M., Delattre, P., Gerstman, L. & Cooper, F. (1956). Tempo of frequency change as a cue for distinguishing classes of speech sounds. *Journal of Experimental Psychology* **52**, 127–37.

Liberman, A. M. & Studdert-Kennedy, M. (1978). Phonetic perception. In *Handbook of Sensory Physiology*, Vol. VIII (R. Held, H. Leibowitz & H.-L. Teuber, eds). Heidelberg: Springer-Verlag.

Lexical access   311

Licklider, J. C. R. (1952). On the process of speech perception. *Journal of the Acoustical Society of America* **24**, 590–4.

Lieberman, P. (1967). *Intonation, Perception, and Language.* Cambridge, MA: MIT Press.

Lindblom, B. (1978). Phonetic aspects of linguistic explanation. *Studia Linguistica* (in press).

Lowerre, B. T. (1976). The HARPY speech recognition system. Ph.D. Dissertation, Carnegie-Mellon Univ., unpublished.

Lowerre, B. T. (1977). Dynamic speaker adaptation in the HARPY speech recognition system. In *Conference Record of the 1977 IEEE International Conference on Acoustics, Speech and Signal Processing,* (H. F. Silverman, ed.), Hartford, IEEE Catalog No. 77CH1197-3 ASSP.

Lowerre, B. & Reddy, D. R. (1978). The HARPY speech understanding system. In *Trends in Speech Recognition* (W. A. Lea, ed.). New York: Prentice-Hall.

Marslen-Wilson, W. D. & Welsh, A. (1978). Processing interactions and lexical access during word recognition in continuous speech. *Cognitive Psychology* **100**, 29–63.

Massaro, D. M. (1975). Backward recognition masking. *Journal of the Acoustical Society of America* **58**, 1059–65.

Massaro, D. M. & Cohen, M. M. (1976). The contribution of fundamental frequency and voice onset Time to the /zi/–/si/ distinction. *Journal of the Acoustical Society of America* **60**, 704–7.

Medress, M. (1969). Computer recognition of single-syllable English words. Ph.D. Dissertation. MIT, unpublished.

Miller, G. A. (1962). Decision units in the perception of speech. *IRE Transactions on Information Theory* IT-**8**, 81–3.

Miller, G. A. & Nicely, P. E. (1955). Analysis of perceptual confusions among some English consonants. *Journal of the Acoustical Society of America* **27**, 338–53.

Morton, J. (1970). A functional model for memory. In *Models of Human Memory,* (D. A. Norman, ed.). New York: Academic Press.

Morton, J. & Long, J. (1976). Effect of word transition probability on phoneme identification. *Journal of Verbal Learning and Verbal Behavior* **15**, 43–51.

Newell, A. (1978). HARPY, production systems, and human cognition. In *Perception and Production of Fluent Speech* (R. Cole, ed.). Hillsdale, NJ: Erlbaum Assoc.

Oden, G. C. & Massaro, D. W. (1978). Integration of featural information in speech perception. *Psychological Review* **85**, 172–91.

Ohala, J. J. (1974). Experimental historical phonology. In *Historical Linguistics II: Theory and Description in Phonology* (J. M. Anderson and C. Jones, eds). Amsterdam: North-Holland, 353–89.

Oshika, B., Zue, V. W., Weeks, R. V., Neu, H. & Aurbach, J. (1975). The role of phonological rules in speech understanding research. *IEEE Transactions on Acoustics, Speech, and Signal Processing* ASSP-**23**, 104–12.

Parker, F. (1977). Distinctive features and acoustic cues. *Journal of the Acoustical Society of America* **62**, 1051–4.

Peterson, G. E., Wang, W. & Sivertsen, E. (1958). Segmentation techniques for speech synthesis. *Journal of the Acoustical Society of America* **30**, 739–42.

Pisoni, D. B. (1976). Speech perception. In *Handbook of Learning and Cognitive Processes* (W. K. Estes, ed.). Hillsdale, NJ: Erlbaum Associates.

Pisoni, D. B. & Sawusch, J. R. (1975). Some stages of processing in speech perception. In *Structure and Process in Speech Perception* (A. Cohen & S. G. Nooteboom, eds). New York: Springer-Verlag, 16–35.

Plomp, R. & Mimpen, A. M. (1968). The ear as a frequency analyzer II. *Journal of the Acoustical Society of America* **43**, 764–8.

Port, R. F. (1979). Influence of tempo on stop closure duration as a cue for voicing and place. *Journal of Phonetics,* **7**, 45–56.

Reddy, D. R. (1978). Machine models of speech. In *Perception and Production of Fluent Speech* (R. Cole, ed.). Hillsdale, NJ: Erlbaum Assoc.

Rubin, P., Turvey, M. & Van Gelder, P. (1976). Initial phonemes are detected faster in spoken words than in spoken non-words. *Perception and Psychophysics* **19**, 394–8.

Savin, H. B. & Bever, T. G. (1970). The nonperceptual reality of the phoneme. *Journal of Verbal Learning and Verbal Behavior* **9**, 295–302.

Searle, C., Jacobson, J. Z. & Rayment, S. G. (1979). Stop consonant discrimination based on human audition. *Journal of the Acoustical Society of America* **65**, 799–809.

Shankweiler, D. & Studdert-Kennedy, M. (1967). Identification of consonants and vowels presented to left and right ears. *Journal of Experimental Psychology* **19**, 59–63.

Sharf, B. (1970). Critical bands. In *Foundations of Modern Auditory Theory, Vol.* 1 (J. V. Tobias, ed.), pp. 157–202. New York: Academic Press.

Shattuck-Hufnagel, S. R. & Klatt, D. H. (1979). The limited use of distinctive features and markedness in speech production: evidence from speech error data. *Journal of Verbal Learning and Verbal Behavior* **18**, 41–56

312   *Dennis H. Klatt*

Singh, S. (1971). Perceptual similarities and minimal phonemic differences. *Journal of Speech and Hearing Research* **14**, 113–24.

Stevens, K. N. (1972*a*). The quantal nature of speech: evidence from articulatory-acoustic data. In *Human Communication: A Unified View* (E. E. David & P. B. Denes, eds). New York: McGraw-Hill.

Stevens, K. N. (1972*b*). Segments, features, and analysis by synthesis. In *Language by Eye and by Ear* (J. F. Kavanaugh & I. G. Mattingly, eds). pp. 47–55. Cambridge, MA: MIT Press.

Stevens, K. N. (1972*c*). Sources of inter- and intra-speaker variability in the acoustic properties of speech sounds. *Proc. Seventh Int. Congress of Phonetic Sciences* (A. Rigault & R. Charbonneau, eds), pp. 206–232. The Hague: Mouton.

Stevens, K. N. (1975). On the potential role of property detectors in the perception of consonants. In *Auditory Analysis and the Perception of Speech* (G. Fant & M. A. A. Tatham, eds). New York: Academic Press.

Stevens, K. N. & Halle, M. (1964). Remarks on analysis by synthesis and distinctive features. In *Proc. of the AFCRL Symposium on Models for the Perception of Speech and Visual Form* (W. Wathen-Dunn, ed.). Cambridge, MA: MIT Press.

Stevens, K. N. & Klatt, D. H. (1974). Role of formant transitions in the voiced-voiceless distinction for stops. *Journal of the Acoustical Society of America* **55**, 653–8.

Studdert-Kennedy, M. (1976). Speech perception. In *Contemporary Issues in Experimental Phonetics* (N. J. Lass, ed.). New York: Academic Press.

Studdert-Kennedy, M. (1979). *Language and Speech* (in press).

Studdert-Kennedy, M., Liberman, A. M., Harris, K. S. & Cooper, F. S. (1970). Motor theory of speech perception: a reply to Lane's critical review. *Psychological Review* **77**, 234–49.

Wakita, H. & Kasuya, H. (1977). A study of vowel normalization and identification in connected speech. In *Conference Record of the 1977 IEEE International Conference on Acoustics, Speech and Signal Processing* (H. F. Silverman, ed.), pp. 417–27. Hartford: IEEE Catalog No. 77CH1197-3 ASSP.

Warren, R. M. (1970). Perceptual restoration of missing speech sounds. *Science* **167**, 392–3.

Wickelgren, W. A. (1969). Context-sensitive coding, associative memory, and serial order in (speech) behavior. *Psychological Review* **76**, 1–15.

Wickelgren, W. A. (1976). Phonetic coding and serial order. In *Handbook of Perception*, Vol. VII. New York: Academic Press, 227–64.

Weeks, R. V. (1974). Predictive syllable mapping in a continuous speech understanding system. In *Contributed Papers of the IEEE Symposium on Speech Recognition* (L. D. Erman, ed.). Carnegie-Mellon University: IEEE Catalog No. 74CH0878-9 AE.

Wolf, J. J. & Woods, W. A. (1978). The HWIM speech understanding system. In *Trends in Speech Recognition* (W. A. Lea, ed.). New York: Prentice-Hall.

Woods, W. A. & V. Zue (1976). Dictionary expansion via phonological rules for a speech understanding system. In *Conference Record of the 1976 IEEE International Conference on Acoustics Speech and Signal Processing* (C. Teacher, ed.), pp. 561–4. Philadelphia, PA: IEEE Catalog No. 76CH1067-8 ASSP.

Zue, V. W. (1976). Acoustic characteristics of stop consonants: a controlled study. *Lincoln Laboratory Technical Report No.* **523**, Cambridge, MA: MIT.

Zue, V. W. & Schwartz, R. (1978). Acoustic processing and phonetic analysis. In *Trends in Speech Recognition* (W. A. Lea, ed.). New York: Prentice-Hall.

Zwicker, E., Terhardt, E. & Paulus, E. (1979). Automatic speech recognition using psychoacoustic models. *Journal of the Acoustical Society of America* **65**, 487–498.

Psychological Review
1967, Vol. 74, No. 6, 431–461

PERCEPTION OF THE SPEECH CODE[1]

A. M. LIBERMAN,[2] F. S. COOPER, D. P. SHANKWEILER, AND M. STUDDERT-KENNEDY[3]

Haskins Laboratories, New York, New York

Man could not perceive speech well if each phoneme were cued by a unit sound. In fact, many phonemes are encoded so that a single acoustic cue carries information in parallel about successive phonemic segments. This reduces the rate at which discrete sounds must be perceived, but at the price of a complex relation between cue and phoneme: cues vary greatly with context, and there are, in these cases, no commutable acoustic segments of phonemic size. Phoneme perception therefore requires a special decoder. A possible model supposes that the encoding occurs below the level of the (invariant) neuromotor commands to the articulatory muscles. The decoder may then identify phonemes by referring the incoming speech sounds to those commands.

Our aim is to identify some of the conditions that underlie the perception of speech. We will not consider the whole process, but only the part that lies between the acoustic stream and a level of perception corresponding roughly to the phoneme.[4] Even this, as we will try to show, presents an interesting challenge to the psychologist.

The point we want most to make is that the sounds of speech are a special and especially efficient code on the phonemic structure of language, not a cipher or alphabet. We use the term code,[5] in contrast to cipher or alpha-

[1] The research reported here was aided at its beginning, and for a considerable period afterward, by the Carnegie Corporation of New York. Funds have also come from the National Science Foundation and the Department of Defense. The work is currently supported by the National Institute of Child Health and Human Development, the National Institute of Dental Research, and the Office of Naval Research.

[2] Also at the University of Connecticut.

[3] Also at the University of Pennsylvania.

[4] For our purposes the phoneme is the shortest segment that makes a significant difference between utterances. It lies in the lowest layer of language, has no meaning in itself, and is, within limits, commutable. There are, for example, three such segments in the word "bad"—/b/, /æ/, and /d/—established by the contrasts with "dad," "bed," and

"bat." As commonly defined, a phoneme is an abstract and general type of segment, represented in any specific utterance by concrete and specific tokens, called phones, that may vary noticeably as a function of context. The distinguishable variants so produced are referred to as allophones.

We do not mean to imply that every phoneme is necessarily perceived as one listens to speech. Linguistic constraints of various kinds make it possible to correct or insert segments that are heard wrongly or not at all. Phonemes can be perceived, however, and some number of them must be perceived if the listener is to discover which constraints apply.

[5] We borrow the terms cipher and code from cryptography. A cipher substitutes a symbol for each of the units (letters,

431

432   LIBERMAN, COOPER, SHANKWEILER, AND STUDDERT-KENNEDY

bet, to indicate that speech sounds represent a very considerable restructuring of the phonemic "message." The acoustic cues for successive phonemes are intermixed in the sound stream to such an extent that definable segments of sound do not correspond to segments at the phoneme level. Moreover, the same phoneme is most commonly represented in different phonemic environments by sounds that are vastly different. There is, in short, a marked lack of correspondence between sound and perceived phoneme. This is a central fact of speech perception. It is, we think, the result of a complex encoding that makes the sounds of speech especially efficient as vehicles for the transmission of phonemic information. But it also poses an important question: by what mechanism does the listener decode the sounds and recover the phonemes?

In this paper we will (a) ask whether speech could be well perceived if it were an alphabet or acoustic cipher, (b) say how we know that speech is, in fact, a complex code, (c) describe some properties of the perceptual mode that results when speech is decoded, (d) consider how the encoding and decoding might occur, and (e) show that the speech code is so well matched to man as to provide, despite its complexity, a uniquely effective basis for communication.

---

usually) of the original message. In a code, on the other hand, the units of the original and encoded forms do not correspond in structure or number, the encoded message typically containing fewer units. Since these distinctions are relevant to our purpose here, we have adopted the terms cipher and code as a convenient way to refer to them. We should add, however, that the arbitrary relation between the original and encoded forms of a message, so usual in cryptography, is not a feature of the encoding of phonemes into syllables.

COULD SPEECH BE ALPHABETIC?

There are reasons for supposing that phonemes could not be efficiently communicated by a sound alphabet—that is, by sounds that stand in one-to-one correspondence with the phonemes. Such reasons provide only indirect support for the conclusion that speech is a code rather than an alphabet. They are important, however, because they indicate that the encoded nature of speech may be a condition of its effectiveness in communication. More specifically, they tell us which aspects of the code are likely to be relevant to that effectiveness.

Phoneme Communication and the Properties of the Ear

Of the difficulties we might expect to have with a sound alphabet, the most obvious concerns rate. Speech can be followed, though with difficulty, at rates as high as 400 words per minute (Orr, Friedman, & Williams, 1965). If we assume an average of four to five phonemes for each English word, this rate yields about 30 phonemes per second. But we know from auditory psychophysics (Miller & Taylor, 1948) that 30 sounds per second would overreach the temporal resolving power of the ear: discrete acoustic events at that rate would merge into an unanalyzable buzz; a listener might be able to tell from the pitch of the buzz how fast the speaker was talking, but he could hardly perceive what had been said. Even 15 phonemes per second, which is not unusual in conversation, would seem more than the ear could cope with if phonemes were a string of discrete acoustic events.

There is at least one other requirement of a sound alphabet that would be hard to satisfy: a sufficient number of identifiable sounds. The number of phonemes, and hence the number of acoustic shapes required, is in the dozens. In English there are about 40. We should, of course, be able to find 40 identifiable sounds if we could pattern the stimuli in time, as in the case of melodies. But if we are to communicate as rapidly as we do, the phoneme segments could last no longer than about 50 milliseconds on the average. Though it is not clear from research on auditory perception how many stimuli of such brief duration can be accurately identified, the available data suggest that the number is considerably less than 40 (Miller, 1956a, 1956b; Nye, 1962; Pollack, 1952; Pollack & Ficks, 1954). We will be interested, therefore, to see whether any features of the encoding and decoding mechanisms are calculated to enhance the identifiability of the signals.

Results of Attempts to Communicate Phonemes by an Acoustic Alphabet

That these difficulties of rate and sound identification are real, we may see from the fact that it has not been possible to develop an efficient sound alphabet despite repeated and thoroughgoing attempts to do so. Thus, international Morse code (a cipher as we use the term here) works poorly in comparison with speech, even after years of practice. But Morse is surely not the best example; the signals are one-dimensional and therefore not ideal from a psychological standpoint. More interesting, if less well known, are the many sound alphabets that have been tested in the attempt to develop reading machines for the blind (Coffey, 1963; Cooper, 1950a; Freiberger & Murphy, 1961; Nye, 1964, 1965; Studdert-Kennedy & Cooper, 1966; Studdert-Kennedy & Liberman, 1963). These devices convert print into sound, the conversion being made typically by encipherment of the optical alphabet into one that is acoustic. The worth of

these devices has been limited, not by the difficulty of converting print to sound, but by the perceptual limitations of their human users. In the 50-year history of this endeavor, a wide variety of sounds has been tried, including many that are multidimensional and otherwise appropriately designed, it would seem, to carry information efficiently. Subjects have practiced with these sounds for long periods of time, yet there has nowhere emerged any evidence that performance with these acoustic alphabets can be made to exceed performance with Morse, and that is little more than a tenth of what can be achieved with speech.

Reading and Listening

We hardly need say that language can be written and read by means of an alphabet, but we would emphasize how different are the problems of communicating phonemes by eye and by ear, and how different their relevance to a psychology of language. In contrast to the ear, the eye should have no great difficulty in rapidly perceiving ordered strings of signals. Given the eye's ability to perceive in space, we should suppose that alphabetic segments set side by side could be perceived in clusters. Nor is there reason to expect that it might be difficult to find identifiable optical signals in sufficient number. Many shapes are available, and a number of different alphabets are, indeed, in use. Thus, written language has no apparent need for the special code that will be seen to characterize language in its acoustic form. In writing and reading it is possible to communicate phonemes by means of a cipher or alphabet; indeed, there appears to be no better way.

Spoken and written language differ, then, in that the former must be a complex code while the latter can be a simple cipher. Yet perception of speech is universal, though reading is not. In the history of the race, as in the development of the individual, speaking and listening come first; writing and reading come later, if at all. Moreover, the most efficient way of writing and reading—namely, by an alphabet—is nevertheless so unnatural that it has apparently been invented only once in all history (Gelb, 1963). Perceiving the complex speech code is thus basic to language, and to man, in a way that reading an alphabet is not. Being concerned about language, we are therefore the more interested in the speech code. Why are speech sounds, alone among acoustic signals and in spite of the limitations of the ear, perceived so well?

Acoustic Cues: A Restructuring of Phonemes at the Level of Sound

To know in what sense speech sounds are a code on the phonemes, we must first discover which aspects of the complex acoustic signal underlie the perception of particular phonemes. For the most part, the relevant data are at hand. We can now identify acoustic features that are sufficient and important cues for the perception of almost all the segmental phonemes.[6] Much remains to be learned, but we know enough to see that the phonemic message is restructured in the sound stream and, from that knowledge, to make certain inferences about perception.

[6] For the discussion that follows we shall rely most heavily on the results of experiments with synthetic speech carried out at Haskins Laboratories. The reader will understand that a review of the relevant literature would refer to many other studies, including, in particular, those that rest on analysis of real speech. For recent reviews and discussions, see Stevens and House, in press; Kozhevnikov and Chistovich, 1965, Chapter 6.

An Example of Restructuring

To illustrate the nature of the code, we will describe an important acoustic cue for the perception of the voiced stop /d/. This example is important in its own right and also broadly representative. The phoneme /d/, or something very much like it, occurs in all the languages of the world.[7] In English, and perhaps in other languages, too, it carries a heavy load of information, probably more than any other single phoneme (Denes, 1963); and it is among the first of the phonemelike segments to appear in the vocalizations of the child (Whetnall & Fry, 1964, p. 84). The acoustic cue we have chosen to examine—the second-formant transition[8]—is a major cue for all the consonants except, perhaps, the fricatives /s/ and /š/, and is probably the single most important carrier of linguistic information in the speech signal (Delattre, 1958, 1962; Delattre, Liberman, & Cooper, 1955, 1964; Harris, 1958; Liberman, 1957;

[7] Some form of a voiceless unaspirated stop having a place of production in the alveolar-dental region is universal (Hockett, 1955; Joseph Greenberg, personal communication, November, 1966). The particular example, /d/, used here is a member of that class in almost all important respects. Even in regard to voicing, it is a better fit than might at first appear, since it shares with the voiceless, unaspirated stop of, say, French or Hungarian, the same position on the dimension of voice-onset-time, which is a most important variable for phonemic differences in voicing. (Lisker & Abramson, 1964a, 1964b).

[8] A formant is a concentration of acoustic energy within a restricted frequency region. Three or four formants are usually seen in spectrograms of speech. In the synthetic, hand-painted spectrograms of Figures 1 and 2, only the lowest two are represented. Formants are referred to by number, the first being the lowest in frequency, the second, the next higher, and so on. A formant transition is a relatively rapid change in the position of the formant on the frequency scale.

Liberman, Delattre, Cooper, & Gerstman, 1954; Liberman, Ingemann, Lisker, Delattre, & Cooper, 1959; Lisker, 1957; O'Connor, Gerstman, Liberman, Delattre, & Cooper, 1957).

Context-conditioned variations in the acoustic cue. Figure 1 displays two highly simplified spectrographic patterns that will, when converted into sound, be heard as the syllables /di/ and /du/ (Liberman, Delattre, Cooper, & Gerstman, 1954). They exemplify the results of a search for the acoustic cues in which hand-drawn or "synthetic" spectrograms were used as a basis for experimenting with the complex acoustic signal (Cooper, 1950, 1953; Cooper, Delattre, Liberman, Borst, & Gerstman, 1952; Cooper, Liberman, & Borst, 1951). The steady-state formants, comprising approximately the right-hand two-thirds of each pattern, are sufficient to produce the vowels /i/ and /u/ (Delattre, Liberman, & Cooper, 1951; Delattre, Liberman, Cooper, & Gerstman, 1952). At the left of each pattern are the relatively rapid changes in frequency of the formants—the formant transitions—that are, as we indicated, important acoustic cues for the perception of the consonants. The transition of the first, or lower, formant, rising from a very low frequency to the level appropriate for the vowel, is a cue for the class of voiced stops /b,d,g/ (Delattre, Liberman, & Cooper, 1955; Liberman, Delattre, & Cooper, 1958). It would be exactly the same for /bi, bu/ and /gi, gu/ as for /di, du/. Most generally, this transition is a cue for the perception of manner and voicing. The acoustic feature in which we are here interested is the transition of the second formant, which is, in the patterns of Figure 1, a cue for distinguishing among the voiced stops, /b,d,g/; that is to say, the second-formant transition for /gi/ or /bi/, as well as /gu/ or

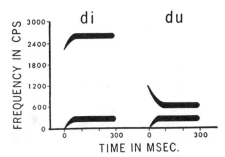

FIG. 1.   Spectrographic patterns sufficient for the synthesis of /d/ before /i/ and /u/.

/bu/, would be different from those for /di/ and /du/ (Liberman, Delattre, Cooper, & Gerstman, 1954). In general, transitions of the second formant carry important information about the place of production of most consonants (Delattre, 1958; Liberman, 1957; Liberman, Delattre, Cooper, & Gerstman, 1954).

It is, then, the second-formant transitions that are, in the patterns of Figure 1, the acoustic cues for the perception of the /d/ segment of the syllables /di/ and /du/. We would first note that /d/ is the same perceptually in the two cases, and then see how different are the acoustic cues. In the case of /di/ the transition rises from approximately 2200 cps to 2600 cps; in /du/ it falls from about 1200 to 700 cps. In other words, what is perceived as the same phoneme is cued, in different contexts, by features that are vastly different in acoustic terms. How different these acoustic features are in nonspeech perception can be determined by removing them from the patterns of Figure 1 and sounding them in isolation. When we do that, the transition isolated from the /di/ pattern sounds like a rapidly rising whistle or glissando on high pitches, the one from /du/ like a rapidly falling whistle on low pitches.[9]

[9] This is true of the patterns shown in Figure 1 as converted to sound by the Pattern Playback. When the formants correspond

436   Liberman, Cooper, Shankweiler, and Studdert-Kennedy

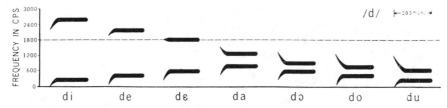

Fig. 2.   Spectrographic patterns sufficient for the synthesis of /d/ before vowels.   (Dashed line at 1800 cps shows the "locus" for /d/.)

These signals could hardly sound more different from each other.   Furthermore, neither of them sounds like /d/ nor like speech of any sort.

The disappearance of phoneme boundaries: Parallel transmission. We turn now to another, related aspect of the code: the speech signal typically does not contain segments corresponding to the discrete and commutable phonemes. There is no way to cut the patterns of Figure 1 so as to recover /d/ segments that can be substituted one for the other.   Nor can we make the commutation simply by introducing a physical continuity between the cut ends, as we might, for example, if we were segmenting and recombining the alphabetic elements of cursive writing.

Indeed, if we could somehow separate commutability from segmentability, we should have to say that there is no /d/ segment at all, whether commutable or not.   We cannot cut either the /di/ or the /du/ pattern in such a way as to obtain some piece that will produce /d/ alone.   If we cut progressively into the syllable from the right-hand end, we hear /d/ plus a vowel, or a nonspeech sound; at no point will we hear only /d/.   This is so because the formant transition is, at every instant,

more closely in their various constant features to those produced by the human vocal apparatus, the musical qualities described above may be harder to hear or may disappear altogether.   So long as the second-formant transitions of /di/ and /du/ are not heard as speech, however, they do not sound alike.

providing information about two phonemes, the consonant and the vowel— that is, the phonemes are being transmitted in parallel.

The Locus: An Acoustic Invariant?

The patterns of Figure 2 produce /d/ in initial position with each of a variety of vowels, thus completing a series of which the patterns shown in Figure 1 are the extremes.   If one extrapolates the various second-formant transitions backward in time, he sees that they seem to have diverged from a single frequency.   To find that frequency more exactly, and to determine whether it might in some sense be said to characterize /d/, we can, as in Figure 3, pair each of a number of straight second formants with first formants that contain a rising transition sufficient to signal a voiced stop of some kind.   On listening to such patterns, one hears an initial /d/ most strongly when the straight second formant is at 1800 cps.   This has been called the /d/ "locus" (Delattre, Liberman, & Cooper, 1955).   There are, correspondingly, second-formant loci for other consonants, the frequency position of the locus being correlated with the place of production.   In general, the locus moves somewhat as a function of the associated vowel, but, except for a discontinuity in the case of /k, g, ŋ/), the locus is more nearly invariant than the formant transition (Delattre, Liberman, & Cooper, 1955; Ohman, 1966; Stevens & House, 1956).

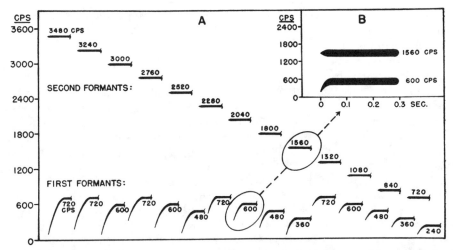

Fig. 3. Schematic display of the stimuli used in finding the second-formant loci of /b/, /d/, and /g/. (A—Frequency positions of the straight second formants and the various first formants with which each was paired. B—A typical test pattern, made up of the first and second formants circled in A. The best pattern for /d/ was the one with the straight second formant at 1800 cps. Figure taken from Delattre, Liberman, and Cooper, 1955.)

Is there, then, an invariant acoustic cue for /d/? Consider the various second formants that all begin at the 1800-cycle locus and proceed from there to a number of different vowel positions, such as are shown in Figure 4.

We should note first that these transitions are not superimposable, so that if they are to be regarded as invariant acoustic cues, it could only be in the very special and limited sense that they start at the same point on the frequency

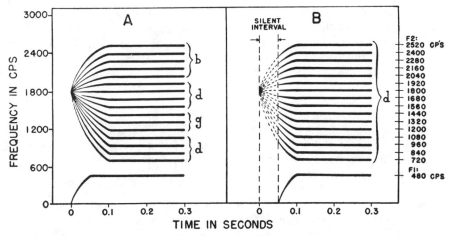

Fig. 4. A—Second-formant transitions that start at the /d/ locus and B—comparable transitions that merely "point" at it, as indicated by the dotted lines. (Those of A produce syllables beginning with /b/, /d/, or /g/, depending on the frequency-level of the formant; those of B produce only syllables beginning with /d/. Figure taken from Delattre, Liberman, and Cooper, 1955.)

438   Liberman, Cooper, Shankweiler, and Studdert-Kennedy

scale. But even this very limited invariance is not to be had. If we convert the patterns of Figure 4 to sound, having paired each of the second formants in turn with the single first formant shown at the bottom of the figure, we do not hear /d/ in every case. Taking the second formants in order, from the top down, we hear first /b/, then /d/, then /g/, then once again /d/, as shown in the figure. In order to hear /d/ in every case, we must erase the first part of the transition, as shown in Figure 4B, so that it "points" at the locus but does not actually begin there. Thus, the 1800-cps locus for /d/ is not a part of the acoustic signal, nor can it be made part of that signal without grossly changing the perception (Delattre, Liberman, & Cooper, 1955).

Though the locus can be defined in acoustic terms—that is, as a particular frequency—the concept is more articulatory than acoustic, as can be seen in the rationalization of the locus by Stevens and House (1956). What is common to /d/ before all the vowels is that the articulatory tract is closed at very much the same point. According to the calculations of Stevens and House, the resonant frequency of the cavity at the instant of closure is approximately 1800 cps, but since no sound emerges until some degree of opening has occurred, the locus frequency is not radiated as part of the acoustic signal. At all events it seems clear that, though the locus is more nearly invariant with the phoneme than is the transition itself, the invariance is a derived one, related more to articulation than to sound. As we will see later, however, the locus is only a step toward the invariance with phoneme perception that we must seek; better approximations to that invariance are probably to be had by going farther back in the chain of articulatory events,

beyond the cavity shapes that underlie the locus, to the commands that produce the shapes.

How General Is the Restructuring?

Having dealt with the restructuring of only one phoneme and one acoustic cue, we should say now that, with several interesting exceptions yet to be noted, it is generally true of the segmental phonemes that they are drastically restructured at the level of sound.[10] We will briefly summarize what is known in this regard about the various types of cues and linguistic classes or dimensions.

Transitions of the second formant. For the second-formant transition—the cue with which we have been concerned and the one that is, perhaps, the most important for the perception of consonants according to place of production—the kind of invariance lack we found with /d/ characterizes all the voiced stops, voiceless stops, and nasal consonants (Liberman, Delattre, Cooper, & Gerstman, 1954; Malecot, 1956). Indeed, the invariance problem is, if anything, further complicated in these other phonemes. In the case of /g, k, ŋ), for example, there is a sudden and considerable shift in the locus as between the unrounded and rounded vowels, creating a severe lack of correspondence between acoustic sig-

---

[10] Somewhat similar complications arise in the suprasegmental domain. For data concerning the relation between the acoustic signal and the perception of intonation see Hadding-Koch and Studdert-Kennedy, 1964a, 1964b.
Lieberman (1967) has measured some of the relevant physiological variables and, on the basis of his findings, has devised a hypothesis to account for the perception of intonation, in particular the observations of Hadding-Koch and Studdert-Kennedy. Lieberman's account of perception in the suprasegmental domain fits well with our own views about the decoding of segmental phonemes, discussed later in this paper.

nal and linguistic perception that we mentioned earlier in this paper and that we have dealt with in some detail elsewhere (Liberman, 1957).

With the liquids and semivowels /r, l, w, j/ the second-formant transition originates at the locus—as it cannot in the case of the stop and nasal consonants—so the lack of correspondence between acoustic signal and phoneme is less striking, but even with these phonemes the transition cues are not superimposable for occurrences of the same consonant in different contexts (Lisker, 1957; O'Connor, Gerstman, Liberman, Delattre, & Cooper, 1957).

Transitions of the third formant. What of third-formant transitions, which also contribute to consonant perception in terms of place of production? Though we know less about the third-formant transitions than about those of the second, such evidence as we have does not suggest that an invariant acoustic cue can be found here (Harris, Hoffman, Liberman, Delattre, & Cooper, 1958; Lisker, 1957b; O'Connor, Gerstman, Liberman, Delattre, & Cooper, 1957). In fact, the invariance problem is further complicated in that the third-formant transition seems to be more or less important (relative to the second-formant transition, for example) depending on the phonemic context. In the case of our /di, du/ example (Figure 1), we find that an appropriate transition of the third formant contributes considerably to the perception of /d/ in /di/ but not at all to /d/ in /du/. To produce equal—that is, equally convincing—/d/'s before both /i/ and /u/, we must use acoustic cues that are, if anything, even more different than the two second-formant transitions we described earlier in this section.

Constriction noises. The noises produced at the point of constriction—as in the fricatives and stops—are another set of cues for consonant perception according to place of production, the relevant physical variable being the frequency position of the band-limited noise. When these noises have considerable duration—as in the fricatives —the cue changes but little with context. Since the cue provided by these noises is of overriding importance in the perception of /s/ and /š/, we should say that these consonants show little or no restructuring in the sound stream (Harris, 1958; Hughes & Halle, 1956). (This may not be true when the speech is rapid.) They therefore constitute an exception to the usual strong dependence of the acoustic signal on its context—that is, to the effects of a syllabic coding operation.

On the other hand, the brief noise cues—the bursts, so called—of the stop consonants display as much restructuring as do the transitions of the second formant (Liberman, Delattre, & Cooper, 1952). Bursts of noise that produce the best /k/ or /g/ vary over a considerable frequency range depending on the following vowel. The range is so great that it extends over the domain of the /p, b/ burst, creating the curiosity of a single burst of noise at 1440 cps that is heard as /p/ before /i/ but as /k/ before /a/.[11] We should also note that the relative importance of the bursts, as of the transitions, varies greatly for the same stop in different contexts. For example, /g/ or /k/, which are powerfully cued by a second-formant transition before the vowel /æ/, will likely require a burst at an appropriate frequency if they are to be well perceived in front of /o/.[12]

[11] This result was obtained in the experiment (Liberman, Delattre, & Cooper, 1952) with synthetic speech referenced above and verified for real speech in a tape-cutting experiment by Carol Schatz (1954).

[12] This can be seen in the results of experiments on the bursts and transitions as

440   LIBERMAN, COOPER, SHANKWEILER, AND STUDDERT-KENNEDY

Thus, the same consonant is primarily cued in two different contexts by signals as physically different as a formant transition and a burst of noise.

Manner, voicing, and position. In describing the complexities of the relation between acoustic cue and perceived phoneme, we have so far dealt only with cues for place of production and only with consonants in initial position in the syllable. A comparable lack of regularity is also found in the distinctions of manner and voicing and in the cues for consonants in different positions (Abramson & Lisker, 1965; Delattre, 1958; Delattre, Liberman, & Cooper, 1955; Liberman, 1957; Liberman, Delattre, & Cooper, 1958; Liberman, Delattre, Cooper, & Gerstman, 1954; Liberman, Delattre, Gerstman, & Cooper, 1956; Lisker, 1957a, 1957b; Lisker & Abramson, 1964b; Ohman, 1966). We will not consider these cues in detail since the problems they present are similar to those already encountered. Indeed, the cues we have discussed as examples of encoding are merely a subset of those that show extensive restructuring as a function of context: it is the usual case that the acoustic cues for a consonant are different when the consonant is paired with different vowels, when it is in different positions (initial, medial, or final) with respect to the same vowels, and for all types of cues (manner or voicing, as well as place). Thus, for example, the cues for manner, place, and voicing of /b/ in /ba/ are acoustically different from those of /b/ in /ab/, the transitional cues for place being almost mirror images; further, the preceding set of cues differs from

cues for the stops (Liberman, Delattre, & Cooper, 1952; Liberman, Delattre, Cooper, & Gerstman, 1954). It is confirmed whenever one attempts, by using all possible cues, to synthesize the best stops.

corresponding sets for /b/ with each of the other vowels.

The vowels. We should remark, finally, on the acoustic cues for the vowels. For the steady-state vowels of Figures 1 and 2, perception depends primarily on the frequency position of the formants (Delattre, Liberman, & Cooper, 1951; Delattre, Liberman, Cooper, & Gerstman, 1952). There is, for these vowels, no restructuring of the kind found to be so common among the consonant cues and, accordingly, no problem of invariance between acoustic signal and perception.[13]

However, vowels are rarely steady state in normal speech; most commonly these phonemes are articulated between consonants and at rather rapid rates. Under these conditions vowels also show substantial restructuring—that is, the acoustic signal at no point corresponds to the vowel alone, but rather shows, at any instant, the merged influences of the preceding or following consonant (Lindblom & Studdert-Kennedy, in press; Lisker, 1958; Shearme & Holmes, 1962; Stevens & House, 1963).

In slow articulation, then, the acoustic cues for the vowels—and, as we saw earlier, the noise cues for fricatives —tend to be invariant. In this respect they differ from the cues for the other phonemes, which vary as a function of context at all rates of speaking. However, articulation slow enough to permit the vowels and fricatives to avoid being encoded is probably artificial and rare.

[13] The absolute formant **frequencies of the** same vowel are different for men, women, and children, and for different individuals, partly as a consequence of differences in the sizes of vocal tracts. This creates an invariance problem very different from the kind we have been discussing and more similar, perhaps, to the problems encountered in the perception of nonspeech sounds, such as the constant ratios of musical intervals.

Phoneme segmentation. We return now to the related problem of segmentation, briefly discussed above for the /di, du/ example. We saw there that the acoustic signal is not segmented into phonemes. If one examines the acoustic cues more generally, he finds that successive phonemes are most commonly merged in the sound stream. This is, as we will see, a correlate of the parallel processing that characterizes the speech code and is an essential condition of its efficiency. One consequence is that the acoustic cues cannot be divided on the time axis into segments of phonemic size.[14]

The same general conclusion may be reached by more direct procedures. Working with recordings of real speech, Harris (1953) tried to arrive at "building blocks" by cutting tape recordings into segments of phoneme length and then recombining the segments to form new words. "Experiments indicated that speech based upon one building block for each vowel and consonant not only sounds unnatural but is mostly unintelligible . . . [p. 962]." In a somewhat similar attempt to produce intelligible speech by the recombination of parts taken from previously recorded utterances, Peterson, Wang, and Sivertsen (1958) concluded that the smallest segments one can use are of roughly half-syllable length. Thus, it has not been possible, in general, to synthesize speech from prerecorded segments of phonemic dimen-

[14] This is not to say that the sound spectrogram fails to show discontinuities along the time axis. Fant (1962a, 1962b) discusses the interpretation to be given these abrupt changes and the temporal segments bounded by them. He warns: "Sound segment boundaries should not be confused with phoneme boundaries. Several adjacent sounds of connected speech may carry information on one and the same phoneme, and there is overlapping in so far as one and the same sound segment carries information on several adjacent phonemes [1962a, p. 9]."

sions. Nor can we cut the sound stream along the time dimension so as to recover segments that will be perceived as separate phonemes. Of course, there are exceptions. As we might expect, these are the steady-state vowels and the long-duration noises of certain fricatives in which, as we have seen, the sounds show minimal restructuring. Apart from these exceptions, however, segments corresponding to the phonemes are not found at the acoustic level.

We shall see later that the articulatory gestures corresponding to successive phonemes—or, more precisely, their subphonemic features—are overlapped, or shingled, one onto another. This parallel delivery of information produces at the acoustic level the merging of influences we have already referred to and yields irreducible acoustic segments of approximately syllabic dimensions. Thus, segmentation also exhibits a complex relation between linguistic structure or perception, on the one hand, and the sound stream on the other.

PERCEPTION OF THE RESTRUCTURED
PHONEMES: THE SPEECH MODE

If phonemes are encoded syllabically in the sound stream, they must be recovered in perception by an appropriate decoder. Perception of phonemes that have been so encoded might be expected to differ from the perception of those that have not and also, of course, from nonspeech. In this section we will suggest that such differences do, in fact, exist.

We have already seen one example of such a difference in the transition cues for /d/ in /di/ and /du/. Taken out of speech context, these transitions sound like whistles, the one rising through a range of high pitches and the other falling through low pitches; they do not sound like each other, nor

442   Liberman, Cooper, Shankweiler, and Studdert-Kennedy

even like speech. This example could be multiplied to include the transition cues for many other phonemes. With simplified speech of the kind already shown, the listener's perception is very different depending on whether he is, for whatever reason, in the speech mode or out of it (Brady, House, & Stevens, 1961).

Even on the basis of what can be heard in real speech, one might have suspected that the perception of encoded and unencoded phonemes [15] is somehow different. One has only to listen carefully to some of the latter in order to make reasonably accurate guesses about the auditory and acoustic dimensions that are relevant to their perception. The fricatives /s/ and /š/, for example, obviously differ in manner from other phonemes in that there is noise of fairly long duration; moreover, one can judge by listening that they differ from each other in the "pitch" of the noise—that is, in the way the energy is distributed along the frequency scale. Consider, on the other hand, the encoded phonemes /b,d,g/. No amount of listening, no matter how careful, is likely to reveal that an important manner cue is a rapidly rising frequency at the low end of the frequency scale (first formant), or that these stops are distinguished from each other primarily by the direction and extent of a rapid frequency glide in the upper frequency range (second and third formants).

[15] There is a need, in much that follows, for a convenient way to refer to classes of phonemes that show much—or little—restructuring of their acoustic cues as a function of context. The former are, indeed, encoded. We shall refer to the latter as "unencoded phonemes," implying only that they are found at the other end of a continuum on degree of restructuring; we do not wish to imply differences in the processes affecting these phonemes, whether or not such differences can be inferred from their perceptual characteristics.

These observations of perceptual differences between speech and nonspeech sounds, and even among classes of phonemes, do not stand alone. Controlled experiments can show more accurately, if sometimes less directly, the differences in perception. We will next consider some of these experiments.

Tendencies toward Categorical and Continuous Perception

Research with some of the encoded phonemes has shown that they are categorical, not only in the abstract linguistic sense, but as immediately given in perception. Consider, first, that in listening to continuous variations in acoustic signals, one ordinarily discriminates many more stimuli than he can absolutely identify. Thus, we discriminate about 1200 different pitches, for example, though we can absolutely identify only about seven. Perception of the restructured phonemes is different in that listeners discriminate very little better than they identify absolutely; that is to say, they hear the phonemes but not the intraphonemic variations.

The effect becomes clear impressionistically if one listens to simplified, synthetic speech signals in which the second-formant transition is varied in relatively small, acoustically equal steps through a range sufficient to produce the three stops, /b/, /d/, and /g/. One does not hear steplike changes corresponding to the changes in the acoustic signal, but essentially quantal jumps from one perceptual category to another.

To evaluate this effect more exactly, various investigators have made quantitative comparisons of the subjects' ability to identify the stimuli absolutely and to discriminate them on any basis whatsoever. For certain consonant distinctions it has been found that the mode of perception is, in fact, nearly categorical: listeners can discriminate only slightly better than they can identify absolutely. In greater or lesser degree, this has been found for /b,d,g/ (Eimas, 1963; Griffith, 1958; Liberman, Harris, Hoffman, & Griffith, 1957; Studdert-Kennedy, Liberman, & Stevens, 1963, 1964); /d,t/ (Liberman, Harris, Kinney, & Lane, 1961)[16]; /b,p/ in intervocalic position (Liberman, Harris, Eimas, Lisker, & Bastian, 1961), and presence or absence of /p/ in *slit* vs. *split* (Bastian, Delattre, & Liberman, 1959; Bastian, Eimas, & Liberman, 1961; Harris, Bastian, & Liberman, 1961).

The perception of unencoded steady-state vowels is quite different from the perception of stops.[17] To appreciate this difference one need only listen to synthetic vowels that vary, as in the example of the stops, in relatively small and acoustically equal steps through a range sufficient to produce three adjacent phonemes—say /i/, /I/, and /ɛ/. As heard, these vowels change step-by-step, much as the physical stimulus changes: the vowel /i/ shades into /I/, and /I/ into /ɛ/. Immediate perception is more nearly continuous than categorical and the listener hears many intraphonemic variations. More precise measures of vowel perception indicate that, in contrast to the stops, listeners can discriminate many more

stimuli than they can identify absolutely (Fry, Abramson, Eimas, & Liberman, 1962; Stevens, Ohman, & Liberman, 1963; Stevens, Ohman, Studdert-Kennedy, & Liberman, 1964). Similar studies of the perception of vowel duration (Bastian & Abramson, 1962) and tones in Thai (Abramson, 1961), both of which are phonemic in that language, have produced similar results. We should suppose that steady-state vowels, vowel duration, and the tones can be perceived in essentially the same manner as continuous variations in nonspeech signals. The results of a direct experimental comparison by Eimas (1963) suggest that this is so.

We emphasize that in speaking of vowels we have so far been concerned only with those that are isolated and steady state. These are, as we have said, unencoded and hence not necessarily perceived in the speech mode. But what of the more usual situation we described earlier, that of vowels between consonants and in rapid articulation? Stevens (1966) has supposed that the rapid changes in formant position characteristic of such vowels would tend to be referred in perception to the speech mode, and he has some evidence that this is so, having found that perception of certain vowels in proper dynamic context is more nearly categorical than that of steady-state vowels. Inasmuch as these rapidly articulated vowels are substantially restructured in the sound stream, Stevens' results may be assumed to reflect the operation of the speech decoder.

Lateral Differences in the Perception of Speech and Nonspeech

The conclusion that there is a speech mode, and that it is characterized by processes different from those underlying the perception of other sounds,

[16] Studies of this distinction (and of the corresponding ones for the other stops) in 11 diverse languages indicate that it tends to be categorical also in production. (Abramson & Lisker, 1965; Lisker & Abramson, 1964a, 1964b.)

[17] In experiments with mimicry, Ludmilla Chistovich and her colleagues have obtained differences between vowels and consonants that are consistent with the differing tendencies toward categorical and continuous perception described here. (Chistovich, 1960; Chistovich, Klaas, & Kuz'min, 1962; Galunov & Chistovich, 1965; Kozhevnikov & Chistovich, 1965.)

444   LIBERMAN, COOPER, SHANKWEILER, AND STUDDERT-KENNEDY

is strengthened by recent indications that speech and nonspeech sounds are processed primarily in different hemispheres of the brain. Using Broadbent's (1954) method of delivering competing stimuli simultaneously to the two ears, investigators have found that speech stimuli presented to the right ear (hence, mainly to the left cerebral hemisphere) are better identified than those presented to the left ear (hence, mainly to the right cerebral hemisphere), and that the reverse is true for melodies and sonar signals (Broadbent & Gregory, 1964; Bryden, 1963; Chaney & Webster, 1965; Kimura, 1961, 1964, 1967). In the terminology of this paper, the encoded speech signals are more readily decoded in the left hemisphere than in the right. This suggests the existence of a special left-hemisphere mechanism different from the right-hemisphere mechanism for the perception of sounds not similarly encoded. It is of interest, then, to ask whether the encoded stops and the unencoded steady-state vowels are, perhaps, processed unequally by the two hemispheres. An experiment was carried out (Shankweiler & Studdert-Kennedy, 1967b) designed to answer this question, using synthetic speech syllables that contrasted in just one phoneme. A significantly greater right-ear advantage was found for the encoded stops than for the unencoded steady-state vowels. The fact that the steady-state vowels are less strongly lateralized in the dominant (speech) hemisphere may be taken to mean that these sounds, being unencoded, can be, and presumably sometimes are, processed as if they were nonspeech. In another experiment (Shankweiler & Studdert-Kennedy, 1967a), the consonant and vowel comparisons were made with real speech. Different combinations of the same set of consonant-vowel-consonant syllables were used

for both tests. As before, a decisive right-ear advantage was found for contrasting stop consonants, and again there was no difference for vowels, even though these were here articulated in dynamic context between consonants. We will be interested to determine what happens to lateral differences in vowel perception when the vowels are very rapidly articulated. Such vowels are, as has been said, necessarily restructured to some extent and may be correspondingly dependent on the speech decoder for their perception.

Perception of Speech by Machine and by Eye

If speech is, as we have suggested, a special code, its perception should be difficult in the absence of an appropriate decoder such as we presumably use in listening to speech sounds. It is relevant, therefore, to note how very difficult it is to read visual transforms of speech or to construct automatic speech recognizers.

Consider, first, a visual transform— for example, the spectrogram. As we have already seen, the spectrographic pattern for a particular phoneme typically looks very different in different contexts. Furthermore, visual inspection of a spectrogram does not reveal how a stretch of speech might be divided into segments corresponding to phonemes, or even how many phonemes it might contain: the eye sees the transformed acoustic signal in its undecoded form. We should not be surprised, then, to discover that spectrograms are, in fact, extremely difficult to read.

Some part of the difficulty may be attributed to inadequacies of the transform or to lack of training. But an improved transform, if one should be found, would not by itself suffice to make spectrograms readable, since it would not obviate the need to decode.

SCHEMA FOR PRODUCTION

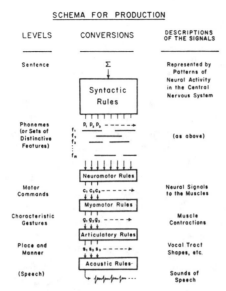

Fig. 5.   Schematic representations of assumed stages in speech production.

Nor is training likely to overcome the difficulty. Many persons have had considerable experience with spectrograms, yet none has found it possible to read them well.[18] Ideally, training in "reading" spectrograms should cause the transitions for /d/ in /di/ and /du/ to look alike. The speech decoder, after all, makes them sound alike when speech is perceived by ear; moreover, it seems obvious that if the decoder did not do this, speech would be much more difficult to perceive. If, as we suspect, training alone cannot make the acoustic cues for the same phoneme *look* alike, then we should, perhaps, conclude that the speech decoder, which makes them *sound* alike, is biologically tied to an auditory input.

[18] "As a matter of fact I have not met one single speech researcher who has claimed he could read speech spectrograms fluently, and I am no exception myself [Fant, 1962a, p. 4]." Spectrograms are, even so, less difficult to read than oscillograms—whence their popular name, "visible speech," and much of the early enthusiasm for them (Potter, Kopp, & Green, 1947).

How, then, do machines fare in recognizing the encoded sounds of speech? If speech were a cipher, like print, it would be no more difficult to build a speech recognizer than a print reader. In fact, the speech recognizer has proved to be more difficult, and by a very wide margin, largely because it needs an appropriate decoder, as a print reader does not, and because the design of that decoder is not easily accomplished—a conclusion confirmed by two decades of intensive effort. We might repeat, in passing, that for human beings the difficulty is the other way around: perceiving speech is far easier than reading.

Encoding and Decoding: From Phoneme to Sound and Back

Conversions from Phoneme to Sound

Having considered the evidence that speech is a code on the phonemes, we must ask how the encoding might have come about. The schema in Figure 5 represents the various conversions that presumably occur as speech proceeds from sentence, through the empty segments at the phoneme level, to the final acoustic signal. The topmost box, labeled Syntactic Rules, would, if properly developed, be further broken down into phrase-structure rules, transformation rules, morphophonemic rules, and the like. (See, for example, Chomsky, 1964.) These processes would be of the greatest interest if we were dealing with speech perception in the broadest sense. Here, however, we may start with the message in the form of an ordered sequence of phonemes (or, as we will see, their constituent features) and follow it through the successive converters that yield, at the end, the acoustic waveform.

Subphonemic features: Their role in production. First, we must take account of the fact that the phonemes

446   Liberman, Cooper, Shankweiler, and Studdert-Kennedy

are compounded of a smaller number of elements, and, indeed, shift the emphasis from the phoneme to these subphonemic features.[19] The total gesture in the articulation of /b/, for example, can be broken down into several distinctive elements: (a) closing and opening of the upper vocal tract in such a way as to produce the manner feature characteristic of the stop consonants; (b) closing and opening of the vocal tract specifically at the lips, thus producing the place feature termed bilabiality; (c) closing the velum to provide the feature of orality; and (d) starting vocal fold vibration simultaneously with the opening of the lips, appropriate to the feature of voicing. The phoneme /p/ presumably shares with /b/ features 1, 2, and 3, but differs as to feature 4, in that vocal fold vibration

[19] The term "feature" has varied uses, even in this paper. Thus, in this paragraph, we describe a particular speech gesture in conventional phonetic terms, referring to how the articulators move and where the constrictions occur as the manner and place features that, taken together, characterize the gesture. Two paragraphs later, the description of a possible model for speech production identifies subphonemic features as implicit instructions to separate and independent parts of the motor machinery. Viewed in this way, the distinctive features of a phoneme are closely linked to specific muscles and the neural commands that actuate them.

Distinctive features of this kind are clearly different from those so well known from the work of Jakobson and his colleagues. See Jakobson, Fant, and Halle (1952) and the various revisions proposed by the several authors (Fant, 1967; Halle, 1964; Jakobson & Halle, 1956; Stevens & Halle, in press). We are, nevertheless, deeply indebted to them for essential points—in particular, that the phonemes can be characterized by sets of features which are few in number, limited to a very few states each, and maintained throughout several phonemes. Other important characteristics for an ideal system of distinctive features include mutual independence, clear correspondences with physiological—or acoustic—observables, and as much universality across languages as parsimony for a single language will allow.

begins some 50 or 60 milliseconds after opening of the lips; /m/ has features 1, 2, and 4 in common with /b/, but differs in feature 3, since the velum hangs open to produce the feature of nasality; /d/ has features 1, 3, and 4 in common with /b/, but has a different place of articulation; and so on.

That subphonemic features are present both in production and perception has by now been quite clearly established.[20] Later in this paper we will discuss some relevant data on production. Here we merely note that we must deal with the phonemes in terms of their constituent features because the existence of such features is essential to the speech code and to the efficient production and perception of language. We have earlier remarked that high rates of speech would overtax the temporal resolving power of the ear if the acoustic signal were merely a cipher on the phonemic structure of the language. Now we should note that *speaking* at rates of 10 to 15 phonemes per second would as surely be impossible if each phoneme required a separate and distinct oral gesture. Such rates can be achieved only if separate parts of the articulatory machinery— muscles of the lips, tongue, velum, etc. —can be separately controlled, and if the linguistic code is such that a change of state for any one of these articulatory entities, taken together with the current state of the others, is a change to another element of the code—that is, to another phoneme. Thus, dividing the load among the articulators allows each to operate at a reasonable pace, and tightening the code keeps the information rate high. It is this kind of parallel processing that makes it possible to get high-speed performance

[20] For discussions of the psychological reality of phoneme segments and subphonemic features, see Kozhevnikov and Chistovich, 1965; Stevens and House, in press; Wickelgren, 1966.

with low-speed machinery. As we will see, it also accounts for the overlapping and intermixing of the acoustic signals for the phonemes that is characteristic of the speech code.

A model for production. The simplest possible model of the production process would, then, have the phonemes of an utterance represented by sets of subphonemic features, and these in turn would be assumed to exist in the central nervous system as implicit instructions [21] to separate and independent parts of the motor machinery. The sequence of neural signals corresponding to this multidimensional string of control instructions may well require, for its actualization, some amplitude adjustments and temporal coordination, in the box labeled "Neuromotor Rules," in order to yield the neural impulses that go directly to the selected muscles of articulation and cause them to contract. If we are to continue to make the simplest possible assumption, however, we must suppose that reorganization of the instructions at this stage would be limited to such coordination and to providing supplementary neural signals to insure cooperative activity of the remainder of the articulatory apparatus; there would be no reorganization of the commands to the "primary" actuators for the selected features. In that case, the neural signals that emerge would bear still an essentially one-to-one correspond-

ence with the several dimensions of the subphonemic structure. Indeed, this is a necessary condition for our model, since total reorganization at this stage would destroy the parallel processing, referred to earlier, on which high-speed reception depends, or else yield a syllabic language from which the phoneme strings could not be recovered.

The next conversion, from neural command (in the final common paths) to muscle contraction, takes place in the box labeled "Myomotor Rules." If muscles contract in accordance with the signals sent to them, then this conversion should be essentially trivial, and we should be able not only to observe the muscle contractions by looking at their EMG signals, but also to infer the neural signals at the preceding level.

It is at the next stage—the conversion from muscle contraction to vocal tract shapes by way of Articulatory Rules—that a very considerable amount of encoding or restructuring must surely occur. If we take into account the structure and function of the articulatory system, in particular the intricate linkages and the spatial overlap of the component parts, we must suppose that the relation between contraction and resulting shape is complex, though predictable. True encoding occurs as a consequence of two further aspects of this conversion; the fact that the subphonemic features can be, and are, put through in parallel means that each new set of contractions (*a*) starts from whatever configuration then exists (as the result of the preceding contractions) and (*b*) typically occurs before the last set has ended, with the result that the shape of the tract at any instant represents the merged effects of past and present instructions. Such merging is, in effect, an encoding operation according to our use of that term, since it involves an extensive restructuring of the output—in this case, the

---

[21] These instructions might be of two types, "on-off" or "go to," even in a maximally simple model. In the one case, the affected muscle would contract or not with little regard for its current state (or the position of the articulator it moves); in the other, the instruction would operate via the γ-efferent system to determine the degree of contraction (hence, the final position of the articulator, whatever its initial position). Both types of instruction—appropriate, perhaps, to fast and slow gestures, respectively—may reasonably be included in the model.

shape of the tract. The relation of message units to code becomes especially complex when temporal and spatial overlaps occur together. Thus, the conversion from muscle contraction to shape is, by itself, sufficient to produce the kinds of complex relation between phoneme and sound that we have found to exist in the overall process of speech production, that is, a loss of segmentability together with very large changes in the essential acoustic signals as a function of context. Given the structure of the articulatory apparatus, these complexities appear to be a necessary concomitant of the parallel processing that makes the speech code so efficient.

The final conversion, from shape to sound, proceeds by what we have in Figure 5 called Acoustic Rules. These rules, which are now well understood,[22] are complex from a computational standpoint, but they operate on an instant-by-instant basis and yield (for the most part) one-to-one relations of shape to sound.

Does the Encoding Truly Occur in the Conversion from Command to Shape?

We have supposed that, of the four conversions between phoneme and sound, one at least—the conversion from contractions to tract shape—is calculated to produce an encoding of the kind we found when earlier we examined the acoustic cues for phoneme perception. But does it, in fact, produce that encoding, and if so, does it account for all of it? Downstream from this level there is only the conversion from shape to sound, and that, though complex, does not appear to involve encoding. But what of the upstream conversions, particularly the one

[22] The dependence of speech sound on vocal tract shape (and movement) has, of course, been studied by many workers and for many years. A landmark in this field, and justification for our statement, is the book by Fant (1960).

that lies between the neural representations of the phonemes and the commands to the articulatory muscles? We cannot at the present time observe those processes, nor can we directly measure their output—that is, the commands to the muscles. We can, however, observe some aspects of the contractions—for example, the electromyographic correlates—and if we assume, as seems reasonable, that the conversion from command to contractions is straightforward, then we can quite safely infer the structure of the commands.[23] By determining to what extent those inferred commands (if not the electromyographic signals themselves) are invariant with the phoneme we can, then, discover how much of the encoding occurs in the conversion from contraction to shape (Articulatory Rules) and how much at higher levels.

[23] For commands of the on-off type (see Footnote 21), we would expect muscle contractions—and EMG potentials—to be roughly proportional to the commands; hence, the commands will be mirrored directly by the EMG potentials when these can be measured unambiguously for the muscles of interest. All these conditions are realizable, at least approximately, for a number of phoneme combinations—for example, the bilabial stops and nasal consonants with unrounded vowels, as described in later paragraphs.

Commands of the "go to" type, which may well be operative in gestures that are relatively slow and precise, would presumably operate via the γ-efferent system to produce only so much contraction of the muscle as is needed to achieve a target length. The contraction—and the resulting EMG signal—would then be different for different starting positions, that is, for the same phoneme in different contexts. Even so, the significant aspects of the command can be inferred, since presence versus absence and sequential position (if not the relative timing) of the EMG signal persist despite even large changes in its magnitude.

For general discussions of the role of electromyography in research on speech, see the reviews by Cooper (1965) and Fromkin and Ladefoged (1966).

Motor commands as presumed invariants. Before discussing the electromyographic evidence, we should say what kind of invariance with the subphonemic features (hence, with the phonemes) we might, at best, expect to find. It should be clear from many of the data presented in this paper that language is no more a left-to-right process at the acoustic level than it is syntactically. As we have seen, the acoustic representations of the successive phonemes are interlaced. Some control center must therefore "know" what the syllable is to be in order that its component subphonemic features may be appropriately combined and overlapped. There are other grounds than the data we have cited for inferring such syllabic organization. Temporal relations between syllables may be adjusted for slow or rapid speech and for changes in syllable duration such as Lindblom has reported for a given syllable placed in different polysyllabic contexts. But these changes in syllable duration do not affect all portions of the syllable equally: timing relations within the syllable are also adjusted according to context (Lindblom, 1964), and this must entail variation in the relative timing of the component subphonemic features, as is suggested by Kozhevnikov and Chistovich's (1965) analysis of the articulatory structure of consonant clusters. Ohman (1964, 1966) has proposed a model for syllable articulation consistent with this analysis. Such contextual variations preclude the invariance of all the features that comprise a phoneme in a particular context. The most that we can expect is that some subset of these features, and so of the neural signals to the muscles (after operation of the Neuromotor Rules of Figure 5), will be invariant with the phoneme; there will then be for each subphonemic feature charac-

teristic neuromotor "markers," implicating only one or a few component parts of the system, perhaps only the contraction of a single specific muscle. These characteristic components of the total neural activity we will refer to as "motor commands."[24] We should also emphasize that we refer here to the phoneme as perceived, not as an abstract linguistic entity serving primarily a classificatory function.

Indications from electromyography. What, then, do we find when we look at the electromyographic (EMG) correlates of articulatory activity? Recent research in our laboratory and several others has been directed specifically to the questions raised in the preceding paragraphs, but the data are, as yet, quite limited. As we see these data, they do, however, permit some tentative conclusions.

When two adjacent phonemes are produced by spatially separate groups of muscles, there are essentially invariant EMG tracings from the characteristic gestures for each phoneme, regardless of the identity of the other.[25]

[24] Thus, the motor commands are, in one sense, abstract "-eme" type entities, with invariance assumed and observation directed to their discovery and enumeration; in another sense, and to the degree that observation justifies the assumption about invariance, motor commands constitute the essential subset of real neural signals with which a general model of production and perception should be principally concerned.

[25] It is not, of course, necessary that the EMG signals be precisely the same since invariance is expected only of the motor commands inferred from them. In the minimally complicated cases cited in this paragraph, the commands do transform into EMG potentials that are essentially the same (in different contexts), aside from some differences in magnitude.

Magnitude differences do occur, however, variously for the individual and context, and may have linguistic significance attributed to them. Thus, Fromkin (1966) concludes, mainly from EMG data on the lip-closing gestures of her principal speaker:

450   LIBERMAN, COOPER, SHANKWEILER, AND STUDDERT-KENNEDY

This has been found for /f/, for example, followed by /s/, /t/, /ts/, /θ/, or /θs/ and preceded by /i/, /il/, or /im/ (MacNeilage, 1963). Similarly, invariance has been found for /b/, /p/, and /m/ regardless of the following vowel (Fromkin, 1966; Harris, Lysaught, & Schvey, 1965). Here it is easy to associate the place and manner features with the contractions of specific muscles, and to equate the EMG signals for a specific feature wherever it occurs, at least within this limited set of phonemes. We should emphasize that corresponding invariance is not to be found in the acoustic signal: for /f/ the duration of the noise varies over a range of two to one in the contexts listed above; the vast differences in acoustic cue for /b/ or /p/ before various vowels were described in an earlier section.

When the temporally overlapping gestures for successive phonemes involve more or less adjacent muscles that control the same structures, it is of course more difficult to discover whether there is invariance or not.[26]

The results of the present investigation do not support the hypothesis that a simple one-to-one correspondence exists between a phoneme and its motor commands. For the bilabial stops /b/ and /p/ different motor commands produce different muscular gestures for these consonants occurring in utterance initial and final positions [p. 195].

Harris, Lysaught, and Schvey (1965) report, on the contrary, that differences in EMG signal for the lip-closing gesture did not reach statistical significance for two groups of five subjects each in two experiments, one of which overlapped Fromkin's study. They noted, though, that each of the subjects showed an individual pattern of small but consistent variations of EMG signal with context. (For a discussion of these differences in the interpretation of basically similar data, see Cooper, 1966.)

[26] A practical difficulty exists in allocating observed EMG potentials to specific muscles when more than one muscle is close to a

This is the situation for the /di, du/ examples we used earlier. In our own studies of such cases we find essentially identical EMG signals from tongue-tip electrodes for the initial consonant; however, the signal for a following phoneme that also involves the tongue tip may show substantial changes from its characteristic form (Harris, 1963; Harris, Huntington, & Sholes, 1966). Such changes presumably reflect the execution of position-type commands (see Footnotes 21 and 23) rather than reorganization at a higher level. True reorganization of the neural commands is not excluded by such data—indeed, we have some data that might be so interpreted (MacNeilage, DeClerk, & Silverman, 1966)—but the evidence so far is predominantly on the side of invariance.

If the commands—or, indeed, signals of any kind—are to be invariant with the phonemes, they must reflect the segmentation that is so conspicuously absent at the acoustic level. Do we, then, find such segmentation in the EMG records? Before answering that question, we should remind ourselves that the activity of a single muscle or muscle group does not, in any case, reflect a phoneme but only a subphonemic feature, and that a change from one phoneme to another may require a change in command for only one of several features. We should not expect, therefore, that all the subphonemic features will start and stop at each phoneme boundary, and, in fact, they do not. We do find, however, in the onsets and offsets of EMG activity in various muscles a segmentation like that of the several dimensions that constitute the phoneme. One can see, then, where the phoneme boundaries

---

surface electrode. Needle electrodes will often resolve such ambiguities, but they pose other problems of a practical nature.

must be.[27] This is in striking contrast to what is found at the acoustic level. There, as we have earlier pointed out, almost any segment we can isolate contains information about—and is a cue for—more than one phoneme. Thus in the matter of segmentation, too, the EMG potentials—and even more the motor commands inferred from them— bear a simpler relation to the perceived phonemes than does the acoustic signal.

In summary we should say that we do not yet know precisely to what extent motor commands are invariant with the phonemes. It seems reasonably clear, however, that they are more nearly invariant than are the acoustic signals, and we may conclude, therefore, that a substantial part of the restructuring occurs below the level of the commands. Whether some significant restructuring occurs also at higher levels can only be determined by further investigation.

Decoding: From Sound to Phoneme

If speech were a simple cipher one might suppose that phoneme perception could be explained by the ordinary principles of psychophysics and discrimination learning. On that view, which is probably not uncommon among psychologists, speech consists of sounds, much like any others, that happen to signal the phoneme units of the language. It is required of the listener only that he learn to connect each sound with the name of the appropri-

ate phoneme. To be sure, the sounds must be discriminably different, but this is a standard problem of auditory psychophysics and poses no special difficulty for the psychologist. It would follow that perception of speech is not different in any fundamental way from perception of other sounds (assuming sufficient practice), and that, as Lane (1965) and Cross, Lane, and Sheppard (1965) suppose, no special perceptual mechanism is required.

The point of this paper has been, to the contrary, that speech is, for the most part, a special code that must often make use of a special perceptual mechanism to serve as its decoder.[28] On the evidence presented here we should conclude, at the least, that most phonemes can not be perceived by a straightforward comparison of the incoming signal with a set of stored phonemic patterns or templates, even if one assumes mechanisms that can extract simple stimulus invariances such as, for example, constant ratios. To find acoustic segments that are in any reasonably simple sense invariant with linguistic (and perceptual) segments— that is, to perceive without decoding— one must go to the syllable level or higher. Now the number of syllables, reckoned simply as the number of permissible combinations and permutations of phonemes, is several thousand in English. But the number of acoustic patterns is far greater than that, since the acoustic signal varies considerably with the speaker and with the stress, intonation, and tempo of his speech

---

[27] In some cases the boundaries are sharply marked by a sudden onset of EMG signal for a particular muscle. Usually, though, the onsets are less abrupt and activity persists for a few hundred milliseconds. This might seem inadequate to provide segmentation markers for the rapid-fire phoneme sequences; indeed, precise time relationships may be blurred in normal articulation, but without obscuring the sequential order of events and the separateness of the channels carrying information about the several features.

[28] We referred earlier to perception in the speech mode and indicated that it was not operative—or, at least, not controlling—for some speech sounds as well as all nonspeech sounds. It need hardly be said, then, that the speech decoder provides only one pathway for perception; nonspeech sounds obviously require another pathway, which may serve adequately for the unencoded aspects of speech as well.

(Cooper, Liberman, Lisker, & Gaitenby, 1963; Liberman, Ingemann, Lisker, Delattre, & Cooper, 1959; Lindblom, 1963, Peterson & Sivertsen, 1960; Peterson, Wang, & Sivertsen, 1958; Sivertsen, 1961). To perceive speech by matching the acoustic signal to so many patterns would appear, at best, uneconomical and inelegant. More important, it would surely be inadequate, since it must fail to account for the fact that we do perceive phonemes. No theory can safely ignore the fact that phonemes are psychologically real.

How, then, is the phoneme to be recovered? We can imagine, at least in general outline, two very different possibilities: one, a mechanism that operates on a purely auditory basis, the other, by reference to the processes of speech production.

The case for an auditory decoder. The relevant point about an auditory decoder is that it would process the signal in *auditory* terms—that is, without reference to the way in which it was produced—and successfully extract the phoneme string. On the basis of what we know of speech, and of the attempts to build an automatic phoneme recognizer, we must suppose such a device would have to be rather complex. There is, to be sure, some evidence for the existence of processing mechanisms in the auditory system that illustrate at a very simple level one kind of thing that an auditory decoder might have to do. Thus, Whitfield and Evans (1965) have found single cells in the auditory cortex of the cat that respond to frequency changes but not to steady tones. Some of these cells responded more to tones that are frequency modulated upward and others to tones modulated downward. Such specificity of response also exists at lower levels in the auditory nervous system (Nelson, Erulkar, & Bryant, 1966). These findings are examples of a kind of auditory processing that might, perhaps, be part of a speech decoder, but one that would have to go beyond these processes—to more complex ones—if it were to deal successfully with the fact that very different transitions will, in different contexts, cue the same phoneme. But if this could be accomplished, and if it were done independently of motor parameters, we should have a purely auditory decoder.

The case for mediation by production. Though we cannot exclude the possibility that a purely auditory decoder exists, we find it more plausible to assume that speech is perceived by processes that are also involved in its production. The most general and obvious motivation for such a view is that the perceiver is also a speaker and must be supposed, therefore, to possess all the mechanisms for putting language through the successive coding operations that result eventually in the acoustic signal.[29] It seems unparsimonious to assume that the speaker-listener employs two entirely separate processes of equal status, one for encoding language and the other for decoding it. A simpler assumption is that there is only one process, with appropriate linkages between sensory and motor components.[30]

[29] We have noted that training in reading speech spectrograms has so far not succeeded in developing in the trainee a visual decoder for speech comparable to the one that works from an auditory input. This may well reflect the existence of special mechanisms for the speech decoder that are lacking for its visual counterpart. In general, a theory about the nature of the speech decoder—and, in particular, a motor theory—must be concerned with the nature of the mechanism, though not necessarily with the question of how it was acquired in the history of the individual or the race. This is an interesting, but separate, question and is not considered here.

[30] We should suppose that the links between perception and articulation exist at

Apart from parsimony, there are strong reasons for considering this latter view. Recall, for example, the case of /di, du/. There we saw that the acoustic patterns for /d/ were very different, though the perception of the consonantal segment was essentially the same. Since it appears that the /d/ gesture—or, at least, some important, "diagnostic" part of it—may also be essentially the same in the two cases, we are tempted to suppose that one hears the same /d/ because perception is mediated by the neuromotor correlates of gestures that are the same. This is basically the argument we used in one of our earliest papers (Liberman, Delattre, & Cooper, 1952) to account for the fact that bursts of sound at very different frequencies are required to produce the perception of /k/ before different vowels. Extending the argument, we tried in that same paper to account also for the fact that the same burst of sound is heard as /p/ before /i/ but as /k/ before /a/, the point being that, because of temporal overlap (and consequent acoustic encoding), very different gestures happen to be necessary in these different vowel environments in order to produce the same acoustic effect (the consonant burst). The argument was applied yet again to account for a finding about second-formant transitions as cues: that the acoustic cues for /g/ can be radically different even when the consonant is paired with closely related vowels (i.e., in the syllables /ga/ and /gɔ/), yet the perception and the articulation are essentially the same (Liberman, 1957). But these are merely striking examples of what must be seen now as a general rule: there is typically a lack of correspondence between acoustic cue and perceived phoneme, and in all these cases it appears that perception mirrors articulation more closely than sound.[31] If this were not so, then for a listener to hear the same phoneme in various environments, speakers would have to hold the acoustic signal constant, which would, in turn, require that they make drastic changes in articulation. Speakers need not do that—and in all probability they cannot—yet listeners nevertheless hear the same phoneme. This supports the assumption that the listener uses the inconstant sound as a basis for finding his way back to the articulatory gestures that produced it and thence, as it were, to the speaker's intent.

The categorical perception of stop consonants also supports this assumption.[32] As described earlier in this paper, perception of these sounds is categorical, or discontinuous, even when the acoustic signal is varied continuously. Quite obviously, the required articulations would also be discontinuous. With /b,d,g/, we can vary the acoustic cue along a continuum, which corresponds, in effect, to closing the vocal tract at various points along its length. But in actual speech the closing is accomplished by discontinuous or categorically different gestures: by the lips for /b/, the tip of the tongue for /d/, and the back of the tongue for /g/. Here, too, perception appears to be tied to articulation.

---

relatively high levels of the nervous system. For information about, or reference to, motor activity, the experienced organism need not rely—at least not very heavily and certainly not exclusively—on proprioceptive returns from the periphery, for example, from muscular contractions. (See von Holst & Mittelstadt, 1950.)

[31] For further discussion of this point, see Liberman, 1957; Cooper, Liberman, Harris, and Grubb, 1958; Lisker, Cooper, and Liberman, 1962; Liberman, Cooper, Harris, MacNeilage, and Studdert-Kennedy, in press.

[32] For further discussion of this point, see Liberman, Cooper, Harris, and MacNeilage, 1962.

454   Liberman, Cooper, Shankweiler, and Studdert-Kennedy

The view that speech is perceived by reference to production is receiving increased attention. Researchers at the Pavlov Institute in Leningrad have adduced various kinds of evidence to support a similar hypothesis (Chistovich, 1960; Chistovich, Klaas, & Kuz'min, 1962). Ladefoged (1959) has presented a motor-theoretical interpretation of some aspects of speech perception. More recently, Ladefoged and McKinney (1963) have found in studies of stress that perception is related more closely to certain low-level aspects of stress production than it is to the acoustic signal. And in a very recent study Lieberman (1967) has found interesting evidence for a somewhat similar conclusion in regard to the perception of some aspects of intonation.

The role of productive processes in models for speech perception. In its most general form, the hypothesis being described here is not necessarily different in principle from a model for speech perception called "analysis-by-synthesis" that has been advanced by Stevens (1960) and by Halle and Stevens (1962; Stevens & Halle, in press) following a generalized model proposed by MacKay (1951). In contrast, perhaps, to the computer-based assumptions of analysis-by-synthesis, we would rather think in terms of overlapping activity of several neural networks—those that supply control signals to the articulators and those that process incoming neural patterns from the ear—and to suppose that information can be correlated by these networks and passed through them in either direction. Such a formulation, in rather general terms, has been presented elsewhere (Liberman, Cooper, Studdert-Kennedy, Harris, & Shankweiler, in press).

The most general form of the view that speech is perceived by reference to production does not specify the level at which the message units are recovered. The assumption is that at some level or levels of the production process there exist neural signals standing in one-to-one correspondence with the various segments of the language—phoneme, word, phrase, etc. Perception consists in somehow running the process backward, the neural signals corresponding to the various segments being found at their respective levels. In phoneme perception—our primary concern in this paper—the invariant is found far down in the neuromotor system, at the level of the commands to the muscles. Perception by morphophonemic, morphemic, and syntactic rules of the language would engage the encoding processes at higher levels. The level at which the encoding process is entered for the purposes of perceptual decoding may, furthermore, determine which shapes can and cannot be detected in raw perception. The invariant signal for the different acoustic shapes that are all heard as /d/, for example, may be found at the level of motor commands. In consequence, the listener is unaware, even in the most careful listening, that the acoustic signals are, in fact, quite radically different. On the other hand, a listener can readily hear the difference between tokens of the morphophoneme {S} when it is realized as /s/ in cats and as /z/ in dogs, though he also "knows" that these two acoustic and phonetic shapes are in some sense the same. If the perception of that commonality is also by reference to production, the invariant is surely at a level considerably higher than the motor commands.

THE EFFICIENCY OF THE SPEECH CODE

Speech can be produced rapidly because the phonemes are processed in parallel. They are taken apart into their constituent features, and the features belonging to successive phonemes are overlapped in time. Thus the load is divided among the many largely independent components of the articulatory system. Within the phonological constraints on combinations and sequences that can occur, a speaker produces phonemes at rates much higher than those at which any single articulatory component must change its state.[33]

In the conversion of these multidimensional and overlapping articulatory events into sound, a complex encoding occurs. The number of dimensions is necessarily reduced, but the parallel transmission of phonemic information is retained in that the cues for successive phonemes are imprinted on a single aspect of the acoustic signal. Thus, the movement of articulators as independent as the lips and the tongue both affect the second formant and its transitions: given an initial labile consonant overlapped with a tongue shape appropriate for the following vowel, one finds, as we have already shown, that the second-formant transition si-

multaneously carries information about both phonemic segments.[34]

If the listener possesses some device for recovering the articulatory events from their encoded traces in the sound stream, then he should perceive the phonemes well and, indeed, evade several limitations that would otherwise apply in auditory perception. As we pointed out early in this paper, the temporal resolving power of the ear sets a relatively low limit on the rate at which discrete acoustic segments can be perceived. To the extent that the code provides for parallel processing of successive phonemes, the listener can perceive strings of phonemes more rapidly than he could if the acoustic signals for them were arranged serially, as in an alphabet. Thus, the parallel processing of the phonemes is as important for efficient perception as for production.

We also referred earlier to the difficulty of finding a reasonable number of acoustic signals of short duration that can be readily and rapidly identified. This limitation is avoided if the decoding of the acoustic signal enables the listener to recover the articulatory events that produced it, since perception then becomes linked to a system of physiological coordinates more richly multidimensional—hence more distinctive—than the acoustic (and auditory) signal.

Having said of the speech code that it seems particularly well designed to circumvent the shortcomings of the ear, we should consider whether its ac-

[33] The phonological constraints may, in fact, play an essential part in making the decoding operation fast and relatively free of error. Since the set of phonemes and phoneme sequences that is used in any particular language is far smaller than the possible set of feature combinations—smaller even than the combinations that are physiologically realizable—information about the allowable combinations of features could be used in the decoding process to reestablish temporal relationships that may have been blurred in articulation (see Footnote 27). Such a "recutting" operation would ease the requirements on precision of articulation and so allow faster communication; also, it would make unambiguous the segmentation into phonemes, thereby qualifying them as units of immediate perception. One may speculate, further, that the serial string of reconstituted phonemes is useful—perhaps essential—in the next operation of speech reception, namely, gaining immediate access to an inventory of thousands of syllable- or word-size units.

[34] Fant (1962a) makes essentially the same point:

The rules relating speech waves to speech production are in general complex since one articulation parameter, e.g., tongue height, affects several of the parameters of the spectrogram. Conversely, each of the parameters of the spectrogram is generally influenced by several articulatory variables [p. 5].

456   LIBERMAN, COOPER, SHANKWEILER, AND STUDDERT-KENNEDY

compliments stop there. As we pointed out earlier, these shortcomings do not apply to the eye, for example, and we do indeed find that the best way to communicate language in the visual mode is by means of an alphabet or cipher, not a code. But we also noted that the acoustic code is more easily and naturally perceived than is the optical alphabet. Perhaps this is due primarily to the special speech decoder, whose existence we assumed for the conversion of sound to phoneme. We would suggest an additional possibility: the operations that occur in the speech decoder—including, in particular, the interdependence of perceptual and productive processes—may be in some sense similar to those that take place at other levels of grammar. If so, there would be a special compatibility between the perception of speech sounds and the comprehension of language at higher stages. This might help to explain why, so far from being merely one way of conveying language, the sounds of speech are, instead, its common and privileged carriers.

REFERENCES

ABRAMSON, A. S. Identification and discrimination of phonemic tones. *Journal of the Acoustical Society of America,* 1961, 33, 842. (Abstract)

ABRAMSON, A. S., & LISKER, L. Voice onset time in stop consonants: Acoustic analysis and synthesis. *Reports of the Fifth International Congress on Acoustics,* 1965, Ia, Paper A51.

BASTIAN, J., & ABRAMSON, A. S. Identification and discrimination of phonemic vowel duration. *Journal of the Acoustical Society of America,* 1962, 34, 743. (Abstract)

BASTIAN, J., DELATTRE, P. C., & LIBERMAN, A. M. Silent interval as a cue for the distinction between stops and semivowels in medial position. *Journal of the Acoustical Society of America,* 1959, 31, 1568. (Abstract)

BASTIAN, J., EIMAS, P. D., & LIBERMAN, A. M. Identification and discrimination of a

phonemic contrast induced by silent interval. *Journal of the Acoustical Society of America,* 1961, 33, 842. (Abstract)

BRADY, P. T., HOUSE, A. S., & STEVENS, K. N. Perception of sounds characterized by a rapidly changing resonant frequency. *Journal of the Acoustical Society of America,* 1961, 33, 1337–1362.

BROADBENT, D. E. The role of auditory localization in attention and memory span. *Journal of Experimental Psychology,* 1954, 47, 191–196.

BROADBENT, D. E., & GREGORY, M. Accuracy of recognition for speech presented to the right and left ears. *Quarterly Journal of Experimental Psychology,* 1964, 16, 359–360.

BRYDEN, M. P. Ear preference in auditory perception. *Journal of Experimental Psychology,* 1963, 65, 103–105.

CHANEY, R. B., & WEBSTER, J. C. Information in certain multidimensional acoustic signals. Report No. 1339, 1965. United States Navy Electronics Laboratory Reports, San Diego, Calif.

CHISTOVICH, L. A. Classification of rapidly repeated speech sounds. *Akusticheskii Zhurnal,* 1960, 6, 392–398. (Trans. in *Soviet Physics-Acoustics,* New York, 1961, 6, 393–398).

CHISTOVICH, L. A., KLAAS, Y. A., & KUZ'MIN, Y. I. The process of speech sound discrimination. *Voprosy Psikhologii,* 1962, 8, 26–39. (Research Library, Air Force Cambridge Research Laboratories, Bedford, Mass. TT-64-13064 35-P)

CHOMSKY, N. Current issues in linguistic theory. In J. A. Fodor & J. J. Katz (Eds.), *The structure of language.* Englewood Cliffs, N. J.: Prentice Hall, 1964. Pp. 50–118.

COFFEY, J. L. The development and evaluation of the Battelle Aural Reading Device. *Proceedings of the International Congress on Technology and Blindness I.* New York: American Foundation for the Blind, 1963. Pp. 343–360.

COOPER, F. S. Research on reading machines for the blind. In P. A. Zahl (Ed.), *Blindness: Modern approaches to the unseen environment.* Princeton, N. J.: Princeton University Press, 1950. Pp. 512–543. (a)

COOPER, F. S. Spectrum analysis. *Journal of the Acoustical Society of America,* 1950, 22, 761–762. (b)

COOPER, F. S. Some instrumental aids to research on speech. *Report on the Fourth Annual Round Table Meeting on Lin-*

guistics and Language Teaching. Monograph Series No. 3. Washington: Georgetown University Press, 1953. Pp. 46–53.

COOPER, F. S. Research techniques and instrumentation: EMG. *American Speech and Hearing Association Reports,* 1965, **1**, 153–158.

COOPER, F. S. Describing the speech process in motor command terms. *Journal of the Acoustical Society of America,* 1966, **39**, 1221 (Abstract) (*Status Report of Speech Research, Haskins Laboratories, SR-5/6,* 1966, 2.1–2.27— text.)

COOPER, F. S., DELATTRE, P. C., LIBERMAN, A. M., BORST, J., & GERSTMAN, L. J. Some experiments on the perception of synthetic speech sounds. *Journal of the Acoustical Society of America,* 1952, **24**, 597–606.

COOPER, F. S., LIBERMAN, A. M., & BORST, J. M. The interconversion of audible and visible patterns as a basis for research in the perception of speech. *Proceedings of the National Academy of Sciences,* 1951, **37**, 318–325.

COOPER, F. S., LIBERMAN, A. M., HARRIS, K. S., & GRUBB, P. M. Some input-output relations observed in experiments on the perception of speech. *Proceedings of the Second International Congress of Cybernetics, 1958.* Namur, Belgium: Association Internationale de Cybernetique. Pp. 930–941.

COOPER, F. S., LIBERMAN, A. M., LISKER, L., & GAITENBY, J. Speech synthesis by rules. *Proceedings of the Speech Communication Seminar,* Stockholm, 1962. Stockholm: Royal Institute of Technology, 1963. F2.

CROSS, D. V., LANE, H. L., & SHEPPARD, W. C. Identification and discrimination functions for a visual continuum and their relation to the motor theory of speech perception. *Journal of Experimental Psychology,* 1965, **70**, 63–74.

DELATTRE, P. C. Les indices acoustiques de la parole: Premier rapport. *Phonetica,* 1958, **2**, 108–118, 226–251.

DELATTRE, P. C. Le jeu des transitions des formants et la perception des consonnes. *Proceedings of the Fourth International Congress of Phonetic Sciences, Helsinki, 1961.* s-Gravenhage: Mouton, 1962. Pp. 407–417.

DELATTRE, P. C., LIBERMAN, A. M., & COOPER, F. S. Voyelles synthétiques à deux formants et voyelles cardinales. *Le Maître Phonétique,* 1951, **96**, 30–37.

DELATTRE, P. C., LIBERMAN, A. M., & COOPER, F. S. Acoustic loci and transitional cues for consonants. *Journal of the Acoustical Society of America,* 1955, **27**, 769–773.

DELATTRE, P. C., LIBERMAN, A. M., & COOPER, F. S. Formant transitions and loci as acoustic correlates of place of articulation in American fricatives. *Studia Linguistica,* 1964, **18**, 104–121.

DELATTRE, P. C., LIBERMAN, A. M., COOPER, F. S., & GERSTMAN, L. J. An experimental study of the acoustic determinants of vowel color: Observations on one- and two-formant vowels synthesized from spectrographic patterns. *Word,* 1952, **8**, 195–210.

DENES, P. B. On the statistics of spoken English. *Journal of the Acoustical Society of America,* 1963, **35**, 892–904.

EIMAS, P. D. The relation between identification and discrimination along speech and non-speech continua. *Language and Speech,* 1963, **6**, 206–217.

FANT, C. G. M. *Acoustic theory of speech production.* 's-Gravenhage: Mouton, 1960.

FANT, C. G. M. Descriptive analysis of the acoustic aspects of speech. *Logos,* 1962, **5**, 3–17. (a)

FANT, C. G. M. Sound spectrography. *Proceedings IV International Congress on Phonetic Sciences, Helsinki, 1961.* 's-Gravenhage: Mouton, 1962. Pp. 14–33. (b)

FANT, C. G. M. Theory of distinctive features. *Speech Transmission Laboratory Quarterly Progress and Status Report,* Royal Institute of Technology (KTH), Stockholm, January 15, 1967. Pp. 1–14.

FREIBERGER, J., & MURPHY, E. F. Reading machines for the blind. *IRE Professional Group on Human Factors in Electronics,* 1961, **HFE-2**, 8–19.

FROMKIN, V. A. Neuro-muscular specification of linguistic units. *Language and Speech,* 1966, **9**, 170–199.

FROMKIN, V. A., & LADEFOGED, P. Electromyography in speech research. *Phonetica,* 1966, **15**, 219–242.

FRY, D. B., ABRAMSON, A. S., EIMAS, P. D., & LIBERMAN, A. M. The identification and discrimination of synthetic vowels. *Language and Speech,* 1962, **5**, 171–189.

GALUNOV, V. I., & CHISTOVICH, L. A. Relationship of motor theory to the general problem of speech recognition (review). *Akusticheskii Zhurnal,* 1965, **11**, 417–426. (Trans. in *Soviet Physics-Acoustics,* New York, 1966, **11**, 357–365.)

GELB, I. J. *A study of writing.* Chicago: University of Chicago Press, 1963.

GRIFFITH, B. C. A study of the relation between phoneme labeling and discrimina-

458   LIBERMAN, COOPER, SHANKWEILER, AND STUDDERT-KENNEDY

bility in the perception of synthetic stop consonants. Unpublished doctoral dissertation, University of Connecticut, 1958.

HADDING-KOCH, K., & STUDDERT-KENNEDY, M. An experimental study of some intonation contours. *Phonetica,* 1964, **11,** 175–185. (a)

HADDING-KOCH, K., & STUDDERT-KENNEDY, M. Intonation contours evaluated by American and Swedish test subjects. *Proceedings of the Fifth International Congress of Phonetic Sciences,* Munster, August 1964. (b)

HALLE, M. On the bases of phonology. In J. A. Fodor & J. J. Katz (Eds.), *The structure of language.* Englewood Cliffs, N. J.: Prentice-Hall, 1964. Pp. 324–333.

HALLE, M., & STEVENS, K. N. Speech recognition: A model and a program for research. *IRE Transactions on Information Theory JT-8,* 1962, **2,** 155–159.

HARRIS, C. M. A study of the building blocks in speech. *Journal of the Acoustical Society of America,* 1953, **25,** 962–969.

HARRIS, K. S. Cues for the discrimination of American English fricatives in spoken syllables. *Language and Speech,* 1958, **1,** 1–7.

HARRIS, K. S. Behavior of the tongue in the production of some alveolar consonants. *Journal of the Acoustical Society of America,* 1963, **35,** 784. (Abstract)

HARRIS, K. S., BASTIAN, J., & LIBERMAN, A. M. Mimicry and the perception of a phonemic contrast induced by silent interval: Electromyographic and acoustic measures. *Journal of the Acoustical Society of America,* 1961, **33,** 842. (Abstract)

HARRIS, K. S., HOFFMAN, H. S., LIBERMAN, A. M., DELATTRE, P. C., & COOPER, F. S. Effect of third-formant transitions on the perception of the voiced stop consonants. *Journal of the Acoustical Society of America,* 1958, **30,** 122–126.

HARRIS, K. S., HUNTINGTON, D. A., & SHOLES, G. N. Coarticulation of some disyllabic utterances measured by electromyographic techniques. *Journal of the Acoustical Society of America,* 1966, **39,** 1219. (Abstract)

HARRIS, K. S., LYSAUGHT, G., & SCHVEY, M. M. Some aspects of the production of oral and nasal labial stops. *Language and Speech,* 1965, **8,** 135–147.

HOCKETT, C. F. *A manual of phonology.* Baltimore: Waverly Press, 1955.

HUGHES, G. W., & HALLE, M. Spectral properties of fricative consonants. *Journal of the Acoustical Society of America,* 1956, **28,** 303–310.

JAKOBSON, R., FANT, G., & HALLE, M. *Preliminaries to speech analysis. The distinctive features and their correlates.* Technical Report No. 13, 1952, Acoustics Laboratory, M.I.T. (Republished, Cambridge, Mass.: M.I.T. Press, 1963.)

JAKOBSON, R., & HALLE, M. *Fundamentals of language.* 's-Gravenhage: Mouton, 1956.

KIMURA, D. Cerebral dominance and perception of verbal stimuli. *Canadian Journal of Psychology,* 1961, **15,** 166–171.

KIMURA, D. Left-right differences in the perception of melodies. *Quarterly Journal of Experimental Psychology,* 1964, **16,** 355–358.

KIMURA, D. Functional asymmetry of the brain in dichotic listening. *Cortex,* 1967, **3,** in press.

KOZHEVNIKOV, V. A., & CHISTOVICH, L. A. *Rech' Artikuliatsia i vospriiatie.* Moscow-Leningrad, 1965. (Trans. in *Speech: Articulation and perception.* Washington: Joint Publications Research Service, 1966, **30,** 543.)

LADEFOGED, P. The perception of speech. In *mechanization of thought processes,* 1959. London: H. M. Stationery Office. Pp. 397–409.

LADEFOGED, P., & McKINNEY, N. P. Loudness, sound pressure, and sub-glottal pressure in speech. *Journal of the Acoustical Society of America,* 1963, **35,** 454–460.

LANE, H. Motor theory of speech perception: A critical review. *Psychological Review,* 1965, **72,** 275–309.

LIBERMAN, A. M. Some results of research on speech perception. *Journal of the Acoustical Society of America,* 1957, **29,** 117–123.

LIBERMAN, A. M., COOPER, F. S., HARRIS, K. S., & MACNEILAGE, P. F. A motor theory of speech perception. *Proceedings of the Speech Communication Seminar,* Stockholm, 1962. Stockholm: Royal Institute of Technology, 1963, D3.

LIBERMAN, A. M., COOPER, F. S., HARRIS, K. S., MACNEILAGE, P. F., & STUDDERT-KENNEDY, M. Some observations on a model for speech perception. *Proceedings of the AFCRL Symposium on Models for the Perception of Speech and Visual Form,* Boston, November 1964. Cambridge: Massachusetts Institute of Technology Press, in press.

LIBERMAN, A. M., COOPER, F. S., STUDDERT-KENNEDY, M., HARRIS, K. S., & SHANKWEILER, D. P. Some observations on the efficiency of speech sounds. Paper presented at the XVIII International Congress of Psychology, Moscow, August 1966. *Zeitschrift für Phonetik, Sprachwissenschaft und Kommunikations-forschung*, in press.

LIBERMAN, A. M., DELATTRE, P. C., & COOPER, F. S. The role of selected stimulus variables in the perception of the unvoiced-stop consonants. *American Journal of Psychology*, 1952, **65**, 497–516.

LIBERMAN, A. M., DELATTRE, P. C., & COOPER, F. S. Some cues for the distinction between voiced and voiceless stops in initial position. *Language and Speech*, 1958, **1**, 153–167.

LIBERMAN, A. M., DELATTRE, P. C., COOPER, F. S., & GERSTMAN, L. J. The role of consonant-vowel transitions in the perception of the stop and nasal consonants. *Psychological Monographs*, 1954, **68**(8, Whole No. 379).

LIBERMAN, A. M., DELATTRE, P. C., GERSTMAN, L. J., & COOPER, F. S. Tempo of frequency change as a cue for distinguishing classes of speech sounds. *Journal of Experimental Psychology*, 1956, **52**, 127–137.

LIBERMAN, A. M., HARRIS, K. S., EIMAS, P. D., LISKER, L., & BASTIAN, J. An effect of learning on speech perception: The discrimination of durations of silence with and without phonemic significance. *Language and Speech*, 1961, **4**, 175–195.

LIBERMAN, A. M., HARRIS, K. S., HOFFMAN, H. S., & GRIFFITH, B. C. The discrimination of speech sounds within and across phoneme boundaries. *Journal of Experimental Psychology*, 1957, **54**, 358–368.

LIBERMAN, A. M., HARRIS, K. S., KINNEY, J. A., & LANE, H. The discrimination of relative onset time of the components of certain speech and nonspeech patterns. *Journal of Experimental Psychology*, 1961, **61**, 379–388.

LIBERMAN, A. M., INGEMANN, F., LISKER, L., DELATTRE, P. C., & COOPER, F. S. Minimal rules for synthesizing speech. *Journal of the Acoustical Society of America*, 1959, **31**, 1490–1499.

LIEBERMAN, P. *Intonation, perception and language*. Cambridge: Massachusetts Institute of Technology Press, 1967.

LINDBLOM, B. Spectrographic study of vowel reduction. *Journal of the Acoustical Society of America*, 1963, **35**, 1773–1781.

LINDBLOM, B. Articulatory activity in vowels. *Journal of the Acoustical Society of America*, 1964, **36**, 1038. (Abstract)

LINDBLOM, B., & STUDDERT-KENNEDY, M. On the role of formant transitions in vowel recognition. *Speech transmission laboratory quarterly progress and status report*, Royal Institute of Technology (KTH), Stockholm, in press. (Also Status report of speech research. Haskins Laboratories, in press.)

LISKER, L. Closure duration and the voiced-voiceless distinction in English. *Language*, 1957, **33**, 42–49. (a)

LISKER, L. Minimal cues for separating /w,r,l,j/ in introvocalic production. *Word*, 1957, **13**, 257–267. (b)

LISKER L,. Anatomy of unstressed syllables. *Journal of the Acoustical Society of America*, 1958, **30**, 682. (Abstract)

LISKER, L., & ABRAMSON, A. S. A cross-language study of voicing in initial stops: Acoustical measurements. *Word*, 1964, **20**, 384–422. (a)

LISKER, L., & ABRAMSON, A. S. Stop categories and voice onset time. *Proceedings of the Fifth International Congress of Phonetic Sciences*, Munster, August, 1964. (b)

LISKER, L., COOPER, F. S., & LIBERMAN, A. M. The uses of experiment in language description. *Word*, 1962, **18**, 82–106.

MACKAY, D. M. Mindlike behavior in artefacts. *British Journal for the Philosophy of Science*, 1951, **2**, 105–121.

MACNEILAGE, P. F. Electromyographic and acoustic study of the production of certain final clusters. *Journal of the Acoustical Society of America*, 1963, **35**, 461–463.

MACNEILAGE, P. F., DECLERK, J. L., & SILVERMAN, S. I. Some relations between articulator movement and motor control in consonant-vowel-consonant monosyllables. *Journal of the Acoustical Society of America*, 1966, **40**, 1272. (Abstract)

MALECOT, A. Acoustic cues for nasal consonants. *Language*, 1956, **32**, 274–284.

MILLER, G. A. The magical number seven, plus or minus two, or, some limits on our capacity for processing information. *Psychological Review*, 1956, **63**, 81–96. (a)

MILLER, G. A. The perception of speech. In M. Halle (Ed.), *For Roman Jakobson*. 's-Gravenhage: Mouton, 1956. Pp. 353–359. (b)

MILLER, G. A., & TAYLOR, W. G. The perception of repeated bursts of noise. *Journal of the Acoustical Society of America*, 1948, **20**, 171–182.

NELSON, P. G., ERULKAR, S. D., & BRYAN, S. S. Responses of units of the inferior-colliculus to time-varying acoustic stimuli. *Journal of Neurophysiology*, 1966, **29**, 834–860.

460   Liberman, Cooper, Shankweiler, and Studdert-Kennedy

Nye, P. W. Aural recognition time for multidimensional signals. *Nature*, 1962, **196**, 1282–1283.

Nye, P. W. Reading aids for blind people—a survey of progress with the technological and human problems. *Medical Electronics and Biological Engineering*, 1964. **2**, 247–264.

Nye, P. W. An investigation of audio outputs for a reading machine. February, 1965. Autonomics Division, National Physical Laboratory, Teddington, England.

O'Connor, J. D., Gerstman, L. J., Liberman, A. M., Delattre, P. C., & Cooper, F. S. Acoustic cues for the perception of initial /w,j,r,l/ in English. *Word*, 1957. **13**, 25–43.

Ohman, S. E. G. Numerical model for coarticulation, using a computer-simulated vocal tract. *Journal of the Acoustical Society of America*, 1964, **36**, 1038. (Abstract)

Ohman, S. E. G. Coarticulation in VCV utterances: Spectrographic measurements. *Journal of the Acoustical Society of America*, 1966, **39**, 151–168.

Orr, D. B., Friedman, H. L., & Williams, J. C. C. Trainability of listening comprehension of speeded discourse. *Journal of Educational Psychology*, 1965, **56**, 148–156.

Peterson, G. E., & Sivertsen, E. Objectives and techniques of speech synthesis. *Language and Speech*, 1960, **3**, 84–95.

Peterson, G. E., Wang, W. S.-Y., & Sivertsen. E. Segmentation techniques in speech synthesis. *Journal of the Acoustical Society of America*, 1958, **30**, 739–742.

Pollack, I. The information of elementary auditory displays. *Journal of the Acoustical Society of America*, 1952, **24**, 745–749.

Pollack, I., & Ficks, L. Information of elementary multidimensional auditory displays. *Journal of the Acoustical Society of America*, 1954, **26**, 155–158.

Potter, R. K., Kopp, G. A., & Green, H. C. *Visible speech.* New York: Van Nostrand, 1947.

Schatz, C. The role of context in the perception of stops. *Language*, 1954, **30**, 47–56.

Shankweiler, D., & Studdert-Kennedy, M. An analysis of perceptual confusions in identification of dichotically presented CVC syllables. *Journal of the Acoustical Society of America*, 1967, in press. (Abstract) (a)

Shankweiler, D., & Studdert-Kennedy, M. Identification of consonants and vowels presented to left and right ears. *Quarterly Journal of Experimental Psychology*, 1967, **19**, 59–63. (b)

Shearme, J. N., & Holmes, J. N. An experimental study of the classification of sounds in continuous speech according to their distribution in the formant 1-formant 2 plane. In *Proceedings of the Fourth International Congress of Phonetic Sciences*, Helsinki, 1961. 's-Gravenhage: Mouton, 1962. Pp. 234–240.

Sivertsen, E. Segment inventories for speech synthesis. *Language and Speech*, 1961, **4**, 27–61.

Stevens, K. N. Toward a model for speech recognition. *Journal of the Acoustical Society of America*, 1960, **32**, 47–55.

Stevens, K. N. On the relations between speech movements and speech perception. Paper presented at the meeting of the XVIII International Congress of Psychology, Moscow, August, 1966. (*Zeitschrift fur Phonetik, Sprachwissenschaft und Kommunikations-forschung*, in press.)

Stevens, K. N., & Halle, M. Remarks on analysis by synthesis and distinctive features. *Proceedings of the AFCRL Symposium on Models for the Perception of Speech and Visual Form*, Boston, November 1964. Cambridge: M.I.T. Press, in press.

Stevens, K. N., & House, A. S. Studies of formant transitions using a vocal tract analog. *Journal of the Acoustical Society of America*, 1956, **28**, 578–585.

Stevens, K. N., & House, A. S. Perturbation of vowel articulations by consonantal context: An acoustical study. *Journal of Speech and Hearing Research*, 1963, **6**, 111–128.

Stevens, K. N., & House, A. S. Speech perception. In J. Tobias & E. Schubert (Eds.), *Foundations of modern auditory theory.* New York: Academic Press, in press.

Stevens, K. N., Ohman, S. E. G., & Liberman, A. M. Identification and discrimination of rounded and unrounded vowels. *Journal of the Acoustical Society of America*, 1963, **35**, 1900. (Abstract)

Stevens, K. N., Ohman, S. E. G., Studdert-Kennedy, M., & Liberman, A. M. Cross-linguistic study of vowel discrimination. *Journal of the Acoustical Society of America*, 1964, **36**, 1989. (Abstract)

Studdert-Kennedy, M., & Cooper, F. S. High-performance reading machines for the blind; psychological problems, technological problems, and status. Paper presented at the meeting of St. Dunstan's International Conference on Sensory Devices for the Blind, London, June 1966.

STUDDERT-KENNEDY, M., & LIBERMAN, A. M. Psychological considerations in the design of auditory displays for reading machines. *Proceedings of the International Congress on Technology and Blindness,* 1963. Pp. 289–304.

STUDDERT-KENNEDY, M., LIBERMAN, A. M., & STEVENS, K. N. Reaction time to synthetic stop consonants and vowels at phoneme centers and at phoneme boundaries. *Journal of the Acoustical Society of America,* 1963, **35,** 1900. (Abstract)

STUDDERT-KENNEDY, M., LIBERMAN, A. M., & STEVENS, K. N. Reaction time during the discrimination of synthetic stop consonants. *Journal of the Acoustical Society of America,* 1964, **36,** 1989. (Abstract)

VON HOLST, E., & MITTELSTADT, H. Das reafferenzprinzip. *Naturwissenschaft,* 1950, **37,** 464–476.

WHETNALL, E., & FRY, D. B. *The deaf child.* London: Heinemann, 1964.

WHITFIELD, I. C., & EVANS, E. F. Responses of auditory cortical neurons to stimuli of changing frequency. *Journal of Neurophysiology,* 1965, **28,** 655–672.

WICKELGREN, W. A. Distinctive features and errors in short-term memory for English consonants. *Journal of the Acoustical Society of America,* 1966, **39,** 388–398.

(Received June 19, 1967)

Cognition, 21 (1985) 1–36

1

The motor theory of speech perception revised*

ALVIN M. LIBERMAN

*Haskins Laboratories, University of
Connecticut and Yale University*

IGNATIUS G. MATTINGLY

*Haskins Laboratories and University of
Connecticut*

Abstract

*A motor theory of speech perception, initially proposed to account for results
of early experiments with synthetic speech, is now extensively revised to accommodate recent findings, and to relate the assumptions of the theory to those
that might be made about other perceptual modes. According to the revised
theory, phonetic information is perceived in a biologically distinct system, a
'module' specialized to detect the intended gestures of the speaker that are the
basis for phonetic categories. Built into the structure of this module is the
unique but lawful relationship between the gestures and the acoustic patterns
in which they are variously overlapped. In consequence, the module causes
perception of phonetic structure without translation from preliminary auditory
impressions. Thus, it is comparable to such other modules as the one that
enables an animal to localize sound. Peculiar to the phonetic module are the
relation between perception and production it incorporates and the fact that it
must compete with other modules for the same stimulus variations.*

Together with some of our colleagues, we have long been identified with a
view of speech perception that is often referred to as a 'motor theory'. Not
the motor theory, to be sure, because there are other theories of perception
that, like ours, assign an important role to movement or its sources. But the

---
*The writing of this paper was supported by a grant to Haskins Laboratories (NIH-NICHD HD-01994).
We owe a special debt to Harriet Magen for invaluable help with the relevant literature, and to Alice Dadou-
rian for coping with an ever-changing manuscript. For their patient responses to our frequent requests for
information and criticism, we thank Franklin Cooper, Jerry Fodor, Carol Fowler, Scott Kelso, Charles Liber-
man, Robert Remez, Bruno Repp, Arthur Samuel, Michael Studdert-Kennedy, Michael Turvey, and Douglas
Whalen. We also acknowledge the insightful comments of an anonymous reviewer.
   Reprint requests should be sent to: Alvin Liberman, Haskins Laboratories, 270 Crown Street, New Haven,
CT 06511, U.S.A.

theory we are going to describe is only about speech perception, in contrast to some that deal with other perceptual processes (e.g., Berkeley, 1709; Festinger, Burnham, Ono, & Bamber, 1967) or, indeed, with all of them (e.g., Washburn, 1926; Watson, 1919). Moreover, our theory is motivated by considerations that do not necessarily apply outside the domain of speech. Yet even there we are not alone, for several theories of speech perception, being more or less 'motor', resemble ours to varying degrees (e.g., Chistovich, 1960; Dudley, 1940; Joos, 1948; Ladefoged & McKinney, 1963; Stetson, 1951). However, it is not relevant to our purposes to compare these, so, for convenience, we will refer to *our* motor theory as *the* motor theory.

We were led to the motor theory by an early finding that the acoustic patterns of synthetic speech had to be modified if an invariant phonetic percept was to be produced across different contexts (Cooper, Delattre, Liberman, Borst, & Gerstman, 1952; Liberman, Delattre, & Cooper, 1952). Thus, it appeared that the objects of speech perception were not to be found at the acoustic surface. They might, however, be sought in the underlying motor processes, if it could be assumed that the acoustic variability required for an invariant percept resulted from the temporal overlap, in different contexts, of correspondingly invariant units of production. In its most general form, this aspect of the early theory survives, but there have been important revisions, including especially the one that makes perception of the motor invariant depend on a specialized phonetic mode (Liberman, 1982; Liberman, Cooper, Shankweiler & Studdert-Kennedy, 1967; Liberman & Studdert-Kennedy, 1978; Mattingly & Liberman, 1969). Our aim in this paper is to present further revisions, and so bring the theory up to date.

The theory

The first claim of the motor theory, as revised, is that the objects of speech perception are the intended phonetic gestures of the speaker, represented in the brain as invariant motor commands that call for movements of the articulators through certain linguistically significant configurations. These gestural commands are the physical reality underlying the traditional phonetic notions—for example, 'tongue backing,' 'lip rounding,' and 'jaw raising'—that provide the basis for phonetic categories. They are the elementary events of speech production and perception. Phonetic segments are simply groups of one or more of these elementary events; thus [b] consists of a labial stop gesture and [m] of that same gesture combined with a velum-lowering gesture. Phonologically, of course, the gestures themselves must be viewed as groups of features, such as 'labial,' 'stop,' 'nasal,' but these features are attributes of the gestural events, not events as such. To perceive an utterance, then, is to perceive a specific pattern of intended gestures.

We have to say 'intended gestures,' because, for a number of reasons (coarticulation being merely the most obvious), the gestures are not directly manifested in the acoustic signal or in the observable articulatory movements. It is thus no simple matter (as we shall see in a later section) to define specific gestures rigorously or to relate them to their observable consequences. Yet, clearly, invariant gestures of some description there must be, for they are required, not merely for our particular theory of speech perception, but for *any* adequate theory of speech production.

The second claim of the theory is a corollary of the first: if speech perception and speech production share the same set of invariants, they must be intimately linked. This link, we argue, is not a learned association, a result of the fact that what people hear when they listen to speech is what they do when they speak. Rather, the link is innately specified, requiring only epigenetic development to bring it into play. On this claim, perception of the gestures occurs in a specialized mode, different in important ways from the auditory mode, responsible also for the production of phonetic structures, and part of the larger specialization for language. The adaptive function of the perceptual side of this mode, the side with which the motor theory is directly concerned, is to make the conversion from acoustic signal to gesture automatically, and so to let listeners perceive phonetic structures without mediation by (or translation from) the auditory appearances that the sounds might, on purely psychoacoustic grounds, be expected to have.

A critic might note that the gestures do produce acoustic signals, after all, and that surely it is these signals, not the gestures, which stimulate the listener's ear. What can it mean, then, to say it is the gestures, not the signals, that are perceived? Our critic might also be concerned that the theory seems at first blush to assign so special a place to speech as to make it hard to think about in normal biological terms. We should, therefore, try to forestall misunderstanding by showing that, wrong though it may be, the theory is neither logically meaningless nor biologically unthinkable.

An issue that any theory of speech perception must meet

The motor theory would be meaningless if there were, as is sometimes supposed, a one-to-one relation between acoustic patterns and gestures, for in that circumstance it would matter little whether the listener was said to perceive the one or the other. Metaphysical considerations aside, the proximal acoustic patterns might as well be the perceived distal objects. But the relationship between gesture and signal is not straightforward. The reason is that the timing of the articulatory movements—the peripheral realizations of the gestures—is not simply related to the ordering of the gestures that is implied by the strings of symbols in phonetic transcriptions: the movements for gestures implied by a single symbol are typically not simultaneous, and the movements implied by successive symbols often overlap extensively. This coarticulation means that the changing shape of the vocal tract, and hence the resulting signal, is influenced by several gestures at the same time. Thus, the relation between gesture and signal, though certainly systematic, is systematic in a way that is peculiar to speech. In later sections of the paper we will consider how this circumstance bears on the perception of speech and its theoretical interpretation. For now, however, we wish only to justify consideration of the motor theory by identifying it as one of several choices that the complex relation between gesture and signal faces us with. For this purpose, we will describe just one aspect of the relation, that we may then use it as an example.

When coarticulation causes the signal to be influenced simultaneously by several gestures, a particular gesture will necessarily be represented by different sounds in different phonetic contexts. In a consonant–vowel syllable, for example, the acoustic pattern that contains information about the place of constriction of the consonantal gesture will vary depending on the following vowel. Such context-conditioned variation is most apparent, perhaps, in the transitions of the formants as the constriction is released. Thus, place information for a given consonant is carried by a rising transition in one vowel context and a falling transition in another (Liberman, Delattre, Cooper, & Gerstman, 1954). In isolation, these transitions sound like two different glissandi or chirps, which is just what everything we know about auditory perception leads us to expect (Mattingly, Liberman, Syrdal, & Halwes, 1971); they do not sound alike, and, just as important, neither sounds like speech. How is it, then, that, in context, they nevertheless yield the same consonant?

Auditory theories and the accounts they provide

The guiding assumption of one class of theories is that ordinary auditory processes are sufficient to explain the perception of speech; there is no need to invoke a further specialization for language, certainly not one that gives the listener access to gestures. The several members of this class differ in principle, though they are often combined in practice.

One member of the class counts two stages in the perceptual process: a first stage in which, according to principles that apply to the way we hear all sounds, the auditory appearances of the acoustic patterns are registered, followed by a second stage in which, by an act of sorting or matching to prototypes, phonetic labels are affixed (Crowder & Morton, 1969; Fujisaki

& Kawashima, 1970; Oden & Massaro, 1978; Pisoni, 1973). Just why such different acoustic patterns as the rising and falling transitions of our example deserve the same label is not explicitly rationalized, it being accounted, presumably, a characteristic of the language that the processes of sorting or matching are able to manage. Nor does the theory deal with the fact that, in appropriate contexts, these transitions support phonetic percepts but do not also produce such auditory phenomena as chirps. To the contrary, indeed, it is sometimes made explicit that the auditory stage is actually available for use in discrimination. Such availability is not always apparent because the casual (or forgetful) listener is assumed to rely on the categorical labels, which persist in memory, rather than on the context-sensitive auditory impressions, which do not; but training or the use of more sensitive psychophysical methods is said to give better access to the auditory stage and thus to the stimulus variations—including, presumably, the differences in formant transition—that the labels ignore (Carney, Widin, & Viemeister, 1977; Pisoni & Tash, 1974; Samuel, 1977).

Another member of the class of auditory theories avoids the problem of context-conditioned variation by denying its importance. According to this theory, speech perception relies on there being at least a brief period during each speech sound when its short-time spectrum is reliably distinct from those of other speech sounds. For an initial stop in a stressed syllable, for example, this period includes the burst and the first 10 ms. after the onset of voicing (Stevens & Blumstein, 1978). That a listener is nevertheless able to identify speech sounds from which these invariant attributes have been removed is explained by the claim that, in natural speech, they are sometimes missing or distorted, so that the child must learn to make use of secondary, context-conditioned attributes, such as formant transitions, which ordinarily co-occur with the primary, invariant attributes (Cole & Scott, 1974). Thus, presumably, the different-sounding chirps develop in perception to become the same-sounding (nonchirpy) phonetic element with which they have been associated.

The remaining member of this class of theories is the most thoroughly auditory of all. By its terms, the very processes of phonetic classification depend directly on properties of the auditory system, properties so independent of language as to be found, perhaps, in all mammals (Kuhl, 1981; Miller, 1977; Stevens, 1975). As described most commonly in the literature, this version of the auditory theory takes the perceived boundary between one phonetic category and another to correspond to a naturally-occurring discontinuity in perception of the relevant acoustic continuum. There is thus no first stage in which the (often) different auditory appearances are available, nor is there a process of learned equivalence. An example is the claim that the distinction between voiced and voiceless stops—normally cued by a complex of acoustic differences caused by differences in the phonetic variable known as voice-onset-time—depends on an auditory discontinuity in sensitivity to temporal relations among components of the signal (Kuhl & Miller, 1975; Pisoni, 1977). Another is the suggestion that the boundary between fricative and affricate on a rise-time continuum is the same as the rise-time boundary in the analogous nonspeech case—that is, the boundary that separates the nonspeech percepts 'pluck' and 'bow' (Cutting & Rosner, 1974; but see Rosen & Howell, 1981). To account for the fact that such discontinuities move as a function of phonetic context or rate of articulation, one can add the assumption that the several components of the acoustic signal give rise to interactions of a purely auditory sort (Hillenbrand, 1984; but see Summerfield, 1982). As for the rising and falling formant transitions of our earlier example, some such assumption of auditory interaction (between the transitions and the remainder of the acoustic pattern) would presumably be offered to account for the fact that they sound like two different glissandi in isolation, but as the same (non-glissando-like) consonant in the context of the acoustic syllable. The clear implication of this theory is that, for all phonetic contexts and for every one of the many acoustic cues that are known to be of consequence for each phonetic segment, the motivation for articulatory and coarticulatory maneuvers is to produce just those acoustic patterns that fit the language-independent characteristics of the auditory system. Thus, this last auditory theory is auditory in two ways: speech perception is governed by auditory principles, and so, too, is speech production.

The account provided by the motor theory

The motor theory offers a view radically different from the auditory theories, most obviously in the claim that speech perception is not to be explained by principles that apply to perception of sounds in general, but must rather be seen as a specialization for phonetic gestures. Incorporating a biologically based link between perception and production, this specialization prevents listeners from hearing the signal as an ordinary sound, but enables them to use the systematic, yet special, relation between signal and gesture to perceive the gesture. The relation is systematic because it results from lawful dependencies among gestures, articulator movements, vocal-tract shapes, and signal. It is special because it occurs only in speech.

Applying the motor theory to our example, we suggest what has seemed obvious since the importance of the transitions was discovered: the listener uses the systematically varying transitions as information about the coarticulation of an invariant consonant gesture with various vowels, and so perceives this gesture. Perception requires no arbitrary association of signal with phonetic category, and no correspondingly arbitrary progression from an auditory stage (e.g., different sounding glissandi) to a superseding phonetic label. As Studdert-Kennedy (1976) has put it, the phonetic category 'names itself'.

By way of comparison with the last of the auditory theories we described, we note that, just as this theory is in two ways auditory, the motor theory is in two ways motor. First, because it takes the proper object of phonetic perception to be a motor event. And, second, because it assumes that adaptations of the motor system for controlling the organs of the vocal tract took precedence in the evolution of speech. These adaptations made it possible, not only to produce phonetic gestures, but also to coarticulate them so that they could be produced rapidly. A perceiving system, specialized to take account of the complex acoustic consequences, developed concomitantly. Accordingly, the theory is not indifferently perceptual *or* motor, implying simply that the basis of articulation and the object of perception are the same. Rather, the emphasis is quite one-sided; therefore, the theory fully deserves the epithet 'motor'.

How the motor theory makes speech perception like other specialized perceiving systems

The specialized perceiving system that the motor theory assumes is not unique; it is, rather, one of a rather large class of special systems or 'modules'. Accordingly, one can think about it in familiar biological terms. Later, we will consider more specifically how the phonetic module fits the concept of modularity developed recently by Fodor (1983); our concern now is only to compare the phonetic module with others.

The modules we refer to have in common that they are special neural structures, designed to take advantage of a systematic but unique relation between a proximal display at the sense organ and some property of a distal object. A result in all cases is that there is not, first, a cognitive representation of the proximal pattern that is modality-general, followed by translation to a particular distal property; rather, perception of the distal property is immediate, which is to say that the module has done all the hard work. Consider auditory localization as an example. One of several cues is differences in time of arrival of particular frequency components of the signal at the two ears (see Hafter, 1984, for a review). No one would claim that the use of this cue is part of the general auditory ability to perceive, as such, the size of the time interval that separates the onsets of two different signals. Certainly, this kind of general auditory ability does exist, but it is no part of auditory localization, either psychologically or physiologically. Animals perceive the location of sounding objects only by means of neural structures specialized to take advantage of the systematic but special relation between proximal stimulus and distal location (see, for example, Knudsen, 1984). The relation is systematic for obvious reasons; it is special because it depends on the circumstance that the animal has two ears, and that the ears are set a certain distance apart. In the case of the human, the only species for which the appropriate test can be made, there is no translation from perceived disparity in time because there is no perceived disparity.

Compare this with the voicing distinction (e.g., [ba] vs. [pa]) referred to earlier, which is cued in part by a difference in time of onset of the several formants, and which has therefore been said by some to rest on a general auditory ability to perceive temporal disparity as such (Kuhl & Miller, 1975; Pisoni, 1977). We believe, to the contrary, that the temporal disparity is only the proximal occasion for the unmediated perception of voicing, a distal gesture represented at the level of articulation by the relative timing of vocal-tract opening and start of laryngeal vibration (Lisker & Abramson, 1964). So we should expect perceptual judgments of differences in signal onset-time to have no more relevance to the voicing distinction than to auditory localization. In neither case do general auditory principles and procedures enlighten us. Nor does it help to invoke general principles of auditory interaction. The still more general principle that perception gives access to distal objects tells us only that auditory localization and speech perception work as they are supposed to; it does not tell us how. Surely the 'how' is to be found, not by studying perception, even auditory perception, in general, but only by studying auditory localization and speech perception in particular. Both are special systems; they are, therefore, to be understood only in their own terms.

Examples of such biologically specialized perceiving modules can be multiplied. Visual perception of depth by use of information about binocular disparity is a well-studied example that has the same general characteristics we have attributed to auditory localization and speech (Julesz, 1960, 1971; Poggio, 1984). And there is presumably much to be learned by comparison with such biologically coherent systems as those that underlie echolocation in bats (Suga, 1984) or song in birds (Marler, 1970; Thorpe, 1958). But we will not elaborate, for the point to be made here is only that, from a biological point of view, the assumptions of the motor theory are not bizarre.

How the motor theory makes speech perception different from other specialized perceiving systems

Perceptual modules, by definition, differ from one another in the classes of distal events that form their domains and in the relation between these events and the proximal displays. But the phonetic module differs from others in at least two further respects.

Auditory and phonetic domains

The first difference is in the locale of the distal events. In auditory localization, the distal event is 'out there', and the relation between it and the proximal display at the two ears is completely determined by the principles of physical acoustics. Much the same can be said of those specialized modules that deal with the primitives of auditory quality, however they are to be characterized, and that come into play when people perceive, for example, whistles, horns, breaking glass, and barking dogs. Not so for the perception of phonetic structure. There, the distal object is a phonetic gesture or, more explicitly, an 'upstream' neural command for the gesture from which the peripheral articulatory movements unfold. It follows that the relation between distal object and proximal stimulus will have the special feature that it is determined not just by acoustic principles but also by neuromuscular processes internal to the speaker. Of course, analogues of these processes are also available as part of the biological endowment of the listener. Hence, some kind of link between perception and production would seem to characterize the phonetic module, but not those modules that provide auditory localization or visual perception of depth. In a later section, we will have more to say about this link. Now we will only comment that it may conceivably resemble, in its most general characteristics, those links that have been identified in the communication modules of certain nonhuman creatures (Gerhardt & Rheinlaender, 1982; Hoy, Hahn, & Paul, 1977; Hoy & Paul, 1973; Katz & Gurney, 1981; Margolish, 1983; McCasland & Konishi, 1983; Nottebohm, Stokes, & Leonard, 1976; Williams, 1984).

The motor theory aside, it is plain that speech somehow informs listeners about the phonetic intentions of the talker. The particular claim of the motor theory is that these intentions are represented in a specific form in the talker's brain, and that there is a perceiving module specialized to lead the listener effortlessly to that representation. Indeed, what is true of speech in this respect is true for all of language, except, of course, that the more distal object for language is some representation of linguistic structure, not merely of gesture, and that access to this object requires a module that is not merely phonetic, but phonological and syntactic as well.

Competition between phonetic and auditory modes

A second important difference between the phonetic module and the others has to do with the question: how does the module cooperate or compete with others that use stimuli of the same broadly defined physical form? For auditory localization, the key to the answer is the fact that the module is turned on by a specific and readily specifiable characteristic of the proximal stimulus: a particular range of differences in time of arrival at the two ears.

Obviously, such differences have no other utility for the perceiver but to provide information about the distal property, location; there are no imaginable ecological circumstances in which a person could use this characteristic of the proximal stimuli to specify some other distal property. Thus, the proximal display and the distal property it specifies only complement the other aspects of what a listener hears; they never compete.

In phonetic perception, things are quite different because important acoustic cues are often similar to, even identical with, the stimuli that inform listeners about a variety of nonspeech events. We have already remarked that, in isolation, formant transitions sound like glissandi or chirps. Now surely we don't want to perceive these as glissandi or chirps when we are listening to speech, but we do want to perceive them so when we are listening to music or to birdsong. If this is true for all of the speech cues, as in some sense it presumably is, then it is hard to see how the module can be turned on by acoustic stigmata of any kind—that is, by some set of necessary cues defined in purely acoustic terms. We will consider this matter in some greater detail later. For now, however, the point is only that cues known to be of great importance for phonetic events may be cues for totally unrelated nonphonetic events, too. A consequence is that, in contrast to the generally complementary relation of the several modules that serve the same broadly defined modality (e.g., depth and color in vision), the phonetic and auditory modules are in direct competition. (For a discussion of how this competition might be resolved, see Mattingly & Liberman, 1985.)

Experimental evidence for the theory

Having briefly described one motive for the motor theory—the context-conditioned variation in the acoustic cues for constant phonetic categories—we will now add others. We will limit ourselves to the so-called segmental aspects of phonetic structure, though the theory ought, in principle, to apply in the suprasegmental domain as well (cf. Fowler, 1982).

The two parts of the theory—that gestures are the objects of perception and that perception of these gestures depends on a specialized module—might be taken to be independent, as they were in their historical development, but the relevant data are not. We therefore cannot rationally apportion the data between the parts, but must rather take them as they come.

A result of articulation: The multiplicity, variety, and equivalence of cues for each phonetic percept

When speech synthesis began to be used as a tool to investigate speech perception, it was soon discovered that, in any specific context, a particular local property of the acoustic signal was sufficient for the perception of one phonetic category rather than another and, more generally, that the percept could be shifted along some phonetic dimension by varying the synthetic stimulus along a locally-definable acoustic dimension. For example, if the onset frequency of the transition of the second formant during a stop release is sufficiently low, relative to the frequency of the following steady state, the stop is perceived as labial; otherwise, as apical or dorsal (Liberman et al., 1954). A value along such an acoustic dimension that was optimal for a particular phonetic category, or, more loosely, the dimension itself, was termed an 'acoustic cue'.

Of course, the fact that particular acoustic cues can be isolated must, of itself, tell us something about speech perception, for it might have been otherwise. Thus, it is possible to imagine a speech-perception mechanism, equipped, perhaps, with auditory templates, that would break down if presented with anything other than a wholly natural and phonetically optimal stimulus. Listeners would either give conflicting and unreliable phonetic judgments or else not hear speech at all. Clearly, the actual mechanism is not of this kind, and the concept of cue accords with this fact.

Nevertheless, the emphasis on the cues has, perhaps, been unfortunate, for the term 'cue' might seem to imply a claim about the elemental units of speech perception. But 'cue' was simply a convenient bit of laboratory jargon referring to acoustic variables whose definition depended very much on the design features of the particular synthesizers that were used to study them. The cues, as such, have no role in a theory of speech perception; they only describe some of the facts on which a theory might be based (cf. Bailey & Summerfield, 1980). There are, indeed, several generalizations about the cues—some only hinted at by the data now available, others quite well founded—that are relevant to such a theory.

One such generalization is that every 'potential' cue—that is, each of the many acoustic events peculiar to a linguistically significant gesture—is an *actual* cue. (For example, every one of 18 potential cues to the voicing distinction in medial position has been shown to have some perceptual value; Lisker, 1978.) All possible cues have not been tested, and probably never will be, but no potential cue has yet been found that could not be shown to be an actual one.

A closely related generalization is that, while each cue is, by definition, more or less sufficient, none is truly necessary. The absence of any single cue, no matter how seemingly characteristic of the phonetic category, can be compensated for by others, not without some cost to naturalness or even intelligibility, perhaps, but still to such an extent that the intended category is, in fact, perceived. Thus, stops can be perceived without silent periods, fricatives without frication, vowels without formants, and tones without pitch (Abramson, 1972; Inoue, 1984; Remez & Rubin, 1984; Repp, 1984; Yeni-Komshian & Soli, 1981).

Yet another generalization is that even when several cues are present, variations in one can, within limits, be compensated for by offsetting variations in another (Dorman, Studdert-Kennedy, & Raphael, 1977; Dorman, Raphael, & Liberman, 1979; Hoffman, 1958; Howell & Rosen, 1983; Lisker, 1957; Summerfield & Haggard, 1977). In the case of the contrast between fricative-vowel and fricative-stop-vowel (as in [sa] vs. [sta]), investigators have found that two important cues, silence and appropriate formant transitions, engage in just such a trading relation. That this bespeaks a true equivalence in perception was shown by experiments in which the effect of variation in one cue could, depending on its 'direction', be made to 'add to' or 'cancel out' the effect of the other (Fitch, Halwes, Erickson, & Liberman, 1980). Significantly, this effect can also be obtained with sine-wave analogues of speech, but only for subjects who perceive these signals as speech, not for those who perceive them as nonspeech tones (Best, Morrongiello, & Robson, 1981).

Putting together all the generalizations about the multiplicity and variety of acoustic cues, we should conclude that there is simply no way to define a phonetic category in purely acoustic terms. A complete list of the cues—surely a cumbersome matter at best—is not feasible, for it would necessarily include all the acoustic effects of phonetically distinctive articulations. But even if it were possible to compile such a list, the result would not repay the effort, because none of the cues on the list could be deemed truly essential. As for those cues that might, for any reason, be finally included, none could be assigned a characteristic setting, since the effect of changing it could be offset by appropriate changes in one or more of the others. This surely tells us something about the design of the phonetic module. For if phonetic categories were acoustic patterns, and if, accordingly, phonetic perception were properly auditory, one should be able to describe quite straightforwardly the acoustic basis for the phonetic category and its associated percept. According to the motor theory, by contrast, one would expect the acoustic signal to serve only as a source of information about the gestures; hence the gestures would properly define the category. As for the perceptual equivalence among diverse cues that is shown by the trading relations, explaining that on auditory grounds requires ad hoc assumptions. But if, as the motor theory would have it, the gesture is the distal object of perception, we should not wonder that the several sources of information about it are perceptually equivalent, for they are products of the same linguistically significant gesture.

A result of coarticulation: I. Segmentation in sound and percept
Traditional phonetic transcription represents utterances as single linear sequences of symbols, each of which stands for a phonetic category. It is an issue among phonologists whether such transcriptions are really theoretically adequate, and various alternative proposals have been made in an effort to provide a better account. This matter need not concern us here, however, since all proposals have in common that phonetic units of some description are ordered from left to right. Some sort of segmentation is thus always implied, and what theory must take into account is that the perceived phonetic object is thus segmented.

Segmentation of the phonetic percept would be no problem for theory if the proximal sound were segmented correspondingly. But it is not, nor can it be, if speech is to be produced and perceived efficiently. To maintain a straightforward relation in segmentation between phonetic unit and signal would require that the sets of phonetic gestures corresponding to phonetic units be produced one at a time, each in its turn. The obvious consequence would be that each unit would become a syllable, in which case talkers could speak only as fast as they could spell. A function of coarticulation is to evade this limitation. There is an important consequence, however, which is that there is now no straightforward correspondence in segmentation between the phonetic and acoustic representations of the information (Fant, 1962; Joos, 1948). Thus, the acoustic information for any particular phonetic unit is typically overlapped, often quite thoroughly, with information for other units. Moreover, the span over which that information extends, the amount of overlap, and the number of units signalled within the overlapped portion all vary according to the phonetic context, the rate of articulation, and the language (Magen, 1984; Manuel & Krakow, 1984; Öhman, 1966; Recasens, 1984; Repp, Liberman, Eccardt, & Pesetsky, 1978; Tuller, Harris, & Kelso, 1982).

There are, perhaps, occasional stretches of the acoustic signal over which there is information about only one phonetic unit—for example, in the middle of the frication in a slowly articulated fricative-vowel syllable and in vowels that are sustained for artificially long times. Such stretches do, of course, offer a relation between acoustic patterns and phonetic units that would be transparent if phonetic perception were merely auditory. But even in these cases, the listener automatically takes account of, not just the transparent part of the signal, but the regions of overlap as well (Mann & Repp, 1980, 1981; Whalen, 1981). Indeed, the general rule may be that the phonetic percept is normally made available to consciousness only after all the relevant acoustic information is in, even when earlier cues might have been sufficient (Martin & Bunnell, 1981, 1982; Repp et al., 1978).

What wants explanation, then, is that the percept is segmented in a way that the signal is not, or, to put it another way, that the percept does not mirror the overlap of information in the sound (cf. Fowler, 1984). The motor theory does not provide a complete explanation, certainly not in its present state, but it does head the theoretical enterprise in the right direction. At the very least, it turns the theorist away from the search for those unlikely processes that an auditory theory would have him seek: how listeners learn phonetic labels for what they hear and thus re-interpret perceived overlap as sequences of discrete units; or how discrete units emerge in perception from interactions of a purely auditory sort. The first process seems implausible on its face, the second because it presupposes that the function of the many kinds and degrees of coarticulation is to produce just those combinations of sounds that will interact in accordance with language-independent characteristics of the auditory system. In contrast, the motor theory begins with the assumption that coarticulation, and the resulting overlap of phonetic information in the acoustic pattern, is a consequence of the efficient processes by which discrete phonetic gestures are realized in the behavior of more or less independent articulators. The theory suggests, then, that an equally efficient perceptual process might use the resulting acoustic pattern to recover the discrete gestures.

A result of coarticulation: II. Different sounds, different contexts, same percept
That the phonetic percept is invariant even when the relevant acoustic cue is not was the characteristic relation between percept and sound that we took as an example in the first section. There, we observed that variation in the acoustic pattern results from overlapping of putatively invariant gestures, an observation that, as we remarked, points to the gesture, rather than the acoustic pattern itself, as the object of perception. We now add that the articulatory variation due to context is pervasive: in the acoustic representation of every phonetic category yet studied there are context-conditioned portions that contribute to perception and that must, therefore, be taken into account by theory. Thus, for stops, nasals, fricatives, liquids, semivowels, and vowels, the always context-sensitive transitions are cues (Harris, 1958; Jenkins, Strange, & Edman, 1983; Liberman et al., 1954; O'Connor, Gerstman, Liberman, Delattre, & Cooper, 1957; Strange, Jenkins, & Johnson, 1983). For stops and fricatives, the noises that are produced at the point of constriction are also known to be cues, and, under some circumstances at least, these, too, vary with context (Dorman et al., 1977; Liberman et al., 1952; Whalen, 1981).

An auditory theory that accounts for invariant perception in the face of so much variation in the signal would require a long list of apparently arbitrary assumptions. For a motor theory, on the other hand, systematic stimulus variation is not an obstacle to be circumvented or overcome in some arbitrary way; it is, rather, a source of information about articulation that provides important guidance to the perceptual process in determining a representation of the distal gesture.

A result of coarticulation: III. Same sound, different contexts, different percepts

When phonetic categories share one feature but differ in another, the relation between acoustic pattern and percept speaks, again, to the motor theory and its alternatives. Consider, once more, the fricative [s] and the stop [t] in the syllables [sa] and [sta]. In synthesis, the second- and third-formant transitions can be the same for these two categories, since they have the same place of articulation; and the first-formant transition, normally a cue to manner, can be made ambiguous between them. For such stimuli, the perception of [sta] rather than [sa] depends on whether there is an interval of silence between the noise for the [s] and the onsets of the transitions.

Data relevant to an interpretation of the role of silence in thus producing different percepts from the same transition come from two kinds of experiments. First are those that demonstrate the effectiveness of the transitions as cues for the place feature of the fricative in fricative-vowel syllables (Harris, 1958). The transitions are not, therefore, masked by the noise of the [s] friction, and thus the function of silence in a stop is not, as it might be in an auditory theory, to protect the transitions from such masking. The second kind of experiment deals with the possibility of a purely auditory interaction—in this case, between silence and the formant transitions. Among the findings that make such auditory interaction seem unlikely is that silence affects perception of the formant transitions differently in and out of speech context and, further, that the effectiveness of silence depends on such factors as continuity of talker and prosody (Dorman et al., 1979; Rakerd, Dechovitz, & Verbrugge, 1982). But perhaps the most direct test for auditory interaction is provided by experiments in which such interaction is ruled out by holding the acoustic context constant. This can be done by exploiting 'duplex perception', a phenomenon to be discussed in greater detail in the next section. Here it is appropriate to say only that duplex perception provides a way of presenting acoustic patterns so that, in a fixed context, listeners hear the same second- or third-formant transitions in two phenomenally different ways simultaneously: as nonspeech chirps and as cues for phonetic categories. The finding is that the presence or absence of silence determines whether formant transitions appropriate for [t] or for [p], for example, are integrated into percepts as different as stops and fricatives; but silence has no effect on the perception of the nonspeech chirps that these same transitions produce (Liberman, Isenberg, &

Rakerd, 1981). Since the latter result eliminates the possibility of auditory interaction, we are left with the account that the motor theory would suggest: that silence acts in the specialized phonetic mode to inform the listener that the talker completely closed his vocal tract to produce a stop consonant, rather than merely constricting it to produce a fricative. It follows, then, that silence will, by its presence or absence, determine whether identical transitions are cues in percepts that belong to the one manner or the other.

An acoustic signal diverges to phonetic and auditory modes

We noted earlier that a formant transition is perceptually very different depending on whether it is perceived in the auditory mode, where it sounds like a chirp, or in the phonetic mode, where it cues a 'nonchirpy' consonant. Of course, the comparison is not entirely fair, since acoustic context is not controlled: the transition is presented in isolation in the one case, but as an element of a larger acoustic pattern in the other. We should, therefore, call attention to the fact that the same perceptual difference is obtained even when, by resort to a special procedure, acoustic context is held constant (Liberman, 1979; Rand, 1974). This procedure, which produces the duplex percept referred to earlier, goes as follows. All of an acoustic syllable except only the formant transition that decides between, for example, [da] and [ga] is presented to one ear. By itself, this pattern, called the 'base', sounds like a stop-vowel syllable, ambiguous between [da] and [ga]. To the other ear is presented one or the other of the transitions appropriate for [d] or [g]. In isolation, these sound like different chirps. Yet, when base and transition are presented dichotically, and in the appropriate temporal relationship, they give rise to a duplex percept: [da] or [ga], depending on the transition, and, simultaneously, the appropriate chirp. (The fused syllable appears to be in the ear to which the base had been presented, the chirp in the other.)

Two related characteristics of duplex perception must be emphasized. One is that it is obtained only when the stimulus presented to one ear is, like the 'chirpy' transition, of short duration and extremely unspeechlike in quality. If that condition is not met, as, for example, when the first two formants are presented to one ear and the entire third formant to the other, perception is not duplex. It is, on the contrary, simplex; one hears a coherent syllable in which the separate components cannot be apprehended. (A very different result is obtained when two components of a musical chord are presented to one ear, a third component to the other. In that case, listeners can respond to the third component by itself and also to that component combined with the first two (Pastore, Schmuckler, Rosenblum, & Szczesiul, 1983).

The other, closely related characteristic of duplex perception is that it is precisely duplex, not triplex. That is, listeners perceive the nonspeech chirp and the fused syllable, but they do not also perceive the base—that is, the syllable, minus one of the formant transitions—that was presented to one ear (Repp, Milburn, & Ashkenas, 1983). (In the experiment with musical chords by Pastore et al., 1983, referred to just above, there was no test for duplex, as distinguished from triplex, perception.)

The point is that duplex perception does not simply reflect the ability of the auditory system to fuse dichotically presented stimuli and also, as in the experiment with the chords, to keep them apart. Rather, the duplex percepts of speech comprise the only two ways in which the transition, for example, can be heard: as a cue for a phonetic gesture and as a nonspeech sound. These percepts are strikingly different, and, as we have already seen, they change in different, sometimes contrasting ways in response to variations in the acoustic signals—variations that must have been available to all structures in the brain that can process auditory information. A reasonable conclusion is that there must be two modules that can somehow use the same input to produce simultaneous representations of two distal objects. (For speculation about the mechanism that normally prevents perception of this ecologically impossible situation, and about the reason why that highly adaptive mechanism might be defeated by the procedures used to produce duplex perception, see Mattingly & Liberman, 1985.)

Acoustic and optical signals converge on the phonetic mode

In duplex perception, a single acoustic stimulus is processed simultaneously by the phonetic and auditory modules to produce perception of two distal objects: a phonetic gesture and a sound. In the phenomenon to which we turn now, something like the opposite occurs: two different stimuli—one acoustic, the other optical—are combined by the phonetic module to produce coherent perception of a single distal event. This phenomenon, discovered by McGurk and McDonald (1976), can be illustrated by this variant on their original demonstration. Subjects are presented acoustically with the syllables [ba], [ba], [ba] and optically with a face that, in approximate synchrony, silently articulates [bɛ], [vɛ], [ðɛ]. The resulting and compelling percept is [ba], [va], [ða], with no awareness that it is in any sense bimodal—that is, part auditory and part visual. According to the motor theory, this is so because the perceived event is neither; it is, rather, a gesture. The proximal acoustic signal and the proximal optical signal have in common, then, that they convey information about the same distal object. (Perhaps a similar convergence is implied by the finding that units in the optic tectum of the barn owl are bimodally sensitive to acoustic and optical cues for the same distal property, location in space; Knudsen, 1982).

Even prelinguistic infants seem to have some appreciation of the relation between the acoustic and optical consequences of phonetic articulation. This is to be inferred from an experiment in which it was found that infants at four to five months of age preferred to look at a face that articulated the vowel they were hearing rather than at the same face articulating a different vowel (Kuhl & Meltzoff, 1982). Significantly, this result was not obtained when the sounds were pure tones matched in amplitude and duration to the vowels. In a related study it was found that infants of a similar age looked longer at a face repeating the disyllable they were hearing than at the same face repeating, another disyllable, though both disyllables were carefully synchronized with the visible articulation (MacKain, Studdert-Kennedy, Spieker, & Stern, 1983). Like the results obtained with adults in the McGurk–MacDonald kind of experiment, these findings with infants imply a perception–production link and, accordingly, a common mode of perception for all proper information about the gesture.

The general characteristics that cause acoustic signals to be perceived as speech
The point was made in an earlier section that acoustic definitions of phonetic contrasts are, in the end, unsatisfactory. Now we would suggest that acoustic definitions also fail for the purpose of distinguishing in general between acoustic patterns that convey phonetic structures and those that do not. Thus, speech cannot be distinguished from nonspeech by appeal to surface properties of the sound. Surely, natural speech does have certain characteristics of a general and superficial sort—for example, formants with characteristic bandwidths and relative intensities, stretches of waveform periodicities that typically mark the voiced portion of syllables, peaks of intensity corresponding approximately to syllabic rhythm, etc.—and these can be used by machines to detect speech. But research with synthesizers has shown that speech is perceived even when such general characteristics are absent. This was certainly true in the case of many of the acoustic patterns that were used in work with the Pattern Playback synthesizer, and more recently it has been shown to be true in the most extreme case of patterns consisting only of sine waves that follow natural formant trajectories (Remez, Rubin, Pisoni, & Carrell, 1981). Significantly, the converse effect is also obtained. When reasonably normal formants are made to deviate into acoustically continuous but abnormal trajectories, the percept breaks into two categorically distinct parts: speech and a background of chirps, glissandi, and assorted noises (Liberman & Studdert-Kennedy, 1978). Of course, the trajectories of the formants are determined by the movements of the articulators. Evidently, those trajectories that conform to possible articulations engage the phonetic module; all others fail.

We conclude that acoustic patterns are identified as speech by reference to deep properties of a linguistic sort: if a sound can be 'interpreted' by the specialized phonetic module as the result of linguistically significant gestures, then it is speech; otherwise, not. (In much the same way, grammatical sentences can be distinguished from ungrammatical ones, not by lists of surface properties, but only by determining whether or not a grammatical derivation can be given.) Of course, the kind of mechanism such an 'interpretation' requires is the kind of mechanism the motor theory presumes.

Phonetic and auditory responses to the cues
Obviously, a module that acts on acoustic signals cannot respond beyond the physiological limits of those parts of the auditory system that transmit the signal to the module. Within those limits, however, different modules can be sensitive to the signals in different ways. Thus, the auditory-localization module enables listeners to perceive differences in the position of sounding objects given temporal disparity cues smaller by several orders of magnitude than those required to make the listener aware of temporal disparity as such (Brown & Deffenbacher, 1979, chap. 7; Hirsh, 1959). If there is, as the motor theory implies, a distinct phonetic module, then in like manner its sensitivities should not, except by accident, be the same as those that characterize the module that deals with the sounds of non-speech events.

In this connection, we noted in the first section of the paper that one form of auditory theory of speech perception points to auditory discontinuities in differential sensitivity (or in absolute identification), taking these to be the natural bases for the perceptual discontinuities that characterize the boundaries of phonetic categories. But several kinds of experiments strongly imply that this is not so.

One kind of experiment has provided evidence that the perceptual discontinuities at the boundaries of phonetic categories are not fixed; rather, they move in accordance with the acoustic consequences of articulatory adjustments associated with phonetic context, dialect, and rate of speech. (For a review, see Repp & Liberman, in press.) To account for such articulation-correlated changes in perceptual sensitivities by appeal to auditory processes requires, yet again, an ultimately countless set of ad hoc assumptions about auditory interactions, as well as the implausible assumption that the articulators are always able to behave so as to produce just those sounds that conform to the manifold and complex requirements that the auditory interactions impose. It seems hardly more plausible that, as has been suggested, the discontinuities in phonetic perception are really auditory discontinuities that were caused to move about in phylogenetic or ontogenetic development as a result of experience with speech (Aslin & Pisoni, 1980). The difficulty with this assumption is that it presupposes the very canonical form of the cues that does not exist (see above) and, also, that it implies a contradiction in assuming, as it must, that the auditory sensitivities underwent changes in the development of speech, yet somehow also remained unchanged and nonetheless manifest in the adult's perception of nonspeech sounds.

Perhaps this is the place to remark about categorical perception that the issue is not, as is often supposed, whether nonspeech continua are categorically perceived, for surely some do show tendencies in that direction. The issue is whether, given the same (or similar) acoustic continua, the auditory and phonetic boundaries are in the same place. If there are, indeed, auditory boundaries, and if, further, these boundaries are replaced in phonetic perception by boundaries at different locations (as the experiments referred to above do indicate), then the separateness of phonetic and auditory perception is even more strongly argued for than if the phonetic boundaries had appeared on continua where auditory boundaries did not also exist.

Also relevant to comparison of sensitivity in phonetic and auditory modes are experiments on perception of acoustic variations when, in the one case, they are cues for phonetic distinctions, and when, in some other, they are perceived as nonspeech. One of the earliest of the experiments to provide data about the nonspeech side of this comparison dealt with perception of frequency-modulated tones—or 'ramps' as they were called—that bear a close resemblance to the formant transitions. The finding was that listeners are considerably better at perceiving the pitch at the end of the ramp than at the beginning (Brady, House, & Stevens, 1961). Yet, in the case of stop consonants that are cued by formant transitions, perception is better syllable-initially than syllable-finally, though in the former case it requires information about the beginning of the ramp, while in the latter it needs to know about the end. Thus, if one were predicting sensitivity to speech from sensitivity to the analogous nonspeech sounds, one would make exactly the wrong predictions. More recent studies have made more direct comparisons and found differences in discrimination functions when, in speech context, formant transitions cued place distinctions among stops and liquids, and when, in isolation, the same transitions were perceived as nonspeech sounds (Mattingly et al., 1971; Miyawaki, Strange, Verbrugge, Liberman, Jenkins, & Fujimura, 1975).

More impressive, perhaps, is evidence that has come from experiments in which listeners are induced to perceive a constant stimulus in different ways. Here belong experiments in which sinewave analogues of speech, referred to earlier, are presented under conditions that cause some listeners to perceive them as speech and others not. The perceived discontinuities lie at different places (on the acoustic continuum) for the two groups (Best et al., 1981; Best & Studdert-Kennedy, 1983; Studdert-Kennedy & Williams, 1984; Williams,

Verbrugge, & Studdert-Kennedy, 1983). Here, too, belongs an experiment in which the formant-transitions appropriate to a place contrast between stop consonants are presented with the remainder of a syllable in such a way as to produce the duplex percept referred to earlier: the transitions cue a stop consonant and, simultaneously, nonspeech chirps. The result is that listeners yield quite different discrimination functions for exactly the same formant transitions in exactly the same acoustic context, depending on whether they are responding to the speech or nonspeech sides of the duplex percept; only on the speech side of the percept is there a peak in the discrimination function to mark a perceptual discontinuity at the phonetic boundary (Mann & Liberman, 1983).

Finally, we note that, apart from differences in differential sensitivity to the transitions, there is also a difference in absolute-threshold sensitivity when, in the one case, these transitions support a phonetic percept, and when, in the other, they are perceived as nonspeech chirps. Exploiting, again, the phenomenon of duplex perception, investigators found that the transitions were effective (on the speech side of the percept) in cueing the contrast between stops at a level of intensity 18 db lower than that required for comparable discrimination of the chirps (Bentin & Mann, 1983). At that level, indeed, listeners could not even hear the chirps, let alone discriminate them; yet they could still use the transitions to identify the several stops.

The several aspects of the theory

For the purpose of evaluating the motor theory, it is important to separate it into its more or less independent parts. First, and fundamentally, there is the claim that phonetic perception is perception of gesture. As we have seen, this claim is based on evidence that the invariant source of the phonetic percept is somewhere in the processes by which the sounds of speech are produced. In the first part of this section we will consider where in those processes the invariant might-be found.

The motor theory also implies a tight link between perception and production. In the second part of this section we will ask how that link came to be.

Where is the invariant phonetic gesture?

A phonetic gesture, as we have construed it, is a class of movements by one or more articulators that results in a particular, linguistically significant deformation, over time, of the vocal-tract configuration. The linguistic function of the gesture is clear enough: phonetic contrasts, which are of course the basis of phonological categories, depend on the choice of one particular gesture rather than another. What is not so clear is how the gesture relates to the actual physical movements of articulators and to the resulting vocal-tract configurations, observed, for example, in X-ray films.

In the early days of the motor theory, we made a simplifying assumption about this relation: that a gesture was effected by a single key articulator. On this assumption, the actual movement trajectory of the articulator might vary, but only because of aerodynamic factors and the physical linkage of this articulator with others, so the neural commands in the final common paths (observable with electromyographic techniques) would nevertheless be invariant across different contexts. This assumption was appropriate as an initial working hypothesis, if only because it was directly testable. In the event, there proved to be a considerable amount of variability which the hypothesis could not account for.

In formulating this initial hypothesis, we had overlooked several serious complications. One is that a particular gesture typically involves not just one articulator, but two or more; thus 'lip rounding', for example, is a collaboration of lower lip, upper lip, and jaw. Another is that a single articulator may participate in the execution of two different gestures at the same time; thus, the lips may be simultaneously rounding and closing in the production of a labial stop followed by a rounded vowel, for example, [bu]. Prosody makes additional complicating demands, as when a greater displacement of some or all of the active articulators is required in producing a stressed syllable rather than an unstressed one; and linguistically irrelevant factors, notably speaking rate, affect the trajectory and phasing of the component movements.

These complications might suggest that there is little hope of providing a rigorous physical definition of a particular gesture, and that the gestures are hardly more satisfactory as perceptual primitives than are the acoustic cues. It might, indeed, be argued that there is an infinite number of possible articulatory movements, and that the basis for categorizing one group of such movements as 'lip rounding' and another as 'lip closure' is entirely a priori.

But the case for the gesture is by no means as weak as this. Though we have a great deal to learn before we can account for the variation in instances of the same gesture, it is nonetheless clear that, despite such variation, the gestures have a virtue that the acoustic cues lack: instances of a particular gesture always have certain topological properties not shared by any other gesture. That is, for any particular gesture, the same sort of distinctive deformation is imposed on the current vocal-tract configuration, whatever this 'underlying' configuration happens to be. Thus, in lip rounding, the lips are always slowly protruded and approximated to some appreciable extent, so that the anterior end of the vocal tract is extended and narrowed, though the relative contributions of the tongue and lips, the actual degrees of protrusion and approximation, and the speed of articulatory movement vary according to context. Perhaps this example seems obvious because lip rounding involves a local deformation of the vocal-tract configuration, but the generalization also applies to more global gestures. Consider, for example, the gesture required to produce an 'open' vowel. In this gesture, tongue, lips, jaw, and hyoid all participate to contextually varying degrees, and the actual distance between the two lips, as well as that between the tongue blade and body and the upper surfaces of the vocal tract, are variable; but the goal is always to give the tract a more open, horn-shaped configuration than it would otherwise have had.

We have pointed out repeatedly that, as a consequence of gestural overlapping, the invariant properties of a particular gesture are not manifest in the spectrum of the speech signal. We would now caution that a further consequence of this overlapping is that, because of their essentially topological character, the gestural invariants are usually not obvious from inspection of a single static vocal-tract configuration, either. They emerge only from consideration of the configuration as it changes over time, and from comparison with other configurations in which the same gesture occurs in different contexts, or different gestures in the same context.

We would argue, then, that the gestures do have characteristic invariant properties, as the motor theory requires, though these must be seen, not as peripheral movements, but as the more remote structures that control the movements. These structures correspond to the speaker's intentions. What is far from being understood is the nature of the system that computes the topologically appropriate version of a gesture in a particular context. But this problem is not peculiar to the motor theory; it is familiar to many who study the control and coordination of movement, for they, like us, must consider whether, given context-conditioned variability at the surface, motor acts are nevertheless governed by invariants of some sort (Browman & Goldstein, 1985; Fowler, Rubin, Remez, & Turvey, 1980; Tuller & Kelso, 1984; Turvey, 1977).

The origin of the perception–production link

In the earliest accounts of the motor theory, we put considerable emphasis on the fact that listeners not only perceive the speech signal but also produce it. This, together with doctrinal behaviorist considerations, led us to assume that the connection between perception and production was formed as a wholly learned association, and that perceiving the gesture was a matter of picking up the sensory consequences of covert mimicry. On this view of the genesis of the perception–production link, the distinguishing characteristic of speech is only that it provides the opportunity for the link to be established. Otherwise, ordinary principles of associative learning are adequate to the task; no specialization for language is required.

But then such phenomena as have been described in this paper were discovered, and it became apparent that they differed from anything that association learning could reasonably be expected to produce. Nor were these the only relevant considerations. Thus, we learned that people who have been pathologically incapable from birth of controlling their articulators are nonetheless able to perceive speech (MacNeilage, Rootes, & Chase, 1967). From the research pioneered by Eimas, Siqueland, Jusczyk and Vigorito (1971), we also learned that prelinguistic infants apparently categorize phonetic distinctions much as adults do. More recently, we have seen that even when the distinction is not functional in the native language of the subjects, and when, accordingly, adults have trouble perceiving it, infants nevertheless do quite well up to about one year of age, at which time they begin to perform as poorly as adults (Werker & Tees, 1984). Perhaps, then, the sensitivity of infants to the acoustic consequences of linguistic gestures includes all those gestures that could be phonetically significant in any language, acquisition of one's native language being a process of losing sensitivity to gestures it does not use. Taking such further considerations as these into account, we have become even more strongly persuaded that the phonetic mode, and the perception–production link it incorporates, are innately specified.

Seen, then, as a view about the biology of language, rather than a comment on the coincidence of speaking and listening, the motor theory bears at several points on our thinking about the development of speech perception in the child. Consider, first, a linguistic ability that, though seldom noted (but see Mattingly, 1976), must be taken as an important prerequisite to acquiring the phonology of a language. This is the ability to sort acoustic patterns into two classes: those that contain (candidate) phonetic structures and those that do not. (For evidence, however indirect, that infants do so sort, see Alegria & Noirot, 1982; Best, Hoffman, & Glanville, 1982; Entus, 1977; Molfese, Freeman, & Palermo, 1975; Segalowitz & Chapman, 1980; Witelson, 1977; but see Vargha-Khadem & Corballis, 1979). To appreciate the bearing of the motor theory on this matter, recall our claim, made in an earlier section, that phonetic objects cannot be perceived as a class by reference to acoustic stigmata, but only by a recognition that the sounds might have been produced by a vocal tract as it made linguistically significant gestures. If so, the perception–production link is a necessary condition for recognizing speech as speech. It would thus be a blow to the motor theory if it could be shown that infants must develop empirical criteria for this purpose. Fortunately for the theory, such criteria appear to be unnecessary.

Consider, too, how the child comes to know, not only that phonetic structures are present, but, more specifically, just what those phonetic structures are. In this connection, recall that information about the string of phonetic segments is overlapped in the sound, and that there are, accordingly, no acoustic boundaries. Until and unless the child (tacitly) appreciates the gestural source of the sounds, he can hardly be expected to perceive, or ever learn to perceive, a phonetic structure. Recall, too, that the acoustic cues for a phonetic category vary with phonetic factors such as context and with extra-phonetic factors such as rate and vocal-tract size. This is to say, once again, that there is no canonical cue. What, then, is the child to learn? Association of some particular cue (or set of cues) with a phonetic category will work only for a particular circumstance. When circumstances change, the child's identification of the category will be wrong, sometimes grossly, and it is hard to see how he could readily make the appropriate correction. Perception of the phonetic categories can properly be generalized only if the acoustic patterns are taken for what they really are: information about the underlying gestures. No matter that the child sometimes mistakes the phonological significance of the gesture, so long as that which he perceives captures the systematic nature of its relation to the sound; the phonology will come in due course. To appreciate this relation is, once again, to make use of the link between perception and production.

How 'direct' is speech perception?

Since we have been arguing that speech perception is accomplished without cognitive translation from a first-stage auditory register, our position might appear similar to the one Gibson (1966) has taken to regard to 'direct perception'. The similarity to Gibson's views may seem all the greater because, like him, we believe that the object of perception is motoric. But there are important differences, the bases for which are to be seen in the following passage (Gibson, 1966, p. 94):

> An articulated utterance is a source of a vibratory field in the air. The source is biologically 'physical' and the vibration is acoustically 'physical'. The vibration is a potential stimulus, becoming effective when a listener is within range of the vibratory field. The listener then *perceives* the articulation because the invariants of vibration correspond to those of articulation. In this theory of speech perception, the units and parts of speech are present both in the mouth of the speaker and in the air between the speaker and listener. Phonemes are in the air. They

can be considered physically real if the higher-order invariants of sound waves are admitted to the realm of physics.

The first difference between Gibson's view and ours relates to the nature of the perceived events. For Gibson, these are actual movements of the articulators, while for us, they are the more remote gestures that the speaker intended. The distinction would be trivial if an articulator were affected by only one gesture at a time, but, as we have several times remarked, an articulatory movement is usually the result of two or more overlapping gestures. The gestures are thus control structures for the observable movements.

The second difference is that, unlike Gibson, we do not think articulatory movements (let alone phonetic structures) are given directly (that is, without computation) by 'higher-order invariants' that would be plain if only we had a biologically appropriate science of physical acoustics. We would certainly welcome any demonstration that such invariants did exist, since, even though articulatory movement is not equivalent to phonetic structure, such a demonstration would permit a simpler account of how the phonetic module works. But no higher-order invariants have thus far been proposed, and we doubt that any will be forthcoming. We would be more optimistic on this score if it could be shown, at least, that articulatory movements can be recovered from the signal by computations that are purely analytic, if nevertheless complex. One might then hope to reformulate the relationship between movements and signal in a way that would make it possible to appeal to higher-order invariants and thus obviate the need for computation. But, given the many-to-one relation between vocal-tract configurations and acoustic signal, a purely analytic solution to the problem of recovering movements from the signal seems to be impossible unless one makes unrealistic assumptions about excitation, damping, and other physical variables (Sondhi, 1979). We therefore remain skeptical about higher-order invariants.

The alternative to an analytic account of speech perception is, of course, a synthetic one, in which case the module compares some parametric description of the input signal with candidate signal descriptions. As with any form of 'analysis-by-synthesis' (cf. Stevens & Halle, 1967), such an account is plausible only if the number of candidates the module has to test can be kept within reasonable bounds. This requirement is met, however, if, as we suppose, the candidate signal descriptions are computed by an analogue of the production process—an internal, innately specified vocal-tract synthesizer, as it were (Liberman, Mattingly, & Turvey, 1972; Mattingly & Liberman, 1969)—that incorporates complete information about the anatomical and physiological characteristics of the vocal tract and also about the articulatory and acoustic consequences of linguistically significant gestures. Further constraints become available as experience with the phonology of a particular language reduces the inventory of possible gestures and provides information about the phonotactic and temporal restrictions on their occurrence. The module has then merely to determine which (if any) of the small number of gestures that might have been initiated at a particular instant could, in combination with gestures already in progress, account for the signal.

Thus, we would claim that the processes of speech perception are, like other linguistic processes, inherently computational and quite indirect. If perception seems nonetheless immediate, it is not because the process is in fact straightforward, but because the module is so well-adapted to its complex task.

The motor theory and modularity

In attributing speech perception to a 'module,' we have in mind the notion of modularity proposed by Fodor (1983). A module, for Fodor, is a piece of neural architecture that performs the special computations required to provide central cognitive processes with representations of objects or events belonging to a natural class that is ecologically significant for the organism. This class, the 'domain' of the module, is apt also to be 'eccentric,' for the domain would be otherwise merely a province of some more general domain, for which another module must be postulated anyway. Besides domain-specificity and specialized neural architecture, a module has other characteristic properties. Because the perceptual process it controls is not cognitive, there is little or no possibility of awareness of whatever computations are carried on within the module ('limited central access'). Because the module is specialized, it has a 'shallow' output, consisting only of rigidly definable, domain-relevant representations; accordingly, it processes only the domain-relevant information in the input stimulus. Its computations are thus much faster than those of the less specialized processes of central cognition. Because of the ecological importance of its domain for the organism, the operation of the module is not a matter of choice, but 'mandatory'; for the same reason, its computations are 'informationally encapsulated', that is, protected from cognitive bias.

Most psychologists would agree that auditory localization, to return to an example we have mentioned several times, is controlled by specialized processes of some noncognitive kind. They might also agree that its properties are those that Fodor assigns to modules. At all events, they would set auditory localization apart from such obviously cognitive activities as playing chess, proving theorems, and recognizing a particular chair as a token of the type called 'chair'. As for perception of language, the consensus is that it qualifies as a cognitive process par excellence, modular only in that it is supported by the mechanisms of the auditory modality. But in this, we and Fodor would argue, the consensus is doubly mistaken: the perception of language is neither cognitive nor auditory. The events that constitute the domain of linguistic perception, however they may be defined, must certainly be an ecologically significant natural class, and it has been recognized since Broca that linguistic perception is associated with specialized neural architecture. Evidently, linguistic perception is fast and mandatory; arguably, it is informationally encapsulated—that is, its phonetic, morphological and syntactic analyses are not biased by knowledge of the world—and its output is shallow—that is, it produces a linguistic description of the utterance, and only this. These and other considerations suggest that, like auditory localization, perception of language rests on a specialization of the kind that Fodor calls a module.

The data that have led us in the past to claim that 'speech is special' and to postulate a 'speech mode' of perception can now be seen to be consistent with Fodor's claims about modularity, and especially about the modularity of language. (What we have been calling a phonetic module is then more properly called a linguistic module.) Thus, as we have noted, speech perception uses all the information in the stimulus that is relevant to phonetic structures: every potential cue proves to be an actual cue. This holds true even across modalities: relevant optical information combines with relevant acoustic information to produce a coherent phonetic percept in which, as in the example described earlier, the bimodal nature of the stimulation is not detectable. In contrast, irrelevant information in the stimulus is *not* used: the acoustic properties that might cause the transitions to be heard as chirps are ignored—or perhaps we should say that the auditory consequences of those properties are suppressed—when the transitions are in context and the linguistic module is engaged. The exclusion of the irrelevant extends, of course, to stimulus information about voice quality, which helps to identify the speaker (perhaps by virtue of some other module) but has no phonetic importance, and even to that extraphonetic information which might have been supposed to help the listener distinguish sounds that contain phonetic structures from those that do not. As we have seen, even when synthetic speech lacks the acoustic properties that would make it sound natural, it will be treated as speech if it contains sufficiently coherent phonetic information. Moreover, it makes no difference that the listener knows, or can determine on auditory grounds, that the stimulus was not humanly produced; because linguistic perception is informationally encapsulated and mandatory, he will hear synthetic speech as speech.

As might be expected, the linguistic module is also very good at excluding from consideration the acoustic effects of unrelated objects and events in the environment; the resistance of speech perception to noise and distortion is well known. These other objects and events are still perceived, because they are dealt with by other modules, but they do not, within surprisingly wide limits, interfere with speech perception (cf. Darwin, 1984). On the other hand, the module is not necessarily prepared for nonecological conditions, as the phenomenon of duplex perception illustrates. Under the conditions of duplex perception the module makes a mistake it would never normally make: it treats the same acoustic information both as speech and as nonspeech. And, being an informationally encapsulated and mandatorily operating mechanism, it keeps on making the same mistake, whatever the knowledge or preference of the listener.

Our claim that the invariants of speech perception are phonetic gestures is much easier to reconcile with a modular account of linguistic perception than with a cognitive account. On the latter view, the gestures would have to be inferred from an auditory representation of the signal by some cognitive process, and this does not seem to be a task that would be particularly congenial to cognition. Parsing a sentence may seem to bear some distant resemblance to the proving of theorems, but disentangling the mutually confounding auditory effects of overlapping articulations surely does not. It is thus quite reasonable for proponents of a cognitive account to reject the possibility that the invariants are motoric and to insist that they are to be found at or near the auditory surface, heuristic matching of auditory tokens to auditory prototypes being perfectly plausible as a cognitive process.

Such difficulties do not arise for our claim on the modular account. If the invariants of speech are phonetic gestures, it merely makes the domain of linguistic perception more suitably eccentric; if the invariants were auditory, the case for a separate linguistic module would be the less compelling. Moreover, computing these invariants from the acoustic signal is a task for which there is no obvious parallel among cognitive processes. What is required for this task is not a heuristic process that draws on some general cognitive ability or on knowledge of the world, but a special-purpose computational device that relates gestural properties to the acoustic patterns.

It remains, then, to say how the set of possible gestures is specified for the perceiver. Does it depend on tacit knowledge of a kind similar, perhaps, to that which is postulated by Chomsky to explain the universal constraints on syntactic and phonological form? We think not, because knowledge of the acoustic-phonetic properties of the vocal tract, unlike other forms of tacit knowledge, seems to be totally inaccessible: no matter how hard they try, even post-perceptually, listeners cannot recover aspects of the process—for example, the acoustically different transitions—by which they might have arrived at the distal object. But, surely, this is just what one would expect if the specification of possible vocal-tract gestures is not tacit knowledge at all, but rather a direct consequence of the eccentric properties of the module itself. As already indicated, we have in earlier papers suggested that speech perception is accomplished by virtue of a model of the vocal tract that embodies the relation between gestural properties and acoustic information. Now we would add that this model must be part of the very structure of the language module. In that case, there would be, by Fodor's account, an analogy with all other linguistic universals.

Perception and production: One module or two?

For want of a better word, we have spoken of the relation between speech perception and speech production as a 'link', perhaps implying thereby that these two processes, though tightly bonded, are nevertheless distinct. Much the same implication is carried, more generally, by Fodor's account of modularity, if only because his attention is almost wholly on perception. We take pains, therefore, to disown the implication of distinctness that our own remarks may have conveyed, and to put explicitly in its place the claim that, for language, perception and production are only different sides of the same coin.

To make our intention clear, we should consider how language differs from those other modular arrangements in which, as with language, perception and action both figure in some functional unity: simple reflexes, for example; or the system that automatically adjusts the posture of a diving gannet in accordance with optical information that specifies the time of contact with the surface of the water (Lee & Reddish, 1981). The point about such systems is that the stimuli do not resemble the responses, however intimate the connection between them. Hence, the detection of the stimulus and the initiation of the response must be managed by separate components of the module. Indeed, it would make no great difference if these cases were viewed as an input module hardwired to an output module.

Language is different: the neural representation of the utterance that determines the speaker's production is the distal object that the listener perceives; accordingly, speaking and listening are both regulated by the same structural constraints and the same grammar. If we were to assume two modules, one for speaking and one for listening, we should then have to explain how the same structures evolved for both, and how the representation of the grammar acquired by the listening module became available to the speaking module.

So, if it is reasonable to assume that there is such a thing as a language module, then it is even more reasonable to assume that there is only one. And if, within that module, there are subcomponents that correspond to the several levels of linguistic performance, then each of these subcomponents must deal both with perception and production. Thus, if sentence planning is the function of a particular subcomponent, then sentence parsing is a function of the same subcomponent, and similarly, *mutatis mutandis*, for speech production and speech perception. And, finally, if all this is true, then the corresponding input and output functions must themselves be as computationally similar as the inherent asymmetry between production and perception permits, just as they are in man-made communication devices.

These speculations do not, of course, reveal the nature of the computations that the language module carries out, but they do suggest a powerful constraint on our hypotheses about them, a constraint for which there is no parallel in the case of other module systems. Thus, they caution that, among all plausible accounts of language input, we should take seriously only those that are equally plausible as accounts of language output; if a hypothesis about parsing cannot be readily restated as a hypothesis about sentence-planning, for example, we should suppose that something is wrong with it.

Whatever the weaknesses of the motor theory, it clearly does conform to this constraint, since, by its terms, speech production and speech perception are both inherently motoric. On the one side of the module, the motor gestures are not the means to sounds designed to be congenial to the ear; rather, they are, in themselves, the essential phonetic units. On the other side, the sounds are not the true objects of perception, made available for linguistic purposes in some common auditory register; rather, they only supply the information for immediate perception of the gestures.

References

Abramson, A.S. (1972) Tonal experiments with whispered Thai. In A. Valdman (Ed.), *Papers in Linguistics and Phonetics to the Memory of Pierre Delattre*, 31–44. The Hague: Mouton.

Alegria, J., & Noirot, E. (1982) Oriented mouthing activity in neonates: Early development of differences related to feeding experiences. In J. Mehler, S. Franck, E.C.T. Walker and M. Garrett (Eds.), *Perspectives on Mental Representation*. Hillsdale, NJ: Erlbaum.

Aslin, R.N., & Pisoni, D.B. (1980) Some developmental processes in speech perception. In G.H. Yeni-Komshian, J.F. Kavanagh, & C.A. Ferguson (Eds.), *Child Phonology*. New York: Academic Press.

Bailey, P.J., & Summerfield, Q. (1980) Information in speech: Observations on the perception of [s]-stop clusters. *Journal of Experimental Psychology: Human Perception and Performance, 6*, 536–563.

Bentin, S. & Mann, V.A. (1983) Selective effects of masking on speech and nonspeech in the duplex perception paradigm. *Haskins Laboratories Status Report on Speech Research, SR-76*, 65–85.

Berkeley, G. (1709) *An essay towards a new theory of vision*. Dublin: Printed by Aaron Rhames for Jeremy Pepyal.

Best, C.T., Hoffman, H., & Glanville, B.B. (1982) Development of infant ear asymmetries for speech and music. *Perception and Psychophysics, 31*, 75–85.

Best, C.T., Morrongiello, B., & Robson, R. (1981) Perceptual equivalence of acoustic cues in speech and nonspeech perception. *Perception and Psychophysics, 29*, 191–211.

Best, C.T. & Studdert-Kennedy, M. (1983) Discovering phonetic coherence in acoustic patterns. In A. Cohen & M.P.R. van den Broecke (Eds.), *Abstracts of the Tenth International Congress of Phonetic Sciences*. Dordrecht, The Netherlands: Foris Publications.

Brady, P.T., House, A.S., & Stevens, K.N. (1961) Perception of sounds characterized by a rapidly changing resonant frequency. *Journal of the Acoustical Society of America, 33*, 1357–1362.

Browman, C.P. & Goldstein, L.M. (1985) Dynamic modeling of phonetic structure. In V. Fromkin (Ed.),

32   *A.M. Liberman and I.G. Mattingly*

Phonetic Linguistics. New York: Academic Press.

Brown E.L. & Deffenbacher, K. (1979) *Perception and the Senses.* New York: Oxford University Press.

Carney, A.E., Widin, G.P., & Viemeister, N.F. (1977) Noncategorical perception of stop consonants differing in VOT. *Journal of the Acoustical Society of America, 62,* 961–970.

Chistovich, L.A. (1960) Classification of rapidly repeated speech sounds. *Akustichneskii Zhurnal, 6,* 392–398. Trans. in *Soviet Physics-Acoustics, 6,* 393–398 (1961).

Cole, R.A. & Scott, B. (1974) Toward a theory of speech perception. *Psychological Review, 81,* 348–374.

Cooper, F.S., Delattre, P.C., Liberman, A.M., Borst, J.M., & Gerstman, L.J. (1952) Some experiments on the perception of synthetic speech sounds. *Journal of the Acoustical Society of America, 24,* 597–606.

Crowder, R.G. & Morton, J. (1969) Pre-categorical acoustic storage (PAS). *Perception and Psychophysics, 5,* 365–373.

Cutting, J.E. & Rosner, B.S. (1974) Categories and boundaries in speech and music. *Perception and Psychophysics, 16,* 564–570.

Darwin, C.J. (1984) Perceiving vowels in the presence of another sound: Constraints on formant perception. *Journal of the Acoustical Society of America, 76,* 1636–1647.

Dorman, M.F., Raphael, L.J., & Liberman, A.M. (1979) Some experiments on the sound of silence in phonetic perception. *Journal of the Acoustical Society of America, 65,* 1518–1532.

Dorman, M.F., Studdert-Kennedy, M., & Raphael, L.J. (1977) Stop consonant recognition: Release bursts and formant transitions as functionally equivalent, context-dependent cues. *Perception and Psychophysics, 22,* 109–122.

Dudley, H. (1940) The carrier nature of speech. *Bell Systems Technical Journal, 19,* 495–515.

Eimas, P., Siqueland, E.R., Jusczyk, P., & Vigorito, J. (1971) Speech perception in early infancy. *Science, 171,* 304–306.

Entus, A.K. (1977) Hemispheric asymmetry in processing dichotically presented speech and nonspeech stimuli by infants. In S.J. Segalowitz and F.A. Greber (Eds.), *Language Development and Neurological Theory.* New York: Academic Press.

Fant, C.G.M. (1962) Descriptive analysis of the acoustic aspects of speech. *Logos, 5,* 3–17.

Festinger, L., Burnham, C.A., Ono, H., & Bamber, D. (1967) Efference and the conscious experience of perception. *Journal of Experimental Psychology Monograph, 74,* (4, Pt. 2).

Fitch, H.L., Halwes, T., Erickson, D.M., & Liberman, A.M. (1980) Perceptual equivalence of two acoustic cues for stop consonant manner. *Perception and Psychophysics, 27,* 343–350.

Fodor, J. (1983) *The Modularity of Mind.* Cambridge, MA: MIT Press.

Fowler, C.A. (1982) Converging sources of evidence on spoken and perceived rhythms of speech: Cyclic production of vowels in monosyllabic stress feet. *Journal of Experimental Psychology: General, 112,* 386–412.

Fowler, C.A. (1984) Segmentation of coarticulated speech in perception. *Perception and Psychophysics, 36,* 359–368.

Fowler, C.A., Rubin, P., Remez, R.E., & Turvey, M.T. (1980) Implications for speech production of a general theory of action. In B. Butterworth (Ed.), *Language Production.* New York: Academic Press.

Fujisaki, M. & Kawashima, T. (1970) Some experiments on speech perception and a model for the perceptual mechanism. *Annual Report of the Engineering Research Institute* (Faculty of Engineering, University of Tokyo), *29,* 207–214.

Gerhardt, H.C. & Rheinlaender, J. (1982) Localization of an elevated sound source by the green tree frog. *Science, 217,* 663–664.

Gibson, J.J. (1966) *The Senses Considered as Perceptual Systems.* Boston: Houghton Mifflin.

Hafter, E.R. (1984) Spatial hearing and the duplex theory: How viable is the model? In G.M. Edelman, W.E. Gall, & W.M. Cowan (Eds.), *Dynamic Aspects of Neocortical Function.* New York: Wiley.

Harris, K.S. (1958) Cues for the discrimination of American English fricatives in spoken syllables. *Language and Speech, 1,* 1–7.

Hillenbrand, J. (1984) Perception of sine-wave analogs of voice onset time stimuli. *Journal of the Acoustical Society of America, 75,* 231–240.

Hirsh, I.J. (1959) Auditory perception of temporal order. *Journal of the Acoustical Society of America, 31*, 759–767.

Hoffman, H.S. (1958) Study of some cues in the perception of the voiced stop consonants. *Journal of the Acoustical Society of America, 30*, 1035–1041.

Howell, P. & Rosen, S. (1983) Closure and frication measurements and perceptual integration of temporal cues for the voiceless affricate/fricative contrast. *Speech Hearing and Language Work in Progress.* University College London, Department of Phonetics and Linguistics.

Hoy, R., Hahn, J., & Paul, R.C. (1977) Hybrid cricket auditory behavior: Evidence for genetic coupling in animal communication. *Science, 195*, 82–83.

Hoy, R. & Paul, R.C. (1973) Genetic control of song specificity in crickets. *Science, 180*, 82–83.

Inoue, A. (1984) A perceptual study of Japanese voiceless vowels and its implications for the phonological analysis of voiceless consonants. Unpublished manuscript.

Jenkins, J.J., Strange, W., & Edman, T.R. (1983) Identification of vowels in 'voiceless' syllables. *Perception and Psychophysics, 34*, 441–450.

Joos, M. (1948) Acoustic phonetics. *Language Monograph 23*, Supplement to *Language, 24*.

Julesz, B. (1960) Binocular depth perception of computer-generated patterns. *Bell System Technical Journal 39*, 1125–1162.

Julesz, B. (1971) *Foundations of Cyclopean Perception.* Chicago: University of Chicago Press.

Katz, L.C. & Gurney, M.E. (1981) Auditory responses in the zebra finch's motor system for song. *Brain Research, 221*, 192–197.

Knudsen, E.I. (1982) Auditory and visual maps of space in the optic tectum of the owl. *Journal of Neuroscience, 2*, 1117–1194.

Knudsen, E.I. (1984) Synthesis of a neural map of auditory space in the owl. In G.M. Edelman, W.E. Gall, & W.M. Cowan, *Dynamic Aspects of Neocortical Function.* New York: Wiley.

Kuhl, P.K. (1981) Discrimination of speech by nonhuman animals: Basic auditory sensitivities conducive to the perception of speech-sound categories. *Journal of the Acoustical Society of America, 70*, 340–349.

Kuhl, P.K. & Meltzoff, A.N. (1982) The bimodal perception of speech in infancy. *Science, 218*, 1138–1144.

Kuhl, P.K. & Miller, J.D. (1975) Speech perception by the chinchilla: Voiced-voiceless distinction in alveolar plosive consonants. *Science, 190*, 69.

Ladefoged, P. & McKinney, N. (1963) Loudness, sound pressure, and subglottal pressure in speech. *Journal of the Acoustical Society of America, 35*, 454–460.

Lee, D.N. & Reddish, P.E. (1981) Plummeting gannets: A paradigm of ecological optics. *Nature, 293*, 293–294.

Liberman, A.M. (1979) Duplex perception and integration of cues: Evidence that speech is different from nonspeech and similar to language. In E. Fischer-Jorgensen, J. Rischel, & N. Thorsen (Eds.), *Proceedings of the IXth International Congress of Phonetic Sciences.* Copenhagen: University of Copenhagen.

Liberman, A.M. (1982) On finding that speech is special. *American Psychologist, 37*, 148–167.

Liberman, A.M., Cooper, F.S., Shankweiler, D.P., & Studdert-Kennedy, M. (1967) Perception of the speech code. *Psychological Review, 74*, 431–461.

Liberman, A.M., Delattre, P.C., & Cooper, F.S. (1952) The role of selected stimulus-variables in the perception of the unvoiced stop consonants. *American Journal of Psychology, 65*, 497–516.

Liberman, A.M., Delattre, P.C., Cooper, F.S., & Gerstman, L.J. (1954) The role of consonant–vowel transitions in the perception of the stop and nasal consonants. *Psychological Monographs, 68*, 1–13.

Liberman, A.M., Isenberg, D., & Rakerd, B. (1981) Duplex perception of cues for stop consonants: Evidence for a phonetic mode. *Perception and Psychophysics, 30*, 133–143.

Liberman, A.M., Mattingly, I.G., & Turvey, M. (1972) Language codes and memory codes. In A.W. Melton and E. Martin (Eds.), *Coding Processes and Human Memory.* Washington, DC: Winston.

Liberman, A.M., & Studdert-Kennedy, M. (1978) Phonetic perception. In R. Held, H.W. Leibowitz, & H.-L. Teuber (Eds.), *Handbook of Sensory Physiology, Vol. VIII: Perception.* New York: Springer-Verlag.

Lisker, L. (1957) Closure duration, first-formant transitions, and the voiced-voiceless contrast of intervocalic stops. *Haskins Laboratories Quarterly Progress Report, 23*, Appendix 1.

Lisker, L. (1978) Rapid vs. rabid: A catalogue of acoustic features that may cue the distinction. *Haskins Laboratories Status Report on Speech Research, SR-54*, 127–132.

Lisker, L. & Abramson, A. (1964) A cross-language study of voicing in initial stops: Acoustical measurement. *Word, 20*, 384–422.

MacKain, K.S., Studdert-Kennedy, M., Spieker, S., & Stern, D. (1983) Infant intermodal speech perception is a left hemisphere function. *Science, 219*, 1347–1349.

MacNeilage, P.F., Rootes, T.P., & Chase, R.A. (1967) Speech production and perception in a patient with severe impairment of somesthetic perception and motor control. *Journal of Speech and Hearing Research, 10*, 449–468.

Magen, H. (1984) Vowel-to-vowel coarticulation in English and Japanese. *Journal of the Acoustical Society of America, 75*, S41.

Mann, V.A. & Liberman, A.M. (1983) Some differences between phonetic and auditory modes of perception. *Cognition, 14*, 211–235.

Mann, V.A. & Repp, B.H. (1980) Influence of vocalic context on the perception of [ʃ]-[s] distinction: I. Temporal factors. *Perception and Psychophysics, 28*, 213–228.

Mann, V.A. & Repp, B.H. (1981) Influence of preceding fricative on stop consonant perception. *Journal of the Acoustical Society of America, 69*, 548–558.

Manuel, S.Y. & Krakow, R.A. (1984) Universal and language particular aspects of vowel-to-vowel coarticulation. *Haskins Laboratories Status Report on Speech Research, SR-77/78*, 69–78.

Margolish, D. (1983) Acoustic parameters underlying the responses of song specific neurons in the white-crowned sparrow. *Journal of Neuroscience, 3*, 1039–1057.

Marler, P. (1970) Birdsong and speech development: Could there be parallels? *American Scientist, 58*, 669–673.

Martin, J.G. & Bunnell, H.T. (1981) Perception of anticipatory coarticulation effects in /stri, stru/ sequences. *Journal of the Acoustical Society of America, 69*, S92.

Martin, J.G. & Bunnell, H.T. (1982) Perception of anticipatory coarticulation effects in vowel-stop consonant-vowel sequences. *Journal of Experimental Psychology: Human Perception and Performance, 8*, 473–488.

Mattingly, I.G. (1976) Phonetic prerequisites for first-language acquisition. In W. Von Raffler-Engel, & Y. Lebrun (Eds.), *Baby Talk and Infant Speech*. Lisse, The Netherlands: Swets & Zeitlinger.

Mattingly, I.G. & Liberman, A.M. (1969) The speech code and the physiology of language. In K.N. Leibovic (Ed.), *Information Processing in the Nervous System*. New York: Springer-Verlag.

Mattingly, I.G. & Liberman, A.M. (1985) Verticality unparalleled. *The Behavioral and Brain Sciences, 8*, 24–26.

Mattingly, I.G., Liberman, A.M., Syrdal, A.M., & Halwes, T. (1971) Discrimination in speech and nonspeech modes. *Cognitive Psychology, 2*, 131–157.

McCasland, J.S. & Konishi, M. (1983) Interaction between auditory and motor activities in an avian song control nucleus. *Proceedings of the National Academy of Sciences, 78*, 7815–7819.

McGurk, H. & MacDonald, J. (1976) Hearing lips and seeing voices. *Nature, 264*, 746–748.

Miller, J.D. (1977) Perception of speech sounds in animals: Evidence for speech processing by mammalian auditory mechanisms. In T.H. Bullock (Ed.), *Recognition of Complex Acoustic Signals* (Life Sciences Research Report 5), p. 49. Berlin: Dahlem Konferenzen.

Miyawaki, K., Strange, W., Verbrugge, R., Liberman, A.M., Jenkins, J.J., & Fujimara, O. (1975) An effect of linguistic experience: the discrimination of [r] and [l] by native speakers of Japanese and English. *Perception and Psychophysics, 18*, 331–340.

Molfese, D.L., Freeman, R.B., & Palermo, D.S. (1975) The ontogeny of brain lateralization for speech and nonspeech stimuli. *Brain and Language, 2*, 356–368.

Nottebohm, F., Stokes, T.M., & Leonard, C.M. (1976) Central control of song in the canary, Serinus canarius. *Journal of Comparative Neurology, 165*, 457–486.

O'Connor, J.D., Gerstman, L.J., Liberman, A.M., Delattre, P.C., & Cooper, F.S. (1957) Acoustic cues for the perception of initial /w, r, l/ in English. *Word, 13*, 25–43.

Oden, G.C. & Massaro, D.W. (1978) Integration of featural information in speech perception. *Psychological Review*, *85*, 172–191.

Ohman, S.E.G. (1966) Coarticulation in VCV utterances: Spectrographic measurements. *Journal of the Acoustical Society of America*, *39*, 151–168.

Pastore, R.E., Schmuckler, M.A., Rosenblum, L., & Szczesiul, R. (1983) Duplex perception with musical stimuli. *Perception and Psychophysics*, *33*, 469–474.

Pisoni, D.B. (1973) Auditory and phonetic memory codes in the discrimination of consonants and vowels. *Perception and Psychophysics*, *13*, 253–260.

Pisoni, D.B. (1977) Identification and discrimination of the relative onset of two component tones: Implications for the perception of voicing in stops. *Journal of the Acoustical Society of America*, *61*, 1352–1361.

Pisoni, D.B. & Tash, J. (1974) Reaction times to comparisons within and across phonetic categories. *Perception and Psychophysics*, *15*, 285–290.

Poggio, G.F. (1984) Processing of stereoscopic information in primate visual cortex. In G.M. Edelman, W.E. Gall, & W.M. Cowan (Eds.), *Dynamic Aspects of Neocortical Function*. New York: Wiley.

Rakerd, B., Dechovitz, D.R., & Verbrugge, R.R. (1982) An effect of sentence finality on the phonetic significance of silence. *Language and Speech*, *25*, 267–282.

Rand, T.C. (1974) Dichotic release from masking for speech. *Journal of the Acoustical Society of America*, *55*, 678–680.

Recasens, D. (1984) Vowel-to-vowel coarticulation in Catalan VCV sequences. *Journal of the Acoustical Society of America*, *76*, 1624–1635.

Remez, R.E., Rubin, P.E., Pisoni, D.B., & Carrell, T.D. (1981) Speech perception without traditional speech cues. *Science*, *212*, 947–950.

Remez, R.E. & Rubin, P.E. (1984) On the perception of intonation from sinusoidal signals: Tone height and contour. *Journal of the Acoustical Society of America*, *75*, S39.

Repp, B.H. (1984) The role of release bursts in the perception of [s]-stop clusters. *Journal of the Acoustical Society of America*, *75*, 1219–1230.

Repp, B.H. & Liberman, A.M. (in press) Phonetic categories are flexible. In S. Harnad (Ed.), *Categorical Perception*. Cambridge: Cambridge University Press.

Repp, B.H., Liberman, A.M., Eccardt, T., & Pesetzky, D. (1978) Perceptual integration of acoustic cues for stop, fricative and affricate manner. *Journal of Experimental Psychology: Human Perception and Performance*, *4*, 621–637.

Repp, B.H., Milburn, C., & Ashkenas, J. (1983) Duplex perception: Confirmation of fusion. *Perception and Psychophysics*, *33*, 333–337.

Rosen, S.M. & Howell, P. (1981) Plucks and bows are not categorically perceived. *Perception and Psychophysics*, *30*, 156–168.

Sondhi, M.M. (1979) Estimation of vocal-tract areas: the need for acoustical measurements. *IEEE Transactions on Acoustics, Speech and Signal Processing*, ASSP-27, 268–273.

Samuel, A.G. (1977) The effect of discrimination training on speech perception: Noncategorical perception. *Perception and Psychophysics*, *22*, 321–330.

Segalowitz, S.J. & Chapman, J.S. (1980) Cerebral asymmetry for speech in neonates: A behavioral measure. *Brain and Language*, *9*, 281–288.

Stetson, R.H. (1951) *Motor Phonetics: A Study of Speech Movements in Action*. Amsterdam: North-Holland.

Stevens, K.N. (1975) The potential role of property detectors in the perception of consonants. In G. Fant & M.A. Tatham (Eds.) *Auditory Analysis and Perception of Speech*. New York: Academic Press.

Stevens, K.N. & Halle, M. (1967) Remarks on analysis by synthesis and distinctive features. In W. Wathen-Dunn (Ed.). *Models for the Perception of Speech and Visual Form*. Cambridge, MA: MIT Press.

Stevens, K.N. & Blumstein, S.E. (1978) Invariant cues for place of articulation in stop consonants. *Journal of the Acoustical Society of America*, *64*, 1358–1368.

Strange, W., Jenkins, J.J., & Johnson, T.L. (1983) Dynamic specification of coarticulated vowels. *Journal of the Acoustical Society of America*, *74*, 695–705.

36   *A.M. Liberman and I.G. Mattingly*

Studdert-Kennedy, M. (1976) Speech perception. In N.J. Lass (Ed.), *Contemporary Issues in Experimental Phonetics*. New York: Academic Press.

Studdert-Kennedy, M. & Williams, D.R. (1984) Range effects for speech and nonspeech judgments of sine wave stimuli. *Journal of the Acoustical Society of America, 75*, S64.

Suga, N. (1984) The extent to which bisonar information is represented in the auditory cortex. In G.M. Edelman, W.E. Gall, & W.M. Cowan (Eds.), *Dynamic Aspects of Neocortical Function*. New York: Wiley.

Summerfield, Q. (1982) Differences between spectral dependencies in auditory and phonetic temporal processing: Relevance to the perception of voicing in initial stops. *Journal of the Acoustical Society of America, 72*, 51–61.

Summerfield, Q. & Haggard, M. (1977) On the dissociation of spectral and temporal cues to the voicing distinction in initial stop consonants. *Journal of the Acoustical Society of America, 62*, 436–448.

Thorpe, W.H. (1958) The learning of song patterns by birds, with especial reference to the song of the chaffinch, *Fringilla coelebs. Ibis, 100*, 535–570.

Tuller, B., Harris, K., & Kelso, J.A.S. (1982) Stress and rate: Differential transformations of articulation. *Journal of the Acoustical Society of America, 71*, 1534–1543.

Tuller, B. & Kelso, J.A.S. (1984) The relative timing of articulatory gestures: Evidence for relational invariants. *Journal of the Acoustical Society of America, 76*, 1030–1036.

Turvey, M. (1977) Preliminaries to a theory of action with reference to vision. In R. Shaw & J. Bransford (Eds.), *Perceiving, Acting, and Knowing: Toward an Ecological Physiology*. Hillsdale, NJ: Erlbaum.

Vargha-Khadem, F. & Corballis, M. (1979) Cerebral asymmetry in infants. *Brain and Language, 8*, 1–9.

Washburn, M.F. (1926) Gestalt Psychology and Motor Psychology. *American Journal of Psychology, 37*, 516–520.

Watson, J.B. (1919) *Psychology from the Standpoint of a Behaviorist*. Philadelphia: J.B. Lippincott Co.

Werker, J.F. & Tees, R.C. (1984) Cross-language speech perception: Evidence for perceptual organization during the first year of life. *Infant Behavior and Development, 7*, 49–63.

Whalen, D.H. (1981) Effects of vocalic formant transition and vowel quality on the English [s]-[š] boundary. *Journal of the Acoustical Society of America, 69*, 275–282.

Williams, H. (1984) *A motor theory of bird song perception*. Unpublished doctoral dissertation. The Rockefeller University.

Williams, D.R., Verbrugge, R.R., & Studdert-Kennedy, M. (1983) Judging sine wave stimuli as speech and nonspeech. *Journal of the Acoustical Society of America, 74*, S66.

Witelson, S. (1977) Early hemisphere specialization and interhemispheric plasticity: An empirical and theoretical review. In S.J. Segalowitz & F.A. Gruber (Eds.), *Language Development and Neurological Theory*. New York: Academic Press.

Yeni-Komshian, G.H. & Soli, S.D. (1981) Recognition of vowels from information in fricatives: Perceptual evidence of fricative-vowel coarticulation. *Journal of the Acoustical Society of America, 70*, 966–975.

Résumé

Une théorie motrice de la perception proposée initialement pour rendre compte des résultats des premières expériences avec de la parole synthétique a été largement révisée afin d'interpréter les données récentes et de relier les propositions de cette théorie à celles que l'on peut faire pour d'autres modalités de perception. La révision de cette théorie stipule que l'information phonétique est fournie par un système biologique distinct, un 'module' spécialisé pour détecter les gestes que le locuteur a eu l'intention de faire: ces gestes fondent les catégories phonétiques. La relation entre les gestes et les patterns acoustiques dans lesquels ceux-ci sont imbriqués de façon variée est unique mais régulée. Cette relation est construite dans la structure du module. En conséquence le module provoque la perception de la structure phonétique sans traduction à partir d'impressions auditives préliminaires. Ce module est ainsi comparable à d'autres modules tels que celui qui permet à l'animal de localiser les sons. La particularité de ce module tient à la relation entre perception et production qu'il incorpore et au fait qu'il doit rivaliser avec d'autres modules pour de mêmes variations de stimulus.

Phonetic Universals in Vowel Systems

BJÖRN LINDBLOM

INTRODUCTION

Phonetic Explanation of Language Universals

From an evolutionary point of view, it does not appear unnatural to assume that language form is forged by the sociobiological conditions of its use. Thus spoken language tends to evolve sound systems and grammars that can be explained, at least in part, with reference to the fact that it is spoken. It uses the vocal-auditory channel and ought therefore to exhibit adaptations to the developmental and adult mechanisms of speech production and speech perception. This point of view implies furthermore that the structuring of sign language should similarly reflect the constraints of its transmission medium, the gestural-visual channel, and that comparative study of speech and sign would be capable of offering important insights into the mechanisms of language (Bellugi & Studdert-Kennedy 1980).

The present chapter is a contribution to the paradigm aiming at the phonetic explanation of language universals (Ohala, forthcoming), and thus it exemplifies the functional perspective described above. It investigates the extent to which certain universal aspects of vowel systems can be said to be consequences of similarly universal properties of speech production, human hearing, and speech perception.

13

EXPERIMENTAL PHONOLOGY

14   BJÖRN LINDBLOM

Table 2.1

Vowel Categories[a]

Front		Central		Back		
i	ü	ɨ	u̇	ɯ	u	high
I	Ü	ɪ	U̇	Ï	U	lower-high
e	ö	ė	ȯ	ë	o	higher-mid
E	Ö	ə	Ȯ	Ɛ̇	O	mid
ɛ	ɔ̈	ɛ̇		ʌ	ɔ	lower-mid
æ		æ̇			ɒ	higher-low
ä		a	à	ɑ	ɑ	low

[a]From Crothers (1978).

SOME FACTS ABOUT VOWEL SYSTEMS

The source of the data on vowel systems used in this paper is Crothers (1978), who presents a typology based on an "areally and genetically representative" sample of 209 languages taken from the Phonology Archive of the Stanford Project on Language Universals. Crothers (henceforth C; in addition, data, tables, and appendices from C are referred to as C-data, C-appendix, etc.) uses the "classical phonemic method," adding a distinction between marginal phonemes and full phonemes. His analyses are based principally on the fully phonemic vowels and their major phonetic realization (i.e., a fairly narrow transcription of the primary member of the phoneme, see C-Appendix III). Vowel quality is quantized in terms of 37 categories, as shown in Table 2.1.

Figure 2.1 demonstrates some gross trends in the C-data (unnormalized, C-Appendix III). It shows as a proportion of all systems examined how often a given phonetic symbol occurs (observations below 5% excluded). The data pertain to all vowel systems containing three through nine vowels and have been arranged in Table 2.1 in the form of a quasiacoustic vowel chart. We note that [i], [a], and [u] are particularly favored. Peripheral qualities, notably [e], [ɛ], [o], and [ɔ], are next in rank. In third place we find two central vowels, [ɨ] and [ə]; two front rounded vowels, [ü] and [ø]; one back unrounded vowel, [ɯ] (we use C's vowel symbols in this chapter, supplemented by standard IPA symbols, some of which are defined acoustically in Table 2.3). Why Figure 2.1 should look the way it does can be understood in light of the following information. These remarks are based entirely on C's work.

Table 2.2 lists the vowel system types most frequently observed in the C-corpus. The symbols indicate broad transcriptions, since this count was apparently made after applying normalization, that is, turning [I], [ɯ], and [ü] into /i/, /u/, and /ɨ/, respectively.

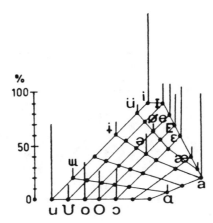

Figure 2.1 Occurrence of phonetic symbols expressed as a proportion of the total number of languages examined (about 200). The data are based on systems containing three through nine vowels (adapted from Crothers, 1978, Appendix III). The phonetic qualities of the unlabeled points are left out for clarity (scores below 5%) but can be inferred with the aid of Table 2.1.

Except for a few cases of two-vowel systems, all languages have /i/a/u/. As systems containing more than these basic three are examined, we first encounter /ɨ/, /ɛ/, or /ɔ/. The vowels /e/ and /o/ occur in larger systems (≥ 7 vowels). A pattern of five basic vowel qualities appears to be the norm, the most common systems being those with close to that number of basic vowels. C further notes that (1) the number of height distinctions is typically equal to or greater than the number of front–back distinctions, (2) the number of interior vowels (e.g., /ü ɨ ə/) cannot exceed the number in the front or back columns, and (3) the number of height distinctions in front vowels is equal to or greater than the number of back vowels. Although Figure 2.1 was constructed without regard to cooccurrence dependencies among the units, the generation of groups of vowels by applying a criterion of highest rank will result in systems that share some of the characteristics that C lists as universals.

Some Previous Attempts to Predict Vowel Systems

Among the first attempts to systematize vowel-system data are those of Troubetzkoy (1929) and Hockett (1955). These studies present typological data and discuss various regularities. The implicational laws of Jakobson (1941) make statements about possible contrasts in the phonological systems of children and in the languages of the world. The gradual unfolding of the vowel contrasts (and other oppositions) is said to obey a rule which we shall here use predictively, namely, the principle of maximal contrast.

In their discussion of the concept of 'markedness', Chomsky and Halle

16   BJÖRN LINDBLOM

Table 2.2

Common Vowel Systems Types[a]

Number of vowels in system	Frequency of occurrence in corpus	Vowel qualities (normalized)
3	23	i a u
4	13	i ɛ a u
	9	i ɨ a u
5	55	i ɛ a u ɔ
	5	i ɛ ɨ a o
6	29	i ɛ i a u ɔ
	7	i e ɛ u o ɔ
7	14	i e i ə a u o
	11	i e ɛ a u o ɔ
9	7	i e ɛ i ə a u o ɔ

[a]From Crothers (1978 p. 105).

(1968;409–411) explore how the complexity of a given vowel system can be measured in terms of the marking conventions and the marked–unmarked status of the vowels in the lexicon on the one hand and certain system conditions on the other. Donegan (1978; Donegan-Miller 1972) presents an account of vowel inventories developed within the framework of natural phonology (Stampe 1973). The regularities of such inventories are seen as "manifestations of phonetically-motivated natural processes." Systems are generated (and evaluated with respect to complexity) by applying context-free and hierarchically organized processes (raising, bleaching, lowering, coloring, and so on) in various patterns of interaction.

PRESENT APPROACH TO THE THEORY OF VOWEL SYSTEMS

Axiomatic and Deductive Definitions of Phonological Constructs

The present approach differs from the above-mentioned accounts in a number of respects. We share with Donegan the belief that phonetically motivated natural processes may underlie many vowel-system regularities. Likewise, we do not deny that bleaching, coloring, and so on sometimes have a certain intuitive appeal in natural vowel phonology when seen as 'fortition' and 'lenition' processes (i.e., processes facilitating perception and production, respectively). Nevertheless we find that, although in many respects insightful, Donegan's framework—like Jackobson's implicational rules and the Chomsky and Halle markedness theory—leaves largely unresolved the theoretically fundamental questions of specifying more precisely the nature of these processes, their independent motivation, and their consequences for linguistic form. Central issues are what causes these dimensions of contrast to arise and what causes bleaching, coloring, and other such processes. It may be objected that these questions are premature, that the prospects of replacing many *axiomatically postulated* constructs in current phonology (such as distinctive features, processes, and rules) by derived concepts rigorously and *deductively obtained* and explicitly anchored in speech behavior appear utterly remote at present. However, since in any scientific field the question of independent motivation is the crucial one in the search for explanations, research priorities seem quite clear. The prospects of such a program scoring rapid and easy success may indeed appear remote, but this circumstance should lead to an intensification of efforts rather than a deferral of action and a search for shortcuts (Lindblom 1980, Ohala 1978).

Hypothetical Universals Shaping Vowel Systems

Several hypotheses about universals that influence the shape of vowel systems are presented below and are developed in three steps and deal with the following topics: (1) the definition of the notion of 'possible vowel,' (2) the processes of normal speech perception, and (3) evolutionary constraints on vowel systems.

NOTION OF 'POSSIBLE VOWEL'

'Possible vowel' is defined articulatorily, acoustically, and perceptually. This is done by capturing "possibilities" in terms of the notion of space and by applying this notion in turn to articulation, acoustics, and perception.

A physiologically oriented model, Lindblom and Sundberg (1971) (hereafter L&S), is used to provide a definition of *possible vowel articulation*. In the L&S model, the parameters that control the shape of the vocal tract are as follows: labial width and labial height, mandible position, tongue body (front-back position and deviation from neutral position), tongue blade (elevation and front-back position), and larynx position. A first intermediate representation is constructed from specifications of these parameters in the form of an articulatory profile similar to a tracing of a lateral X ray of the midsagittal outline of the vocal tract. The class of all such profiles defines the space hypothesized to be the universal articulatory space for vowels.

The L&S model can also be used to define the corresponding *acoustic space* (Figure 2.2). The steps involved in its derivation are as follows: A second intermediate representation is generated from the profile. It represents the

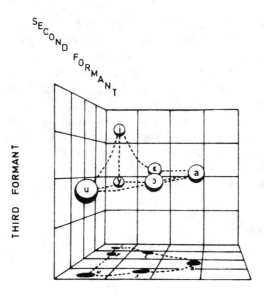

Figure 2.2   Three-dimensional illustration of a hypothetic universal: the acoustic vowel space.

cross-sectional areas along the tract, the so-called vocal tract area function. This is a quantification of the cavity shapes. It is used to derive the end product, the formant frequencies associated with the input articulatory configuration. The class of all formant patterns defines the acoustic vowel space.

The perceptual vowel space is obtained by mapping acoustic onto auditory representations. This has been done in two ways. In a preliminary implementation of the present framework (Liljencrants & Lindblom 1972), henceforth L&L) we substituted the physical frequency scale used in formant specifications for a perceptually more satisfactory dimension, namely, the quasilogarithmic mel scale (Fant 1973).

In the current version we go several steps farther and incorporate a numerical model of the human hearing system that is due to Schroeder, Atal, and Hall (1979). This acoustic-to-auditory transformation is described below.

NORMAL SPEECH PERCEPTION

Human listeners appear capable of making at least the following two types of judgment when listening to a native speaker of their own language: they are able to determine *what* was said (to judge the structure and meaning of an utterance) and to say something about *how* it was said (to judge speech-quality features such as a foreign accent or the phonetic symptoms of patho-

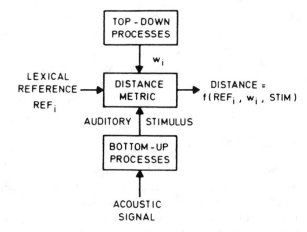

Figure 2.3 Conceptualization of speech perception. An identification depends on the relative distance between stimulus and reference patterns weighted by the grammatical-semantic plausibility of the reference patterns.

logical speech). One approach to the conceptualization of these aspects of a listener's behavior is illustrated in Figure 2.3. Stimulus-controlled (bottom-up) processes refer to the series of transformations that the acoustic signal undergoes in the auditory periphery. These processes are universal in that by definition they are independent of language and cognitive conditions. Some examples are the frequency analysis and the spatio-temporal coding of neural impulses that the peripheral stages of the auditory system pass on to the brain for conceptual analysis (see the auditory model described below). There are also conceptually determined (top-down) processes that delimit a range of alternative candidates for identification in a given context as defined by grammatical structure, "expectations," presuppositions about the speaker, and so on.

How can these phenomena be modeled? Assume that a listener matches the auditory-neural representation of a given speech signal against reference patterns that he retrieves from lexical storage and derives on-line under the influence of grammatical, conceptual, and pragmatic constraints. His judgment of what was said is based on that reference pattern which best fulfills a combination of two criteria: phonetic similarity and grammatical-conceptual plausibility. This matching presupposes a perceptual *distance metric*: phonetic similarity is quantified in terms of the "distance" between the auditory stimulus (STIM in Figure 2.3) and a given reference pattern (REF). This distance is weighted by a coefficient, w_i reflecting grammatical-conceptual-pragmatic plausibility. It is this weighting that introduces top-down effects and aims at describing phenomena such as phonemic restorations and our ability to listen non-physically—that is, our ability occasionally to hear only what we "want" to hear.

A listener's judgment of how something was said is possible because the concept of distance accounts for the identification of an utterance not in terms of a perfect match but in terms of the match that is best relatively speaking. Thus, the highest scoring interpretation may quite commonly be achieved by a distance which is greater than zero or might occur when a listener understands what is being said but furthermore notices that, for instance, the speaker has a heavy accent or exhibits symptoms of dysarthria.

EVOLUTIONARY CONSTRAINTS

We hypothesize that vowel systems tend to evolve so as to make the process of speech understanding efficient and to ensure speech intelligibility under a variety of conditions and disturbances. Such efficiency depends in part on vowel identification, which can be assumed to be facilitated by the ontogenetic and diachronic development of perceptual difference among the targets of a vowel system that are maximally, or, perhaps, sufficiently large (see Jakobson 1941). Our work explores measures of both maximal and sufficient perceptual contrast.

Since the notion of perceptual distance used here depends not only on stimulus-related but also on conceptual factors, it must be pointed out that all calculations reported below were undertaken on the assumption of equal top-down probabilities of vowel-system members. We strongly suggest that such an assumption would be at variance with the facts of everyday speech communication. We know that in individual languages certain vowel contrasts are found more frequently than others, a notion explored under the concept of 'functional load.' However, within the present framework, computational experiments incorporating non-uniform functional load can easily be accommodated. To test the model more fully against data from individual languages it will indeed be necessary to undertake such studies. The trouble appears to be how to define functional load quantitatively (see Wang 1967; King 1967). Nevertheless, since assumptions about unequal top-down probabilities must necessarily introduce language-specific conditions, they have been left aside in the present attempt to explore the influence of universal conditions.

IMPLEMENTATION OF THE FRAMEWORK

A Phonetic-Phonological Paradox:
The Lesson of the L&L Model

An early attempt to implement some of the ideas presented above was made in L&L. That study differs from the present one primarily in the following three respects. First, the three-dimensional acoustic space of Figure 2.2 was represented by a two-dimensional approximation. Second, the perceptual space was obtained by translating the two dimensions of the acoustic representation—that is, the first formant frequency, F_1, and an effective upper formant frequency, F_2', both calibrated in Hz—into the perceptual parameters M1 and M2' specified in auditorily relevant units, mels. Third, the perceptual distance between two arbitrary vowels i and j was defined as the Euclidean distance between the points representing their location in the perceptual plane. Thus perceptual distance, D_{ij}, was defined as

$$D_{ij} = [(M1_i - M1_j)^2 + (M2_i' - M2_j')^2]^{1/2} \tag{1}$$

Vowel systems were then derived according to a criterion of maximal perceptual contrast which was defined in terms of all the possible vowel pairs of an n-vowel system. Thus Equation 1 is applied to all pairs. After the inversion and squaring of D_{ij}, summation occurs across all cells of the triangular vowel-by-vowel matrix. We have

$$\sum_{i=2}^{n} \sum_{j=1}^{i-1} 1/(D_{ij})^2 \rightarrow \text{minimized} \tag{2}$$

For a given number of vowels, n, a computer algorithm was used to find that combination of formant patterns (that system of vowel qualities) for which intervocalic distances were maximized according to Equation 2.

The results are presented in Figure 2.4, which shows the wedge-shaped vowel plane in terms of linear frequency scales for systems ranging in size from three through twelve vowels. The horizontal and vertical lines correspond to divisions of F_1 at every 200 Hz from 200 to 800 Hz and of F_2 at every 500 Hz from 500 to 2500 Hz. In the top row the rightmost figure shows a superposition of the results for all systems.

For a detailed discussion the reader is referred to the original study (Liljencrants & Lindblom 1972). The predicted systems containing three through six vowels show reasonable agreement with observed facts. The favoring of peripheral vowels is similarly a positive result. However, systems with seven or more vowels turn out to have too many high vowels compared with natural systems. The seven- and eight-vowel systems lack interior mid vowels such as [ø] and exhibit four rather than three or two degrees of backness in the high vowels. The nine-, ten-, eleven-, and twelve-vowel systems have five degrees of backness in the high vowels, which is at least one too many. How do we account for this discrepancy?

In Lindblom (1975), the mel distances between the extreme corners of the vowel space of Figure 2.2 were found to be 850 (i/u), 675 (i/a), and 550 (u/a) using Equation 1. This finding lies at the bottom of the less successful L&L predictions. It is hard to reconcile with data from a typological survey of 150 vowel systems (Sedlak 1969) showing that for about 70% of the languages the preferred number of vowels between /i/ and /u/ is zero and one between

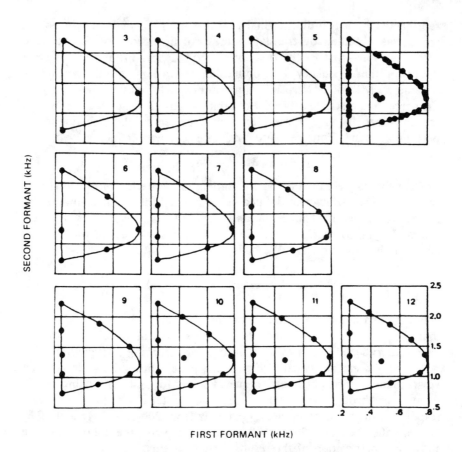

Figure 2.4   Results of vowel system predictions plotted on an F_2/F_1 plane (from Liljencrants & Lindblom 1972).

/a/ and /u/ as well as between /a/ and /i/. This trend is clearly borne out also in the C-data. (See Figure 2.1).

Expressed in acoustic terms, these facts indicate that the dimension of F_1 (a major correlate of articulatory opening and vowel height) is favored in vowel contrasts over higher formants (related mainly to front–back and rounding). Lindblom (1975) argues that if vowel systems had developed security margins guaranteeing a certain amount of perceptual differentiation in communication under noisy conditions, they would be expected to exploit F_1 (height or sonority) more than other formants, since, according to acoustic theory, F_1 is more intense and thus statistically more resistant to noise. Lindblom (1975) contains some revised and more successful predictions obtained by weighting F_1 differences in the distance computations so as to make them a much more important determinant of computed distance than the contribution from higher formants.

Crothers obtains a revision of the L&L model by defining the vowels as circular areas on a two-dimensional vowel chart and by letting the optimal arrangement be "that which allows the maximum diameter for a given number of vowels in the vowel space" (p. 126). He notes that F_1 is much more important perceptually than higher formants and adjusts his vowel space accordingly. Predictions for seven-, eight-, and nine-vowel systems are clearly improved.

A Revised Model and Some New Results

TOWARDS PERCEPTUALLY REALISTIC DISTANCE MEASURES

The L&L study can be criticized on a number of grounds. One decision that we question is the adoption of the formant-based distance measure, Equation 1. While it seems reasonable to suppose that spectral peaks, or their temporal equivalents, play a rather special role as determinants of vowel quality, there is in fact little evidence to suggest that the ear literally tracks formants and discards all other information. Such an idea appears particularly implausible in view of the following two circumstances. First, formants defined as poles in the complex frequency domain are highly elusive in acoustic representations and lack unambiguous spectral correlates owing to the complex interactions associated with voice-source characteristics, aspiration, nasalization, or simply because of a high F_0. Second, there are several studies showing that, along with the formant pattern, the F_0 and local relations among formant levels contribute toward determining phonetic quality. If we intend to apply distance measures not only to ideal zero-free oral vowels but to voiced and voiceless consonants and to nasalized and aspirated segments as well, formant-based, or pole/zero-based, distance measures promise to become rather unwieldly tools, especially if we want to project onto such measures the characteristics of the auditory system.

Bernstein (1976) developed a quantitative representation of vowel perception in order to predict the patterning of vowel systems. Although his study was limited to steady-state synthetic vowels, he concluded that it was not possible to describe his experimental results on subjective vowel dissimilarities solely in terms of the lowest three formant frequencies. Formant levels were found to contribute significantly.

We use Bernstein's finding to further support our conviction that perceptual distance functions defined on acoustic parameters should be abandoned and replaced by distance functions defined in terms of dimensions more directly related to the processes of the *auditory* system.

At this point let us return to describing our current procedure for mapping acoustic onto auditory representations. As pointed out, we do so by means of the mathematical model proposed by Schroeder *et al.* (1979). The input to the model is the harmonic power spectrum of an arbitrary (but possible) vowel. This spectrum is then passed through an auditory filter whose shape is given by psychoacoustical data on pure tone masking. The result of this analysis is a sort of spectrum, an auditory spectrum, that represents theoretically the effect of masking on a pure tone by that vowel. This broadband spectral analysis simulates certain well-known universal aspects of human hearing:

1. *Frequency resolution.* The auditory filters, or critical bands, increase in width as a function of frequency. Formants forming a part of a high-frequency formant complex may therefore not always be individually resolved in the auditory representation. These bandwidth variations are modeled by choosing a single auditory filter shape and an auditory frequency scale that is calibrated in Bark units (each of them one critical band wide) and brings about a quasi-logarithmic transformation of the physical frequency scale.

2. *Asymmetrical masking characteristics.* Lower frequencies tend to mask higher frequencies more than conversely (this is known as 'upward spread of masking'). This effect is introduced by the use of an asymmetrical filter shape.

Other features of the model are

3. *Nonlinear frequency response.* The intensity of sound pressure level (SPL) of a pure tone that is just audible varies as a function of frequency. This measurement defines the threshold of hearing. The SPL of two tones of different frequencies that appear to sound equally loud (or equivalently stated, to have the same loudness level—a quantity measured in phons) may differ considerably depending on the frequency separation. These facts, the equal loudness level contours and the threshold of hearing (which is the zero loudness-level curve), give what is known as the Fletcher-Munson curves when plotted on an SPL versus frequency diagram and are nonlinear functions of frequency. When corrections for such nonlinearities are applied to the output of the auditory filter, their main effect on a vowel is to reduce the contribution of the low-frequency components.

4. *Loudness.* We suggested previously that spectral peaks may be more conspicuous than spectral valleys in the perceptual analysis of vowel quality and should therefore undergo special processing in simulations. Psycho-

acoustics does in fact offer a scale that relates physical intensity of a sound to its subjective strength. That is the loudness scale. It should be clear that the loudness of a tone must depend on its intensity; however, this would not be its absolute sound pressure level because the relevant measure is the number of dB above hearing threshold. It is also dependent on its frequency since, as we saw in the preceding section, the ear's sensitivity to different frequencies is rather nonuniform. We also mentioned that if the intensity value is expressed in terms of phons, the tone is described in a way that takes the ear's nonlinear frequency response into consideration. Consequently psychoacousticians use numbers calibrated in phons to calculate loudness, which is given in 'sones.' The relation is $S = 2^{(L-40)/10}$, which says that, at 40 phons or above, loudness (S, in sones) is doubled by every increase of ten phons (L). It follows indirectly also that between 0 and 40 phons (a range calling for another formula), loudness grows slowly from zero to one. We conclude that a difference of 10 phons in a spectral valley is going to be reflected by a much smaller loudness difference than the corresponding difference in two pronounced peaks. Thus by incorporating loudness calculation into the model, we take some steps toward formally representing the idea that peaks should carry greater weight perceptually than valleys. The present algorithm is a somewhat modified version of the model proposed by Schroeder *et al.* (1979). It is described in greater detail in Bladon and Lindblom (1981, henceforth B&L).

We can now summarize the steps involved in deriving the auditory representation of a steady-state vowel (steps 5 through 8, below) from its acoustic specification (steps 1 through 4).

1. Specification of formant frequencies.
2. Computation of formant bandwidths (Fant 1972).
3. Derivation of the harmonic spectrum using standard assumptions about voice source, radiation, and higher-pole correction (Fant 1960).
4. Absolute calibration: specification of SPL and dB.
5. Conversion of Hz into Bark (B&L).
6. Auditory filtering: Schroeder's equation for the 'smearing' induced by basilar membrane mechanics and neural processing is used. The input power spectrum is convolved with the filter function to produce an excitation pattern calibrated in dB/Bark versus Bark.
7. Correction for nonlinear frequency response. Calibration of auditory spectrum in phon/Bark versus Bark.
8. Derivation of the loudness density plot. Calibration in sones/Bark versus Bark.

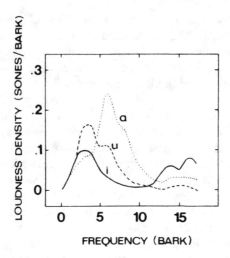

Figure 2.5 Loudness density plots (auditory spectra) of [i, u, ɑ].

Examples of this type of representation are shown in Figure 2.5

As a point of departure in developing distance metrics, we begin by considering a measure adapted from Plomp (1970):

$$D_{ij} = [c \int_{0}^{24.5} |E_i(x) - E_j(x)|^p dx]^{1/p} \qquad (3)$$

where $E(x)$ stands for the auditory representation of a vowel (calibrated in sones/Bark (E) versus Bark (x)), indices refer to the members of a given vowel pair, c is a constant, and 0–24.5 Bark is the interval of integration (i.e., the audio range). When this measure is computed and compared with perceptual dissimilarity judgments, fairly high correlations ($r \geq .85$) have been observed (B&L; Carlson & Granström 1979; Nord & Sventelius 1979). These results are encouraging, although they also indicate that a number of problems in devising perceptually realistic distance metrics still await their final solution.

Our first application of the distance notion is a comparison of data obtained from Equations 1 and 3 for a given set of vowels (Table 2.3). Equation 1 was modified to accommodate M3 also. These vowels were obtained by quantizing a mel-scale version of the three-dimensional acoustic spaces of Figure 2..2. Roughly equal quantization steps were chosen individually for M1, M2, and M3. Table 2.3 lists the corresponding Hz values and gives approximate phonetic labels for this set of quasi-cardinal vowels.

Table 2.3

Formant Frequencies of Quasi-Cardinal Vowels
Used in Vowel System Simulations[a]

	F_1	F_2	F_3	F_4
[i]	255	2191	3112	3594
[y]	263	2191	2482	3594
[ü]	269	1693	2331	3594
[ʉ]	276	1256	2331	3594
[ɯ]	283	897	2331	3594
[u]	290	625	2331	3594
[e][a]	364	2260	2811	3594
[ø]	371	1860	2413	3594
[ə]	377	1400	2413	3594
[ɤ]	384	1014	2413	3594
[o]	392	690	2413	3594
[ɛ]	481	1979	2681	3594
[œ]	489	1514	2593	3594
[ʌ]	495	1121	2506	3594
[ɔ]	502	790	2425	3594
[æ]	610	1732	2568	3594
[Œ]	616	1293	2553	3594
[ɑ]	621	924	2538	3594
[a]	750	1250	2521	3594

[a][e] is an empirically motivated modification of the
model-based vowel space (Fant 1973).

Figure 2.6 shows the results of the computations. To enable the reader
to replicate our results we need to add that the SPL of [a] is set at 70 db,
the vowels have their inherent intensities, $F_0 = 100$ Hz, and $p = 2$ in Equation 3. Formant-based distances are given along the abscissa and auditory
spectrum distances along the ordinate. The presentation has been limited to
distances from the vowel [i]. We can see that the largest distance computed
according to Equation 1 is the [i]/[u] distance, D_{iu}, which is several hundred
mels larger than D_{ia} and $D_{iɔ}$. For the auditory model measure plotted along
the ordinate the results are different: D_{iu} is nearly half as great as D_{ia} and
$D_{iɔ}$. What do these results mean?

They imply that as we substitute the spectrum-based for the formant-based
measure we achieve a warping of the perceptual space that can be visualized
in terms of the two-dimensional projection of the vowel space. We bring about
a compression of the two-dimensional plane in what corresponds to the
front–back dimension. In other words, height, or sonority, is caused to span
a wider relative range than backness. How does this come about?

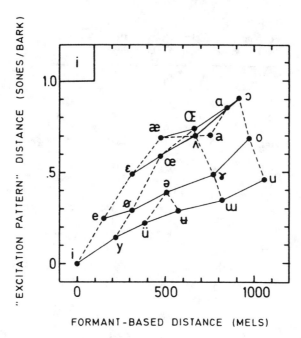

Figure 2.6 Comparison of formant-based (abscissa) and spectrum-based (ordinate) distances computed for a given set of vowels (Table 2.3). All values represent distances in relation to [i].

To suggest an answer, let us examine once more the auditory spectra of Figure 2.5. Comparing $E_i(x)$, $E_u(x)$, and $E_a(x)$ and making an informal visual judgment, we obtain the answer to the preceding question: There is a closer resemblance between the curves of [i] and [u] than between those of [i] and [a]. This impression is captured by Equation 3, which for $p = 1$ equates D_{ij} with the area enclosed between the curves. (For $p \neq 1$, D_{ij} will correspond only indirectly to this area; see B&L.)

We also note that the peak corresponding to F_1 dominates these spectra. The reason for this is partly acoustic (F_1 is already strong in the harmonic spectra), partly psychoacoustic (the transformation into sones/Bark enhances this effect).

In conclusion, we find that by adopting an auditorily somewhat more realistic distance measure we derive a perceptual vowel space that appears to have precisely those properties that were lacking in the L&L model. Now what do predictions based on this new space look like?

DERIVED SYSTEMS: MAXIMAL AND SUFFICIENT CONTRAST

From a more detailed exploration of the present algorithm and of a more approximate model based on a set of $\frac{1}{3}$-octave filters (Plomp 1970), we have learned that the relative reduction of D_{iu} is brought about by a combination of conditions: (1) vowel spectra should retain their inherent intensity variations; (2) filtering and a spectrum-based distance measure must be adopted. The conversion into loudness density is thus not the primary cause of the reduction of D_{iu}. For this reason we decided to include two interpretations of $E(x)$ in Equation 3: (1) $E(x)$ = loudness density pattern in sones/Bark versus Bark (the Schroeder representation), and (2) $E(x)$ = output of the auditory filter in dB/Bark (relative to threshold) versus Bark (the Plomp approximation).

The question arises which of these two interpretations represents a better approximation of the neural excitation pattern. It is by no means an established fact that timbre (vowel quality) and loudness judgments use identical inputs. They might tap partly parallel and partly different processes (Møller 1978). However, assuming that they do use the same input, we choose hypothesis (1), which implies that the auditory cues of vowel quality are those present in a loudness density plot. Assuming that they do not, we adopt hypothesis (2), which means that the auditory cues of vowel quality are better represented in the (pure-tone, simultaneous) masking curve generated by a vowel masker. The present results do not provide evidence for the resolution of this issue. Still more sophisticated auditory models are required to simulate truly realistic neural excitation patterns. For our present purposes, however, we regard hypotheses (1) and (2) as approximations of such patterns.

In the style of L&L (see Figure 2.4), Figures 2.7 and 2.8 show the results of computations based on Equations 3 and 2. In the calculations for Figure 2.7, $E(x)$ of Equation 3 is defined as the loudness density pattern of the vowel (step 8, above). In those for Figure 2.8, it is interpreted as the output of the auditory filter (step 6) defined relative to the threshold of hearing. As described above, the former definition has the effect of enhancing formant peaks somewhat, particularly F_1. The diagrams show optimal vowel systems, that is, given the vowel inventory of Table 2.3, the computer program made an exhaustive search and identified that combination of vowels for which the criterion of *maximal system contrast*, Equation 2, was met. Table 2.4 presents the results in terms of the vowel symbols of Table 2.3. (In this table we repeat for ease of comparison the C-data from Table 2.2; where C listed two vowel inventories for a system of a given size, both are listed and labeled C-1 for the more frequently occurring system and C-2 for the less common system. For eight vowels per system C observed only a few cases.)

Comparing the results of Figure 2.7 with those of L&L (Figure 2.4), we note that the revised interpretation of perceptual vowel representation (= loudness density plot) does indeed reduce the number of high vowels in systems with large numbers of vowels. Moreover, while it was true for L&L that all systems had [i] and [u] but not always [a], the reverse is the case in Figure 2.7. The back-vowel series now appears favored (possibly because of an F_1-F_2 proximity and a concomitant enhancement along the loudness

30   BJÖRN LINDBLOM

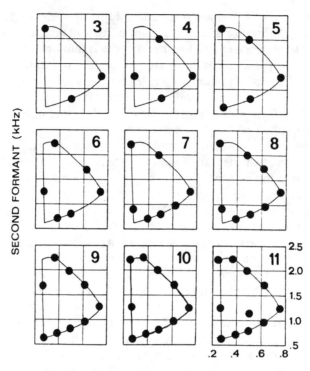

SECOND FORMANT (kHz)

FIRST FORMANT (kHz)

Figure 2.7   Revised predictions analogous to those of Figure 2.4. Auditory representation of vowel = loudness density plot.

scale). Figures 2.4 and 2.7 are similar in that a mid-central vowel appears only for the very largest systems.

Turning to a comparison between Figures 2.4 and 2.8, we can make the observation that in the latter the second revision of the perceptual vowel representation (output of the auditory filter) also reduces the number of high vowels in large systems, although not so drastically as the first. All systems have [i], [a], and [u]. A mid central vowel appears somewhat earlier than in Figures 2.4 and 2.7. Regretably we are unable to present a comparison between predictions and facts in terms of acoustic measurements. In any case, had formant frequency data been available for the languages of the C-data, in spite of many recent contributions, we would have had trouble selecting a linguistically and perceptually valid normalization procedure capable of separating language-specific from speaker-idiosyncratic determinants of such data (Disner 1980). We accordingly make the comparison in terms of pho-

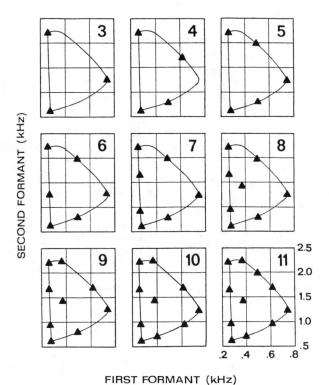

Figure 2.8   Revised predictions analogous to those of Figure 2.4. Auditory representation of vowel = output of auditory filter.

netic symbols. The following observations refer to Figures 2.7 and 2.8 and Table 2.4.

Three vowels: Facts and predictions are in agreement. Systems containing [i, a, o], as suggested in Figure 2.7, have been reported.

Four vowels: The L-prediction (loudness density) is more similar to C-2. Closest match: [ɪ a ɯ o] (Amahuaca) and [e a ʌ o] (Squamish). The F-prediction (auditory filter) is more similar to C-1. Closest match: [i æ u ɑ] (Chamorro).

Five vowels: Both the L- and F-predictions are in good agreement with C-1.

Six vowels: F-prediction is in good agreement with C-1. L-prediction yields a pattern very atypical owing to the lack of [i] and [u].

Seven vowels: Mid, central vowel of C-1 is missing in the patterns predicted

Table 2.4
C-data of Table 2.2 Compared with
Derived Optimal Systems

No. of vowels	System type	Vowel qualities
3	C	i a u
	L[a]	i a ɔ
	F[b]	i a u
4	C₁	i ɛ a u
	C₂	i ɨ a u
	L	ɛ ɐ a ɔ
	F	i æ ɔ u
5	C₁	i ɛ a ɔ u
	C₂	i ɛ i a o
	L	i ɛ a ɔ u
	F	i ɛ a ɔ u
6	C₁	i ɛ ɨ a ɔ u
	C₂	i e ɛ u o ɔ
	L	e æ ɐ o ɑ ɔ
	F	i ɛ ɐ a ɔ u
7	C₁	i e i ə a u o
	C₂	i e ɛ a u o ɔ
	L	i ɛ ɯ a ɑ o ɔ
	F	i ü ɛ a u ɯ ɔ
9	C	i e ɛ i ə a u o ɔ
	L	e ɛ æ ü a ɑ u o ɔ
	F	i e æ ü ə a u ɯ ɔ

[a]Loudness density patterns.
[b]Output spectra of an auditory filter.

by both F and L. Closest match (L): [i ɛ ɯ ʌ u ɔ ɑ] (Dafla). Criterion of sufficient contrast (see below) applied to F gives good agreement with C-1.

Eight vowels: Closest match (L): [i e ɛ ə u o ɔ] (Javanese, Mianka). Closest match (F): [i ɛ ü ɔ̈ a ɯ u O] (Turkish).

Nine vowels: The pattern predicted by L is atypical owing to the lack of [i]. Closest match (F): [i y u e ʉ o ɛ ø ɑ] (Norwegian).

By and large, the revised sets of predictions give somewhat more satisfactory results than L&L, but certain systematic discrepancies remain. The L-predictions are not obviously superior to the F-predictions although they do incorporate additional psychoacoustic facts and ought, therefore, currently at least, to be a better representation of the auditory spectrum. Languages offer a rich variety of phonetic realizations for a given size and type of vowel system (C-Appendix III). This quality variation suggests that predictions should not be restricted to the criterion of *maximal* perceptual contrast which gives one unique configuration per system of size n. The C-data clearly show that for a given n there can be several types of systems (see the classification with respect to number of interior vowels, for example, 7:0, 7:2, where the number to the left of the colon indicates the total number of vowels and that to the right, the number of this total which are interior vowels) as well as phonetic variations in the implementation of a given type. The question then arises whether some of these effects could also be deduced within the present framework.

To investigate this question we introduce the criterion of *sufficient contrast*. One way of defining this notion is to have the algorithm enumerate, say, the best m systems for each value of n. Another approach which seems preferable is to make a quantitative estimate of sufficient system contrast, keep it independent of system size, and study its effect on the predictions. We chose the former method, letting $m = 50$. We have studied the structure of the best 50 systems with respect to both phonetic variation and type. The results were obtained by means of the F model.

Suppose that sufficient contrast does operate in real systems and that it tends to be invariant across languages and system sizes. It follows from this assumption that the phonetic values of vowel phonemes should exhibit more variation in small than in large systems. We find this expectation supported by the C-data when we examine how C transcribes the vowels that function as /i/, /a/, and /u/ in systems varying in size. For instance, in the three-vowel systems we find [i ɪ e] for /i/, [u o ʊ ɯ] for /u/, and [a ɛ ä æ æ̈] for /a/. In the nine-vowel systems, on the other hand, /u/ is [u] or [ʊ]. Figure 2.9 shows the percentage of occurrences of the extreme [i], [u], and [a] qualities as a function of n. Also shown is the percentage of occurrence of the corresponding vowels in the best 50 simulated systems. For [i] and [u] the C-data support the notion of sufficient contrast. In the computed results the frequency of the corner vowels increases with system size.

How well do predictions match the C-data with respect to favored system types? Table 2.5 compares the distributions of interior vowels (indicated by the number following the colon). In the C-data, an interior vowel is defined as a vowel that is nonperipheral, that is, is not found in the leftmost or rightmost columns or in the bottom row of Table 2.1. In the computer simulations this concept was similarly defined. With reference to Table 2.3, the following vowels are interior: 2–5, 8–10, 13–14, 17. (Exception: in the absence of the vowels numbered 1, 6, or 19, the vowels numbered 2, 5, or 17, respectively, were not classified as interior.)

In the C-data, the eight- and nine-vowel systems are particularly small samples. Caution is also advisable in the use of Table 2.5, since the criterion

34   BJÖRN LINDBLOM

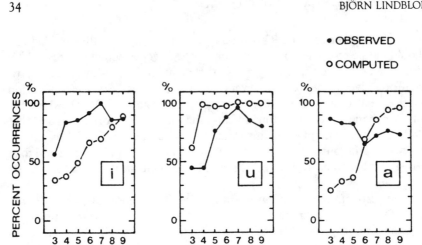

Figure 2.9 Occurrences of [i], [u], and [a]. Filled circles show the extreme vowels [i], [u], and [a] as realizations of /i/, /u/, and /a/ in Crothers' data (1978, Appendix III); open circles show the same vowels, based on simulations.

of sufficient contrast is interpreted in a rather ad hoc fashion. The major point is rather that predictions of system type can be made.

Figure 2.10 shows the distribution of predicted vowel systems belonging to the 7:2 type. The dots indicate the optimal system as given in Figure 2.7. The majority of the 50 predicted systems have [ɨ] and [ə] as the favored interior vowels this is shown by the centrally located peaks in the distributional profiles. This is a case where the optimal system differs from the most common among those meeting the condition of sufficient contrast. Figure 2.10 underlines the necessity to consider a wider range of solutions to the problem of optimizing system contrast.

In concluding this section, we find that the present framework generates vowel systems sharing a number of essential characteristics with natural systems. If the frequency of occurrence in the simulations was investigated for each individual vowel category, it would be possible to construct a diagram analogous to Figure 2.1. These figures would be highly similar.

However, we must also draw attention to one of the more conspicuous negative findings. Although the current predictions are much more satisfactory than those of L&L with regard to high vowels in large systems, it is somewhat problematic that the fairly popular 7:0 system (e.g., that of Italian and Bengali) is still absent. By setting the criterion of system contrast so generously that 7:0 instances *are* produced, we also generate many cases of 7:2

Table 2.5

Comparison of Observed (C) and Predicted (F) Vowel System Types

System type	3:0	3:1	4:0	4:1	5:0	5:1	6:0	6:1	6:2	7:0	7:1	7:2	8:0	8:1	8:2	8:3	9:2	9:3
C(%)	100	0	59	41	87	13	22	73	5	39	11	50	0	44	22	33	73	36
F(%)	76	24	38	62	10	80	0	68	32	0	12	82	0	4	50	44	16	76

36   BJÖRN LINDBLOM

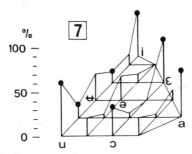

Figure 2.10   Distribution of predicted qualities in the best 50 seven-vowel systems. Dots refer to the optimal predicted system.

systems where, unfortunately, according to the data, the "2" represents two high vowels (e.g., [ü/ɯ], rather than a high/mid pair (e.g., [ɨ/ə]). Thus we see that to some extent there are still too many high vowels and that we must look for still further ways of constraining the space of vowel contrasts.

EXTENSIONS AND LIMITATIONS

Diphthongs

Would it be possible to apply the present framework also to diphthongs? Edström (1971) examined diphthongs of over 80 languages reported to have diphthongs. In view of the secondhand and heterogeneous nature of the data, few generalizations can be made. However, one trend that ought to survive further diphthong typologies is presented in Table 2.6, which indicates that diphthongs like [aj] and [aw] are favored over [ej] and [ow], which are in turn used more often than [uj] and [iw]. We can restate this and say that diphthongs are favored according to the degree of sonority of their nuclei. Alternatively, visualizing the diphthongs as trajectories in acoustic space, we see that their frequency of occurrence is positively correlated with the extent of the diphthong trajectory in the *revised* F_1-dominated space.

Quantal Aspects of the Vowel Space

One of the more striking features of language, including its phonological aspect, is its structuring in terms of *discrete* and hierarchically organized units. We have nevertheless made the present predictions with the aid of a *continuous* space. This is deliberate, since explanatory phonology ought to aim at

Table 2.6

Percentage of Languages for which the Indicated Vowel is the Nucleus of a Nucleus + Glide (Palatal or Velar) Sequence $(N = 83)$[a]

a/ɑ	o/ɔ	e/ɛ	u	i
83%	34%	25%	18%	7%

[a]From Edström (1971).

giving a deductive account of the quantal nature of speech. There are no doubt numerous reasons for speech being quantal (Stevens 1972; Studdert-Kennedy & Lane 1980). The present work bears on this issue by demonstrating a possible origin of universally favored vowel quality categories such as [i], [a], [u], [ɛ], and [ɔ]. In our results these vowels recur in a stable manner and practically independently of system size. Thus, even though based on a continuous space, the procedure favors certain vowel qualities more than others. Given such a distribution rather than a uniform one, the phonetic space will appear quantal.

Acquired Similarity and the Language Dependence of the Vowel Space

By definition, our vowel space is a hypothetical universal. It remains fixed. 'Similarity' is a function defined in terms of the space. Let us briefly examine this assumption critically.

Everyday experience shows that things that at first looked very similar may after a while cease to look so. It is also rich in situations where we find ourselves in disagreement over similarity judgments, sometimes because we tend to limit our perception of a person or an object to certain features rather than the whole, and our selective samplings may differ more than hypothetical Gestalt impressions.

Similar considerations can also be made in the case of speech-sound perception. Does the strategy of feature extractions occur in normal speech perception? Are vowel similarities partly acquired? If we say "yes," it may be because we believe that different languages require listeners to attend to and learn different cues whose similarity relations may be subjectively different from those of the wholes.

These remarks have implications both for the predictions of vowel systems and for the empirical verification of the vowel space by perceptual experiments. It would seem that if the space is to a large extent malleable during acquisition, we would perhaps expect social and cultural rather than universal factors to shape vowel systems. Furthermore, such elasticity would make it very hard to observe the space experimentally in its language-innocent state (see Terbeek & Harshman 1972).

Figure 2.11 is based on perceptual data on Swedish from Hanson (1967: Table 9.1), and our calculations derived from Hanson's stimulus specifications (Table 10.1). The results are presented for nine vowels in a three-by-three matrix, each cell comparing a given vowel (insert) with all the remaining vowels. There are thus eight dots in each diagram. (In the [o:] plot there are nine, since it includes a comparison between [o:] and [ɔ], a reference point assigned a dissimilarity of 5.) Each such dot represents a given vowel pair and a comparison between computed and observed dissimilarity values. The point is that, if we assume that listeners' similarity judgments are language-independent and describable by a unique function of the acoustic stimulus attributes, we would expect to be able to fit this unique function, that is, a *single line*, to the nine individual vowel plots of Figure 2.11. Clearly, we cannot. What we have done is to use three best-fitting lines, one for each column of graphs. There is, significantly, a larger intercept and a less-steep slope for the front vowels.

What does this difference between front and back lines tell us? It says that for a vowel pair with a small spectral distance, the predicted perceptual dissimiliarity must be made dependent on whether the vowels are front or back. For instance, although [y:] and [ø:] may have a spectral distance similar to that for [u:] and [o:], the front pair is heard as more dissimilar. It is as if listeners make their space more spacious at the point where the universal perceptual space seems most crowded.

The lesson appears to be that the more language-dependent plasticity the subjective vowel space possesses, the greater we should expect the discrepancies to be between natural systems and systems derived from a theoretical universal baseline.

Universal Phonetic Space = Articulatory Space * Perceptual Space

We have tried to justify the present framework primarily with reference to the criterion of perceptual contrast. What about production? Having introduced the concept of sufficient contrast, we have in principle invited the interaction of other processes, for example, mechanisms of memory and speech motor control that might contribute systematic effects under the heading of sufficient perceptual differentiation.

It makes sense, in fact, to talk about sufficient contrast also in the contexts of memory retrieval operations and the feedback control of speech gestures (perhaps particularly with regard to speech development). If we were to look at the optimization of vowel systems from this broader perspective, an optimal system might be one that meets not only perceptual but also

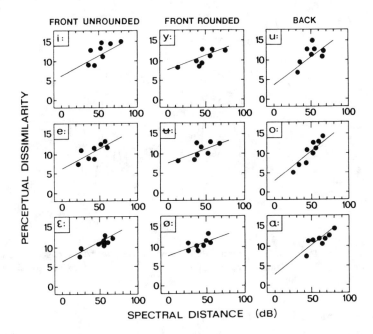

Figure 2.11 Perceptual dissimilarity estimates (Hanson 1967) plotted against computed distances for the nine long Swedish vowels.

memory-based and sensori-motor conditions of distinctiveness. For instance, how, in that case, could the detailed geometry of the articulatory (= sensori-motor) space influence the design of sound inventories?

Let us draw attention to three sets of matching facts: (1) Articulators have greater mobility at the front of the mouth (e.g., lips, tongue tip). (2) There appears to be a richer supply of structures for sensory control at anterior vocal tract locations (Hardcastle 1970). (3) Acoustic-perceptual effects are greater at the front than at the back, given geometrically comparable articulatory perturbations and conditions typical of, for example, voiceless consonants (Stevens 1968). Is there a fourth set of matching facts, namely, the data on consonant inventories that indicate (by Hardcastle's hypothesis) that languages exhibit a richer variety of front than back consonants (see also Figure 2.12)? If so, does the asymmetry of vocal tract sensori-motor representation also manifest itself in vowel systems? Does it contribute to the primacy of height (sonority or F_1) over front–back (chromaticity or F_2) distinctions and the favoring of vowel contrasts produced in anterior articulatory regions that have expanded sensory representations? Hopefully, these are empirical questions.

40   BJÖRN LINDBLOM

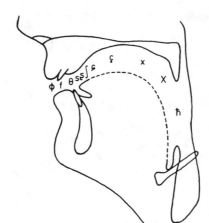

Figure 2.12   The set of IPA symbols used to describe voiceless fricatives shown on a vocal tract profile to illustrate an asymmetry with respect to how languages exploit the articulatory space (Hardcastle 1970).

Role of Sequential Constraints: [iᶻ] and [ɚ]

It is clear that the present definition of 'possible vowel' is too restricted and should at least be extended to include also dimensions such as nasalization, retroflexion, apicalization, length, phonation type, and so on. Let us briefly comment on [iᶻ] (the apicalized or coronal vowel of Chinese and certain Swedish dialects) and retroflex [ɚ]. Formant patterns for these qualities might be those given below:

	F_1	F_2	F_3
[iᶻ]	310	1610	2775
[ɚ]	500	1350	1700

A revision of Figure 2.2 modified to include these vowels would show two peaks in high-vowel territory: one for [i] and one for [iᶻ]. Owing to the extreme low F_3 value of [ɚ], it would also have a marked minimum hanging down from the center. By the present definitions of perceptual contrast, these vowels are highly distinctive. Exploratory work on predicting systems from inventories containing also these qualities indicates that they tend to be favored and are often capable of ousting many dorsal competitors.

This result appears to weaken the force of the present conclusions since, in fact, these vowels are quite rare in the languages of the world. On the other hand, it brings out an observation that parallels a principle noted previously in studies of consonant clusters (Elert 1970): differentiation of articulatory place. The parallel is the fact that vowels tend to be primarily dorsal, whereas the typical consonant system (Nartey 1979) exploits the anterior articulators more fully.

It does not seem unreasonable to suggest that in the disfavoring of [i^Z] and [$ɚ$]—which often seem to originate as contextual variants when they do occur—we see the operation of a dynamic articulatory constraint having to do with the facilitation of the coarticulatory integration of successive gestures. The implication of this is that vowel systems tend to become s*yntagmatically* as well as *paradigmatically* optimized, that is, as different as possible not only with respect to other vowels but also with respect to the consonants they appear next to.

"Maximal Utilization of Available Features"

Ohala (1980) applies the notion of space and the principle of maximum perceptual contrast to consonant systems. He convincingly argues that this principle would predict systems with rather preposterous and counterfactual properties. As an alternative principle he suggests 'maximum utilization of the available distinctive features,' which would make many consonants perceptually very similar and would create minimal rather than maximal differences with respect to number of distinctive features. His reasoning leads him to ask whether consonant inventories are structured according to different principles from those which apply to vowel inventories.

His point is well taken. We do not try to respond to it fully here but simply offer a tentative and methodologically motivated "no." It is not hard to believe that the discovery of features and the generalization of such features to yield new phonemes may play an important role in the acquisition of phonology and that such processes apply also to the development of vowel systems. Given, say [i ɛ a ɔ u], by perceptual criteria and some abstract and discrete recoding of the associated component articulations (i.e., into features), a child might discover and conquer new contrasts by recombining the articulatory gestures mastered so far. This strategy supported and elaborated with the aid of empirical observations would be worth exploring along with other constraints (sufficient perceptual contrast) in the predictions of future vowel systems. A major difficulty, though, is to give a substantive, *deductive account* of the features.

In response to Ohala's query, then, our comment is that, insofar as the integration of several speech behavior constraints can be achieved within the present framework for describing vowels, it may well be that the principles underlying consonant systems on the one hand and vowel inventories on the

42   BJÖRN LINDBLOM

other might turn out to be more similar than Ohala, for the sake of argument, wanted to imply.

The Distance Metric

It would be misleading to conclude this discussion section without making a few critical comments on the above presentation of the distance metric. Implicit in our model of speech perception is the idea that it would in principle be possible to formulate a complete and realistic theory of vowel perception in terms of the notion of distance. Upon further reflection we realize that this represents a rather strong claim about the power of such a metric. It must account for, among other things, formant-frequency-difference limen data, the effect of F_0, level, and spectral tilt, and duration on vowel quality across speakers having different vocal tract geometries. We do not at present have a unified theory that explains these and other systematic phenomena (Ainsworth 1980) and there are accordingly no distance measures and auditory models capable of comprehensively imitating natural vowel perception.

Much work remains to be done on breaking in distance measures and constructing auditory models. Therefore the present results are preliminary and serve the primary purpose of illustrating the possibility of a substance-based, deductive approach to phonological questions.

ACKNOWLEDGMENTS

The author is grateful to Peter Ladefoged and John Ohala for many helpful comments on the manuscript of this chapter.

REFERENCES

Ainsworth, W. (1980). *Summary of the session on Vowel perceeption, Gotland Workshop* (Quarterly Progress and Status Report 1/1980), 8–12. Stockholm: Speech Transmission Laboratory, Royal Institute of Technology, Stockholm.

Bellugi, U., & M. Studdert-Kennedy, eds. 1980. *Sign language and spoken language: Biological constraints on linguistic form.* Dahlem Workshop, Weinheim: Verlag Chemie.

Bernstein, J. C. 1976. *Vocoid psychoacoustics, articulation and vowel phonology* (Natural Language Studies No. 23). Ann Arbor: Phonetics Laboratory, University of Michigan.

Bladon, R. A. W., & B. Lindblom. (1981). Modeling the judgment of vowel quality differences. *Journal of the Acoustical Society of America* 69:1414–1422.

Carlson, R., & B. Granström. (1979). Model predictions of vowel dissimilarity. (Quarterly Progress and Status Report 3–4/1979), 84–104. (Stockholm: Speech Transmission Laboratory, Royal Institute of Technology.)

Chomsky, N., & M. Halle. 1968. *The sound pattern of English*. New York: Harper & Row.

Crothers, J. 1978. Typology and universals of vowel systems. In J. H. Greenberg, C. A. Ferguson, & E. A. Moravcsik, eds., *Universals of human language. Vol. 2: Phonology*, 93-152. Stanford: Stanford University Press.

Disner, S. F. 1980. Evaluation of vowel normalization procedures. *Journal of the Acoustical Society of America* 67:253-261.

Donegan, P. J. 1978. *The natural phonology of vowels* Dissertation, (Working Papers in Linguistics 28). Columbus: Ohio State University.

Donegan-Miller, P. J. 1972. Some context-free processes affecting vowels (Working Papers in Linguistics 23). Columbus: Ohio State University.

Edström, B. 1971. Diphthong systems. Stockholm University. Unpublished paper.

Elert, C.-C. 1970. *Ljud och Ord i Svenskan:*. Stockholm, Almqvist & Wiksell.

Fant, G. 1960. *Acoustic theory of speech production*. The Hague: Mouton.

Fant, G. 1972. Vocal tract wall effects, losses and resonance bandwidths. (Quarterly Progress and Status Reports 2-3/1972), 28-52. Stockholm: Speech Transmission Laboratory, Royal Institute of Technology.

Fant, G. 1973. *Speech sounds and features*. Cambridge, MA: MIT Press.

Hanson, G. 1967. *Dimensions in speech sound perception*. Ericsson Technics 23.

Hardcastle, W. J. 1970. The role of tactile and proprioceptive feedback in speech production (Work in progress 4), 100-112. Department of Linguistics, Edinburgh University.

Hockett, C. 1955. A manual of phonology. *International Journal of American Linguistics*, Memoir 11.

Jakobson, R. 1941. *Kindersprache, Aphasie und allgemeine Lautgesetze*. (*Språkvetenskapliga Sällskapets i Uppsala Förhandlingar 1940-1942*) Uppsala: Almqvist & Wiksell. (Reprinted in R. Jakobson. 1962. *Selected writings I*, 328-401. The Hague: Mouton.

King, R. D. (1967). Functional load and sound change. *Language* 43:831-852.

Liljencrants, J., & B. Lindblom. (1972). Numerical simulation of vowel quality systems: The role of perceptual contrast. *Language* 48:839-862.

Lindblom, B. 1975. Experiments in sound structure. Plenary address, 8th International Congress of Phonetic Sciences, Leeds. (Also in *Revue de Phonétique Appliquée* 51:155-189. Université de l'Etat Mons, Belgique.

Lindblom, B. 1980. The goal of phonetics, its unification and application. In *Proceedings of the Ninth International Congress of Phonetic Sciences*. (Vol. 3) 3-18. Copenhagen: Institute of Phonetics.

Lindblom, B., & J. Sundberg. 1971. Acoustic consequences of lip, tongue, jaw and larynx movement. *Journal of the Acoustical Society of America* 50: 1166-1179.

Møller, A. R. 1978. Neurophysiological basis of discrimination of speech sounds. *Audiology* 17:1-9.

Nartey, J. N. A. 1979. A study in phonemic universals—especially concerning fricatives and stops 46. (Working papers in phonetics University of California at Los Angeles).

Nord, L., and E. Sventelius. 1979. Analysis and prediction of difference limen data for formant frequencies (Quarterly Progress and Status Report 3-4/1979), 60-72. Stockholm: Speech Transmission Laboratory, Royal Institute of Technology.

Ohala, J. J. 1978. Phonological notations as models. In W. U. Dressler & W. Meid, eds., *Proceedings of the 12th International Congress of Linguists* (Vienna, Aug. 28-Sept. 2, 1977), 811-816. Innsbruck: Innsbrucker Beiträge zur Sprachwissenschaft.

Ohala, J. J. 1980. Moderator's introduction to Symposium on Phonetic Universals in Phonological Systems and their Explanation. *Proceedings of the Ninth International Congress of Phonetic Sciences (Vol. 3)* 181-185. Copenhagen: Institute of Phonetics.

Ohala, J. J. Forthcoming. *The origin of sound patterns in language*.

Plomp, R. 1970. Timbre as a multidimensional attribute of complex tones. In R. Plomp & G. F. Smoorenburg, eds., *Frequency analysis and periodicity detection in hearing*, 397–414. Leiden: Sijthoff.

Schroeder, M. R., B. S. Atal, & J. L. Hall. 1979. Objective measure of certain speech signal degradations based on masking properties of human auditory perception. In B. Lindblom & S. Öhman, eds., *Frontiers of speech communication research*, 217–229. London: Academic Press.

Sedlak, P. 1969. Typological considerations of vowel quality systems. (Working Papers in Language Universals 1) 1–40. Stanford: Stanford University.

Stampe, D. 1973. A dissertation on natural phonology. Ph.D. diss., University of Chicago.

Stevens, K. N. 1968. Acoustic correlates of place of articulation for stop and fricative consonants (Quarterly Progress Report 89), 199–205. Cambridge, MA: MIT.

Stevens, K. N. 1972. The quantal nature of speech: Evidence from articulatory-acoustic data. In P. B. Denes & E. E. David Jr., eds., *Human communication: A unified view*, 51–66. New York: McGraw-Hill.

Studdert-Kennedy, M., & H. Lane. 1980. Clues from the differences between signed and spoken language. In U. Bellugi and M. Studdert-Kennedy, eds., *Signed language and spoken language: Biological constraints on linguistic form* Dahlem Workshop, 29–39. Weinheim: Verlag Chemie.

Terbeek, D., & R. Harshman. 1972. Is vowel perception non-Euclidean? (Working Papers in Phonetics 22) 13–29. University of California at Los Angeles.

Troubetzkoy, N. S. 1929. Zur allgemeinen Theorie der phonologischen Vokalsysteme. *Travaux du Cercle Linguistique de Prague* 1:39–67.

Wang, W. S-Y. 1967. The measurement of functional load. *Phonetica* 16:36–54.

COGNITIVE PSYCHOLOGY **18**, 1–86 (1986)

The TRACE Model of Speech Perception

JAMES L. MCCLELLAND

Carnegie–Mellon University

AND

JEFFREY L. ELMAN

University of California, San Diego

We describe a model called the TRACE model of speech perception. The model is based on the principles of interactive activation. Information processing takes place through the excitatory and inhibitory interactions of a large number of simple processing units, each working continuously to update its own activation on the basis of the activations of other units to which it is connected. The model is called the TRACE model because the network of units forms a dynamic processing structure called "the Trace," which serves at once as the perceptual processing mechanism and as the system's working memory. The model is instantiated in two simulation programs. TRACE I, described in detail elsewhere, deals with short segments of real speech, and suggests a mechanism for coping with the fact that the cues to the identity of phonemes vary as a function of context. TRACE II, the focus of this article, simulates a large number of empirical findings on the perception of phonemes and words and on the interactions of phoneme and word perception. At the phoneme level, TRACE II simulates the influence of lexical information on the identification of phonemes and accounts for the fact that lexical effects are found under certain conditions but not others. The model also shows how knowledge of phonological constraints can be embodied in particular lexical items but can still be used to influence processing of novel, nonword utterances. The model also exhibits categorical perception and

---

The work reported here was supported in part by a contract from the Office of Naval Research (N-00014-82-C-0374), in part by a grant from the National Science Foundation (BNS-79-24062), and in part by a Research Scientists Career Development Award to the first author from the National Institute of Mental Health (5-K01-MH00385). We thank Dr. Joanne Miller for a very useful discussion which inspired us to write this article in its present form. David Pisoni was extremely helpful in making us deal more fully with several important issues, and in alerting us to a large number of useful papers in the literature. We also thank David Rumelhart for useful discussions during the development of the basic architecture of TRACE and Eileen Conway, Mark Johnson, Dave Pare, and Paul Smith for their assistance in programing and graphics. Send requests for reprints to James L. McClelland, Department of Psychology, Carnegie–Mellon University, Schenley Park, Pittsburgh, PA 15213.

1

the ability to trade cues off against each other in phoneme identification. At the word level, the model captures the major positive feature of Marslen-Wilson's COHORT model of speech perception, in that it shows immediate sensitivity to information favoring one word or set of words over others. At the same time, it overcomes a difficulty with the COHORT model: it can recover from underspecification or mispronunciation of a word's beginning. TRACE II also uses lexical information to segment a stream of speech into a sequence of words and to find word beginnings and endings, and it simulates a number of recent findings related to these points. The TRACE model has some limitations, but we believe it is a step toward a psychologically and computationally adequate model of the process of speech perception.   © 1986 Academic Press, Inc.

Consider the perception of the phoneme /g/ in the sentence "She received a valuable gift." There are a large number of cues in this sentence to the identity of this phoneme. First, there are the acoustic cues to the identity of the /g/ itself. Second, the other phonemes in the same word provide another source of cues, for if we know the rest of the phonemes in this word, there are only a few phonemes that can form a word with them. Third, the semantic and syntactic context further constrain the possible words which might occur, and thus limit still further the possible interpretation of the first phoneme in "gift."

There is ample evidence that all of these different sources of information are used in recognizing words and the phonemes they contain. Indeed, as Cole and Rudnicky (1983) have recently noted, these basic facts were described in early experiments by Bagley (1900) over 80 years ago. Cole and Rudnicky point out that recent work (which we consider in detail below) has added clarity and detail to these basic findings but has not lead to a theoretical synthesis that provides a satisfactory account of these and many other basic aspects of speech perception.

In this paper, we describe a model whose primary purpose is to account for the integration of multiple sources of information, or constraint, in speech perception. The model is constructed within a framework which appears to be ideal for the exploitation of simultaneous, and often mutual, constraints. This framework is the interactive activation framework (McClelland & Rumelhart, 1981; Rumelhart & McClelland, 1981, 1982). This approach grew out of a number of earlier ideas, some coming first from research on spoken language recognition (Marslen-Wilson & Welsh, 1978; Morton, 1969; Reddy, 1976) and others arising from more general considerations of interactive parallel processing (Anderson, 1977; Grossberg, 1978; McClelland, 1979).

According to the interactive-activation approach, information processing takes place through the excitatory and inhibitory interactions among a large number of processing elements called units. Each unit is a very simple processing device. It stands for a hypothesis about the input being processed. The activation of a unit is monotonically related to the strength of the hypothesis for which the unit stands. Constraints among hypotheses are represented by connections. Units which are mutually consistent are mutually excitatory, and units that are mutually inconsistent are mutually inhibitory. Thus, the unit for /g/ has mutually excitatory connections with units for words containing /g/, and has mutually inhibitory connections with units for other phonemes. When the activation of a unit exceeds some threshold activation value, it begins to influence the activation of other units via its outgoing connections; the strength of these signals depends on the degree of the sender's activation. The state of the system at a given point in time represents the current status of the various possible hypotheses about the input; information processing amounts to the evolution of that state, over time. Throughout the course of processing, each unit is continually receiving input from other units, continually updating its activation on the basis of these inputs, and, if it is over threshold, it is continually sending excitatory and inhibitory signals to other units. This "interactive-activation" process allows each hypothesis both to constrain and be constrained by other mutually consistent or inconsistent hypotheses.

Criteria and Constraints on Model Development

There are generally two kinds of models of the speech perception process. One kind of model, which grows out of speech engineering and artifical intelligence, attempts to provide a machine solution to the problem of speech recognition. Examples of this kind of model are HEARSAY (Erman & Lesser, 1980; Reddy, Erman, Fennell, & Neely, 1973) HWIM (Wolf & Woods, 1978), HARPY (Lowerre, 1976), and LAFS/SCRIBER (Klatt, 1980). A second kind of model, growing out of experimental psychology, attempts to account for aspects of psychological data on the perception of speech. Examples of this class of models include Marslen-Wilson's COHORT Model (Marslen-Wilson & Tyler, 1980; Marslen-Wilson & Welsh, 1978; Nusbaum & Slowiaczek, 1982); Massaro's feature integration model (Massaro, 1981; Massaro & Oden, 1980a, 1980b; Oden & Massaro, 1978); Cole and Jakimik's (1978, 1980) model of auditory word processing, and the model of auditory and phonetic memory espoused by Fujisaki and Kawashima (1968) and Pisoni (1973, 1975).

Each approach honors a different criterion for success. Machine models are judged in terms of actual performance in recognizing real speech. Psychological models are judged in terms of their ability to account for details of human performance in speech recognition. We call these two criteria *computational* and *psychological* adequacy.

In extending the interactive activation approach to speech perception, we had essentially two questions: First, could the interactive-activation

approach contribute toward the development of a computationally sufficient framework for speech perception? Second, could it account for what
is known about the psychology of speech perception? In short, we wanted
to know, was the approach fruitful, both on computational and psychological grounds.

Two facts immediately became apparent. First, spoken language introduces many challenges that make it far from clear how well the interactive-activation approach will serve when extended from print to speech.
Second, the approach itself is too broad to provide a concrete model,
without further assumptions. Here we review several facts about speech
that played a role in shaping the specific assumptions embodied in
TRACE.

Some Important Facts about Speech

Our intention here is not to provide an extensive survey of the nature
of speech and its perception, but rather to point to several fundamental
aspects of speech that have played important roles in the development
of the model we describe here. A very useful discussion of several of
these points is available in Klatt (1980).

Temporal nature of the speech stimulus. It does not, of course, take a
scientist to observe one fundamental difference between speech and
print: speech is a signal which is extended in time, whereas print is a
stimulus which is extended in space. The sequential nature of speech
poses problems for a modeler, in that to account for context effects, one
needs to keep a record of the context. It would be a simple matter to
process speech if each successive portion of the speech input were processed independently of all of the others, but in fact, this is clearly not
the case. The presence of context effects in speech perception requires
a mechanism that keeps some record of that context, in a form that allows
it to influence the interpretation of subsequent input.

A further point, and one that has been much neglected in certain
models, is that it is not only prior context but also subsequent context
that influences perception. (This and related points have recently been
made by Grosjean & Gee, 1984; Salasoo & Pisoni, 1985; and Thompson,
1984). For example, Ganong (1980) reported that the identification of a
syllable-initial speech sound that was constructed to be between /g/ and
/k/ was influenced by whether the rest of the syllable was /Is/ (as in
"kiss") or /Ift/ (as in "gift"). Such "right context effects" (Thompson,
1984) indicate that the perception of what comes in now both influences
and is influenced by the perception of what comes in later. This fact
suggests that the record of what has already been presented cannot not
be a static representation, but should remain in a malleable form, subject
to alteration as a result of influences arising from subsequent context.

TRACE MODEL   5

Lack of boundaries and temporal overlap. A second fundamental point
about speech is that the cues to successive units of speech frequently
overlap in time. The problem is particularly severe at the phoneme level.
A glance at a schematic speech spectrogram (Liberman, 1970; Fig. 1)
clearly illustrates this problem. There are no separable packets of information in the spectrogram like the separate feature bundles that make up
letters in printed words.

Because of the overlap of successive phonemes, it is difficult and, we
believe, counterproductive to try to divide the speech stream up into
separate phoneme units in advance of identifying the units. A number of
other researchers (e.g., Fowler, 1984; Klatt, 1980) have made much the
same point. A superior approach seems to be to allow the phoneme identification process to examine the speech stream for characteristic patterns, without first segmenting the stream into separate units.

The problem of overlap is less severe for words than for phonemes,
but it does not go away completely. In rapid speech, words run into each
other, and there are no pauses between words in running speech. To be
sure, there are often cues that signal the locations of boundaries between
words—stop consonants are generally aspirated at the beginnings of
stressed words in English, and word initial vowels are generally preceded
by glottal stops, for example. These cues have been studied by a number
of investigators, particularly Lehiste (e.g., Lehiste, 1960, 1964) and Nakatani and collaborators. Nakatani and Dukes (1977) demonstrated that
perceivers exploit some of these cues but found that certain utterances
do not provide sufficient cues to word boundaries to permit reliable perception of the intended utterance. Speech errors often involve errors of

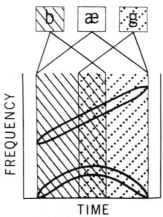

FIG. 1. A schematic spectrogram for the syllable "bag," indicating the overlap of the
information specifying the different phonemes. Reprinted with permission from Liberman
(1970).

word segmentation (Bond & Garnes, 1980), and certain segmentation decisions are easily influenced by contextual factors (Cole & Jakimik, 1980). Thus, it is clear that word recognition cannot count on an accurate segmentation of the phoneme stream into separate word units, and in many cases such a segmentation would perforce exclude from one of the words a shared segment that is doing double duty in each of two successive words.

Context-sensitivity of cues. A third major fact about speech is that the cues for a particular unit vary considerably with the context in which they occur. For example, the transition of the second formant carries a great deal of information about the identity of the stop consonant /b/ in Fig. 1, but that formant would look quite different had the syllable been "big" or "bog" instead of "bag." Thus the context in which a phoneme occurs restructures the cues to the identity of that phoneme (Liberman, 1970). The extent of the restructuring depends on the unit selected and on the particular cue involved. But the problem is ubiquitous in speech.

Not only are the cues for each phoneme dramatically affected by preceding and following context, they are also altered by more global factors such as rate of speech (Miller, 1981), by morphological and prosodic factors such as position in word and in the stress contour of the utterance, and by characteristics of the speaker such as size and shape of the vocal tract, fundamental frequency of the speaking voice, and dialectical variations (see Klatt, 1980, and Repp & Liberman, 1984, for discussions).

A number of different approaches to the problem have been tried by different investigators. One approach is to try to find relatively invariant—generally relational—features (e.g., Stevens & Blumstein, 1981). Another approach has been to redefine the unit so that it encompasses the context and therefore becomes more invariant (Fujimura & Lovins, 1982; Klatt, 1980; Wickelgren, 1969). While these are both sensible and useful approaches, the first has not yet succeeded in establishing a sufficiently invariant set of cues, and the second may alleviate but does not eliminate the problem; even units such as demisyllables (Fujimura & Lovins, 1982), context-sensitive allophones (Wickelgren, 1969), or even whole words (Klatt, 1980) are still influenced by context. We have chosen to focus instead on a third possibility: that the perceptual system uses information from the context in which an utterance occurs to alter connections, thereby effectively allowing the context to retune the perceptual mechanism on the fly.

Noise and indeterminacy in the speech signal. To compound all the problems alluded to above, there is the additional fact that speech is often perceived under less than ideal circumstances. While a slow and careful speaker in a quiet room may produce sufficient cues to allow correct perception of all of the phonemes in an utterance without the aid of lexical or other higher level constraints, these conditions do not always obtain. People can correctly perceive speech under quite impoverished conditions, if it is semantically coherent and syntactically well formed (G. Miller, Heise, & Lichten, 1951). This means that the speech mechanisms must be able to function, even with a highly degraded stimulus. In particular, as Thompson (1984), Norris (1982), and Grosjean and Gee (1984) have pointed out, the mechanisms of speech perception cannot count on accurate information about any part of a word. As we shall see, this fact poses a serious problem for one of the best current psychological models of the process of spoken word recognition (Marslen-Wilson & Welsh, 1978).

Many of the characteristics that we have reviewed differentiate speech from print—at least, from very high quality print on white paper—but it would be a mistake to think that similar problems are not encountered in other domains. Certainly, the sequential nature of spoken input sets speech apart from vision, in which there can be some degree of simultaneity of perception. However, the problems of ill-defined boundaries, context sensitivity of cues, and noise and indeterminacy are central problems in vision just as much as they are in speech (cf. Ballard, Hinton, and Sejnowski, 1983; Barrow & Tenenbaum, 1978; Marr, 1982). Thus, though the model we present here is focussed on speech perception, we would hope that the ways in which it deals with the challenges posed by the speech signal are applicable in other domains.

The Importance of the Right Architecture

All four of the considerations listed above played an important role in the formulation of the TRACE model. The model is an instance of an interactive activation model, but it is by no means the only instance of such a model that we have considered or that could be considered. Other formulations we considered simply did not appear to offer a satisfactory framework for dealing with these four aspects of speech (see Elman & McClelland, 1984, for discussion). Thus, the TRACE model hinges as much on the particular processing architecture it proposes for speech perception as it does on the interactive activation processes that occur within this architecture.

Interactive-activation mechanisms are a class too broad to stand or fall on the merits of a single model. To the extent that computationally and psychologically adequate models can be built within the framework, the attractiveness of the framework as a whole is, of course, increased, but the adequacy of any particular model will generally depend on the particular assumptions that model embodies. It is no different with interactive-

8   MC CLELLAND AND ELMAN

activation models than with models in any other computational frame-work, such as expert systems or production systems.

THE TRACE MODEL

Overview

The TRACE model consists primarily of a very large number of units, organized into three levels, the *feature, phoneme,* and *word* levels. Each unit stands for a hypothesis about a particular perceptual object occurring at a particular point in time defined relative to the beginning of the ut-terance.

A small subset of the units in TRACE II, the version of the model we focus on in this paper, is illustrated in Figs. 2, 3, and 4. Each of the three figures replicates the same set of units, illustrating a different property of the model in each case. In the figures, each rectangle corresponds to a separate processing unit. The labels on the units and along the side indicate the spoken object (feature, phoneme, or word) for which each unit stands. The left and right edges of each rectangle indicate the portion of the input the unit spans.

At the feature level, there are several banks of feature detectors, one for each of several dimensions of speech sounds. Each bank is replicated for each of several successive moments in time, or time slices. At the phoneme level, there are detectors for each of the phonemes. There is one copy of each phoneme detector centered over every three time slices. Each unit spans six time slices, so units with adjacent centers span over-lapping ranges of slices. At the word level, there are detectors for each word. There is one copy of each word detector centered over every three feature slices. Here each detector spans a stretch of feature slices cor-responding to the entire length of the word. Again, then, units with ad-jacent centers span overlapping ranges of slices.

Input to the model, in the form of a pattern of activation to be applied to the units at the feature level, is presented sequentially to the feature-level units in successive slices, as it would if it were a real speech stream, unfolding in time. Mock-speech inputs on the three illustrated dimensions for the phrase "tea cup" (/tik^p/) are shown in Fig. 2. At any instant, input is arriving only at the units in one slice at the feature level. In terms of the display in Fig. 2, then, we can visualize the input being applied to successive slices of the network at successive moments in time. However, it is important to remember that all the units are continually involved in processing, and processing of the input arriving at one time is just begin-ning as the input is moved along to the next time slice.

The entire network of units is called "the Trace," because the pattern of activation left by a spoken input is a trace of the analysis of the input at each of the three processing levels. This trace is unlike many traces,

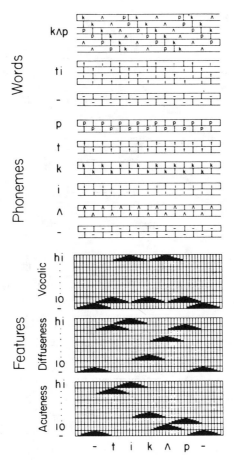

FIG. 2. A subset of the units in TRACE II. Each rectangle represents a different unit. The labels indicate the item for which the unit stands, and the horizontal edges of the rectangle indicate the portion of the Trace spanned by each unit. The input feature specifications for the phrase "tea cup," preceded and followed by silence, are indicated for the three illustrated dimensions by the blackening of the corresponding feature units.

though, in that it is dynamic, since it consists of activations of processing elements, and these processing elements continue to interact as time goes on. The distinction between perception and (primary) memory is completely blurred, since the percept is unfolding in the same structures that serve as working memory, and perceptual processing of older portions of the input continues even as newer portions are coming into the system. These continuing interactions permit the model to incorporate right context effects, and allow the model to account directly for certain aspects

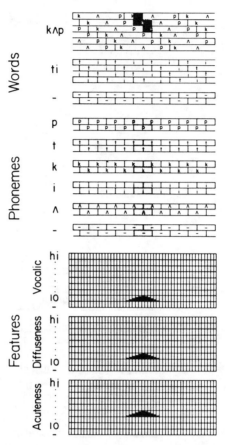

Fig. 3. The connections of the unit for the phoneme /k/, centered over Time Slice 24. The rectangle for this unit is highlighted with a bold outline. The /k/ unit has mutually excitatory connections to all the word- and feature-level units colored either partly or wholly in black. The more coloring on a units' rectangle, the greater the strength of the connection. The /k/ unit has mutually inhibitory connections to all of the phoneme-level units colored partly or wholly in grey. Again, the relative amount of inhibition is indicated by the extent of the coloring of the unit; it is directly proportional to the extent of the temporal overlap of the units.

of short-term memory, such as the fact that more information can be retained for short periods of time if it hangs together to form a coherent whole.

Processing takes place through the excitatory and inhibitory interactions of the units in the Trace. Units on different levels that are mutually consistent have mutually excitatory connections, while units on the same

TRACE MODEL   11

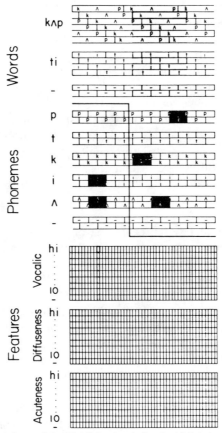

FIG. 4. The connections of the highlighted unit for the high value on the Vocalic feature dimension in Time Slice 9 and for the highlighted unit for the word /kʌp/ starting in Slice 24. Excitatory connections are represented in black, inhibitory connections in grey, as in Fig. 3.

level that are inconsistent have mutually inhibitory connections. All connections are bidirectional. Bidirectional excitatory and inhibitory connections of the unit for /k/ centered over Feature-slice 24 (counting from 0) are shown in Fig. 3; connections for the high value of the feature Vocalic in Slice 9 and for the word /kʌp/ with the /k/ centered over Slice 24 are shown in Fig. 4.

The interactive activation model of visual word recognition (McClelland & Rumelhart, 1981) included inhibitory connections between each unit on the feature level and letters that did not contain the feature, and between each letter unit and the words that did not contain the letter. Thus the units for *T* in the first letter position inhibited the units for all words that did not begin with *T*. However, more recent versions of the visual model eliminate these between-level inhibitory connections, since these connections can interfere with successful use of partial information (McClelland, 1985; McClelland, 1986). Like these newer versions of the visual model, TRACE likewise contains no between-level inhibition. We will see that this feature of TRACE plays a very important role in its ability to simulate a number of empirical phenomena.

Sources of TRACE's architecture. The inspiration for the architecture of TRACE goes back to the HEARSAY Speech understanding system (Erman & Lesser, 1980; Reddy et al., 1973). HEARSAY introduced the notion of a Blackboard, a structure similar to the Trace in the TRACE model. The main difference is that the Trace is a dynamic processing structure that is self-updating, while the Blackboard in HEARSAY was a passive data structure through which antonomous processes shared information.

The architecture of TRACE bears a strong resemblance to the "neural spectrogram" proposed by Crowder (1978, 1981) to account for interference effects between successive items in short-term memory. Like our Trace, Crowder's neural spectrogram provides a dynamic working memory representation of a spoken input. There are two important differences between the Trace and Crowder's neural spectrogram, however. First of all, the neural spectrogram was assumed only to represent the frequency spectrum of the speech wave over time; the Trace, on the other hand, represents the speech wave in terms of a large number of different feature dimensions, as well as in terms of the phonemes and words consistent with the pattern of activation at the feature level. In this regard TRACE might be seen as an extension of the neural spectrogram idea. The second difference is that Crowder postulates inhibitory interactions between detectors for spectral components spaced up to several hundred milliseconds apart. These inhibitory interactions extend considerably farther than those we have included in the feature level of the Trace. This difference does not reflect a disagreement with Crowder's assumptions. Though we have not found it necessary to adopt this assumption to account for the phenomena we focus on in this article, lateral extension of inhibition in the time domain might well allow the TRACE framework to incorporate many of the findings Crowder discusses in the two articles cited.

Context-Sensitive Tuning of Phoneme Units

The connections between the feature and phoneme level determine what pattern of activations over the feature units will most strongly activate the detector for each phoneme. To cope with the fact that the features representing each phoneme vary according to the phonemes surrounding them, the model adjusts the connections from units at the feature level to units at the phoneme level as a function of activations at the phoneme level in preceding and following time slices. For example, when the phoneme /t/ is preceded or followed by the vowel /i/, the feature pattern corresponding to the /t/ is very different than it is when the /t/ is preceded or followed by another vowel, such as /a/. Accordingly, when the unit for /i/ in a particular slice is active, it changes the pattern of connections for units for /t/ in preceding and following slices.

TRACE I and TRACE II

In developing TRACE, and in trying to test its computational and psychological adequacy, we found that we were sometimes led in rather different directions. We wanted to show that TRACE could process real speech, but to build a model that did so it was necessary to worry about exactly what features must be extracted from the speech signal, about differences in duration of different features of different phonemes, and about how to cope with the ways in which features and feature durations vary as a function of context. Obviously, these are important problems, worthy of considerable attention. However, concern with these issues tended to obscure attention to the fundamental properties of the model and the model's ability to account for basic aspects of the psychological data obtained in many experiments.

To cope with these conflicting goals, we have developed two different versions of the model, called TRACE I and TRACE II. Both models spring from the same basic assumptions, but focus on different aspects of speech perception. TRACE I was designed to address some of the challenges posed by the task of recognizing phonemes from real speech. This version of the model is described in detail in Elman and McClelland (in press). With this version of the model, we were able to show that the TRACE framework could indeed be used to process real speech—albeit from a single speaker uttering isolated monosyllables at this point. We were also able to demonstrate the efficacy of the idea of adjusting feature to phoneme connections on the basis of activations produced by surrounding context. With connection strength adjustment in place, the model was able to identify the stop consonant in 90% of a set of isolated monosyllables correctly, up from 79% with an invariant set of connections. This level of performance is comparable to what has been achieved by other machine-based phoneme identification schemes (e.g., Kopec, 1984) and illustrates the promise of the connection strength adjustment scheme for coping with variability due to local phonetic context. Ideas for extending the connection strength adjustment scheme to deal with the ways in which cues to phoneme identification vary with global variables (rate, speaker characteristics, etc.) are considered in the general discussion.

TRACE II, the version described in the present paper, was designed to account primarily for lexical influences on phoneme perception and for what is known about on-line recognition of words, though we use it to illustrate how certain other aspects of phoneme perception fall out of the TRACE framework. This version of the model is actually a simplified version of TRACE I. Most importantly, we eliminated the connection-strength adjustment facility, and we replaced the real speech inputs to TRACE I with mock speech. This mock speech input consisted of over-lapping but contextually invariant specifications of the features of successive phonemes. Obviously, then, TRACE II sidesteps many fundamental issues about speech. But it makes it much easier to see how the mechanism can account for a number of aspects of phoneme and word recognition. A number of further simplifying assumptions were made to facilitate examination of basic properties of the interactive activation processes taking place within the model.

The following sections describe TRACE II in more detail. First we consider the specifications of the mock-speech input to the model, and then we consider the units and connections that make up the Trace at each of the three levels.

Mock-Speech Inputs

The input to TRACE II was a series of specifications for inputs to units at the feature level, one for each 25-ms time slice of the mock utterance. These specifications were generated by a simple computer program from a sequence of to-be-presented segments provided by the human user of the simulation program. The allowed segments consisted of the stop consonants /b/, /p/, /d/, /t/, /g/, and /k/, the fricatives /s/ and /S/ (``sh`` as in ``ship``), the liquids /l/ and /r/, and the vowels /a/ (as in ``pot``), /i/ (as in ``beet``), /u/ (as in ``boot``), and /^/ (as in ``but``). /^/ was also used to represent reduced vowels such as the second vowel in ``target.`` There was also a ``silence`` segment represented by /−/. Special segments, such as a segment halfway between /b/ and /p/, were also used; their properties are described in descriptions of the relevant simulations.

A set of seven dimensions was used in TRACE II to represent the feature-level inputs. Five of the dimensions (Consonantal, Vocalic, Diffuseness, Acuteness, and Voicing) were taken from classical work in phonology (Jakobson, Fant, & Halle, 1952), though we treat each of these dimensions as continua, in the spirit of Oden and Massaro (1978), rather than as binary features. A sixth dimension, Power, was included because it has been found useful for phoneme identification in various machine systems (e.g., Reddy, 1976), and it was incorporated here to add an additional dimension to increase the differentiation of the vowels and consonants. The seventh dimension, the amplitude of the burst of noise that occurs at the beginning of word initial stops, was included to provide an additional basis for distinguishing the stop consonants, which otherwise differed from each other on only one or two dimensions. Of course, these dimensions are intentional simplifications of the real acoustic structure of speech, in much the same way that the font used by McClelland and Rumelhart (1981) in the interactive-activation model of visual word recognition was an intentional simplification of the real structure of print.

Each dimension was divided into eight value ranges. Each phoneme was assigned a value on each dimension; the values on the Vocalic, Diffuseness, and Acuteness dimensions for the phonemes in the utterance /tik^p/ are shown in Fig. 2. The full set of values are shown in Table 1. Numbers in the cells of the table indicate which value on the indicated dimension was most strongly activated by the feature pattern for the indicated phoneme. Values range from 1 = *very low* to 8 = *very high*. The last two dimensions were altered for the categorical perception and trading relations simulations.

Values were assigned to approximate the values real phonemes would have on these dimensions and to make phonemes that fall into the same phonetic category have identical values on many of the dimensions. Thus, for example, all stop consonants were assigned the same values on the Power, Vocalic, and Consonantal dimensions. We do not claim to have captured the details of phoneme similarity exactly. Indeed, one cannot do so in a fixed feature set because the similarities vary as a function of context. However, the feature sets do have the property that the feature pattern for one phoneme is more similar to the feature pattern for other phonemes in the same phonetic category (stop, fricative, liquid, or vowel) than it is to the patterns for phonemes in other categories. Among the stops, those phonemes sharing place of articulation or voicing are more similar than those sharing neither attribute.

The correlations of the feature patterns for the 15 phonemes used are shown in Table 2. It is these correlations of the patterns assigned to the

TABLE 1
Phoneme Feature Values Used in TRACE II

Phoneme	Power	Vocalic	Diffuse	Acute	Cons.	Voiced	Burst
p	4	1	7	2	8	1	8
b	4	1	7	2	8	7	7
t	4	1	7	7	8	1	6
d	4	1	7	7	8	7	5
k	4	1	2	3	8	1	4
g	4	1	2	3	8	7	3
s	6	4	7	8	5	1	—
S	6	4	6	4	5	1	—
r	7	7	1	2	3	8	—
l	7	7	2	4	3	8	—
a	8	8	2	1	1	8	—
i	8	8	8	8	1	8	—
u	8	8	6	2	1	8	—
^	7	8	5	1	1	8	—

TABLE 2
Correlations of Feature Patterns of the Different Phonemes Used in Trace II

Phoneme	p	b	t	d	k	g	s	S	r	l	a	i	u	^
p	—	.76	.71	.56	.60	.46	.30							
b	.76	—	.56	.71	.46	.60								
t	.71	.56	—	.76	.56	.42	.35							
d	.56	.71	.76	—	.42	.56								
k	.60	.46	.56	.42	—	.77		.24						
g	.46	.60	.42	.56	.77	—								
s	.30		.35				—	.65						
S					.24		.65	—					.20	
r									—	.80	.29		.20	.37
l									.80	—	.32		.32	.32
a									.29	.32	—	.65	.75	.67
i											.65	—	.65	.49
u								.20	.20	.32	.75	.65	—	.59
^									.37	.32	.67	.49	.59	—

Note. Correlations of less than .20 have been replaced by blanks.

different phonemes, rather than the actual values assigned to particular phonemes or even the labels attached to the different mock-speech dimensions, that determine the behavior of the simulation model, since it is these correlations that determine how much an instance of one phoneme will tend to excite the detector for another.

The feature patterns were constructed in such a way that it was possible to create feature patterns that would activate two different phonemes in the same category (stop, liquid, fricative, or vowel) to an equal extent by averaging the values of the two phonemes on one or more dimensions. In this way, it was a simple matter to make up ambiguous inputs, halfway between two phonemes, or to construct continua varying between two phonemes on one or more dimensions.

The feature specification of each phoneme in the input stream extended over 11 time slices of the input. The strength of the pattern grew to a peak at the 6th slice and fell off again, as illustrated in Fig. 2. Peaks of successive phonemes were separated by 6 slices. Thus, specifications of successive phonemes overlapped, as they do in real speech (Fowler, 1984; Liberman, 1970).

Generally, there were no cues to word boundaries in the speech stream—the feature specification for the last phoneme of one word overlapped with the first phoneme of the next in just the same way feature specifications of adjacent phonemes overlap within words. However, entire utterances presented to the model for processing—whether they were individual syllables, words, or strings of words—were preceded and followed by silence. Silence was not simply the absence of any input; rather, it was a pattern of feature values, just like the phonemes. Thus, a ninth value on each of the seven dimensions was associated with silence. These values were actually outside the range of values which occurred in the phonemes themselves, so that the features of silence were completely uncorrelated with the features of any of the phonemes used.

Feature Level Units and Connections

The units at the feature level are detectors for features of the speech stream at particular moments in time. In TRACE II, there was a unit for each of the nine values on each of the seven dimensions in each time slice of the Trace. The figures show three sets of feature units in several time slices. Units for features on the same dimension within the same time slice are mutually inhibitory. Thus, the unit for the high value of the Vocalic dimension in Time Slice 9 inhibits the units for other values on the same dimension in the same time slice, as illustrated in Fig. 4. This figure also illustrates the mutually excitatory connections of this same feature unit with units at the phoneme level. In the next section we redescribe these connections from the point of view of the phoneme level.

The Phoneme Level and Feature—Phoneme Connections

At the phoneme level, there is a set of detectors for each of the 15 phonemes listed above. In addition, there is a set of detectors for the presence of silence. These silence detectors are treated like all other phoneme detectors. Each member of the set of detectors for a particular phoneme is centered over a different time slice at the feature level, and the centers are spaced three time slices apart. The unit centered over a particular slice received excitatory input from feature units in a range of slices, extending both forward and backward from the slice in which the phoneme unit is located. It also sends excitatory feedback down to the same feature units in the same range of slices.

The connection strengths between the feature-level units and a particular phoneme-level unit exactly match the feature pattern the phoneme is given in its input specification. Thus, as illustrated in Fig. 3, the strengths of the connections between the node for /k/ centered over Time Slice 24 and the nodes at the feature level are exactly proportional to the pattern of input to the feature level produced by an input specification containing the features of /k/ centered in the same time slice.

There are inhibitory connections between units at the phoneme level. Units inhibit each other to the extent that the speech objects they stand for represent alternative interpretations of the content of the speech stream at the same point in the utterance. Note that, although the feature specification of a phoneme is spread over a window of 11 slices, successive phonemes in the input have their centers 6 slices apart. Thus each phoneme-level unit is thought of as spanning 6 feature-level slices, as illustrated in Fig. 3. Each unit inhibits others in proportion to their overlap. Thus, a phoneme detector inhibits other phoneme detectors centered over the same slice twice as much as it inhibits detectors centered 3 slices away, and inhibits detectors centered 6 or more slices away not at all.

Word Units and Word—Phoneme Connections

There is a unit for every word in every time slice. Each of these units represents a different hypothesis about a word identity and starting location in the Trace. For example, the unit for the word /kˆp/ in Slice 24 (highlighted in Fig. 4) represents the hypothesis that the input contains the word "cup" starting in Slice 24. More exactly, it represents the hypothesis that the input contains the word "cup" with its first phoneme centered in Time Slice 24.

Word units receive excitation from the units for the phonemes they contain in a series of overlapping windows. Thus, the unit for "cup" in Time Slice 24 will receive excitation from /k/ in slices neighboring Slice

24, from /ˆ/ in slices neighboring Slice 30, and from /p/ in slices neighboring Slice 36. As with the feature–phoneme connections, these connections are strongest at the center of the window and fall off linearly on either side.

The inhibitory connections at the word level are similar to those at the phoneme level. Again, the strength of the inhibition between two word units depends on the number of time slices in which they overlap. Thus, units representing alternative interpretations of the same stretch of phoneme units are strongly competitive, but units representing interpretations of nonoverlapping sequences of phonemes do not compete at all.

TRACE II has detectors for the 211 words found in a computerized phonetic word list that met all of the following constraints: (a) the word consisted only of the phonemes listed above; (b) it was not an inflection of some other word that could be made by adding "-ed," "-s," or "-ing"; (c) the word together with its "-ed," "-s," and "-ing" inflections occurred with a frequency of 20 or more per million in the Kucera and Francis (1967) word count. It is not claimed that the model's lexicon is an exhaustive list of words meeting this criterion, since the computerized phonetic lexicon was not complete, but it is reasonably close to this. To make specific points about the behavior of the model, detectors for the following three words not in the main list were added: "blush," "regal," and "sleet." The model also had detectors at the word level for silence (/–/), which was treated like a one-phoneme word.

Presentation and Processing of an Utterance

Before processing of an utterance begins, the activations of all of the units are set at their resting values. At the start of processing, the input to the initial slice of feature units is applied. Activations are then updated, ending the initial time cycle. On the next time cycle, the input to the next slice of feature units is applied, and excitatory and inhibitory inputs to each unit resulting from the pattern of activation left at the end of the previous time slice are computed.

It is important to remember that the input is applied, one slice at a time, proceeding from left to right as though it were an ongoing stream of speech "writing on" the successive time slices of the Trace. The interactive-activation process is occurring throughout the Trace on each time slice, even though the external bottom-up input is only coming into the feature units one slice at a time. Processing interactions can continue even after the left to right sweep through the input reaches the end of the Trace. Once this happens, there are simply no new input specifications applied to the Trace; the continuing interactions are based on what has already been presented. This interaction process is assumed to continue indefinitely, though for practical purposes it is always terminated after some predetermined number of time cycles has elapsed.

Details of Processing Dynamics

The interactive activation process in the Trace model follows the dynamic assumptions laid out in McClelland and Rumelhart (1981). Each unit has a resting activation value arbitrarily set at 0, a maximum activation value arbitrarily set at 1.0, and a minimum activation set at − .3. On every time cycle of processing, all the weighted excitatory and inhibitory signals impinging upon a unit are added together. The signal from one unit to another is just the extent to which its activation exceeds 0; if its activation is less than 0, the signal is 0.[1] Global level-specific excitatory, inhibitory, and decay parameters scale the relative magnitudes of different types of influences on the activation of each unit. Values for these parameters are given below.

After the net input to each unit has been determined based on the prior activations of the units, the activations of the units are all updated for the next processing cycle. The new value of the activation of the unit is a function of its net input from other units and its previous activation value. The exact function used (see McClelland & Rumelhart, 1981) keeps unit activations bounded between their maximum and minimum values. Given a constant input, the activation of a unit will stabilize at a point between its maximum and minimum that depends on the strength and sign (excitatory or inhibitory) of the input. With a net input of 0, the activation of the unit will gradually return to its resting level.

Each processing time cycle corresponds to a single time slice at the feature level. This is actually a parameter of the model—there is no intrinsic reason why there should be a single cycle of the interactive-activation process synchronized with the arrival of each successive slice of the input. A higher rate of cycling would speed the percolation of effects of new input through the network relative to the rate of presentation.

Output Assumptions

Activations of units in the Trace rise and fall as the input sweeps across the feature level. At any time, a decision can be made based on the pattern of activation as it stands at that moment. The decision mechanism can, we assume, be directed to consider the set of units located within a small window of adjacent slices within any level. The units in this set then

[1] At the word level, the inhibitory signal from one word to another is just the square of the extent to which the sender's activation exceeds zero. This tends to smooth the effects of many units suddenly becoming slightly activated, and of course it also increases the dominance of one active word over many weakly activated ones.

constitute the set of response alternatives, designated by the identity of the item for which the unit stands (note that with several adjacent slices included in the set, several units in the alternative set may correspond to the same overt response). Word identification responses are assumed to be based on readout from the word level, and phoneme identification responses are assumed to be based on readout from the phoneme level. As far as phoneme identification is concerned, then, a homogeneous mechanism is assumed to be used with both word and nonword stimuli. The decision mechanism can be asked to make a response either (a) at a criterial time during processing or (b) when a unit in the alternative set reaches a criterial strength relative to the activation of other alternative units. Once a decision has been made to make a response, one of the alternatives is chosen from the members of the set. The probability of choosing a particular alternative i is then given by the Luce (1959) choice rule:

$$p(R_i) = \frac{S_i}{\sum_j S_j}$$

when j indexes the members of the alternative set, and

$$S_i = e^{ka_i}.$$

The exponential transformation ensures that all activations are positive and gives great weight to stronger activations, and the Luce rule ensures that the sum of all of the response probabilities adds up to 1.0. Substantially the same assumptions were used by McClelland and Rumelhart (1981).

Minimizing the Number of Parameters

At the expense of considerable realism, we have tried to keep TRACE II simple by using homogeneous parameters wherever possible. Thus, as already noted, the feature specifications of all phonemes were spread out over the same number of time slices, effectively giving all phonemes the same duration. The strength of the total excitation coming into a particular phoneme unit from the feature units was normalized to the same value for all phonemes, thus making each phoneme equally excitable by its own canonical pattern. Other simplifying assumptions should be noted as well. For example, there were no differences in connections or resting levels for words of different frequency. It would have been a simple matter to incorporate frequency as McClelland and Rumelhart (1981) did, and a complete model would, of course, include some account for the ubiquitous effects of word frequency. We left it out here to facilitate an examination of the many other factors that appear to influence the process of word recognition in speech perception.

Even with all the simplifications described above, the TRACE model still has a number of free parameters. These parameters are listed in Table 3. It should be noted that parameters are not in general directly comparable across levels. For example, phoneme-to-phoneme and word-to-word inhibition are not directly comparable to each other or to feature-to-phoneme inhibition, since feature-level units compete only within a single slice, while phoneme and word units compete in proportion to their overlap.

There was some trial and error in finding the set of parameters used in the reported simulations, but, in general, the qualitative behavior of the model was remarkably robust under parameter variations, and no systematic search of the space of parameters was necessary. Generally, manipulations of parameters simply influence the magnitude or the timing of one effect or another without changing the basic nature of the effects observed. For example, stronger bottom-up excitation speeds things up and can indirectly influence the size of top-down effects, since, for example, stronger word level activations produce stronger feedback to the phoneme level. Stronger top-down excitation, of course, directly influences the magnitude of lexical effects. The one parameter that appeared to influence the qualitative behavior of the model was the strength of within-level inhibition. Stronger within-level inhibition make the model commit itself more strongly to slight early differences in activation among competing alternatives. There was, therefore, some tuning of this parameter to avoid early overcommitment that would prevent right context from exerting an influence under some circumstances. Finally, a low rate of feature-level decay was used to allow feature-level activations to persist after the input moved on to later slices.

The parameter values were held constant at the values shown in the

TABLE 3
Parameters of TRACE II

Parameter	Value
Feature–phoneme excitation	.02
Phoneme–word excitation	.05
Word–phoneme excitation	.03
Phoneme–feature excitation	.00
Feature-level inhibition	.04
Phoneme-level inhibition[a]	.04
Word-level inhibition[a]	.03
Feature-level decay	.01
Phoneme-level decay	.03
Word-level decay	.05

[a] Per three time-slices of overlap.

table throughout the simulations, except in the simulations of categorical perception and trading relations. Since we were not explicitly concerned with the effects of feedback to the feature level in any of the other simulations, we set the feedback from the phoneme level to the feature level to zero to speed up the simulations in all other cases. In the categorical perception and trading relations simulations this parameter was set at .05. Phoneme-to-feature feedback tended to slow the effective rate of decay at the feature level and to increase the effective distinctiveness of different feature patterns. Rate of decay of feature-level activations and strength of phoneme-to-phoneme competition were set to .03 and .05 to compensate for these effects. No lexicon was used in the categorical perception and trading relations simulations, which is equivalent to setting the phoneme to word excitation parameter to zero.

THE DYNAMICS OF PHONEME PERCEPTION

In the introduction, we motivated the approach taken in the TRACE model in general terms. In this section, we see that the simple concepts that lead to TRACE provide a coherent and synthetic account of a large number of different kinds of findings on the perception of phonemes. Previous models have been able to provide fairly accurate accounts of a number of these phenomena. For example, Massaro and Oden's feature integration model (Massaro, 1981; Massaro & Oden, 1980a, 1980b; Oden & Massaro, 1978) accounts in detail for a large body of data on the influences of multiple cues to phoneme identity, and the Pisoni/Fujisaki–Kawashima model of categorical perception (Fujisaki & Kawashima, 1968; Pisoni, 1973, 1975) accounts for a large body of data on the conditions under which subjects can discriminate sounds within the same phonetic category. Marslen-Wilson's COHORT model can account for the time course of lexical influences on phoneme identification. What we hope to show here is that TRACE brings these phenomena, and several others not considered by either model, together into a coherent picture of the process of phoneme perception as it unfolds in time.

The present section consists of three main parts. The first focuses on lexical effects on phoneme identification and the conditions under which these effects are obtained. Here, we see how TRACE can account for the basic lexical effect, and we make it clear why lexical effects are only obtained under some conditions. The second part of this section focuses on the question of the role of phonotactic rules—that is, rules specifying which phonemes can occur together in English—in phoneme identification. Here, we see how TRACE mimics the apparently rule-governed behavior of human subjects, in terms of a "conspiracy" of the lexical items that instantiate the rule. The third part focuses on two aspects of phoneme identification often considered quite separately from lexical ef-

24   MC CLELLAND AND ELMAN

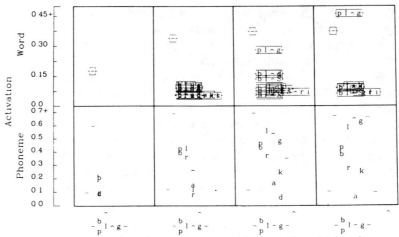

FIG. 5. Phoneme- and word-level activations at several points in the unfolding of a segment ambiguous between /b/ and /p/, followed by /l/, /ˆ/, and /g/. See text for a full explanation.

fects—namely, the contrasting phenomena of cue tradeoffs in phoneme perception and categorical perception. Here we see that TRACE provides an account of both effects as well as details of their time course. All three parts of this section illustrate how the simple mechanisms of mutual excitation and inhibition among the processing units of the Trace provide a natural way of accounting for the relevant phenomena. The section ends with a brief consideration of the ways in which TRACE might be extended to cope with several other aspects of phoneme identification and perception.

Lexical Effects

You can tell a phoneme by the company that it keeps.[2] In this section, we describe a simple simulation of the basic lexical effect on phoneme identification reported by Ganong (1980). We start with this phenomenon because it, and the related phonemic restoration effect, were among the primary reasons why we felt that the interactive-activation approach would be appropriate for speech perception as well as visual word recognition and reading.

For the first simulation, the input to the model consisted of a feature specification which activated /b/ and /p/ equally, followed by (and partially overlapping with) the feature specifications for /l/, then /ˆ/, then /g/. Figure 5 shows phoneme and word-level activations at several points in the unfolding of this input specification. Each panel of the figure represents

[2] This title is adapted from the title of a talk by David E. Rumelhart on related phenomena in letter perception. These findings are described in Rumelhart and McClelland (1982). We thank Dave for his permission to adapt the title.

a different point in time during the presentation and concomitant processing of the input. The upper portion of each panel is used to display activations at the word level; the lower panel is used for activations at the phoneme level. Each unit is represented by a rectangle, labeled with the identity of the item the unit stands for. The horizontal extension of the rectangle indicates the portion of the input spanned by the unit. The vertical position of the rectangle indicates the degree of activation of the unit. In this and subsequent figures, activations of the phoneme units located between the peaks of the input specifications of the phonemes (at Slices 3, 9, 15, etc.) have been deleted from the display for clarity (the activations of these units generally get suppressed by the model, since the units on the peaks tend to dominate them). The input itself is indicated below each panel, with the successive phonemes positioned at the temporal positions of the centers of their input specifications. The /^/ along the x axis represents the point in the presentation of the input stream at which the snapshot was taken.

The figure illustrates the gradual buildup of activation of the two interpretations of the first phoneme, followed by gradual buildups in activation for subsequent phonemes. As these processes unfold, they begin to produce word-level activations. It is difficult to resolve any word-level activations in the first few frames, however, since in these frames, the information at the phoneme level simply has not evolved to the point where it provides enough constraint to select any one particular word. In this case, it is only after the /g/ has come in that the model has information telling it whether the input is closer to "plug," "plus," "blush," or "blood" (TRACE's lexicon contains no other words beginning with /pl^/ or /bl^/). After that point, as illustrated in the fourth panel, "plug" wins the competition at the word level and, through feedback support to /p/, causes /p/ to dominate /b/ at the phoneme level. The model, then, provides an explicit account for the way in which lexical information can influence phoneme identification.

Two things about the lexical effect observed in this case are worthy of note. First, the effect is rather small. Second, it does not emerge until well after the ambiguous segment itself has come and gone. There is a slight advantage of /p/ over /b/ in Frames 2 and 3 of the figure. In these cases, however, the advantage is not due to the specific information that this item is the word "plug"—the model can have no way of knowing this at these points in processing. The slight advantage for /p/ at these early points is due to the fact that there are more words beginning with /pl/ than /bl/ in the model's lexicon, and in particular, there are more beginning with /pl^/ than /bl^/. So, when the input is /?l^d/, with the ? standing for the ambiguous /b/–/p/ segment, the model must actually overcome this slight /p/-ward bias. Eventually, it does so.

Figure 6 shows the temporal course of buildup of the strength of the

26   MC CLELLAND AND ELMAN

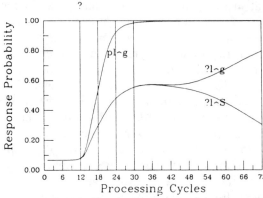

FIG. 6. The time course of the buildup in the strength of the /p/ response based on activations of phoneme units in Slice 12. in processing an ambiguous /b/–/p/ segment in /_l^g/,
and the same segment in /–l^S/. The ambiguous segment is indicated by the "?". Also
shown is the buildup of response strength for processing an unambiguous /p/ segment in
/pl^g/. The vertical line topped with "?" indicates the point in time corresponding to the
center of the initial segment in the input stream. Successive vertical lines indicate centers
of successive phonemes.

/p/ response based on activations of the phoneme units in Slice 12 for
two cases in which the initial segment is ambiguous between /p/ and /b/.
In one case, the ambiguous segment is followed by /l^g/ (as in "plug");
in the other, it is followed by /l^S/ (as in "blush"). Given the model's
restricted lexicon, which does not contain the word "plush," the lexical
effect should lead to eventual dominance of the /p/ response in the first
case, but a suppression of the /p/ response in the second case. The differences between the contexts do not begin to show up until after the
center of the final phoneme, which occurs at Slice 30. The reason for this
is simply that the information is not available until that point, because
the phoneme that signals what the word will be comes at the very end of
the word. The effect takes another few time slices to begin to influence
the activation of the initial phoneme, because it percolates to the first
phoneme by way of the feedback from the word or words that contain it.

Elimination of the lexical effect by time pressure. Fox (1982) has reported that the lexical effect on word initial segments is eliminated if
subjects are given a deadline to respond within 500 ms of the ambiguous
segment. Though they can correctly identify unambiguous segments in
responses made before the deadline, these early responses show no sensitivity to the lexical status of the alternatives. Similar findings are also
reported by Fox (1984).

Our model is completely consistent with Fox's results. Indeed, we have already seen that the activations in the Trace only begin to reflect the lexical effect about one phoneme or so after the phoneme that establishes the lexical identity of the item. Given that this segment does not occur, in Fox's experiments, until the second or third segment after the ambiguous segment, there is no way that a lexical effect could be observed in early responses.

But what about the fact that early responses to unambiguous segments can be accurate? TRACE accounts for this too. In Figure 7 we show the state of the Trace at various different points after the unambiguous /b/ in /blˆg/. Here, the /b/ dominates the /p/ from the earliest point. The analogous result is obtained, when the stimulus is /p/ in /plˆg/, and the activation for the initial phoneme is quite independent of whether or not the item is a word. The response strength for the case when /plˆg/ is presented in Fig. 6 shows that the probability of choosing /p/ is near unity within 12 processing cycles, or 300 ms of the initial segment, well before the deadline would be reached—and well before word identity specifying information is available.

Lexical effects late in a word. In the model, lexical effects on word-initial segments develop rather late, at least in the case where there is no context preceding the word. Of course, the exact timing of the development of any lexical effect would be dependent upon the set of words activated by the stimulus; if one word predominated early on, a lexical effect could develop rather earlier. In general, though, word-initial ambiguities will require time to resolve on the basis of lexical information.

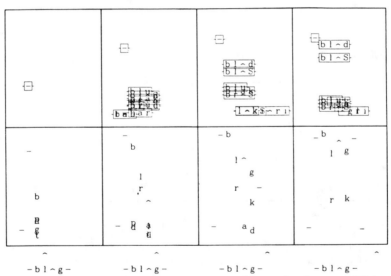

FIG. 7. The state of the Trace at various stages of processing the stream /blˆg/.

28   MC CLELLAND AND ELMAN

However, when the ambiguous segment comes late in the word, and the information that precedes the ambiguous segment has already established which of the two alternatives for the ambiguous segment is correct, TRACE shows a lexical effect that develops as the direct perceptual information relevant to the identity of the target segment is being processed. This phenomenon is illustrated in Fig. 8, which shows the state of the Trace at several points in time relative to an ambiguous final segment that could be a /t/ or a /d/, at the end of the context /targ^/. Within the duration of a single phoneme after the center of the ambiguous segment, /t/ already has an advantage over /d/. We therefore predict that Fox's results would come out differently, were he to use word-final, as opposed to word-initial, ambiguous segments. In such a case we would expect the lexical effect to show up well within the 500-ms deadline.

Dependence of the lexical effect on phonological ambiguity. One further aspect of the lexical effect that was noted by Ganong (1980) deserves comment. This is the fact that the lexical effect on the identity of a phoneme only occurs with segments which fall in the boundary region between two phonemes. For segments which are unambiguous examples of one category or the other, the effect is not obtained. TRACE is entirely consistent with this aspect of the data. The influence of the lexicon is simply another source of evidence, like that coming from the feature

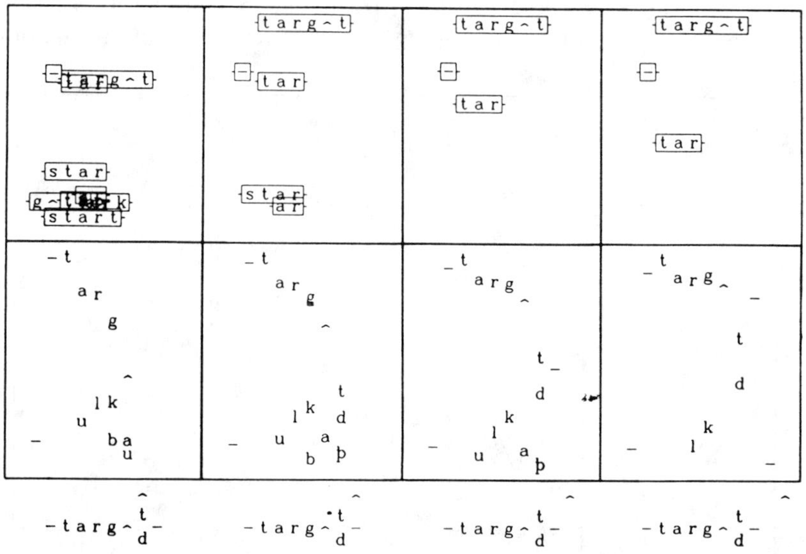

FIG. 8. The state of the Trace at several stages of processing the stream consisting of /targ^/ followed by a segment ambiguous between /t/ and /d/.

level. influencing the activation of one phoneme unit or another. When the bottom-up input is decisive, it can preempt any lexical bias effects. We have verified this in simulations presenting unambiguous tokens of /p/ or /b/, followed either by /l^g/ or /l^S/. In these simulations, the unit for the presented initial segment reaches a very high level of activation, independent of the following context. When the segment comes at the end of the word, the context exerts stronger effects, thus accounting for the fact that speech distortions are easier to detect when they come early in a word than when they come late (Marslen-Wilson & Welsh, 1978). However, even there, it is possible to override lexically based activations with clear bottom-up signals, although there may be some slowing of the activation process which would probably show up in reaction times.

It should be noted that TRACE's account of lexical effects is quite similar to the account offered by the feature integration theory of Massaro and Oden (1980a). Indeed, Massaro and Oden's model provides quantitative fits to Ganong's findings. We will make some mention of the slight differences in quantitative assumptions between the models below. For now, we note a more crucial difference: TRACE incorporates specific assumptions about the time course of processing which allows it to account for the conditions under which lexical effects will be obtained, as well as for the influence (or a lack thereof) of lexical effects on reaction times, to which we now turn.

Absence of lexical effect in some reaction-time studies. Foss and Blank (1980) presented some results which seemed to pose a challenge to interactive models of phoneme identification in speech perception. They gave subjects the task of listening to spoken sentences for occurrences of a particular phoneme in word-initial position. Reaction time to press a response key from the onset of the target phoneme was the dependent variable. In one example, the target was /g/ and the sentence was, *At the end of last year, the government.* . . . The subject's task was simply to press the response key upon hearing the /g/ at the beginning of the word *government.*

The principle finding of Foss and Blank's study was that it made no difference whether the target came at the beginning of a word or a nonword. Later studies by Foss and Gernsbacher (1983) indicate that other experiments which have found lexical or even semantic and syntactic context effects on monitoring latencies are flawed, and that monitoring times for word-initial phonemes are primarily influenced by acoustic factors affecting phoneme detectability, rather than lexical, semantic, or syntactic factors.

The conclusion that phoneme monitoring is unaffected by the lexical status of the target-bearing phoneme string seems at variance with the spirit of the TRACE model, since in TRACE, the lexical level is always involved in the perceptual process. However, we have already seen that there are conditions under which the lexical level does not get much of a chance to exert an effect. In the previous section we saw that there is no lexical effect on identification of ambiguous word-initial targets when the subject is under time pressure to respond quickly, simply because the subject must respond before information is even available that would allow the model—or any other mechanism—to produce a lexical effect.

In the Foss and Blank situation, there is even less reason to expect a lexical effect, since the target is not an ambiguous segment. We already saw that activation curves rise rapidly for unambiguous segments; in the present case, they can reach near-peak levels well before the acoustic information that indicates whether the target is in a word or nonword has reached the subject's ear.

The results of a simulation run illustrating these points are shown in Fig. 9. For this example, we imagine that the target is /t/. Note how during the initial syllable of both streams, little activation at the word level has been established. Even toward the end of the stream, where the information is just coming in which determines that "trugus" is not a word, there is little difference, because in both cases, there are several active word-level candidates, all supporting the word-initial /t/. It is only after the end of the stream that a real chance for a difference has occurred. Well before this time arrives, the subject will have made a response, since the strength of the /t/ response reaches a level sufficient to guarantee a high accuracy by about Cycle 30, well before the end of the word, as illustrated in Fig. 10.

Even though activations are quite rapid for unambiguous segments, these can still be influenced by lexical effects, provided that the lexical information is available in time. In Fig. 11, we illustrate this point for the phoneme /t/ in the streams /sikrˆt/ (the word "secret") and /gˆldˆt/ ("guldut," a nonword). The figure shows the strength of the /t/ response as a function of processing cycles, relative to all other responses based on activations of phoneme units at Cycle 42, the peak of the input specification for the /t/. Clearly, response strength grows faster for the /t/ in /sikrˆt/ than for the /t/ in /gˆldˆt/; picking an arbitrary threshold of .9 for response initiation, we find that the /t/ in /sikrˆt/ reaches criterion about 3 cycles or 75 ms sooner than the /t/ in /gˆldˆt/.

Studies showing lexical effects in reaction times. Marslen-Wilson (1980) has reported an experiment that demonstrates the existence of lexical effects in phoneme monitoring for phonemes coming at later points in words. For phonemes coming at the beginning of a word or at the end of the first syllable, he found no facilitation for phonemes in words rel-

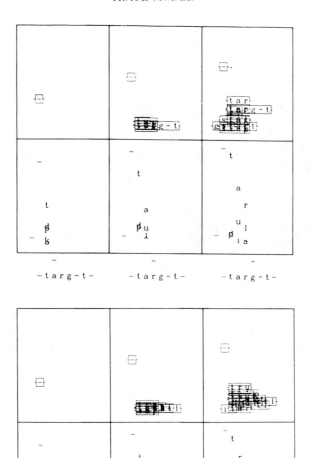

FIG. 9. State of the Trace at three different points during the processing of the word "target" (/targ˄t/) and the nonword "trugus" (/tr˄g˙s/).

ative to phonemes in nonwords (in fact there was a nonword advantage for these early target conditions). For targets occurring at the end of the second syllable of a two-syllable word (like "secret"—though the stimuli in this particular experiment were Dutch) Marslen-Wilson found an 85-

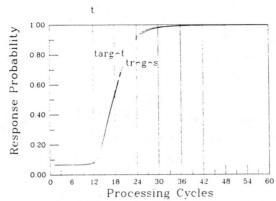

FIG. 10. Time course of growth in the probability of the /t/ response based on activations of phoneme units in Slice 12, during processing of /targˆt/ and /trˆgˆs/. The vertical lines indicate the peaks on the feature patterns corresponding to the successive phonemes of the presented word.

ms advantage compared to corresponding positions in nonwords. This compares quite closely with the value of about 75 ms we obtained for the /sikrˆt/–/gˆldˆt/ example. At the ends of even longer words, the word advantage increased in size to 185 ms. Marslen-Wilson's result thus confirms that there are indeed lexical effects in phoneme monitoring—even for unambiguous inputs—but underscores the fact that there is no word advantage for phonemes whose processing can be completed long before lexical influences would have a chance to show up.

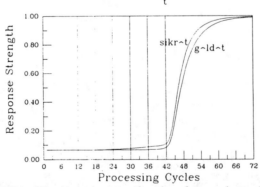

FIG. 11. Probability of the /t/ response as a function of processing cycles, based on activation of phoneme units at Cycle 42, for the stream /sikrˆt/ (''secret'') and /gˆldˆt/ (''guldut''). Vertical lines indicate the peaks of the input patterns corresponding to the successive phonemes in either stream.

The TRACE model and Marslen-Wilson's COHORT model (Marslen-Wilson & Tyler, 1980; Marslen-Wilson & Welsh, 1978) offer fairly similar interpretations of lexical effects in phoneme monitoring. Both models account for the growth in the effect as a function of position in the word. As in COHORT, lexical effects in TRACE depend on the point at which the pattern of activation at the word level begins to specify the identities of the phonemes. In COHORT, there is a discrete moment when this occurs—when the cohort of items consistent with the input is reduced to a single item. In TRACE, things are not quite so discrete. However, it will still generally be the case in TRACE that the size of the lexical effect will vary with the location of the "unique point," the point at which the bottom-up input remains consistent with only a single word. However, since Marslen-Wilson's experiments were performed with Dutch words, we have not been able to simulate his experimental demonstration of this effect in detail.

TRACE and COHORT make similar predictions in some situations, but not in all. In the next section, we consider a phenomenon which TRACE accounts for via the same mechanisms it uses to account for the lexical effects we have been considering. Here, the graded feedback from the word level to the phoneme level allows TRACE to account for an effect that would not be predicted by COHORT, unless additional assumptions were made.

Are Phonotactic Rule Effects the Result of a Conspiracy?

Recently, Massaro and Cohen (1983) have reported evidence they take as support for the use of phonotactic rules in phoneme identification. In one experiment, Massaro and Cohen's stimuli consisted of phonological segments ambiguous between /r/ and /l/ in different contexts. In one context (/t_i/) /r/ is permissible in English, but /l/ is not. In another context (/s_i/) /l/ is permissible in English but /r/ is not. In a third context (/f_i/) both are permissible, and in a fourth (/v_i/) neither is permissible. Massaro and Cohen found a bias to perceive ambiguous segments as /r/ when /r/ was permissible or as /l/ when /l/ was permissible. No bias appeared in either of the other two conditions.

With most of these stimuli, phonotactic acceptability is confounded with the actual lexical status of the item; thus /fli/ and /fri/ ("flee" and "free") are both words, as is /tri/ but not /tli/. In the /s_i/ context, however, neither /sli/ or /sri/ are words, yet Massaro and Cohen found a bias to hear the ambiguous segment as /l/, in accordance with phonotactic rules.

It turns out that TRACE produces the same effect, even though it lacks phonotactic rules. The reason is that the ambiguous stimulus produces

34   MC CLELLAND AND ELMAN

partial activations of a number of words ("sleep" and "sleet" in the model's lexicon; it would also activate "sleeve," "sleek," and others in a model with a fuller lexicon). None of these word units gets as active as it would if the entire word had been presented. However, all of them (in the simulation, there are ony two, but the principle still applies) are partially activated, and all conspire together and contribute to the activation of /l/. This feedback support for the /l/ allows it to dominate the /r/, just as it would if /sli/ were an actual word, as shown in Fig. 12.

The hypothesis that phonotactic rule effects are really based on word activations leads to a prediction: that we should be able to reverse these effects if we present items that are supported strongly by one or more lexical items even if they violate phonotactic rules. A recent experiment by Elman (1983) confirms this prediction. In this experiment, ambiguous phonemes (for example, halfway between /b/ and /d/) were presented in three different types of contexts. In all three types, one of the two (in this case, the /d/) was phonotactically acceptable, while the other (the /b/) was not. However, the contexts differed in their relation to words. In one case, the legal item actually occurred in a word ("bwindle"–"dwindle"). In a second case, neither item made a word, but the illegal item was very close to a word ("bwacelet"–"dwacelet"). In a third case, neither item

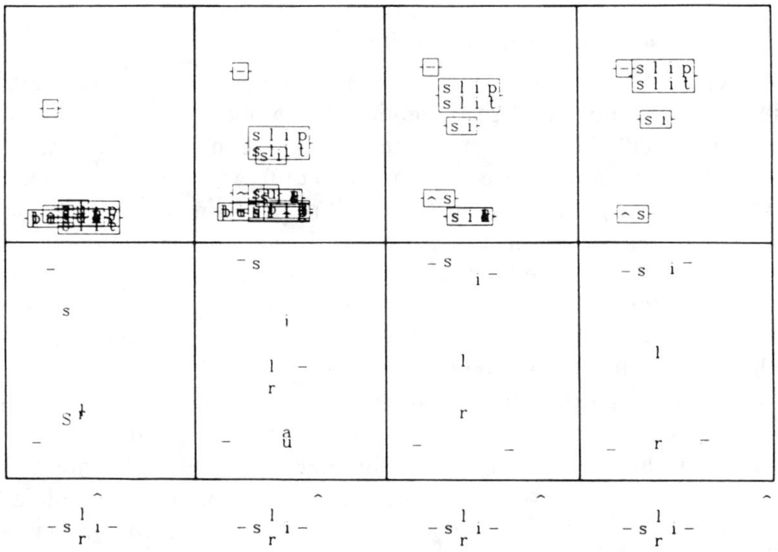

FIG. 12. State of the Trace at several points in processing a segment ambiguous between /l/ and /r/, in the context /s_i/. The units for "sleep" (/slip/) and "sleet" (/slit/) are boxed together since they take on identical activation values.

was particularly close to a word ("bwiffle"–"dwiffle"). Results of the experiment are shown in Table 4. The existence of a word identical to one of the two alternatives or differing from one of the alternatives by a single phonetic feature of one phoneme strongly influenced the subject's choices between the two alternatives. Indeed, in the case where the phonotactically irregular alternative ("bwacelet") was one feature away from a particular lexical item ("bracelet"), subjects tended to hear the ambiguous item in accord with the similar lexical item (that is, as a /b/) even though it was phonotactically incorrect.

To determine whether the model would also produce such a reversal of the phonotactic rule effects with the appropriate kinds of stimuli, we ran a simulation using a simulated input ambiguous between /p/ and /t/ in the context /_luli/. /p/ is phonotactically acceptable in this context, but /t/ in this context makes an item that is very close to the word "truly." The results of this run, at two different points during processing, are shown in Fig. 13. Early on in processing, there is a slight bias in favor of the /p/ over the /t/, because at first a large number of /pl/ words are slightly more activated than any words beginning with /t/. Later, though, the /t/ gets the upper hand as the word "truly" comes to dominate at the word level. Thus, by the end of the word or shortly thereafter, the closest word has begun to play a dominating role, causing the model to prefer the phonotactically inappropriate interpretation of the ambiguous initial segment.

Of course, at the same time the word "truly" tends to support /r/ rather than /l/ for the second segment. Thus, even though this segment is not ambiguous, and the /l/ would suppress the /r/ interpretation in a more neutral context, the /r/ stays quite active.

Trading Relations and Categorical Perception

In the simulations considered thus far, phoneme identification is influenced by two different kinds of factors, featural and lexical. When one sort of information is lacking, the other can compensate for it. The image

TABLE 4
Percentage Choice of Phonotactically Irregular Consonant

Stimulus type	Example	Percentage of identifications as "illegal" phoneme[a]
Legal word/illegal nonword	dwindle/bwindle	37
Legal nonword/illegal nonword	dwiffle/bwiffle	46
Legal nonword/illegal nearword	dwacelet/bwacelet	55

[a] $F_{(2,34)} = 26.414$, $p < .001$.

that emerges from these kinds of findings is of a system that exhibits great flexibility by being able to base identification decisions on different sources of information. It is, of course, well established that within the featural domain each phoneme is generally signaled by a number of different cues, and that human subjects can trade these cues off against each other. The TRACE model exhibits this same flexibility, as we detail shortly.

But there is something of a paradox. While the perceptual mechanisms exhibit great flexibility in the cues that they rely on for phoneme identification, they also appear to be quite "categorical" in nature. That is, they produce much sharper boundaries between phonetic categories than we might expect based on their sensitivity to multiple cues; and they appear to treat acoustically distinct feature patterns as perceptually equivalent, as long as they are identified as instances of the same phoneme.

In this section, we illustrate that in TRACE, just as in human speech perception, flexibility in feature interpretation—specifically, the ability to trade one feature of a phoneme off against another—coexists with a strong tendency toward categorical perception.

For these simulations, the model was stripped down to the essential minimum necessary, so that the basic mechanisms producing cue trade-

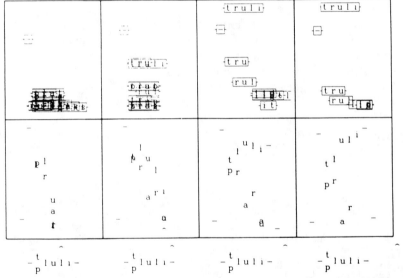

FIG. 13. State of the Trace at several points in processing an ambiguous /p/–/t/ segment followed by /uli/.

offs and categorical perception could be brought to the fore. The word level was eliminated altogether, and at the phoneme level there were only three phonemes, /a/, /g/, and /k/, plus silence (/−/). From these four items, inputs and percepts of the form /−ga−/ and /−ka−/ could be constructed. The following additional constraints were imposed on the feature specifications of each of the phonemes: (1) the /a/ and /−/ had no overlap with either /g/ or /k/, so that neither /a/ nor /−/ would bias the activations of the /g/ and /k/ phoneme units where they overlapped with the consonant; (2) /g/ and /k/ were identical on five of the seven dimensions, and differed only on the remaining two dimensions.

The two dimensions which differentiated /g/ and /k/ were voice onset time (VOT) and the onset frequency of the first formant (F1OF). These dimensions replaced the voicing and burst amplitude dimensions used in all of the other simulations. Figure 14 illustrates how F1OF tends to increase as voice onset time is delayed.

Summerfield and Haggard (1977) have shown that subjects are sensitive both to VOT and to F1OF and that it is possible to trade one of these cues off against the other. Thus, the boundary between /ga/ and /ka/ shifts to longer VOTs when F1 starts off lower rather than higher.

Categorical perception and trading relations among cues have been studied on a variety of different continua by a variety of different investigators. We have chosen to focus on the VOT and F1OF features, as exemplified by the /ga/−/ka/ continuum, because there is data on trade-offs between these cues (Summerfield & Haggard, 1977), and because

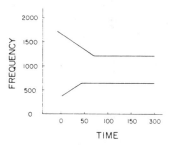

FIG. 14. Schematic diagram of a syllable that will be heard as /ga/ or /ka/, depending on the point in the syllable at which voicing begins. Prior to the onset of voicing, F2 (top curve) is energized by aperiodic noise sources, and F1 is "cut back" (the noise source has little or no energy in this range). Because of the fact that F1 rises over time after syllable onset (as the vocal tract moves from a shape consistent with the consonant into a shape consistent with the vowel), its frequency at the onset of voicing is higher for later values of VOT. Parameters used in constructing this schematic syllable are derived from Kewley-Port's (1982) analysis of the parameters of formants in natural speech, and are similar to those used in many perceptual experiments.

several categorical perception studies of VOT continua (using /g/–/k/, /d/–/t/, or /b/–/p/ stimuli) have covaried both VOT and F1OF, if only because F1OF tends to covary with VOT when realistic stimuli are used (e.g., Pisoni & Lazarus, 1974; Samuel, 1977). Though the simulations use a /g/–/k/ continuum, we consider several categorical perception experiments using /d/–/t/ and /b/–/p/ continua, since the same dimensions can differentiate the two members of both of these other pairs. We also consider data obtained in experiments on other continua, using other cues. We could easily have repeated the simulations with other sets of continua; however, the general qualitative form of the results would be the same. What would vary from case to case would be the magnitude of the effect of a step along a given dimension.

The pattern of excitatory input to the VOT and F1OF detectors produced by the canonical mock speech /g/ and /k/ used in the simulations are illustrated in Fig. 15.

Trading relations. TRACE quite naturally tends to produce trading relations between features, since it relies on the weighted sum of the excitatory inputs to determine how strongly the input will activate a particular phoneme unit. All else being equal, the phoneme unit receiving the largest sum bottom-up excitation will be more strongly activated than any other, and will therefore be the most likely response when a choice must be made between one phoneme and another. Since the net bottom-up input is just the sum of all of the inputs, no one input is necessarily decisive in this regard.

Generally, experiments demonstrating trading relations between two or more cues manipulate each of the cues over a number of values ranging between a value more typical of one of two phonemes and a value more typical of the other. Summerfield and Haggard did this for VOT and F1OF, and found the typical result, namely that the value of one cue that gives rise to 50% choices of /k/ was affected by the value of the other cue: the higher the value of F1OF, the shorter the value of VOT needed for 50% choices of /k/. Unfortunately, they did not present full curves relating phoneme identification to the values used on each of the two dimensions. In lieu of this, we present curves in Fig. 16 from a classic trading relations experiment, by Denes (1955). Similar patterns of results have been reported in other studies, using other cues (e.g., Massaro, 1981, Figs. 4 and 5), though the transitions are often somewhat steeper (see below for a discussion of the issue of steepness). We have chosen to present the shallower curves reported by Denes because in them we see clearly that there are cases in which a cue that favors one of the two phonemes to a moderate degree will give rise to the perception of the other phoneme when paired up with a strong cue that favors the other

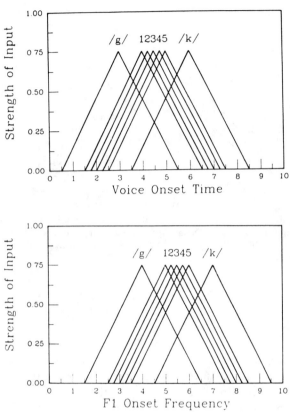

FIG. 15. Canonical feature-level input for /g/ and /k/, on the two dimensions that distinguish them, and the patterns used for the five intermediate values used in the trading relations simulation. Along the abscissa of each dimension the nine units for the nine different value ranges of the dimension are arrayed. The curves labeled /g/ and /k/ indicate the relative strength of the excitatory input to each of these units, produced by the indicated phoneme. The canonical curves also indicate the strengths of the feature-to-phoneme connections for /g/ and /k/ on these dimensions. That is, the canonical input pattern for each phoneme exactly matches the strengths of the corresponding feature–phoneme connections. Numbered curves on each dimension show the feature patterns used in the trading relations simulation.

phoneme. An additional finding is the bowing of the curves; they tend to be approximately linear through the middle of their range, but to level off at both ends, where the values on both dimensions agree in pointing to one alternative or the other.

To see if TRACE would simulate the basic trade-off effect obtained by Summerfield and Haggard, and to see if it would produce the same shape

40   MC CLELLAND AND ELMAN

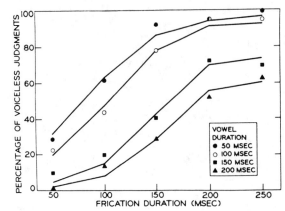

FIG. 16. Results of an experiment demonstrating the trade-off between two cues to the identity of /s/ and /z/. Data from Denes, 1955, fitted by the model of Massaro and Cohen, 1977. ●, 50 ms; ○, 100 ms; ■, 150 ms; ▲, 200 ms. Reprinted with permission from Massaro and Cohen (1977).

trade-off curves as have been generally reported, we generated a set of 25 intermediate phonetic segments made up by pairing each of five different intermediate patterns on the VOT dimension with each of five different intermediate patterns on the F1OF dimension. The different feature patterns used on each dimension are shown in Fig. 15, along with the canonical feature patterns for /g/ and /k/ on each of the two dimensions. On the remaining five dimensions, the intermediate segments all had the common canonical feature values for /g/ and /k/.

The model was tested with each of the 25 stimuli, preceded by silence (/–/) and followed by /a–/. In this and all subsequent simulations we report in this paper, the peak of the initial silence phoneme occurred at Time Slice 6 in the input, and the peaks of successive phoneme segments occurred at six slice intervals. Thus, for these stimuli, the peak on the intermediate phonetic segment occurred at Slice 12, the peak of the following vowel occurred at Slice 18, and the peak of the final silence occurred at Slice 24. For each input presented, the interactive activation process was allowed to continue through a total of 60 time slices, well past the end of the input. The state of the Trace at various points in processing, for the most /g/-like of the 25 stimuli, is shown in Fig. 17. At the end of the 60th time slice, we recorded the activation of the units for /g/ and /k/ in Time Slice 12 and the probability of choosing /g/ based on these activations. (It makes no difference to the qualitative appearance of the results if a different decision time is used; earlier decision times are associated with smaller differences in relative activation between the /g/ and /k/ phoneme units, and later ones with larger differences, but the general pattern is the same.)

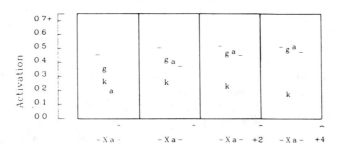

FIG. 17. The state of the Trace at various points during and after the presentation of a syllable consisting of the most /g/-like of the 25 intermediate segments used in the trading relations experiment, represented by /X/, preceded by silence and followed by /a/, then another silence.

Response probabilities were computed using the formulas given earlier for converting activations to response strengths and strengths into probabilities. The resulting response probabilities, for each of the 25 conditions of the experiment, are shown in Fig. 18. The pattern of results is quite similar to that obtained in Denes (1955) experiment on the /s/–/z/ continuum. The contribution of each cue is approximately linear and additive in the middle of the range, but the curves flatten out at the extremes, as in the Denes (1955) experiment. More importantly, the model's behavior exhibits the ability to trade one cue off against another. For example, there are three different combinations of feature values which lead to a probability between .82 and .85 of choosing /k/: (1) the neutral value of the VOT dimension coupled with the most /k/-like value on the F1OF dimension; (2) the neutral value on the F1OF dimension coupled with the most /k/-like value of the VOT dimension; and (3) the somewhat

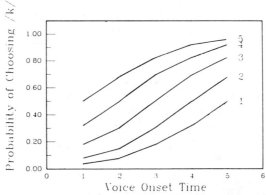

FIG. 18. Simulated probability of choosing /k/ at Time Slice 60, for each of the 25 stimuli used in the trading relations simulation experiment. Numbers next to each curve refer to the intermediate pattern on the F1OF continuum used in the five stimuli contributing to each curve. Higher numbers correspond to higher values of F1OF.

/k/-like values on both dimensions. In terms of Summerfield and Haggard's measure, the value of VOT needed to achieve 50% probability of reporting /k/, we can see that the VOT needed increases as the F1OF decreases, just as these investigators found.

Cue trade-offs in phoneme identification are accounted for in detail by the feature integration model of Oden and Massaro (1978; Massaro, 1981; Massaro and Oden, 1980a, 1980b). While we have shown how TRACE can account for the basic trade-off effect and the general form of the trade-off curves, we have not yet attempted the kinds of detailed fits that Massaro, Oden, and collaborators have reported in a number of studies. However, the models are quite similar, so it seems rather unlikely that cue trade-off data would be able to discriminate between them. And both make special assumptions about lack of invariance of cues to phoneme identity across contexts.

One apparent dissimilarity between the models deserves comment. Whereas cue strengths are combined multiplicatively in the determination of response strengths in the feature integration model, they are combined additively in the bottom-up inputs to the units in TRACE. However, in TRACE, two further computational steps take place before these inputs result in response strengths. First, the interactive-activation process enhances differences between competing units. Second, the resulting unit activations are subjected to an exponential transformation. Just this second step by itself would transform influences that have additive effects on unit activations into influences that have multiplicative effects on response strength. Thus, the models would be mathematically equivalent if the interactive activation process were simply replaced by a linear, additive combination of inputs to the units. In quantitative formulations of the interactive activation process closely related to the ones we use (Grossberg, 1978), what the interactive activation process does is simply rescale the unit activations, preserving the ratios of their bottom-up activation but keeping them bounded. Though our version of these equations does not do this exactly, the ways in which it deviates from this would be difficult to use as the basis for an empirical distinction between the TRACE approach and the feature integration model. Thus, up to a point, we can see TRACE as (approximately) implementing the computations specified in Oden and Massaro's model. The models differ, though, in that TRACE is dynamic and in that it incorporates feedback to the phoneme level. This allows TRACE to account for categorical perception in a different way.

Categorical perception. In spite of the fact that TRACE is quite flexible in the way it combines information from different features to determine the identity of a phoneme, the model is quite categorical in its overt responses. This is illustrated in two ways: first, the model shows a much sharper transition in its choices of responses as we move from /g/ to /k/

along the VOT and F1OF dimensions than we would expect from the slight changes in the relative excitation of the /g/ and /k/ units. Second, the model tends to obliterate differences between different inputs which it identifies as the same phoneme, while sharpening differences between inputs assigned to different categories. We will consider each of these two points in turn, after we describe the stimuli used in the simulations.

Eleven different consonant feature patterns were used, embedded in the same simulated /–a–/ context as in the trading relations simulation. The stimuli varied from very low values of both VOT and F1OF, more extreme than the canonical /g/, through very high values on both dimensions, more extreme than the canonical /k/. All the stimuli were spaced equal distances apart on the VOT and F1OF dimensions. The locations of the peak activation values on each of these two continua are shown in Fig. 19.

Figure 20 indicates the relative initial bottom-up activation of the /g/ and /k/ phoneme units for each of the 11 stimuli used in the simulation. The first thing to note is that the relative bottom-up excitation of the two phoneme units differ only slightly. For example, the canonical feature pattern for /g/ sends 75% as much excitation to /g/ as it sends to /k/. The feature pattern two steps toward /g/ from /k/ (Stimulus 5), sends 88% as much activation to /g/ as to /k/.

The figure also indicates, in the second panel, the resulting activations

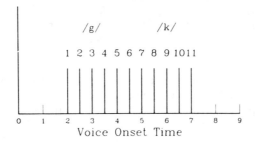

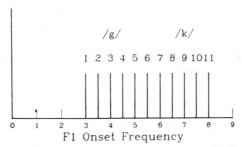

FIG. 19. Locations of peak activations along the VOT and F1OF dimensions, for each of the 11 stimuli used in the categorical perception simulation.

44   MC CLELLAND AND ELMAN

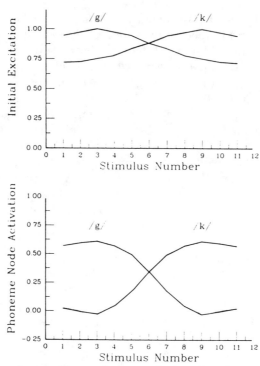

FIG. 20. Effects of competition on phoneme activations. The first panel shows relative amounts of bottom-up excitatory input to /g/ and /k/ produced by each of the 11 stimuli used in the categorical perception simulation. The second panel shows the activations of units for /g/ and /k/ at Time Cycle 60. Stimuli 3 and 9 correspond to the canonical /g/ and /k/, respectively.

of the units for /g/ and /k/ at the end of 60 cycles of processing. The slight differences in net input have been greatly amplified, and the activation curves exhibit a much steeper transition than the relative bottom-up excitation curves.

There are two reasons why the activation curves are so much sharper than the initial bottom-up excitation functions. The primary reason is *competitive inhibition*. The effect of the competitive inhibition at the phoneme level is to greatly magnify the slight difference in the excitatory inputs to the two phonemes. It is easy to see why this happens. Once one phoneme is slightly more strongly activated than the other, it exerts a stronger inhibitory influence on the other than the other can exert on it. The net result is that "the rich get richer." This general property of competitive inhibition mechanisms was discussed by McClelland and Rumelhart (1981), following earlier observations by Grossberg (see Grossberg, 1978, for a discussion) and Levin (1976); it is also well known as one possible basis of edge enhancement effects in low levels of visual information processing. A second cause of the sharpening of the activation curves is the phoneme-to-feature feedback, which we consider in detail in a moment.

The identification functions that result from applying the Luce choice rule to the activation values shown in the second panel of Fig. 20 are shown in Fig. 21 along with the *1BX* discrimination function, which is discussed below. The identification functions are even sharper than the activation curves; there is only a 4% chance that the model will choose /k/ instead of /g/ for Stimulus 5, for which /k/ receives 88% as much bottom-up support as /g/. The increased sharpness is due to the properties of the response strength assumptions. These assumptions essentially implement the notion that the sensitivity of the decision mechanism, in terms of d' for choosing the most strongly activated of two units, is a linear function of the difference in activation of the two units. When the activations are far enough apart, d' will be sufficient to ensure near-100% correct performance, even though both units have greater than 0 activation. Of course, the amount of separation in the activations that is necessary for any given level of performance is a matter of parameters; the relevant parameter here is the scale factor used in the exponential transformation of activations. The value used for this parameter in the present simulations (10) was the same as that used in all other cases where we translate activation into response probability, including the trading relations simulation.

Some readers may be puzzled as to why TRACE II exhibits a sharp identification function in the categorical perception experiment, but shows a much more gradual transition between /g/ and /k/ in the trading relations simulation. The reason is simply that finer steps along the VOT and F1OF continua were used in the trading relations simulation. All of the stimuli for the trading relations simulation lie between Stimuli 6 and 4 in the categorical perception simulation.

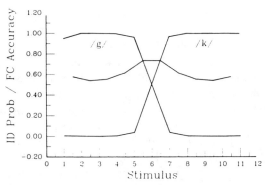

FIG. 21. Simulated identification functions and forced-choice accuracy in the *ABX* task.

This obviously brings out the fact that the apparent steepness of the identification function depends on the grain of the sampling of different points along the continuum between two stimuli, as well as a host of other factors (Lane, 1965). Whether an empirical or simulated identification function looks steep or not depends on the selection of stimuli by the experimenter or modeler. However, it is worth noting that the steepness of the identification function is independent of the presence of trading relations, at least in the simulation model. That is, if we had used more widely separated steps along the VOT and F1OF dimension, we would have obtained much steeper identification functions. The additivity of excitatory inputs would still apply, and thus it would still be possible to trade cues off against each other.

In TRACE, the categorical output of the model comes about only after an interactive competition process that greatly sharpens the differences in the activation of the detectors for the relevant units. This interactive process takes time. In the simulation results reported here, we assumed that subjects waited a fixed time before responding. But, if we assume that subjects are able to respond as soon as the response strength ratio reaches some criterial level, we would find that subjects would be able to respond more quickly to stimuli near the prototype of each category than they can to stimuli near the boundary. This is exactly what was found by Pisoni and Tash (1974).

The sharpening the model imposes on the identification function, in conjunction with the fact that it can trade one feature off against another, shows how the model, like human perceivers of speech, can be both flexible and decisive at the same time. These aspects of TRACE are shared with the feature integration model (Massaro, 1981). However, the TRACE model's decisiveness extends even further than we have observed thus far; feedback from the phoneme to the feature level tends to cause the model to obliterate the differences between input feature patterns that result in the identification of the same phoneme, thus allowing the model to provide an account not only for sharp identification functions, but also for the fact that discriminability of speech sounds is far poorer within categories than it is between categories.

Strictly speaking, at least as defined by Liberman, Cooper, Shankweiler, and Studdert-Kennedy (1967), true categorical perception is only exhibited when the ability to discriminate different sounds is no better than could be expected based on the assumption that the only basis a listener has for discrimination is the categorical assignment of the stimulus to a particular phonetic category. However, it is conceded that "true" categorical perception in this sense is never in fact observed (Studdert-Kennedy, Liberman, Harris, & Cooper, 1970). While it is true that the discrimination of sounds is much better for sounds which perceivers assign to different categories than for sounds they assign to the same category, there is also at least a tendency for discrimination to be somewhat better than predicted by the identification function, even between stimuli which are always assigned to the same category. TRACE II produces this kind of approximate categorical perception.

The way it works is this. When a feature pattern comes in, it sends more excitation to some phoneme units than others; as they become active, they begin to compete, and one gradually comes to dominate the others. This much we have already observed. But as this competition process is going on, there is also feedback from the phoneme level to the feature level. Thus, as a particular phoneme becomes active, it tends to impose its canonical pattern of activation on the feature level. The effect of the feedback becomes particularly strong as time goes on, since the feature input only excites the feature units very briefly; the original pattern of activation produced by the phoneme units is, therefore, gradually replaced by the canonical pattern imposed by the feedback from the phoneme level. The result is that the pattern of activation remaining at the feature level after 60 cycles of processing has become assimilated to the prototype. In this way, feature patterns for different inputs assigned to the same category are rendered nearly indistinguishable.

An impression of the magnitude of this effect is illustrated in Fig. 22, which shows how different the feature patterns of adjacent stimuli are at the end of 60 cycles of processing. The measure of difference is simply $1 - r_{ab}$, where r_{ab} stands for the correlation of the patterns produced by stimuli a and b. Only the two dimensions which actually differ between the canonical /g/ and /k/ are considered in the difference measure. Furthermore, the correlation considers only the feature pattern on the feature

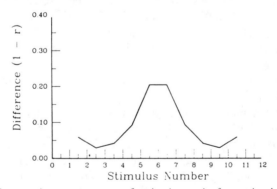

FIG. 22. Differences between patterns of activation at the feature level at Cycle 60, for pairs of stimuli one step apart along the /g/–/k/ continuum used for producing the identification functions shown previously in Fig. 21. The difference measure is the correlation of the two patterns, subtracted from 1.0; thus, if the two patterns correlated perfectly, their difference would be 0.

units in Time Slice 12, right at the center of the input specification. If all dimensions are considered, the values of the difference measure are reduced overall, but the pattern is the same. Inclusion of feature patterns from surrounding slices likewise makes little difference.

To relate the difference between two stimuli to probability correct choice performance in the *ABX* task generally used in categorical perception experiments, we once again use the Luce (1959) choice model. The probability of identifying stimulus *x* with alternative *a* in is given by

$$p(R_{(x=a)}) = \frac{S_{ax}}{S_{ax} + S_{bx}},$$

where S_{ax} is the "strength" of the similarity between *a* and *x*. This is given simply by the exponential of the correlation of *a* and *x*:

$$S_{ax} = e^{k_r r_{ax}},$$

and similarly for S_{bx}. (The exponential transformation is required to translate correlations, ranging from +1 to −1, into positive values, so that Luce's ratio rule can be used. The same transformation is used for translating activations into response strengths in identification tasks.) Here k_r is the parameter that scales the relation between correlations and strengths. These assumptions are consistent with the choice assumptions made for identification responses. The resulting response probabilities, for one choice of the parameter k_r (5) are shown in Fig. 21 (the exponentiation parameter k_r is different than the parameter k used in generating identification probabilities from activations because correlations and activations are not on equivalent scales).

Basically, the figure shows that the effect of feedback is to make the feature patterns for inputs well within each category more similar than those for inputs near the boundary between categories. Differences between stimuli near the prototype of the same phoneme are almost obliterated. When two stimuli straddle the boundary, the feature-level patterns are much more distinct. As a result, the probability of correctly discriminating stimuli within a phoneme category is much lower than the probability of discriminating stimuli in different categories.

The process of "canonicalization" of the representation of a speech sound via the feedback mechanism takes time. During this time, two things are happening: one is that the activations initially produced by the speech input are decaying; another is that the feedback, which drives the representation toward the prototype, is building up. In the simulations, we allowed a considerable amount of time for these processes before computing similarities of different activation patterns to each other. Obviously, if we had left less time, there would not have been as much of an opportunity for these forces to operate. Thus, TRACE is in agreement with the finding that there tends to be an increase in within-category discrimination when a task is used which allows subjects to base their responses on judgments of the similarity of stimuli spaced closely together in time (Pisoni & Lazarus, 1974).

It should be noted that it would be possible to account for categorical perception in TRACE without invoking feedback from the phoneme level to the feature level. All we would need to do is assume that the feature information that gives rise to phoneme identification is inaccessible, as proposed by the motor theory of speech perception (Liberman et al., 1967), or is rapidly lost as proposed by the "dual-code" model (Fujisaki & Kawashima, 1968; Massaro, 1975, 1981; Pisoni, 1973, 1975.) The dual-code model, which has had considerable success accounting for categorical perception data, assumes that phoneme identification can be based either on precategorical information or on the results of the phoneme identification process. Since it is assumed that feature information decays rapidly (especially for consonant features—see below), responses must often be based solely on the output of the phoneme identification process, which is assumed to provide a discrete code of the sequence of phonemes. This interpretation accounts for much of the data on categorical perception quite well. Indeed, it is fairly difficult to find ways of distinguishing between a feedback model and one that attributes categorical perception to a loss of information from the feature level coupled with a reliance on a more abstract code. Both feedback models and dual code models can accommodate the fact that vowels show less of a tendency toward categorical perception than consonants (Fry, Abramson, Eimas, & Liberman, 1962; Pisoni, 1973). It is simply necessary to assume that vowel features are more persistent than consonant features (Crowder, 1978, 1981; Fujisaki & Kawashima, 1968; Pisoni, 1973, 1975). However, the two classes of interpretations do differ in one way. The feedback account seems to differ most clearly from a limited feature access account in its predictions of performance in discriminating two stimuli, both away from the center of a category, but still within it. Here, TRACE tends to show greater discrimination than it shows between stimuli squarely in the middle of a category.

Standard interpretations of categorical perception can account for increases in discriminability near the boundary between two categories (where identification may in fact be somewhat variable), simply in terms of the fact that marginal stimuli are more likely to give rise to different category labels. But TRACE can account for increases in discriminability at extreme values of feature continua which would not give rise to different category labels. In TRACE, the reason for this increase in discriminability is that the activation of the appropriate item at the phoneme level is weaker, and therefore the feedback signal is weaker, than it is when the input occurs near the center of the category. For example, Stimulus 1 in our simulations falls below the canonical /g/ stimulus, and therefore activates the /g/ phoneme detector less strongly than stimuli closer to the canonical /g/. A similar thing happens with the /k/. This results in less "canonicalization" of the extreme stimuli, and produces a "W"-shaped discrimination function, as shown in Fig. 22.

There is some evidence bearing on this aspect of TRACE's account of categorical perception. Samuel (1977) has reported *ABX* discrimination data that show noticeable minima in the discrimination function near the canonical stimuli within each category on a /d/–/t/ continuum. Indeed, Samuel's account of this effect, though not couched in terms of interactive activation processes, has a great deal of similarity to what we see in TRACE; he suggests that near-canonical items are more strongly assimilated to the canonical pattern. Unfortunately the effect we seek is fairly subtle, and so it will be difficult to separate from noise. In Samuel's experiment, the effect is fairly clear-cut at both extremes of the VOT continuum in three observers at the end of extensive training, as shown in Fig. 23, and even unpracticed subjects tend to show the effect toward the high end of the VOT continuum, well past the prototype for /t/.

In summary, TRACE appears to provide a fairly accurate account of the phenomena of cue trade-offs and categorical perception of speech sounds. It accounts for categorical perception without relying on the notion that the phenomenon depends on readout from an abstract level of processing; it assumes instead that the feature level, like other levels of the system, is subject to feedback from higher levels which actually changes the representation as it is being retained in memory, pushing it toward a canonical representation of the phoneme most strongly activated by the input.

Other Phenomena at the Phoneme Level

The literature on phoneme perception includes several further findings we have not yet been able to consider in detail. The next few paragraphs consider one of these findings and how it might be accommodated in the TRACE model.

Effects of global and local context on phoneme identification. In our simulations of trading relations, we have shown that the criterial value needed on one dimension of stimulus variation can be affected by other dimensions. Thus, when the onset of F1 is relatively high, shorter voicing latencies are needed to perceive a sound as unvoiced. Other factors also influence the phoneme perceived as a result of a particular featural input.

TRACE MODEL   51

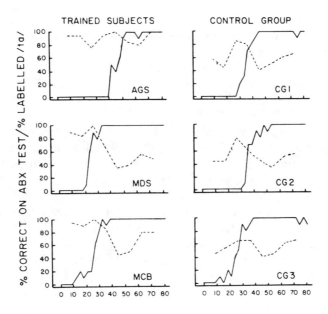

VOICE ONSET TIME (msec)

FIG. 23. Identification (solid curves) and *ABX* discrimination data (dashed curves) from three practiced and three naive subjects. Simplified and reprinted, with permission, from Samuel (1977).

The identity of phonemes surrounding a target phoneme, the rate of speech of a syllable in which a particular feature value occurs, as well as characteristics of the speaker and the language being spoken all influence the interpretations of features. See Repp and Liberman (1984) for a discussion of all of these sorts of influences on the boundaries between phonemes.

It has been suggested by Miller, Green, and Schermer (1984) and by Repp and Liberman (1984) that these different effects may have different sources. In particular, Miller et al. (1984) suggest that lexical effects and semantic and syntactic influences on the one hand may be due to a different mechanism than influences such as speech rate and coarticulatory influences due to local phonetic context.

The assumptions we have incorporated into TRACE make a similar distinction. In TRACE I, we have accounted for effects of phonetic context by allowing activations of units to influence the feature-to-phoneme connections in adjacent time slices (see Elman & McClelland, in press, for details). In the discussion, we consider ways of extending the connection modulation idea to accommodate effects of variations in rate and speaker parameters. Our main point here is that connection modulation is quite a different mechanism than the simple additive combination of excitatory influences that underlies the way TRACE accounts for trade-offs among the cues to a single phoneme or for the effects of top-down influences on the phoneme boundary.

Summary of Phoneme Identification Simulations

We have considered a number of phenomena concerning the identification and perception of phonemes. These include lexical influences on phoneme identification, and the lack thereof, both in reaction time and in response choice measures; "phonotactic rule" effects on phoneme identification and the role of specific lexical items in influencing these effects; the integration of multiple cues to phoneme identity and the categorical nature of the percept that results from this integration. TRACE integrates all of these phenomena into a single account that incorporates aspects of the accounts offered for particular aspects of these results by other models. In the next section, we show how TRACE can also encompass a number of phenomena concerning the recognition of spoken words.

THE TIME COURSE OF WORD RECOGNITION

The study of spoken word recognition has a long history, and many models have been proposed. Morton's now-classic logogen model (Morton, 1969) was the first to provide an explicit account of the integration of contextual and sensory information in word recognition. Other models of this period (e.g., Broadbent, 1967) concentrated primarily on effects of word frequency. Until the mid 1970s, however, there was little explicit consideration of the time course of spoken word recognition. Several studies by Marslen-Wilson and his collaborators (Marslen-Wilson, 1973; Marslen-Wilson & Tyler, 1975) and by Cole and his collaborators (Cole, 1973; Cole & Jakimik, 1978, 1980) pioneered the investigation of this problem.

Marslen-Wilson's COHORT model (Marslen-Wilson & Tyler, 1980; Marslen-Wilson & Welsh, 1978) of speech perception was based on this early work on the time course of spoken word recognition. The COHORT model was one of the sources of inspiration for TRACE, for two main reasons. First, it provided an explicit account of the way top-down and bottom-up information could be combined to produce a word recognition mechanism that actually worked in real time. Second, it accounted for the findings of a number of important experiments demonstrating the "on-line" character of the speech recognition process. However, several deficiencies of the COHORT model have been pointed out, as we shall see.

Because TRACE was motivated in large part by a desire to keep what is good about COHORT and improve upon its weaknesses, we begin this section by considering the COHORT model in some detail. First we review the basic assumptions of the model, then consider its strengths and weaknesses. There appear to be four basic assumptions of the COHORT model.

1. The model uses the first sound (in Marslen-Wilson & Tyler, 1980, the initial consonant cluster-plus-vowel) of the word to determine which words will be in an initial cohort or candidate set.

2. Once the candidate set is established, the model eliminates words from the cohort immediately, as each successive phoneme arrives, if the new phoneme fails to match the next phoneme in the word. Words can also be eliminated on the basis of semantic constraints, although the initial cohort is assumed to be determined by acoustic input alone.

3. Word recognition occurs immediately, as soon as the cohort has been reduced to a single member; in an auditory lexical decision task, the decision that an item is a nonword can be made as soon as there are no remaining members in the cohort.

4. Word recognition can influence the identification of phonemes in a word only after the word has been recognized.

There is a considerable body of data that supports various predictions of the COHORT model. It has been observed in a variety of paradigms that lexical influences on phoneme identification responses are much greater later in words than at their beginnings (Bagley, 1900; Cole and Jakimik, 1978, 1980; Marslen-Wilson, 1980; Marslen-Wilson and Welsh, 1978). We considered some of this evidence in earlier sections. Another important finding supporting COHORT is the fact that the reaction time to decide that an item is a nonword is constant, when measured from the occurrence of the first phoneme that rules out the last remaining word in the cohort (Marslen-Wilson, 1980).

Perhaps the most direct support for the basic word recognition assumptions of COHORT comes from the gating paradigm, introduced first by Grosjean (1980). In this paradigm, subjects are required to guess the identity of a word after hearing successive presentations of the word. The first presentation is cut off so that the subject hears only the first N ms ($N = 30$ to 50 in different studies). Later presentations are successively lengthened in N-ms increments until eventually the whole word is presented. The duration at which half the subjects correctly identify the word is called the "isolation point." Considerably more input is required before subjects are reasonably sure of the identity of the word; that point is termed the "acceptance point." Grosjean's initial study confirmed many basic predictions of COHORT, though it also raised a few difficulties for it (see below). In a more recent study using the same method, Tyler and Wessels (1983) carried out a very close analysis of the relation between the empirically determined isolation point and the point at which the input the subject has received is consistent with one and only one remaining item, the point at which recognition would be expected to occur in the COHORT model. They report that the isolation point falls very close to this theoretically derived recognition point, strongly supporting the basic immediacy assumptions of the COHORT model.

It should be noted that the gating task is not a timed task, and so it does not provide a direct measure of what the subject knows as the speech input is unfolding. However, it is now in fairly wide use, and Cotton and Grosjean (1984) have established that the basic patterns of results obtained in Grosjean's (1980) pioneering gating experiment do not depend on the presentation of successively longer and longer presentations of the same stimulus.

A dilemma for COHORT. Though the COHORT model accounts for a large body of data, there are several difficulties with it. We consider first the one that seems the most serious: as stated, COHORT requires accurate, undistorted information about the identity of the phonemes in a word up to the isolation point. Words cannot enter into consideration unless the initial consonant cluster plus vowel is heard, and they are discarded from it as soon as a phoneme comes along that they fail to match. No explicit procedure is described for recovering words into the cohort once they have been excluded from it, or when the beginning of the word is not accurately perceived due to noise or elision.

These aspects of COHORT make it very difficult for the model to explain recognition of words with distorted beginnings, such as ''dwibble'' (Norris, 1982), or words whose beginnings have been replaced by noise (Salasso & Pisoni, 1985). From a computational point of view, this makes the model an extremely brittle one; in particular it fails to deal with the problem of noise and underspecification which is so crucial for recognition of real speech (Thompson, 1984).

The recognizability of distorted items like ''dwibble'' might be taken as suggesting that what we need to do is liberalize the criterion for entering and retaining words in the cohort. Thus, the cohort could be defined as the set of words consistent with what has been heard or mild (e.g., one or two features) deviations from what has been heard. This would allow mild distortions like replacing /r/ with /w/ not to disqualify a word from the cohort. It would also allow the model to cope with cases where the beginning of the word is underspecified; in these cases, the initial cohort would simply be larger than in the case where the input clearly specified the initial phonemes.

However, there is still a problem. Sometimes we need to be able to rule out items which mismatch the input on one or two dimensions and sometimes we do not. Consider the items ''pleasant'' and ''blacelet.'' In the first case, we need to exclude ''present'' from the cohort, so the slight difference between /l/ and /r/ must be sufficient to rule it out; in the second case, we do not want to lose the word "bracelet," since it provides the best fit overall to the input. Thus, in this case, the difference between /l/ and /r/ must not be allowed to rule a word candidate out.

Thus the dilemma: on the one hand, we want a mechanism that will be able to select the correct word as soon as an undistorted input specifies it uniquely, to account for the Tyler and Wessels results. On the other hand, we do not want the model to completely eliminate possibilities which might later turn out to be correct. We shall shortly see that TRACE provides a way out of this dilemma.

Another problem for COHORT. Grosjean (1985) has recently pointed out another problem for COHORT, namely, the possibility that the subject may be uncertain about the location of the beginning of each successive word. A tacit assumption of the model is that the subject goes into the beginning of each word knowing that it is the beginning. In the related model of Cole and Jakimik (1980) this assumption is made explicit. Unfortunately, it is not always possible to know in advance where one word starts and the next word ends. As we discussed in the introduction, acoustic cues to juncture are not always reliable, and in the absence of acoustic cues, even an optimally efficient mechanism cannot always know that it has heard the end of one word until it hears enough of the next to rule out the possible continuations of the first word.

What is needed, then, is a model that can account for COHORT's successes, and overcome these two important deficiencies. The next two sections show that TRACE does quite well on both counts. The first of these sections examines TRACE's behavior in processing words whose beginnings and endings are clearly deliniated for it by the presence of silence. The second considers the processing of multiword inputs, which the model must parse for itself.

One Word at a Time

In this section we see how TRACE resolves the dilemma facing CO-HORT, in that it is immediately sensitive to new information but is still able to cope with underspecified or distorted word beginnings. We also consider how the model accounts for the preference for short-word responses early in processing a long word. The section concludes with a discussion of ways the model could be extended to account for word frequency and contextual influences.

Competition vs bottom-up inhibition. TRACE deals with COHORT's dilemma by using competition, rather than phoneme-to-word inhibition. The essence of the idea is simply this. Phoneme units have excitatory connections to all the word units they are consistent with. Thus, whenever a phoneme becomes active in a particular slice of the Trace, it sends excitation to all the word units consistent with that phoneme in that slice. The word units then compete with each other; items that contain each successive phoneme dominate all others, but if no word matches perfectly, a word that provides a close fit to the phoneme sequence can eventaully win out over words that provide less adequate matches. The exact metric of "closeness of fit" depends, of course, on a large number of details. In the absence of such a metric, a simple count of the number of acoustic features differing between a lexical item and a presented stimulus can provide a useful first approximation, but other factors such as stress, location of differences within the word, and discriminability of the differing features will of course come into play.

Consider, from this point of view, our two items "pleasant" and "blacelet" again. In the first instance, "pleasant" will receive more bottom-up excitation than "present," and so will win out in the competition. We have already seen, in our analysis of categorical perception at the phoneme level, how even slight differences in initial bottom-up excitation can be magnified by the joint effects of competition and feedback. But the real beauty of the competition mechanism is that this action is contingent on the activation of other word candidates. Thus, in the case of "blacelet", since there is no word "blacelet," "bracelet" will not be suppressed. Initially, it is true, words like "blame" and "blatant" will tend to dominate "bracelet," but since the input matches "bracelet" better than any other word, "bracelet" will eventually come to dominate the other possibilities.

This behavior of the model is illustrated using examples from its restricted lexicon in Fig. 24. In one case, the input is "legal," and the word "regal" is completely dominated by "legal." In the other case, the input is "lugged," and the word "rugged" eventually dominates, because there is no word "lugged" (pronounced to rhyme with "rugged"—the word "lug" is not in the model's lexicon). Here "rugged" must compete with other partial matches of "lugged," of course, and it is less effective in this regard than it would be if the input exactly matched it, but it does win out in the end.

It should be noted that the details of what word will be most strongly activated in such cases depend on a number of factors, including, in particular, the distinctiveness of mismatching phonemes. Also, it is possible to find cases in which a word that correctly spans a part of a longer string dominates a longer word that spans the whole string but misses out on a phoneme in one place or another. An item like "vigorette" may or may not be a case in point. In such cases, though, the most important thing might not turn out to be winning and losing, but rather the fact that both tend to stay in the game. Such neologisms can suggest a poetic

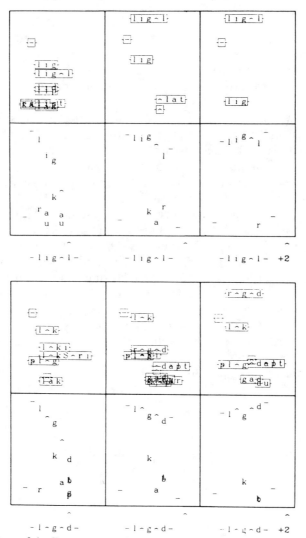

Fig. 24. State of the Trace at two points during processing of "legal" and "lugged."

conjunction of meanings, if used just right: "He walked briskly down the street, puffing his vigorette."

Time course of word recognition in TRACE. So far we have shown how TRACE overcomes a dificulty with the COHORT model in cases where the beginning of a word has been distorted. In earlier sections on phoneme processing, some of the simulations illustrate that the model is capable of recognizing words with underspecified (i.e., ambiguous) initial

58   MC CLELLAND AND ELMAN

phonemes. In this section, we examine how well TRACE emulates the
COHORT model, in cases where the input is an undistorted representation of some particular word. In particular, we wanted to see how close
TRACE would come to behaving in accord with COHORT's assumption
that incorrect words are dropped from the cohort of active candidates as
soon as the input diverges from them.

To examine this process, we considered the processing of the
word "product" (/prad^ct/). Figure 25 shows the state of the Trace at
various points in processing this word, and Fig. 26 shows the response
strengths of several units relative to the strength of the word "product"
itself, as a function of time relative to the arrival of the successive phonemes in the input. In this figure, the response strength of "product" is
simply set to 1.0 at each time slice and the response strengths of units
for other words are plotted in terms of the ratio of their strength, divided
by the strength of "product." The curves shown are for the words "trot,"
"possible," priest," "progress," and "produce"; these words differ
from the word "product" (according to the simulation program's stress-
less encoding of them!) in the 1st, 2nd, 3d, 4th, and 5th phonemes, respectively. Figure 26 shows that these items begin to drop out of "contention" just after each successive phoneme comes in. Of course, there
is nothing hard and fast or absolute about dropping a candidate in
TRACE. What we see instead is that mismatching candidates simply
begin to fade as the input diverges from them in favor of some other
candidate. This is just the kind of behavior the COHORT model would

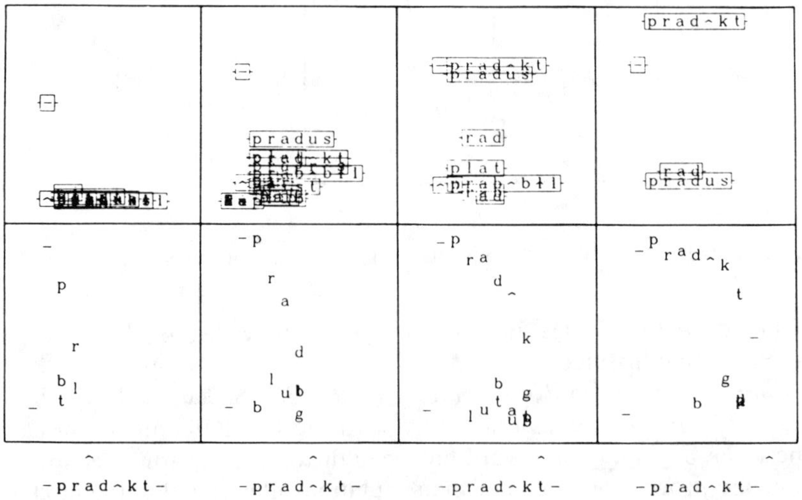

FIG. 25. State of the Trace at various points in processing the word "product" (/prad˙kt/).

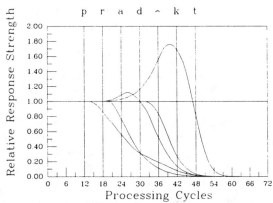

FIG. 26. Response strengths of the units for several words relative to the response strength of the unit for "product" (/prad'kt/), as a function of time relative to the peak of the first phoneme that fails to match the word. The successive curves coming off of the horizontal line representing the normalized response strength of "product" are for the words "trot," "possible," "priest," "progress," and "produce," respectively. In our lexicon they are rendered as /trat/, /pas'b'l/, /prist/, /pragr's/, and /pradus/, respectively.

produce in this case, though of course the drop-off would be assumed to be an abrupt, discrete event.[3]

There is one aspect of TRACE's behavior which differs from that of COHORT: among those words that are consistent with the input up to a particular point in time, TRACE shows a bias in favor of shorter words over longer words. Thus, "priest" has a slight advantage before the /a/ comes in, and "produce" is well ahead of "product" until the /ˆ/comes in (in phonemes, "produce" is one shorter than "product").

This advantage for shorter words is due to the competition mechanism. Recall that word units compete with each other in proportion to the overlap of the sets of time slices spanned by each of the words. Overlap is, of course, symmetrical, so long and short words inhibit each other to an equal extent. But longer words suffer more inhibition from other long words than short words do. For example, "progress" and "probable" inhibit "product" more than they inhibit "priest" and "produce." Thus, units for longer words are generally subjected to extra inhibition, particularly early on when many candidates are active, and so they tend to suffer in comparison to short words as a result.

---

[3] The data reported by Tyler and Wessels actually appears to indicate an even more immediate drop-off than is seen in this simulation. However, it should be remembered that the curves shown in Fig. 26 are on-line response strength curves, and thus reflect the lags inherent in the percolation of input from the feature to the word level. The gating task, on the other hand, does not require subjects to respond on-line. If the input is simply turned off at the peak of each phoneme's input specification, and then allowed to run free for a few cycles, the dropout point shifts even earlier.

We were at first somewhat disturbed by this aspect of the model's behavior, but it turns out to correspond quite closely with results obtained in experiments by Grosjean (1980) and Cotton and Grosjean (1984) using the gating paradigm. Both papers found that subjects hearing the beginnings of words like "captain" tended to report shorter words consistent with what they had heard (e.g., "cap"). However, we should observe that in the gating paradigm, when the word "captain" is truncated just after the /p/, it will sound quite a bit like "cap" followed by silence. In TRACE, this silence would activate silence units at the phoneme and word levels, and the word-level silence units would compete with units for words that extend into the silence. It will reinforce the preference of the model for short-word interpretations, because the detection of the silence will inhibit the detector for the longer word. Thus, there are actually two reasons why TRACE might favor short-word interpretations over long-word interpretations in a gating experiment. Whether human subjects show a residual preference for shorter interpretations over longer ones in the absence of a following silence during the course of processing is not yet clear from available data.

We should point out that the experimental literature indicates that the advantage of shorter words over longer ones holds only under the special circumstances of gated presentation and then only with early gates, when shorter words are relatively more complete than longer ones would be. It has been well known for a long time that longer words are generally more readily recognized than shorter ones when the whole word is presented for identification against a background of noise (Licklider & Miller, 1951). Presumably, the reason for this is simply that longer words generally provide a larger number of cues than shorter words do and hence are simply less confusable.

Frequency and context effects. There are, of course, other factors which influence when word recognition will occur beyond those we have considered thus far. Two very important ones are word frequency and contextual predictability. The literature on these two factors goes back to the turn of the century (Bagley, 1900). Morton's (1969) logogen model effectively deals with several important aspects of this huge literature, though not with the time course of these effects.

We have not yet included either word frequency or higher level contextual influences in TRACE, though of course we believe they are important. Word frequency effects could be accommodated, as they were in the interactive-activation model of word recognition, in terms of variation in the resting activation level of word units, or in terms of variation in the strength of phoneme-to-word connections. Contextual influences can be thought of as supplying activation to word units from even higher levels of processing than the word level. In this way, basic aspects of these two kinds of influences can be captured. We leave it to future research, however, to determine to what extent these elaborations of TRACE would provide a detailed account of the data on the roles of these factors. For now, we turn to the problem of determining where one word ends and the next one begins.

Lexical Basis of Word Segmentation

How do we know when one word ends and the next word begins? This is by no means an easy task, as we noted in the introduction. To recap our earlier argument, there are some cues in the speech stream, but as several investigators have pointed out (Cole & Jakimik, 1980; Grosjean & Gee, 1984; Thompson, 1984), they are not always sufficient, particularly in fluent speech. It would thus appear that there is an important role for lexical knowledge to play in determining where one word ends and the next word begins, as well as in identifying the objects that result from the process of segmentation. Indeed, as Reddy (1976) has suggested, segmentation and identification may be joint results of the mechanisms of word recognition.

Cole and Jakimik (1980) discuss these points and present evidence that semantic and syntactic context can guide segmentation in cases where the lexicon is consistent with two readings ("car go" vs "cargo"). Our present model lacks syntactic and semantic levels, so it cannot make use of these higher level constraints; but it can make use of its knowledge about words, not only to identify individual words in isolation, but to pick out a sequence of words in continuous streams of phonemes. Word identification and segmentation emerge together from the interactive-activation process, as part and parcel of the process of word activation.

This section considers several aspects of the way in which word segmentation emerges from the interactive-activation process, as observed in simulations with TRACE II. Before we consider these, it is worth recalling the details of some of the assumptions made about the bottom-up activation of word units and about competitive inhibition between word units. First, the extent to which a particular phoneme excites a particular word unit is independent of the length of the word. Second, the extent to which a particular word unit inhibits another word unit is proportional to the temporal overlap of the two word units. This means that words which do not overlap in time will not inhibit each other, but will gang up on other words that partially overlap each of them. These two assumptions form most of the basis of the effects we observe in the simulations.

The boundary is in the ear of the "behearer." First, we consider the basic fact that the number of words we hear in a sequence of phonemes can depend on our knowledge of the number of words the sequence makes. Consider the two utterances, "she can't" and "secant". Though we can say either item in a way that makes it sound like a single word or like two words, there is an intermediate way of saying them so that the first seems to be two words and the second seems like only one.

To see what TRACE II would do with single- and multiple-word inputs, we ran simulation experiments with each individual word in the main 211-word lexicon preceded and followed by silence, and then with 211 pairs of words, with a silence at the beginning and at the end of the entire stream. The pairs were made by simply permuting the lexicon twice and then abutting the two permutations so that each word occurred once as the first word and once as the second word in the entire set of 211 pairs. We stress, of course, that real speech would tend to contain cues that would mark word boundaries in many cases; the experiment is simply designed to show what TRACE would do in cases where these cues are lacking.

With the individual words, TRACE made no mistakes—that is, by a few slices after the end of the word, the word that spanned the entire input was more strongly activated than any other word. An example of this is shown using the item /parti/ in Fig. 27. The stream /parti/ might be either one word ("party") or two ("par tea" or "par tee"—the model knows of only one word pronounced /ti/). At early points in processing the word, "par" dominates over "party" and other longer words, for reasons discussed in the previous section. By the time the model has had a chance to process the end of the word, however, "party" comes to dominate.

Why does a single longer word eventually win out over two shorter

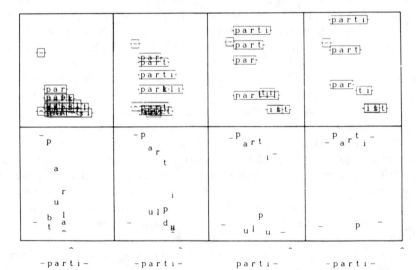

FIG. 27. The state of the Trace at various points during processing of /parti/.

ones in TRACE? There are two main reasons. First of all, a longer word eventually receives more bottom-up support than either shorter word, simply because there are more phonemes activating the longer word than the shorter word. The second reason has to do with the sequential nature of the input. In the case of /parti/, by the time the /ti/ is coming in, the word "party" is well enough established that it keeps /ti/ from getting as strongly activated as it would otherwise, as illustrated in Fig. 27. This behavior of the model leads to the prediction that short words embedded in the ends of longer words should not get as strongly activated as shorter words coming earlier in the longer word. This prediction could be tested using the gating paradigm, or a cross-modal priming paradigm such as the one used by Swinney (1982).

However, it should be noted that this aspect of the behavior of the model can be overridden if there is bottom-up information favoring the two-word interpretation. Currently, this can only happen in TRACE through the insertion of a brief silence between the "par" and the "tea." As shown in Fig. 28, this results in "par" and "tea" dominating all other word candidates.

What happens when there is no long word that spans the entire stream, as in /barti/? In this case, the model settles on the two-word interpretation "bar tea," as shown in Fig. 28. Note that other words, such as "art," that span a portion of the input, are less successful than either "bar" or "tea." The reason is that the interpretations "bar" and "art" overlap with each other, and "art" and "tea" overlap with each other, but "bar"

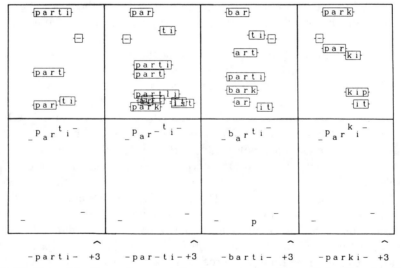

FIG. 28. State of the Trace after processing the streams /parti/, /par-ti/, /barti/, and /parki/.

and "tea" do not overlap. Thus, "art" receives inhibition from both "bar" and "tea," while "bar" and "tea" each receive inhibition only from "art." Thus two words that do not overlap with each other can gang up on a third each overlaps with partly and drive it out.

These remarkably simple mechanisms of activation and competition do a very good job of word segmentation, without the aid of any syllabification, stress, phonetic word boundary cues, or semantic and syntactic constraints. In 189 of the 211 word pairs tested in the simulation experiment, the model came up with the correct parse, in the sense that no other word was more active than either of the two words that had been presented. Some of the failures of the model occurred in cases where the input was actually consistent with two parses, either a longer spanning word rather than a single word (as in "party") or a different parse into two words, as in "part rust" for "par trust." In such cases TRACE tends to prefer parses in which the longer word comes first. There were, however, some cases in which the model did not come up with a valid parse, that is, a pattern that represents complete coverage of the input by a set of nonoverlapping words. For example, consider the input /parki/. Though this makes the two words "par" and "key," the word "park" has a stronger activation than either "par" or "key," as illustrated in Fig. 28.

This aspect of TRACE II's behavior indicates that the present version of the model is far from the final word on word segmentation. A complete model would also exploit syllabification, stress, and other cues to word identity to help eliminate some of the possible interpretations of TRACE II's simple phoneme streams. The activation and competition mechanisms in TRACE II are sufficient to do quite a bit of the word segmentation work, but we do not expect them to do this perfectly in all cases without the aid of other cues.

Some readers may be troubled by a mechanism that does not insist upon a parse in which each phoneme is covered by one and only one word. Actually, though, this characteristic of the model is often a virtue, since in many cases the last phoneme of a word must do double duty as the first phoneme of the next, as in "hound dog" or "brush shop." While speakers tend to signal the doubling in careful speech, the cues to single vs double consonants are not always sufficient for disambiguation, as is clear when strings with multiple interpretations are used as stimuli. For example, an utterance intended as "no notion" will sometimes be heard as "known notion" (Nakatani & Dukes, 1977). The model is not inclined to suppress activations of partially overlapping words, even when a nonoverlapping parse is available. This behavior of TRACE is illustrated with /bˆstap/ ("bus top" or "bus stop") in Fig. 29. In this case, higher levels could provide an additional source of information that would help the model choose between overlapping and nonoverlapping interpretations.

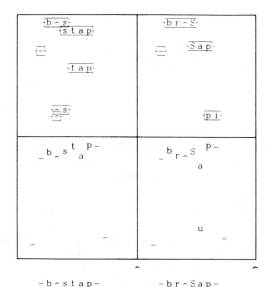

FIG. 29. State of the Trace at the end of the streams /bustap/ ("bus stop" or "bus top") and /bruSap/ ("brush shop").

The simulations we have reported show that the word activation/competition mechanism can go a long way toward providing a complete interpretation of the input stream as a sequence of words. As a word is beginning to come in, the model tends to prefer shorter words consistent with the input stream over longer ones. As the input unfolds through time, however, the model tends to prefer to interpret streams of phonemes as single longer words rather than as a sequence of short words; and it tends to find parses that account for each phoneme once. But it does not insist upon this, and will occasionally produce an interpretation that leaves part of the stream of phonemes unaccounted for or which accounts for part of the stream of phonemes twice. Often enough, it will also leave an alternative to its "preferred parse" in a strong position, so that both the preferred parse and the alternative would be available to higher levels and subject to possible reinforcement by them.

Thus far in this section, we have considered the general properties of the way in which TRACE uses lexical information to segment a speech stream into words, but we have not considered much in the way of empirical data that these aspects of the model shed light on. However, there are two findings in the literature which can be interpreted in accordance with TRACE's handling of multiword speech streams.

Where does a nonword end? A number of investigators (e.g., Cole & Jakimik, 1980) have suggested that when one word is identified, its identity can be used to determine where it ends and therefore where the next word begins. In TRACE, the interactive activation process can often establish where a word will end even before it actually does end, particularly in the case of longer words or when activations at the word level are aided by syntactic and semantic constraints. However, it is much harder to establish the end of a nonword, since the fact that it is a nonword means that we cannot exploit any knowledge of where it should end to do so.

This fact may account for the finding of Foss and Blank (1980) that subjects are much slower to respond to target phonemes at the beginning of a word preceded by a nonword than at the beginning of a word preceded by a word. For example, responses to detect word initial /d/ were faster in stimuli like the following:

At the end of last year, the government decided . . .

than they were when the word preceding the target (in this case government) was replaced by a nonword such as "gatabont." It should be noted that the targets were specified as word-initial segments. Therefore, the subjects had not only to identify the target phoneme, they had to determine that it fell at the beginning of a word, as well, The fact that reaction times were faster when the target was preceded by a word suggests that subjects were able to use their knowledge of where the word "government" ends to help them determine where the next word begins.

An example of how TRACE allows one word to help establish where its successor begins is illustrated in Fig. 30. In the example, the model receives the stream "possible target" or "pagusle target," and we imagine that the target is word-initial /t/. In the first case, the word "possible" is clearly established and competitors underneath it have been completely crushed by the time the initial /t/ in "target" becomes active at the phoneme level (second panel in the upper part of the figure), so there is no ambiguity about the fact that this /t/ is at the beginning of the next word. (The decision mechanism would, of course, be required to note that the model had established the location of the end of the preceding word. We have not yet incorporated explicit assumptions about how this would be done.) In the second case, words beginning and ending at a number of different places, including some that overlap with the location of the /t/, are partly activated. Thus, the subject would have to wait until he is well into the word "target" before it becomes clear that the first /t/ in target is in fact a word-initial /t/.

In reality, the situation is probably not as bleak for the perceiver as it appears in this example, because in many cases there will be cues in the manner of pronunciation and the syllabification of the input that will help to indicate the location of the word boundary. However, given the imprecision and frequent absence of such cues, it is not surprising that the

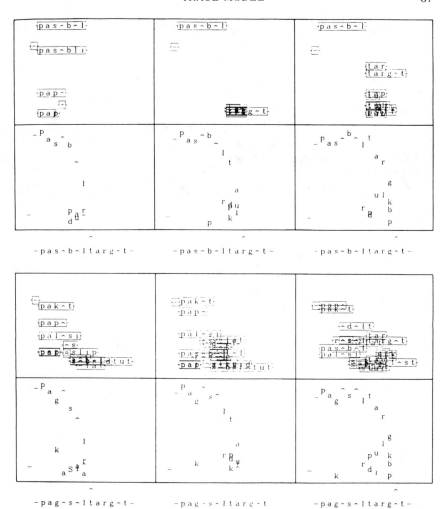

FIG. 30. State of the Trace at several points during the processing of "possible target" and "pagusle target."

lexical status of one part of a speech stream plays an important role in determining where the beginning of the next word must be.

The long and short of word identification. One problematic feature of speech is the fact that it is not always possible to identify a word unambiguously until one has heard the word after it. Consider, for example, the word "tar." If we are listening to an utterance and have gotten just to the /r/ in "The man saw the tar box," though "tar" will tend to be the preferred hypothesis at this point, we do not have enough information to say unequivocally that the word "tar" will not turn out to be "target" or "tarnished" or one of several other possibilities. It is only after more time has passed, and we have perceived either a silence or enough of the next word to rule out any of the continuations of /tar/, that we can decide we have heard the word "tar." This situation, as it arises in TRACE with the simple utterance /tarbaks/ ("tar box") is illustrated in Fig. 31. Though "tar" is somewhat more active than the longer word "target" when the /r/ is coming in, it is only when the word "box" emerges as the interpretation of the phonemes following "tar" that the rival "target" finally fades as a serious contender.

With longer words the situation is different. As we have already seen in another example, by the time the end of a longer word is reached it is

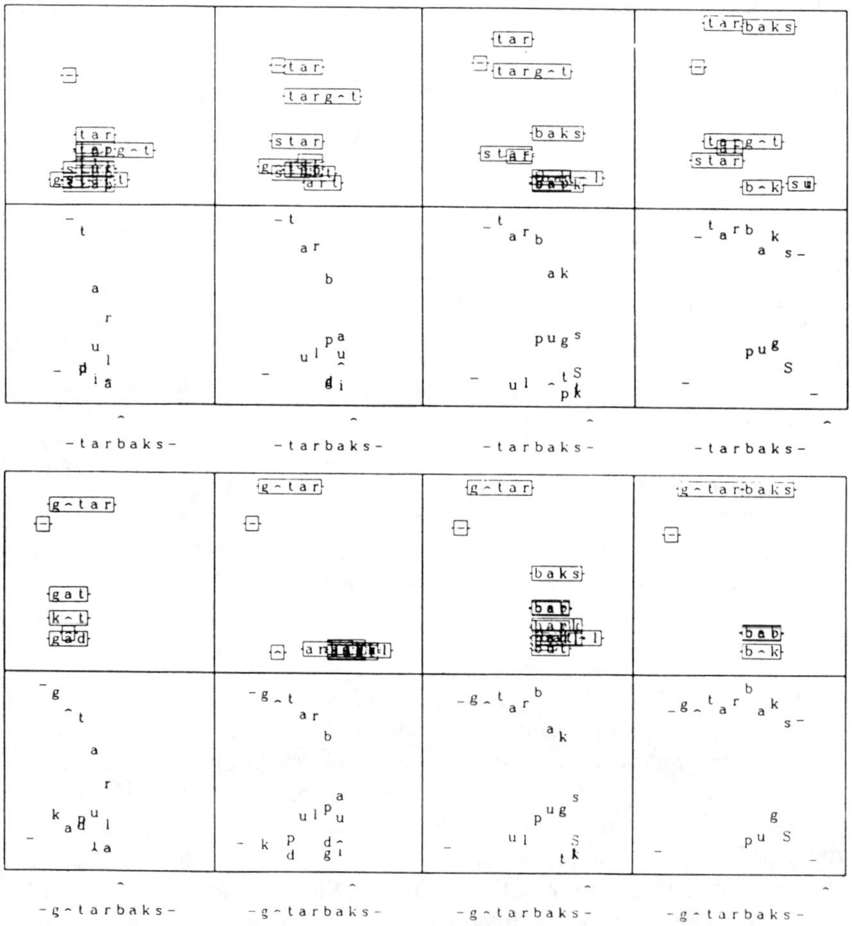

FIG. 31. State of the Trace at several points in processing "tar box" and "guitar box."

much more likely that only one word candidate will remain. Indeed, with longer words it is often possible to have enough information to identify the word unambiguously well before the end of the word. An illustration of this situation is provided by a simulation using the utterance "guitar box" /gˆtarbaks/. By the time the /r/ has registered, "guitar" is clearly dominant at the word level, and can be unambiguously identified without further ado.

Recently, an experiment by Grosjean (1985) has demonstrated these same effects empirically. Grosjean presented subjects with long or short words followed by a second word and measured how much of the word and its successor the subject needed to hear to identify the target. With longer words, subjects could usually guess the word correctly well before the end of the word, and by the end of the word they were quite sure of the word's identity. With monosyllabic words, on the other hand, many of the words could not be identified correctly until well into the next word. On the average, subjects were not sure of the word's identity until about the end of the next word, or the beginning of the one after. As Grosjean (1985) points out, a major reason for this is simply that the spoken input often does not uniquely specify the identity of a short word. In such cases, the perceptual system is often forced to process the short word, and its successor, at the same time.

Recognizing the words in a short sentence. One last example of TRACE II's performance in segmenting words is illustrated in Fig. 32. The figure shows the state of the Trace at several points during the processing of the stream /SiSˆtˆbaks/. By the end, the words of the phrase "She shut a box," which fits the input perfectly with no overlap, dominate all others.

This example illustrates how far it is sometimes possible to go in parsing a stream of phonemes into words, without even considering syntactic and semantic constraints, or stress, syllabification, and juncture cues to word identification. The example also illustrates the difficulty the model has in perceiving short, unstressed words like "a". This is, of course, just an extreme version of the difficulty the model has in processing monosyllabic words like "tar," and is consistent with Grosjean's data on the difficulty subjects have with identifying short words. In fact, Grosjean and Gee (1984) report pilot data indicating that these difficulties are even more severe with function words like "a" and "of." It should be noted that TRACE makes no special distinction between content and function words, per se, and neither do Grosjean and Gee. However, function words are usually unstressed and considerably shorter than content words. Thus, it is not necessary to point to any special mechanisms for closed versus open class morphemes to account for Grosjean and Gee's results.

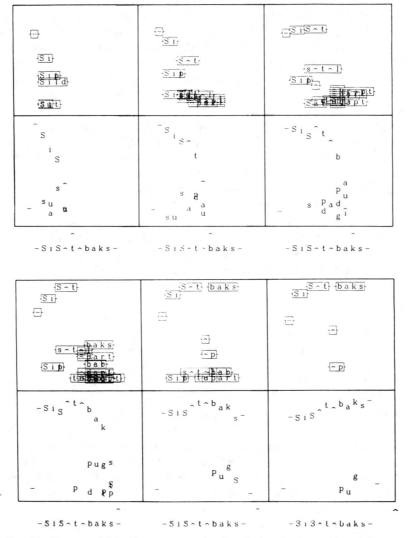

FIG. 32. The state of the Trace at several points during the processing of the stream /Sisˆtˆbaks/ (''She shut a box'').

Summary of Word Identification Simulations

While phoneme identification has been studied for many years, data from on-line studies of word recognition is just beginning to accumulate. There is an older literature on accuracy of word identification in noise, but it has only been quite recently that useful techniques have been developed for studying word recognition in real time.

What evidence there is, though indicates the complexity of the word identification process. While the word identification mechanism is sensitive to each new incoming phoneme as it arrives, it is nevertheless robust enough to recover from underspecification or distortion of word beginnings. And it appears to be capable of some simultaneous processing of successive words in the input stream. TRACE appears to capture these aspects of the time course of word recognition. In these respects, it improves upon the COHORT model, the only previously extant model that provides an explicit account of the on-line process of word recognition. And the mechanisms it uses to accomplish this are the same ones that it used for the simulations of the process of phoneme identification described in the preceding section.

GENERAL DISCUSSION

Summary of TRACE's Successes

In this article, we have seen that TRACE can account for a number of different aspects of human speech perception. We begin by listing the major correspondences between TRACE and what we know about the human speech understanding process.

1. TRACE, like humans, uses information from overlapping portions of the speech wave to identify successive phonemes.

2. The model shows a tendency toward categorical perception of phonemes, as do human subjects. The model's tendency toward categorical perception is affected by many of the same parameters which affect the degree of categorical perception shown by human subjects; in particular, the extent to which perception will be categorical increases with time between stimuli that must be compared.

3. The model combines feature information from a number of different dimensions, and exhibits cue trade-offs in phoneme identification. These characteristics of human speech perception have been demonstrated in a very large number of studies.

4. The model augments information from the speech stream with feedback from the lexical level in reaching decisions about the identity of phonemes. These lexical influences on phoneme identification occur in conditions similar to those in which lexical effects have been reported, but do not occur in conditions in which these effects have not been obtained.

5. Like human subjects, the model exhibits apparent phonotactic rule effects on phoneme identification, though it has no explicit representation of the phonotactic rules. The tendency to prefer phonotactically regular interpretations of ambiguous phonemes can be overridden by particular lexical items, just as it can in the human perceiver.

6. In processing unambiguous phoneme sequences preceded by si-

lence, the model exhibits immediate sensitivity to information favoring one word interpretation over another. It shows an initial preference for shorter words relative to longer words, but eventually a sequence of phonemes that matches a long word perfectly will be identified as that word, overturning the initial preference for the short-word interpretation. These aspects of the model are consistent with human data from gating experiments.

7. Though the model is heavily influenced by word beginnings, it can recover from underspecification or distortion of a word's beginning.

8. The model can use its knowledge of the lexicon to parse sequences of phonemes into words, and to establish where one word ends and the next one begins when cues to word boundaries are lacking.

9. Like human subjects, the model sometimes cannot identify a word until it has heard part of the next word. Also like human subjects, it can better determine where a word will begin when it is preceded by a word rather than a nonword.

10. The model does not demand a parse of a phoneme sequence that includes each phoneme in one and only one word. This allows it to cope gracefully with elision of phonemes at word boundaries. It will often permit several alternative parses to remain available for higher level influences to choose among.

In addition to these characteristics observed in the present paper, our simulations with TRACE I show several further correspondences between the model and human speech perception. Most important of these is the fact that the model is able to use activations of phoneme units in one part of the Trace to adjust the connection strengths determining which features will activate which phonemes in adjacent parts of the Trace. In this way the model can adjust as human subjects do to coarticulatory influences on the acoustic properties of phonemes (Fowler, 1984; Mann & Repp, 1980).

There is, of course, more data on some of these points than others. It will be very interesting to see how well TRACE will hold up against the data as further empirical studies are carried out.

Some of the Reasons for the Successes of TRACE

To what does the TRACE model owe its success in simulating human speech perception? Some of TRACE's successes simply depend on its ability to make use of the information as it comes it. For example, it fails to show context effects only when a response must be made, or can be made with high accuracy, before contextual information is available.

There are several other reasons for TRACE's success. One, we think, is the use of continuous activation and competition processes in place of discrete decisive processes such as segmentation and labeling. Activation and competition are matters of degree and protect TRACE from catastrophic commitment in marginal cases, and they provide a natural means for combining many different sources of information. Of course, this feature of the model is shared with several other models (e.g., Morton, 1969; Oden & Massaro, 1978), though only Nusbaum and Slowiaczek (1982) have previously incorporated these kinds of assumptions in a model of the time course of word recognition.

Part of the success of TRACE is specifically due to the use of competitive inhibitory interactions instead of bottom-up (or top-down) inhibition. Competition allows the model to select the best interpretation available, settling for an imperfect one when no better one is available, but overriding poor ones when a good one is at hand. These and other virtues of competitive inhibition have been noted before (e.g., Feldman & Ballard, 1982; Grossberg, 1973; Levin, 1976; Ratliff, 1965; von Bekesy, 1967) in other contexts. Their usefulness here attests to the general utility of the competitive inhibition mechanism.

The elimination of between-level inhibition from the interactive activation mechanism puts us in a very nice position with respect to one general critique of interactive-activation models. It is often said that activation models are too unconstrained and too flexible to be anything more than a language for conveniently describing information processing. We are now in a position to suggest that a restricted version of the framework is not only sufficient but superior. Interactive-activation models could exploit both excitatory and inhibitory connections both between and within levels, but in the original interactive-activation model of letter perception, only inhibitory interactions were allowed within a level. In more recent versions of the visual model (McClelland, 1985, 1986), and in TRACE, we have gone even further, allowing only excitatory connections between levels and only inhibitory connections within levels. From our experience, it appears that models which adhere to these constraints work as well as or better than members of the more general class that do not. We hasten to add that we have no proof that this is true. We have, however, no reason to feel that we could improve the performance of our model by allowing either between-level inhibitory interactions or within-level excitation.

Other aspects of the successes of TRACE depend on its use of feedback from higher to lower levels. Feedback plays a central role in the accounts of categorical perception, lexical effects on phoneme identification, and "phonotactic rule" effects.

We do not claim that any of these phenomena, taken individually, require the assumption of a feedback mechanism. For example, consider the phenomenon of categorical perception. We use feedback from the phoneme to the feature level to drive feature patterns closer to the prototype of the phoneme they most strongly activate. This mechanism, coupled with the competition mechanism at the phoneme level, accounts for better discrimination between than within categories. However, we could account for categorical perception by suggesting that subjects do not have access to the acoustic level at all, but only to the results of the phoneme identification process. Similarly, lexical effects on phoneme identification can be accounted for by assuming that subjects (sometimes) read out from the word level and infer the identity of phonemes from the lexical code (Marslen-Wilson, 1980; Marslen-Wilson & Welsh, 1978; Morton, 1979). In the case of "phonotactic rule" effects, other interpretations are of course available as well. One could, for example, simply suppose that subjects use knowledge of the phonotactic constraints, perhaps captured in units standing for legal phoneme pairs, and that it is the output of such units that accounts for the influence of phonotactic regularity on phoneme identification.

We know of no single convincing empirical reason to prefer feedback accounts to other possibilities. However, we have two theoretical reasons for preferring to retain top-down as well as bottom-up interactions in our activation models. One reason has to do with the simplicity of the resulting decision mechanisms. Feedback allows higher level considerations to influence the outcome of processing at lower levels in just the same way that lower level considerations influence the outcome of processing at higher levels. The influences of lexical and other constraints on phoneme identification need not be pushed out of the theory of speech perception itself into decision processes, but are integrated directly into the perceptual process in a unified way. Given top-down as well as bottom-up processing, the decision mechanisms required for generating overt responses that reflect lexical and other contextual influences are greatly simplified; no special provision needs to be made for combining lexical and phonetic outputs in the decision mechanism.

A second reason for retaining feedback comes up when we consider the problem of learning. Although we have not discussed how learning might occur in TRACE, we have assumed that the mechanisms of speech perception are acquired through modification of connection strengths. Very roughly, in many learning schemes, connections between units are strengthened when two units tend to be activated simultaneously, at the expense of connections between units that tend not to be activated at the same time (cf. Grossberg, 1978; Rosenblatt, 1962; Rumelhart & Zipser, 1985). In such schemes, however, there is a serious problem if activation is entirely bottom-up; for in that case, once a particular unit has been "tuned" to respond to a particular pattern, it is difficult to retune it; it fires when its "expected" pattern is presented, and when it fires, its tendency to respond to that pattern only increases. Feedback provides a way to break this vicious cycle. If higher levels insist that a particular phoneme is present, then the unit for that phoneme can become activated even if the bottom-up input would normally activate some other phoneme instead; then the learning mechanism can "retune" the detector for the phoneme so that it will need to depend less on the top-down input the next time around.

In general, the use of feedback appears to place more of the intelligence required for perception and perceptual learning into the actual perceptual mechanism itself, and to make the mechanisms which exhibit this intelligence explicit. As formulated here, these mechanisms are incredibly simple; yet they appear to buy quite a lot which often gets pushed into unspecified "decision" and "postperceptual guessing" processes (e.g., Forster, 1976).

Finally, the success of TRACE also depends upon its architecture, rather than the fundamental computational principles of activation and competition, or the decision to include feedback. By architecture, we mean the organization of the Trace structure into layers consisting of units corresponding to items occurring at particular times within the utterance. As we noted in the introduction, this architecture is one we decided upon only after several other kinds of architecture had failed.

There are three principle positive consequences of the TRACE architecture. First, it keeps straight what occurred when in the speech stream. Competition occurs only between units competing to represent the same portion of the input stream. Multiple copies of the same phoneme and word units can be active at the same time without producing confusion. Furthermore, the architecture permits the same competition mechanism that chooses among alternative word interpretations of a single-word utterance to segment longer utterances into words. No separate control structure, resetting the mechanism at the beginning of each new word, is required.

Second, the architecture permits both forward and backward interactions. Backward interactions are absolutely essential if the model is to account for the fact that the identity of a phoneme (or a word; Warren & Sherman, 1974) can be influenced by what comes after it as well as what comes before it. Some kind of record of the past is necessary to capture these kinds of influences, as well as to provide a clear picture of the sources of the more conventional effects of preceding context, and the Trace construct lays this out in a way that is both comprehensible and efficient.

Third, the Trace structure provides an explicit mechanism which instantiates the idea that there may be no distinction between the mechanisms which carry out perceptual processing and those which provide a working memory for the results of the perceptual process. At one and the same time, the Trace is a perceptual processing system and a memory system. As a result, the model automatically accounts for the fact that coherent memory traces persist longer than incoherent ones. The coherent ones resonate through interactive (that is, bottom-up and top-down) activation, while incoherent ones fail to establish a resonance and therefore die away more rapidly.

Several of these aspects of TRACE overlap with assumptions made in other models, as mentioned in previous sections; continuity between working memory and the perceptual processing structures has been suggested by a number of other authors (e.g., Conrad, 1962), and the notion that working memory is a dynamic processing structure rather than a passive data structure has previously been advocated by Crowder (1978, 1981) and Grossberg (1978). Indeed, Grossberg has noted that resonating activation/competition processes can both enhance a perceptual representation and increase the retention of a representation; his analysis of interactive-activation processes in perception and memory captures the continuity of perception and memory as well as many other desirable properties of interactive-activation mechanisms.

Some Deficiencies of TRACE

Although TRACE has had a number of important successes, it also has a number of equally important deficiencies. A number of these deficiencies relate to simplifying assumptions of the simulation model. It is important to be clear that such deficiencies are not intrinsic to the basic structure of the model but to the simplifications we have imposed upon it to increase our ability to understand its basic properties. Certain deficiencies—such as the assumption that all phonemes are the same length, that all features are equally salient and useful and overlap an equal amount from one phoneme to another—are not present in TRACE I. Obviously a fully realistic model would take account of such differences. Other factors that should be incorporated in a more complete model include some provision for effects of word frequency, and some mechanisms for exploiting available cues to word boundaries.

Another deficiency of the model is that the decision mechanisms have not been fully enough elaborated. For example, as it stands the model does not provide a mechanism for deciding when a nonword has been presented. Nor have we specified how decision processes would actually use the information available at the word level to locate word-initial phonemes. A related problem is the lack of an explicit provision for variability in the activation and/or readout processes. Incorporating variability directly into a simulation model would greatly increase the complexity of the simulation process, but would also increase the model's ability to capture the detailed properties of reaction time distributions and errors (Ratcliff, 1978).

So far we have considered deficiencies which we would attribute to simplifying assumptions adopted to keep TRACE as simple and transparent in its behavior as possible. However, there are some problems that are intrinsic to the basic structure of the model.

One fundamental deficiency of TRACE is that fact that it requires massive duplication of units and connections, copying over and over again the connection patterns that determine which features activate which phonemes and which phonemes activate which words. As we already noted, learning in activation models (e.g., Ackley, Hinton, & Sejnowski, 1985; Grossberg, 1976; Rumelhart & Zipser, 1985) usually involves the retuning of connections between units depending on their simultaneous activation. Given TRACE's architecture, such learning would not generalize from one part of the Trace to another and so would not be accessible for inputs arising at different locations in the Trace. A second problem is that the model, as is, is insensitive to variation in global parameters, such as speaking rate, speaker characteristics and accent, and ambient acoustic characteristics. A third deficiency is that it fails to account for the fact that one presentation of a word has an effect on the perception of it a very short time later (Nusbaum & Slowiaczek, 1982). These two presentations, in the current version of the model, simply excite separate tokens for the same word in different parts of the Trace.

All these deficiencies reflect the fact that the TRACE consists of a large set of independent tokens of each feature, phoneme, and word unit. What appears to be called for instead is a model in which there is a single stored representation of each phoneme and each word in some central representational structure. If this structure is accessed every time the word is presented, then we could account for repetition priming effects. Likewise, if there were a single central structure, learning could occur in just one set of units, as could dynamic returning of feature–phoneme and phoneme–word connections to take account of changes in global parameters or speaker characteristics.

However, it remains necessary to keep straight the relative temporal location of different feature, phoneme, and word activations. Thus it will not do to simply abandon the Trace in favor of a single set of units consisting of just one copy of each phoneme and one copy of each word.

It seems that we need to have things both ways: we need a central representation that plays a role in processing every phoneme and every word and that is subject to learning, retuning, and priming. We also need to keep a dynamic trace of the unfolding representation of the speech stream, so that we can continue to accommodate both left and right contextual effects.

We are currently beginning to develop a model that has these properties, based on a scheme for using a central network of units to tune the connections between the units in the Trace in the course of processing, thereby effectively programing it "on the fly." Similar ideas have already been applied to visual word recognition (McClelland, 1985, 1986). Our hope is that a new version of the model based on these ideas will preserve the positive features of TRACE I and TRACE II, while overcoming their principle deficiencies.

Some General Issues in Speech and Language Perception

There are a number of general issues in speech and language perception. Four questions in particular appear to lie close to the heart of our conception of what speech perception is all about. First, what are the basic units in speech perception? Second, what is the percept, and which aspects of the processing of spoken language should be called perceptual? Third, what is the representation of linguistic rules? Fourth, is there anything unique or special about speech perception? We conclude this article by considering each issue from the perspective we have developed through the course of our explorations of TRACE.

What is the perceptual unit? Throughout this article, we have considered three levels of processing—feature, phoneme, and word. At each level, individual processing units stand for hypotheses about the features, phonemes, and words that might be present at different points in the input stream. It is worth noting that most aspects of the model's performance are independent of the specific assumptions that we have made about the units, or even the levels. Thus, if we replaced the phoneme level with demisyllables (Fujimura & Lovins, 1978) or phoneme triples (Wickelgren, 1969), very little of the behavior of the model would change. These units can capture some of the coarticulatory influences on phoneme identity, and they would reduce some of the word-boundary ambiguities faced by the current version of the model, but neither coarticulatory influences nor word boundary ambiguities would disappear altogether (see Elman & McClelland, in press, for further discussion).

In fact, interactive activation models like TRACE can be formulated in which each perceptual object is represented, not by a single unit, but by a pattern of activation over a collection of units. For example, the phoneme units in each time slice of TRACE might be replaced by a different set of units which did not have a one-to-one correspondence to phonemes. A phoneme would be represented by a particular pattern of activation over the set of units (each representing, perhaps, to some conjunction of lower level features) rather than by a single unit in the set.

There are some computational advantages of distributed representation compared to our "one unit one concept" assumption (Hinton, Mc-

Clelland, & Rumelhart, in press), but it is very difficult to find principled ways of distinguishing between local and distributed representational schemes empirically. Indeed, in certain cases there is an exact mapping and, in general, it is possible to approximate most aspects of the behavior of a local scheme with a distributed one and vice versa (Smolensky, 1986). In light of this, our use of local as opposed to distributed representations is not perhaps as significant as it might appear at first glance. What is essential is the information that the representation captures, rather than whether it does so via distributed or local representation. The use of local representations, with each unit (at the phoneme and word levels, anyway) representing a mutually exclusive alternative makes it much easier to relate the states of the processing system to overt response categories but is not otherwise a fundamental feature of the structure of the model.

What is the percept? At a number of points in this article, we have alluded to ways in which our conception of perception differs from the usage of other authors. Such concepts as perception are inherently tied to theory, and only derive their meaning with respect to particular theoretical constructs. Where does the TRACE model place us, then, with respect to the question, what is speech perception?

For one thing, TRACE blurs the distinction between perception and other aspects of cognitive processing. There is really no clear way in TRACE to say where perceptual processing ends and conceptual processes or memory begin. However, following Marr's (1982) definition of visual perception, we could say that speech perception is the process of forming representations of the stimulus—the speaker's utterance—at several levels of description. TRACE provides such a set of representations, as well as processes to construct them. On this view, then, the Trace is the percept, and interactive activation is the process of perception.

Aspects of this definition are appealing. For example, on this view, the percept is a very rich object, one that refers both to abstract, conceptual entities like words and perhaps at higher levels even meanings, as well as to more concrete entities like acoustic signals and features. Perception is not restricted to one or a subset of levels, as it is in certain models (e.g., Marslen-Wilson, 1980; Morton, 1979).

On the other hand, the definition seems overly liberal, for there is evidence suggesting that perceptual experience and access to the results of perceptual processing for the purposes of overt responding may not be completely unconstrained. A number of experiments, both in speech (e.g., Foss & Swinney, 1973; McNeil & Lindig, 1973) and reading (Drewnowski & Healy, 1977; Healy, 1976) suggest that under certain conditions lower levels of processing are inaccessible, or are at best accessed only with extra time or effort. On this evidence, if perception is to form representations, and if the representations are anything like those postulated in TRACE, then perception is quite independent of the experience of the perceiver and of access to the percept. Put another way, we may choose to define the Trace as the percept, but it is not the perceptual experience. This does not seem to be a very satisfactory state of affairs.

One coherent response to these arguments would be to say that the Trace is not the experience itself, but that some part or parts of it may be the *object* of perceptual experience. It seems sensible, for example, to suppose that the percept itself consists of that part of the Trace under scrutiny by the decision mechanisms. On this view, it would not be incoherent to suppose that representations might be formed which would nevertheless be inaccessible either to experience or to overt response processes. It would be a matter separate from the analysis of the interactive-activation process itself to specify the scope and conditions of access to the Trace. In our simulations, we have assumed that the decision mechanism could be directed with equal facility to all levels, but this may turn out to be an assumption that does not apply in all cases.

How are rules represented? It is common in theories of language to assume without discussion that linguistic rules are represented *as such* in the mind of the perceiver, and that perception is guided primarily by consultation of such rules. However, there are a number of difficulties associated with this view. First, it does not explain how exceptions are handled; it would seem that for every exception, there would have to be a special rule that takes precedence over the more general formulation. Second, it does not explain aspects of rule acquisition by children learning language, particularly the fact that rules appear to be acquired, at least to a large extent, on a word by word basis; acquisition is marked by a gradual spread of the rule from one lexical item or set of lexical items to others. Third, it does not explain how rules come into existence historically; as with acquisition, it appears that rules spread gradually over the lexicon. It is difficult to reconcile several of these findings with traditional rule-based accounts of language knowledge and language processing.

Models like TRACE and the interactive-activation model of word recognition take a very different perspective on the issue of linguistic rules. They are not represented as such, but rather they are built into the perceptual system via the excitatory and inhibitory connections needed for processing the particular items which embody these rules. Such a mechanism appears to avoid the problem of exceptions without difficulty, and to hold out the hope of accounting for the observation that rule acquisition and rule change are strongly tied to particular items which embody the rules.

What is special about speech? We close by raising a question that often comes up in discussions of the mechanisms of speech perception. Is speech special? If so, in what ways? It has been argued that speech is special because of the distinctive phenomenon of categorical perception; because of the encodedness of information about one phoneme in those portions of the speech stream that are generally thought to represent other phonemes; because the information in the speech stream that indicates the presence of a particular phoneme appears not to be invariant at any obvious physical level; because of the lack of segment boundaries, and for a variety of other reasons.

Over the last several years, a number of empirical arguments have been put forward that suggest that perhaps speech may not be so special, or at least, not unique. Cue trade-offs and contextual influences are, of course, present in many other domains (Medin & Barsalou, in press), and a large number of studies have reported categorical perception in other modalities (see Repp, 1984, for a discussion). Computational work on problems in vision have made clear that information that must be extracted from visual displays is often complexly encoded with other information (Barrow & Tenenbaum, 1978; Marr, 1982), and the lack of clear boundaries between perceptual units in vision is notorious (Ballard et al., 1983; Marr, 1982). Thus, the psychological phenomena that characterize human speech perception, and the computational problems that must be met by any mechanism of speech perception, are not, in general, unique to speech. To be sure, the particular constellation of problems that must be solved in speech perception is different than the constellation of problems faced in any other particular case, but most of the individual problems themselves do appear to have analogs in other domains.

We therefore prefer to view speech as an excellent test bed for the development of an understanding of mechanisms which might turn out to have considerably broader application. Speech is special to us, since it so richly captures the multiplicity of the sources of constraint which must be exploited in perceptual processing, and because it so clearly indicates the powerful influences of the mechanisms of perception on the constructed perceptual representation. We see the TRACE model as an example of a large class of massively parallel, interactive models that holds great promise to provide a deeper understanding of the mechanisms generally used in perception.

REFERENCES

Ackley, D., Hinton, G., & Sejnowski, T. (1985). Boltzmann machines: Constraint satisfaction networks that learn. *Cognitive Science*, 9, 113–147.

Anderson, J. A. (1977). Neural models with cognitive implications. In D. LaBerge & S. J. Samuels (Eds.), *Basic processes in reading: Perception and comprehension*. Hillsdale, NJ: Erlbaum.

Bagley, W. C. (1900). The apperception of the spoken sentence: A study in the psychology of language. *American Journal of Psychology*, 12, 80–130.

Ballard, D. H., Hinton, G. E., & Sejnowski, T. J. (1983). Parallel visual computation. *Nature (London)*, 306, 21–26.

Barrow, H. G., & Tenenbaum, J. M. (1978). In A. R. Hanson & E. M. Riseman (Eds.), *Computer vision systems* (pp. 3–26). New York: Academic Press.

von Bekesy, G. (1967). *Sensory inhibition*. Princeton, NJ: Princeton Univ. Press.

Bond, Z. S., & Garnes, S. (1980). Misperceptions of fluent speech. In R. Cole (Ed.), *Perception and production of fluent speech*. Hillsdale, NJ: Erlbaum.

Broadbent, D. E. (1967). Word frequency effect and response bias. *Psychological Review*, 74, 1–15.

Cole, R. A. (1973). Listening for mispronunciations: A measure of what we hear during speech. *Perception & Psychophysics*, 13, 153–156.

Cole, R. A., & Jakimik, J. (1978). Understanding speech: How words are heard. In G. Underwood (Ed.), *Strategies of information processing*. New York: Academic Press.

Cole, R. A., & Jakimik, J. (1980). A model of speech perception. In R. Cole (Ed.), *Perception and production of fluent speech*. Hillsdale, NJ: Erlbaum.

Cole, R. A., & Rudnicky, A. (1983). What's new in speech perception? The research and ideas of William Chandler Bagley, 1874–1946. *Psychological Review*, 90, 94–101.

Conrad, R. (1962). An association between memory errors and errors due to acoustic masking of speech. *Nature (London)*, 196, 1314–1315.

Cotton, S., & Grosjean, F. (1984). The gating paradigm: A comparison of successive and individual presentation formats. *Perception & Psychophysics*, 35, 41–48.

Crowder, R. G. (1978). Mechanisms of auditory backward masking in the stimulus suffix effect. *Psychological Review*, 85, 502–524.

Crowder, R. G. (1981). The role of auditory memory in speech perception and discrimination. In T. Myers, J. Laver, & J. Anderson (Eds.), *The cognitive representation of speech* (pp. 167–179). New York: North-Holland.

Denes, P. (1955). Effect of duration on the perception of voicing. *Journal of the Acoustical Society of America*, 27, 761–764.

Drewnowski, A., & Healy, A. (1977). Detection errors on *the* and *and*: Evidence for readings units larger than the word. *Memory & Cognition*, 5, 636–647.

Elman, J. L. (1983). Unpublished results.

Elman, J. L., & McClelland, J. L. (1984). The interactive activation model of speech perception. In Norman Lass (Ed.), *Language and speech* (pp. 337–374). New York: Academic Press.

Elman, J. L., & McClelland, J. L. (in press). Exploiting the lawful variability in the speech wave. In J. S. Perkell, & D. H. Klatt (Eds.), *Invariance and variability of speech processes* Hillsdale, NJ: Erlbaum.

Erman, L. D., & Lesser, U. R. (1980). The Hearsay-II speech understanding system: A tutorial. In W. A. Lea, *Trends in speech recognition* (pp. 361–381). Englewood Cliffs, NJ. Prentice-Hall.

Feldman, J. A., & Ballard, D. H. (1982). Connectionist models and their properties. *Cognitive Science*, 6, 205–254.

Forster, K. I. (1976). Accessing the mental lexicon. In R. J. Wales & E. Walker (Eds.), *New approaches to language mechanisms*. Amsterdam: North-Holland.

Foss, D. J., & Blank, M. A. (1980). Identifying the speech codes. *Cognitive Psychology* 12, 1–31.

Foss, D. J., & Gernsbacher, M. A. (1983). Cracking the dual code: Toward a unitary model of phoneme identification. *Journal of Verbal Learning and Verbal Behavior*, 22, 609–633.

Foss, D. J., & Swinney, D. A. (1973). On the psychological reality of the phoneme: Perception, identification, and consciousness. *Journal of Verbal Learning and Verbal Behavior, 12,* 246–257.

Fowler, C. A. (1984). Segmentation of coarticulated speech in perception. *Perception & Psychophysics, 36,* 359–368.

Fox, R. (1982). Unpublished manuscript. Vanderbilt University.

Fox, R. A. (1984). Effect of lexical status on phonetic categorization. *Journal of Experimental Psychology: Human Perception and Performance, 10,* 526–540.

Fry, D. B., Abramson, A. S., Eimas, P. D., & Liberman, A. M. (1962). The identification and discrimination of synthetic vowels. *Language and Speech, 5,* 171–189.

Fujimura, O., & Lovins, J. B. (1982). Syllables as concatenative phonetic units. In A. Bell & J. B. Hooper (Eds.), *Syllables and segments* (pp. 107–120). Amsterdam: North-Holland.

Fujisaki, H., & Kawashima, T. (1968, August). The influence of various factors on the identification and discrimination of synthetic speech sounds. *Reports of the 6th International Congress on Acoustics.* Tokyo.

Ganong, W. F. (1980). Phonetic categorization in auditory word perception. *Journal of Experimental Psychology: Human Perception and Performance, 6,* 110–125.

Grosjean, F. (1980). Spoken word recognition processes and the gating paradigm. *Perception & Psychophysics, 28,* 267–283.

Grosjean, F. (1985). The recognition of a word after its acoustic offset: Evidence and implications. Working paper, Northeastern University, Boston.

Grosjean, F., & Gee, J. (1984). Another view of spoken word recognition. Working paper, Northeastern University, Boston.

Grossberg, S. (1973). Contour enhancement, short-term memory, and constancies in reverberating neural networks. *Studies in Applied Mathematics, 52,* 217–257.

Grossberg, S. (1976). Adaptive pattern classification and universal recoding, 1: Parallel development and coding of neural feature detectors. *Biological Cybernetics, 23,* 121–134.

Grossberg, S. (1978). A theory of visual coding, memory, and development. In E. L. J. Leeuwenberg & H. F. J. M. Buffart (Eds.), *Formal theories of visual perception.* New York: Wiley.

Healy, A. F. (1976). Detection errors on the word *the:* Evidence for reading units larger than letters. *Journal of Experimental Psychology: Human Perception and Performance, 2,* 235–242.

Hinton, G. E., McClelland, J. L., & Rumelhart, D. E. (1986). Distributed representations. In D. E. Rumelhart, J. L. McClelland, and the PDP Research Group, *Parallel distributed processing: Explorations in the microstructure of cognition: Vol. 1.* Cambridge, MA: Bradford Books.

Jakobson, R., Fant, G., & Halle, M. (1952). *Preliminaries to speech analysis.* Cambridge: MIT Press.

Kewley-Port, D. (1982). Measurement of formant transitions in naturally produced stop consonant–vowel syllables. *Journal of the Acoustical Society of America, 72,* 379–389.

Klatt, D. H. (1980). Speech perception: A model of acoustic–phonetic analysis and lexical access. In R. Cole (Ed.), *Perception and production of fluent speech* (pp. 243–288). Hillsdale, NJ: Erlbaum.

Kopec, G. E. (1984). Voiceless stop consonant identification using LPC spectra. *Proceedings of the IEEE International Conference on Acoustics, Speech, and Signal Processing* (pp. 42.1.1–42.1.4). San Diego, CA.

84   MC CLELLAND AND ELMAN

Kucera, H., & Francis, W. (1967). *Computational analysis of present-day American English*. Providence, RI: Brown Univ. Press.

Lane, H. L. (1965). The motor theory of speech perception: A critical review. *Psychological Review* 72, 275–309.

Lehiste, I. (1960). An acoustic–phonetic study of internal open juncture. *Phonetica*, 5, 1–54.

Lehiste, I. (1964). Juncture. *Proceedings of the 5th International Congress of Phonetic Sciences, Munster* (pp. 172–200). Basel/New York: S. Karger.

Levin, J. A. (1976). *Proteus: An activation framework for cognitive process models* (ISI/WP-2). Marina del Rey, CA: Information Sciences Institute.

Liberman, A. M. (1970). The grammars of speech and language. *Cognitive Psychology*, 1, 301–323.

Liberman, A. M., Cooper, F. S., Shankweiler, D., & Studdert-Kennedy, M. (1967). Perception of the speech code. *Psychological Review*, 84, 452–471.

Licklider, J. C. R., & Miller, G. A. (1951). The perception of speech. In S. S. Stevens (Ed.), *Handbook of Experimental Psychology*. New York: Wiley.

Lowerre, B. T. (1976). *The HARPY speech recognition system*. Unpublished doctoral dissertation, Carnegie–Mellon University, Pittsburgh.

Luce, R. D. (1959). *Individual choice behavior*. New York: Wiley.

Mann, V. A., & Repp, B. H. (1980). Influence of vocalic context on perception of the [s]–[š] distinction. *Perception & Psychophysics*, 28, 213–228.

Marr, D. (1982). *Vision*. San Francisco: Freeman.

Marslen-Wilson, W. D. (1973). Linguistic structure and speech shadowing at very short latencies. *Nature (London)*, 244, 522–523.

Marslen-Wilson, W. D. (1980). Speech understanding as a psychological process. In J. C. Simon, (Ed.), *Spoken language generation and understanding* (pp. 39–67). New York: Reidel.

Marslen-Wilson, W. D., & Tyler, L. K. (1975). Processing structure of sentence perception. *Nature (London)*, 257, 784–786.

Marslen-Wilson, W. D., & Tyler, L. K. (1980). The temporal structure of spoken language understanding. *Cognition*, 8, 1–71.

Marslen-Wilson, W. D., & Welsh, A. (1978). Processing interactions and lexical access during word recognition in continuous speech. *Cognitive Psychology*, 10, 29–63.

Massaro, D. W. (1975). *Experimental psychology and information processing*. Chicago: Rand McNally.

Massaro, D. W. (1981). Sound to representation: An information-processing analysis. In T. Myers, J. Laver, & J. Anderson (Eds.), *The cognitive representation of speech* (pp. 181–193). New York: North-Holland.

Massaro, D. W., & Cohen, M. M. (1977). The contribution of voice-onset time and fundamental frequency as cues to the /zi/–/si/ distinction. *Perception & Psychophysics*, 22, 373–382.

Massaro, D. W., & Cohen, M. M. (1983). Phonological constraints in speech perception. *Perception & Psychophysics*, 34, 338–348.

Massaro, D. W., & Oden, G. C. (1980a). Speech perception: A framework for research and theory. In N. Lass (Ed.), *Speech and language: Advances in basic research and practice* (Vol. 3, pp. 129–165). New York: Academic Press.

Massaro, D. W., & Oden, G. C. (1980b). Evaluation and integration of acoustic features in speech perception. *Journal of the Acoustical Society of America*, 67, 996–1013.

McClelland, J. L. (1979). On the time relations of mental processes: An examination of systems of processes in cascade. *Psychological Review*, 86, 287–330.

McClelland, J. L. (1985). Putting knowledge in its place: A scheme for programming parallel processing structures on the fly. *Cognitive Science*, **9**, 113–146.

McClelland, J. L. (1986). The programmable blackboard model of reading. In J. L. McClelland, D. E. Rumelhart, and the PDP Research Group, *Parallel distributed processing: Explorations in the microstructure of cognition: Vol. 2*. Cambridge, MA: Bradford Books.

McClelland, J. L., & Rumelhart, D. E. (1981). An interactive activation model of context effects in letter perception. Pt. I: An account of basic findings. *Psychological Review*, **88**, 375–407.

McNeil, D., & Lindig, K. (1973). The perceptual reality of phonemes, syllables, words, and sentences. *Journal of Verbal Learning and Verbal Behavior*, **12**, 419–430.

Medin, D. L., & Barsalou, L. W. (in press). Categorization processes and categorical perception. In S. Harnad (Ed.), *Categorical perception*. Cambridge, England: Cambridge Univ. Press.

Miller, G., Heise, G., & Lichten, W. (1951). The intelligibility of speech as a function of the context of the test materials. *Journal of Experimental Psychology*, **41**, 329–335.

Miller, J. L. (1981). Effects of speaking rate on segmental distinctions. In P. D. Eimas & J. L. Miller (Eds.), *Perspectives on the study of speech* (pp. 39–74). Hillsdale, NJ: Erlbaum.

Miller, J. L., Green, K., & Schermer, T. M. (1984). A distinction between the effects of sentential speaking rate and semantic congruity on word identification. *Perception & Psychophysics*, **36**, 329–337.

Morton, J. (1969). Interaction of information in word recognition. *Psychological Review*, **76**, 165–178.

Morton, J. (1979). Word recognition. In J. Morton & J. C. Marshall (Eds.), *Psycholinguistics 2: Structures and processes* (pp. 107–156). Cambridge, MA: MIT Press.

Nakatani, L., & Dukes, K. (1977). Locus of segmental cues for word juncture. *Journal of the Acoustical Society of America*, **62**, 714–719.

Norris, D. (1982). Autonomous processes in comprehension: A reply to Marslen-Wilson and Tyler. *Cognition*, **11**, 97–101.

Nusbaum, H. C., & Slowiaczek, L. M. (1982). An activation model of auditory word recognition. *Research on speech perception, progress rep. No. 8* (pp. 289–305). Department of Psychology, Indiana University.

Oden, G. C., & Massaro, D. W. (1978). Integration of featural information in speech perception. *Psychological Review*, **85**, 172–191.

Pisoni, D. B. (1973). Auditory and phonetic memory codes in the discrimination of consonants and vowels. *Perception & Psychophysics*, **13**, 253–260.

Pisoni, D. B. (1975). Auditory short-term memory and vowel perception. *Memory & Cognition*, **3**, 7–18.

Pisoni, D., & Lazarus, J. H. (1974). Categorical and non-categorical modes of speech perception along the voicing continuum. *Journal of the Acoustical Society of America*, **55**, 328–333.

Pisoni, D. B., & Tash, J. (1974). Reaction times to comparisons within and across phonetic categories. *Perception & Psychophysics*, **15**, 285–290.

Ratcliff, R. (1978). A theory of memory retrieval. *Psychological Review*, **85**, 59–108.

Ratliff, F. (1965). *Mach bands: Quantitative studies on neural networks in the retina*. San Francisco: Holden Day.

Reddy, D. R. (1976). Speech recognition by machine: A review. *Proceedings of the IEEE*, **64**, 501–531.

Reddy, D. R., Erman, L. D., Fennell, R. D., & Neely, R. B. (1973). The Hearsay speech

86   MC CLELLAND AND ELMAN

understanding system: An example of the recognition process. *Proceedings of the International Conference on Artificial Intelligence* (pp. 185–194). Stanford, CA.

Repp, B. H. (1984). Categorical perception: Issues, methods, findings. In J. Lass (Ed.), *Speech and Language* (Vol. 10). New York: Academic Press.

Repp, B. H., & Liberman, A. M. (1984). Phonetic categories are flexible. *Haskins Laboratories Status Report on Speech Research*, SR-77/78, 31–53.

Rosenblatt, F. (1962). *Principles of neurodynamics*. New York: Spartan Books.

Rumelhart, D. E., & McClelland J. L. (1981). Interactive processing through spreading activation. In C. Perfetti & A. Lesgold (Eds.), *Interactive processes in reading*. Hillsdale NJ: Erlbaum.

Rumelhart, D. E., & McClelland, J. L. (1982). An interactive activation model of context effects in letter perception. Pt. II: The contextual enhancement effect and some tests and extensions of the model. *Psychological Review*, 89, 60–84.

Rumelhart, D. E., & Zipser, D. (1985). Competitive learning. *Cognitive Science*, 9, 75–112.

Salasoo, A., & Pisoni, D. (1985). Interaction of knowledge sources in spoken word identification. *Journal of Memory and Language*, 24, 210–231.

Samuel, A. G. (1977). The effect of discrimination training on speech perception: Noncategorical perception. *Perception & Psychophysics*, 22, 321–330.

Smolensky, P. (1986). Neural and conceptual interpretation of PDP models. In J. L. McClelland, D. E. Rumelhart, and the PDP Research Group, *Parallel distributed processing: Explorations in the microstructure of cognition: Vol. II*. Cambridge, MA: Bradford Books.

Stevens, K., & Blumstein, S. (1981). The search for invariant acoustic correlates of phonetic features. In P. D. Eimas & J. L. Miller (Eds.), *Perspectives on the study of speech* (pp. 1–38). Hillsdale, NJ: Erlbaum.

Studdert-Kennedy, M., Liberman, A. M., Harris, K. S., & Cooper, F. S. (1970). Motor theory of speech perception: A reply to Lane's critical review. *Psychological Review*, 77, 234–249.

Summerfield, Q., & Haggard, M. (1977). On the dissociation of spatial and temporal cues to the voicing distinction in initial stop consonants. *Journal of the Acoustical Society of America*, 62, 435–448.

Swinney, D. A. (1982). The structure and time-course of information interaction during speech comprehension: Lexical segmentation, access, and interpretation. In J. Mehler, E. C. T. Walker, & M. Garret (Eds.), *Perspectives on mental representation*. Hillsdale, NJ: Erlbaum.

Thompson, H. (1984). Word recognition: A paradigm case in computational (psycho-)linguistics. *Proceedings of the Sixth Annual Meeting of the Cognitive Science Society*, Boulder, CO.

Tyler, L. K., & Wessels, J. (1983). Quantifying contextual contributions to word-recognition processes. *Perception & Psychophysics*, 34, 409–420.

Warren, R. M., & Sherman, G. (1974). Phonemic restorations based on subsequent context. *Perception & Psychophysics*, 16, 150–156.

Wickelgren, W. A. (1969). Context-sensitive coding, associative memory and serial order in (speech) behavior. *Psychological Review*, 76, 1–15.

Wolf, J. J., & Woods, W. A. (1978). The HWIM speech understanding system. In W. A. Lea (Ed.), *Trends in speech recognition*. Englewood Cliffs, NJ: Prentice–Hall.

(Accepted July 25, 1985)

Psychological Review
1978, Vol. 85, No. 3, 172–191

Integration of Featural Information in Speech Perception

Gregg C. Oden and Dominic W. Massaro
Univeristy of Wisconsin—Madison

A model for the identification of speech sounds is proposed that assumes that (a) the acoustic cues are perceived independently, (b) feature evaluation provides information about the degree to which each quality is present in the speech sound, (c) each speech sound is defined by a propositional prototype in long-term memory that determines how the featural information is integrated, and (d) the speech sound is identified on the basis of the relative degree to which it matches the various alternative prototypes. The model was supported by the results of an experiment in which subjects identified stop-consonant–vowel syllables that were factorially generated by independently varying acoustic cues for voicing and for place of articulation. This experiment also replicated previous findings of changes in the identification boundary of one acoustic dimension as a function of the level of another dimension. These results have previously been interpreted as evidence for the interaction of the perceptions of the acoustic features themselves. In contrast, the present model provides a good description of the data, including these boundary changes, while still maintaining complete noninteraction at the feature evaluation stage of processing.

Although considerable progress has been made in the field of speech perception in recent years, there is still much that is unknown about the details of how speech sounds are perceived and discriminated. In particular, while there has been considerable success in isolating the dimensions of acoustic information that are important in perceiving and identifying speech sounds, very little is known about how the information from the various acoustic dimensions is put together in order to actually accomplish identification. The present article proposes and tests a model of these fundamental integration processes that take place during speech perception.

Much of the study of features in speech has focused on the stop consonants of English. The stop consonants are a set of speech sounds that share the same manner of articulation: Their production begins with a buildup of pressure behind some point in the vocal tract, following which is a sudden release of that pressure. In terms of their production, the six stops in English can be classified using the two featural dimensions of place of articulation and voicing. *Place of articulation* refers to the point in the oral cavity at which the air flow is blocked or occluded. *Voicing* refers to whether or not vocal-cord vibration occurs during the period of occlusion and release. The six stops of English consist of three cognate pairs that share place of articulation but differ in voicing: The consonants /p/ and /b/ are labial, /t/ and /d/ are alveolar, and /k/ and /g/ are velar. The first member of each pair is voiceless and the second is voiced.

The above classification based on speech *production* follows from the idea that place of articulation can be described independently of voicing. Analogously, much of the research on speech *perception* has operated on the corresponding idea that the perception of place of articulation can occur independently of the perception of voicing. Data supporting this premise were accumulated in research using the pattern playback synthesizer (Delattre, Liberman, & Cooper, 1955; Liberman, Delat-

This research was supported in part by National Institute of Mental Health Grant MH 19399 and grants from the Wisconsin Alumni Research Foundation. James Bryant, Michael Cohen, and David Warner provided assistance in performing the experiment and the members of the Wisconsin Human Information Processing Program (WHIPP), especially Lola Lopes, provided useful comments on this research.

Requests for reprints should be sent to Gregg C. Oden or Dominic W. Massaro, Department of Psychology, University of Wisconsin, Madison, Wisconsin 53706.

tre, & Cooper, 1958). This research revealed that perception of place of articulation was primarily a function of one set of acoustic cues, whereas perception of voicing was primarily a function of another set of cues. Perception of voicing was shown to be influenced by the voice onset time (VOT), the time between the onset of the release burst and the onset of vocal-cord vibration, and also by the degree of aspiration during the VOT period (Liberman et al., 1958). On the other hand, perception of place of articulation was shown to be primarily a function of the second and third formant (F_2 and F_3) transitions and of the burst frequency (Delattre et al., 1955; Harris et al., 1958; Hoffman, 1958). Another type of data that was taken to support the independent processing of speech features was the pattern of confusion errors obtained when subjects listened to speech sounds presented against various levels of noise (Miller & Nicely, 1955).

Although these early experiments supported the perceptual independence of place and voicing, more recent research appears to indicate that there is some dependence in the perception of place and voicing information (Abramson & Lisker, 1973; Haggard, 1970; Lisker & Abramson, 1970; Smith, 1973). Lisker and Abramson (1970), for example, using synthesized speech sounds, showed that voicing judgments in English were critically dependent on place of articulation. The boundary between voiced and voiceless sounds, measured in terms of VOT, was about 23 msec for labials, 37 msec for alveolars, and 42 msec for velars. These perceptual results agreed rather well with the range of VOT values derived from acoustical measurements of natural speech (Klatt, 1975; Lisker & Abramson, 1964). As Miller (1977) points out, however, the duration of the formant transitions in Lisker and Abramson's synthetic stimuli differed for the different places of articulation. These duration differences may, therefore, be directly responsible for the differences in VOT boundaries. Eliminating this problem, Miller still found significant differences, although the change in the VOT boundary was now only about one fourth as large (4.75 msec) as that reported by Lisker and Abramson.

The change in the VOT boundary with place of articulation might seem to be evidence against the perceptual independence of place and voicing in stop consonants. However, whether or not such changes in the voicing boundary constitute evidence against perceptual independence depends on the underlying model of speech perception that is assumed. It is possible that the acoustic features of place and voicing may be perceived independently and that changes in the voicing boundary may simply result from the way in which features are evaluated, combined, and matched against memorial representations of the alternative consonants.

The model proposed in the present article provides a detailed description of the processes that may be involved in using featural information to identify speech sounds. This model will be tested directly by using the procedures of information integration theory (Anderson, 1974). In the present case, these procedures involve the formulation of a model consisting of a set of algebraic rules to describe the integration processes. This model is then tested with identification data for synthetic speech stimuli that have been factorially generated by independently varying acoustic cues for voicing and for place of articulation.

The proposed integration model, which will be described in detail in the next section, can be articulated within the framework of a more general auditory information-processing model (Massaro, 1975a, 1975b). Figure 1 presents a schematic diagram of the auditory recognition process in Massaro's model. According to this model, the auditory stimulus is transduced by the auditory receptor system and acoustic features are detected and stored in preperceptual auditory storage (PAS). The features stored in PAS are a direct consequence of the properties of the auditory stimulus and the auditory receptor system. It is assumed that the feature detection process cannot be modified by learning or by the listener's knowledge or expectations. The features are assumed to be independent; the value of one feature does not influence the value of another at this stage of processing.

The primary recognition process evaluates each of the acoustic features in PAS and compares or matches these features to those that define perceptual units in long-term memory

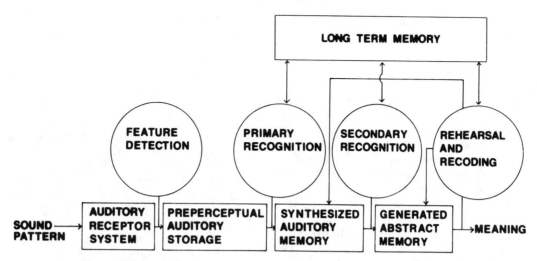

Figure 1. Schematic diagram of the general auditory information processing model.

(LTM). Every perceptual unit has a representation in LTM, which is called a *sign* or *prototype*. The prototype of a perceptual unit is specified in terms of the acoustic features that define the ideal acoustic information as it would be represented in PAS. The recognition process operates to find the prototype in LTM that best matches the acoustic features in PAS. It should be stressed that the primary recognition operation is not simply a pure template matching of features. In speech perception, there is good evidence for a normalization process that adjusts for variations in the voice quality of different speakers, speaking rate, and so on (see Massaro, 1975b, pp. 88–92, for a review of the evidence concerning voice quality). In our view, the adjustment operation does not have a direct influence on the evaluation of the acoustic features but occurs at the later prototype matching stage (see below). For the present, the allowance of this top–down influence should comfort those who are justifiably skeptical of the sufficiency of only bottom–up processes. In addition, as will be described below, the prototypes are not simply loose conglomerations of features but rather are propositions that may be, in principle, arbitrarily rich in logical structure.

The perceptual outcome of primary recognition is held in synthesized auditory memory (SAM). In contrast to feature evaluation, the outcome of the primary recognition process is influenced by the listener's knowledge and ex-

pectations and can be modified by learning experience. The secondary recognition process translates the perceptual code in SAM into an abstract code in generated abstract memory (GAM). The critical difference between SAM and GAM is in terms of the properties of the stored information. The synthesized percept of a friend's voice can be thought of as the actual sound experience, whereas the abstract encoding might be in terms of defining characteristics such as low and harsh. This model has previously been evaluated primarily with experiments on the dynamics of auditory information processing and speech perception. Within this context, the goal of the present work is to extend and quantify the model to describe how the listener integrates the various acoustic features in the identification of a speech sound.

Fuzzy Logical Model of Phoneme Identification

According to the proposed integration model, there are three conceptually distinct operations involved in phoneme identification: (a) The *feature evaluation* operation determines the degree to which each feature is present in PAS, (b) the *prototype matching* operation determines how well each candidate phoneme provides an absolute match to the speech sound, and (c) the *pattern classification* operation determines which phoneme provides the best match to the speech sound relative to the other phonemes under consideration.

Feature Evaluation

The feature evaluation process provides information about the degree to which each feature is present in the speech sound. Rather than assuming that the listener simply detects presence or absence, we assume that the feature is perceptually more or less present. This assumption is supported by the results of recent studies that, in contrast to the earlier work on categorical perception, have shown that acoustic features are perceived continuously rather than in an all-or-none fashion. Barclay (1972) required subjects to identify consonants as either /b/ or /g/ even though phonetically all were instances of /d/. Under these conditions, subjects more often identified a sound as /b/ the closer it was to the labial end of the place dimension. Pisoni and Tash (1974) found that the latency for deciding whether two sounds are the same phoneme is dependent on their *degree* of similarity with respect to VOT. Using a discrimination task that minimized the sensory interference from successive stimuli, Pisoni and Lazarus (1974) and Carney, Widin, and Viemeister (1977) demonstrated that subjects can reliably discriminate speech sounds that are acoustically different but phonetically the same. McNabb's (Note 1) subjects were more confident in their phonetic classifications for stimuli that were more extreme on the acoustic dimension. All of these results are consistent with the assumption that listeners can hear the degree to which acoustic features are present in speech sounds.

The assumption of continuous acoustic features contrasts with the traditional description of binary all-or-none distinctive features (Jakobson, Fant, & Halle, 1961) but corresponds to the more recent treatment of distinctive features provided by Chomsky and Halle (1968). They distinguish between the classificatory and phonetic function of distinctive features. The features are envisioned as binary (+ or −) only in their classificatory function. In their phonetic or descriptive function, they are multivalued features that relate to aspects of the speech sounds and the per-

ceptual representation (Chomsky & Halle, 1968, p. 298). Similarly, Ladefoged (1975) distinguishes between the phonetic and phonemic level of description. A feature describing the phonetic quality of a sound has a value along a continuous scale, whereas a feature classifying the phonemic oppositions is given a discrete value. In terms of our model, the representation of acoustic features in PAS would be comparable to the continuous values of their phonetic features. Even though place and voicing would be expressed as continuous rather than discrete, the phonemic judgment may still be discrete. That is to say, the listener can hear the degree of voicing but the listener's judgment in a forced-choice classification task with the six stops as alternatives will be either voiced or voiceless. Analogously, the degree of alveolarity of a stop consonant can be perceived, but the classification will be labial, alveolar, or velar.

Since acoustic features vary continuously from one speech sound to another, they can be represented as predicates that may be more or less true rather than only absolutely true or false (Goguen, 1969; Zadeh, 1975). These so-called *fuzzy predicates* represent the feature evaluation process: Each predicate is applied to the speech sound and specifies the degree to which it is true that the sound has the relevant acoustic characteristic. For example, if we use the notation t(A) to signify the truth value of Proposition A, then

$$t[\text{VOICED}(S_{ij})] = .65 \qquad (1)$$

represents the fact that it is .65 true that a given speech sound (S_{ij}), from the ith row and jth column of the factorial stimulus design, is perceived to be voiced. Similarly,

$$t[\text{ALVEOLAR}(S_{ij})] = .30 \qquad (2)$$

signifies that it is .30 true that the speech sound is perceived to be alveolar. To simplify the notation, let

$$A_i = t[\text{ALVEOLAR}(S_{ij})] \qquad (3)$$

and

$$V_j = t[\text{VOICED}(S_{ij})], \qquad (4)$$

so that A_i and V_j are subjective values that specify the degree to which the speech sound is perceived to be alveolar and voiced, respectively.

Prototype Matching

Each phoneme is defined by a prototype in long-term memory corresponding to a proposition such as

/b/: (LABIAL) AND (VOICED), (5)

/p/: (LABIAL) AND [NOT (VOICED)], (6)

/d/: (ALVEOLAR) AND (VOICED), (7)

and

/t/: (ALVEOLAR) AND [NOT (VOICED)]. (8)

Proposition 5 says simply that /b/ is labial *and* voiced, Proposition 6 specifies that /p/ is labial *and* not voiced, and so on. We actually assume that the relevant prototypes in LTM correspond to consonant–vowel syllables rather than stop consonants. The acoustic cues to stop-consonant phonemes depend critically on vowel context, and this lack of invariance disqualifies the stop-consonant phoneme as a perceptual unit prototype in long-term memory (Massaro, 1975b). However, for ease of exposition and because the vowel is constant, we will refer to the classification of these sounds as *phoneme identification*.

These simple propositions are themselves not fuzzy and are identical to the traditional, discrete featural definitions of these phonemes. However, in the fuzzy logical model, these prototypes are translated directly into fuzzy propositions that are the matching functions that specify the degree to which a given speech sound matches the LTM prototype of each of the associated phonemes. The translation from prototype to matching function involves two steps. First, the features in the prototypes must be replaced with the fuzzy featural predicates from the feature evaluation stage. Second, conjunction and negation must be defined for the fuzzy case. On the basis of previous work in speech perception (Massaro & Cohen, 1976, 1977; Oden, in press) and also in other cognitive domains (Oden, 1977), we assume that conjunction and negation follow Equations 9 and 10, respectively:

$$t(A \land B) = t(A) * t(B) \qquad (9)$$

and

$$t(\neg A) = 1 - t(A), \qquad (10)$$

where A and B are arbitrary propositions.

Consequently, the four matching functions corresponding to the prototypes given above are

$$B(S_{ij}) = L_i V_j, \qquad (11)$$

$$P(S_{ij}) = L_i(1 - V_j), \qquad (12)$$

$$D(S_{ij}) = A_i V_j, \qquad (13)$$

and

$$T(S_{ij}) = A_i(1 - V_j). \qquad (14)$$

For example, the degree to which a perceived speech sound will match the prototype of /b/ is specified by the matching function $B(S_{ij})$. According to Equation 11, this matching function for /b/ is equal to the degree to which the sound is labial multiplied by the degree to which the sound is voiced. Equations 12–14 define matching functions that specify the degree to which the speech sound matches the prototypes for /p/, /d/, and /t/, respectively.

Pattern Classification

In the final operation, the speech sound is classified on the basis of the relative degree to which it matches the various alternative phoneme prototypes as specified by the matching functions. It is assumed that the person classifies the sound as being an instance of whichever phoneme provides the best match. However, since perception is a noisy process in which a given physical stimulus will be perceived differently at different times, phoneme classification is necessarily a probabilistic process. Probabilistic choice processes of this sort may be modeled in a number of theoretically different ways that are formally similar (e.g., Luce, 1959; Thurstone, 1927). For the purposes of the present article, it will be assumed that the choice process follows Luce's model. Thus, for example, in the present experiment in which listeners were asked to identify the initial consonant of the speech sounds as /b/, /p/, /d/, or /t/, the probability that a given speech sound is identified as /b/ rather than /p/, /d/, or /t/ should be

$$p(b | S_{ij})$$
$$= \frac{B(S_{ij})}{B(S_{ij}) + P(S_{ij}) + D(S_{ij}) + T(S_{ij})}. \qquad (15)$$

In general, the probability of identifying a sound to be a particular phoneme should be equal to the goodness of the match of the sound to that phoneme relative to the sum of the goodness-of-match values for all of the phonemes being considered.

If we expand Equation 15 by inserting the equations for the various matching functions, the result is

$$p(b \mid S_{ij})$$
$$= \frac{L_i V_j}{L_i V_j + L_i(1 - V_j) + A_i V_j + A_i(1 - V_j)}. \quad (16)$$

In this case, however, the denominator is simply equal to $L_i + A_i$, and this will, of course, therefore be the case for the other three phonemes as well. Thus, with the fuzzy logical model, the probabilities that a given speech sound will be identified to be /b/, /p/, /d/, or /t/ are given by the following equations:

$$p(b \mid S_{ij}) = L_i V_j / (L_i + A_i), \quad (17)$$

$$p(p \mid S_{ij}) = L_i(1 - V_j) / (L_i + A_i), \quad (18)$$

$$p(d \mid S_{ij}) = A_i V_j / (L_i + A_i), \quad (19)$$

and

$$p(t \mid S_{ij}) = A_i(1 - V_j) / (L_i + A_i). \quad (20)$$

Test of the Model

Unfortunately, very little of the previous experimental work on speech perception can be used to test the model. Most of these studies do not address the integration problem, since only a single acoustic dimension was used in a given experiment. There are a number of reasons that may explain why this procedure has been used almost exclusively. First, most formal linguistic representations of a given dimension are discrete rather than continuous (Jakobson et al., 1961). For example, a stop consonant is considered to be either completely voiced or completely voiceless rather than, say, .7 voiced and .3 voiceless. With such a binary representation, the integration of information from the place and voicing dimensions would simply be logical conjunction: The consonant /b/ is represented as voiced *and* labial, /t/ is voiceless *and* alveolar, and so on. Within this framework, the identification of sounds involving a number of dimensions would be expected to follow directly from the results of the

relevant single-dimension experiments. For example, if the discrete feature hypothesis were correct, the results when a subject is asked to make voicing judgments within a particular place of articulation could be expected to generalize to the more natural situation in which the subject must integrate information across both voicing and place of articulation.

A second possible reason why only single-dimension experiments were carried out is that it is traditional in psychophysical research to vary a single dimension while holding all other dimensions constant. It is only recently that data reduction techniques such as analysis of variance have been used in this work. With the few factorial speech perception experiments that were done earlier, the data analyses were effectively reduced to single-dimensional analyses, since no analyses of interactions were performed (Harris et al., 1958; Hoffman, 1958). Thus, the critical information that might have shed some light on the integration problem was essentially left unused.

Massaro and Cohen (1976, 1977) were concerned with integration processes that take place prior to the integration of voicing and place of articulation information. Specifically, they addressed the question of how the various acoustic cues are integrated to arrive at a *single* acoustic phonetic distinction, such as the difference between voiced and voiceless sounds. Previous research has shown that voicing of initial stop consonants can be cued by a variety of acoustic features. These features include VOT; the presence versus absence of aspiration during VOT; the fundamental frequency (F_0) at the onset of vocal-cord vibration; the presence or absence of significant F_1 transitions at the onset of vocal-cord vibration; the frequency of F_1 at the onset of vocal-cord vibration; and the frequency, intensity, and duration of the aperiodic information in the release burst at the onset of the stop consonant.

Massaro and Cohen (1976) utilized a similar framework to the one presented here to study how two acoustic dimensions are evaluated and integrated in the perception of the single feature of voicing. Rather than varying just a single dimension, they simultaneously varied two or more dimensions through several values in a factorial design. Listeners were asked to rate the degree to which the speech sound was heard as /si/ relative to /zi/. In one experiment, the stimuli were generated by crossing several levels of VOT with several levels of F_0. The stimuli were heard as more /zi/-like with decreases in VOT and decreases in F_0. The quantitative results were used to test the predictions of the model presented here. The assumption that acoustic dimensions were combined multiplicatively as in Equations 11–14 provided a significantly better description than the assumption of an additive combination. This experiment and others (Massaro & Cohen, 1977) provide solid support for the model in the domain in which multiple acoustic cues contribute to one phonetic distinction.

A study by Sawusch and Pisoni (1974) was one of the first to systematically vary voicing and place of articulation in order to examine the nature of the featural integration process. This experiment consisted of four parts that were run separately. In Part 1, all of the stimuli were voiced consonant syllables, but the acoustic cues to place of articulation were varied and the subjects identified the syllables as either /ba/ or /da/. In Part 2, all of the speech sounds were labial, but VOT was varied, and the subjects identified these syllables either as /ba/ or /pa/. In Parts 3 and 4, voicing and place of articulation were covaried from labial–voiced to alveolar–voiceless. With this technique, the sound was made more alveolar as it was made more voiced. In Part 3, these syllables had to be classified by the subjects as either /ba/ or /ta/; whereas in Part 4, the subjects were allowed to classify the syllables as /ba/, /da/, /pa/, or /ta/. On the basis of the results of this experiment, Sawusch and Pisoni rejected a simple additive feature model and proposed a more complex model including a cross-product term. This latter model provided a better account for the data.

Recently, Oden (in press) has shown that the fuzzy logical model provides an even better account for the data of Sawusch and Pisoni (1974). Of particular interest is the series of sounds for which both place and voicing were covaried and which was presented to the subjects twice, once to make a forced choice to identify each sound as either /ba/ or /ta/ and the other time to identify the sounds

as either /ba/, /pa/, /da/, or /ta/. According to the fuzzy logical model, the feature evaluation and prototype matching operations should not change under these two conditions. All that should change, for example, for the probability of identifying a sound to be /ba/, is which terms are included in the denominator of the equation for the pattern classification operation. The fuzzy logical model was successful in describing the data of Sawusch and Pisoni's experiment, including the data for these different response conditions. However, while this experiment did vary both voicing and place of articulation, it does not provide a thorough test of the fuzzy logical model, since these dimensions were not independently varied.

Experiment

In order to adequately test the proposed fuzzy logical model, it is necessary to have subjects identify phonemes for which the degree of voicing and the degree of place of articulation are varied independently. In the present experiment, subjects identified the initial phoneme of synthesized consonant–vowel syllables as being either /b/, /p/, /d/, or /t/. Acoustic cues to voicing and to place of articulation were independently varied through several values.

Method

Stimuli. Each stimulus was a syllable of 320-msec duration consisting of a stop consonant followed by the vowel /ae/ as in "bat." The acoustic cues to the voicing and the place of articulation of the consonant part of the syllables were varied independently in a 5 × 7 factorial design. The five different degrees of voicing were produced by varying VOT in 10-msec steps from 0 to 40 msec. The seven different levels on the place-of-articulation dimension were produced by varying the frequencies at which the second and third formants (F_2 and F_3) began. The actual values for the various levels of this factor are listed in Table 1, and Figure 2 presents spectrograms of two of the stimuli.

For each syllable, the fundamental frequency (F_0) was 126 Hz and remained at this value throughout the syllable until a linear decrease to 112 Hz during the last 120 msec of the syllable. The first formant (F_1) started at 200 Hz and increased to 734 Hz in a negatively accelerated manner over the first 30 msec of the sound. During the first 70 msec, F_2 and F_3 increased or decreased (in a negatively accelerating manner), respectively, to reach the frequencies of F_2 (1,600 Hz) and F_3 (2,851 Hz) of the vowel. The fourth and fifth formants (F_4 and F_5) were constant at 3,500 and 4,000 Hz, respectively.

The energy source for the initial part of the stop-consonant transition period depended on the VOT value. For a VOT value of 0 msec, the voicing source was turned on at the onset of the syllable and increased linearly to full amplitude in 20 msec. For VOT values greater than 0, the syllable began with the onset of aspiration, which served as the energy source for the F_1 through F_5 formants. The aspiration reached full amplitude instantaneously and remained on during the VOT interval. At the end of the VOT interval, the aspiration source was turned off with a linear fall time of 20 msec. Although VOT of a synthetic speech sound is defined to be the interval between the onset of the speech sound and the onset of the buzz source, the immediate rise time and the 20-msec fall time of the amplitude of aspiration mean that the perceived VOT interval was probably somewhat longer than the nominal value. Figure 2 shows the resulting transitions for 0- and 40-msec VOTs, respectively.

Procedure. On each trial a syllable was randomly selected without replacement from the 5×7 stimulus design. The stimulus was presented to the subject and followed by a 2-sec response interval, which ended with the onset of a 250-msec visual signal to the subject. The subject identified the stimulus as /b/, /p/, /d/, or /t/ and indicated his response by pushing an appropriately labeled button. The presentation of the next test stimulus followed the end of the previous response interval by 1 sec. On the first day, the subject was read the instructions and was given a practice session of a block of 35 trials. The subject was then asked if he had any questions, and his responses were checked to insure that he had responded on each practice trial. This was followed by two experimental sessions with roughly 10-minute breaks between sessions. On the second day, the subject was run through two more experimental sessions. Each session consisted of 10 blocks of the full set of 35 speech sounds in the stimulus design, for a total of 40 responses per subject to each of the 35 sounds. The experiment took about 1 hour each day, and each subject was tested on 2 consecutive days.

Table 1
Starting Frequencies (Hz) of F_2 *and* F_3
Formants of the Seven Different Speech Sounds

Stimulus	F_2	F_3
1	1,270	2,263
2	1,345	2,397
3	1,425	2,614
4	1,510	2,770
5	1,600	2,934
6	1,695	3,020
7	1,796	3,200

Note. Steady-state values for F_2 and F_3 are 1,600 and 2,851 Hz, respectively.

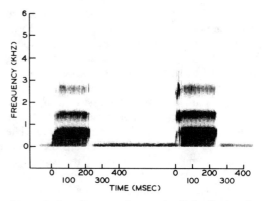

Figure 2. Spectrograms of two stimuli (a /ba/ and a /pa/).

Apparatus and subjects. All stimuli were produced on-line during the experiment by a formant series resonator speech synthesizer (FONEMA OVE-IIId) controlled by a PDP-8/L computer (Cohen & Massaro, 1976). The stimuli were specified as concatenations of steady-state and transition segments. Synthesizer control parameters (e.g., F_0) indicated at each segment boundary the parameter values that were to be changed for a given interval. Segment durations were always multiples of 10 msec. Intermediate values within a segment were computed with linear or nonlinear interpolation as appropriate and were output to the synthesizer every 10 msec. The output of the speech synthesizer was amplified with a McIntosh MC-50 amplifier and presented over headphones (Koss Model 4AA) at a comfortable listening intensity (about 76 dB SPL). Four subjects could be tested simultaneously in separate sound-attenuated rooms.

Sixteen subjects served in the experiment. The subjects were solicited from the University of Wisconsin community and were paid $4 for their participation.

Results and Discussion

Figure 3 presents the data from this experiment. Each panel gives the data for a given level of VOT; and within each panel, the four curves give the identification probabilities for the four phonemes. As can be seen in Figure 3, the shapes of these curves change markedly but in a systematic fashion from panel to panel. The total pattern of data presented in all five panels provides the important information about how place and voicing information is integrated. However, this manner of presenting the data makes it difficult to determine how well the model fits the data.

Figure 4 plots the same data with separate panels for each of the four phonemes. This

FEATURAL INFORMATION IN SPEECH PERCEPTION   180

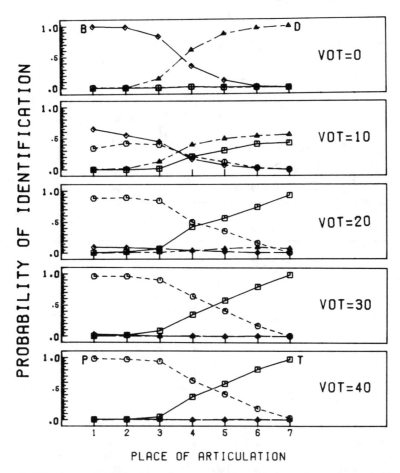

Figure 3. Identification probabilities for each response alternative for each speech sound. (Each panel presents the data for a given level of voice onset time [VOT]. Diamonds, triangles, circles, and squares represent the data for /b/, /d/, /p/, and /t/, respectively.)

figure also gives the predictions of the fuzzy logical model when fitted to the data. In this and the following figures of this type, the data are the points and the predictions are represented by the curves. In this experiment, the predictions are obtained by fitting the model separately for each individual subject and then averaging these predictions over subjects. Thus, the data for each subject are fitted individually, and both the data and the predictions in this figure are averaged over all 16 subjects. In each panel of the graph, the spacing of the levels along the abscissa is proportional to the spacing of the marginal means across the seven levels of the formant transitions. This spacing was computed separately for each of the four response types and then averaged over response types, so that the spacing along the

abscissa is the same for all four panels. Spacing the levels of the abscissa in this way allows the pattern of the predictions of the model to be more easily seen.

To fit the model to the data of each subject, the computer subroutine STEPIT (Chandler, 1969) was used. This subroutine iteratively adjusts the values of the parameters until it finds that set of values which results in predictions of the model that come closest to fitting the data. *Closeness of fit* was defined in terms of the sum of the squared deviations of the data from the model. Fitting the model required 12 parameters: 5 to specify the degree of voicing for each level of VOT and 7 to specify the degree of labiality for each level of the place-of-articulation factor.

As can be seen in Figure 4, the model pro-

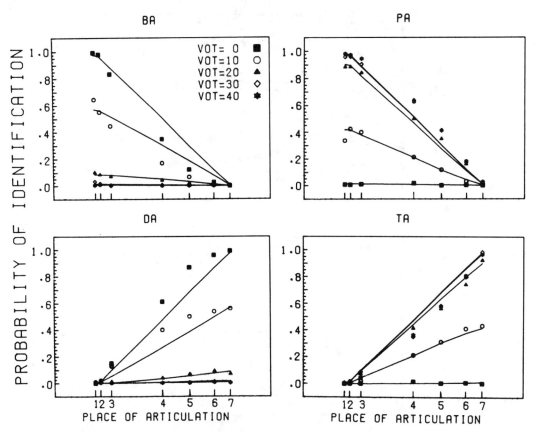

Figure 4. Identification probabilities and predictions of the simple fuzzy logical model. (Each panel presents the data for a given response alternative. Note that the spacing along the abscissa is proportional to the spacing of the subjective place values. VOT = voice onset time.)

vides a general account of the data but deviates systematically from the data. Not many of the deviations are very large and the grand root mean squared deviation of the model from the data is .092, which is fairly small considering that 105 independent data points are fitted for each subject using only 12 free parameters. Of the 140 data points, only 105 are independent because the four response probabilities must sum to one for each of the 35 separate stimuli. In this experiment, for the range of stimuli used, it was assumed that a sound was perceived to be alveolar to the degree that it was not perceived to be labial, that is, $L_i = 1 - A_i$. (Relaxing this assumption had virtually no effect on the fit of the model.) Accordingly, it was only necessary to estimate the seven values of A_i to account for the place features.

Because of the large number of degrees of freedom (93) for this test of the model, the relatively good fit can be taken as general support of the fuzzy logical model. However, it is possible that other models with an equivalent number of parameters might do just as well. Accordingly, an alternative model based on additive rather than multiplicative feature combinations was fitted to the data using the identical procedures. In this model, the matching functions given in Equations 11–14 are replaced by the following:

$$B(S_{ij}) = L_i + V_j, \tag{21}$$

$$P(S_{ij}) = L_i + (1 - V_j), \tag{22}$$

$$D(S_{ij}) = A_i + V_j, \tag{23}$$

and

$$T(S_{ij}) = A_i + (1 - V_j). \tag{24}$$

The rest of the model remains the same. Thus, this alternative "additive feature integration" model uses exactly the same number of parameters as with multiplicative feature integration and, therefore, is equivalent in simplicity and power. Nevertheless, it was unable to provide a satisfactory account of the data as is reflected in its root mean squared deviation of .247.

The performance of the additive feature model indicates that the substantially better fit of the comparable fuzzy logical model should be taken as support for this latter model. However, despite this success, the fact that of the deviations of the data from the fuzzy logical model those which are of any size are clearly systematic, both within and between panels of Figure 4, indicates that there are important effects that are left unaccounted for by the model as formulated so far. Therefore, a more complex version of the model was developed in an attempt to provide a more complete account of the data.

Featural modification in the phoneme prototypes. The simple version of the fuzzy logical model assumes that each feature is treated the same for each of the alternative phonemes that have that particular feature. This is the simplest case and is what is implicitly assumed in discrete feature theories. However, there are reasons to suppose that, in fact, some of the features may be expected on the average to take on more extreme values for some phonemes than for others. For example, the typical voice onset time of voiceless stop consonants produced under natural conditions is longer for alveolar than for labial stop consonants (Lisker & Abramson, 1970). Consequently, it may be that the actual subjective prototype in long-term memory incorporates information about the necessary extremity of the various features for the idealized phoneme. For example, the prototypes for /b/ and /d/ might more accurately be defined as

$$\text{/b/}: \quad (\text{LABIAL}) \text{ AND } [\text{VERY (VOICED)}] \quad (25)$$

and

$$\text{/d/}: \quad (\text{ALVEOLAR}) \text{ AND } [\text{MODERATELY (VOICED)}]. \quad (26)$$

These modifiers do not mean that a *perfect* /b/ is now considered to be any more voiced than is a *perfect* /d/. What the modifiers do signify is that extremity on these features is more

important for /b/ than for /d/; that is, that with Equation 25, the goodness of the match to the ideal /b/ falls off more rapidly as the speech sound becomes less voiced.

If such modifiers are psychologically real, then they must somehow be allowed for within the model. The problem is how the modifiers are manifested in the matching functions of the prototypes. Zadeh (1972, 1975) has proposed that modifiers of this sort should be represented as power functions. For example, Zadeh suggests that "very" may be defined as

$$t[\text{VERY}(A)] = t(A)^2, \quad (27)$$

where A is any proposition. In the general case, modifiers (mod) of this sort will be represented by exponents:

$$t[\text{mod}(A)] = t(A)^q, \quad (28)$$

where q may take on any value depending on whether the actual subjective modifier corresponds to "very," "extremely," "moderately," "somewhat more than moderately," or perhaps some modifier for which we have no common phrase.

Thus, in the general form, the matching function for /b/ may be represented as

$$B(S_{ij}) = (L_i)^q (V_j)^r, \quad (29)$$

where the subscripts on L_i and V_j indicate that they vary as the speech sound (S_{ij}) varies; whereas, in contrast, the exponents q and r have no subscripts, since they are constant for a given phoneme and over all speech sounds.

The basic nature of the pattern classification operation of the model remains unchanged with the addition of these modifiers. The probability of identifying a syllable to be /b/ will still follow from Equation 15. Of course, when Equation 15 and the equations for the other phonemes are expanded by inserting the equations for the matching functions, the resulting formulae will be much more complex than Equations 17 through 20. Despite this greater mathematical complexity, however, the complex fuzzy logical model is conceptually very nearly the same as the simple fuzzy logical model. The only substantive change is the addition of the modifiers to the prototypes. All of the other changes in the equations are superficial and follow directly given the structure of the psychological model.

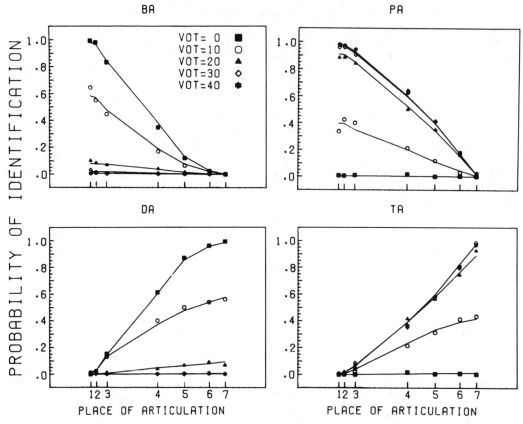

Figure 5. Identification probabilities and predictions of the complex fuzzy logical model. (Note that the spacing along the abscissa is proportional to the spacing of the subjective place values. VOT = voice onset time.)

To determine whether the observed results could be better described by the addition of modifiers to the prototype definitions, the complex version of the fuzzy logical model was also fitted to the data of this experiment. The complex version of the model required an additional 8 parameters for the modifier exponents, for a total of 20. Figure 5 presents the data along with the predictions of the complex fuzzy logical model. As is clear from this figure, the complex version of the model provides a very close fit to the data. This conclusion is also evident from the grand root mean squared deviation of .039 for this model. Thus, the data provide very strong support for the fuzzy logical model of phoneme identification and also for the necessity of including modifiers in the definitions of the phoneme prototypes.

Again, it is useful to compare the performance of the complex fuzzy logical model with that of other models with the same number of parameters. For example, featural weighting can also be included in the additive featural model. In the case of additive combination rules, it is most natural to make the weights multiply their respective features, such as

$$B(S_{ij}) = qL_i + rV_j. \qquad (30)$$

The addition of weights improved the fit of the additive feature model, resulting in a root mean squared deviation of .161. This is, of course, not nearly as good a fit as the complex fuzzy logical model, even though it uses the same number of parameters. In fact, this weighted additive features model still does not account for the data as well as the simple fuzzy logical model.

It might be thought that it is the exponents per se that allow the complex fuzzy logical model to provide such a good fit to the data.

Table 2

Parameter Estimates for the Complex Fuzzy Logical Model: Average Values of Phoneme Prototype Modifiers

Phoneme	Dimension	
	Voicing	Place of articulation
/b/	2.44	2.79
/p/	2.37	1.04
/d/	2.04	1.69
/t/	1.95	2.21

However, when exponential weights are incorporated into the additive feature model to produce matching functions such as

$$B(S_{ij}) = (L_i)^q + (V_j)^r, \qquad (31)$$

the root mean squared deviation is .230, which is not even as good a fit as with the multiplicatively weighted additive feature model.

One more model was fitted to the data. This was a version of the complex fuzzy logical model, but instead of using 12 parameters to represent the five degrees of voicing and the seven degrees of labiality, these values were obtained as simple functions of the levels of the corresponding factor of the design. Thus, for example, the degrees of labiality were given by the following equation:

$$L_i = \frac{x_i^c}{x_i^c + (1 - x_i)^c}, \quad \text{where} \quad c \geq 1, \quad (32)$$

which is ogival in form when the x_i parameters are constrained to fall between zero and one. The larger the c parameter, the steeper is the middle section of the ogive. The x_i values were obtained by a simple linear function of the level of the factor, that is,

$$x_i = ai + b, \qquad (33)$$

except that values less than zero were set to zero and values greater than one were set to one. Taken together, Equations 32 and 33 specify an ogival type of curve in three parameters: a, b, and c. The first two allow the ogive to shift linearly along the place factor to position the boundary at the proper place and the third determines the sharpness of the boundary. A similar three-parameter ogival function was used to obtain the degree of voicing values from the levels of the voicing

factor. Thus, altogether there were three place parameters, three voicing parameters, and eight exponential weight parameters for a total of 14 and a saving of six from the original complex fuzzy logical model.

Despite this considerable decrease in the number of parameters, this version of the model fit the data nearly as well as the full 20-parameter version (root mean squared deviation = .045). It is especially interesting to note that although this version of the model requires only two more parameters than the simple fuzzy logical model, the fit is still more than twice as good in terms of the root mean square criterion. Thus, the point is reemphasized that the success of the model is not simply due to the number of parameters used, but rather to the fact that the parameters are combined in a way that captures the structure of the underlying psychological processes.

Details of the effects of featural modification. It is interesting to note in Figure 5 the effect of including the exponents corresponding to the modifiers in the prototypes. In contrast to the curves representing the model predictions in Figure 4, those in Figure 5 are not diverging fans of straight lines. Rather, these curves display a marked bowed shape, whose direction depends on the actual modifiers of a given phoneme prototype relative to those for the other phonemes. The values obtained for the exponents corresponding to these modifiers are given in Table 2. The parameters for voicing and degree of alveolarity are shown in Table 3. These values are averages of the values obtained for each subject that were used in fitting the model to the subject's data.

Table 3

Parameter Estimates for the Complex Fuzzy Logical Model: Average Degrees of Voicing and Alveolarity for Levels of Stimulus Design

Level of voicing factor	Degree of voicing	Level of place factor	Degree of alveolarity
1	0	1	.01
2	0	2	.06
3	.01	3	.18
4	.57	4	.52
5	.93	5	.76
		6	.99
		7	1.00

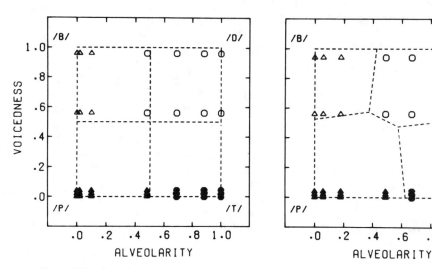

Figure 6. Psychological parameter spaces for the simple and complex fuzzy logical models. (The dashed lines partition the parameter spaces into regions in which a given response alternative is predicted by the respective model to be most likely. Each point represents the subjective position of a stimulus and specifies what phoneme it was most often identified to be, with open triangles, closed triangles, open circles, and closed circles standing for /b/, /p/, /d/, and /t/, respectively.)

Another useful way to represent the effect of the exponents in the complex fuzzy logical model is given in Figure 6. The two panels of this figure each represent the *psychological* parameter space of the stimuli in terms of the two critical acoustic dimensions. The four corners of each square represent the ideal points for the four phonemes. It should be stressed that these diagrams represent the psychological, not the physical, parameter space. For example, the vertical dimension represents the subjective degree of voicing not some arbitrary physical measure such as VOT.

In each square of Figure 6, the dashed lines indicate the boundaries separating those stimuli most likely to be identified as one phoneme from those most likely to be identified as another phoneme. The left panel of the figure gives the partitioning of the parameter space as predicted by the simple version of the model. In this case, if the value for alveolarity is greater than .5, the stimulus will be identified more often as alveolar no matter what the value of voicing and so on. The right panel gives the partitioning as predicted by the complex version of the model. Here, the effects

of the modifiers are clear: The large exponents associated with extreme modifiers such as "very" or "quite" cause a restriction of the region in which the stimuli are identified to be instances of that phoneme. In the description of the present results, the alternatives /b/ and /t/ now include less of the total parameter space.

The panels of Figure 6 also show in another fashion that the complex version of the model provides a superior account of the data. The stimuli used in the experiment are shown in each panel of the figure as open and filled circles and triangles. These points are positioned in their respective positions in the parameter space as determined from the parameter values used in fitting the respective version of the model to the data.[1] The points classify each stimulus according to the phoneme it was

---

[1] Note that the parameter values for place and for voicing are not the same for the two versions of the model (see Figure 6). This is because with the simple model, these parameters are influenced by the effects in the data that are accounted for in the complex model by the exponents.

most often identified to be. Of particular interest is the fourth level of alveolarity, counting from the left of the figure. For this level, the two most voiced stimuli were most often identified as /d/, the *alveolar voiced* phoneme; whereas the other three stimuli were most often identified as /p/, the *labial unvoiced* phoneme. This change in the boundary along the place dimension as a function of voicedness may also be seen in Figure 3.

Miller (1977) and Repp (Note 2) also found large differences in the place boundary for voiced and voiceless labial and alveolar stop consonants. The changeover from labial to alveolar responses shifts toward the alveolar end as the speech sounds are made more voiceless. This kind of boundary change clearly cannot be accounted for by either noninteractive, discrete feature theories or by the simple fuzzy logical model. However, as the right-hand panel of Figure 6 shows, this effect is nicely accounted for by the complex fuzzy logical model. It is simply a natural manifestation of the modifiers in the phoneme prototypes. Thus, it is additional evidence in support of this model that it is able to provide a good account for this "phonetic boundary

shift" and that it is able to do so without having to resort to explanations about complex feature interactions.

The three-dimensional graphs in Figure 7 illustrate this same partitioning of the parameter space in a more complete and less abstract fashion. These are graphs of the degree to which each of the four phoneme prototypes matches each possible stimulus specified in terms of subjective values. To make the graphs more legible, only the upper part of each matching function, where it provides a better match to the stimuli than do the alternative matching functions, is shown. That is, the matching function of a given phoneme is shown only for the region of the parameter space where that phoneme is predicted to be preferred. The left-hand three-dimensional graph illustrates the characteristics of the simple model: The matching functions are identical in shape for each of the phonemes and increase to the optimal point at each corner in a relatively gradual manner. In contrast, the right-hand graph shows that with the complex model, some of the functions increase much more steeply than others and, in general, more steeply than with the simple

SIMPLE MODEL

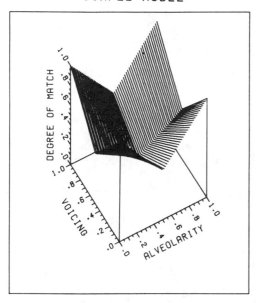

COMPLEX MODEL

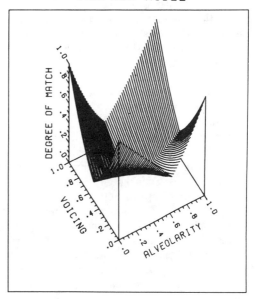

Figure 7. Hypothetical matching functions for the simple and complex fuzzy logical models. (The matching function for each phoneme specifies the degree to which the prototype for that phoneme matches each possible speech sound. Each matching function is shown only for that part of the parameter space where the corresponding phoneme is predicted to be the most frequent response.)

model. Note also that the places where the functions intersect, that is, the bottom of the "valleys," are the boundaries that were presented in Figure 6.

General Discussion

Related Approaches to Pattern Identification

One of the most important conceptual forebears of the fuzzy logical model is Selfridge's (1959) Pandemonium model. Selfridge proposed four levels of processing, the lowest of which, that consisting of "data demons," was simply the level of reception and sensory storage. The other three levels correspond directly to the three stages of the fuzzy logical model: The "computational demons" perform feature evaluation, the "cognitive demons" do kinds of featural integration that are analogous to the present prototype matching, and the "decision demon" chooses among the alternatives just as is done in the pattern classification stage of the fuzzy logical model. Pandemonium also shares with the present model the characteristics of parallel processing within each level of computation, of logical combination rules for featural integration, and of featural evaluation processes that result in information about the *degree* to which features are present in the stimulus. Selfridge gave particular emphasis to this latter aspect of Pandemonium and illustrated the concept with diagrams (Selfridge, 1959, p. 525) that are strikingly similar to those of fuzzy predicates that appear in the fuzzy logic literature (e.g., Zadeh, 1972).

However, whereas the fuzzy logical model is intended to describe the cognitive processes that are actually used by humans to identify speech sounds, Selfridge (1959) was primarily interested in the problem of learning to make correct identifications. Thus, Selfridge concentrated on how Pandemonium might be made to come to discover the appropriate features and feature integration rules over the course of training trials. In contrast, the present article relied on intuition and on the analytic linguistic description of the phonemes to formulate the corresponding prototype specifications.

Another closely related approach is that of Morton (1969), who developed a model of word

identification based on signal detection theory (Green & Swets, 1966). In this model, the evidence for each candidate word is accumulated in parallel; for each word, the accumulation is compared against a criterion that is determined in part by the degree to which that word is expected. While Morton does not explicitly consider how the information from separate features is put together to determine the evidence for a given word, the obvious assumption is that each feature contributes independent evidence that is simply accumulated along with the rest. With this assumption, Morton's model leads to equations of the same form as those of the simple version of the fuzzy logical model.

In the area of speech perception, the models of Sawusch and Pisoni (1974) and of Repp (1977) are similar in several respects to the fuzzy logical model. Sawusch and Pisoni propose a model with three stages: auditory analysis that results in a set of acoustic cues, acoustic cue combination that produces the phonetic features such as those of place and voicing, and phonetic feature combination that results in the final identification. The phonetic featural information is considered to be continuous proportions of the nominal features. Sawusch and Pisoni propose and test a number of rules for combining the phonetic features. In all of these rules, the proportions are weighted by multiplicative weights and then combined to produce the predicted response probabilities directly. The combination rules that were considered were either strictly additive or else contained cross-product terms added in with the individual featural information. Of most importance is that all of these rules treat the featural information as continuous rather than discrete.

Repp's (1977) model of featural integration in speech perception is based on a spatial representation of speech sounds. In this model, the features correspond to dimensions in a euclidean space. Thus, both the prototypes and the stimulus can be considered to be points in this space, and the degree of match of each prototype to the stimulus is, therefore, an inverse function of the distance from prototype to stimulus. Thus, this model is identical to the fuzzy logical model in overall structure in that it considers identification to be a process of choosing the phoneme with the highest degree of match. However, Repp's model differs from the present model primarily in its use of the euclidean distance function to describe the combined influence of the features.

Feature Independence

The assumption of independent acoustic features has been supported for a variety of speech stimuli. Not all acoustic manipulations will result in independence, however. Massaro and Cohen (1977) manipulated independently the duration of the frication period and the amplitude of vocal-cord vibration during the frication period on a /si/ to /zi/ continuum. Intuitively, these manipulations might not be expected to have independent effects, since other experiments have shown that the cue value of frication duration depends on whether or not vocal-cord vibration is present. Increasing the duration of frication without vocal-cord vibration makes the sound more voiceless, whereas frication duration with vocal-cord vibration has very little effect on perceived voicing. Accordingly, it seems reasonable to assume that the acoustic feature to voicing is the composite sound spectrum composed of both the high frequency noise and the harmonic energy produced by vocal-cord vibration. A version of the fuzzy logical model based on this single-composite feature idea was contrasted with one based on independent acoustic features. The description of the data was better for the composite features model than for the independent features model. This result shows two things: First, the independent features model is not too general, that is, it can be disconfirmed; second, a logical analysis of the stimulus situation is helpful in understanding how various acoustic manipulations will be processed in terms of acoustic features.

Phoneme Versus Syllable Prototypes

We have assumed that the relevant prototypes in LTM correspond to consonant–vowel syllables rather than stop-consonant phonemes. Given that no test of this assumption is possible in the present experiment, it is important to consider other sources of evidence. Acoustic cues to consonant phonemes depend critically on vowel context, and any normalization process that depends on vowel context is not easily handled by phoneme–unit models. In contrast, the necessary normalization is easy to build into syllable prototypes in LTM. Consider the classic example of the large differences in the second formant transitions in the stop consonant syllables /di/ and /du/. The second formant rises from approximately 2,200 Hz to 2,600 Hz in /di/, whereas it falls from approximately 1,200 Hz to 700 Hz in /du/. The second formant then remains relatively constant at these values during the steady-state vowel.

This example makes it apparent that the stop consonant /d/ cannot be invariantly defined by a phoneme prototype in LTM. However, the problem is easily solved by consonant–vowel syllable prototypes. Simplifying the situation, assume that two ordered features, the onset frequency of the second formant and its steady-state value, are sufficient acoustic features for distinguishing the syllables /di/ and /du/. In this case, /di/ would be defined as having a rising transition and a high steady-state vowel, whereas /du/ would be defined as having a falling transition and a low steady-state vowel. Consonant–vowel prototypes, then, solve the gross problem of the lack of acoustic invariance of stop consonants.

Another problem with phoneme prototypes is that the vowel sometimes provides direct acoustic cues to the identity of the consonantal portion of the syllable. As an example, vowel duration has a large influence on the perception of voicing of a vowel–consonant syllable in word-final position. Denes (1955), for example, carried out an experiment to evaluate the contribution of vowel duration and frication duration in the perception of voicing in word-final position. The test alternatives were the two pronunciations of the homograph "use" as in the noun "the use" and the verb "to use." Four durations of the synthetically produced vowel were independently varied with five durations of frication taken from real speech. No vocal-cord vibration was present during the frication period. The results showed that the proportion of voiceless responses decreased with increases in vowel duration and increased with increases in frication duration. Massaro and Cohen (1977) provided a quantitative description of these results in terms of the simple fuzzy logical model. It was assumed that vowel duration and frication duration are perceived independently and combined multiplicatively as in the fuzzy logical model. The good fit of the model and the meaningful parameter estimates simultaneously support the fuzzy logical model and the accompanying assumption of syllable prototypes in LTM.

Prototype modifiers. The inclusion of modifiers in the prototypes represents a fairly large deviation from the traditional way of thinking about phonemes. However, it would seem to be unlikely that there is no interaction at all between the articulations associated with the various acoustic dimensions. For voiced stops, for example, VOT increases as the place of articulation moves from labial to alveolar to velar points of closure. The difference in VOT follows directly from the time course of the pressure developed across the oral closure following release (Klatt, 1975). The release period is longer for velars than for labials, since the velar release involves the whole tongue body, whereas only the lips move in labials. Given that there are effects of this sort, then it also would seem most reasonable for the listener to come to expect some voiced phonemes to be subjectively more voiced than others. It is this kind of knowledge that the phoneme prototype modifiers represent.

An additional phenomenon that the phoneme prototype modifiers may be able to help interpret is the learning of dialects. It is, at first, difficult to understand people whose dialects are strongly different than one's own. However, after a period of listening, it becomes much easier and automatic. This process of "educating your ear" might be a matter of changing the modifiers on various phonemes, that is, restructuring the prototypes of perceptual units in long-term memory.

Phonetic boundary changes. Previous work (e.g., Lisker & Abramson, 1970) has found evidence for changes in the voicing boundary as a function of place of articulation. This result was obtained in the present experiment in terms of the quantitative predictions of the complex fuzzy logical model. The present experiment also obtained evidence of the same sort in support of the existence of changes in *place* boundaries as a function of *voicing*. In

addition, these latter changes were also indicated by a qualitative effect: The crossover point between labial and alveolar phonemes occurred between different levels of the place factor depending upon the particular value of VOT.

Such boundary changes are sometimes (e.g., Haggard, 1970) taken to be evidence of interaction in the perception of the acoustic features themselves. However, once it is recognized that the qualities of place and voicing are continuous, then featural interaction becomes potentially an infinitely complex problem. If we had to allow arbitrary interaction between the feature evaluation operations, so that the perception of one feature depended in an idiosyncratic way not only on the value of its own specific acoustic cues (which under natural conditions are highly correlated) but also on all of the other cues that might be varied independently, then the task of specifying how phoneme identification takes place would be even more formidable than it is at present. Happily, as the present article has demonstrated, the existence of changes in the boundaries need not lead us to accept the featural interaction hypothesis. Rather, it appears that the acoustic featural information is obtained independently but combined together by an integration rule of a form that produces the overall observed interaction. In fact, the success of the complex fuzzy logical model in accounting for the data, including all of the phonetic boundary changes, while still maintaining complete noninteraction of feature evaluation, may be taken to be strong evidence for the independence of acoustic feature perception during phoneme identification.

Conclusions

The following three main conclusions may be reached from the present work:

1. The fuzzy logical model provides a good description of the processes used in integrating information about voicing and place of articulation during phoneme identification.

2. Some phonemes require more extreme values on one or both acoustic dimensions than do other phonemes, and therefore, phoneme prototype definitions must allow for modifiers.

3. There are changes in the voicing boundary

as a function of place and also changes in the place boundaries as a function of voicing. However, these effects do not require that there be any interaction in the perception of the acoustic features but rather may result simply from the nature of the prototype representations of the speech sounds in long-term memory.

Reference Notes

1. McNabb, S. D. *Using confidence ratings to determine the sensitivity of phonetic feature detectors.* Paper presented at the meeting of the Midwestern Psychological Association, Chicago, May 1976.

2. Repp, B. H. *Interdependence of voicing and place decisions.* Unpublished manuscript, Haskins Laboratories, New Haven, Conn., September 1977.

References

Abramson, A. S., & Lisker, L. Voice-timing perception in Spanish word-initial stops. *Journal of Phonetics,* 1973, *1,* 1–8.

Anderson, N. H. Information integration theory: A brief survey. In D. H. Krantz, R. C. Atkinson, R. D. Luce, & P. Suppes (Eds.), *Contemporary developments in mathematical psychology* (Vol. 2). San Francisco: W. H. Freeman, 1974.

Barclay, J. R. Non-categorical perception of a voiced stop: A replication. *Perception & Psychophysics,* 1972, *11,* 269–273.

Carney, A. E., Widin, G. P., & Viemeister, N. F. Non-categorical perception of stop consonants differing in VOT. *Journal of the Acoustical Society of America,* 1977, *62,* 961–970.

Chandler, J. P. Subroutine STEPIT-Finds local minima of a smooth function of several parameters. *Behavioral Science,* 1969, *14,* 81–82.

Chomsky, N., & Halle, M. *The sound pattern of English.* New York: Harper & Row, 1968.

Cohen, M. M., & Massaro, D. W. Real-time speech synthesis. *Behavior Research Methods and Instrumentation,* 1976, *8,* 189–196.

Delattre, P. C., Liberman, A. M., & Cooper, F. S. Acoustic loci and transitional cues for consonants. *Journal of the Acoustical Society of America,* 1955, *27,* 769–773.

Denes, P. Effect of duration on the perception of voicing. *Journal of the Acoustical Society of America,* 1955, *27,* 761–764.

Goguen, J. A. The logic of inexact concepts. *Synthese,* 1969, *19,* 325–373.

Green, D. M., & Swets, J. A. *Signal detection theory and psychophysics.* New York: Wiley, 1966.

Haggard, M. P. The use of voicing information. *Speech Synthesis and Perception,* 1970, *2,* 1–15.

Harris, K. S., Hoffman, H. S., Liberman, A. M., Delattre, P. C., & Cooper, F. S. Effect of third-formant transitions on the perception of the voiced stop consonants. *Journal of the Acoustical Society of America,* 1958, *30,* 122–126.

Hoffman, H. S. Studies of some cues in the perception of the voiced stop consonants. *Journal of the Acoustical Society of America,* 1958, *30,* 1035–1041.

Jakobson, R., Fant, C. G. M., & Halle, M. *Preliminaries to speech analysis: The distinctive features and their correlates.* Cambridge, Mass.: MIT Press, 1961.

Klatt, D. H. Voice onset time, frication, and aspiration in word-initial consonant clusters. *Journal of Speech and Hearing Research,* 1975, *18,* 686–706.

Ladefoged, P. *A course in phonetics.* New York: Harcourt Brace Jovanovich, 1975.

Liberman, A. M., Delattre, P., & Cooper, F. S. Distinction between voiced and voiceless stops. *Language and Speech,* 1958, *1,* 153–167.

Lisker, L., & Abramson, A. S. A cross-language study of voicing in initial stops: Acoustical measurements. *Word,* 1964, *20,* 384–423.

Lisker, L., & Abramson, A. S. The voicing dimension: Some experiments in comparative phonetics. In *Proceedings of the Sixth International Congress of Phonetic Sciences* (1967). Prague, Czechoslovakia: Academic, 1970.

Luce, R. D. *Individual choice behavior.* New York: Wiley, 1959.

Massaro, D. W. *Experimental psychology and information processing.* Chicago: Rand-McNally, 1975. (a)

Massaro, D. W. (Ed.). *Understanding language: An information processing analysis of speech perception, reading and psycholinguistics.* New York: Academic Press, 1975. (b)

Massaro, D. W., & Cohen, M. M. The contribution of fundamental frequency and voice onset time to the /zi/–/si/ distinction. *Journal of the Acoustical Society of America,* 1976, *60,* 704–717.

Massaro, D. W., & Cohen, M. M. The contribution of voice-onset time and fundamental frequency as cues to the /zi/–/si/ distinction. *Perception & Psychophysics,* 1977, *22,* 373–382.

Miller, G. A., & Nicely, P. E. An analysis of perceptual confusions among some English consonants. *Journal of the Acoustical Society of America,* 1955, *26,* 338–352.

Miller, J. L. Nonindependence of feature processing in initial consonants. *Journal of Speech and Hearing Research,* 1977, *20,* 519–528.

Morton, J. Interaction of information in word recognition. *Psychological Review,* 1969, *76,* 165–178.

Oden, G. C. Integration of fuzzy logical information. *Journal of Experimental Psychology: Human Perception and Performance,* 1977, *3,* 565–575.

Oden, G. C. Integration of place and voicing information in the identification of synthetic stop consonants. *Journal of Phonetics,* in press.

Pisoni, D. B., & Lazarus, J. H. Categorical and non-categorical modes of speech perception along the voicing continuum. *Journal of the Acoustical Society of America,* 1974, *55,* 328–333.

Pisoni, D. B., & Tash, J. Reaction times to comparisons within and across phonetic categories. *Perception & Psychophysics,* 1974, *15,* 285–290.

Repp, B. H. Dichotic competition of speech sounds: The role of acoustic stimulus structure. *Journal of*

Experimental Psychology: Human Perception and Performance, 1977, *3*, 37–50.

Sawusch, J. R., & Pisoni, D. B. On the identification of place and voicing features in synthetic stop consonants. *Journal of Phonetics*, 1974, *2*, 181–194.

Selfridge, O. G. Pandemonium: A paradigm for learning. In D. Blake & A. Utteley (Eds.), *Symposium on the mechanization of thought processes*. London: H. M. Stationary Office, 1959.

Smith, P. T. Feature-testing models and their application to perception and memory for speech. *Quarterly Journal of Experimental Psychology*, 1973, *25*, 511–534.

Thurstone, L. L. A law of comparative judgment. *Psychological Review*, 1927, *34*, 273–286.

Zadeh, L. A. A fuzzy-set-theoretic interpretation of linguistic hedges. *Journal of Cybernetics*, 1972, *2*, 4–34.

Zadeh, L. A. The concept of a linguistic variable and its application to approximate reasoning (II). *Information Sciences*, 1975, *8*, 301–357.

Received July 16, 1977 ■

Invariant cues for place of articulation in stop consonants

K. N. Stevens

Research Laboratory of Electronics, Massachusetts Institute of Technology, Cambridge, Massachusetts 02139

S. E. Blumstein

Department of Linguistics, Brown University, Providence, Rhode Island 02912
(Received 1 February 1978; revised 18 July 1978)

In a series of experiments, identification responses for place of articulation were obtained for synthetic stop consonants in consonant–vowel syllables with different vowels. The acoustic attributes of the consonants were systematically manipulated, the selection of stimulus characteristics being guided in part by theoretical considerations concerning the expected properties of the sound generated in the vocal tract as place of articulation is varied. Several stimulus series were generated with and without noise bursts at the onset, and with and without formant transitions following consonantal release. Stimuli with transitions only, and with bursts plus transitions, were consistently classified according to place of articulation, whereas stimuli with bursts only and no transitions were not consistently identified. The acoustic attributes of the stimuli were examined to determine whether invariant properties characterized each place of atriculation independent of vowel context. It was determined that the gross shape of the spectrum sampled at the consonantal release showed a distinctive shape for each place of articulation: a prominent midfrequency spectral peak for velars, a diffuse-rising spectrum for alveolars, and a diffuse-falling spectrum for labials. These attributes are evident for stimuli containing transitions only, but are enhanced by the presence of noise bursts at the onset.

PACS numbers: 43.70.Dn, 43.70.Ve

INTRODUCTION

A great deal of research has been devoted to the study of the acoustic properties that signal to a listener the place of articulation for stop consonants. This research has followed two paths. One of these directions examines the listener identification of sounds whose acoustic parameters are systematically manipulated. The range of parameter values that leads to a particular consonant response is taken to define the acoustic cues for that consonantal place of articulation. The other approach is to carry out acoustic analysis of tokens of real speech utterances. The measured acoustic attributes associated with a particular consonant are taken to define the acoustic correlates of that place of articulation.

Early studies of the perception of synthetic speech sounds have examined the role of various acoustic attributes as cues for place of articulation. For example, several investigators have noted that the spectrum of the burst of acoustic energy occurring at consonantal release provides a cue for place of articulation.[1-5] Other studies have examined the role of the second- and third-formant starting frequencies, or loci, as place-of-articulation cues.[6] Still others have suggested that place of articulation is signaled by the direction of rapid spectrum change within a few tens of ms following consonantal release.[7,8]

For the most part, this work failed to find a set of acoustic properties that are invariant for a particular place of articulation, independent of the following vowel. The burst spectrum appears to differ somewhat from one vowel environment to another for a given place of articulation. The starting points of the transitions of the second and higher formants for a given consonant place of articulation show considerable variation from one vowel context to another (although there tends to be a fixed second-formant locus, if the locus is defined by extrapolating the formant contour back beyond the onset of voicing[6]). The direction of the second-formant transition likewise is not invariant, as evidenced, for example, by the fact that this formant falls following consonant release in the syllables [du] and [dɑ], but rises in [di].

The conclusion that has been drawn from these studies is that the identification of place of articulation for a stop consonant requires that a series of context-dependent cues must be extracted and interpreted in a different way for each phonetic context in which the consonant appears. Either the phonetic context must first be identified and the stop-consonant cues interpreted in relation to this context, or the various combinations of cues that identify a particular place of articulation must be decoded through some kind of special computation or lookup process (see, for example, Liberman *et al.*[9] and Stevens and Halle[10]).

Although the various acoustic attributes associated with different places of stop-consonant articulation are separately observable on a spectrographic representation, it is by no means clear that the auditory system processes the signal by examining each of these attributes independently. The possibility that stop consonants are characterized by more global properties has been noted by several investigators who have carried out acoustic analyses of these consonants.[5,7,11,12] These global properties reflect the configuration of acoustic events that occur at the release of a stop consonant— acoustic events that are a consequence of a particular place of articulation. It has been suggested[7,12-14] that the auditory system responds to these properties in an integrated manner rather than by processing each of a number of simpler properties and combining these at a later stage. Furthermore, several researchers[5,7,12] have hypothesized that the integrated property or properties associated with a particular phonetic feature provide acoustic invariance in the sense that they are independent of the context in which the feature occurs.

The purpose of this paper is to explore this concept of integrated acoustic properties through a series of experiments in which several acoustic characteristics of synthetic stop consonants in different phonetic environments are systematically manipulated, and identification responses are obtained. The range of acoustic characteristics that yield a particular consonantal response in various phonetic environments is examined, and an attempt is made to specify integrated acoustic properties that define each place of articulation independent of vowel context.

On the basis of these studies, we shall suggest that the auditory system samples the short-term spectrum at stimulus onset for a stop consonant, and that identification of place of articulation for the consonants is based on attributes of the gross shape of this spectrum. This onset spectrum is determined both by the burst spectrum and by the formant frequencies at the onset of voicing.

I. THEORETICAL INTERPRETATION OF THE ACOUSTIC CHARACTERISTICS OF STOP CONSONANTS

The shape of the onset spectrum for different burst frequencies and formant starting frequenceis can be predicted from theoretical considerations.[12] Thus before discussing the individual experiments, we shall review this theoretical background.

When the articulatory structures achieve a particular configuration, the acoustic cavities formed by these structures have certain natural frequencies. For example, when the cross-sectional area of the vocal tract is uniform along its length (corresponding roughly to a schwa or neutral vowel), the formant frequencies are regularly spaced at frequencies that are approximately $c/4l$, $3c/4l$, $5c/4l$, etc., where $c = $ speed of sound, and $l = $ vocal tract length. The spectrum envelope for a vowel with these formant frequencies shows the amplitudes of the spectral peaks decreasing with increasing frequency, according to well-established theoretical principles.[15] When a constriction is made in the tube corresponding to a consonant closure in the oral cavity, acoustic theory shows that there is always a lowering of the first-formant frequency. Depending on the position and shape of the constriction, the second and higher formants also undergo displacements upwards and downwards relative to their frequencies for a uniform vocal tract. The spectrum envelope due to a lowered frequency of $F1$ with no shifts in the other formants is illustrated in the upper panel of Fig. 1. There is a decrease in the amplitude of the higher formants relative to the amplitude of the spectral peak associated with $F1$.

Shifting of the frequencies of $F2$, $F3$, and higher formants downwards (keeping $F1$ at the same frequency) causes a decrease in the amplitudes of the higher formants in relation to the lower formants, as shown in the upper panel of Fig. 1. Such a downward shift in the formant frequencies occurs when a constriction is made at the lips, and hence this is the short-time spectrum that is to be expected at the onset of voicing for a labial consonant immediately after release of the constriction. On the other hand, an upward shift of the frequencies of $F2$, $F3$, and $F4$ relative to the values for the neutral vowel results in an increase of the amplitudes of the higher formants (e.g., $F4$ and $F5$) in relation to the lower formants (e.g., $F2$), as is also shown in the figure. This configuration of formants is expected on theoretical grounds for an alveolar consonant. Thus the spectra at the onset of voicing for a labial and an alveolar consonant differ not only with respect to the frequencies of the spectral peaks or formants at voicing onset, but also with respect to the overall shape of the spectrum as determined by the relative amplitudes of the spectral peaks.

At the release of a syllable-initial alveolar voiced consonant in English, a burst of turbulence noise is generated at the constriction, usually just prior to the onset of voicing. This noise source excites the higher

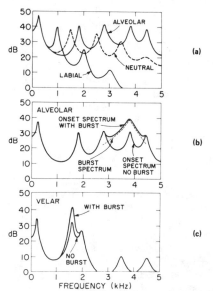

FIG. 1. (a) The dashed line represents the theoretical spectrum obtained with a voice source and with a low first-formant frequency and the second and higher formants located at the neutral positions of 1500, 2500, 3500, and 4500 Hz. Also shown are theoretical spectra for formant locations corresponding to an alveolar consonant (upward shifts of $F2$, $F3$, and $F4$) and a labial consonant (downward shifts of $F2$ and higher formants). (b) The spectrum of voice-source excitation of formants corresponding to an alveolar consonant is shown (from the upper panel), together with a theoretical spectrum for a noise burst at the release of an alveolar consonant (dashed line), and a composite spectrum obtained with both sources. (c) The theoretical spectrum for voice-source excitation of formants corresponding to a velar consonant is shown, together with the modified spectrum when noise is present.

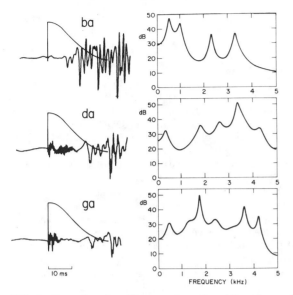

FIG. 2. Examples of waveforms and spectra at the release of three voiced stop consonants as indicated. Superimposed on each waveform is the time window (of width 26 ms) that is used for sampling the spectrum. Short-time spectra are determined for the first difference of the waveform (sampled at 10 kHz) and are smoothed using a linear prediction algorithm, i.e., they represent all-pole spectra that provide a best fit to the calculated short-term spectra with preemphasis.

vocal-tract resonances (usually $F4$, $F5$, and higher), resulting in a burst spectrum like that shown by the dashed line in the middle panel of Fig. 1. If we select a time window with a duration that is sufficient to encompass both the burst and the initial 10 or so ms at voicing onset, then the onset spectrum has the appearance shown by the solid line in the figure. The higher amplitudes of the high-frequency peaks in relation to the lower peaks are accentuated by the presence of the burst. That is, the burst contributes to this overall property of the gross spectrum shape. For the labial consonant, the burst is relatively weak, and does not greatly influence the overall spectrum shape at the onset of the consonant, shown in the upper panel of the figure.

In the case of the velar consonant, the second and third formants are usually relatively close together at onset, because the resonances of the cavities anterior and posterior to the point of constriction are roughly equal. This proximity of two formants enhances the amplitudes of both spectral peaks in relation to the amplitudes of higher formants, as shown in the lower panel of Fig. 1. The noise burst at the release of a velar stop consonant excites the resonance of the vocal-tract cavity anterior to the constriction, which is usually continuous with the second or third formant of the following vowel (depending on whether it is a back or front vowel). Thus the spectrum of the burst has a relatively narrow peak that is in the vicinity of the proximate second and third formants at the onset of voicing, and the presence of the burst causes an enhancement of the spectral energy concentration in this midfrequency

region. This enhancement of the spectral peak is shown in the lower portion of Fig. 1, in which the spectra at onset with and without burst are compared.

The absolute positions of the formants in Figs. 1(a), 1(b), and 1(c) may be shifted up or down within certain limits without affecting the gross spectral shapes, as long as the relative positions of the formants remain roughly the same. These kinds of formant shifts at consonantal release are to be expected when a given consonant is followed by different vowels.

These theoretical notions suggest that relatively invariant acoustic properties should exist for the various places of articulation for stop consonants independent of the following vowel if these properties are based on the gross shape of the short-term spectrum sampled at the consonantal release. This spectrum should, after all, come close to reflecting the articulatory configuration at the release, and it is known that certain aspects of that configuration (such as the region of contact between lower articulators and upper structures) remain relatively invariant independent of the following vowel. The time course of the formant transitions, on the other hand, depends both on the starting formant frequencies, which are determined by the consonantal configuration, and on the frequencies towards which these formants are moving, which are determined by the following vowel. Thus the spectrum sampled at onset is more likely to provide a context-independent indication of the consonantal place of articulation than are the trajectories of the formants.

Whether the auditory system actually assesses the gross shape of the short-term spectrum at a stimulus onset or discontinuity is a question that can only be answered through further research. Zhukov et al.[16] have proposed such a mechanism, and provide some experimental support for this view.

Examples of spectra measured at the onsets for the stop consonants [b], [d], and [g] followed by the vowel [ɑ], as produced by an adult male speaker, are shown in Fig. 2. These are linear prediction spectra obtained by preemphasizing the high frequencies and using a 26-ms time window beginning at the consonantal release.[17] The spectrum at the release of a stop consonant can, of course, be influenced by the duration and shape of the window that is selected for examining the spectrum. The selection of a 26-ms window with the shape indicated in Fig. 2 (which has an effective duration of somewhat less than 26 ms) is based on a preliminary study of onset spectra for a number of consonant–vowel syllables using different window lengths. The 26-ms window seemed to give spectra for which the gross attributes associated with the different places of articulation were most salient, although these spectral attributes were not strongly dependent on window length. It is evident, however, that the selection of an appropriate window for sampling the spectrum must in the long run be based on a more systematic examination of the properties of the auditory system,[18] as well as the effects of different window lengths on the spectrum shape for various onset phenomena in speech.

The spectrum for [g] in Fig. 2 shows a pronounced

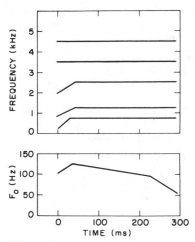

FIG. 3. The upper panel shows the trajectories of the first five formants for a synthetic syllable with no burst--the syllable that is identified as [ba]. The lower panel shows the fundamental-frequency contour that was used for all stimuli.

peak in the midfrequency range. There is a more diffuse spread of spectral energy for the [b] and [d] spectra, and the overall shapes of the spectra for these two consonants are quite different, as the theory would predict.

The theoretical discussion noted above should also apply to the spectrum sampled at the offset or at the instant of vocal-tract closure in a vowel-consonant syllable. There is no burst at this instant of time (although there could be a release burst some tens of ms later), but the formant frequencies do approach target values appropriate to the consonantal place of articulation, and consequently the spectrum shape should be similar to one of the theoretically derived spectra illustrated in Fig. 1. Thus a perceptual mechanism that samples spectra at both onsets and offsets, and interprets these spectra in terms of attributes of their gross shape could, in principle, classify both syllable-initial and syllable-final consonants.

It is important to note that the concept of an onset spectrum, as described here, implies some kind of continuity of spectrum change as the onset burst merges into the formant transitions, which in turn merge into the vowel. Thus, for example, if the spectrum of a burst is not consistent with the spectrum at the onset of voicing (as might occur if a [g] burst were appended to formant onsets appropriate for [d]), then two discontinuities would occur: one at the release of the burst and one at the onset of voicing, and the listener would be exposed to conflicting cues for place of articulation. Several experiments of this type have been conducted, and have shown that the phonetic label attributed to a particular burst spectrum changes as a consequence of the context which follows. [2,3,19]

II. EXPERIMENT

The general procedure was to synthesize a number of different series of consonant-vowel stimuli in which bursts and formant transitions were manipulated systematically, and to present these stimuli to listeners for identification of the initial consonant. The results of these identification tests were then examined to determine what acoustic properties give rise to each place of articulation.

A. Stimuli

Altogether 13 different series of stimuli were produced on the synthesizer designed by Dennis Klatt. [20] These included continua which ranged from [b] to [d] to [g] or [b] to [g] in the environment of the vowels [ɑ i u]. The vowels were generated by a digital representation of a cascade connection of tuned circuits, with a sampling rate of 10 kHz. For all stimuli, the duration of voicing was 250 ms and in some stimuli, a 5-ms noise burst was appended 5–15 ms prior to voicing onset. The fundamental-frequency contour for all stimuli is shown at the bottom of Fig. 3. The vowels [i] and [u] were slightly diphthongized to provide greater naturalness for these vowels. The frequencies of the first four formants (in Hz) for the vowels were as follows:

vowel [ɑ]: 720, 1240, 2500, 3600

vowel [i]: 330–270, 2000–2300, 3000, 3600

vowel [u]: 370–330, 1100–1000, 2350, 3200.

The frequency ranges for [i] and [u] indicate the extent of diphthongal formant motion throughout the vowel.

1. Transition-only stimulus series

For six of the series of stimuli, there were transitions of the formants during the initial 20–40 ms, and the source of excitation of the vowel resonators was turned on abruptly, the first glottal pulse coinciding with the beginning of the formant transitions. Based on theoretical considerations, the first-formant transition for all stimuli was rising; the $F1$ starting frequency was 200 Hz for [ɑ] syllables and 180 Hz for [i] and [u] syllables. The duration of the $F1$ transition was 15–30 ms for [i] syllables, 20–45 ms for [ɑ] syllables, and 15 ms for [u] syllables. For those $F1$ transitions which varied in duration along the continuum, the faster transitions were at the [b] end of the stimulus series, and the slower transitions at the [g] end. The durations of the transitions for all other formants were always 40 ms, with a linear formant trajectory from the starting frequency to the steady-state value for the vowel.

In constructing a stimulus series, the starting frequencies of $F2$, $F3$, and, in the case of [i] syllables, $F4$, were systematically manipulated through the series of values, [21] so that the characteristics of the spectrum at onset varied through the gross shapes predicted by the acoustic theory outlined above. In three of the series, these changes in the formant starting frequencies passed through ranges known to be appropriate for the consonants [b], [d], and [g], whereas in the other three the values ranged from [b] through [g] without an intervening [d]. Thus at the [b] end of a stimulus continuum, the second and higher formants started at relatively low frequencies; for the alveolar anchor point on the continuum, the starting frequencies were relatively high, and for the velar anchor point, two of the formants

TABLE I. Starting frequencies of $F2$, $F3$ and $F4$ (in Hz) for the various full and partial-cue stimulus series. For series with vowels [a] and [u], the starting frequencies of $F4$ were 3600 and 3200 Hz, respectively.

		F2	F3			F2	F3	F4			F2	F3
[ba da ga]	1	900	2000	[bi di gi]	1	1800	2600	3200	[bu du gu]	1	800	2000
	2	1010	2110		2	1833	2633	3317		2	933	2117
	3	1120	2220		3	1867	2667	3433		3	1067	2233
	4	1240	2340		4	1900	2700	3550		4	1200	2350
	5	1350	2450		5	1933	2733	3667		5	1333	2467
	6	1470	2570		6	1967	2767	3783		6	1467	2583
	7	1580	2680		7	2000	2800	3900		7	1600	2700
	8	1700	2800		8	2067	2833	3817		8	1567	2583
	9	1680	2630		9	2133	2867	3733		9	1533	2467
	10	1670	2460		10	2200	2900	3650		10	1500	2350
	11	1650	2280		11	2267	2933	3567		11	1467	2233
	12	1640	2100		12	2333	2967	3483		12	1433	2117
	13	1620	1920		13	2400	3000	3400		13	1400	2000
	14	1610	1750									
[ba ga]	1	900	2000	[bi gi]	1	1800	2600	3400	[bu gu]	1	800	2000
	2	1010	2000		2	1916	2666	3400		1	900	2000
	3	1120	2000		3	2033	2733	3400		3	1000	2000
	4	1240	2000		4	2150	2800	3400		4	1100	2000
	5	1350	2000		5	2266	2866	3400		5	1200	2000
	6	1470	2000		6	2383	2933	3400		6	1300	2000
	7	1580	2000		7	2500	3000	3400		7	1400	2000
										8	1500	2000

started close together to form a narrow spectral prominence. These extreme values are roughly similar to the values observed in real speech, although some details may be different. The formant trajectories for a typical stimulus with transitions only are shown in the upper section of Fig. 3.

The formant starting frequencies for the six stimulus series are listed in Table I. The number of stimuli in the [b d g] series was 13 or 14, and in the [b g] series it was 7 or 8.

Because a cascade configuration was used for the formant synthesizer, it was unnecessary to specify the amplitudes of individual formants—the formant amplitudes are dependent on their frequencies, just as they are in natural speech. Thus changes in the relative amplitudes of the formants at voicing onset will occur as the starting frequencies of the transitions take on different values for different stimuli, as has been discussed above in connection with Fig. 1.

2. Stimuli with bursts

In order to generate a stimulus continuum with initial bursts, it might appear at first glance that an appropriate strategy would be to generate a burst in which spectral energy is concentrated in a restricted frequency range, and to manipulate systematically the frequency of the burst. Such a procedure would, however, violate conditions of continuity of burst and vowel formants. In real speech, bursts are generated by noise excitation of certain vocal-tract resonances. When voicing begins after a burst, the glottal source excites the same resonances, albeit with different relative amplitudes. Thus peaks in the spectrum of the burst should be roughly continuous with at least some of the spectral peaks or formants at the onset of voicing in the following vowel. In the various stimulus series containing bursts and transitions, this condition was achieved by always locating the spectral peaks of a burst at the starting frequencies of formants in the adjacent vowel. A series of stimuli was generated by systematically adjusting the amplitude of the spectral peak associated with one formant in relation to that associated with another formant. In natural speech, at least for velars and alveolars, one spectral peak in the burst corresponding to one of the formants is usually the most prominent, although it is recognized that other formants are excited to a lesser extent by the frication noise. In the case of the labials, generation of the burst by noise excitation of just one formant gives only a rough approximation of the burst spectrum, since in natural speech there are usually weak energy peaks distributed throughout the spectrum.[12]

The timing of the burst in relation to the onset of voicing followed roughly the characteristics of natural speech, i.e., shortest voice onset time (5 ms) for labials, and longest (15 ms) for velars. The burst amplitudes were selected to enhance the shapes of the onset spectra in the manner illustrated in Fig. 1. These burst amplitudes (at least for alveolars and velars) are roughly in accord with amplitudes found to be optimal on the basis of perceptual experiments.[23]

Consider, for example, a [ba da ga] series containing both bursts and transitions. The formant specifications of the [ba da ga] stimuli given in Table I were used as starting points, and bursts were appended to these stimuli. For stimulus 8 in the series (the one with the highest $F3$ value), the burst was produced by exciting a resonator centered at 3600 Hz with a 5-ms segment of white noise, beginning 10 ms prior to the onset of voicing. Thus the burst frequency is continuous with $F4$ of the adjacent vowel. For stimulus number 14 in the series, at the [g] end of the continuum, the burst was produced by exciting a resonator centered at 1610 Hz

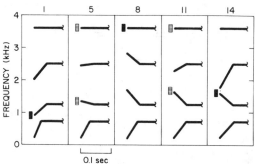

FIG. 4. Schematic spectrographic representations of the initial portions of some of the burst-plus-transition stimuli in the [ba da ga] continuum. The filled rectangles preceding particular formants indicate the frequency-time locations of full-amplitude bursts for stimulus 1 (left panel), stimulus 8 (third panel), and stimulus 14 (right panel), from Table I. The shaded rectangles represent burst components of lower amplitude adjacent to F2 and F4 onsets for the intermediate stimulus 5 (second panel) and stimulus 11 (fourth panel).

(the starting frequency of the F2 transition) with a 5-ms segment of white noise, beginning 15 ms prior to voicing onset. To generate the bursts for stimuli between 8 and 14, both F4 (which remained at 3600 Hz in this series) and F2 (which varied from one stimulus to the next) were excited by 5-ms segments of noise, but the relative amplitudes of the high- and low-frequency components were systematically changed to values that were interpolated (on a logarithmic amplitude scale) between the end-point amplitudes given by stimuli 8 and 14. A similar interpolation procedure was used for generating bursts for stimuli 1–8. The end-point stimulus 1 was generated with the noise burst exciting formant 2, in this case initiated 5 ms prior to voicing. The change in amplitude of a spectral peak for the burst from one stimulus to the next in this series (and in other others that were generated with different vowels) was in the range of 4–6 dB. A consequence of this interpolation is that for stimuli intermediate between the extreme points, there are two peaks in the spectrum of the burst, and the overall amplitude of the burst is of the order of 10 dB lower than that for the extreme stimuli. The manner in which the bursts were generated is illustrated in the schematized spectrographic representation of several of the burst-plus-transition stimuli in the [ba da ga] series, shown in Fig. 4.

The burst-plus-transition stimuli in the [bu du gu] series were generated in the same manner as the [ba da ga] series. For the [bi di gi] series with bursts, the transition-only stimuli of Table I were used as a starting point, but in this case the burst for the end-point [g] stimulus (number 13) was generated by exciting the third rather than the second formant. This procedure for generating the [g] burst is in accord with known phonetic facts, which show that velar consonants before back vowels have bursts near F2, while those before front vowels have bursts at F3 (or even F4 in some cases).

In addition to the three burst-plus-transition series (which we shall call *full-cue* stimuli), several stimulus series were generated with bursts only, followed by

steady higher-formant frequencies, i.e., with no higher-formant transitions but with the F1 transition the same as before. (The F1 transition is, of course, necessary to provide the cues for voicing and manner of articulation of the stop, but contributes little information about place of articulation.) Stimuli in one of these series were produced by generating the bursts in the manner just described for the [ba da ga] stimuli, but then straightening the transitions. Informal listening to these burst-only stimuli showed that place of articulation could not be identified. The quality of the consonant seemed to improve significantly, however, if the onset of voicing was delayed an additional 10 ms relative to the onset of the burst. Thus all burst-only stimuli modeled on the [ba da ga] and the [bu gu] series were produced with this modification. Three other series of burst-only stimuli with no transitions were modeled on the [b g] series of Table I. In all of these stimuli, the burst duration was 5 ms and its onset occurred 15 ms prior to voicing onset. In the case of the [ba ga] and the [bu gu] series, the center frequency of the burst was always at the frequency given in Table I as the starting frequency of F2, but the higher formants had no transitions. For the [bi gi] burst-only stimuli, the burst spectrum also had a single spectral peak, but the frequency position of this peak varied in equal logarithmic steps from 1400 Hz at one end of the continuum to 3000 Hz at the other end. Again, the transitions of the formants were straightened for the [bi gi] series. For all these burst-only stimuli therefore, the frequency of a spectral peak for the burst was usually not contiguous with one of the higher formants, in contrast to the examples in Fig. 4 for stimuli with both bursts and transitions. This violation of continuity led to unnatural stimuli and inconsistent responses, as the results will demonstrate.

TABLE II. Percentage of subjects who were able to label the test continua according to the phonetic categories investigated. Percentages are based on 20 subjects for all stimulus series, except for the burst-cue [ba da ga] series, for which 25 subjects were used.

Full-Cue stimuli		Percentage
ba-da-ga		95
bi-di-gi		100
bu-du-gu		75
	Mean	90

Transition-Only Stimuli		Percentage
ba-da-ga		100
ba-ga		70
bi-di-gi		85
bi-gi		65
bu-du-gu		65
bu-gu		100
	Mean	81

Burst-Cue Stimuli		Percentage
ba-da-ga		36
ba-ga		0
bi-gi		30
bu-gu		5
	Mean	18

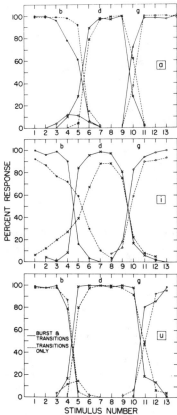

FIG. 5. Identification functions for stimuli on [b d g] continua with three different vowels. Solid lines represent data for stimuli with bursts and transitions; dashed lines for transition-only stimuli. Data are based on numbers of subjects indicated in Table II.

The left-hand column of Table II summarizes the 13 stimulus series: the three full-cue series containing both bursts and transitions, the six partial-cue series containing transitions only, and the four burst-cue series with no transitions. Each of the 13 series of stimuli was organized into an identification test in which each stimulus was presented 10 times in a random order. There was a three-second interstimulus interval. Prior to the presentation of the test tape for each stimulus series, subjects heard the sequence of stimuli twice. Two practice trials preceded the beginning of the test. All these recorded tests were presented binaurally over headphones at a comfortable listening level to groups of listeners, who were instructed to identify the consonants as either [b], [d], or [g] in the case of the [b d g] series, or as [b] or [g] in the case of the [b g] series.

B. Subjects

Twenty listeners participated in each test, except in the [ba da ga] burst-only test series in which there were 25 subjects. For the most part, different groups of listeners were used in the different tests; however, there was some overlap of subjects across the various tests. The listeners were all graduate and undergrad-

uate students at Brown University who were paid for their participation.

III. RESULTS AND DISCUSSION

Each subject's identification function for each test was analyzed separately. As our primary goal was to determine the range of stimuli defining each phonetic category, we eliminated subjects who were unable to label the stimuli according to the phonetic categories investigated, i.e., either [b], [d], and [g], or [b] and [g]. Our criteria for dropping subjects were fairly conservative. In the case of the [b d g] identification series, subjects simply had to have three different ranges of responses. However, we were not concerned if category identification scores of the subject were consistently high or if the slopes of the phonetic boundaries were sharp. Similar criteria were used for the [b g] identification continua, except that in this case the subjects had to have two different ranges of responses. Thus, we basically eliminated only those subjects who responded randomly or who identified the stimuli as belonging to one phonetic category.

Table II shows the total percent of subjects who were included in the final data analysis. On the whole, most subjects were able to identify the full- and partial-cue stimuli, with the full-cue stimuli being identified by more subjects. In contrast, only 18% of the subjects were able to identify the burst-cue stimuli with any consistency. Comparison across vowel contexts for the full- and partial-cue stimuli shows that 88% of the subjects were able to identify the consonants in the [a] series, 83% in the [i] series, and 80% in the [u] series. Thus the synthetic continua generated seemed to be fairly comparable across the three vowel contexts.

Mean identification functions for the full and partial [b d g] series across the three vowel contexts are presented in Fig. 5. With the exception of the [b] category for the [a] series, the responses to the individual stimuli are generally more consistent and the shapes of the functions are more categorical (in the sense that the slopes at the phonetic boundaries are sharper) for the full-cue than for the partial-cue stimuli, although the boundaries are about the same. Figure 6 shows the mean responses of the subjects to the partial [b g] series. Inspection of the graphs indicates that the identification functions have similar shapes across the three series.

In order to determine whether there are unique acoustics properties underlying each of the phonetic dimensions independent of vowel environments, we now examine the acoustic attributes that characterize the stimuli in each of the [b d g] response regions of Figs. 5 and 6. In accord with earlier studies[1,6,24] the data show that absolute onset frequencies of the formants, directions of formant motion, or burst frequencies fail to provide invariant characterizations of the different phonetic categories. Although these attributes alone cannot uniquely characterize each place of articulation, it is possible to select combinations of these attributes that reflect more directly the gross properties of the onset spectra as discussed earlier.

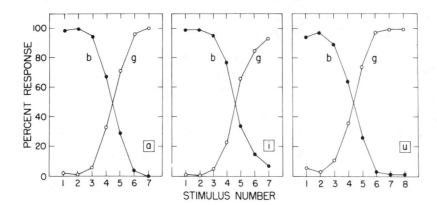

FIG. 6. Identification functions for stimuli on [b g] continua with three different vowels. Stimuli contain transitions only with no bursts. Data are based on number of subjects indicated in Table II.

Figure 7 shows the attributes of the stimuli on the burst-plus-transition continuum plotted in relation to two dimensions: the difference between $F3$ and $F2$ onset frequencies, and the frequency of the component of the burst with greater intensity. The $F3-F2$ dimension provides a measure of mid-frequency prominence in the onset spectrum, and the burst frequency indicates the region of the onset spectrum that is enhanced by the burst (cf. Fig. 1). A stimulus point is included only if 75% of the responses to that stimulus are in the same phonetic category. As the figure shows, the continua divide into three discrete phonetic categories with no area of overlap. Stimuli are labeled as [g] when the difference between $F3$ and $F2$ is 780 Hz or less. For these stimuli, the burst is in the region of $F2$ or $F3$, and it enhances the midfrequency spectral prominence due to the proximity of $F2$ and $F3$. For the categories [b] and [d], the spacing between $F2$ and $F3$ onset frequencies is greater than it is for [g], and [d] is distin-

guished from [b] by the frequency of the burst, with [d]'s characterized by greater high-frequency energy and [b]'s by low-frequency energy.

The measures depicted in Fig. 7 represent a first approximation to the characterization of the shape of the onset spectrum. It has been suggested in the introductory discussion that this spectrum has a distinctive gross shape for stimuli corresponding to different places of articulation. It is of some interest, therefore, to interpret the data of Figs. 5 and 6 directly in terms of the gross shapes of the onset spectra, rather than in terms of selected attributes that contribute to these shapes. In particular, it is instructive to examine these spectra for stimuli that lie both in the middle of each phonetic category, where the relevant acoustic property is presumably more salient, and at the boundary between two categories, where the acoustic properties are weakly representative of both phonetic categories.

We have computed the onset spectra for all of the stimuli used in the various stimulus continua, using the same procedures as those described in connection with Fig. 2. From these spectra we have selected items corresponding to (1) stimuli that represent the best prototypes for [b], [d], and [g], and (2) stimuli close to the phonetic boundaries. These spectra are displayed in Fig. 8. Each panel of the figure shows three onset spectra: two corresponding to tokens for which the response to a particular phonetic category is close to 100%, and one corresponding to a stimulus close to the phonetic boundary. Data are shown for the [b]–[d], [d]–[g], and [b]–[g] pairs for each of the three vowel environments. In the case of the [b]–[d] and [d]–[g] pairs, spectra for the burst-plus-transition stimuli are shown; for the [b]–[g] pair, only the transition-only stimuli were tested, and hence only spectra for these stimuli are shown.

We examine first the various groups of onset spectra corresponding to the [b]–[d] pairs with the three different following vowels. For all of the spectra in these panels forming the left column of the figure, we observe that there is a diffuse spread of energy over the mid-frequency range from 1–3 kHz. That is, there is more than one spectral peak in this range, and no single peak

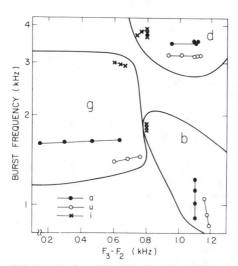

FIG. 7. Display of identification data of Fig. 5, with stimulus characteristics specified in terms of burst frequency and difference between $F3$ and $F2$ at onset of voicing. Each point represents a stimulus that was identified as [b], [d], or [g] for 75% or more of the responses. Ranges of stimulus characteristics corresponding to each response category are indicated by the contours.

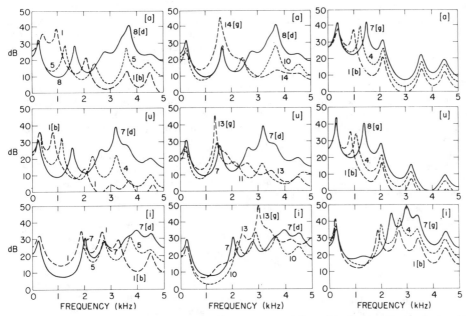

FIG. 8. Short-term spectra sampled at onset for various stimuli used in the identification tests. Each panel shows three spectra corresponding to three stimuli on the continuum, ranging from one response category to an adjacent response category. Two of the spectra (the solid line and the long-dashed line) represent stimuli in the middle of a phonetic category, for which the responses were close to 100% [b], [d], or [g], as indicated. The third spectrum in each panel (short-dashed line) represents a stimulus between phonetic categories, for which responses were equivocal. The panels in the left column and in the middle column show spectra for stimuli from the [b d g] series containing both bursts and transitions. The panels in the right column show spectra for the transition-only [b g] series. Spectra are calculated and smoothed in the manner described in connection with Fig. 2, i.e., they are spectra calculated using a linear prediction algorithm, with a high-frequency preemphasis, and with a time window of width 26 ms centered at the onset.

stands out prominently from the other peaks. The onset spectra for stimuli identified as [d] show a general rise in the amplitudes of the spectral peaks from $F2$ to $F3$ to $F4$, the largest peak being in the vicinity of the fourth formant. For [d] followed by [a] and [u] there is a rather prominent peak at high frequencies, due to the burst that is located in the vicinity of the fourth formant, but the frequency is above the range we define as the middle range (1–3 kHz). In contrast to [d], the [b] stimuli show a decrease in the amplitudes of spectral peaks corresponding to successively higher formants above $F2$. Spectra for stimuli at the phonetic boundary between [b] and [d] show neither a rising nor a falling trend for the amplitudes of spectral peaks corresponding to $F2$, $F3$, and $F4$. The $F3$ is either lower or higher in amplitude than the $F2$ and $F4$ peaks. Thus the onset spectra for [b] can be characterized as diffuse and falling (or grave), whereas the spectra for [d] are diffuse and rising (or acute). [12,25]

Turning next to the spectra that include [g] as one of the endpoints, we observe that the [g] spectra all exhibit a prominent spectral peak in the midfrequency range from 1–3 kHz, for the stimuli both in the full-cue [b d g] series and in the partial-cue [b g] series. This peak is prominent in the sense that the amplitude of the peak is well above the amplitudes of other peaks in the spectrum. In the case of [g] before back vowels, the frequency of the prominent peak is at the lower end of the range, whereas for [g] before [i] it is at the upper end

of the range. These spectra are said to be characterized by the feature of compactness. [25] In all sections of Fig. 8 the contrast between the compact [g] spectrum and the diffuse [b] or [d] spectrum is evident, since in the spectrum for [b] and [d] the peaks are distributed throughout the midfrequency range without any single dominant peak. The spectra for stimuli at the phoneme boundary are, as expected, intermediate between the diffuse and compact shapes. That is, they are characterized neither by a prominent midfrequency peak, nor by a diffuse spread of energy.

Spectra similar to those in Fig. 8 have been measured for stimuli in the partial-cue [b d g] series. The attributes of these spectra are similar to those obtained for the full-cue [b d g] stimuli, except that in the case of the full-cue stimuli the burst enhances the properties inherent in the first 5 or 10 ms of the onset of the formant transitions.

The characterization of spectra as being compact or diffuse, or as grave or acute, is based here on qualitative observations of the gross spectral shape. More precise definition of these properties is needed, and must await the collection and interpretation of data on onset spectra from a number of utterances from real speech. [17,26]

If we were to examine spectra at the onsets of the burst-only stimuli, we would find gross spectral shapes similar to those depicted in Fig. 8, since the bursts are the same as those in the full-cue stimuli. Why, then, do most listeners fail to classify these burst-only stimuli consistently? As noted above, we suggest that the burst-only stimuli are characterized by two onsets— one at the onset of the burst and the other at the onset of voicing. The short-time spectrum does not undergo a smooth and continuous change as the stimulus proceeds from the initial onset into the vowel (as it does in natural speech or in the synthetic full-cue stimuli), but rather, there are, in effect, two onsets in sequence. The cues provided by these two onsets are conflicting, and can lead to inconsistent responses, depending upon which onset is weighted more heavily. This finding underlines the requirement that the spectrum at onset must not only have a gross shape appropriate for a particular place of articulation, but must also undergo a smooth and continuous change in shape during the transition into the vowel.

IV. CONCLUSION

We postulate in this paper that the place of articulation for a syllable-initial stop consonant can be identified, independent of vowel context, on the basis of the gross shape of the spectrum sampled at the consonantal release. The characteristics of this onset spectrum are determined both by the burst of acoustic energy at the release and by the initial portions of the formant transitions at voicing onset. This point of view was suggested many years ago by Fant[12] and by Halle, Hughes, and Radley,[11] and emphasized the importance of the spectrum sampled at the consonantal release rather than the trajectories of the formants during their transitions into the vowel. Results of this study support this interpretation and further suggest that invariant cues for place of articulation for stop consonants can be characterized independent of the following vowel by an *event*, i.e., the spectrum at stimulus onset occurring at a point in time, rather than by a sequence of events over time. In this view, then, the formant transitions are *not* the primary cues signaling place of articulation. Instead, their primary function, as has been postulated by Cole and Scott,[5] seems to be to join the onset spectrum to the vowel smoothly without introducing any additional discontinuities. Such discontinuites would, of course, signal new onsets, as noted above.

The implication of this hypothesis is that the auditory system is endowed with a mechanism that detects the presence of an abrupt onset of energy and assigns certain simple properties to the spectrum sampled at this onset. Experimental evidence from auditory psychophysics and from auditory physiology suggests that a signal undergoes some kind of special processing at an abrupt onset,[27,28] but there is little detailed information concerning the nature of this processing (see Zhukov *et al.*[16] for discussion of these questions).

While data presented in this paper are consistent with this theoretical view concerning the detection of spectral properties at onsets and offsets, they do not constitute a strong test of the theory. There are several possible experiments which could provide such a test. For example, brief stimuli in which only the onsets of consonant-

vowel syllables are preserved could be presented to listeners to determine whether the information contained in these onsets is sufficient to identify place of articulation. Some experiments along these lines have already been carried out, with results that support the hypothesis.[4,29] A stronger test of the theory would be to determine whether perception of place of articulation depends on attributes of the gross shape of the spectrum at onset, independent of fine details such as burst characteristics and formant onset frequencies. Thus, for example, the relative amplitudes of the formants at the onset of a particular CV syllable could be manipulated to yield a different gross spectrum shape without changing the onset frequencies. The question would be whether perception goes with the formant onset frequencies or with the gross spectrum shape at onset. Details such as how an abrupt onset is defined, the time window for sampling the spectrum, and the spectral resolution could be worked out on the basis of such experiments.

If indeed the auditory system is endowed with these types of detectors, then there is an explanation for the ability of young infants to discriminate stimuli with different places of articulation, particularly when these stimuli are produced with the full cues consisting of bursts and transitions.[30] These stimuli represent clear tokens of the compact-diffuse and grave-acute properties. Similarly, infants have shown the ability to discriminate place of articulation when signaled by three-formant patterns without a preceding burst.[31-33] As discussed above, these stimuli still contain the onset characteristics representing the compact-diffuse and grave-acute phonetic distinctions. However, there is evidence that discrimination of place of articulation by infants is improved when full-cue stimuli are used.[30]

On the other hand, it is known that adult listeners can identify place of articulation for stimuli containing only the first two formants.[1,6] Clearly, these stimuli do not possess the general properties noted above. The context-independent properties for place of articulation, however, do occur in conjunction with acoustic attributes which are in themselves context-dependent—in particular, such attributes as the directions of the formant transitions and the formant frequencies of the following vowel. Although these secondary attributes are not invariant, they could be invoked in the identification of stimuli when the primary invariant attribute is absent or distorted, as has been suggested by Cole and Scott.[5] Thus, two- or three-formant patterns could be identified by a process that requires reference to attributes of the following vowel. According to this view, then, the context-dependent cues are secondary, learned presumably by the child as attributes which co-occur with the primary invariant context-independent cues for place of articulation.

Although the concept of invariant spectral properties associated with place of articulation has been discussed here in the context of voiced stop consonants in consonant–vowel syllables in English, its extension to other classes of consonants and to other phonetic environments can be readily envisioned. Reference has already been made to the fact that spectra sampled at the vowel offset of a vowel–consonant syllable should exhibit the same properties as the onset spectrum for a given place of consonant articulation, since the formant transitions for initial and final consonants begin and end at about the same frequencies. Onset spectra for voiceless stops and spectra sampled immediately following the release of nasal consonants would probably show characteristics similar to those for voiced stops in initial position, since the burst for a voiceless stop has properties similar to that for the voiced cognate, and since the starting points of the formant transitions for a nasal consonant are similar to those for a voiced stop with the same place of articulation. Thus a particular place of articulation can be characterized in terms of invariant acoustic properties for different manners of articulation and across different syllabic contexts. Further experimental data need to be collected, however, in order to test these hypotheses, and to further elaborate the theory.

ACKNOWLEDGMENTS

This work was supported in part by the National Institutes of Health, Grant NS-04332. Dr. Blumstein's participation was supported in part by the John Simon Guggenheim Foundation and the Radcliffe Institute. Measurement and display of the linear-prediction spectra were accomplished using a program written by Dennis Klatt, whose help is gratefully acknowledged. The assistance of Georgia Nigro in running the experimental subjects is acknowledged with thanks.

[1] F. S. Cooper, P. C. Delattre, A. M. Liberman, J. M. Borst, and L. J. Gerstman, "Some experiments on the perception of synthetic speech sounds," J. Acoust. Soc. Am. 24, 597–606 (1952).

[2] C. D. Schatz, "The role of context in the perception of stops," Language, 30, 47–56 (1954).

[3] E. Fischer-Jorgensen, "Perceptual studies of Danish stop consonants," Ann. Rep. Inst. Phonet. Univ. Copenhagen 6, 75–168 (1972).

[4] H. Winitz, M. E. Scheib, and J. A. Reeds, "Identification of stops and vowels for the burst portion of /p,t,k/ isolated from conversational speech," J. Acoust. Soc. Am. 51, 1309–1317 (1972).

[5] R. A. Cole and B. Scott, "Toward a theory of speech perception," Psychol. Rev. 81, 348–374 (1974).

[6] P. C. Delattre, A. M. Liberman, and F. S. Cooper, "Acoustic loci and transitional cues for consonants," J. Acoust. Soc. Am. 27, 769–773 (1955).

[7] K. N. Stevens, "The potential role of property detectors in the perception of consonants," in Auditory Analysis and Perception of Speech, edited by G. Fant and M. A. A. Tatham (Academic, New York, 1975), pp. 303–330.

[8] K. N. Stevens, and S. E. Blumstein, "Quantal aspects of consonant production and perception: A study of retroflex consonants," J. Phonet. 3, 215–234 (1975).

[9] A. M. Liberman, F. S. Cooper, D. P. Shankweiler, and M. Studdert-Kennedy, "Perception of the speech code," Psychol. Rev. 74, 431–461 (1967).

[10] K. N. Stevens and M. Halle, "Remarks on analysis by synthesis and distinctive features," in Models for the Perception of Speech and Visual Form, edited by W. Wathen-Dunn (MIT Press, Cambridge, MA, 1967), pp. 88–102.

[11] M. Halle, G. W. Hughes, and J-P. A. Radley, "Acoustic properties of stop consonants," J. Acoust. Soc. Am. 29, 107–116 (1957).

[12] G. Fant, Acoustic Theory of Speech Production (Mouton, The Hague, 1960).

[13] E. Fischer-Jorgensen, "Acoustic analysis of stop consonants," Miscellanea Phonetica II, 42–59 (1954).

[14] G. Fant, "Stops in CV syllables," Speech Transmission Laboratory QPSR, Royal Institute of Technology, Stockholm, No. 4, 1–25 (1969).

[15] G. Fant, "On the predictability of formant levels and spectrum envelope from formant frequencies," in For Roman Jakobson, edited by M. Halle et al., pp. 109–120 (Mouton, The Hague, 1956).

[16] S. Ya. Zhukov, M. G. Zhukova, and L. A. Chistovich, "Some new concepts in the auditory analysis of acoustic flow," Sov. Phys. Acoust. 20, 237–240 (1974) [Akust. Zh. 20, 386–392 (1974)].

[17] S. E. Blumstein and K. N. Stevens, "Acoustic invariance for place of articulation in stops and nasals across syllabic contexts," J. Acoust. Soc. Am. 62, S26(A) (1977).

[18] C. L. Searle, J. Z. Jacobson, and B. Kimberly, Speech as patterns in the 3-space of time and frequency. In Perception and Production of Fluent Speech, edited by R. A. Cole (Erlbaum, Hillsdale, NJ) (in press).

[19] M. F. Dorman and L. J. Raphael, "Onset spectra and stop consonant recognition," J. Acoust. Soc. Am. 62, S78(A) (1977).

[20] D. Klatt, "Acoustical theory of terminal analog speech synthesis," in Proceedings of the 1972 International Conference on Speech Communication and Processing, Boston, MA (1972).

[21] The inclusion of F4 transitions for the front vowel [i] is consistent with what is known about the important role of F4 in the perception of that vowel[22] and the high relative amplitude of that formant in the vowel. For the back vowels [a] and [u], the fourth formant is much weaker, and the F4 transitions are not expected to play a significant role in providing cues for place of articulation (except for retroflex consonants).

[22] R. Carlson, G. Fant, and B. Granstrom, "Two-formant models, pitch, and vowel perception," in Auditory Analysis and Perception of Speech, edited by G. Fant and M. A. A. Tatham (Academic, New York, 1975), pp. 55–82.

[23] M. A. Bush, "Integration of cues in the perception of stop consonants," SM thesis (MIT, 1977) (unpublished).

[24] H. S. Hoffman, "Study of some cues in the perception of the voiced stop consonants," J. Acoust. Soc. Am. 30, 1035–1041 (1958).

[25] R. Jakobson, G. Fant, and M. Halle, Preliminaries to Speech Analysis (MIT Press, Cambridge, MA, 1963).

[26] V. W. Zue, "Acoustic characteristics of stop consonants: A controlled study," Ph.D. thesis (MIT, 1976) (unpublished).

[27] N. Y-S. Kiang, T. Watanabe, E. C. Thomas, and L. F. Clark, Discharge Patterns of Single Fibers in the Cat's Auditory Nerve (MIT, Cambridge, MA, 1965).

[28] B. Leshowitz and E. Cudahy, "Masking patterns for continuous and gated sinusoids," J. Acoust. Soc. Am. 58, 235–242 (1975).

[29] S. E. Blumstein and K. N. Stevens, "Perceptual invariance and onset spectra for stop consonants in different vowel environments," J. Acoust. Soc. Am. 60, S90(A) (1976).

[30] M. Bush and K. L. Williams, "Infant place discrimination of voiced stop consonants with and without release bursts," J. Acoust. Soc. Am. 61, S64(A) (1977).

[31] A. Moffitt, "Consonant cue perception by twenty- to twenty-four-week-old infants," Child Dev. 42, 717–732 (1971).

[32] P. Morse, "The discrimination of speech and nonspeech stimuli in early infancy," J. Exp. Child Psychol. 14, 477–492 (1972).

[33] P. Eimas, "Auditory and linguistic processing of cues for place of articulation by infants," Percept. Psychophys. 16, 513–521 (1974).

Received 30 October 1969   9.5, 9.7

Hemispheric Specialization for Speech Perception

Michael Studdert-Kennedy* and Donald Shankweiler†

Haskins Laboratories, 270 Crown Street, New Haven, Connecticut 06510

Earlier experiments with dichotically presented nonsense syllables had suggested that perception of the sounds of speech depends upon unilateral processors located in the cerebral hemisphere dominant for language. Our aim in this study was to pull the speech signal apart to test its components in order to determine, if possible, which aspects of the perceptual process depend upon the specific language processing machinery of the dominant hemisphere. The stimuli were spoken consonant–vowel–consonant syllables presented in dichotic pairs which contrasted in only one phone (initial stop consonant, final stop consonant, or vowel). Significant right-ear advantages were found for initial and final stop consonants, nonsignificant right-ear advantages for six medial vowels, and significant right-ear advantages for the articulatory features of voicing and place of production in stop consonants. Analysis of correct responses and errors showed that consonant features are processed independently, in agreement with earlier research employing other methods. Evidence is put forward for the view that specialization of the dominant hemisphere in speech perception is due to its possession of a linguistic device, not to specialized capacities for auditory analysis. We have concluded that, while the general auditory system common to both hemispheres is equipped to extract the auditory parameters of a speech signal, the dominant hemisphere may be specialized for the extraction of linguistic features from those parameters.

INTRODUCTION

Man is a language-using animal with skeletal structure and brain mechanisms specialized for language. For more than a century, it has been known that language functions are, to a considerable extent, unilaterally represented in one or the other of the cerebral hemispheres, most commonly the left. The evidence of cerebral lateralization and localization argues powerfully for the existence of neural machinery specialized for language, but the exact nature of the language function, and characteristics of the neural mechanisms that serve it, remain to be specified. Most studies of the neural basis of language have dealt with higher-level language functions and their dissolution. An alternative approach, which may prove more fruitful, is to investigate the lower-level language functions, that is, to focus on the production and perception of speech sounds.

Study of the evolution of the vocal tract in relation to the physiological requirements for producing the sounds of speech suggests that man has evolved special structures for speech production and has not simply appropriated existing structures designed for eating and breathing (Lieberman, 1968; Lieberman, Klatt, and Wilson, 1969). We may reasonably suppose that he has also evolved matching mechanisms for speech perception. There is, in fact, much evidence that speech perception entails peculiar processes, distinct from those of nonspeech auditory perception (for a review of the evidence, see Liberman, Cooper, Shankweiler, and Studdert-Kennedy, 1967). There are also grounds for believing that the sounds of speech are integral to the hierarchial structure of language (Lieberman, 1967; Mattingly and Liberman, 1970). We might, therefore, expect that among the language processes lateralized in the dominant hemisphere are mechanisms for the perception of speech. Evidence of this is not easily gathered from normal subjects with intact nervous systems. But recently a plausible technique has become available and is put to work in the present study.

Kimura (1961a), using a task similar to one described by Broadbent (1954), showed that, if pairs of contrasting digits were presented simultaneously to right and left ears, those presented to the right were more accurately reported. She attributed the effect to functional prepotency of the contralateral pathway from the right ear to language-dominant left hemisphere (Kimura, 1961b). There is evidence for stronger contralateral than ipsilateral auditory pathways in dog (Tunturi, 1946), cat (Rosenzweig, 1951; Hall and Goldstein, 1968), and man (Bocca, Calearo, Cassinari,

Volume 48, Number 2 (Part 2), 1970.

STUDDERT-KENNEDY AND SHANKWEILER

and Migliavacca, 1955), and for inhibition of the ipsi-lateral signal in man during dichotic presentation (Milner, Taylor, and Sperry, 1968; Sparks and Geschwind, 1968). The right-ear advantage for verbal materials has now been repeatedly confirmed, and attempts to account for it solely in terms of memory, attention, or various response factors have been found inadequate (for reviews, see Bryden, 1967, and Satz, 1968). Kimura's attribution of the effect to cerebral dominance has received support from several other pieces of evidence. She herself (1961b) showed that the effect was reversed—a left-ear advantage appeared —in subjects known to have language dominance in the right hemisphere. She and others (Kimura, 1964; Chaney and Webster, 1965; Curry, 1967) showed that the effect was also reversed for nonspeech materials (melodies, sonar signals, environmental noises). The reversal of the effect for dichotically presented non-speech fits with other indications that perception of auditory patterns and their attributes typically depends more upon right-hemisphere mechanisms than upon left (Milner, 1962; Spreen, Benton, and Fincham, 1965; Shankweiler, 1966a,b; Vignolo, 1969).

Kimura's contention that ear advantages in di-chotic listening reflect dual cerebral asymmetries of function in perception of verbal and nonverbal ma-terials is thus supported by much evidence from a variety of sources. Dichotic listening techniques, there-fore, seem to offer a new way to raise the question of the status of speech (in the narrow sense) and its relation to language. If speech is indeed integral to language, we might expect this fact to be reflected in the neural machinery for its perception. Specifically, we may ask: Are the sounds of speech processed by the dominant hemisphere, by the minor hemisphere along with music, or equally by both hemispheres? All the dichotic speech studies referred to above used meaning-ful words as stimuli and therefore did not speak to this question. Studies using nonsense speech have, however, been carried out in order to discover whether the right-ear advantage depends upon the stimuli being meaningful. The results show clearly that it does not (Shankweiler and Studdert-Kennedy, 1966; Curry, 1967; Curry and Rutherford, 1967; Kimura, 1967; Kimura and Folb, 1968; Darwin, 1969; Haggard, 1969). We were therefore encouraged to make further use of dichotic listening experiments as a device for probing in some detail the processes of speech per-ception. Our general plan was to pull the speech signal apart and to test its components (consonants, vowels, isolated formants, and so on) in order to determine, if possible, which aspects of the perceptual process depend upon lateralized mechanisms, and by looking for in-formation contained in perceptual errors to guess at some of the characteristics of the processing machinery.

In a study employing synthetic speech (Shankweiler and Studdert-Kennedy, 1967), we compared synthetic CV syllables and steady-state vowels. Our choice of stimuli was dictated by the repeated finding at Haskins Laboratories that the identification of stop consonants and vowels engage different perceptual processes, stop consonants being "categorically," and vowels "con-tinuously," perceived (for discussion and summary of this evidence, see Liberman et al., 1967; Lane, 1965; Studdert-Kennedy, Liberman, Harris, and Cooper, 1970). In our dichotic study of these two classes of phonemes, we found a significant right-ear advantage for the stop consonants and a small, but not significant right-ear advantage for the vowels. We also found evidence implicating the articulatory features of voicing and place of production in stop consonant perception and lateralization. The present study[1] was designed to press our analysis of speech perception further by testing the lateralization of "natural" speech rather than synthetic, of final consonants as well as initials, of vowels embedded in CVC syllables rather than steady-state, and of the consonant features of voicing and place.

I. METHOD

A. Test Construction

We wished to study dichotic effects in the perception of initial and final stop consonants followed or preceded by various vowels, and of medial vowels followed or preceded by various stop consonants. We constructed four dichotic tests: two consonant and two vowel tests. The stimuli consisted of consonant–vowel–consonant (CVC) syllables formed by pairing each of the six stop consonants, /b, d, g, p, t, k/, with each of the six vowels, /i, ɛ, æ, ɑ, ɔ, u/. In one consonant and one vowel test, all syllables ended with the consonant /p/ [initial-consonant-varying (IC) tests], while in the other pair of tests all syllables began with the consonant /p/ [final-consonant-varying (FC) tests].

The syllables were spoken by a phonetician. He was given two randomized lists of 36 CVC syllables (six consonants × six vowels), one with initial consonants varying, one with final consonants varying. He was asked to read each list once at an even intensity (monitored on a VU meter), and to release the final stop. His utterances were recorded, a spectrogram was made of each syllable, and its duration was measured. The durations averaged around 400 msec, with a range of about 300–500 msec. Most of the variability arose from differences in the "natural" length of the vowels and from differences in the delay of the final stop release. For some few syllables, which seemed not perfectly intelligible, the phonetician was asked to make a new recording.

As an example of test construction, we will describe the procedure for the dichotic consonant test in which the initial consonant varied. The 36 recorded syllables were dubbed several times with a two-channel tape

HEMISPHERIC SPECIALIZATION OF SPEECH

recorder: half the syllables were assigned to one track of the tape and half to the other, so that each consonant was recorded equally often on each track. The syllables were then spliced into tape loops. Each loop carried a pair of syllables contrasting only in their initial consonants (e.g., /bap/–/dap/), one on each tape track. There were 90 such loops: each consonant was paired once with every consonant other than itself (15 combinations) followed by each of the six vowels.

The next task was to synchronize the onsets of the two syllables on a loop. This was accomplished by playing the loop on a special two-channel tape deck, modified to permit the length of leader tape passing between two playback heads to be varied, until the onsets of the two syllables coincided. Onset was defined on a permanent oscillographic record, obtained from a Honeywell 1508 Visicorder, as the first excursion above noise level that was sustained and followed by clear periodicity. Synchronization of onsets was determined from a three-channel Visicorder record, with two channels displaying the speech waves and the third a 100-Hz sine wave. Figure 1 reproduces the Visicorder record of two syllables with synchronous onsets.

Once the playback of two syllables on a loop had been synchronized, the pair was dubbed on parallel tracks using an Ampex PR-10 recorder. The input channels were matched for peak intensity on the VU meter, and the pair was recorded four times, each syllable going twice to channel 1 and twice to channel 2. In view of the arduous process of construction, this master tape of synchronized, contrasting syllables, distributed evenly over channels, was preserved uncut, as a source of stimuli in possible future experiments. From it, each syllable pair was recorded twice, once in each of its two channel orientations, on an Ampex PR-10. Thus 90 loops, made from dubbings of 36 parent recordings, yielded 180 third-generation stimuli in which each consonant was paired with every consonant other than itself followed by each of the six vowels, once on each tape track.

These stimuli were then spliced into a random order with the restriction that each consonant pair should appear once with each vowel in the first half and once with each vowel in the second half of the test. There was a 6-sec interval between stimuli, a 10-sec interval after every 10th stimulus, and a 30-sec interval after the 90th.

The IC vowel test was constructed from the original 36 recordings in exactly the same way as the IC consonant test, with the single difference that the tape loops were formed from pairs of syllables contrasting only in their vowels.

The FC consonant and vowel tests were constructed in a similar manner. Here the difference was in the alignment procedure: these syllables were synchronized at their final releases. Selecting the exact point of release on an oscillographic record proved a singularly

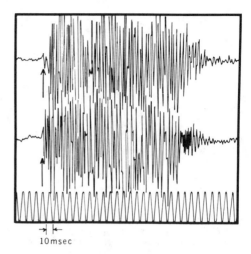

10 msec

FIG. 1. Temporal alignment of syllables for dichotic presentation.

difficult task. Many arbitrary decisions had to be made and the resulting alignments were almost certainly less precise than those of the corresponding IC pairs.

B. Subjects

There were 12 subjects: seven women and five men, aged between 18 and 26 years. Audiograms were taken separately on left and right ears. All subjects had normal hearing, considered themselves right-handed, and had no left-handed members of their immediate families. They served for four sessions of 45–50 min each and were paid for their work.

C. Procedure

Subjects took the tests individually in a quiet room, listening, over matched PDR-8 earphones, to the output of an Ampex PR-10 two-channel tape recorder.

The order in which the tests were given was counterbalanced. All subjects took a vowel test in their first and fourth sessions: half took the IC, half the FC on each occasion. All subjects took a consonant test in their second and third sessions: half of those who had taken the IC vowel test in their first session took the FC consonant test in their second and the IC consonant test in their third. The orders for the other subgroups of subjects were appropriately reversed. One subject (BZ) did not come for his final session and so gave no data on the IC vowel test.

The experimenter began a session by playing a steady-state calibrating tone (1000 Hz), spliced to the beginning of each test, on both recorder channels and adjusting the outputs to the voltage equivalent of approximately 70 dB SPL. The subject was then given the following, or analogous, instructions to read:

This is an experiment in speech perception. You are going to listen over earphones to a series of monosyllables—consonant–vowel–consonant monosyllables, such as "pet," "bap," "doop," "pawg," and so on. They

STUDDERT–KENNEDY AND SHANKWEILER

will be presented in *simultaneous pairs*, one to the left ear, one to the right. In any pair, the two syllables will have the same consonants, but different vowels. *The two vowels will always be different*, and will be drawn from the set of six given below.

Your task is to *identify both vowels*. Opposite the appropriate trial number on your answer sheet you should write *two* of the following:

ee	(as in beet)
eh	(as in bet)
ae	(as in bat)
ah	(as in father)
aw	(as in bought)
oo	(as in boot)

You should always write *two* vowels, *even if you have to guess*. Write them in order of confidence. That is to say, *write the one you are more sure of first, the one your are less sure of second*. There are 180 trials in the first test. You will have a short rest after 90, a longer rest after the 180. Then you will do a second test of the same length.

Each batch of 90 trials takes about 10 min, and the task may not be easy. But you are asked to *give it your fullest possible attention*. Don't worry if you think you are missing a lot. Just make careful guesses, and then get ready for the next trial. There are about 6 sec between trials.

Any questions? If not, put the earphones on and adjust them so that they fit comfortably on your head.

For the consonant test, the specified responses were: b, d, g, p, t, k. Appropriate changes in instructions were made for the FC tests.

Subjects wrote their responses on two 90-item response sheets, at the top of which the set of letters from which responses were to be selected was displayed. Upon completion of the 180-item test, subjects took a short rest, reversed the orientation of the earphones and took the test again. For each of the four dichotic tests, half the subjects heard channel 1 in their right ear first and half heard it in their left ear first. Channels were switched across ears by phone reversal rather than electrically so that bias due to channel and phone characteristics or phone position on the head would not be confounded with ear performance.

D. Summary

The elaborate procedure of test construction and presentation described above yielded 360 dichotic trials for each subject on each test, that is, 24 judgments on each of the 15 contrasting phoneme combinations or 60 judgments on each phoneme by each ear. Any bias due to neighboring vowel (or consonant), imprecise synchronization of onsets or offsets, recorder channels, earphone characteristics, or position of earphones on the head or sequence of testing was distributed equally over the ears of the entire group of subjects.

II. RESULTS

A. Over-All Performance

Table I summarizes the raw data and provides percentage bases for subsequent tables. Over-all performance on both ears was considerably higher for the IC vowels (82%) than for the IC consonants (68%); FC consonant performance (74%) falls midway.[2] For reasons that will become apparent (see below: an index of the laterality effect), we distinguished between trials on which both syllables were correctly identified and trials on which only one syllable was correctly identified. The distribution of total correct into the two categories is shown in the two right-hand columns of Table I. The difficulty of the IC consonant test as compared with the vowel is again shown by its lower percentage of both-correct trials (43% for consonants, 69% for vowels) and its higher percentages of one-correct trials (25% for consonants, 14% for vowels).

B. Ear Advantage

Table II presents percentage correct on the three tests, by preference and by ear, for individual subjects and for the group.

On the initial-consonant test, every subject shows a total right-ear advantage of between 4% (SB, JH) and 22% (AL). The mean total right-ear advantage of 12%

TABLE I. Over-all performance: initial consonants, medial vowels, and final consonants.

Test	No. of syllable combinations	No. of syllable presentations per ear per subject	No. of subjects	No. of syllable presentations per ear for group	No. of syllable presentations for group (both ears)	Total correct	No. correct on trials with both correct	No. correct on trials with only one correct
Initial consonants	15	360	12	4320	8640	5858 (68%)[a]	3702 (43%)	2156[b] (25%)
Medial vowels (IC)	15	360	11	3960	7920	6516 (82%)	5442 (69%)	1074[b] (14%)
Final consonants	15	360	12	4320	8640	6394 (74%)	4505 (52%)	1889 (22%)

[a] All percentages in this table are based on number of syllable presentations for group (both ears).
[b] Group percentage bases for trials on which only one syllable was correctly identified.

HEMISPHERIC SPECIALIZATION OF SPEECH

TABLE II. Percentage correct by preference and by ear for individual subjects.

Subject ear	Initial consonants						Medial vowels						Final consonants					
	1st Pref.		2nd Pref.		Total		1st Pref.		2nd Pref.		Total		1st Pref.		2nd Pref.		Total	
	L	R	L	R	L	R	L	R	L	R	L	R	L	R	L	R	L	R
SB	42	37	25	35	68	72	42	44	35	33	77	77	40	44	27	26	67	70
JH	40	42	23	25	63	67	45	47	40	36	85	83	36	49	23	23	59	72
MJ	27	46	18	16	45	62	34	48	29	24	63	72	41	45	19	14	60	59
NK	43	45	26	29	69	74	44	44	34	33	78	77	37	44	22	25	59	69
AL	33	21	18	52	51	73	47	10	10	54	57	64	53	14	13	62	66	76
BL	23	59	43	24	67	84	64	34	28	62	92	96	37	57	46	32	83	89
LN	21	65	45	17	65	82	40	59	58	40	98	99	32	62	42	27	74	89
HW	34	44	24	23	58	67	50	46	40	47	90	93	55	38	18	32	73	70
JW	30	50	23	18	53	68	32	37	24	23	56	60	37	54	28	20	65	74
BZ	25	57	42	26	67	83	—	—	—	—	—	—	41	52	43	36	84	88
SZ	33	52	38	28	71	81	58	42	40	57	98	99	37	55	43	30	80	85
JWn	28	53	34	21	62	74	45	54	52	42	97	96	39	52	41	31	81	83
Mean	32	48	30	26	62	74	46	42	35	41	81	83	40	47	31	30	71	77
$\bar{R}-\bar{L}$	16		−4		12		−4		6		2		7		−1		6	

is significant on a two-tailed matched pairs t-test ($t=7.19$, $p<0.001$).

For the final consonants, right-ear advantages are smaller and more variable. Ten subjects show a total right-ear advantage of between 2% (JWn) and 15% (LN). Two subjects (MJ, HW) show left-ear advantages of 1% and 3%, respectively. The mean total right-ear advantage of 6% is significant on a two-tailed matched pairs t-test ($t=3.84$, $p<0.01$).

The vowel results are again variable. Seven subjects show right-ear advantages, three (JH, NK, JWn) show small left-ear advantages and one (SB) shows no advantage. The mean total right-ear advantage of 2% falls short of significance on a two-tailed test at the 0.05 level ($t=2.16$, $p<0.06$).

Over-all performance is higher on first preferences than on second for all three tests and, for both initial and final consonants, the total right-ear advantage is derived from first preferences (although some subjects— SB and AL on initials, HW and AL on finals—show their larger ear advantage on second preferences). That the right-ear advantage on consonants does not arise from a general tendency to report the right ear first, while the left-ear signal decays in storage, is shown by the fact that the ear advantage on first preferences for the vowels is to the left. Furthermore, the higher over-all performance on first preferences is due almost entirely to the right ear on initial consonants, to the left ear on vowels.[3] The tendency to attach greater confidence to correct responses combined with the relatively large number of trials on which both responses were correct leads to nonsignificant reversals of the consonant-ear advantages on second preferences.

C. An Index of the Laterality Effect

The laterality effect has been shown to be a function, under certain circumstances, of task difficulty (Satz, Achenbach, Pattishall, and Fennell, 1965; Bartz, Satz, and Fennell, 1967; Satz, 1968), and a ceiling is neces-

sarily imposed upon it by very high or very low over-all performance (Halwes, 1969). Since the vowels evidently set the listeners an easier task than the consonants, we sought a method of data analysis by which the two levels of difficulty might be equated. We found this in trials on which only one of the syllables was correctly identified. All such trials are presumably, in some sense, of equal difficulty, and over-all performance on the subset is necessarily equal (50%) for consonants and vowels. No ear advantage can, in any event, be detected on trials for which the syllables are either both correct,[4] or both incorrect, so that restriction of a laterality measure to the trials on which only one syllable was correctly identified (see Table I, last column) confines attention to the only occasions on which the effect has an opportunity to appear. Our null hypothesis for these one-correct trials is then that the single correct syllables are identified equally often by right and left ears. Deviation from this 50–50 distribution may be expressed as a percentage: $(R-L)/(R+L)\,100$, where R (or L) is the number of trials on which the correctly identified syllable was delivered to the right (or left) ear. The index will range from 0 (50–50 distribution) to ±100 (0–100 distribution), with negative values indicating a left-ear advantage, positive values a right-ear advantage. Its significance may be tested on the null hypothesis that $R/(R+L) = L/(R+L) = 0.50$, using the normal curve as an approximation to the binomial.

Table III presents values of this index, based on one-correct-only trials, for individual subjects, on initial consonants, final consonants, and vowels. For initial consonants, the mean-percentage laterality effect is 26. Each subject contributes between 150 and 208 trials. For nine subjects, the index is positive and significant; for three subjects (SB, JH, NK), the index is positive, but not significant.

For final consonants, the mean percentage laterality effect is 17. Each subject contributes between 89 and 237 trials. For seven subjects, the index is positive and

STUDDERT-KENNEDY AND SHANKWEILER

TABLE III. Individual percentage ear advantages for initial stop consonants, final stop consonants, and medial vowels based on trials containing only one correct response.

Subject	Initial consonants		$\frac{R-L}{R+L}$ — 100	P	Medial vowels		$\frac{R-L}{R+L}$ — 100	P	Final consonants		$\frac{R-L}{R+L}$ — 100	P
	R−L[a]	R+L			R−L	R+L			R−L	R+L		
SB	15	171	9	NS[b]	2	134	1	NS	10	182	5	NS
JH	18	200	9	NS	−5	99	−5	NS	54	196	28	<0.0001
MJ	62	208	30	<0.0001	33	191	17	<0.02	−3	237	−1	NS
NK	20	178	11	NS	−1	143	−1	NS	37	205	18	<0.01
AL	94	204	46	<0.0001	26	192	14	<0.06	37	177	21	<0.01
BL	62	150	41	<0.0001	4	32	12	NS	21	89	24	<0.05
LN	58	178	33	<0.0001	4	8	50	NS	52	122	43	<0.0001
HW	32	186	17	<0.05	8	50	16	NS	−10	184	−5	NS
JW	55	207	27	<0.0001	13	191	7	NS	32	188	17	<0.05
BZ	55	153	36	<0.0001	—	—	—	—	15	95	16	NS
SZ	36	156	23	<0.01	1	9	0	NS	20	106	19	<0.06
JWn	43	165	26	<0.001	−1	25	−4	NS	12	108	11	NS
Total	550	2156			84	1074			277	1889		
			Mean 26				Mean 10				Mean 17	

[a] R = Number of trials on which only the right-ear stimulus was correctly identified. L = Number of trials on which only the left-ear stimulus was correctly identified.
[b] NS = Not significant at 0.10 level.

significant; for three subjects (SB, BZ, JWn), the index is positive but not significant; for two subjects (MJ, HW), the index is negative and not significant.

For the vowels, the mean-percentage laterality effect is 10, but the reliability of this is low. Subjects vary widely in their indices and in their numbers of one-correct trials. Subject LN, for example, has an index of 50, based on only 8 trials, subject NK an index of −1 based on 143 trials, subject MJ an index of 17 based on 191 trials. For only two subjects (MJ, AL) is the index significant.

D. Laterality Effect for Individual Stop Consonants and Vowels

Up to this point, we have treated stop consonants and vowels as undifferentiated classes. But do all members of these classes show a laterality effect of the same degree? To answer this question, the group data were broken down by phonemes, and the laterality index was computed for each consonant and vowel. Figure 2 presents the results. The indices are arranged from left to right in order of decreasing magnitude. Consonants and vowels are perfectly segregated by this arrangement. /b/ and /g/ have the highest indices, and the voiced consonant at a given place value is always

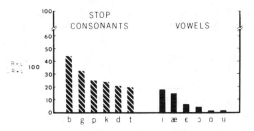

FIG. 2. The right-ear advantage for individual stop consonants and vowels on single-error trials. For explanation of the index plotted against the ordinate, see text.

higher than its unvoiced counterpart. But the right-ear advantage is present for the whole class of initial stop consonants, and all indices are significant with $p < 0.0001$: lateralization is strong and consistent. For the vowels, on the other hand, lateralization is weak and inconsistent: all indices are positive, but only one (for /i/) is significant with $p < 0.01$, and one (for /æ/) with $p < 0.10$.

E. Laterality Effect and Item Difficulty

We eliminated task difficulty as a variable affecting the apparent lateralization of consonants and vowels by analyzing one-correct trials only. But it would still be possible for differences in the lateralization of individual phonemes on these trials to be linked to item difficulty. Consonants were therefore ranked according to difficulty, measured by total number of errors (order: /k, b, t, g, p, d/) and the value of their indices (order: /b, g, p, k, d, t/). Kendall's tau (Siegel, 1956) was computed and gave a nonsignificant value of 0.20. Vowels ranked according to their levels of difficulty (/æ, ɔ, ɑ, u, ɛ, i/) and indices (/i, æ, ɛ, ɔ, ɑ, u/) yielded a nonsignificant tau of −0.13. There is, therefore, no evidence here for a relation between the observed laterality effect and item difficulty.

F. Identification of Consonant Feature Values

Having found that each of the six stop consonants is significantly lateralized, we may now ask whether the same is true of the articulatory features of which they are composed. Logically prior to this, however, is the question of whether these features are even perceived. Their psychological validity is, in fact, attested by the results of scaling the perceived distances among the stop consonants, /b, d, g, p, t, k/ (Greenberg and Jenkins, 1964), and analyses of errors in perception and

HEMISPHERIC SPECIALIZATION OF SPEECH

short-term memory have suggested that the features are separately extracted and stored (Miller and Nicely, 1955; Singh, 1966, 1969; Wickelgren, 1966; Klatt, 1968). Experiments with dichotic listening offer a new approach to study of the perceptual process.

Each of the six stop consonants may be specified in terms of two articulatory features: voicing and place of production. In English, place of production has three values (labial, alveolar, velar), while voicing has only two (voiced, voiceless), so that we can specify each of the stops uniquely within a 2×3 matrix. The dichotic pairs may then contrast in voicing (/b, p/, /d, t/, /g, k/), in place (/b, d/, /b, g/, /d, g/, /p, t/, /p, k/, /t, k/), or in voicing and place (/b, t/, /b, k/, /d, p/, /d, k/, /g, p/, /g, t/). In each of these three blocks of trials, each consonant occurs equally often at each ear. If consonants are perceptually irreducible wholes and their component features no more than useful descriptive devices, we would expect performance to display only chance variation across blocks of trials for which articulatory features were the basis of classification. But, in fact, we find, as in our earlier experiment (Shankweiler and Studdert-Kennedy, 1967b), that performance does vary significantly. Table IV shows that when a feature value is common to both ears (that is, when the dichotic pair contrasts in only one feature), an error is less likely to be made and both responses are more likely to be correct than when no feature value is common (that is, when the dichotic pair provides a double contrast, a contrast in both voicing and place). Furthermore, performance varies according to which feature is shared: more advantage accrues from shared place than from shared voicing.[5] Or, in opposite terms, the feature more adversely affected by conditions of dichotic competition is place: even when voicing is shared, the contrast in place depresses performance. The outcome confirms the perceptual reality of the features: voicing and place values are indeed separately extracted.

The same conclusion is suggested by an analysis of errors. Even if a consonant is wrongly identified, one of its feature values may be correctly identified and appropriate analysis will permit inferences about the perceptual process. The analysis is confined to trials on which a single error was made, since it is only for these that we can assign an error to its ear and stimulus. To ensure that no differential advantage accrues through a shared feature value, the analysis is also confined to

TABLE IV. Percentage of different trial outcomes as a function of feature composition of dichotic pairs.

Feature having a value shared by the dichotic pair	Trial outcomes (percent)		
	Both correct	One correct	Neither correct
Place	61	37	2
Voice	43	52	5
Neither	33	55	12

TABLE V. Number and percentage of features correct on single-error responses in double-contrast trials.

Feature correct	Number	Percent
Voice alone	678	72
Place alone	184	19
Neither	83	9
Total	945	100

trials on which each ear receives a different value of both voicing and place, that is, to double contrast trials. For these trials we may then determine the frequency with which each feature was correctly identified on erroneous responses and we may compare this frequency with that expected by chance. To make the procedure clear, suppose that the stimulus pair is /b, t/ and that the subject correctly identifies /b/, so that we know his error is on /t/. His erroneous response may then be correct on voicing (/p/ or /k/), correct on place (/d/), or correct on neither feature (/g/). Correct guesses, if made on the perceptually unanalyzed phonemes without regard to their component features, would then be distributed in the proportions 2:1:1 for voicing, place, and neither feature correct. Table V shows that, in fact, voicing alone is correctly identified an overwhelmingly large proportion of times. Chi-square for this table equals 200.34, which, with 2 degrees of freedom (df), is highly significant (p<0.001).

We may be confident, then, that the features are separately processed, and that voicing values are more accurately identified than place. But some advantage may yet accrue to the identification of one feature from the correct identification of the other. In other words, the two perceptual processes may be at least partially dependent. The degree of their independence may be estimated by combining correct responses and errors into a single confusion matrix and carrying out an information analysis (Miller and Nicely, 1955; Attneave, 1959). The procedure has the additional advantage of providing a comparison between voicing and place identification in which the unequal guessing probabilities for the two features may be discounted by expressing, for each feature, the information transmitted as a percentage of the maximum possible transmitted information.

Three confusion matrices were therefore constructed: a 2×2 voicing matrix in which stimuli and responses were grouped into voiced and voiceless; a 3×3 place matrix in which stimuli and responses were grouped into labial, alveolar, and velar; and a 6×6 matrix for the six individual consonants. Entries into these tables could use only those trials on which at least one phoneme was correctly perceived, since, when neither phoneme is correct, the erroneous responses cannot be assigned to their appropriate stimuli. This has two consequences for the analysis. First, since all double errors are excluded, it leads to an overestimate of the

STUDDERT-KENNEDY AND SHANKWEILER

TABLE VI. Information in bits, and percentage of maximum possible information transmitted for each feature separately, and for the features combined in individual consonants.

	Absolute amount of information transmitted in bits				Percentage of maximum possible information transmitted			
	Voice	Place	(V+P)	Combined	Voice	Place	$\left[\dfrac{V+P}{2}\right]$	Combined
	0.38	0.41	(0.79)	0.86	38	26	(32)	33
Maximum possible	1	1.58		2.58				

transmitted information for the experiment as a whole. But, since the purpose of the analysis is to compare the features and to estimate their degree of independence rather than to make a reliable estimate of information transmission, this need not concern us. A second consequence is that not all phonemes, or classes of phonemes, are equally represented in the trials to be analyzed, so that the presented information (and hence the possible transmitted information) is reduced from the value that it would have if the sample were representative of the whole set of stimuli. However, the reduction in presented information proved to be only a few thousandths of a bit for each matrix, so that maximum possible transmitted information remained effectively 1 bit on voicing, 1.58 bits on place, and 2.58 bits on the individual consonants.

The actual information transmitted was computed for each matrix and the results are displayed on the left side of Table VI. If the features of voicing and place were independently identified, the sum of the information transmitted for voicing and place separately would equal the information transmitted for the individual consonants in which the two features are combined (McGill, 1954; Miller and Nicely, 1955). Table VI shows that the required additivity holds to a close approximation. The independent perception of these features, demonstrated by previous investigators (Miller and Nicely, 1955; Singh, 1966) is again confirmed.

Table VI (right side) also expresses information transmitted as a percentage of maximum possible information transmitted on the two features, thus correcting for their unequal guessing probabilities. We again see the superiority of voicing over place identification: 12% more of the available voicing information is transmitted than of the available place information.

TABLE VII. Percentage correct responses on each feature value for trials with at least one correct response.

Feature	Value	Percent correct
Place	Labial	64
	Alveolar	82
	Velar	63
Voicing	Voiced	85
	Voiceless	83

The general superiority of voicing over place identification, shown by the three data analyses described above, may not, of course, hold for all feature values. As a rough test for the homogeneity of the effect, we can compute the percentage correct on each feature value for all trials having at least one correct response (double-error trials again being excluded since responses on these trials cannot be assigned to their stimuli). Table VII shows the results of these computations. There is little difference between performance on the labial and velar place values: both are some 20% lower than performances on either of the two voicing values. The joker in the set is the alveolar performance of 82%, suggesting that perception of this place value is no more affected by dichotic stress than is perception of voicing. However, the results must be viewed with caution, since the data reveal a heavy bias toward alveolar responses: 42% of all place responses on these trials were alveolar, as compared with 29% each for labial and velar responses. A similar, though much smaller, bias appears in the data of Miller and Nicely (1955, Table XVIII) for the set of six stop consonants.

The bias probably does not reflect listeners' expectations based on their experience with the language. Even though Denes (1963) estimates alveolar stop consonants to be roughly three times as frequent in English as either labial or velar stops, he also estimates voiceless stops to be very nearly twice as frequent as voiced, and no corresponding bias appears in our data (if anything, the reverse: 53% of listeners' responses on these trials were voiced, 47% voiceless). Furthermore, analysis of errors shows that most alveolar responses are made on trials in which at least one of the stimuli carries the alveolar place value. The "bias" therefore arises when one member of a dichotic pair is alveolar and the other is not: the alveolar value then "dominates" the contrasting labial or velar value. In other words, our first inference seems to be correct: the "bias" has a perceptual basis, and the alveolar stops in this experiment were less susceptible to dichotic stress than labial or velar stops.

G. Lateralization of Feature Perception

We may now ask whether the independence of the two features and the advantage of voicing over place shown in the combined data, holds equally for the two

HEMISPHERIC SPECIALIZATION OF SPEECH

TABLE VIII. Percentage correct responses for the two ears as a function of feature composition of dichotic pairs.

Feature having a value shared by the dichotic pair	Percent correct	
	Left ear	Right ear
Place	74	86
Voice	63	75
Neither	54	67

TABLE IX. Conditional percentages of feature errors for the two ears on single-error responses in double-contrast trials.

Feature in error	Other feature	Percent	
		Left	Right
Place	Voicing correct	86	93
Place	Voicing incorrect	14	7
Voicing	Place correct	67	73
Voicing	Place incorrect	33	27

TABLE X. Percentage correct responses on each feature value for each ear on trials with at least one correct response.

Feature	Value	Percent correct	
		Left ear	Right ear
Place	Labial	59	71
	Alveolar	79	84
	Velar	58	68
Voicing	Voiced	82	89
	Voiceless	80	87

ears. To answer these questions, the data were reanalyzed separately for each ear. We begin with a reanalysis of Table IV. The results are now given in terms of percentage of correct responses for each ear rather than in terms of trial outcomes, since no difference between the ears can appear on trials for which the responses were either both correct or both incorrect. Table VIII shows the outcome of the reanalysis. For both ears the ranking is exactly as in Table IV: performance is highest when place is shared, second highest when voicing is shared, and lowest when neither feature is shared.

We may notice, furthermore, that the right ear has approximately the same advantage over the left ear (about 12%) for each type of dichotic pair. This suggests that the right-ear advantage is the same for both voicing and place—that one feature is not more heavily lateralized than the other. The same conclusion is suggested by an error analysis along the lines of Table V. Again we make use only of double-contrast trials, and, to avoid any bias due to possible interaction between the features (despite their evident independence), we compute for each ear conditional percentages: that is, we compute the percentage correct on voicing, given that place was missed, and the percentage correct on place, given that voicing was missed. Table IX gives the results of these computations: the right-ear advantage is 7% on voicing, 6% on place.

However, equal lateralization of the two features is not evident in every analysis. Table X shows the breakdown of Table VII by ear. The expected right-ear advantage appears for every value of both features, but is somewhat greater for labial and velar place values than for voicing, suggesting stronger lateralization of these place values. [Both ears, incidentally, show a gain in alveolar performance: for the left ear the gain is approximately 20% as against 13%–16% for the right ear, perhaps reflecting a somewhat stronger alveolar preference on the left ear (44% of all left-ear responses, as against 39% of all right ear responses, were alveolar)].

Finally, Table XI displays the results of the information analysis. Both ears transmit a greater percentage of their voicing than of their place information. And for both ears the expected additivity, or independence, of feature information holds quite closely. However, the right-ear advantage is here greater on voicing (18%) than on place (10%). The difference cannot be tested for significance, but the disagreements between Tables VIII and IX (features equivalent in lateralization), Table X (right-ear advantage greater on two place values), and Table XI (right-ear advantage greater on voicing) are obvious.

There is also disagreement between one particular analysis in this and in our earlier study. In that study, we found differing degrees of laterality effect according to which features were shared (or contrasted) between the ears in a dichotic pair. We took this to indicate some

TABLE XI. Information in bits and percentage of maximum possible information transmitted for each feature separately and for the features combined in individual consonants, for right and left ears.

	Absolute amount of information transmitted in bits				Percentage of maximum possible information transmitted			
	Voice	Place	(V+P)	Combined	Voice	Place	$\left\{\dfrac{V+P}{2}\right\}$	Combined
Right ear	0.49	0.50	(0.99)	1.06	49	32	40	41
Left ear	0.31	0.35	(0.66)	0.70	31	22	26	27
Maximum possible	1	1.58	2.58					

difference in the degrees of lateralization of the two features. But in the corresponding analysis of the present study (Table VIII) we found no differences in laterality effect.

We therefore conclude that, while both features are clearly and independently lateralized, reliable estimates of their relative degrees of lateralization have eluded us.

III. DISCUSSION

The results are in general agreement with those of our previous study and of several other investigators (Curry, 1967; Curry and Rutherford, 1967; Kimura, 1967; Darwin, 1969a,b; Haggard, 1969; Halwes, 1969), in demonstrating a laterality effect for the perception of dichotic signals that differ only in their phonetic structure. They show further that the laterality effect extends to the perception of subphonemic features. Before discussing some of the problems that the results present, we briefly consider a possible mechanism of speech lateralization.

A. Mechanism for the Laterality Effect in Speech Perception

As Kimura (1961b, 1964) first suggested, the laterality effect may be accounted for by the assumptions of cerebral dominance and functional prepotency of the contralateral over the ipsilateral auditory pathways. Contralateral prepotency rests upon the greater number of these neurons and upon inhibition of ipsilateral neurons during dichotic stimulation. Strong corroboration of Kimura's argument has come from the work of Milner, Taylor, and Sperry (1968). (See also Sparks and Geschwind, 1968.) They studied right-handed patients (presumably left-brained for language) for whom the main commissures linking the cerebral hemispheres had been sectioned to relieve epilepsy. Under dichotic stimulation, these subjects were able to report verbal stimuli presented to the right ear, but not those presented to the left; under monaural stimulation, they performed equally well with the two ears. Milner *et al.* attribute their results to suppression of the ipsilateral pathway from left ear to left (language) hemisphere during dichotic stimulation and, of course, to sectioning of the callosal pathway that should have carried the left-ear input from right hemisphere to left. Their data justify the inference that, when under dichotic stimulation normal left-brained subjects correctly perceive a left-ear verbal input, the signal has been suppressed ipsilaterally, has traveled the contralateral path to the right hemisphere, and has been transferred across the lateral commissures to the left hemisphere for processing. Inputs to both ears therefore converge on the dominant hemisphere, that from the right ear by the direct contralateral path and that from the left ear by an indirect path, crossing first to the right hemisphere, then laterally to the left. The right-ear advantage in dichotic studies of speech must then

arise because the left-ear input, traveling an indirect path to the left cerebral hemisphere suffers, on certain trials, a disadvantage or "loss" to which the right-ear input, traveling a direct path, is less susceptible.

The locus of this loss can be broadly specified. We first assume that the two contralateral pathways are equivalent, so that the two signals reach their respective hemispheres in equivalent states; there is, of course, ample opportunity for the signals to interact at subcortical levels, but presumably whatever loss such interaction may induce is induced equally on both signals. If we further assume that the two signals upon arrival in the dominant hemisphere are served by the same set of processors (as evidence, discussed below, suggests), loss in the left-ear signal must occur immediately before, during, or after transfer to the dominant hemisphere.

The nature and source of the left-ear loss are matters of great interest to which we return briefly in a later section of the discussion. Here we merely remark that a preliminary attack on the problem might be made through careful comparison of error patterns for right- and left-ear inputs. As we have seen, in the limited data of the present study the general pattern of errors is rather similar for the two ears. This suggests that the left-ear input is subject to stress that differs in degree, but not in kind, from that exerted on the right-ear input. The notion of a generalized auditory stress common to both ears, whatever its source, is encouraged by the fact that the error pattern in this experiment is remarkably similar to that found in other studies. The superiority of voicing identification over place, for example, was observed by Miller and Nicely (1955) and by Singh (1966) in studies of speech perception through masking noise.

B. Nature of Cerebral Dominance in Speech Perception

To speak of cerebral dominance in speech perception is to imply that at least some portion of the perceptual function is performed more efficiently, or even exclusively, by the dominant hemisphere. The problem is to define that portion. That dichotic inputs must, at some point in their time course, converge on a final common path is evident from the fact that the two inputs ultimately activate a single articulatory response mechanism. But how early the inputs converge is the matter of interest. We would like to know, for example, whether convergence occurs before any linguistic analysis of the signal whatever (as would be true if both ears were served by a single set of specialized speech processors in the speech-dominant hemisphere), after partial linguistic analysis (as would be true if, for example, features were separately extracted in the two hemispheres, but were recombined in the dominant hemisphere), or after complete linguistic analysis and immediately before response (as would be true if the two hemispheres were equivalent in their capacities to

HEMISPHERIC SPECIALIZATION OF SPEECH

TABLE XII. Number and percentage of errors on double-contrast trials that arose by blending or not blending features from opposite ears. Trials affording two errors and trials affording one error are distinguished.

Trial outcome	Number of "blend" errors	Number of "nonblend" errors	Total number of errors	Percent "blend" errors
Double error	263	147	410	64
Single error	673	272	945	71
Total	936	419	1355	69

analyze the signal, but were served by a single set of specialized output mechanisms in the speech-dominant hemisphere). More generally, is the signal from the nondominant hemisphere transferred to the dominant hemisphere in a linguistic or in an auditory code? Some leverage on this question may be gained from a further analysis of errors in the present study.

Independent processing of subphonemic features requires that, at some point between input and output, a syllable be broken into its component features and that, at some later point, these features be recombined into a unitary response. If convergence of the two inputs occurs before features are recombined, a feature value has an opportunity to lose its local sign, that is, to lose information about its ear of origin. A correctly perceived feature from one ear might then be incorrectly combined with a correctly perceived feature from the opposite ear. The resulting response would be a "blend" of features from opposite ears. However, if convergence of the two inputs occurs *after* features are recombined, local sign could only be lost for the entire syllable, not for its component features. Blend responses would then occur only by chance. Evidence for greater than chance occurrence of blends is therefore evidence for loss of local sign on features and, by inference, for convergence of the inputs before the features are recombined.

Blends cannot be detected on single-contrast trials: even if the error occurs in combining the features, any resulting response will be correct, since one of the crossed feature values is presented to both ears. But on double-contrast trials, blending errors may be detected. For example, if the stimulus pair is /b, t/, the erroneous responses /p/ or /d/ are blends (drawing place values from one ear and voicing values from the other), while the erroneous responses /g/ and /k/ are not blends. Both classes of error would occur equally often, if there were no tendency for errors of local sign to occur on the features and if subjects were distributing their errors at random. In fact, blending errors occur with high frequency. Table XII shows that, of 410 errors on double-error double-contrast trials, 263 (64%) were blends; of 945 errors on single-error double-contrast trials, 673 (71%) were blends. The over-all percentage of blends (69%) is far in excess of chance expectation (50%). For each row of the table, p<0.0001 on a test of the chance hypothesis by the normal approximation to the binomial.

Errors of local sign on the features do then occur in these data, as in those of Kirstein and Shankweiler (1969), with very high frequency. The result is additional evidence for the independent processing of the features. More importantly, it suggests that inputs to left and right ears converge on a common center at some stage *before* combination of the features into a final unitary response.

We may now ask whether convergence occurs immediately before feature combination or at some earlier stage. In other words, is the signal that is transferred from right hemisphere to left coded into separate linguistic features or is it in some form of nonlinguistic auditory code? If the first were true, features of the left-ear syllable and features of the right-ear syllable would be extracted in separate hemispheres, and the feature composition of one syllable should have no effect on the probability of correctly identifying the other. If the second were true, interaction could occur between auditory parameters of the two inputs during the process of feature extraction, and this interaction should be reflected in performance. In fact, we already know from Tables IV and VIII that a response is more likely to be correct if the two inputs have a feature value in common. Furthermore, the advantage of sharing a feature value accrues more frequently if place is shared than if voicing is shared. We conclude that the inputs converge before rather than after feature extraction, and that duplication of the auditory information conveying the shared feature value gives rise to the observed advantage. In other words, we take the systematic relation between performance and the feature composition of dichotic pairs to be evidence consistent with the hypothesis of interaction during, or immediately before, the actual process of feature extraction.

Also consistent with this interpretation are the similar error patterns for left and right ears that we have already reported. As a further example, Table XIII shows the breakdown of Table XII by ear. (Only single-error trials are considered, since double errors cannot be assigned to their ears. An example of a single-error "blend" would be the response /d/ in the response pair /b, d/, given to stimulus pair /b, t/.) While the percentage of "blend" errors is greater for the right ear (75%) than for the left (69%), the difference is not significant at the 0.05 level, and both ears

TABLE XIII. Number and percentage of errors on double-contrast trials that arose by blending or not blending features from opposite ears, for right and left ears. Single-error trials only.

Ear	Number of "blend" errors	Number of "nonblend" errors	Total number of errors	Percent "blend" errors
Right	268	91	359	75
Left	405	181	586	69
Total	673	272	945	71

show a heavy preponderance of "blend" over "non-blend" errors.

We therefore tentatively conclude that convergence of the two signals in the dominant hemisphere occurs before the extraction of linguistic features, and that it is for this process of feature extraction that the dominant hemisphere is specialized. On this hypothesis, we would assign to the dominant hemisphere that portion of the perceptual process which is truly linguistic: the separation and sorting of a complex of auditory parameters into phonological features. Such a specialized "decoding" operation has been shown, on quite other grounds, to be entailed in speech perception (Liberman et al., 1967).

C. Role of the General Auditory System in Speech Perception

The foregoing argument has suggested that the role of the dominant hemisphere is due to its possession of a special linguistic device rather than to superior capacities for auditory analysis. We should therefore emphasize the distinction between extraction of the auditory parameters of speech and linguistic "interpretation" of those parameters. It is for the latter that specialized processing is required and for which the dominant hemisphere seems to be equipped, while the former is the domain of the general auditory system common to both hemispheres. In other words, the peculiarity of speech may lie not so much in its acoustic structure as in the phonological information that this structure conveys. There is therefore no a priori reason to expect that specialization of the speech perceptual process should extend to the mechanisms by which the acoustic parameters of speech are extracted.

Consider, for example, an acoustic variable underlying the identification of place in stop consonants: the extent and direction of the second formant transition (Liberman, Delattre, Cooper, and Gerstman, 1954). Data bearing on the perception of such frequency transitions in nonspeech have been reported for resonant frequencies (Brady, House, and Stevens, 1961) and, more recently, for tone bursts (Pollack, 1968; Nabelek and Hirsh, 1969). Nabelek and Hirsh determined the optimal glide durations for the discrimination of frequency change to be, in general, between 20 and 30 msec. They remark that these values are "close to the durations that were found by Liberman, Delattre,

Gerstman, and Cooper (1956) to be important for the discrimination of speech sounds" (p. 1518). They conclude that this optimum transition duration "is a general property of hearing and . . . does not only appear in connection with speech sounds" (p. 1518).

Their conclusion does not, of course, imply that there may be no functional differences between the hemispheres in auditory perception. There is, in fact, much evidence that for nonspeech the right nondominant hemisphere plays a greater role than the left in recognition of auditory patterns and in discrimination of their attributes (Milner, 1962; Kimura, 1964; Benton, 1965; Chaney and Webster, 1965; Shankweiler, 1966a,b; Curry, 1967; Vignolo, 1969). But whatever the peculiar auditory capabilities of the right hemisphere may be, there is reason to believe that each hemisphere can perform an auditory pattern analysis of the speech signal without aid from the other. The isolated left hemisphere can, in fact, go further and complete the perceptual process by interpretation of these auditory patterns as sets of linguistic features (as the data of Milner et al. cited in Sec. III-A, show).

Whether the right hemisphere can go so far is open to question. Sperry and Gazzaniga (1967) (see also Smith and Burkland, 1966; Gazzaniga and Sperry, 1967; Sparks and Geschwind, 1968) found that commissurectomized patients, instructed orally to select an object from a concealed tray with the left hand, were able to do so. Since left-hand stereognostic discrimination was known, from other of their tests, to be controlled only by the right hemisphere, it was evident that this hemisphere, in some sense, "perceived" the speech. However, the hemisphere was unaware of what it had "heard": the patients were unable to name the object they had selected and were holding. Similar results have been reported by Milner et al. (1968) for commissurectomized patients to whom instructions had been presented dichotically, thus presumably confining left-hand instructions to the right hemisphere. These authors conclude that "the minor, right hemisphere does show some rudimentary verbal comprehension" (p. 184).

Interpretation of such results is not easy, particularly since these patients had pre-existing epileptogenic lesions in addition to surgical disconnection of the hemispheres. However, it seems possible that the right hemisphere's "rudimentary comprehension" rested on auditory analysis which, by repeated association with

HEMISPHERIC SPECIALIZATION OF SPEECH

the outcome of subsequent linguistic processing, had come to control simple discriminative responses. Certainly, a capacity for the auditory analysis of speech would seem to be the least we can attribute to the right hemisphere.

We therefore conclude that the auditory system common to both hemispheres is probably equipped to track formants, register temporal intervals, and in general extract the auditory parameters of speech. But to the dominant hemisphere may be largely reserved the tasks of linguistic interpretation: for example, selecting from a formant transition the relevant overlapping cues to consonantal place of articulation and to neighboring vowel, or selecting from the infinity of temporal intervals automatically registered in the auditory stream the one interval relevant to the perception of voicing (Lisker and Abramson, 1964; Abramson and Lisker, 1965). Completion of such tasks is presumably prerequisite to conscious perception of speech.

The interpretation of the laterality effect outlined in preceding sections has implications for future work that may best be drawn by first discussing the results for consonants and vowels in the present study.

D. Consonant-Feature Lateralization

Underlying lateralization of consonants are the independent lateralizations of their component features. Since the bulk of consonantal errors is due to the loss of a single feature (see Tables V and IX), any reduction in the laterality effect of one feature would lead to a reduction in the laterality effect of the consonants as a whole. An example of such an effect may have been provided by the final consonants of this study.

The right-ear advantage for the final consonants, though significant, was relatively small. The result is at variance with that of Darwin (1969a,b), who found a strong right-ear advantage for final consonants in dichotically presented synthetic VC syllables.[6] If we accept the difference as genuine and not due to some artifact such as poor synchronization of the final consonants in this study, an interesting explanation might be that our reduced effect arose from reduced place lateralization, and that place lateralization only occurs for cues carried by a formant transition. A formant transition was the sole source of cues in the unreleased synthetic stops used by Darwin, but not in the released "natural" speech stops of the present study, where final bursts may sometimes have provided enough information for clear place identification.

The implication, in light of our previous argument, is that a final burst, standing in relative isolation from the rest of the syllable, may be estimated as well by the minor as by the major hemisphere and that information about its parameters (intensity, duration, frequency band) is liable to relatively little loss during transfer to the dominant hemisphere for feature extraction. A

formant transition, on the other hand, in which cues for both vowel and consonant are delicately implicated, even if correctly estimated auditorily by the minor hemisphere, may be subject to degradation during transfer to the dominant hemisphere. The presence of a formant transition was found by Darwin (1969a,b) in an experiment with synthetic (initial) fricatives (/f, s, ∫, v, z, ʒ/ followed by /ɛp/) to be a necessary condition of right-ear advantage: fricatives synthetized from friction alone, without transition, were clearly identifiable, but gave no right-ear advantage. The likely importance of formant transitions in the laterality effect may also bear on the results for the vowels to which we now turn.

E. Vowel Lateralization

A main purpose of the present study was to determine whether natural vowels embedded in a consonantal frame would show a greater right-ear advantage than the synthetic, isolated, steady-state vowels of our previous study. They did not. Nonetheless, some tendency toward a right-ear advantage for the vowels is evident. In both studies, the mean advantage, though not significant, was to the right (4%, 2%). Of the 21 subjects in the two studies, 13 gave right-ear advantages (two significant), seven gave left-ear advantages (none significant), and one gave no ear advantage. For the six vowels in the present study, all ear advantages were to the right (one significant). In short, the vowels display a weak, variable, right-ear advantage, and by this are distinguished from consonants for which a stronger right-ear advantage is the rule, and also from musical or other nonspeech sounds for which a left-ear advantage is the rule (Kimura, 1964; Shankweiler, 1966a,b; Chaney and Webster, 1965; Curry, 1967).

The vowels studied up till now seem to occupy a position on the margin of speech. But we should note that the vowels of this experiment, though embedded in CVC syllables, were still of relatively long duration, each syllable lasting between 300 and 500 msec. Presumably, were they synthetic, we could push them (or isolated steady-state vowels) toward nonspeech and a left-ear advantage by systematic manipulation of their spectral composition, musicalizing them, perhaps, by reducing the bandwidths of their formants and increasing their duration. But under what conditions might the tentative right-ear advantage be magnified into a full right-ear advantage comparable with that of the consonants?

If the vowels are isolated and steady-state, merely reducing their duration from 150 to 40 msec has no effect: neither the longer nor the shorter vowels show a significant ear advantage (Darwin, 1969a,b), and reduction of duration much below 40 msec is not possible without loss of vowel quality and approach to a nonspeech click. But for vowels placed in CVC syllables the story may be different. We know that the identification of synthetic CVC vowels may be affected by the rate of articulation (Lindblom and Studdert-Kennedy, 1967). Such vowels may be said to be "encoded" (Liberman *et al.*, 1967) in the sense that cues for their identification are provided simultaneously (in parallel) with cues for the identification of their neighboring consonants. Identification of both vowels and consonants entails a judgment, in some form, of the formant transitions. From the dichotic work of Haggard (1969) we know that synthetic semivowels and laterals (/w, r, l, j/), for which important cues are carried by relatively slow formant transitions, may give a right-ear advantage of the same order as that given by stop consonants. And finally, we have the evidence of Darwin (1969a,b), cited above, on the possible importance of formant transitions in the laterality effect for fricatives. We may then reasonably hypothesize that reduced, rapidly articulated, "encoded" vowels in CVC syllables, dependent for their recognition on the perception of formant transitions, would show a significant right-ear advantage. Experiments to test this hypothesis are now being planned.

F. Cerebral Dominance and Information Loss in the Laterality Effect

In the foregoing discussion, we have suggested that differences in right-ear advantage among stops and vowels may be due to differences in the susceptibility of these signal classes to information loss during transmission. In earlier discussions (for example, Shankweiler and Studdert-Kennedy, 1967a; Shankweiler, 1970), we have taken such differences in ear advantage to reflect differences in the degree to which consonants and vowels engage the specialized perceptual mechanisms of the dominant hemisphere. We should now make explicit the reasons for this shift in interpretation and, at the same time, summarize our current understanding of the laterality effect.

There are two necessary conditions of an ear advantage in dichotic listening. First, some part of the perceptual process must depend upon unilateral neural machinery; second, the signal from the ipsilateral ear must undergo a significant loss due either to degradation of the signal during transmission to the dominant hemisphere or to its decay during the time it is held before final processing. Wherever a reliable contralateral ear advantage is observed, both these conditions must have been fulfilled. However, Darwin (1969a,b) and Halwes (1969) have independently pointed out that where an ear advantage is not observed, or is small, the outcome is ambiguous: it may indicate either no unilateral processing or no significant information loss in the ipsilateral signal. In other words, the absence of an ear advantage is not inconsistent with complete lateralization of some portion of the perceptual function, since the outcome may simply indicate that the acoustic materials being studied are

not susceptible to information loss under certain experimental conditions.

This is the interpretation that the reduced effect for final consonants seems to demand, since, in the interests of parsimony, we must suppose that final consonants require the operation of specialized feature extractors in the dominant hemisphere no less than initials. For the vowels, the situation is not so clear. The "continuous" nature of vowel perception (for a recent discussion, see Studdert-Kennedy *et al.*, 1970) may perhaps be related to vowels not engaging discrete feature extractors in the dominant hemisphere. At the same time, transfer of vowel information to the dominant hemisphere for final perceptual response is unavoidable, and the most parsimonious interpretation again seems to be that the reduced or null laterality effect for vowels is also due to reduced information loss rather than to absence of cerebral dominance.

We may, finally, distinguish two broad directions that future research with dichotic materials might take. First, there is research of general auditory interest. Much remains to be learned about the experimental and acoustic conditions of ipsilateral transmission loss. Appropriate research may increase our understanding of those features in the design of the auditory system that make it possible to demonstrate laterality effects. Second, there is research directed primarily to the understanding of speech perception. Wherever a laterality effect for speech materials clearly occurs, we may exploit the effect to infer underlying perceptual processes. Here we should emphasize a point that may easily be missed: the size of the laterality effect is not a measure of its importance or of its value for research. We are not concerned in dichotic experiments to estimate the contribution of a variable to control over perception. We are, rather, exploiting the apparently trivial errors of a system under stress to uncover its functional processes.

IV. CONCLUSIONS

This study of dichotically presented "natural" speech CVC syllables showed: (1) a significant right-ear advantage for initial stop consonants; (2) a significant, though reduced, right-ear advantage for final stop consonants; (3) a nonsignificant right-ear advantage for six medial vowels; and (4) significant and independent right-ear advantages for the articulatory features of voicing and place in initial stop consonants.

We have argued, following Kimura (1961b), that the right-ear advantages are to be attributed to left cerebral dominance and functional prepotency of the contralateral pathways during dichotic stimulation. From analysis of the errors made in perception of the initial stop consonants, we have tentatively concluded that, while the general auditory system may be equipped to extract the auditory parameters of a speech signal, the dominant hemisphere is specialized

HEMISPHERIC SPECIALIZATION OF SPEECH

for the extraction of linguistic features from those parameters. The laterality effect would then be due to a loss of auditory information arising from interhemispheric transfer of the ipsilateral signal to the dominant hemisphere for linguistic processing.

ACKNOWLEDGMENTS

We wish to thank A. M. Liberman, M. P. Haggard, C. J. Darwin, and T. Halwes for many hours of fruitful discussion during the preparation of this paper. Acknowledgment is due to the Charles E. Merrill Publishing Company for permission to reprint Figs. 1 and 2, which are also to appear in Shankweiler (1970). This work was supported in part by a grant to Haskins Laboratories from the National Institute of Child Health and Human Development.

* Also Queens College of the City Univ. of New York, Flushing, N. Y.
† Also Univ. of Connecticut, Storrs, Conn.
[1] Reports of some of the findings of this study were included in a paper read before the Acoustical Society of America (Shankweiler and Studdert-Kennedy, 1967a), and in a presentation by one of us (D.S.) at the ONR conference on Perception of Language, University of Pittsburgh, January 1967. (Shankweiler, 1970).
[2] Main results for the FC consonants are presented in Tables I, II, and III. All further consonant data analysis is for IC consonants only, largely due to our dissatisfaction with the FC stimuli. Accordingly, since vowel data were intended for comparison with consonant, only the IC vowel data have been fully analyzed: all reported vowel results are for this test only.
[3] Order of report effects have been shown to be present, but insufficient to account for the entire laterality effect, in many studies. For reviews, see Bryden (1967), Satz (1968), and Halwes (1969).
[4] A measure of ear advantage might be derived from both-correct trials by use of preference scores, but these trials may not all be of equal difficulty.
[5] We note here a discrepancy between this result and a finding of our earlier study. There, performance was improved by the sharing of voicing (suggesting the greater difficulty of that feature); here, performance was improved by the sharing of place. Since the inference from Table IV of greater difficulty in the perception of place than of voicing is borne out by every other relevant analysis in the present study [as also by the findings of Miller and Nicely (1955) and Singh (1966)], we have discounted the discrepancy in our subsequent discussions.
[6] Trost et al. (1968) report equal right-ear advantages for initial and final consonants in "natural" CVC syllables. But since their test lists included fricatives and liquids, and voiced, voiceless, and nasal stops (not all of which occurred equally often in initial and final position), their results are difficult to compare with those of this study.

REFERENCES

ABRAMSON, A. S., and LISKER, L. (1965). "Voice Onset-time in Stop Consonants: Acoustical Analysis and Synthesis," Int. Congr. Acoust., 5th, Liège, Vol. Ia, p. A51.

ATTNEAVE, F. (1959). *Applications of Information Theory to Psychology* (Holt, Rinehart, and Winston, New York).

BARTZ, W. H., SATZ, P., and FENNELL, E. (1967). "Grouping Strategies in Dichotic Listening: The Effects of Instructions, Rate and Ear Symmetry," J. Exp. Psychol. 74, 132–136.

BENTON, A. L. (1965). "The Problem of Cerebral Dominance," Canad. Psychologist 6, 332–348.

BOCCA, E., CALEARO, C., CASSINARI, V., and MIGLIAVACCA, F. (1955). "Testing 'Cortical' Hearing in Temporal Lobe Tumors," Acta Oto-Laryngol. 45, 289–304.

BRADY, P. T., HOUSE, A. S., and STEVENS, K. N. (1961). "Perception of Sounds Characterized by a Rapidly Changing Resonant Frequency," J. Acoust. Soc. Amer. 33, 1357–1362.

BRANCH, C., MILNER, B., and RASMUSSEN, T. (1964). "Intracarotid Sodium Amytal for the Lateralization of Cerebral Speech Dominance," J. Neurosurg. 21, 399–405.

BROADBENT, D. E. (1954). "The Role of Auditory Localization in Attention and Memory Span," J. Exp. Psychol. 47, 191–196.

BRYDEN, M. P. (1967). "An Evaluation of Some Models of Dichotic Listening," Acta Oto-Laryngol. 63, 595–604.

CHANEY, R. B., and WEBSTER, J. C. (1965). "Information in Certain Multidimensional Signals," U. S. Navy Electron. Lab. Rep. No. 1339, San Diego, Calif.

CURRY, F. K. W. (1967). "A Comparison of Left-handed and Right-handed Subjects on Verbal and Non-verbal Dichotic Listening Tasks," Cortex 3, 343–352.

CURRY, F. K. W., and RUTHERFORD, D. R. (1967). "Recognition and Recall of Dichotically Presented Verbal Stimuli by Right- and Left-handed Persons," Neuropsychologia 5, 119–126.

DARWIN, C. J. (1969a). *Auditory Perception and Cerebral Dominance*, (Unpublished PhD thesis, University of Cambridge).

DARWIN, C. J. (1969b). "Laterality Effects in the Recall of Steady-State and Transient Speech Sounds," J. Acoust. Soc. Amer. 46, 114(A).

DENES, P. B. (1963). "On the Statistics of Spoken English," J. Acoust. Soc. Amer. 35, 892–904.

GAZZANIGA, M. S., and SPERRY, R. W. (1967). "Language after Section of the Cerebral Commissures," Brain 90, 131–148.

GREENBERG, J. H., and JENKINS, J. (1964). "Studies in the Psychological Correlates of the Sound System," Word 20, 157–177.

HAGGARD, M. P. (1969). "Perception of Semi-Vowels and Laterals," J. Acoust. Soc. Amer. 46, 115(A).

HALL, J. L., and GOLDSTEIN, M. H. (1968). "Representation of Binaural Stimuli by Single Units in Primary Auditory Cortex of Unanaesthetized Cats," J. Acount Soc. Amer. 43, 456–461.

HALWES, T. (1969). "Effects of Dichotic Fusion in the Perception of Speech," PhD thesis, University of Minnesota.

KIMURA, D. (1961a). "Some Effects of Temporal Lobe Damage on Auditory Perception," Canad. J. Psychol. 15, 156–165.

KIMURA, D. (1961b). "Cerebral Dominance and the Perception of Verbal Stimuli," Canad. J. Psychol. 15, 166–171.

KIMURA, D. (1964). "Left–Right Differences in the Perception of Melodies," Quart. J. Exp. Psychol. 16, 355–358.

KIMURA, D. (1967). "Functional Asymmetry of the Brain in Dichotic Listening," Cortex 3, 163–178.

KIMURA, D., and FOLB, S. (1968). "Neural Processing of Backwards-Speech Sounds," Science 161, 395–396.

KIRSTEIN, E., and SHANKWEILER, D. (1969). "Selective Listening for Dichotically Presented Consonants and Vowels," Haskins Labs. Status Rep. on Speech Res. SR 17/18, 133–141.

KLATT, D. H. (1968). "Structure of Confusions in Short-Term Memory Between English Consonants," J. Acoust. Soc. Amer. 44, 401–407.

LANE, H. L. (1965). "The Motor Theory of Speech Perception: A Critical Review," Psychol. Rev. 72, 275–309.

LIBERMAN, A. M., COOPER, F. S., SHANKWEILER, D., and STUDDERT-KENNEDY, M. (1967). "Perception of the Speech Code," Psychol. Rev. 74, 431–461.

LIBERMAN, A. M., DELATTRE, P. C., COOPER, F. S., and GERSTMAN, L. J. (1954). "The Role of Consonant–Vowel Transitions in the Perception of the Stop and Nasal Consonants," Psychol. Monogr. 68, No. 379.

LIBERMAN, A. M., DELATTRE, P. C., GERSTMAN, L. J., and COOPER, F. S. (1956). "Tempo of Frequency Change as a Cue for

Distinguishing Classes of Speech Sounds," J. Exp. Psychol. *52*, 127–137.

LIBERMAN, A. M., DELATTRE, P. C., and COOPER, F. S. (**1958**). "Some Cues for the Distinction Between Voiced and Voiceless Stops in Initial Position," Language and Speech *1*, 153–167.

LIEBERMAN, P. (**1967**). *Intonation, Perception and Langauge* (MIT Press, Cambridge, Mass.).

LIEBERMAN, P. (**1968**). "Primate Vocalizations and Human Linguistic Ability," J. Acoust. Soc. Amer. *44*, 1574–1584.

LIEBERMAN, P., KLATT, D. L., and WILSON, W. A. (**1969**). "Vocal Tract Limitations on the Vowel Repertoires of Rhesus Monkey and Other Nonhuman Primates," Science *164*, 1185–1187.

LINDBLOM, B. E. F., and STUDDERT-KENNEDY, M. (**1967**). "On the Role of Fomant Transitions in Vowel Recognition," J. Acoust. Soc. Amer. *42*, 830–843.

LISKER, L., and ABRAMSON, A. S. (**1964**). "A Cross-Language Study of Voicing in Initial Stops: Acoustical Measurements," Word *20*, 384–422.

MATTINGLY, I., and LIBERMAN, A. M. (**1970**). "The Speech Code and the Physiology of Language," in *Information Processing in the Nervous System*, K. N. Leibovic, Ed. (Springer, New York), pp. 97–117.

McGILL, W. J. (**1954**). "Multivariate Information Transmission," Psychometrika *19*, 97–116.

MILLER, G., and NICELY, P. E. (**1955**). "An Analysis of Perceptual Confusions Among Some English Consonants," J. Acoust. Soc. Amer. *27*, 338–352.

MILNER, B. (**1962**). "Laterality Effects in Audition," in *Interhemispheric Relations and Cerebral Dominance*, V. B. Mountcastle, Ed. (Johns Hopkins U. P., Baltimore), pp. 177–195.

MILNER, B., TAYLOR, L., and SPERRY, R. W. (**1968**). "Lateralized Suppression of Dichotically-presented Digits after Commissural Section in Man," Science *161*, 184–185.

NABELEK, I., and HIRSH, I. J. (**1969**). "On the Discrimination of Frequency Transitions," J. Acoust. Soc. Amer. *45*, 1510–1519.

POLLACK, I. (**1968**). "Detection of Rate of Change of Auditory Frequency," J. Exp. Psychol. *77*, 535–541.

ROSENZWEIG, M. R. (**1951**). "Representations of the Two Ears at the Auditory Cortex," Amer. J. Physiol. *167*, 147–158.

SATZ, P. (**1968**). "Laterality Effects in Dichotic Listening," Nature *218*, 277–278.

SATZ, P., ACHENBACH, K., PATTISHALL, E., and FENNELL, E. (**1965**). "Order of Report, Ear Asymmetry and Handedness in Dichotic Listening," Cortex *1*, 377–396.

SATZ, P., FENNELL, E., and JONES, M. B. (**1969**). "Comments on: A Model of the Inheritance of Handedness and Cerebral Dominance," Neuropsychologia *7*, 101–103.

SHANKWEILER, D. (**1966a**). "Defects in Recognition and Reproduction of Familiar Tunes after Unilateral Temporal Lobectomy," Paper read before the 37th Ann. Meeting of the Eastern Psychol. Ass., New York, N. Y.

SHANKWEILER, D. (**1966b**). "Effects of Temporal-Lobe Damage on Perception of Dichotically Presented Melodies," J. Comp. Physiol. Psychol. *62*, 115–119.

SHANKWEILER, D. (**1970**). "An Analysis of Laterality Effects in Speech Perception," in *Perception of Language*, P. Kjeldergaard, Ed. (Chas. E. Merrill, Columbus, Ohio).

SHANKWEILER, D., and STUDDERT-KENNEDY, M. (**1966**). "Lateral Differences in Perception of Dichotically Presented Synthetic Consonant–Vowel Syllables and Steady-State Vowels," J. Acoust. Soc. Amer. *39*, 1256(A).

SHANKWEILER, D., and STUDDERT-KENNEDY, M. (**1967a**). "An Analysis of Perceptual Confusions in Identification of Dichotically Presented CVC Syllables," J. Acoust. Soc. Amer. *41*, 1581(A).

SHANKWEILER, D., and STUDDERT-KENNEDY, M. (**1967b**). "Identification of Consonants and Vowels Presented to Left and Right Ears," Quart. J. Exp. Psychol. *19*, 59–63.

SIEGEL, S. (**1956**). *Non-parametric Statistics*. (McGraw–Hill, New York).

SINGH, S. (**1966**). "Crosslanguage Study of Perceptual Confusions of Plosive Phonemes in Two Conditions of Distortion," J. Acoust. Soc. Amer. *40*, 635–656.

SINGH, S. (**1969**). "Interrelationship of English Consonants," in Proc. Intern. Congr. Phonetic Sci., 6th, Prague, pp. 542–544.

SMITH, A., and BURKLAND, C. W. (**1966**). "Dominant Hemispherectomy: Preliminary Report on Neuropsychological Sequelae," Science *153*, 1280–1282.

SPARKS, R., and GESCHWIND, N. (**1968**). "Dichotic Listening in Man After Section of Neocortical Commissures," Cortex *4*, 3–16.

SPERRY, R. W., and GAZZANIGA, M. S. (**1967**). "Language Following Surgical Disconnection of the Hemispheres," in *Brain Mechanisms Underlying Speech and Language*, C. H. Millikan and F. L. Darley, Eds. (Grune and Stratton, New York), pp. 108–121.

SPREEN, O., BENTON, A. L., and FINCHAM, R. W. (**1965**). "Auditory Agnosia Without Aphasia," Arch. Neurol. *13*, 84–92.

STUDDERT-KENNEDY, M., LIBERMAN, A. M., HARRIS, K. S., and COOPER, F. S. (**1970**). "The Motor Theory of Speech Perception: A Reply to Lane's Critical Review," Psychol. Rev. *77*, 234–249.

TROST, J. E., SHEWAN, C. M., NATHANSON, S. N., and SANT, L. V. (**1968**). "A Dichotic Study of Ear Superiority in Perception of Consonants," Paper read before the 44th Annual Convention of the American Speech and Hearing Association, Denver.

TUNTURI, A. R. (**1946**). "A Study on the Pathway from the Medial Geniculate Body to the Acoustic Cortex in the Dog," Amer. J. Physiol. *147*, 311–319.

VIGNOLO, L. A. (**1969**). "Auditory Agnosia: A Review and Report of Recent Evidence," in *Contributions to Clinical Neuropsychology*, A. L. Benton, Ed. (Aldine, Chicago), pp. 172–208.

WICKELGREN, W. A. (**1966**). "Distinctive Features and Errors in Short-Term Memory for English Consonants," J. Acoust. Soc. Amer. *39*, 388–398.

PERCEPTION OF CONSONANTAL DISTINCTIONS

Paper 11. C. T. Best, B. Morrongiello, and R. Robson (1981), Perceptual equivalence of acoustic cues in speech and nonspeech perception. *Perception & Psychophysics* 29, 191–211.

Paper 12. W. F. Ganong, III (1980), Phonetic categorization in auditory word perception. *Journal of Experimental Psychology: Human Perception and Performance* 6, 110–125.

Paper 13. D. Kewley-Port (1983), Time-varying features as correlates of place of articulation in stop consonants. *Journal of the Acoustical Society of America* 73, 322–335.

Paper 14. P. K. Kuhl and J. D. Miller (1978), Speech perception by the chinchilla: Identification functions for synthetic VOT stimuli. *Journal of the Acoustical Society of America* 63, 905–917.

Paper 15. L. Lisker and A. S. Abramson (1970), The voicing dimension: Some experiments in comparative phonetics. In *Proceedings of the Sixth International Congress of Phonetic Sciences, Prague, 1967*, pp. 563–567. Prague: Academia.

Paper 16. H. McGurk and J. MacDonald (1976), Hearing lips and seeing voices. *Nature* 264, 746–748.

Paper 17. J. D. Miller, C. C. Wier, R. E. Pastore, W. J. Kelly, and R. J. Dooling (1976), Discrimination and labeling of noise-buzz sequences with varying noise-lead times: An example of categorical perception. *Journal of the Acoustical Society of America* 60, 410–417.

Paper 18. J. L. Miller and A. M. Liberman (1979), Some effects of later-occurring information on the perception of stop consonant and semivowel. *Perception & Psychophysics* 25, 457–465.

Paper 19. K. Miyawaki, W. Strange, R. Verbrugge, A. M. Liberman, J. J. Jenkins, and O. Fujimura (1975), An effect of linguistic experience: The discrimination of [r] and [l] by native speakers of Japanese and English. *Perception & Psychophysics* 18, 331–340.

Paper 20. D. B. Pisoni (1977), Identification and discrimination of the relative onset time of two component tones: Implications for voicing perception in stops. *Journal of the Acoustical Society of America* 61, 1352–1361.

Paper 21. B. H. Repp, A. M. Liberman, T. Eccardt, and D. Pesetsky (1978), Perceptual integration of acoustic cues for stop, fricative, and affricate manner. *Journal of Experimental Psychology: Human Perception and Performance* 4, 621–637.

Paper 22. Q. Summerfield (1981), Articulatory rate and perceptual constancy in phonetic perception. *Journal of Experimental Psychology: Human Perception and Performance* 7, 1074–1095.

Paper 23. R. M. Warren (1970), Perceptual restoration of missing speech sounds. *Science* 167, 392–393.

As noted in the Commentary to the section on Theoretical Perspectives, a fundamental problem in research on speech perception has been to discover the processes that allow the listener to derive the phonetic structure (e.g., features, segments, syllables) of the utterance from the acoustic signal. This issue has been approached empirically from a variety of perspectives using a number of different methodologies. The eclectic and controversial nature of the enterprise is apparent in the diverse set of papers in this and the following section, all of which are concerned with some aspect of the listener's ability to perceive the individual consonants and vowels that comprise the lexical items of language. This section includes papers that focus primarily on the perception of consonantal contrasts; the papers in the following section focus primarily on the perception of vowels.

Many investigators have approached the issue of speech perception by attempting to specify in some detail the precise nature of the perceptual mapping between acoustic signal and linguistic representation, with the goal of placing constraints on the kinds of models that can explain the observed phenomena. As illustrated by the papers in this section, although much has been learned about the acoustic properties underlying phonetic distinctions, in this case, consonantal contrasts, just how the listener processes the acoustic information to perceive the intended consonant is far from resolved. For example, Repp, Liberman, Eccardt, and Pesetsky (1978), focusing on the lack of invariance in the speech signal and the diversity of properties specifying a given phonetic distinction, argue that perceptual coherence is provided by a specialized mechanism that takes into account the origin of these cues, namely, the articulatory act [see Liberman and Mattingly (1985) in the section on Theoretical Perspectives]. In contrast, Kewley-Port (1983), working within the same general theoretical framework as Stevens and Blumstein (1978, in the section on Theoretical Perspectives), shows that if time-varying aspects of speech are considered, there is evidence for invariance in the speech signal—presumably eliminating the need for a specialized processing mechanism. The papers by Miller and Liberman (1979) and Summerfield (1981) both concern the way in which listeners accommodate for variation in the speech signal due to changes in speaking rate. Miller and Liberman interpret their results in terms of a mechanism that adjusts for alterations in rate through reference to knowledge of articulation [see Liberman and Mattingly (1985) in the section on Theoretical Perspectives]. Summerfield, on the other hand, discusses his findings within the theoretical framework of event perception [see Fowler (1986) in the section on Theoretical Perspectives], suggesting that the critical information specifying phonetic identity remains invariant across changes in rate, such that "normalization" for rate is unnecessary.

A different approach to the issue of underlying mechanism involves a direct comparison between the perception of speech and nonspeech auditory patterns. Basing their studies on the classic and highly influential investigation of voicing by Lisker and Abramson (1970), Miller, Wier, Pastore, Kelly, and Dooling (1976) and Pisoni (1977) show that the phenomenon of categorical perception, originally believed to be unique to speech, can also be found with nonspeech auditory patterns. Thus, it is argued, the categorical nature of speech perception does not require the operation of a specialized speech mechanism. On the other hand, Best, Morrongiello, and Robson (1981), who focus on the trading relations and perceptual equivalence of multiple cues for phonetic categories, find striking differences between the perception of speech and nonspeech analogs, and propose that speech-specific mechanisms may be involved in these aspects of phonetic perception. The research of Miyawaki, Strange, Verbrugge, Liberman, Jenkins, and Fujimura (1975) also demonstrates a dissociation between the perception of speech and nonspeech auditory patterns. Of particular interest is their finding that long-term linguistic experience altered the perception of a speech contrast, but did not alter the perception of the acoustic information underlying the contrast when taken out of the speech context.

Yet another approach to investigating the mechanisms that mediate the perception of speech involves a direct comparison of humans and nonhumans. Working within this framework, Kuhl and Miller (1978) compared the perception of speech by human and chinchilla; the chinchilla is known to have auditory processing abilities in common with those of humans, but of course does not possess a human language. On the basis of the striking similarities in the human and chinchilla data, Kuhl and Miller conclude that at least some aspects of the human's ability to categorize speech are based not on species-specific, speech-specific mechanisms, but on more general mechanisms, in this case, psychoacoustic processes characteristic of the mammalian auditory system.

In their paper, McGurk and MacDonald (1976) demonstrate that speech perception is not limited to the auditory modality, but may in some situations involve a visual as well as an auditory component. It appears that during speech perception articulatory information from the talker's face is combined with information from the speech signal itself and, importantly, combined in such a way as to yield a unified percept of the speech event. Examples of how theory might accommodate the phenomenon of bimodal speech perception are found in Liberman and Mattingly (1985) and Fowler (1986), both in the section on Theoretical Perspectives.

The nature of the complex relation between speech perception and the lexicon is investigated in the final two papers in the section [see also Klatt (1979) and McClelland and Elman (1986) in the section on Theoretical Perspectives]. In his study on perceptual restoration, Warren (1970) provides an early demonstration of the influence of lexical knowledge on the perception of speech sounds. Ganong (1980) uses a phonetic categorization paradigm to investigate lexical effects further, in particular, to determine the level of perceptual processing at which such effects arise.

Perception & Psychophysics
1981, 29 (3), 191-211

Perceptual equivalence of acoustic cues in speech and nonspeech perception

CATHERINE T. BEST
Haskins Laboratories, New Haven, Connecticut 06510

and

BARBARA MORRONGIELLO and RICK ROBSON
University of Massachusetts, Amherst, Massachusetts 01003

Trading relations show that diverse acoustic consequences of minimal contrasts in speech are equivalent in perception of phonetic categories. This *perceptual equivalence* received stronger support from a recent finding that discrimination was differentially affected by the phonetic cooperation or conflict between two cues for the /slIt/-/splIt/ contrast. Experiment 1 extended the trading relations and perceptual equivalence findings to the /sei/-/stei/ contrast. With a more sensitive discrimination test, Experiment 2 found that cue equivalence is a characteristic of perceptual sensitivity to phonetic information. Using "sine-wave analogues" of the /sei/-/stei/ stimuli, Experiment 3 showed that perceptual integration of the cues was phonetic, not psychoacoustic, in origin. Only subjects who perceived the sine-wave stimuli as "say" and "stay" showed a trading relation and perceptual equivalence; subjects who perceived them as nonspeech failed to integrate the two dimensions perceptually. Moreover, the pattern of differences between obtained and predicted discrimination was quite similar across the first two experiments and the "say"-"stay" group of Experiment 3, and suggested that phonetic perception was responsible even for better-than-predicted performance by these groups. Trading relations between speech cues, and the perceptual equivalence that underlies them, thus appear to derive specifically from perception of phonetic information.

Research with a variety of minimal segmental distinctions in synthetic speech has shown that perception of a phonetic contrast can be cued by appropriate change in the major acoustic property that differentiates that contrast in natural speech (e.g., Liberman, Cooper, Shankweiler, & Studdert-Kennedy, 1967; Liberman, Harris, Hoffman, & Griffith, 1961; Liberman & Studdert-Kennedy, 1978; Studdert-Kennedy, 1976). However, minimal articulatory contrasts result in concurrent differences along more than one acoustic dimension. As this last fact might suggest, perceptual studies indicate that listeners make use of the various acoustic consequences of a given spoken segmental distinction. For example, voicing distinctions in initial, prestress position can be cued not only by changes in voice onset time (VOT—as an acoustic measure), with all else held constant, but also by changes in F1 onset frequency, F0 contour, or aspiration energy (e.g., Haggard, Ambler, & Callow, 1970; Lisker, 1975; Lisker, Liberman, Erickson, Dechovitz, & Mandler, 1977; Repp, 1979; Lisker, Note 1), all of which are acoustic correlates of laryngeal timing distinctions in stop production (Abramson & Lisker, 1965). A variety of acoustic consequences of articulatory distinctions have also been found to serve as cues for place (e.g., Dorman, Studdert-Kennedy, & Raphael, 1977; Harris, Hoffman, Liberman, Delattre, & Cooper, 1958) and manner of articulation (e.g., Dorman, Raphael, & Liberman, 1979; Miller & Liberman, 1979; Repp, Liberman, Eccardt, & Pesetsky, 1978).

The fact that various acoustic properties serve as cues for a phonetic contrast suggests that they provide equivalent information about the distinction involved (cf. Dorman et al., 1977; Repp et al., 1978). If different cues do provide equivalent phonetic information, it should be possible to offset a "weakness"

This work was supported by NICHD Grant HD01994 to the Haskins Laboratories and NINCDS Postdoctoral Fellowship Grant NS5085 to the first author. We thank the following people for their valuable contributions: Alvin M. Liberman, for use of the Haskins facilities, and for helpful advice throughout the project; Rachel Clifton, for use of her auditory perception laboratory at the University of Massachusetts at Amherst and for advice during the initial stages of the project; Terry G. Halwes, for instruction on stimulus development; and Michael Studdert-Kennedy, Bruno H. Repp, Robert E. Remez, Robert Verbrugge, and Steven S. Braddon for helpful discussions and suggestions on earlier drafts of this paper. These findings were presented at the 98th Meeting of the Acoustical Society of America, Salt Lake City, Utah, November 1979. An earlier version of this paper also appears in the *Haskins Laboratories: Status Report on Speech Research*, 1980, SR-62. The senior author is currently at the Neurosciences and Education Program, Box 142, Teachers College, Columbia University, New York, New York 10027.

0031-5117/81/030191-21$02.35/0

in one cue by strengthening the value of another (within limits possibly defined by the acoustic effects of natural articulations). Empirical work has supported this hypothesis—perceptual *trading relations* have been found among diverse cues for voicing (e.g., Summerfield & Haggard, 1977), place (e.g., Bailey & Summerfield, 1980; Hoffman, 1958), and manner distinctions (e.g., Dorman, Raphael, & Isenberg, 1980). However, while trading relations indicate that different acoustic properties may cue a given phonetic category, they cannot support a stronger claim that the cues yield *qualitatively equivalent percepts*. Trading-relation studies have typically used forced-choice identification tests, which merely assess whether any of several acoustic manipulations are *acceptable* as cues for a given contrast. Forced-choice tests do not measure whether the same-category percepts based on different acoustic cues are identical in quality. Qualitative equivalence between percepts based on diverse acoustic cues will be referred to as *perceptual equivalence*.

In a recent experiment on the /slIt/-/splIt/ contrast, Fitch, Halwes, Erickson, and Liberman (1980) conducted a more stringent test of perceptual equivalence between two cues for the medial stop /p/. A trading relation between two synthetic /slIt/-/splIt/ continua showed that when the formant transitions following silent closure were appropriate for a natural "slit" (/slIt/-biased continuum), listeners needed a significantly longer closure gap than when the transitions were appropriate for "split" (/splIt/-biased continuum) in order to hear "split" 50% or more of the time. Thus, additional silence compensated perceptually for "weakness" of the /slIt/-biased spectral cue. If the convergence of the two cues upon a unitary speech percept ("split") was tied to their common articulatory origin, Fitch et al. (1980) reasoned, then differently cued stimuli should be difficult to discriminate within a phonetic category (i.e., they should be perceptually equivalent).

Mere demonstration of poor within-category discriminability between cues would not support perceptual equivalence, however, since the null hypothesis cannot be proven. Therefore, Fitch et al. tested whether discrimination performance would be differentially affected by cooperation or conflict of the two cues along the phonetic dimension, using an oddity procedure that included three types of comparisons between stimuli from the two continua. In "two conflicting cues" comparisons, /slIt/-biased stimuli (spectral bias toward "slit") had longer closures (temporal bias toward "split") than /splIt/-biased stimuli, such that the two cues exactly *cancelled* one another phonetically. In the "two cooperating cues" comparisons, the two cues *complemented* each other phonetically—on all trials the /splIt/-biased stimuli had a longer closure gap (by the same amount of

difference as in "two conflicting cues") than the /slIt/-biased stimuli. In "one-cue" comparisons, the stimuli contrasted only on the spectral dimension.

The "phonetic" hypothesis was that if the two cues showed perceptual equivalence along a single phonetic dimension, /slIt/-biased and /splIt/-biased stimuli would be quite difficult to discriminate when they belonged to the same phonetic category. This would be the case for all "conflicting cues" comparisons. In contrast, /slIt/-biased and /splIt/-biased stimuli should have been comparatively easy to discriminate when they belonged to different phonetic categories; this would be the case for those "one-cue" comparisons that straddled the category boundary. Enhancing the between-category differences should lead to the highest discrimination performance; this was accomplished by those "cooperating cues" comparisons that straddled the phonetic category boundary. The alternative "auditory" hypothesis was that the two cues might remain discriminable on an auditory basis. In that case, performance would be equally high across the board for both "two-cue" comparison types, since they contrasted along two acoustic dimensions, relative to performance on "one-cue" comparisons, which contrasted on only one acoustic dimension. The results clearly supported the "phonetic" hypothesis, indicating that the two acoustic cues were perceptually equivalent along a single dimension in speech.

The three-way oddity results may offer an important contribution to our knowledge about the conditions under which information from diverse acoustic dimensions is integrated in speech perception. However, other phonetic category cues should be explored to assess the extent and reliability of perceptual equivalence among phonetic cues (although, indeed, the many reported trading relations make it unlikely that perceptual equivalence is idiosyncratic to /slIt/-/splIt/). Experiment 1 of this paper extended the trading relations and perceptual equivalence findings to the /sei/-/stei/ contrast,[1] which is simpler than /slIt/-/splIt/ in phonetic, articulatory, and acoustic properties. /Sei/ and /stei/ are dynamically similar, in that each starts (/s/) with the tongue pressed against the inner sides of the upper teeth, tongue-tip nearly in contact with the alveolar ridge and/or the inner side of the juxtaposed front teeth, and each ends (/ei/) with a more open vocal tract. The result is that the vocalic formant transitions are very similar in the two words. The major acoustic consequences of *complete* linguoalveolar (or -dental) closure following /s/ (for /stei/) are the introduction of a silent gap and a lower vocalic F1 onset frequency. (For general accounts of stop closure properties, see Delattre, Liberman, & Cooper, 1955; Fant, 1962; Stevens, 1971, 1974.) In the /slIt/-/splIt/ contrast, on the other hand, bilabial juxtaposition and the consequent labial transitions of the upper formants occur only for /splIt/.

If wider support was to be found (in Experiment 1) for the suggestion that perceptual integration of diverse acoustic cues takes account of their common origin in speech production, then it might be that trading relations and perceptual equivalence between cues are specific to the perception of phonetic information. Experiments 2 and 3 were therefore designed to test two alternatives to the notion that such findings might be unique to phonetic perception.

First, the oddity procedure might not provide the optimal test for true equivalence of the *perceptual* qualities of phonetic cues. It is widely believed that the oddity procedure places heavy demands on auditory short-term memory, which may have encouraged listeners to categorize each stimulus in order to distinguish among the *categorizations*, rather than discriminate finer-grained acoustic qualities that might have been perceptually available prior to categorization. Moreover, since the discrimination test was administered after the forced-choice identification test, test order could also have biased the subjects to categorize stimuli before discriminating them. Experiment 2 minimized these problems by using a discrimination test with lower memory demands, and by collecting discrimination data prior to identification data.

Second, although it has been suggested that perceptual equivalence between diverse speech cues would occur only for perception of phonetic category information (cf. Fitch et al., 1980), no direct studies have been conducted with *non*speech sounds. Experiment 3 tested the "psychoacoustic" alternative that trading relations and perceptual equivalence between cues might occur for nonspeech sounds with complex acoustic properties like those used in our /sei/-/stei/ contrasts.

EXPERIMENT 1

Method

Subjects

The subjects were 15 undergraduate students. Ten subjects from Yale University were tested at Haskins Laboratories and paid $3/h for participation. The other five were from the University of Massachusetts at Amherst, and they received grade-credits toward their introductory psychology courses; they completed the tests in an auditory perception laboratory at their psychology department. All subjects reported having normal hearing in both ears (no diagnosed hearing losses).

Stimuli

Two 290-msec, three-formant vocalic syllables were created on the Haskins parallel-resonance synthesizer. They were stylized versions of the vocalic portions from natural, male utterances of "say" and "stay," and differed from one another only in F1 onset frequency (230 Hz vs. 430 Hz), as the acoustic analyses in the

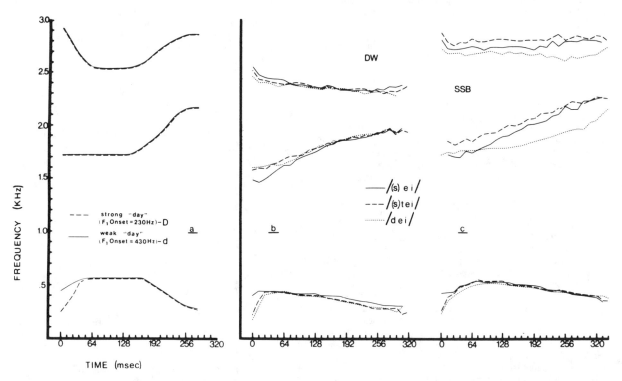

Figure 1. Acoustic measurements of F1, F2, and F3 for the following stimuli, from spectral sections of consecutive 12.8-msec windows: (a) synthetic weak "day" and strong "day," (b) averages of five tokens each of "say," "stay," and "day" by male talker D.W. (Fort Worth, Texas), and (c) by male talker S.S.B. (Brooklyn, New York—variations in S.S.B.'s F2 and F3 frequencies reflect slight vowel color variations among these words in his dialect).

194   BEST, MORRONGIELLO, AND ROBSON

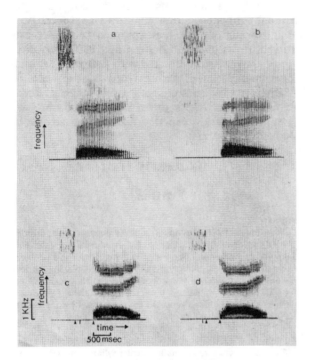

Figure 2. Spectrograms of natural, male utterances of (a) "say," and (b) "stay," by talker S.S.B., and synthesized vocalic tokens of "stay" made from (c) weak "day" and (d) strong "day." The synthetic tokens are preceded by an natural 120-msec /s/, and although they had different silent gap durations, a trading relation showed them to be identified equally consistently as "stay."

left-hand panel of Figure 1 illustrate. The formant amplitudes and overall amplitude envelopes of the stimuli were identical, as were the time-varying frequency characteristics of F2 and F3, and also of F1 beyond the initial 40-msec transition differences (details in Appendix A). Acoustic analyses on five tokens each of "say," "stay," and "day" uttered by two males (center and right-hand panels of Figure 1) showed that the most pronounced spectral difference between the vocalic parts of "say" and "stay" was a lower F1 onset frequency for "stay." The vocalic portion of "stay" and "day" involve nearly identical articulatory gestures[2]; as would be expected, they were virtually identical in formant onset characteristics. Figure 2 shows spectrograms of a natural "say" and "stay," and of "stay" tokens made from the two synthetic syllables by preceding each with a natural /s/ and a silent (closure) interval.

To determine how well the F1 onset frequencies of the two isolated synthetic syllables would support perception of an alveolar stop, 12 additional synthetic syllables were generated for an "ay"-"day" continuum. F1 onset was varied between 160 Hz and the 611-Hz steady state, in 33-Hz steps. A randomized forced-choice identification test (10 judgments/token) with 18 naive listeners (9 from Yale, 9 from University of Massachusetts/Amherst) revealed a fairly sharp category boundary. The test syllable with the 430-Hz F1 onset was perceived as nearly equivocal between "ay" and "day," and will hereafter be called *weak "day,"* abbreviated d. The stimulus with the 230-Hz F1 onset was identified 100% of the time as "day," and will be called *strong "day,"* abbreviated D.

The D and d syllables were each used to generate a "say"-"stay" continuum that incorporated a natural 120-msec /s/ from a male "say" utterance. The /s/ and the synthetic syllable were separated by silent gaps ranging between 0 and 136 msec, in 8-msec increments, resulting in two "say"-"stay" continua with 18 members each (from s[0]d to s[136]d, and from s[0]D to s[136]D).

Procedure

For the forced-choice identification test, a randomized sequence of 360 single-item trials was generated, with 2.5-msec interstimulus intervals (ISIs). The sequence contained 10 repetitions of all items from the two "say"-"stay" continua, and was presented in sound-attenuated test rooms at a comfortable listening level (approximately 75 dB). The subjects identified each stimulus in writing as "say" or "stay."

The subjects took a 15-min break following the identification test, and then completed a three-way oddity discrimination test that included the following comparison types: "one cue," "two cooperating cues," and "two conflicting cues." In the 18 possible "one-cue" comparisons, the three stimuli on each trial had identical gap durations (comparisons covered the entire 0-to-136-msec range), and the "odd" stimulus differed from the other two in its F1 onset frequency (D vs. d). For both two-cue comparison types, a 24-msec gap difference was chosen to compensate phonetically for the F1 difference.[3] In the 15 possible "cooperating cues" comparisons, D stimuli always had a 24-msec longer silent gap (both cues biased toward "stay") than did d stimuli, so that the phonetic complementarity of the cues enhanced the between-category differences; comparisons ranged from s[0]d-s[24]D to s[112]d-s[136]D. For the 15 possible "conflicting cues" comparisons, d stimuli (spectral bias toward "say") had a 24-msec longer gap (temporal bias toward "stay") than did D stimuli, so that phonetic *cancellation* between the cues minimized any between-category differences; these comparisons ranged from s[0]D-s[24]d to s[112]D-s[136]d. Phonetically based discrimination should be facilitated for "cooperating cues" comparisons that straddled the category boundary, because between-category differences were enhanced for those comparisons, relative to "one-cue" comparisons that straddled the boundary. Discrimination of the "conflicting cues" comparisons should be lowest, because between-category differences were minimized in all comparisons of that type—they never straddled the boundary.

The discrimination test was a randomized sequence of all stimulus comparisons for all three comparison types, and included six presentations[4] of each of the 48 possible stimulus comparisons (total items = 288). Within each trial, ISIs were 1 sec, and inter-trial intervals (ITIs) were 3 sec.

Results and Discussion

Identification Test

The results for the forced-choice identification test are shown in Figure 3. The mean category boundary

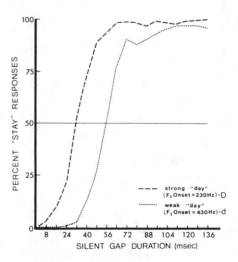

Figure 3. Identification functions for the strong "day" and weak "day" continua in Experiment 1.

(50% "stay" responses) for the strong "day" (D) function fell at 32.4 msec (range = 11.4-52.0 msec), and that for the weak "day" (d) function at 57.1 msec (range = 40.0-94.0 msec); the boundary difference was significant (t = 7.23, p < .001). The average trading relation between the two continua was thus 24.6 msec (range = 9.3-54.0 msec). To be perceived as "stay," the d stimuli required approximately 24 msec more silence between the /s/ and the vocalic syllable than did the D stimuli.

Three-Way Oddity Test

The results for the three-way oddity test are shown in Figure 4. Obtained functions for the three comparison types are represented in the left panel. The right panel represents the corresponding *predicted* functions derived from the identification data (formula in Appendix B), which indicate the limits of the effect of perceived category differences upon discrimination performance. The *obtained* data were submitted to an analysis of variance (ANOVA) crossing 3 comparison types with 15 stimulus pairs, which included only the range of overlap between one-cue and two-cue comparison types (mean gap durations per comparison of 12-128 msec). The Comparison Types effect [F(2,28) = 34.14, p ≪ .001] supported the perceptual equivalence prediction that the order of performance levels would be: "cooperating cues" > "one cue" > "conflicting cues" (see Table 1 for Tukey pairwise contrasts). The "phonetic" argument also predicted improved discrimination performance on comparisons that straddled category boundaries, especially if category differences were enhanced. In line with this prediction, performance near the boundary was higher than within-category performance; that is, there were boundary-related peaks in performance [Stimulus Pairs: F(14,196) = 7.01, p ≪ .001]. In addition, the Comparison Types by Stimulus Pairs interaction [F(28,392) = 3.31, p ≪ .001, broken down by simple effects tests] indicated that the magnitude of peak vs. trough level differences followed the order: "cooperating cues" [F(14,588) = 27.13, p ≪ .001] > "one cue" [F(14,588) = 2.39, p < .005] > "conflicting cues" [F(14,588) = 1.75, p = .05].[5] The "phonetic" predictions were clearly supported.

Analyses were also conducted on the predicted data, obtained vs. predicted comparisons, and individual performance patterns (see details in Appendix C). As Figure 4 shows, the predicted discrimination pattern was essentially the same as the obtained pattern. Obtained performance levels were slightly higher than predicted, but only for stimulus comparisons that were removed from the between-category performance peaks by 16-24 msec or more (i.e., those that did *not* straddle the boundary). Moreover, the residual performance levels (obtained minus predicted level—the performance that was unexplainable by phonetic *category* differences) still followed the "phonetic" order: "cooperating cues" > "one cue" > "conflicting cues." Residual discrimination patterns will be discussed later in the paper, since they are best understood relative to the obtained-predicted differences found in Experiments 2 and 3.

Conclusions

The results of Experiment 1 clearly indicated a trading relation and perceptual equivalence between

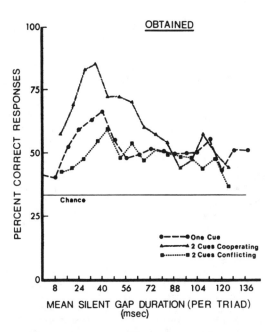
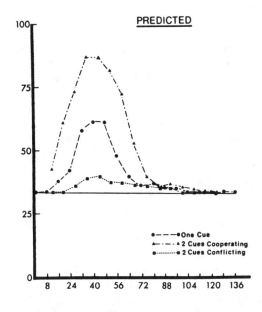

Figure 4. Obtained (left-hand panel) and predicted (right-hand panel) results for the three-way oddity test in Experiment 1.

196   BEST, MORRONGIELLO, AND ROBSON

Table 1
ω **Values of Tukey Tests on Significant Comparison Type (CT) Effects From ANOVAs for Experiments 1, 2, and 3**

	One Cue vs. Cooperating Cues	Cooperating Cues vs. Conflicting Cues	Conflicting Cues vs. One Cue
	Experiment 1 (Represented as Mean Percentages Correct)		
Obtained Data	8.72††	13.16††	4.44*
Predicted Data	9.57†	18.14††	8.58†
Obtained "Peak-Range" Data	17.22††	25.97††	8.75*
Predicted "Peak-Range" Data	25.91††	43.22††	17.31†
	Experiment 2 (Represented as Mean True d′ Values)		
Obtained Data	1.43††	2.04††	.61*
Predicted Data	1.85††	2.13††	.29
Observed "Peak-Range" Data	1.68††	2.88††	1.20**
Predicted "Peak-Range" Data	2.31††	3.32††	1.01**
	Experiment 3 (Represented as Mean Number Correct, Out of Six)		
"Say"-"Stay" Listeners	.72†	1.08††	.36*
"Temporal" Listeners (Peak)	.76*	.91*	.15

*p < .05.   **p < .01.   †p < .005.   ††p < .001.

gap duration and F1 onset frequency as cues for the "say"-"stay" distinction. The Fitch et al. (1980) findings were thus replicated for a different phonetic category contrast. Silent gap duration and F1 onset frequency appeared to have converged on a single dimension in phonetic perception.

EXPERIMENT 2

Although Experiment 1 suggested that the silence and F1 spectral cues for the "say"-"stay" contrast are perceptually equivalent in quality, the oddity task's heavy demands on auditory short-term memory[6] may have biased the subjects to *recode* the rapidly fading sensory information into phonetic category information. Phonetic categorizations are believed to be better retained in memory than are raw acoustic properties, especially in the case of consonants (cf. Crowder, 1971, 1973; Crowder & Morton, 1969; Darwin & Baddeley, 1974; Fujisaki & Kawashima, 1969; Pisoni, 1975; Pisoni & Tash, 1974; Repp, Healy, & Crowder, 1979; Pisoni, Note 2). Thus, the oddity task may not be a sensitive test for qualitative equivalence of cues *at the sensory level*. Experiment 2 used a 2IAX ("same"-"different") discrimination procedure with short ISIs to induce performance that would better reflect perceptual sensitivity to the physical properties of the stimuli. In addition, the identification test was run after the discrimination task, to control against the possibility that obtaining forced-choice identifications before discrimination judgments might have introduced an experimental bias toward phonetic categorization, and thus against comparison of physical properties.

We used the 2IAX procedure to assess perceptual sensitivity, based on several considerations.[7] While standard signal detection theory (SDT—MacMillan, Kaplan, & Creelman, 1977) does not allow estimation of perceptual sensitivity from oddity data, it *does*

permit estimation of perceptual sensitivity from ABX, 4IAX, and 2IAX data, through the use of the d′ sensitivity index. According to SDT predictions (MacMillan et al., 1977), d′ values (hence sensitivity) should be lowest for the 2IAX procedure. This is because that procedure biases observers to give "same" responses for physically different stimulus pairs that are difficult to discriminate, which artificially deflates standard d′ values [computed as z(Hits) − z(False Alarms); Kaplan et al., 1978]. However, the data on actual sensitivities of the paradigms are equivocal.[8] Moreover, a relatively new formula for computing bias-corrected, *true* d′ values from 2IAX data yields sensitivity values at least as high for 2IAX data as for AXB and 4IAX (Kaplan, MacMillan, & Creelman, 1978).[9] Finally, memory demands for making "same"-"different" judgments on two "say"-"stay" stimuli per trial would seem lower than for ABX or 4IAX judgments.

Method

Subjects

A new group of 14 subjects participated in this experiment. Seven were Yale undergraduates; the other seven were undergraduates at the University of Massachusetts/Amherst. All reported having normal hearing in both ears.

Stimuli

The stimuli from Experiment 1 were used again. This time, however, stimuli containing gaps over 96 msec were eliminated from the test, since they had been identified as "stay" nearly 100% of the time in Experiment 1. The truncated "say"-"stay" continua contained 14 stimuli each.

Procedure

The subjects first completed a three-way 2IAX test, which employed 300-msec ISIs and 2.5-sec ITIs. Stimulus pairs for the three types of test comparisons ("one cue," "cooperating cues," and "conflicting cues") were chosen from the truncated "say"-"stay" continua by the same means as described in Experiment 1, with 24-msec silence again used as the temporal compensation value in both two-cue comparison types. In addition, a fourth set of "physically same" catch-trial comparisons was included to provide false-alarm-rate data. There were 11 possible mean gap values each for "one cue" (s[8]d-s[8]D to s[88]d-s[88]D) and "physically same" comparisons (s[8]d-s[8]d and s[8]D-s[8]D, to s[88]d-s[88]d and s[88]D-s[88]D), and 10 possible pairs each for "conflicting cues" (from s[0]D-s[24]d to s[72]D-s[96]d) and "co-operating cues" comparisons (from s[0]d-s[24]d to s[72]d-s[96]D).

Six judgments were obtained for each of the 42 possible stimulus contrasts (total items = 252), randomized across pairings and comparison types. Instructions attempted to focus attention on the differences in acoustic properties of the stimuli, rather than on phonetic categories. The subjects were told that most of the "different" pairs would be tokens of the same word, so they should listen closely for slight *sound* differences between members of same-word pairs.

A randomized 280-trial forced-choice identification test (2.5-msec ISIs), containing 10 repetitions of all stimuli in the truncated continua, was administered after the 2IAX test.

Results and Discussion

Identification Test

The identification results (lower panel, Figure 5) replicated the trading relation found in Experiment 1, this time with a boundary difference of 18.5 msec (range = 5.1-37.3 msec). The somewhat smaller trading relation may have resulted from truncating the continua (stimulus range effect), but was nonetheless significant (t = 8.88, p < .001). The D (strong "day") category boundary fell at 25.3 msec (range = 10.7-51.2 msec), and the d (weak "day") boundary at 43.8 msec (range = 33.6-60.0 msec).

Three-Way 2IAX Test

The three-way 2IAX results (upper panel, Figure 5) showed the "phonetic" order of "different" response levels for the three types of test comparisons ("co-operating cues" > "one cue" > "conflicting cues"), as did the three-way oddity results of Experiment 1. The small peak in percentage of "different" responses for "physically same" and catch trials near the category boundary resulted from the ambiguous identifications of the boundary stimuli.

The true d' values offer a more accurate measure of differential *perceptual sensitivities* than do the raw data; Figure 6 shows the obtained (left-hand panel) and predicted sensitivity functions (right-hand panel) represented by these true d' values (formulas in Appendix D). An ANOVA was run on the obtained true d' data, spanning the overlap among comparison types (12-88-msec mean gaps), for the 3 comparison types by 10 stimulus pairs. The pattern of results (see Table 2, and the Tukey pairwise contrasts in Table 1) essentially replicated the Experiment 1 findings. The results of analyses on the predicted data, obtained vs. predicted comparisons, and individual performance patterns also replicated the previous findings (see Appendix E for details). Once again, detailed discussion of obtained vs. predicted differences will be deferred until later in the paper.

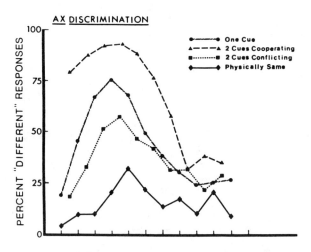

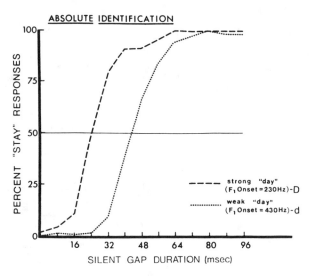

Figure 5. Obtained functions for the three-way 2IAX discrimination test (upper panel) and the forced-choice identification test (lower panel), for Experiment 2.

In contrast with the oddity test of Experiment 1, the 2IAX test produced a small, but significant, performance-level peak (higher d' values) near the category boundary for "conflicting cues" comparisons. However, this "conflicting cues" peak reflects the fact that the trading relation found in Experiment 2 was only 18.5 msec, which did not match the predetermined 24-msec gap compensation value used. Since gap duration and F1 onset differences in the "conflicting cues" comparisons did not precisely cancel one another, there was a small but predictable enhancement of sensitivity near the boundary.

Conclusions

All of the major findings from Experiment 1 were replicated—a trading relation was found between the

198   BEST, MORRONGIELLO, AND ROBSON

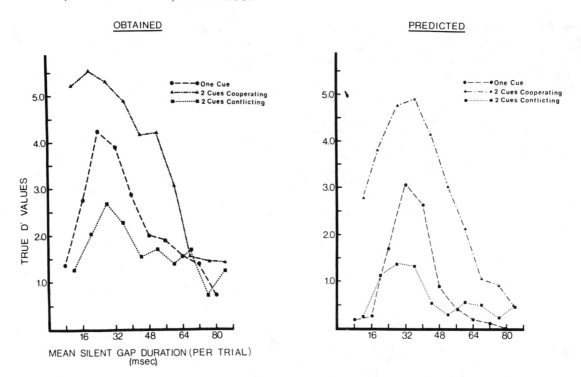

Figure 6. Obtained (left-hand panel) and predicted (right-hand panel) functions for true d′ values on the three-way 2IAX test in Experiment 2.

Table 2

Results From the ANOVAs Performed on the True d′ Values Computed for the Three-Way 2IAX Data From Experiment 2

ANOVA	Effect	df	F	p
Obtained Data (3CT* by 10SP**)	CT	2, 26	41.78	≪.001
	SP	9,117	17.08	≪.001
	CT by SP	18,234	6.48	<.001
CT by SP Simple Effects				
"Cooperating Cues"	SP	9,351	18.43	≪.001
"One Cue"	SP	9,351	8.47	<.001
"Conflicting Cues"	SP	9,351	1.97	<.05
Predicted Data (3CT by 10SP)	CT	2, 26	109.99	≪.001
	SP	9,117	17.88	≪.001
	CT by SP	18,234	9.42	<.001
CT by SP Simple Effects				
"Cooperating Cues"	SP	9,351	26.91	≪.001
"One Cue"	SP	9,351	13.39	<.001
"Conflicting Cues"	SP	9,351	1.83	>.05†
"Cooperating Cues" (2F†† by 10 SP)	F	1, 13	17.26	≪.001
	SP	9,117	37.96	≪.001
	F by SP	9,117	2.09	<.05
"One Cue" (2F by 10SP)	F	1, 13	35.23	≪.001
	SP	9,117	13.02	≪.01
	F by SP	9,117	1.90	>.05‡
"Conflicting Cues" (2F by 10SP)	F	1, 13	21.11	≪.001
	SP	9,117	4.58	<.001
	F by SP	9,117	.49	n.s.
Obtained "Peak-Range" Data‡‡ (3CT)	CT	2, 26	31.66	≪.001
Predicted "Peak-Range" Data (3CT)	CT	2, 26	66.23	≪.001

*Comparison types ("cooperating cues," "one cue," "conflicting cues").   **Stimulus pairs.   †Marginal (.05 cut-off = 1.88).
††Functions (predicted vs. observed).   ‡Marginal (.05 cut-off = 1.96).   ‡‡Mean value for gap durations between 20 and 48 msec (average per AX pair) in each type of test comparison.

F1 onset and silence cues, and the pattern of 2IAX sensitivities fit the "phonetic" predictions. The two acoustic cues for the "say"-"stay" contrast appear to be perceptually equivalent, even under conditions designed to reduce demands on auditory short-term memory and to reduce experimentally induced biases to categorize stimuli before discriminating them. That is, the "phonetic" pattern of three-way discrimination performance seems not to depend on the employment of a task that places heavy demands on memory.

EXPERIMENT 3

The question that now arises, however, is: What is the origin of the equivalence in perceptual sensitivity to the temporal and spectral cues for the "say"-"stay" contrast? At least two possibilities present themselves: (1) the "phonetic" alternative, that the equivalence derives specifically from perception of phonetic information (recall that even in Experiment 2, the subjects perceived the stimuli as "say" and "stay") —that is, it occurs "only for sounds ... being processed as speech" (Fitch et al., 1980, p. 344); or (2) the "psychoacoustic" alternative, that the pattern derives from general (not speech-specific) properties of auditory perception. Although we know of no research on psychoacoustic integration of acoustic cues like those we used in the "say"-"stay" research, the "psychoacoustic" alternative gains converging support from: (a) known tradeoffs in nonspeech perception (e.g., the time-intensity trade in auditory localization: Green, 1976); and (b) speech-relevant discontinuities in perception of changes along a single acoustic dimension in nonspeech stimuli (e.g., categorical perception for rise-time and onset-time nonspeech contrasts: Cutting & Rosner, 1974, 1976; Cutting, Rosner, & Foard, 1976; Miller, Wier, Pastore, Kelly, & Dooling, 1976; Pastore, Ahroon, Baffuto, Friedman, Puleo, & Fink, 1977; Pisoni, 1977).

Therefore, it would be important to determine whether there was some psychoacoustic interaction between the "say"-"stay" cues. For example, it could be that longer gaps were needed for the d stimuli than for the D stimuli to be heard as "stay," because the /s/ offset was closer in frequency to the 430-Hz F1 onset than to the 230-Hz F1 onset (by 3-4 critical bands). This possibility seems unlikely, though, because it contradicts findings that gap sensitivity is *inversely* related to the amount of frequency difference between the acoustic components surrounding the gap (Divenyi, 1979; Divenyi & Danner, 1977; Divenyi & Sachs, 1978). Hence, the cue integration we found in Experiments 1 and 2, and that found by Fitch et al. (1980), may indeed be unique to the perception of phonetic information. Nonetheless, the possibility remained open that the inverse relationship between temporal and spectral sensitivity *might* be reversed, for purely (and as yet unknown) psycho-

acoustic reasons, under certain stimulus and task conditions like those used in the "say"-"stay" tests. A third experiment was run to determine whether the "phonetic" or the "psychoacoustic" alternative would better explain trading relations and perceptual equivalence between phonetic cues.

This test required nonspeech control stimuli that maintained the crucial temporal and spectral properties of the "say"-"stay" stimuli, since the potential psychoacoustic effects might be dependent upon that particular array of physical properties. On the other hand, however, the stimuli had to be dissimilar enough from the "say"-"stay" stimuli that most naive listeners would fail to hear them as speech. We used "sine-wave analogues" of the "say"-"stay" continua for this experiment because they fit both criteria—they were essentially identical to the synthetic speech stimuli, except that their "formants" had bandwidths of 1 Hz. Another recent study employed sine-wave analogues of speech continua, and reported that most naive listeners heard the sine-wave stimuli as nonspeech sounds (e.g., beeps, chimes, slide-guitar notes, electronic tones). Only a few listeners spontaneously perceived them as distorted ("chime-like") speech. Identification tests revealed distinct differences in category boundaries, dependent on whether the sine-wave stimuli were perceived as speech or as nonspeech (Dorman, 1979; Bailey, Summerfield, & Dorman, Note 3). Because sine-wave analogues can be perceived either as speech or as nonspeech, which can affect categorization performance, we grouped our subjects according to their posttest reports of what the stimuli sounded like. The "phonetic" alternative predicted that the trading relation and perceptual equivalence between cues would occur only for subjects who heard the sine-wave analogues as "say" and "stay." In contradistinction, the "psychoacoustic" alternative predicted that those perceptual patterns would occur even for subjects who perceived the sine-wave stimuli as nonspeech.

Method

Subjects
Twenty-two naive listeners completed this experiment. Fifteen were Yale undergraduates and seven were enrolled at the University of Massachusetts/Amherst. All reported normal hearing in both ears.

Stimuli
Sine-wave analogues of the weak "day" (d) and strong "day" (D) speech syllables were made by synthesizing three simultaneous sine waves, using a software program developed for the PDP-11/45 at Haskins Laboratories.[10] In each of the sine-wave "day" analogues, the time-varying amplitude and center frequency characteristics of each of the synthetic speech formants was imitated by a frequency- and amplitude-modulated sine wave (see Figure 7). The sine-wave analogue of D will be termed "strong SW1 transition" (SW), and the analogue of d will be termed "weak SW1 transition" (sw).[11]

The nonspeech analogue of /s/ also had to differ enough from natural /s/ to be heard as a nonspeech sound by most listeners, and yet be similar enough to /s/ that it *could* be heard as speech.

200   BEST, MORRONGIELLO, AND ROBSON

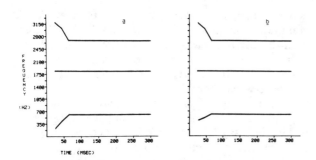

Figure 7. Schematic time-spectrum representations of the three-sine-wave analogues for the synthetic speech syllables used in Experiments 1 and 2: (a) weak "day" analogue: (b) strong "day" analogue.

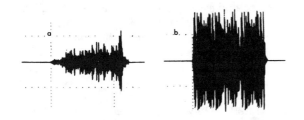

Figure 8. CRT display of digitized waveforms for (a) natural male /s/ (from "stay") used in the "say"-"stay" continua for Experiments 1 and 2, and (b) amplitude-reshaped "hiss" used in the sine-wave continua for Experiment 3.

We used a "hiss" created by changing the rise time and overall amplitude (but not the fall time) of the natural /s/ used in the synthetic "say"-"stay" continua (see Figure 8). The hiss (abbreviated h) had the same frequency and offset properties as the /s/ of Experiments 1 and 2, and thus met the requirements just outlined.

The SW and sw continua were constructed by inserting varying gap durations (in 8-msec steps, from 0 to 96 msec, as in Experiment 2) between h and the sine-wave analogue. Each continuum contained 14 stimuli (h[0]SW to h[96]SW, and h[0]sw to h[96]sw). which most of our naive listeners heard as bizarre electronic sounds or distorted nonspeech sounds, such as beeps, water drips, etc. Only about one-quarter of the subjects perceived them as "chime-like" utterances of "say" and "stay."

Procedure

An AXB identification procedure was used (cf. Bailey et al., 1978; Dorman, 1979), since the labels required for a standard forced-choice identification test might have encouraged subjects to perceive the stimuli as speech. On each trial, the second stimulus (X) had to be identified as being more similar either to the first stimulus (A) or the last stimulus (B). Categories A and B were fixed across trials; A was a sine-wave analogue to natural "say" (h[0]sw, the analogue for s[0]d), and B was the closest analogue to natural "stay" (h[96]SW, the analogue for s[96]D). Each of the 28 possible AXB trials was presented 10 times in a randomized test sequence.

After the AXB test and a subsequent 15-min break, the subjects took a three-way oddity test, which was designed exactly as in Experiment 1. It included "cooperating cues" (10 contrasts: h[0]sw-h[24]SW to h[72]sw-h[96]SW), "one cue" (13 contrasts: h[0]sw-h[0]SW to h[96]sw-h[96]SW), and "conflicting cues" comparisons (10 contrasts: h[0]SW-h[24]sw to h[72]SW-h[96]sw). Six judgments were obtained for each of the 33 possible stimulus contrasts (total = 198), and the test sequence was randomized across all comparison types.[12]

Group assignments. Sixteen subjects (all seven University of Massachusetts subjects and nine of the Yale subjects) were told before testing that the stimuli were computer sounds with two components—a "hiss" followed by a "chime-like" sound, with varying gap lengths between the components. The remaining six Yale subjects were told that the stimuli were distortions of "say" and "stay," and that they should listen for those words as they completed their tasks. We hoped this would induce a "speech perceptual set," and thereby allow us to assess the contribution of speech processing/perception to performance.

Subjects answered a posttest questionnaire on what the stimuli sounded like, and which stimulus properties they had attended to. The subjects were divided into five groups, according to their questionnaire responses. One subgroup included four subjects who claimed to have been guessing or changing their perceptual strategies from trial to trial; their performance was near chance, and appeared haphazard. Another group of three subjects perceived speech contrasts other than "say"-"stay" (i.e., "sleh"-"sreh," the French "un"-"rien," and two Greek words), including one subject who had been instructed to listen for "say" and "stay." The perceptual patterns for these first two groups will not be discussed further. Only the remaining three subgroups will be discussed in more detail. They were:

(1) Five subjects who heard "say" and "stay," either by instruction (three subjects) or spontaneously (two subjects), for even a portion of the test session. Three claimed to have occasionally listened for tone differences (the two "spontaneous" subjects) or for different water drips (one "instructed" subject, who used this strategy throughout most of the three-way oddity test), because at times they "lost touch with" the words. Therefore, this grouping provides a conservative test of the "phonetic" alternative.

(2) Five subjects who focused primarily on nonspeech *temporal* contrasts related to changes in gap duration, including differences in the gaps (two subjects) or spaces (one subject) between the hiss and sine waves, and overall length differences (two subjects).

(3) Five subjects who perceived nonspeech contrasts related to the SW vs. sw *spectral* difference. These subjects generally ignored the hiss and listened for contrasts between two different kinds of water drips (two subjects), two different pitches (one subject), the presence or absence of a ringing quality (one subject), or the presence or absence of electronic "waw" (one subject).

Groups 2 and 3 each included one of the subjects instructed to listen for "say" and "stay"; each reported that they could not hear the words, and had instead perceived a nonspeech contrast.[13] The three groups of subjects will be referred to as: (1) "say"-"stay" listeners, (2) "temporal" listeners, and (3) "spectral" listeners.

Results and Discussion

AXB Identification Test

Group comparisons. The AXB identification data for the three groups are shown in the upper panels of Figures 9-11. To determine whether the AXB differences among the three groups were statistically significant, a two-way ANOVA was performed for 3 groups by 2 continua. The data used in this test were "percent Category B responses" because the majority of AXB functions for the "spectral" group had no 50% crossovers within the range tested. The significant Groups by Continua interaction [$F(2,12) = 14.77$, p < .01] indicates that categorizations of the SW and sw continua contrasted substantially among the three groups of listeners. Only the "say"-"stay" group showed the sort of trading relation found in Experiments 1 and 2.

PERCEPTUAL EQUIVALENCE IN SPEECH AND NONSPEECH   201

"SAY-STAY" LISTENERS

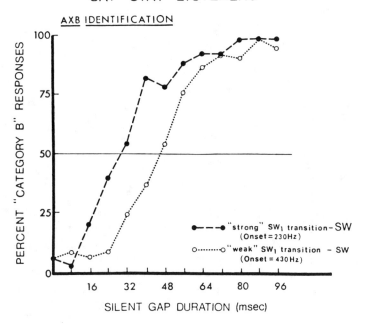

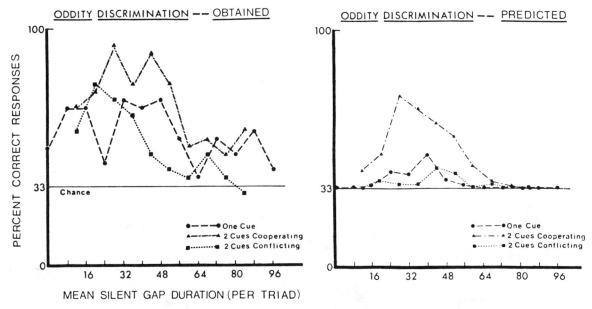

Figure 9. Sine-wave AXB identification functions (upper panel), and obtained (lower left) and predicted (lower right) functions for the three-way oddity test, "say"-"stay" listeneners. Experiment 3.

"Say"-"stay" listeners. The "say"-"stay" listeners showed a 17.8-msec trading relation (range = 7.6-29.6) between gap duration and the SW-sw spectral contrast (upper panel Figure 9), which was a significant boundary difference by a one-way ANOVA [$F(1,4) = 28.8$, $p < .01$]. The crossover value for the sw continuum was 45.8 msec (range = 40.0-52.0 msec); for the SW continuum, it was 27.9 msec (range = 22.4-38.4 msec). The trading relation magnitude and category boundaries were nearly the same as in Experiment 2, which included the same range of gap durations.

"Temporal" listeners. In contrast with the "say"-"stay" group, the "temporal" listeners (upper panel, Figure 10) failed to use the SW-sw contrasts consistently in their categorizations. They categorized stimuli according to duration changes showing a SW boundary at 34.3 msec (range = 26.0-44.8) and a sw boundary at 40.7 msec (range = 32.0-48.0). The 6.4-msec boundary difference (range = −2.65 to +8.0) was not significant.

"Spectral" listeners. In contrast with the other two sine-wave groups, the "spectral" listeners consistently

202   BEST, MORRONGIELLO, AND ROBSON

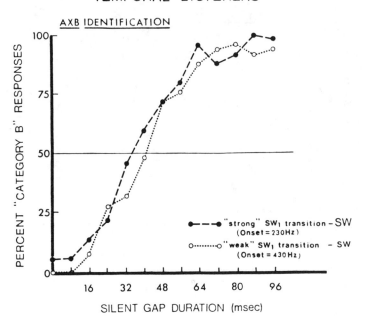

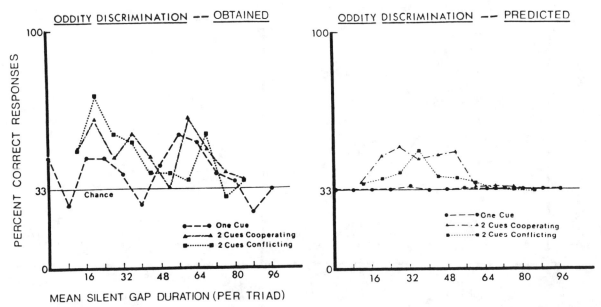

Figure 10. Sine-wave AXB identification functions (upper panel), and obtained (lower left) and predicted (lower right) functions for the three-way oddity test, "temporal" listeners, Experiment 3.

categorized stimuli by SW-sw differences (upper panel, Figure 11), according to their simple effects test for the Groups by Continua interaction [F(1,12) = 60.1, p < .001]. None of the SW stimuli were identified with A more often than chance, nor were the sw stimuli identified with B more often than chance, except for one token categorized as B 65% of the time. Thus, lengthening the gaps did not *completely* compensate for the SW-sw difference. The asymptote of the sw function at long gaps makes it unlikely that

extending the range of the gap durations would have resulted in a complete trading relation for this group.

Three-Way Oddity Test

Group comparisons. There were also group differences in the pattern of three-way oddity discrimination (Figures 9-11) for both the obtained (lower left panels) and the predicted data (lower right panels). To compare discrimination performance among the three groups, mean "peak range" (16-48-msec gaps)

"SPECTRAL" LISTENERS

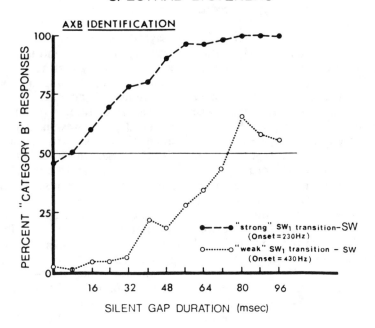

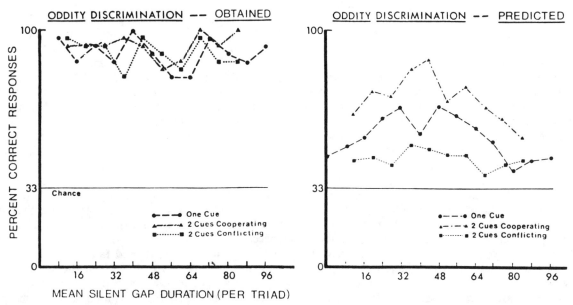

Figure 11. Sine-wave AXB identification functions (upper panel), and obtained (lower left) and predicted (lower right) functions for the three-way oddity test, "spectral" listeners, Experiment 3.

performances were calculated for the three comparison types. The range was extended beyond the 20-48-msec "peak range" used in Experiments 1 and 2 in order to include all the peaks of the "say"-"stay" group (lower left, Figure 9) and the peaks of the "temporal" group at 20 msec (lower left, Figure 10). An ANOVA was performed on these data for 3 groups by 3 comparison types. The order of "peak-range" performance levels differed significantly among the three groups [Groups by Comparison Types: $F(4,24) = 3.49$, p < .025].

"Say"-"stay" listeners. Only the "say"-"stay" group (lower left, Figure 9) showed the "phonetic" pattern found in the previous two experiments [simple effects test for the Groups by Comparison Types interaction: $F(2,24) = 9.4$, p < .01]. An ANOVA was run on their obtained data for 3 comparison types by 10 stimulus pairs (mean gap durations of between 12 and 88 msec). The Comparison Types effect [$F(2,8) = 33.35$, p < .001] supported the performance order: "cooperating cues" > "one cue" > "conflicting cues" (see Tukey pairwise contrasts, Table 1).[14] Peak-level per-

204   BEST, MORRONGIELLO, AND ROBSON

formance was significantly higher than trough-level performance across the three comparison types, according to the Stimulus Pairs effect [F(9,36) = 4.36, p < .001] (see Appendix F for individual patterns).

"Temporal" listeners. The obtained discrimination pattern for this group (lower left, Figure 10) suggested that the "cooperating cues"-"conflicting cues" distinction was moot for them; what mattered were noticeable temporal differences between stimuli. The Stimulus Pairs effect for this group [F(9,36) = 3.08, p < .01] indicates that there were two performance peaks; the level of the 20-msec peak appears higher than the one around 60-68 msec. The order of performance in the 20-msec "peak-range" (simple effects test for the Groups by Comparison Types interaction F(2,24) = 4.86, p < .025] was "conflicting cues" ≥ "cooperating cues" > "one cue" (see Tukey pairwise contrasts, Table 1). This pattern fits the "auditory" prediction that performance for two-cue comparisons would be better than for "one cue."

"Spectral" listeners. The "spectral" listeners, unlike either of the other two sine-wave groups, discriminated the SW-sw contrast nearly perfectly across the board (lower left, Figure 11). Performance was equally high across all three comparison types and at all gap durations.

Obtained vs. Predicted Differences

Because all three groups of listeners in Experiment 3 showed higher obtained than predicted performance, as was found in the previous two experiments, residual performance patterns (obtained minus predicted performance levels) among the three experiments will be discussed here. The Experiment 3 groups differed in their residual performance patterns (see details of analyses in Appendix F). Residual performance for the "temporal" listeners followed the order: "conflicting cues" > "cooperating cues" > "one cue."[15] The "spectral" listeners, in contrast, showed the residual performance pattern of "conflicting cues" > "one cue" > "cooperating cues," which also deviates from the "phonetic" pattern of Experiments 1 and 2. Only the "say"-"stay" listeners replicated the "phonetic" pattern of residual performance levels found in the previous experiments: "cooperating cues" > "one cue" > "conflicting cues." Thus, residual performance patterns were consistent across the "say"-"stay" listener groups from all three experiments. The "say"-"stay" residual performance pattern was distinctly different from the "temporal" and "spectral" patterns in Experiment 3.

These findings suggest that the "say"-"stay" residual performance was due to perception of the subcategorical differences as phonetic, rather than as purely auditory (nonphonetic), distinctions. Had the origin of the residual discriminability been purely auditory, the pattern should have followed the "auditory" prediction, or at least should have followed the "temporal" or "spectral" patterns. Although the residual discrimination performance of the "say"-"stay" listeners cannot be explained by *between*-category phonetic contrasts, it can be explained by *within*-category distinctions *that are nonetheless phonetic* (i.e., relevant to allophonic or articulatory variations). We note here that, for the "say"-"stay" listeners in all three experiments, the position of the obtained peaks was shifted toward the D (or SW) boundary. This shift, coupled with the consistent "day" categorization of D (whose F1 onset was like natural "day" and "stay") and the equivocal categorization of d (whose F1 onset was like natural "say"—see Stimuli, Experiment 1), suggests that residual discrimination was probably based on a distinction such as "clear /t/ closure" vs. "inexact (or weak) /t/ closure." Gap duration and F1 onset frequency differences apparently provided equivalent information about within-category, as well as between-category, phonetic distinctions.

Conclusions

The two most important points to be made about Experiment 3 are: (1) The identification and discrimination patterns of the "temporal" and "spectral" listeners differed substantially from the "say"-"stay" results of Experiments 1 and 2; and (2) the sine-wave "say"-"stay" results were essentially identical to the results of the two earlier experiments with synthetic speech. Only the subjects who perceived "say"-"stay" showed a trading relation and perceptual equivalence between the two acoustic cues. Thus, the trading relation and "phonetic" discrimination pattern appear to occur specifically with perception of *speech* contrasts. They are not attributable to general psychoacoustic sensitivities or interactions, since they did not appear in the two nonspeech groups. The nonspeech listeners focused on only one acoustic dimension (for the most part), and failed to integrate the two into a unitary percept. When the stimuli were perceived as speech, however, gap duration and spectral information were perceptually integrated in a manner that took account of their common origin in speech. Thus, the two cues are integral in speech perception, but separable in auditory perception (cf. Garner & Morton, 1969).

The residual performance patterns of the "temporal" and "spectral" groups were basically consistent with "auditory" predictions, whereas the residual performance pattern of the "say"-"stay" group was consistent with "phonetic" predictions (as were the residual patterns found in Experiments 1 and 2). The discrimination performance on "say"-"stay" contrasts that cannot be explained by phonetic *category* differences may nonetheless results from perception of subcategorical stimulus differences as providing phonetic, rather than purely auditory, information.

SUMMARY AND GENERAL CONCLUSIONS

The three experiments present five major findings that bear on the integration of diverse acoustic properties in speech perception. First, there is a trading relation between the two primary acoustic consequences of the articulatory distinction between "say" and "stay." If unequivocal spectral information about the occurrence of a medial /t/ is provided, listeners hear "stay" when the duration of a silent gap between /s/ and the vocalic syllable minimally specifies a stop closure. However, when spectral information provides only equivocal information about an alveolar stop, listeners need stronger evidence for stop closure from another acoustic cue (e.g., longer closure gap) in order to perceive "stay."

Second, the two cues for the speech distinction, although from different *acoustic* dimensions, are perceptually equivalent. They converge upon a unitary phonetic dimension and provide qualitatively equivalent information about contrastive speech events. Stimulus tokens within a single phonetic category are quite difficult to distinguish perceptually, even though distinct along two different acoustic dimensions ("conflicting cues" comparisons). However, discrimination is comparatively easy when the parameter values for the same two acoustic dimensions are such that the stimuli being discriminated are in different phonetic categories ("cooperating cues").

Third, the qualitative equivalence of the two cues within a single phonetic dimension reflects equivalence in sensitivity to those properties of the speech stimuli. When subjects listen to "say"-"stay" stimuli, the "phonetic" discrimination pattern emerges even under conditions designed to reduce memory demands and eliminate an experimentally induced "set" to categorize stimuli before discriminating them.

Fourth, trading relations and perceptual equivalence between cues derive specifically from the integrated perception of multiple acoustic properties as *phonetic information*, and not from psychoacoustic factors. Those perceptual patterns do not occur when listeners perceive the acoustic variations as nonspeech contrasts. Experiment 3 implies that the perceptual integration of diverse acoustic information is determined by what the listener perceives the stimuli to be, much more than it is by raw stimulus characteristics and/or their interactions with basic properties of the auditory system. Several other recent speech perception findings provide converging support for the notion that performance patterns are determined more by the type of information focused upon than they are by the absolute physical properties of the stimuli. Changes

in identification functions occur not only for sine-wave speech continua, dependent on whether the stimuli are heard as speech or nonspeech (Dorman, 1979; Bailey et al., Note 3), but also for speech continua, dependent on the specific phonetic contrast subjects listen for (Carden, Levitt, Jusczyk, & Walley, 1981). Moreover, discrimination performance for speech continua differs substantially, depending on whether listeners are focusing on phonetic category information or ignoring phonetic categories to focus on purely acoustic properties (Repp, Note 4).

Fifth, the *pattern* of residual performance on "say"-"stay" discriminations suggests that even within a phonetic category, acoustic variations in the two cues are treated perceptually as if they provide phonetic, not simply auditory, information. To our knowledge, this is the first time it has been possible to distinguish empirically between the contributions of auditory and phonetic perception to speech discrimination performance levels that cannot be explained by phonetic *category* differences. For this reason, and also because the differences among the comparison types were small (see Appendices C, E, and F), the effect needs replication. We suggest that the residual discriminability of speech contrasts should most likely reflect phonetic, not auditory, perceptual contributions whenever the acoustic characteristics of the stimuli fall within the range of natural speech variation, and whenever listeners perceive the stimulus properties as information about speech contrasts.

The pattern of perceptual integration of the two cues by the three groups of "say"-"stay" listeners paralleled the pattern of acoustic and articulatory qualities found in natural "say" and "stay" utterances (cf. Experiment 1). That is, "stay" differs from "say" in that only the former word involves a *complete* linguoalveolar closure, which results in a longer closure silence and lower F1 onset frequency than found in the latter word. Perceptual integration of the silence and F1-onset cues indicated that listeners had acted as though both cues provided comparable information about whether a complete linguoalveolar closure had occurred. This pattern of perception-production similarities leads us to agree with the conclusion of Fitch et al. (1980) that trading relations and perceptual equivalence indicate that phonetic perception takes account of the common articulatory origin of diverse cues for a given speech contrast. The perception-production commonalities implied by our results and those of Fitch et al. may suggest that, when listeners attend to the phonetic properties of speech stimuli, they are perceiving articulatory information provided by the acoustic waveform. An excellent discussion of this possibility can be found in Summerfield (1978). Further corroboration for this hypothesis comes from research on the parallel effects of phonetic context on perception and produc-

206   BEST, MORRONGIELLO, AND ROBSON

tion. A variety of context effects indicate that phonetic perception takes account of articulatory consequences —e.g., context-dependent shifts in patterns of perception for consonant contrasts parallel the effects of context on the corresponding articulatory gestures (e.g., Mann, 1980; Mann & Repp, 1980, 1981; Miller & Liberman, 1979).

The "say"-"stay" results reported in this paper appear robust, and reflect the perceptual integrity of the multiple acoustic consequences of articulatory gestures *as phonetic information*. But the possibility that the trading relation/perceptual equivalence pattern may be unique to speech needs further investigation. To learn whether that perceptual pattern is uniquely human, the responses of animals to speech and nonspeech contrasts conveyed by multiple physical cues (even nonauditory) might be studied (cf. Kuhl, 1978; Liberman & Pisoni, 1977; but also compare Kuhl & Miller, 1975, 1978; Morse & Snowdon, 1975; Waters & Wilson, 1976). For example, a recent report of discrimination among natural leaf categories (oak vs. nonoak) by pigeons (Cerella, 1979) suggested that the animals may have treated several dimensions of contrast among leaf outlines as equivalent (e.g., smooth vs. serrated edge, shallow vs. deep notches between lobes, etc.). Further research would be necessary, however, to determine the completeness of the pigeon's perceptual integration of leaf-outline dimensions— that is, to determine whether they would show trading relations and perceptual equivalence among the diverse features.

Also, to assess whether perceptual equivalence is uniquely characteristic of *speech* perception, or whether it may be a more general quality in perception of complex acoustic information for naturally occurring contrastive events, the perceptual integration of multiple cues might be explored for familiar *non*speech events that are rich in dynamic acoustic information. For example, there are probably spectral as well as temporal contrasts between the acoustic products of plucking vs. bowing actions on a violin string (Schelleng, 1973), or between the acoustic consequences of hard vs. soft attack in the playing of piano notes (Weyer, 1976, 1976/1977). Contrastive nonspeech properties such as these might also be perceptually integrated, but it is not clear a priori whether such integration would imply qualitative equivalence among the diverse acoustic cues. Answers to questions about multiple acoustic properties of natural nonspeech events, and about perceptual integration of those (possible) properties, still await empirical exploration.

The strength of the current findings implies that perceptual equivalence among multiple cues for a given phonemic contrast is a key aspect of adult speech perception. Developmental research on trading relations and perceptual equivalence in speech perception may aid in understanding the interplay of maturation, perceptual experience, and articulatory competence in the ontogeny of the general ability to perceive phonetically relevant characteristics of human speech (again, see discussions by Kuhl, 1978; Liberman & Pisoni, 1977). Such research would help in appraising whether certain acoustic contrasts elicit innate or biologically determined perceptual responses, while others gain an effect on perception primarily through receptive and productive language experience. For example, the voiced-voiceless distinction can be cued for adults by contrasts in either VOT or F1 onset frequency (e.g., Lisker, 1975). However, though young children and even very young infants respond to VOT categories much like adults (cf. Jusczyk, 1981; Kuhl, 1978), children do not respond strongly to F1 onset distinctions until they are around 5 years old (Simon & Fourcin, 1978), at which time they may show phonetic trading relations that are smaller in magnitude than the corresponding adult trading relations (Robson, Morrongiello, Best, & Clifton, Note 5). These facts may suggest that the development of trading relations in phonetic perception is dependent on fairly extensive language experience, and would begin to show up only during the preschool-kindergarten years. On the other hand, a recent study of 6-month-olds' perception of the /slIt/-/splIt/ contrast, cued either by the artificial introduction of silence alone or by natural silence plus /p/ bursts and transitions, suggests that even young infants might show some evidence of a phonetic trading relation (Morse, Eilers, & Gavin, Note 6).

REFERENCE NOTES

1. Lisker, L. *Rapid vs. rabid: A catelogue of acoustic features that may cue the distinction* (Status Report on Speech Research, SR-54, 127-132). New Haven, Conn: Haskins Laboratories, 1978.

2. Pisoni, D. B. *On the nature of categorical perception of speech sounds* (Status Report on Speech Research, SR-27, 209-210). New Haven, Conn: Haskins Laboratories, 1971.

3. Bailey, P. J., Summerfield, A. Q., & Dorman, M. F. *On the identification of sinewave analogues of certain nonspeech sounds* (Status Report on Speech Research, SR-51/52, 1-25). New Haven, Conn: Haskins Laboratories, 1977.

4. Repp, B. H. *Two strategies in fricative discrimination.* Manuscript submitted for publication, 1980.

5. Robson, R., Morrongiello, B., Best, C. T., & Clifton, R. K. *Trading relations in the perception of speech by five-year-olds and adults.* Paper presented at the meeting of the Eastern Psychological Association, Hartford, Connecticut, April 1980.

6. Morse, P. A., Eilers, R., & Gavin, W. *Exploring the perception of the "sound of silence" in early infancy.* Paper presented at the second meeting of the International Conference on Infant Studies, New Haven, Connecticut, April 1980.

7. Pastore, R. E. Personal communication, 1980.

8. Remez, R. E. Personal communication, 1979.

9. Repp, B. H. Personal communication, 1979.

10. Summerfield, A. Q. Personal communication, 1979.

REFERENCES

ABRAMSON, A. S., & LISKER, L. Voice onset time in stop consonants: Acoustic analysis and synthesis. In D. E. Commins

(Ed.), *Proceedings of the 5th Congress of International Acoustics.* Liège, Belgium: Thone, 1965.

BAILEY, P. J., & SUMMERFIELD, A. Q. Information in speech: Observations on the perception of [s]-stop clusters. *Journal of Experimental Psychology: Human Perception and Performance,* 1980, **6**, 536-563.

CARDEN, G., LEVITT, A. G., JUSCZYK, P. W., & WALLEY, A. Evidence for phonetic processing of cues to place of articulation: Perceived manner affects perceived place. *Perception & Psychophysics,* 1981, **29**, 26-36.

CERELLA, J. Visual classes and natural categories in the pigeon. *Journal of Experimental Psychology: Human Perception and Performance,* 1979, **5**, 68-77.

CREELMAN, C. D., & MacMILLAN, N. A. Auditory phase and frequency discrimination: A comparison of nine methods. *Journal of Experimental Psychology: Human Perception and Performance,* 1979, **5**, 146-156.

CROWDER, R. G. The sound of vowels and consonants in immediate memory. *Journal of Verbal Learning and Verbal Behavior,* 1971, **10**, 587-596.

CROWDER, R. G. Representation of speech sounds in precategorical acoustic storage. *Journal of Experimental Psychology,* 1973, **1**, 14-24.

CROWDER, R. G., & MORTON, J. Pre-categorical acoustic storage (PAS). *Perception & Psychophysics,* 1969, **5**, 365-373.

CUTTING, J. E., & ROSNER, B. S. Categories and boundaries in speech and music. *Perception & Psychophysics,* 1974, **16**, 564-570.

CUTTING, J. E., & ROSNER, B. S. Discrimination functions predicted from categories in speech and music. *Perception & Psychophysics,* 1976, **20**, 87-88.

CUTTING, J. E., ROSNER, B. S., & FOARD, C. F. Perceptual categories for musiclike sounds: Implications for theories of speech perception. *Quarterly Journal of Experimental Psychology,* 1976, **28**, 361-378.

DARWIN, C. J., & BADDELEY, A. D. Acoustic memory and the perception of speech. *Cognitive Psychology,* 1974, **6**, 41-60.

DELATTRE, P. C., LIBERMAN, A. M., & COOPER, F. S. Acoustic loci and transitional cues for consonants. *Journal of the Acoustical Society of America,* 1955, **27**, 769-773.

DIVENYI, P. L. Some psychoacoustic factors in phonetic analysis. *Proceedings of the 9th International Congress of Phonetic Sciences.* Copenhagen: Stougaard Jensen, 1979.

DIVENYI, P. L., & DANNER, W. F. Discrimination of time intervals marked by brief acoustic pulses of various intensities and spectra. *Perception & Psychophysics,* 1977, **21**, 125-142.

DIVENYI, P. L., & SACHS, R. M. Discrimination of time intervals bounded by tone bursts. *Perception & Psychophysics,* 1978, **24**, 429-436.

DORMAN, M. F. On the identification of sineway analogues of CV syllables. *Proceedings of the 9th International Congress of Phonetic Sciences* (Vol. 2). Copenhagen: Stougaard Jensen, 1979.

DORMAN, M. F., RAPHAEL, L. J., & ISENBERG, D. Acoustic cues for the fricative/affricate contrast in word-final position. *Journal of Phonetics,* 1980, **8**, 397-405.

DORMAN, M. F., RAPHAEL, L. J., & LIBERMAN, A. M. Some experiments on the sound of silence in phonetic perception. *Journal of the Acoustical Society of America,* 1979, **65**, 1518-1532.

DORMAN, M. F., STUDDERT-KENNEDY, M., & RAPHAEL, L. J. Stop consonant recognition: Release bursts and formant transitions as functionally equivalent, context-dependent cues. *Perception & Psychophysics,* 1977, **22**, 109-122.

FANT, C. G. M. Descriptive analysis of the acoustic aspects of speech. *Logos,* 1962, **5**, 3-17.

FITCH, H. L., HALWES, T. G., ERICKSON, D. M., & LIBERMAN, A. M. Perceptual equivalence of two acoustic cues for stop consonant manner. *Perception & Psychophysics,* 1980, **27**, 343-350.

FUJISAKI, H., & KAWASHIMA, T. On the modes and mechanisms of speech perception. *Annual Report of the Audio Engineering Society,* 1969, **28**, 67-73.

GARNER, W. R., & MORTON, J. Perceptual independence: Definitions, models, and experimental paradigms. *Psychological Bulletin,* 1969, **72**, 233-259.

GREEN, D. M. *An introduction to hearing.* New York: Wiley, 1976.

HAGGARD, M. P., AMBLER, S., & CALLOW, M. Pitch as a voicing cue. *Journal of the Acoustical Society of America,* 1970, **47**, 613-617.

HARRIS, K. S., HOFFMAN, H. S., LIBERMAN, A. M., DELATTRE, P. C., & COOPER, F. S. Effect of third-formant transitions on the perception of the voiced stop consonants. *Journal of the Acoustical Society of America,* 1958, **30**, 122-126.

HOFFMAN, H. S. Study of some cues in the perception of the voiced stop consonants. *Journal of the Acoustical Society of America,* 1958, **30**, 1035-1041.

JUSCZYK, P. W. Infant speech perception: A critical appraisal. In P. D. Eimas & J. A. Miller (Eds.), *Perspectives on the study of speech.* Hillsdale, N.J: Erlbaum, 1981.

KAPLAN, H. L., MacMILLAN, N. A., & CREELMAN, C. D. Methods and designs: Tables of d' for variable-standard discrimination paradigms. *Behavior Research Methods & Instrumentation,* 1978, **10**, 796-813.

KUHL, P. K. Predispositions for perception of speech-sound categories: A species-specific phenomenon? In F. D. Minifie & L. L. Lloyd (Eds.), *Communicative and cognitive abilities—Early behavioral assessment.* Baltimore, Md: University Park Press, 1978.

KUHL, P. K., & MILLER, J. D. Speech perception by the chinchilla: Voiced-voiceless distinction in alveolar plosive consonants. *Science,* 1975, **190**, 69-72.

KUHL, P. K., & MILLER, J. D. Speech perception by the chinchilla: Identification functions for synthetic VOT stimuli. *Journal of the Acoustical Society of America,* 1978, **63**, 905-917.

LIBERMAN, A. M., COOPER, F. S., SHANKWEILER, D. P., & STUDDERT-KENNEDY, M. Perception of the speech code. *Psychological Review,* 1967, **74**, 430-460.

LIBERMAN, A. M., HARRIS, K. S., HOFFMAN, H. S., & GRIFFITH, B. C. The discrimination of speech sounds within and across phoneme boundaries. *Journal of Experimental Psychology,* 1961, **61**, 379-388.

LIBERMAN, A. M., & PISONI, D. B. Evidence for a special speech-perceiving subsystem in the human. In T. H. Bullock (Ed.), *Recognition of complex acoustic signals.* Berlin: Dahlem Konferenzen, 1977.

LIBERMAN, A. M., & STUDDERT-KENNEDY, M. Phonetic perception. In H. L. Teuber (Ed.), *Handbook of sensory physiology* (Vol. 8) *Perception.* Berlin: Springer-Verlag, 1978.

LISKER, L. Is it VOT or a first-formant transition detector? *Journal of the Acoustical Society of America,* 1975, **57**, 1547-1551.

LISKER, L., LIBERMAN, A. M., ERICKSON, D. M., DECHOVITZ, D., & MANDLER, R. On pushing the voice-onset-time (VOT) boundary about. *Language and Speech,* 1977, **20**, 209-216.

MacKAIN, K. S., BEST, C. T., & STRANGE, W. Native language effects on liquid perception. *Journal of the Acoustical Society of America,* 1980, 67 (Suppl.), S27. (Abstract K12)

MacMILLAN, N. A., KAPLAN, H. L., & CREELMAN, C. D. The psychophysics of categorical perception. *Psychological Review,* 1977, **84**, 452-471.

MANN, V. A. Influence of preceding liquids on stop-consonant perception. *Journal of the Acoustical Society of America,* 1980, 67 (Suppl.). S99, (Abstract QQ1)

MANN, V. A., & REPP, B. H. Influence of vocalic context on perception of the [ʃ]-[s] distinction. *Perception & Psychophysics,* 1980, **28**, 213-228.

MANN, V. A., & REPP, B. H. Influence of preceding fricative on stop consonant perception. *Journal of the Acoustical Society of America,* 1981, **69**, 548-558.

McGOVERN, K., & STRANGE, W. The perception of /r/ and /l/

in syllable-initial and syllable-final position. *Perception & Psychophysics*, 1977, **21**, 162-170.

MILLER, J. A., & LIBERMAN, A. M. Some effects of later-occurring information on the perception of stop consonant and semivowel. *Perception & Psychophysics*, 1979, **25**, 457-465.

MILLER, J. D., WIER, C. C., PASTORE, R. E., KELLY, W. J., & DOOLING, R. J. Discrimination and labeling of noise-buzz sequences with varying noise-lead times: An example of categorical perception. *Journal of the Acoustical Society of America*, 1976, **60**, 410-417.

MORSE, P. A., & SNOWDON, C. T. An investigation of categorical speech discrimination by rhesus monkeys. *Perception & Psychophysics*, 1975, **17**, 9-16.

PASTORE, R. E., AHROON, W. A., BAFFUTO, K. J., FRIEDMAN, C., PULEO, J. S., & FINK, E. A. Common factor model of categorical perception. *Journal of Experimental Psychology: Human Perception and Performance*, 1977, **4**, 686-696.

PASTORE, R. E., FRIEDMAN, C. J., & BAFFUTO, K. J. A comparative evaluation of the AX and two ABX procedures. *Journal of the Acoustical Society of America*, 1976, **60** (Suppl.), S120. (Abstract)

PISONI, D. B. Auditory short term memory and vowel perception. *Memory & Cognition*, 1975, **3**, 7-18.

PISONI, D. B. Identification and discrimination of the relative onset time of two-component tones: Implications for voicing perception in stops. *Journal of the Acoustical Society of America*, 1977, **61**, 1352-1361.

PISONI, D. B., & LAZARUS, J. H. Categorical and noncategorical modes of speech perception along the voicing continuum. *Journal of the Acoustical Society of America*, 1974, **55**, 328-333.

PISONI, D. B., & TASH, J. Reaction times to comparisons within and across phonetic boundaries. *Perception & Psychophysics*, 1974, **15**, 285-290.

REPP, B. H. Relative amplitude of aspiration noise as a voicing cue for syllable-initial stop consonants. *Language and Speech*, 1979, **22**, 173-189.

REPP, B. H., HEALY, A. F., & CROWDER, R. G. Categories and context in the perception of isolated steady-state vowels. *Journal of the Acoustical Society of America*, 1979, **5**, 129-145.

REPP, B. H., LIBERMAN, A. M., ECCARDT, T., & PESETSKY, D. Perceptual integration of temporal cues for stop, fricative, and affricate manner. *Journal of Experimental Psychology: Human Perception and Performance*, 1978, **4**, 621-637.

REPP, B. H., & MANN, V. A. Perceptual assessment of fricative-stop coarticulation. *Journal of the Acoustical Society of America*, 1980, **67** (Suppl.), S100. (Abstract QQ8)

SCHELLENG, J. C. The bowed string and the player. *Journal of the Acoustical Society of America*, 1973, **53**, 26-41.

SIMON, C., & FOURCIN, A. J. Cross-language study of speech-pattern learning. *Journal of the Acoustical Society of America*, 1978, **63**, 925-935.

STEVENS, K. N. The role of rapid spectrum changes in the production and perception of speech. In L. L. Hammerich & R. Jakobson (Eds.), *Form and substance: Festschrift for Eli Fischer-Jørgensen*. Copenhagen: Akademisk Forlag, 1971.

STEVENS, K. N. The quantal nature of speech: Evidence from articulatory-acoustic data. In L. Pinson & D. Denes (Eds.), *Human communication: A unified view*. Cambridge, Mass: M.I.T. Press, 1974.

STUDDERT-KENNEDY, M. Speech perception. In N. J. Lass (Ed.), *Contemporary issues in experimental phonetics*. New York: Academic Press, 1976.

SUMMERFIELD, A. Q. Perceptual learning and phonetic perception. *Interrelations of the communicative senses. Proceedings of the NSF Conference at Asilomar*. Washington, D.C: NSF Publication, 1978.

SUMMERFIELD, A. Q., & HAGGARD, M. P. On the dissociation of spectral and temporal cues to the voicing distinction in initial stop consonants. *Journal of the Acoustical Society of America*, 1977, **62**, 435-448.

WATERS, R. S., & WILSON, W. A. Speech perception by rhesus monkeys: The voicing distinction in synthesized labial and velar stop consonants. *Perception & Psychophysics*, 1976, **19**, 285-289.

WEYER, R. D. Time-frequency-structures in the attack transients of piano and harpsichord sounds—1. *Acustica*, 1976, **35**, 233-252.

WEYER, R. D. Time-varying amplitude-frequency-structures in the attack transients of piano and harpsichord sounds—II. *Acustica*, 1976-77, **36**, 241-252.

NOTES

1. The use of these words might have introduced a lexical bias (frequency counts for "say" and "stay" are not equal), although the effect of that bias on performance could not have interfered with our test results, since it should have involved both "say"-"stay" continua equally. Moreover, although neither /sɛ/ nor /stɛ/ is a word, and neither is phonologically permissible in American English because of the final lax vowel, our pilot work with that contrast showed a trading relation between silence and F1 onset.

2. The /t/ in "stay" is unaspirated ([t] as opposed to [tʰ]). When an unaspirated /t/ follows an /s/ in American English, as in "stay," it is identified in context as "t" ("stay"). However, if the /s/ is removed from "stay" (leaving a vocalic syllable similar to our synthetic stimuli with low F1 onset frequency), the isolated unaspirated [teɪ] is identified as "day" rather than "tay" because word-initial voiceless stops in spoken American English are nearly always aspirated (i.e., [tʰeɪ]).

3. Pilot testing had indicated that subjects would need an additional 24 msec of silent gap (approximately) to begin hearing "stay" for the d continuum, relative to the D continuum.

4. Although 12-18 judgments per comparison are typically obtained in discrimination tests, we used only six judgments per comparison in order to compare identification and discrimination results gathered within a single moderate-length test session, hoping thereby to minimize changes in response criteria, attention level, etc. In addition, since we were most interested in the subjects' "natural" or "normal" perception of the stimuli, we kept presentations per stimulus at the smallest number likely to yield reliable response functions. These concerns also related to our use of 10, rather than the usual 20, judgments per token in the identification test. This situation thus provides a conservative test of our hypotheses, because the potential for response variability was higher than usual.

5. The Stimulus Pairs simple effect for the "conflicting cues" comparisons did not support a performance peak near the category boundary: instead, it indicated lower discrimination performance for the extreme endpoints from the two continua (s[0]D vs. s[24]d, s[8]D vs. s[32]d, and s[112]D vs. s[136]d) than for all other comparisons.

6. Although the oddity task is commonly assumed to have higher memory demands than other discrimination procedures used in auditory research, and hence to yield the lowest performance level, no direct comparisons of oddity vs. other tasks are known (Pastore, Note 7; Remez, Note 8; Repp, Note 9), with one recent exception. MacKain, Best, and Strange (1980) found slightly higher above-chance performance for an AXB than an oddity task, using a synthetic /rak/-/lak/ continuum. Their finding corroborates the common intuitions about the relative difficulty (memory demands) of the oddity task.

7. We refer here to variable-standard rather than fixed-standard discrimination designs. Although fixed-standard designs yield higher performance than variable-standard designs, according both to theoretical models (SDT analysis: MacMillan et al., 1977) and to empirical work with nonspeech stimuli (Creelman & MacMillan, 1979), those task differences may be very small for discrimination of speech (Repp, Note 4). Furthermore, we were limited to a variable-standard design because the three-way discrimination design dictated that the magnitude of within-pair

differences be fixed and that stimulus comparisons should cover the range of the two continua.

8. Higher d′ values have been obtained through AXB than 4IAX tests for frequency (Creelman & MacMillan, 1979) and intensity discriminations (Pastore, Friedman, & Baffuto, 1976), but 4IAX tasks have obtained higher d′ values than ABX for phase (Creelman & MacMillan, 1979) and speech discriminations (e.g., Pisoni, 1975; Pisoni & Lazarus, 1974; Pisoni, Note 2). These discrepancies may indicate that two 4IAX observer strategies are logically possible, one of which is more sensitive; which strategy listeners will adopt appears to be unpredictable (Creelman & MacMillan, 1979; MacMillan et al., 1977).

9. True d′ values from 2IAX data are equal to or slightly higher than ABX or 4IAX d′ values for frequency discriminations, and may be even more improved for phase discriminations, relative to the latter two paradigms. Compare variable-standard designs in Figure 4 with the interrelation of Figure 1 and Table 2 (Creelman & MacMillan, 1979, pp. 151-152), which show the same pattern of ABX-4IAX performance level differences found in speech discrimination tests (e.g., Pisoni, 1975, Note 2).

10. Thanks are extended to Philip Rubin for his helpful modifications of the sine-wave synthesis program originally written by Rod McGuire at Haskins Laboratories.

11. The two sine-wave syllables lacked the final diphthongization from /e/ to /i/ because the additional frequency modulation seemed to make their speech-like qualities too obvious, and were physically more analogous to /dɛ/ than to /dei/. However, the offset of the three sine waves was such that they sounded like "day" rather than "deh" to most listeners who heard them as speech.

12. It was especially important in Experiment 3 to keep testing time and stimulus repetition low in order to minimize the possibility that nonspeech listeners might spontaneously begin to hear the stimuli as speech after prolonged exposure, and consequently shift their perceptual behavior.

13. As these descriptions of the subgroups suggest, there was great variation in individual perceptions of these stimuli, and attempts to impose perceptual characterizations did not work consistently. Both the individual variation and the inconsistent response to "perceptual instruction" seem to be characteristic of tests with sine-wave speech analogues, inasmuch as they have been noted before (e.g., Bailey et al., Note 3; Summerfield, Note 10).

14. The functions appeared a bit rough because of the small number of subjects, the difficulty that three of the subjects had in keeping "tuned" to "say" and "stay" throughout the test, and especially because of the subject who reported listening for different water drips through most of the three-way oddity test; all of these factors make interpretation of any visual irregularities difficult. For example, there is an apparent bimodality in the "cooperating cues" peak, but the "dip" between the two highest points represents a total drop of only 4-5 correct responses. Furthermore, the "double-peak" pattern was shown by only two subjects, each of whom showed a "dip" of two responses in magnitude. One of these subjects was a "spontaneous" "say"-"stay" listener, and had the noisiest data of this group.

15. The "temporal" group's obtained boundary-related peak (20 msec) was shifted from the predicted peak (36 msec), and their function showed a second unexpected obtained peak (60-68 msec), suggesting that the oddity and AXB tests may have tapped different perceptual processes—they may have been using three categories, rather than two. The shallow slopes of the AXB functions suggest that the two prototype categories (A and B) might not have been the most appropriate for these listeners. The 20-msec peak hints that one perceived contrast may have been "contiguity between hiss and sine wave" vs. "delay between hiss and sine wave," which would be consistent with the general psychoacoustic boundary at 20 msec for detection of temporal differences between components of two-part signals (e.g., Miller et al., 1976; Pastore et al., 1977; Pisoni, 1977). The later peak (60-68 msec) may distinguish "a two-component signal" vs. "two separate signals."

Although the pattern of performance around this second peak (56-88 msec) indicated that in that range the "temporal" listeners must have responded to SW-sw differences, the drop in performance between 72 and 96 msec makes it unlikely that they had merely focused on the spectral contrasts at longer gap durations. It is more likely that they were still attending to temporal information, and that sensitivity to gap changes in that range may have been differentially affected by the SW vs. sw onset spectra (and/or that discrimination as a function of gap duration is nonmonotonic).

APPENDIX A

In both stimuli, there was a 25-msec rise time and a 50-msec fall time; the parameter values for the amplitudes of F2 and F3 throughout the stimuli were 4/5 that of F1. The F0 contour began at 120 Hz and remained at that frequency for 240 msec, after which it fell linearly to 90 Hz during the final 50 msec. F3 began with a linear 40-msec transition from 3,196 to 2,694 Hz (somewhat exaggerated with respect to natural stimuli), and remained at the latter frequency for 130 msec, after which it rose linearly to 3,029 Hz during the ensuing 70 msec. F2 remained at 1,840 Hz for the initial 150 msec, and rose linearly to 2,298 Hz during the following 90 msec. F2 and F3 remained at their last-named frequencies during the final 50 msec. F1 reached 611 Hz at the end of the initial 40-msec transitions, remained at that frequency for 110 msec, then fell linearly to 304 Hz during the final 90 msec.

APPENDIX B

We used the following formula to predict each subject's performance for each of the 44 stimulus comparisons tested (from McGovern & Strange, 1977):

$$Pcorr = [1 + 2(Pa - Pb)2]/3,$$

where Pcorr is predicted probability of correct responses for a given stimulus comparison, Pa is obtained proportion of "stay" responses to stimulus a, and Pb is the observed proportion of "stay" responses to stimulus b in the comparison. Chance level responding was 33%.

APPENDIX C

Predicted Data

To determine whether the obtained pattern derived from the phonetic category judgments, an ANOVA was performed on the predicted data for 3 comparison types by 15 stimulus pairs. Figure 4 shows that the results from this ANOVA were essentially the same as for the obtained data [Stimulus Pairs, $F(14,196) = 10.72$, $p \ll .001$; Comparison Types, $F(2,28) = 29.60$, $p \ll .001$—see Table 1 for Tukey pairwise contrasts]. The Comparison Types by Stimulus Pairs interaction [$F(28,392) = 33.13$, $p \ll .001$] was also highly similar to the obtained results [simple effects tests: "cooperating cues," $F(14,588) = 17.76$, $p \ll .001$; "one cue," $F(14,588) = 4.36$, $p < .001$; "conflicting cues," $F(14,588) = .22$, n.s.].

Obtained vs. Predicted Differences

Although the obtained and predicted data showed similar *patterns*, Figure 4 suggests that obtained discrimination was slightly better than predicted, particularly beyond the immediate neighborhood of the performance "peaks" that had been expected for clear between-category comparisons. This observation was supported by ANOVAs for each of the three comparison types, which crossed the 2 functions (obtained vs. predicted) with 15 stimulus pairs (12-128-msec range). The three significant functions effects showed that obtained performance was better than predicted for "cooperating cues" [$F(1,14) = 8.82$, $p < .025$], "one cue" $F(1,14)$ $= 12.22$, $p < .005$], and "conflicting cues" comparisons [$F(1,14) = 19.39$, $p < .001$]. Significant Functions by Stimulus Pairs interactions for "one cue" [$F(17,238) = 2.54$, $p < .001$] and "cooperating cues" comparisons [$F(17,238) = 4.56$, $p \ll .001$] revealed that obtained performance was higher than predicted *only* for comparisons distant from the between-category performance peak by 16-24 msec or more; performance on between-category comparisons was fully determined by the identification functions. These interactions also indicated that the obtained peaks were shifted toward the D boundary (highest performance levels in the "cooperating cues" and "one cue" comparisons at approximately 36-40 msec), relative to the predicted peak positions, which were at the average of the crossover boundary values for the two continua (highest performance levels at approximately 44-48 msec).

Because differences between obtained and predicted performance were not found for between-category comparisons, the pattern of *within*-category differences was examined. For this purpose, within-category refers to all comparisons whose predicted level was 39% or less ($\leqslant 6\%$ above chance), since in each of those comparisons the stimuli being compared never differed by more than 10% in their category assignments in the identification test. This "within-category" range included "conflicting cues" comparisons with mean gap durations of between 12 and 44 msec and between 60 and 128 msec, "one cue" comparisons with gaps of between 0 and 16 msec and between 56 and 136 msec, and "cooperating cues" comparisons with mean gap durations of between 76 and 128 msec. The pattern of mean above-chance discrimination for these within-category comparisons was "cooperating cues" (mean correct = 49.2%) > "one cue" (48.2%) > "conflicting cues" (47.0%). If we consider only the within-category obtained performance that was unaccounted for by phonetic category identifications (residual performance = obtained mean minus predicted mean), the pattern remains: "cooperating cues" (residual performance = 14.0%) > "one cue" (13.0%) > "conflicting cues" (11.7%).

Individual Patterns

Consistency of the "phonetic" perceptual equivalence pattern in individuals was also examined, for stimulus comparisons with average gap durations near the two identification boundaries (between 20 and 48 msec), henceforth termed the "peak range." This analysis was based on the mean percent correct obtained responses for "one cue" comparisons between s[24]D-s[24]d and s[48]D-s[48]d, "cooperating cues" comparisons between s[32]D-s[8]d and s[56]D-s[32]d, and "conflicting cues" comparisons between s[32]d-s[8]D and s[56]d-s[32]D. Ten of the 15 subjects showed the order "cooperating cues" > "one cue" > "conflicting cues," a proportion (67%) significantly better than chance by binomial test ($p < .002$). For the

other five subjects, "one cue" performance was equal to or lower than "conflicting cues" performance. However, the key criterion for "phonetic" perceptual equivalence is that "peak-range" performance be better for "cooperating cues" than for "conflicting cues," since both involve contrast on two acoustic dimensions. This latter criterion was met by all 15 subjects, a proportion that is far beyond chance expectation by binomial test, $p \ll .001$. Two one-way ANOVAs performed on these obtained and predicted "peak-range" means, for the two comparison types, supported the "phonetic" predictions even more strongly than did the overall group ANOVAs. For the obtained "peak-range" data, the comparison types effect was significant [$F(2,28) = 36.59$, $p \ll .001$], as it was for the predicted "peak-range" data [$F(2,28) = 81.51$, $p < .001$] (see Table 1 for Tukey pairwise contrasts).

APPENDIX D

To determine true d' values for obtained and predicted data in the 2IAX test, it was necessary to calculate P[H] (probability of a hit) and P[FA] (probability of a false alarm). These were derived by the following formulas:

$$P[H] = P(``S''/S)$$

for the obtained hit rate, where P is probability or proportion, "S" is "same" responses, and /S is "given a physically identical AX pair";

$$P[H] = P(``stay''/A)^2 + P(``stay''/X)^2$$

for the predicted hit rate, where P("stay"/A) is proportion of "stay" responses to stimulus A in the identification test, and likewise for stimulus X in P("stay"/X);

$$P[FA] = P(``D''/S)$$

for the obtained false alarm rate, where "D" is "different" responses; and

$$P[FA] = P(``stay''/A) \cdot P(``say''/A) + P(``stay''/X)$$
$$P(``say''/X)$$

for predicted false alarm rate. These values of P[H] and P[FA] were used to look up true d' values in the table provided by Kaplan et al. (1978). Because this table (and the computational formula used to derive the tabled values) does not allow for P[H] and P[FA] of either 0.00 or 1.00, we substituted 0.01 and 0.99, respectively, for occurrences of those values in our data. Thus, the true d' values were artificially constrained (although to a small extent) at the high and low extremes ($d'max = 6.93$; $d'min = 0.00$).

APPENDIX E

Predicted data

An ANOVA was also performed on the predicted data, for the 3 comparison types by 10 stimulus pairs (12-88-msec mean gaps). The results are listed in Table 2, with the Tukey pairwise contrasts presented in Table 1. As Figure 6 indicates, the pattern of predicted results was quite similar in form to the pattern of obtained results.

RESIDUAL SENSITIVITY

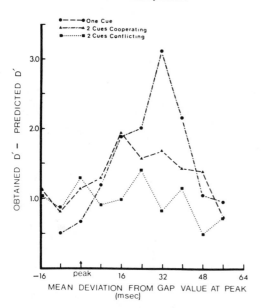

Figure E1. Residual sensitivity (obtained d′ minus predicted d′) found in the three-way 2IAX test, Experiment 2.

Obtained vs. Predicted Differences

In order to compare obtained and predicted true d′ values, ANOVAs were conducted for each of the three comparison types, for the 2 functions (obtained vs. predicted) by 10 stimulus pairs (12-88-msec mean gaps). The pattern of differences between obtained and predicted functions was virtually the same as in Experiment 1 (see Table 2, "Cooperating cues," "One cue," and "Conflicting cues"), demonstrating a higher sensitivity for obtained than for predicted data, particularly for comparisons beyond the immediate range of the between-category performance peaks. Mean residual sensitivities were calculated (obtained true d′ minus predicted true d′) for the three comparison types, across all comparisons in which the pair members had deviated from one another by less than 10% in proportion of "stay" identifications (roughly "within-category" pairs, as defined in Experiment 1); included were "conflicting cues" comparisons with mean gap durations (per pair) of 12 msec and between 44 and 84 msec, "one cue" comparisons with gaps of 8 msec and between 48 and 88 msec, and "cooperating cues" comparisons with mean gaps of between 60 and 84 msec. These obtained-predicted difference values followed the order "cooperating cues" (mean residual sensitivity = 1.49) ≥ "one cue" (1.46) > "conflicting cues" (1.37). However, because of the shift in positions of the obtained peaks relative to the predicted peaks, we recalculated residual sensitivity values (obtained-predicted differences) according to deviations in gap duration from the value at the peak. The order of these residual sensitivities (Figure E1) was "cooperating cues" (1.58) > "one cue" (1.38) > "conflicting cues" (.98).

Individual Patterns

The individual patterns of mean "peak-range" sensitivities were virtually identical to those found in Experiment 1. Nine of the 14 subjects (p < .001 by binomial test) showed the expected order: "cooperating cues" > "one cue" > "conflicting cues." However, the key criterion ("cooperating cues" > "conflicting cues") was met by all 14 subjects (p < .0002). As in Experiment 1, the ANOVAs performed on the "peak-range" data (20-48-msec mean gaps—cf. Appendix C, Experiment 1) for both the obtained and the predicted true d′ values upheld the individual analyses (see Table 2).

APPENDIX F

Individual Analysis: "Say"-"Stay" Listeners

Four of the five listeners in this group met the crucial criterion for "phonetic" perceptual equivalence ("cooperating cues" > "conflicting cues"; p < .04 by binomial test). The subject who failed had listened for "different water drips" during most of the discrimination test; her data show much the same pattern as the "spectral" group (described below). All four listeners who had more consistently perceived "say" and "stay" met the criterion (p < .01).

Obtained-Predicted Differences

Group comparisons. All three groups of listeners showed better obtained than predicted discrimination (compare lower left panels and the corresponding lower right panels, Figures 9-11). However, the pattern of obtained-predicted differences varied among the groups. To directly compare the group patterns, mean percentages of performance unexplained by AXB categorizations (residual performance = obtained mean minus predicted mean) were calculated for the entire range, within each comparison type.

"Temporal" listeners. The residual performance levels for the "temporal" group were small, and followed a different pattern from that observed in the two previous "say"-"stay" experiments: "conflicting cues" (mean residual performance = 8.4%) > "cooperating cues" (7.0%) > "one cue" (6.3%).

"Spectral" listeners. Residual performance for this group was very high, unaffected by between-category vs. within-category considerations, and showed the order: "conflicting cues" (mean residual performance = 43.9%) > "one cue" (35.2%) > "cooperating cues" (22.3%). This residual performance pattern was constrained by near-ceiling obtained performance for all three comparison types (artificially reducing the residual performance level, especially for "cooperating cues").

"Say"-"Stay" listeners. The residual performance pattern for the sine-wave "say"-"stay" group was like the patterns found in the two previous "say"-"stay" experiments: "cooperating cues" (mean residual performance = 19.5%) ≥ "one cue" (19.4%) > "conflicting cues" (14.6%). Also, the positions of the obtained peaks were slightly shifted toward the SW category boundary, relative to the positions of the predicted peaks, just as the obtained peaks in the first two experiments had shifted toward the D boundary.

(Received for publication October 15, 1980; accepted November 4, 1980.)

Journal of Experimental Psychology:
Human Perception and Performance
1980, Vol. 6, No. 1, 110–125

Phonetic Categorization in Auditory Word Perception

William F. Ganong III
Brown University

To investigate the interaction in speech perception of auditory information and lexical knowledge (in particular, knowledge of which phonetic sequences are words), acoustic continua varying in voice onset time were constructed so that for each acoustic continuum, one of the two possible phonetic categorizations made a word and the other did not. For example, one continuum ranged between the word *dash* and the nonword *tash*; another used the nonword *dask* and the word *task*. In two experiments, subjects showed a significant lexical effect—that is, a tendency to make phonetic categorizations that make words. This lexical effect was greater at the phoneme boundary (where auditory information is ambiguous) than at the ends of the continua. Hence the lexical effect must arise at a stage of processing sensitive to both lexical knowledge and auditory information.

Linguistic context has long been known to aid and bias the identification of speech. For example, the identification of sequences of words in noise is substantially aided if the words form sentences (Miller, Heise, & Lichten, 1951). The phoneme restoration effect (Warren, 1970) shows that context can control the perception of individual segments: When a single phone of an utterance is replaced by a noise burst or a cough, a listener is not aware which phone was replaced. Both previous and subsequent context influence this effect (Warren & Sherman, 1974). Perception is influenced not only by immediate linguistic context (e.g., the role a word plays in a sentence) but also by the frequency of a word's use in the language. For example, there is a large word-frequency effect in the identification of words presented in noise (Broadbent, 1967).

This article examines the influence on phonetic categorization of a rather simple linguistic variable: the lexical status of a phonetic sequence (i.e., whether the phonetic sequence is a word). Lexical status is already known to influence phonetic processing. Reaction time for phoneme detection is faster if the target appears in a word than if it appears in a nonword (Rubin, Turvey, & Van Gelder, 1976). Presumably this word advantage reflects a perceptual bias in favor of words similar to the perceptual bias that favors high-frequency words over low-frequency words in noise. The purpose of this article is to determine the stage in the perceptual process at which the biasing effect of lexical status appears. Does it follow phonetic categorization, or, alternatively, can it influence the interpre-

This work was supported by Grant HD 05331 from the National Institute of Child Health and Human Development to Peter D. Eimas, by National Science Foundation (NSF) Grant BMS 75 08439 to Richard B. Millward, by National Institutes of Health Grant NO1 HD 12420 to Haskins Laboratories, and by an NSF postdoctoral fellowship to the author (SMI 77-12336).

Alvin Liberman made the facilities of Haskins Laboratories available to me. Terry Halwes's and Patricia Keating's aid in generating the stimuli was essential, and discussion with them, Susan Carey, and Peter D. Eimas helped to clarify the issues discussed here. Several reviewers, including Neal Macmillan, Bruno Repp, and Michael Posner, made comments that improved the presentation of this material. I thank them all. This work was reported at the 95th meeting of the Acoustical Society of America at Providence, Rhode Island, May 1978.

Requests for reprints should be sent to William F. Ganong III, who is now at the Department of Psychology, University of Pennsylvania, 3815 Walnut Street, Philadelphia, Pennsylvania 19104.

tation of acoustic cues, which underlies phonetic categorization?

Asking this question presupposes that there is a stage of processing in normal speech perception that carries out phonetic categorization. This is a substantive assumption—it is possible, for example, to construct models for word perception that do not include a stage of phonetic categorization (Klatt, 1979). But the assumption must certainly be correct for experiments in which subjects are required to make phonetic categorizations. Evidence for this assumption in other experimental contexts derives primarily from work on categorical perception. The first psychologists to investigate the perception of synthetically constructed stop consonants discovered that listeners were able to discriminate with ease only those stimuli that they perceived as belonging to different phonetic categories (Liberman, Harris, Hoffman, & Griffith, 1957). Discrimination of stimuli from the same phonetic category was only slightly above chance. This phenomenon was named categorical perception because subjects acted as if the only information available was the phonetic category of each stimulus.

The concept of categorical perception has since undergone modification. It is now clear that subjects can use some auditory information as well as information about phonetic categories in discrimination (Carney, Widin, & Viemeister, 1977; Fujisaki & Kawashima, 1970), but under many conditions, the perception of speech, especially the stop consonants, is very nearly categorical. Is this auditory information of any use in the normal course of speech perception (the purpose of which is clearly the identification of words and sentences, not their discrimination)? Liberman, Mattingly, and Turvey (1972) proposed, instead, that the role of phonetic categorization is the substitution of a phonetic label for the auditory information representing a stop consonant in order to facilitate higher level linguistic processing.[1]

The phonetic categorization of an acoustic continuum between different stop consonants is typically characterized by two unambiguous regions (which are consis-

tently given one or another phonetic categorization) separated by a narrow boundary region containing phonetically ambiguous stimuli. An acoustic variable frequently used to construct such acoustic continua is voice onset time (VOT). VOT is an acoustic cue for voicing in syllable-initial stops in many languages (Lisker & Abramson, 1964). Perception of such a continuum is often described by a single number, the locus of the phoneme boundary, which is the (interpolated) point on the acoustic continuum that would receive each phonetic categorization on half of the trials. For an English-speaking subject, the phoneme boundary between d and t responses for a [da–ta] continuum is at about 35-msec VOT. Stimuli with VOT of less than 30 msec are consistently labelled d, and stimuli with VOT greater than 40 msec are consistently labeled t.

A model in which lexical status affects phonetic processing only after phonetic categorization has occurred can be called a *categorical* model. In an *interactive* model, lexical status would be allowed to direct and bias the processing of the auditory information specifying phonetic categories. One example of such a model is the *criterion-shift* model, in which lexical status would

---

[1] The situation is clearly different for noncategorical phonetic distinctions. Many phonetic distinctions (such as differences between vowels) are conveyed by large acoustic differences that can be easily discriminated regardless of phonetic category. Context can bias the interpretation of these differences in words. In an experiment on the perception of disyllabic words in noise, Pollack (1959) showed that some additional auditory information beyond a simple phonetic transcription is available to subjects for a few seconds after a word is presented. He had subjects identify words from a response set given at various delays after the stimulus. For delays under 5 sec, performance depended on the delay between presentation of the stimulus and the response set and was better than performance based on subjects' immediate identification of the stimulus presented. Thus, some form of auditory memory must have been involved. However, Pollack's stimuli differed in both consonants and vowels. The auditory memory used may have been primarily memory for vowels. The present experiment extends Pollack's results to the class of speech sounds that are least likely to allow such auditory memory: the stop consonants.

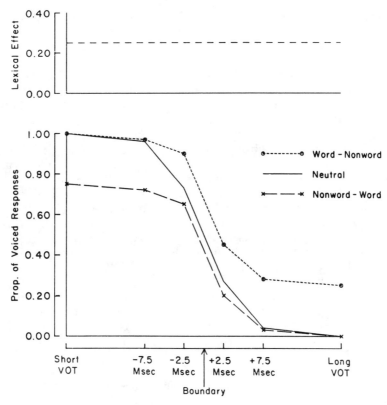

Figure 1. The lexical effect, as predicted by the categorical model. (The lower portion of the graph shows the proportion of stimuli given a voiced phonetic categorization as a function of voice onset time (VOT) for three different types of continua. The solid line shows idealized data from a neutral continuum, whose perception is not biased by lexical effects. The line with short dashes shows the the categorical model's prediction of a lexical effect on a continuum whose voiced end is a word and whose voiceless end is a nonword. Similarly, the line with long dashes shows the result of a post-categorical tendency to make phonetic categorizations voiceless, on a continuum in which voiceless responses make words. The top part of the figure shows, as a function of VOT, a measure of the lexical effect.)

change the criterion by which the auditory information is judged. The categorical model can be tested by determining whether the effect of lexical status is concentrated at the phoneme boundary.

In the categorical model, a bias toward phonetic categorizations that make words would operate as a correction process. Candidate phonetic categorizations that did not happen to make words would be changed to phonetic categorizations that did make words. Thus, subjects presented with speech stimuli for phonetic classification as beginning with [d] or [t] might, upon hearing the nonword *tash*, correct the [t] categorization to [d] so as to make the word *dash*. Since a strict categorical model

assumes no acoustic information is available when lexical status has its effect (i.e., after phonetic categorization), for a particular acoustic continuum between words and nonwords, the probability of a categorization being corrected depends only on the categorization and not on the acoustic information that specified it. A formal description of this model is given in Appendix A.

In the present experiment, the phonetic categorization of a lexically biased continuum is not compared with the categorization of an unbiased continuum, but with a continuum biased in the opposite direction. Figure 1 shows the result of such biases, according to the categorical model

The figure shows a hypothetical phonetic categorization function (the solid line) based on a cumulative normal function, assuming a difference of 5-msec VOT corresponds to a z score difference of 1.2. The categorical model's predictions for the shape of the identification functions, assuming a probability of correcting a nonword response of .25, is also shown. In the top panel of Figure 1 is the resulting lexical-effect function, which is simply the difference between the two identification functions. The shape of this lexical-effect function, as predicted by the categorical model, is derived in Appendix A. In Figure 1 it is assumed that the two lexical biases are equal, so the lexical-effect function does not depend on VOT. If the biases are not equal, the resulting lexical-effect function will be a monotonic function of VOT, and its value at the phoneme boundary will be the average of the values at the ends of the continuum.

In a criterion-shift model, on the other hand, a bias toward hearing words could affect the interpretation of acoustic information at a stage of processing before phonetic categorization. The criterion for making a phonetic categorization would depend on lexical status. This change in criterion would produce a shift in the location of the phoneme boundary. For example, a subject whose phoneme boundary for a [da-ta] continuum was at 35-msec VOT might require 40-msec VOT to hear a [t] in the environment _ash (because dash is a word and tash is not). Such a shift in the location of the phoneme boundary would not produce a uniform effect throughout the continuum but would produce an effect concentrated near the phoneme boundary, just as a change in threshold affects the probability of detection of near-threshold stimuli far more than subthreshold or suprathreshold stimuli. The categorization of stimuli far from the phoneme boundary would not be influenced much because the shift in criterion would not affect the interpretation of unambiguous acoustic evidence. However, for the acoustically ambiguous stimuli near the boundary, a change in criterion would produce large effects on categoriza-

tion. Such a change could shift a stimulus from the ambiguous region to the word region or from the part of the nonword phonetic category near the boundary into the ambiguous region. This model is also described quantitatively in Appendix A.

Figure 2 shows the predictions of the criterion-shift model. This figure assumes equal but opposite direction lexical biases for the two continua, as did Figure 1. Assuming that the phonetic categorization function is sigmoid, with the steepest slope near the phoneme boundary, the lexical-effect function will generally reach a maximum in the neighborhood of the phoneme boundary and thus be greater near the phoneme boundary than at either end of the continuum. This is unlike the shape of the lexical-effect function according to the categorical model, for which the value at the boundary must be between the values at the ends of the continua. Thus, to test the categorical model, it is only necessary to determine whether the effect of lexical bias is spread equally throughout the continuum (as the categorical model predicts) or concentrated at the phoneme boundary (as the criterion-shift model predicts.)

The most direct way to determine whether lexical effects are stronger near the phoneme boundary would be to compare phonetic categorizations of lexically biased acoustic continua with the phonetic categorizations of neutral continua, which are not biased by lexical factors. Alexander (Note 1) has done this with limited success.[2] The present study, instead, compared categorizations of matched pairs of continua chosen so that lexical biases on the two continua operate in opposite directions. Pairs of VOT continua between monosyllabic words and nonwords were synthesized so that the voiced end of one continuum of each pair was a word and the voiceless end

---

[2] The problem with this approach is that biases in the perception of the neutral continuum against which the lexically biased series are judged can confuse and hide lexical effects. This seems to have happened in Alexander's (Note 1) study. It showed an overall bias toward phonetic categorizations that make words, but this bias was not reliable across continua.

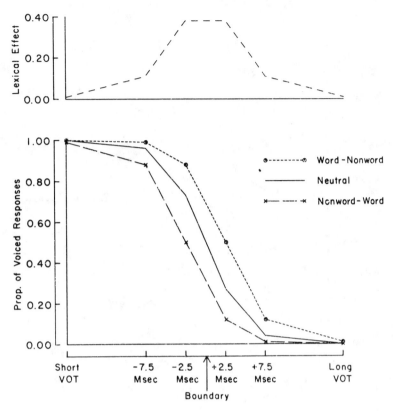

Figure 2. The lexical effect, as predicted by the criterion-shift model. (This figure is analogous to Figure 1, except that it shows predictions of the criterion-shift model.)

was not, and vice versa for the other continuum. For example, one continuum ranged from the word *dash* to the nonword *tash*, and its matched pair ranged from *dask* (nonword) to *task* (word). Thus, it is only possible to measure the lexical effect for the two continua combined. The continua of each pair were carefully matched to have the same vowel and to be as similar as possible in postvocalic consonants.

Experiment 1

Method

Stimuli. Seven pairs of continua were synthesized using the Haskins Laboratories speech synthesis by rule program, FOVE (Ingemann, Note 2). Four alveolar continuum pairs were synthesized. One pair was based on the words *dash* and *task* (that is, one continuum ranged between the word *dash* and the nonword *tash*; the other ranged between the nonword *dask* and the word *task*). Other continuum pairs were based on *dust* and *tuft*, *dirt* and *turf*, and *dose*

and *toast*. Three velar continua, based on *gift* and *kiss*, *geese* and *keep*, and *gush* and *cusp* were also synthesized. Each continuum had seven members, with VOTs of 15, 25, 30, 35, 40, 45, and 55 msec. The stimuli were recorded on audiotape in the format that subjects later heard. The alveolar and velar stimuli were presented in different blocks. Thus, there was a block containing a randomization of all the alveolar stimuli (presented with a 3-sec interstimulus interval), which was followed by a block containing all the velar stimuli. This pattern was repeated six times. Another tape was constructed that contained all the endpoint stimuli, with a 5-sec interstimulus interval.

Procedure. Seventeen subjects[3] (paid volunteers from the psychology department's subject pool) participated in the experiment. First, they were presented with a block of trials containing each stimulus from the alveolar continua. The subjects were instructed to write, for each stimulus, their first impression as to whether the syllable began with d or t. This was followed by a block of velar trials. Six

---

[3] An 18th subject, who refused to categorize any of the velar stimuli as g or k, was immediately dropped.

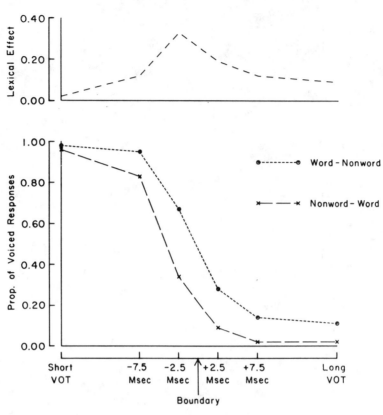

Figure 3. Results of Experiment 1. (Phonetic categorizations pooled as described in the text.)

blocks of alveolar and six blocks of velar trials were presented to each subject. The subjects were not told which words and nonwords would be presented.

Unfortunately, FOVE does not always produce perfectly intelligible speech. To be able to show an advantage for phonetic categorizations that make words, a subject must hear the words as words. Hence, in a second condition, (which always followed the first) the endpoints of the continua were presented and subjects spelled out the words and nonwords they heard. The subjects were instructed to spell words correctly and to make a rough guess for the spelling of nonwords. The data from the second condition were used to determine which continua each subject heard correctly. For each subject, the phonetic categorization data were analyzed for only those continuum pairs for which the lexical status (e.g., word or noword) of three of the four endpoint stimuli was correctly identified.

Results

Application of the criterion to subject's spelling of the words and nonwords resulted in elimination of from 0 to 3 of the 7 continuum pairs for each subject, for a total

of 22 of the 119 continuum pairs (18%). Different continuum pairs passed the criteria to quite different degrees. The most successful pair, dash–task, was spelled acceptably by all of the 17 subjects, whereas the geese–keep pair was spelled correctly by only 6 of the subjects.

The results of phonetic categorization, pooled across subjects and continua, are shown in Figure 3. Phoneme boundaries differed across subjects and across continua. Thus, each subject's data from a given continuum pair was pooled, and the phoneme boundary for that subject on that continuum pair was determined. The position of each phoneme boundary was estimated by finding the VOT that received the proportion of voiced responses closest to one half. Henceforth, the data are considered relative to the position of these phoneme boundaries. The line with short dashes in the figure shows the proportion of voiced responses to continua whose voiced end is a word, and the line with long dashes shows responses to continua whose voiceless end is a word. The leftmost and rightmost points of each line show responses to the endpoints of the continua: stimuli with VOTs of 15 and 55 msec. The four middle points of each line show responses to stimuli with various differences in VOT from the phoneme boundary. For example, the third point from the left in each line was determined by pooling data from the first stimulus to the left of each subject's phoneme boundary for each continuum pair. There was a small but consistent lexical effect in all seven continuum pairs ($p < .01$, sign test). This effect was also consistent across subjects (pooling data across different continua); 16 of the 17 subjects showed a lexical effect ($p < .001$, sign test).

In Figure 3, the lexical effect seems to be stronger at the voiceless end of the continua than at the voiced end. This pattern was reliable across subjects (11 subjects had stronger effects at the voiceless end, 2 at the voiced end, and 4 had equal-size effects; $p < .05$, sign test) but not across continua (five continua showed the effect, one did not, and one showed equal-size effects). Most of the effect was caused by the gift–kiss continuum pair. Most subjects categorized almost all of the stimuli from the gift–kift continuum as beginning with g.

The data were next examined to determine whether the lexical effect was spread throughout the continuum, as predicted by the categorical model, or concentrated at the phoneme boundary, as predicted by the interactive model. For each subject, the size of the lexical effect exhibited at the phoneme boundary was compared with the sum of the two lexical effects measured at the ends of the continuum. Sixteen of the subjects showed more lexical effect at the phoneme boundary than at either endpoint, and 1 showed the opposite tendency ($p < .005$, sign test). Five of the seven continuum pairs showed more of an effect at the boundaries than at the endpoints. One showed equal-size effects (the dose–toast pair), and one (the problematical geese–keep pair) showed the opposite ef-

fect. Only 6 of the subjects passed the (quite weak) screening criteria for this continuum, and none of them heard all four of the endpoint stimuli from these continua correctly. The concentration of the lexical effect at the phoneme boundary is, then, not significant across continua ($p > .1$). However, this failure to obtain significance is probably due to the small number of different continuum pairs tested and to the poor quality of the geese–keep pair.

Experiment 2

Experiment 2 was designed to provide a replication of Experiment 1, with more continuum pairs, to determine whether the lexical effect arises the first time a subject hears stimuli from a particular continuum,[4] and to determine whether the effect is robust enough to appear even if subjects know the stimulus set.

Method

Stimuli. The stimuli for Experiment 2 were produced by digitally cross splicing tokens of natural speech. Any stimulus with a positive VOT contains two acoustic segments: a voiceless, noisy segment (consisting of a burst and aspiration) and a voiced segment which begins, by definition, at the voice onset time. In VOT continua produced with a speech synthesizer (as used in most previous experiments on the perception of VOT), the voiceless segment is produced by passing aspiration noise through the formant filters. At the onset of voicing, glottal pulsing replaces aspiration noise as the source for the formant filters, and a voiced segment results. For the stimuli for Experiment 2, these two segments were excised from natural speech rather than produced synthetically (Lisker, 1976; Spencer & Halwes, Note 3). Thus the stimuli were considerably more intelligible than those of Experiment 1.

For each continuum pair, two voiced stimuli with exactly the same acoustic waveform for the first 100 msec were constructed by digital splicing. Two voiceless endpoints were similarly constructed. These tokens were used to supply the voiced and aspirated segments to construct the stimuli with different VOTs.

---

[4] This condition was included to assure that the lexical effect is truly perceptual, that is, that it arises before subjects have learned the set of continua used in the experiment. Otherwise, the lexical effect might be due to processes peculiar to a situation in which a closed set of words and nonwords is presented repeatedly.

For each continuum, six stimuli were produced by cross splicing. One had the shortest VOT possible using the particular natural tokens on which the stimuli were based. The next four stimuli for each continuum were chosen to span the phoneme boundary (as measured in a pilot experiment) in approximately 5-msec steps. The sixth stimulus had the longest VOT possible given the tokens used. The VOTs of the first, second, and sixth stimulus of each continuum are given in Table 1. The VOTs of the third, fourth, and fifth stimuli were approximately 5, 10, or 15 msec more than the VOT of the second stimulus. The details of the construction and selection of these stimuli is given in Appendix B.

Eighteen new subjects (again, paid volunteers from the psychology department's subject pool) participated in Experiment 2. The experiment was conducted using a PDP-8 minicomputer, which generated the stimuli on-line by digital splicing, presented the stimuli to subjects (at a 10-kHz sampling rate) and collected responses. Subjects were run in groups of 3 or fewer. They heard stimuli presented over headphones and typed their responses. Each subject was assigned to one of six groups, each group containing 3 subjects. All subjects in each group heard the stimuli in the same order.

Each subject participated in one session consisting of seven blocks of trials. In the first block of trials, subjects were presented with a randomization of all 48 labial stimuli and pushed the b or p keys to indicate their first impression of the first segment of each stimulus. The order in which stimuli were presented was constrained so that for each stimulus of each continuum, one of the six groups of subjects heard that stimulus before they heard the other stimuli from the same continuum. The second and third blocks presented the alveolar and velar stimuli in an analogous fashion for phonetic categorization.

The fourth block was a whole-syllable identification condition. Subjects were presented with endpoint stimuli from all of the continua in a random order and responded by indicating whether the stimulus was a word or nonword (by pushing the w or n keys) and spelling out the stimulus.

In the fifth through seventh blocks, subjects again phonetically categorized the labial, alveolar, and velar stimuli. However, this time the stimuli were presented in groups of trials containing only stimuli from a particular continuum pair, and the first four stimuli of each such group of trials were the four endpoints of the two continua. Within each block, the different groups of trials were not explicitly separated, but the way in which the stimuli were grouped was explained to the subjects. Throughout the experiment, each stimulus was presented 3 sec after the last subject finished responding to the previous stimulus.

Results

The same criteria used in Experiment 1 were applied to subjects' identification of the lexical status of the endpoints (col-

Table 1
Stimuli for Experiment 2

Word		Voice onset times		
		Stimulus		
Voiced	Voiceless	1	2	6
Labials				
bash	past	10.0	19.0	61.7
boat	pope	8.6	18.0	42.8
babe	page	7.2	16.2	59.4
beef	peace	8.0	16.7	56.1
Alveolars				
dark	tarp	18.6	36.6	84.4
deep	teach	22.1	36.0	89.0
depth	text	19.3	46.9	82.6
dirt	turf	19.5	52.2	86.0
Velars				
garb	cars	18.2	40.6	64.3
gorge	corpse	35.4	53.2	86.1
gulp	cult	35.6	39.4	69.8
gout	couch	14.9	37.9	66.7
gift	kiss	23.1	40.6	85.1
geese	keep	21.9	39.0	88.8

Note. Stimuli 1 and 6 had the shortest and longest voice onset times (VOTs) possible, given the particular tokens used. Stimuli 2, 3, 4, and 5 were chosen to span the phoneme boundary in 5-msec steps. Thus the voice onset times (VOTs) of stimuli 3, 4, and 5 can be obtained by adding 5, 10, or 15 msec to the VOT for Stimulus 2.

lected in the fourth block). The stimuli for Experiment 2 were more successful than those of Experiment 1—only 24 of the 252 continuum pairs were eliminated (10%). Figure 4 shows the phonetic categorization data, pooled in the same way as the data of Figure 3 (i.e., with respect to phoneme boundary locations for each continuum pair), for the first three blocks of trials, in which the stimuli were presented in random order for phonetic categorization. Again, there is a lexical effect that is significant across subjects (17 of 18, $p < .001$, sign test) and across continua (14 of 14, $p < .001$). This time the effect is significantly stronger at the boundary than at the end of each continuum, showing a larger effect both for subjects (15 of the 18 subjects show the effect, $p < .005$) and for continua (14 of 14, $p < .001$). Thus, in Experiment

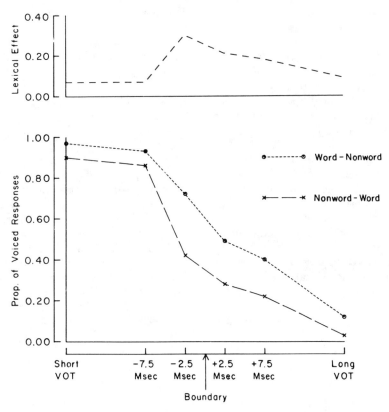

Figure 4. Results of Experiment 2. (Phonetic categorizations of each subject during the first three blocks of the experiment, when stimuli from different continua were presented together in random order.)

2 as in Experiment 1, there is a lexical effect concentrated at the phoneme boundary.

The data were next examined to see if the lexical effect was present the first time that subjects heard a stimulus from a particular continuum. Figure 5 shows the resulting data, pooled with respect to phoneme boundary location tor the first three blocks of trials. Again, there is a significant lexical effect across continua (nine continua show the lexical effect, one shows the opposite effect, and four show no effect, $p <$ .05, by a sign test), and, again, it appears stronger at the phoneme boundary than at the ends of the continua.

Finally, data gathered in the last three blocks of trials were examined. Responses pooled in the usual way are shown in Figure 6. Again, there is a significant lexical effect that is stronger at the boundary than at the endpoints. This effect is not apparently

different from the effects during the first blocks.

The failure of blocking to reduce or eliminate the word advantage was surprising, since most previous studies of the word advantage in vision or word frequency effects in auditory word perception have found that the effects are eliminated when the message set is known. However, the word advantage in visual perception can be maintained in the face of perfect knowledge of the stimulus set (Smith & Haviland, 1972) if the visual angle of the words is small enough (Purcell, Stanovich, & Spector, 1978).

In Figure 4 (as in Figure 3), there seems to be a slightly larger lexical effect for the voiceless stimuli than for the voiced stimuli. On closer examination, however, this tendency is not reliable across subjects (of the 14 subjects showing different amounts of lexical bias at the ends of the continua, 7 showed more effect at the voiced end) nor continua (five of the nine unequally affected continuum pairs showed stronger effects at the voiced end). The tendency for the lexical effect to be greater at the voiceless end of the continuum in Experiment 1 thus seems to have been a product of the particular words or speech-synthesis strategy used there.

The data were also examined to determine whether the size of the lexical effect is correlated with the frequency of occurrence of the words defining the continua. The sum of the logarithm of the frequency of occurrence (as measured using the Kucera & Francis, 1967, norms) of the words defining each continuum pair was correlated with the size of the lexical effect measured at the phoneme boundary for each pair. The correlation coefficient (−.04) was not reliably different from zero. Thus, no word-frequency effect is apparent in these data. However, the experiment was not designed to test for word-frequency effects, so little importance should be attached to this result.

Discussion

It is clear from the results of Experiments 1 and 2 that lexical status affects phonetic categorizations much more for acoustically ambiguous (i.e., boundary) stimuli than for acoustically unambiguous (endpoint) stimuli. Hence, lexical status has an effect before acoustic information is replaced by a phonetic categorization. This demonstration that lexical effects are stronger at the boundary than at the endpoints does not rule out the possibility that some lexical effects occur after phonetic categorization. However, the concentration of the lexical effect at the phoneme bound-

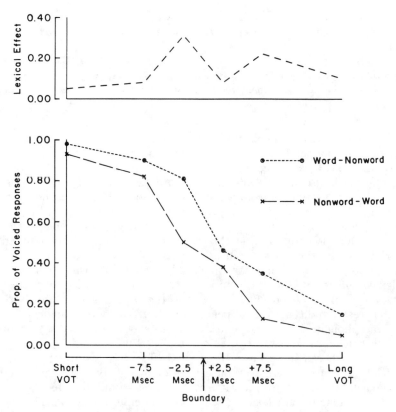

Figure 5. Phonetic categorization when stimuli are unfamiliar. (These data represent subjects' responses to the first stimulus presented to them from each continuum.)

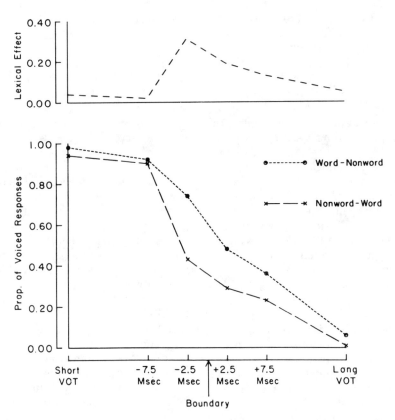

Figure 6. Phonetic categorization with grouped presentation of stimuli. (The results of the last three blocks of Experiment 2, when stimuli from each continuum pair were presented in the same group of trials.)

ary certainly does show that some acoustic information is available when lexical knowledge comes into play. So the categorical model is incorrect, although there may be postcategorical effects as well as precategorical ones.[5]

Lexical status is a fairly simple form of higher level linguistic knowledge that might be expected to affect the interpretation of acoustic evidence. Other studies have shown effects comparable to the results reported here, using semantic (rather than lexical) information to bias phonetic categorizations. Garnes and Bond (1977) showed that sentence context can bias phonetic categorization, and Spencer and Halwes (Note 3) have shown that the size of these effects depends, to some extent at least, on subjects' expectations about and knowledge of the experimental situation. Similarly, Marslen-Wilson and Welsh

(1978) and Cole and Jakimik (1978) have shown that the detection and shadowing of mispronunciations depends on the predictability (on syntactic and semantic grounds) of the mispronounced word. Thus, it seems that the additional auditory information tapped by the lexical effect can interact with much higher level linguistic constraints.

There are at least three different levels at which this information could be coded. The information could be coded as extra candidate phonetic categorizations; it could be

_____

[5] It could be argued that the results of the present experiments are "merely" due to response bias. But this claim is irrelevant to the question under consideration here: The categorical model prohibits response bias (or any other tendency to perceive speech sounds as words) from being concentrated at the phoneme boundary.

kept in a raw, uninterpreted form; or it could be coded as confidence ratings for various phonetic categorizations.

In a simple version of sophisticated guessing theory, the extra information would be represented as a set of possible phonetic categorizations (Catlin, 1969). In the case of stimuli from an acoustic continuum, this is equivalent to adding a third categorization, *don't know*, to the two possible categorizations of the continuum. To account for the lexical effect's concentration at the phoneme boundary, this model must assume that only items labeled as ambiguous are susceptible to lexical effects and that the probability of an item receiving an ambiguous categorization increases near the phoneme boundary. Of the various possible representations of the additional auditory information, this is the most linguistic.

At the opposite pole is the possibility that the perceptual system stores the additional auditory information in a raw, unprocessed, echoic form. In this model, when the output of the phonetic recognizer is not a word, the acoustic evidence specifying that phonetic sequence would be reexamined to determine whether the evidence was consistent with any phonetic strings that were words. This model would explain the concentration of the lexical effect near the phoneme boundary by postulating that stimuli far from the phoneme boundary would be consistent with only one phonetic categorization. Stimuli near the boundary, on the other hand, would allow two categorizations, and the one that made a word would be favored.

It is necessary to posit the existence of an echoic store not only to explain the evidence for the stimulus suffix effect (Crowder & Morton, 1969) but also to explain the trading relations shown in the integration of different acoustic cues into a phonetic percept (Repp, Liberman, Eccardt, & Pesetsky, 1978). There are two problems with the assumption that the additional auditory information involved in the lexical effect is stored in echoic memory. One is the apparent coarseness of the code in echoic memory. Distinctions among stop consonants cannot be retrieved from the precategorical acoustical store. Thus, a stimulus suffix interferes with memory for acoustically dissimilar vowels but not for acoustically similar vowels (Darwin & Baddeley, 1974) or stop consonants (Crowder, 1971). Another potential problem is the short duration over which information stored in echoic memory is available. Estimates vary, but the duration of echoic memory for consonants is probably under one second.

A third form of coding, intermediate in processing depth between the candidate phonetic categorizations of sophisticated guessing theory and the raw sensory information of the echoic store, would use goodness of fit ratings of different possible phonetic categorizations. In this model, a bias toward categorizations that make words would show up as a lower rating threshold for words than for nonwords. For stimuli near the phoneme boundary, this difference in thresholds would affect phonetic categorization. However, the phonetic categorization of stimuli far from the boundary would not be influenced by these differences in threshold because the ratings of the correct phonetic categorization would be quite high. Information in this form is neither strictly phonetic nor auditory but, rather, expresses the relation between the auditory data and the phonetic possibilities in a succinct way. It is interesting that the most successful speech understanding system to date, HARPY, works in this way (Klatt, 1977; Lowerre & Reddy, in press).

Also, implicit confidence rating responses of this sort have been used in many models of linguistic processing. Morton's (1969) logogens measure the acoustic/phonetic fit of each word in the language to the stimulus.[6] Marslen-Wilson and Welsh's (1978) modifications of the logogen view preserve this feature. And Massaro's (Note 4) model of the integration of information

---

[6] The logogen model, as stated by Morton (1969), simply counts phonetic features. To account for the data presented here, the model must be slightly modified to sum the goodness of fit ratings of each segment of the word. This modification seems in the spirit of the original logogen model.

from different knowledge sources also provides estimates of the goodness of fit of various options. Massaro's work is of particular interest because he has carried out experiments on reading that are analogous to the experiments described here. He has examined the visual perception of letterlike forms drawn from a (visual) continuum from the letter c to the letter e (Naus & Shillman, 1976). The perception of such stimuli is biased in favor of orthographically regular strings, just as in the present experiment phonetic categorization is biased toward words.

Deciding between these different representations of the additional auditory information will be a difficult task because they are all modifications of the simple categorical model with the same goal. They can perhaps best be distinguished by examining the way in which the processing of phonetically ambiguous items is influenced by later arriving biasing information. All of the work described above on syntactic and semantic context in phonetic decisions provides the biasing context before the phonetic ambiguity. Providing the biasing information at various delays after the ambiguous item should provide information about the nature of the coding of this additional auditory information. If the information is stored in some sort of echoic store, phonetic categorization of the ambiguous acoustic information should only be susceptible to bias over a short period of time, regardless of the linguistic structure of the utterance. On the other hand, if the information is stored as confidence ratings or as sets of possible phonetic categorizations, the linguistic structure of the utterance (particularly, whether the ambiguous information and biasing information are in the same clause) would be of great importance.

Reference Notes

1. Alexander, D. *The effect of semantic value on perceived b-p boundary.* Unpublished manuscript. Massachusetts Institute of Technology, 1972.

2. Ingemann, F. *Speech synthesis by rule using the FOVE program.* Paper presented at the International Congress of Phonetic Sciences, Miami, 1977.

3. Spencer, N. J., & Halwes, T. *Relating categorical speech perception to ordinary language: Boundary shifts on a "t" to "d" continuum in nonsense, word, and sentence context.* Manuscript in preparation, 1978.

4. Massaro, D. W. *Reading and listening* (Tech. Rep. 423). Madison: University of Wisconsin, Wisconsin Research and Development Center for Cognitive Learning, December, 1977.

References

Broadbent, D. E. Word-frequency effect and response bias. *Psychological Review*, 1967, *74*, 1–15.

Carney, A. E., Widin, G. P., & Viemeister, N. F. Noncategorical perception of stop consonants differing in VOT. *Journal of the Acoustical Society of America*, 1977, *62*, 961–970.

Catlin, J. On the word-frequency effect. *Psychological Review*, 1969, *76*, 504–506.

Cole, R. A., & Jakimik, J. Understanding speech: How words are heard. In G. Underwood (Ed.), *Strategies of information processing.* London: Academic Press, 1978.

Crowder, R. G. The sound of vowels and consonants in immediate memory. *Journal of Verbal Learning and Verbal Behavior*, 1971, *10*, 587–596.

Crowder, R. G., & Morton, J. Precategorical acoustic storage (PAS). *Perception & Psychophysics*, 1969, *5*, 365–373.

Darwin, C. J., & Baddeley, A. D. Acoustic memory and the perception of speech. *Cognitive Psychology*, 1974, *6*, 41–60.

Fujisaki, H., & Kawashima, T. Some experiments on speech perception and a model for the perceptual mechanism. *Annual Report of the Engineering Research Institute* (University of Tokyo), 1970, *29*, 207–214.

Garnes, S., & Bond, Z. S. The relationship between semantic expectation and acoustic information. In W. Dressler, O. Pfeiffer, & T. Herok (Eds.), *Phonologica 1976 Akten der dritten Internationalen Phonologie-Tagung Wien, 1.–4. September, 1976.* Innsbruck: Institut für Sprachwissenschaft der Universität Innsbruck, 1977.

Klatt, D. H. Review of the ARPA speech understanding project. *Journal of the Acoustical Society of America*, 1977, *62*, 1345–1366.

Klatt, D. H. Speech perception: A model of acoustic-phonetic analysis and lexical access. *Journal of Phonetics*, 1979, *7*, 279–312.

Kucera, H., & Francis, W. N. *Computational analysis of present-day American English.* Providence, R.I.: Brown University Press, 1967.

Liberman, A. M., Harris, K. S., Hoffman, H. S., & Griffith, B. C. The discrimination of speech sounds within and across phoneme boundaries. *Journal of Experimental Psychology*, 1957, *54*, 358–368.

Liberman, A. M., Mattingly, I. G., & Turvey, M. T. Language codes and memory codes. In A. W. Melton & E. Martin (Eds.), *Coding processes in*

123   WILLIAM F. GANONG III

human memory. Washington, D.C.: V. H. Winston, 1972.

Lisker, L. Stop voicing production: Natural outputs and synthesized inputs. In, *Haskins Laboratories: Status report on speech research, 1976, SR-47.* (ERIC Document Reproduction Service No. ED-128-870; NTIS No. AD A031789)

Lisker, L., & Abramson, A. Cross-language study of voicing in initial stops. *Word,* 1964, *30,* 384–422.

Lowerre, B., & Reddy, D. R. The HARPY speech understanding system. In W. Lea (Ed.), *Trends in speech recognition.* Englewood Cliffs, N.J.: Prentice-Hall, in press.

Marslen-Wilson, W. D., & Welsh, A. Processing interaction and lexical access during word recognition in continuous speech. *Cognitive Psychology,* 1978, *10,* 29–63.

Miller, G. A., Heise, G., & Lichten, W. The intelligibility of speech as a function of the context of the test materials. *Journal of Experimental Psychology,* 1951, *41,* 329–335.

Morton, J. A. Interaction of information in word perception. *Psychological Review,* 1969, *76,* 165–178.

Myerow, S., & Millward, R. SPLIT—A sound editor for a PDP-8 computer. *Behavior Research Methods and Instrumentation,* 1978, *10,* 281–284.

Naus, M. J., & Shillman, R. J. Why a Y is not a V. A new look at the distinctive features of letters.

Journal of Experimental Psychology: Human Perception and Performance, 1976, *2,* 394–400.

Pollack, I. Message uncertainty and message reception. *Journal of the Acoustical Society of America,* 1959, *31,* 1500–1508.

Purcell, D. G., Stanovich, K. E., & Spector, A. Visual angle and the word superiority effect. *Memory & Cognition,* 1978, *6,* 3–8.

Repp, B. H., Liberman, A. M., Eccardt, T., & Pesetsky, D. Perceptual integration of cues for stop, fricative, and affricate manner. *Journal of Experimental Psychology: Human Perception and Performance,* 1978, *4,* 621–637.

Rubin, P., Turvey, M. T., & Van Gelder, P. Initial phonemes are detected faster in spoken words than in spoken nonwords. *Perception & Psychophysics,* 1976, *19,* 394–398.

Smith, E. E., & Haviland, S. E. Why words are perceived more accurate.y than nonwords. *Journal of Experimental Psychology,* 1972, *92,* 59–64.

Stevens, K. N., & Klatt, D. H. Role of formant transitions in the voice-voiceless distinction for stops. *Journal of the Acoustical Society of America,* 1974, *55,* 653–659.

Warren, R. M. Perceptual restoration of missing speech sounds. *Science,* 1970, *167,* 392–393.

Warren, R. M., & Sherman, G. L. Phonemic restoration based on subsequent context. *Perception & Psychophysics,* 1974, *16,* 150–156.

Appendix A

This appendix describes quantitatively the predictions of the categorical and criterion-shift models.

The categorical model can be described by two equations. For a continuum C1, for which a response of d makes a word and t does not (such as the *dash–tash* series), the categorical model predicts

$$P(d|v) = P_0(d|v) + P_{change:C1}*[1 - P_0(d|v)]$$

where $P(d|v)$ is the probability of responding d to a stimulus with voice onset time (VOT) v, $P_0(d|v)$ is the probability of a response of d to a stimulus with VOT $= v$ in an unbiased situation (which is also the probability of an internal response of d before the correction process), and $P_{change:C1}$ is the probability of correcting a t response to d for Continuum C1. Similarly, the predictions for a continuum in which a t response makes a word (such as the *dask–task* continuum) are given by

$$P(d|v) = (1 - P_{change:C2})*P_0(d|v).$$

The lexical effect function $L(v)$ is simply the difference in response probabilities for the two continua of a matched pair. Thus,

$$L(v) = P_0(d|v) + P_{change:C1}*[1 - P_0(d|v)]$$
$$- (1 - P_{change:C2})*P_0(d|v)$$
$$= P_{change:C1} + P_0(d|v)*(P_{change:C2} - P_{change:C1})$$

In Figure 1, it is assumed that $P_{change:C2} = P_{change:C1}$, so $L(v)$ is constant (i.e., does not depend on v). This is not an essential feature of the model; there is no reason to think biases are equal. However, for any value of $P_{change:C2} - P_{change:C1}$, the value of $L(v)$ at the boundary (where $P_0(v) = .5$) will be equal to the mean of the values of $L(v)$ at the ends of the continuum and certainly less than their sum.

The quantitative predictions of the criterion-shift model are described by

$$P(d|v) = P_0(d|v + b_{C1}),$$

where $P_0(d|x)$ is the probability of responding d to a stimulus with VOT $= x$ in a situation in which there is no lexical bias, and b_{C1} is the criterion shift for this continuum. b_{C1} will be negative when the voiced end of Continuum C1 is a word (resulting in more voice responses) and positive when the voiceless end is a word.

The shape of $L(v)$, according to the criterion shift model, is simply

$$L(v) = P_0(d|v + b_{C1}) - P_0(d|v + b_{C2}).$$

Figure 2 shows the predictions of the criterion-shift model, assuming that $P_0(d|v)$ is a cumulative normal function. Figure 2 assumes equal but opposite direction lexical biases for the two continua, as did Figure 1. Assuming that $P_0(d|v)$ is sigmoid, with steepest slope near the phoneme boundary, $L(v)$ will generally reach a maximum in the neighborhood of the phoneme boundary and, thus, be greater near the phoneme boundary than at either end of the continuum. This is unlike the shape of $L(v)$ according to the categorical model, for which the value at the boundary must be between the values at the ends of the continuum.

Appendix B

I am aware of only two previous studies (Lisker, 1976; Spencer & Halwes, Note 3) that used voice onset time (VOT) continua produced by cross splicing natural speech. Since these studies are not readily available, it seems important to describe the technique in some detail.

The splicing method uses segments cut from voiced and voiceless natural tokens to supply the aspirated and voiced segments of each stimulus. Good tokens of each stimulus are recorded and digitized, and pitch periods are marked in the voiced stimulus. Stimuli from the VOT continuum are produced by replacing the segment before a particular pitch period in the voiced token with an equal duration segment from the beginning of the voiceless token. (For these purposes, the beginning of a pitch period is taken to be the last upward-going zero crossing before a pitch pulse. This choice minimizes clicks due to splicing and assures that a pitch pulse occurs at each nominal VOT. Stimuli produced by this method can only have VOTs at times that are the beginnings of pitch periods in the voiced stimulus.)

For the present experiment, tokens of the voiced and voiceless syllables used to construct the continua were spoken by a female phonetician, in the sentence environment "Now say . . .," and recorded on audiotape. Her fundamental frequency was approximately 200 Hz at the beginning of each syllable. The tokens were digitized on a PDP-8 minicomputer, using a sampling rate of 10 kHz and a 4.5-kHz lowpass filter. The waveform editing program SPLIT (Myerow & Millward, 1978) was used to edit tokens out of the carrier phrase, and the beginning of each token's burst was carefully determined. Zero crossings before pitch periods were located by examining an oscillographic display. The digitized tokens and the locations of the pitch periods were used to generate the spliced tokens that subjects heard.

Tokens were digitized for 22 continua pairs. The endpoint stimuli from those continua were presented to 13 subjects for identification of the whole syllable (not just the initial segment). Those continua pairs for which more than five of the endpoints were incorrectly identified were eliminated. The errors in identification rarely involved the voicing of the initial segment. Often errors were due to misperceptions of the vowel or final consonants. The remaining 16 continua pairs were used in a pilot experiment. Two of these pairs contributed many more errors in identification of the endpoints than did the other pairs, so these 2 pairs were also eliminated. The remaining continua pairs (whose word endpoints and VOTs are given in Table 1) were used in Experiment 2. It is important to note that the selection of stimuli was on grounds independent of whether they produced the lexical effect. The excluded continua were not eliminated because they failed to show a word bias, but simply because the endpoint stimuli were not intelligible enough. Thus, there is no reason to think that the remaining continua pairs are not a representative sample from the set of intelligible continua pairs for English.

In the pilot experiment, there was considerable variation in the position of phoneme boundaries within the pairs of continua. One source of this variation could be random fluctuations in the particular aspiration and voicing waveforms used. Random variations in the amplitude of segments of aspiration noise or glottal pulses could influence the position of the phoneme boundary. Therefore, it was decided to use exactly the same aspiration and voicing waveforms to construct the stimuli of both continua of each pair. The first pitch pulse more than 100 msec after stimulus onset was found in the voiced token of one of the continua. In both voiced and voiceless tokens, the initial segment of this duration was replaced with a comparable segment from the corresponding member of the other continuum. The tokens produced sounded perfectly natural but produced pairs of continua that used exactly the same aspiration and voicing sequences for the first 100 msec of the stimuli. For half of the continua pairs, the initial segments were taken from the continuum whose voiced end was a word, and vice versa for the other half.

One objection to the use of stimuli produced in this manner can be raised. Although VOT is clearly controlled by this method, other acoustic cues (e.g., formant transition duration, Stevens & Klatt, 1974) that are known to affect the voicing decision for stops are not controlled systematically. This objection is correct but irrelevant to the purposes of the present study. If the goal for the study were to investigate just the acoustic cue VOT (and not other acoustic cues), this would be a serious problem. But in the present study, it is only important to relate the perception of stimuli varying along some acoustic variable to other factors; it is not important that this variable be any particular acoustic cue. As long as subjects' perceptions of the stimuli depend on the acoustic variable (as they evidently did in this experiment), the stimuli will be sufficient for examining the relation between acoustic information and higher order knowledge.

Received January 12, 1979 ■

Time-varying features as correlates of place of articulation in stop consonants

Diane Kewley-Port

Department of Psychology, Indiana University, Bloomington, Indiana 47405

(Received 1 July 1981; accepted for publication 12 July 1982)

Running spectral displays derived from linear prediction analysis were used to examine the initial 40 ms of stop-vowel CV syllables for possible acoustic correlates to place of articulation. Known spectral and temporal properties associated with the stop consonant release gesture were used to define a set of three-time-varying features observable in the visual displays. Judges identified place of articulation using these proposed features from running spectra of the syllables /b,d,g/ paired with eight vowels produced by three talkers. Average correct identification of place was 88%; identification was better for the male talkers (92%) than the one female talker (78%). *Post hoc* analyses suggested, however, that simple rules could be incorporated in the feature definitions to account for differences in vocal tract size. The nature of the information contained in linear prediction running spectra was analyzed further to take account of known properties of the peripheral auditory system. The three proposed time-varying features were shown to be displayed robustly in auditory filtered running spectra. The advantages of describing acoustic correlates for place from the dynamically varying temporal and spectral information in running spectra is dicussed with regard to the static template matching approach advocated recently by Blumstein and Stevens [J. Acoust. Soc. Am. **66**, 1001–1017 (1979)].

PACS numbers: 43.70.Dn, 43.70.Gr, 43.66.Fe

INTRODUCTION

Recently a number of investigators have developed speech processing techniques which incorporate or model known spectral and temporal processing characteristics of the peripheral auditory system. Studies of auditory physiology by Kiang (1980), Kiang *et al.* (1979), Delgutte (1980, 1981), Sachs and Young (1979, 1980), and Young and Sachs (1979) have shown how the rapidly changing speech signal is represented in the neural signals output from the peripheral auditory system. Information gathered from this and other psychophysical research has been implemented in specific speech processing systems by several other investigators. Word recognition systems using auditory filters for processing the speech signal have been developed by Zwicker *et al.* (1979) and Klatt (1979). On a more limited scale, Bladon and Lindblom (1979) and Carlson and Granstrom (1980) have designed and experimentally evaluated auditory filters for classifying vowel spectra. Another application has included the development of speech vocoders which incorporate properties of auditory processing (Schroeder *et al.*, 1979; Flanagan, 1980; Flanagan and Christensen, 1980).

The present research was inspired directly by the recent work of Searle and his colleagues (1979, 1980). Searle *et al.* developed a frequency-by-amplitude analysis based on peripheral auditory filters approximated by analog 1/3-octave filters, updated at 1.6-ms intervals. Their approach emphasized not only the auditory transformation of the speech signal, but also the dynamic changes in the transformation. Their analyses permitted them to construct a three-dimensional representation, displaying the running spectra of a speech signal as it changed over time. In a preliminary study of the properties of stop consonants observed in these running spectra, Searle *et al.* were very successful in identifying cues to voicing for stop consonants, but only partially successful in identifying cues to place. The idea of examining distinctive cues in running spectral displays provided the basis for developing a similar analysis technique in this investigation to study several long-standing questions concerning acoustic invariance in stop consonants.

In particular, the present research examined the problem of identifying invariant cues for place of articulation in initial stop consonants. Although this issue has been one of great interest in speech research, only recently have investigators actually claimed to have solved the problem. Stevens and Blumstein (1978, 1981; Blumstein and Stevens, 1979, 1980) in a series of articles have attempted to describe and experimentally verify the existence of static integrated acoustic cues for place of articulation in stops. They have argued that invariant acoustic properties for place can be found in the overall gross shape of the spectrum at the onset of the release burst. Stevens and Blumstein claim that a unique spectral shape can be found for each particular place of articulation. Furthermore, they have argued that these spectral shapes are correlates of the phonologically distinctive features that define place of articulation which can be observed across syllable position, consonant manner class, and talker (Jakobson *et al.*, 1952).

Stevens and Blumstein have developed specific templates of the gross spectral shapes for each place of articulation. These templates were derived from single 25.6-ms spectral sections taken at the onset of stop-vowel syllables and smoothed by linear prediction. Blumstein and Stevens (1979) have also carried out several experimental tests to assess the adequacy of these templates to identify place of articulation for syllable-initial and final stops produced in five vowel contexts by six talkers. Their results showed that the templates were fairly successful in identifying the place of articulation of stops in syllable-initial position, but not of stops in syllable-final position.

Stevens and Blumstein also carried out two further studies to verify experimentally that the overall shape of the onset spectra contained important perceptual cues for identifying place of articulation. Both studies used synthetic CV syllables (Stevens and Blumstein, 1978; Blumstein and Stevens, 1980). The synthetic stimuli varied in overall duration from relatively long CV syllables to very brief truncated stimuli, although they were all constructed using the same synthesis principles. These principles involved preserving the natural details of the burst, VOT, and voiced formant transitions in their "full-cue" set. All these parameters were then manipulated to produce a stop consonant-vowel continuum from /b/ to /d/ to /g/ before three vowels. Subjects were able to identify some of these stimuli as /b/, /d/, or /g/ on 100% of the trials in a forced choice task, whereas other stimuli were identified ambiguously. Stevens and Blumstein then observed, in an informal way, that the onset spectra for the unambiguously identified stimuli were in agreement with the proposed gross spectral shapes. From these findings they argued that the gross shape of the spectrum at onset contains the perceptually distinctive acoustic information to identify place of articulation in stops.

Although many other experimental conditions were included in their two reports, the basic strategy for verifying the role of gross spectral properties in synthetic CV syllables remained basically the same. By their own admission, these data "do not constitute a strong test of the theory" (Stevens and Blumstein, 1978, p. 1367). Indeed, their experimental procedures appear to be unsatisfactory as a way of verifying whether the gross spectral shapes are sufficient perceptual cues for place of articulation, primarily because acoustic properties of the stimulus set were not manipulated in terms of the gross onset spectral properties themselves, but rather in terms of burst frequency, VOT, and formant transitions. Nevertheless, Stevens and Blumstein argued that invariant acoustic cues for specifying place of articulation can be located in the first 10–20 ms of a stop waveform. These particular claims motivated several aspects of the present investigation.

The research undertaken in this report examines the initial portion of the acoustic waveform, as Stevens and Blumstein have suggested, but used running spectral displays for the spectral representation. These running spectra differed considerably from Searle's running spectra since they were calculated digitally using linear prediction analysis (Markel and Gray, 1976). Linear prediction running spectra produced with a carefully chosen set of analysis parameters can in fact provide a good spectral representation for speech, with fine resolution of the formant structure in the frequency-by-amplitude domain and good temporal resolution by appropriately updating the analysis in the time domain. Continuous running spectral representations of speech are presumably a better model of the spectral information output from the peripheral auditory system than are Stevens' single integrated spectral sections. That is, the most basic property of auditory neural signals is that they vary directly with the time variations of the input acoustic signal. In fact, Schroeder et al. (1979) have modeled the spectral processing properties of the ear in a manner quite analogous to our calculation of a running spectrum. In their model, Schroeder et al. state: "The inner ear...performs a running short-time spectral analysis in which the frequency coordinate f is represented by a spatial coordinate x along the length of the basilar membrane. We approximate this process by short-time Fourier transformations over successive 20-ms time windows" (p. 1647).

Figure 1 shows six typical running spectral displays of stops in different vowel contexts. The first frame effectively displays 5 ms of the burst release. Subsequent frames are offset at 5-ms intervals. Further details of how these displays were generated are provided in Sec. IIA below.

Underlying the analysis of invariant cues to place of articulation used by Stevens and Blumstein is the assumption that the information specifying place is contained primarily in the first 10–20 ms of the stop-vowel waveform. While this assumption has enjoyed wide support over the years (cf. Jakobson et al., 1952; Fant, 1960; Cole and Scott, 1974; Tekieli and Cullinan, 1979), competing accounts have also been proposed. Liberman and his colleagues at Haskins (Cooper et al., 1952; Liberman et al., 1954, 1967) have emphasized the importance of the voiced formant transitions in

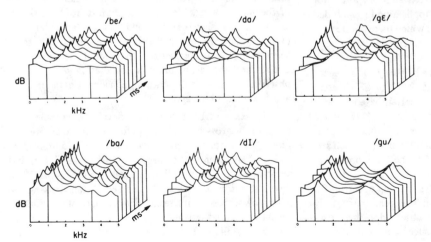

FIG. 1. Running spectral displays for the first eight frames of six stop-vowel syllables. Each frame is offset by 5 ms.

carrying place of articulation information. Liberman's argument has been that an essential property of speech is that it is *dynamic*. Formant transitions of stop-vowel syllables appeared to be the appropriate cues to place because they capture the important time-varying changes associated with both the underlying articulatory gestures and the resulting acoustic signal. Recent research, however, has cast doubt on the hypothesis that formant transitions are the most important cues to place of articulation in natural speech. Dorman *et al.* (1977) obtained poor identification of place of articulation from only the formant transition plus vowel segments edited from natural syllables. Furthermore, Kewley-Port (1980, 1982) measured numerous parameters of formant transitions in natural CV's and was unable to reliably distinguish place of articulation based on these measures across all eight vowel contexts studied.

Examination of the running spectral displays in the present investigation revealed that emphasis on properties of the voiced formant transitions was due, in part, to the representation of CV's in the spectrographic analysis typically used in earlier studies (Potter *et al.*, 1947; Liberman *et al.*, 1954). The running spectral displays of the present investigation showed continuous changes in the spectral prominences from the release burst into the voiced formant transitions. As can be seen in Fig. 1, the onset of voicing in these displays is indicated by the abrupt appearance of a well defined $F1$ peak at low frequencies, while the upper formants are more nearly continuous into the burst. The voiced formant transitions do not stand out visually as isolated distinctive segments of the speech signal in the running spectral displays.

Visual examination of numerous stop-vowel syllables from a male talker revealed several time-varying acoustic features or attributes that could potentially distinguish place of articulation in the running spectral displays. This observation led to pilot studies (Kewley-Port, 1979a, b) of running spectra which suggested that some of these features might specify place invariantly over different vowel contexts. The earlier feature definitions were carefully considered and redefined for the larger and more formal experiment presented here. The features that we developed were similar to acoustic features derived from the acoustic theory of speech production as proposed by Fant and to the features used by Stevens (Stevens, 1975; Stevens and Blumstein, 1978) in his research. In fact, as will be seen below, the features have strong roots in the distinctive feature theory of Jakobson *et al.* (1952). The important aspect of these features, however, is that they are time varying and preserve the essential dynamic characteristics of the stop-vowel syllable.

I. TIME-VARYING FEATURES OF PLACE OF ARTICULATION

The time-varying features proposed in this experiment are similar to the acoustic correlates for place described by Fant (1960, 1973) and Stevens (Stevens and Blumstein, 1978, 1981). For both Fant and Stevens the acoustic correlates of place directly reflect the underlying articulatory gestures according to the principles of the acoustic theory of speech production. Furthermore, since the articulatory gesture for a given consonant is assumed to be relatively fixed, the corresponding acoustic cues for place should be invariant. The

running spectral features proposed in the present study are similar to the relational, invariant features originally suggested by Fant and Stevens. A general description of the time-varying properties associated with each place of articulation follows below.

The first property observed in the running spectra was the tilt of the burst. In the running spectral displays, the spectrum of the first 5 ms of the burst was displayed in the first spectral section or frame. According to the predictions of the acoustic theory of speech production, both Fant (1960) and Stevens (1975; Stevens and Blumstein, 1978) have proposed that burst spectra for labials emphasize low frequencies with a general downward tilt of spectral energy from the low to the high frequencies. This can be seen in the running spectra in Fig. 1 as a flat or falling tilt of spectral energy in the burst frame for /be/ and /ba/. Alveolars, on the other hand, were predicted to have a generally rising tilt of energy from low to high frequencies which can be seen in the running spectra of /da/ and /dɪ/ in Fig. 1. Velar bursts have not been characterized as rising or falling because burst energy shifts from high to low as the vowel context moves from front to back (Halle *et al.*, 1957; Fant, 1960; Stevens, 1975).

Although the tilt of burst property discussed above is purely a *spectral* property, there is an implied temporal property necessary for locating the burst itself. In this experiment, as in most earlier studies of stop consonants, the burst frame was located visually in the waveform by the experimenter. In ongoing speech processing, however, the occurrence of the burst itself must also be detected. A time-varying acoustic feature for locating the burst in running speech has already been proposed by Stevens who suggested that the release burst can be detected when an abrupt change in energy occurs (Stevens, 1980; Stevens and Blumstein, 1981). This proposal corresponds well with physiological studies which have shown that the auditory system responds uniquely to abrupt changes at signal onset (Zhukov *et al.*, 1974; Delgutte, 1980, 1981). We suggest that an abrupt change in energy can be observed easily in running spectra which include the low energy frames occurring in the stop closure preceding the burst.

While velar place of articulation is not characterized by burst tilt, Fant and Stevens have proposed that the essential spectral property of velar bursts is the presence of a compact or prominent peak of energy in the mid-frequency region (see /ge/ and /gu/ in Fig. 1). Stevens and Blumstein (1978, 1981; Blumstein and Stevens, 1979) argue that this spectral property is sufficient to identify velar place when captured in a static onset spectrum. However, Fant has pointed out that the burst release has temporal properties as well (Fant, 1960, 1973). Labial and alveolar bursts are said to be between 5 and 10 ms in length which is shorter than the 20–30 ms velar bursts. Furthermore, velars are described as having a compact spectrum which lasts throughout the longer burst. This compact spectrum arises from a resonant pole produced in the cavity in front of the velar constriction. Fant (1973) pointed out that the velar release is relatively slow so that this resonance is sustained for approximately 30 ms. Therefore a distinctive property of velars is that only slow changes in spectral energy are observed over this interval compared to the more rapid changes observed for labials and alveolars. The running spectral analysis as proposed here also captures these temporal properties of the release bursts. The 5-ms burst frame is quite prominent in this analysis and clearly displays the tilt of the bursts. As the linear prediction window slides along in succeeding frames for labials and alveolars, transient energy is encountered and a rapid change in spectra can be observed (see Fig. 1). For velars, however, successive spectra following the burst show little change in the prominent mid-frequency spectra.

One other feature appeared prominently in our visual examination of the running spectral displays. This correlate of place articulation was the delay in the onset of voicing relative to the burst. In the running spectra, the frame in which the $F1$ peak onsets relative to the burst is a direct measure of VOT (voice-onset-time). Vot has been shown to increase in length from labials to alveolars to velars (Lisker and Abramson, 1964; Zue, 1976). In running spectral displays, our earlier pilot work indicated that a delay of 20 ms (i.e., four frames) or more in the onset of voicing was strongly associated with velar place (see Fig. 1).

The observations of spectral and temporal features associated with labial, alveolar, and velar place were formalized for evaluation in an earlier pilot study (Kewley-Port, 1979a, b). Based on these results, three time-varying features having binary feature categories were defined for examination in this experiment. These definitions, in conjunction with an assignment matrix, were used by judges to determine place of articulation in running spectral displays as follows.

Feature 1: *Tilt of the spectrum at burst onset*: Tilt was estimated by visually fitting a straight line to the first frame between 0 and 3500 Hz. The feature categories were R = rising and F = flat or falling.

Feature 2: *Late onset of low-frequency energy*. Late onset was defined as the occurrence of high amplitude, low-frequency peaks ($F1$ peaks) starting in the fourth frame of the display or later. Feature categories were L = late onset and N = no late onset.

Feature 3: *Mid-frequency peaks extending over time*. This feature was defined as the presence of a single, prominent peak between 1000 and 3500 Hz occurring for three or more frames, although not necessarily consecutive frames. The feature categories were Y = yes, peaks exist and N = no, no such peaks are present.

After the feature categories were specified, place of articulation was assigned by the judges as /b/, /d/, or /g/ in accordance with the assignment matrix in Table I. An entry of "?" in the assignment matrix meant that either feature category could occur for that stop. The "*" by the feature L

indicated that in ambiguous cases, the presence of L was sufficient to assign the stop g.

Our earlier pilot study had examined stops before only the front vowels from one talker. In the present experiment we added more vowels and more speakers to the original data base. The purpose of this study was to determine if the features and new assignment matrix could adequately describe the invariant visual properties of running spectra for identifying place of articulation in stop consonants.

II. EXPERIMENT
A. Stimuli

Three talkers, two males (RP and TF) and one female (NL), produced the set of consonant–vowel syllables that were analyzed in this study. Syllables from talker RP, a phonetician, were a subset of those analyzed in a separate study of formant transitions (see Kewley-Port, 1980, 1982). Three repetitions each of the syllables /b,d,g/ paired with /i, ɪ, e, ɛ, æ, a, o, u/ were used in this study. The data base was then expanded by adding an additional male talker TF, and a female talker NL, both of whom were phonetically naive. They produced the syllables /b,d,g/ paired with /i, e, a, o, u/. All syllables were embedded in the carrier sentence, "Teddy said CV." Sentences were read from randomly ordered lists. Talkers were recorded in a sound attenuated IAC booth on an Ampex AG–500 tape recorder using an Electro-Voice D054 microphone. Three repetitions of each syllable were digitized for analysis from the middle of the ten lists recorded. Waveforms were first low-pass filtered at 4.9 kHz and then sampled at 10.0 kHz using a 12-bit A/D converter. The total number of syllables examined in this experiment was 162, 72 from speaker RP, and 45 each from speakers TF and NL.

All syllables were analyzed on a PDP 11/34 computer using the SPECTRUM program (Kewley-Port, 1979c) to produce running spectral displays such as those shown in Fig. 1. The waveforms were edited and first differenced (pre-emphasized). A Hamming window was then positioned so that the burst onset of the CV was located in the center of the window. Linear prediction coefficients were calculated for each window using the autocorrelation method of Markel and Gray (1976). Since this method requires at least two pitch pulses to fall within the analysis window, 20-ms windows were used for RP and NL, but TF, having a lower fundamental frequency, required a 25-ms window. Smoothed spectra were calculated by means of a discrete Fourier transform of the reflection coefficients with added zeros using the algorithm of Markel (1971; also see Markel, 1972). The resulting 256-point spectrum has a 19.5-Hz bandwidth. This narrow bandwidth reflects the potential accuracy of specifying formant frequency information when the linear prediction analysis parameters have been appropriately chosen. Monsen (1981) has recently shown that accuracy of measuring vowel formants was poorer than predicted at approximately 60 Hz.

A new spectral section or frame was calculated at 5-ms intervals. The 20- and 25-ms Hamming windows used in this analysis have effective durations of about 10 and 12.5 ms, respectively. Thus the 5-ms update interval produced some

TABLE I. Matrix used by judges to assign place of articulation from specific feature categories.

Tilt of burst	Late onset	Mid-frequency peaks	Assigned consonant
F	N	N	b
R	?	N	d
?	L*	Y	g

spectral overlap between frames without severe oversampling as can be seen in Fig. 1. These temporal parameters were originally selected to preserve the onsets of formant transitions as accurately as possible within the limits of the linear prediction method (see Kewley-Port, 1982).

In these running spectral displays, the Hamming window was positioned visually by the experimenter in such a way that the first frame encompassing the burst had an effective duration of about 5 ms. Therefore the first frame can be said to display spectral energy from the release burst only. Very often the first several frames analyzed were voiceless, i.e., missing the $F1$ peak. According to Markel and Gray (1976), fewer linear prediction coefficients are needed to specify the spectrum adequately in voiceless than in voiced frames. Spectral sections calculated with fewer coefficients had smoother peaks, closer to the underlying fricative spectrum, than did the rippled peaks often produced by extra coefficients. Therefore, in this analysis, four fewer coefficients were used in analyzing the voiceless frames. Fourteen coefficients were used to calculate voiced frames for the males with five formant peaks; 12 coefficients were used for the female with four formant peaks.

A running spectral display was then plotted for the first eight frames—or 40 ms—for each CV. Using a Tektronics hard-copy unit (Model 4631), an 8-1/2- by 11-in. display was produced for each of the 162 CV's. All the CV's were randomized, coded by number, and placed in looseleaf notebooks for examination by the judges in this experiment.

B. Judges

Three members of the laboratory served as judges. Phonetically sophisticated judges were required for this task because the descriptions of both the displays and the phonetic features employed standard acoustic and phonetic terminology. The judges were not, however, familiar with running spectral displays or the specific nature of the present experiment. Two of the judges (ACW and TDC) were graduate students in Psychology; the third was a post-doctoral fellow (SEK) with a Ph.D. in Speech and Hearing Sciences.

C. Procedure

The present experiment consisted of three parts: (1) training, (2) independent judging, and (3) collaborative judging. The training session was used to acquaint the judges with the feature definitions and the assignment matrix to be used to identify place of articulation from running spectral displays. A typewritten page containing the feature definitions and assignment matrix for consonant identification as described earlier was given to each judge. A 20-min training session was conducted by the experimenter with 15 examples of running spectra, none of which were included in the 162 test displays. Figure 1 shows the six primary examples used in the training phase. Table II shows the correct feature responses and consonants on a facsimile of a response sheet.

During the training phase, judges learned to identify each feature category for a display independently and write corresponding letters on their response sheets. The judges were then asked to assign a consonant according to the entries in the assignment matrix. It was noted that the assignment matrix did not include all possible combinations of features. The judges were told, however, that combinations not represented in the matrix would probably occur infrequently. If they occurred, judges were instructed to assign a consonant in whatever way they could.

After training, the judges were asked to respond to each of the 162 displays *independently*. Each judge viewed half of the displays in the looseleaf notebooks in two separate 1-h sessions on different days. The response sheets from the independent sessions were scored for correct consonant identification only. One or more incorrect responses occurred on 46 of the 162 displays. To resolve errors which may have resulted from careless judgments, a collaborative judging session was arranged one week after the independent judging sessions were completed. The three judges met together as a group with the experimenter present and were given the feature definition sheets and additional instructions for rescoring the 46 displays in which errors occurred. Judges were instructed to write down on a separate response sheet whether they unanimously agreed or disagreed for a given display. When judges disagreed, they were asked to indicate in what ways the features or matrix were ambiguous. The displays were judged in a 1-1/2-h session which was taperecorded for later analysis.

D. Results

In the collaborative judging, 20 of the 46 displays were unanimously assigned to the correct consonant, while ten of the displays were unanimously identified incorrectly. The remaining 16 were judged to be ambiguous. To obtain an overall score for correct identification, all unanimous assignments from the independent and the succeeding collaborative judgments were used in the final results. For the 16 ambiguous displays, the forced choice responses from the independent judging were used since the consonants had not

TABLE II. Correct responses for the training examples seen in Fig. 1.

| Syllable | Features | | | Assigned consonant |
	Tilt of burst	Late onset	Mid-frequency peaks	
/be/	F	N	N	b
/da/	R	N	N	d
/gɛ/	R	L	Y	g
/ba/	F	N	N	b
/dɪ/	R	L	N	d
/gu/	R	L	Y	g

TABLE III. Results of assigning consonants to running spectral displays using three judges.

Talker	No. errors	(N)	% Correct	% Correct by sex
RP	14	(216)	94	Male = 92
TF	14	(135)	90	
NL	30	(135)	78	Female = 78
Total	58	(486)	88	

been assigned for ambiguous cases in the collaborative judging.

Table III shows the overall results for consonant identification. Consonants were correctly identified 88% of the time from the running spectral displays. The errors were not uniformly distributed by talker. Specifically there was a large difference in correct identification depending on the sex of the talker, 92% correct for male talkers, but only 78% correct for the female talker.

The distribution of errors by consonant and vowel is shown in Table IV. Overall, /d/ was identified most accurately, with performance at 93%. The consonant /b/ was identified in most contexts except in syllables containing the high vowels /i,e,u/. Most errors occurred for /b/ syllables produced by the female speaker. Analysis of the collaborative judging errors indicated that the tilt of the burst was ambiguous or slightly rising for bilabial stops before high vowels. The consonant /g/ was poorly identified in the syllable /gi/ with 56% correct. Most of these errors were also contributed by the female speaker whose mid-frequency peaks occurred above the 3500-Hz limit imposed in the original feature definitions. Additional /g/ errors occurred because the otherwise prominent mid-frequency peaks were not clearly "single" peaks in the display.

Table V displays the pattern of errors for the consonants identified in the running spectral displays. /b/ consonants were frequently mistaken as /d/'s, but not the converse. Bilabials and velars were rarely mistaken for one another. /g/'s were frequently mistaken for /d/'s.

The feature categories assigned for each CV were analyzed to determine whether the judges had reliably and consistently categorized the features. Judges were said to disagree on feature assignment when they had not unanimously assigned the same feature categories. The results showed that when the judges correctly identified the consonant in the independent judging, only 2% feature disagreement occurred. In the collaborative judging of the other 46 displays, only 8% feature disagreement was observed. Therefore an overall score of 5% feature disagreement was obtained from the three judges. These results indicate that it was relatively easy for the judges to categorize the features in the running spectral displays as specified by our feature definitions.

The specification of the original assignment matrix was based primarily on running spectra from a male speaker, RP.

TABLE V. Percentage of response errors obtained for a given consonant in running spectral displays.

Displayed	Assigned consonant		
	b	d	g
b	...	14%	2%
d	2%	...	5%
g	0%	13%	...

To check the validity of the feature matrix for assigning stops for all three talkers, the percentage of feature assignments made by all three judges in the independent judging was calculated. These results are given in Table VI, where percentages are entered in terms of the categories as they appeared on the feature definition sheet.

It can be seen from the data in this table that the percent judgment of feature categories other than "?" was quite high, averaging 92%. The two entries of "?," which signified that either category might occur, were assigned equally to the categories. These results indicate that the original assignment matrix was appropriate for the features examined in this experiment. The slightly lower assignments of correct categories for Tilt of burst (85% and 88%) and the presence of Mid-frequency peaks for /g/ (83%) suggest that some improvement of these feature definitions may be needed in future studies.

Not all possible permutations of the feature categories were listed in the assignment matrix. As a consequence, there were possible combinations of feature categories which led to ambiguous consonant assignments. Most of these occurred for the 46 displays in which a consonant error occurred. These were dealt with in the analysis of the collaborative judging data. However, for the displays judged unanimously correct, only 1% of the responses resulted from ambiguous feature combinations. Thus possible ambiguities in the assignment matrix were not a problem in this study.

Only ten of the displays (6%) were unanimously assigned the incorrect place of articulation. The incorrect assignments for these displays provide some insights into problems with the current feature definitions. Four of the ten displays were /b/'s before front vowels. Because the burst tilt was rising, judges assigned d's to these displays. Three other displays were the female talker's /gi/'s each having a

TABLE IV. Percent correct identification of consonant by vowel for all talkers. Note, vowels /ɪ, ɛ, æ/ were produced by only one talker.

Vowel	(N)	b	d	g	Total
i	(81)	67	93	56	72
e	(81)	70	81	89	80
a	(81)	100	93	100	96
o	(81)	93	96	100	96
u	(81)	78	96	100	91
ɪ	(27)	89	100	100	96
ɛ	(27)	100	100	67	89
æ	(27)	100	100	67	89
Total	(486)	84	93	87	88

TABLE VI. Percent of feature assignments obtained in independent judging. They are listed according to the feature categories appearing in the feature matrix used for consonant assignment.

Consonant	Tilt of burst	Late onset	Mid-frequency peaks
b	F = 85	N = 96	N = 98
d	R = 88	?N = 59 ?L = 41	N = 96
g	?F = 35 ?R = 65	L = 96	Y = 83

small mid-frequency compact peak at or above the 3500-Hz frequency limit used in the feature definitions. Judges also incorrectly assigned /d/'s to these displays. Analysis of the remaining three displays (2%), however, showed unusual compact peaks for these /g/ syllables.

Some special attention should be given to the feature Late onset of $F1$. All three features in this experiment were defined as binary. Since only two binary features are necessary to specify the three consonants, this feature system is redundant. However, the feature of Late onset was so prominent in the running spectral displays that we thought that it ought to play some role in distinguishing place of articulation among the stops, especially /g/ from /b,d/. In particular, since Mid-frequency peaks were sometimes difficult to identify for /g/, it was thought that in ambiguous cases, the additional feature of Late onset of $F1$ might facilitate the correct identification of the stop category. This was incorporated in the feature definition sheet using "L *" in the matrix for /g/. Post hoc analysis revealed, however, that the Late onset feature was actually used by the judges to disambiguate /g/ in only three cases (0.6% of the judgments). Thus the current feature definition system did not adequately capture the intended usefulness of Late onset, even though Late onset was present in 96% of the /g/'s.

As a consequence, the running spectra were re-examined to determine if an alternative definition for Late onset could be developed. The frame in which the onset of $F1$ occurred was determined visually by the experimenter for the 162 displays. In doing this, we found that approximately 50% of the /g/ displays had $F1$ onset after 30 or more milliseconds, compared to only one /d/ display and no /b/ displays. This observation suggests a new definition for Late onset, namely, that the category L refers to onset of $F1$ peaks after 30 ms (six or more frames). An informal examination of the present running spectra indicated that the proposed change in the Late onset feature would produce only a small overall improvement in consonant identification if incorporated in the analysis. However, the proposed change represents a much better implementation of the concept which was intended for the Late onset of $F1$ feature, namely, that the presence of the Late onset of $F1$ (i.e., a long VOT) is strongly associated with the consonant /g/. Such a feature can be useful in disambiguating /g/ in running spectral displays where Mid-frequency peaks may not be clearly present.

III. COMPARISON OF LINEAR PREDICTION AND AUDITORY FILTERED RUNNING SPECTRA

The results from this study have demonstrated that human observers can reliably identify place of articulation from visual features displayed in running spectra. Place of articulation was identified using time-varying features observed in the initial portions of the stop-vowel waveform which were independent of the following vowel context. While such findings were reliable and consistent across three judges for a large number of natural speech tokens, there still remains the question of the relation between linear prediction running spectra and spectral processing of speech by the human auditory system. Specifically, we were interested in

determining if the time-varying features used in the visual experiment would be as robust in auditory spectral representations as they were in linear prediction spectra.

Several investigators have constructed auditory processing models to produce spectral representations of speech signals. In some cases, the output of these models has been examined for the presence of spectral cues for speech recognition. In particular, as noted earlier, the research of Searle and his colleagues (Searle et al., 1979, 1980) using running spectra to search for place and voicing cues in stops inspired the present study. Although Searle et al. explicitly advocated the development and use of auditory processing techniques for speech, analysis techniques currently implemented in speech research are simply not adequate models of known psychophysical properties of the human auditory system. In the case of Searle et al.'s study, a standard, commercial set of 1/3-octave filters was chosen as the basis of their speech processor. Design characteristics of 1/3-octave filters were developed to meet a set of engineering standards for commercial filters (American National Standards Institute ANSI S1.11–1966 class III). The popularity of 1/3-octave filters for speech processing (e.g., Klein et al., 1970; Schouten and Pols, 1979) derives from their general availability and speed (i.e., analog processing). As we shall see below, however, 1/3-octave filter characteristics are only a gross approximation to the actual filtering properties of the human auditory system.

Before evaluating the success of several recent processing techniques, it will be useful to compare the properties of running spectral displays with several of the known properties of mammalian auditory systems as well as with other auditory processing models currently employed in speech analysis. In terms of the individual smoothed spectra, we will briefly discuss the characteristics of the analyzing filters (e.g., linear prediction, FFT, 1/3-octave filter banks) and the representation of the frequency dimension (e.g., linear, log, bark).

Differences in design characteristics of the filters for processing speech signals can produce quite different spectral displays. Based on psychophysical measures, the frequency resolution in the human auditory system has been described in terms of a set of critical bands (Scharf, 1970). A critical-band analysis corresponds roughly to the frequency analysis of a set of bandpass filters whose bandwidth is constant (about 100 Hz) below 500 Hz, and then becomes successively broader as frequency increases above 500 Hz. Bandwidth, however, is only one property of a bandpass filter. Two other properties less frequently discussed are the shape of the filter itself (e.g., rectangular versus Hamming) and the slopes of the skirts of the filter. While these two properties of auditory filters have generally been fitted by simple functions, Patterson and Nimmo-Smith (1980) have specified a unique, two-part filter shape to account for their data. The discussion that follows, however, emphasizes differences in bandwidth since it has received the most attention in the psychophysical literature. (See Klatt, 1976 and 1979, for a comprehensive list of appropriate design characteristics for critical-band filters for speech processing.)

Research has produced two sets of estimates for the

bandwidth of critical-band filters, one about one-half as wide as the other (see Sever and Small, 1979). This range varies approximately from 0.1 to 0.18 times the center frequency of the filter. Estimates of the well-known bark critical-band filters used by Zwicker (1961; Zwicker *et al.*, 1979) are compared with other filter bandwidths in Fig. 2. The hatched area includes bandwidths most often reported in the psychophysical literature. One-third-octave filters have bandwidths approximately 0.23 times the center frequency. Thus the bandwidths of 1/3-octave filters are considerably broader than estimates of the critical bandwidths derived from psychophysical data. This means that 1/3-octave filters provide poorer frequency resolution in the important mid-frequency range used in speech than does the human auditory system. As a consequence, 1/3-octave filtering of speech signals probably represents a lower limit on the poorest frequency resolution that the human auditory system might display. One-sixth-octave filters have been used in the speech analysis systems developed by Schroeder *et al.* (1979) and Flanagan and Christensen (1980). While 1/6-octave filter bandwidths are narrower than Zwicker's (1961) estimates as seen in Fig. 2, they correspond well with more recent

bandwidth estimates, especially those of Patterson (1976; Patterson and Nimmo-Smith, 1980). [See Flanagan and Christensen (1980) for a demonstration of mid-frequency differences between 1/3-octave filters and 1/6-octave filters.]

On the other hand, linear prediction spectra used in the present study are theoretically capable of providing a constant frequency resolution of 19.5 Hz (but see Monsen, 1981). As can be seen in Fig. 2, this resolution is considerably narrower than that of the auditory system, particularly at higher frequencies. We should note, however, that frequency resolution as measured in discharge patterns of auditory-nerve fibers in cats can be extremely accurate under optimal signal conditions. The analyses carried out recently by Delgutte (1980, 1981) and Young and Sachs (1979; Sachs and Young, 1979, 1980) have shown considerable accuracy in determining formant frequencies of synthetic vowels under certain conditions. It is not known if such precise formant frequency information is available under normal listening conditions for human speech recognition. However, linear prediction spectra when displayed on a log-frequency axis appear roughly similar in frequency resolution to many of the vowel-formant figures reported in both Sachs and Young (1980, cf. Fig. 13) and Delgutte (1981, Chap. 1). These figures represent vowel spectra in log frequency as a function of interval measures of the discharge patterns of auditory-nerve fibers. Thus linear prediction spectra may be considered as providing an upper limit on the best possible frequency resolution the human auditory system might display.

With spectrally analyzed speech, several possible representations of the frequency-by-amplitude dimensions can be chosen. Linear prediction spectra are typically represented on a linear frequency scale. In the auditory system, however, frequency on the basilar membrane is equally distributed in approximately bark intervals (Zwicker, 1961; Schroeder *et al.*, 1979), which is often approximated by a simple log-frequency scale. Thus, for research employing auditory filters, a bark frequency or modified log scale (technical Mel) is probably more appropriate for displaying frequency than is a linear scale.

Another property of running spectral displays is the representation of time. We know that the auditory system can closely track time variations in waveforms in terms of synchrony of discharge firings with the input signal (Kiang, 1980). Apparently, the important acoustic distinctions in speech vary much more slowly than the temporal processing capabilities of the ear. Therefore the limits of the representation of the time dimension for processing speech spectra should be set according to the observed rates of change in the speech signal. For speech, this limit would be placed somewhere between 1 and 20 ms. Searle *et al.* (1979) originally used a 1.6-ms time frame for running spectra. This time frame seemed to present too much detail, so they used averaged time frames of 8 ms in their feature analysis. The running spectra in the present study were 5 ms apart, while Klatt's (1979) spectra were 10 ms apart. Thus the time intervals between spectra currently employed by different investigators are in the 5- to 10-ms range.

The question originally posed in this section was

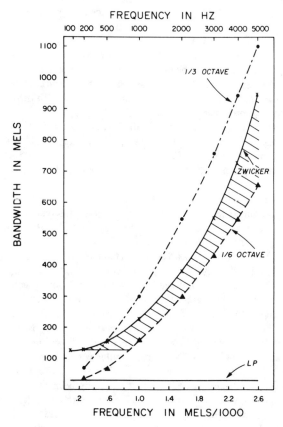

FIG. 2. Four different filter bandwidths as a function of frequency are displayed using the technical Mel scale. 1/3- and 1/6-octave filter bandwidths are shown according to ANSI standards. The function labeled Zwicker is derived from his definition of critical bands in terms of barks (Zwicker, 1961). The function LP is the constant 19.5-Hz bandwidth of our linear prediction spectra. The hatched area represents critical bandwidths typically reported in psychoacoustic research (see text).

whether running spectral features would be prominently displayed in auditory filter representations of running spectral displays. To explore this problem further, we decided to re-examine the stimuli in our data base with two auditory filter representations. SPECTRUM was modified so that a set of programmable, sliding filters could be applied to the previously computed spectral sections. Two properties of the filters were adjustable: bandwidth and the slopes of the skirts. Fixed properties included symmetry in a log-frequency space and a flat top giving an overall trapezoidal shape. These fixed filter properties were chosen to match 1/3-octave filter bank specifications. The filters were overlapped in close frequency intervals in order to produce smooth spectra. Pilot work showed that for the spectra used in this experiment, the convolution of the programmable filters with the smoothed linear prediction spectra produced filtered spectra almost identical to those produced by convolution with the equivalent 200-point FFT. Thus the smoothed linear prediction spectra were used as input to the programmable filters in this analysis.

The programmable filters were selected as follows. One-third-octave filters were chosen because they have frequently been used in speech processing, most recently by Searle et al. (1979, 1980), and they represent a frequency resolution which is probably poorer than that of the human auditory system. The 1/3-octave filters were digitally defined according to the ANSI S1.11–1966 class III standard, with a bandwidth constant of 0.23 times the center frequency, and skirts having a 50 dB/oct rolloff. The other filters, although similar to the auditory filters of Bladon and Lindblom (1979) and Klatt (1979), were patterned more closely

after the narrower filters proposed by Patterson (1976) and the 1/6-octave filters of Flanagan and Christensen (1980). The bandwidth constant was 0.13 and the skirts had a 75 dB/oct rolloff. Below 400 Hz, regardless of the bandwidth constant, the bandwidth was fixed at 95 Hz in keeping with standard critical-band measurements as shown in Fig. 2.

The running spectral display was also altered for spectra processed by the auditory filters by implementing a log-frequency scale. Amplitude was still displayed in decibels, and the time frame rate was kept at 5 ms. The 1/3-octave running spectra produced by this digital method are not directly comparable to 1/3-octave filter bank running spectra (see Searle et al., 1979). In an analog filter bank, as well as in the ear, the time constant for high-frequency spectral components is shorter than that for low-frequency components. Thus rapid change in high-frequency information has a finer temporal resolution than low-frequency change. This relationship is not preserved in a digital analysis based on windowing where rapid changes in high frequencies are averaged over the window duration. This should not be a serious problem for our linear prediction analysis because our window size and the 5-ms frame rate appear to preserve the temporal variation observed the speech waveform as discussed earlier. Nonetheless, the 1/3-octave and auditory filter running spectra presented below are only approximations to true filter bank analyses.

With these programming changes, the running spectra that we previously examined could be redisplayed using 1/3-octave filters or auditory filters. Figure 3 compares three linear prediction running spectra with auditory filter displays. Figure 4 compares three different linear prediction

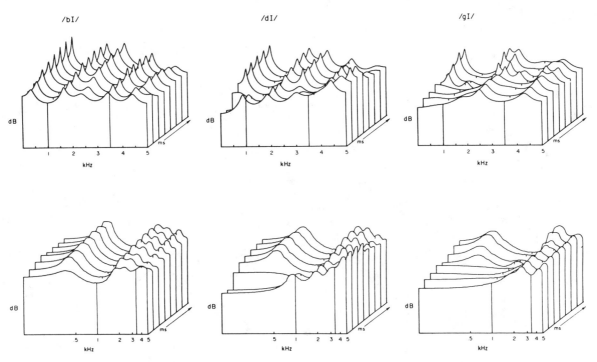

FIG. 3. Comparison of running spectral displays produced by either linear prediction analysis (top), or smoothed by auditory filtering of the Patterson type (bottom) for three stop-vowel syllables.

running spectra with 1/3-octave filter displays.

We re-examined the displays computed earlier using both types of filters to determine the extent to which the three visual features used to identify place were still present. In carrying out these analyses, we were interested in determining how such filtering would potentially alter our earlier feature descriptions. Approximately half of the 116 displays which had been correctly identified by all three judges in the independent judging were examined first. Then all 46 displays from the collaborative judging were redisplayed and examined visually by the experimenter.

An examination of Figs. 3 and 4 reveals that an auditory filter representation changes the frequency space in three important ways. First, the low-frequency region of $F1$ is more prominently displayed. Second, filtering alters the spectral tilt of each spectral section. Because bandwidths are broader at higher frequencies, more energy is averaged into the high-frequency filters causing an upward spectral tilt. Thus both auditory filters and 1/3-octave filters result in a nonlinear transformation of spectral tilt which emphasizes high-frequency energy in comparison to the linear prediction spectra due to the imposed constant bandwidth of the filters at low frequencies (see Fig. 2). Finally, the spectral peaks move toward higher frequencies because the filters are symmetrical in log-frequency space, which means that they include more high-frequency energy than low-frequency energy in a linear frequency domain. Klatt (1979) has recently implemented Patterson's hypothesis (1974; Patterson and Nimmo-Smith, 1980) that auditory filters are symmetrical in linear frequency, but the log-frequency symmetry has been more commonly used. As a result of this shift, the feature

definitions referring to the 3500-Hz marks shown on the displays should probably be altered to approximately 4000 Hz in the following discussion.

The results of our examination of the auditory filter representations of running spectra may now be compared to the earlier feature definitions based on linear prediction spectra. The Tilt of burst category definitions are altered in a similar way using either 1/3-octave or auditory filters due to the high-frequency emphasis. The categories should now be *strongly rising* for /d/ versus *moderately rising* for /b/. Looking at running spectra on which an error occurred such that a /b/ had been misclassified as /d/, the filtering appeared to disambiguate these cases specifically because of the high-frequency emphasis. However, the current auditory filter representations did not incorporate a transformation of the present amplitude dimension from decibels to sones or some other measure of equal loudness. While the effects of implementing equal loudness contours on the Tilt of burst feature are yet to be explored, we note that this would alter *relative* amplitude. Since the Tilt feature is itself relative, we may presume that its specific definition might change, but not its effectiveness as a feature. To summarize our observations, both the 1/3-octave and auditory filter representations of the Tilt of burst categories appeared to be as successful as the earlier linear prediction displays.

The definition of the Late onset feature is not altered significantly by filter representations of running spectra. The $F1$ peak, as shown in Figs. 3 and 4, is described as a broad, well-formed, low-frequency peak. Otherwise, no other aspects of this feature appeared to change for either 1/3-octave or auditory filters.

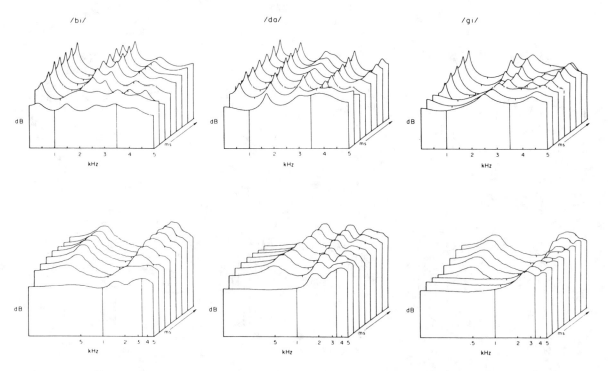

FIG. 4. Comparison of running spectral displays produced by either linear prediction analysis (top), or smoothed by 1/3-octave filters (bottom) for three stop-vowel syllables.

The visual display of the Mid-frequency peak feature changed quite a bit under the two types of filtering. Single prominent peaks were still readily observable for /g/'s, but they were narrower, had more "ripple," and appeared in more spectral sections (see Fig. 3). A significant problem occurred for the 1/3-octave filters which did not occur for the auditory filters. Many /b/'s analyzed by 1/3-octave filters acquired prominent mid-frequency peaks like those shown for /bi/ on Fig. 4. These peaks would cause them to be misclassified as /g/'s. For these same /b/ stimuli, auditory filtering did not produce mid-frequency peaks. Auditory filtering appeared to disambiguate many /g/ displays which had previously been misclassified either because two smaller peaks were superimposed on the prominent peak, or because the prominent peaks occurred on fewer than three spectra. Thus the results from this analysis indicate that mid-frequency peaks for /g/'s are more salient in running spectral displays using auditory filtering than in those using linear prediction filtering. However, the 1/3-octave filter representations would cause many more /b,g/ confusions.

In summary, the present study demonstrated that three acoustic features could be used to accurately identify place of articulation from linear prediction running spectra prepared for *visual* inspection. However, linear prediction spectra provide a much finer spectral resolution than the human auditory system carries out. Therefore two other spectral representations were used to construct running spectral displays. In the 1/3-octave filter representation, all features were preserved in the visual displays, but, unfortunately, too many mid-frequency peaks were erroneously produced for /b/'s. Thus it appears that 1/3-octave filtering may eliminate some spectral properties that are important for speech analysis. These filters generate spectra having a poorer frequency resolution than that of the human auditory system. The other filter representation was representative of a class of auditory filters currently used by other investigators. The original features proposed in this study were all displayed robustly in auditory filter running spectra, and, in some cases, appeared to display place of articulation more successfully than did the linear prediction running spectra. Thus it appears that the proposed time-varying features can be used to classify place of articulation in initial stop syllables displayed in two different spectral representations of speech, namely, linear prediction and auditory filtered running spectra.

IV. EXTENSIONS OF RUNNING SPECTRAL ANALYSIS FOR PLACE CUES

Based on the results of this study and on the preceding discussion, it is now possible to recommend specific changes in both the definitions of the features and the analysis procedures which can be used in future extensions of this research. Special attention will be given to the problem of vocal-tract normalization, i.e., accounting for the differences obtained between the male and female talkers in this study.

In terms of analysis techniques which compute the running spectra, further exploration of the auditory filter representations should be carried out. Since the human auditory system is the best speech processing device currently available, implementation of analogous spectral processing capabilities may make the task of locating reliable acoustic cues for speech easier. This appeared to be the case for the auditory filters examined in this study.

Turning to the individual feature definitions, we begin with the feature of Mid-frequency peaks extending in time. The frequency range of 1000–3500 Hz used in the Mid-frequency peaks definition was determined from the earlier pilot study using male speaker RP. The results of the present investigation demonstrated that this range was unsuitable for the female talker because all potential peaks for /gi/ fell outside this range. Fant (1973) has already provided an explanation of this problem. Fant presented a table showing which formant is associated with the compact resonance peaks observed for /g/. For /i/ and /e/, the compact peak is associated with both $F3$ and $F4$. That is, for high front vowels, the more palatal constriction for /g/ produces a short vocal-tract resonance cavity. The formant peak of this cavity is high and close to $F3$ and $F4$. Thus, in order to capture a prominent peak for /g/, the mid-frequency range must be placed higher than $F4$ by approximately 500 Hz. The frequency range for $F4$ is, of course, dependent on a talker's vocal-tract size and that will have to be considered in future analyses.

Likewise, the lower value of the mid-frequency range was originally set at 1000 Hz based on talker RP's velar peaks. The lowest peaks for velars occur before the vowels /o/ and /u/ which are associated with the talker's $F2$ resonance (see /gu/ on Fig. 1). Although the prominent peaks for /o/ and /u/ are continuous with $F2$, they fall from a higher frequency in the burst into the steady state $F2$ for the vowel. Based on these observations, it appears that a simple rule to account for vocal-tract size can be implemented in the definition of the frequency range for Mid-frequency peaks which can solve this problem. The lower frequency limit should be placed at the lower frequency of a talker's $F2$ for /o/ or /u/, and the upper limit should be placed 500 Hz higher than a talker's $F4$. These values are for linear prediction spectra. If auditory filtering is used, the lower limit would not change, but the upper limit should be set about 1000 Hz higher than the talker's $F4$ because of the spectral averaging of the higher frequencies.

Next consider the Tilt of burst feature. We noted earlier that more /b/ errors occurred for the high vowels than the low vowels, and more errors occurred for the female than the male talkers. That is, rising spectral tilts were sometimes obtained in the 5-ms, burst-only spectra for /b/, apparently due to high-frequency energy associated with certain vowel contexts. Earlier in this discussion we suggested that this problem might be solved by changing the definition of rising tilt to be rising more prominently for /d/'s. We also note that with auditory filtering an emphasis of high frequencies was observed which had the beneficial effect of sorting more clearly /b/'s from /d/'s, particularly for the more ambiguous high vowel cases. We should note, however, that the Tilt of burst definition also includes an upper frequency limit, previously set to 3500 Hz. This limit was imposed because the burst-only spectra for /d/ are *not* in fact "diffuse rising" up to 5000 Hz as Stevens and Blumstein (1978) have suggested. Rather, for /d/ before back vowels, a vowel dependent peak in the spectra occurs for males at about 3000 Hz so that the spectra fall above this frequency. Both Zue (1976) and Klatt (1980) have previously reported this spectral property. This peak is vowel dependent and therefore varies with vocal-tract size. Thus the upper frequency limit for the Mid-frequency peaks and Tilt of burst features must take into account vocal-tract size, and probably can be set to the same value using the previously suggested rule. The problems in the feature analysis discussed above arose from an interaction of vowel context effects and differences in vocal-tract size. The specific solution proposed here is that by properly accounting for differences in vocal-tract size in the feature definitions, the features will automatically specify place of articulation independent of the vowel context.

Finally, the feature of Late onset of $F1$, as previously discussed, should be considered as a secondary feature for separating velars with long VOT's from bilabials and alveolars. Suggestions for a new definition of this feature and the resulting matrix were previously given at the end of Sec. IID. Treating delay in voicing onset as a secondary correlate to place of articulation has also been proposed by Fant (1973, p. 136). If Late onset can be used as a secondary cue to place, it might be worthwhile to determine if any empirical evidence could be found for the use of this feature in the perception of place of articulation. Several studies have already demonstrated that identification of place of articulation changes when the VOT of the stimuli was manipulated (Sawusch and Pisoni, 1974; Miller, 1977; Oden and Massaro, 1978). All three of these studies, however, used synthetic stop-vowel syllables without release bursts. Therefore a more careful synthesis study using velar syllables with bursts containing the important Mid-frequency peaks feature is needed to verify the specific role of the Late onset feature in perception of place of articulation.

The adequacy of these three features for specifying place of articulation was determined using human observers who examined visual displays of running spectra. The presence of the three features in the running spectra could, in principle, be determined algorithmically by computer. However, since this experiment was an initial study of these features, human observers were used to obtain feedback about possible ambiguities in the definitions or procedures in the collaborative judging session. In future experimentation with these features, a machine implementation of the feature definitions will certainly be included.

V. DISCUSSION AND CONCLUSIONS

The results of this study demonstrate that invariant features for identifying place of articulation in initial stop consonants are readily observable in continuous running spectral displays of CV syllables. This experiment was an initial attempt to establish the adequacy of the analysis procedures and proposed feature descriptions for identifying place across a large number of vowel contexts and several talkers. Although this research has a theoretical framework very similar to that of Stevens and Blumstein (1978, 1981; Blum-

stein and Stevens, 1979), our analysis differs from theirs in a very important way: running spectral features incorporate the *time* dimension whereas Stevens and Blumstein onset spectra are basically static spectral "snapshots" of the continuously changing speech signal. Indeed, Blumstein and Stevens (1979, p. 1013) have acknowledged that the time dimension might have to be incorporated into their analysis. After our pilot work was completed (Kewley-Port, 1979a,b), Blumstein and Stevens (1979, p. 1013) suggested that an analysis procedure similar to the running spectra of Searle *et al.* (1979) might be an improvement over their single-spectrum static template procedure. The present findings demonstrate that this suggestion is correct.

Our running spectral analysis contrasts with the static template analysis proposed by Stevens and Blumstein in several ways. For example, by integrating energy over a 26-ms time window into a single onset spectrum, important spectral differences that are present for the labial and alveolar bursts are obscured. A 26-ms window will always include some transitional information about the vowel (aspirated or voiced) along with the energy in the burst. Furthermore, a single, fixed integration window cannot account for the differences in the *temporal* properties of the release burst as described previously by Fant (1960, 1973). The rapidly changing spectra following the burst for bilabials and alveolars cannot be observed in only a single 26-ms onset spectra. But more importantly, the velar property of a *slowly varying* compact spectrum extending in time cannot be represented in only a single onset spectrum having no temporal dimension. Blumstein and Stevens have stated in their recent publications that the compact spectra for velars must persist in time for listeners to identify velars correctly (1979, p. 1002; 1980, p. 652). Nevertheless, their single onset spectra cannot, in principle, represent this acoustic information adequately.

In fact, the velar template constructed by Blumstein and Stevens (1979) is essentially a peak detector. However, in carrying out their analysis, they discovered that simple integration of the first 26 ms of spectral energy produced numerous spectra containing prominent peaks which were not velars. To be precise, 27% of the alveolar consonants had spectral peaks near the $F2$ locus at 1800 Hz. This observation prompted Stevens and Blumstein to modify the original diffuse rising template so as to exclude peaks occurring around 1800 Hz (1979, p. 1005). Furthermore, alveolar peaks said to arise from subglottal resonances also occurred in the 800–1600-Hz region. These peaks were also arbitrarily excluded from the diffuse-rising template (1979, p. 1005). Moreover, a problem for the compact template was the presence of double peaks. Blumstein and Stevens (1979, p. 1006) apparently treated two spectral peaks separated by less than 500 Hz as a single peak. Thus it appears that attempts to locate the spectral feature compact as a simple peak in a single, 26-ms integrated spectrum have given rise to numerous exceptions and the postulation of *ad hoc* decision rules. Similar problems did not arise in our analysis of running spectral displays. We suspect that the problems were present for Stevens and Blumstein because the temporal dimension of the speech signal was eliminated in their static onset spectra analysis.

The present investigation was limited to the initial voiced stops /b,d,g/ and several other phonetic parameters still await investigation. Foremost is voicing. In particular, it is of some interest to determine if our analysis will correctly identify place of articulation for /ptk/ as well as /bdg/. Clearly, the two primary features, Tilt of burst and Mid-frequency peaks, are located mostly in the burst portion of the spectral displays. Since this portion of the spectra should be very similar for voiced and voiceless consonants, we may confidently predict that our proposed features will successfully identify place in /ptk/. The secondary feature of Late onset of $F1$, on the other hand, will probably need some further modification. Only research with both the voiced and voiceless consonants will determine whether the Late onset feature can be defined in such a way that it can act as a reliable secondary cue for identifying /g/ in various vowel contexts.

The features used in this study were used to identify place in what has been called *initial* stops. Initial in the context of this experiment means *syllable initial* since, in fact, all CV's examined here were originally extracted from the carrier sentence "Teddy said CV." No claims or hypothesis are being proposed on the basis of this experiment for presence of these features in running spectra of syllable final stops, or in running spectra of segments from other manner classes such as nasals or fricatives. For example, the Tilt of burst feature, as discussed, contains as part of its definition the location of a burst following a closure interval. Since this sequence of acoustic events is not found in nasals, the feature would not apply to the class of nasal consonants. This conclusion is quite different from the proposals made by Stevens and Blumstein (1978, 1981). The invariant acoustic cues they propose in terms of onset spectra are linked to the general notion of distinctive features for place as proposed by Jakobson *et al.* (1952) and Chomsky and Halle (1968). Thus Stevens and Blumstein specifically claim that onset spectra can and should correctly specify place for final stops and nasals. However, their own research provides little convincing evidence to support this claim. For final stops in the Blumstein and Stevens' template study (1979), the average correct identification of place at closure was 53%, and identification of the final burst (which is not typically present in running fluent speech) was 76%. In the preliminary study of [n] versus [m], average place identification was 76%. However, [n]'s were accepted by both the labial and alveolar template 67% of the time, so that the unique identification of [n]'s was at best only about 33%. Therefore the combined results of uniquely identifying [n] versus [m] was near the 50% chance level for two choices. These results do not support the strong claims of Stevens and Blumstein that static onset-spectra templates can reliably capture the invariant properties for the distinctive feature of place in all environments or across several manner classes.

In conclusion, we have proposed three time-varying, relational acoustic features as a principled solution to the problem of invariant acoustic cues for place of articulation in initial stop consonants. These features are clearly observable in visual representations of running spectral displays of naturally produced CV syllables. The present study evaluated this proposed analysis for voiced stops before a large number of vowels produced by three talkers. From our results, it appears that these features are invariant over vowel context, and with the addition of two simple rules, appear to be invariant over vocal-tract size as well. The running spectra used in this study appropriately model some of the peripheral processing characteristics of the human auditory system. The time-varying features used to specify place of articulation in this experiment were also shown to be robustly displayed in another visual representation which more closely approximated the filtering properties of the auditory system. Although the features examined in this experiment may be ultimately limited to identifying place in syllable-initial, voiced and voiceless stops, it is fully expected that examination of auditory spectral representations of speech signals in which the time dimension is properly preserved will also be successful in determining the acoustic correlates of other classes of speech sounds as well.

ACKNOWLEDGMENTS

I am very grateful to David B. Pisoni who encouraged me to pursue this research as part of a doctoral dissertation submitted to the Graduate Center of The City University of New York. I am particularly indebted to him for the time and support he gave while conducting the research and in preparing the manuscript. In addition, I wish to thank Michael Studdert-Kennedy, Dennis H. Klatt, Katherine S. Harris, and Donald Robinson for carefully reading earlier versions of this manuscript. Some of the results of this research was presented before the Acoustical Society of America at the 97th meeting in Cambridge, MA and the 100th meeting in Los Angeles, CA. This research was supported by the National Institutes of Health, Research Grant NS–12179–05 and the National Institute of Mental Health, Research Grant MH–24027–06 to Indiana University in Bloomington.

Bladon, R. A. W., and Lindblom, B. (**1979**). "Auditory modeling of vowels," in *Speech Communication Papers Presented at the 97th Meeting of the Acoustical Society of America*, edited by J. J. Wolf and D. H. Klatt (Acoustical Society of America, New York), pp. 1–4.

Blumstein, S. E., and Stevens, K. N. (**1979**). "Acoustic invariance in speech production: Evidence from measurements of the spectral characteristics of stop consonants," J. Acoust. Soc. Am. **66**, 1001–1017.

Blumstein, S. E., and Stevens, K. N. (**1980**). "Perceptual invariance and onset spectra for stop consonants in different vowel environments," J. Acoust. Soc. Am. **67**, 648–662.

Carlson, R., and Granstrom, B. (**1980**). "Model predictions of vowel dissimilarity," Q. Prog. Status Rep. **STL–QPRS 3–4**, Speech Transmission Laboratory, Stockholm, 84–104.

Chomsky, N., and Halle, M. (**1968**). *The Sound Pattern of English* (Harper and Row, New York).

Cole, R. A., and Scott, B. (**1974**). "The phantom in the phoneme: Invariant cues for stop consonants," Percept. Psychophys. **15**, 101–107.

Cooper, F. S., Delattre, P. C., Liberman, A. M., Borst, J. M., and Gerstman, L. J. (**1952**). "Some experiments on the perception of synthetic speech sounds," J. Acoust. Soc. Am. **24**, 597–606.

Delgutte, B. (**1980**). "Representations of speech-like sounds in the discharge patterns of auditory-nerve fibers," J. Acoust. Soc. Am. **68**, 843–857.

Delgutte, B. (**1981**). "Representation of speech-like sounds in the discharge patterns of auditory-nerve fibers," unpublished doctoral thesis, MIT, Cambridge, MA.

Dorman, M. F., Studdert-Kennedy, M., and Raphael, L. J. (**1977**). "Stop-consonant recognition: Release bursts and formant transitions as functionally equivalent, context-dependent cues," Percept. Psychophys. **22**, 109–122.

Fant, G. (**1980**). *Acoustical Theory of Speech Production* (Mouton, The Hague, The Netherlands).

Fant, G. (**1973**). "Stops in CV-syllables," in *Speech Sounds and Features*, edited by G. Fant (MIT, Cambridge, MA), pp. 110–139.

Flanagan, J. L. (**1980**). "Parametric coding of speech spectra," J. Acoust. Soc. Am. **68**, 412–419.

Flanagan, J. L., and Christensen, S. W. (**1980**). "Computer studies on parametric coding of speech spectra," J. Acoust. Soc. Am. **68**, 420–430.

Halle, M., Hughes, G. W., and Radley, J. P. A. (**1957**). "Acoustic properties of stop consonants," J. Acoust. Soc. Am. **29**, 107–116.

Jakobson, R., Fant, C. G. M., and Halle, M. (**1952**). *Preliminaries to Speech Analysis* (MIT, Cambridge, MA).

Kewley-Port, D. (**1979a**). "Continuous spectral change as acoustic cues to place of articulation," Res. Speech Percept., Prog. Rep. No. 5, Indiana University, 327–346.

Kewley-Port, D. (**1979b**). "Spectral continuity of burst and formant transitions as cues to place of articulation in stop consonants," in *Speech Communication Papers Presented at the 97th Meeting of The Acoustical Society of America* (Acoustical Society of America, New York), pp. 175–178.

Kewley-Port, D. (**1979c**). "Spectrum: A program for analyzing the spectral properties of speech," Res. Speech Percept., Prog. Rep. No. 5, Indiana University, 475–492.

Kewley-Port, D. (**1980**). "Representations of spectral change as cues to place of articulation in stop consonants," Res. Speech Percept., Tech. Rep. No. 3, Indiana University.

Kewley-Port, D. (**1982**). "Measurements of formant transitions in naturally produced stop consonant-vowel syllables," J. Acoust. Soc. Am. **72**, 379–389.

Kiang, N. Y. S. (**1980**). "Processing of speech by the auditory nervous system," J. Acoust. Soc. Am. **68**, 830–835.

Kiang, N. Y. S., Eddington, D. K., and Delgutte, B. (**1979**). "Fundamental considerations in designing auditory implants," Acta Otolaryngol. **87**, 204–218.

Klatt, D. H. (**1976**). "A digital filter bank for spectral matching," in *Conference Record of the 1976 IEEE International Conference on Acoustics Speech and Signal Processing*, edited by C. Teacher (IEEE Catalog No. 76CH1067-8 ASSP, Philadelphia, PA), pp. 537–540.

Klatt, D. H. (**1979**). "Speech perception: A model of acoustic-phonetic analysis and lexical access," J. Phonet. **7**, 279–312.

Klatt, D. H. (**1980**). "Software for a cascade/parallel formant synthesizer," J. Acoust. Soc. Am. **67**, 971–995.

Klein, W., Plomp, R., and Pols, L. C. W. (**1970**). "Vowel spectra, vowel spaces, and vowel identification," J. Acoust. Soc. Am. **48**, 999–1009.

Liberman, A. M., Cooper, F. S., Shankweiler, D. P., and Studdert-Kennedy, M. (**1967**). "Perception of the speech code," Psychol. Rev. **74**, 431–461.

Liberman, A. M., Delattre, P. C., Cooper, F. S., and Gerstman, L. J. (**1954**). "The role of consonant-vowel transitions in the perception of the stop and nasal consonants," Psychol. Monogr. **68** (8, Whole No. 379), 1–13.

Lisker, L., and Abramson, A. S. (**1964**). "A cross-language study of voicing in initial stops: Acoustical measurements," Word **20**, 384–422.

Markel, J. D. (**1971**). "FFT pruning," IEEE Trans. Audio Electroacoust. **AU–19**, 305–311.

Markel, J. D. (**1972**). "Digital inverse filtering—a new tool for formant trajectory estimation," IEEE Trans. Audio Electroacoust. **AU–20**, 129–137.

Markel, J. D., and Gray, A. H. (**1976**). *Linear Prediction of Speech* (Springer-Verlag, New York).

Miller, J. L. (**1977**). "The perception of voicing and place of articulation in initial stop consonants: Evidence for the nonindependence of feature pro-

cessing," J. Speech Hear. Res. **20**, 519–528.

Monsen, R. B. (**1981**). "Accuracy of formant frequency estimation by spectrograms and by linear prediction analysis," J. Acoust. Soc. Am. Suppl. 1 **69**, S17.

Oden, G. C., and Massaro, D. W. (**1978**). "Integration of featural information in speech perception," Psychol. Rev. **85**, 179–191.

Patterson, R. D. (**1974**). "Auditory filter shape," J. Acoust. Soc. Am. **55**, 802–809.

Patterson, R. D. (**1976**). "Auditory filter shapes derived with noise stimuli," J. Acoust. Soc. Am. **59**, 640–654.

Patterson, R. D., and Nimmo-Smith, I. (**1980**). "Off-frequency listening and auditory-filter asymmetry," J. Acoust. Soc. Am. **67**, 229–245.

Potter, R. K., Kopp, G. A., and Green, H. C. (**1947**). *Visible Speech* (Van Nostrand, New York).

Sachs, M. B., and Young, E. D. (**1979**). "Encoding of steady-state vowels in the auditory nerve: Representations in terms of discharge rate," J. Acoust. Soc. Am. **66**, 470–479.

Sachs, M. B., and Young, E. D. (**1980**). "Effects of nonlinearities on speech encoding in the auditory nerve," J. Acoust. Soc. Am. **68**, 858–875.

Sawusch, J. R., and Pisoni, D. B. (**1974**). "On the identification of place and voicing features in synthetic stop consonants," J. Phon. **2**, 181–194.

Scharf, B. (**1970**). "Critical bands," in *Foundations of Modern Auditory Theory*, Vol. 1, edited by J. V. Tobias (Academic, New York), pp. 157–202.

Schouten, M. E. H., and Pols, L. C. W. (**1979**). "CV- and VC-transitions: A spectral study of coarticulation—Part II," J. Phonet. **7**, 205–224.

Schroeder, M. R., Atal, B. S., and Hall, J. L. (**1979**). "Optimizing digital speech coders by exploiting masking properties of the human ear," J. Acoust. Soc. Am. **66**, 1647–1652.

Searle, C. L., Jacobson, J. Z., and Rayment, S. G. (**1979**). "Stop consonant discrimination based on human audition," J. Acoust. Soc. Am. **65**, 799–809.

Searle, C. L., Jacobson, J. Z., and Kimberly, B. P. (**1980**). "Speech as patterns in the 3-space of time and frequency," in *Perception and Production of Fluent Speech*, edited by R. A. Cole (Erlbaum, Hillsdale, NJ), pp. 73–102.

Sever, J. C., and Small, A. M. (**1979**). "Binaural critical masking bands," J. Acoust. Soc. Am. **66**, 1343–1350.

Stevens, K. N. (**1975**). "The potential role of property detectors in the perception of consonants," in *Auditory Analysis and Perception of Speech*, edited by G. Fant and M. A. A. Tatham (Academic, New York), pp. 303–330.

Stevens, K. N. (**1980**). "Acoustic correlates of some phonetic categories," J. Acoust. Soc. Am. **68**, 836–842.

Stevens, K. N., and Blumstein, S. E. (**1978**). "Invariant cues for place of articulation in stop consonants," J. Acoust. Soc. Am. **64**, 1358–1368.

Stevens, K. N., and Blumstein, S. E. (**1981**). "The search for invariant acoustic correlates of phonetic features," in *Perspectives on the Study of Speech*, edited by P. D. Eimas and J. Miller (Erlbaum, Hillsdale, NJ), pp. 1–38.

Tekieli, M. E., and Cullinan, W. L. (**1979**). "The perception of temporally segmented vowels and consonant-vowel syllables," J. Speech Hear. Res. **22**, 103–121.

Young, E. D., and Sachs, M. B. (**1979**). "Representations of steady-state vowels in the temporal aspects of the discharge patterns of populations of auditory-nerve fibers," J. Acoust. Soc. Am. **66**, 1381–1403.

Zhukov, S. Ya., Zhukova, M. G., and Chistovich, L. A. (**1974**). "Some new concepts in the auditory analyis of acoustic flow," Sov. Phys. Acoust. **20**, 237–240 [*Akust. Z.* **20**, 386–392 (**1974**)].

Zue, V. W. (**1976**). "Acoustic characteristics of stop consonants: A controlled study," Tech. Rep. **523**, Lincoln Laboratory, MIT, Cambridge, MA.

Zwicker, E. (**1961**). "Subdivision of the audible frequency range into critical bands (Frequenzgruppen)," J. Acoust. Soc. Am. **33**, 248.

Zwicker, E., Terhardt, E., and Paulus, E. (**1979**). "Automatic speech recognition using psychoacoustic models," J. Acoust. Soc. Am. **65**, 487–498.

Speech perception by the chinchilla: Identification functions for synthetic VOT stimuli

Patricia K. Kuhl[a] and James D. Miller

Central Institute for the Deaf, St. Louis, Missouri 63110
(Received 11 May 1977; revised 2 November 1977)

In an attempt to clearly differentiate perceptual effects that are attributable to "auditory" and "phonetic" levels of processing in speech perception we have undertaken a series of experiments with animal listeners. Four chinchillas (Chinchilla laniger) were trained to respond differently to the "endpoints" of a synthetic alveolar speech continuum (0 ms VOT and +80 ms VOT) and were then tested in a generalization paradigm with the VOT stimuli between these endpoints. The resulting identification functions were nearly identical to those obtained with adult English-speaking listeners. To test the generality of this agreement, the animals were then tested with synthetic stimuli that had labial and velar places of articulation. As a whole, the functions produced by the two species were very similar; the same relative locations of the phonetic boundaries, with lowest VOT boundaries for labial stimuli and highest for velar stimuli, were obtained for each animal and human subject. No significant differences between species on the absolute values of the phonetic boundaries were obtained, but chinchillas produced identification functions that were slightly, but significantly, less steep. These results are discussed with regard to theories of speech perception, the evolution of a speech-sound repertoire, and current interpretations of the human infant's perceptual proclivities with regard to speech-sound perception.

PACS numbers: 43.70.Dn, 43.66.Gf, 43.80.Lb

INTRODUCTION

Current theories of speech perception (Stevens and House, 1972; Studdert-Kennedy, 1974, 1976; Fant, 1973) consider the sound-to-meaning transformation a hierarchically organized process with many levels between the acoustic waveform and a perceived "message." At some stage in the processing of speech, the acoustic waveform is transformed into a phonetic feature matrix (Studdert-Kennedy, 1974, 1976). This process has typically been considered a complex one involving considerable recoding and restructuring of the information in the acoustic waveform because the acoustic cues for speech sounds appear to be highly context dependent (Liberman et al., 1967). Speech research, therefore, has been directed toward identifying the essential acoustic characteristics which identify phonetic units, the levels involved in the transformation from the acoustic waveform to a phonetic matrix, the nature of the transformations of the acoustic signal which occur at each processing level, and the processing levels and accompanying transformations that are uniquely involved when the acoustic signal is speech.

In attempting to account for the data obtained in speech experiments, many theorists have found it useful to distinguish between what they have called "auditory" levels of processing, ones that are not specific to speech signals, and "phonetic" levels of processing, which are presumed to be unique to speech-sound processing (Studdert-Kennedy, 1974, 1976; Pisoni, 1977; Liberman, 1970). The evidence often cited as supporting a dichotomy between auditory and phonetic levels of processing consists of (1) a lack of acoustic invariance between the acoustic cues and our percepts (Liberman et al., 1967) such that the same acoustic cue can be perceived as a different phoneme in different contexts (Liberman, Delattre, and Cooper, 1952) and different acoustic cues can be perceived as the same phoneme in different contexts (Liberman et al., 1954); (2) the discovery of perceptual behaviors, like categorical perception, which appeared to be unique to speech-sound processing (Studdert-Kennedy et al., 1970); and (3) evidence from studies of selective adaptation suggesting that "phonetic feature detectors" may be operating in adult human listeners (Eimas and Corbit, 1973; Eimas, Cooper, and Corbit, 1973).

Conceptually, auditory processes were thought to be those which produced simple, straightforward frequency-over-time transforms of the signal, similar to those produced by a sound spectrograph, while phonetic processes somehow converted these widely diverse acoustic patterns into an invariant percept. More recently, however, the typical arguments that led to the conceptualization of a clear dichotomy between auditory and phonetic processes have been questioned. First, more sophisticated spectral analysis of speech has suggested that invariant cues for stop consonants, at least in syllable-initial position, may be found in the dynamic "configurations" of spectral energy over time (Fant, 1973; Stevens, 1975; Stevens and Blumstein, 1976). These cues are abstract and relational, but Stevens (1975) has argued that auditory "property detectors" would account for their differentiation. Second, perceptual behaviors thought to be unique to speech, such as categorical perception, have now been demonstrated for complex nonspeech signals (Cutting and Rosner, 1974; Miller et al., 1976; Pastore, 1976; Pisoni, 1977). And third, the effects of selective adaptation, thought to provide evidence for exclusively "phonetic" feature detectors (Eimas and Corbit, 1973; Eimas et al., 1973) now appear to be more reasonably attributed to auditory, and what may be called abstract auditory, levels of pro-

[a] The author is presently an Assistant Professor in the Department of Speech and Hearing Sciences at the University of Washington, Seattle, WA 98195.

906   P. K. Kuhl and J. D. Miller: VOT perception by the chinchilla   906

cessing (Blumstein, Stevens, and Nigro, 1977; Diehl, 1975; Ganong, 1975; Sawusch, 1976). Evidence from selective adaptation studies in support of a detector mechanism that responds to a phonetic feature regardless of its position in a word (/ba/ adapting /ab/, for example) is lacking (Ades, 1974).

Ideally, the solution to determining the nature and number of the level(s) of processing, and attributing each level to mechanisms that are "auditory" or "phonetic" in nature, requires experimental methods that somehow allow one to intervene at various stages in the processing of sound to observe the restructuring of the information that has occurred at each stage. Lacking strategies for direct intervention, researchers have adopted a variety of experimental techniques, such as selective adaptation, that allow one to make inferences about the various levels involved. We (Kuhl and Miller, 1975; Burdick and Miller, 1975; Miller and Kuhl, 1976; Miller, 1977) have proposed a completely different solution to the problem, one that provides a direct test (probably the only direct test) of the distinction between auditory and phonetic levels of processing. The solution is to use an animal listener, one, who by definition, has no phonetic resources. Our approach is to systematically examine the perceptual phenomena, thought to be unique to the perception of speech by human listeners, in an animal listener, one whose psychoacoustic capabilities are fairly similar to man's but who does not bring to the task any of the phylogenetic predispositions that are peculiarly linguistic in nature. The rationale for this "comparative approach" is to tease out the perceptual effects that are attributable to general perceptual mechanisms from those that are unique to speech-sound processing. Liberman's (1970) forecast of the outcome of these experiments was dictated by current theories. "Unfortunately, nothing is known about the way nonhuman animals perceive speech...however, we should suppose that, lacking the speech-sound decoder, animals would not perceive speech as we do, even at the phonetic level" (p. 320). More specifically, Liberman, Mattingly, and Turvey (1972) forecast, "They should not hear categorically...and they should not hear the /di/-/du/ patterns ...as two-segment syllables that have the first segment in common" (p. 324).

The voicing feature was an ideal target for initiating these investigations. This phonetic distinction is widespread, if not universal, in the languages of the world (Jakobson, Fant, and Halle, 1969; Chomsky and Halle, 1968) and it is realized in different, though consistent, ways across languages (Lisker and Abramson, 1964). Many of its acoustic correlates in initial position have been examined using synthetic speech, including voice-onset time (VOT) (Abramson and Lisker, 1970), the presence of a voiced transition at the onset of voicing (Liberman, Delattre, and Cooper, 1958; Stevens and Klatt, 1974), a pitch change prior to voicing onset (Haggard, Ambler, and Callow, 1970), and the frequency of the first formant at voicing onset (Lisker, 1975a; Summerfield and Haggard, 1977). Some research has been directed at nonspeech stimuli in which the absolute timing cues, frequency cues, and intensity differ-

ences of two signals are systematically manipulated (Divenyi, Sachs, and Grant, 1976).

Lisker and Abramson (1964) demonstrated that VOT measurements of naturally produced plosive consonants in the initial position of words served to distinguish voiced and voiceless tokens spoken by native talkers of 11 different languages. The VOT values were trimodally distributed, that is, talkers tended to produce three kinds of plosives: those in which voicing substantially preceded the release of the plosive burst (prevoiced); those in which voicing closely followed the plosive burst (voiceless unaspirated); and those in which voicing considerably lagged the release of the plosive burst (aspirated). Some languages employ two of the three categories while others employ all three. In Spanish, for example, only two of the three categories (prevoiced and voiceless-unaspirated plosives) occur and aspirated plosives are not produced (Williams, 1977). English also utilizes two of the three categories, but not the same two that Spanish does; voiceless-unaspirated plosives contrast with aspirated plosives. Prevoiced plosives are in free variation with voiceless-unaspirated sounds (Lisker and Abramson, 1964). Cantonese and Danish are similar to English; Kikuyu, French, and German are similar to Spanish. Some languages, such as Thai, utilize all three phonetic categories.

When English-speaking adults are presented with computer-synthesized stimuli ranging in VOT from −100 to +100 ms and instructed to label them as /da/ or /ta/, perception changes abruptly from voiced to voiceless at approximately +35 ms VOT (Abramson and Lisker, 1970). This "boundary" VOT value divides the distributions of VOT values of voiced and voiceless tokens that are naturally produced by English-speaking adults (Lisker and Abramson, 1964). For the stimuli originally synthesized by Abramson and Lisker at Haskins Laboratories, the boundary VOT value shifts with the place of articulation of the voiced–voiceless pair, such that the bilabial, alveolar, and velar boundaries are located between +20 and +45 ms VOT, typically in the above order (Abramson and Lisker, 1970). Again, the boundary locations for alveolar and velar stimuli divide the distributions of VOT values for voiced and voiceless tokens produced naturally by English-speaking adults.

When these synthetic stimuli are arranged in ABX trials for discrimination, performance on stimulus pairs that were labeled differently is near perfect, while performance on stimulus pairs that were labeled similarly is near chance (Abramson and Lisker, 1970). This correlation between the location of the phonetic boundary and a peak in discrimination performance was termed categorical perception, and has been traditionally thought to be a direct result of phonetic categorization and thus considered unique to the processing of speech sounds (Liberman et al., 1967; Studdert-Kennedy et al., 1970). Recent data on nonspeech signals demonstrate that this is not the case.

Cutting and Rosner (1974) demonstrated categorical perception for sawtooth-wave stimuli varying in rise time that were perceived as musical instruments being "plucked" or "bowed." Miller *et al.* (1976) demonstrated categorical perception for noise-buzz sequences designed to simulate the gross spectral characteristics of stop consonant-vowel syllables without being perceived as speech. Pisoni (1977) varied the onset times of two pure tones in a stepwise fashion and demonstrated categorical perception; and finally, Pastore (1976) reported categorical perception for visual stimuli in which a light-emitting diode was gated on and off at various frequencies to produce "flicker" or "fusion." While we are far from understanding the nature of all of the factors critical in obtaining categorical perception, it is clear that memory constraints and stimulus uncertainty, as well as the nature of the psychophysical continuum, play an important role (see Kuhl, 1978 for review).

Infants cannot "label" stimuli but when it was demonstrated that an infant discriminated stimulus pairs drawn from different adult-defined categories and did not discriminate stimulus pairs that were drawn from the same adult-defined categories, and this has now been demonstrated for a voiced-voiceless (Eimas *et al.*, 1971), a liquid (Eimas, 1975), and a place of articulation (Eimas, 1974a) continuum, the infant was thought to be perceiving these stimuli in a "linguistic mode" (Eimas, 1974b; Morse, 1974). In addition, infants may categorically discriminate voicing contrasts that are not phonemic in the infant's linguistic environment. The English voiceless-unaspirated versus voiceless-aspirated pair (/pa/ versus /pʰa/) is discriminated by two-month-old Kikuyu (Streeter, 1976) and Spanish (Lasky, Syrdal-Lasky, and Klein, 1975) infants even though this contrast is not phonemic in either language. On the other hand, the case for discrimination of the Spanish prevoiced /ba/ from the voiceless-unaspirated /pa/ by American infants is not quite as clear. While Spanish infants (Lasky, Syrdal-Lasky, and Klein, 1975) and Kikuyu infants (Streeter, 1976) have been shown to discriminate VOT's of − 30 and 0 ms, there is no evidence to suggest that American infants discriminate this pair (Eimas, 1974b; Eilers *et al.*, 1978). Eimas (1974b) concluded, however, that there was a strong suggestion that American infants could discriminate VOT's of − 70 and +10 ms. We hasten to add, though, that no one has examined perception of these contrasts by infants of different linguistic backgrounds in the same laboratory setting. Considering the nature of the acoustic cue being manipulated in these synthetic patterns there is good reason to attend to the effects that different loudspeakers and signal-to-noise ratios may have. Also, no one has examined this contrast using a pair of naturally produced signals.

Taken as a whole, the cross-language data on infants suggests that young infants demonstrate perceptual sensitivities that optimize the discrimination of speech-sound pairs. These perceptual proclivities have been interpreted to mean that infants have innate knowledge of speech cues. But while the infant's perceptual proclivities are "linguistically relevant," their origins may reflect constraints that are psychoacoustic, that is, more general in nature, rather than specifically linguistic (Kuhl, 1978). The fact that infants discriminate non-

speech sounds categorically (Jusczyk *et al.*, 1977) would support this contention.

In this report we review our initial results on an identification task obtained with synthetic stimuli from an alveolar voiced-voiceless continuum (Kuhl and Miller, 1975) and extend these results to stimuli which differ with respect to place of articulation. The animal chosen for these comparative experiments is the chinchilla (*Chinchilla laniger*), a rodent commonly used in auditory behavioral and physiologic experiments, whose audibility curve is nearly identical to that of man (Miller, 1970), whose detection thresholds for complex sounds are similar to man's (Luz, 1969), but whose ability to resolve differences in frequency is poorer than that of man (Miller, 1970). The results obtained with alveolar stimuli are reported in experiment I; results obtained with labial and velar stimuli are reported in experiments II and III, respectively. Experiment IV is a report of results obtained when the stimuli from all three continua were used.

I. EXPERIMENT I

A. Method

1. Stimuli

The speech sounds were synthesized at the Haskins Laboratories on the parallel-resonance synthesizer in accordance with the parameter files developed by Abramson and Lisker (1970). Spectrograms of the resulting stimuli are shown in Fig. 1 and the courses of the center frequencies of the three formants during the first 100 ms of the synthetic syllables are shown in Fig. 2. Each synthetic syllable was 435 ms in duration and during voiced excitation of the resonators the fundamental frequency was 114 Hz until the last 100 ms when the fundamental fell to 70 Hz at the rate of 44 Hz/s. The rules for synthesis were as follows: For a specified VOT, the upper two formants were excited with thermal noise for the duration of the interval specified by the

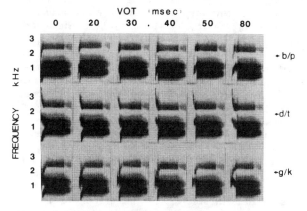

FIG. 1. Spectrograms of synthetic sounds used in these experiments. The voice-onset times (VOT's) are shown across the top of the figure (note that VOT's of 10, 60, and 70 ms are omitted). Each row represents a different place of articulation. These are the stimuli developed by Abramson and Lisker (1970).

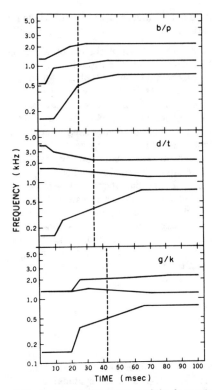

FIG. 2. Center frequencies of the formants as a function of time for the b/p-, d/t-, and g/k-stimuli. Only the first 100 ms of the 453-ms stimuli are shown. During the period of the voice-onset time (VOT), the upper formants are excited by noise while the first formant is off. At the onset of voicing all three formants are excited by time-locked periodic pulses (see text for additional detail). The dashed vertical lines are placed at the average values (humans and chinchillas) of the boundaries between the voiceless-unaspirated and voiceless-aspirated plosive consonants.

VOT value; at the end of this interval, these two formants were excited with periodic pulses. The first formant was effectively "off" throughout the VOT interval. In addition, however, the first formant was effectively "off" during the first 5 ms for b/p and d/t stimuli, and the first 20 ms of g/k stimuli, regardless of the specified VOT (see spectrograms in Fig. 1). This "F_1-off" technique at VOT's near zero stimulates the transient and friction sounds that occur at and just after the moment of stop release, while synthesis techniques associated with the longer VOT's are designed to simulate aspiration sounds (Fant, 1973; Klatt, 1975). In any case, it is important for the reader to understand that the lines shown in Fig. 2 represent the values programmed for the formants. The earliest portions of the curves for the first formant are never realized because they are not excited. As the VOT is increased, the center frequency of the first formant at the onset of "voicing" rises until the steady-state values that we indicated in Figs. 1 and 2 are achieved.

A single token of each stimulus, VOT's from 0 to +80 ms in 10-ms steps, was recorded on a full-track tape recorder (Nagra, type 4.2) and then re-recorded onto a

disk pack (Control Data, model 846-2-16) of the Random-Access Programmable Recorder of Complex Sounds (RAP), a self-contained digital recorder which provides random access to all stimuli via a number of peripheral controls (Spenner et al., 1974). The speech sounds were presented at 60 dB SPL against a continuously presented speech-shaped masking noise of 12 dB SPL.

2. Subjects

Four chinchillas (*Chinchilla laniger*), each about two years of age, were the animal subjects. Each animal was housed individually in the animal colony at Central Institute for the Deaf (CID) and had continuous access to food, but water was available only during test sessions.

Two of the four animals had been previously trained to categorize naturally produced alveolar tokens as either voiced (/d/) or voiceless (/t/) syllables (Kuhl and Miller, 1975). The other two animals had never been trained in behavioral experiments. Four English-speaking adults, the authors and two CID research assistants, also served as subjects.

3. Apparatus

The test booth and behavioral apparatus have been described elsewhere (Miller, 1970; Burdick and Miller, 1973, 1975). Briefly, a double-grille cage is suspended below a loudspeaker (Altec, 605A) in a sound-treated booth. The cage is divided by a midline barrier and has a door buzzer mounted at one end. A metal drinking tube is mounted at one end such that the animal can just reach it with his tongue. The metal drinking tube is connected by plastic tubing through a solenoid-operated valve to a bottle of distilled water. The flow of water is regulated by the number of licks required to open the solenoid-operated valve. Lights are mounted at each end of the midline barrier and directly over the drinking tube.

Presentation of a speech sound was initiated by the experimenter and controlled by punched paper tape and a high-speed paper-tape reader. The punched tape was prepared according to the randomization specifications described below. Trials were timed and contingencies delivered using standard relays, timers, and counters. The experimenter monitored the animal by closed-circuit television.

4. Training and testing procedures

a. Maintaining a background activity. Drinking at the water tube was the background activity maintained throughout the experiment. Several days before the experiment began each animal's water intake was restricted to a small amount given once daily. After the animal's body weight had dropped approximately 10%, each animal was brought to the experimental chamber once daily and trained to lick the water tube mounted on the cage for his daily ration of water (approximately 6 ml). Each animal was weighed before and after each session and we attempted to maintain their body weights at approximately 90% of their predeprivation levels. Discrimination training began when an animal drank steadily for 10–15 min each day.

b. Discrimination training. The instrumental avoidance technique used to train the animals has been described (Burdick and Miller, 1975). Trials were presented at approximately 10–15 s intervals while the animal was drinking. Each trial consisted of two repetitions of the same synthetic syllable separated by a 500-ms silent interval. On *positive* trials, the animal had to flee the drinking tube and cross the midline barrier to avoid a mild shock and the sounding of the buzzer. The *trial interval* was 2.5 s in duration; that is, the animal had 2.5 s (1 s after the second syllable) to cross the midline barrier to avoid shock. If he crossed within the 2.5-s trial interval, the barrier lights were briefly (500 ms) lit and the animal successfully avoided shock. If he failed to cross within the 2.5-s trial interval, shock and the buzzer were presented until the animal crossed the barrier. On *negative trials*, the animal could remain at the drinking tube. If the animal successfully inhibited the crossing response throughout the 2.5-s trial interval, he was rewarded with "free" water; that is, the solenoid-operated valve was opened and the water poured freely for 1 s. During the "free" water period, the lights above the drinking tube were lit. Buzzer and shock were never presented on negative trials.

For two of the animals /t/ (+80 ms VOT) was the positive stimulus and /d/ (0 ms VOT) was the negative stimulus; for the other two animals these roles were reversed. During discrimination training only these two syllables (0 ms VOT and +80 ms VOT) were presented. One of the animals for whom /t/ was the positive stimulus and one of the animals for whom /d/ was the positive stimulus had been trained on naturally produced /t/- and /d/- CV syllables (Kuhl and Miller, 1975). At the end of that experiment, these two animals had learned to classify correctly the voiced and voiceless CV syllables produced by eight different talkers in six different vowel contexts. The other two animals were novices and had never participated in behavioral experiments.

In the first stage of discrimination training, only negative trials were presented until the animal continued to drink throughout the trial interval and drank the "free" water. Positive trials were then gradually introduced, first on 25% of the trials, then 40% of the trials, and finally on 50% of the trials. Randomization of positive and negative trials was accomplished by computer-punched paper tapes with the stipulation that no more than four positive or negative trials occurred consecutively.

Crossing the midline barrier during the 2.5-s trial interval was a correct response (hit) on positive trials and an error (false alarm) on negative trials. Failure to cross the midline barrier during the 2.5-s trial interval was an error (miss) on positive trials and a correct response (correct rejection) on negative trials. The percent-correct score for each session was the number of hits and correct rejections divided by the total number of trials, and multiplied by 100.

There were 28 trials in each daily session. Two of these trials were "training trials" and were not scored. They were designed to counteract the animal's tendency to make increasingly longer latency responses on positive trials and to make false alarms after misses. For these two trials, one of which was positive and one of which was negative, the trial interval was shortened from 2.5 to 2.0 s, so that shock (on the positive-training trial) and "free" water (on the negative-training trial) were presented 0.5 s earlier. The positive training trial occurred on the first positive trial after one with a latency greater than 2.0 s; the negative training trial followed the positive training trial, or followed a miss, whichever occurred first.

When performance for each animal remained at or above 96% correct for four consecutive days, generalization testing commenced.

c. Generalization testing. During generalization sessions, the "endpoint" stimuli, 0 and +80 ms VOT, were randomly presented on half of the trials, and the stimuli between these endpoints, +10 to +70 ms VOT in 10-ms steps, were randomly presented on the other half of the trials. During the endpoint trials, all the contingencies previously described were in effect. That is, shock was presented when an animal failed to cross on a positive trial and free water occurred when an animal correctly refrained from crossing on a negative trial. But when generalization stimuli were presented, shock was never presented and all feedback was arranged to tell the animal he was always "correct," no matter what he did. If he crossed, the barrier lights were lit; if he refrained from crossing, the free water occurred.

The generalization tests were run in ten consecutive days. Each day 28 trials were presented, 14 "endpoint" trials (two of which were training trials) and 14 generalization trials (two for each generalization stimulus). Presentation was random with the stipulation that no more than four endpoint trials or four generalization trials could occur in consecutive order. A total of ten observations for each generalization stimulus were obtained for each animal.

d. Testing human subjects. Each of the four human subjects was tested once daily for ten consecutive days. They sat in the same sound-treated booth such that their heads were in the approximate position that the animal's head was in while drinking. The trial structure was exactly the same for adult and animal subjects since the same punched paper tapes were used for both groups. That is, 28 trials were given daily, 14 of which were endpoint trials and 14 of which were the stimuli between the endpoints (two observations of each). Listeners were instructed to label the stimuli as /da/ or /ta/ and they wrote down their responses.

B. Results

1. Location of the phonetic boundaries

The mean percent of the observations labeled /da/ for both human and chinchilla subjects for each stimulus is plotted in Fig. 3. The fitted curves were obtained by drawing a straight line on probability paper which provided the best visual fit to the obtained data points. The 50% points (phonetic boundaries) of those fitted curves are 35.2 ms VOT for English-speaking adults and 33.3

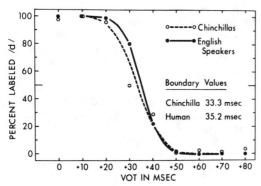

FIG. 3. Mean percentage of /d/ responses by chinchilla and human subjects to synthetic speech sounds constructed to simulate a continuum ranging from /da/ to /ta/. The animals were trained on the two "endpoint" stimuli (0 and +80 ms VOT). and then tested with stimuli ranging from +10 to +70 ms in a generalization paradigm (feedback always arranged to indicate a correct response).

ms VOT for chinchillas. The location of the boundary for English-speaking subjects is in good agreement with that reported by Abramson and Lisker (1970).

When the data for individual subjects are examined, the boundary values range from 29.9 ms VOT to 42.0 ms VOT for humans and from 26.7 ms VOT to 36.0 ms VOT for chinchilla subjects, a range of 12.1 ms for humans and 9.3 ms for chinchillas.

Exposure to natural speech had no effect on the location of the boundary. The two animals trained in the natural-speech experiment had a mean boundary value of 31.4 ms VOT while the two animals who had no previous training had a mean boundary value of 32.8 ms VOT.

2. Boundary width

To examine the differences in the slopes of the functions for human and animal subjects, we matched each subject's fitted curve at the 50% point. These curves are shown in Fig. 4. The difference in ms between the 75% point and the 25% point was calculated for each subject; the mean boundary width was 9.0 ms for chinchillas and 5.1 ms for humans. Prior training on natural speech had no effect on the width of the boundary region.

II. EXPERIMENT II

A. Method

1. Stimuli

The stimuli were synthesized at Haskins Laboratories to simulate labial plosives and were recorded under the exact same conditions as previously described. The stimuli ranged from 0 ms VOT to +80 ms VOT, in 10-ms steps.

2. Subjects

Two of the four chinchillas used in experiment I served as subjects, one for whom the voiced stimulus had been positive and one for whom the voiceless stimulus had been positive; one had originally been trained

on natural speech while the other had been trained only on the synthetic tokens. The same four English-speaking adults were tested.

3. Apparatus

The apparatus was identical to that described in experiment I.

4. Procedure

a. Discrimination training. Immediately after the final session of experiment I, the animal began training sessions on the "endpoint" stimuli of the labial continuum, 0 ms VOT and +80 ms VOT, which were presented randomly with 0.50 probability from the start.

When performance for each animal remained at or above 96% correct for four consecutive days, generalization testing began.

b. Generalization testing. The generalization sessions were run exactly as before, the labial "endpoint" stimuli, 0 ms VOT and +80 ms VOT, were randomly presented on half of the trials, and the stimuli between these endpoints, +10 to +70 ms VOT in 10-ms steps, were randomly presented on the other half of the trials. As before, all the contingencies previously described were in effect during the endpoint trials, but during generalization trials all feedback was arranged to tell the animal he was always correct, no matter what he did.

Generalization tests were run in ten consecutive days, each day 28 trials (14 endpoint trials, two of which were training trials, and 14 generalization trials) were run. A total of ten observations of each generalization stimulus was obtained for each animal.

B. Results

1. Transfer to stimuli with a labial place of articulation

The transfer from the alveolar stimuli to the labial "endpoints" appeared to be relatively easy. Both animals performed nearly as accurately on the first exposure to the labial stimuli as they had on the alveolar stimuli, suggesting that they were responding to a set

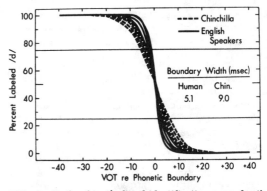

FIG. 4. Each subject's fitted identification curve for the /da/-/ta/ continuum is matched at the 50% point and the difference in ms between the 75% point and the 25% point (boundary width) is calculated. The slopes of the functions for chinchilla subjects are slightly less steep than those of the human subjects.

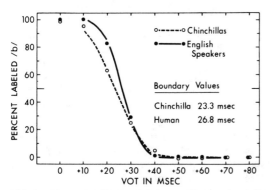

FIG. 5. Mean percentage of /b/ responses by chinchilla and human subjects to synthetic speech sounds constructed to simulate a continuum ranging from /ba/ to /pa/. The animals were trained on the two "endpoint" stimuli (0 and +80 ms VOT), and then tested with stimuli ranging from +10 to +70 ms in a generalization paradigm (feedback always arranged to indicate a correct response).

of abstract acoustic cues which characterize both sets of stimuli.

2. Location of the phonetic boundaries

The mean percent of the observations labeled /ba/ for each stimulus is plotted in Fig. 5 for both groups of subjects. The fitted curves were obtained by drawing a straight line on probability paper which provided the best visual fit to the obtained data points. The 50% points (phonetic boundaries) of those fitted curves are 26.8 ms VOT for English-speaking adults and 23.3 for chinchillas. This location of the boundary for English-speaking subjects is in good agreement with that reported by Abramson and Lisker (1970).

The boundary values for individual subjects ranged from 21.3 ms VOT to 29.5 ms VOT for human subjects and were 21.3 ms VOT and 24.5 ms VOT for the two chinchilla subjects.

3. Boundary width

Each subject's fitted curve was matched at the 50% point and these curves are displayed in Fig. 6. The difference in ms between the 75% point and the 25% point was calculated for each subject; the mean boundary width was 9.4 ms for chinchillas and 6.2 ms for humans.

III. EXPERIMENT III

A. Method

1. Stimuli

The stimuli were synthesized at Haskins Laboratories to simulate velar plosive consonants and were recorded under the exact same conditions described in experiment I. The stimuli ranged from 0 ms VOT to +80 ms VOT, in 10-ms steps.

2. Subjects

The subjects described in experiment II were run in experiment III.

3. Apparatus

The apparatus was identical to that described in experiment I.

4. Procedure

a. *Discrimination training*. Immediately after the final session of experiment II, the animal began training sessions on the "endpoint" stimuli of the velar continuum, 0 ms VOT and +80 ms VOT, which were presented randomly with 0.50 probability.

When performance for each animal remained at or above 96% correct for four consecutive days, generalization testing began.

b. *Generalization testing*. The generalization sessions were run exactly as before; the velar "endpoint" stimuli, 0 ms VOT and +80 ms VOT were randomly presented on half of the trials, and the stimuli between these endpoints, +10 to +70 ms VOT in 10-ms steps, were randomly presented on the other half of the trials. As before, all the contingencies previously defined were in effect during the endpoint trials but during generalization trials, all feedback was arranged to tell the animal he was always correct, no matter what he did.

Generalization tests were run in ten consecutive days; each day 28 trials (14 endpoint trials, two of which were training trials, and 14 generalization trials) were run. A total of ten observations for each generalization stimulus was obtained for each animal.

B. Results

1. Transfer to stimuli with a velar place of articulation

As before, the transfer from one place of articulation (labial) to another (velar) appeared to be relatively easy. Both animals performed nearly as accurately on the first exposure to the velar endpoint stimuli as they had on the labial stimuli, again suggesting that they were responding to an acoustic cue for voicing that was not specific to any one place of articulation.

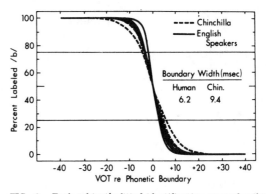

FIG. 6. Each subject's fitted identification curve for the /ba/–/pa/ continuum is matched at the 50% point and the difference in ms between the 75% point and the 25% point (boundary width) is calculated. The slopes of the functions for chinchilla subjects are slightly less steep than those of the human subjects.

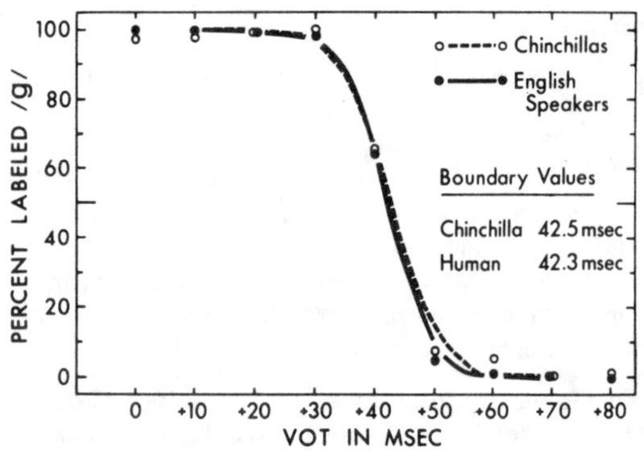

FIG. 7. Mean percentage of /g/ responses by chinchilla and human subjects to synthetic speech sounds constructed to simulate a continuum ranging from /ga/ to /ka/. The animals were trained on the two "endpoint" stimuli (0 and +80 ms VOT), and then tested with stimuli ranging from +10 to +70 ms in a generalization paradigm (feedback always arranged to indicate a correct response).

2. Location of the phonetic boundaries

The mean percent of the observations labeled /ga/ for both groups of subjects for each stimulus is plotted in Fig. 7. The fitted curves were obtained by drawing a straight line on probability paper which provided the best visual fit to the obtained data points. The 50% points (phonetic boundaries) of those fitted curves are 42.3 ms VOT for English-speaking adults and 42.5 ms VOT for chinchillas. The location of the boundary for human subjects is in good agreement with that reported by Abramson and Lisker (1970).

The boundary values for individual subjects ranged from 37.2 ms VOT to 47.5 ms VOT for humans and were 41.0 ms VOT and 43.7 ms VOT for the two animal subjects.

3. Boundary width

Each subject's fitted curve was matched at the 50% point and these curves are displayed in Fig. 8. The difference in ms between the 75% point and the 25% point was calculated for each subject; the mean boundary width was 6.9 ms for chinchillas and 4.2 ms for humans.

IV. EXPERIMENT IV

A. Method

1. Stimuli

The labial, alveolar, and velar stimuli previously described were used.

2. Subjects

A single animal, the one for whom voiced stimuli were positive, was run.

3. Apparatus

The apparatus was identical to that described in previous experiments.

4. Procedure

a. Discrimination training. Immediately after the final session of experiment III the animal began training on the endpoint stimuli (0 ms VOT and +80 ms VOT) of all three continua which were randomly presented. When performance reached criterion ($\geq$ 96% correct for four consecutive days) generalization tests began.

b. Generalization testing. The generalization sessions were run exactly as before with the exception that six endpoint stimuli (0 ms VOT and +80 ms VOT from the labial, alveolar, and velar continua) were randomly presented on half of the trials and the 21 stimuli between the endpoints (+10 ms VOT to +70 ms VOT from the labial, alveolar, and velar continua) were randomly presented on the other half of the trials. In other words, the animal was reporting whether the stimulus was voiced or voiceless regardless of the place of articulation of the stimulus. All of the previously described contingencies were in effect during the endpoint trials but during generalization trials feedback was arranged to tell the animal he was always correct, no matter what he did.

Generalization tests were run in 30 consecutive days; as before, 28 trials were given each day (14 endpoint trials and 14 generalization trials). A total of ten observations for each generalization stimulus was obtained.

B. Results

1. Location of the phonetic boundaries

The animal's fitted curves that were obtained when place of articulation was held constant (experiments I, II, and III) are contrasted with those obtained when place of articulation was randomly varied (experiment IV) in Fig. 9. Most importantly, the relative locations of the three boundaries did not change when place of articulation was varied randomly. The phonetic boundaries obtained when place of articulation was held constant were 21.3 ms VOT, 26.7 ms VOT, and 41.0 ms VOT for the labial, alveolar, and velar stimuli, respectively. The boundaries obtained when place of articulation was ran-

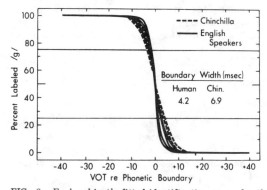

FIG. 8. Each subject's fitted identification curve for the /ga/–/ka/ continuum is matched at the 50% point and the difference in ms between the 75% point and the 25% point (boundary width) is calculated. The slopes of the functions for chinchilla subjects are slightly less steep than those of the human subjects.

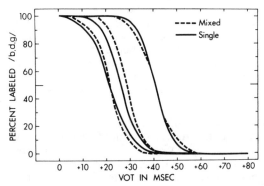

FIG. 9. The fitted curves obtained for one chinchilla subject are compared under two experimental conditions: (1) when the place of articulation of the stimuli is held constant within testing sessions (experiments I, II, and III); and (2) when the place of articulation of the stimuli is randomly varied within testing sessions (experiment IV).

domized were almost identical in the labial and velar case and differed by 2 ms VOT in the alveolar case.

2. Boundary width

The boundary widths of the fitted curves for the data obtained when place of articulation was held constant (experiments I, II, and III) are very similar to those obtained when place of articulation was randomly varied (experiment IV). The random presentation resulted in an identical boundary width for the alveolar stimuli, a slightly narrower boundary width (steeper function) for the labial stimuli, and a slightly wider boundary width for the velar stimuli.

V. STATISTICAL ANALYSES

A. Phonetic boundary

The phonetic boundary values for all subjects in all conditions were subjected to a two-factor (species x place of articulation) Analysis of Variance (Lindquist, 1953). While the main effect of species was not significant ($F = 0.376$), the main effect of place of articulation was highly significant ($F = 47.3$; $p < 0.001$). There were no significant interactions.

B. Boundary width

The boundary widths for all subjects in all conditions were subjected to a two-factor (species x places of articulation) Analysis of Variance (Lindquist, 1953). Both the main effect of species ($F = 10.65$; $p < 0.05$) and of places of articulation ($F = 8.59$; $p < 0.05$) were significant. Again, no significant interactions were found. For both groups of subjects, the steepest slopes for the identification functions were obtained with the velar stimuli and the shallowest slopes were found with the labial stimuli.

A composite of the identification functions is displayed in Fig. 10. The data reflect the results of the statistical analyses; the boundary values appear to be quite similar for the two species while the slopes of the func-

tions are slightly but consistently less steep for the animal listeners.

VI. DISCUSSION

A. Comparison of the "labeling" functions for human and nonhuman listeners

The identification functions for the animal listeners are remarkably similar to those for the English-speaking adults, with the exception that the slopes are slightly less steep. This result is similar to that obtained by Zlatin and Koenigsknecht (1975) in that the labeling functions they obtained for synthetic stimuli with two year olds have significantly larger boundary widths than those obtained with six year olds and adult subjects. One could argue that the increased steepness in the functions for adults reflects perceptual "tuning" with repeated exposure to the language. Streeter and Landauer (1975) have demonstrated that the discrimination of synthetic voiceless-unaspirated from voiceless-aspirated syllables by children improves with exposure to English. On the other hand, young children and animals tend to be less than perfect experimental subjects and their responses are sometimes governed by things other than the nature of the stimulus. For example, while the animals' behaviors lead us to predict that they are capable of identifying 0 ms VOT and +80 ms VOT with 100% accuracy, they made errors on 1.5% of the endpoint trials; adult listeners made no errors. We believe, then, that at least part of this difference in slope is attributable to our less than perfect control over their behavior.

The fact that good agreement between the identification functions for humans and animals was obtained for all three stimulus sets, and that the boundary values shift with the place of articulation similarily for the two groups of subjects, refutes the notion that the animals simply divided the continuum "in the middle." For all three sets of stimuli the endpoints remained the same, 0 ms VOT and +80 ms VOT, but the boundaries for the animal subjects shifted from a mean of 23.3 ms VOT to a mean of 42.5 ms VOT.

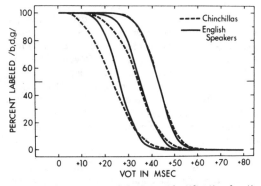

FIG. 10. A composite of the mean identification functions for chinchilla and human subjects that were obtained with bilabial, alveolar, and velar synthetic stimuli. No significant differences between species on the absolute values of the phonetic boundaries were obtained, but chinchillas produced identification functions that were slightly, but significantly, less steep.

Why these boundary locations change with the place of articulation is not entirely clear but a variety of experiments with English-speaking listeners point to acoustical—auditory factors. First, the boundary values obtained in the recent examples of categorical perception of nonspeech continua, in which the temporal onsets of a noise and a buzz (Miller *et al.*, 1976) or of two pure tones (Pisoni, 1977) are manipulated, are in general agreement with the locations of boundaries between voiced and voiceless syllables, strongly suggesting that basic psychoacoustic constraints, such as the perception of temporal order (Hirsh, 1959), play a role in the placement of a boundary in the region of 20–50 ms. But within this range a variety of acoustic details are capable of producing changes in the exact location of the boundary. For example, it has been shown that shifts in the d/t boundary from a VOT near 20 ms to one near 50 ms can be achieved by altering the duration of the first formant transition (Stevens and Klatt, 1974; Lisker *et al.*, 1975). That the critical factor in these produced shifts are due to the absolute frequency of F_1 at voicing onset and not the F_1-transition detector hypothesized by Stevens and Klatt (1974) is suggested by a variety of experiments. Lisker (1975a) demonstrated that the presence of a voiced F_1 transition is neither necessary nor sufficient to induce the perception of a voiced stop and that the role attributed to F_1 is largely due to its frequency at voicing onset. Data gathered by Summerfield and Haggard (1977) support and further refine the notion by demonstrating a complementary relation between VOT and the F_1-onset frequency; the lower the effective onset frequency of the first formant, the greater the VOT required for the perception of a voiceless-aspirated plosive. As the authors point out, this relationship also holds in speech production; longer VOT's are generally obtained in /i/-vowel contexts than in /a/-vowel contexts (Klatt, 1975).

If, however, the time courses of the first formants of b/p, d/t, and g/k continua are held constant, and a single vowel context (/a/) is used, there is no consistent increase in the crossover point as the place of articulation moves from front to back; in fact, the crossover points are nearly identical (Lisker, 1975b).

Taking all of these things into account for the synthetic stimuli we have used, the fact that the b/p boundary is located at a smaller VOT than the d/t and g/k boundaries is probably related to the rapid rise programmed for the first formant of the labial stimuli in relation to that of the alveolar and velar stimuli (see Figs. 1 and 2), such that the frequency of F_1 for a given VOT value in the short lag region is always higher for the labial stimuli than for the alveolar or velar stimuli. On the other hand, the difference in our data between the d/t and g/k boundaries cannot be so explained since their first formants are identical in the region of interest. Lisker's (1975a) data demonstrate that differences in the synthesis of the upper formants can alter the locations of these boundaries. The exact way in which they do so is suggested by experiments on nonspeech stimuli. For example, Divenyi and Danner (1975) demonstrated that for nonspeech stimuli the degree of spectral overlap between a noise and a following periodic signal, as well

as the intensity differences between the two, modify the separation interval between the two signals which is required to produce the maximum sensitivity to a change. In other words, the relative salience or prominence of the aspiration noise will depend upon how it relates, spectrally and intensively, to its acoustic context, and these factors will influence the location of the perceptual boundary.

Unfortunately, the complete story of how the acoustic details interact to influence the voiced—voiceless boundary for syllable-initial English plosives is not yet known even for the case of adult, English-speaking listeners. In the case of the chinchilla, even less is known, but it seems sensible to us that factors such as pitch, formant locations, relative levels and durations of friction-like sounds, relative levels and duration of aspiration-like sounds, and so on would operate in a qualitatively similar way for chinchilla as for man.

B. Implications for theories of speech perception and the evolution of a speech-sound repertoire

Taken as a whole, these data suggest that a mammal with the appropriate auditory capabilities and no linguistic experience is predisposed to hear an abrupt qualitative change in the short voicing-lag region of the VOT continuum. These data can be thought of as "labeling" data since they were obtained under conditions that are typical for identification tasks. But in the absence of discrimination data they do not provide a clear case of "categorical perception" by the criteria established by Studdert-Kennedy *et al.* (1970). We expect, however, that the animal's discrimination data will show the peaks in performance near the boundary that are characteristic of categorical perception and, in fact, preliminary data (Kuhl, 1976) suggest that this is the case.

Taken together, the labeling and discrimination data for the chinchilla suggest that certain acoustic continua produce what we might call "natural" categories where small acoustic changes are not detected until a kind of "threshold" occurs producing an abrupt qualitative change in the percept. It would have made sense in the evolutionary scheme of things to select sounds such that they fell on opposite sides of these natural boundaries.

The general notion that speech sounds form "natural categories" is supported by other data demonstrating an animal's ability to categorize naturally produced tokens in which both the critical cues, and many irrelevant aspects of the signals, are allowed to vary. Research in our laboratory has shown that chinchillas can learn to categorize correctly (1) the sustained vowels /a/ and /i/ produced by 24 different talkers, both male and female (Burdick and Miller, 1975), (2) CV syllables beginning with /t/ versus /d/ produced in six different vowel contexts by eight different talkers (Kuhl and Miller, 1975), and (3) CV syllables beginning with /b/ versus /d/ in eight different vowel contexts produced by 12 different talkers (Miller and Kuhl, 1976). The success of a rodent in these tasks is remarkable considering our difficulties (and failures) in attempting to specify invariant acoustic cues for these categories.

The suggestion provided by these experiments is that

some speech-sound categories can be described by their configurational acoustic properties, even though we have yet to specify these cues precisely (Miller, 1977). Mammalian hearing appears to operate on the same general properties with primary differences in the range of frequencies detected and the degree of resolution within that range (Bekesy, 1960). These configurational properties may be generally obvious to the mammalian ear even though our analog to peripheral analysis (sound spectrograph) does not reveal them.

While these arguments emphasize the psychoacoustic considerations in the selection of candidates for a speech-sound repertoire, they are not meant to underplay the articulatory considerations that formed a complementary selective pressure on the process. Stevens (1972) has recently demonstrated that certain articulatory postures produce acoustic characteristics that are relatively insensitive to articulatory perturbations around that posture. He expresses the notion that "...all phonetic features occurring in language have their roots in acoustic attributes with these characteristics. Language seeks out these regions, as it were, and from them assembles an inventory of phonetic elements that are used to form the code for communication by language" (Stevens, 1972, p. 64). We have emphasized another point that Stevens makes, namely, that the selection of preferred regions of articulation must have been guided not only by the relative stability of acoustic dimensions (such as F_1 and F_2) but by the relative stability of their *psychoacoustic* attributes, that is, the stability of the signal after processing by the auditory mechanism. We suggest that speech sounds were selected to exploit the perceptual discontinuities that are a natural result of the functions of the mammalian auditory system.

If this view is correct, one would expect to find that all universal phonetic contrasts are based on these natural psychophysical boundaries and that animals whose psychoacoustic capabilities are grossly similar to those of humans will give evidence of these boundaries. In other words, we would expect to find another psychophysical boundary in the prevoicing region of the VOT continuum which accounts for the phonemic distinction upheld by Spanish and Thai listeners.

C. Interpretations of the human infant's perceptual behavior

These notions also lead one to predict that human infants, regardless of the linguistic environment in which they are raised and prior to any extensive linguistic exposure, would discriminate these universals. If so, their accomplishments, though "linguistically relevant," might simply reflect psychoacoustic predispositions that are favorable to speech-sound perception (Kuhl, 1978).

If infants come into the world with similar perceptual proclivities how, then, can we account for the differences in perception among adult listeners of different languages? While it is clear that linguistic experience alters the identification and discrimination functions characteristic of categorical perception, it is not clear

exactly what this means. For example, Spanish-speaking adults demonstrate enhanced sensitivity in the prevoiced region of the VOT continuum, corresponding to the location of their perceived phonetic boundary (Williams, 1977); but English-speaking adults do not demonstrate enhanced discrimination in this region (Abramson and Lisker, 1970). And Japanese adults, tested in the traditional ABX or oddity discrimination task, do not show an increase in sensitivity for pairs of stimuli which straddle the English /r-l/ phonetic boundary (Miyawaki *et al.*, 1975). Whether these effects reflect a true difference in the listener's sensory capabilities or whether they reflect a change in a listener's ability to code and remember stimuli is unknown, since the psychophysical procedures typically used (ABX or oddity discrimination) require that the listener code and remember the stimuli (Pisoni, 1973; Pisoni and Lazarus, 1974). Our biases lead us to predict that the latter is true. That is, we would predict that Japanese adults tested with methods that put fewer constraints on memory, such as repeating-standard technique (Sinnott *et al.*, 1976), would demonstrate increased sensitivity at the phonetic boundary; one could then systematically examine how increases in memory load and/or stimulus uncertainty modify that performance.

D. Exploring the nature of complex auditory perception using an "animal model"

Should further experiments demonstrate the generality of the findings we have discussed, the advantages of an "animal model" to explore the psychoacoustic nature of speech-sound processing are obvious. Techniques that are not possible for use with human subjects, such as those requiring physiologic intervention, are appropriate with animal subjects and may eventually reveal the neurologic correlates of auditory property detectors responsible for speech-sound differentiations. More immediately, the effects of a hearing loss, induced by noise exposure or ototoxic drugs, on the perception of speech-sound categories may be assessed. The evaluation of cochlear implants on complex auditory perception or the effects of early auditory experience on complex auditory perception, are made possible with animal subjects.

It is doubtful that a rodent such as the chinchilla, or a primate for that matter, will ever "decode" on-going speech. He supposedly has no syntactic or semantic talents to rely on and what we know of the decoding process suggests that the human listener uses his syntactic and semantic resources in the process (Miller, Heise, and Lichten, 1951; Pickett and Pollack, 1963; Pollack and Pickett, 1963), and suggests, in fact, that the human listener is not capable of a strict phoneme-by-phoneme analysis of running discourse. Shockey and Reddy (1974) have shown that phonetically trained listeners identify only 70% of the phonetic segments in sentence-length strings when they are listening to a foreign language. We do not know if a chinchilla would do as well, but these findings make us curious about the limits of an animal's abilities and the nature of the "breakdown" when it occurs; toward this goal, we intend to systematically explore an animal's perception of speech using stimulus sets that are thought to require progressively more "phonetic" processing.

ACKNOWLEDGMENTS

This research was supported by NIH grant NS 03856 to Central Institute for the Deaf and NIH grant RR 00396 to the Biomedical Computer Laboratory of Washington University, St. Louis, Missouri. The authors gratefully acknowledge the cooperation of the Haskins Laboratories (NIH contract NIH-71-2420) in providing the computer-synthesized stimuli. The authors also wish to thank A. M. Engebretson and W. J. Kelly for programming assistance.

Abramson, A., and Lisker, L. (1970). "Discrimination along the voicing continuum: Cross-language tests," in *Proceedings of the* 6th *International Congress of Phonetic Science, Prague*, 1967 (Academic, Prague), pp. 569–573.

Ades, A. E. (1974). "How phonetic is selective adaptation? Experiments on syllable position and vowel environment," Percept. Psychophys. 16, 61–67.

Békésy, G. von (1960). *Experiments in Hearing* (McGraw-Hill, New York).

Blumstein, S. E., Stevens, K. N., and Nigro, G. N. (1977). "Property detectors for bursts and transitions in speech perception," J. Acoust. Soc. Am. 61, 1301–1313.

Burdick, C. K., and Miller, J. D. (1973). "New procedure for training chinchillas for psychoacoustic experiments," J. Acoust. Soc. Am. 54, 789–792.

Burdick, C. K., and Miller, J. D. (1975). "Speech perception by the chinchilla: discrimination of sustained /a/ and /i/," J. Acoust. Soc. Am. 58, 415–427.

Chomsky, N., and Halle, M. (1968). *The Sound Pattern of English* (Harper and Row, New York).

Cutting, J. E., and Rosner, B. S. (1974). "Categories and boundaries in speech and music," Percept. Psychophys. 16, 564–570.

Diehl, R. L. (1975). "The effect of selective adaptation on the identification of speech sounds," Percept. Psychophys. 17, 48–52.

Divenyi, P. L., and Danner, W. F. (1975). "Nonmonotonic discrimination functions for time intervals: Implications for VOT perception," J. Acoust. Soc. Am. 58, S36(A).

Divenyi, P. L., Sachs, R. M., and Grant, K. W. (1976). "Stimulus correlates in the perception of voice onset time (VOT): I. Discrimination of the time interval between tone bursts of different intensities and frequencies," J. Acoust. Soc. Am. 60, S91(A).

Eilers, R. E., Wilson, W. R., and Moore, J. M. (1978). "Speech discrimination in the language-innocent and the language-wise: A study in the perception of voice onset time," J. Child Lang. (in press).

Eimas, P. D. (1974a). "Auditory and linguistic processing of cues for place of articulation by infants," Percept. Psychophys. 16, 513–521.

Eimas, P. D. (1974b). "Linguistic processing of speech by young infants," in *Language Perspectives—Acquisition Retardation, and Intervention*, edited by R. L. Schiefelbusch and L. L. Lloyd (University Park, Baltimore), pp. 55–74.

Eimas, P. D. (1975). "Auditory and phonetic coding of the cues for speech: discrimination of the /r-l/ distinction by young infants," Percept. Psychophys. 18, 341–347.

Eimas, P. D., Cooper, W. E., and Corbit, J. D. (1973). "Some properties of linguistic feature detectors," Percept. Psychophys. 13, 247–252.

Eimas, P. D., and Corbit, J. D. (1973). "Selective adaptation of linguistic feature detectors," Cog. Psychol. 4, 99–109.

Eimas, P. D., Siqueland, E. R. Jusczyk, P., and Vigorito, J. (1971). "Speech perception in infants," *Science* 171, 303–306.

Fant, G. (1973). *Speech Sounds and Features* (MIT, Cambridge, MA).

Ganong, W. F. (1975). "An experiment on 'phonetic adaptation,'" RLE Progress Report 116, 206–210.

Haggard, M., Ambler, S., and Callow, M. (1970). "Pitch as a voicing cue," J. Acoust. Soc. Am. 47, 613–617.

Hirsh, I. J. (1959). "Auditory perception of temporal order," J. Acoust. Soc. Am. 31, 759–767.

Jakobson, R., Fant, C. G. M., and Halle, M. (1969). *Preliminaries to Speech Analysis: The Distinctive Features and their Correlates* (MIT, Cambridge, MA).

Jusczyk, P., Rosner, B., Cutting, J., Foard, C., and Smith, L. (1977). "Categorical perception of nonspeech sounds by 2-month-old infants." Percept. Psychophys. 21, 50–54.

Klatt, D. (1975). "Voice onset time, frication, and aspiration in word-initial consonant clusters," J. Speech Hear. Res. 18, 686–706.

Kuhl, P. K. (1978). "Predispositions for the perception of speech-sound categories: A species-specific phenomenon?," in *Communicative and Cognitive Abilities—Early Behavioral Assessment*, edited by R. L. Schiefelbusch and L. L. Lloyd (University Park, Baltimore) (in press).

Kuhl, P. K. (1976). "Speech perception by the chinchilla: Categorical perception of synthetic alveolar plosive consonants," J. Acoust. Soc. Am. 60, S81(A).

Kuhl, P. K., and Miller, J. D. (1975). "Speech perception by the chinchilla: Voiced–voiceless distinction in alveolar plosive consonants," Science 190, 69–72.

Lasky, R. E., Syrdal-Lasky, A., and Klein, R. E. (1975). "VOT discrimination by four- to six-and-a-half-month-old infants from Spanish environments," J. Exp. Child Psychol. 20, 215–225.

Liberman, A. M. (1970). "The grammars of speech and language," Cog. Psychol. 1, 301–323.

Liberman, A. M., Cooper, F. S., Shankweiler, D. P., and Studdert-Kennedy, M. (1967). "Perception of the speech code," Psychol. Rev. 74, 431–461.

Liberman, A. M., Delattre, P. C., and Cooper, F. S. (1952). "The role of selected stimulus variables in the perception of the unvoiced stop consonants," Am. J. Psychol. 65, 497–516.

Liberman, A. M., Delattre, P. C., and Cooper, F. S. (1958). "Some cues for the distinction between voiced and voiceless stops in initial position," Lang. Speech 1, 153–167.

Liberman, A. M., Delattre, P. C., Cooper, F. S., and Gerstman, L. J. (1954). "The role of consonant-vowel transitions in the perception of the stop and nasal consonants," Psychol. Mono. 68, 1–13.

Liberman, A. M., Mattingly, I. G., and Turvey, M. T. (1972). "Language codes and memory codes," in *Coding Processes in Human Memory*, edited by A. W. Melton and E. Martin (Winston and Wiley, New York), pp. 307–334.

Lindquist, E. F. (1953). *Design and Analysis of Experiments in Psychology and Education* (Houghton Mifflin, Boston).

Lisker, L. (1975a). "Is it VOT or a first-formant transition detector?" J. Acoust. Soc. Am. 57, 1547–1551.

Lisker, L. (1975b). "In (qualified) defense of VOT," Haskins Labs. Stat. Rep. Speech Res. SR-44, 109–117.

Lisker, L., and Abramson, A. (1964). "A cross-language study of voicing in initial stops: Acoustical measurements," Word 20, 384–422.

Lisker, L., Liberman, A. M., Erickson, D. M., and Dechovitz, D. (1975). "On pushing the voice onset time boundary about," Haskins Labs. Stat. Rep. Speech Res.

SR42/43, 257–264.

Luz, G. A. (1969). "Conditioning the chinchilla to make avoidance responses to novel sounds," J. Comp. Physiol. Psychol. 68, 348–354.

Miller, G., Heise, G., and Lichten, W. (1951). "The intelligibility of speech as a function of the context of the test materials," J. Exp. Psychol. 41, 329–335.

Miller, J. D. (1970). "Audibility curve of the chinchilla," J. Acoust. Soc. Am. 48, 513–523.

Miller, J. D. (1977). "Perception of speech sounds in animals: Evidence for speech processing by mammalian auditory mechanisms," in *Recognition of Complex Acoustic Signals*, edited by T. H. Bullock (Abakon Verlags-gesellschaft, Berlin), pp. 49–58.

Miller, J. D., and Kuhl, P. K. (1976). "Speech perception by the chinchilla: A progress report on syllable-initial voiced-plosive consonants," J. Acoust. Soc. Am. 59, S54(A).

Miller, J. D., Wier, C. C., Pastore, R. E., Kelly, W. J., and Dooling, R. J. (1976). "Discrimination and labeling of noise-buzz sequences with varying noise-lead times: An example of categorical perception," J. Acoust. Soc. Am. 60, 410–417.

Miyawaki, K., Strange, W., Verbrugge, R., Liberman, A., Jenkins, J., and Fujimura, O. (1975). "An effect of linguistic experience: The discrimination of /r/ and /l/ by native speakers of Japanese and English," Percept. Psychophys. 18, 331–340.

Morse, P. A. (1974). "Infant speech perception: A preliminary model and review of the Literature," in *Language Perspectives—Acquisition, Retardation, and Intervention* (University Park, Baltimore), pp. 19–54.

Pastore, R. E. (1976). "Categorical perception: A critical re-evaluation," in *Hearing and Davis: Essays Honoring Hallowell Davis*, edited by S. K. Hirsh, D. H. Eldredge, I. J. Hirsh, and S. R. Silverman (Washington University, St. Louis), pp. 253–264.

Pickett, J. M., and Pollack, J. (1963). "Intelligibility of excerpts from fluent speech: Effects of rate of utterance and duration of excerpt," Lang. Speech 6, 151–164.

Pisoni, D. B. (1973). "Auditory and phonetic memory codes in the discrimination of consonants and vowels," Percept. Psychophys. 13, 253–260.

Pisoni, D. B. (1977). "Identification and discrimination of the relative onset time of two-component tones: Implications for voicing perception in stops," J. Acoust. Soc. Am. 61, 1352–1361.

Pisoni, D. B., and Lazarus, J. H. (1974). "Categorical and noncategorical modes of speech perception along the voicing continuum," J. Acoust. Soc. Am. 55, 328–333.

Pollack, I., and Pickett, J. M. (1963). "The intelligibility of excerpts from conversation," Lang. Speech 6, 165–171.

Sawusch, J. R. (1976). "The structure and flow of information in speech perception: Evidence from selective adaptation of stop consonants," Ph.D. dissertation (Indiana University) (unpublished).

Shockey, L., and Reddy, D. R. (1974). "Transcription of unfamiliar language material," J. Acoust. Soc. Am. 55, S88(A).

Sinnott, J. M., Beecher, M. D., Moody, D. B., and Stebbins, W. C. (1976). "Speech sound discrimination by monkeys and humans," J. Acoust. Soc. Am. 60, 687–695.

Spenner, B. F., Engebretson, A. M., Miller, J. D., and Cox, J. R. (1974). "Random-access programmable recorder of complex sounds (RAP): A digital instrument for auditory research," J. Acoust. Soc. Am. 55, 427.

Stevens, K. N. (1972). "The quantal nature of speech: Evidence from articulatory-acoustic data," in *Human Communication: A Unified View*, edited by E. E. David, Jr., and P. B. Denes (McGraw–Hill, New York), pp. 51–66.

Stevens, K. N. (1975). "The potential role of property detectors in the perception of consonants," in *Auditory Analysis and Perception of Speech*, edited by G. Fant and M. A. A. Tatham (Academic, London), pp. 191–196.

Stevens, K. N., and Blumstein, S. E. (1976). "Context-independent properties for place of articulation in stop consonants," J. Acoust. Soc. Am. 59, S40(A).

Stevens, K. N., and House, A. S. (1972). "Speech Perception," in *Foundations of Modern Auditory Theory*, edited by J. V. Tobias (Academic, New York), Vol. II, pp. 3–62.

Stevens, K. N., and Klatt, D. H. (1974). "Role of formant transitions in the voiced–voiceless distinction for stops," J. Acoust. Soc. Am. 55, 653–659.

Streeter, L. A. (1976). "Language perception of 2-month-old infants shows effects of both innate mechanisms and experience," Nature 259, 39–41.

Streeter, L. A., and Landauer, T. K. (1975). "Effects of learning English as a second language on the acquisition of a new phonemic contrast," J. Acoust. Soc. Am. 57, S49(A).

Studdert-Kennedy, M. (1974). "The perception of speech," in *Current Trends in Linguistics*, edited by T. A. Sebeck (Monton, The Hague, Netherlands), Vol. 12, pp. 2349–2385.

Studdert-Kennedy, M. (1976). "Speech perception," in *Contemporary Issues in Experimental Phonetics*, edited by N. J. Lass (Academic, New York), pp. 243–293.

Studdert-Kennedy, M., Liberman, A., Harris, K. S., and Cooper, F. S. (1970). "Motor theory of speech perception," Psychol. Rev. 77, 234–249.

Summerfield, Q., and Haggard, M. (1977). "On the dissociation of spectral and temporal cues to the voicing distinction in initial stop consonants," J. Acoust. Soc. Am. 62, 435–448.

Williams, L. (1977). "The perception of stop consonant voicing by Spanish–English bilinguals," Percept. Psychophys. 21, 289–297.

Zlatin, M. A., and Koenigsknecht, R. A. (1975). "Development of the voicing contrast I: Perceptual status of voice onset time," J. Speech Hear. Res. 18, 541–553.

THE VOICING DIMENSION: SOME EXPERIMENTS IN COMPARATIVE PHONETICS*

LEIGH LISKER**—ARTHUR S. ABRAMSON***

Speech synthesis has made it possible to produce controlled variations along acoustic dimensions to test their perceptual relevance for phonemic distinctions. Zones of perceptual ambiguity are compared with boundaries between ranges of acoustic values measured in speech. We are interested in doing this in cross-language comparisons. For each of the languages we want to know the number of phonological categories along a dimension used in common. For languages with the same number of categories the boundaries need not be the same.

Our research has led us to believe that in many languages some phoneme categories are distinguished by the timing of glottal adjustments relative to supraglottal articulation, and that this timing relation determines not only the voicing state as narrowly defined, but the degree of aspiration and certain features associated with the so-called force of articulation as well. For word-initial stops in non-whispered speech, this relation is realized acoustically by what we have called voice onset time (VOT), i.e., the interval between the release burst and the onset of laryngeal pulsing.[1] A recent pilot study with synthetic speech demonstrated the distinctive power of VOT.[2] The present study takes a closer look at its perceptual relevance in three languages, English, Spanish and Thai. The resulting data also furnish a basis for discrimination experiments.

We used the Haskins Laboratories parallel resonance synthesizer, which has three

* This research was supported by the National Institute of Child Health and Human Development of the National Institutes of Health and the Information Systems Branch of the Office of Naval Research.

** University of Pennsylvania and Haskins Laboratories. New York, N. Y.

*** University of Connecticut and Haskins Laboratories, New York, N. Y.

[1] L. Lisker and A. S. Abramson, "A Cross-Language Study of Voicing in Initial Stops: Acoustical Measurements," *Word* 20 (1964), 384—422; L. Lisker and A. S. Abramson. "Stop Categorization and Voice Onset Time", *Proc. 5th Intl. Cong. Phon. Sci.*, E. Zwirner and W. Bethge, eds. (Basel. 1965), pp. 389—391.

[2] A. S. Abramson and L. Lisker, "Voice Onset Time in Stop Consonants: Acoustic Analysis and Synthesis", *Proc. 5th Intl. Cong. on Acoustics*, D. E. Commins. ed. (Liège, 1965), Vol. Ia, Paper A 51. See also A. M. Liberman, P. C. Delattre, and F. S. Cooper. "Some Cues for the Distinction between Voiced and Voiceless Stops in Initial Position", *Language and Speech* 1 (1958), 153—166.

Proceedings of the Sixth International Congress of Phonetic Sciences, Prague 1967.
© 1970 by Academia, Publishing House of the Czechoslovak Academy of Sciences.

formant generators with variable frequencies and amplitudes, a choice of buzz or hiss excitation, or a mixture of the two, and control of the overall amplitude and fundamental frequency.

Our basic pattern was built on three steady-state formants for a vowel of the type [a]. Labial, apical and velar stops were made by adding appropriate release bursts and formant transitions to the beginning. We synthesized 37 VOT variants, ranging from 150 msec. before the release to 150 msec. after it. For voicing before the release (voicing lead), we used only low-frequency harmonics of the buzz source. For voice onset after release (voicing lag), the interval between burst and onset of pulsing was excited by hiss alone, with suppression of the first formant to simulate the effects of an open glottis. Calling the release zero time, we gave negative numbers to voicing lead and positive numbers to lag. The stimuli varied in 10 msec. steps, except for the range from —10 to +50, where we made them in 5 msec. steps. Each variant had a fundamental frequency of 114 cps. with a drop toward the end. The 37 variants were recorded in eight random orders, with two occurrences of each on each tape. The test subjects were five native speakers of Latin American Spanish, twelve of American English, and eight of Thai. Using their own orthographies, the subjects identified the stimuli with their stop phonemes.

Figs. 1—3 give the identification curves as functions of VOT values. The bars show frequency distributions of VOT values measured in speech. All the expected categories emerge, but the perceptual crossover zones do not always match very well the zones between the ranges of measured values. In Spanish (Fig. 1), (bdg) are produced with voicing lead, while (ptk) have zero VOT or short lag. The three perceptual crossovers occur to the right of these boundaries, suggesting that some other features, perhaps burst and hiss intensities or formant transitions, were not optimally set. In Fig. 2 the productions of English (bdg) show a small scattering of lead values but a concentration at zero or just after it, while (ptk) all show lag. The boundaries between ranges match the perceptual crossovers well, although there are slight discrepancies in the labials and apicals. For all three places of articulation the English perceptual crossovers have higher VOT values than the Spanish, though the differences are less than expected. Thai was chosen because for two of its places of closure it has three categories, usually called voiced, voiceless unaspirated and voiceless aspirated; the velars have only the latter two. The categories lie in the regions of voicing lead, zero VOT or short lag, and long lag respectively. The match between speech and perception (Fig. 3) is good for the left-hand boundary for the labials and apicals, showing great sensitivity to voicing lead; the right-hand boundary, however, shows the same kind of mismatch as the Spanish and English. For the velars, nevertheless, the match is perfect.

For all three languages the stop categories occupy distinct ranges along the VOT dimension. To be sure, the match between our production and labelling data is somewhat less than perfect, but this is scarcely surprising in view of the severely restricted number of variables involved in the experiment. However, despite the

564

likelihood that other acoustic features play a role in fixing the category boundaries
studied, it seems quite clear that the timing of voice onset is a major factor in de-

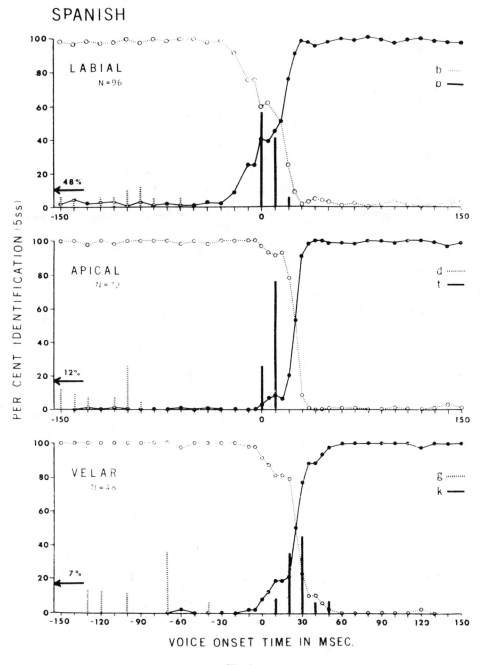

Fig. 1.

termining the location of those boundaries in languages as diverse phonetically as Spanish. English and Thai.

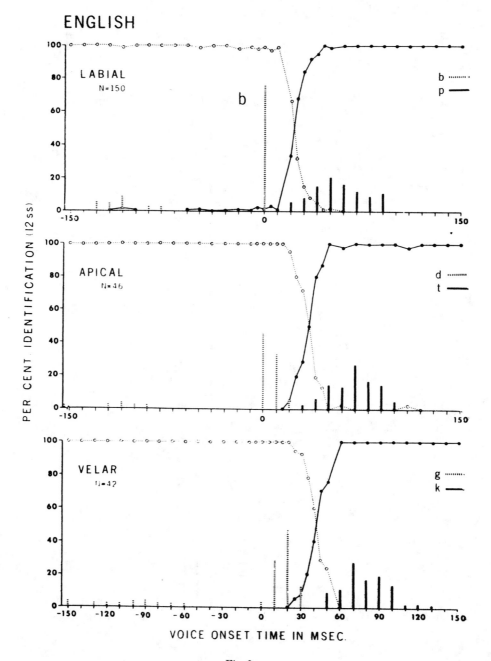

Fig. 2.

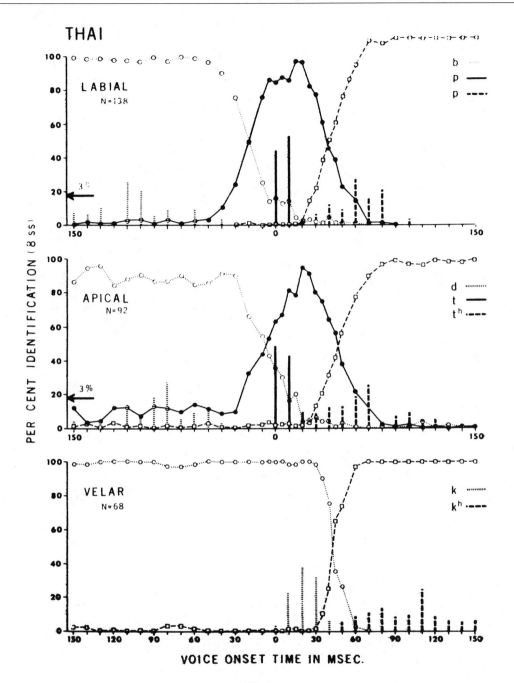

Fig. 3.

(Reprinted from Nature, Vol. 264, No. 5588, pp. 746–748, December 23/30, 1976)

© Macmillan Journals Ltd., 1976

Hearing lips and seeing voices

MOST verbal communication occurs in contexts where the listener can see the speaker as well as hear him. However, speech perception is normally regarded as a purely auditory process. The study reported here demonstrates a previously unrecognised influence of vision upon speech perception. It stems from an observation that, on being shown a film of a young woman's talking head, in which repeated utterances of the syllable [ba] had been dubbed on to lip movements for [ga], normal adults reported hearing [da]. With the reverse dubbing process, a majority reported hearing [bagba] or [gaba]. When these subjects listened to the soundtrack from the film, without visual input, or when they watched untreated film, they reported the syllables accurately as repetitions of [ba] or [ga]. Subsequent replications confirm the reliability of these findings; they have important implications for the understanding of speech perception.

To further confirm and generalise the original observation, new materials were prepared. A woman was filmed while she fixated a television camera lens and repeated ba-ba, ga-ga, pa-pa or ka-ka. Each utterance was repeated once per second, with an interval of approximately 0.5 s between repetitions. From this master recording four dubbed video-records were prepared in which the original vocalisations and lip movements were combined as follows: (1) ba-voice/ga-lips; (2) ga-voice/ba-lips; (3) pa-voice/ka-lips; (4) ka-voice/pa-lips. Dubbing was carried out so as to ensure, within the temporal constraints of telerecording equipment, that

For the purpose of analysis, a correct response was defined as an accurate repetition of the auditory component of each recording. Under the auditory-only condition accuracy was high, with averages of 91, 97 and 99% for pre-school, school age and adult subjects respectively; errors were unsystematic. Under the auditory visual condition, where subjects heard the original soundtrack, errors were substantial. For pre-school subjects average error rate was 59%, for school children 52% and for adults 92%.

Subsequent analysis was confined to detailed consideration of responses to the auditory–visual presentations. Responses were first categorised according to the operational definations illustrated in Table 1.

The meaning of 'auditory' and 'visual' categories is self-evident. A 'fused' response is one where information from the two modalities is transformed into something new with an element not presented in either modality, whereas a 'combination' response represents a composite comprising relatively unmodified elements from each modality. Responses which could not be unambiguously assigned to one of these four categories were allocated to a small, heterogeneous 'other' category. Table 2 presents the percentage of responses in each category.

Table 2 shows that the original observation of the effect of [ba]/[ga] presentations on adult responses is highly replicable; 98% of adult subjects gave fused responses to the ba-voice/ga-lips presentation and 59% gave combination responses to its complement. The effect is also generalisable, at least to other stop

---

Table 1 Stimulus conditions and definition of response categories from auditory–visual condition

| Stimuli | | Response Categories | | | | |
Auditory component	Visual component	Auditory	Visual	Fused	Combination	Other
ba-ba	ga-ga	ba-ba	ga-ga	da-da	—	—
ga-ga	ba-ba	ga-ga	ba-ba	da-da	gabga bagba baga gaba	dabda gagla etc.
pa-pa	ka-ka	pa-pa	ka-ka	ta-ta	—	tapa pta kafta etc.
ka-ka	pa-pa	ka-ka	pa-pa	—	kapka pakpa paka kapa	kat kafa kakpat etc.

---

there was auditory–visual coincidence of the release of the consonant in the first syllable of each utterance. Each recording comprised three replications of its auditory–visual composite. Four different counterbalanced sequences of recordings (1)–(4) were prepared, each with a ten-second gap of blank film between successive segments. The recordings were suitable for relay via a 19-inch television monitor; audio–visual reproduction was of good quality.

Twenty-one pre-school children (3–4 y), 28 primary school children (7–8 yr) and 54 adults (18–40 yr) were tested. The adult sample was predominantly male; there were approximately equal numbers of boys and girls in the younger samples. Subjects were individually tested under two conditions: (1) auditory–visual, where they were instructed to watch the film and repeat what they heard the model saying, and (2) auditory only, where they faced away from the screen and again had to repeat the model's utterances. Every subject responded to all four recordings ((1)–(4) above) under each condition, each time in a different sequence; sequence of presentation was counterbalanced across subjects.

consonants; 81% of adults gave a fused response to pa-lips/ka-voice and 44% gave combination responses to its complement. The effects, however, are more pronounced with [ba]/[ga] than with [pa]/[ka] combinations; the latter comment applies to all ages.

The data in Table 2 also illustrate that the auditory perception of adult subjects is more influenced by visual input than is that of subjects in the two younger groups; the latter do not differ consistently from each other. It is interesting to note that where responses are dominated by a single modality, this tends to be the auditory for children and the visual for adults. However, it should also be noted that the frequency of fused responses to ba-voice/ga-lips, and pa-voice/ka-lips presentations is at a substantial level for pre-school and school children alike. These auditory–visual illusions, therefore, are observable across a wide age span, although there clearly are age-related changes in susceptibility to them, particularly between middle childhood and adulthood.

Appropriate analyses confirm that the various effects reported for the auditory–visual condition are statistically significant. Alone, however, the data fail to testify to the powerful nature of the

Table 2 Percentage of responses in each category in the auditory visual condition

Stimuli Auditory	Visual	Subjects	Responses Auditory	Visual	Fused	Combination	Other
ba-ba	ga-ga	3–5 yr (n = 21)	19	0	81	0	0
		7–8 yr (n = 28)	36	0	64	0	0
		18–40 yr (n = 54)	2	0	98	0	0
ga-ga	ba-ba	3–5 yr (n = 21)	57	10	0	19	14
		7–8 yr (n = 28)	36	21	11	32	0
		18–40 yr (n = 54)	11	31	0	54	4
pa-pa	ka-ka	3–5 yr (n = 21)	24	0	52	0	24
		7–8 yr (n = 28)	50	0	50	0	0
		18–40 yr (n = 54)	6	7	81	0	6
ka-ka	pa-pa	3–5 yr (n = 21)	62	9	0	5	24
		7–8 yr (n = 28)	68	0	0	32	0
		18–40 yr (n = 54)	13	37	0	44	6

illusions. We ourselves have experienced these effects on many hundreds of trials; they do not habituate over time, despite objective knowledge of the illusion involved. By merely closing the eyes, a previously heard [da] becomes [ba] only to revert to [da] when the eyes are open again.

Contemporary, auditory-based theories of speech perception are inadequate to accommodate these new observations; a role for vision (that is, perceived lip movements) in the perception of speech by normally hearing people is clearly illustrated. Our own observations and those of others[1] indicate that, in the absence of auditory input, lip movements for [ga] are frequently misread as [da], while those for [ka] are sometimes misread as [ta]; [pa] and [ba] are often confused with each other but are never misread as [ga, da, ka or ta]. It is also known that, in auditory terms, vowels carry information for the consonants which immediately preceed them[2]. If we speculate that the acoustic waveform for [ba] contains features in common with that for [da] but not with [ga], then a tentative explanation for one set of the above illusions is suggested. Thus, in a ba-voice/ga-lips presentation, there is visual information for [ga] and [da] and auditory information with features common to [da] and [ba]. By responding to the common information in both modalities, a subject would arrive at the unifying percept [da]. Similar reasoning would account for the [ta] response under pa-voice/ka-lips presentations.

By the same token, it could be argued that with ga-voice/ba-lips and ka-voice/pa-lips combinations the modalities are in conflict, having no shared features. In the absence of domination of one modality by the other, the listener has no way of deciding between the two sources of information and therefore oscillates between them, variously hearing [babga], [papka], and so on.

The *post facto* nature of this interpretation is acknowledged. More refined experimentation is required to clarify the nature and ontogenetic development of the illusions and their generality needs further investigation. We are at present working on these issues but believe that the finding now reported are of some interest in their own right.

Full details of the dubbing procedure are available from us. We thank the staff of the University of Surrey AVA Unit for their technical assistance in preparing materials and also Susan Ballantyne whose lip movements we filmed.

HARRY MCGURK
JOHN MACDONALD

*Department of Psychology,
University of Surrey, Guildford,
Surrey GU2 5XH, UK*

Received July 15; accepted November 11, 1976.

[1] Binnie, C. A., Montgomery, A. A. and Jackman, P. L., *J. Speech Hearing Res.*, **17**, 619–630 (1974).
[2] Liberman, A. M., Delattre, P. C., and Cooper, F. S., *Am. J. Psych.*, **65**, 497–516 (1952).

Discrimination and labeling of noise–buzz sequences with varying noise-lead times: An example of categorical perception*

James D. Miller, Craig C. Wier,[†] Richard E. Pastore,[‡] William J. Kelly, and Robert J. Dooling§

Central Institute for the Deaf, St. Louis, Missouri 63110
(Received 26 September 1974; revised 19 March 1976)

The onset of a noise [0.9–2.1 kHz, 55 dB SPL (A weighted)] preceded that of a buzz [100 Hz, 0.5–3.0 kHz, 70 db SPL (A weighted), 500 msec] by −10 to +80 msec and both terminated simultaneously. Eight adults discriminated among noise-lead times in an oddity task. In separate sessions, they labeled singly presented stimuli with either of the two responses: "no noise" or "noise." The results are highly similar to those reported for the categorical perception of synthetic plosive consonants differing in voice-onset time. On the average, discrimination was best across a noise-lead-time boundary of about 16 msec, where labeling also shifted abruptly. These results and those of categorical perception, generally, are interpreted in terms of Weber's law as applied to a single component within a stimulus complex. It is concluded that categorical perception of sounds is not unique to speech and suggested that it may be a general property of sensory behavior.

Subject Classification: [43] 65.75; [43] 70.30.

INTRODUCTION

The ideal form of categorical perception was recently described by Studdert-Kennedy *et al.* (1970) thus: "...a mode by which stimuli are responded to, and *can only be responded to, in absolute terms.* Successive stimuli drawn from a physical continuum are not perceived as forming a continuum, but as members of discrete categories. They are identified absolutely, that is, independently of the context in which they occur. Subjects asked to discriminate between pairs of such "categorical" stimuli are able to discriminate between stimuli drawn from different categories, but not between stimuli drawn from the same category. In other words, discrimination is limited by identification: subjects can only discriminate between stimuli that they can identify differently."

Categorical perception also has been described as a special property of the perception of speech sounds. According to Mattingly *et al.* (1971) it is "...unusual, if not unique, since in the perception of nonspeech sounds, many more stimuli can be discriminated than can be identified." The experiments reported here are directed to the question of whether categorical perception is a unique perceptual mode used by humans when listening to speech or whether categorical perception may be a general property of sensory behavior.

I. METHODS AND PROCEDURES

A. Subjects

There were eight subjects. Four were the authors (excluding R. E. Pastore), and four were experienced listeners from the Signal Detection Laboratory of Central Institute for the Deaf, who typically make superior scores on auditory discrimination tasks. The author-subjects were, of course, aware of the research questions. The others were not.

B. Stimuli

Thermal noise was filtered with a bandpass of ~900 to ~2700 Hz and adjusted to 55 dB SPL in a 6-cc coupler followed by an *A*-weighting network. The buzz was a 1-msec square wave with a 100-Hz repetition rate, filtered with a band pass of 500–3000 Hz and adjusted to 70 dB measured in the same way as the noise. An individual stimulus was formed by gating the noise with a 5-msec rise-and-fall at various times in relation to the gating of the buzz. This was done without regard for the phase of the 100-Hz buzz. For this reason, a nominal noise-lead time of 20 msec actually varied randomly between 20–29 msec with an average value that was about 24 msec. All reported values of noise-lead times are nominal. The duration of the buzz was always 500 msec with 5-msec rise-and-fall times. The noise and buzz were always terminated simultaneously. Nominal noise-lead times were varied from −10 to +80 msec in 5-msec steps.

C. Discrimination testing

An oddity task was used. Three stimuli were presented with an interstimulus interval of about 0.5 sec. Lead times of −10 to +80 msec (10-msec steps) were selected in groups of four (−10, 0, +10, +20; 0, +10, +20, +30; and so on). Random pairings were made of the lead times and presented in the oddity format. On each trial two identical and one different lead times were presented and the subjects voted whether the odd stimulus was first, second, or third. Feedback was given after each oddity trial. Easy discriminations were thus interspersed with difficult discriminations, for example, in the set 0, 10, 20, and 30, the pair (0, 30) is easy while the pair (20, 30) is more difficult. The major part of the discrimination data were collected prior to the labeling experiment. However, some additional discrimination data (see below) and all control data were collected after the labeling experiments had been completed.

D. Labeling experiments

Single stimuli with nominal noise-lead times of −10 to +80 msec (10-msec steps) were presented to the subjects for labeling as no-noise or noise. These labels were chosen because of the observation that the noise was nearly inaudible for short lead times and clearly audible for long lead times. The intertrial interval was 3 sec and no feedback was given.

E. Control experiments

The control experiments were discrimination and labeling of noises that varied in duration but had the same spectral characteristics as the noises in the noise–buzz sequences. Discrimination and labeling of noises with durations equal to the leading portions of the noise–buzz sequences were "short controls." Discrimination and labeling of noises with durations equal to the total durations of the noise–buzz sequences were "long controls." Discrimination and labeling tests were identical to those for the noise-buzz sequences except that the labels were "short noise" and "long noise" for the control experiments. These experiments were done to determine whether the results for the noise–buzz sequences could be explained in terms of the duration of the leading noise by itself (short controls) or in terms of the total duration of the noise–buzz sequences (long controls).

II. RESULTS

The percent-correct performance for discrimination of 10-msec differences in noise-lead times for the four author–subjects is shown in Fig. 1. Discriminations (circles) are from 10-msec step comparisons in the oddity task with noise-buzz sequences. These functions have maxima and near chance performance away from

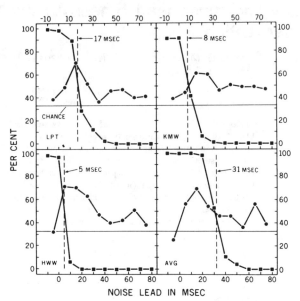

FIG. 2. Discrimination and labeling by the "experienced listeners." The procedure and stimulus ensemble are the same as described for Fig. 1.

the maxima. Each filled circle is based on about 160 trials. The open circles are from additional experiments run after the labeling data had been collected and they are based on about one-third as many trials. Data from randomly ordered presentations of individual stimuli to be labeled as "no noise" or "noise" are also shown (squares). Each point is based on 100 trials. The lead time where "no-noise" and "noise" responses are equally probable is marked by the vertical line; this is the category boundary. It is apparent that the labeling functions are steep[1] and that the category boundaries are near the peaks in the discrimination functions.

The performance for our four experienced signal-detection subjects, who were unaware of the purpose of the experiment, is shown in Fig. 2. The discrimination functions represent coarser sampling of noise-lead times; nevertheless, these data are no different in kind from those of the author–subjects.

The "short control" experiments (Fig. 3) yielded labeling functions similar in form to those of the noise–buzz sequences. The best discrimination performance for the short-control stimuli is as that for the noise–buzz sequences. However, the discrimination functions for the "short control" stimuli do not approach chance on either side of a maximum as do similar functions for noise–buzz sequences.

The "long control" experiments (Fig. 4) result in near chance discrimination and shallow labeling functions totally unlike those for the noise–buzz sequences.

The data of Figs. 3 and 4 are from the author–subjects. Similar results were obtained for the other four subjects but they are not shown.

Following the ideal form of categorical perception presented in the introduction, discrimination functions

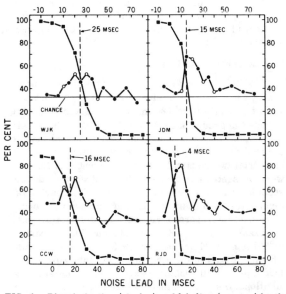

FIG. 1. Discrimination (circles) and labeling (squares) by the author–subjects. Discriminations are from 10-msec step comparisons in the oddity task with noise-buzz sequences. The labeling data are from randomly-ordered presentations of the individual stimuli to be labeled as "no-noise" or "noise."

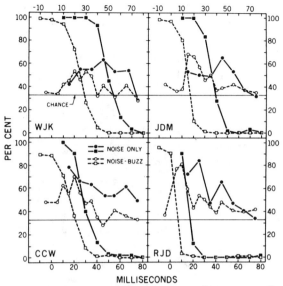

FIG. 3. Discrimination and labeling of the "short control" stimuli. The stimuli are noises with the durations of 10–80 msec, and in the labeling tests the responses were "short" or "long." Data for the same subjects from noise–buzz experiments (Fig. 1) are replotted here as open symbols.

can be predicted from the labeling data (Liberman *et al.*, 1957).[2] Table I shows the predicted and obtained values based on the median-across-subject performance on the labeling task. The predicted values for the noise-buzz sequences are peaked with maxima near the obtained maxima, and the overall level of performance is underestimated, particularly for stimulus conditions where the lead is longer than those values at or near the peak. The predicted values for the short-control stimuli show a small peak for noise bursts about 30 msec in duration, but the discrimination data do not show any peaking. Both the predicted and obtained values for the long-control stimuli are consistently near chance.

III. DISCUSSION

A. Categorical perception with speech and nonspeech sounds

The degree to which the discrimination values predicted from the labeling data correspond to the discrimination values obtained directly has been suggested as a test for the presence of categorical perception. Typically, for synthetic-speech stimuli, the obtained values exceed the predicted values indicating there exists some basis for discrimination between stimuli within categories. However, Studdert-Kennedy *et al.* (1970) argue that "the deviation of the obtained from the predicted is so much greater for some continua than others that we are justified in maintaining a distinction (p. 235)." They proceed to provide three necessary criteria for categorical perception: (1) there should be "peaks" or regions of high discriminability in the discrimination function; (2) there should be "troughs" or regions where discriminability is near chance; and (3)

the peaks and troughs should correspond to the shape of the identification functions, peaks should occur at the identification boundaries and troughs within categories.

The predicted and obtained discrimination data for the noise-buzz stimuli shown in Table I display a form typical of such data for synthetic speech. The peaks are reasonably well predicted, and the within-category discrimination is underestimated. The data approach chance near the upper bound of the lead times tested. The short-control data obtained do not show the predicted peaks and there are no regions of close agreement between predicted and obtained values. The long-control data are well predicted by the model but of little interest since both values are consistently near chance.

Neither the short-control nor the long-control data can be described as representing categorical perception. The noise-buzz data, however, appear to be quite similar to that described as categorical perception in the case of synthetic speech. The degree to which the noise-buzz data resemble data for synthetic speech may best be seen by direct comparison.

Figure 5 contains some of the results of Liberman *et al.* (1961) plotted along with some of those from the noise-buzz experiments described above. The Liberman data are for the discrimination of synthetic /to/ and /do/ where a voicing lead is changed to a voicing lag at the same time as F_1 is delayed relative to F_2.[3] Labeling functions are referred to the left-hand ordinates and discrimination data are referred to the right-hand ordinates, which are deviations from chance. There is no difference in the qualities of peaked dis-

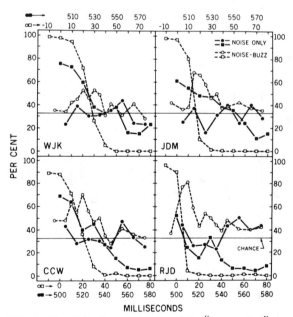

FIG. 4. Discrimination and labeling of the "long control" stimuli. The stimuli are noise alone with the durations (500–580 msec) noted on the abscissa, and in the labeling tests the responses were "short" or "long." Data for the same subjects from the noise-buzz experiments (Fig. 1) are replotted as open symbols.

TABLE I. Predicted and obtained discrimination scores (proportions of correct responses). Obtained scores are medians for all subjects tested while the predicted scores are calculated from the median labeling functions.

Midpoints of stimulus pairs in milliseconds

	Step size (msec)	P(C)	−5	0	5 / 505	10 / 510	15 / 515	20 / 520	25 / 525	30 / 530	35 / 535	40 / 540	45 / 545	50 / 550	55 / 555	60 / 560	65 / 565	70 / 570	75 / 575
Noise–Buzz[a]	10	Predicted	0.33	0.34	0.36	0.45	0.55	0.42	0.35	0.34	0.33	0.33	0.33	0.33	0.33	0.33	0.33	0.33	0.33
	10	Obtained	0.38	—	0.47	0.52	0.65	0.60	0.55	0.49	0.47	0.36	0.44	—	0.42	—	0.41	—	0.39
	10	Difference	0.05	—	0.11	0.07	0.10	0.18	0.20	0.15	0.11	0.03	0.11	—	0.09	—	0.08	—	0.06
	20	Predicted	—	0.37	0.49	0.74	0.75	0.67	0.48	0.36	0.34	0.34	0.34	0.33	0.33	0.33	0.33	0.33	0.33
	20	Obtained	—	0.57	—	0.84	0.80	0.92	0.79	0.77	0.69	0.66	—	0.57	—	0.53	—	0.42	—
	20	Difference	—	0.20	—	0.10	0.05	0.25	0.31	0.41	0.35	0.32	—	0.24	—	0.20	—	0.09	—
	30	Predicted	—	—	0.75	0.81	0.90	0.86	0.71	0.49	0.36	0.34	0.34	0.34	0.33	0.33	0.33	0.33	0.33
	30	Obtained	—	—	0.94	—	0.97	0.97	0.98	0.95	0.89	—	0.76	0.82	0.74	0.72	0.64	0.54	—
	30	Difference	—	—	0.19	—	0.07	0.11	0.27	0.46	0.53	—	0.42	0.46	0.41	0.39	0.31	0.21	—
Short controls[b]	10	Predicted	—	—	—	—	0.34	0.37	0.45	0.41	0.39	0.38	0.36	0.34	0.33	0.33	0.33	0.33	0.33
	10	Obtained	—	—	—	—	0.73	—	0.66	—	0.54	—	0.60	—	0.53	—	0.46	—	0.36
	10	Difference	—	—	—	—	0.39	—	0.21	—	0.15	—	0.24	—	0.20	—	0.13	—	0.03
	20	Predicted	—	—	—	—	—	0.50	0.57	0.68	0.57	0.48	0.41	0.36	0.34	0.33	0.33	0.33	0.33
	20	Obtained	—	—	—	—	—	0.93	—	0.93	—	0.81	—	0.82	—	0.72	—	0.54	—
	20	Difference	—	—	—	—	—	0.43	—	0.25	—	0.33	—	0.46	—	0.39	—	0.21	—
	30	Predicted	—	—	—	—	—	—	0.76	0.81	0.87	0.66	0.49	0.42	0.36	0.34	0.33	—	—
	30	Obtained	—	—	—	—	—	—	1.00	—	1.00	—	0.97	—	0.88	—	0.90	—	—
	30	Difference	—	—	—	—	—	—	0.24	—	0.13	—	0.48	—	0.52	—	0.57	—	—
Long controls[b]	10	Predicted	—	—	0.34	0.35	0.35	0.34	0.33	0.34	0.34	0.34	0.34	0.34	0.34	0.34	0.34	0.33	0.34
	10	Obtained	—	—	0.35	—	0.31	—	0.29	—	0.30	—	0.38	—	0.45	—	0.36	—	0.32
	10	Difference	—	—	0.01	—	0.04	—	0.04	—	0.04	—	0.04	—	0.11	—	0.02	—	0.02
	20	Predicted	—	—	—	0.39	0.36	0.36	0.35	0.34	0.36	0.36	0.35	0.36	0.35	0.35	0.36	0.33	—
	20	Obtained	—	—	—	0.36	—	0.37	—	0.39	—	0.39	—	0.32	—	0.33	—	0.37	—
	20	Difference	—	—	—	0.03	—	0.01	—	0.05	—	0.03	—	0.04	—	0.02	—	0.04	—
	30	Predicted	—	—	—	—	0.40	0.39	0.39	0.37	0.37	0.38	0.39	0.38	0.38	0.36	0.34	—	—
	30	Obtained	—	—	—	—	0.41	—	0.39	—	0.46	—	0.40	—	0.36	—	0.37	—	—
	30	Difference	—	—	—	—	0.01	—	0.00	—	0.09	—	0.01	—	0.02	—	0.04	—	—

[a] The column headings refer to nominal noise-lead times which are midway between those being tested.
[b] The column headings refer to the durations of the noise bursts which are midway between those being tested.

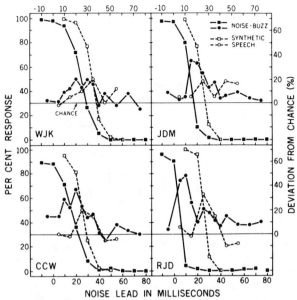

FIG. 5. Discrimination and labeling of noise–buzz sequences and synthetic speech. The author–subjects data from Fig. 1 are plotted together with the data of four subjects from experiments on voice-onset time with synthetic speech (Liberman *et al.*, 1961).

crimination functions and sharply changing labeling functions for the two sets of data. They do differ in the uniformity of the location of the category boundary or threshold. This difference may be accounted for in that Liberman *et al.* used selected subjects, response categories that are highly overlearned, and delayed "F_1-plus-triangular-patch" to induce the change at the boundary.

Figure 6 contains the data of Abramson and Lisker (1970) along with the comparable 20-msec step comparisons from our data. In the experiment of Abramson and Lisker the discrimination is among differences in voice-onset times of synthetic syllables (labial stop followed by /a/), while in our experiment the discrimination is among noise-lead times of the noise–buzz stimuli.

The upper panel is for pooled data and the lower panel is for two individual subjects—one of Abramson and Lisker, the other ours. The data from both experiments appear to approach chance at about the same rate and lead-time value. If the noise–buzz data were shifted to take into account the average 4-msec increase in the nominal lead time, the fit at the peak would be even closer. Abramson and Lisker do not provide discrimination values predicted from identification data. Nonetheless, since their obtained discrimination scores and their category boundaries are so similar to those for the noise–buzz condition, it is reasonable to assume the relations between predicted and observed discrimination scores for synthetic /pa/–/ba/ stimuli would be very similar to those for noise–buzz stimuli as shown in Table I.

Thus, labeling, discrimination, and their interrela-

tions for noise–buzz sequences heard as nonspeech[4] can be similar to those heard as speech.

Although early attempts to demonstrate categorical perception with non-speech stimuli were unsuccessful (see Mattingly *et al.*, 1971 and references therein), more recently Cutting and Rosner (1974) found categorical performance for certain musical sounds. Thus, our results and those of Cutting and Rosner (1974) firmly establish that categorical perception similar to that found for synthetic plosive consonants is not unique to speech or to a special perceptual set such as the "speech mode."

B. An approach to categorical perception

The relevant tests for the demonstration of categorical perception described by Studdert-Kennedy *et al.* (1970) are typically applied to a set of stimuli arranged in equal physical steps along a continuum. These steps are measured in linear dimensions and no ratio transform is used. The use of equal physical steps in discrimination testing implies, of course, that where Weber's law applies, discriminability will decline as the magnitude of the variable is increased since a constant ratio of Δx to x is required for equal discriminability. It is also probably important to note that where categorical perception is demonstrated, it is a

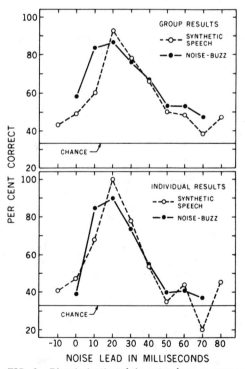

FIG. 6. Discrimination of the noise–buzz sequences and of synthetic speech. The upper panel displays the pooled data from the author–subject group in the present experiments for 20-msec-step comparisons compared with the analagous data for synthetic-speech stimuli (Abramson and Lisker, 1970). The lower panel displays the performance for the same conditions of one subject from the noise–buzz experiment and one subject from the synthetic-speech experiment.

single component of a *stimulus complex* that is the variable. It is likely that the unchanged or constant part of the stimulus complex provides an immediate stimulus context against which the effects of the changed component are judged. The frequently cited examples of categorical perception (Studdert-Kennedy *et al.*, 1970) involve just such changes in intrastimulus relations while the frequently cited examples of noncategorical perception (for example, judgments of series of pure tones differing in frequency or intensity) do not. This fact suggests that modifications in Weber's law required to provide "peaks" and "troughs" in the discrimination function may, in part, be related to the interactions between the constant part of the stimulus complex and the component that is varied. Consider the judgment of temporal order of the onsets of two tones—one of high pitch, the other low. As the high tone is started more and more in advance of the low, one may notice a change from apparent simultaneity to nonsimultaneity with uncertain order, to a definite Gestalt-like sequence of high leading low, to a clear temporal separation wherein the high-tone and low-tone onsets are heard as distinct events with the high starting ahead of the low (Hirsh, 1974; Hirsh, 1959; and Hirsh and Sherrick, 1961). Thus, as the amount by which the high tone precedes the low is increased, perceptual boundaries or thresholds are crossed corresponding to the perceptual effects of nonsimultaneity, Gestalt sequence with obvious ordering, and ordered onsets of two distinct percepts. Clearly, if the low tone were deleted from the experiment, then the discrimination of the different high tones would be described by Weber's law as applied to duration. The low tone provides a stimulus context against which the duration of the high tone can be judged in terms of the listed perceptual effects and correspondingly one would expect to find perturbations in the Weber fraction at the perceptual boundaries. This line of reasoning does *not* rule out the effects of attention, set, or training since a subject's performance undoubtedly will depend on all of these (Gengel and Hirsh, 1970).

By way of simplification, we argue that categorical perception may be usefully approached in terms of psychophysical boundaries or thresholds for perceptual effects that are encountered as one component of a stimulus complex is changed relative to the remainder of the complex. In the region of a threshold the effects of the varied component undergo rapid changes in detectability, discriminability, clarity, or perceived magnitude. Once across a threshold further changes in the magnitude of the component can be expected to follow Weber's law unless, of course, another threshold is encountered.

A simple example may illustrate the argument. Suppose a series of tones with constant differences in their *powers* is prepared and each is mixed with a noise burst of constant power. If these stimuli are presented to listeners for labeling, the labeling function will abruptly change from "noise alone" to "tone-plus-noise" at the masked threshold for the tone. In discrimination tests those stimuli with the tone below threshold will be discriminated poorly as should be the case for subthreshold stimuli. The discriminability of those stimuli with the tones above the masked threshold will de-

cline with the power of the tones since constant differences are tested and Weber's law requires constant ratios.

However, those stimulus pairs that straddle the masked threshold will be discriminated well. Otherwise said, below the masked threshold the Weber fraction for the tone (in noise) is very large while above the masked threshold the Weber fraction quickly reaches values similar to those for tones in isolation. The arrangement of the tones in a series with constant differences in their powers necessarily implies a reduction of the discriminability of such differences as their power is increased. Thus, in this example, the labeling function changes at the threshold, which is not surprising since this is a common operational definition of a threshold. The peaking of the discrimination function is easily explained in that subthreshold changes are difficult to discriminate and suprathreshold changes follow Weber's law. Furthermore, notice that the sharp peak in the discrimination function and the sharp change in the labeling function would not occur if the same tones were presented without the noise. One might have subjects label these same tones (without noise) as "soft" and "loud" and also discriminate them. While extensive training at a particular "loud–soft" boundary might cause some slight peaking of the discrimination function and "sharpen" the labeling function, such an experiment would probably never produce results as "categorical" as those with noise as a stimulus context. Obviously, this approach has no difficulty with the finding that changes in some components of synthetic speech result in categorical perception only when embedded in the context of a synthetic syllable and do not result in categorical perception when presented in isolation. The removal of the component from the speech context in fact includes a change in the stimulus context which may well change the location or existence of the relevant thresholds, the relevant Weber fractions, or both.

The categorical perception of the noise–buzz sequences of the present experiments can be simply understood in terms of the general notions presented above. Suppose that the noise lead is "difficult-to-detect" or "hard-to-hear" when it is below threshold and that the noise lead is "easy-to-hear" or a "clear noise" when it exceeds a threshold. (Without specific training, of course, different subjects may choose slightly different perceptual thresholds. For example, some may listen for "nonsimultaneous onsets" of noise and buzz, others for a clear sequence of noise preceding buzz, while others might require that the noise reach a certain level of loudness or clarity. All of these thresholds fall in the range of the obtained results, that is, noise leads of milliseconds or tens of milliseconds.) Beyond the threshold for "clear noise" the subject discriminates differences in the durations of the lead times. According to the previous argument the results can be understood in terms of the difficulty of discriminating "subthreshold" pairs and "suprathreshold" pairs with the best discrimination occurring when the pair straddles the threshold region.

In emphasizing the importance of the stimulus configuration, we do not wish to imply that training, attention, or memory are irrelevant or unimportant. Indeed, as Lane (1965) emphasizes, there are parallels between experiments on categorical perception and those on training and generalization (Mostofsky, 1965). The available data and general psychological knowledge make it reasonable to assume that training on any arbitrary categorization of a set of stimuli may "sharpen" the boundary and enhance discrimination of stimuli that straddle the boundary. However, this is a matter of degree and we suggest that the best examples of categorical perception are those that are based on perceptual thresholds which have been further "sharpened" by appropriate training, psychological set, and attention. We would also suggest that those thresholds that mark the emergence of a new perceptual quality, rather than a just-noticeable change in the magnitude of a quality, are probably the best candidates for the establishment of categorical perception.

It has also been noted by several authors (Fujisaki and Kawashima, 1969, 1970; Barclay, 1972; Pisoni, 1973; and Pisoni and Lazarus, 1974) that when tests of discrimination favor comparisons of responses such as names rather than comparisons of sensory traces, then it is more likely that the results will be categorical. Long intratrial intervals, overlearned responses or labels for the stimuli, and other setting factors such as instructions probably increase the chances that the subjects will compare labels or names of the stimuli rather than their sensory traces during discrimination tests.

In summary, it is suggested that categorical perception can be fruitfully approached with familiar concepts from learning, memory, and psychophysics. Special emphasis is given to the relation of the varied stimulus component to the remainder of the stimulus complex. Categorical perception can be expected in the region of a perceptual threshold and the degree of "categoricalness" will depend on intrastimulus relations, the nature of the sensory system, training, attention, and other setting factors. This view carries the implication that examples of categorical perception abound in general sensory psychophysics (the region of a masked threshold, the region of the threshold for temporal order, and many others serve as good candidates) and that one only needs to take the time to collect the prescribed data in order to demonstrate the existence of numerous cases of categorical perception for nonspeech stimuli. But it is also true that both previous research and the present discussion support the view that categorical perception in its nearly ideal form will occur only when certain combinations of stimulus configurations as well as training and perceptual-cognitive factors obtain. For example, it is known that boundary between voiced and voiceless categories of plosive consonants depends on the listener's language and the details of synthesis (Abramson and Lisker, 1970; Williams, 1974; Liberman *et al.*, 1958), and we suspect that eventual explanation of these facts will involve interactions among the factors mentioned above.

The continued search for the factors underlying categorical perception and its degree remains important in our view, not because it is unique to human speech, but rather because the notion of categorical perception may aid in the understanding of perception generally and because it seems to be particularly relevant to the analysis and design of biological communications systems whether auditory or nonauditory and whether human or nonhuman.

ACKNOWLEDGMENT

We gratefully acknowledge the importance of discussion with Dr. Charles S. Watson during the planning and conduct of the experiments and his suggestions for improvement of the manuscript.

[*]This research was supported by a Public Health Service Grant (NS 03856) from the National Institute of Neurological and Communicative Disorders and Stroke to the Central Institute for the Deaf. An earlier report of these findings was presented at the 86th Meeting of the Acoustical Society of America, Los Angeles, CA [J. Acoust. Soc. Am. 55, 390 (A) (1974)].

[†]Present address: Laboratory of Psychophysics of Harvard University, Cambridge, MA 02139.
[‡]Present address: Department of Psychology, State University of New York, Binghamton, NY 13901.
[§]Present address: Field Research Center of Rockefeller University, Millbrook, NY 12545.

[1]By "steep" we mean labeling functions that charge 3%–13% per millisecond.

[2]The predicted discrimination scores $P(\hat{c})$ for the oddity task were obtained by summing the appropriate joint probabilities. There are six ways (t_j) to present two different stimuli S_1 and S_2 in an oddity triad. There are eight ways (l_i) for an observer to label a triad, and probabilities of each are calculated from his labeling data. Further, partitioning for those responses scored as correct yields:

$$P(\hat{c}) = \sum_{i=1}^{8} \sum_{j=1}^{6} P(t_j)\, P(l_i \mid t_j)\, P(c \mid t_j l_i),$$

where $\hat{c}$ is a correct response.

[3]The stimuli used by Liberman *et al.* (1961) are not usually described in this manner. The authors themselves describe the changing aspect of the stimuli as "...the delay of the onset of the first formant relative to the second and third," p. 380, and later as "first-formant cutback," p. 382. Careful examination of their Figure 1 reveals, however, that the entire pattern of voice-bar ("triangular patch") and first-formant is delayed relative to the second and third formant. In an early paper by Liberman, Delattre and Cooper (1958) "cutback" and "delay" are clearly distinguished and a footnote describes the stimuli, apparently identical (with the exception of an added burst of high frequency noise) to those of Fig. 1 of the 1961 paper, as follows: "... the triangular patch just below and to the left of the first formant was added because it was found, in this special case, to increase the realism of the sound. It may function as a voice bar or possibly, in combination with the first formant, as a transition. In either event its position is constant in relation to the first formant, and the only difference among the patterns is in the time of onset of the first formant-plus-triangular patch" (p. 161).

[4]The author–subjects did not hear "speech" when listening to noise–buzz sequences and the other subjects did not comment. In our opinion, the noise–buzz stimuli are correclty described as nonspeech sounds.

Abramson, A. S., and Lisker, L. (1970). "Discrimination Along the Voicing Continuum: Cross-Language Tests," in

Proceedings of the 6th International Congress of Phonetic Science, Prague, 1967 (Academiac, Prague), pp. 569–573.

Barclay, J. R. (1972). "Noncategorical Perception of a Voiced Stop: A Replication," Percept. Psychophys. 11, 269–273.

Cutting, J. E., and Rosner, B. S. (1974). "Categories and Boundaries in Speech and Music," Percept. Psychophys. 16, 564–570.

Fujisaki, H., and Kawashima, T. (1969). "On the Modes and Mechanisms of Speech Perception," Sogoshikenjo-Nenpo 28, 67–73.

Fujisaki, H., and Kawashima, T. (1970). "Some Experiments on Speech Perception and a Model for the Perceptual Mechanism," Annu. Rept. Eng. Res. Inst., Fac. Eng., U. Tokyo, 29, pp. 207–214.

Gengel, R. W., and Hirsh, I. J. (1970). "Temporal Order: The Effect of Single Versus Repeated Presentations, Practice, and Verbal Feedback," Percept. Psychophys. 7, 209–211.

Hirsh, I. J. (1959). "Auditory Perception of Temporal Order," J. Acoust. Soc. Am. 31, 757–767.

Hirsh, I. J. (1974). "Temporal Order and Auditory Perception," in *Sensation and Measurement*, edited by H. R. Moskowitz, B. Scharf, and J. C. Stevens (D. Reidel, Dordrecht, Holland).

Hirsh, I. J., and Sherrick, C. E. (1961). "Perceived Order in Different Sense Modalities," J. Exp. Psychol. 62, 423–432.

Lane, H. (1965). "The Motor Theory of Speech Perception: A Critical Review," Psychol. Rev. 72, 275–309.

Liberman, A. M., Delattre, P. C., and Cooper, F. S. (1958), "Some Cues for the Distinction between Voiced and Voiceless Stops in Initial Position," Language Speech 1, 153–167.

Liberman, A. M., Harris, K. S., Hoffman, H. S., and Griffith, B. C. (1957). "The Discrimination of Speech Sounds within and across Phoneme Boundaries," J. Exp. Psychol. 54, 358–368.

Liberman, A. M., Harris, K. S., Kinney, J. A., and Lane, H. (1961). "The Discrimination of Relative Onset-Time of the Components of Certain Speech and Nonspeech Patterns," J. Exp. Psychol. 61, 379–388.

Mattingly, I. G., Liberman, A. M., Syrdal, A. K., and Halwes, T. (1971). "Discrimination in Speech and Nonspeech Modes," Cognit. Psychol. 2, 121–157.

Mostofsky, D. I., Ed. (1965). *Stimulus Generalization* (Stanford University, Stanford, CA, 1965), pp. 389.

Pisoni, D. B. (1973). "Auditory and Phonetic Memory Codes in the Discrimination of Consonants and Vowels," Percept. Psychophys. 13, 253–260.

Pisoni, D. B., and Lazarus, J. H. (1974). "Categorical and Non-categorical Modes of Speech Perception along the Voicing Continuum," J. Acoust. Soc. Am. 55, 328–333.

Studdert-Kennedy, M., Liberman, A. M., Harris, K. S., and Cooper, F. S. (1970). "The Motor Theory of Speech Perception: A Reply to Lane's Critical Review," Psychol. Rev. 77, 234–249.

Williams, L. (1974). "Speech Perception and Production as a Function of Exposure to a Second Language," Ph. D. dissertation (Harvard University), 140 pp. (unpublished).

Perception & Psychophysics
1979, Vol. 25 (6), 457-465

Some effects of later-occurring information on the perception of stop consonant and semivowel

JOANNE L. MILLER
Northeastern University, Boston, Massachusetts 02115

and

ALVIN M. LIBERMAN
Haskins Laboratories, 270 Crown Street, New Haven, Connecticut 06511

In three experiments, we determined how perception of the syllable-initial distinction between the stop consonant [b] and the semivowel [w], when cued by duration of formant transitions, is affected by parts of the sound pattern that occur later in time. For the first experiment, we constructed four series of syllables, similar in that each had initial formant transitions ranging from one short enough for [ba] to one long enough for [wa], but different in overall syllable duration. The consequence in perception was that, as syllable duration increased, the [b-w] boundary moved toward transitions of longer duration. Then, in the second experiment, we increased the duration of the sound by adding a second syllable, [da], (thus creating [bada-wada]), and observed that lengthening the second syllable also shifted the perceived [b-w] boundary in the first syllable toward transitions of longer duration; however, this effect was small by comparison with that produced when the first syllable was lengthened equivalently. In the third experiment, we found that altering the structure of the syllable had an effect that is not to be accounted for by the concomitant change in syllable duration: lengthening the syllable by adding syllable-final transitions appropriate for the stop consonant [d] (thus creating [bad-wad]) caused the perceived [b-w] boundary to shift toward transitions of shorter duration, an effect precisely opposite to that produced when the syllable was lengthened to the same extent by adding steady-state vowel. We suggest that, in all these cases, the later-occurring information specifies rate of articulation and that the effect on the earlier-occurring cue reflects an appropriate perceptual normalization.

In exploratory work with synthetic speech, we chanced on a phenomenon that seemed to hold promise for the study of two related perceptual effects: most directly, how later-occurring aspects of the speech signal modify the perception of an earlier-occurring cue and, by implication, how duration of the syllable specifies, inter alia, the articulatory rate to which the listener must adjust. Following the early findings of Liberman, Delattre, Gerstman, and Cooper (1956), we had used the duration of the initial consonant-vowel transitions to produce the perceived distinction in manner between stop-vowel ([ba]) and semivowel-vowel ([wa]) syllables. Then we varied the duration of the syllable—by extending the steady-state portion of the vowel—and observed that perception

of the transition cue was, in consequence, quite markedly affected: when we made the syllable longer, the manner boundary, as we perceived it, was displaced toward a longer duration of transition.

We were reminded, then, of a series of studies by Summerfield (1975, Note 1) that dealt with the effect of rate of articulation on the perception of the voicing distinction in stop-vowel syllables. Having put his attention on the location of the perceptual boundary along a continuum of voice onset times, a major cue for the distinction in question, Summerfield found that variations in the articulatory rate of the sentence frame caused the perceptual boundary for the target phone to be displaced. More to the point of our interest here, he also found that the rate effect can be quite local, so local, indeed, that it was observed when the syllable containing the target (syllable-initial) phone was isolated and the rate information was conveyed only by variations in the duration of that syllable. If is, of course, just there that Summerfield's results with voicing anticipate ours with manner.

This research was supported by NINCDS Grant NS 14394 to J. L. Miller, HEW Biomedical Research Support Grant RR 07143 to Northeastern University, and NICHD Grant HD 01994 to Haskins Laboratories. Portions of the research were presented at the 95th meeting of the Acoustical Society of America, Providence, 1978. A. M. Liberman is also at the University of Connecticut and Yale University.

0031-5117/79/060457-09$01.15/0

It is, perhaps, to be expected that a cue like voice onset time should be affected by rate of articulation, for the cue is temporal in nature. Indeed, other temporal cues have been shown to be perceived in relation to speech rate. These include, for example, the following: silence duration as a cue for voicing in intervocalic stop consonants (Port, 1976, Note 2) and as a cue for single vs. double consonants (Pickett & Decker, 1960); frication duration and silence duration as cues for the fricative-affricate manner distinction (Repp, Liberman, Eccardt, & Pesetsky, 1978; Dorman, Raphael, & Liberman, Note 3); and vowel duration as a cue for vowel quality (Ainsworth, 1972, 1974; Verbrugge, Strange, Shankweiler, & Edman, 1976; Verbrugge & Shankweiler, Note 4). Since the transition cue for the [b-w] distinction is essentially temporal, it, too, should be perceived in relation to articulatory rate. That it is, in fact, so perceived is indicated by a study carried out concurrently with those we are reporting here. That study (Minifie, Kuhl, & Stecher, Note 5) found that varying the articulatory rate of a sentence frame did affect whether a word within the sentence was heard as beginning with [b] or [w]. Moreover, investigations into the production of syllable-initial consonants at various rates of articulation have revealed changes in the speed with which the relevant gestures are made and also in the durations of the resulting acoustic transitions (Gay, 1978; Gay & Hirose, 1973; Gay, Ushijima, Hirose, & Cooper, 1974). Given that changes in transition duration occur with changes in rate, we should expect that the listener would make the appropriate normalization when using transition duration to cue a phonetic distinction.

We will here report three experiments designed to enlighten us further about the phenomenon described in our opening paragraph, namely, that the perceived distinction between syllable-initial stop and semi-vowel, as cued by duration of transitions, is affected by acoustic information that occurs later in time. In the first experiment, we are concerned primarily to establish the phenomenon more securely than our preliminary observations can have done. In the second experiment, we ask whether the effect of later-occuring information is confined to a single syllable. The point of the third experiment is to see if the effect of the later-occurring aspects of the signal is only by changes in syllable duration, or whether it is also influenced by the structure of the syllable.

EXPERIMENT 1

That duration of the steady-state portion of the syllable-final vowel affects the perceived boundary between syllable-initial stop and semivowel was, as we have pointed out, reasonably apparent from our initial observations. But those were based on stimulus variations that were not so systematic as they might have been, and the judgments were made only by us. It is appropriate, then, that we do the experiment properly, the more so in order to delimit the range of durations over which the effect can be found.

Method

Stimuli. The stimuli for all experiments we report in this paper were synthetic speech patterns generated on the Haskins Laboratories parallel-resonance synthesizer. For Experiment 1, we synthesized four series of syllables that ranged from [ba] to [wa]. The syllables were three-formant patterns, consisting of a fixed initial 20 msec of prevoicing (first formant only), a variable duration of formant transition appropriate for [b] or [w], and a subsequent period of steady-state formants. To create each series, we varied the transition duration from 16 to 64 msec in 4-msec steps, for a total of 13 stimuli per series. Syllables with relatively short transitions were perceived as [ba] and those with longer transitions as [wa]. As we increased the duration of transitions in 4-msec steps, we decreased the duration of the steady-state formants by the same amount; thus, within a given series, all stimuli had the same overall duration. The four [ba-wa] series differed from each other in the overall duration of the syllables, specifically, in the duration of the steady-state formants. These syllable durations were: 80, 152, 224, and 296 msec.

For all stimuli, the first formant (F1) started at 234 Hz and rose linearly to a steady-state value of 769 Hz, while the second formant (F2) began at 616 Hz and rose linearly to a final value of 1,232 Hz. The third formant (F3) remained constant at 2,862 Hz. The overall amplitude of each syllable had a gradual onset, increasing by 28 dB over the course of the prevoicing and the formant transitions, and remained constant thereafter.[1]

Each of the 52 stimuli (4 series × 13 stimuli per series) was digitized at a 10-kHz sampling rate by the pulse code modulation (PCM) system at the Haskins Laboratories. These stimuli were then used to make three randomized test orders, each containing eight instances of each stimulus. All stimuli were recorded with an interstimulus interval of 3 sec.

Procedure. All subjects listened to the three test orders over the course of two sessions. They were informed that they would hear computer-generated syllables, [ba]-like or [wa]-like, and of variable duration. They were asked to decide about each syllable whether it was [ba] or [wa], guessing if necessary, and to indicate the decision by marking an appropriately formatted response sheet. The stimuli were presented to the subjects through earphones at approximately 78 dB SPL, measured for the peak intensity of the vowel.

Subjects. The subjects were eight college students who were paid for their participation in the experiment. None reported a history of a speech or hearing disorder.

Results

As is apparent from Figure 1, there was a systematic effect of syllable duration on the identification of the stop consonant [b] and the semivowel [w]: as syllable duration increased, an increasingly longer transition was required to perceive [w]. To obtain a summary account of the effect, we calculated for each subject the location of the [b-w] phonetic boundary for each of the four syllable durations, using the procedure introduced by Eimas, Cooper, and Corbit (1973). That procedure calls for transforming the percentages of [b] responses to z scores, fitting a regression line to the transformed data by finding a

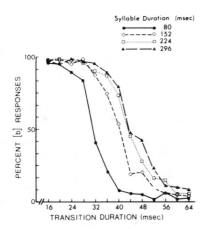

Figure 1. Effect of syllable duration on the [b-w] distinction as cued by transition duration.

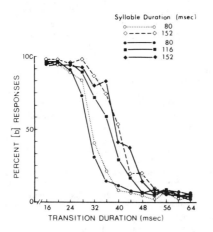

Figure 2. Replication and extension of the effect of syllable duration on the [b-w] distinction. The data from the main study are shown by open symbols and the data from the auxiliary study by filled symbols.

least-mean-squares solution and then taking the boundary to be the stimulus value corresponding to a z score of zero. Averaged across subjects, the mean boundary locations for the 80-, 152-, 224-, and 296-msec series proved to be at transition durations of 31.9, 41.3, 44.7, and 46.6 msec, respectively. Thus, over the range of syllable durations tested, we obtained a shift of about 15 msec in the location of the boundary. As one can see either by examining the calculated boundaries or by inspecting the identification functions of Figure 1, the largest boundary shifts were at the shortest syllable durations, with increasingly smaller shifts occurring as syllable duration increased. A consequence is that the gap between the functions for the 80- and 152-msec series—about 9 msec of difference in the location of the boundary—is quite large.

In order to fill that gap, and at the same time to test the replicability of our initial findings, we conducted an auxiliary study in which we included the two shortest syllable durations (80 and 152 msec) of the initial study, together with a new condition of syllable duration (116 msec) lying midway between them. (These new syllables were constructed by extending the steady-state vowel of each syllable in the 80-msec series by 36 msec.) The subjects for this auxiliary experiment were the same eight students who had participated in the initial one. In Figure 2, we see the results of the three syllable-duration conditions of the auxiliary experiment and, for comparison, the results of the two corresponding conditions of the initial study. It is plain that the two corresponding conditions of the two studies did indeed produce essentially the same results and that the new, intermediate condition produced an intermediate result.

The combined data from the two studies, shown in Figure 3, clearly indicate that, as syllable duration increases, there is a perfectly regular change in the way our subjects identified the patterns as [ba] and [wa]: the longer the duration of the syllable, the longer the duration of transition needed in order to hear [wa]. Using the same combined data, we calculated, for each subject, the location of the [b-w] boundary for each of the five syllable durations. Those data are presented in Table 1, where we see that the effect of syllable duration, shown in Figure 3, occurred for every subject in nearly every syllable-duration condition. The mean boundary values are shown, as a function of syllable duration, in Figure 4. There we see, as we might have inferred from Figure 3, that the transition duration at the boundary is a smooth and negatively accelerated function of the duration of the syllable.

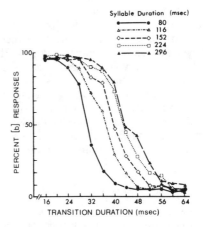

Figure 3. Combined results of the two studies of the effect of syllable duration on the [b-w] distinction. (The identification functions for the 80- and 152-msec series are based on data from both studies of Experiment 1).

460   MILLER AND LIBERMAN

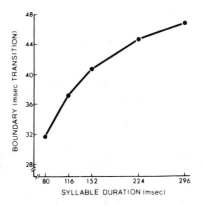

Figure 4. Effect of syllable duration on the location of the [b-w] boundary. (The boundary values for the 80- and 152-msec series are based on data from both studies of Experiment 1).

EXPERIMENT 2

In Experiment 1, we found that later-occurring information in the syllable affected the perception of an earlier-occurring cue: the duration of the syllable determined whether the initial formant transitions of different durations were perceived as [b] or [w]. Now we mean to find out whether such effects are contained within syllable boundaries. What is the effect, if any, of adding a second syllable of variable duration to the one containing the transition cue?

There is reason to believe that the effect of adding a second syllable will be small. We have in mind the experiments by Summerfield (1975, Note 1) described in the introduction to this paper. As the reader may recall, Summerfield found that perception of an important temporal cue for voicing (voice onset time) was affected by variations in the rate at which the utterance was articulated and, further, that the effect was quite local. That is, rate information closer to the target phone had more effect on its perception than rate information that occurred farther away. A similar result has been reported by Port (Note 2) for the intervocalic voicing distinction as cued by duration of intersyllabic silence. If we assume about the results of Experiment 1 that syllable duration had its effect because it specified the rate of articulation, then we might suppose that, following the Summerfield and Port studies, the most important duration would be that of the syllable containing the target phone.

Method

Stimuli. For this experiment, we used stimuli that were identical to some of those used in Experiment 1, except that a [da] was added to each syllable. To create these disyllables, we selected from the stimuli of Experiment 1 just those that had durations of 80 and 224 msec. The reader will recall that stimuli of both durations—let us call them the 80-msec series and the 224-msec series—had initial formant transitions that ranged from 16 to 64 msec in steps of 4 msec, and were perceived, depending on the duration

of the formant transitions, as [ba] or [wa]. For the purposes of this experiment, we added to each of those patterns a synthetic syllable, [da], 72 msec in duration. Thus, we had one series containing stimuli composed of an 80-msec [ba] or [wa] followed by a 72-msec [da], which we will refer to as the 80-72-msec series, and one series with stimuli consisting of a 224-msec [ba] or [wa] followed by a 72-msec [da], which we will refer to as the 224-72-msec series. Next, we created two additional [bada-wada] series by extending the steady-state formants of the [da] so as to make the syllable 216 (instead of 72) msec long. These will be referred to as the 80-216-msec series and the 224-216-msec series. Note that a comparison of performance on the two series containing a short [ba] or [wa] (the 80-72- and 80-216-msec series) with performance on the two series containing a long [ba] or [wa] (the 224-72- and 224-216-msec series) will allow us to assess the effect of lengthening the syllable containing the transition cue for [b-w]. On the other hand, comparing performance on the two series containing the short [da] (the 80-72- and 224-72-msec series) with that on the series containing the long [da] (the 80-216- and 224-216-msec series) will show the effect of lengthening not the target syllable, but the one following.

Each of the two [da]s contained an initial 24 msec of transition followed by steady-state formants, 48 msec in length for the 72-msec [da] and 192 msec in length for the 216-msec [da]. The starting frequency values for the [da] transitions were 234 Hz (F1), 1,541 Hz (F2), and 3,195 Hz(F3), and the steady-state formant frequency values for the [da] were the same as those for the [ba] or [wa], namely, 769 Hz (F1), 1,232 Hz (F2), and 2,862 Hz (F3). As for the amplitude of the [da], it increased by 10.5 dB over the initial transition segment, reaching and maintaining a level equal to that of the first syllable ([ba]) or ([wa]). Fundamental frequency for [da] was also set equal to that of the first syllable.

Each of the 52 stimuli (4 series × 13 stimuli per series) was digitized at a 10-kHz sampling rate, using the PCM system. We then generated three randomized test orders, each containing eight instances of each of these 52 tokens. These orders were recorded on audio tape with an interstimulus interval of 3 sec.

Procedure. The subjects were presented with the three test orders over the course of two sessions. They were informed that they would hear computer-generated disyllables, [bada] or [wada], and that the durations of both syllables would vary. They were asked to decide whether the first syllable of each stimulus was [ba] or [wa], guessing if necessary, and to indicate their choice by writing B or W on an answer sheet. All subjects heard the stimuli through earphones at approximately 78 dB SPL, measured for the peak intensity of the vowel in the first syllable.

Subjects. Fourteen paid listeners participated in this experiment, including three subjects who served as listeners in the first experiment. All were college students or staff who reported no history of a speech or hearing disorder.

Results

In Figure 5 are plotted the data from the four [bada-wada] series. We should first examine the effect on the [b-w] boundary of changing the duration of the first syllable—that is, the one containing the target [b] or [w] phone—while holding constant the duration of the second syllable ([da]). Clearly, lengthening the first syllable (from 80 to 224 msec) shifted the [ba-wa] boundary to a longer duration of transition, and this was true whether the duration of the second syllable was 72 or 216 msec. Calculating the boundary values by the method described in Experiment 1, we obtained values (in milliseconds of transition) for the four disyllables as follows: 80-72 = 33.0, 80-216 = 35.9, 224-72 = 40.7, and 224-216 = 41.9. The average boundary value for the two series with a short [ba] or [wa] (80-72 and 80-216) is 34.4 msec, and that for the two series with a long [ba] or [wa] (224-72 and 224-216) is 41.3 msec. Thus the boundary shift attributable to the difference in duration of the first syllable is about 7 msec. The reliability of this difference was confirmed by an analysis of variance, First Syllable by Second Syllable by Subject, performed on the boundary scores, that showed a significant effect of first syllable (p < .001) but no significant interaction. Thus, the magnitude of shift resulting from lengthening the first syllable did not depend on the duration of the second syllable.

Consider, next, the effect on the [b-w] boundary of changing the duration of the second syllable ([da]) from 72 to 216 msec. Making the appropriate comparisons in Figure 5, we see that there was, indeed, an effect and, further, that the effect was in the same direction as that produced by variation in the duration of the first syllable. Moreover, the analysis of variance on the boundary scores, mentioned above, showed that the effect of lengthening the second syllable was reliable (p < .01). Again, the lack of a reliable interaction between First Syllable and Second Syllable indicated that the effect of lengthening [da] did not differ as a function of the duration of the first syllable. Of particular relevance to our purposes, however, is the fact that the boundary shift produced by changing the duration of the second syllable, when averaged over the two durations of the first syllable, proved to be only 2 msec, smaller by fair margin than the 7-msec boundary shift produced by varying the duration of the first syllable. A difference in that direction was, in fact, found with 13 of the 14 subjects; the remaining subject showed no difference.

We move now to comparisons that permit us to see more directly whether the location of the [b-w] boundary is determined primarily by the duration of the first syllable, as the results so far suggest, or, alternatively, by the duration of the entire disyllable. For that purpose we reproduce some of the results of Experiment 1 and set them alongside some of the results of Experiment 2, with which we are now concerned. That is done in Figure 6. Now we are able to take advantage of an aspect of our experimental design. It is that the durations of two of the [bada-wada] patterns were so chosen as to create disyllables having the following characteristics: (1) their overall durations (152 and 296 msec) are equal to the durations of two of the four monosyllables of Experiment 1, while (2) the duration of the first syllable of each of these disyllables (80 msec) is equal to another of the monosyllables of Experiment 1. If the boundary is determined primarily by the duration of the first syllable, then the results obtained with both of the disyllables, whether the durations are 80-plus-72 or 80-plus-216, would be like those for the 80-msec condition of Experiment 1. But if it is the duration

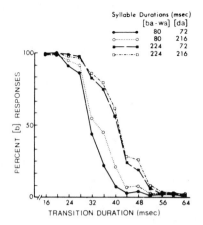

Figure 5. Effect of duration of a first and second syllable on perception of the [b-w] distinction in initial position in the first syllable.

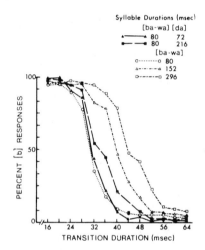

Figure 6. Comparison of the effect of varying the duration of a first and second syllable on perception of the [b-w] distinction in initial position in the first syllable.

of the disyllable that is important, then the results with the disyllables should compare with those obtained in Experiment 1 when the monosyllables were 152 and 296 msec. We see from Figure 6 that, in fact, the results with the disyllables lie quite close to those of the 80-msec monosyllables, closer certainly than to the monosyllables whose durations (152 and 296 msec) are equal to the overall durations of the disyllables. Plainly, then, the location of the boundary for a syllable-initial [b-w] contrast is primarily determined by the duration of the syllable that contains the target phone.

EXPERIMENT 3

In Experiments 1 and 2, we found that perception of a syllable-initial transition-duration cue for the

462   MILLER AND LIBERMAN

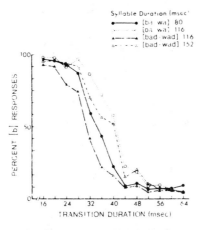

Syllable Duration (msec)
- ●——● [ba-wa] 80
- ○········○ [ba-wa] 116
- ▲——▲ [bad-wad] 116
- △-·-·-△ [bad-wad] 152

Figure 7. Comparison of the effect on the [b-w] distinction of lengthening the syllable by extending the steady-state formants and by adding transitions that cue a final consonant.

distinction between [b] and [w] was affected by the duration of the syllable containing the target phone and, to a lesser extent, by the duration of a following syllable. Putting our attention now again on the syllable containing the target phone, we ask whether its internal structure, as well as its duration, has an effect. To find out, we have compared two ways of changing syllable duration: by extending the steady-state formants, as we had done in the earlier experiments, and by adding transitions appropriate for a syllable-final stop consonant.

If we assume, as we have before, that the effect of syllable duration is via an adjustment (by the listener) for the rate of articulation it specifies, we might suppose that the internal structure of the syllable would have an effect independently of its duration. Thus, for example, two syllables that have the same overall duration but different internal structures—one ending in a voiced stop and the other ending in a vowel—would presumably have been produced at different rates of articulation. For such different syllables, then, the [b-w] boundary should be located at different durations of transitions.

Method

Stimuli. The stimuli for this study comprised four series of synthetic syllables. Two of these, identical with some that were used in Experiment 1, consisted of prevoicing and initial formant transitions (appropriate for [b] or [w]) of variable duration (16 to 64 msec in steps of 4 msec), followed by steady-state formants (appropriate for [a]) of variable duration, to yield CV syllables with total stimulus durations of 80 msec in the case of one series and 116 msec in the other. We will refer to these "old" series as the [ba-wa]-80 and the [ba-wa]-116 series. The two new series were formed by simply adding to the end of each of the "old" patterns 36 msec of formant transitions appropriate for a syllable-final [d]. Consequently, these syllables sounded like [bad] or [wad] and had a duration of 116 msec in the case of the one series ([bad-wad]-116) and 152 msec in the other ([bad-wad]-152). Across the final [d] transition, the first formant fell linearly from its

steady-state value of 769 to 234 Hz, as the second and third formants rose linearly from their steady-state levels of 1,232 and 2,862 Hz to 1,541 and 3,363 Hz, respectively. During this period, the overall amplitude fell 4.5 dB.

Using the PCM system, we digitized the stimuli (10-kHz sampling rate) and then created three test orders, each containing random arrangements of eight tokens of each of the 52 stimulus types (4 series × 13 stimuli per series). The interstimulus interval was 3 sec.

Procedure. The three test orders were presented to the subjects in two sessions. The subjects were told that they would hear one of four syllables—[ba], [wa], [bad], or [wad]—and that these would vary in duration. They were asked to indicate for each syllable whether it began with [b] or [w], and to guess if necessary. The syllables were presented through earphones at approximately 78 dB SPL, measured for the peak intensity of the vowel.

Subjects. The subjects were 10 paid college students who reported no speech or hearing disorders. Two of the listeners had participated in one or more of our previous experiments with [b-w].

Results

Having in mind that half of this experiment was an exact repetition of Experiment 1, we should first make the appropriate comparison of results. For that purpose we look, in Figure 7, at the functions that were obtained with the two [ba-wa] series. We observe that, as in Experiment 1, lengthening the steady-state vowel caused the [b-w] boundary to shift toward a longer duration of transition. As determined by the method referred to in Experiment 1, the phonetic boundaries were found to lie at 36.1 msec for the syllables with overall durations of 80 msec ([ba-wa]-80) and at 41.8 msec for those with durations of 116 msec ([ba-wa]-116). These are to be compared with boundaries of 31.8 and 37.2 msec that were obtained for the same conditions in Experiment 1 (see Table 1). Thus, the magnitude of the boundary shift owing to the 36-msec change in syllable duration was approximately equal in the two experiments, but in Experiment 3 all boundaries fell at longer transition durations. We do not know why. The only differences

Table 1
Individual and Mean [b-w] Boundary Values, in Milliseconds of Transition Duration, for the Several Syllable Durations of Experiment 1

Subject	Syllable Duration				
	80	116	152	224	296
1	28.8	35.2	40.0	47.2	48.0
2	33.6	36.0	40.8	43.2	46.4
3	38.4	45.6	46.4	48.8	48.0
4	28.8	32.0	37.6	40.8	41.6
5	28.8	36.0	39.2	45.6	46.4
6	33.6	36.0	42.4	48.8	50.4
7	28.8	35.2	39.2	44.0	44.8
8	33.6	41.6	41.6	39.2	47.2
Mean	31.8	37.2	40.9	44.7	46.6

Note—The scores for the 80- and 152-msec durations are the averages of the scores from the main and auxiliary studies.

were in the subjects and in the overall contexts in which the stimuli were presented.

In all of the experimental results so far presented, the target syllable—that is, the one containing the syllable-initial [b] or [w]—had the structure CV. It is of interest, then, to examine the effect of varying the duration of the steady-state vowel in a CVC syllable. To see that effect, we look at the two remaining functions in Figure 7—that is, those for the [bad-wad] series having durations of 116 msec ([bad-wad]-116) and 152 msec ([bad-wad]-152). We observe that with the CVC syllable, as with the CV, increasing the duration of the steady-state vowel causes the [b-w] boundary to shift toward longer durations of transition. Calculating these boundaries as we have the others, we obtained locations of 32.5 and 39.4 msec for the [bad-wad]-116 and [bad-wad]-152 series, respectively.

Having now seen the effect of increasing the duration of the syllable by adding steady-state vowel (in both CV and CVC structures), we can turn to the question that is of greatest interest to us in this experiment—namely, how does this effect compare with that which is obtained when the same increases in syllable duration are produced by adding, not steady-state vowel, but syllable-final formant transitions appropriate for a stop? To answer that question, we should use the functions shown in Figure 7 to make two comparisons. The first is between [ba-wa]-80 and [bad-wad]-116. We see, then, that the phonetic boundary for [bad-wad]-116 is at a *shorter* transition duration than that for [ba-wa]-80. Recall, now, that the effect of increasing syllable duration by adding 36 msec of steady-state vowel was to shift the phonetic boundary toward a *longer* duration of syllable-initial transition. Thus, the two ways of increasing syllable duration—adding steady-state vowel or adding syllable-final (stop) transitions—have exactly opposite effects.

The second comparison we want to make is between [ba-wa]-116 and [bad-wad]-152. Here we see the same effect that we observed in the comparison we just made between [ba-wa]-80 and [bad-wad]-116—namely, that lengthening the syllable by adding 36 msec of syllable-final transitions shifted the phonetic boundary for the [b-w] distinction toward shorter durations of syllable-initial transitions. Since we do not have, in this experiment, a condition of [ba-wa]-152, we cannot directly compare the effect of lengthening the syllable by the two different means, as we did above for the cases of [ba-wa]-80, [ba-wa]-116, and [bad-wad]-116. However, we know from the results of Experiment 1 that changing syllable duration from 116 to 152 msec by adding 36 msec of steady-state vowel did, in fact, shift the boundary toward longer durations of transitions. Thus, we have further evidence that adding 36 msec of steady-state vowel and

the same amount of syllable-final transition have opposite effects.[2] This conclusion is supported by an analysis of variance performed on the individual boundary scores, Adding Steady-State Vowel by Adding Formant Transitions by Subject. The opposite effects of Adding Steady-State Vowel and Adding Formant Transitions were both significant (p < .001 and p < .05, respectively), and the interaction between these two effects was not significant (p > .10).

DISCUSSION

Our three experiments show that information occurring later in the speech stream affects the perception of an earlier-occurring cue. When considered, most generally, as an after-going effect, our finding is one of a class that is common in speech perception. For example, it has been found by several investigators that perception of cues for stop and fricative consonants depends in some instances on the nature of the following vowel (e.g., Cooper, Delattre, Liberman, Borst, & Gerstman, 1952; Dorman, Studdert-Kennedy, & Raphael, 1977; Fischer-Jorgensen, 1954; Kunisaki & Fujisaki, Note 6; Repp & Mann, Note 7). Moreover, the effect is not confined within a single syllable, since information present in a following syllable can affect the perception of phonetic segments that belong to the preceding one (e.g., Repp, 1978; Repp et al., 1978; Dorman, Raphael, Liberman, & Repp, Note 8). Such after-going effects are important, because they imply that phonetic perception is not accomplished, phone by phone, in a simple progression through the acoustic signal. Apparently, the perceiver operates over relatively long stretches of sound, integrating into unitary phonetic percepts a numerous variety of acoustic cues that are quite widely distributed in time and thoroughly overlapped with cues for other phones (cf. Liberman, Cooper, Shankweiler, & Studdert-Kennedy, 1967).

Of the after-going effects reported in the literature, most are associated with the way articulatory and coarticulatory maneuvers smear the acoustic information for the discrete and successive segments of the phonetic message. Thus, the cues for a single phone may be spread through several acoustic segments as, for example, when stop-consonant closure and opening into a following vowel produce a period of silence, a transient burst of sound, a period of frication, some aspiration, and, finally, the onset of voicing, usually at some point during the formant transitions into the vowel (cf. Fant, 1973; Fischer-Jorgensen, 1954; Halle, Hughes, & Radley, 1957). Or, in apparently opposite fashion, coarticulation may cause cues for successive phonetic segments to be collapsed into a single segment of sound and conveyed simultaneously on the same acoustic para-

464   MILLER AND LIBERMAN

meter as, for example, when the initial formant transitions convey information both about the initial consonant and the following vowel of a CV syllable (Liberman et al., 1967).

The after-going effects we have reported in this paper are, however, of a different sort, in that they are apparently owing to a different cause: normalization for the consequences of changes in rate of articulation. As we pointed out in the introduction to this paper, there is reason to believe that different rates of articulation produce different durations of formant transition in syllable-initial consonants. There is, moreover, considerable basis for supposing that information about rate of articulation is provided by syllable duration, one of the variables of our experiment (cf. Gay, 1978; Klatt, 1976; Peterson & Lehiste, 1960; Gaitenby, Note 9). We conclude, therefore, that the result of the first two experiments—namely, that the perceived [b-w] boundary shifted as a function of syllable-duration—is to be interpreted as an appropriate adjustment by the listener for changes in articulatory rate.

Having in mind that one of the rate-specifying variables in our experiments was simply duration of the syllable, we should take note here of those cases in which duration is a cue in its own right. There is, for example, the distinction between voiced and voiceless stops in syllable-final position (e.g., [ɛd] vs [ɛt]). In that case, the syllable is longer, other things being equal, when the final stop is voiced, and there is evidence that listeners use the duration appropriately in identifying the voicing value of the final segment (e.g., Denes, 1955; Raphael, 1972). Or, as is well known, a similar situation exists for certain vowel distinctions. Thus, [æ] is inherently longer than [ɛ] and here, too, duration is, per se, a cue for the phonetic identity of the vowel (e.g., Peterson & Lehiste, 1960; Mermelstein, Liberman, & Fowler, Note 10; cf. Verbrugge & Shankweiler, Note 4).

Thus duration can, in fact, specify duration and not, as in our experiment, rate of articulation. Accordingly, it is of interest to know what happens in such cases when, as in our third experiment, duration is increased, not by extending the steady-state vowel but by adding formant transitions appropriate for a stop consonant. Such experiments have shown that adding (stop-consonant) formant transitions has the same effect as adding a certain duration of steady-state vowel (Mermelstein et al., Note 10; Raphael, Dorman, and Liberman, Note 11; cf. Mermelstein, 1978). That is, when duration, qua duration, is being specified, formant transitions contribute to it, just as we should expect, given the impossibility of dividing a syllable into acoustic segments (transitions and steady-state) that correspond one-to-one with the phonetic segments. In contrast, as the reader will recall, we found in our third study that increasing the duration of the syllable by adding formant transitions had an effect precisely opposite to that produced by adding the same amount of steady state.[3] This suggests that, in our experiments, duration itself was not the cue; its effect was presumably owing instead to its role in specifying rate of articulation. In that case, we should have expected that the structure of the syllable as well as its duration would be important.

The experiments reported here have demonstrated that the effect of transition duration as a cue for the [b-w] distinction is influenced by the duration and structure of the syllable containing the cue and, to a lesser extent, by the duration of a subsequent syllable. In our view, this after-going effect reflects an adjustment by the listener to the articulatory rate of the speaker: the duration and structure of the syllable provide information about rate, and the listener uses this information when making a phonetic judgment of [b] vs. [w].

REFERENCE NOTES

1. Summerfield, A. Q. *On articulatory rate and perceptual constancy in phonetic perception.* Unpublished manuscript, 1978.

2. Port, R. F. *Effects of word-internal versus word-external tempo on the voicing boundary for medial-stop closure.* Paper presented at the 95th meeting of the Acoustical Society of America, Providence, R.I., 1978.

3. Dorman, M. F., Raphael, L. J., & Liberman, A. M. *Further observations on the role of silence in the perception of stop consonants.* Paper presented at the 91st meeting of the Acoustical Society of America, Washington, D.C., 1976.

4. Verbrugge, R. R., & Shankweiler, D. P. *Prosodic information for vowel identity.* Paper presented at the 93rd meeting of the Acoustical Society of America, University Park, 1977.

5. Minifie, F., Kuhl, P., & Stecher, B. *Categorical perception of [b] and [w] during changes in rate of utterance.* Paper presented at the 94th meeting of the Acoustical Society of America, Miami, 1977.

6. Kunisaki, O., & Fujisaki, H. *On the influence of context upon perception of voiceless fricative consonants.* Research Institute of Logopedics and Phoniatrics, University of Tokyo, Annual Bulletin No. 11, 1977, 85-91.

7. Repp, B. H., & Mann, V. A. *Influence of vocalic context on perception of the [s]-[ʃ] distinction.* Paper presented at the 96th meeting of the Acoustical Society of America, Honolulu, 1978.

8. Dorman, M. F., Raphael, L. J. Liberman, A. M., & Repp, B. *Some maskinglike phenomena in speech perception.* Paper presented at the 89th meeting of the Acoustical Society of America, Austin, Tex., 1975.

9. Gaitenby, J. *The elastic word.* In Haskins Laboratories Status Report on Speech Research, SR-2, 1965.

10. Mermelstein, P., Liberman, A. M., & Fowler, A. *Perceptual assessment of vowel duration in consonantal context and its application to vowel identification.* Paper presented at the 94th meeting of the Acoustical Society of America, Miami, 1977.

11. Raphael, L. J., Dorman, M. F., & Liberman, A. M. *The perception of vowel duration in VC and CVC syllables.* Paper presented at the 89th meeting of the Acoustical Society of America, Austin, Tex., 1975.

12. Suzuki, H. *Mutually complementary effect of rate and amount of formant transition in distinguishing vowel, semi-vowel, and stop-consonant.* Research Laboratory of Electronics, Quarterly Progress Report No. 96, 1970, M.I.T., 164-172.

REFERENCES

AINSWORTH, W. A. Duration as a cue in the recognition of synthetic vowels. *Journal of the Acoustical Society of America*, 1972, **51**, 648-651.

AINSWORTH, W. A. The influence of precursive sequences on the perception of synthesized vowels. *Language and Speech*, 1974, **17**, 103-109.

COOPER, F. S., DELATTRE, P. C., LIBERMAN, A. M., BORST, J. M., & GERSTMAN, L. J. Some experiments on the perception of synthetic speech sounds. *Journal of the Acoustical Society of America*, 1952, **24**, 597-606.

DENES, P. Effect of duration on the perception of voicing. *Journal of the Acoustical Society of America*, 1955, **27**, 761-764.

DORMAN, M. F., STUDDERT-KENNEDY, M., & RAPHAEL, L. J. Stop-consonant recognition: Release bursts and formant transitions as functionally equivalent, context-dependent cues. *Perception & Psychophysics*, 1977, **22**, 109-122.

EIMAS, P. D., COOPER, W. E., & CORBIT, J. D. Some properties of linguistic feature detectors. *Perception & Psychophysics*, 1973, **13**, 247-252.

FANT, G. *Speech sounds and features.* Cambridge: MIT Press, 1973.

FISCHER-JORGENSEN, E. Acoustic analysis of stop consonants. *Miscellanea Phonetica*, 1954, **2**, 42-59.

GAY, T. Effect of speaking rate on vowel formant transitions. *Journal of the Acoustical Society of America*, 1978, **63**, 223-230.

GAY, T., & HIROSE, H. Effect of speaking rate on labial consonant production. *Phonetica*, 1973, **27**, 44-56.

GAY, T., USHIJIMA, T., HIROSE, H., & COOPER, F. S. Effect of speaking rate on labial consonant-vowel articulation. *Journal of Phonetics*, 1974, **2**, 47-63.

HALLE, M., HUGHES, G. W., & RADLEY, J. P. A. Acoustic properties of stop consonants. *Journal of the Acoustical Society of America*, 1957, **29**, 107-116.

KLATT, D. H. Linguistic uses of segmental duration in English. *Journal of the Acoustical Society of America*, 1976, **59**, 1208-1221.

LIBERMAN, A. M., COOPER, F. S., SHANKWEILER, D. P., & STUDDERT-KENNEDY, M. Perception of the speech code. *Psychological Review*, 1967, **74**, 431-461.

LIBERMAN, A. M., DELATTRE, P. C., GERSTMAN, L. J., & COOPER, F. S. Tempo of frequency change as a cue for distinguishing classes of speech sounds. *Journal of Experimental Psychology*, 1956, **52**, 127-137.

MERMELSTEIN, P. On the relationship between vowel and consonant identification when cued by the same acoustic information. *Perception & Psychophysics*, 1978, **23**, 331-336.

PETERSON, G. E., & LEHISTE, I. Duration of syllable nuclei in English. *Journal of the Acoustical Society of America*, 1960, **32**, 693-703.

PICKETT, J. M., & DECKER, L. R. Time factors in perception of a double consonant. *Language and Speech*, 1960, **3**, 11-17.

PORT, R. F. *The influence of speaking tempo on the duration of stressed vowel and medial stop in English trochee words.* Unpublished PhD thesis, University of Connecticut, 1976.

RAPHAEL, L. J. Preceding vowel duration as a cue to the perception of the voicing characteristic of word-final consonants in American English. *Journal of the Acoustical Society of America*, 1972, **51**, 1296-1303.

REPP, B. H. Perceptual integration and differentiation of spectral cues for intervocalic stop consonants. *Perception & Psychophysics*, 1978, **24**, 471-485.

REPP, B. H., LIBERMAN, A. M., ECCARDT, T., & PESETSKY, D. Perceptual integration of acoustic cues for stop, fricative, and affricate manner. *Journal of Experimental Psychology: Human Perception and Performance*, 1978, **4**, 621-637.

SUMMERFIELD, A. Q. *Information processing analysis of perceptual adjustments to source and context variables in speech.* Unpublished PhD thesis, Queen's University of Belfast, 1975.

VERBRUGGE, R. R., STRANGE, W., SHANKWEILER, D. P., & EDMAN, T. R. What information enables a listener to map a talker's vowel space? *Journal of the Acoustical Society of America*, 1976, **60**, 198-212.

NOTES

1. Since the starting and terminating formant-frequency values of the transition segment were kept constant as its duration was changed, its rate was necessarily changed as well. That is, as transition duration varied from short ([ba]) to long ([wa]), transition rate varied from fast to slow. Given that Liberman et al. (1956) have shown that transition duration, and not rate, appears to be the effective cue for the [b-w] contrast, we will refer to the stimulus manipulation in our experiments as one of duration (cf. Suzuki, Note 12).

2. Summerfield (Note 1) has reported a similar finding for the syllable-initial voiced-voiceless boundary as cued by voice onset time (VOT). Specifically, he found that the boundary was shifted toward a longer VOT value as the syllable was lengthened by extending the steady-state vowel, but that it was shifted toward a shorter value when the syllable was lengthened by adding a final fricative.

3. We should point out a difference between the experiments of Mermelstein et al. (Note 10) and Raphael et al. (Note 11), on the one hand, and those conducted by us, on the other. In their experiments, the transitional information was added to the beginning of the syllable (thus, for example, changing [ɛd] vs. [ɛt] to [dɛd] vs. [dɛt]), whereas we added the consonantal transitions to the end of the syllable (so that [ba] vs. [wa] became [bad] vs. [wad]). Although unlikely, it may be that the added transitions functioned differently in their experiments and ours because of this difference in where in the syllable they were added.

(Received for publication October 30, 1978;
revision accepted March 13, 1979.)

Perception & Psychophysics
1975, Vol. 18 (5), 331-340

An effect of linguistic experience:
The discrimination of [r] and [l] by native speakers
of Japanese and English

KUNIKO MIYAWAKI
University of Tokyo, Tokyo, Japan

WINIFRED STRANGE and ROBERT VERBRUGGE
University of Minnesota, Minneapolis, Minnesota 55455

ALVIN M. LIBERMAN
Haskins Laboratories, New Haven, Connecticut 06510

JAMES J. JENKINS
University of Minnesota, Minneapolis, Minnesota 55455

and

OSAMU FUJIMURA
University of Tokyo, Tokyo, Japan

To test the effect of linguistic experience on the perception of a cue that is known to be effective in distinguishing between [r] and [l] in English, 21 Japanese and 39 American adults were tested on discrimination of a set of synthetic speech-like stimuli. The 13 "speech" stimuli in this set varied in the initial stationary frequency of the third formant (F3) and its subsequent transition into the vowel over a range sufficient to produce the perception of [r a] and [l a] for American subjects and to produce [r a] (which is not in phonemic contrast to [l a]) for Japanese subjects. Discrimination tests of a comparable set of stimuli consisting of the isolated F3 components provided a "nonspeech" control. For Americans, the discrimination of the speech stimuli was nearly categorical, i.e., comparison pairs which were identified as different phonemes were discriminated with high accuracy, while pairs which were identified as the same phoneme were discriminated relatively poorly. In comparison, discrimination of speech stimuli by Japanese subjects was only slightly better than chance for all comparison pairs. Performance on nonspeech stimuli, however, was virtually identical for Japanese and American subjects; both groups showed highly accurate discrimination of all comparison pairs. These results suggest that the effect of linguistic experience is specific to perception in the "speech mode."

One way to examine the effect of linguistic experience on the perception of speech is to compare the discrimination of phonetic segments by two groups of speakers: one group speaks a language in which the segments under study are functionally distinctive, the other does not. In that circumstance, a difference in the ability to discriminate can be attributed to the linguistic use of the distinction in the one case and lack of such linguistic use in the other.

Two cross-language studies of the kind described above are relevant to the experiment reported in this paper. One study deals with vowels (Stevens, Liberman, Studdert-Kennedy, & Ohman, 1969) and one deals with the voicing distinction in stops (Abramson & Lisker, 1970). In the vowel study, linguistic experience appeared to have no effect. Discrimination of synthetic vowels was the same for Swedish and American listeners, though the vowels were phonemically distinct for the one group and not for the other. The voicing distinction in stops yielded an opposite result. More accurate discrimination was observed at those positions on the stimulus continuum that corresponded to the different positions of the voicing boundary for the language spoken by the subjects (Thai or English).

This research was supported by grants to the following: Haskins Laboratories, National Institute of Child Health and Human Development (HD-01994); the Center for Research in Human Learning, National Institute of Child Health and Human Development (HD-01136) and the National Science Foundation (GB 35703X); and James J. Jenkins, National Institute of Mental Health (MH-21153). Dr. Liberman received support from the Japan Society for the Promotion of Science for his contribution to this research. The authors wish to express their appreciation to Thomas Edman for testing the second group of American subjects and to Arthur Abramson and Leigh Lisker for their assistance in constructing the speech stimuli. Robert Verbrugge is now at the Human Performance Center, University of Michigan, Ann Arbor; Osamu Fujimura is now the Head of the Linguistics and Speech Analysis Department, Bell Laboratories, Murray Hill, New Jersey. Requests for reprints should be sent to Winifred Strange, Center for Research in Human Learning, University of Minnesota, Minneapolis, Minnesota 55455.

The difference in discriminability obtained with vowels and stops may be related to articulatory, acoustic, and perceptual differences between these two classes of sounds. For the stops, the articulatory gestures are relatively rapid movements to and from closures of the vocal tract. For the vowels, the movements are slower and the vocal tract is more nearly open. The acoustic cues for the stops are, correspondingly, characterized by rapid changes in amplitude and frequency within a relatively short interval (Delattre, Liberman, & Cooper, 1955), while the cues for the vowels can be (and were in the experiment referred to above) associated with steady-state signals of longer durations (Fry, Abramson, Eimas, & Liberman, 1962). It may also be relevant that the cues for the stops are complexly encoded in the sound stream in the sense that they are merged on the same acoustic parameter with cues for succeeding (or preceding) segments, while in the case of vowels there can be (and were in the experiment referred to above) stretches of sound that carry cues for only one (vowel) segment (Liberman, Cooper, Shankweiler, & Studdert-Kennedy, 1967). In the perceptual domain, two differences between vowels and stops have been found. First, in the comparison with steady-state vowels, stops show a greater tendency toward categorical perception (Fry et al., 1962; Liberman, Harris, Hoffman, & Griffith, 1957; Pisoni, 1973, 1975; Stevens et al., 1969; Vinegrad, 1972; Fujisaki & Kawashima, Note 1). Second, stops yield a larger right-ear advantage in dichotic listening tests, presumably due to a greater reliance on the left-hemisphere processing (Shankweiler & Studdert-Kennedy, 1967).

The experiment reported here is intended to investigate the effect of linguistic usage on the perception of yet another class of phones, the liquids [r] and [l]. There are several reasons why an investigation of these phones is of interest.

First, the perception of [r] and [l] is an obvious choice for a cross-language study of Japanese and English, since the distinction between these phones is phonemic in English but not in Japanese. In syllable-initial position, which is the only context we will be concerned with, [r] and [l] are in minimal contrast in English, as in "red" vs. "led." The articulation of these phones is hard to characterize because reasonably stable acoustic results can be achieved by a variety of articulatory strategies. Typically, however, the English [r] in syllable initial position is articulated with the tongue tip turned up against the post-alveolar region of the hard palate—the lateral palato-lingual contact spreading medially without forming a closure—while the medio-dorsum of the tongue maintains a concave shape (Miyawaki, Note 2). A syllable-initial [l], on the other hand, is articulated with the tongue tip in contact with only the medial portion of the alveolar ridge, forming no palato-lingual contact laterally. In

both cases, the voicing continues throughout the articulation (Heffner, 1952; Jones, 1956). Acoustically, a sufficient and important cue for the distinction between [r] and [l] is the initial steady-state and transition of the third formant. For [r], the third formant originates just slightly above the starting frequency of the second-formant transition, while for [l], it starts from a much higher frequency, equal to or even higher than the steady-state frequency of the third formant of the adjoining vowel (O'Connor, Gerstman, Liberman, Delattre, & Cooper, 1957).

In Japanese, [r] and [l] do not constitute a phonemic contrast. The phone that is referred to as a Japanese [r] is typically a loose alveolar stop in initial position or the so-called "flapped-r"—the tongue tip making a very brief contact with the alveolar ridge—in intervocalic position. To an American listener, the Japanese [r] often sounds like [d]. In some cases, the phone is produced with "lateral" articulation, usually with a tendency of retroflexing, and it might sound to an American like an [l] or an [r]. There is no apparent allophonic distribution of [r] and [l] in different contexts (Miyawaki, 1973).

Acoustically, in contrast to the American liquids, the Japanese [r] tends to have little or no initial steady state. The starting point and the transition of the third formant seem to vary unsystematically over a range of values sufficient to distinguish the American [r] and [l], although it appears that in most cases F3 assumes relatively lower values more like the American [r] than [l]. It is important to note that both English [l] and English [r] are perceived by Japanese speakers as the same consonant, their /r/, and there is no other English consonant that shares this characteristic in word-initial position.

Second, a cross-language study of [r] and [l] is of interest because these phones form an articulatory manner class (liquids) that is not only different from the two classes previously studied (stops and vowels), but in some ways intermediate between them. Thus, the liquids are not articulated with the complete closure of the vocal tract that characterizes the stops, nor with the open vocal tract of the vowels. Also, their articulation is not so fast as that of the stops, nor so slow as the vowels. As for their acoustic characteristics, liquids in initial position typically have short steady-state portions with an appreciable amount of sound energy preceding the formant transitions, while stop consonants have only transitions with little or no sound energy preceding them and vowels can be produced entirely with steady-state formants.

From the standpoint of distribution, liquids in English are intermediate between vowels and stops in terms of their phonotactic property, viz, vowel affinity (Fujimura, 1975). In Japanese /r/, the only liquid, behaves as a consonant from a functional point of view.

A third reason for a cross-language study of [r] and [l] is that it is quite easy to isolate the distinguishing acoustic cue for these phones. Thus, we can determine how the two language groups discriminate this cue, not only in a speech context, but also in isolation, when it is not perceived as speech. On this basis, we can judge whether the effect of linguistic experience, if any, is limited in the perceptual domain to speech or whether, alternatively, it extends to nonlinguistic auditory processes.

For these reasons, it is interesting to examine any difference between the Americans and the Japanese in the pattern of discrimination of this class of sounds. In addition, our study has a final point of interest in that it provides data relevant to some questions about tendencies toward continuous and categorical perception. So far, these questions have been asked about vowels and stops, but not about the liquids, the class of phones that we will study here.

METHOD

Stimulus Materials

A series of 15 three-formant speech patterns was generated with the parallel-resonance synthesizer at Haskins Laboratories. The structure of the third formant (F3) varied over a range sufficient to produce perception of the consonant-vowel syllables, [ra] and [la]. The stimuli consisted of three contiguous parts: an initial 50-msec steady-state portion, a 75-msec transition of the formant frequencies between the initial and final steady states, and a final steady-state vowel portion of 375 msec duration.

The 15 stimuli differed only in the frequency values of the third formant within the initial steady-state and transition portions. Initial steady-state values of F3 varied in 15 roughly equal steps from 1,362 to 3,698 Hz. Transitions of the formant frequency were linear functions of time from each initial steady-state value to the common steady-state value of 2,525 Hz for the vowel.

Frequency values of the first formant (F1) and second formant (F2) were identical for all 15 stimuli. F1 was set to a frequency of 311 Hz during the initial steady state, then was changed linearly during the transition to a frequency of 769 Hz for the vowel. F2 remained at a constant frequency of 1,232 Hz throughout the entire syllable.

Within the final 400 msec of each syllable, amplitudes of F2 and F3 were set to -3 and -15 dB relative to F1, respectively. The amplitude of F1 at its onset was -12 dB relative to its final value and increased as a decelerated function over the first 100 msec of the syllable. F2 amplitude over the first 100 msec was -3 dB relative to its final steady-state value. F3 amplitude remained constant throughout the syllable. Superimposed on these amplitude values was an overall amplitude contour on the first 50 msec of the syllable, which began 15 dB below its final value and rose linearly. The syllable had a gradually falling fundamental frequency contour from 114 to 96 Hz.

For comparison with the speech patterns, a set of nonspeech stimuli was generated which consisted of the 15 different F3 patterns in isolation. The stimuli were generated by setting the F1 and F2 amplitudes to zero throughout the syllable, so the resultant F3 patterns may be considered as acoustically identical to the F3 patterns *within* the speech stimuli. These stimuli did not sound like speech, but rather light high-pitched glissandos followed by a steady pitch. Figure 1 illustrates the two pairs of examples at nearly extreme F3 values. Stimuli are numbered consecutively with the lowest F3 initial value labeled "1."

Two types of tests were constructed from the speech stimulus set: an identification test and an oddity discrimination test. The former was constructed by recording the speech patterns one at a time in

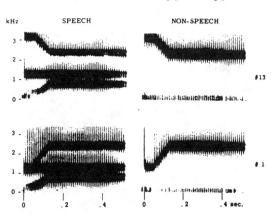

Figure 1. Spectrograms of speech and nonspeech stimuli—[la] upper and [ra] lower.

random order with a 1.5-sec interstimulus interval. Each stimulus appeared 10 times for a total of 150 trials. Trials occurred in blocks of 30 with a 5-sec interval between blocks. This test will be referred to as the identification test.

For oddity discrimination tests, Stimuli 14 and 15 were deleted.[1] Ten pairs of stimuli were selected such that each pair (AB) differed by three steps (i.e., 1-4, 2-5, ..., 10-13). For each pair, triads were constructed by duplicating one stimulus of the pair; all six permutations (AAB, ABA, BAA, ABB, BAB, BBA) were generated. Thus, the oddity test consisted of 60 triads, six permutations for each of 10 comparison pairs. The triads were recorded in random order with a 1-sec interstimulus interval and a 3-sec intertriad interval. Two such randomizations were recorded on audio tape for presentation to subjects. These will be referred to as Speech Tests 1 and 2, respectively.

Oddity discrimination tests of the nonspeech F3 patterns were constructed in the same way as the speech tests. This was accomplished by substituting the corresponding F3 stimulus for each speech stimulus. Thus, the pairing of stimuli and order of triads was the same as that in the speech tests. The two randomizations of 60 triads each will be referred to as Nonspeech Tests 1 and 2, respectively.

For purposes of familiarizing the subjects with the stimuli, two additional recordings were generated. The speech familiarization tape contained the following sequences: the speech stimulus set presented in succession from No. 1 to No. 15, the set repeated in reverse order, the patterns presented in random order with each stimulus occurring two times, and Stimuli 4 and 10 presented five times each. (The latter were judged to be the "best" tokens of [ra] and [la] by an experienced phonetician.) A nonspeech familiarization tape included a set of randomly presented F3 patterns, with each stimulus occurring twice and the two nonspeech patterns, Stimuli 4 and 10, recorded five times each. All experimental materials were then rerecorded and the second-generation recordings used in the experiment.

Subjects

Subjects were 39 native speakers of American English and 21 native speakers of Japanese. The American subjects, undergraduate students at the University of Minnesota, were tested at different times and under somewhat different procedures. Nineteen of the American subjects were students in introductory psychology classes offered during the summer session; this group is referred to as Americans I. The remaining 20 subjects were students in introductory psychology classes during the regular fall quarter; they are referred to as Americans II. The students received monetary reimbursement and extra credit points toward their course grade. All subjects reported having normal hearing.

334   MIYAWAKI, STRANGE, VERBRUGGE, LIBERMAN, JENKINS, AND FUJIMURA

The Japanese subjects were students and staff at the University of Tokyo. Every member of the group had received at least 10 years of formal English language training. Two subjects had lived abroad from the age of 12 years to 16 years. K.M. attended English-speaking schools in Ceylon; S.A. attended school in Germany. Data obtained for these subjects are discussed separately in the results. (It should be understood that English teaching in Japan usually tends to stress reading and writing; conversational English is not emphasized.) Subjects were paid for their participation in the experiment. All subjects reported having normal hearing.

Procedure

The experimental procedures were basically the same for all three groups of subjects, Americans I and II and Japanese. This section describes the basic procedure; in Appendix A, detailed procedural information for each group is given. The experiment consisted of three parts: familiarization, discrimination tests, and identification tests (for the Americans only).

Familiarization. The procedure for speech familiarization was as follows: Subjects listened to the ordered series without being told what speech sounds were represented. They were then informed that the stimuli were several instances of the English syllables [ra] and [la], and were presented the random series. Finally, they heard the five repetitions of Stimuli 4 and 10, which were described by the experimenter as the "best" instances of the two syllables.

For nonspeech familiarization, subjects were told that the stimuli were "related" to the speech sounds, but would probably not sound like speech. They heard the random series and were asked to describe them as best they could. They were then presented the repetitions of Stimuli 4 and 10 and asked if they could tell them apart easily.

Discrimination. Subjects were told that they would hear triplets of sounds in which two were always identical and one different, and they were to indicate on printed score sheets whether the different one occurred first, second, or third in the triad. They were instructed to respond on every triad, even if they had to guess. They were told they could use any criterion to make the difference judgment.

All subjects completed two repetitions of Tests 1 and 2 (240 trials) for each stimulus set (speech and nonspeech) on the first day of testing. On Day 2, subjects were reminded of the procedure and again completed two repetitions of Tests 1 and 2 for each stimulus series. Thus, subjects completed a total of 480 trials, 48 judgments for each AB comparison pair, for both the speech stimuli and the nonspeech stimuli.

Identification (American subjects only). On the third day of testing, the American subjects were instructed to listen to each speech stimulus, and mark down on printed score sheets whether the syllable began with an "r" or an "l." They were told to identify every stimulus and were limited to the two response alternatives. They completed two repetitions of the identification test for a total of 300 trials, comprising 20 judgments for each of 15 stimuli.

RESULTS

Comparison of American and Japanese Discrimination of the [r-l] Contrast

Most relevant to the purposes of this study are the data, shown in the lower half of Figure 2, on the discrimination of [r-l] by the two language groups. But before comparing those data, we should note, in the upper half of the figure, the results of the identification test which was given only to the Americans. There, where the percent of "r" responses is plotted for each of the 13 stimuli[2] of the "speech" series, we see that the American subjects did, in fact, divide the stimuli rather neatly into the two phoneme categories that our synthetic patterns were designed to embrace and, further, that the boundary between the categories is in the neighborhood of Stimulus 7.

Looking now at the lower graph, where percent correct in the discrimination task is plotted against the stimulus pair being tested, we see immediately that the performance by the two groups was markedly different. The American subjects discriminated well between those stimuli that were drawn from different phoneme categories, that is, those that straddle or include the one (Stimulus 7) closest to the boundary between [r] and [l]. However, they discriminated rather poorly those that were given the same category assignment in the identification test. The Japanese, on the other hand, showed no such increase in discrimination at the phoneme boundary; for the stimuli that lay within a phoneme class, their discrimination was close to that of the Americans.

Examination of the discrimination functions for individual subjects revealed that 34 of the 39 American subjects were highly accurate in discriminating pairs whose members were labeled as different phonemes (especially Pairs 5-8 and 6-9). Discrimination of pairs whose members were labeled as the same phoneme was considerably less accurate, although still above the 33% chance level. (A discussion of differences in discrimination data for the Americans I and Americans II groups is included in Appendix A.)

Examination of the data for the Japanese subjects, however, found little evidence of such accurate discrimination. Only three subjects showed distinct

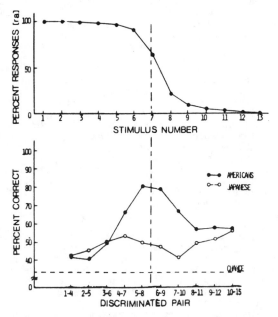

Figure 2. Upper graph: Pooled identification of speech stimuli by Americans. Lower graph: Pooled discrimination by Americans (closed circles) and Japanese (open circles).

peaks in discrimination in the vicinity of the phoneme boundary indicated in the American identification data. One of these subjects, S.A. (23 years) lived in Germany between the ages of 12 and 16 and is a fluent speaker of German. Subject K.M. (23 years) lived in Ceylon between the ages of 12 and 16 and is a fluent speaker of English. Subject M.S. (43 years) received regular English training in Japan with an emphasis on reading and writing, starting at the age of 12. (Discrimination data for each of these subjects and for the remainder of the sample are given in Appendix B.)

Discrimination of the [r-l] Cue in Isolation [Nonspeech]—Americans and Japanese

As we pointed out in the introduction, it was possible in this experiment to compare the discrimination of the relevant acoustic cue (the F3 transition in this case) under two conditions: when it is the only basis for the perceived distinction (if any) between the speech sounds, and when it is presented in isolation and does not sound like speech at all. This comparison is of some interest even in the study of speech-sound discrimination that does not make a cross-language comparison. Thus, given an increase in the speech-sound discrimination at the phoneme boundary, as there was for the American subjects in our experiment, the nonspeech discrimination function helps us to know whether the discrimination peak is part of our general auditory perception or whether, alternatively, it is somehow peculiar to the speech context—that is, to perception in the speech mode. In the case of a cross-language comparison, the nonspeech discrimination data are potentially even more interesting. Having found a difference in speech-sound discrimination between the two language groups, as we did in our experiment, we can see in the nonspeech data where the difference might lie. If we assume, as we do, that the difference between the language groups reflects an effect of linguistic experience, then we can look to the nonspeech functions to help us decide whether that effect was at the auditory level or whether, alternatively, it was somehow specific to perception in the speech mode. If the effect were on auditory perception quite generally, we should expect the two groups to differ similarly on both the speech and nonspeech discrimination. Alternatively, if the effect is specific to the speech mode, we should expect the two groups to discriminate the nonspeech stimuli in similar fashion, however much they might differ in discrimination of the speech sounds. In all cases, a result that tends to put the effect in the speech mode could, of course, be interpreted alternatively as a purely auditory interaction between the cue and the constant acoustic context to which it is always added in the speech patterns. But such an interpretation is empty unless one can make sense of it in terms of what is known, on other grounds, about auditory perception.

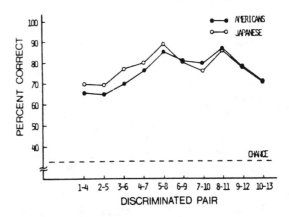

Figure 3. Pooled discrimination of nonspeech stimuli by Americans (closed circles) and Japanese (open circles).

In the case of cross-language comparisons, the results of the relevant nonspeech discrimination provide a useful check on the procedures as well. If there are no differences between groups for the nonspeech stimuli, we can be more confident that the differences in discrimination of the speech sounds were not due to some uncontrolled methodological factors in the conduct of the experiment.

The pooled data for discrimination of the F3 cue in isolation are shown in Figure 3 for both the American and Japanese subjects. Looking first at the results for the American subjects, we see that the shape of the function is quite different from that obtained when the same acoustic variable was perceived in a speech context where it cued the distinction between [r] and [l]. The difference between speech and nonspeech discrimination functions is similar to the finding of an earlier experiment on place distinctions in voiced stops (Mattingly, Liberman, Syrdal, & Halwes, 1971), where the relevant cue was tested in and out of speech context. In both experiments, it is apparent that the discrimination peak obtained in the speech context is peculiar to that context and is not, more generally, characteristic of the way we perceive the relevant acoustic variable.

But it is the nonspeech discrimination function obtained with the Japanese subjects that is of particular interest. We see very clearly that the Japanese do not differ from the Americans on any of the comparison pairs. The nonspeech discrimination functions are virtually identical for the two groups of subjects. We conclude, then, that the differences between the groups on the speech stimuli are a function of processes specific to the perception of speech, or at least speech-like stimuli such as ours, as opposed to stimuli that cannot be identified as phonological units. Also, the results suggest that the procedures for testing the two groups were comparable, and that the differences on speech discrimination cannot be attributed to uncontrolled methodological factors.

It is interesting to note that, for both groups,

discrimination for all nonspeech comparison pairs is quite accurate (ranging from 66% to 89%). That is, both Japanese and Americans were able to discriminate differences in F3 patterns when they were presented in isolation. This suggests that the poor discrimination by Japanese for all speech comparison pairs and by Americans for within-category pairs is not due to the acoustic differences per se being indiscriminable, but rather has something to do with the phonemic identity of the speech patterns which contain these F3 patterns. However, two factors may have contributed to the relatively better discrimination of the isolated formants: the F3 patterns were presented at a much higher amplitude than the F3 components within the speech patterns, and it is possible that the lower formants in the speech patterns masked the F3 component to some extent. More research that measures the effects of intensity and masking on the perception of nonspeech is needed to explore these factors.

In both the Japanese and American nonspeech functions, two comparison pairs appear to be discriminated slightly better than the others. It is interesting to note that each of these pairs contains Stimulus 8 (5-8 and 8-11). Stimulus 8 is unique in that its F3 does not contain a frequency transition. In other words, this pattern is a steady state in contrast to Stimuli 1 through 7, which contain rising transitions, and Stimuli 9 through 13, which have falling transitions. It appears that subjects were able to distinguish between "no transition" vs. "some transition" slightly better than between transitions with different slopes.

Categorical Perception of [r] and [l]

We may now turn to a consideration of the relation between the identification and discrimination functions obtained for the stimuli presented to the American subjects. A reexamination of Figure 2

shows a striking correspondence between the sharp change in identification of the stimuli as [r] and [l] and the peak in the discrimination function. The close relation between identification and discrimination is similar to that found for stop consonants, and has been referred to as "categorical perception" (Liberman et al., 1957). In contrast, the correlation between identification and discrimination does not always hold for other speech sounds, such as steady-state vowels (Fry et al., 1962).

A strong test for the presence of categorical perception may be made by predicting the shape of the discrimination function. If one makes the extreme assumption that subjects are able to discriminate speech stimuli only when they label them differently, it is possible to predict their discrimination functions from their identification performance. Each of the two stimuli in an oddity triad has a probability of being labeled as "r" or as "l," as determined in the identification test. From these data, it is possible to calculate the probability of the triad being heard as each of the possible sequences of the two phonemes. Only some of these perceived sequences will result in correct choices of the odd member, and those probabilities may be summed for each stimulus order. The probability of correct discrimination for a stimulus pair will be an average of the probabilities for the six possible orders. If Pr is the probability of one member being heard as "r" and Pr' is the probability of the other member being heard as "r," then the average probability of correct discrimination is found to be Pcorr = $[1 + 2(Pr - Pr')^2]/3$.

The predicted discrimination function for the pooled data is shown in Figure 4. As is typical of such functions, the location and extent of the discrimination peak is fairly accurately predicted, while within-category discrimination is under-estimated. This suggests that even though subjects labeled the stimuli as the same phoneme, they were able to discriminate intraphonemic variants to some extent. This point also conforms with the observation that the discrimination by Japanese subjects, even though poor, was better than chance.

DISCUSSION

Returning now to the questions that prompted this study, we may conclude that rather clear answers have been obtained. We note, first, that familiarity with the [r-l] distinction obviously has a major impact on the ability to make correct discriminations in an oddity test. In this respect, the findings are overwhelming. American subjects show a peak of highly accurate discrimination at the point where stimuli from different phonetic classes are being contrasted. Japanese subjects show no such accurate discrimination at any point along the stimulus dimension. Moreover, the results are consistent for individuals, not merely characteristic of group

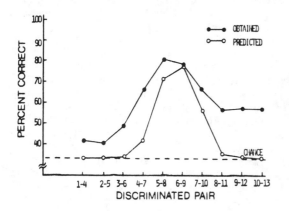

Figure 4. Obtained (closed circles) and predicted (open circles) functions for pooled discrimination by Americans. (See text for explanation of predicted function.)

averages. Of the 39 American subjects, 34 showed clear discrimination peaks in their individual protocols, while only 3 of the 21 Japanese subjects did. Furthermore, two of the three Japanese subjects who did show discrimination peaks learned languages with the relevant liquid contrast as early adolescents. It is reasonable to conclude, therefore, that considerable experience with the linguistic distinction is prerequisite to successful performance on the discrimination test with synthetic speech stimuli such as we have employed. Also, since all Japanese subjects had studied English extensively, it is tempting to hazard the hypothesis that discrimination requires effective *phonetic* experience at a relatively early age, say early adolescence.

The finding that Japanese subjects cannot for the most part discriminate [r] and [l] over this range of synthetic stimuli confirms the observation of Goto (1971) that native Japanese speakers who are highly fluent in English cannot perceive the distinction between [r] and [l] produced by other speakers (both Japanese and American). Even more interesting, Goto reports that his subjects cannot distinguish reliably *their own* tokens of [r] and [l], even when American speakers judge the tokens to be appropriate instances of the two phones. Thus, the lack of discrimination of synthetic stimuli covering a range of variation is in harmony with what is known about the properties of perception of real speech in normal contexts. This does not mean, however, that training after adolescence does not help at all. In fact, some of our Japanese subjects may not fail in discriminating natural utterances of [ra] and [la]. The stimuli compared on the discrimination test are undoubtedly much more similar to each other than optimal instances of the phonemes. Also, there may be other cues for the distinction in natural utterances which some Japanese subjects may depend on more heavily than do Americans.

Second, it is apparent that the difference in discrimination performance is limited to the speech-like condition. No difference appeared between the American and Japanese groups in the discrimination of the acoustic cue for [r] vs. [l] when it was presented in isolation. This finding is consistent with the argument that speech perception is a special mode of auditory perception that is accomplished in quite a different manner from general auditory perception. In all cases, such an argument must, as we said earlier, leave room for the fact that even though the acoustic cue being discriminated was always the only variable, it was presented by itself in the nonspeech case, while in the speech case, it was added to a fixed auditory pattern, thus creating the possibility of an auditory interaction. In this experiment, comparison of the speech and nonspeech discrimination functions must also take into account the differences in amplitude of the F3-transition cue in the two cases and the possibility that in the speech context the F3 cue was to some degree masked by the constant F1 and F2.

Finally, the study yielded results concerning the "categorical perception" of liquids in initial position in English. While American listeners make more correct discriminations of stimuli than would be predicted from a strict categorical perception hypothesis, the match between predicted and obtained discrimination functions resembles more closely that obtained for stop consonants than that obtained for vowels (Fry et al., 1962; Liberman et al., 1957).

Since the present study was performed, Eimas (in press) has studied how 2- and 3-month-old infants perceive the stimuli utilized in this study. Using a habituation paradigm, he tested the discrimination of speech stimuli both within and between the [l] and [r] categories. The infant discriminations were remarkably parallel to those we obtained with American adults. Infants who were habituated to stimuli from one side of the adult boundary and then switched to stimuli from the other side of the boundary showed impressive recovery from habituation. Within-class shifts of stimuli produced much less recovery. However, shifts within the [l] category produced greater recovery than shifts within the [r] category, reflecting the tendency shown by American subjects to discriminate within the [l] category better than within the [r] category. Infants tested with comparable shifts in the nonspeech stimuli (F3 alone) failed to show significantly different recovery from habituation in all conditions. Thus, the infant data are parallel in all respects to the American adult data that we have presented here. Obviously, it would be of great interest now to follow the course of habituation-discrimination in Japanese children.

APPENDIX A

Specific Procedures

Americans I. Subjects were assigned to one of two counterbalanced conditions according to convenience in scheduling test sessions. Ten subjects were tested in the speech-first condition, nine subjects in the nonspeech-first condition. During an initial session, all subjects were given familiarization on both stimulus series. Discrimination testing began the following day, after subjects were again familiarized with the task by listening to 10 triads of the first test without responding. The procedures in speech-first and nonspeech-first conditions were identical except for the order of presentation of the stimulus series for discrimination. For the speech-first subjects, the order for the first day was as follows: Speech Tests 1 and 2, Nonspeech Tests 1 and 2, Speech Tests 1 and 2, Nonspeech Tests 1 and 2. For nonspeech-first subjects, the order was reversed, i.e., Nonspeech Tests 1 and 2, Speech Tests 1 and 2, etc. The order of presentation on the second day of discrimination testing was the same as for Day 1 for each group. Both groups completed identification tests on the third day.

Subjects were tested in small groups (from one to four) in sessions which lasted about 2 h. Testing was conducted in a quiet experimental room. Stimuli were reproduced on a Crown CS 822 tape recorder and presented to subjects binaurally over Koss Pro-600A earphones. Signal levels were monitored with a Heathkit IM21 AC VTVM at the output to the earphones. Both speech and nonspeech stimuli were presented at a sound level approximately

338   MIYAWAKI, STRANGE, VERBRUGGE, LIBERMAN, JENKINS, AND FUJIMURA

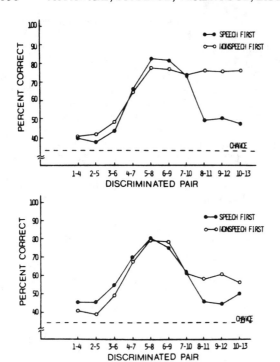

Figure 5. Pooled discrimination of speech stimuli for Americans I (upper graph) and Americans II (lower graph), speech-first and nonspeech-first conditions.

70 dB above threshold. The playback amplitude for the nonspeech stimuli was increased to make the isolated F3 patterns equal in peak amplitude to the three-formant speech patterns. Thus, the amplitude of the isolated F3 patterns was far greater than the amplitude of the comparable F3 components *within* the three-formant patterns. However, the *total* signal for each set of stimuli was equal in amplitude and duration.

Americans II. The 20 subjects were divided into two groups of 10 each according to convenience in scheduling test sessions. The groups were tested in two counterbalanced conditions, speech first and nonspeech first, in a manner similar to the Americans I, except for the following. While the Americans I groups were presented Speech and Nonspeech Tests 1 and 2 alternately within a single session of discrimination testing, the Americans II groups completed two repetitions of Tests 1 and 2 for the first stimulus series before proceeding to the other stimulus series. Thus, on Day 1 the speech-first group completed *two* repetitions of Speech Tests 1 and 2, then completed two repetitions of Nonspeech Tests 1 and 2. The order on Day 2 was identical to that of Day 1 for each group.

Another difference in procedure from the Americans I was in familiarization. For the Americans II groups, familiarization took place for each stimulus series just prior to the first discrimination test in that series. After discrimination tests were completed for the first series (i.e., Tests 1, 2, 1, 2), subjects were given familiarization on the other stimulus series and then proceeded with the tests. No familiarization was given on Day 2; subjects were merely reminded of the test procedure and told what series they would be listening to first.

Subjects were tested in a sound-attenuated experimental room using the same equipment and procedures as for the Americans I. Speech stimuli were presented at a sound level about 70 dB above threshold. Nonspeech stimuli were presented at -5 dB relative to the speech. (The absolute amplitude of the isolated F3 patterns was still far above that of the F3 component within the speech patterns.)

Japanese. All 21 subjects were tested using the Americans II nonspeech-first presentation order. That is, the order on Day 1 was: nonspeech familiarization, Nonspeech Tests 1, 2, 1, 2, speech familiarization, Speech Tests 1, 2, 1, 2. Day 2 was the same as Day 1, except that no familiarization was given.

Subjects were tested individually in a sound-attenuated experimental room. Stimuli were reproduced on a TEAC-type tape recorder and presented to subjects binaurally over Iwatsu DR-305 stereo earphones. Speech stimuli and nonspeech stimuli were output from the tape recorder at about 74 and 76 dB above threshold, respectively. However, each subject adjusted the signal level at his earphones by means of an Ando SAL-20 attenuator, which had a range of 20 dB in 2-dB steps. Attenuation levels that subjects selected as "most comfortable" varied from -2 to -16 dB. The average listening level for speech was approximately 68 dB above threshold; for the nonspeech stimuli, the average was approximately 70 dB above threshold. Thus, as was the case for the American subjects, the isolated F3 patterns were heard at a much higher absolute level than the F3 component within the speech patterns.

Comparison of Results for Speech-First and Nonspeech-First Groups

The upper panel of Figure 5 presents the results of speech discrimination tests for the Americans I speech-first and nonspeech-first groups. The major difference between the groups is their discrimination of comparison pairs within the "l" category. The nonspeech-first subjects were able to discriminate these pairs as accurately as they did the between-category pairs. This could not be predicted from their identification performance, which was very similar to that of the speech-first subjects. An inspection of individual subjects' functions showed that six of the nine subjects produced functions with the elevated within-"l" discrimination. The other three subjects produced functions similar to the speech-first results.

The lower panel of Figure 5 presents the comparable discrimination results for the Americans II speech-first and nonspeech groups. Again, the only difference between the groups is their performance on the within-"l" comparison pairs. However, the difference is much smaller than for the Americans I subjects. The Americans II nonspeech-first subjects showed more nearly "categorical" performance; i.e., in spite of better discrimination of the within-"l" pairs than the within-"r" pairs, performance within either category was still inferior to that for between-category pairs.

Two differences in procedure might have contributed to the different results for Americans I and Americans II nonspeech groups. First, recall that for the Americans I group, familiarization took place in a separate session the day before discrimination testing. Speech familiarization was always given before nonspeech familiarization. Thus, for these subjects, both nonspeech familiarization and testing (Tests 1 and 2) intervened between speech familiarization and the initial speech discrimination tests. In addition, both discrimination testing sessions began with the nonspeech stimuli. These factors apparently caused some "interference" in the speech discrimination task. Subjects may have adopted a "nonspeech" listening strategy, since they were told to use any criteria they could to discriminate the odd member of the triads. Once having established a strategy, the subjects seem to have maintained it throughout testing, since the data for the first and second halves of each day's testing, and the data for Day 1 and Day 2, are very consistent.

In contrast, the Americans II nonspeech-first group received their speech familiarization immediately prior to speech discrimination tests on the first day of testing. This might have helped to establish a "speech" listening strategy for these subjects. None of the 10 subjects produced speech functions like the Americans I nonspeech-group function, although most showed some elevation in discrimination of the within-"l" category pairs.

A second difference in procedure might have contributed in a related manner. The Americans I group switched from nonspeech to speech stimuli twice within a testing session, whereas the

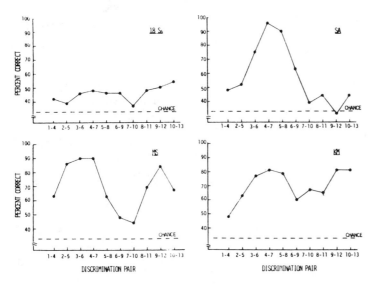

Figure 6. Pooled discrimination of speech stimuli by 18 Japanese subjects (upper left) and individual discrimination functions for three exceptional Japanese subjects. (See text for explanation of exceptional subjects.)

Americans II group completed all nonspeech tests before going on to speech tests. Again, the former procedure may have biased subjects toward a "nonspeech" listening strategy, whereas the latter procedure provided a clear distinction between the two series of stimuli. Additional support for the notion that the high discriminability of the within-"l" category pairs is a nonspeech phenomenon is given by the results of some of the Japanese subjects on the speech discrimination trials. The average curve for Japanese subjects climbs at the "l" end. (See Figure 2.) Most of this is accounted for by five subjects whose individual discrimination functions showed relatively more accurate discrimination of Pairs 8-11, 9-12, and 10-13.

The Japanese pooled data may be compared with the Americans II nonspeech-first group (compare Figures 2 and 5), since the order of presentation is identical for these groups. The difference in discrimination in the region of the Americans' category boundary is clearly present in this comparison.

APPENDIX B

The discrimination data for the three Japanese subjects who showed peaks of high discrimination are given in Figure 6. As adolescents, K.M. and S.A. learned languages employing the phonemic distinction between [r] and [l]. M.S. did not. The upper left panel shows the pooled speech discrimination data for the remaining 18 Japanese subjects.

REFERENCE NOTES

1. Fujisaki, H., & Kawashima, T. *On the modes and mechanisms of speech perception.* Research on Information Processing, Annual Report No. 2, University of Tokyo, Division of Electrical Engineering, Engineering Research Institute, 1969, 67-73.
2. Miyawaki, K. *A preliminary study of American English /r/ by use of dynamic palatography.* Annual Bulletin, Research Institute of Logopedics and Phoniatrics, Faculty of Medicine, University of Tokyo, 1972, **6**, 19-24.

REFERENCES

Abramson, A. S., & Lisker, L. Discriminability along the voicing continuum: Cross-language tests. In *Proceedings of the 6th International Congress of Phonetic Sciences* (Prague, 1967). Prague: Academia, 1970. Pp. 569-573.

DeLattre, P. C., Liberman, A. M., & Cooper, F. S. Acoustic loci and transitional cues for consonants. *Journal of the Acoustical Society of America*, 1955, **27**, 769-773.

Eimas, P. D. Developmental aspects of speech perception. In R. Held, H. Leibowitz, & H. L. Teuber (Eds.), *Handbook of sensory physiology.* New York: Springer-Verlag, in press.

Fry, D. B., Abramson, A. S., Eimas, P. D., & Liberman, A. M. The identification and discrimination of synthetic vowels. *Language and Speech*, 1962, **5**, 171-189.

Fujimura, O. Syllable as a unit of speech recognition. *IEEE Transactions on Acoustics, Speech, and Signal Processing*, 1975, **23**, 82-87.

Goto, H. Auditory perception by normal Japanese adults of the sounds "L" and "R." *Neuropsychologia*, 1971, **9**, 317-323.

Heffner, R.-M. S. *General phonetics.* Madison: University of Wisconsin Press, 1952.

Jones, D. *An outline of English phonetics.* Cambridge Mass: Heffer, 1956.

Liberman, A. M., Cooper, F. S., Shankweiler, D. P., & Studdert-Kennedy, M. Perception of the speech code. *Psychological Review*, 1967, **74**, 431-461.

Liberman, A. M., Harris, K. S., Hoffman, H. S., & Griffith, B. C. The discrimination of speech sounds within and across phoneme boundaries. *Journal of Experimental Psychology*, 1957, **54**, 358-368.

Mattingly, I. G., Liberman, A. M., Syrdal, A. K., & Halwes, T. Discrimination in speech and nonspeech modes. *Cognitive Psychology*, 1971, **2**, 131-157.

Miyawaki, K. *A study of lingual articulation by use of dynamic palatography.* Masters thesis, Department of Linguistics, University of Tokyo, March 1973.

O'Connor, J. D., Gerstman, L. J., Liberman, A. M., DeLattre, P. C., & Cooper, F. S. Acoustic cues for the perception of initial /w, j, r, l/ in English. *Word*, 1957, **13**, 25-43.

Pisoni, D. B. Auditory and phonetic memory codes in the discrimination of consonants and vowels. *Perception & Psychophysics*, 1973, **13**, 253-260.

Pisoni, D. B. Auditory short-term memory and vowel perception. *Memory & Cognition*, 1975, **3**, 7-18.

Shankweiler, D. P., & Studdert-Kennedy, M. Identification of consonants and vowels presented to left and right ears. *Quarterly Journal of Experimental Psychology*, 1967, **19**, 59-63.

Stevens, K. N., Liberman, A. M., Studdert-Kennedy, M.,

340   MIYAWAKI, STRANGE, VERBRUGGE, LIBERMAN, JENKINS, AND FUJIMURA

& OHMAN. S. E. G. Cross-language study of vowel perception. *Language and Speech*, 1969, **12**, 1-23.

VINEGRAD, M. D. A direct magnitude scaling method to investigate categorical versus continuous modes of speech perception. *Language and Speech*, 1972, **15**, 114-121.

NOTES

1. These two stimuli had such extreme values of F3 that some pilot subjects heard them as [ra], with a noisy glide superimposed on it.

2. Since Stimuli 14 and 15 were deleted from discrimination, the identification data for these stimuli were not included in the analysis.

(Received for publication April 11, 1975;
revision received August 11, 1975.)

Identification and discrimination of the relative onset time of two component tones: Implications for voicing perception in stops*

David B. Pisoni

Research Laboratory of Electronics, Massachusetts Institute of Technology, Cambridge, Massachusetts 02139
(Received 28 July 1976; revised 12 January 1977)

Experiments on the voiced–voiceless distinction in stop consonants have shown sharp and consistent labeling functions and categorical-like discrimination functions for synthetically produced speech stimuli differing in voice-onset time (VOT). Other research has found somewhat comparable results for young infants and chinchillas as well as cross-language differences in the perception of these same synthetic stimuli. In the present paper, four experiments were carried out to investigate a possible underlying basis of these seemingly diverse results. All of the experiments employed a set of nonspeech tonal stimuli that differed in the relative onset time of their components. In the first experiment identification and discrimination functions were obtained with these signals which showed strong evidence for categorical perception: the labeling functions were sharp and consistent, the discrimination functions showed peaks and troughs which were correlated with the labeling probabilities. Other experiments provided evidence foir the presence of three distinct categories along this nonspeech stimulus continuum which were separated by narrow regions of high discriminability. Based on these findings a general account of voicing perception for stops in initial position is proposed in terms of the discriminability of differences in the temporal order of the component events at onset.

PACS numbers: 43.70.Dn

INTRODUCTION

Within the last few years considerable attention has been devoted to the study of the voicing feature in stop consonants, particularly in terms of the dimension of voice onset time (VOT). The important work of Lisker and Abramson[1,2] has shown that the voicing and aspiration differences among stop consonants in a wide diversity of languages can be characterized by changes in VOT, which, in turn, reflect differences in the timing of glottal activity relative to supralaryngeal events. According to Lisker and Abramson[1] it appears that there are three primary modes of voicing in stops: (1) Prevoiced stops in which voicing onset precedes the release burst, (2) shortlag voiced stops in which voicing onset is simultaneous or briefly lags behind the release burst, and (3) long-lag voiceless stops in which the voicing onset lags behind the release burst. From acoustic measurements, Lisker and Abramson[1] found relatively little overlap in the modal values of VOT for the voicing distinctions that occurred in the 11 languages that they studied. Moreover, in perceptual experiments with synthetic stimuli they found that subjects identify and discriminate differences in VOT in a categorical-like manner that reflects the phonological categories of their language.[2–4] That is, subjects show consistent labeling functions with a sharp crossover point from one phonological category to another and discontinuities in discrimination that are correlated with the abrupt changes in the labeling functions. Subjects can discriminate two synthetic stimuli drawn from different phonological categories better than two stimuli selected from the same phonological category.[5,6]

The categorical perception of these synthetic stimuli has been interpreted as evidence for the operation of a special mode of perception, a speech mode, that is unique to the processing of speech signals.[7–9] The argument for the presence of a specialized speech mode is based primarily on three empirical findings. First, nonspeech signals are typically perceived in a continuous mode; discrimination is monotonic with the physical scale. It is well known that subjects can discriminate many more differences than they can reliably label on an absolute basis. Second, until recently, no convincing demonstrations of categorical perception had been obtained with nonspeech signals. Third, it has generally been assumed that the nonmonotonic discrimination functions are entirely the result of labeling processes associated with phonetic categorization. Indeed, the nonspeech control experiments carried out by Liberman et al.[6] and Mattingly, Liberman, Syrdal, and Halwes[10] were designed specifically to determine whether the discontinuities in the speech discrimination functions were due to the acoustic or psychophysical attributes of the signals themselves rather than some speech-related labeling process. Since both of these studies failed to find peaks in the nonspeech discrimination functions at phoneme boundaries, it was concluded that the discrimination functions for the speech stimuli were attributable to phonetic categorization resulting from the stimuli being perceived as speech.

Additional support for the existence of a specialized speech perception mode has come from the results of Eimas and his associates who found that two- and three-month-old infants could discriminate synthetic speech sounds varying in VOT in a manner comparable to that of English-speaking adults.[11] The infants could discriminate between two speech sounds selected from across an adult phoneme boundary but failed to discriminate two stimuli selected from within an adult phonological category even though the acoustic differences between the pairs of stimuli were apparently constant. The implication of these findings is that the infants have access to mechanisms of phonetic categorization at an extremely early age. Furthermore, it has been suggested that these mechanisms are in some way innately determined or develop very rapidly after birth. The important point is that it has been assumed that infants are responding to differences in VOT in a "linguistically relevant" manner which is a consequence of phonetic coding of these signals rather than responding to psychophysical differences prior to phonetic categorization (however, see Stevens and Klatt[12]). If this claim is true, or even partly true, it would provide very strong support for an account of phonological perception based on a set of universal phonetic features which are innately determined. It would also suggest that the environment plays a secondary role in phonological development.

Several recent studies, however, have provided some strong evidence for reevaluating this interpretation of the infant data, as well as, the more general claims associated with a specialized mode of speech perception. These results are based on perceptual experiments with chinchillas,[13] two cross-language experiments with young infants,[14,15] and a study involving more complex nonspeech signals.[16] The common property of these seemingly diverse studies is that they have focused on the voicing distinction in stop consonants, specifically VOT.

Kuhl and Miller[13] showed that chinchillas could be trained to respond differentially to the consonants /d/ and /t/ in syllables produced by four talkers in three vowel contexts. More importantly, however, was the finding that the training generalized to a continuum of synthetically produced stimuli varying in VOT. The identification functions for chinchillas were quite similar to human data: The synthetic stimuli were partitioned into two discrete categories with a sharp crossover point. The phoneme boundary for chinchilla occurred at almost precisely the same place as for humans which suggests a psychophysical rather than a phonetic basis for the labeling behavior. Since chinchillas presumably have no spoken language and consequently have no phonological coding system, Kuhl and Miller assumed that the labeling behavior in response to synthetic stimuli would be determined exclusively by the acoustic attributes and psychophysical properties of these signals. The results of this study indicate that the boundary between voiced and voiceless labial stops that occurs at about +25 msec is probably a "natural" region of high sensitivity along the VOT continuum and, at least in the case of the chinchilla, has little to do with phonetic coding.

Following Eimas's work with infants from English-speaking environments, two crosslanguage studies were conducted recently using similar methodology and comparable synthetic stimuli differing in VOT. Lasky et al.[14] studied four- to six-and-one-half-month-old infants born to Spanish-speaking parents and found evidence for the presence of three categories in their discrimination functions. One boundary occurred in the region of +20– +60 msec which corresponds to the English voiced–voiceless distinction, whereas the other boundary occurred in the region between roughly –20 and –60 msec. These results are interesting because Spanish

has only one phoneme boundary separating its voiced–voiceless stops and this boundary does not coincide with either of the two boundaries found in the infant data of Lasky et al. (see for example, Abramson and Lisker[17] for relevant adult Spanish data). One conclusion that can be drawn from these findings is that the environment probably plays only a minor role in phonological development at this age and that the infants are more likely to be responding to some set of acoustic attributes independently of their phonetic status.

In another related study Streeter[15] found that Kikuyu infants also show evidence of three categories of voicing for labial stops. This result is important because in Kikuyu there are no voicing contrasts for labial stops although there are contrasts at other places of articulation. Since this particular distinction is not phonemic in the adult language, it probably never occurred in the language environment of these infants. As a consequence, the infants' discrimination performance must be due entirely to the acoustic and psychophysical attributes of the stimuli. This conclusion is supported by the fact that the categories and boundaries found in this study were quite comparable to those obtained in the Lasky et al. study.

The results of both cross-language investigations of voicing perception are quite similar and indicate that infants can discriminate differences in VOT. Moreover, the pattern of results suggests that infants have the ability to deal with at least three modes of voicing. The basis of these distinctions, however, may be the result of naturally defined regions of high discriminability along the VOT continuum rather than processes of phonetic categorization. Thus, the infants may not be responding to these signals linguistically as suggested by the earlier interpretation of Eimas, but instead may be responding to some complex psychophysical relation that occurs between the components of the stimulus at each of these modes of voicing. In anticipation, one such relation is strongly suggested by the results of the present series of nonspeech experiments in terms of changes in sensitivity to differences in temporal order between two components of a stimulus complex. The infants may be responding simply to differences between simultaneous and successive events.

In another study, Miller et al.[16] generated a set of nonspeech control signals that were purported to be analogous to VOT stimuli. The stimuli differed in the duration of a noise burst preceding a buzz. Identification and discrimination functions were obtained with adults in a manner comparable to those collected in the earlier adult speech-perception experiments. For discrimination, the stimuli were presented in an oddity paradigm, whereas for labeling the subjects responded with two choices, either "no noise" or "noise" present before the onset of the buzz. The results of this study revealed identification and discrimination functions that were similar to those found with stop consonants differing in VOT. Discrimination was excellent for stimuli selected from between categories and quite poor for stimuli from within a category. The labeling functions were sharp and consistent; the peak in discrimination occurred at roughly the boundary between the two categories.

Miller *et al.*[16] offered a psychophysical account of these categorical-like results in terms of the presence of a perceptual threshold at the boundary between two perceptually distinctive categories. According to Miller *et al.*, in the case of noise-buzz stimuli, there is a certain value of noise-lead time below which subjects can no longer detect the presence of the noise preceding a buzz. At values below this duration the stimuli are perceived as members of one category and subjects cannot discriminate differences in duration between stimuli because they are below threshold. At noise durations slightly above this value there are marked changes in sensitivity and response bias as a threshold is crossed and a new perceptual quality emerges from the stimulus complex. Miller *et al.* suggest that discrimination of differences above this threshold value follow Weber's law and, consequently, constant ratios are needed rather than constant differences in order to maintain the same level of discriminability. The boundary between these categories separates distinct sets of perceptual attributes and results in the partitioning of the stimulus continuum into equivalence classes. These equivalence classes for most purposes are categorical: the relation defining membership in a class is symmetrical, reflexive, and transitive.[18]

The account of the labeling and discrimination data offered by Miller *et al.* suggests the presence of naturally determined boundaries at specific regions along the VOT continuum. These boundaries occur at places where a new perceptual attribute emerges in the course of continuous variations in one or more parameters of a complex signal. In the Miller *et al.* study the experimental variable was the duration of a noise burst preceding a buzz which was varied over a relatively small range of values. Based on their suggestion we generated a set of nonspeech signals that differed in the temporal order of the onsets of two component tones of different frequencies. The stimuli varied over a range from −50 msec where the lower tone leads the higher tone, through simultaneity, to +50 msec where the lower tone lags behind the higher tone. Our goal in producing these stimuli was to have a set of nonspeech stimuli that differed on a variable known to play an important role in the perception of voicing, namely the relative timing between two events. A well-known and important cue to voicing in stops is laryngeal timing. One of several cues to laryngeal timing is the onset of the first formant relative to the second, the "cutback cue."[19] Thus, in using nonspeech signals such as these, we hoped to learn something about how the timing relations in stop consonants are perceived. Moreover, we hoped that these results would provide the basis for a more general account of the diverse findings obtained with adults, infants and chinchillas on VOT stimuli, as well as an account of the results obtained with the nonspeech stimuli.

EXPERIMENT I

In this experiment, subjects were trained to identify stimuli selected from a nonspeech auditory continuum

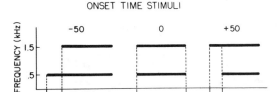

FIG. 1. Schematic representations of three stimuli differing in relative onset time: leading (−50 msec), simultaneous (0 msec), and lagging (+50 msec).

by means of a disjunctive conditioning procedure.[20] The results of this study serve as the baseline for our subsequent experiments.

A. Method

1. Subjects

Eight paid volunteers served as subjects. They were recruited by means of an advertisement in a student newspaper and were paid at a base rate of $2.00 per hour plus whatever they could earn during the course of the experiment. All were right-handed native speakers of English.

2. Stimuli

The stimuli consisted of 11 two-tone sequences that were generated digitally with a computer program that permits the user to specify the amplitude and frequency of two sinusoids at successive moments in time.[21] Schematic representations of three of the signals are shown in Fig. 1. The lower tone was set at 500 Hz, the higher tone at 1500 Hz. The amplitude of the 1500-Hz tone was 12 dB lower than the 500-Hz tone to preserve the amplitude relations found for a neutral vowel. The experimental variable under consideration was the onset time of the lower tone relative to the higher tone. For the −50-msec stimulus, the lower tone leads the higher by 50 msec, for the 0-msec condition both tones were simultaneous, and for the +50-msec condition the lower-tone lags the higher tone by 50 msec. All the remaining intermediate values, which differed in 10-msec steps from −50 to +50 msec, were also generated. Both tones were terminated together. In all cases, the duration of the 1500-Hz tone was held constant at 230 msec and only the duration of the 500-Hz tone was varied to produce these stimuli. The eleven stimuli were recorded on audio tape and later digitized via an A-D converter and stored in digital form.

3. Procedure

All experimental events involving the presentation of stimuli, collection of responses, and feedback were controlled by a small laboratory computer. The digitized waveforms of the test signals were reconverted to analog form via a D-A converter and presented to subjects binaurally through Telephonics (TDH-39) matched and calibrated headphones. The stimuli were presented at a comfortable listening level of about 80 dB (*re* 0.0002 dyn/cm²) which was maintained consistently throughout all the experiments to be reported here.

Speech Perception

418

TABLE I. Order of presentation of training and test sequences for experiment I.

Day	Type of session	Sequence description	Feedback	Number of trials
1	Training	Initial shaping sequence (−50, +50)	Yes	160
1	Training	Identification training (−50, +50)	Yes	160
1	Training	Identification training (−50, −30; +30, +50)	Yes	160
2	Training	Warmup sequence (−50, +50)	Yes	80
2	Labeling	Identification sequence (all 11 stimuli)	No	165
2	Discrimination	ABX Discrimination (9 two-step comparisons)	Yes	252

The present experiment consisted of two 1-h sessions which were conducted on separate days. All subjects were run in small groups. The order of presentation of the test sequences is given in Table I. On day 1 subjects received identification training sequences; on day 2 they were tested for identification and ABX discrimination.

In the initial training sessions, subjects were presented with the end point stimuli, −50, and +50, in a random order and were told to learn which one of two buttons was associated with each sound. Immediate feedback for the correct response was provided by turning on a light above the response button although no explicit coding or labeling instructions were given. Subjects were free to adopt their own strategies. After 320 trials, two additional intermediate stimuli (−30 and +30) were included as training stimuli. Immediate feedback was maintained throughout the training conditions.

For identification, subjects were presented with all 11 stimuli in random order and told to respond in this condition exactly as before. However, no feedback was provided in this condition. In ABX discrimination all nine two-step pairs along the continuum were arranged

in the four ABX permutations and presented to subjects with feedback for the correct response. Subjects were told to determine whether the third sound was most like the first sound or the second sound. Timing and sequencing in the experiment were self-paced to the slowest subject in a given session.

B. Results and discussion

All eight subjects learned to respond to the endpoint stimuli with a probability of greater than 0.90 during the training sessions. The results of the identification and ABX-discrimination tests are shown in Fig. 2. The labeling functions are shown by the filled circles and triangles connected by solid lines. For five of the eight subjects (S1, S2, S4, S7, and S8), the labeling functions are extremely sharp and consistent and show only a very small region of ambiguity between the two response categories. For the remaining three subjects (S3, S5, and S6), the labeling functions are less consistent although with additional training these functions would probably have leveled out. For the most part, however, the labeling data for these nonspeech signals are quite good, given the modest number of training trials (560) over the two-day experiment.

The crossover points for the category boundary (CB) for six of the eight subjects do not occur precisely at the 0 onset-time value but are displaced towards the category containing lagging stimuli. These are shown separately for each subject in Fig. 2. This asymmetry might be due to either the relatively greater masking of high frequencies by low frequencies or to some limitation on processing temporal order information. In order to test the masking interpretation, we ran a pilot study in which the amplitude of the 1500-Hz tone was varied over a 24-dB range from −12 to +12 dB relative to the amplitude of the 500-Hz tone. If the asymmetry in the labeling function is caused by masking of the higher tone by the lower tone, we would expect increases in the amplitude of the higher tone to produce systematic

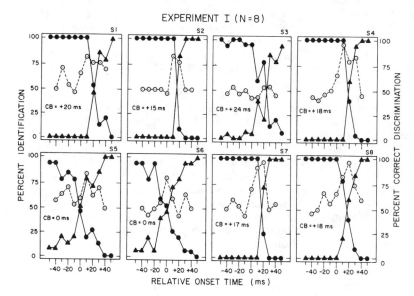

FIG. 2. Labeling functions are shown by the filled circles and triangles (left ordinate) and ABX discrimination function by open circles (right ordinate) for individual subjects in experiment I.

TABLE II. Observed and predicted ABX discrimination scores and chi-square values for goodness of fit.

Subject		−50/−30	−40/−20	−30/−10	−20/0	−10/+10	0/+20	+10/+30	+20/+40	+30/+50	Sum
1	Observed (O)	0.50	0.71	0.54	0.46	0.68	0.82	0.79	0.79	0.71	
	Predicted (P)	0.50	0.50	0.50	0.50	0.50	0.61	0.88	0.56	0.51	
	O−P	0	0.21	0.04	0.04	0.18	0.21	0.09	0.23	0.20	
	Chi-square	0	5.04	0	0	3.64	5.32	1.96	5.88	4.76	26.6 [a]
2	Observed	0.50	0.50	0.50	0.50	0.46	0.86	0.79	0.50	0.50	
	Predicted	0.50	0.50	0.50	0.50	0.50	0.88	1.00	0.51	0.50	
	O−P	0	0	0	0	−0.04	0.02	0.21	0.01	0	
	Chi-square	0	0	0	0	0	0	0	0	0	0
3	Observed	0.46	0.54	0.46	0.50	0.43	0.43	0.54	0.54	0.46	
	Predicted	0.50	0.50	0.50	0.50	0.55	0.51	0.61	0.68	0.50	
	O−P	−0.04	0.04	−0.04	0	0.12	0.08	0.07	0.14	−0.04	
	Chi-square	0	0	0	0	1.68	0.56	0.56	2.52	0	5.4
4	Observed	0.43	0.39	0.46	0.50	0.68	0.96	0.79	0.82	0.43	
	Predicted	0.50	0.50	0.50	0.50	0.50	0.68	0.94	0.58	0.50	
	O−P	−0.07	−0.11	−0.04	0	0.18	0.28	−0.15	0.24	−0.07	
	Chi-square	0.56	1.12	0	0	3.64	10.36	10.36	6.72	0.56	33.3 [a]
5	Observed	0.57	0.64	0.71	0.54	0.61	0.82	0.64	0.71	0.50	
	Predicted	0.51	0.50	0.50	0.58	0.68	0.52	0.50	0.54	0.51	
	O−P	0.06	0.14	0.21	−0.04	−0.07	0.30	0.14	0.17	0.01	
	Chi-square	0.56	2.24	5.04	0.28	0.56	10.80	2.24	3.64	0	24.6
6	Observed	0.50	0.43	0.50	0.57	0.82	0.61	0.43	0.68	0.50	
	Predicted	0.51	0.50	0.52	0.58	0.56	0.56	0.52	0.51	0.50	
	O−P	−0.01	−0.07	−0.02	−0.01	0.26	0.05	−0.09	0.17	0	
	Chi-square	0	0.56	0	0	7.84	0.28	0.84	0.28	0	9.8
7	Observed	0.50	0.61	0.54	0.43	0.71	0.93	0.96	0.50	0.57	
	Predicted	0.50	0.50	0.50	0.50	0.50	0.77	1.00	0.54	0.50	
	O−P	0	0.11	0.04	−0.07	0.21	0.16	−0.04	−0.04	0.07	
	Chi-square	0	1.12	0	0.56	5.04	3.92	0	0	0.56	11.2
8	Observed	0.46	0.50	0.68	0.57	0.68	0.79	0.96	0.75	0.61	
	Predicted	0.50	0.50	0.50	0.50	0.52	0.68	0.72	0.58	0.51	
	O−P	−0.04	0	0.18	0.07	0.16	0.11	0.24	0.17	0.10	
	Chi-square	0	0	3.58	0.56	2.80	1.40	8.12	3.36	1.12	20.9

[a] $p < 0.001$, df = 8.

shifts in the locus of the category boundary towards progressively shorter onset-time values. No such shift was observed in the pilot experiment, which suggests that the temporal order account is the more likely cause of the asymmetry in the placement of the category boundary. The results of the subsequent experiments reported below also support this conclusion.

The observed two-step ABX-discrimination functions are shown by open circles and broken lines and are plotted over the corresponding labeling functions for comparison. Most subjects show evidence of categorical-like discrimination: there is a peak in the discrimination function at the category boundary and there are troughs within both categories. Subject S2 is the most extreme example in the group, showing very nearly the idealized form of categorical perception.[9]

The labeling data and the discrimination functions indicate that categorical perception can be obtained with these nonspeech signals. To test the strength of these results against the categorical perception model, the ABX predictions from the labeling probabilities were compared with the observed discrimination functions.[5]

A χ^2 test was used to assess the goodness of fit between the expected discrimination functions and the observed functions.[22] The observed and predicted discrimination scores, as well as the individual χ^2 values for each subject are given in Table II.

The fit of the observed and prediction functions is quite good in several cases such as S2 and S6 as shown by the low chi squares. In other cases, however, the fits are poor and the chi squares reach a very conservative level of significance (i.e., S1 and S4). In the case of S4 the discrimination function is the right shape and level but is just shifted slightly from the discrimination functions predicted from the labeling probabilities.

In general, however, the data from the present experiment show categorical-perception effects that are at least as comparable as those obtained with speech sounds, particularly stop consonants. Thus, the results of this study serve as another demonstration of categorical perception with nonspeech signals and suggest that this form of perception is not unique to speech stimuli.[23] But what is the basis for the present cate-

EXPERIMENT II (N=12)

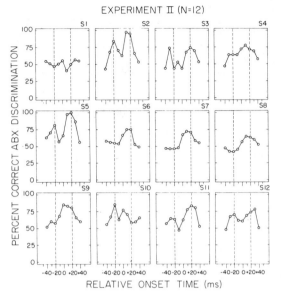

FIG. 3. ABX discrimination functions for individual subjects in experiment II. Broken lines have been drawn through −20 and +20 msec to mark off three regions of onset time.

gorical-perception results? Are these findings due to some labeling process brought about by the training procedures as Lane[20] has argued or is there a simpler psychophysical explanation? In order to rule out the labeling explanation, it is necessary to obtain ABX-discrimination functions before any training experience. If peaks in discrimination still remain in the absence of any labeling experience we will have reason to suspect some psychophysical basis to the observed discrimination functions. The next experiment was carried out to test this hypothesis.

EXPERIMENT II

A. Method

1. Subjects

Twelve volunteers served as subjects. They were recruited in the same way as the subjects from the previous experiment and met the same selection requirements.

2. Stimuli

The eleven stimuli of experiment I were also used in the present experiment.

3. Procedure

The procedures for the ABX-discrimination tests were identical to those used in the previous experiment. The experiment consisted of two 1-h sessions held on separate days. On each day the subjects received 360 ABX trials with immediate feedback provided for the correct response. In the course of the experiment each of the nine two-step stimulus comparisons was responded to 80 times by each subject.

B. Results and discussion

The ABX-discrimination functions for all 12 subjects are shown in Fig. 3. Except for S1 whose performance is close to chance, all of the other subjects show one of two patterns of discrimination performance. Four of the subjects show evidence of a single peak in the discrimination function at approximately +20 msec, whereas the rest of the subjects show discrimination functions with two peaks. For this group one peak occurs at approximately +20 msec, whereas a second peak occurs at approximately −20 msec. Broken vertical lines have been drawn through the discrimination functions at values of −20 and +20 msec to facilitate these comparisons.

The peak in discrimination at +20 msec is comparable to that found in the previous experiment. A re-examination of Fig. 2 also shows some evidence of a smaller peak in the −20-msec range for several subjects in experiment I, although the major peak occurs at +20 msec and is correlated with changes in the labeling function.

It is clear from the results of the present experiment that the peaks in discrimination do not arise solely from the training procedures employed in experiment I and the associated labels. Rather, it appears that natural categories are present at places along the stimulus continuum that are marked by narrow regions of high sensitivity. Based on these results, it is possible to describe three categories within the −50 to +50-msec region. Going from left to right, the first category contains stimuli with the lower tone leading by 20 msec or more; the second category contains stimuli in which both tones occur more-or-less simultaneously within the −20 to +20-msec region, whereas the third category contains stimuli in which the lower-tone lags behind the higher tone by 20 msec or more. Within the context of this experiment, the three regions correspond, respectively, to leading, simultaneous and lagging temporal events.

The presence of peaks in the ABX-discrimination functions for these nonspeech stimuli is in sharp contrast to the results obtained previously by Liberman et al.[6] and Mattingly et al.[10] who found marked differences in discrimination between speech and nonspeech signals. In these experiments, nonspeech control stimuli were created that nominally contained the same acoustic properties of speech but, nevertheless, did not sound like speech. For example, in the Liberman et al.[6] study, the synthetic spectrograms of the /do/−/to/ stimuli were inverted before being converted to sound on the pattern playback. In the Mattingly et al.[10] study, the second-formant transitions (i.e., chirps) were isolated from the rest of the stimulus pattern since it was assumed that these acoustic cues carry the essential information for place of articulation. When these nonspeech stimuli were presented to subjects in a discrimination task the discrimination functions that were obtained failed to show peaks and troughs that corresponded to those found with the parallel set of speech stimuli from which they were derived. The discrimination functions were flat and very nearly close to chance in most of the cases, especially in the earlier study by Liberman and his co-workers.

The failure to find peaks and troughs in the discrimination functions of the nonspeech control stimuli may have been due to the lack of familiarity with these stimuli and the absence of any feedback during the discrimination task. With complex multidimensional signals it may be difficult for subjects to attend to the relevant attributes that distinguish these stimuli. For example, if the subject is not specifically attending to the initial portion of the stimulus but focusses instead on other properties, his discrimination performance may be no better than chance. Indeed, the Liberman et al.[6] results indicate precisely this. Moreover, without feedback in experiments such as this the subject may focus on one aspect or set of attributes on a given trial and a different aspect of the stimulus on the next trial. As a result, the subject may respond to the same stimulus quite differently at different times during the course of the experiment. The results of the present experiment strongly indicate that nonspeech signals can be responded to consistently and reliably from trial to trial when the subject is provided with information about the relevant stimulus parameters that control his response.

The argument for the presence of three natural categories and our interpretation of the previous nonspeech control experiments would be strengthened if it could be demonstrated that subjects can classify these same stimuli into three distinct categories whose boundaries occur at precisely these regions on the continuum. We addressed this question in the next experiment.

EXPERIMENT III

In this experiment we used the same training procedures as in the first experiment except that subjects were now required to use three response categories instead of two. Our aim was to determine whether subjects would partition the stimulus continuum consistently into three distinct categories and whether the boundaries would lie at the same points of high discriminability identified in the previous experiment.

A. Method

1. Subjects

Eight additional subjects were recruited for the present experiment. They were obtained from the same

TABLE III. Order of presentation of training and test sequences for experiment III.

Day	Type of session	Sequence description	Feedback	Number of trials
1	Training	Initial shaping sequence (−50, 0, +50)	Yes	180
1	Training	Identification training (−50, 0, +50)	Yes	300
2	Training	Warmup sequence (−50, 0, +50)	Yes	90
2	Labeling	Identification sequence (all 11 stimuli)	No	165

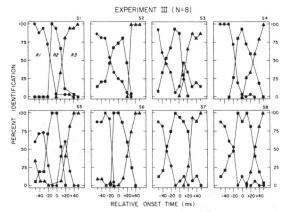

FIG. 4. Labeling functions for individual subjects after training on −50-, 0-, and +50-msec stimuli as representative of each of the three categories, R1, R2, and R3.

source and met the same requirements as the subjects used in the previous experiments.

2. Stimuli

The same basic set of 11 tonal stimuli were also used in the present experiment.

3. Procedure

The experiment took place on two separate days. The first day was devoted to shaping and identification training with three stimuli; on the second day the labeling tests were conducted. Subjects were not given any explicit labels to use in the task and, as in the previous experiment, were free to adopt their own coding strategies. The procedure used in this experiment was similar to that used in experiment I. Subjects were presented with three training stimuli, −50, 0, and +50 msec and were told to learn to respond differentially to these signals by pressing one of three buttons located on a response box. The order of presentation of the test sequences is given in Table III. Immediate feedback was provided for the correct response in each case.

B. Results and discussion

The identification functions for the eight subjects are shown in Fig. 4. As shown here, all subjects partitioned the stimulus continuum into three well-defined categories. As anticipated, the boundaries between categories occur at approximately −20 and +20 msec. While there is some noise in the data when compared to the results of the first experiment, it is clear that subjects could reliably and consistently use the three responses and associate them with three distinct sets of attributes along the stimulus continuum. There is very little confusion or overlap between the three response categories although the results are not nearly as consistent as those obtained with the stop consonants by Liberman and others.[5, 10, 22]

The identification data from this experiment would probably have been more consistent if additional members of each category were used during training as in the first experiment and if the range of stimuli was expanded slightly. Because of time constraints we used only one exemplar of each category during training. Further experiments are currently under way to resolve these issues.

In this experiment we did not explicitly provide subjects with an appropriate set of labels to use in encoding these sounds, although it is likely that they invented ones of their own. We assumed that by training subjects on representative members of a category we could reveal some aspects of the underlying categorization process, and therefore gain some insight into the basis for defining category membership. The results of these experiments have revealed the presence of three natural categories that can be defined by the presence of certain distinct perceptual attributes at onset. For many subjects these categories are separated by regions of high discriminability corresponding more or less to what might be called a perceptual threshold. We suggested earlier that the three categories observed along this continuum could be characterized by the subject's ability to discriminate differences in temporal order among the components of a stimulus complex. Thus, the middle category corresponds to stimuli that listeners judge to be more or less simultaneous at onset, whereas both of the two other categories contain stimuli that are judged to contain two distinct events at onset, separated by a discriminable temporal interval.[24]

In order to provide additional support for this account, we carried out another experiment in which subjects were required to determine whether there were one or two distinct events at stimulus onset. The results of this study should provide information bearing on the potential range of attributes that define the perceptual qualities which result from continuous variations in the relative onset of the two tonal components.

EXPERIMENT IV

A. Method

1. Subjects

Eight additional volunteers were recruited as subjects. None had participated in the previous experiments nor had any of them taken part in a previous psychophysical experiment. Thus, they were experimentally naive observers.

2. Stimuli

The same 11 tonal stimuli were also used in the present experiment.

3. Procedure

The experiment was conducted in a single 1-h experimental session. Each of the 11 stimuli was presented singly, in a random order. There were 40 replications of each stimulus, which gave a total of 440 trials. Subjects were told to listen to each sound carefully and then to determine whether they could hear one or two events at stimulus onset. They were told that on some trials the two tones would be simultaneous at onset, whereas on other trials they could be successive. Sub-

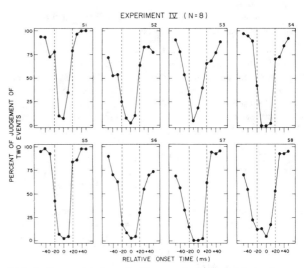

FIG. 5. Per cent judgment of two events for individual subjects as a function of relative onset time of the two components. Broken lines have been drawn through −20 and +20 msec to permit comparisons.

jects were provided with a response box and told to press the button labeled "1" for one event at onset or the button "2" for two events at onset. No feedback was given at any time during the experiment. There was a short break after the first 220 trials.

B. Results and discussion

The results for each of the eight subjects are shown in Fig. 5 where the per-cent judgments of two events are displayed as a function of the stimulus value. All subjects showed similar U-shaped functions with fairly sharp crossover points between categories. There is a region in the center of the continuum, bounded by −20 and +20 msec, which was judged by every subject to contain stimuli whose components are predominantly simultaneous. On the other hand, there are two distinct regions at either end of the continuum in which subjects can reliably judge the presence of two distinct temporal events at stimulus onset, one leading and one lagging. Thus, the results of this experiment, as well as the findings of the other experiments, indicate the presence of three natural categories that may be distinguished by the relative discriminability of the temporal order of the component events. These judgments appear to be relatively easy to make and are consistent from subject to subject. The findings suggest the presence of a fairly robust perceptual effect for processing temporal order information which may also underlie the perception of voicing distinctions in stop consonants in initial position.

V. GENERAL DISCUSSION

The results of the present series of experiments are consistent with the finding of Hirsh,[24] Hirsh and Sherrick,[25] and more recently Stevens and Klatt[12] who found that 20 msec is about the minimal difference in onset time needed to identify the temporal order of two distinct events. Stimuli with onset times greater than about 20 msec are perceived as successive events; stimuli with onset times less than about 20 msec are perceived as simultaneous events.

Based on the results of the present set of experiments with nonspeech stimuli differing in relative onset time, we would like to offer a general account of the labeling and discrimination data that can handle the four seemingly diverse sets of findings that have been previously reported in the literature. To review briefly, these four sets of findings are the perceptual results obtained for: (1) infants, (2) adults, (3) chinchillas with synthetic speech sounds differing in VOT, and (4) the recent findings obtained for adults with nonspeech control stimuli differing in noise-lead time. Although specific accounts have been proposed to handle these findings individually, in our view a more general account of voicing perception is preferable.

We suggest that the four sets of findings may simply reflect a basic limitation on the ability to process temporal-order information. In the case of the voicing dimension, the time of occurrence of an event (i.e., onset of voicing) must be judged in relation to the temporal attributes of other events (i.e., release from closure). The fact that these events, as well as others involved in VOT, are ordered in time implies that highly distinctive and discriminable changes will be produced at various regions along the temporal continuum. Although continuous variations in the temporal relations may nominally be present in these stimuli, at least according to the experimenter's operational criteria, the only perceptual change to which the listener is sensitive appears to be the presence or absence of a discrete attribute rather than the magnitude of difference between events. Thus, the discrimination of small temporal differences in tasks such as these is relatively poor, whereas the discrimination of discrete attributes is excellent. This, of course, is the implication of the previous categorical-perception experiments. Phonological systems apparently have exploited this principle during the evolution of language. As Stevens and Klatt[12] have remarked, the inventory of phonetic features used in natural languages is not a continuous variable but rather consists of the presence or absence of sets of attributes or cues. This seems also to be the case with nonspeech stimuli having temporal properties similar to speech.

The account of voicing perception proposed here does not minimize the importance of the F1 transition cue[12, 26] or of the duration of aspiration noise preceding voicing onset,[16] as well as the numerous other cues to the voiced-voiceless distinction.[1] We would suggest that these cues are simply special cases of the more general process underlying voicing distinctions, namely, whether the events at onset are perceived as simultaneous or successive and if successive what their temporal order is.

It should be pointed out, however, that while the line of argument in this paper has emphasized the temporal domain, there is also strong evidence for some temporal-spectral interaction in voicing perception.[27] A

complete account of voicing perception in stops will, of necessity, have to deal with the findings that the voiced-voiceless boundary varies as a function of the place of articulation of the consonant and the following vowel context. Additional experiments with comparable nonspeech signals are currently in progress to see whether these differences are a consequence of phonetic categorization or some more general psychophysical process.

The range of values found in the present experiments between −20 and +20 msec probably represents the lower limits on the region of perceived simultaneity. We assume that experience in the environment probably serves to tune and align the voicing boundaries in different languages and, accordingly, there will be some slight modification of the precise values associated with different regions along a temporal continuum such as VOT. It is also possible, as in the case of English voicing contrasts, that if appropriate experience is not forthcoming with the particular distinction, its discriminability will be substantially reduced. The exact mechanism underlying these processes, as well as their developmental course, is under extensive investigation.[28,29]

In summary, the results of these four experiments suggest a general explanation for the perception of voicing contrasts in initial position in terms of the relative discriminability of the temporal order between two or more events. These findings may be thought of as still another example of how languages have exploited the general properties of sensory systems to represent phonetic distinctions. As Stevens[30] has suggested, all phonetic features of language probably have their roots in acoustic attributes with well-defined properties. We suggest that one of these properties corresponds to simultaneity at stimulus onset as reflected in the perception of voicing contrasts in stops.

ACKNOWLEDGMENTS

I thank Jerry Forshee and Judy Hupp for their assistance in carrying out these experiments at Indiana while I was on leave at MIT. I am also grateful to Professor Kenneth Stevens and Dr. Dennis Klatt for their interest and advice at various stages of this project.

*Reprints may be obtained from the author who has now returned to the Department of Psychology, Indiana University, Bloomington, IN 47401. This research was supported, in part, by NIH grants Nos. NS-07040 and NS-04332 to the Research Laboratory of Electronics, M. I. T. and, in part, by NIMH grant No. MH-24027 and NIH grant No. NS-12179 to Indiana University.

[1]L. Lisker and A. S. Abramson, "A cross language study of voicing in initial stops: Acoustical measurements," Word 20, 384–422 (1964).

[2]L. Lisker and A. S. Abramson, "The voicing dimension: Some experiments in comparative phonetics," in *Proceedings of the 6th International Congress of Phonetic Sciences* (Academia, Prague, 1970), pp. 563–567.

[3]A. S. Abramson and L. Lisker, "Voice onset time in stop consonants: Acoustic analysis and synthesis," in *Proceedings of the 5th International Congress of Acoustics* (Rapports, Liège, 1965).

[4] A. S. Abramson and L. Lisker, "Discriminability along the voicing continuum: Cross-language tests," in *Proceedings of the* 6th *International Congress of Phonetic Sciences* (Academia, Prague, 1970), pp. 569–573.

[5] A. M. Liberman, K. S. Harris, H. S. Hoffman, and B. C. Griffith, "The discrimination of speech sounds within and across phoneme boundaries," J. Exp. Psychol. 54, 358–368 (1957).

[6] A. M. Liberman, K. S. Harris, J. A. Kinney, and H. L. Lane, "The discrimination of relative onset time of the components of certain speech and non-speech patterns," J. Exp. Psychol. 61, 379–388 (1961).

[7] A. M. Liberman, F. S. Cooper, D. P. Shankweiler, and M. Studdert-Kennedy, "Perception of the speech code," Psychol. Rev. 74, 431–461 (1967).

[8] A. M. Liberman, "Some characteristics of perception in the speech mode," in *Perception and Its Disorders, Proceedings of A.R.N.M.D.*, edited by D. A. Hamburg (Williams & Wilkins, Baltimore, 1970), pp. 238–254.

[9] M. Studdert-Kennedy, A. M. Liberman, K. S. Harris, and F. S. Cooper, "The motor theory of speech perception: A reply to Lane's critical review," Psychol. Rev. 77, 234–249 (1970).

[10] I. G. Mattingly, A. M. Liberman, A. K. Syrdal, and T. G. Halwes, "Discrimination in speech and non-speech modes," Cognitive Psychol. 2(2), 131–157 (1971).

[11] P. D. Eimas, E. R. Siqueland, P. Jusczyk, and J. Vigorito, "Speech Perception in infants," Science 171, 303–306 (1971).

[12] K. N. Stevens and D. H. Klatt, "The role of formant transitions in the voiced–voiceless distinction for stops," J. Acoust. Soc. Am. 55, 653–659 (1974).

[13] P. K. Kuhl and J. D. Miller, "Speech perception by the chinchilla: Voiced-voiceless distinction in alveolar plosive consonants," Science 190, 69–72 (1975).

[14] R. E. Lasky, A. Syrdal-Lasky, and R. E. Klein, "VOT discrimination by four to six and a half month old infants from Spanish environments," J. Exp. Child Psychol. 20, 213–225 (1975).

[15] L. A. Streeter, "Language perception of 2-month old infants shows effects of both innate mechanisms and experience," Nature 259, 39–41 (1976).

[16] J. D. Miller, C. C. Wier, R. Pastore, W. J. Kelly, and R. J. Dooling, "Discrimination and labeling of noise-buzz sequences with varying noise-lead times: An example of categorical perception," J. Acoust. Soc. Am. 60, 410–417 (1976).

[17] A. S. Abramson and L. Lisker, "Voice-timing perception in Spanish word-initial stops," J. Phonetics 1, 1–8 (1973).

[18] J. S. Bruner, J. J. Goodnow, and G. A. Austin, *A study of thinking* (Wiley, New York, 1956).

[19] A. M. Liberman, P. C. Delattre, and F. S. Cooper, "Some cues for the distinction between voiced and voiceless stops in initial position," Lang. Speech 1(3), 153–167 (1958).

[20] H. L. Lane, "The motor theory of speech perception: A critical review," Psychol. Rev. 72, 275–309 (1965).

[21] I am indebted to Dr. Dennis Klatt for his help with the program used to generate these stimuli.

[22] D. B. Pisoni, "On the nature of categorical perception of speech sounds," Ph.D. thesis (University of Michigan, 1971); *Supplement to Status Report on Speech Research*, SR-27 (Haskins Laboratories, New Haven, 1971), pp. 1–101.

[23] J. E. Cutting and B. S. Rosner, "Categories and boundaries in speech and music," Percept. Psychophys. 16, 564–570 (1974).

[24] I. J. Hirsh, "Auditory perception of temporal order," J. Acoust. Soc. Am. 31, 759–767 (1959).

[25] I. J. Hirsh and C. E. Sherrick, "Perceived order in different sense modalities," J. Exp. Psychol. 62, 423–432 (1961).

[26] L. Lisker, "Is it VOT or a first-formant transition detector?" J. Acoust. Soc. Am. 57, 1547–1551 (1975).

[27] A. Q. Summerfield, "Information-Processing Analyses of Perceptual Adjustments to Source and Context Variables in Speech," Ph.D. thesis (Queen's University of Belfast, 1975) (unpublished).

[28] P. D. Eimas, "Auditory and phonetic coding of the cues for speech: Discrimination of the r-l distinction by young infants," Percept. Psychophys. 18, 341–347 (1975).

[29] P. D. Eimas, "Developmental aspects of speech perception," in *Handbook of Sensory Physiology: Perception*, edited by R. Held, H. Leibowitz, and H. L. Teuber (Springer–Verlag, New York, 1977).

[30] K. N. Stevens, "The quantal nature of speech: Evidence from articulatory-acoustic data," in *Human Communication: A Unified View*, edited by E. E. David, Jr. and P. B. Denes (McGraw–Hill, New York, 1972), pp. 51–66.

Journal of Experimental Psychology:
Human Perception and Performance
1978, Vol. 4, No. 4, 621-637

Perceptual Integration of Acoustic Cues for Stop, Fricative, and Affricate Manner

Bruno H. Repp, Alvin M. Liberman, Thomas Eccardt,
and David Pesetsky
Haskins Laboratories, New Haven, Connecticut

Introducing a short interval of silence between the words SAY and SHOP causes listeners to hear SAY CHOP. Another cue for the fricative–affricate distinction is the duration of the fricative noise in SHOP (CHOP). Now, varying both these temporal cues orthogonally in a sentence context, we find that, within limits, they are perceived in relation to each other: The shorter the duration of the noise, the shorter the silence necessary to convert the fricative into an affricate. On the other hand, when the rate of articulation of the sentence frame is increased while holding noise duration constant, a longer silent interval is needed to hear an affricate, as if the noise duration, but not the silence duration, were effectively longer in the faster sentence. In a second experiment, varying noise and silence durations in GRAY SHIP, we find that given sufficient silence, listeners report GRAY CHIP when the noise is short but GREAT SHIP when it is long. Thus, the long noise in the second syllable disposes listeners to displace the stop to the first syllable, so that they hear not a syllable-initial affricate (i.e., stop-initiated fricative) but a syllable-final stop (followed by a syllabe-initial fricative). Repeating the experiment with GREAT SHIP as the original utterance, we obtain the same pattern of results, together with only a moderate increase in GREAT responses. In all such cases, the listeners integrate a numerous, diverse, and temporally distributed set of acoustic cues into a unitary phonetic percept. These several cues have in common only that they are the products of a unitary articulatory act. In effect, then, it is the articulatory act that is perceived.

When a speaker makes an articulatory gesture appropriate for a phonetic segment, the acoustic consequences are typically numerous, diverse, and distributed over a relatively long span of the signal. In the articulation of an intervocalic stop consonant, for example, the characteristically rapid closing and opening of the vocal tract has acoustic consequences that include, among others, the following: various rising and falling transitions of the several formants; a period of significantly reduced sound intensity; and then a second, acoustically different set of formant transitions, plus (in the case of voiceless stops in iambic stress patterns) a transient burst of sound, a delayed onset of the first formant, and, for the duration of that delay, band-limited noise in place of periodic sound in the higher formants.

Despite their obvious diversity and their distribution over periods as long as 300

This research was supported by National Institute for Child Health and Human Development Grant HD01994 and by BRSG Grant RR05596. We would like to thank Georgann Witte for her help in data analysis. A short version of this paper was presented at the 94th meeting of the Acoustical Society of America in Miami Beach, Florida, December 1977. Additional affiliations of the authors are as follows: Alvin M. Liberman, University of Connecticut and Yale University; Thomas Eccardt, Yale University; David Pesetsky, Massachusetts Institute of Technology.

Request for reprints should be sent to Bruno H. Repp, Haskins Laboratories, 270 Crown Street, New Haven, Connecticut 06510.

msec (Repp, Note 1), these acoustic features—usually referred to as "cues"—are nevertheless integrated into the unitary perception of a phonetic segment. In such cases of integration we find trading relations among the several cues that take part: Within limits, one cue can be exchanged for another without any change in the phonetic percept; in that sense, the cues are perceptually equivalent, though they may differ greatly in acoustic (and presumably auditory) terms and be quite far removed from each other in time.

To find the basis for the perceptual integration and for the perceptual equivalence it implies, we should first ask what it is that these diverse features have in common. As already implied, we have not far to look: Each is one of the normal products of the same linguistically significant act. Given that commonality, and given the convergence on a unitary phonetic percept, we find it most parsimonious to suppose that the acoustic cues are processed by a system specialized to perceive the phonetically significant act by which they were produced. On that assumption, the boundaries of the integration would be set not by the number, diversity, or temporal distribution of the cues but rather by a decision that they do (or do not) plausibly specify an articulatory act appropriate for the production of a single phonetic segment.

Just how the various cues contribute, separately and in various combinations, to the integrated phonetic percept has been the subject of the many experimental studies of speech perception carried out over the last 30 years. These have established the more or less important roles of the cues and, either directly or by implication, have outlined the trading realtions—hence perceptual equivalences—among them. In one of the most recent of these studies, Summerfield and Haggard (1977) made explicit how a trading relation among the cues for the voicing distinction is to be understood by taking account of the fact that they are the common products of the same articulatory act. A more general discussion of this matter, with examples of the several classes of cues that engage in such trading relations,

is to be found in Liberman and Studdert-Kennedy (in press).

In the experiments reported here, we put our attention on simple cues of a temporal sort: duration of silence and duration of fricative noise. We examined their integration in the perception of the distinction between fricative and affricate, and we also investigated the effect on that integration of a still more widely distributed temporal variable, namely, the rate at which the surrounding speech is articulated. In the second experiment, we studied the effects of those same temporal cues, but now in connection with the perception of juncture. That provided us with an opportunity to examine a case in which the integration occurs across syllable boundaries: A syllable-final stop is perceived or not, depending on a cue in the next syllable that simultaneously determines whether the initial segment in that syllable is taken to be a fricative or an affricate.

Experiment 1

In this experiment we selected two cues for study, both temporal in nature and both relevant to the fricative–affricate distinction. One of them is silence. A short period of silence (or near silence) in the acoustic signal tells the listener that the speaker has closed his vocal tract, a gesture characteristic of stop consonants and affricates. That silence is a powerful and often sufficient cue for the perception of stop or affricate manner can be experimentally demonstrated by inserting silence at the appropriate place in an utterance. So, for example, SLIT can be converted into a convincing SPLIT by inserting a sufficient amount of silence between the fricative noise and the vocalic (LIT) portion. That was done originally in tape-splicing experiments (Bastian, Eimas, & Liberman, 1961; Bastian, Notes 2 & 3). For the same phonetic contrast, investigators have more recently explored the range of effective silence durations (Dorman, Raphael, & Liberman, Note 4) and, in another study, revealed a trading relation between silence and a spectral cue (Erickson, Fitch, Halwes, & Liberman, Note 5).

Other contrasts—similar in that they, too, are based on the presence or absence of stop or stoplike manner—have also been found to depend in important ways on the silence cue. Thus, with appropriate insertions of silence, SI can be made to sound like SKI, or SU like SPU (Bailey & Summerfield, Note 6). Silence can also be sufficient to cue the fricative–affricate contrast in, for example, SAY SHOP versus SAY CHOP (Dorman et al., Note 4); it is this contrast that concerns us here.[1]

For the fricative–affricate contrast, there are, as always, other cues besides silence. The one we used in our experiment is duration of (fricative) noise, a cue shown originally by Gerstman (1957) to be important. Thus, we had two temporal cues, duration of silence and duration of noise, and we shall see how they are integrated to produce the perception of affricate manner. Then we shall examine the effect on that integration of a variable that is also temporal in nature: rate of articulation. Our interest in introducing that variable springs from several sources. We might expect, first of all, that the effect of articulatory rate would be especially apparent on cues that are themselves durational in nature. Several studies tend to confirm that expectation (e.g., Ainsworth, 1974; Fujisaki, Nakamura, & Imoto, 1975; Pickett & Decker, 1960; Summerfield, Note 7). Indeed, one of these studies dealt with the same fricative–affricate contrast we studied, and it reported a seemingly paradoxical effect: Having determined that increasing the duration of silence between SAY and SHOP was sufficient to convert the utterance PLEASE SAY SHOP to PLEASE SAY CHOP, Dorman et al. (Note 4) found that when the rate of the precursor PLEASE SAY was increased, more silence was needed to produce the affricate in CHOP. We wished to test for that effect at each of several durations of the fricative noise, and in a larger sentence context. The results may then bear on an interpretation of the paradoxical effect that is consistent with the hypothesis we have advanced to account for the integration of the segmental cues themselves— namely, that perception takes account of production.

To appreciate the point, we should take note of the claim by students of speech production (e.g., Kozhevnikov & Chistovich, 1965) that changes in rate of articulation do not stretch or compress all portions of the speech signal proportionately. In that connection, the data most relevant to our purposes are owing to Gay (1978). He found that durations of silence associated with stop consonants change less with rate than do the durations of the surrounding vocalic portions. It is possible, then, that the somewhat corresponding cue elements of our experiment—duration of silence and duration of fricative noise—are, in like fashion, differentially affected by changes in speaking rate. If so, and if perception is indeed guided, as it were, by tacit knowledge of the consequences of articulation, then we should expect that the perceptual integration of the two cues would reflect such inequalities as the production may have caused.

Method

Subjects. Seven paid volunteers (Yale University undergraduates) participated, as did three of the authors (Repp, Eccardt, & Pesetsky). All except Repp are native speakers of American English (he learned German as his first language). The results of all 10 subjects were combined since there were no substantial differences among them.

Stimuli. A male talker recorded the sentence WHY DON'T WE SAY SHOP AGAIN at two different speaking rates, using a monotone voice and avoiding emphatic stress on any syllable. The fast sentence lasted 1.26 sec, and the slow sentence lasted 2.36 sec—a ratio of .53. The sentences were low-pass filtered at 4.9 kHz and digitized at a sampling rate of 10 kHz. This was done with the Haskins Laboratories Pulse Code Modulation (PCM) system. Monitoring the waveforms on high-resolution oscillograms, we excerpted the SH noise of the slow utterance (110 msec in duration) and substituted it for the SH noise in the fast utterance (originally 92 msec). Thus, the two utterances had identical noise portions.

---

[1] It may be noted that the stop consonants (affricates) in the three examples given have different places of articulation. Perceptual information about place of articulation is provided by spectral cues preceding and following the silence (Bailey & Summerfield, Note 6). In our experiments we are concerned only with cues for stop manner and not with place distinctions. Therefore, we pass over the question why, in the last example, listeners hear SAY CHOP (SAY TSHOP) and not SAY PSHOP or SAY KSHOP.

Knowing that rate of onset of the fricative noise is an important cue for the fricative–affricate distinction (Cutting & Rosner, 1974; Gerstman, 1957), we were concerned that it be not too extreme. Preliminary observations suggested that the noise onset in our stimuli was so gradual as to bias the perception strongly toward fricative and even perhaps to override the effects of the two duration cues we wished to study. To remove, or at least reduce, that bias, we removed the initial 30 msec of the noise, leaving 80 msec. That maneuver had the effect of creating a more abrupt onset.[2]

We used the PCM system to vary the two temporal cues under study: noise duration and silence duration. Three different noise durations were created by either duplicating or removing 20 msec from the center of the 80-msec noise, leaving the onset and offset unchanged. Thus, the noise durations were 60, 80, and 100 msec in both sentence frames. In each of the resulting six sentences, varying amounts of silence were inserted before the fricative noise. Silence duration was varied from 0 to 100 msec in 10-msec steps. Eleven silence durations, three noise durations, and two speaking rates resulted in 66 sentences. These were recorded in five different randomizations, with 2 sec intervening between successive sentences.

To determine how the different noise durations were perceived outside the sentence context, we prepared a separate tape containing isolated SHOP (CHOP) words excerpted from the test sentences. (The stimuli consisted of the portion from the beginning of the fricative noise to the beginning of the P-closure.) Three different noise durations and two speaking rates yielded six stimuli; these were duplicated 10 times and recorded in a random sequence, separated by 3-sec intervals. The different speaking rates were reflected in the durations of the vocalic portions of the test words; they were 140 msec (slow) and 113 msec (fast).

Procedure.   The subjects listened in a quiet room over an Ampex Model 620 amplifier-speaker, as the tapes were played back on an Ampex Model AG-500 tape recorder. Intensity was set at a comfortable level. All subjects listened to the isolated words first, except for the three authors, who took this brief test at a later date. The task was to identify each word as either SHOP or CHOP, using the letters s and c for convenience in writing down the responses and guessing when uncertain. The same responses were required in the sentence test. The listeners were informed about the different speaking rates but not about the variations in noise and silence duration (obviously this does not apply to those authors who participated). After a pause, the sentence test was repeated, so that 10 responses per subject were obtained for each sentence.

Results

Consider first the results obtained for isolated words. Although the original utterance had contained SHOP, the isolated words were predominantly perceived as CHOP. Presumably, this was a consequence of our having cut back the original fricative noise and thus creating not only a shorter noise duration but also a more abrupt onset; both changes would be expected to bias perception toward affricate manner (Gerstman, 1957). Despite the bias, there was a clear effect of the variations in noise duration: The percentages of CHOP responses to the three noise durations (60, 80, and 100 msec) were 99, 91, and 81 (slow rate) and 99, 90, and 73 (fast rate), respectively. Thus, as expected, the probability of hearing an affricate decreased as noise duration increased. In addition, there seemed to be a slight effect of vowel duration at the longest noise duration, again in the expected direction: When the vocalic portion was shorter— this being the only manifestation of the faster speaking rate in the isolated words— the probability of hearing CHOP was lower, which indicated that the noise duration was to some extent effectively longer at the fast speaking rate.

We turn now to the results of the main experiment. That silence was an effective cue for the fricative–affricate distinction in sentence context is shown in Figure 1. There we see that the listeners heard SHOP or CHOP, depending on the duration of the silence that separated the fricative noise from the syllable (SAY) immediately preceding it. This replicates earlier findings (Dorman et al., Note 4). If, as is reasonable, we consider an affricate to be a stop-initiated fricative, then our result is also perfectly consistent with those of other investi-

---

[2] This manipulation merely created a situation favorable for obtaining the desired effect and in no way affected the validity of the experiment. In fact, our cutting back the noise resulted in a moderate bias in the opposite direction, toward hearing an affricate (CHOP). It should be noted in this connection that not only does SAY SHOP turn into SAY CHOP when silence is inserted but that a natural SAY CHOP can also be turned into SAY SHOP by removing the silence that precedes the fricative noise. Both effects have limits, however: A noise with an extremely abrupt onset will not easily be heard as a fricative even in the absence of silence, and a noise with an extremely gradual onset will not easily be heard as an affricate even if sufficient silence is present.

gators who have found silence to be important in the perception of stop-consonant manner.

We see, further, that duration of fricative noise had a systematic effect, as indicated by the horizontal displacement of the three functions in each panel of Figure 1. The proportion of SHOP responses increased significantly with noise duration, $F(2, 18) = 32.36$, $p < .001$. That effect establishes a trading relation between silence and noise durations: As noise duration increases, more silence is needed to convert SHOP into CHOP.[3]

The effect of speaking rate can be seen by comparing the two panels of Figure 1.

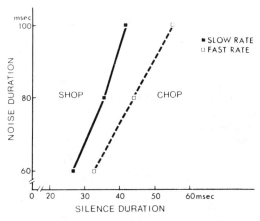

Figure 2. Boundaries between perceived fricative (SHOP) and affricate (CHOP) at each speaking rate as joint functions of the duration of silence and the duration of fricative noise.

We see that the paradoxical effect first discovered by Dorman et al. (Note 4) was indeed replicated: For equivalent noise durations, more silence was needed in the fast sentence frame than in the slow sentence frame to convert the fricative into an affricate, $F(1, 9) = 16.35$, $p < .01$.

The foregoing results are represented more concisely in Figure 2 where the data points are the SHOP–CHOP boundaries (i.e., the 50% crossover points of the six labeling functions) as estimated by the method of probits (Finney, 1971). This procedure fits cumulative normal distribution functions to the data; it also yields estimates of standard deviations and standard errors of the

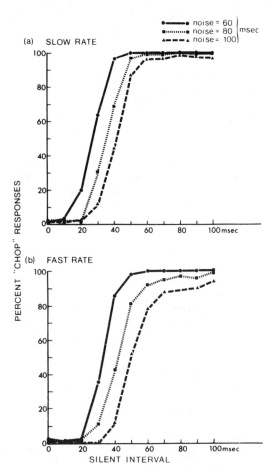

Figure 1. Effect of duration of silence and duration of fricative noise on the perceived distinction between fricative (SHOP) and affricate (CHOP). (This is shown for each of the two rates at which the sentence frame was articulated.)

[3] Strictly speaking, the term "trading relation" may not be appropriate for a positve relation between two cues, but for want of a better term, we use it. The positive covariation of the two perceptual cues is a direct consequence of their negative covariation in production: Fricatives have a long noise duration and no silence, whereas affricates have a shorter noise duration preceded by a closure interval. Genuine perceptual trading relations (negative covariation) are observed when two acoustic properties are positively correlated in production, such as, for example, silence and the extent of the first formant transition as cues for stop manner (Bailey & Summerfield, Note 6). In any case, a positive trading relation can be turned into a negative one by simply reversing the directionality of the scale on which one of the cues is measured.

626   REPP, LIBERMAN, ECCARDT, AND PESETSKY

boundaries.[4] To show the trading relation between the temporal cues more clearly, Figure 2 plots the SHOP–CHOP boundaries (abscissa) as a function of noise duration (ordinate) and speaking rate (the two separate functions). Each function describes a trading relation between noise duration and silence duration by connecting all those combinations of silence and noise durations for which SHOP and CHOP responses are equiprobable. The joint dependence of perceptual judgments on both durational cues is indicated by the fact that the trading functions are neither perfectly vertical nor perfectly horizontal but have intermediate slopes. Both functions are strikingly linear.

Although an increase in speaking rate left the linear form of the trading relation unchanged, it shifted the function toward longer silence durations, simultaneously changing its slope and indicating that rate of articulation had a differential effect on the effective durations of silence and noise. In fact, the trading functions in Figure 2 coincide well with straight lines through the origin of the coordinate system, which means that within each speaking-rate condition, the fricative–affricate boundary is associated with a constant ratio between silence and noise durations—approximately .44 at the slow rate and .55 at the fast rate. A separate analysis of variance of silence/noise ratios showed only a significant effect of speaking rate, $F(2, 18) = 14.60, p < .01$; the effect of noise duration and the interaction term were far from significance. Thus, the consequence of changing the rate of articulation was a change in the ratio of silence to noise required for the same phonetic perception.[5]

Discussion

It is not novel to find that variations in rate of articulation have an effect on the perception of temporal cues in speech. Nor is it entirely novel to find, as we have, that variations in rate have an unequal effect on the several temporal cues— duration of silence and duration of noise—that are effective in the perception of the fricative–affricate distinction; as we pointed out in

the introduction, that conclusion was suggested by an experiment that is owing to Dorman et al. (Note 4). What we have done is to extend that finding. Having varied both the duration of silence and the duration of noise, we saw that the inequality is not peculiar to a particular duration of noise, and we saw, moreover, a trading relation between the two duration cues. That trading relation becomes now a component of one interpretation of the seemingly paradoxical rate effect.

To appreciate that interpretation in its broadest form, we should take note once again of the comments by several students of speech production that variations in rate of articulation do not affect all portions of the speech signal equally. To the extent that this is so, a listener cannot adjust for rate variations by applying a simple scale factor but must rather make a more complex correction, one that embodies a tacit knowledge, as it were, of the inequalities in the signal that rate variations generate. Perhaps the results of our experiment are an instance of that correction and that tacit knowledge. Suppose that in the case of utterances like those of our experiment, variations in rate of articulation cause the duration of the fricative noise to change more than the duration of the silence. If the listener's perception reflects an accurate understanding of that inequality, then he or she should expect that given an increase in rate, the noise would shorten more than the silence. But on hearing, as in some of the conditions of our experiment, that the noise duration remains constant when the rate increases, the listener would assign to the

---

[4] The boundary estimates obtained from the average data of all subjects were virtually identical with the averages of the estimates for individual subjects, so the former have been plotted in Figure 1. The response function for the longest noise seemed to reach asymptote below 100% CHOP responses, especially at the fast speaking rate. This caused the estimated boundaries to fall at somewhat longer silence durations than the 50% intercepts shown in Figure 1.

[5] It must be kept in mind that this description is true only within the limits of the present experiment. Had the noise duration been increased beyond 100 msec, a point would have been reached where no amount of silence would have led to a substantial percentage of CHOP responses (cf. Experiment 2).

noise an effectively greater (relative) length. As we know, a longer noise duration biases the perception toward fricative, though, as shown by the trading relation in our results, that bias can be overcome by an increase in the duration of silence. A consequence of all that would be just the effect of rate we found in our experiment: When the rate was increased as the duration of noise was held constant, listeners required more silence to perceive an affricate.

The foregoing interpretation depends, among other considerations, on a determination that variations in rate do, in fact, produce the particular inequality we are here concerned with. As we pointed out earlier, Gay (1978) found in utterance types somewhat analogous to ours that rate variations produced smaller variations in the silence associated with stop consonants than in the durations of the surrounding vocalic portions. There are no data, unfortunately, on exactly those utterances we used in our experiment. We have made efforts in that direction, but the results so far are inconclusive. Until such time as we know more clearly just what happens in speech production, the interpretation we have offered here is, of course, quite tentative.

The interpretation must be tentative for yet another reason: It does not reckon with the possibility that certain other cues for the fricative–affricate distinction might have been at work in ways that we do not yet thoroughly understand. We have in mind, in particular, the rise time of the fricative noise. From the work of Gerstman (1957) and of Cutting and Rosner (1974), we know that it is a relevant cue. Dorman, Raphael, and Liberman (Note 8) recently varied noise rise time and silence duration to produce the distinction between DISH and DITCH, which is essentially similar to the SAY SHOP—SAY CHOP contrast investigated here, and showed that the two cues engage in an orderly trading relation, as we might have expected. However, we do not know how, or even whether, noise rise time varies with rate of articulation. Information on this matter might conceivably affect our interpretation of the present results.

Returning now to the most important re-sults of our experiment, we should emphasize that there are two. The one has to do with the trading relation between duration of silence and duration of noise as joint cues for the fricative–affricate distinction. It is to us provocative that these cues, diverse and distributed as they seem, are nevertheless integrated into the unitary phonetic percept we call fricative or affricate. In our view, this integration occurs because cues such as these converge through a single decision process that takes account of their common origin: They are the consequences of the same articulatory act. The other result, which we have already discussed at some length, is that the two duration cues were affected unequally by a change in rate of articulation. We would now simply emphasize the inequality, which is a very reliable effect, for it does imply that perceptual correction for variations in rate is not made in this case by applying a simple scale factor but that it may rather require some more sophisticated computation that, like the integration of the duration cues, takes account of particular facts about speech production.

Experiment 2

While exploring the boundaries of the phenomenon reported in Experiment 1, we observed an effect that we have undertaken to investigate more systematically in Experiment 2. We reported in Experiment 1 that with increases in the duration of silence between SAY and SHOP, the fricative in SHOP changed to the affricate in CHOP. However, when the fricative noise was at its longest (100 msec), it occasionally seemed to us that CHOP changed back to SHOP and that the stoplike effect was displaced to the end of the preceding syllable, converting SAY to SAYT. If confirmed, that effect would be interesting from our point of view because it bespeaks an integration of perceptual cues across syllable (word) boundaries. It is also relevant to the problem of "juncture," so long a concern of linguists (see Lehiste, 1960).

Our concern, then, is with the perceptual integration of the cues that affect perception and placement of stop-consonant man-

628   REPP, LIBERMAN, ECCARDT, AND PESETSKY

ner, either as a final segment added to one syllable or as the conversion of the first segment of the next syllable from fricative to affricate. The cues we examined were the same as those of Experiment 1, duration of silence between the syllables and duration of the fricative noise at the beginning of the second syllable. However, there are two changes. To offer maximum opportunity for the stoplike effect to be transferred from the second syllable to the first, we included durations of fricative noise longer than those used in Experiment 1, thus providing a stronger bias against affricate percepts; and to make the alternative responses equally plausible to our subjects, we used a new sentence, DID ANYBODY SEE THE GRAY (GREAT) SHIP (CHIP). The sentence context was employed to make the test as natural as possible. (Rate of articulation was not a variable in this experiment.)

In a second part of the experiment (Experiment 2b), we assessed the effects of those spectral and durational cues that distinguish GRAY and GREAT. For that purpose, we investigated how the results depend on whether, in the original recording, the word was pronounced as GRAY or as GREAT.

Method

Subjects.   The subjects were the same as in Experiment 1.

Stimuli: Experiment 2a.   The sentence DID ANYBODY SEE THE GRAY SHIP was produced by a male speaker in a monotone voice and recorded in digitized form. Using the editing facilities of the Haskins Laboratories PCM System, we varied the duration of silence inserted before the word SHIP for 0 to 100 msec in steps of 10 msec. The duration of the fricative noise in SHIP was also varied. Starting with the duration of the noise as recorded, which was 122 msec, we excised or duplicated 20-msec portions from its center, thus shortening or lengthening it without changing the characteristics of its onset or offset. In this way we created four durations of noise—62, 102, 142, and 182 msec—for use in the experiment. Four noise durations and 11 silence durations led to 44 test utterances. These were recorded in five different randomizations, with intervals of 2 sec between sentences.

To see how the fricative–affricate distinction is affected by noise duration alone, we excised the word SHIP (CHIP) and varied the duration of the noise as described above, but in steps of 20 rather than 40 msec. These isolated words were recorded in a randomized sequence containing 10 repetitions of each stimulus. The interstimulus interval was 3 sec.

Stimuli: Experiment 2b.   A second sentence, DID ANYBODY SEE THE GREAT SHIP, was recorded by the same speaker who had produced the sentence, DID ANYBODY SEE THE GRAY SHIP, of Experiment 2a. He attempted to imitate the intonation and speaking rate of the first-produced sentence. That he succeeded well was suggested by our own listening and by comparison of the waveforms. Using the PCM System, we excerpted the fricative noise from the SHIP of Experiment 2a and substituted it for the noise in the corresponding word of the new sentence. Thus, the two stimulus sentences had exactly the same fricative noise in the final word SHIP. Both sentences were used in Experiment 2b: the original sentence, DID ANYBODY SEE THE GRAY SHIP, and the new sentence, DID ANYBODY SEE THE GREAT SHIP; the important difference was simply in the opposition between the words GRAY and GREAT.

Inspection of waveforms and spectrograms revealed that there was only a slight difference in duration between the two utterances; this difference was almost entirely accounted for by the additional closure period between GREAT and SHIP in the second sentence. The final transitions of the second and third formants were, as expected, somewhat steeper in GREAT than in GRAY. Also, the GREAT syllable had a longer duration (210 msec, not including the following closure period) than GRAY (187 msec).[6] Their offset characteristics were similar.

Only two noise durations, 82 and 142 msec, were used, as against the four (62, 102, 142, and 182 msec) of Experiment 2a. There were more silence durations, on the other hand, covering the (wider) range from 0 to 150 msec in steps of 10 msec. Thus, with 2 noise durations, 16 silence durations, and 2 sentence frames, there were 64 test sentences in all. These were recorded in five randomized sequences.

Procedure.   Experiments 2a and 2b were conducted in a single session of about 2-hours duration. The isolated word sequence was presented first (the response alternatives being SHIP and CHIP), followed by the sentences of Experiments 2a and 2b, in that order. Each set of sentences was repeated once, so that each subject gave a total of 10 responses to each sentence. The subjects chose from four response alternatives, using letter codes in writing down their responses: A = GRAY SHIP, B = GREAT SHIP, C = GRAY CHIP, D = GREAT CHIP. No subject had any difficulties in using this system.

Results

Experiment 2a.   In Figure 3 are shown the effects of the two cues, duration of si-

---

[6] Our intuition may tell us that GRAY should have been longer than GREAT. However, these intuitions are based on the pronunciation of these words in isolation, where word-final lengthening extends the vowel in GRAY. When followed by SHIP, on the other hand, the longer duration of GREAT is quite plausible. However, we do not know whether this observation has any generality.

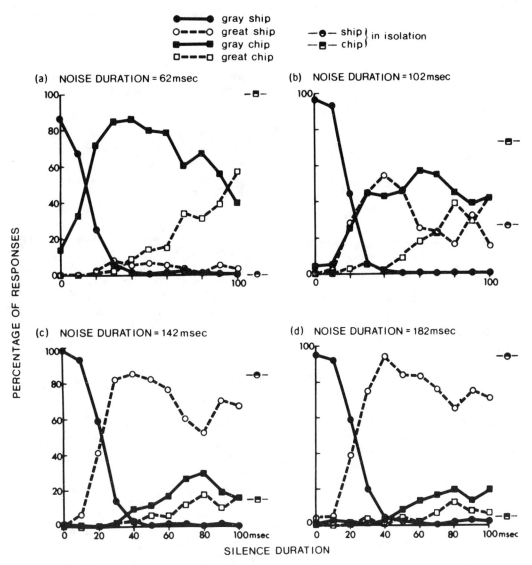

Figure 3. The effect of duration of silence, at each of four durations of fricative noise, on the perception and placement of stop (or affricate) manner.

lence and duration of fricative noise, on the perception of stop or stoplike manner in the utterance DID ANYBODY SEE THE GRAY (GREAT) SHIP (CHIP). Duration of silence is the independent variable; the four panels correspond to the durations of fricative noise. At the right of each panel, we also show the results obtained when the second of the key words, SHIP (CHIP), was presented in isolation.

Let us consider first the responses to the isolated word SHIP (CHIP). At noise dura-

tions of 62, 102, 142, and 182 msec—those used in the experiment—the percentages of CHIP responses were 100, 73, 16, and 6, respectively. Thus, as we had every reason to expect, duration of the noise is a powerful cue for the fricative–affricate distinction. The SHIP-CHIP boundary was estimated to be at 119 msec of noise duration. In contrast to the stimuli of Experiment 1, whose noise durations all fell below this boundary and therefore were predominantly heard as affricates, those of the present experiment

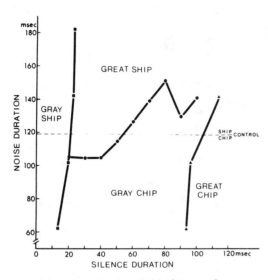

Figure 4. Boundaries that divide the several response categories, represented as joint functions of duration of silence and duration of fricative noise.

spanned the entire range from affricate to fricative.

The more important results of the experiment are seen by examining the graphs that tell us how the stimuli were perceived in the sentence context. We note first that when the silence was of short duration (less than 20 msec), the subjects perceived primarily GRAY SHIP. At those very short durations of silence, no stoplike effect was evident, either as an affricate at the beginning of the second syllable (CHIP) or as a stop consonant at the end of the first syllable (GREAT). With increasing durations of silence, a stoplike effect emerged. As in Experiment 1, somewhat more silence was required at the longer noise durations for this stoplike effect to occur, $F(3, 27) = 6.93$, $p < .01$.

Perhaps the most interesting result was that once a stop was heard, its perceptual placement in the utterance depended crucially on the duration of the fricative noise: At short noise durations, the listeners reported predominantly GRAY CHIP; at longer noise durations, GREAT SHIP. This resulted in a significant response category by noise duration interaction, $F(9, 81) = 71.52$, $p < .001$.

We also see that the response percentages were in fair agreement with the results for isolated words. When the critical word was

heard as CHIP in isolation, it was generally heard as (GRAY or GREAT) CHIP in sentence context, too—provided, of course, that it was preceded by at least 30 msec of silence —and words heard as SHIP in isolation were generally heard as (GREAT) SHIP. Responses in the GREAT CHIP category occurred at the longer silence durations when the noise was short, but even at the longest silence duration and shortest noise such responses reached only about 50%.

A more concise representation of the results, showing perceptual boundaries as determined by the probit method, is to be found in Figure 4. There we see three functions, each of which links those combinations of silence duration and noise duration that are precisely balanced between certain response alternatives, as we specify below. The dashed horizontal line represents the SHIP–CHIP boundary for isolated words.

Consider first the nearly vertical function at the left (squares). This function characterizes the boundary between GRAY SHIP and all other responses. In other words, at each combination of silence and noise durations on this function, listeners were just as likely to hear a stoplike effect as they were to hear no stop at all. The lower part of this function, which represents the boundary between GRAY SHIP and GRAY CHIP, corresponds directly to the SAY SHOP—SAY CHOP boundary functions of Experiment 1 (cf. Figure 2). As in Experiment 1, this part of the function is slanted and thus reflects a trading relation between silence and noise durations. Moreover, again in agreement with Experiment 1, the trading relation can be described as a constant ratio of silence to noise. However, this ratio (about .20) is considerably smaller than that obtained in Experiment 1 at a comparable speaking rate (.44). This is presumably due to the fact that in the present experiment less silence was needed to obtain a stoplike effect. The reason for that was suggested by listening to the words preceding the silence when taken out of context. The SAY of Experiment 1 actually sounded like SAY (not SAYT) in isolation, but the excised word GRAY of the present experiment, although correctly pronounced in the original sentence, sounded much more like GREAT. Thus, the vocalic portion preceding the silence contained stronger stop-manner cues in the present experiment than in Experiment 1, so that less silence was required to hear a stoplike effect. These observations provide indirect evidence for yet another trading relation between two cues for stop manner: the (spectral and temporal) characteristics of the vocalic portion preceding the silence, and silence duration itself.

Returning to the boundary function at the left of Figure 4, we note that the function changes from slanted at short noise durations to completely vertical at longer noise durations. In other words, the trading relation between silence and noise durations which characterizes the GRAY SHIP versus GRAY CHIP distinction disappears as the distinction changes to GRAY SHIP versus GREAT SHIP. This phonetic contrast, located in the first syllable, is apparently not affected by further increases in noise duration in the second syllable but depends only on silence duration.

We turn now to the second function in Figure 4, that connecting the circles. This function represents the boundaries between GREAT SHIP, on the one hand, and GRAY CHIP or GREAT CHIP on the other. (GRAY SHIP responses did not enter into the calculation of these boundaries.) Since GREAT CHIP responses occurred primarily at long silence durations, the major part of the boundary function represents the distinction between GREAT SHIP and GRAY CHIP, that is, the perceived location of juncture. It is clear that noise duration was the major juncture cue, as we should have expected given earlier observations of Lehiste (1960) and Nakatani and Dukes (1977). Had it been the only cue, the boundary function would have been perfectly horizontal. As we see, however, the function shows a clear rise at intermediate silence durations (40–80 msec): GREAT SHIP responses were more frequent at short silence durations, and GRAY CHIP responses were more frequent at longer silence durations. Thus, silence duration was a secondary cue for the location of the word boundary (cf. Christie, 1974, for a related result).

The third function in Figure 4—that connecting the triangles—represents the boundary between GRAY CHIP and GREAT CHIP, excluding other responses. There was no obvious dependency of this boundary on noise duration; the uppermost data point, which may suggest such a dependency, was based on only a few observations, since at this noise duration (142 msec) GREAT SHIP responses predominated (cf. Figure 3). We note that a fairly long period of silence (about 100 msec) was required to hear both a syllable-final stop and an affricate.

Experiment 2b. By using the sentence containing the word GRAY as the "source" for half of the stimuli, Experiment 2b partially replicated Experiment 2a. These results are shown in the top panels of Figure 5. They may be contrasted with the results obtained with the new GREAT source, shown in the bottom panels. For each source, the effects of noise and silence duration were similar to those observed in Experiment 2a; therefore, they need no further comment. The change in the response pattern as a function of noise duration was again highly significant, $F(3, 27) = 58.95$, $p < .001$.

The effect of primary interest was that of source. It can be seen that more GREAT (both GREAT SHIP and GREAT CHIP) responses occurred when the source was GREAT, as shown by a significant Source × Response Categories interaction, $F(3, 27) = 10.11$, $p < .01$. However, this effect did not substantially change the overall response pattern. At silence durations of less than 20 msec, the listeners still reported GRAY SHIP; at longer silence durations GRAY CHIP was heard when the noise was short, even though the original utterance had been GREAT. Thus, the cues for stop manner in the word GREAT were readily integrated with the intial consonant of the next word if the short noise biased perception toward hearing an affricate.

As in Experiment 2a, we calculated three kinds of perceptual boundaries (cf. Figure 4).[7] These are shown in Figure 6, where they

_____
[7] The GRAY SHIP versus GRAY CHIP (+ GREAT CHIP) boundary estimates were based on only two data points (noise durations). To obtain probit

632   REPP, LIBERMAN, ECCARDT, AND PESETSKY

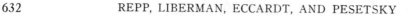

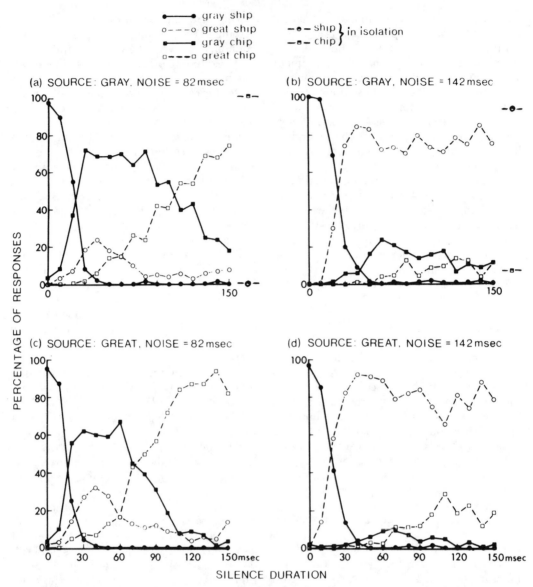

Figure 5. Effects of varying the "source" (original pronunciation as GRAY or GREAT) on the perception and placement of stop (or affricate) manner. (These are shown at each of two durations of noise and represented as the percentage of occurrence of the several responses plotted against the duration of silence.)

are plotted, separately for each "source," as joint functions of silence duration and noise duration. We see that the boundary between GRAY SHIP and the other responses

(squares) shifted significantly to the left as the source changed from GRAY to GREAT, $F(1, 9) = 33.66$, $p < .01$. In other words, less silence was needed to hear a stoplike effect (regardless of whether it was placed at the end of the first or at the beginning of the second syllable) when the original utterance had contained the word GREAT. Note that the stop-manner cues preceding

_____

estimates, we added two hypothetical anchor points: 22 msec (of noise) with 0% GREAT SHIP responses, and 202 msec (of noise) with 100% GREAT SHIP responses.

a relatively short silence were readily integrated with those following the silence: Within the range of silence (and noise) durations in which the subjects' responses were either GRAY SHIP or GRAY CHIP, the frequency of GRAY CHIP responses actually was increased when the source was changed from GRAY to GREAT.

The second boundary function—that separating GREAT SHIP from GRAY CHIP and GREAT CHIP responses (circles)—also showed an interesting pattern of source effects. At shorter silence durations, in which the distinction was mainly between GREAT SHIP and GRAY CHIP, the change in source from GRAY to GREAT increased GREAT SHIP responses and decreased GRAY CHIP responses. This is reasonable, although it provides a counterexample to the recent conclusion by Nakatani and Dukes (1977) that cues in the first word have no effect on the perceived location of the word boundary. At long silence durations (beyond 100 msec), on the other hand, the phonetic distinction was primarily between GREAT SHIP and GREAT CHIP; there, source ceased to have any effect. Thus, when the silent interval exceeded about 100 msec, stop-manner cues

preceding the silence were no longer integrated with those that followed it.

The third boundary, GRAY CHIP versus GREAT CHIP (triangles), showed by far the largest source effect. Since the phonetic contrast was located here in the word that was actually changed in pronunciation and since, because of the relatively long silence duration, the stop-manner cues preceding the silence were perceived independently of the cues following it, the large effect is readily understandable. On the other hand, the effect is not trivial, since, as we pointed out earlier, the word GRAY from the GRAY source actually sounded like GREAT in isolation. That the stimuli derived from the GRAY source received any GREAT CHIP responses at all was probably due to the presence of relatively strong stop-manner cues in the word GRAY.

General Discussion

The most interesting aspect of the data, in our view, is that whether a syllable-final stop consonant was perceived (GRAY vs. GREAT) depended on the duration of the noise following the silence—an acoustic event occurring much later in time. There

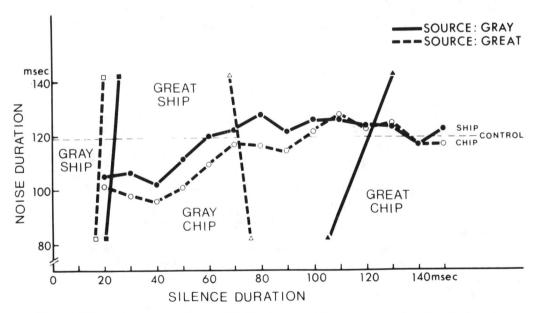

Figure 6. Effects of varying the "source" (original pronunciation as GRAY or GREAT) on the boundaries that divide the several response categories.

are three questions we may ask about this temporal integration: Why does it occur? What are its limits? And when does the listener reach a decision about what he has heard? We consider these questions in turn.

Why does temporal integration occur? We have seen that cues as diverse and as widely distributed as (a) the spectral and temporal properties of the vocalic portion preceding the silence, (b) the silence duration itself, and (c) the spectral and temporal properties of the noise portion following the silence are all integrated into a unitary phonetic percept. Can we explain such integration on a purely auditory basis? Auditory integration does occur—for example, it is responsible for the perceptual coherence of homogeneous events such as the fricative noise—and surely we have much more to learn about such integration, especially in the case of complex acoustic signals. But it seems to us quite implausible to suppose that purely auditory principles could ever account for perceptual integration of acoustic cues as heterogeneous and temporally spread as those we have dealt with here.

We encounter similar problems when we seek to explain our results in terms of feature detectors as they have been postulated by several contemporary theorists (e.g., Blumstein, Stevens, & Nigro, 1977; Eimas & Corbit, 1973; Miller, 1977). Consider again the case in which the perception of a syllable-final stop consonant (GREAT vs. GRAY) depends on whether the fricative noise following the silence extends beyond a certain duration. If a single phonetic feature detector were responsible for the syllable-final stop, then its integrative power and complexity would have to be so great as to remove from the concept of feature detector the simplicity that is its chief attraction. Alternatively, there might be many simple auditory feature detectors, each responsive to elementary properties of the signal, whose outputs are integrated by a higher level phonetic decision mechanism (cf. Massaro & Cohen, 1977). But that view fails to provide any principled reason why the outputs of certain feature detectors feed into a single phonetic decision in the way they do. Without reference to the articulatory system that produced the speech signal, the rules by which the detector outputs might be integrated would seem entirely arbitrary.

One might suppose, of course, that the diverse cues have become integrated into a unitary percept as a result of learning. Surely, the cues have frequently been associated in the production and perception of speech. But would such association be sufficient to cause them eventually to sound alike, as the integration (and various trading relations) indicate that they do? Common experience and common sense suggest that it would not. Consider, for example, a listener who has for many years heard a bell and a buzzer, each of a particular kind, always sounded in close temporal and spatial contiguity. It is reasonable to expect that these very different stimuli (or rather their corresponding percepts) would become associated in his or her mind: On hearing one he or she would expect to hear the other, and either would presumably become a sufficient sign for whatever it was that the two, taken together, normally signified. But it seems implausible that they would ever be integrated into a unitary percept, the components of which are no longer readily available to introspection. Nor does it seem plausible that a change in, say, the duration of the buzz could be compensated for by a simultaneous change in the duration or frequency of the sound of the bell so as to produce exactly the same integrated percept. Yet that is exactly what is true of the diverse acoustic cues that converge on a unitary phonetic percept. At all events, we think it implausible to attribute the perceptual integration of the acoustic cues simply to learning by association.

As we pointed out in the introduction, we believe that the guiding principle of temporal integration in phonetic perception is to be found in the articulatory act that underlies the production of the relevant phonetic segment. By an *articulatory act* we mean not a particular articulatory gesture but all articulatory maneuvers that result from the speaker's "intention" to produce a given segment, for example, a stop consonant. Thus, our definition of the articulatory act is intimately tied to the hypothesis that units of phoneme size are physiologically real at some early level in speech production. At the later articulatory level, we can distinguish individual gestures (such as closing and opening the jaw, raising the tongue tip) that form the components of the articulatory act. It is, of course, these several gestures that produce the several (and sometimes even more numerous) acoustic cues. The perceptual process by which the acoustic cues are integrated into a unitary phonetic percept somehow recaptures the gestures and also mirrors the processes by which they unfolded from a unitary phonetic intention (or motor program). We find it plausible to suppose that speech perception, as a unique biological capacity, has in fact evolved to reflect the equally species-specific capacity for speech production. The consequence is that, in a very real sense, the listener perceives directly the speaker's "intent"—the phonetically significant articulatory act (for views related to ours in their emphasis on the perception of articulatory events but different from ours in other respects, see Fowler, 1977; Bailey & Summerfield, Note 6; Summerfield, Note 7).

We turn now to our second question, that about the limits of temporal integration. From the data of our experiments, we obtain an estimate according to the following considerations. The boundary between GRAY CHIP and GREAT CHIP indicates the longest period of time over which the stop-manner cues preceding the silence are still integrated with the cues following the silence into a single stoplike percept (affricate). Although the exact temporal interval varied with the strength of the stop-manner cues preceding the silence (cf. Figure 6), a silence duration of 100 msec is a reasonably typical value. To this must be added the approximate temporal extent of the relevant cues preceding and following the silence—at least 100 msec for the duration of both the vocalic portion and the fricative noise. We thus arrive at a temporal range of 300—350 msec for the integration of stop-manner cues. This estimate is in good agreement with results on the single-

geminate distinction for intervocalic stop consonants (e.g., TOPIC vs. TOP PICK), since, as Pickett and Decker (1960) and Repp (Note 1) have shown, that boundary occurs around 200 msec of silence at normal rates of speech. Inasmuch as the manner cues following the closure interval (the formant transitions of the second vocalic portion) are shorter in this case (perhaps 50 msec), we arrive again at an integration period of about 350 msec. This coincidence is not surprising since the articulatory gesture underlying an intervocalic stop consonant is similar to that for a stop consonant embedded between a vowel and a fricative. In our view, the range of temporal integration in perception reflects not an auditory limitation—such as the duration of a pre-perceptual auditory store (Massaro, 1975)—but the longest acceptable duration of the underlying articulatory act. Different articulatory acts may well be associated in perception with different ranges of temporal integration.

We thus arrive at our third question: When do the listeners decide what they have heard? Before we can answer that question, we must point out that there are two logically distinct decisions the listener must make: (a) *What* phoneme has occurred? (b) *Where* does it belong? Thus, in the case of the GREAT SHIP—GRAY CHIP distinction, the listener must decide first that a stop consonant has occurred and, then, whether it belongs with the first or the second syllable. We see three possibilities for the temporal organization of the listener's decisions: (a) Both the What and Where decisions occur after all relevant cues have been integrated; (b) the What decision occurs as soon as sufficient cues are available, but the Where decision is delayed until the end of the integration period; and (c) both a What decision and a Where (default) decision are made as soon as sufficient cues are available, but the Where decision may be revised in the light of later information. We discuss these hypotheses in turn.

The first hypothesis implies, in the case of GREAT SHIP, that listeners do not know whether they have heard a stop consonant until they have processed at least the first

636   REPP, LIBERMAN, ECCARDT, AND PESETSKY

120 msec of the fricative noise. This seems implausible on intuitive grounds. It is more likely that phonetic information accumulates continuously from the speech signal and that What decisions can be made, in principle at least, before all cues have been processed (cf. Remington, 1977; Repp, Note 1). If this were not so, we should have to assume that the relevant cues are integrated at a prephonetic level and thus are held in a temporary auditory memory—precisely the argument we do not wish to make. On the other hand, if temporally separate cues (such as those preceding and following the silence in GRAY CHIP) are immediately translated into phonetic representations, temporal integration merely combines identical phonetic codes within a certain time span and thus is not dependent on auditory limitations. In terms of our experiment, this means that the listener already "knew" at the end of the vocalic portion of GRAY (which, as the reader may remember, contained sufficient stop-manner cues to be perceived as GREAT in isolation) that a stop had occurred; the silence duration cue (if less than about 100 msec) and the noise duration cue (if less than about 120 msec) merely confirmed this perceptual knowledge.

The remaining two hypotheses differ in their assumptions about when the Where decision occurs. According to one hypothesis, listeners do not know whether they have heard GRAY or GREAT until they have processed the fricative noise; in other words, the Where decision is postponed until all relevant cues have been integrated. The alternative hypothesis assumes that listeners group the stop consonant automatically with the preceding syllable until later information leads them to revise that decision. This leads to the paradoxical prediction that in an utterance heard as GRAY CHIP, listeners actually perceive GREAT for the brief moment that extends from the end of the vocalic portion to the end of the fricative noise, as they would have if CHIP had never occurred. We hope to conduct experiments in the future that will shed more light on these questions.

Reference Notes

1. Repp, B. H. *Perception of implosive transitions in VCV utterances* (Status Report on Speech Research, SR-48). New Haven, Conn.: Haskins Laboratories, 1976.

2. Bastian, J. *Silent intervals as closure cues in the perception of stop consonants.* (Quarterly Progress Report No. 33, Appendix 1.) New Haven, Conn.: Haskins Laboratories, 1959.

3. [Bastian, J.] *Silent intervals and formant transitions as cues in the perception of stop phonemes* (Quarterly Progress Report No. 35, Appendix 2.) New Haven, Conn.: Haskins Laboratories, 1960.

4. Dorman, M. F., Raphael, L. J., & Liberman, A. M. *Further observations on the role of silence in the perception of stop consonants* (Status Report on Speech Research, SR-48). New Haven, Conn.: Haskins Laboratories, 1976.

5. Erickson, D., Fitch, H. L., Halwes, T. G., & Liberman, A. M. *A trading relation in perception between silence and spectrum.* Unpublished manuscript, 1978.

6. Bailey, P. J., & Summerfield, A. Q. *Some observations on the perception of [s] + stop clusters* (Status Report on Speech Research, SR-53, Vol. 2). New Haven, Conn.: Haskins Laboratories, 1978.

7. Summerfield, A. Q. *On articulatory rate and perceptual constancy in phonetic perception.* Unpublished manuscript, 1977.

8. Dorman, M. F., Raphael, L. J., & Liberman, A. M. *Some experiments on the sound of silence in phonetic perception.* Unpublished manuscript, 1978.

References

Ainsworth, W. A. The influence of precursive sequences on the perception of synthesized vowels. *Language and Speech*, 1974, *17*, 103–109.

Bastian, J., Eimas, P. D., & Liberman, A. M. Identification and discrimination of a phonemic contrast induced by silent interval. *Journal of the Acoustical Society of America*, 1961, *33*, 842. (Abstract)

Blumstein, S. E., Stevens, K. N., & Nigro, G. N. Property detectors for bursts and transitions in speech perception. *Journal of the Acoustical Society of America*, 1977, *61*, 1301–1313.

Christie, W. M., Jr. Some cues for syllable juncture perception in English. *Journal of the Acoustical Society of America*, 1974, *55*, 819–821.

Cutting, J. E., & Rosner, B. S. Categories and boundaries in speech and music. *Perception & Psychophysics*, 1974, *16*, 564–570.

Eimas, P. D., & Corbit, J. D. Selective adaptation of linguistic feature detectors. *Cognitive Psychology*, 1973, *4*, 99–109.

Finney, D. J. *Probit analysis* (3rd ed.). Cambridge, England: Cambridge University Press, 1971.

Fowler, C. A. *Timing control in speech production.* Unpublished doctoral dissertation, University of Connecticut, 1977.

Fujisaki, H., Nakamura, K., & Imoto, T. Auditory perception of duration of speech and non-speech stimuli. In G. Fant & M. A. A. Tatham (Eds.), *Auditory analysis and perception of speech.* London: Academic Press, 1975.

Gay, T. Effect of speaking rate on vowel formant movements. *Journal of the Acoustical Society of America,* 1978, *63,* 223–230.

Gerstman, L. *Cues for distinguishing among fricatives, affricates, and stop consonants.* Unpublished doctoral dissertation, New York University, 1957.

Kozhevnikov, V. A., & Christovich, L. A. *Speech, articulation, and perception* (NTIS No. JPRS-305430) Washington, D.C.: U.S. Dept. of Commerce, 1965.

Lehiste, I. An acoustic-phonetic study of internal open juncture. *Phonetica Supplement,* 1960, *5,* 1–54.

Liberman, A. M., & Studdert-Kennedy, M. Phonetic perception. In R. Held, H. Leibowitz, & H.-L. Teuber (Eds.), *Handbook of sensory physiology: Vol. 8. Perception.* Heidelberg: Springer-Verlag, in press.

Massaro, D. W. Preperceptual images, processing time, and perceptual units in speech perception. In D. W. Massaro (Ed.), *Understanding language: An information-processing analysis of speech perception, reading, and psycholinguistics.* New York: Academic Press, 1975.

Massaro, D. W., & Cohen, M. M. Voice onset time and fundamental frequency as cues to the /zi/–/si/ distinction. *Perception & Psychophysics,* 1977, *22,* 373–382.

Miller, J. L. Properties of feature detectors for VOT: The voiceless channel of analysis. *Journal of the Acoustical Society of America,* 1977, *62,* 641–648.

Nakatani, L. H., & Dukes, K. D. Locus of segmental cues for word juncture. *Journal of the Acoustical Society of America,* 1977, *62,* 714–719.

Pickett, J. M., & Decker, L. R. Time factors in the perception of a double consonant. *Language and Speech,* 1960, *3,* 11–17.

Remington, R. Processing of phonemes in speech: A speed–accuracy study. *Journal of the Acoustical Society of America,* 1977, *62,* 1279–1290.

Summerfield, Q., & Haggard, M. On the dissociation of spectral and temporal cues to the voicing distinction in initial stop consonants. *Journal of the Acoustical Society of America,* 1977, *62,* 435–448.

Received February 2, 1978 ∎

Journal of Experimental Psychology:
Human Perception and Performance
1981, Vol. 7, No. 5, 1074-1095

Articulatory Rate and Perceptual Constancy in Phonetic Perception

Quentin Summerfield
Queen's University, Belfast, Northern Ireland, United Kingdom, and
Haskins Laboratories, New Haven, Connecticut

The perception of syllable-initial stop consonants as voiced (/b/, /d/, /g/) or voiceless (/p/, /t/, /k/) was shown to depend on the prevailing rate of articulation. Reducing the articulatory rate of a precursor phrase causes a greater proportion of test consonants to be identified as voiced. Subsequent experiments demonstrated that this effect depends almost entirely on variation in the duration of the syllable immediately preceding the test syllable; this, the duration of the intervening silent stop closure, and the duration of the test syllable itself all influenced the identification of the stop as voiced or voiceless. Variation in the tempo of a nonspeech melody produced no effect on the perception of embedded test syllables. Those manipulations which produce the major part of the influence of rate do so not by changing the context in which the stop is perceived, but rather by changing temporal concomitants of the constriction, occlusion, and release phases of the articulation of the stop itself. For this reason, an explanation for such effects based on *extrinsic* timing in perception is found to be wanting. Timing should, in the main, be regarded as *intrinsic* to the acoustical specifications of phonetic events, a view that is compatible with recent reformulations of the problem of timing control in speech production.

One achievement of perceptual systems is to detect what is constant in objects and events despite transformations applied to them. Visually, for instance, we perceive a rotating object as rigid; auditorily, we perceive the same word spoken in different voices. In such situations, the stimulation to the sensory receptors is resolved to yield a description of the object or event plus a description of the transformation. Paradoxically, although the transformation may complicate a physical specification of the proximal stimulation, its introduction often dispels rather than exacerbates ambiguity: On awakening in a dimly lit room, for instance, one may not be able to identify even familiar objects until one moves one's head. An analogous strategy—of deliberately introducing a transformation so as to identify what remains constant—was applied in the experiments reported here. They were designed to refine and extend our understanding of the acoustical information specifying contrasts in voicing for English stop consonants articulated in prestress, prevocalic position. The technique identified acoustical parameters predisposing percepts of voiced (/b/, /d/, /g/) or voiceless (/p/, /t/, /k/) stops under a set of transforms approximating those achieved by natural variations in rate of articulation.

Increases in rate of articulation engender a reorganization, rather than a simple speed-

The first three experiments reported here were conducted at Queen's University with the support of Grants AT/2058/021/HQ from the Joint Speech Research Unit and B/RG/1466 from the Science Research Council, U.K. The subsequent experiments were performed at Haskins Laboratories with the support of Grant HD-01994 from the National Institute of Child Health and Human Development while the author was supported by a North Atlantic Treaty Organisation postdoctoral research fellowship from the Science Research Council, U.K. This paper was prepared at the MRC Institute of Hearing Research. Experiments 2 and 3 were described in a paper presented to the 91st Meeting of the Acoustical Society of America, Washington D.C., 1976. Experiments 1, 4, 5, and 7 were summarized as Summerfield (1979).

I thank Mark Haggard, Alvin Liberman, Bruno Repp, and Peter Bailey for advice and encouragement, and two anonymous reviewers for their comments on an earlier version of this paper.

Requests for reprints should be sent to Quentin Summerfield who is now at the MRC Institute of Hearing Research, University of Nottingham, Nottingham NG7 2RD, United Kingdom.

ing-up, of the pattern of electromyographic activity at the articulators (Gay, Ushijima, Hirose, & Cooper, 1974). This is accompanied by a restructuring of the acoustics (Klatt, 1976; Kozhevnikov & Chistovich, 1965) and so appears to compound the lack of invariance generally believed to exist between acoustic segments and the phonetic percepts they induce. Accordingly, it has often been suggested that a tacit knowledge of articulatory dynamics must mediate an acoustic–phonetic translation in perception (e.g., Liberman, Cooper, Shankweiler, & Studdert-Kennedy, 1967; Liberman & Pisoni, 1977). In one version of this view, the acoustical specifications of rate and phonetic identity are independent up to a certain stage. Phonetic perception would proceed by first determining articulatory rate and then use this knowledge to normalize those segment durations that are phonetically distinctive. However, an alternative possibility exists. Here, the essential acoustical qualities of phonetic identity would be preserved despite variation in rate of articulation, so that a knowledge of rate would not be a necessary precursor to the determination of phonetic identity. This second orientation demands of the theorist a more complex description of the acoustical specifications of phonemes and, by implication, of the processes of speech production. However, it would simplify models describing the process of perceiving phonetic identity. Although the data reported here cannot refute one class of explanation in favor of the other, they suggest that the second view provides the currently more useful theoretical framework and new factual detail on perceptual sensitivities to phonetic dimensions.

Precursive Influences on the Perception of Voicing Contrasts

Lisker and Abramson (e.g., 1964, 1971) proposed that contrasts in stop consonant voicing are achieved in the production of speech by coordinating the timing of glottal abduction and adduction with supralaryngeal constriction, occlusion, and release. This proposition rationalizes the diverse acoustic concomitants of the voicing contrast articulated in different phonetic contexts: as a change in vowel duration postvocalically (e.g., /æb-æp/); as a change in closure duration in medial, poststress position (e.g., /ræbId-ræpId/); and, in particular, as a change in voice onset time (VOT) summarizing the multiple acoustical consequences of producing the contrast in prevocalic position (e.g., /bæ-pæ/).

The acoustic consequences of stepwise increments in VOT can be implemented in successive members of continua of synthetic consonant–vowel (CV) syllables. When English-speaking listeners categorize the members of such continua according to the identity of the initial consonant, they place phoneme boundaries close to those values of VOT that optimally segregate voiced from voiceless stops in productions of their language (Lisker & Abramson, 1967). Summerfield and Haggard (Note 1) sought to determine whether the perceptual VOT boundary is fixed, or whether it varies according to the prevailing rate of speech. A VOT continuum, consisting of a series of syllables ranging from /gIl/ to /kIl/, was synthesized and was presented to speakers of British English in carrier phrases for identification as either "You'll hear 'gill' again" or "You'll hear 'kill' again." By varying the synthesis time base it was possible to present the carrier phrase at two different articulatory rates. For each rate, a set of identifications of the two stimuli that spanned each listener's phoneme boundary was obtained.

The results suggested that VOT might not be perceived absolutely: Increasing the articulatory rate of both the carrier phrase and the test syllable increased the probability that a test syllable with a given VOT would be perceived as "kill." The result was replicated with more sophisticated synthesis and experimental control—Summerfield (Note 2) showed that the positions of phoneme boundaries on both a /ga-ka/ and a /gi-ki/ continuum shifted to shorter VOTs as the articulatory rate of an introductory precursor phrase was increased. The direction of the result is perceptually useful. In speech production the mean of the distribution of VOTs characterizing syllable-initial voiceless stops shifts to shorter VOTs as rate of articulation increases, while the mean of the voiced distribution is essentially unchanged

1076   QUENTIN SUMMERFIELD

(Diehl, Souther, & Convis, 1980; Summerfield, 1975). The class of phenomena wherein phonetic identity has been shown to depend upon contextual articulatory rate, of which these results provide an instance, has been comprehensively reviewed by Miller (in press) and by Nooteboom (in press). The experiments reported here were intended to replicate and extend the results obtained by Summerfield (1975, Note 2).

General Method

Theoretically, it is possible to draw a distinction between rate of articulatory movement and syllable duration (e.g., Haggard, 1979). The distinction requires a somewhat unnatural view of syllables, however. A consonant-vowel syllable, for instance, must be regarded in articulatory terms as a rapid opening gesture generating formant transitions followed by a static configuration producing a steady-state vowel. Rate of articulatory movement and syllable duration can then be manipulated independently by changing separately the durations of the transitions and the steady state. Although syllables are often synthesized in this form, connected speech is characterized by continuous movement of most of the articulators and, as a result, of the accompanying formant structure. Generally, rate of articulatory movement and syllable duration are inversely, though nonlinearly, correlated. Here, these two factors will not be dissociated. A change in both rate of articulatory movement and syllable duration implied by compressing or expanding a syllable in time will be referred to as a change in *articulatory rate*.

Experiments 1, 2, and 3 were carried out in the Department of Psychology at the Queen's University of Belfast and used an OVE IIIb serial resonance synthesizer. These experiments were run on-line. Stimuli were generated and subjects' responses were automatically collected at run time (Draper, 1973). Stimuli were presented binaurally through AKG K-60 headphones at an average peak level of 75 dB (SPL).

Experiments 4, 5, 6, and 7 were carried out at the Haskins Laboratories, New Haven, Connecticut, and used an OVE IIIc serial resonance synthesizer. These experiments were run off-line. Stimulus sequences were recorded on audiotape and presented to listeners binaurally through Telephonics TDH39 headphones at an average peak level of 75 dB. All stimuli were 5-formant synthetic speech sounds. VOT continua were created by first constructing a CV syllable with a VOT of O msec and then decreasing the level of the output of the pulse generator, increasing the level of the output of the noise generator, and maximally widening the bandwidth of F1 (to approximately 300 Hz) from the start of the syllable to the desired onset of voicing. This procedure simulates the acoustical consequences of opening the vocal cords and coupling the pharynx and the trachea. It is the approximate equivalent with a serial resonance synthesizer of exciting the higher formants with noise and "cutting back" the first formant with a parallel resonance synthesizer (cf. Liberman, Delattre, & Cooper, 1958). The fundamental frequency at the onset of voicing was fixed at 100 Hz in all stimuli so that no co-variation of this cue to voicing with VOT would occur.

Experiment 1

Experiment 1 was designed to test the generality of the findings reported by Summerfield (Note 2) by examining effects of a varying precursive articulatory rate on the perception of bilabial (/b-p/) and alveolar (/d-t/), in addition to velar (/g-k/), stops synthesized in combination with each of the vowels /a/, /ɜ/, and /i/. If the earlier results reflect a general sensitivity to speech rate in the perception of stop voicing, as opposed to some idiosyncrasy of the velar contrast, then phoneme boundaries on all these continua should shift to shorter values of VOT as the articulatory rate of an introductory phrase is increased.

Method

Stimuli. Stimuli consisted of precursor phrases and test syllables. Two precursors, one of which will be labeled "slow" (P1) and the other "fast" (P2), were derived from a copy-synthesis version of the phrase "A bird in the hand is worth two in the. . . ."[1] The duration of P1 was 1,840 msec. P2 was created by selectively reducing the synthesis time base in those portions of P1 corresponding to more open configurations of the vocal tract and in which little or no spectral change was occurring in either the first (F1) or the second (F2) formant. This procedure produced a second, faster precursor whose acoustical relation to P1 approximated that which accompanies a natural increase in rate of articulation. The duration of P2 was 1,472 msec. The ratio of the overall durations of P1 and P2, 1:1.25, is much smaller than that which can occur across different rates of articulation in natural speech (Grosjean & Lane, 1976). Because a more complicated set of acoustic-phonetic factors would have been introduced by modeling an extreme range of natural rates, variation in articulatory rate was constrained here so that it would not be accompanied by any covariation in naturalness. Six experimental precursors were derived from P1 and P2 by adjusting the contours of F2 and F3 over the final 10 msec of the phrase to produce slight coarticulation appropriate for the place of production of the following test syllable.

The test syllables comprised nine CV VOT continua representing the combination of the bilabial, alveolar, and velar places of articulation with the vowels /a/, /ɜ/, and /i/. The durations of the initial formant tran-

---

[1] This phrase clearly provided an anomalous semantic context for the test syllables. It was used because its set of synthesis control parameters had previously been copied from spectrographic analyses of natural speech to generate a very natural-sounding multisyllable utterance.

sitions were 30, 40, and 50 msec in bilabial, alveolar, and velar continua, respectively, reflecting the variation found in natural productions (Fant, 1973; Perkell, 1969). The overall amplitude and fundamental frequency contours were the same in all syllables. Their duration was 332 msec. Each of the nine continua was composed of six syllables. VOT ranges, selected on the basis of pilot tests to span the phoneme boundaries of most listeners, were: bilabial (/a/, /ɜ/, and /i/), +6 to +36 msec; alveolar (/a/, /ɜ/, and /i/), +10 to +40 msec; velar (/a/ and /ɜ/), +12 to +42 msec and (/i/), +20 to +50 msec. The pitch–pulse generator in the synthesizer was free running, thereby producing statistical, but not absolute, pitch synchrony to the intended VOT of every stimulus.

Subjects and procedure. A heterogeneous group of 16 people composed of high school, undergraduate, and postgraduate students served as listeners. They ranged in age from 16 yr. to 26 yr., declared themselves to have normal hearing in both ears, and to have learned English as their first language in the British Isles.

There were six blocks of 180 trials. Within each block the place of articulation of the consonant in the test syllable was held constant, while the vowel in the test syllable and the articulatory rate of the precursor phrase varied randomly. A 50-msec silence separated precursors from test syllables. The silence represented the closure interval during which the supralaryngeal vocal tract is constricted at the place of production and air flow has ceased. In every block, each of the 36 combinations of precursors and test syllables occurred 5 times. There were two blocks for each place of production so that, in total, each combination was presented 10 times.

Subjects were instructed to attend to the entire sentence on each trial, to identify the initial consonant of the test syllable, and to rank its degree of approximation to /b, d, g/ or /p, t, k/ on a 9-point rating scale presented as a row of nine buttons on a response box. Each reponse was made by pressing one button and was scored as an integer in the range −4 to +4. Negative numbers corresponded to voiceless percepts, zero to a completely ambiguous percept, and positive numbers to voiced percepts. Increasing modulus of response indicated increasing category goodness. Prior to listening to the experimental sequences, listeners practiced using the response categories with each continuum of test syllables.

Results and Discussion

For the present analysis, the 10 responses made by each listener to each precursor/ test-syllable combination were reduced to a binary (voiced or voiceless) classification and summed to obtain an identification function for each continuum at each rate. An integrated normal ogive was fitted to each function by the Probit method (Finney, 1971), and the mean and the standard deviation of the normal distribution underlying each fitted function were determined. The mean provides an estimate of the phoneme boundary—the VOT of a hypothetical stimulus for which voiced and voiceless responses would

have been equiprobable. The standard deviation reflects the slope of the fitted function in the region of the boundary, which in turn indicates the width of the region of uncertainty on the stimulus continuum between the two response categories.[2]

The results are summarized in Figure 1. The positions of phoneme boundaries in milliseconds of VOT estimated with the fast and slow precursors averaged over the 16 listeners are plotted against the vertical axis for each of the nine continua that are arrayed horizontally. A rectangle is plotted for each continuum. Its extremities indicate the positions of the two boundaries. The arrow contained within the rectangle indicates the direction of the shift between the faster and slower conditions.

Nondirectional *t* tests showed that each shift in the position of the boundary was significant ($p < .02$). At least 12 of the 16 subjects displayed an effect in the direction of the majority with each test continuum.

Two major results are evident. First, phoneme boundaries consistently shifted to shorter VOTs as the articulatory rate of the precursor phrase increased, showing that the effects of articulatory rate demonstrated by Summerfield and Haggard (Note 1) and by Summerfield (Note 2) do generalize across place and vocalic contexts. Second, as shown by Lisker and Abramson (1967), phoneme boundaries fell at increasingly longer values of VOT for bilabial, alveolar, and velar stops. Additionally, within each place of production, boundaries fell at increasingly longer values of VOT with the vowels /a/, /ɜ/, and /i/. Summerfield (Note 2) and Cooper (1974) have also reported that phoneme boundaries fall at longer VOTs with /i/ compared to /a/.[3]

The effects of both place and vocalic context primarily reflect the influence of ma-

---

[2] Boundary width was not constant, but correlated positively with the position of the VOT boundary. Implications of this subsidiary finding are discussed in Summerfield (Note 8).

[3] Since the identification of members of VOT continua is susceptible to range effects (Darwin, 1976), the spread of boundaries obtained here may have been exaggerated by the use of different VOT ranges in different continua. However, analogous differences in the positions of phoneme boundaries have been obtained without concomitant differences in stimulus range (Summerfield, Note 2; Summerfield & Haggard, 1977).

1078   QUENTIN SUMMERFIELD

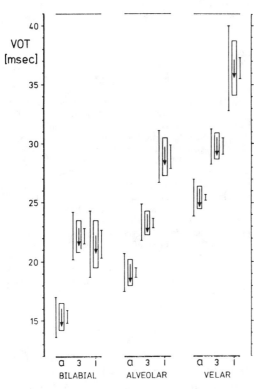

Figure 1. Results of Experiment 1 averaged over 16 subjects.

nipulations of a spectral parameter, the frequency of the first formant at the onset of voicing. Low first-formant onset frequencies in CV syllables favor voiced percepts and predispose voicing boundaries at longer values of VOT (Lisker, 1975; Summerfield & Haggard, 1977; cf. Stevens & Klatt, 1974). In natural speech, the first formant typically starts at about 200 Hz in a syllable-initial voiced stop consonant and then rises to a frequency appropriate for the following phone. This formant usually rises progressively more rapidly in this order: velars, alveolars, and bilabials (e.g., Fant, 1973). The synthetic test syllables used here were derived from exemplars with VOTs of 0 msec in which F1 started at 200 Hz and rose to steady-state frequencies of 277 Hz for /i/, 504 Hz for /ɜ/, and 664 Hz for /a/. The duration of this transition, and of those in the higher formants, was 30 msec (bilabials), 40 msec (alveolars), and 50 msec (velars). Thus, at any particular VOT, syllables necessarily incorporated progressively lower

first-formant onset frequencies before /a/, /ɜ/, and /i/. Similarly, as the overall duration of the initial formant transitions increased from bilabial to alveolar to velar, so progressively lower first-formant onset frequencies accompanied bilabials, alveolars, and velars, within any vocalic context. This rationalization was confirmed by Lisker (Note 3) and by Miller (1977) who demonstrated that when differences in the contour of F1 between different places of production are eliminated in synthetic syllables, differences in voicing boundaries are substantially reduced.

The major interest here, however, is with the shift in boundary itself, rather than the interrelation of its position with place and vocalic contexts. The shifts displayed in Figure 1 are small, ranging between approximately 2 and 5 msec, but their direction is consistent. The effect could be rationalized by the simple model illustrated in Figure 2: VOT is timed by a perceptual "clock" (e.g., Allen, 1973; Creelman, 1962) whose rate is set or whose output is weighted by the articulatory rate in the precursor phrase. Faster precursors cause the clock to run more rapidly and result in a given absolute VOT being judged longer and hence increase the likelihood of the stop in the test syllable being judged as voiceless. This will be called the *extrinsic feed-forward* account of timing in the perception of voicing contrasts. One concern of this paper is to examine two aspects

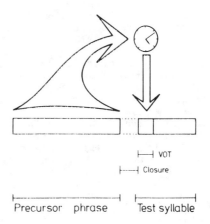

Figure 2. A simple model of extrinsic timing in the perception of stop-consonant voicing that superficially accounts for the results of Experiment 1.

of this account. First, does the influence of articulatory rate operate solely in the feed-forward fashion schematized in Figure 2? Second, is it legitimate to suggest that temporal properties of the acoustic speech stream can be extracted and used to normalize the durations of segments such as VOTs that are putatively critical for phonetic distinctions?

Experiment 2

Experiment 2 was designed to establish the temporal limits on the effect of articulatory rate demonstrated in Experiment 1. Its first aim was to measure the maximum size of the shift in VOT boundary that can be obtained by varying precursive articulatory rate. Its second aim was to determine whether extreme differences in articulatory rate between precursor phrases and test syllables destroy their coherence and neutralize the effect of precursive articulatory rate.

Method

Stimuli. Nine precursor phrases and a single continuum of test syllables were synthesized. The precursors were derived from the same copy-synthesis version of "A bird in the hand is worth two in the . . ." used in Experiment 1. It consisted of 157 time slices of 10-msec duration and 135 slices of 2-msec duration. In 92 of the 10-msec slices the frequencies of neither F1 nor F2 differed by more than 1.5% from their values in the previous slice. Four additional precursors were generated by changing the time base in these slices to 2, 6, 14, and 18 msec, respectively. An additional extremely slow precursor was created by increasing the time base of all the 10-msec slices to 20 msec. Three extremely fast precursors were created by setting the durations of these same slices to 2, 3, and 4 msec. The total durations in milliseconds of the nine precursors were: P1:586, P2:743, P3:900, P4:1,106, P5:1,474, P6:1,842, P7:2,210, P8:2,570, P9:3,412. Informal listening suggested that P4 to P8 covered the natural range of rate variation, while P1 to P3 were unnaturally fast and P9 was unnaturally slow.

The test syllables comprised a single /gi-ki/ continuum. They were derived from a CV syllable whose initial formant transitions in F2 and F3 were linear in frequency-time over their duration of 44 msec. F2 started at 2.4 kHz and reached a steady state at 2.0 kHz. F3 started at 2.6 kHz and reached a steady state at 3.0 kHz. F1 was fixed at 275 Hz with no initial transition. Any VOT in the range 0 msec and to +80 msec could be imposed on this basic stimulus using the procedure described previously. Any test syllable so derived could be combined with any of the nine precursors. A silent closure interval of 50 msec linked the two.

Subjects and procedure. Six adult listeners took part in the experiment. They declared themselves to have normal hearing and to have learned English as their first language in the British Isles.

Stimuli were presented under the control of an interactive threshold-determining algorithm derived from procedures for parameter estimation by sequential testing (PEST) (Taylor & Creelman, 1967) implemented as described by Summerfield and Haggard (1977). Phoneme boundaries for each precursor were estimated by randomly interleaving presentations from two PEST runs originating from starting VOTs approximately evenly balanced about the expected boundary region. Runs terminated when the step size of each was less than or equal to 1 msec and the two boundary estimates were also within 5 msec of each other.

Listeners were tested individually in a sound-damped cubicle. Each listener estimated phoneme boundaries on the test continuum twice with each of the nine precursors. At the start, the middle, and the end of the experiment, boundaries on the test continuum were estimated in the absence of a precursor. Each of these baseline estimates was obtained from four interleaved PEST runs. They were included to indicate whether any drift in subjects' boundaries occurred during the course of the experiment.

Results

The means of the boundary estimates averaged over the six listeners for each of the nine precursors are plotted in Figure 3. Each point represents the mean of 24 estimates. Filled circles plot points corresponding to the range of precursor rates judged to be natural, P4 to P8. Open circles plot points corresponding to P1–P3 and P9, which represented unnaturally fast and slow extremes of articulatory rate, respectively. The length of the error bar indicates the average standard deviation of the four estimates made by each subject with each combination of precursors and test syllables. The three isolated points plotted on the extreme left represent the means of the boundary estimates determined in the absence of a precursor at the start (S), middle (M), and end (E) of the experiment. Again, each point plots the mean of 24 estimates, four having been provided by each listener.

The main result of Experiment 2 is that the effect of precursive speech rate on the perception of stop voicing is essentially monotonic over the range of rates examined (with the exception of a single reversal between P3 and P4). The phoneme boundary on the continuum of test syllables systematically moved to longer VOTs as the overall duration, and hence the articulatory rate, of the precursor phrase was reduced from un-

1080   QUENTIN SUMMERFIELD

naturally fast to unnaturally slow productions. Increasing the duration of the precursor from 586 msec (P1) to 3,412 msec (P9) produced a mean shift in the position of the boundary of 11.6 msec, ranging among listeners from 4.7 msec to 15.7 msec. The empirical function relating boundary position to precursor duration is sigmoidal, asymptoting at its extremes but not folding back on itself. Neither unnaturalness of the precursor nor an unnatural relation of articulatory rates between precursor and test syllable destroyed their coherence. Variation in precursor rate between P4 and P8, the range of rates judged to be natural, produced a significant shift in the position of the boundary, $F(4, 20) = 21.70$, $p < .001$. Boundaries estimated with the three unnaturally fast precursors (P1, P2, and P3) did not differ significantly from one another ($p > .1$). Planned comparisons between the extreme precursors and their adjacent natural precursors also showed no significant differences ($p > .1$). Finally, there were no significant differences among the three baseline estimates ($p > .1$). In summary, Experiment 2 demonstrated that shifts in voicing boundaries of about 10 msec of VOT can be obtained consistently across listeners by using an extended range of precursor rates and that variations in acoustic–phonetic naturalness do not unduly prejudice the effect.

Experiment 3

The influence of precursive articulatory rate was sustained over the 50-msec silent closure interval that linked precursors and test syllables in Experiments 1 and 2. Experiment 3 was designed to determine whether the influence is modified as the duration of the closure interval is increased. If, as implied in Figure 2, the precursor calibrates a perceptual mechanism invoked in the registration of voicing contrasts, then, conceivably, a particular state of calibration could be sustained for an appreciable length of time. In a situation in which a similar calibration could be said to have occurred, Cole, Coltheart, and Allard (1974) found that the advantage in reaction time to make same–different judgments of letter names spoken in the same, as opposed to a different, voice was sustained for up to 8 sec.

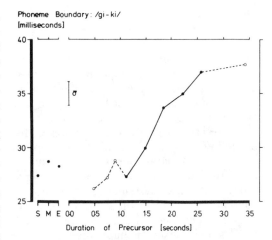

Figure 3. Results of Experiment 2 averaged over 6 subjects.

Alternatively, the effect of speech-rate variation could diminish as the closure interval is increased. The diminution could be related to the passage of time per se and could reflect the gradual reversion to a baseline state of calibration. Alternatively, or in addition, silence here could play either or both of two specifically linguistic roles. First, silences greater than about 250 msec could indicate that a juncture (i.e., a break in the articulatory flow) had occurred between precursors and test syllables. Possibly, effects of introductory speech rate are only manifest when precursors and test syllables are perceived to cohere as a single continuous articulation. If so, effects of precursive articulatory rate may be absent or diminished when the "closure interval" is greater than about 250 msec.

In its second linguistic role, the duration of the closure interval could directly influence the categorization of test syllables by acting as a cue to voicing. This is the case in poststress intervocalic position, where voiced stops are typically characterized by shorter closures than are voiceless stops. This difference in duration possesses cue value: /ræpId/ can be converted into /ræbId/ by reducing the duration of the silent closure (Lisker, 1957; Port, 1979). In prestress initial position it has sometimes been reported that no difference in closure duration exists between voiced and voiceless stops (Klatt,

1973; Lisker, Note 4). However, Westbury (Note 5) reported that voiceless stops are characterized by closures about 20 msec longer than those in voiced stops. Prosody could determine the mapping of acoustic cues into phonetic categories and not permit an acoustic cue possessing potency in one context to produce an effect in another.

There is no a priori reason, however, for expecting this organization in perceptual processing. A parameter with cue value in one prosodic context could have some potency if it varies systematically in another context related to the first by a transform of stress. Thus, increases in closure duration may contribute to an impression of voicelessness even in prestress stops. If this is the case, phoneme boundaries could shift initially to shorter VOTs as the duration of the silent closure interval linking precursor phrases with test syllables is increased in the range of short closure durations from 50 msec to 250 msec.

In summary, the objective of Experiment 3 was to examine the influence of increasing the duration of the silent closure interval between precursors and test syllables on the effect of changing precursive speech rate. There are three nonexclusive roles that silence could play. First, as the duration of silence increases, a state of perceptual adjustment to a particular introductory rate of speech induced by the precursor could revert to a baseline state of calibration. Second, in the range from about 50 to 250 msec, silence could act as a cue to voicing, with longer durations increasing the likelihood of voiceless percepts. Third, in the range beyond about 250 msec, silence could indicate a juncture and reduce the effect of precursive speech rate by implying a break in the articulatory coherence of precursor phrases and test syllables.

Method

Stimuli and procedure. Two of the precursors and the continuum of test syllables used in Experiment 2 were used again. The precursors were P4 and P8, which represented the extremes of the natural range of variation in articulatory rate and had produced a consistent shift in the VOT boundary.

Phoneme boundaries were estimated on the continuum of test syllables under eight conditions distinguished by the duration of the silent closure interval linking the precursor to the test syllable. These intervals were 50, 100, 250, 500, 1,000, 2,000, 4,000, and 8,000 msec. The four listeners who had produced the most consistent differences in boundary between P4 and P8 in Experiment 2 took part. For each listener in each condition, the interval between precursor and test syllable was held constant and two boundaries on the test continuum were estimated by two interleaved PEST runs. The four listeners served in two sessions during which they made a total of four boundary estimates with each combination of precursors and closure intervals. Each listener provided four baseline boundary estimates, one at the beginning and end of each session, each estimated from four interleaved PEST runs with the test syllables presented in isolation.

Results

The four boundaries estimated by each listener in each condition were averaged to provide a single phoneme boundary. In Table 1, the mean difference between boundaries obtained with the two precursors is tabulated for each closure interval. The difference is largest at closure intervals of 50 and 100 msec, is substantially reduced at an interval of 250 msec, and decreases to an asymptote of about 2 msec at an interval of 1,000 msec.

Figure 4 displays plots which relate closure interval and boundary position for the individual precursors. Nondirectional *t* tests for each closure interval assessed the significance of the difference in mean boundary position between the two precursors. The differences at 50, 100, 250, and 4,000 msec were significant ($p < .05$). There were no systematic differences among the baseline

Table 1
Results of Experiment 3

Separation	Difference
50	11.3
100	9.6
250	4.2
500	3.3
1,000	2.3
2,000	1.8
4,000	2.2
8,000	2.0

Note. Mean differences (in milliseconds) between the positions of the phoneme boundary on a /gi-ki/ continuum estimated with a faster and a slower precursor phrase for eight separations (in milliseconds) of precursors and test syllables.

1082   QUENTIN SUMMERFIELD

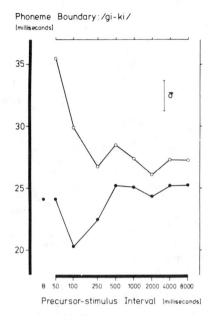

Figure 4. Results of Experiment 3 averaged over four subjects.

estimates ($p > .1$). The error bar indicates the mean standard deviation of the four boundary estimates made for each listener with each combination of precursor rate and closure interval. These deviations did not vary with either rate ($p > .2$) or closure interval ($p > .1$).

Discussion

As the closure interval separating the precursor phrase from the test syllable was increased from 50 msec, the influence of variation in the articulatory rate of the precursor diminished. It was substantially reduced at an interval of 250 msec, and reached an asymptote at an interval of about 1 sec. Possibly, the influence of precursive articulatory rate is determined by the temporal pattern of articulation in a traveling window. As the window sweeps off the end of the precursor, the information determining the prevailing state of perceptual calibration changes. The view through the window is now of silence, and the state of perceptual calibration reverts to that typically found when test syllables are presented in isolation.

However, this explanation does not do justice to the complexity of the role played by

closure. The two functions illustrated in Figure 4 corresponding to the individual precursor phrases do not simply decay to baseline. Rather, with both precursors, boundaries shifted initially to shorter VOTs and then lengthened, depending on the articulatory rate of the precursor, before tending to baseline. Figure 4 shows that the effect occurred more prominently with the slower precursor, though in fact, for each subject and with each precursor, voicing boundaries shifted first to shorter VOTs—with extensions of the closure up to 100 msec in the fast condition and up to 250 msec in the slow condition—and then shifted back to longer VOTs with the next extension in closure duration. While closure duration is a less potent cue to voicing here than in poststress, intervocalic position, its roles in the two contexts appear to be qualitatively similar: Longer closures favor voiceless percepts.

Increases in the duration of silence beyond about 250 msec caused the effect of changing introductory speech rate to diminish rapidly. This result could reflect reversion to a baseline state of calibration. Alternatively, the absence of coherence between precursors and test syllables implied by silent intervals of this duration may have largely eliminated the effect of speech rate. The second, linguistic, interpretation is favored by the observations (a) that shorter silences do play a linguistic role as a cue to voicing and (b) that asymptotic performance was reached at a shorter interval of silence with the faster precursor, implying that a shorter interval is sufficient to indicate a juncture at the faster rate of speech. At the longest intervals, the two functions did not revert to the same asymptote and exhibited a difference even at the longest closure interval. Apparently, the influence of precursive articulatory rate does contain a small long-lasting component.

The results of Experiment 3 suggest that the major influence of precursive articulatory rate is modified by increases in closure duration, not through the decay of a rate-induced state of perceptual calibration, but rather because the duration of the closure interval is itself linguistically informative. The simple extrinsic feed-forward account of timing in the perception of voicing contrasts illustrated in Figure 2 is inadequate to account for this finding. Prior to modifying the model, however, it will be informative to determine which aspect of the precursor appears to provide information about articulatory rate.

Experiment 4

From where in the precursor does the supposed feed-forward influence derive? Three alternatives can be distinguished. The influence could stem from the average articulatory rate over the entire precursor phrase and, as a result, be shown to depend upon the overall duration of the precursor. In contrast, the origin of the influence could be local to that portion of the precursor immediately abutting the test syllable—it could depend only upon the articulatory rate of the final syllable in the precursor. Between these two extremes exists the possibility of a graduated influence wherein the effect of varying the rate of a syllable in the precursor increases in proportion to its proximity to the test syllable.

Method

Stimuli and procedure. The phrase "Why are you . . ." was synthesized, as it is produced naturally, with no discontinuities separating the three syllables. Successive thirds of the phrase will be identified with the syllables "why," "are," and "you" only for descriptive convenience. By setting the duration of each syllable to either 220 msec (slow: S) or 110 msec (fast: F), six versions of the phrase, varying in overall duration from 660 msec (SSS) to 330 msec (FFF), were created as illustrated in Figure 5. The arrangement permits the influence of a change in the duration of each syllable on the perception of voicing in a following test syllable to be estimated. For instance, the influence of the final third (you) can be estimated by comparing the positions of phoneme boundaries produced with Precursors 1 (SSS) and 2 (SSF), and also by comparing the effects of Precursors 5 (FFS) and 6 (FFF). In a similar fashion, two comparisons can be made to measure the influence of the rate of each of the other two syllables, and so allow the influence of the total duration of the precursor to be estimated.

Figure 5 outlines four hypotheses for the rank ordering of the obtained boundaries. If the precursive effect depends upon the entire duration of the phrase (Hypothesis A), voicing boundaries should rank in decreasing order according to precursor number $1 > 2 = 3 > 4 = 5 > 6$. Alternatively, if the influence derives only from the final syllable in the precursor (Hypothesis B), the rank order should be $1 = 3 = 5 > 2 = 4 = 6$. Hypotheses C and D moderate Hypothesis B by predicting

that the precursive effect derives from a window within which the influence of the duration of any particular syllable is inversely proportional to its proximity to the test syllable. Hypothesis C ($1 = 3 > 5 > 2 > 4 = 6$) predicts the outcome if the influence extends over the final two syllables in the precursor, while Hypothesis D predicts the outcome if the influence extends over all three syllables. Hypothesis D predicts the order $1 > 3 > 5 > 2 > 4 > 6$.

A single 10-member /biz-piz/ test continuum was synthesized whose members ranged in VOT from +5 msec to +50 msec. In accordance with a suggestion from Fant (1973) for increasing naturalness, the duration of the vocalic portions of the test syllables was held constant as VOT increased. The duration of the first test syllable with a VOT of +5 msec was 230 msec, while that of the 10th syllable with a VOT of +50 msec was 275 msec. Any of the six precursor phrases could introduce any of the 10 test syllables. A constant closure interval of 100 msec linked the two. Thus the stimulus presented on any trial was an exemplar of either "Why are you bees?" or "Why are you peas?"

Nine listeners took part in the experiment. Their qualifications were similar to those of earlier listeners except that they declared themselves to have learned English as their first language in the United States. They were tested either singly or in pairs in a sound-attenuated room. Listeners heard a set of familiarization and practice trials in which they identified instances of /biz/ and /piz/ first in isolation and then in the context of the precursor phrases. The experiment comprised 600 trials, which included 10 instances of each combination of precursor and test syllable. The trials were presented in three blocks of 200 with an interstimulus interval of 3 sec and additional pauses every 20 trials. The listeners were instructed to attend to the entire phrase on each trial and to identify the initial consonant of the test syllable as either /b/ or /p/ by writing either B or P.

Results and Discussion

Cumulative normal ogives were fitted to the identification data provided by each listener with each precursor according to the Probit method to determine phoneme boundaries and boundary widths. Boundary width averaged about 7 msec and did not vary systematically. In the upper part of Figure 6, the phoneme boundaries corresponding to each precursor, averaged over the nine listeners, have been ranked. Their order corresponds to the graduated prediction of Hypothesis D in which the influence of any particular segment in the precursor increases with its proximity to the test syllable. The lower part of the figure displays the extent of the shift in the phoneme boundary on the test continuum induced by a change in the duration, and hence the articulatory rate, of each of the three syllables comprising the

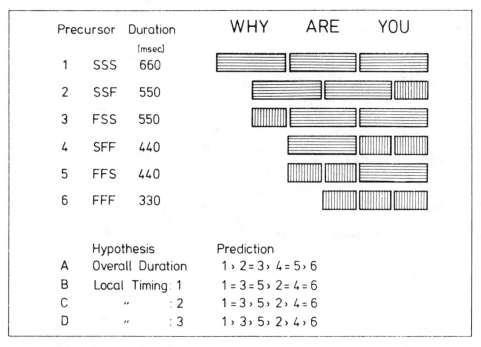

Figure 5. Schematic descriptions of the six precursor phrases used in Experiment 4. (S = slow; F = fast.)

precursor. The mean of each of these differences is positive and in a directional *t* test differs significantly from zero ($p < .05$).

Although the overall influence is graduated throughout the precursor phrase, two thirds of the total effect derives from the duration of the final syllable "you." A posteriori comparisons made according to the criteria recommended by Scheffé (1959) show that the size of shift attributable to the syllable "you" is significantly greater than those due to either of the two preceding syllables ($p < .05$).

In summary, the major component (67%) of the precursive influence of articulatory rate on stop voicing derives from events occurring in the 110–220 msec immediately prior to the closure for the stop. A much smaller component (14%) is related to events occurring 440–660 msec prior to the closure. A comparable result has been obtained for stop voicing in the intervocalic, poststress position (Port, Note 6). The demonstration that the effect is largely local to the stop closure prompts the question of whether an influence on the perception of stop voicing will also derive from the articulatory rate of

the test syllable itself: That is, does the position of the phoneme boundary on a VOT continuum vary as a function of the duration of the syllables that comprise the continuum? This question was examined in Experiment 5.

Postcursive Influences on the Perception of Voicing Contrasts

Experiment 5

Method

Stimuli and procedure. Four 10-member /biz-piz/ continua were synthesized as illustrated in the upper part of Figure 7. They ranged in VOT from +5 to +50 msec and were distinguished by the duration of the vowel. The stimuli incorporated a constant-frequency first formant set to 300 Hz. The second and third formants were configured naturally with no arbitrary discontinuities between initial transitions, steady-state vowel, and final transitions leading into the postvocalic frication. As VOT increased, the total duration of periodic excitation was held constant by duplicating synthesis parameters in the middle of the vowel. In the first continuum the duration of the vocalic portion was 87.5 msec. The duration of the fricative was constant in all continua at 62.5 msec. Thus, the total duration of the members of the first continuum increased from 155 msec to 200 msec as VOT increased from +5 to +50 msec.

The durations of the vocalic portions of the other three continua were 162.5, 237.5, and 312.5 msec. A randomization of these 40 syllables was recorded in the same format as that used in Experiment 4 and with each syllable occurring 10 times. The same nine listeners who had served in Experiment 4 listened to this randomization and indicated whether they perceived the initial consonant of each syllable as /b/ or /p/.

Results

Cumulative normal ogives were fitted to the identification data using Probit analysis, and the averages of the underlying means estimating the positions of the phoneme boundaries have been plotted in the lower part of Figure 7. The mean boundary posi-

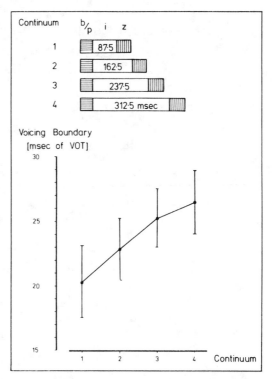

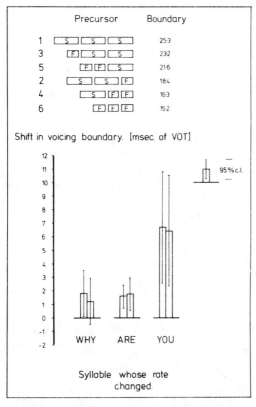

Figure 6. Results of Experiment 4 averaged over 9 subjects. (Upper panel: Precursor phrases ranked according to the position of the phoneme boundary on the /biz-piz/ continuum that they introduced. Lower panel: Shifts in the boundary induced by doubling the articulatory rate of each third of the precursor. The pairs of precursors compared to compute the six shifts were, from left to right, [WHY] P1-P3, P4-P6; [ARE] P3-P5; P2-P4; [YOU] P1-P2, P5-P6. VOT = voice onset time; S = slow; F = fast.)

Figure 7. Upper panel: Schematic representations of members of the four continua of test syllables used in Experiment 5. Lower panel: Results of Experiment 5 averaged over 9 subjects showing the positions of the phoneme boundaries on four /biz-piz/ voice onset time [VOT] continua distinguished by the duration of the vowel. (The error bars indicate the 95% confidence limits of the means.)

tions differ significantly from one another, $F(3, 24) = 12.01$, $p < .001$. The voicing boundary between /biz/ and /piz/ is not fixed. It shifts monotonically to longer values of VOT as the duration of the vowel in the test syllable increases. Thus, as with the precursive influence examined in Experiments 1–4, longer, more slowly articulated syllables increase the probability of voiced percepts. The result confirms earlier claims that vowel duration can influence the position of the phoneme boundary on a VOT continuum. Summerfield and Haggard (Note 1) found that by extending the duration of the vowel in near-boundary members of a /gIl-kIl/ continuum, they increased the likelihood that those syllables would be identified as /gIl/. The effect appeared to be important in that experiment: The same proportional change in articulatory rate produced a larger effect postcursively than precursively. Similarly, Ainsworth (1973) mentioned that variation in vowel duration shifted the positions of the phoneme boundaries on a /si-ti-di/ continuum.

Logically, one would now wish to determine whether postcursive influences extend beyond the test syllable. Just as Experiment 4 sought to estimate the temporal range of the precursive influence, so it should be possible to delimit the extent of the postcursive effect. This was the intention of Experiment 6.

Experiment 6

Method

Stimuli and procedure. The objective of this experiment was to delimit the range of the postcursive influence of articulatory rate on the perception of prevocalic voicing contrasts. It had two component goals. The first was to determine whether an influence derives from the articulatory rate of syllables that follow the test syllable. To this end, two versions of the word *again* were synthesized and appended to the members of the second continuum (C2) used in Experiment 5, creating continua BAG1 and BAG2. The duration of the word *again* was 375 msec in BAG1 and 560 msec in BAG2. The second goal of the experiment was to determine whether the postcursive effect depends simply upon the duration of periodicity in the test syllable or if the particular form in which periodicity is manifest is important. To answer this question, three continua were synthesized. One was created by removing the fricative segment from each of the members of C2 leaving a /bi-pi/ continuum which will be identified by the letter B. A fricative /z/ of 37.5-msec duration was appended to each member of B to create a /biz-piz/ continuum, BZ1. Finally, Continuum BZ2 was created by adding a /z/ of 87.5 msec to each member of Continuum B.

Thus, the stimuli for Experiment 6 comprised five /b-p/ continua each of which ranged from +5 to +50 msec of VOT. The initial CV portions of stimuli with the same VOT in different continua were specified by the same sequence of synthesis control parameters. Two predictions can be made for the outcome of the experiment. First, if the position of the voicing boundary depends on the articulatory rate of syllables following the test syllable in the same way as on those preceding it, then the boundary should fall at a shorter VOT on Continuum BAG1 than on BAG2. Second, if the influence of the rate of the syllable that includes the VOT derives from its total duration of periodic excitation, including both the vowel and the final voiced fricative, then boundaries should fall at progressively longer VOTs on Continua B, BZ1, and BZ2. A randomization in which each of the 50 stimuli occurred 10 times was recorded and presented to the same nine listeners who had taken part in Experiments 4 and 5. Once again they were instructed to identify the initial consonant of the test syllable or phrase as either /b/ or /p/.

Results

The data were analyzed in Probit analyses. Estimates of the positions and widths of the boundaries on the five continua, averaged over the nine listeners, are tabulated in Table 2. There were no systematic differences among the boundary widths. The boundary positions were examined in an analysis of variance and shown to differ systematically, $F(4, 32) = 4.71, p < .01$. A posteriori comparisons showed that the boundary on Continuum B fell at a significantly longer VOT than did the boundaries on BZ1, BZ2, and BAG1 ($p < .05$) and BAG2 ($p < .1$). The latter four boundaries did not differ systematically from one another.

Discussion

The results of Experiment 6 are surprising. Experiment 5 had shown that if the duration of the vocalic portion of syllables comprising a VOT continuum is increased, the voicing boundary moves to a longer VOT. In Experiment 6, adding periodic excitation to each syllable in the form of /z/ friction produced the opposite effect: The phoneme boundary moved to a shorter VOT. This change appears to depend categorically upon whether there is a /z/; changing the actual duration of the friction between Continua BZ1 and BZ2 produced no effect. Similarly, no effect was produced by manipulating the duration of syllables in the word *again* that followed the test syllable.

To confirm this unexpected finding, eight new listeners were recruited. They identified the initial consonants of the members of six VOT continua: two /bi-pi/ continua distin-

Table 2
Results of Experiment 6

Continuum	PB	BW
B	23.0	7.8
BZ1	20.6	6.8
BZ2	20.2	7.5
BAG1	20.8	8.2
BAG2	20.6	7.1

Note. Averages over nine listeners of phoneme boundaries (PB) and boundary widths (BW) on five VOT continua (in milliseconds).

guished by the duration of their vocalic portions (90 and 165 msec); two /biz-piz/ continua formed by adding 60 msec of aperiodically excited frication to the members of the /bi-pi/ continua; and two /bis-pis/ continua formed by adding 160 msec of aperiodically excited frication. It was possible to synthesize distinct /biz-piz/ and /bis-pis/ continua because fricative duration is a sufficient cue to fricative voicing in syllable-final position (Harris, 1958). The average positions of the phoneme boundaries and boundary widths on these nine continua have been tabulated in Table 3.

The paradoxical result of Experiment 6 was replicated. Once again, boundaries fell at longer VOTs on the /bi-pi/ continua and at shorter VOTs on the /biz-piz/ and /bis-pis/ continua, whose boundaries did not differ significantly. An analogous effect has been reported by Miller and Liberman (1979). They synthesized a /ba-wa/ continuum by systematically increasing the duration of the initial formant transitions and showed that the position of the phoneme boundary moves to longer transition durations as the duration of the vowel /a/ is increased. However, appending periodically excited formant transitions appropriate for a postvocalic /d/ caused the /b-w/ boundary on the resulting /bad-wad/ continuum to fall at a shorter duration of the initial formant transitions.

Given contemporary knowledge of articulatory dynamics, it is difficult to explain why the addition of a syllable-final consonant should moderate the perception of syllable-initial consonants in this way. The present result and that of Miller and Lib-

erman emphasize the inadequacy of any account of speech perception that posits only strictly serial processing (as Miller and Liberman noted) and, as such, refute the feed-forward model of perceptual voice-onset timing illustrated in Figure 2. The demonstration of complex postcursive effects requires that the model be elaborated to include a feed-back component. The issue is further complicated by the results of Experiment 3 which showed that increases in the durations of the stop closure between precursors and test syllables in the range from 50 to 250 msec increased the likelihood that the stop would be perceived as voiceless. In that experiment, further increases in closure duration led to the perception of a pause, and the test syllables were perceived essentially as if they had been presented in isolation. However, the closure duration corresponding to the minimum, in the empirical function relating closure duration and voicing boundary, was found to vary with the articulatory rate of the precursor phrase. The result stressed how elaborate the extrinsic timing model would have to be to accommodate the data even in qualitative terms. It would be necessary to explain how, for instance, feed-forward and feed-back effects interact. In addition, feed-forward effects within precursor phrases would presumably moderate one another. The logical untidiness of the class of explanation based on extrinsic timing is illustrated in Figure 8. Possibly a different and more elegant explanation should be sought. Indeed, is time, per se, a controlling variable in phonetic perception?

In What Sense Is Time an Ingredient of the Process of Phonetic Perception?

The experiments described here embody an implicit distinction between *cues* for phonetic contrasts and *contextual variables* that appear to modify the interpretaion of cues. However, the implied functional distinction between a cue and its context may be false. It is not obvious how cue and context can be distinguished objectively, since both are simply parameters of a speech signal whose systematic manipulation produces a change in the phonetic interpretation of the signal. (See Weisstein, 1973, and Bailey and Sum-

Table 3
Results of a Partial Replication of Experiment 6

Continuum	Shorter vowel		Longer vowel	
	PB	BW	PB	BW
/bi-pi/	28.1	7.1	29.5	6.6
/bis-pis/	23.5	6.7	26.4	6.2
/biz-piz/	22.8	5.9	26.5	5.8

Note. Averages over eight listeners of phoneme boundaries (PB) and boundary widths (BW) on six VOT continua (in milliseconds).

1088 QUENTIN SUMMERFIELD

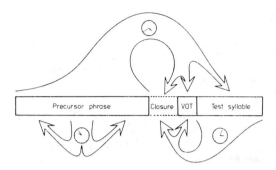

| Precursor phrase | Closure | VOT | Test syllable |

Figure 8. An elaboration of Figure 2 illustrating the complexities with which a complete account of extrinsic timing for the perception of voicing contrasts would have to contend. (VOT = voice onset time.)

merfield, 1980, for elaborations of this argument.)

Just as descriptions of speech production emphasize coarticulation and the temporal ramifications of phonetic elements, so an alternative account of the results described here might stress listeners' sensitivity to an analogous temporal distribution of information specifying phonetic identity. The production of a stop consonant entails the constriction, the occlusion, and the release of the supralaryngeal vocal tract. These maneuvers must be coordinated with ongoing gestures responsible for the production of surrounding vowels and, in the case of voiceless stops, with the abduction and adduction of the vocal cords. Manipulations of the signal that change the acoustical specifications of constriction, occlusion, and release and their coordination with other articulatory events should influence the identity of a stop as voiced or voiceless. Thus, effects on the perception of stop voicing might be expected to follow from changes in the acoustical specification of the syllable containing the constriction phase of the event as in Experiments 1, 2, and 4, the occlusion phase as in Experiment 3, and the syllable containing the release phase as in Experiments 5 and 6. The temporal "window" from which the influence of speech rate derives should be both short and, for the most part, local to the time course of the articulatory maneuvers generating the stop.

This was the implication of the results of Experiments 1–6, though some explanation is also required for the small but consistent influence of more distant syllables found in Experiment 4 and by Port (Note 6). The general conclusion is comparable with that reached by Repp, Liberman, Eccardt, and Pesetsky (1978) regarding the temporal distribution of information specifying stop manner. It appears that extrinsic variables such as time, rhythm, or tempo may not have caused the major effects described here. Time is necessarily intrinsic to articulatory events but may not be a variable controlling their enactment or their perceptual registration.

This apparently radical stance predicts that if Experiment 1 were to be repeated with a precursor devised so that temporal information were dissociated from information specifying articulatory maneuvers, then no effect on the perception of voicing contrasts should result. Experiment 7 was designed to test an instance of this hypothesis by embedding synthetic test syllables drawn from a VOT continuum into a tune composed from synthetic, nonspeech buzzes. Will changes in the tempo of the tune influence the perception of voicing in the consonant that initiates the embedded test syllable? If the cause of the precursive speech rate effect is properly to be attributed to variations in prevailing tempo, then shifts in the voicing boundary should accompany changes in the tempo of the melody. Equally, if the proper explanation is that the durations of acoustic segments that occur in a stream are registered relative to one another, as suggested by Ainsworth (1973), then changes in the tempo of the carrier should generate systematic changes in the perception of the test syllables. However, if the effects are not mediated by changes in tempo or relative duration, but by changes in the acoustical specifications of the articulation of stop consonants, then changes in carrier tempo should produce no effect here. In confirming the hypothesis of no change, it would be necessary to ensure that listeners were not simply insensitive to temporal variations. Control for that contingency can be incorporated in the experiment by using test syllables of two different durations. Regardless of any effects of the tempo of the carrier, listeners should place phoneme boundaries at a longer VOT on the continuum formed

from the more slowly articulated test syllables.

Experiment 7

Method

Stimuli and procedure. The stimuli used in Experiment 7 are illustrated schematically in the upper portion of Figure 9. The carrier consisted of four bars of
the tune that normally accompanies the Christmas carol
"Good King Wenceslaus" (i.e., /CC/CD/CC/G /AG/
AB/C /C /). The crochets were synthesized as 200-
msec notes followed by 50 msec of silence. The minims
were synthesized as 450-msec notes also followed by 50
msec of silence. In each note the first formant was set
to 1.0 kHz and the third formant to 3.0 kHz. The second
formant oscillated between 1.5 kHz and 2.5 kHz, changing frequency every 10 msec. These notes were ma-
chinelike buzzes rather than sung vowels. The melody
was carried on the fundamental. A second version of the
carrier tune was created by reducing the duration of
each crochet to 75 msec and each minim to 200 msec.
With 50 msec of silence intervening between each note,
the tempo of this version of the melody was twice that
of the first.

Two nine-member /biz-piz/ continua were created,
ranging in VOT from 0 to +40 msec. In one, the duration
of the syllables was 450 msec; in the other it was 200
msec. The fundamental frequency of each syllable was
constant. When embedded in the carrier in the place of
the seventh note, the impression was of proper melodic
and rhythmic coherence, but of a clear change in source
between a single sung test syllable and the surrounding
tune. Two additional combinations of carrier tunes and
test syllables were created by crossing the slow syllables
with the fast carrier and vice versa.

Nine new listeners took part in the experiment. They
listened to a randomization that included 10 instances
of each of the 36 combinations of carrier tunes and test
syllables and identified the initial consonant of each test
syllable as either /b/ or /p/.

Results

The average positions of phoneme boundaries obtained with each combination of test
continuum and carrier tune were determined
by Probit analysis. The results are displayed
in the lower part of Figure 9 in the same
format as was employed earlier in Figure 1.
An analysis of variance showed that voicing
boundaries did not shift significantly with
changes in the tempo of the carrier tune,
$F(1, 8) = .18$, $p > .2$, but did shorten significantly as the duration of the embedded
test syllables was reduced, $F(1, 8) = 14.58$,
$p < .01$.

Discussion

The outcome of Experiment 7 supports the
contention that the precursive influence of
articulatory rate, earlier interpreted as reflecting the influence of extrinsic timing,
may be better described as the result of
manipulations applied to the intrinsic time
course of the acoustical concomitants of the
event of stop consonant production itself.
However, it could be argued that the failure
of tempo in a nonspeech melody to influence
the perception of a speech sound is to be
expected on the grounds that speech and
music receive separate perceptual processing
(e.g., Kimura, 1967). A stronger test would
be one in which carrier and test syllables
specified different acoustical sources, as they
did in Experiment 7, but were both speech.

Diehl et al. (1980) have reported the results of such an experiment. They replicated
the basic effect of speech rate shown here
in Experiments 1 and 2 with stimuli representing the speech of an adult male.[4] They
then proceeded to rescale the formant frequencies and to change the mean fundamental frequency in precursor phrases and
test syllables independently. These manipulations resulted in the impression that precursors and test syllables had been spoken
by two different talkers, one male and one
female, so that there was a switch in source
between precursors and test syllables. In this
condition, effects of varying precursive speech
rate were significantly reduced.

The hypothesis that changes in speech
tempo are responsible for the precursive effect does not explain this result. It predicts
that changes in the identification of members
of the test continuum will occur regardless
of the apparent sources of precursor phrases
and test syllables. The result of Diehl et al.
is predicted by the alternative argument that
precursive effects follow from manipulations
applied to the intrinsic time course of the
articulation of the consonant perceived as
initiating the test syllable. According to this
argument no effect should be obtained when
a change in source between precursor and
test syllable is specified because the constric-

---

[4] Surprisingly—and inexplicably—with precursors and
test syllables representing a female talker, the direction
of the boundary shift was reversed.

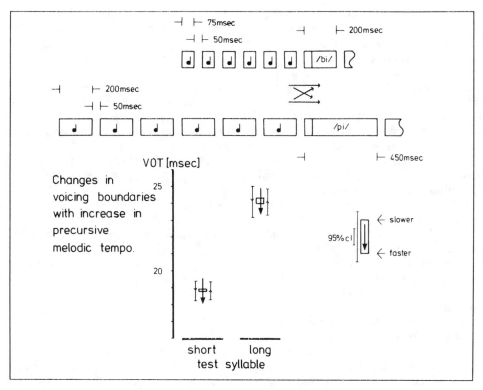

Figure 9. Upper panel: Schematic illustrations of the first two bars of the faster and slower versions of the melody used as a carrier in Experiment 8. Lower panel: Results of Experiment 8 averaged over 9 listeners.

tion phase of the stop (specified in the precursor) and the release phase (specified in the test syllable) represent different articulations.[5]

General Discussion

The experiments reported in this paper have shown that variations in contextual articulatory rate systematically influence the identification of syllable-initial stop consonants as voiced or voiceless. Increases in contextual rate increase the likelihood that a stop will be identified as voiceless. The major part of the effect derives from changes local to the test syllable. A small component derives from changes several seconds or several syllables prior to the test syllable.

The major effect suggests that the "window of influence" through which information specifying articulatory rate might be presumed to emerge encompasses little more than the time span of the acoustical concom-

itants of the articulatory events involved in the production of the stop consonant itself. At an average rate of speech, movements of the articulators responsible for the constriction, occlusion, and release of the supralaryngeal vocal tract occur over about 400 msec (Gay, 1977; Perkell, 1969; Sussman, McNeilage, & Hanson, 1973). The greater proportion of the effects of articulatory rate revealed in Experiments 4 and 5 derived from changes in the acoustical specification

---

[5] An apparently conflicting result was reported by Summerfield (Note 8) who found no significant diminution of the effect of precursive articulatory rate when precursor phrases and test syllables were synthesized to represent the outputs of vocal tracts of different lengths. However, only small differences in average formant frequencies were used to imply a difference in vocal-tract length; there was no difference in fundamental frequency—the perceptually dominant indicant of different voices. Reexamination of the stimuli suggests that listeners may not have perceived a change in talker. The result of Diehl et al. (1980) appears to be more conclusive, therefore.

of events occurring within this time span. Thus, in the case of prestressed stop consonants at least, the window that provides the view of contextual articulatory rate essentially coincides with the duration of the articulatory event that this rate is meant to normalize. The acoustical substrate for the direct perception of rate is the same as the acoustical elements whose interpretation rate must mediate. This observation implies that rate cannot mediate the interpretation of the elements; the event must be self-normalizing. Indeed, to speak of normalization as in an engineering approach to speech recognition is unnecessary, because it appears that timing is largely intrinsic to the acoustical specification of phonetic identity.

Explanations are still required for the small but consistent influence of more distant syllables in Experiment 4 and in Port (Note 6), and for the residual influence remaining when precursor and test syllables were separated by up to 8 sec in Experiment 3. Intrinsic timing, as expressed here, cannot explain these effects. In the absence of better motivated explanations, they must be presumed to reflect extrinsic timing of the kind implied in Figure 2. The paragraphs that follow concentrate on the major effects that appear to warrant explanation in terms of intrinsic timing.

The conclusion that timing is largely intrinsic to the acoustical specification of phonetic events has two related implications. The first is that there may exist a greater commonality among the acoustical bases for the perception of voicing contrasts articulated in different phonetic contexts than has traditionally been emphasized. The second relates the present, essentially intrinsic account of timing in phonetic perception to an emerging reformulation of the problems of temporal coordination and seriation in speech production.

Commonalities in Perceptual Sensitivity to the Acoustical Consequences of Voicing Contrasts Articulated in Different Phonetic Contexts

Tradition has asserted the lack of invariance of the acoustical manifestations of phonetic elements. It has been stressed (e.g., Liberman et al., 1967) and recently reemphasized (Liberman & Pisoni, 1977) that the perception of contrasts in stop voicing, for instance, demands sensitivity to different acoustic cues in different phonetic contexts. Although stemming from similar coordinations of laryngeal and supralaryngeal maneuvers (e.g., Lisker & Abramson, 1971), postvocalic contrasts were observed to be cued by changes in vowel duration, intervocalic poststress contrasts by changes in closure duration, and prevocalic prestress contrasts by changes in voice onset time. However, inspection of the present results, in relation to those reported by others, indicates that these contextual variations are differences of degree rather than of kind. Manipulations of the same acoustical parameters predispose voiced or voiceless percepts in each of the contexts catalogued previously.

Consider first the syllable containing the occlusive maneuver. With all other acoustical parameters held constant, an increase in the duration of this syllable increases the likelihood of voiced percepts of postvocalic stops (e.g., Raphael, 1972), intervocalic poststress stops (Port, 1979, Note 6), and intervocalic prestress stops (Summerfield, 1974, and the present Experiments 1, 2, and 4). Similarly, an increase in the duration of the stop closure relative to that of the preceding (and where possible, the following) vocalic segment increases the likelihood of voiceless percepts of postvocalic released stops (Wajskop & Sweerts, 1973), intervocalic poststress stops (Lisker, 1957; Port, 1979, Note 6), and intervocalic prestress stops (Experiment 3). Increases in VOT increase the likelihood of voiceless percepts of both intervocalic poststress stops (Lisker, Note 7) and intervocalic prestress stops (Lisker & Abramson, 1967). Finally, an increase in the duration of the syllable containing the release maneuver increases the probability of voiced percepts of both intervocalic poststress stops (Port, 1979, Note 6) and intervocalic prestress stops (Experiment 5). Inspection of spectral parameters reveals a similar picture (Klatt, 1975). A low-frequency first formant abutting stop closure predisposes percepts of voiced stops postvocalically (Wolf, 1978), intervocalically poststress (Lisker, Note 7), and intervocalically prestress (Lisker, 1975; Summerfield & Haggard, 1977).

A list of operational similarities is not a specification of acoustic invariance. However, such similarities in sensitivity to the acoustical surface structure of articulatory events may underlie the appreciation of a single phonetic contrast despite contextual variation, and further inspection may reveal an abstract and relational acoustical invariance of the type proposed by some (e.g., Gibson, 1966) as the necessary basis for perceptual constancy.

In illustration of that claim, it can be seen that in both the intervocalic prestress context examined in the experiments described in this paper, and the other contexts discussed previously, a general rule for increasing the probability of a voiced stop percept is to increase the proportion of the devoiced interval (i.e., the sum of the stop closure and the VOT) to the surrounding voiced interval encompassing the abutting vowels. Superficially, this statement implies little more than the fact that voiceless stops are produced by properly coordinating vocal cord abduction and adduction with supralaryngeal occlusion, constriction, and release. However, emphasizing a relational basis for the contrast in acoustical terms can help to rationalize the form in which the contrast is realized in different linguistic environments. In American English, for instance, the difference in duration between the vowels in productions of /ab/ and /ap/ does not result directly from the control of laryngeal–supralaryngeal coordination; in adults, the contrast appears to be controlled by sustaining the activity in the muscles involved in the production of the vowel (Raphael, 1975), although the linguistic evolution of the difference may have included the need to abduct the vocal cords earlier in relation to vocal tract occlusion in the production of voiceless stops to avoid voicing during the closure. Klatt (1975) uses this argument to support his contention that the difference in vowel duration has been incorporated in American English as a phonological rule.

The results of the present experiments and those of Port suggest that the rule is not arbitrary. Rather, it coheres with and capitalizes on a general rule for specifying the voiced value of the feature by decreasing the ratio of aperiodic to periodic acoustical energy over the time course of supralaryngeal occlusion, constriction, and release. This relational property is potentially invariant over changes in stress and rate, and so could specify the voicing distinction in all contexts. However, while the experiments reported here suggest the possibility of its existence, rigorous specification of such an invariant relation remains elusive.

Timing in Speech: Extrinsic or Intrinsic?

The account of extrinsic timing in speech perception suggested by the results of Experiment 1 and illustrated in Figures 2 and 8 is logically akin to many accounts of speech production. Kozhevnikov and Chistovitch (1965), for instance, felt that since continuous variation in articulatory rate appears to be possible, it would be uneconomical for rate to be included in the plan for an act of speaking. If rate were included, a different plan would be required for every enunciation. Rather, these authors suppose that rate should be the concern of the executor of the plan. Similarly, Shaffer (1976) has written that "we can consider the articulatory coherence of a syllable as the consequence of a timing pattern imposed upon a group of (invariant) phoneme commands" (p. 387). These two accounts and others (e.g., Lindblom, 1975; Mackay, 1970) belong to a class of theories that Fowler (1980) has identified as models of extrinsic timing in speech production.

The conclusion drawn from the perceptual experiments reported here is that time is essentially intrinsic to the acoustical specifications of contrasts in stop voicing and is not an independent parameter controlling phonetic perception. An account of speech production in which time was considered to be intrinsic to the plan for an act of speaking would be compatible with this orientation. Appropriate support can be found in formulations of the general theory of action (Turvey, 1977; Turvey, Shaw, & Mace, 1978) and in the application of an action-theoretical perspective to the problem of timing control in speech production (Fowler, Rubin, Remez, & Turvey, 1980).

These authors observe that during skilled actions, muscle systems behave as instances of critically damped nonlinear oscillatory systems (e.g., Asatryan & Fel'dman, 1965; Kelso, 1977). Within its elastic range, a critically damped oscillatory system reaches the same resting position whenever it is released following displacement. The position does not depend on the initial degree of compression or expansion; the system attains its equilibrium configuration regardless of the starting conditions. Fowler et al. (1980) suggest that it would be economical for the oral musculature to be similarly organized during acts of speaking. An articulatory target configuration appropriate for a particular vowel or consonant would be approached by establishing parameters for the muscles of the mouth as an instance of a particular mass–spring system. The same parameters, for instance, would then result both in the downward and backward movement of the body of the tongue when the vowel /ε/ is produced after the high front vowel /i/, and in the upward and forward movement when the same vowel /ε/ follows the low back vowel /a/.

Pertinent to the results of the present experiment is the observation that no temporal executor is required to realize the acts that a mass–spring system can perform. The intercoordination and calibration of articulators can occur with respect to the phase of critically damped cycles. Thus, movement over time occurs, but time is not a variable that controls movement.

Logically, the parameters over which talkers exercise control to produce phonetic contrasts would be those having specific acoustical consequences that listeners can detect to distinguish members of one phonetic class from another. Ideally, therefore, accounts of speech perception and speech production should converge on a single set of descriptors applicable to both perception and production. If extrinsic timing is the appropriate metaphor for speech production, then temporal normalization should be expected in speech perception. To the extent that the results of the present experiments confound the expectations of extrinsic timing, the al-ternative view—that timing is intrinsic to the control of articulatory gestures and to the acoustical information for phonetic perception—is supported and warrants further scrutiny.

Reference Notes

1. Summerfield, Q., & Haggard, M. P. *Speech rate effects in the perception of stop voicing.* Speech Synthesis and Perception No. 6, 1972, 1–12. Progress Report, Psychological Laboratory, University of Cambridge.
2. Summerfield, Q. *Towards a detailed model for the perception of voicing contrasts.* Speech Perception No. 3, 1974, 1–26. Progress Report, Department of Psychology, Queen's University of Belfast.
3. Lisker, L. *In (qualified) defence of VOT.* Status Report on Speech Research, SR-44. New Haven, Conn.: Haskins Laboratories, 1975.
4. Lisker, L. *Stop duration and voicing in English.* Status Report on Speech Research, SR-19/20. New Haven, Conn.: Haskins Laboratories, 1969.
5. Westbury, J. R. *Temporal control of medial stop-consonant clusters in English.* Paper presented at the 93rd Meeting of the Acoustical Society of America, State College, Pennsylvania, June 1977.
6. Port, R. F. *Effects of word-internal vs. word-external tempo on the voicing boundary for medial stop closure.* Status Report on Speech Research, SR-55/56. New Haven, Conn.: Haskins Laboratories, 1978.
7. Lisker, L. *Rabid vs. rapid: A catalogue of acoustic features that may cue the distinction.* Status Report on Speech Research, SR-54. New Haven, Conn.: Haskins Laboratories, 1978.
8. Summerfield, Q. *Cues, contexts, and complications in the perception of voicing contrasts.* Speech Perception No. 4, 1975, 99–130. Progress Report, Department of Psychology, Queen's University of Belfast.

References

Ainsworth, W. Durational cues in the perception of certain consonants. *Proceedings of the British Acoustical Society (Vol. 2),* 1973, 1–4.
Allen, G. Segmental timing control in speech production. *Journal of Phonetics,* 1973, *1,* 219–237.
Asatryan, D. G., & Fel'dman, A. G. Functional tuning of the nervous system with control of movement or maintenance of a steady posture—1. Mechanographic analysis of the work on the joint on execution of a posturai task. *Biophysics,* 1965, *10,* 925–935.
Bailey, P. J., & Summerfield, A. Q. Information in speech: Observations on the perception of [s]-stop clusters. *Journal of Experimental Psychology: Human Perception and Performance,* 1980, *6,* 536–563.
Cole, R. A., Coltheart, M., & Allard, F. Memory of a speaker's voice: Reaction time to same- or different-voice letters. *Quarterly Journal of Experimental Psychology,* 1974, *26,* 1–7.
Cooper, W. E. Contingent feature analysis in speech

1094 QUENTIN SUMMERFIELD

perception. *Perception & Psychophysics*, 1974, *16*, 201-204.

Creelman, C. D. Human discrimination of auditory duration. *Journal of the Acoustical Society of America*, 1962, *34*, 229-234.

Darwin, C. J. The perception of speech. In E. C. Carterette & M. P. Friedman (Eds.), *Handbook of perception* (Vol. 7): *Language and speech*. New York: Academic, 1976.

Diehl, R. L., Souther, A. F., & Convis, C. L. Conditions on rate normalisation in speech perception. *Perception & Psychophysics*, 1980, 27, 435-443.

Draper, G. SPEX: A system to run speech perception experiments. *Proceedings of the 9th DECUS Europe Seminar*. Maynard, Mass.: Digital Equipment Corporation, 1973.

Fant, G. Stops in CV syllables. In G. Fant (Ed.), *Speech sounds and features*. Cambridge Mass.: MIT Press, 1973.

Finney, D. J. *Probit analysis*. New York: Cambridge University Press, 1971.

Fowler, C. A. Coarticulation and theories of extrinsic timing. *Journal of Phonetics*, 1980, *8*, 113-133.

Fowler, C. A., Rubin, P., Remez, R. E., & Turvey, M. T. Implications for speech production of a general theory of action. In B. Butterworth (Ed.), *Language production*. New York: Academic Press, 1980.

Gay, T. Articulatory movements in VCV sequences. *Journal of the Acoustical Society of America*, 1977, *62*, 183-193.

Gay, T., Ushijima, T., Hirose, H., & Cooper, F. S. Effects of speaking rate on labial consonant-vowel articulation. *Journal of Phonetics*, 1974, *2*, 47-63.

Gibson, J. J. *The senses considered as perceptual systems*. Boston, Mass.: Houghton Mifflin, 1966.

Grosjean, F., & Lane, H. How the listener integrates the components of speaking rate. *Journal of Experimental Psychology: Human Perception and Performance*, 1976, *2*, 538-543.

Haggard, M. P. Experience and perspectives in articulatory synthesis. In B. Lindblom & S. Ohman (Eds.), *Frontiers of speech communication research*. London: Academic, 1979.

Harris, K. S. Cues for the discrimination of American-English fricatives in spoken syllables. *Language & Speech*, 1958, *1*, 1-17.

Kelso, J. A. S. Motor control mechanisms underlying human movement reproduction. *Journal of Experimental Psychology: Human Perception and Performance*, 1977, *3*, 529-543.

Kimura, D. Functional asymmetry of the brain in dichotic listening. *Cortex*, 1967, *3*, 163-178.

Klatt, D. H. Interaction between two factors that influence vowel duration. *Journal of the Acoustical Society of America*, 1973, *43*, 1102-1104.

Klatt, D. H. Voice onset time, frication, and aspiration in word-initial consonant clusters. *Journal of Speech and Hearing Research*, 1975, *18*, 686-706.

Klatt, D. H. The linguistic uses of segment duration in English: Acoustic and perceptual evidence. *Journal of the Acoustical Society of America*, 1976, *59*, 1208-1221.

Kozhevnikov, V. A. & Chistovich, L. A. *Speech, artic-

ulation, and perception* (NTIS No. JPRS-305430) Washington, D.C.: U.S. Dept. of Commerce, 1965.

Liberman, A. M., Cooper, F. S., Shankweiler, D. P., & Studdert-Kennedy, M. The perception of the speech code. *Psychological Review*, 1967, *74*, 431-461.

Liberman, A. M., Delattre, P. C., & Cooper, F. S. Some cues for the distinction between voiced and voiceless stops in initial position. *Language and Speech*, 1958, *1*, 153-167.

Liberman, A. M., & Pisoni, D. B. Evidence for a special speech-perceiving subsystem in the human. In T. H. Bullock (Ed.), *Recognition of complex acoustic signals*. Berlin: Abakon, 1977.

Lindblom, B. E. F. Some temporal regularities of spoken Swedish. In G. Fant and M. A. A. Tatham (Eds.), *Auditory analysis and perception of speech*. New York: Academic, 1975.

Lisker, L. Closure duration and the intervocalic voiced-voiceless distinction in English. *Language*, 1957, *33*, 42-49.

Lisker, L. Is it VOT or an F1 transition detector? *Journal of the Acoustical Society of America*, 1975, *57*, 1547-1551.

Lisker, L., & Abramson, A. S. A cross-language study of voicing in initial stops: acoustical measurements. *Word*, 1964, *20*, 329-422.

Lisker, L., & Abramson, A. S. The voicing dimension: Some experiments in comparative phonetics. In *Proceedings of the Sixth International Congress of Phonetic Sciences*. Prague: Academia, 1967.

Lisker, L., & Abramson, A. S. Distinctive features and laryngeal control. *Language*, 1971, *47*, 767-785.

Mackay, D. G. Spoonerisms: The structure of errors in the serial order of speech. *Neuropsychologia*, 1970, *8*, 323-350.

Miller, J. L. Nonindependence of feature processing in initial consonants. *Journal of Speech and Hearing Research*, 1977, *20*, 519-528.

Miller, J. L. The effect of speaking rate on segmental distinctions: Acoustical variation and perceptual compensation. In P. D. Eimas & J. L. Miller (Eds.), *Perspectives in the study of speech*. Hillsdale, N.J.: Erlbaum, in press.

Miller, J. L., & Liberman, A. M. Some effects of later occurring information on the perception of stop consonant and semivowel. *Perception & Psychophysics*, 1979, *25*, 457-465.

Nooteboom, S. G. Speech rate and segmental perception or the role of words in phoneme identification. In T. Myers (Ed.), *The cognitive representation of speech*. London: Academic, in press.

Perkell, J. S. *Physiology of speech production: Results and implications of a quantitative cineradiographic study*. Cambridge, Mass.: MIT Press, 1969.

Port, R. F. The influence of tempo on stop closure duration as a cue for voicing and place. *Journal of Phonetics*, 1979, *7*, 45-56.

Raphael. L. J. Preceding vowel duration as a cue to the perception of the voicing characteristic of word-final consonants in American English. *Journal of the Acoustical Society of America*, 1972, *51*, 1296-1303.

Raphael, L. J. The physiological control of durational differences between vowels preceding voiced and voiceless consonants in English. *Journal of Phonetics,* 1975, *3,* 25–34.

Repp, B. H., Liberman, A. M., Eccardt, T., & Pesetsky, D. Perceptual integration of acoustic cues for stop, fricative and affricate manner. *Journal of Experimental Psychology: Human Perception and Performance,* 1978, *4,* 621–637.

Shaffer, L. H. Intention and performance. *Psychological Review,* 1976, *83,* 375–393.

Scheffé, H. *The analysis of variance.* New York: Wiley, 1959.

Stevens, K. N., & Klatt, D. H. Role of formant transitions in the voiced-voiceless distinction for stops. *Journal of the Acoustical Society of America,* 1974, *55,* 653–659.

Summerfield, Q. How a detailed account of segmental perception depends on prosody and vice versa. In A. Cohen and S. G. Nooteboom (Eds.), *Structure and process in speech perception.* New York: Springer, 1975.

Summerfield, Q. Timing in phonetic perception: Extrinsic or intrinsic? In K. J. Kohler and W. J. Barry (Eds.), *"Time" in the production and the perception of speech.* Arbeitsberichte Nr. 12. University of Kiel: Kiel, West Germany, 1979.

Summerfield, Q., & Haggard, M. P. On the dissociation of spectral and temporal cues to the voicing distinction in initial stop consonants. *Journal of the Acoustical Society of America,* 1977, *62,* 435–448.

Sussman, H., MacNeilage, P. F., & Hanson, R. J. Labial and mandibular dynamics during the production of bilabial consonants: Preliminary observations. *Journal of Speech and Hearing Research,* 1973, *16,* 397–420.

Taylor, M. M., & Creelman, C. D. PEST: Efficient estimates on probability functions. *Journal of the Acoustical Society of America,* 1967, *41,* 782–787.

Turvey, M. T. Preliminaries to a theory of action with reference to vision. In R. Shaw & J. Bransford (Eds.), *Perceiving, acting and knowing: Toward an ecological psychology.* Hillsdale, N.J.: Erlbaum, 1977.

Turvey, M. T., Shaw, R., & Mace, W. Issues in the theory of action: Degrees of freedom, coordinative structures, and coalitions. In J. Requin (Ed.), *Attention and performance VIII.* Hillsdale, N.J.: Erlbaum, 1978.

Wajskop, M., & Sweerts, J. Voicing cues in oral stop consonants. *Journal of Phonetics,* 1973, *1,* 121–130.

Weisstein, N. Beyond the yellow-volkswagen detector and the grandmother cell: A general strategy for the exploration of operations in human pattern recognition. In R. L. Solso (Ed.), *Contemporary issues in cognitive psychology: The Loyola symposium.* Washington, D.C.: Wiley, 1973.

Wolf, C. G. Voicing cues in English final stops. *Journal of Phonetics,* 1978, *6,* 299–310.

Received March 21, 1980 ∎

Reprinted from
23 January, volume 167, pages 392-393

SCIENCE

Perceptual Restoration of Missing Speech Sounds

Abstract. *When an extraneous sound (such as a cough or tone) completely replaces a speech sound in a recorded sentence, listeners believe they hear the missing sound. The extraneous sound seems to occur during another portion of the sentence without interfering with the intelligibility of any phoneme. If silence replaces a speech sound, the gap is correctly localized and the absence of the speech sound detected.*

We frequently listen to speech against a background of extraneous sounds. Individual phonemes may be masked, yet comprehension is possible. In a study of the effect of transient masking sounds, it was found that replacement of a phoneme in a recorded sentence by a cough resulted in illusory perception of the missing speech sound. Further, the cough did not seem to coincide with the restored sound.

In the first experiment exploring this phonemic restoration effect, 20 undergraduate psychology students were tested. The stimulus was a tape recording of the sentence, "The state governors met with their respective legislatures convening in the capital city," with a 120-msec section deleted and replaced with a recorded cough of the same duration. The speech sound removed (as determined by slow movement past the playback head and confirmed by a sound spectrograph) was the first "s" in the word "legislatures" together with portions of the adjacent phonemes which might provide transitional cues to the missing sound. The subjects were told that, after listening to a cough occurring somewhere in a sentence, they would be given a typewritten statement of the sentence so that they could circle the exact position at which the cough occurred. They were told also that they would be asked whether or not the cough replaced completely the circled sounds. The stimulus was heard binaurally through headphones in an audiometric room at 80 db (peak), and the cough was heard at 86 db (peak) above 0.0002 microbars.

Nineteen subjects reported that all speech sounds were present (the single subject reporting a missing phoneme selected the wrong one). The illusory perception of the absent phoneme was in keeping with the observations of others (graduate students and staff), who, despite knowledge of the actual stimulus, still perceived the missing phoneme as distinctly as the clearly pronounced sounds actually present.

No subject identified correctly the position of the cough, and half the subjects circled positions beyond the boundaries of the word "legislatures." The median distance separating responses from the true position was five phonemes. These errors were rather symmetrically distributed in time, with 11 subjects placing the cough early, and 9 late.

In order to determine whether phonemic restorations could be obtained with another extraneous sound, a second group of 20 subjects was tested under the same procedure except that the cough was replaced by a 1000-hz tone (intensity equal to the peak intensity of the cough). Results similar to those of the first experiment were obtained.

Every subject reported that all speech sounds were present, and no subject identified the position of the tone correctly. Eight subjects circled positions beyond the boundaries of the word "legislatures," the median distance separating responses from the true position was three phonemes, and most subjects (13) placed the tone earlier than its actual position, although this tendency to early placement was not statistically significant.

The inability to identify the position of extraneous sounds in sentences has been reported (1). In these studies very brief intrusive sounds (clicks and hisses) were used, and, as considerable care was taken to ensure that no phoneme was obliterated or masked phonemic restorations were not observed. Inability to identify temporal order is more general than had been thought; it occurs with sequences consisting solely of nonspeech sounds such as hisses, tones, and buzzes. It was suggested that accurate perception of order may be restricted to items which may be linked temporally to form speech or music (2).

Phonemic restorations are linked to language skills, which enable the listener to replace the correct sound. The experiments involving the deletion of the first "s" in "legislatures" did not permit the listener familiar with English any choice (that is, no other sound could produce an English word). But, Sherman (3) found that when a short cough was followed immediately by the sounds corresponding to "ite," so that the word fragment could have been derived from several words, such as "kite" or "bite," the listener used other words in the sentence to determine the phonemic restoration; when the preceding and following context indicated that the incomplete word was a verb referring to the activity of snarling dogs, the ambiguous fragment was perceived quite clearly as either "bite" or "fight."

Phonemic restorations are not restricted to single phonemes, but may involve deleted clusters of two or three sounds. Also, extraneous sounds other than coughs and tones (for example, buzzes) may be used to produce the illusion. But, when a speech sound was deleted and not replaced with an extraneous sound, the gap was recognized in its proper location, and illusory perception of the missing sound did not occur. Of course, unlike extraneous sounds, a silence would not occur normally unless produced by the speaker. Also, silent intervals have functions akin to phonemes, requiring their accurate identification and localization for speech comprehension.

The ability to understand speech with masked phonemes is not surprising; the redundancy of language can account readily for this. However, our lack of awareness of restorative processes—our illusory perception of the speaker's utterance rather than the stimulus actually reaching our ears—reflects characteristics of speech perception which may help us understand the perceptual mechanisms underlying verbal organization.

RICHARD M. WARREN*
*Department of Psychology,
University of Wisconsin-Milwaukee,
Milwaukee 53201*

References and Notes

1. P. Ladefoged and D. E. Broadbent, *Quart. J. Exp. Psychol.* **12**, 162 (1960); T. G. Bever, J. R. Lackner, R. Kirk, *Percept. Psychophys.* **5**, 225 (1969).
2. R. M. Warren, C. J. Obusek, R. M. Farmer, R. P. Warren, *Science* **164**, 586 (1969).
3. G. Sherman, unpublished study.
4. Supported by PHS grant NB05998-03 and by the University of Wisconsin-Milwaukee Graduate School. I thank C. J. Obusek for assistance.
* Visiting Scientist until August 1970 at the Institute of Experimental Psychology, Oxford University, Oxford, England.
12 November 1969

PERCEPTION OF VOCALIC DISTINCTIONS

As in the case of consonants, much of the research on vowel perception has focused on issues of variability and context-dependency. A central goal has been to explain the processes by which a listener is able to perceive the intended vowel of the speaker, despite the fact that the absolute formant frequencies of vowels change radically as a function of a number of factors, including phonetic context, speaker and speaking rate.

Various approaches to this problem are represented in this section. One approach involves a solution based on normalization. Ladefoged and Broadbent (1957) offer evidence that perceived vowel quality may arise from a normalization process wherein listeners treat formant frequencies of a target vowel not in an absolute manner, but in relation to the other vowels in the sentence context. Building in part on psychoacoustic studies of vowel perception by Chistovich and her colleagues, exemplified by Chistovich and Lublinskaya (1979), Syrdal and Gopal (1986) offer a model in which the auditory system transforms the formant frequency values of vowels in such a way as to reduce variability across speakers; this auditory transform, in conjunction with a decision metric, yields relatively accurate vowel identification. On this view, normalization is inherent in the transformation and classification processes for individual vowels.

The papers noted above all assume, at least tacitly, that it is the steady-state (or quasi-steady-state) portion of a vowel that is the basis for vowel identification—that the critical "slice" for perception is the section within the vowel nucleus that most closely approaches the vowel target. There is an alternative view, in which the critical information for vowel perception resides not in the vowel nucleus but instead in dynamic spectral information that is distributed across the entire syllable. Lindblom and Studdert-Kennedy (1967) offer evidence for this view by demonstrating that the trajectories of the formant transitions "into" and "out of" the vowel nucleus play an important role in vowel perception. Strange, Jenkins, and Johnson (1983) take the dynamic view further by showing that appropriately aligned formant transitions can lead to highly accurate vowel identification across speakers, even when the vowel nucleus itself is removed from the syllable. On the basis of their findings, Strange *et al.* speculate that the time-varying spectral properties of vowels may remain invariant across such contextual factors as speaker and speaking rate. Such invariant information would obviate the need for a normalization process [see Stevens and Blumstein (1978) in the section on Theoretical Perspectives and Summerfield (1981) in the section on Perception of Consonantal Distinctions].

Two additional issues are addressed in the two remaining papers in this section. In the first, Pisoni (1973) exemplifies the long-standing tradition in speech research of explicitly comparing the perception of consonants and vowels [another instance can be found in Studdert-Kennedy and Shankweiler (1970) in the section on Theoretical Perspectives]. More specifically, Pisoni uses an information-processing framework to investigate the relative roles of auditory and phonetic short-term memory in the perception of these two classes of phonetic segments. Finally, Darwin (1984) uses vowel perception as an occasion to investigate a more general issue in speech perception: How it is that the listener is able to isolate the speech of a particular talker when produced in concert with the speech of other talkers, as well as with other sounds. Although this problem has received relatively little attention to date, it is of prime importance. An adequate model of speech perception must explain not only perception in a controlled laboratory setting, but also perception in the noisy natural world.

Hearing Research, 1 (1979) 185–195   185

© Elsevier/North-Holland Biomedical Press

THE 'CENTER OF GRAVITY' EFFECT IN VOWEL SPECTRA AND CRITICAL DISTANCE BETWEEN THE FORMANTS: PSYCHOACOUSTICAL STUDY OF THE PERCEPTION OF VOWEL-LIKE STIMULI

LUDMILLA A. CHISTOVICH and VALENTINA V. LUBLINSKAYA

Pavlov Institute of Physiology, Academy of Sciences of the U.S.S.R., Leningrad, U.S.S.R.

(Received 27 August 1978; accepted 25 February 1979)

A two-formant synthetic vowel with closely spaced formants (F_1 and F_2 being fixed) can be made perceptually similar to a single-formant stimulus with $F^\star = (F_1 + F_2)/2$ by adjusting the A_2/A_1-amplitude ratio of the formants. The critical distance between the formants (Δz_c) that corresponds to the disappearance of this 'center of gravity' effect was found to be equal to 3.0–3.5 Bark. A close to continuous relation between A_2/A_1 and $F^\star$ of a single-formant matching stimulus was found for stimuli with $\Delta z < \Delta z_c$. A clear discontinuous relationship between A_2/A_1 and $F^\star$ was observed for stimuli with $\Delta z > \Delta z_c$. For stimuli with $\Delta z > \Delta z_c$, the formant amplitudes appeared to be of minor importance, the vowel quality being determined by the frequency locations of the formant peaks in the vowel spectrum. Formant peaks can be detected even if they are represented by very small spectral irregularities. Possible relations between peak extraction and 'center of gravity' effects are discussed.

Key words: vowels; spectrum shape; auditory processing.

Early studies of synthetic vowel perception suggest that vowel quality is determined by something close to the 'center of gravity' of formant clusters [7,10,20]. Data in favor of the 'center of gravity' hypothesis have been presented in more recent reports [4,3]. Bedrov et al. [2] looking for as simple and convincing as possible manifestations of the 'center of gravity' effect, used single-formant stimuli ($F^\star$ — variable) and two-formant stimuli with closely spaced formants ($F_2 - F_1 = 350$ Hz); in their experiments the position of formants along the frequency scale was varied, and two values of A_2/A_1 were used. The change of A_2/A_1 was found to be equivalent to the displacement of the stimulus spectrum along the frequency scale; maximum similarity of single-formant stimuli appeared to correspond to a condition of $F_1 < F^\star < F_2$, with $F^\star$ being closer to F_1 if $A_1 > A_2$, and $F^\star$ being closer to F_2 if $A_1 < A_2$.

The data presented in refs. 7, 10, 20, 4 and 3 seem to indicate that the 'center of gravity' refers to some local properties of spectrum shape — to the gross maxima or to the formant cluster location. If this is the case, the manifestations of the 'center of gravity' effect are bound to disappear when the formant distance exceeds some critical value. In this study we tried to obtain some preliminary estimations of this expected critical distance and to investigate the amplitude vs. frequency relationships for stimuli with less — and more — than critical separation of the formants.

186

PROCEDURE

The subjects were sitting in a sound-proof booth, and the stimuli were presented periodically in pairs. Each stimulus had a duration of 320 ms. The interval between the pairs was 600 ms. The stimuli within the pairs were separated by 320 ms. The method of adjustment, with some modifications, was used in all the experiments. The subject could control one of the parameters of the second stimulus in the pair. The experimenter selected in random order one of the prescribed sets of the standard parameter values. After each adjustment, the signal was switched off for about 30 s.

The excitation source to synthesize both the standard and the variable sound was 30 μs square wave pulses, with a repetition rate of 100 Hz. Two independent filtering systems were used to shape the spectrum, each consisting of two parallel formant channels. The formant filters consisted of two series connected bandpass filters with a slope of about 30 dB per octave on both sides of the maxima. Formant frequency could be controlled either in steps (by the experimenter) or continuously (by the subject).

Formant amplitude was controlled by means of attenuators. When the difference in attenuation in the formant channels was less than about 25 dB it truly reflected the level difference between formant peaks of the stimulus spectrum. Some deformations of the spectrum shape in the vicinity of the weak formant frequency were observed for higher attenuation differences, owing to the phase responses of the filters. These deformations were pronounced only for stimuli with the second formant being the weak one (see the text). A heterodyne spectrum analyzer C5-3 with an H-110 level recorder was used for spectrum analysis.

Stimuli were presented monaurally through a TD-6 earphone, with a cushion for an AR-03 speech audiometer. The frequency response of the earphone as measured in a NBS 9-A coupler was flat up to 5 kHz. For an additional check of the cushion, the auditory thresholds were measured for the same subjects using our earphone as well as a TDH-39 earphone, calibrated on 9-A coupler, with an MX41/AR cushion. No significant differences in thresholds could be observed.

The two authors served as subjects. They had normal hearing and were highly experienced in psychoacoustical measurements.

RESULTS

Critical distance between the formants in two-formant stimuli

The critical distance between the formants can be estimated by studying the relation between F^* of a single-formant matching stimulus and F_1 of a two-formant standard, F_2 being fixed and $A_1 \approx A_2$. When $F_2 - F_1$ is small enough, the decrease of F_1 is accompanied by a decrease of F^*. At some point this relationship disappears with a sudden increase of the spread of F^* settings (Chistovich and Sheikin, in press). Unfortunately this approach is too time-consuming. The approach applied in this study was based on the reversion of the matching procedure and on making use of the subject's ability to introspect. Single-formant stimuli with $F^* = (F_1 + F_2)/2$ were used as the standards; the subject was to control A_2/A_1 of the two-formant variable, F_1 and F_2 being fixed. The task of the subject was to find out whether by moving the variable along the A_2/A_1 continuum it was possible to locate the point where the variable was closer to the standard than at the end-points of the continuum, the end-points corresponding to complete suppression of either the first or the second formant. If the variable at one end-point was, for instance, preceived as [u], and at another end-point as [a], with the standard being perceived as [o], the subject had to find out whether it was possible to change the variable into an [o]-like vowel. F_2 was held fixed during the experiment; the experimenter chose one of the preselected F_1 values of the variable and the corresponding $F^* = (F_1 + F_2)/2$ value of the standard. The subject was allowed as much time as he needed to reach a reliable 'yes' or 'no' decision.

Fig. 1 shows the percentage of 'no' decisions averaged over both subjects as a function of F_1, F_2 being the parameter of the curve. An F_1 value corresponding to the 50% point on the curve and the F_2 value for this curve were converted from Hz into Bark [21]. An approximation of $z(f)$ function by $z = 6.7 \times \text{Arsh} \, ((f - 20)/600)$ was used [18]. The difference between these two z values was regarded as an estimation of Δz_c, the critical distance between the formants. The following three Δz_c values were thus obtained: 3.0 Bark for $F_2 = 0.7$ kHz, 3.4 Bark for $F_2 = 1.0$ kHz and 3.2 Bark for $F_2 = 1.3$ kHz. They are rather close to each other and do not contradict the estimations obtained by Chistovich and Sheikin (in press): $3.3 < \Delta z_c < 4.3$ for $F_2 = 1.4$ kHz and $3.1 < \Delta z_c < 4.0$ for $F_2 = 1.8$ kHz. It seems reasonably safe to conclude that the critical distance between the formants is around 3.0–3.5 Bark.

Single-formant to two-formant matching

The first attempt to study the quantitative relation between the formant amplitude ratio and the frequency of the matching formant was made by Mushnikov et al. [14]. Three-formant stimuli ($F_1 = 0.3$ kHz, $F_2 = 1.5$ kHz, $F_3 = 2.5$ kHz) with a varied amplitude of the third formant were used as the standards. Two-formant stimuli with $F_1 = 0.3$ kHz and F_2^* controlled by the subject served as the matching variable. The results failed to support the 'center of gravity' hypothesis. A clearly discontinuous relation between F_2^* and A_3 was observed in the data from at least one of three subjects participating in the

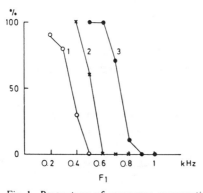

Fig. 1. Percentage of responses representing subject's failure to find a match between two-formant stimuli and a single-formant one as a function of formant spacing. Each curve corresponds to the set of two-formant stimuli with fixed F_2: 1 – 0.7 kHz; 2 – 1.0 kHz; 3 – 1.3 kHz.

188

experiment: the subject adjusted F_2^* either close to F_2 or close to F_3, the proportion of these choices was influenced by the A_3 value (see ref. 6, pp. 270–272, for discussion). The next attempt was made by Chistovich and Sheikin (in press) who used the two-formant standards ($F_1 = 1.5$ kHz, $F_2 = 2.5$ kHz; A_2/A_1 being varied) and the single-formant variable. A close to continuous relationship between F^* and A_2/A_1 was found. The contradictory results obtained in these two studies might result from the unfortunate choice of the distance between the formants – it was equal to 3.3 Bark, thus being close to Δz_c found in our experiments. Bearing this in mind in this study we used three sets of two-formant standards: two sets with $\Delta z < \Delta z_c$ ($F_1 = 0.4$ kHz, $F_2 = 0.7$ kHz and $F_1 = 0.8$ kHz, $F_2 = 1.3$ kHz) and one set with $\Delta z > \Delta z_c$ ($F_1 = 0.6$ kHz, $F_2 = 1.3$ kHz).

The experimenter changed A_2/A_1 by decreasing either the A_1 or the A_2 level from its initial 75 dB SPL value. As the two-formant standards with $A_1 \approx A_2$ were louder than the single-formant variable, the subject was instructed first to adjust the overall level of the variable and then to go on with the matching. The best match in vowel quality was to be used as a criterion for the F^* adjustment. From 5 to 10 F^* adjustments were made by the subject for each of the A_2/A_1 values. Arithmetic mean, $\overline{F}$, and range of spread, $F_{max}^* - F_{min}^*$, were used as parameters of adjustments. In the case of a clearly bimodal distribution, two $\overline{F}^*$ values were computed.

Fig. 2 shows the results obtained for stimuli with $\Delta z < \Delta z_c$ as well as for the stimuli with $\Delta z > \Delta z_c$. Both sets of stimuli differ only in F_1, F_2 being the same. (The data obtained for the second set of stimuli with $\Delta z < \Delta z_c$ appeared to be practically similar to that presented in Fig. 2, left column, and are thus omitted.) Apparently continuous relations between F^* and A_2/A_1 exist for stimuli with $\Delta z < \Delta z_c$. ($F_{max}^* - F_{min}^*$) values are rather small, especially in the V.L. data (bottom left). There is no great difference in performance between the subjects – individual $\overline{F}^*$ values are close enough to the averaged curve shown in Fig. 2, top left and bottom left. The data show that the range of formant level differences where the F^* location is influenced by both formants is about 40 dB wide.

Clear discontinuous relations between F^* and A_2/A_1 are seen in L.Ch. data for stimuli with $\Delta z > \Delta z_c$. F^* is adjusted either close to F_1 or close to F_2. The shift from the F_1 preference to the F_2 preference does not correspond to the equality of the formant amplitudes; it occurs when the second formant is about 10 dB lower.

The $\overline{F}^*$ vs. A_2/A_1 relation for V.L. could be approximated by a smooth curve, but the enormous spread of F^* settings points to an almost random behaviour of the subject. In the middle range of A_2/A_1 the values of ($F_{max}^* - F_{min}^*$) in Fig. 2, bottom right, are ten times higher than those in Fig. 2, bottom left.

There is no doubt that at least two parameters are needed to describe the vowel quality of stimuli with $\Delta z > \Delta z_c$. One of these parameters must correspond to the frequency of the dominating formant. Experiments on single-formant matching cannot reveal the nature of the other parameters.

Two-formant to two-formant matching

According to ref. 7, the variation of the first formant amplitude of a front vowel does not effect the vowel quality. The timbre can only be made duller or sharper. If this is true

189

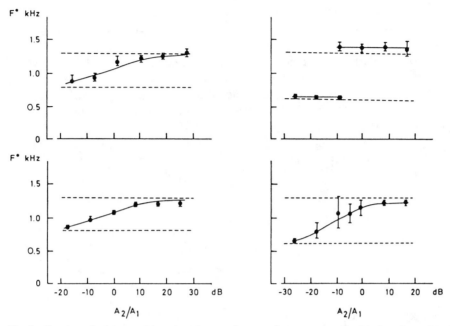

Fig. 2. Results of the matching experiments for two-formant stimuli with less-than-critical (left column) and more-than-critical (right column) formant spacing. Points correspond to $\bar{F}^{\star}$, vertical bars to $(F^{\star}_{max} - F^{\star}_{min})$. Broken lines indicate F_1 and F_2 of two-formant stimuli. Rows: subject L.Ch. (top) and subject V.L. (bottom).

for all stimuli with $\Delta z > \Delta z_c$, then the variable shown in Fig. 3 I, bottom, ought to be most similar to the standard (Fig. 3 I, top) on the condition that the F_1 of the variable is equal to F_1 of the standard. It is self-evident that such a relationship must cease to obtain when the A_1 of the standard is made so small that the first formant peak cannot be detected in the spectrum of the standard.

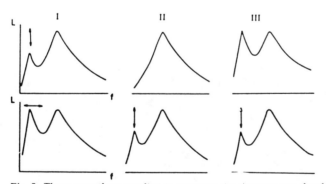

Fig. 3. Three procedures applied to measure the first formant threshold. Top: the first stimulus in the pair controlled by the experimenter. Bottom: the second stimulus in the pair controlled by the subject.

190

Two sets of standards with $\Delta z > \Delta z_c$ ($F_1 = 0.3$ kHz, $F_2 = 1.0$ kHz and $F_1 = 0.5$ kHz, $F_2 = 1.3$ kHz) were used in our experiments. In the experiments on F_1^* matching, the experimenter changed A_1 in the standard trying to find the threshold and to obtain no less than 10 F_1^* adjustments for each of the A_1 values around the threshold. F_2 of the variable was equal to F_2 of the standard, and both formants of the variable were of equal amplitudes. The subject was allowed to change the overall intensity of the variable to make both stimuli equally loud before starting the matching. A similar procedure was applied in the F_2^* matching experiments.

Figs. $4a_1-d_1$ show the F_1^* vs. A_1/A_2 relationships obtained. The clear threshold-like effect is evident: up to some decrease of the A_1 level all the matches group around F_1. An

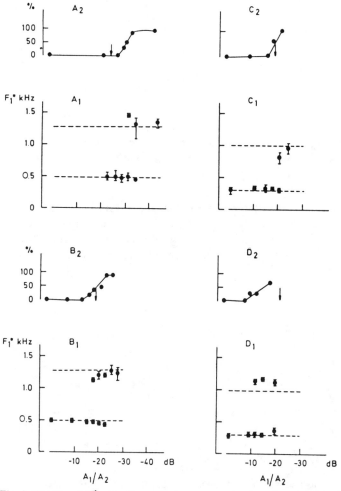

Fig. 4. Results of F_1^* adjusting experiments. a_1-d_1 show location of F_1^* settings; a_2-d_2 show the percentage of cases when F_1^* was set close to F_2. Broken lines indicate F_1 and F_2 of the standard.

additional decrease of A_1 causes some F_1^* matches to approach F_2. Figs. $4a_2 - d_2$ show the percentage of F_1^* being close to F_2 as a function of the first formant level. Although statistically reliable psychometric functions cannot be obtained there is no doubt that the uncertainty range is rather wide.

Similar results were found in the experiments on F_2^* matching (Fig. 5). The data for the stimuli with $F_1 = 0.5$ kHz, $F_2 = 1.3$ kHz are not quite reliable because the A_2 threshold appeared to be close to a degree of attenuation in the second formant channel accompanied by a deformation of the spectrum shape of the standard in the F_2 region. The single spectral peak at the F_2 frequency was replaced by two peaks in the vicinity of F_2 —

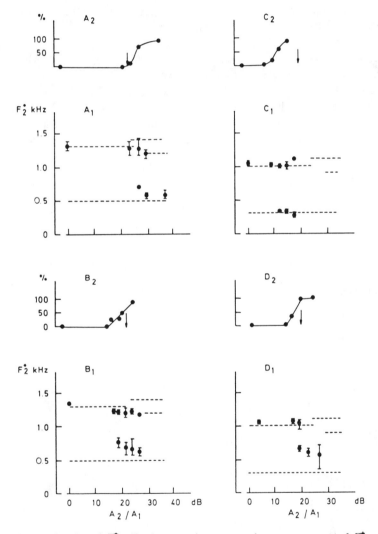

Fig. 5. Results of F_2^* adjusting experiments. $a_1 - d_1$ show location of F_2^* settings; $a_2 - d_2$ show the percentage of cases when F_2^* was set close to F_1.

192

see broken lines in Figs. $5a_1$, b_1. The same effect was observed for stimuli with $F_1 = 0.3$ kHz, $F_2 = 1.0$ kHz, but in this case it had no influence on the results — the A_2 threshold appeared to be higher.

The data in Fig. 4 and Fig. 5 suggest three perceptual categories for two-formant stimuli varying in A_2/A_1, F_1 and F_2 being fixed, and $\Delta z > \Delta z_c$. One category corresponds to stimuli with both formants above the threshold. The vowel quality of these stimuli is determined by the frequencies of both formants. Two other categories correspond to 'single-formant' stimuli with F^* being equal either to F_1 or to F_2. If this is true, the formant threshold could be measured also by adjusting the formant amplitude corresponding to the boundary between 'two-formant' and 'single-formant' categories; the value of the threshold measured by this method ought to be close to the value corresponding to the 50% point in Figs. $4a_2 - d_2$ or Figs. $5a_2 - d_2$.

Figs. 3 II, III show two procedures of formant threshold measurement by means of A_1 adjusting. In both cases the subject had to control A_1 in the variable (F_1, F_2 and A_2 were fixed) and try to locate the boundary between a given back vowel and a vowel close either to [t] ($F_1 = 0.3$ kHz, $F_2 = 1.0$ kHz) or to a low [ə] ($F_1 = 0.5$ kHz, $F_2 = 1.3$ kHz). The subject was presented with a standard, which he was instructed to ignore, corresponding in one case to a single-formant stimulus with $F^* = F_2$ and in another case, to a two-formant stimulus with the same formant frequencies as in the variable and with equal amplitudes

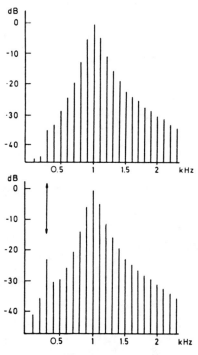

Fig. 6. Examples of spectra with just detectable first formant $F_0 = 100$ Hz, $F_1 = 300$ Hz, $F_2 = 1000$ Hz.

of both formants. Similar procedures were used in the experiments on A_2 adjusting.

Thresholds were computed as arithmetic means of 10 settings; the standard deviation of the settings ranged from 1.4 to 3.3 dB.

In all 8 cases (4 stimuli conditions, two subjects) the thresholds measured by the first procedure (single-formant standard) appeared to be lower than those measured by the second procedure; the average difference in thresholds was equal to 12.4 dB. That means that some parameters of formant peak detection are context-sensitive.

Arrows in Fig. 4 and Fig. 5 represent the thresholds averaged over two procedures. In 4 out of 8 cases they are quite close to the 50% points, in two cases they are displaced to the right, and in two cases to the left of 50% points. It seems possible to conclude that the detection of the formant peak is automatically accompanied by receiving the information about the location of this peak along the frequency scale.

Taking into account the values of the averaged thresholds for A_1 and A_2 one can estimate the dynamic range of A_2/A_1 corresponding to the 'two-formant' vowel category. It is about 45–50 dB wide, thus being only a little wider than the dynamic range for the 'center of gravity' (see Fig. 2).

Fig. 6 shows two examples of spectra with just detectable first formants. One of them (above) corresponds to the threshold measured by the most sensitive procedure — using the single-formant standard. The first formant is represented in this case by a small irregularity on the spectrum envelope. This is in good agreement with the previously reported data [13,5]. The second example (below) corresponds to the averaged threshold. In this case the spectral peak is quite pronounced.

DISCUSSION

The data obtained for two-formant stimuli with widely spaced formants suggest that if the formant peaks are detected, the relative amplitudes of the formants are of minor importance for vowel quality. Stimuli with quite different overall spectrum shape are perceived as most similar if their formant frequencies coincide. This is in agreement with the results reported in refs. 11 and 12 but is not compatible with the suggestion [15,16] that vowel parameters correspond to some low-frequency components of the whole spectrum shape curve.

The values of Δz_c obtained in this study as well as the fact of monotonic relations between F^* and A_2/A_1 for stimuli with $\Delta z < \Delta z_c$ could help to explain the data on single-formant and two-formant approximation of vowels [7,10,4,3] by reference to the formant structure of natural vowels [8,9].

In back vowels the distance between F_1 and F_2 is less than Δz_c, the relative amplitude of the second formant increases from [u] to [a]. Thus the single-formant approximation must be possible, with F^* being most close to F_1 in [u] and being displaced toward F_2 in [a]. These effects have been described by Delattre et al. [7].

In front vowels the distance between F_1 and F_2 exceeds Δz_c, but the distance between F_2 and F_3 (F_4) is less than Δz_c. In the most front vowel [i] A_2 is less than A_3. Thus to approximate front vowels two-formant stimuli are needed. F_2^* must be most displaced upward from F_2 in a two-formant [i]. These effects have been observed in a number of studies [7,10,20,4,3].

194

Both the minor importance of the formant amplitudes when the formants are widely spaced and the equivalence of amplitude changes to frequency shifts for closely spaced formants point to positional coding of spectrum shape — description of the pattern by indicating the locations of some 'objects' (maxima, irregularities) discovered on this pattern. Taking into account the 'center of gravity' effect and Δz_c values, one might expect that the 'objects' detected on the spectrum contour correspond to gross spectral maxima. The data obtained for stimuli with $\Delta z > \Delta z_c$ clearly disagree with this idea — just detectable formants may be represented by quite small irregularities on the spectrum shape. It seems that the only model which can conform both with the 'center of gravity' effect and with the small formant peak detection would be a model that performs a serial processing of spectral information; first it extracts the peaks and then it averages the results over wide intervals of the frequency scale. A lateral inhibition model adjusted to fit the psychoacoustical data on formant peak detection has been described [6,18]. Here we shall discuss only the problem concerning the averaging of data along the frequency scale.

One approach to simulate the 'center of gravity' effect is to use a row of many summators with highly overlapping summation intervals and with closely spaced central frequencies. The most unpleasant problem in this approach concerns the procedure of selecting the elements with maximal output: the locations of these elements would represent the 'center of gravity' positions.

Another aproach is to use a set of rather few summators with a spacing of central frequencies comparable to the width of the summation interval. The output information in this case must not be strictly positional — along with the location of 'excited' elements, the amount of 'excitation' in adjacent elements is to be available.

The relation between the frequency of the input single-formant stimulus and the output response of such a set can be described as a locally-continuous scale.

The subject's impression in the matching experiments is that he is using a scale with the end points corresponding to two adjacent vowels compatible with the standard. In changing the variable he is trying to minimize the difference in the positions between the variable and the standard along the scale. This seems to be rather close to what could be expected from the observer having at his disposal the above-mentioned set of summators and using this set to match the stimuli.

Assuming that each summator corresponds to a vowel (or a class of vowels), it is possible to use the frequency of a single-formant stimulus best approximating this vowel as estimation of the central frequency of the summator. All back vowels [u], [o], [ɔ], [ɑ] and [a] can be approximated by single-formant stimuli. The best F^* value for [u] is around 0.3 kHz, and the best F^* value for [a] is around 1.2 kHz [7]. The average inter-vowel interval is equal to 1.5–1.6 Bark. Assuming that Δz_c corresponds to the interval of summation, we can conclude that the spacing is equal to about half the summation interval. For an estimation of the inter-vowel interval in the high frequency region, the data on two-formant approximation of the vowels [ɪ], [ʉ], [y], [i] can be used. All these vowels can be synthesized using the same F_1 value [11,17]. Data on mimicking [1] and on similarity scaling [19] suggest that the users of quite different languages can differentiate between all the corresponding natural vowels although this differentiation is not perfect. The best F_2^* for [i] is around 2.9–3.2 kHz [7,3,17], the best F_2^* for [ɪ] is around 1.4–1.5 kHz [17]. This corresponds to an average inter-vowel interval 1.1–1.25 Bark wide.

195

These considerations suggest that the 'center of gravity' perhaps does not really exist as an intermediate variable extracted from the speech signal. The 'center of gravity' effect might reflect the spatial organization of the neural net that performs the spectral data processing.

REFERENCES

[1] Avakjan, R.V. (1976): Study of isolated vowel perception by Russian language users (normal persons and persons with 'sensory' and 'motor' aphasia). Fisiologia Cheloveka 2, 81–89.

[2] Bedrov, Ja.A., Chistovich, L.A. and Sheikin, R.L. (1976): Frequency location of the 'center of gravity' of the formants as the useful parameter in vowel perception. Akust. Zh. 24, 480–486.

[3] Carlson, R., Fant, G. and Granström, B. (1975): Two-formant models, pitch, and vowel perception. In: Auditory Analysis and Perception of Speech, pp. 55–82. Editors: G. Fant and M.R.A. Tatham. Academic Press, New York.

[4] Carlson, R., Granström, B. and Fant, G. (1970): Some studies concerning perception of isolated vowels. STL-QPSR 2–3, 19–35.

[5] Chistovich, L.A. (1971): Auditory processing of speech stimuli – evidences from psychoacoustics and neurophysiology. In: Proc. 7th Int. Congress on Acoustics, Budapest, Vol. 1, pp. 27–42.

[6] Chistovich, L.A., Ventsov, A.V., Granstrem, M.P. et al. (1976): Fiziologia Rechi. Vosprijatie Rechi Chelovekom (Physiology of Speech. Speech Perception). Nauka, Leningrad.

[7] Delattre, P., Liberman, A.M., Cooper, F.S. and Gerstman, L.J. (1952): An experimental study of the acoustic determinants of vowel colour: observations on one- and two-formant vowels synthesized from spectrographic patterns. Word 8, 195–210.

[8] Fant, G. (1973): Speech sounds and features. MIT Press, Cambridge, Mass.

[9] Fant, G. (1975): Non-uniform vowel normalization. STL-QPSR 2–3, 1–19.

[10] Miller, R. (1953): Auditory tests with synthetic vowels. J. Acoust. Soc. Am. 25, 114–121.

[11] Lindqvist, J. and Pauli, S. (1968): The role of relative spectrum levels in vowel perception. Report of the 6th Int. Congress on Acoustics, Tokyo, Vol. 2, B 91–94.

[12] Mushnikov, V.N. and Chistovich, L.A. (1971): Auditory representation of the vowel. I. Cues for [i] and [e] distinction. In: Analyz Rechevych Signalov Chelovekom, pp. 5–10. Nauka, Leningrad.

[13] Mushnikov, V.N. and Chistovich, L.A. (1971): Auditory representation of the vowel II. Detection of the second formant in the synthetic vowel. In: Analyz Rechevych Signalov Chelovekom, pp. 11–19. Nauka, Leningrad.

[14] Mushnikov, V.N., Slepokurova, N.A. and Zukov, S.Ja. (1974): On the auditory correlates of the second formant of vowels. Preprints of the 8th Int. Congress on Acoustics, London, p. 323.

[15] Plomp, R. (1975): Auditory analysis and timbre perception. In: Auditory Analysis and Perception of Speech, pp. 7–22. Editors: G. Fant and M.A.A. Tatham. Academic Press, New York.

[16] Pols, L.C.W. (1977): Spectral analysis and identification of Dutch vowels in monosyllabic words. Institute for Perception, TNO, Soesterberg, The Netherlands.

[17] Sheikin, R.L. and Golusina, A.G. (1971): Scaling of vowels in reference to 'male–female' voices. In: Sensory Systems, Vol. 2, pp. 83–91. Nauka, Leningrad.

[18] Tjomov, V.L. (1971): A model to describe the results of psycho-acoustical experiments on steady-state stimuli. In: Analyz Rechevych Signalov Chelovekom, pp. 36–49. Nauka, Leningrad.

[19] Terbeek, D. (1977): A cross-language multidimensional scaling study of vowel perception. p. 37. Working Papers in Phonetics, University of California, Los Angeles.

[20] Warshawskij, L.A. and Litvak, I.M. (1955): Study of the formant structure and some other characteristics of Russian speech sounds. In: Problemy Fisiologicheskoj Akustiki Leningrad 3, 5–17.

[21] Zwicker, E. and Feldtkeller, R. (1967): Das Ohr als Nachrichtenempfänger, 2nd edn. Verlag Hirzel, Stuttgart.

Perceiving vowels in the presence of another sound: Constraints on formant perception

C. J. Darwin

Laboratory of Experimental Psychology, University of Sussex, Brighton, BN1 9QG, England

(Received 9 February 1984; accepted for publication 15 June 1984)

Speech is normally heard against a background of other sounds, yet our ability to isolate perceptually the speech of a particular talker is poorly understood. The experiments reported here illustrate two different ways in which a listener may decide whether a tone at a harmonic of a vowel's fundamental forms part of the vowel. First, a tone that starts or stops at a different time from a vowel is less likely to be heard as part of that vowel than if it is simultaneous with it; moreover, this effect occurs regardless of whether the tone has been added to a normal vowel, or to a vowel that has already been reduced in energy at the tone's frequency. Second, energy added simultaneously with a vowel, at a harmonic frequency near to the vowel's first formant, may or may not be fully incorporated into the vowel percept, depending on its relation to the first formant: When the additional tone is just below the vowel's first formant frequency, it is less likely to be incorporated than energy that is added at a frequency just above the first formant. Both experiments show that formants may only be estimated after properties of the sound wave have been grouped into different apparent sound sources. The first result illustrates a general auditory mechanism for performing perceptual grouping, while the second result illustrates a mechanism that may use a more specific constraint on vocal-tract transfer functions.

PACS numbers: 43.70.Dn, 43.66.Jh

INTRODUCTION

It is a curious fact that most experiments on the perception of speech have used only speech as a stimulus. The fact is curious since in the normal course of events we hear speech in the presence of other sounds and other voices. Studying the perception of the speech of a single speaker in isolation has told us a great deal about which acoustic consequences of a speaker's articulation are necessary or sufficient for the appropriate percept, but we know very little about how these acoustic properties are actually extracted from the raw sound wave. The problem is severe, since for any speech recorded outside of the soundproof, anechoic chamber, properties of the recorded soundwave will not correspond in a simple way with properties of the spoken soundwave. Other sound sources and echoes will also contribute to the recording.

A conceptual distinction needs to be made (cf. Bregman, 1978) between properties of the raw soundwave and derived properties that may be *source specific*. The large literature on speech perception has addressed itself to the problem of what source-specific properties are perceptually salient but has almost entirely ignored the problem of how such properties could be extracted from the raw acoustic signal. Yet the problem lies at the very heart of successful speech recognition and has radical theoretical implications. What constraints need to be applied by a process that can separate the speech of a single speaker from other sounds? Are they speech specific or can constraints that apply to sounds in general do the trick? In order to answer these questions, experiments need to be considered on the perception of speech in the presence of other structured sounds.

A. Perceptual grouping of speech sounds

Most experiments on the perception of speech in the presence of other sounds have used one of two types of additional sound—either random noise (Miller and Nicely, 1955; Pickett, 1957) or an additional formant (Darwin, 1981) or voice (Brokx and Nooteboom, 1982; Darwin, 1981; Scheffers, 1983). With random noise, the main perceptual problem is the detection of structure, whereas with an additional formant or voice, the main problem is to group evident structure appropriately (cf. Bregman, 1978; McAdams, 1980; McAdams and Bregman, 1979).

In performing appropriate grouping of formants, it is clear that a common harmonic spacing is influential. Sentences synthesized on a different fundamental frequency from an interfering passage of speech are more intelligible than those of the same fundamental (Brokx and Nooteboom, 1982). The same is true for pairs of simultaneous isolated vowel sounds (Scheffers, 1983); the intelligibility of the vowels is slightly higher when they are synthesized on different fundamentals (80%) than when they are synthesized on the same fundamental (68%). Similarly, when four formants may be grouped in two alternative ways to give both a three-formant syllable and a separate single formant, listeners tend to group together the three formants that share a common fundamental (Darwin, 1981, experiment IV).

The size of the grouping effect by a common fundamental is not large in some experiments, and clearly can have no effect in voiceless speech, or for formants in which the individual harmonics are too close together, relative to the critical bandwidth, to be resolved (but see Bregman *et al.*, 1983). It is likely that other factors also play a role. In Scheffers' experiment, for example, listeners could identify 68% of vowels presented in pairs on the same fundamental frequency. Grouping by fundamental is of no use in separating the different vowels in this experiment, yet listeners still performed substantially above chance. Constraints other than fundamental frequency must have been used to separate out those formants that could form one of the nine different vowels used in the experiment.

Another factor that could be important in grouping together different formants in running speech is onset time. A formant that starts at a different time from others is less likely to contribute to the phonetic quality of a syllable than if it starts at the same time as the others (Darwin, 1981 experiment IV; cf. Bregman and Pinker, 1978; Dannenbring and Bregman, 1978; Rasch, 1978). A difference in onset time is not, of itself, sufficient reason to separate one formant from the remainder: The first formant of an aspirated stop typically starts later than the higher formants, yet it is well integrated into the vowel. Rather, a difference in onset time provides the potential for a separate perceptual group.

B. Estimating *F*1 frequency

The experiments described in this paper form part of a series (see also Darwin, 1983; Darwin and Sutherland, 1984); examining the perception of sounds that differ in their first formant frequency, in the presence of extra energy at one of the harmonic frequencies close to the first formant. The first formant is of particular interest in the context of the extraction of speech features, since its value almost always has to be inferred from the raw spectral data presented by the ear to the brain. In the first formant region, the individual harmonics of voiced speech are generally spaced by substantially more than the critical bandwidth as recently described (Moore and Glasberg, 1983) and so are resolved as separate peaks. In general, there is no actual peak present at the frequency corresponding to the first formant frequency. Yet it is clear that the percept of vowel quality is not given by the frequency of the most intense harmonic (Karnickaya *et al.*, 1975; Carlson *et al.*, 1975; Assmann and Nearey, 1983); rather, some smoothing function is applied to the spectral peaks or some weighted average formed of them in order to estimate the formant frequency. The need to derive the formant frequency raises the following question: Which frequencies should be included in the estimation procedure? Can some of the frequency components present at a particular time be excluded from the estimation procedure by virtue of, for example, their having a different starting time from the other frequencies present in the vowel? Our recent experiments have indeed shown that they can.

C. Perceptual grouping of first formant harmonics

When extra energy is added to a vowel at a harmonic frequency close to the first formant, the vowel quality changes, indicating that the extra energy is being perceived as part of the vowel and is contributing to the estimated frequency of the first formant. However, if this extra energy is made to start earlier than the main vowel, listeners can perceptually subtract it out from the vowel, yielding the original vowel quality (Darwin, 1983). Such perceptual sub-

traction of a leading tone could be due to two types of mechanism: peripheral adaptation at the frequency of the leading tone (cf. Summerfield *et al.*, 1981, 1984), or perceptual grouping on the basis of onset-time differences. Darwin and Sutherland (1984) have argued that perceptual grouping plays a substantial role in the effect on the following grounds. First, an additional (500 Hz) tone can be separated from a *short* vowel when it starts at the same time as the vowel but continues after it; with longer vowels, the perceptual separation produced by a leading tone is unchanged, but that produced by a lagging tone is weaker (presumably because the listener has already decided on the vowel quality by the time the tone is heard sticking out at the end of the vowel). Second, the perceptual separation of a leading tone (at 500 Hz) from the following vowel is reduced if the leading portion of the tone is accompanied by a second (1000 Hz) tone that starts at the same time as the leading tone, but which stops as the vowel starts; the 1000-Hz tone tends to form a new perceptual group with the leading portion of the 500-Hz tone, leaving the remainder of the 500-Hz tone free to be incorporated again into the vowel. This result cannot be explained by adaptation.

In the experiments reported here, we pursue two questions relating to the perceptual separation of a tone from a vowel. First, does the perceptual separation due to timing differences only hold when the sound that results from subtracting out the extra energy has a more "normal" vowel spectrum? Second, what are the limits on the amount of energy that may be added at a harmonic frequency and that will still be incorporated into the vowel percept?

I. EXPERIMENT 1

We have shown previously that the change in vowel quality, produced by adding extra energy to a harmonic near the first formant frequency, can be reduced or abolished when the energy starts (Darwin, 1983) at a different time from the main vowel. It is not clear to what extent our results reflect a tendency on the part of subjects to prefer simple vowels (as produced by a formant synthesizer with conventional buzz excitation) over those whose harmonics have been modified in intensity. The previous experiments showed that subjects can use onset and offset time to separate a normally synthesized vowel from an additional tone. But what if a vowel sound is used that gives a normal spectrum *before* the additional tone has been subtracted; will perceptual separation occur, giving an abnormal vowel percept?

In order to assess whether perceptual separation of the tone and vowel is influenced by the resulting vowel spectrum, experiment 1 compares the case where energy is added to a harmonic of a normal vowel, with the case where energy is added to a vowel that has already been *depleted* in energy at that frequency. If a subjective preference for a particular type of vowel spectrum is influencing our results, then we would expect to find that temporal offsets had less of an effect on the separation of energy added to a depleted vowel than on the separation of energy added to a normal vowel. In the former case, *retaining* the extra energy as part of the vowel percept gives a normal vowel spectrum, while in the latter, *separating* the energy gives the normal spectrum.

A. Method

Perceived vowel quality is estimated by measuring the phoneme boundary between /I/ and /ɛ/ along a continuum of sounds differing in their first formant. We refer to the first formant frequency that was used to synthesize a sound as its *nominal F* 1. When we add energy to a harmonic of a vowel, its *nominal F* 1 stays constant by definition. Phoneme boundaries for the various conditions are measured in terms of this nominal *F* 1. So, if the addition of energy to a vowel has no perceptual effect on its quality, then the phoneme boundary will stay at the same nominal *F* 1 value. However, if adding energy produces the percept of a higher *F* 1 frequency, then the phoneme boundary will appear at a *lower* nominal *F* 1 value along the continuum. Conversely, if adding energy produces the percept of a lower *F* 1 frequency, then the phoneme boundary will appear at a *higher* nominal *F* 1 value.

1. Synthesis techniques

The basic continuum of sounds was produced by Klatt's software parallel-formant speech synthesis program (Klatt, 1980). The additional 500-Hz tones were produced for each member of a continuum by digitally filtering each member of the original vowel continuum (with an appropriate duration) twice through a 101-coefficient Finite Impulse Response filter, attenuating harmonics other than 500 Hz by at least 56 dB, and leaving the 500-Hz component unchanged in intensity. To produce continua with different levels of additional energy at 500 Hz, the tones so produced were digitally added to or subtracted from the vowels of the original continuum. The filtering introduced a time delay of 10 ms, so, before adding in the filtered tone, the original vowel was also shifted by 10 ms. These digital signal processing operations were all performed with ILS software on the laboratory's VAX 11/780 computer.

2. Stimulus continua

There were 11 different continua, the original continuum and ten others derived from it. Five were made by adding to each member of the original continuum various 500-Hz tones which could either be simultaneous with the vowel or start or stop at different times from it. Each tone raised by 6 dB the level of the 500-Hz component in the vowel to which it was added.

Five more continua were made in a similar way, but this time the tone was added to a vowel continuum which had already been reduced in energy at 500 Hz. The effect of adding in the extra tone was to bring the energy at 500 Hz back to its original level during the vowel.

a. Original vowel. The original vowel continuum had seven members whose first formants differed in equal steps between 375 and 500 Hz. The vowels were synthesized on a constant fundamental frequency of 125 Hz, so that the first formant fell between the third and fourth harmonics. The first formant bandwidth parameter of the Klatt synthesizer was fixed at 70 Hz. The second through fifth formant frequencies were fixed at 2300, 2900, 3800, and 4600 Hz. The vowels were 56 ms long, including a 16-ms rise and fall time, so that the steady state was 24 ms (or three pitch pulses). Short (56 ms) vowels are used in the experiment in order to give offset-time effects a chance to appear.

b. Original vowel plus tone. Five more continua (each with seven members) were constructed from the original continuum by adding a 500-Hz tone to each member. Each 500-Hz tone had the same amplitude and phase as the 500-Hz component of the vowel to which it was added. So each vowel in the new continua had 6 dB more energy at 500 Hz than the vowel in the original continuum from which it was derived. In one continuum, the extra tone was simultaneous with the original vowel; we will refer to this as the *augmented* vowel continuum. The remaining four continua were constructed in a manner similar to the augmented but with different durations and temporal alignments of the added tone. The tone was always present during the vowel; it could either (i) start 32 or 240 ms before the vowel but stop at the same time as the vowel, or (ii) start with the vowel but stop 32 or 240 ms after it. The spectra of the resulting vowels were checked to ensure that the phase relations between the additional tone and the vowel stayed constant to produce the required (6 dB) increase in level. Schematic waveform envelopes and spectra for a sound from near the middle of the original vowel continuum (nominal *F* 1 450 Hz), and the corresponding sound with extra energy starting 32 ms before the vowel are shown on the left of Fig. 1.

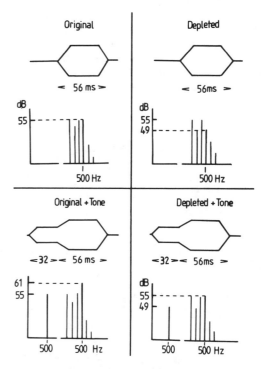

FIG. 1. Spectra and schematic waveform envelopes for stimuli near the middle of four continua used in experiment 1. In the bottom-left panel a tone at 500 Hz has been added to the original vowel (top-left). In the bottom-right panel a 500-Hz tone has been added to a vowel that has already been depleted in energy at 500 Hz (top-right), so that adding in the tone restores the 500-Hz component to its level in the original vowel.

c. Depleted vowel. The *depleted* continuum was constructed from the original by reducing the level of the 500-Hz component of each member by 6 dB. The depletion was accomplished by subtracting from each member of the original continuum one-half of its 500-Hz component.

d. Depleted vowel plus tone. Four more continua were constructed from the depleted continuum by adding various 500-Hz tones. The intensity of the tone added to each sound was appropriate to bring the total level at 500 Hz back to its original value. The tones had the same onset and offset times relative to the main vowel as in the conditions described in Sec. I B. Note that the simultaneous condition here is identical to the original vowel; the original vowel continuum was used in order to reduce the number of conditions to be taken by the subjects.

Schematic waveform envelopes and spectra for a sound from near the middle of the depleted vowel continuum, and the corresponding sound with extra energy starting 32 ms before the vowel are shown on the right of Fig. 1.

3. Procedure

Twelve student subjects, all native speakers of British English and without hearing problems, were tested individually in a soundproof booth over Sennheiser HD-414 headphones. The level of the member of the basic continuum with the lowest first formant was approximately 58 dB(A).

The sounds were produced on line by the laboratory's VAX 11/780 computer (via a microprocessor controlled peripheral—the DEC LPA-11K—at a sampling frequency of 10 kHz, low-pass filtered at 4.5 kHz and 48 dB/oct). Subjects responded on a conventional terminal keyboard with either of the two identification responses ("I" for /I/ and "E" for /ɛ/). If they were not sure of a sound's category on first hearing, they could press "R" to repeat it. Following each key press, the appropriate next sound was played after a

pause of 1 s. If the key press occurred while the current sound was being played, the 1-s pause started at the end of that sound. The terminal screen showed the allowed response keys and the current trial number, as well as castigating the use of other keys.

The main experiment was preceded by a demonstration of the basic continuum, the augmented continuum, and the depleted continuum, followed by a practice identification session using ten successive random orderings of those three continua. After the practice session, subjects were told that they might now hear tones mixed in with the vowels, but they were to ignore them and simply report the vowel that they heard. For the main experiment, each subject heard ten successive random sequences of the 77 items (11 continua × 7 steps) and was free to take a rest at any time.

B. Results

Identification functions pooled across the 12 subjects for the 11 continua are shown in Figs. 2 and 3. They are expressed as the percentage of /I/ responses given to each sound, where each sound is referred to by its *nominal* first formant frequency. If additional energy made no difference to vowel quality, the phoneme boundary would be at the same nominal first formant frequency. There are, however, clear differences between the conditions.

In order to pool across subjects without confounding between-subject variability in boundary position with the slope of the individual identification functions, the curves of the individual subjects were aligned around each curve's 50% boundary before averaging. The resulting averaged curve was then plotted at the mean boundary. The slope of each plotted curve thus gives the average slope of the individual identification functions. The slopes do not change substantially across conditions.

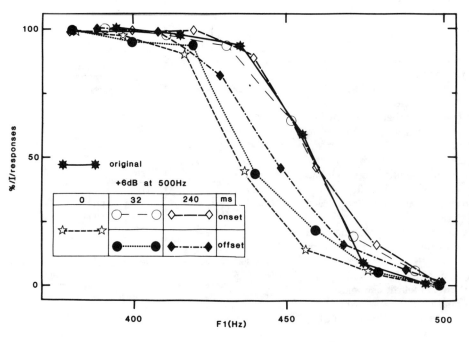

FIG. 2. Mean identification functions from experiment 1 for 12 subjects for *F*1 continua differing in the onset (open symbols) and offset times (filled symbols) of + 6 dB of energy at 500 Hz added to the original vowel continuum.

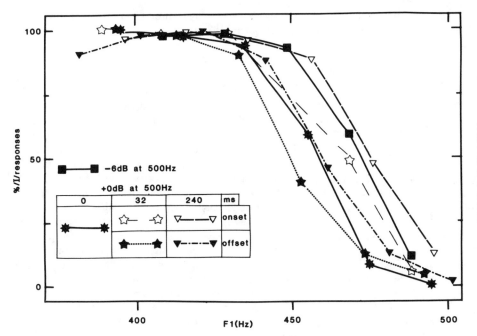

FIG. 3. Mean identification functions from experiment 1 for 12 subjects for $F1$ continua differing in the onset (open symbols) and offset times (filled symbols) of $+6$ dB of energy at 500 Hz added to a vowel continuum that has been depleted by 6 dB at 500 Hz.

The phoneme boundaries for each subject in each condition were found by probit analysis, and the average phoneme boundaries with their standard errors are shown in Fig. 4 for all 11 conditions. The variability of the phoneme boundary across subjects increases in the conditions with added tone compared with the original condition. The standard deviation of particular condition's boundary across the 12 subjects ranged from 9.7 Hz for the original condition to 18.7 Hz for one of the long offset-time conditions.

1. Onset differences

First, this experiment confirms previous findings that a harmonic that starts before the main vowel makes less of a contribution to vowel quality than one that starts at the same time as the remaining harmonics. In Fig. 4(a), the original vowel continuum gives a phoneme boundary at the value shown by the filled triangle and the horizontal line. Adding energy at 500 Hz that starts and stops at the same time as the

main vowel augments the energy at 500 Hz by 6 dB. This augmented continuum gives a phoneme boundary with a nominally lower $F1$ value $[t(11) = 6.76; p < 0.001]$ showing that the extra energy is making a contribution to the quality of the vowel. But when the additional energy starts 32 or 240 ms earlier than the main vowel (solid lines), it ceases to make any contribution to the vowel quality—the phoneme boundary moves back from the augmented value $[t(11) = 5.71, p < 0.001$ ms; $t(11) = 5.95, p < 0.001$ for 240 ms] to regain its original position.

Second, the present experiment shows a similar result when the removal of extra energy leads away from, rather than back towards, the originally synthesized vowel. Figure 4(b) shows results from the case where 6 dB of energy is first removed from the 500-Hz harmonic, giving a vowel continuum with a boundary at a *higher* nominal frequency than the original $[t(11) = 5.01, p < 0.001]$. Adding back in the missing 6 dB to this depleted continuum, of course, returns us to the original vowel quality. But now, if the tone corresponding to the missing 6 dB starts earlier than the main vowel (solid lines), the vowel quality moves *away* from the original $[t(11) = 6.40, p < 0.001]$ to that appropriate to the condition depleted by 6 dB. Thus vowel quality changes with onset time in the same direction and by approximately the same amount whether the perceptual removal of the tone moves the vowel's spectrum towards or away from the originally synthesized vowel. It is thus likely that the shift with onset time *towards* the original vowel quality, that we have previously found and replicate here, does not reflect simply a preference for the original vowel.

2. Offset differences

First, this experiment confirms that a harmonic that stops at a different time from the remainder of a vowel makes less of a contribution to its quality than if it were simulta-

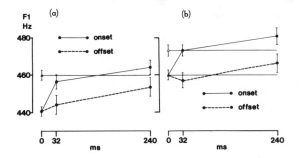

FIG. 4. Mean phoneme boundaries with standard error across 12 subjects from experiment 1. In (a) extra energy has been added to the original vowel continuum, starting or stopping at different times from the vowel. The filled triangle and horizontal line indicate the boundary value for the original continuum. In (b) energy has been added to a vowel continuum depleted in energy by 6 dB relative to the original. The depleted continuum's boundary is shown with an open triangle.

neous. In Fig. 4(a), there is a significant shift in the phoneme boundary away from the augmented condition towards the original continuum's boundary when the extra energy stops 240 ms after the vowel [$t(11) = 3.1, p < 0.01$], but not when it stops 32 ms after [$t(11) < 1.0$]. There is a similar trend in Fig. 4(b). Combining the data from the two halves of Fig. 4 in an analysis of variance showed that the offset effect at 240 ms is significant overall [$F(1,11) = 7.2, p = 0.02$], and there is no difference in its size between the two halves of the figure.

3. Comparison of onset and offset effects

An obvious feature of Fig. 4 is that there is an almost constant change in vowel quality between the 32- and 240-ms conditions irrespective of the original vowel quality (normal or depleted) and onset versus offset. Analysis of variance on the relevant eight conditions confirms this with a significant effect of time [$F(1,11) = 7.16, p = 0.02$] that does not interact with either onset/offset or vowel quality.

On the other hand, there *is* a clear difference between onset and offset conditions when we compare the boundary shift between 0 and 32 ms [$F(1,11) = 22.2, p < 0.002$]. A 32-ms onset-time difference has a larger effect compared with the simultaneous case than does a 32-ms offset-time difference. The normal and depleted vowels are similar in this respect.

C. Discussion

This experiment has confirmed our previous findings and produced a clear answer to the new question that it addressed. It confirms our previous findings that a harmonic that starts or stops at a different time from the rest of a vowel can be perceptually segregated from that vowel. Since offset-time differences are effective in producing some perceptual segregation, our previous claim (Darwin and Sutherland, 1984) is confirmed that the perceptual separation is not simply due to adaptationlike mechanisms. Rather, we must appeal to some mechanism such as perceptual grouping to explain the results. A tone that starts or stops at a different time from the main vowel forms its own perceptual stream and so makes a reduced contribution to the vowel quality. Such streaming is clearly present at the smallest onset-time difference of 32 ms, but longer offset-time differences are required to give a clear effect. The difference between onset and offset effects might perhaps be reduced if even shorter vowels than those used here (56 ms) were used.

The main question that the experiment addressed was whether the perceptual separation of a tone from an accompanying vowel was influenced by whether the vowel spectrum was more normal before or after the tone had been perceptually separated from it. The results clearly show that the perceptual segregation of a synchronous tone is *not* influenced by whether the spectrum that remains after the tone has segregated is a normal vowel, or one depleted in energy at the tone's frequency. The effect cannot, therefore, be explained as being due to a preference for a particular type of spectral profile. Rather, the effect appears to be due to general auditory grouping mechanisms that use onset and offset asynchronies as an indication that different sound sources

may be present (cf. Bregman and Pinker, 1978; Dannenbring and Bregman, 1978).

II. EXPERIMENT 2

The finding that a difference in onset time can serve to segregate perceptually two sound sources raises a paradox for the perception of normal speech. We have shown that a harmonic that starts at a different time from the rest of a vowel makes little contribution to the vowel's phonetic quality. But in normal speech the harmonics of the voice become audible and inaudible at different times as a formant peak sweeps across the harmonics of a varying fundamental. How then do we ever manage to group them together? The answer is not entirely clear, but one way out of the apparent paradox is to note that, in our experiment, the tone that is potentially separable on the basis of time differences, is *not* a speechlike sound. Speech does not consist of pure tones alternating with vowels. The *potential* separation afforded by the difference in onset time becomes an *actual* separation because the separable sounds could not be from the same speech source. What then determines whether sounds *are* from the same speech source? It could be simply that the sounds share a common pitch (cf. Darwin and Bethell-Fox, 1977), or it may be a more complex attribute concerning possible articulatory maneuvers. The question is an empirical one and is under investigation.

According to the above view, then, onset time differences *allow* perceptual segregation to occur, but they are not *sufficient* for it to occur. Are they *necessary*? Can a harmonic that is strictly simultaneous with the rest of a vowel make a reduced contribution to it simply by virtue of the fact that to include it would give a spectrum that was not speechlike?

In the next experiment, we investigate the effect on vowel quality of adding to the members of an /I/–/ɛ/ continuum different amounts of extra energy at one of two harmonic frequencies, 375 and 500 Hz. The effect of the added energy on the perceived first formant frequency is assessed by measuring the shift in the phoneme boundary produced by the added energy. The obtained shift is then compared with the shift expected according to two different ways of estimating the first formant frequency from the spectrum. If the perceptual shift is the same as that estimated from the spectrum, then we can be confident that *all* the extra energy is being incorporated into the vowel percept.

A. Method

The stimuli and measurement techniques were essentially similar to those used in the first experiment. Different amounts of energy at one of two different harmonic frequencies (375 and 500 Hz) were added to an original vowel continuum and the consequent changes in the /I/–/ɛ/ phoneme boundary were measured.

1. Stimuli

Eleven different vowel continua were used in the experiment. Ten of them differed in the amount of extra energy that had been added to the original vowel continuum at either 375 or 500 Hz (the third and fourth harmonics of the

125-Hz fundamental). They were synthesized using the methods described for experiment 1.

The original continuum varied in first formant frequency with nine values of *F*1 between 375 and 542 Hz in roughly 21-Hz steps. (Five more values of the first formant were used in deriving other continua; they had frequencies of 312, 333, 354, 563, and 584 Hz.)

The other ten continua were derived from the original continuum by adding to each member of the continuum extra energy at either 375 or 500 Hz. The tones that provided the additional energy were produced as in experiment 1 by filtering the appropriate member of the original continuum to isolate a particular harmonic and then adding it back with variable intensity into its parent sound to produce different amounts of gain. The added energy increased the level of the appropriate harmonic in each member of a continuum by 3, 6, 9, 12, or 15 dB.

Each continuum had nine members, but the range of first formant values in the original continuum used to produce each of the derived continua varied so that the phoneme boundary could be estimated efficiently. Those conditions with first formant ranges other than 375–542 Hz were as follows: with additional energy at 375 Hz: + 9 dB, 396–563 Hz; + 12 dB and + 15 dB, 417–584 Hz; with additional energy at 500 Hz: + 3 dB, 354–521 Hz; + 6 dB, 333–500 Hz; + 9 dB, + 12 dB and + 15 dB, 312–479 Hz. Since sounds from the different continua were randomized together in the experiment, range effects (see, e.g., Brady and Darwin, 1978) could not have influenced the results.

B. Procedure

The subjects' task in this experiment was simply to label each sound they heard as an /I/ or an /ɛ/. Seventeen subjects (the data of five were subsequently rejected) were tested individually as in experiment 1. In the main experiment,

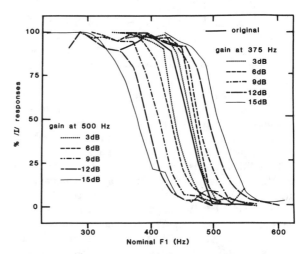

FIG. 5. Mean identification functions from experiment 2 for 12 subjects for *F*1 continua differing in the amount of extra energy added at either 375 or 500 Hz.

each subject heard ten successive random sequences of the 99 items (11 conditions × 9 continuum steps) and was free to take a rest at any time.

C. Results

The data of five subjects were discarded since they did not allow the phoneme boundary of each of the 11 conditions to be estimated reliably. The problem conditions were usually those where a high level of energy at 375 Hz had been added. One subject's boundaries in two conditions fell too far outside the range of sounds used to be estimated accurately; the other four gave markedly nonmonotonic identification functions in one or more condition. Identification functions pooled across the remaining 12 subjects for the 11 continua are shown in Fig. 5. The curves are plotted as in experiment

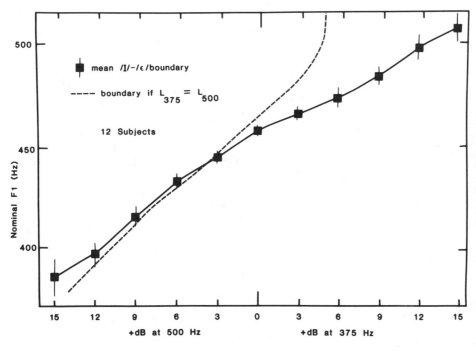

FIG. 6. Mean phoneme boundaries and standard error across 12 subjects for vowel continua with different levels of additional simultaneous energy at 375 or 500 Hz in experiment 2. The dashed line shows the nominal *F*1 values corresponding to equal levels of 375 and 500 Hz in the different conditions.

1; their slopes are the average slopes of the 12 subjects and do not change substantially across the conditions.

As before, the phoneme boundaries for individual subjects were estimated by probit analysis and are shown together with their standard errors across subjects in Fig. 6. The phoneme boundaries are plotted in terms of the *nominal* first formant frequency used to synthesize the sound from the *original* continuum from which the boundary sound for each condition was derived. If the additional energy has no effect on vowel quality, the results will appear as a horizontal line. If the addition of energy gives the percept of a lower $F1$, then the phoneme boundary will move to a higher nominal F value. Conversely, a higher $F1$ percept will give a boundary at a lower nominal $F1$. We would expect and indeed find that increasing the level of the 375-Hz component of the vowel leads to higher nominal $F1$ values, whereas increasing the level of the 500-Hz component leads to lower nominal $F1$ values. It is clear that there is a marked shift in the boundary as energy is added at either 375 or 500 Hz, reflecting the fact that the extra energy is being treated to *some* extent as part of the vowel.

The shift in the nominal $F1$ boundary produced by changing the amount of extra energy at 375 or 500 Hz is approximately linear in Fig. 6. This simple result might lead one to suppose that all the additional energy was being incorporated into the vowel. But, if we look at the spectra of sounds that fall on the phoneme boundary in the various conditions, we see a more complicated picture emerging.

Eleven new sounds were produced that lay exactly on the average boundaries of the 11 different continua. The boundary stimulus for a particular condition was made by first synthesizing a new token along the original continuum with the appropriate nominal first formant value, and then adding to it the appropriate amount of energy at either 375 or 500 Hz for that condition. The conditions in which extra energy has been added at 500 Hz (Fig. 7, right-hand panel) give boundary sounds whose spectra look broadly similar;

the level of the formant rises with increased additional energy, but the relative levels of harmonics around the formant peak are similar across conditions. By contrast, the conditions in which extra energy has been added at 375 Hz (Fig. 7, left-hand panel) give more heterogeneous boundary sounds. Their spectra have very different envelopes, with an increasingly prominent peak at 375 Hz. Why should these very different spectra all be heard as similar? Subjects were, after all, free to label all the sounds from a continuum with high levels of additional energy at 375 Hz as /I/. The answer appears to be that not all the extra energy at 375 Hz is being incorporated perceptually into the vowel, perhaps because of subjects' knowledge about vocal tract transfer function constraints.

The *actual* extent to which extra energy is being perceived as part of the vowel has been estimated in two ways. The first way uses only local information around the formant peak, while the second uses information from the whole spectrum. Both methods allow the same conclusion: Subjects are not using all of the additional 375-Hz energy when estimating the first formant frequency.

1. Weighting two local harmonic levels

The phoneme boundary in the *original* continuum happens to occur at a first formant frequency for which the 375- and 500-Hz components have almost identical levels. If we assume that only these two harmonics are used in computing the position of the first formant, then we can estimate to what extent the extra tone is being incorporated into the vowel by comparing the observed first formant boundaries with those necessary to give equal intensity at 375 and 500 Hz. The dashed line in Fig. 6 shows the expected values. It follows the listeners' values closely when energy is added at 500 Hz, but deviates markedly when 375-Hz energy is added.

To help in understanding possible reasons for the difference between energy added at 375 and at 500 Hz, the continuous lines in Fig. 8 show how the level of those two harmonics in the *original* vowel continuum would change as a function of the nominal $F1$ frequency. The phoneme boundary is marked by a vertical line. If subjects were estimating the first formant simply by comparing the amplitudes of those two frequencies, then it is clear that adding energy at 500 Hz can readily be compensated for by moving to a lower nominal $F1$ value. Lower $F1$ sounds in the original continuum have up to 10 dB less energy at 500 Hz than does the boundary sound. The filled circles indicate the levels of the 500-Hz component at the perceptual boundary for the five continua that have additional energy at 500 Hz. They stay close to the level of the corresponding 375-Hz component. But adding energy at 375 Hz cannot be compensated for by moving the nominal $F1$ to higher frequencies than the original boundary value, since the level of the 375-Hz component only drops by about 3 dB.

If subjects were adopting the simple strategy of weighting the two harmonics closest to the peak in order to estimate the first formant, then they would not show phoneme boundaries for any continuum that had 6 dB or more added to the 375-Hz tone. Yet all of the 17 subjects tested gave clear boundaries when up to 9 dB was added at 375 Hz and 13 out

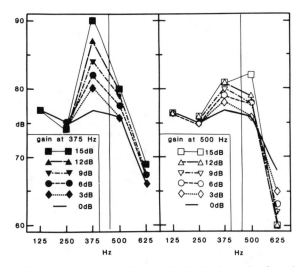

FIG. 7. Levels (in arbitrary dB units) of the first five harmonics of sounds synthesized to be at the phoneme boundary for each condition in experiment 2. The conditions differ in the amount of energy added to either the 375- or the 500-Hz component.

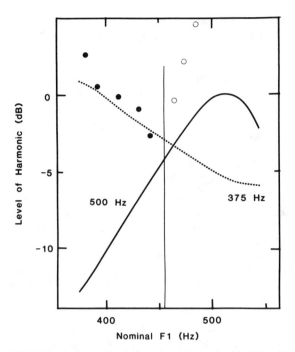

FIG. 8. The continuous lines indicate the relative levels of the 375- and 500-Hz components of the original vowel continuum as a function of the synthesized nominal $F1$ value. The filled circles show the levels of the 500-Hz component for boundary sounds in continua that have had that component increased by 3, 6, 9, 12, or 15 dB. The unfilled circles show the corresponding levels of the 375-Hz component from continua with that component boosted by 3, 6, and 9 dB. The 12- and 15-dB points lie off the graph.

of the total of 17 subjects tested gave estimable boundaries out to 15 dB. The open circles in Fig. 8 show the level of the 375-Hz component at the perceptual boundary for the first three conditions with added energy at 375 Hz. The points are all substantially above the 500-Hz component curve. The remaining two points lie off the graph. It is clear then that if subjects were adopting a local strategy for estimating formant frequency, some of the energy at 375 Hz would have to be discounted.

2. LPC estimation of first formant frequency

The second estimate uses an operation that takes into account the whole spectrum rather than just the two harmonics closest to the first formant peak. Linear predictive analysis (LPC) finds the best fitting all-pole spectrum to a given sound. It provides a good estimate of formant frequencies for simple (non-nasal) vowel sounds spoken in isolation. For each subject's data in each condition, a vowel token was synthesized that lay on the probit-estimated boundary. A 12-coefficient LPC analysis (with 95% pre-emphasis, using ILS software) was made of each of these sounds and the first formant frequency estimated from the resulting poles. If the extra energy were being entirely incorporated into the vowel and listeners were using a method equivalent to LPC analysis to estimate $F1$, we would expect that the LPC-estimated first formant of sounds synthesized to be on the perceptual boundary would remain approximately constant across conditions. On the other hand, if only part of the extra energy is being incorporated into the vowel, we would expect the LPC-estimated first formant to vary across the different conditions. Specifically, if the 375-Hz component is not being fully incorporated into the vowel, we would expect the first formant of a boundary sound, as estimated by LPC analysis, to be at a lower frequency than the LPC-estimated first formant from the original condition.

The mean LPC-estimated first formant values of boundary sounds from the 11 continua are shown in Fig. 9. For the original continuum, the mean LPC estimate of the first formant of each subject's boundary sound is exactly the synthesized value (456 Hz). The boundary sounds from the conditions in which extra energy has been added at 500 Hz give mean estimated $F1$ boundaries that are not significantly different (across subjects) from 456 Hz, except for the 15-dB condition [$t(11) = 2.8, p < 0.02$]. If listeners were using LPC analysis to estimate $F1$ frequency, then they would also be incorporating all the additional energy at 500 Hz into the vowel, except in the 15-dB condition. With extra energy added at 375 Hz, though, a very different picture emerges. Now the mean LPC-estimated first formant frequencies of the

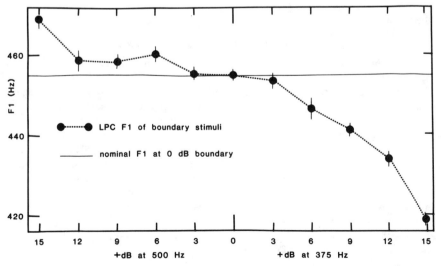

FIG. 9. Means (and their standard errors) of first formant frequencies estimated by LPC analysis from sounds synthesized to be at the perceptual boundary between /I/ and /ɛ/ in experiment 2. The 11 conditions differ in the amounts of energy added to the 375- or 500-Hz components. The horizontal line lies at the $F1$ phoneme boundary for the original condition with no extra energy.

boundary sounds fall significantly below 456 Hz in all but the 3-dB condition. If the human listener were using a method equivalent to LPC analysis, he would first have had to discount some of the 375-Hz energy in the four most intense conditions.

It is, of course, a matter of empirical test what precise method is being used by listeners to estimate the first formant, but it is hard to see how any simple weighting function, when applied to the spectra of Fig. 7 could yield a constant estimate of the first formant frequency. Both methods that we have used lead to the same conclusion: Some of the 375-Hz energy must have been discounted by the listener.

D. Discussion

Experiment 2 has set some limits to the mechanisms underlying first formant frequency estimation. On the one hand, it is clear that extra energy added to the simple spectrum that results from a formant synthesizer excited by a conventional glottal source *can* be incorporated into a vowel percept, changing the perceived formant frequency. We have shown that up to 12 dB of harmonic energy at 500 Hz can be incorporated into a vowel whose first formant lies *below* 500 Hz. On the other hand, additional energy at 375 Hz is only partially incorporated into the formant frequency estimate. What might be the reason for the asymmetry? Is it due to some psycho-acoustic factor such as masking, or must it be attributed to a higher-level constraint?

Upward spread of masking from an intense 375-Hz component could not be responsible for the effect since masking would make the 500-Hz frequency component less audible, and so would tend to produce a lower first formant frequency; the result that we find is that the perceived first formant is higher in frequency than would be expected from the levels of the harmonics.

A possible higher-level reason for the difference between the 375- and 500-Hz conditions in this experiment lies in the shape of the vocal tract transfer function. The function must pass through a gain of 0 dB at 0 Hz, constraining the amplitude changes that can be achieved in harmonics that lie below the first formant peak more than those that lie above it. The resulting constraint on harmonic intensities around a first formant peak has already been discussed and is illustrated in Fig. 8. It is arguable whether such a constraint should be described as specific or not, since many other acoustic systems have transfer functions that are similarly constrained. Constraints that are more specific to speech, such as those on average formant spacing and on formant bandwidths, may prove necessary to explain thoroughly the effect that we have found, but this testing must await further empirical data.

The actual spectrum of a vowel is, or course, a combination of the vocal tract transfer function with the source spectrum. So it is possible that additional low-frequency energy could be regarded as coming from a prominent peak in the source spectrum rather than from the vocal tract transfer function itself. Subjects could be removing part of the 375-Hz energy from the formant frequency calculation in one of two ways. First, they could be interpreting the extra energy at 375 Hz as arising from a different voice quality, rather than from a different vocal tract configuration. Second, they could be rejecting the extra energy completely from the vowel percept, hearing it as a separate tone.

It is likely that some additional energy was rejected completely from the vowel percept by the subjects, since many were aware of extra tones present along with the speech. We have not yet been able to develop a paradigm that would allow us to measure the loudness of the perceived extra tones.

III. GENERAL DISCUSSION

The experiments described here have made two points: (i) A difference in onset or offset time can be used to segregate energy at a harmonic frequency from a vowel regardless of whether the segregation leads towards or away from a normal spectral envelope; (ii) additional energy at a harmonic frequency that is slightly above the first formant frequency is incorporated into a vowel percept at higher energy levels than is energy at a harmonic frequency slightly below the first formant frequency.

The first result, we would maintain, reflects *general auditory* mechanisms of perceptual grouping, while the second reflects the operation of a higher-level constraint that may be speech specific.

Similar results to those found in experiment 1 have been reported in the perception of nonspeech sounds by Dannenbring and Bregman (1978) and by Bregman and Pinker (1978). Dannenbring and Bregman found that a harmonic that started or stopped at a slightly different time from the rest of a harmonic complex was more likely to form a perceptual group with another tone of similar frequency that alternated with the complex than one that was simultaneous. Similarly, Bregman and Pinker showed that the rated richness of a harmonic complex was reduced when one of its components had been segregated out in this manner.

The results of our experiment 2, however, show that energy at a harmonic frequency may still be excluded from a vowel percept when the harmonic is simultaneous with the vowel. There are limits on what energy can be included in formant frequency estimation. Such limits probably reflect a listener's knowledge of constraints on vocal-tract transfer functions.

A. Levels of description in speech perception

The speech perception literature consists, for the most part, of descriptions of the relationship between properties of entities such as formant, burst, voice-onset time, and silence, on the one hand, and linguistic units such as phoneme or distinctive feature, on the other. The experiments that have established such relationships have used the speech of a single talker, natural or synthetic, so that there is no experimental distinction between properties of the sound wave and properties that are specific to a particular sound source.

The main theoretical thrust of the experiments reported here and of previous experiments in a similar vein (Darwin, 1981, 1983; Darwin and Bethell-Fox, 1977; Darwin and Sutherland, 1984) is to establish a case for two different levels of description for auditory information. An initial level describes sound in terms of properties that are evident in the waveform. Such properties may be used subsequently to establish more abstract properties that could be due to a single sound source. The more abstract properties are those that should make contact with stored phonetic knowledge on the attributes of phonetic categories.

The earlier level of description must capture explicitly both those properties of the sound that can be used in assigning features to different putative sources, as well as properties that will subsequently be used to identify a sound's category. It could be viewed as the auditory equivalent of Marr's (1982) primal sketch.

Marr identifies four different representational stages in the process of identifying three-dimensional objects in vision. The first stage is the image, which simply represents the intensity of light at each point; the final stage is a model-based description of 3-D objects. Between these stages lie two more, the primal sketch and the 2 1/2-D sketch. The primal sketch makes explicit important information about the two-dimensional image such as intensity changes and their geometrical organization. It deals in such primitives as edge segments, terminations, discontinuities, and virtual lines and is computed from the image by using general constraints on the way that surfaces and edges of objects structure light. The 2 1/2-D sketch interprets the primal sketch in terms of explicit surfaces with specific orientations relative to the viewer.

Each level of representation makes explicit different types of property—intensity, edges, surface orientation or shape, and different constraints on the nature of the physical world are exploited in moving from one level to the next. Information about the raw intensity levels present in the image representation never makes contact with information about the three-dimensional properties of particular objects, since a particular property of a specific object can result in many very different values in the intensity of light in the image depending on such factors as the level and direction of illumination, the object's distance from the viewer, occlusion by other objects, and so on.

For the same reasons it is a mistake to allow raw spectral information from the soundwave, or even properties extracted directly from the soundwave, to make immediate contact with stored knowledge on the properties of phonetic categories. Knowledge about the properties of phonetic categories must be represented by properties of the sound produced by a single (though not necessarily any particular) speaker. Yet properties that are apparent in the raw waveform are not specific to a single speaker or sound source; they are properties that are due to whatever sound sources are present at the time. For example, the silence necessary to cue an intervocalic stop consonant is silence of a single sound source; there may be no actual silence present in the waveform (see Darwin and Bethell-Fox, 1977). Raw spectral features are also influenced by other phonetically irrelevant factors such as the transfer function between the talker and the listener (Fant, 1980).

The lower level of auditory analysis should capture, for example, information about spectral peaks, local direction of movement in amplitude and frequency of energy regions,

time of onset of energy in different regions, and so on. Such a description should then serve as a rich data base for the operation of processes that can identify appropriate, more abstract structures. General auditory and more specialized phonetic knowledge can be brought to bear to interpret the data in terms of specific sound sources. It is only after such processes have worked over the initial representation that we may sensibly talk of such source-specific cues to phone identity as formants, silence, voice-onset time, and the like. The experiments described here provide some experimental evidence for the distinction between the two levels and suggest two different types of knowledge that might mediate between them.

ACKNOWLEDGMENTS

The research was supported by grant GR/A 83977 from the UK SERC to Professor N. S. Sutherland and, subsequently, by grant GR/C 6009.9 to the author. John Doyle and Ian Winter helped to run the experiments while employed on Sutherland's grant. Arthur G. Samuel's comments on an earlier draft helped substantially to clarify my arguments and presentation.

Assmann, P. F., and Nearey, T. M. (**1983**). "Perception of height differences in vowels," J. Acoust. Soc. Am. Suppl 1 **74**, S89.

Brady, S. A., and Darwin, C J. (**1978**). "Range effect in the perception of voicing," J. Acoust. Soc. Am. **63**, 1556–1558.

Bregman, A. S. (**1978**). "The formation of auditory streams," in *Attention and Performance VII*, edited by J. Requin (Erlbaum, Hillsdale, NJ), pp. 63–76.

Bregman, A. S., Abramson, J., and Darwin, C. J. (**1983**). "Effect of amplitude modulation upon fusion of spectral components," J. Acoust. Soc. Am. Suppl. 1 **74**, S9.

Bregman, A. S., and Pinker, S. (**1978**). "Auditory streaming and the building of timbre," Can. J. Psychol. **32**, 19–31.

Brokx, J.P.L., and Nooteboom, S. G. (**1982**). "Intonation and the perceptual separation of simultaneous voices," J. Phonet. **10**, 23–36.

Carlson, R., Fant, G., and Granstrom, B. (**1975**). "Two-formant models, pitch and vowel perception," in *Auditory Analysis and Perception of Speech*," edited by G. Fant and M. A. A. Tatham (Academic, London), pp. 55–82.

Dannenbring, G. L., and Bregman, A. S. (**1978**). "Streaming vs fusion of sinusoidal components of complex tones," Percept. Psychophys. **24**, 369–376.

Darwin, C. J. (**1981**). "Perceptual grouping of speech components differing in fundamental frequency and onset time," Q. J. Exp. Psychol. **33A**, 185–207.

Darwin, C. J. (**1983**). "Auditory processing and speech perception," in *Attention and Performance X*, edited by D. G. Bouwhuis (Erlbaum, Hillsdale, NJ).

Darwin, C. J., and Bethell-Fox, C. E. (**1977**). "Pitch continuity and speech source attribution," J. Exp. Psychol.: Hum. Percept. Perf. **3**, 665–672.

Darwin, C. J., and Sutherland, N. S. (**1984**). "Grouping frequency components of vowels: when is a harmonic not a harmonic?" Q. J. Exp. Psychol. **36A**, 193–208.

Fant, G. (**1980**). "Perspectives in speech research," Speech Transmission Laboratory, Stockholm, QPSR 1980/2–3, 1–16.

Karnickaya, E. G., Mushnikov, V. N., Slepokurova, N. A., and Zhukov, S. Ja. (**1975**). "Auditory processing of steady-state vowels," in *Auditory Analysis and Perception of Speech*," edited by G. Fant and M. A. A. Tatham (Academic, London), pp. 37–53.

Klatt, D. H. (**1980**). "Software for a cascade/parallel formant synthesizer,"

J. Acoust. Soc. Am. **67**, 971–995.

Marr, D. (**1982**). *Vision* (Freeman, San Francisco).

McAdams, S. (**1980**). "Spectral fusion and the creation of auditory images," in *Music, Mind and Brain: the Neuropsychology of Music*, edited by M. Clynes (Plenum, New York).

McAdams, S., and Bregman, A. S. (**1979**). "Hearing musical streams," Comp. Music J. **3**(4), 26–43, 60.

Miller, G. A., and Nicely, P.E. (**1955**). "An analysis of perceptual confusions among some English consonants," J. Acoust. Soc. Am. **27**, 338–352.

Moore, B. C. J., and Glasberg, B. R. (**1983**). "Suggested formulae for calculating auditory-filter bandwidths and excitation patterns," J. Acoust.

Soc. Am. **74**, 750–753.

Pickett, J. M. (**1957**). "Perception of vowels heard in noise of various spectra," J. Acoust. Soc. Am. **29**, 613–620.

Rasch, R. A. (**1978**). "Perception of simultaneous notes such as in polyphonic music," Acustica **40**, 21–33.

Scheffers, M. T. M. (**1983**). "Sifting vowels: auditory pitch analysis and sound segregation," Doctoral dissertation, Groningen University.

Summerfield, A. Q., Foster, J., Gray, S., and Haggard, M. P. (**1981**). "Perceiving vowels from 'flat spectra'," J. Acoust. Soc. Am. Suppl. 1 **69**, S116.

Summerfield, A. Q., Haggard, M. P., Foster, J., and Gray, S. (**1984**). "Perceiving vowels from uniform spectra: phonetic exploration of an auditory after-effect," Percept. Psychophys. **35**, 203–213.

THE JOURNAL OF THE ACOUSTICAL SOCIETY OF AMERICA   VOLUME 29, NUMBER 1   JANUARY, 1957

Information Conveyed by Vowels

PETER LADEFOGED, *Phonetics Department, University of Edinburgh, Scotland*

AND

D. E. BROADBENT, *Medical Research Council Applied Psychology Unit, Cambridge, England*

(Received June 12, 1956)

Most speech sounds may be said to convey three kinds of information: linguistic information which enables the listener to identify the words that are being used; socio-linguistic information, which enables him to appreciate something about the background of the speaker; and personal information which helps to identify the speaker. An experiment has been carried out which shows that the linguistic information conveyed by a vowel sound does not depend on the absolute values of its formant frequencies, but on the relationship between the formant frequencies for that vowel and the formant frequencies of other vowels pronounced by that speaker. Six versions of the sentence *Please say what this word is* were synthesized on a Parametric Artificial Talking device. Four test words of the form *b-*(vowel)*-t* were also synthesized. It is shown that the identification of the test word depends on the formant structure of the introductory sentence. Some psychological implications of this experiment are discussed, and hypotheses are put forward concerning the ways in which all three kinds of information are conveyed by vowels.

IN recent years a great deal of research has been directed towards the specification of the "information-bearing elements of speech."[1] It seems that at the moment much of this research is hampered through lack of consideration of the kinds of information that are conveyed by speech. For the sake of convenience in exposition we may consider this information to be of three kinds. Firstly, when we listen to a person talking, we can receive information about what he is saying; in other words, we can appreciate the linguistic significance of the utterance. Secondly, in addition to the information we receive as a result of considering an utterance in terms of a linguistic system, we also receive information of a different kind about the general background of the speaker; thus we can usually infer something about a speaker's place of origin and his social status from his accent. This kind of information may be termed socio-linguistic; it is conveyed by the features of a person's speech which he acquires through the influence of the particular groups of which he is (or was) a member. Lastly there is the kind of information conveyed by the idiosyncratic features of a person's speech. These, like the group and linguistic features, may be part of an individual's learned speech behavior; but, unlike the other features, idiosyncratic features may also be due to anatomical and physiological considerations, such as the particular shape of the vocal

cavities. The information which these features convey may be termed personal information. The relations between these three kinds of information are summarized in Fig. 1.

It is possible to arrange experimental situations which will elicit responses with respect to each of these three kinds of information. Thus one can ask a subject: Were these two sounds pronounced by the same speaker? (personal information); or: Is there any difference of accent between these two speakers? (socio-linguistic information); or: Do these two utterances consist of the same words used in the same way? (linguistic information). It is also possible to arrange a situation where the socio-linguistic information and the linguistic information will be assessed concurrently. These two kinds of information taken together are sometimes said to be equivalent to the phonetic value of a sound.[2] This point of view, however, is disputed by others who believe that "The phonetic

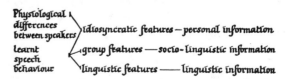

FIG. 1. Differences in utterances and the information that they convey.

---

[1] G. E. Peterson, J. Acoust. Soc. Am. 24, 629–637 (1952).

[2] Peter Ladefoged, Lingua 5, 113–127 (1956).

value of a speech sound is independent of language and meaning."[1]

In this article an experiment is discussed which is concerned with those features of vowel quality which convey linguistic information. This has led to some consideration of both the group and the idiosyncratic features of vowel quality, and tentative conclusions are reached concerning the ways in which all three kinds of information are conveyed.

DEVELOPMENT OF EXPERIMENTAL MATERIAL

It has been supposed for almost a century now that the variations in the formants, or regions of the auditory spectrum in which there is a relatively large amount of spectral energy, are responsible for most of the information conveyed by vowels. However, there is as yet no general agreement on the precise properties of the formants which convey the information. There are differences of opinion as to whether the value of a given vowel depends on the absolute values of certain properties of its formants, or whether it depends on the relation between these values and the values for other vowels pronounced by the same speaker. As a proponent of the first view, we may instance G. E. Peterson, who analyzed a group of matched vowels obtained by recording the sounds produced by speakers trying to imitate the phonetic quality of the vowels in two reference words. He came to the general conclusion that "front vowels could be rather readily identified by observing the positions in frequency of the peaks of the first three formants." [1] Contrasting with this view is the theory propounded by M. Joos,[3] to the effect that the phonetic quality of a vowel depends on the relationship between the formant frequencies for that vowel and the formant frequencies of other vowels pronounced by that speaker.

A necessary part of Joos' theory is that whenever a listener to speech has to identify a vowel without the benefit of any clues from the context, he utilizes whatever knowledge he has of the speaker's formant frequencies in other words. Even when the vowel which the listener is considering is quite unlike any that he has ever heard that speaker produce before, he nevertheless focuses his attention not on the absolute values of the frequencies of the formants, but on the relations between those frequencies and the general ranges of frequencies which seem to be characteristic of the speaker. Thus unknown vowels are identified in terms of the way in which their acoustic structure fits into the pattern of sounds that the listener has been able to observe.

This part of the theorem has now been verified in an experimental situation. It has been found that subjects hearing a test word immediately after hearing a specified introductory sentence are greatly influenced

in their identification of the test word by the range of the formant frequencies in the introductory sentence.

In order to carry out this experiment it was first of all necessary to obtain introductory sentences which were identical except in the ranges of their formants. This cannot of course be done by recording different people saying the same sentence, because the utterances are bound to differ in many ways. Accordingly it was decided to use synthesized speech, which can be precisely controlled in all respects. The particular instrument used for the purpose was the Edinburgh University Phonetics Department's copy of the Parametric Artificial Talking Device[4] developed at the Ministry of Supply Signals Research and Development Establishment. The essential parts of the device are a generator producing a pulse corresponding to the larynx pulse which serves to excite the vocal tract; four formant generators which respond to the pulse excitation; and a generator which will produce noise corresponding to the excitation in fricative sounds. This instrument will synthesize speech which can be specified in terms of six variables, but which nevertheless sounds so natural that recordings of some sentences are always confused with recordings of normal speech. The six variables which are normally specified are the intensity and frequency of the pulse excitation, the frequencies of the lowest three formants, and the intensity of the fricative noise. In order to set up the synthesizer so that it will produce an utterance, information depicting these variables as functions of time is painted on a glass slide. The slide is then scanned by a mechanism which produces six controlling voltages which vary with time. The voltages control the appropriate generators of the synthesizer so that a sequence of speech-like sounds is produced.

As well as the factors which are specified by the information painted on the glass slide, it is also possible to vary other factors, such as the frequency of the fourth formant, and the amplitudes and damping constants of all four formants; but no provision is made for controlling these factors as functions of time, and they were not in fact varied in the course of the experiment. In addition, it is possible to alter the frequency range over which each of the formant generators is operating. It was this facility that was used to produce the necessary variations in the introductory sentences.

Six versions of the sentence *please say what this word is* were synthesized with the PAT device. This sentence was chosen as a suitable introductory context because the formant frequencies of the sounds vary over a wide range. Formant one varies between the low value necessary to produce the /i/ in *Please* to the high value required for the /ɐ/ in *what*; and formant two varies

---

[3] M. Joos, *Acoustic Phonetics*, Supplement to Language 24 (1948).

[4] W. Lawrence, "The synthesis of speech from signals which have a low information rate," in *Communication Theory*, W. Jackson, editor (Butterworths Scientific Publications, London, 1955), Chap. 34.

TABLE I. Differences in the six versions of the introductory sentence: *Please say what this word is.*

Sentence version	Differences from sentence 1	Frequency range in cps	
		Formant 1	Formant 2
1	...	275–500	600–2500
2	F. 1. down	200–380	600–2500
3	F. 1. up	380–660	600–2500
4	F. 2. down	275–500	400–2100
5	F. 2. up	275–500	800–2900
6	F. 1. down F. 2. up	200–380	800–2900

between the high value in the /i/ of *please* and the low value at the beginning of the /w/ in *word*.

In making all six versions of the introductory sentence the synthesizer was controlled by a single slide. Consequently the versions were identical with one another except for the variations which were introduced in the ranges over which the formant generators operated. The variations are summarized in Table I, which shows the highest and lowest values both of formant one and of formant two that actually occurred in each version of this sentence.

It is interesting to note at this point that despite the great acoustic differences between the versions they were all readily identifiable as the same sentence. Moreover, all the trained phoneticians who listened to the different versions agreed that the variations which had been introduced did not appear to make any significant difference in either the linguistic or the socio-linguistic information which was being conveyed. With the exception of version six, which did sound rather unnatural and could not be judged as a sample of normal speech, all the different versions sounded like the same sentence pronounced by people who had the same accent but differed in their personal characteristics.

In addition to these introductory sentences, four test words were synthesized. Each of these was of the form *b*-(vowel)-*t*. The formant frequencies for the middle of the vowel in each of these words are shown in Table II. The vowels in each of these test words were of comparatively short duration.

TEST PROCEDURE

A short listening test was devised with the aid of recordings of the material which has been described in the previous section. This test was taken by sixty

TABLE II. The frequencies of the first two formants in the four test words.

Test word	Frequency in cps	
	Formant one	Formant two
A	375	1700
B	450	1700
C	575	1700
D	600	1300

subjects. The first part of the test consisted of recordings of the test words *A*, *B*, *C*, and *D* arranged in a random order. There were ten items in this part of the test. Subjects were told that they would hear ten words, each of which might be either *bit*, *bet*, *bat* or *but*. They were instructed to tick the appropriate word on the answer sheets with which they had been provided. The means of the responses in respect of each test word are shown in Table III.

Between each of the first five words in the listening test there was a short pause during which subjects were requested to count aloud from one to ten. This was done in an attempt to prevent the identification of a test word being unduly influenced by the auditory memory of the preceding word. The efficacy of this procedure is discussed in a subsequent section.

In the second part of the recording the test words occurred immediately after the various versions of the introductory sentence. Subjects were given the following written instructions:

You will now hear a voice saying *Please say what this word is.* This will be followed immediately by one of the words: *bit, bet, bat, but.* Please tick the

TABLE III. Means of the responses of 60 subjects for the ten words in the first part of the listening test.

Test word	Number of subjects identified as:			
	bit	*bet*	*bat*	*but*
A	52	8	...	...
B	14	46	...	...
C	...	27	33	...
D	...	1	14	45

appropriate word on the answer sheet below. There are twelve test sentences in this part of the recording; after answering in respect of each, there will be a short pause, during which you will be requested to count aloud, slowly, from one to ten.

The twelve items were arranged so that the predicted responses occurred in a random order. The results of this part of the test are shown in Fig. 2.

DISCUSSION OF RESULTS

It will be seen from Fig. 2 that subjects are undoubtedly influenced in their identification of the test word by the auditory context in which it occurs. Thus word *A* is identified as *bit* by 87% of the subjects when it is preceded by version one of the introductory sentence; but as *bet* by 90% of the subjects when it is preceded by version two in which the first formant varies over a lower range. All that remains to be shown is that the influence of the introductory sentence is in accordance with the theory put forward by Joos concerning the relative nature of this aspect of vowel quality.

The relations between the formant structures of the

vowels in a number of words can be conveniently represented by means of a formant chart which shows the frequency of the first formant at a time in the word when the formant structure is changing at a minimum rate plotted against the frequency of the second formant at the same time. In order to provide a basis for discussion, some of the vowels of one of the authors (P.L.) are shown in this form in Fig. 3. The symbols used are /ɪ/ as in *bit*, /ɛ/ as in *bet*, /a/ as in *bat*, /ʌ/ as in *but*, /i/ as in *please*, /e/ as in *say*, /ɐ/ as in *what*, and /ɜ/ as in *word*. The axes in this and the subsequent diagrams have been arranged so that these acoustic charts can be easily compared with the vowel diagrams used by phoneticians. The scale used throughout is the Koenig scale.

The pattern formed by the vowels shown in Fig. 3 may be taken as a representation of one of the kinds of relationships which can occur. Bearing this in mind, we may now consider the relationships between the vowels in each of the six versions of the introductory sentence and the test words with which they were designed to be associated. Figure 4 presents these data; solid points lettered *A*, *B*, *C*, and *D* represent the test words, and the open circles indicate the vowels in the different versions of the introductory sentence.

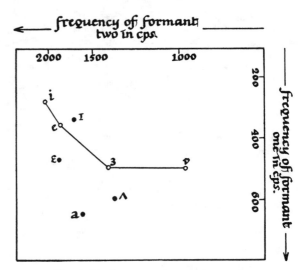

FIG. 3. The formant structure of some of the vowels of one of the authors (P.L.).

It will be seen from a comparison of Figs. 3 and 4 that when the test word *A* is associated with version one of the introductory sentence its relative position is similar to that of P.L.'s *bit*; and, in fact 87.5% of the subjects did identify it as *bit*. But when this word occurs in association with version two its relative position is more like that of P.L.'s *bet*; which accounts for the shift in identification whereby 90% of the subjects now consider it to be *bet*. Similar reasoning explains the change in identification of word *B* when it is associated with version one (92% *bet*) as opposed to version three (97% *bit*). But we must also note in connection with word *B* that when it was associated with versions two and six of the introductory sentence by far the majority of the subjects still identified it in the same way (i.e., as *bet*) as when it was associated with version one. The probable reason for this is that the relative position of the vowel /ɛ/ as in *bet* can be anywhere in a comparatively large area. As Daniel Jones[5] has noted: "The vowel (sc. /ɛ/) varies a good deal with different speakers." Presumably, therefore, the shifts in its relative position due to its being associated with versions two and six were not great enough to move it out of the part of the vowel pattern in which it is reasonable to expect to find a vowel of the /ɛ/ type.

The results shown in Fig. 2 indicate that there is a considerable amount of disagreement concerning the identification of word *C*. Some of the reasons for this can be appreciated from a comparison of the data presented in Figs. 3 and 4. Only when it is associated with version three of the introductory sentence does the vowel in this word have a relative position which is comparable with any of the relative positions of P.L.'s vowels. In these circumstances 80% of the subjects did identify it as the same word, *bet*. But when it occurs in

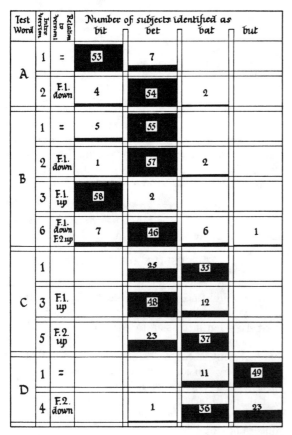

Test Word	Intro. Version	Relation to version	bit	bet	bat	but
A	1	=	**53**	7		
A	2	F.1. down	4	**54**	2	
B	1	=	5	**55**		
B	2	F.1. down	1	**57**	2	
B	3	F.1. up	**58**	2		
B	6	F.1. down E.2 up	7	**46**	6	1
C	1			25	**35**	
C	3	F.1. up		**48**	12	
C	5	F.2. up		23	**37**	
D	1	=			11	**49**
D	4	F.2. down		1	**36**	23

FIG. 2. Means of the responses of sixty subjects identifying the test words *A*, *B*, *C*, and *D* preceded by different versions of the introductory sentence.

[5] Daniel Jones, *An Outline of English Phonetics* (W. Heffer, Cambridge, England, 1956).

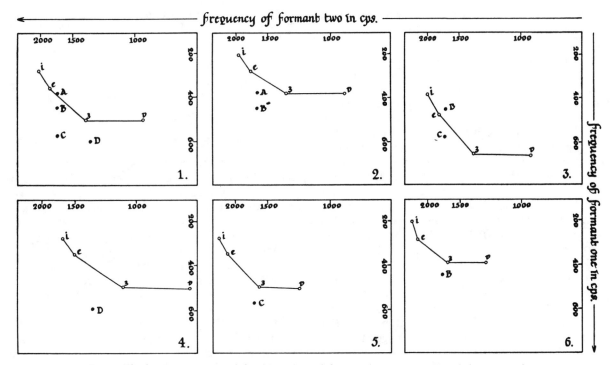

FIG. 4. The formant structure of the six versions of the introductory sentence and the test words that they were each designed to be associated with.

association with version one, where it occupies a relative position only slightly nearer the point in the pattern occupied by P.L.'s *bat* than his *bet*, it is not surprising that 58% of the subjects identify it as *bat* and 42% as *bet*. The results obtained from the association of this word with version five, however, are not so readily understandable. It might be expected that at least a small proportion of the subjects would identify this word as *but* in these circumstances. But in fact this did not happen, perhaps because this simplified treatment in terms of the frequencies of only two formants is not sufficient to account for the differences between these two words. On the other hand, tests with word *D* show that it is possible for the auditory context to influence the identification of a given test word so that it can be taken to be either *bat* or *but*. When this word was associated with version one, the majority of the subjects identified it as *but* (82%) as opposed to *bat* (18%); but in association with version four, in which the second formant was comparatively lower, then the results were *bet* (2%) *bat* (60%), and *but* (38%). Thus word *D* illustrates the fact that shifts in the range of the second formant in the introductory sentence can produce alterations in the identification of the test word which are of the same order as those produced by variations in the range of the first formant.

Taken all together, the results of this test seem to shown quite conclusively that, as Joos has said, the linguistic information conveyed by a given vowel is largely dependent on the relations between the frequencies of its formants and the frequencies of the formants of other vowels occurring in the same auditory context. It is, therefore, only of limited service to look for common points in the acoustic structure of equivalent vowels spoken by different speakers.

PSYCHOLOGICAL IMPLICATIONS

It is obvious that this experiment provides a demonstration of perceptual constancy in the auditory field; that is an auditory phenomenon somewhat parallel to the visual case in which the response evoked by a stimulus is influenced by the stimuli with which it is closely associated. An example is the correct identification of the color of an object in widely differing illuminations. Consequently it is hoped that further investigation of the auditory phenomenon will provide data which are of general psychological interest.

There are many factors which have not been considered in any way in the course of the present experiment. For example, at the moment nothing is known about the length of the introductory sentence which is necessary in order to influence the identification of the test word. Nor do we know to what extent it is necessary to use an introductory sentence containing a wide variety of vowels which may serve as reference points. In addition, further evidence is required concerning the necessary degree of proximity between the auditory context and the stimulus word. A preliminary experiment has been reported[6] in which it is shown that if there is a ten-second silent interval

---

[6] Broadbent, Ladefoged, and Lawrence, Nature, **178**, 815–816 (1956).

between the introductory sentence and the test word, then the influence of the introductory sentence is significantly less. But the precise temporal limitations of the phenomenon have not yet been established.

Further research is also needed to determine the value of the procedure of counting between items in a test in order to weaken the auditory memory of the preceding words. Subjects were requested to count aloud between the first five items presented in the test. But despite this they were probably influenced in their identifications of the fifth word presented to them by their memory of the previous items. Both the first and fifth items were word *A*. When they first heard this word 45 subjects identified it as *bit* and 15 as *bet*; but when it occurred as the fifth item (i.e., after they had heard other test words) all 60 subjects identified word *A* as *bit*. On the other hand, counting items had a significant effect on some occasions. Word *C* was identified as *bet* by 37 subjects and as *bat* by 23 subjects when it occurred as the fourth item in the test, and could not directly be compared with word *B*; but when word *C* occurred immediately after word *B* it seems likely that the two words were judged together, since in these circumstances 10 subjects identified word *B* as *bit* and 50 as *bet*, and 8 subjects identified word *C* as *bet* and 52 as *bat*.

SOCIO-LINGUISTIC AND PERSONAL INFORMATION

All the responses demanded by the listening test which has been described above are specifically related to linguistic information. But, on the basis of this test, two points may be noted concerning the socio-linguistic and personal information conveyed by vowels. Firstly, as we have mentioned, there do not appear to be any differences in the socio-linguistic information conveyed by the different versions of the introductory sentence. It therefore seems to be a plausible hypothesis that socio-linguistic information does not depend on the absolute values of the formant frequencies, but is, like linguistic information, a matter of the relative formant structure of vowels. Secondly, there is tentative evidence that subjects belonging to different socio-linguistic groups gave different responses to some of the test material. Consideration of the precise criteria that were used in dividing subjects into groups in accordance with their accents is, unfortunately, outside the scope of this article. It must suffice to state that there were three main groups: in one there were seven subjects who had what is known as a Basic Scots vowel system[7]; in the second there were nineteen Scottish speakers who had vowel systems that had been slightly modified due to the influence of the English of England: and in the third there were nineteen subjects who were speakers of the form of English of England known as R.P. Table IV shows the responses of each of these three groups in respect of test word *D* preceded by

TABLE IV. Identifications of test word *D* in association with version one of the introductory sentence by different groups of subjects.

Number in group	Character of group	Identified as:	
		bat	*but*
7	Scots	3	4
19	English influenced Scots	4	15
19	English (R.P.)	1	18

version one of the introductory sentence. It can be seen that there is a greater tendency among the Scottish speakers to favor the identification of this word as *bat*, presumably because in their speech the relative position of the vowel in *bat* is similar to that of the vowel in the test word. The relation between accent and type of response is only just statistically significant, using tau,[8] $p = 0.05$, and further confirmation is desirable.

On this basis it seems at least possible that both the linguistic and the socio-linguistic information conveyed by vowels depend largely on the relative positions of the formants. When we consider that a speaker has vowel sounds which are typical of a Scottish speaker (i.e., when we interpret the socio-linguistic information conveyed by his vowels), we probably do so by appreciating the relative formant structure of the vowels.

On the other hand, the personal information conveyed by vowels does seem to depend partly on the absolute values of the formant frequencies. Thus all the versions of the introductory sentence sounded as if they had been spoken by different voices. The reasons for this are best understood by reference to the articulatory processes involved in speech. The formants of a sound are essentially properties of the shape of the vocal tract. Consequently the ranges over which a speaker's formants can vary depend to a great extent on the size of his head. Because the ranges cannot be altered at will, they are not part of a speaker's learned speech behavior, and can therefore convey only personal information. Additional personal information is, of course, conveyed by the relative positions of some of a speaker's vowels, insofar as these are idiosyncratic features of his speech and not aspects which identify him as belonging to a particular group.

Finally, it is interesting to consider the current usages of the term "phonetic quality" in the light of the hypotheses that have been put forward above in connection with the ways in which all three kinds of information are conveyed. It seems that when phoneticians talk about the quality of a speech sound they do not always mean the same thing. When teaching the pronunciation of the vowels of a foreign language, for instance, they assess their pupils' utterances in terms of the linguistic and socio-linguistic information that they convey; they are therefore concerned with the relative formant structure only.

---

[7] D. Abercrombie and A. J. Aitken, *A Scots Phonetic Reader*, (to be published).

[8] J. W. Whitfield, Biometrika **34**, 292–296 (1947).

104   P. LADEFOGED AND D. E. BROADBENT

But on other occasions when observing utterances, particularly in field-work situations, phoneticians seem to imply that vowel quality can be judged in relation to certain absolute standards. Many phoneticians believe that it is possible to describe the quality of a vowel in an isolated monosyllable spoken by an informant, even if they have no other information concerning the speaker.

It is not yet known whether the cardinal vowels which serve as reference points for phoneticians are really precise points with fixed acoustic specifications, or whether they are only a set of vowels which have the same relative formant structure when pronounced by different phoneticians. But whatever their nature,

it seems that the whole theory underlying the methods which are used in practice for describing vowels needs restating, so that it is made clear whether linguistic and socio-linguistic criteria are being used in making assessments of quality, or whether an attempt is being made to classify speech sounds in terms of purely auditory criteria.

ACKNOWLEDGMENTS

The authors would like to acknowledge the help of many of their colleagues. In particular, W. Lawrence, D. Abercrombie, and J. Anthony have been of great assistance.

9.5   Received 1 May 1967

On the Róle of Formant Transitions in Vowel Recognition

B. E. F. LINDBLOM*

Department of Speech Communication, Royal Institute of Technology (KTH), Stockholm 70, Sweden

M. STUDDERT-KENNEDY†

Haskins Laboratories, New York, New York 10017

An inventory of speechlike sounds was synthesized displaying systematic variations of the rate and direction of formant transitions. These sounds were specified by a set of vowel formant patterns selected along a continuum varying from [ʊ] to [ɪ]; they were assigned to isolated, steady-state vowels, and to the points of zero rate of formant frequency change in symmetrical consonant–vowel–consonant syllables. The time variations of formant frequencies were made convex and concave by the choice of two consonantal frames: [w-w] and [j-j]. The results obtained in a series of vowel identification experiments indicate that a listener's categorization of the continuum varied as a function of the environment and the duration of the vowel. These findings suggest that, in the recognition of monosyllabic nonsense speech, the identity of a vowel is determined not solely by the formant-frequency pattern at the point of closest approach to target, but also by the direction and rate of adjacent formant transitions. In general, subjects adjusted their categorizations of the continuum in the consonantal contexts in such a way that complete transitions between loci and vowel target were not necessary: the transitions were permitted to undershoot the target frequencies for the vowel. In particular, the excursions of formants in the [w-w] syllables tended to be overestimated. Thus, there was a tendency for the categorizations to be made so as to compensate for the formant-frequency undershoot associated with vowel reduction [B. Lindblom, "Spectrographic Study of Vowel Reduction," J. Acoust. Soc. Am. 35, 1773–1781 (1963)]. The effects observed are discussed in terms of an active model of vowel recognition, peripheral auditory analysis, distinctive features, and previously reported observations on vowel perception.

I. PROBLEM OF VOWEL RECOGNITION

THIS study deals with an aspect of human vowel recognition. Basic to the exploration of this process is an understanding of the conditions under which the mechanisms underlying recognition operate. For the vowel system of a given language, these conditions are determined by the relation between the sounds to be decoded and the categories to be recognized. This relation, in turn, is dependent on how the acoustic realizations of vowels are constrained in the generation of speech. In this article, we begin with a brief examination of the mechanism of speech production in order to point out a problem inherent in the recognition of vowel sounds generated by this mechanism. The results of an experiment on vowel identifica-

tion will then be presented and discussed in the light of this problem.

The range of acoustic shapes characteristic of vowels is limited by the constraints of speech production. For a given articulatory system, constants and physical laws set certain margins of performance beyond which the system cannot go. Within these limits, the available degrees of freedom are used in two ways. On the one hand, there are articulatory control mechanisms related to the categories and processes postulated in the formal description of a language: these mechanisms exploit the available physiological apparatus for linguistic purposes. On the other hand, there are extralinguistic mechanisms, such as those producing variations in speaking rate, vocal effort, etc., or reflecting the play of psychological variables: these mechanisms tend to perturb the former basic underlying processes. It is hypothesized herein that, in terms of the substrate of linguistically determined *articulatory control*, an utterance is organized as a succession of vocal-tract states, there being a low

* During the initial stages of this work guest researcher at the Res. Lab. Electron., MIT, Cambridge, Mass., and Haskins Laboratories, New York.
† Present address: Inter-American University, San German, P. R.

RÔLE OF FORMANT TRANSITIONS IN VOWEL RECOGNITION

number of such states associated with each phoneme. At the level of *articulatory performance*, however, the picture is different, for the gestures invoked to actualize these states are relatively slow: They merge spatially and temporally into a continuous process that often only approximates the intended states and continually exhibits instances of coarticulation. For experimental data compatible with these ideas and similar views of speech production, see Refs. 1–8. When the control is relaxed or perturbed by extralinguistic variables, these effects become even more marked so that ellipsis and reduction may result. For syllable production, a super-ordinate timing mechanism is required to control the relative moments at which maneuvers towards adjacent consonant and vowel goals are initiated. Since there are physiological and mechanical limitations on the rates at which such maneuvers can be carried out, the extent of the articulatory movements within a given syllable can vary as a function of the temporal pattern of syllabic gesture initiation. A consequence of this organization for the pronunciation of a vowel is that the speech organs sometimes undershoot the articulatory target of the vowel. As the temporal proximity of adjacent gesture initiations increases, the undershoot effect observed in the vowel of, for example, a consonant–vowel–consonant (CVC) syllable tends also to increase. Acoustically, the typical vowel segment will then appear as a continuously varying event. Only rarely will its formants reach a steady state. At some point during the segment, however, they will approach the pattern corresponding to the underlying target more closely than at other instants. Formant frequencies sampled at this moment, may be considerably displaced from their target values owing to the undershoot and perturbation effects. (Refs. 2, 3, 4, and 6.)

The acoustic information on a vowel phoneme generally present in the speech wave can be stylized as a sequence of three elements: transition+pattern at point of closest approach to target+transition. We have pointed out that these elements are subject to

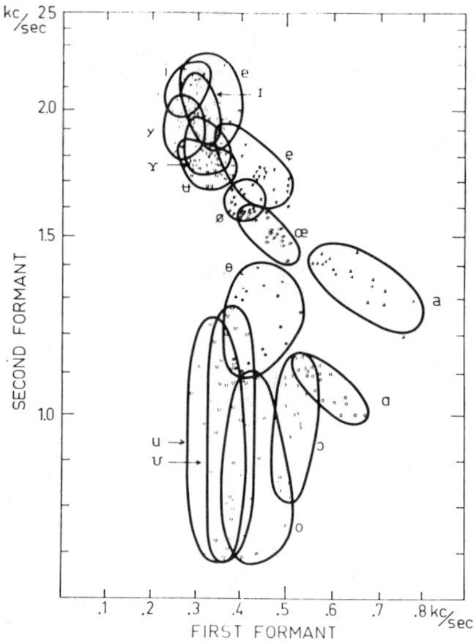

Fig. 1. Ambiguity of raw first and second formant data sampled at points of closest approach to target (Swedish).

considerable contextual modification. These modifications sometimes make the middle element ambiguous. An illustration of such ambiguity is given in Fig. 1. This figure is based on spectrographic measurements of the formant frequencies of eight long and eight short Swedish vowels pronounced by one talker. The data refer to samples at points of closest approach to target. The immediate environment of these sounds was [ɛ'd–d], preceded by a carrier phrase. The talker was instructed to attempt to vary his rate of speaking in synchrony with a timing signal presented to him over an earphone. Each vowel was repeated about 18 times at different rates. In an F_1–F_2 plot, it can be seen that the sampling procedure used causes considerable overlap of the vowel areas. Taking the third formant into account reduces this overlap somewhat, especially in the front and close vowel region, but is far from removing it completely. There is every reason to believe that, for normal conversational speech, similar data would show even greater overlap. In a language with a rich vowel system such as Swedish, the risk of ambiguity would seem to be particularly great. But in other types of languages such as Japanese, ambiguity has also been shown to occur.[9] For ambiguity in American English vowels, see Figs. 5 and 6, which are discussed later.

From the point of view of the above single-sample specifications, the problem of vowel recognition is to recover the identity of the underlying target in the face of ambiguity and large perturbation effects. Obviously, in human recognition of speech this problem is normally

[1] M. Halle and K. N. Stevens, "Speech Recognition: A Model and a Program for Research," IRE Trans. Inform. Theory **IT-8**, 155–159 (1962).
[2] K. N. Stevens and A. S. House, "Perturbation of Vowel Articulations by Consonantal Context: An Acoustical Study," J. Speech & Hearing Res. **6**, 111–128 (1963).
[3] B. Lindblom, "Spectrographic Study of Vowel Reduction," J. Acoust. Soc. Am. **35**, 1773–1781 (1963).
[4] B. Lindblom, "Articulatory Activity in Vowels," Speech Transmission Lab. QPSR **2**, p. 1 (1964).
[5] S. E. G. Öhman, "Coarticulation in VCV Utterances: Spectrographic Measurements," J. Acoust. Soc. Am. **39**, 151–168 (1966).
[6] K. N. Stevens, A. S. House, and A. P. Paul, "Acoustical Description of Syllabic Nuclei: An Interpretation in Terms of a Dynamic Model of Articulation," J. Acoust. Soc. Am. **40**, 123–132 (1966).
[7] S. E. G. Öhman, "Numerical Model of Coarticulation," J. Acoust. Soc. Am. **41**, 310–320 (1967).
[8] W. L. Henke, "Dynamic Articulatory Model of Speech Production Using Computer Simulation," PhD thesis, MIT, Sept. 1966.

[9] O. Fujimura and K. Ochiai, "Vowel Identification and Phonetic Contexts," J. Acoust. Soc. **35**, 1889 (A) (1963).

LINDBLOM AND STUDDERT-KENNEDY

coped with. To explain how, we might argue that a listener relies on "context." For instance, he may use the more absolutely identifiable cues in longer segments of speech to infer the identity of the reduced vowels from various phonological, syntactic, and semantic constraints. Or again, perhaps our selection of an isolated, acoustic vowel attribute gives a misleading perspective of the vowel recognition problem: Other information in the short-term acoustic context, such as the direction and rate of adjacent formant transitions, may also be important in the auditory representation of the signal and the processes of symbol assignment. It is precisely this latter possibility that is examined in the present paper.

An identification experiment was performed in order to investigate the relative rôles that formant transitions and the formant pattern at the point of closest approach to target play in vowel recognition, and to ascertain whether operations contributing to the "solution" of the vowel-recognition problem, as formulated above, are invoked at the level of monosyllabic nonsense speech. In the experiment, American English listeners were asked to identify vowel sounds presented under steady-state conditions and in symmetrical CVC syllables. The vowel-formant patterns assigned to the points of closest approach to target were selected from a continuum ranging from [ɪ] to [ʊ]. The rate and direction of the adjacent transitions were systematically varied by the choice of two consonantal frames: [w-w] and [j-j]. Two main possible outcomes of the experiment were anticipated. It was argued that a listener might categorize the vowel continuum in one of two ways.

● *Context-free case:* Categorization would be the same for the #V#, [w], and [j] contexts. As long as two stimuli had identical formant frequencies at their midpoints they would be perceptually equivalent no matter how different the adjacent formant frequency transitions. This result would indicate that sampling occurs at zero rate of change of formants, and that the measurement of the midpoint formant frequencies can be made by the auditory system irrespective of transitional context. Symbol assignment would be based on a straightforward classification of auditory patterns.

● *Context-dependent case:* Categorization would vary: The boundary between [ɪ] and [ʊ] vowels would shift as a function of context. The interpretation of this result would depend on the details of the boundary displacements.

II. STIMULUS SPECIFICATION

The stimuli were constructed, according to the above three-element model, so as to contain an initial transition, a pattern of closest approach to target, and a final transition. The basic building blocks were 20 points along a vowel-formant continuum and two sets of

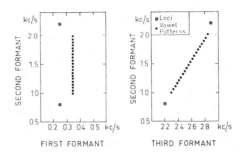

FIG. 2. Formant frequencies of vowels and consonants used to generate synthetic stimuli of #V# and CVC structure.

consonantal loci. The loci served as starting points for the initial transitional segment and the vowel patterns as the terminals of this segment. The final segment was always the mirror image of the first half of the stimulus. Thus, these syllables were of symmetrical CVC structure. At the start of the stimulus, formant frequencies remained stationary at locus frequencies for about 20 msec, then moved on to one of the vowel patterns, and from there symmetrically back to the same locus frequencies again. A 20-msec steady-state pattern at these frequencies terminated the syllable. In this way, each set of loci was combined with each vowel formant pattern.

The vowel patterns were selected along a continuum in the F_1-F_2-F_3 space as follows:

$$F_1 = 350,$$
$$F_2 = 1000 + [(n-1) \cdot 1000]/19,$$
$$F_3 = 2300 + [(n-1) \cdot 525]/19,$$

where n represents stimulus number. Thus, F_1 is constant, while F_2 varies in linear steps of about 53 cps from 1000 to 2000 cps, and F_3 varies between 2300 and 2825 cps in steps of approximately 28 cps. Perceptually, at the extremes of this continuum, the vowel sounds approach American English [ɪ] and [ʊ]. The sets of loci chosen were a [j] set in which $F_1 = 250$, $F_2 = 2200$, $F_3 = 2900$ cps, and a [w] set where $F_1 = 250$, $F_2 = 800$, $F_3 = 2200$ cps. The information on vowels and loci is represented graphically in Fig. 2.

The relative locations of the loci and the vowel continuum were selected so as to produce initial F_2 and F_3 movements that would always exhibit either positive slopes ([w] series) or negative slopes ([j] series). The general form of the formant-frequency variation throughout the entire vowel segment was parabolic. Thus, in the [j] series, the F_2 and F_3 transitions were symmetrical parabolas, *concave* upward in a frequency–time display. The vowel continuum patterns in this set were assigned to points of zero rate of frequency change, where F_2 and F_3 reached their *minimum* values. In the [w] series the F_2 and F_3 transitions were also symmetrical parabolas, but *convex* upward. Again, the vowel patterns occurred at points

ROLE OF FORMANT TRANSITIONS IN VOWEL RECOGNITION

of zero rate of change, but at these points F_2 and F_3 now reached their *maximum* values. The course of F_1 was identical in the two series: It was convex upward and always reached its maximal value at the zero rate of change point. The case of zero slope of all transitions was also included to produce 20 steady-state versions of the vowel patterns. Finally, duration was introduced as a variable, the vowel segments being either 200- or 100-msec long. Twenty vowel patterns, two sets of consonant loci, one steady-state frame, and two rates give a total of $(20 \cdot 2 \cdot 2 + 20 \cdot 2) = 120$ stimuli.

These syllables were synthesized on OVE II at the Department of Speech Communication (Speech Transmission Laboratory), KTH, Stockholm. The spectral shape of the source and radiation factors were simulated by a single real-axis pole at 50 cps producing a slope of -6 dB/oct. The correction for higher poles that is introduced by means of the KH and F5' circuits was at the standard settings of 4 kcps. The frequency of the fourth formant was fixed at 3500 cps and formant bandwidths as follows: $B_1 = 50$, $B_2 = 60$, $B_3 = 80$, and $B_4 = 125$ cps. A monotone fundamental frequency of 100 cps was used. The OVE II formant circuits are connected in series.[10,11]

In the stationary vowel series, formant frequencies were adjusted manually: Only the ON and OFF sets of the A_0, or voice source intensity, gate were programmed from the OVE II function generator. In the CVC syllables, two control patterns for the parameters were used to generate the stimuli, one for each consonantal environment. The appropriate frequency values for the loci and vowel patterns were obtained by calibrating the frequency range of the formant in question. This was done to improve the accuracy of frequency control. A frequency analysis of each formant circuit—repeated before each syllable was synthesized—indicated that formant frequencies were within ± 5 cps of the desired frequencies. Spectrograms of each individual test stimulus were examined before the preparation of test tapes. Figure 3 presents spectrographic illustrations of some of the stimuli generated.

III. EXPERIMENTAL PROCEDURES

The method used to study the perception of the vowels was a two-alternative forced-choice identification task. Two groups of American English listeners were asked to label the vowel sounds as either [ɪ] or [ʊ]. Data are available from six subjects run at Haskins Laboratories (CA, KE, FE, KR, SO, AD), New York, and four subjects run at KTH, Stockholm (HW, DW, MS, JH). All listeners were native speakers of American

[10] G. Fant, "Acoustic Analysis and Synthesis of Speech with Applications to Swedish," Ericsson Tech. No. 1, **15**, 3–108 (1959).
[11] G. Fant, J. Mártony, U. Rengman, and A. Risberg, "OVE II Synthesis Strategy," in *Proceedings of the Speech Communication Seminar Stockholm 1962* (Royal Institute of Technology, Speech Transmission Laboratory, Stockholm, 1963), Vol. 2, paper F5.

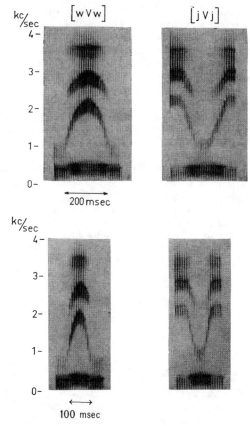

FIG. 3. Spectrographic illustrations of stimuli in the [w-w] and [j-j] series.

English, of fairly homogeneous dialectal backgrounds and without obvious speech or hearing defects. With the exception of one subject (JH), they had had no previous experience in auditory and psychophysical tasks. No one was informed what the test was about either before or during the course of the testing. Subjects were paid for their work. The tests were distributed over a period of 10 days with one session per day, and the listening material assigned to each session lasted, at most, 50 min, exclusive of interruptions and breaks. The stimuli were arranged in four major groups: slow [w] and [j] series, fast [w] and [j] series, slow #V# series and fast #V# series. Four different randomizations of the stimuli in each series were used. Each series began with five buffer stimuli that were not used in subsequent processing of the data. On a given test tape, there were four 3–4 min series, one representative from each major group; the order of the various CVC and #V# tests was counterbalanced across the tapes. The total number of responses to each individual stimulus obtained from each listener was at least 15. On the average, each observer made

LINDBLOM AND STUDDERT-KENNEDY

about 2000 responses in all. The New York and Stockholm subjects were run under almost identical conditions. They were seated in quiet rooms or booths and listened to the stimuli over earphones. To estimate the absolute level of the stimuli at the subjects' ears, the beginning of each tape had a 1000-cps sinusoidal signal that had been recorded at the level of the maximum reading for the vowel stimuli on the occasion of the synthesis. The gain of the tape-recorder playback for this tone was adjusted to give a voltage across the earphones equivalent to 80 dB *re* 0.0002 dyn/cm². The instructions read to the listeners were as follows:

"This is an experiment in speech perception. You are going to hear a sequence of vowel sounds. You are asked to identify each one as either [ɪ], as in 'bit,' or [ʊ], as in 'book.' In the first two tests, you will hear each vowel placed between two semiconsonantal sounds. Sometimes you will hear them between two [w]'s, as in [wɪw] or [wʊw]; other times you will hear them between two [j]'s, as in [jɪj] or [jʊj]. But whatever their context, you are asked to identify only the vowel sound in the middle. If you think the vowel is more like the [ɪ] in 'bit,' write *i* on your answer sheet opposite the appropriate stimulus number; if you think the vowel is more like the [ʊ] in 'book,' write *oo* on your answer sheet opposite the appropriate stimulus number.

"There are 45 stimuli in each of the first two tests with a 4-second interval between stimuli and a 9-second interval after the 15th, 25th, and 35th stimuli. So, each test will last for about 3 or 4 minutes. We will pause for a moment between tests and you will be warned when the second one is going to begin.

"In the next two tests you will again hear the vowels, but this time you will hear them alone without any surrounding context. Again you are asked to identify each vowel as either [ɪ], as in 'bit,' or [ʊ], as in 'book,' and to record your judgment opposite the appropriate stimulus number on your answer sheet.

"There are 25 stimuli in each of the next two tests with a 4-second interval between stimuli. So each test will last about two minutes. We will pause for a moment between tests and you will be warned when the second one is going to begin."

These instructions were read to the participants before the first four tests with appropriate pauses for writing the symbols and key words on the blackboard, and for questions and answers. Between every four tests, a longer break of about 5 min was normally taken. At subsequent sessions, the full instructions were not repeated, but a summary was given: "The tests today are similar to those of previous days. Remember, you are asked to identify each vowel as either [ɪ], as in 'bit,' or [ʊ], as in 'book.'"

IV. EXPERIMENTAL RESULTS I

A. Slow Stimuli (Vowel Duration: 200 msec)

Data were plotted for the observers individually in the form shown in Fig. 4. This figure shows the percentage of [ɪ] responses (dots) and [ʊ] responses (crosses) as a function of the stimulus continuum. Low-stimulus numbers refer to vowel patterns with low F_2 and F_3 values (see Section on stimulus specification, above). Reading from the top, the graphs show the

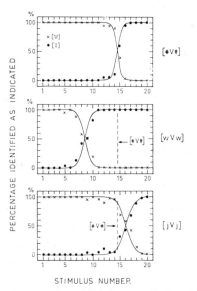

FIG. 4. The percentage of [ɪ] responses (dots) and [ʊ] responses (crosses) for one subject as a function of stimulus number and vowel environment.

results in the #V#, [wVw], and [jVj] contexts for one subject (JH). To present the results in a fairly compact form, a quantification of the data has been attempted. On the assumption that the probability of making a given response increases (or decreases) in the region of a phoneme boundary, according to the function of an integrated normal distribution, ogives were fitted to the individual identification graphs as shown in Fig. 4. The mean value of the distribution corresponds to the boundary, or the 50% crossover point along the continuum. Its standard deviation is inversely related to the steepness of the cumulative curve. Mean values $\bar{x}$ and standard deviations σ for such distributions are presented in Table I for individual observers and for the three stimulus conditions #V#, [wVw], and [jVj]. The duration of the vowel segment was 200 msec in this material. To establish $\bar{x}$ and σ, the data were also plotted on normal-probability graph paper and a best-fitting straight-line approximation was determined in the region of the phoneme boundary by visual inspection.[12] This transformation of percentages into σ or z units has the effect of magnifying the importance of "noise" inherent in data points close to the asymptotes of the distribution, whereas errors of equal magnitude at more and more central values are given successively less weight. This fact was considered in the curve-fitting procedure by restricting it to the transitional segment between asymptotes.

Before considering the boundary locations, something should be said about the variability of the data. It

---

[12] A somewhat different procedure was used for the [w] data. It is described later in Sec. VI.

RÔLE OF FORMANT TRANSITIONS IN VOWEL RECOGNITION

TABLE I. Fifty percent crossovers or boundary locations ($\bar{x}$) and standard deviations (σ) of identification functions fitted to the vowel responses obtained for steady-state condition ($\bar{x}_v$ and σ_v), the [w-w] context ($\bar{x}_w$ and σ_w) and the [j-j] context ($\bar{x}_j$ and σ_j). The numbers are in terms of stimulus numbers ($\bar{x}$) and continuum steps (σ). Duration of vowel stimuli: 200 msec.

Subject	$\bar{x}_v$	σ_v	$\bar{x}_w$	σ_w	$\bar{x}_j$	σ_j
CA	13.7	2.8	6.7	5.0	...	...
KE	12.7	2.3	9.0	3.5	14.5	3.7
FE	13.2	2.2	8.3	3.5	14.9	3.0
KR	12.9	2.4	9.6	4.7	14.4	2.4
SO	14.4	2.2	10.4	4.3	...	...
AD	13.0	2.6	12.3	4.0	14.3	4.0
JH	14.7	0.9	8.6	1.3	16.2	1.7
MS	14.8	0.8	13.2	1.7	11.8	1.2
DW	12.3	1.2	12.1	0.9	9.0	2.0
HW	14.0	1.3	17.1	4.2	11.0	3.3

TABLE II. Data from Table I. Displacement of boundaries for CVC stimuli in relation to #V# stimuli. Positive numbers indicate downward shifts, negative numbers upward shifts.

Subject	$\bar{x}_v$-$\bar{x}_w$	$\bar{x}_v$-$\bar{x}_j$
CA	7.0	...
KE	3.7	−1.8
FE	4.9	−1.7
KR	3.3	−1.5
SO	4.0	...
AD	0.7	−1.3
JH	6.1	−1.5
MS	1.6	3.0
DW	0.1	3.3
HW	−3.1	3.0
Median	3.5	−1.4

appears from Table I that the σ values are somewhat larger for the consonantal contexts than for the #V# situation. This result may be taken to indicate that subjects found it more difficult to make the judgments in the former cases. It is not unlikely that the consonantal stimuli struck some observers as more unnatural than the sustained vowels. For, though (by some stretch of the imagination) a [wVw] stimulus might roughly sound somewhat like *will* or *wool*, it is hard to find any English words to match the [jVj] stimuli. The difficulty of the consonant environments can also be inferred from the fact that three subjects failed altogether to show crossovers in the CVC situations, as did subjects CA and SO in the [j] environment. These data deviate from those of the others either in that the percentages of [ɪ] and [ʊ] answers fluctuate around 50% all along the stimulus continuum, or in that the subject favors a single response close to 100% of the time. Since cumulative ogives serve no descriptive purpose in such cases, these data are not tabulated. For the remainder of the material, clear crossovers were obtained. Yet some subjects showed uncertainty as to the identity of the vowel, even in clearly "asymptotic" regions of the stimulus continuum, and would, in such cases, produce asymptotes closer to 10% and 90% rather than to the expected 0% and 100%. It is, thus, clear that observers differed markedly in the case with which they made the identifications.

An examination of the boundary locations for the three experimental conditions indicates that for most of the subjects the [w] environment shifts the boundary towards low-stimulus numbers in relation to its position in the #V# situation. This general tendency is brought out most clearly in Table II where the distances between the boundaries for the consonant and the steady-state vowel contexts are presented for the observers individually and in terms of median values. The median boundary displacement for the [w] context is 3.5 continuum steps in the direction of low-stimulus numbers, and that for the [j] context is smaller (1.4 steps) but occurs in the opposite direction. These

shifts, when expressed in terms of the frequency steps of the second formant, are approximately 185 cps ([w]) and 75 cps ([j]). Hence, there is a clear tendency for the boundary location to vary with context: it shifts in the direction of the consonantal loci. The [j] stimuli yield less consistent results in that the shifts occur towards both high- and low-stimulus numbers. The data of subject HW differ most markedly from the general trend of the material both in the direction and in the magnitude of the shifts.

In Fig. 4, the boundary shifts have the same directions as the median displacements discussed above. It is apparent that a larger displacement is obtained for the [w] context than for the [j] context. The [w] stimuli were those with convex frequency-time variation in the second and third formants, so that the initial transitional segment always contained positive or rising transitions. The midpoint vowel patterns at the termination of these segments invariably represented the frequency *maximum* of the formant in question (F_1 included). In terms of steps along the continuum, the boundary shift is about 320 cps in F_2. Describing this effect in terms of [ɪ] responses alone, it can be said that in 100% of the cases stimulus No. 11 in the [w] series appeared equivalent to stimulus No. 17 in the #V# series, as regard vowel identity. Thus, in the [w] context, the pattern of maximal extent of the formant transitions need only be about $F_1=350$, $F_2=1525$, and $F_3=2575$ for it to be consistently labeled [ɪ], whereas, in the #V# situation, a more "acute" pattern of $F_1=350$, $F_2=1845$, $F_3=2740$ is required to elicit equally consistent [ɪ] responses. The [j] stimuli had second and third formants that varied in a concave fashion as a function of time, so that the initial transitions were falling (except for the first formant transitions that were identical in the [w] and [j] series and exhibited a rise–fall or convex time variation). At the point of zero rate of change, formants (F_2 and F_3) reached their *minimum* frequency values. The boundary shift brought about by the [j] context is much smaller than for [w], only about 1.5 continuum steps as compared with 6 for [w]. On the whole, the identity changes

LINDBLOM AND STUDDERT-KENNEDY

I told you you <u>will</u> woo her

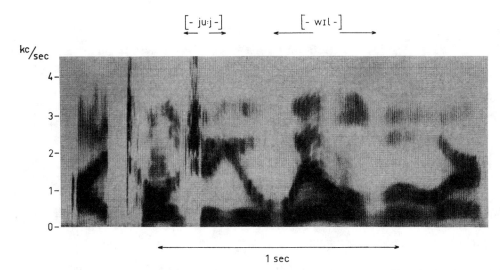

FIG. 5. Spectrogram of *I told you you will woo her* pronounced naturally with contrastive stress on *will* and reduced stress on the first *you*. Notice the small difference between the central F_2 values in [ju:j] and [wɪl]. Compare this utterance with that in Fig. 6.

are most extreme in the region of Vowel Patterns **11, 12, 13,** and **14,** where symbol assignment shifts radically from 100% [ɪ] responses in the [w] context to nearly 100% [ʊ] judgments in the [j] environment.

V. DISCUSSION

A. Complementarity of Vowel Production and Vowel Perception

The results of the identification experiment suggest that vowel stimuli that were identical with respect to midpoint formant frequencies, but differed with respect to formant transitions, were not perceptually equivalent. One purpose of the experiment was to investigate the relative rôles of formant transitions and such midpoint patterns in vowel recognition. The present results appear to indicate that the identity of a vowel stimulus is determined not only by the formant pattern at the point of closest approach to target, but also by the direction of the adjacent formant transitions. A second objective was to ascertain whether operations contributing to the reduction of ambiguity can be invoked in the recognition of monosyllabic nonsense speech. Do the particular effects observed in this experiment serve this purpose?

That, in fact, they do appears from the following considerations. As mentioned earlier, formant frequencies at the center of vowels may undershoot their target values and be displaced away from the values observed for steady-state conditions in the direction of adjacent consonantal loci. (Refs. 2, 3, 4, and 6.) In the production of syllables like [wɪw] and [wʊw],

formants will, thus, be shifted towards their values for [w]; and for syllables like [jɪj] and [jʊj], towards their values for [j]. An illustration of such effects is given in Figs. 5 and 6, which show spectrograms of the utterances *I told you you will woo her* and *I told you you will woo her*, pronounced by a native male speaker of American English. The utterances contain the phonetic segments [−ju:j−] and [−wɪl−] under different conditions of stress that approximate some of the test syllables used. Table III shows differences between F_2

TABLE III. Differences in cycles per second between the second formant values of [ɪ] and [u:] in "null" environments and context (F_2 undershoot).

	Stressed	Unstressed	Context
[u:]	0	−660	[j-j]
[ɪ]	+420	+970	[w-l]

values for [ɪ] and [u:] in a "say hVd again" environment and the above segments. Each value is based on 10 measurements and has been sampled at points of closest approach to target. These data confirm the results of earlier investigations by demonstrating that formant undershoot occurs in the direction of the immediately adjacent loci and increases with shorter duration and decreasing prominence (Refs. 3 and 4). There is an asymmetry between the magnitudes of undershoot observed in the [j-j] and [w-l] environments, the displacement being greater in the [w-l] environment for both conditions of stress. This result may indicate a

RÔLE OF FORMANT TRANSITIONS IN VOWEL RECOGNITION

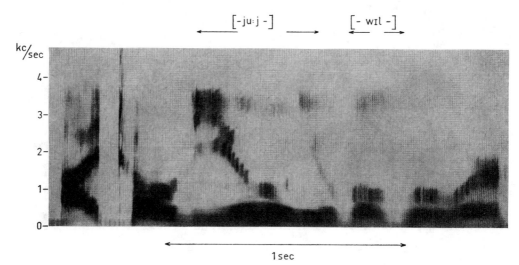

FIG. 6. Spectrogram of *I told you you will woo her* with contrastive stress on the first *you* and reduced stress on *will*. F_2 samples taken in the middle of the vowels of [ju:j] and [wɪl] are almost identical.

difference between the time constants of the movements involved, but may also be related to differences in locus-target distances, vowel duration, and stress.[13]

As noted earlier, the boundary shifts observed in Fig. 4 also occur in the direction of the loci. In terms of the stimulus continuum the [w] boundary is located six steps away from the position of the #V# boundary: It has been shifted toward low-stimulus numbers, that is, toward the [w] loci. Similarly, the [j] boundary has been slightly displaced toward the [j] loci. For this subject, it is clear that *categorization of the continuum is adjusted* in the different environments *so as to compensate for an undershoot effect* in the vowel stimuli. From the point of view of certain acoustic attributes of vowels, it would appear that the processes of vowel production and vowel recognition have complementary rôles: recognition compensates for production.

B. Active Recognition Model

The complementarity between production and recognition at the level of the nonsense syllable can be shown to be compatible with, for instance, an "active" perceptual analysis. By an active strategy, it is meant one that embodies an internal replication of the stimulus. The speech recognition model proposed by MacKay,[15,16] analysis by synthesis (Ref. 2),[17,18] and the motor theory[15,20] fall in this category. The steps by which the recognition of syllables like [jɪj], [wʊw], etc. might proceed according to such a scheme are as follows: The stimulus undergoes peripheral auditory analysis. A decision is made as to the contextual frame: Is it #V#, [wVw], or [jVj]? A computation is made of the auditory consequences of realizing an [ɪ] articulatorily and acoustically in the selected context. The result of this replication is compared with the input stimulus. The error is measured. The vowel [u] is rep-

[13] An interesting question is to what extent the control of the articulatory goals underlying the production of American English vowels remains invariant under changes of stress. Current linguistic analysis of American English[14] postulates a vowel reduction rule that, in certain situations, would replace, for instance, an [ɪ] vowel by and [i] provided that at least tertiary stress had been assigned to the [ɪ] previously in the stress cycle. Whether such a rule reflects a restructuring of the articulatory control of vowel pronunciation or merely describes an automatic physiological consequence of weak stress falls outside the scope of the present discussion.

[14] N. Chomsky and G. A. Miller, "Introduction to the Formal Analysis of Natural Languages," in *Handbook of Mathematical Psychology* (John Wiley & Sons Inc., New York, 1963), Vol. 2, pp. 269–321.

[15] D. M. MacKay, "Mindlike Behaviour in Artefacts," Brit. J. Sci. **2**, 105–121 (1951).

[16] D. M. MacKay, "The 'Active/Passive' Controversy," paper presented at the Seminar on Speech Production and Perception, Leningrad 13–16 Aug. 1966 (to be published in Z. für Phonetik usw.).

[17] K. N. Stevens and M. Halle, "Remarks on Analysis by Synthesis and Distinctive Features," paper presented at the Symposium on Models for the Perception of Speech and Visual Form, Boston, Mass., 11–14 Nov. 1964 (to be published).

[18] K. N. Stevens and A. S. House, "Speech Perception," *Foundations of Modern Auditory Theory*, J. Tobias and E. Schubert, Eds. (to be published).

[19] A. M. Liberman, F. S. Cooper, K. S. Harris, and P. F. MacNeilage, "A Motor Theory of Speech Perception," in *Proceedings of the Speech Communication Seminar Stockholm 1962*, (Royal Institute of Technology, Speech Transmission Laboratory, Stockholm, 1963), Vol. 2, paper D3.

[20] A. M. Liberman, F. S. Cooper, M. Studdert-Kennedy, K. S. Harris, and P. F. MacNeilage, "Some Observations on the Efficiency of Speech Sounds," paper presented at the Seminar on Speech Production and Perception, Leningrad, 13–16 Aug. 1966 (to be published in Z. für Phonetick usw.).

licated in a similar manner in the same context. Again the result is compared with the input. The vowel yielding the smaller error is the response. Accordingly, at the extreme low end of the vowel continuum, it is [ʊ] that gives the smaller error in the #V# context. As the stimulus number increases it is still [ʊ] that gives the better match until stimuli near the boundary are encountered. Here errors are about the same for both alternatives. It is seen from Fig. 4 that, in the #V# context, the boundary occurs, not at the mid-point of the continuum, but around Stimuli 14 and 15. This asymmetry might indicate that the listener in question assigns a more central continuum location to a typical [ʊ] sound than to an [ɪ] which appears to be located at the extreme high end. The same reasoning applies to the other contexts. However, if the process of internal replication is to simulate accurately the transformations from neural commands to sound, coarticulation will be one of the features replicated. Hence, it should predict different formant patterns for the two vowels in the various contexts. Not only will there be transitions in the case of the [w] and [j] environments and more or less steady-state formants for #V#, but the formant pattern at closest approach to target will also be different owing to the undershoot effect.

Consider a vowel formant pattern in the [wVw] context having an intermediate position on the stimulus continuum; Stimulus 11, for instance. The time variations of the second formant of this stimulus are shown to the left in Fig. 7. The ordinate has a mel scale. The internal regeneration mechanism supplies two alternative comparison patterns [wɪw] and [wʊw] (upper right of the figure). It is assumed that these patterns have been computed in accordance with the dynamic laws of speech production. Thus, the point of closest target approach falls short of the intended target frequencies for [ɪ] and [ʊ]. The assumptions underlying the construction of the replicated patterns are: (a) the

TIME VARIATIONS OF SECOND FORMANT

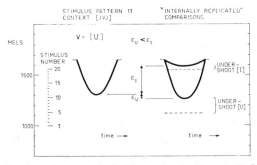

FIG. 8. Analogous to Fig. 7. Stimulus Pattern 11 occurs in the [j-j] context. Notice that it is [jʊj] that now gives the smaller error ($\varepsilon_U < \varepsilon_I$) so the response is [ʊ].

[ʊ] and [ɪ] target patterns correspond to Stimuli 4 and 20, respectively. ([ʊ] is given a slightly more central location than [ɪ]); (b) the undershoot in F_2 depends on the locus–target distance in question and is estimated at 25% of this distance for the present case. For the purposes of the present discussion, the deviation of the theoretically generated alternatives from the stimulus is taken to be defined simply as the difference in mels between these patterns at the instant of closest approach to target. If the mismatch for [ɪ], henceforth denoted ε_I, is larger than that for [ʊ], ε_U, the vowel recognized is [ʊ], and conversely; since in the present case of [wVw] $\varepsilon_I < \varepsilon_U$ the vowel response is [ɪ]. In Fig. 8 is shown the identical vowel formant configuration now in the [jVj] context. The internally generated candidates exhibit the same dynamic features as the previous patterns. It is seen that, although the formant configuration at zero rate of change is the same as before, a comparison of the errors in this context gives the opposite result. Since $\varepsilon_U < \varepsilon_I$, the vowel recognized is [ʊ]. As remarked above, such radical identity changes can be observed in Fig. 4. in the region of Vowel Patterns 11, 12, 13, and 14 for the two consonantal environments. For [wVw], ε_I is smaller than ε_U for stimulus numbers larger than 11, whereas the situation where $\varepsilon_I > \varepsilon_U$ obtains will be approached as lower stimulus numbers are encountered. Accordingly the boundary between [ɪ] and [ʊ] lies *below* Pattern 11 in the [w] environment. Similarly, in the case of [jVj], ε_U is smaller than ε_I for stimulus numbers below 11 and the [ɪ]-[ʊ] boundary, or the switchover from ($\varepsilon_U < \varepsilon_I$) to ($\varepsilon_U > \varepsilon_I$), occurs *above* Stimulus 11. As seen earlier in Fig. 4 and Table II, this is also the direction in which the experimentally observed boundary shifts occur. If the exact locations of the boundaries are taken to be found at a place where $\varepsilon_I = \varepsilon_U$ the expected boundaries occur between 8 and 9 (w), 12 and 13 (#V#), and 15 and 16 (j). The observed locations shown in Fig. 4 are about 8.5 (w), 14.5 (#V#), and 16 (j). The major discrepancy, two continuum steps, is obtained for

TIME VARIATIONS OF SECOND FORMANT

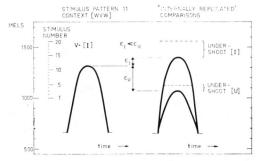

FIG. 7. "Active" analysis of Stimulus Pattern 11 in the [w-w] series (in terms of second formant only). Stimulus Pattern 11 is compared with two "internally computed" candidates for the best match: [wɪw] and [wʊw]. These hypothetical alternatives exhibit undershoot in relation to the targets (dashed). In this case, [wɪw] gives the smaller error ($\varepsilon_I < \varepsilon_U$), which makes [ɪ] the vowel response.

RÔLE OF FORMANT TRANSITIONS IN VOWEL RECOGNITION

#V#. The asymmetrical distribution of the estimated locations is in agreement with the data and is due to the definition of errors in terms of mels and the choice of target values for [ɪ] and [ʊ]. This asymmetry compares favorably with that observed in the formant-undershoot data from natural utterances similar to the present test syllables (Figs. 5 and 6).

VI. EXPERIMENTAL RESULTS II

A. Fast Stimuli (Vowel Duration: 100 msec)

The vowel recognition behavior under analysis is of great complexity. Any attempt to model it at present must be functional rather than structural. Accordingly, little can be said now about the actual mechanisms underlying the boundary shifts. On the other hand, the active model suggested above, although informal, provides a convenient starting-point for a further examination of the complementarity of production and perception at the nonsense syllable level. As used here, complementarity refers to the observation that, from the point of view of the phonetician, mechanisms of production introduce ambiguity at the acoustic level, whereas perceptual mechanisms resolve it. If the dependence of undershoot on the rate of talking (Refs. 3 and 4) were incorporated in the active recognition scheme, the internally predicted undershoot would depend on a measurement of the duration of the vowel. Since there is a general tendency in this material for the boundary shifts to occur in such a direction that they in fact compensate for undershoot in the vowels (whether subconsciously "assumed" or not by the listener), it is reasonable to ask whether a compression of the time scale of the same stimuli patterns would give rise to even larger boundary shifts. These considerations lead to a new experiment that might establish whether recognition at the nonsense-syllable level corrects for the variance and ambiguity in vowels to the same extent as they are introduced by production.

As mentioned earlier, in the Section on stimulus specification, two sets of stimuli were synthesized. One set contained vowels 200-msec long. The experimental results presented so far pertain to this set. During the listening sessions, subjects made responses also to a set of fast stimuli that differed from the slow ones only in that the time scale of the vowel segments had been compressed by a factor of 2 (Fig. 3). Vowel segments were consequently 100-msec long, and the over-all length of the CVC syllables was 140 msec. These sounds were presented under conditions described in the Section on experimental procedures. These conditions were identical for fast and slow stimuli, but the two types of stimuli occurred in separate groups on the test tapes. The data were plotted in the form of identification graphs, and ogives were fitted to the data points. The results of this experiment closely resemble those already discussed. Table IV shows crossover values ($\bar{x}$)

TABLE IV. Fifty percent crossovers ($\bar{x}$) and standard deviations (σ) for data from a supplementary experiment in which vowel stimuli were 100-msec long but otherwise identical to those of Table I.

Subject	$\bar{x}_v$	σ_v	$\bar{x}_w$	σ_w	$\bar{x}_j$	σ_j
CA	12.6	2.5	6.0	3.1	⋯	⋯
KE	12.6	2.2	6.9	2.6	12.0	7.2
FE	12.1	2.2	5.5	3.4	16.2	2.6
KR	12.1	2.0	5.6	2.6	12.5	3.3
SO	13.4	1.8	9.0	1.2	⋯	⋯
AD	12.5	2.5	8.0	4.0	13.3	3.3
JH	14.1	1.0	8.5	1.5	16.9	1.4
MS	14.3	0.8	12.0	3.7	11.8	1.7
DW	11.3	1.2	11.5	1.2	8.8	2.3
HW	14.0	1.4	17.7	3.8	11.0	3.7

and standard deviations (σ) for the three stimulus conditions. Boundary shifts occur as before (Table V): There are substantial downward shifts for [w] and upward shifts for [j]. Exceptions from this tendency are found among subjects who also deviated earlier. In similar agreement with the previous results, standard deviations are somewhat smaller in the #V# context, and Subjects CA and SO have trouble with the [j] stimuli, showing no crossovers.

TABLE V. Data from Table IV. Displacement of boundaries for CVC stimuli in relation to #V# stimuli.

Subject	$\bar{x}_v - \bar{x}_w$	$\bar{x}_v - \bar{x}_j$
CA	6.6	⋯
KE	5.7	0.6
FE	6.6	−4.1
KR	6.5	−0.4
SO	4.4	⋯
AD	4.5	−0.8
JH	5.6	−2.8
MS	2.3	2.5
DW	−0.2	2.5
HW	−3.7	3.0
Median	5.0	0.1

Consider again the active model and the replicated patterns corresponding to [ɪ] in the [w] and [j] contexts. The duration of the vowels is now 100 msec. Let the internal replication mechanism make the same calculations as before, except that the undershoot effect is now assumed to be larger, say, 50% of the locus–target distance. As before, the [ɪ]–[ʊ] boundaries are located at a point on the continuum that yields equally large errors in terms of mels and the midpoint value of the second formant. These conditions now give boundary locations slightly above Stimulus No. 4 for [w], and close to 18 for [j]. The duration decrease of the stimuli should consequently cause a further shift of the boundaries by about four steps for [w] and by two steps for [j] from their previously estimated positions. Wherever a graphical curve-fitting procedure made a significance test of differences between the fast and slow data seem worthwhile, the 50% crossover

TABLE VI. Shifts of the [w-w] and [j-j] boundaries associated with a change of vowel duration in the stimuli. Positive numbers refer to upward shifts and conversely.

Subject	$\Delta \bar{x}_w$	$\Delta \bar{x}_j$
CA	−0.7	⋯
KE	−2.1***	−2.5
FE	−2.9***	+1.3
KR	−3.9***	−1.9
SO	−1.4*	⋯
AD	−4.3***	−1.0
JH	−0.1	+0.7
MS	−1.2***	0.0
DW	−0.6*	−0.2
HW	0.6	0.0

points, or means ($\bar{x}$), and the standard deviations (σ) were established by means of probit analysis.[21,22] According to this method, the best-fitting lines were determined after transforming response percentages to weighted values or probits, a procedure whereby points receive weights depending on both their inherent statistical reliability and their relative location in the distribution. Only the data lying between asymptotic regions were used. The method also provides an estimate of the variance of the crossover points, which makes it possible to use a *t* test to judge the significance of crossover differences. In this test, an infinite number of degrees of freedom was assumed.

Table VI shows the boundary displacement associated with a duration change in the stimuli. The values given refer to the differences between "fast" and "slow" boundary locations. A negative number thus indicates a downward shift, a positive number an upward shift. It is seen that for [w], shifts occur in the expected direction. Their magnitudes are, in general, smaller than estimated. On the other hand, the differences are probably not due to chance as indicated in the Table by the conventional asterisk notation. Only the [w] data seemed worth processing statistically. Thus, Tables I and IV show graphical estimates for #V# and [jVj], and computed estimates for [wVw]. In the case of [jVj], the results are less consistent with respect to the direction of the shifts that are small.

VII. PERIPHERAL REPRESENTATION OF VOWEL SOUNDS

The response of the human auditory system to a sound can be shown to depend appreciably on the acoustic context of this sound. Such dependence is exemplified for instance by adaptation and fatigue phenomena that manifest themselves as a time-varying short-term or more persistent reduction of auditory sensitivity.[23–25] Threshold shifts of this kind introduce a temporary decaying skewness in the frequency response of the ear and have for this reason been considered responsible for certain pitch-shift effects. It has been found, for instance, that the pitch attributed to pure tones tends to be displaced away from a frequency region whose threshold has been temporarily raised by preceding or simultaneous stimulation, towards a more sensitive region (Ref. 23).[26,27] Whereas there is a great deal of information in the literature on such contextual effects in the perception of pure tones, there appear to be few, if any, data on the peripheral representation of spectral shape in complex sounds like vowels and still fewer on the dependence of such representations on various environmental conditions. There is, however, a study by Brady *et al.*[28] on the perception of sounds with a rapidly varying formant frequency that may be of some relevance to the present discussion. In that investigation, listeners were asked to find a best match between a test sound and an adjustable comparison stimulus. Both stimuli were single-formant sounds of equal duration in the range of 20–50 msec and generated by identical periodic excitation. In the test stimulus, the resonant frequency varied linearly over a 500-cps range; the resonant frequency of the comparison stimulus was steady-state, but could be controlled by the observers. The results indicate that the preferred location of the formant frequency of the comparison stimulus was a value close to the terminal frequency of the varying formant. It is of interest to note that this tendency was stronger for a faster rate of frequency change and somewhat more pronounced for upward frequency ramps than for downward ones. In conclusion, the authors suggest that "there may be some overshoot or extrapolation in the processing of brief stimuli characterized by rapidly changing spectra." There are several possible ways in which these results could be interpreted. The foregoing discussion suggests one: The hypothetical overshoot mechanism (whose existence is supported by the tendency to place the comparison resonance still closer to the terminal frequency for a faster rate of frequency change) could tentatively be identified with adaptational processes.

[21] J. P. Guilford, *Psychometric Methods* (McGraw–Hill Book Co., New York, 1954).

[22] D. J. Finney, *Probit Analysis* (Cambridge University Press, Cambridge, England, 1947).

[23] G. von Békésy, *Experiments in Hearing* (McGraw–Hill Book Company, New York, 1960), pp. 366–368.

[24] R. Plomp, *Experiments on Tone Perception* (Institute for Perception RVO–TNO, Soesterberg, The Netherlands, 1966), pp. 20–22.

[25] E. Lüscher and J. Zwislocki, "The Decay of Sensation and the Remainder of Adaptation after Short Pure-Tone Impulses on the Ear," Acta Oto-Laryngol. **35**, 428–445 (1947).

[26] J. P. Egan and D. R. Meyer, "Changes in Pitch of Tones of Low Frequency as a Function of the Pattern of Excitation Produced by a Band of Noise," J. Acoust. Soc. Am. **22**, 827–833 (1950).

[27] J. C. Webster and E. D. Schubert, "Pitch Shifts Accompanying Certain Auditory Threshold Shifts," J. Acoust. Soc. Am. **26**, 754–758 (1954).

[28] P. T. Brady, A. S. House, and K. N. Stevens, "Perception of Sounds Characterized by a Rapidly Changing Resonant Frequency," J. Acoust. Soc. Am. **33**, 1357–1362 (1961).

RÔLE OF FORMANT TRANSITIONS IN VOWEL RECOGNITION

During the test stimulus, auditory events can be grossly pictured as follows: There occurs a continuous change in the sensitivity of the ear owing to adaptation. At any given moment the "tracking" of the formant peak may be shifted towards a region of lower threshold, that is, upwards for an ascending ramp and downwards for descending ramps, the amount of displacement depending on how far adaptation has progressed at that moment. This effect would accordingly be one of the factors contributing to shifting matches closer to the terminal frequencies of the ramps. If verified by future experimentation[29] these speculations invite the conclusion that the peripheral auditory representation of spectral formant peaks depends on the rate of formant frequency change and offer a possible explanation of some of the present rate- and context-dependent boundary shifts. According to this view, vowel production and vowel perception could be said to be complementary in the sense that articulatory activity is characterized by undershoot and perception by overshoot.

VIII. DISTINCTIVE FEATURES

There are various other ways of describing the results obtained, for instance, in terms of distinctive features. If, in a sequence of feature complexes, one of the features takes the values of $+-+$ in one case and $---$ in another, the phonetic correlates of the middle segment need exhibit less pronounced "negativity" in absolute terms in the positive context than in the negative one. In Fig. 4, this is illustrated by the fact that the observer permits $[\upsilon]$ vowels to possess less marked cues of flatness (labialization) and graveness (velarization) in the plain (unrounded) and acute (palatalized) context of $[j]$, and conversely $[\iota]$ vowels to present less trace of plain and acute attributes in the flat and grave environment of $[w]$. This interpretation exemplifies the statement that phonetic features are relational. Their values are specified along scales in relative terms.[30,31] The data may also be examined with respect to their implications about a talker's encoding strategy. In order to produce $[\iota]$ and $[\upsilon]$ sounds that remain distinctive, what is minimally required of him? Suppose that he produces $[\iota]$ and $[\upsilon]$ vowels that are most intelligible when their formant patterns approach the upper and lower ends, respectively, of the vowel continuum. In the $[w\text{V}w]$ context, it is not necessary for an $[\iota]$ vowel to have a formant pattern that lies close to the upper end of the continuum. For example,

F_2 and F_3 at 1525 and 2575 cps will be sufficient to elicit the correct response from the listener of Fig. 4. The situation is reversed, but similar, for the $[j\text{V}j]$ environment and an $[\upsilon]$ vowel. In terms of the extent of formant movements in syllables like $[w\iota w]$ and $[j\upsilon j]$, this, consequently, means that a complete transition from loci to vowel target is not required. The transitions could undershoot their target frequencies for the vowel to a certain extent without distinctiveness being lost. Under such circumstances, it is not necessary for a talker to compensate for the sluggish dynamics of his articulatory mechanism by reorganizing his control of it in such a way that undershoot is avoided. The present findings suggest that there may be recognition processes that compensate for this sluggishness and absence of reorganization. Not only do we "speak to be heard in order to be understood," but we obviously also listen to hear in order to understand.

IX. RÔLE OF EXPECTANCY

It might be argued that the boundary shifts have to do with differences in the predictability of the vowels in the different contexts. According to this view the more probable vowel could be given as a response to stimuli located in an intermediate uncertainty region between clear $[\iota]$ and $[\upsilon]$ alternatives. This bias should have the effect of moving the boundary towards the less probable vowel. It can be objected that such a mechanism would remain insensitive to a tempo change. Since duration-dependent shifts were observed, this view is difficult to defend. Moreover, it is not clear what should be meant by the notion of "more probable vowel" in this connection.

X. PRODUCTION AND PERCEPTION OF DIPHTHONGS

There is an old observation on the perception of diphthongs that appears pertinent in connection with the present results. Jespersen[32] writes: "Fallende Diphthonge. Hier entscheidet oft bloss die Richtung der Bewegung den resultierenden Laut. Statt dass man z.B. in beabsichtigtem $[\alpha i]$ den ganzen Weg von $[\alpha]$ bis $[i]$ geht, begnügt man sich damit, nur ein Stück zu gehen, indem das Ohr leicht *getäuscht wird* (italicized by us, BL/MSK) und die Phantasie leicht das Fehlende ergänzt." Similar remarks can be found in the works of other authors.[33] Thus, Jones states that "the English diphthong *ai* is one which begins at *a* and moves in the direction of *i*. *To give the right effect* (italics ours, BL/MSK) it is not necessary that *i* should be quite reached; the diphthong may, and generally does, end at an opener vowel than this, such as a fairly open variety of *e*." The italicized passages clearly imply that

---

[29] It is believed that information relevant to these questions can be obtained by means of standard psychoacoustical experimental techniques. Several projects designed to elucidate these problems are at present under way.

[30] F. de Saussure, *Cours de linguistique générale* (C. Bally & Sechehaye, Paris, 1916), pp. 1–337.

[31] R. Jakobson and M. Halle, *Fundamentals of Language* (Mouton and Company, 's-Gravenhage, The Netherlands, 1956), pp. 1–87.

[32] O. Jespersen, *Lehrbuch der Phonetik* (Verlag von B. G. Teubner, Leipzig, Germany, 1926), p. 208.

[33] D. Jones, *An Outline of English Phonetics* (W. Heffer & Sons Ltd., Cambridge, England, 1956), pp. 58–59 Sec. 224.

the auditory value of the second element is [i], in the opinion of these phoneticians. Thus, an articulatory movement [ɑe] or [ɑɛ] is heard as [ɑi] by the naïve listener. In terms of the second formant of such sounds, there would be a transition that would have a positive slope and would fall short of an [i] value, thus, terminating at a lower frequency. In spite of this reduced extent, an [i] element is claimed to be heard that is analogous to what was found for [wɪw] in the present material.

XI. SOME PARALLEL OBSERVATIONS

The results of Fujimura and Ochiai (Ref. 9) on vowel identification also bear on our own findings.[34] These investigators gated out 50-msec portions of vowels from Japanese words and made an analysis of listener responses to these segments presented in isolation. In general, the confusions could be explained in terms of coarticulation. Thus, it was found that an [u] from /yuyusii/ was recognized as /i/. If more of the context or the entire word had been presented, confusions would not have occurred to the same extent. The implication of this work (and of our own) is that the assignment of symbols to vowels normally involves some sort of context-sensitive routine. Whether these operations are of short-term (syllabic) and/or long-term (word) nature cannot be inferred from this Japanese investigation. The present findings on the categorization of the [ɪ]–[ʊ] continuum, on the other hand, do not exclude the interpretation that, among other processes, a short-term mechanism might be involved.

In agreement with the present results, Stevens[35] found that listeners tend to categorize a given vowel continuum differently depending on whether the vowels are isolated and steady-state, or embedded in a CVC frame. It is of interest to note that, the boundary shift observed also occurred in a direction so as to compensate for potential undershoot effects.

Fry *et al.*[36] observed a dependence of vowel labeling on context. These investigators asked listeners to identify synthetic steady-state vowels presented in ABX groupings. They conclude that the effect of sequence on vowel identification is considerable. There was a tendency for a given vowel stimulus along an [ɪ]–[ɑe] continuum to be judged as closer (more [ɪ] like) when paired with a more open sounding ([ɑe] like) vowel, and conversely, as more [ɑe] like in the neighborhood of a closer sounding stimulus. Similar context dependence in vowel perception was reported also by Lade-

foged and Broadbent.[37] This study demonstrated that the vowel in a monosyllable could be influenced by the formant patterns used in a preceding carrier sentence. The results of Fry *et al.* appear to indicate that a shift of reference frame in vowel perception may occur although the stimuli do not contain formant transitions and are separated in time by as much as one second (Ref. 36). At present, it cannot be determined whether these contrast effects and the present analogous [ɪ]–[ʊ] boundary shifts are attributable to the same underlying mechanism. It is worth reiterating, however, that mechanisms of perceptual analysis whose operations contribute to enhancing contrast in the above-mentioned sense are precisely the type of mechanisms that seem well suited to their purpose given the fact that the slurred and sluggish manner in which human speech sound stimuli are often generated tends to reduce rather than sharpen such contrast.

XII. SUMMARY AND CONCLUSIONS

1. Listeners were found to categorize a vowel continuum ranging from [ɪ] to [ʊ] differently depending upon whether the context of the vowels was #V#, [w-w], or [j-j].

2. The locations of the boundary between [ɪ] and [ʊ] observed for [w-w] and [j-j] tended to be displaced towards the consonant loci in relation to its position for #V#.

3. The boundary shift was most marked for [w-w].

4. A decrease of the duration of the vowel stimuli gave results similar to those mentioned above but was associated with a slightly larger boundary displacement for [w-w].

There emerges from these two experiments the tentative conclusion that, in the recognition of monosyllabic nonsense speech, the identity of a vowel sound is determined not only by the formant pattern at the point of closest approach to target but also by the *direction* and *rate* of adjacent formant transitions. Boundary shifts in the [w] context occurred in such a direction as to compensate for formant-frequency undershoot in the vowels. Vowel recognition thus compensated for vowel production. In this sense, these processes were found to exhibit complementarity.

ACKNOWLEDGMENTS

We would like to express our deep gratitude to Dr. F. S. Cooper, Haskins Laboratories, New York, to Professor G. Fant, Department of Speech Communication, KTH, Stockholm, and to Professor K. N. Stevens, Massachusetts Institute of Technology, Cambridge,

---

[34] We wish to express our gratitude to Professors Fujimura and Ochiai for putting a prepublication draft of this paper at our disposal.

[35] K. N. Stevens, "On the Relations between Speech Movements and Speech Perception," paper presented at the Seminar on Speech Production and Perception, Leningrad, 13–16 Aug. 1966 (to be published in Z. für Phonetik usw).

[36] D. B. Fry, A. S. Abramson, P. D. Eimas, and A. M. Liberman, "The Identification and Discrimination of Synthetic Vowels," Language and Speech **5**, 171–189 (1962).

[37] P. Ladefoged and D. E. Broadbent, "Information Conveyed by Vowels," J. Acoust. Soc. Am. **39**, 98–104 (1957).

RÔLE OF FORMANT TRANSITIONS IN VOWEL RECOGNITION

Massachusetts, for making it possible for us to do the present research and for their generous support and stimulating interest during all phases of it. We are also greatly indebted to Mrs. S. Felicetti for preparing the manuscript and for editorial aid, to Mr. Å. Florén for technical assistance, and to all other colleagues at the Department of Speech Communication, KTH, and at Haskins Laboratories who helped us in various ways. The cooperation of Professor W. L. Henke and Professor A. S. House during the exploratory stages of this work is gratefully acknowledged. To a considerable extent, the present investigation owes it existence to Professor A. M. Liberman who encouraged us all along and with whom we have had frequent and fruitful discussions. Thanks are due also to Dr. O. Franzén, Professor J. M. Heinz, Dr. A. W. Slawson, and Dr. S. E. G. Öhman for responding with many valuable thoughts and suggestions.

This research was supported by funds for speech research at Haskins Laboratories, at Research Laboratory of Electronics, MIT, and at the Department of Speech Communication, KTH.[38]

---

[38] The Joint Services Electronics Program; The National Science Foundation; the National Aeronautics and Space Administration; the U. S. Air Force Cambridge Research Laboratories; the National Institutes of Child Health and Human Development, the National Institutes of Health, U. S. Department of Health, Education, and Welfare; and the Swedish Technical Research Council (Statens Tekniska Forskingsråd).

Perception & Psychophysics
1973. Vol. 13. No. 2, 253-260

Auditory and phonetic memory codes
in the discrimination of consonants and vowels*

DAVID B. PISONI

Indiana University, Bloomington, Indiana 47401

Recognition memory for consonants and vowels selected from within and between phonetic categories was examined in a delayed comparison discrimination task. Accuracy of discrimination for synthetic vowels selected from both within and between categories was inversely related to the magnitude of the comparison interval. In contrast, discrimination of synthetic stop consonants remained relatively stable both within and between categories. The results indicate that differences in discrimination between consonants and vowels are primarily due to the differential availability of auditory short-term memory for the acoustic cues distinguishing these two classes of speech sounds. The findings provide evidence for distinct auditory and phonetic memory codes in speech perception.

Current theories of speech perception suggest that the perception of speech sounds may involve processes that are in some way basically different from the processes involved in the perception of other sounds (Liberman, Cooper, Shankweiler, & Studdert-Kennedy, 1967). A large body of experimental work indicates that when listeners are exposed to certain classes of speech sounds, their ability to identify and discriminate between them on an auditory basis is limited to a large degree by their linguistic knowledge. Differences in the perception of certain classes of speech sounds have led investigators to propose a "special" speech perception mode to characterize the way these phonetic segments are heard (Liberman, 1970). Other results have suggested that a "special" perceptual mechanism may exist for the processing of speech sounds (Studdert-Kennedy & Shankweiler, 1970; Studert-Kennedy, Liberman, Harris, & Cooper, 1970).

One of the findings that has been cited as evidence for a special speech perception mode is the difference in perception between synthetic stop consonants and steady-state vowels. Stop consonants have been found to be perceived in a categorical mode, unlike other auditory stimuli. Discrimination is limited by absolute identification. Listeners are able to discriminate stimuli drawn from *different* phonetic categories but cannot discriminate stimuli drawn from the *same* phonetic

category, even though the acoustic difference between stimuli is comparable.

For example, Liberman, Harris, Hoffman, and Griffith (1957) found that synthetic speech stimuli that varied in acoustically equal steps through the range sufficient to produce the initial stop consonants /b/, /d/, and /g/ were perceived as members of discrete categories. When listeners were required to discriminate pairs of these stimuli, they were able to discriminate stimuli drawn from different phonetic categories but could not discriminate stimuli drawn from the same phonetic category. The obtained discrimination functions were not monotonic with changes in the physical scale, but showed marked discontinuities at points along the continuum that were correlated with changes in identification.

On the other hand, steady-state vowels have been found to be perceived continuously, much like nonspeech sounds. Listeners are able to discriminate many more differences than would be predicted on the basis of absolute identification. Fry, Abramson, Eimas, and Liberman (1962) reported that synthetic vowel stimuli varying in acoustically equal steps through the range of /I/, /ɛ/, and /æ/ were perceived in a continuous mode. The discrimination functions did not yield discontinuities along the continuum that were related to changes in identification but were relatively constant across the entire continuum. In addition, they reported that listeners could perceive many more intraphonemic differences for the vowel series than for the consonant series. Similar differences between stop consonants and steady-state vowels have been reported more recently by Stevens, Liberman, Studdert-Kennedy, and Ohman (1969) and by Pisoni (1971). The results of these studies have led investigators to propose two different modes for the perception of speech stimuli: a categorical or phonetic mode and a continuous or auditory mode[1] (Liberman et al, 1967; Studdert-Kennedy, 1973; Studdert-Kennedy, Shankweiler, & Pisoni, 1972).

*This paper is based on a portion of a thesis submitted to the University of Michigan in partial fulfillment of the requirements for the PhD degree. I am very grateful to Dr. Franklin S. Cooper and Professor Alvin M. Liberman for making the unique facilities of Haskins Laboratories available to me for preparation of the stimulus materials and for their interest in this work. I am also indebted to Professor Irwin Pollack and Professor Michael Studdert-Kennedy for their help and advice. This research was supported in part by a grant from NICHD to Haskins Laboratories, an NSF grant to Irwin Pollack, and a Rackham Prize Fellowship from the Graduate School of the University of Michigan. A shorter version of this paper was presented at the meetings of the Acoustical Society of America, Denver, Colorado, October 1971.

Although the distinction between categorical and continuous modes of perception has played an important role in theoretical discussions of speech perception, the differences between these two modes of perception are not well understood. Recently, Fujisaki and Kawashima (1969, 1970) proposed a model of the perceptual processes involved in speech discrimination that considers the separate contributions of phonetic and auditory short-term memory. They suggest that the categorical-continuous distinction in speech perception may be related to the degree to which separate auditory and phonetic memory components are employed in the decision process during discrimination.

According to Fujisaki and Kawashima's model, when a listener discriminates two *different* phonetic types, he bases this decision on the derived phonetic properties and features of the auditory stimulus as represented in some type of *phonetic short-term memory*. The listener determines whether the two stimuli have been identified as belonging to the same or different phonetic categories with a binary decision. For example, are the two stimuli the "same" phonetic segment or "different" phonetic segments? Following this strategy, a listener's performance in a discrimination task should be completely predictable from his performance on an identification task and should approach the ideal case of categorical perception. The listener can discriminate two stimuli only to the extent that he can identify the stimuli as being different phonetic segments (Liberman et al, 1957).

Categorical perception, which appears to be unique to certain kinds of speech sounds, may be contrasted with continuous perception where the listener is able to discriminate between two identical phonetic types, or allophones. In order to make a correct decision, the listener must rely on some stored auditory information about the acoustic parameters of the stimuli as represented in *auditory short-term memory*, because he has categorized both stimuli as the same phonetic segment. The listener now makes a comparative judgment rather than an absolute judgment, attending to the specific acoustic properties of the two stimuli. As a consequence, discrimination performance is independent of identification.

The purpose of the present experiment was to test the hypothesis that consonants and vowels differ in the degree to which distinct auditory and phonetic memory codes are employed in discrimination. If categorical perception is related to the differential use of auditory short-term memory in discrimination, it should be possible to demonstrate this by the use of several procedures which have not been employed previously in speech perception experiments. One such procedure is a delayed comparison recognition memory task. In this task, two stimuli are presented with a varying comparison interval between them. The S's task is to indicate whether the two stimuli were the same or different. We can produce a relative preponderance of comparative and absolute judgments and, in turn, a differential reliance on auditory and phonetic memory codes by selecting pairs of stimuli to be discriminated from either "between" phonetic categories or "within" phonetic categories. By examining discrimination performance over a range of comparison intervals, the temporal course of recognition memory for vowel and consonant stimuli may be assessed.

METHOD

Experimental Design

The design of the present experiment involved the manipulation of three independent variables: stimulus conditions (four levels, two classes of vowels, and two classes of consonants); stimulus comparisons (two levels, within phonetic category comparisons and between phonetic category comparisons); and delay interval (0.0, .25, .50, 1.0, and 2.0 sec). Ss were assigned to one of four different stimulus conditions, with the stimulus variable distributed over all levels of the other two independent variables.

Subjects

Sixteen undergraduate students at the University of Michigan served as Ss in the present experiment. The Ss were obtained from the paid S pool at the Mental Health Research Institute. All Ss were right-handed native speakers of English and reported no history of a hearing disorder or speech impediment. Ss were paid for their services at the rate of $2/h. None of the Ss had ever heard any synthetic speech stimuli before the experiment.

Description of Stimuli

The following four sets of synthetic speech stimuli were prepared, and they correspond to the different stimulus conditions in the experiment. All of the stimuli were digitized, and their wave forms were stored on the Pulse Code Modulation System at Haskins Laboratories (Cooper & Mattingly, 1969).

Voiced Stop Consonants (/bæ/-/dæ/)

A set of voiced stop consonant-vowel stimuli were synthesized on the Haskins Laboratories parallel resonance synthesizer. The set consisted of seven three-formant syllables that were 300 msec in duration. The final 220 msec of each stimulus was a steady-state vowel appropriate for an American English /æ/, with the first three formants fixed at 743, 1,620, and 2,862 Hz, respectively. During the initial 40 msec, a period of closure voicing was simulated on the synthesizer by a low-amplitude F_1 at 150 Hz. This period of prevoicing appropriate for the voiced stops was followed immediately by a 40-msec transitional period, during which the first three formants moved toward the steady-state frequencies of the vowel. The experimental variable was the starting frequencies of the second and third formant transitions. Stimulus 1 had second and third formant frequencies, beginning at 1,232 and 2,180 Hz. For successive stimuli in the series, the F_2 and F_3 starting frequency increased in approximately equal steps from 1,232 to 1,695 Hz and from 2,180 to 3,195 Hz, respectively. The change in both F_2 and F_3 transitions from Stimulus 1 to Stimulus 7 has been shown to be the major acoustic cue for distinguishing place of production between the syllables /bæ/ and /dæ/ (Liberman et al, 1967). The fundamental frequency was set at 120 Hz for the entire duration of the syllable.

Bilabial Stop Consonants (/ba/-/pa/)

A set of seven three-formant bilabial stop consonants was also produced on the Haskins synthesizer. The stimuli varied in 10-msec steps along the voice onset time (VOT) continuum from 0 through +60 msec, which distinguishes /ba/ and /pa/. VOT has been defined as the interval between the release of the articulators and the onset of laryngeal pulsing or voicing. Synthesizer control parameter values for these stimuli were similar to those employed by Lisker and Abramson (1967). Each of the seven stimuli had a duration of 300 msec. The final 250 msec of the CV syllable was a steady-state vowel appropriate for an American English /a/. The frequencies of the first three formants were fixed at 769, 1,232, and 2,525 Hz, respectively. During the initial 50-msec transitional period, the first three formants moved upward toward the steady-state frequencies of the vowel. For each successive stimulus in the set, the amplitude of F_1 was "cutback" (amplitude reduced) and the excitation source was switched from buzz (periodic) to hiss (aperiodic) in 10-msec steps. Lisker and Abramson (1967) have showed that changes in amplitude in the lower frequency region and type of excitation characterize the voicing and aspiration differences between /b/ and /p/ in English.

Long Steady-State Vowels (/i/-/I/)

Seven 300-msec steady-state vowels were synthesized on the vocal tract analogue synthesizer at the Research Laboratory of Electronics, M.I.T. The stimuli were arranged so that the first three formants varied in approximately equal logarithmic steps through the English vowels /i/ and /I/. The fourth and fifth formants were fixed at 3,500 and 4,500 Hz, respectively. The formant frequency values employed here were identical to those provided by Stevens et al (1969) in their study of vowel perception.

Short Steady-State Vowels (/i/-/I/)

An additional set of seven vowel stimuli were also produced on the vocal tract analogue synthesizer at M.I.T. These seven stimuli were identical to the long vowels described above, except that their duration was reduced to 50 msec. The 50-msec vowel condition was included because both Fujisaki and Kawashima (1970) and Pisoni (1971) had reported that vowels of very brief duration could be perceived categorically.

Experimental Materials

The experimental materials were produced under computer control. Two types of tests were prepared for each stimulus condition: an identification test and a delayed comparison recognition memory test.

Absolute Identification Tests

Two different 70-item identification tests were prepared for each of the four stimulus conditions. Each identification test contained 10 different randomizations of an entire series of the seven stimuli in the set. The stimuli were recorded singly with a 4-sec interval between presentations and an 8-sec interval after every 10 presentations.

Delayed Comparison Recognition Memory Tests

Four different delayed comparison recognition memory tests were constructed for each of the four stimulus conditions. Each test tape contained two separate replications of 50 trials. A set of 50 trials consisted of 10 basic test pairs at each of five delay intervals. The 10 test pairs were constructed in the following manner. Stimuli 1, 3, 5, and 7 were selected from each of the four original sets of seven stimuli. The four stimuli were arranged

into three AB pairs (i.e., 1 with 3, 3 with 5, and 5 with 7). These three pairs appeared in two permutations (i.e., AB and BA), producing six "different" AB pairs at a given delay interval. Each of the four stimuli was also paired with itself once, resulting in four "same" AA pairs at each delay interval. Each set of 50 trials appeared in a different random arrangement in each test.

The stimuli were recorded in pairs, with a 5-sec interval between successive trials. The delay intervals (0, .25, .50, 1.0, 2.0 sec) were arranged automatically under computer control. A 100-msec 1,000-Hz tone was recorded 750 msec before the onset of the first stimulus in each pair as a ready signal.

Procedure

The experiment was conducted in an anechoic chamber located in the Phonetics Laboratory at the University of Michigan. The experimental tapes were reproduced on an Ampex 351-2 tape recorder and were presented binaurally through Telephonics (TDH-39) matched and calibrated headphones. The gain of the tape recorder was adjusted to give a voltage across the earphones equivalent to 75 dB SPL re 0.0002 dynes/cm^2 for a 1,000-Hz calibration tone. Measurements were made on a Ballantine VTVM (Model 300) before the presentation of each experimental tape.

At the beginning of the experiment, Ss were told that this was an experiment dealing with speech perception and that the sounds they would hear were made by a computer to approximate human speech. The instructions for the identification test were identical to those used in previous speech perception experiments. The Ss were told that the stimuli would be presented individually and that they were required to identify each stimulus as belonging into one of two categories, depending on the particular stimulus condition employed (e.g., /b/ or /d/, /b/ or /p/, /i/ or /I/).

For the delayed comparison recognition memory task, Ss were told that they would hear two stimuli separated by a varying interval on each trial and that their task was to decide whether the two stimuli were the "same" or "different." They were told that approximately half of all the pairs were the same and half of the pairs were different. Ss were encouraged to guess if they were not sure of a judgment. Judgments for both identification and discrimination tests were recorded in prepared booklets containing IBM test sheets for later analyses.

The Ss were tested for 1 h/day on 2 consecutive days. Each session began with a 70-item identification test, which was followed by four 100-trial delayed comparison recognition memory tests. The order of presentation for the delayed comparison tests was reversed on the second day.

RESULTS

Absolute Identification

The average identification function for each of the four stimulus conditions is shown in Fig. 1. Each point is based on 80 judgments summed over the four Ss in each condition.

Inspection of this figure reveals that Ss partitioned each of the stimulus continua into two relatively distinct phonetic segments. The average percent correct discrimination functions summed over all delay intervals are also plotted on the corresponding identification functions in Fig. 1. Two aspects of these data are of interest. First, discrimination performance is better between phonetic categories than within phonetic categories for every stimulus condition. Second,

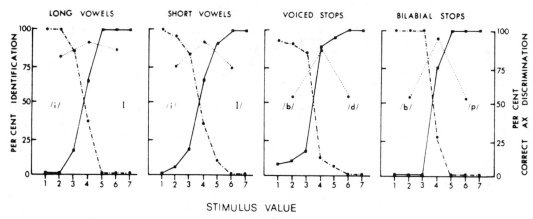

Fig. 1. Average identification functions for each of the four stimulus conditions, with discrimination functions averaged over all delay intervals superimposed on the corresponding identification functions.

within-category discrimination is close to chance for both consonant conditions but well above chance for both vowel conditions. Within-category comparisons for the long-vowel condition also appear to be more discriminable than they are for the short-vowel condition.

Delayed Comparison Recognition Memory

The major stimulus comparisons under consideration are also shown in Fig. 1. Within-category discrimination scores were obtained at each delay interval by averaging the judgments for Stimulus Comparisons 1-3 and 5-7 in each stimulus condition. Between-category discrimination scores were obtained at each delay interval for judgments of Stimulus Comparisons 3-5 in each stimulus condition. Two separate scoring procedures were used to assess recognition memory performance. The first procedure examined only responses to trials in which the two stimuli to be

discriminated were different, i.e., P("D"|D). The second procedure employed a d′ measure, which considered responses to both same and different trials. The d′ measure was employed in order to account for possible response biases which might enter into the same-different task.

P("D"|D) Discrimination Scores

Discrimination probabilities were obtained from conditions in which the pairs of stimuli were different. Figure 2 shows the average probability of a "different" response when the stimuli were different as a function of delay interval. Each point is based on 32 judgments per S at each delay interval. Filled circles represent between phonetic category comparisons, whereas open circles represent within phonetic category comparisons.

The P("D"|D) scores were analyzed by means of a three-factor analysis of variance for mixed designs. F ratios were evaluated against the corresponding mean

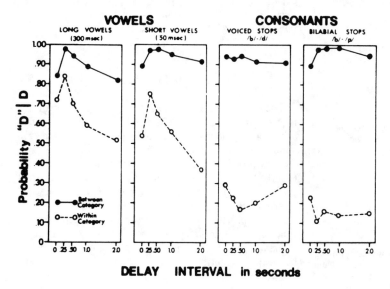

Fig. 2. Average probability of a "different" response when the stimuli within a pair were different [P("D"|D)] as a function of delay interval for each stimulus condition for within and between phonetic categories.

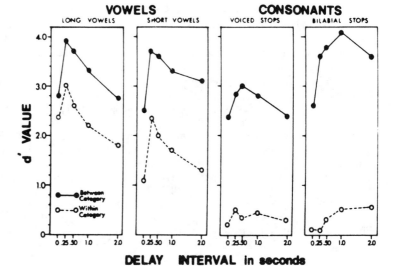

VOWELS **CONSONANTS**

Fig. 3. Average d' scores for within- and between-category comparisons as a function of delay interval for each stimulus condition.

square term including Ss. The main effects of stimulus condition (i.e., vowels vs consonants) [F(3,12) = 16.47, p < .001], delay interval [F(4,48) = 5.58, p < .005], and stimulus comparison (i.e., between vs within) [F(1,12) = 238.35, p < .001] were all significant. Second-order interactions of Stimulus Condition by Delay Interval [F(12,48) = 2.77, p < .01] and Stimulus Condition by Stimulus Comparison [F(3,12) = 16.37, p < .001] were also significant.

The overall P("D" | D) scores for between-category comparisons are quite high and relatively stable across the delay intervals for three of the four stimulus groups. One exception appears to be the long-vowel condition, where there is a slight decline in the between-category discrimination scores as the delay interval increases. However, Newman-Keuls tests on the differences among between-category means for each group indicated that they did not differ significantly from each other.

Inspection of the within-category scores, however, shows very marked differences in discrimination between consonants and vowels. Within-category consonant scores are quite low and do not appear to be related in any way to changes in the delay interval. Newman-Keuls tests showed that there were no significant differences for the consonant means across delay intervals. On the other hand, the within-category vowel scores are much higher and are systematically related to changes in the delay interval. For both vowel stimulus conditions, within-category discrimination is maximum at .25 sec and then decreases with increases in the delay interval. Newman-Keuls tests established that the .25-sec interval was significantly different from the other delay intervals for both vowel conditions.

d' Discrimination Scores

To separate the effects of recognition memory and possible response bias on the observed judgments, a d' score was computed. False alarm rates were obtained from trials on which Ss responded "different" when the pairs of stimuli were the same, i.e., P("D" | S). Since these false alarm rates were available for each stimulus at each delay interval, it was possible to obtain a d' score and use this as a reliable measure of recognition memory that was independent of response bias. The d' value has been used in this manner as a measure of trace strength in recognition memory (Wickelgren, 1966; Massaro, 1970). Figure 3 shows the average d' scores for within- and between-category comparisons as a function of delay interval for each stimulus condition. Better discrimination accuracy is shown by the higher d' levels.

The results presented in Fig. 3 indicate that discrimination accuracy decreases for both within- and between-category comparisons as the delay interval increases beyond .25 sec. The effect also appears to be greater for the vowel conditions than for the consonants. Another three-factor analysis of variance was applied to the d' scores. This analysis revealed essentially the same results as the analysis of variance performed on the P("D" | D) scores. However, one important difference appeared between the two analyses. The Stimulus Condition by Delay Interval interaction, which was significant in the first analysis with the P("D" | D) scores, did not reach significance with the d' scores.

It is clear from the results of both scoring procedures that increases in the delay interval affect vowel discrimination accuracy much more than consonant discrimination. Moreover, the differences that obtain appear to be most pronounced for the within-category vowel comparisons.

DISCUSSION

The overall results of the present experiment strongly support the claim that differences in discrimination between consonants and vowels are related in some way to the differential use of auditory short-term memory for these two classes of speech sounds. Furthermore, the results provide some insight into the temporal course of recognition memory in speech discrimination.

The major findings of this experiment can be illustrated by considering again the two types of discrimination trials employed: within phonetic category comparisons and between phonetic category comparisons. It was argued at the outset that discrimination judgments for these comparisons may be considered to represent two types of memory components: short-term auditory memory and short-term phonetic memory, respectively. The results shown in Fig. 2, based on the P("D" | D) scores, indicated that only within-category vowel discrimination was related to changes in the comparison delay interval. Within-category consonant discrimination was not only quite poor overall, but also showed no relationship to changes in delay interval. These differences indicate that while auditory short-term memory facilitates vowel discrimination within categories, it contributes little to within-category consonant discrimination. On the other hand, the P("D" | D) scores for between-category discrimination were quite high and appeared to be unaffected by changes in the delay interval. Phonetic memory appears to be quite reliable for both vowels and consonants.

The d' analysis, which considered the response bias inherent in the same-different task, revealed several additional findings which were obscured by the P("D" | D) scoring analysis. First, there appears to be some tendency even for the between-category d' scores to decrease with increases in the delay interval. This was most noticeable for the long-vowel condition. Secondly, the absence of a significant Stimulus Condition by Delay Interval interaction with the d' scores suggests that consonant discrimination is also affected to some extent by changes in the delay interval. The conclusion that the course of short-term memory is different for vowels than for consonants is, perhaps, a premature oversimplification. The differences that obtain are entirely due to within-category comparisons, which we have argued are based on auditory short-term memory. For these pairs, large and consistent differences do obtain for consonants and vowels in both the P("D" | D) and d' analyses.

While it may be concluded from these results that auditory short-term memory for consonants is different from auditory short-term memory for vowels, an explanation for the differences is clearly warranted. It is apparent that the acoustic information needed to discriminate two physically different but phonetically identical consonants is somehow not available for use in discrimination, even at very short delay intervals. However, it is not clear why this acoustic information is unavailable for use in discrimination.

One possible explanation has been suggested by Fujisaki and Kawashima (1970). Their explanation may be called the cue-duration hypothesis. According to this hypothesis, the major factor responsible for the inferior auditory short-term memory with consonants is the duration of the critical information in the signal. The acoustic cues that distinguish stop consonants (i.e., formant transitions) are relatively short in duration and presumably cannot be stored well in memory. On the other hand, the acoustic cues that distinguish vowels (i.e., formant frequencies) extend the entire duration of the stimulus. Although Fujisaki and Kawashima (1970) and Pisoni (1971) have reported that short vowels are perceived more categorically than long vowels, their findings must be considered in light of the present experiment. If the cue-duration hypothesis were correct, we would expect, in the present experiment, to find the short vowels to be more similar to the stop consonants than the long steady-state vowels. The recognition memory data of this experiment argue against this prediction. Short vowels of 50 msec duration behave almost identically to the long vowels. Although discrimination is somewhat lower overall in the short-vowel condition, the effect of the delay interval is still present, especially for within-category comparisons.

Since categorical perception can be defined only by examining the relationship between identification and discrimination (see Studdert-Kennedy et al, 1970, for further discussion), short vowels may show a tendency towards categoricalness under certain experimental conditions. However, the type of categorical perception previously found with short vowels may, in fact, be qualitatively different from that found with stop consonants. For example, both Fujisaki and Kawashima (1970) and Pisoni (1971) used an ABX discrimination procedure, which may have prevented a direct comparison between successive stimuli and forced their listeners to use an encoded categorization in discrimination. Thus, the categorical perception observed with short vowels by Fujisaki and Kawashima and by Pisoni may be attributed to the use of the ABX discrimination procedure rather than being inherent in the perceptual processes underlying vowel perception.

Several other findings deserve some comment. First, there was a noticeable decrease in discrimination performance at the 0.0-sec delay interval for both the P("D" | D) and d' scores. It is possible that this decrease represents an interruption of processing at an early stage of perceptual analysis. Using a backward masking paradigm, Massaro (1970) has found that perceptual processing of a brief tone is terminated if a masking tone follows the test tone at very short delay intervals. Massaro suggests that the masking tone interrupts a readout of information from a preperceptual sensory store, which holds the image of a stimulus until the features needed for identification can be extracted. It is interesting to note that the interruption at the 0.0-sec delay interval is more apparent for the within-category vowel comparisons than for the within-category consonant comparisons. Moreover, the interruption is less marked overall for the between-category comparisons than for the within-category comparisons.

The direction of the interruption is that anticipated if the subsequent signal terminated the processing of auditory features, assuming that phonetic processing was more nearly completed.

Secondly, discrimination accuracy for within-category vowel comparisons reaches a maximum at the .25-sec delay interval. Successive increases in the delay interval beyond .25 sec produce a steady decline in discrimination performance. This value may represent the processing time necessary for auditory recognition (see Massaro, 1972). If perceptual processing is completed within .25 sec, then the acoustic information may still be relatively salient for use in subsequent discrimination.

The most important difference between categorically and continuously perceived stimuli appears to rest on the level of within-category discrimination performance. Although the discrimination functions for vowels show a peak at the boundary between phonetic segments, the level of within-category discrimination is still well above chance. These findings suggest that categorization for vowels is not absolute and that purely auditory information is still available for use in discrimination judgments. Since prosodic information is carried almost entirely by vowels, auditory information could be available for use in vowel discrimination.

The situation with respect to the consonants is somewhat peculiar. Although the discrimination functions for the consonants show comparable peaks at phonetic boundaries, the level of within-category discrimination is very close to chance, indicating that categorization is absolute and binding. The extraction of relevant features from the acoustic signal for consonant recognition may preclude the further use of auditory information for nonphonetic judgments. It seems reasonable to conclude from these results that consonant recognition may be mediated by some specialized decoder which is tuned to specific phonetic features (Liberman et al, 1967). However, it is not possible to determine from the outcome of the present experiment whether this mediation involves an overlap with some articulatory-motor component or whether it is due to some inherent limitation of the auditory system.

The differences obtained in this study between consonants and vowels are also related to the findings reported by Crowder (1971) on recency effects in immediate memory. Crowder found that for lists of auditorily presented synthetic stop-vowel syllables, a recency effect is observed in ordered recall if the syllables in the list contrast only on vowels. However, the recency effect is curiously absent if the syllables contrast only on stop consonants. His findings are exactly what we would expect if auditory information about consonants were unavailable for use in later recall as a consequence of phonetic classification. The vowel data indicate that some type of auditory information is still available in memory for later use in immediate recall.

In summary, the results of this experiment suggest that the differences between consonant and vowel discrimination are primarily due to the differential availability of auditory short-term memory for the acoustic cues which distinguish these two classes of speech sounds Vowel discrimination within categories was considerably better than consonant discrimination within categories. As a result, we can conclude that auditory short-term memory for the acoustic properties of vowels is better than auditory short-term memory for the acoustic properties of consonants.

REFERENCES

Cooper, F. S., & Mattingly, I. G. Computer-controlled PCM system for investigation of dichotic speech perception. Status Report on Speech Research (SR-17/18), Haskins Laboratories, New York, 1969, 17-21.

Crowder, R. G. The sound of vowels and consonants in immediate memory. Journal of Verbal Learning & Verbal Behavior, 1971, 10, 587-596.

Fry, D. B., Abramson, A. S., Eimas, P. D., & Liberman, A. M. The identification and discrimination of synthetic vowels. Language & Speech, 1962, 5, 171-189.

Fujisaki, H., & Kawashima, T. On the modes and mechanisms of speech perception. Annual Report of the Engineering Research Institute, Vol. 28, Faculty of Engineering, University of Tokyo, Tokyo, 1969, 67-73.

Fujisaki, H., & Kawashima, T. Some experiments on speech perception and a model for the perceptual mechanism. Annual Report of the Engineering Research Institute, Vol. 29, Faculty of Engineering, University of Tokyo, Tokyo, 1970, 207-214.

Liberman, A. M. Some characteristics of perception in the speech mode. In D. A. Hamburg (Ed.), Perception and its disorders; Proceedings of A.R.N.M.D. Baltimore: Williams & Wilkins, 1970. Pp. 238-254.

Liberman, A. M., Cooper, F. S., Shankweiler, D. P., & Studdert-Kennedy, M. Perception of the speech code. Psychological Review, 1967, 74, 431-461.

Liberman, A. M., Harris, K. S., Hoffman, H. S., & Griffith, B. C. The discrimination of speech sounds within and across phoneme boundaries. Journal of Experimental Psychology, 1957, 54, 358-368.

Lisker, L., & Abramson, A. S. Some experiments in comparative phonetics. Proceedings of the 6th International Congress of Phonetic Sciences, Prague, September 1967.

Massaro, D. W. Retroactive interference in short-term recognition memory for pitch. Journal of Experimental Psychology, 1970, 83, 32-39.

Massaro, D. W. Preperceptual images, processing time, and perceptual units in auditory perception. Psychological Review, 1972, 79, 124-145.

Pisoni, D. B. On the nature of categorical perception of speech sounds. Doctoral thesis, University of Michigan, August 1971.

Stevens, K. N., Liberman, A. M., Studdert-Kennedy, M., & Ohman, S. E. G. Cross-language study of vowel perception. Language & Speech, 1969, 12, 1-23.

Studdert-Kennedy, M. The perception of speech. In T. A. Sebeok (Ed.), Current trends in linguistics. Vol. XII. The Hague: Mouton, 1973.

Studdert-Kennedy, M., Liberman, A. M., Harris, K., & Cooper, F. S. The motor theory of speech perception: A reply to Lane's critical review. Psychological Review, 1970, 77, 234-249.

Studdert-Kennedy, M., & Shankweiler, D. P. Hemispheric specialization for speech perception. Journal of the Acoustical Society of America, 1970, 48, 579-594.

Studdert-Kennedy, M., Shankweiler, D. P., & Pisoni, D. B.

260   PISONI

Auditory and phonetic processes in speech perception: Evidence from a dichotic study. Cognitive Psychology, 1972. 3, 455-466.

Wickelgren. W. A. Phonemic similarity and interference in short-term memory for single letters. Journal of Experimental Psychology, 1966. 71, 396-404.

NOTE

1. In this paper. it is assumed that auditory and phonetic modes of perception reflect processing of information at two distinct stages of perceptual analysis. The auditory stage refers to the analysis of the acoustic wave form into a set of time-varying psychological dimensions (pitch. loudness. timbre). whereas the phonetic stage refers to the transformation of auditory dimensions into abstract phonetic features.

(Received for publication July 31. 1972:
revision received November 17. 1972.)

Dynamic specification of coarticulated vowels

Winifred Strange, James J. Jenkins, and Thomas L. Johnson

Center for Research in Human Learning, University of Minnesota, 75 East River Road, Minneapolis, Minnesota 55455

(Received 21 June 1982; accepted for publication 1 June 1983)

An adequate theory of vowel perception must account for perceptual constancy over variations in the acoustic structure of coarticulated vowels contributed by speakers, speaking rate, and consonantal context. We modified recorded consonant–vowel–consonant syllables electronically to investigate the perceptual efficacy of three types of acoustic information for vowel identification: (1) static spectral "targets," (2) duration of syllabic nuclei, and (3) formant transitions into and out of the vowel nucleus. Vowels in /b/–vowel–/b/ syllables spoken by one adult male (experiment 1) and by two females and two males (experiment 2) served as the corpus, and seven modified syllable conditions were generated in which different parts of the digitized waveforms of the syllables were deleted and the temporal relationships of the remaining parts were manipulated. Results of identification tests by untrained listeners indicated that dynamic spectral information, contained in initial and final transitions taken together, was sufficient for accurate identification of vowels even when vowel nuclei were attenuated to silence. Furthermore, the dynamic spectral information appeared to be efficacious even when durational parameters specifying intrinsic vowel length were eliminated.

PACS numbers: 43.70.Dn, 43.70.Ve

INTRODUCTION

An adequate theory of speech perception must explain how a listener recovers the phonetic segments from the acoustic signal produced by the speaker's articulatory acts. A central goal in understanding this process is to describe the correspondence between parameters of the acoustic signal and phonetic units, that is, to specify the acoustic information that supports the perception of phonetic segments. Several decades of research have shown us that the correspondence is not a simple one-to-one mapping between acoustic features and phonetic features. Many different acoustic patterns give rise to the same phonetic percept; and likewise, the same acoustic pattern may give rise to the perception of different phonetic units, depending upon its relation to the surrounding acoustic context. In other words, speech perception is an instance of the perceptual constancy problem.

The research reported here addresses the problem of the correspondence between the acoustic signal and the phonetic percept for a major class of English phonemes, the vowels. Vowels have traditionally been differentiated in articulatory terms by the static vocal tract shapes attained by positioning the tongue, jaw, and lips in different configurations. These characteristic vocal tract shapes are often referred to as articulatory "targets." The acoustic patterns which are the consequences of these articulatory targets are described in terms of their static spectral characteristics, and are often referred to as acoustic targets. The center frequencies of the first two or three oral speech formants differentiate English vowels when they are spoken as sustained, isolated tokens by a single speaker. Vowels are thus conceived of as points in an acoustic vowel space in which the coordinates are the frequencies of the first and second formants. Multiple tokens of a particular vowel type, spoken by a single speaker as isolated (uncoarticulated) phones, fall into a small region in vowel space, well differentiated from the regions which circumscribe each other vowel type.

The variability in the acoustic patterns for a particular perceived vowel derives from several sources. First, because formant frequencies are a function of the overall size and shape of the supralaryngeal vocal tract, vowels spoken by different speakers vary acoustically in complex ways. The variability is especially great when comparing vowels spoken by men, women, and children, but there is considerable variability even for vowels produced by speakers of the same sex and age (Peterson and Barney, 1952; Strange *et al.*, 1976). Second, when vowels are coarticulated with consonants, as they nearly always are in continuous speech, the spectral characteristics of the acoustic signal vary such that the acoustic targets found in isolated vowels may not be attained in any spectral cross section taken through the changing acoustic pattern (Stevens and House, 1963). This is often referred to as target "undershoot." Third, vowels coarticulated with consonants in ongoing speech may display different amounts of target undershoot, depending upon speaking rate, sentence and word stress, and the individual style of speech (Lindblom, 1963; Gay, 1978).

The influence of any of these factors may result in a set of acoustic patterns in which the static spectral configurations that are characteristic of isolated vowels are not realized. More importantly, the region in vowel space populated by tokens of a particular vowel type produced in all these contexts will often overlap significantly with regions containing tokens of other vowel types. Acoustic vowel targets are thus ambiguous with respect to perceived vowel identity across variations in speakers, phonetic context, speech rate, and stress.

In the face of this perceptual constancy problem, two general types of theories have been offered to account for the perception of vowels, which we refer to here as (1) target normalization theories and (2) dynamic specification theories. They differ in their characterizations of the acoustic information that supports vowel perception and in their accounts of how that information is detected and used in the process of recovering the phonetic sequence from the speech signal.

Target normalization theories assume that the essential information for vowel identity is contained in the asymptotic spectral cross section within the syllabic nucleus, which most closely corresponds to the canonical (isolated) vowel targets. However, since these static spectral patterns are inherently ambiguous across speakers and contexts, the veridical perception of vowels requires complicated normalization processes through which the variable acoustic "input" is recoded in some way to arrive at the invariant percept (see Joos, 1948; Ladefoged and Broadbent, 1957; Lieberman *et al.*, 1972; Stevens and House, 1963). More recently, researchers have attempted to differentiate vowels acoustically on the basis of transformations of the target formant frequencies (Gerstman, 1968; Skinner, 1977; Nearey, 1977). However, it remains the case that all these models take as their acoustic "raw data" a single spectral cross section through the acoustic signal (but see Assmann *et al.*, 1982).

An alternative approach, taken in our laboratory and elsewhere, seeks a characterization of vowel perception that refocuses attention on the whole complex of acoustic consequences of articulating vowels in ongoing speech. In this view, vowels are conceived of as characteristic *gestures* having intrinsic timing parameters (Fowler, 1980). These dynamic articulatory events give rise to a dynamic acoustic pattern in which the changing spectro-temporal configuration provides sufficient information for the identification of the phonetic units. Perception is conceived of as the pickup of that information as it is specified over time in the acoustic signals (see Shankweiler *et al.*, 1977).

The research reported here examines the nature of the acoustic information used by listeners in identifying American English vowels in consonant–vowel–consonant (CVC) syllables. Previous research has shown that vowels spoken in CVC syllables are identified quite accurately by phonetically naive listeners, despite the presence of considerable ambiguity in the static acoustic configurations (targets) produced by differences in speakers, rate of speech, and phonetic context (Verbrugge *et al.*, 1976; Strange *et al.*, 1976; Macchi, 1980). Further studies explored possible sources of dynamic information by investigating perception of vowels produced in CVC, CV, and VC syllable contexts (Strange *et al.*, 1979; Gottfried and Strange, 1980). Results indicated the importance of two sources of information: (1) formant transitions into and out of the "vowel nucleus," and (2) temporal parameters which specify intrinsic vowel length.[1]

While these studies point to the importance of temporal and dynamic spectral information for vowel perception, a general problem with their interpretation derives from the fact that the vowels presented in the different syllable contexts were actually different productions. Thus differences in vowel identifiability across these syllabic conditions, taken as evidence for the relative perceptual efficacy of the differ-

ent acoustic parameters, could have resulted from uncontrolled differences in production.

To circumvent this confounding of perception and production, the present experiments used a different technique to explore the sources of acoustic information that specify vowel identity in a CVC syllable. Starting with syllables produced by adult speakers, digitized waveforms of the syllables were electronically modified in order to delete or alter various spectral and temporal parameters of the acoustic signal while holding others constant. The altered waveforms were then converted back to analog signals and presented to listeners who identified the vowels.

We were particularly interested in examining the relative contributions to vowel identification of three sources of information: (1) the quasi-steady-state formant frequencies of the vowel nucleus that correspond most closely to the canonical acoustic vowel targets, (2) temporal information, including the correlated parameters of length of vocalic nuclei and elapsed time between initial consonant release and final consonant closure, and (3) the formant transitions into and out of the vowel nucleus, which provide what we will refer to as dynamic spectral information. The latter two sources of information cannot be characterized by acoustic parameters available in any single spectral cross section of the syllable, but rather must be described with reference to a temporal interval or a change over time in spectral configuration. As such, they are a function of the dynamic articulatory gestures characteristic of coarticulated vowels.

I. SINGLE-SPEAKER EXPERIMENT

In the first study, CVC syllables spoken "briskly" in citation form by one adult male served as the corpus. Ten English vowels were produced twice each in the consonantal context, /b–vowel–b/. The second repetition of each syllable was spoken at a somewhat faster rate, in order to introduce some variability in the acoustic patterns associated with the vowels. Several modified syllable conditions were generated by altering the digitized waveforms of these 20 syllables. Before describing in detail how the stimulus materials were generated (see Sec. IA) the basic technique and rationale are described here.

Each syllable was divided into three components, as shown in Fig. 1: (a) an initial component, which included prevoicing (if present) and the initial transitions, (b) a center component, which encompassed the entire quasi-steady-state vowel nucleus, and (c) a final component, which included the transitions out of the vowel nucleus and the final stop release, if present. These components were defined as proportions of the total syllable extent from initial consonant release to final consonant closure. Thus their absolute durations varied across syllable tokens and types.

Seven modified syllable tests were generated by selecting various combinations of components and altering the temporal relationships among them. (1) Silent-center syllables were generated by attenuating to silence the center component, leaving the initial and final components intact and in their original temporal relationships. (2) Variable (duration) centers were the converse—both initial and final compo-

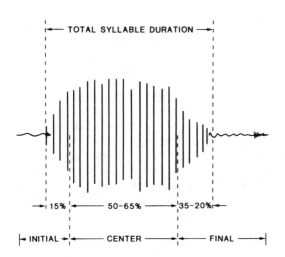

FIG. 1. Schematic representation of the acoustic waveform of a syllable. Each syllable was divided into three components which were proportions of the total syllable length, from initial stop release to final stop closure.

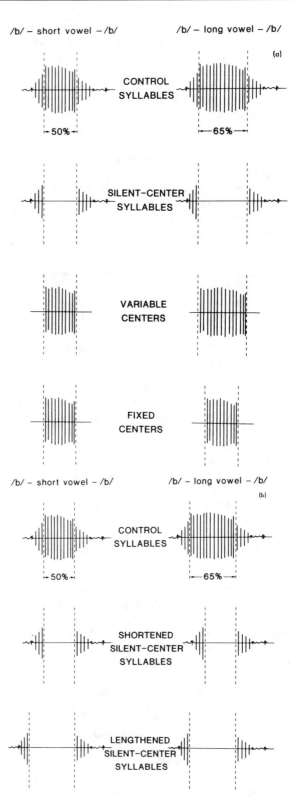

FIG. 2. (a) Schematic representations of the acoustic waveforms of control syllables (top row), silent-center syllables (second row), variable centers stimuli (third row), and fixed centers stimuli (bottom row). (b) Schematic representations of the acoustic waveforms of control syllables (top row), shortened silent-center syllables (middle row), and lengthened silent-center syllables (bottom row).

nents were attenuated to silence, leaving the vowel nucleus of each syllable intact. Three additional tests were generated by altering temporal parameters: (3) Fixed (duration) centers were the same as (2) except that all 20 tokens were "trimmed" to be the same length, that of the shortest stimulus of condition (2). (4) Shortened silent-center syllables were the same as (1) except elapsed-time differences were neutralized by substituting the shortest original silent interval between all 20 initial and final components. (5) Lengthened silent-center syllables were generated similarly, by substituting the longest original interval. Two final modified syllable tests consisted of (6) initial components alone, and (7) final components alone. In addition, a control syllables test contained the unaltered syllables. Figure 2(a) and (b) illustrates examples of stimuli in modified conditions 1 through 5.

Let us consider the kinds of information for vowel identity available in each of these sets of stimuli. The original syllables (control condition) included all sources of information: vowel nuclei containing static target information; initial and final transitions, which carry dynamic spectral information about the initiation and completion of the vowel gesture; differences in vocalic duration and elapsed time between initial consonant release and final consonant closure, which are informative of intrinsic vowel length. The silent-center syllables contained two of these sources of information: dynamic spectral information about the entire vowel gesture, available in the consonant transitions (taken together), and temporal information given by elapsed-time differences. The information missing from these stimuli were the static vowel targets. These syllables can be thought of as "vowel-less" from the standpoint of traditional definitions of vowels (see Jenkins et al., in press).

In contrast, the variable center stimuli contained the vowel targets and also information about intrinsic vowel length, specified by vocalic duration differences. Temporal information was minimized in the fixed centers by equalizing vocalic duration, and in the shortened and lengthened silent-center syllables by essentially equalizing elapsed time between initial consonant release and final consonant closure. Fixed center stimuli thus contained static target information, but essentially no dynamic spectral or temporal information. Stimuli in the shortened and lengthened silent-center syllables conditions contained dynamic spectral information, but neither vowel targets nor durational information about intrinsic vowel length. Likewise, the initial components and final components each contained dynamic spectral information, but only about the initiation or completion of the vowel gesture, respectively. (Previous research indicated that neither component alone was sufficient to specify vowel identity adequately. Thus these conditions were included as controls for the three silent-center conditions.)

According to dynamic specification theory, the identification of coarticulated vowels is accomplished on the basis of information specified over the temporal course of (at least) the syllable-length utterance. Following this model, we would predict that modified stimuli which retained dynamic spectral and temporal sources of information would yield relatively accurate vowel identification, whereas stimuli in which such information was minimized would yield relatively poor identification. Specifically, we hypothesized that the silent-center syllables, in which both dynamic spectral information (about the entire vowel gesture) and temporal information about intrinsic vowel length were available, would fare best of all the modified syllable conditions. Indeed, if dynamic information is sufficient to specify the vowel gesture, we would expect vowels in silent-center syllables to be identified unambiguously, despite the absence of the vowel targets. Target normalization theories, alternatively, would predict a significant decrement in vowel identification for silent-center syllables, since the vowel targets, thought to be the primary "cue" to vowel identity, are not physically instantiated in these stimuli.

The relative contribution of dynamic spectral and temporal information can be assessed by comparing the three silent-center syllable conditions. Vowels in CVC syllables may be perceived accurately primarily because the consonants provide perceptually salient temporal markers specifying intrinsic vowel length. If this were the case, then we would expect significant decrements in identification accuracy for both the shortened and lengthened silent-center syllables, since neither vocalic duration differences nor elapsed time differences were retained in these stimuli. If, however, the transitional components of the acoustic pattern provide perceptually relevant information about the timing of articulatory gestures, vowel identifiability in these two conditions might remain quite good, despite the absence of (ordinarily) correlated durational parameters. Furthermore, if neither the initials nor finals components alone produced accurate vowel identification relative to these silent-center syllables, we could conclude that the dynamic spectral information specifying the vowel was abstract, i.e., defined as a relation over both initial and final transitional parts of the CVC syllable.

Finally, the relative importance of static targets versus vocalic duration information can be assessed by comparing

performance on variable and fixed center stimuli. If, as is often assumed, the targets are the primary cues for vowel identity, we might expect vowel identification in the fixed centers condition to be no worse than in the variable centers condition, in which relative duration differences (and some formant movement) were present. (This constitutes a strong target theory prediction which few researchers would advocate today. However, studies in which single cross sections of syllables are taken as the only input for normalization algorithms imply such a strong position.) Alternatively, dynamic specification theory would predict a decrement in performance in the fixed centers condition, because information about the vowel gesture as coarticulated with the consonants is minimized in this condition.

A. Method

1. Stimulus materials

Twenty /b/–vowel–/b/ syllables containing the vowels /i,ɪ,e,ɛ,æ,ɑ,ʌ,o,ʊ,u/ were spoken by an adult male. Two repetitions of the ten syllables, spoken at slightly different speaking rates, were recorded with a Revox A77 tape recorder and a Spherodyne microphone. The 20 syllables were low-pass filtered (3860-Hz cutoff) and digitized at a 10-kHz sampling rate, using the Haskins Laboratories PCM system.

From visual displays of the waveforms, the total duration from the initial consonant release to the final consonant closure (end of high-frequency energy) was determined for each syllable. Durations ranged from 114 to 202 ms with a mean of 167 ms. Each syllable was then divided into three proportional components in such a way that all the quasi-steady-state vowel was encompassed in the center component (Lehiste and Peterson, 1961). The duration of the initial component of each syllable was defined as the first 15% of the total duration (plus any prevoicing, if present). It contained from three to five pitch periods after the release and was from 22- to 30-ms long, not counting prevoicing.

The proportional duration of the center components varied for different vowel types: for intrinsically short vowels, /ɪ,ɛ,ʌ,ʊ/, 50% of the total duration (following the initial component) was designated the center component. For the intermediate vowels, /i,u/, 60% of the total duration was so designated, and for the intrinsically long vowels, /e,æ,ɑ,o/, the center component was 65% of the total duration. The number of pitch periods in the 20 centers varied from six to 15 and durations ranged from 57 to 127 ms.

The final component of each syllable was the remaining 20% (long vowels), 25% (intermediate vowels), or 35% of the total syllable duration, plus the final consonant release, if present. It contained from four to six pitch periods and was from 33- to 42-ms long. In order to minimize transients produced by abrupt onsets and offsets, all cuts in the waveforms were made at the zero crossing closest to the point determined by the above definitions. However, the integrity of pitch periods was not always preserved.

Acoustical analysis performed after stimulus construction confirmed that none of the quasi-steady-state vowel nucleus remained in the initial or final components, with the exception of the final component of one token of /bʊb/. For all other tokens, one or more of the first three formants were still in transition at the end of the initial and beginning of the final components. That is, formants had not attained their asymptotic frequencies within either component. Many syllables were characterized by formant movement throughout their entire extents. In addition to these spectral criteria, amplitude envelopes showed that all peak amplitude pitch pulses were included within the center components. For initial and final components, amplitude envelopes were rising and falling, respectively.

Silent-center (SC) syllables were produced by attenuating to silence the center component of each syllable, leaving the initial and final components intact and in the appropriate temporal relationship. Thus these syllables each contained a (noticeable) silent interval of from 57- to 127-ms long. Shortened silent-center (ShSC) syllables were constructed by positioning the initial and final components of each of the SC syllables such that the silent interval between them was 57 ms for all 20 syllables. Lengthened silent-center (LoSC) syllables were made by separating the initial and final components of each of the 20 syllables by a 163-ms interval.[2]

Variable (V) centers were constructed by attenuating to silence both initial and final components. Fixed (F) center stimuli were generated by attenuating to silence equal portions from the beginning and end of the V centers such that each stimulus was about 58 ms in duration, and included from five to seven pitch periods.[3] Finally, the Initial (I) stimuli and the final (F) stimuli were generated by attenuating to silence the center and final components and the center and initial components, respectively.

Eight separate test conditions were constructed by randomly arranging four repetitions of each of the 20 appropriate stimuli in an identification test, with a 4-s interstimulus interval, and an 8-s interval between each block of ten stimuli. The control condition consisted of the 20 unmodified syllables each appearing four times in the test order. The SC syllables condition included four repetitions of each of the 20 SC syllables, and so on. Digital waveforms were reconverted to analog signals, low-pass filtered, and recorded on audio tape with a Crown SX tape recorder for playback to subjects.

2. Procedure

Subjects were randomly assigned to the eight stimulus conditions and tested in small groups in a quiet room. Test tapes were presented via a Revox A77 tape recorder, MacIntosh MV49 amplifier, and AR acoustic suspension loudspeaker at a comfortable listening level. Subjects responded by circling key words on a response form. For the V centers and F centers conditions, the response alternatives were key words beginning with the vowel sound: eat, it, ate, Ed, at, odd, up, oat, (h)ook, ooze. For the remaining six conditions, the key words were: beeb, bib, babe, beb, bab, bob, bub, bobe, buub (should), boob.[4] Prior to testing, all subjects were given a familiarization sequence with the task and response forms, using a subset of the control syllables as stimuli. Subjects practiced on the response form on which they would be tested and feedback was given. Following this, each group of subjects was presented 20 stimuli from the test condition in

which they were participating, but no feedback was given. The subjects in the seven modified syllables conditions were told that the syllables had been modified electronically and that they were to try to identify the vowel that had been spoken in the original syllable.

After completing the 80-item test of their assigned experimental condition, subjects in all eight conditions completed a second 80-item test in which the control stimuli were presented. (For the subjects assigned to the control condition, this was a retest on the same materials.) No feedback was given for either test. Data from both tests of any subject who had an error rate greater than 20% on the second (control syllables) test were discarded on the grounds that these listeners could not reliably identify the speaker's vowels even when full acoustic information was available.

3. Subjects

A total of 159 subjects were tested. Data from seven subjects were discarded on the basis of their performance on the second test (no more than three from any one group). Nineteen subjects remained in each of the eight stimulus conditions. All were native speakers of American English and reported no hearing loss. Almost all subjects were natives of the upper Midwest area. They were recruited from introductory psychology courses at the University of Minnesota and had received no training in phonetics.

B. Results and discussion

Data from the first test only for the 19 subjects in each group were included in the analyses presented here. Perceptual performance was first analyzed by comparing the mean number of overall errors in vowel identification in each of the eight stimulus conditions. An error was defined as a vowel response other than the one intended by the speaker in the original production or the omission of a response (the latter occurred only rarely). Figure 3 presents the overall error rates for the eight conditions, expressed as a percentage of total opportunities.

It is readily apparent that performance varied markedly across the eight conditions. A one-way analysis of variance showed the overall difference in mean errors between groups to be highly significant, $F(7,144) = 73.40, p < 0.001$. *Post hoc* comparisons were performed, using a Tukey test of honestly significant differences ($p = 0.05$).

Of primary interest is the finding that vowels in the SC syllables were identified relatively accurately (only 6% errors), despite the fact that the vowel nuclei were missing from the signals. Indeed, identification of the vowels in these "vowel-less" syllables was not significantly worse than identification of the unmodified control syllables. This supports our main hypothesis that dynamic sources of information are sufficient for highly accurate identification of coarticulated vowels (see also Jenkins *et al.*, in press).

Performance in the initials and finals conditions was significantly worse than for any of the other conditions. These extremely high error rates corroborated our expectations that sufficient information for vowel identification was not "contained within" either of the components taken by

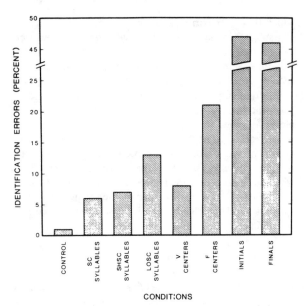

FIG. 3. Average identification errors (expressed as percentages of opportunities) for each stimulus condition in the single-speaker experiment.

TABLE I. Identification errors (in percent) on short, mid, and long vowels in silent-center syllables, shortened silent-center syllables, and lengthened silent-center syllables conditions: single-speaker experiment.

	Vowels			
Condition	Short /ɪ, ɛ, ʌ, ʊ/	Mid /i, u/	Long /e, æ, ɑ, o/	Overall vowels
SC syllables	9%	3%	5%	6%
ShSC syllables	9%	3%	8%	7%
LoSC syllables	21%	6%	9%	13%

itself. We can conclude, then, that the information used by subjects in identifying the vowels in the SC syllables was dynamic (and abstract) in that it was specified as a relational function over the two acoustic components of the stimulus taken as a whole. Indeed, to both subjects and experimenters, the stimuli sounded like single CVC syllables with a "hiccup" or glottal stop in the middle of each vowel.

A comparison of the three SC syllable conditions allows us to separate the relative contribution of temporal information about intrinsic vowel length and dynamic spectral information available in the transitional components of the CVC syllables. If vowel duration, specified in these stimuli by differences in elapsed time from consonantal release to consonant closure, were the primary source of information about the vowel gesture used to differentiate the vowels in the SC syllables, then we would expect error rates on the ShSC and LoSC syllables to be significantly higher, since elapsed time differences among the vowels were essentially neutralized in these conditions. However, Tukey tests showed no significant overall differences among the three conditions, nor did a more lenient test of pairwise comparisons (least significant differences, Keppel, 1973). In fact, errors on ShSC syllables were not significantly greater than errors on control syllables, although vowels in LoSC syllables were misidentified significantly more often than in the control syllables by a Tukey test ($p = 0.05$).

While the overall error rates for the three SC syllable conditions were not different, the pattern of errors shown in a vowel-by-vowel analysis varied somewhat across conditions. Table I gives the percentages of errors for intrinsically short, mid, and long vowels in these three conditions. To the extent that durational information is important for accurate vowel identification, we expected that long vowels in the ShSC syllables condition, and short vowels in the LoSC syllables condition would be misidentified more often than in

the SC syllables condition. As the percentages indicate, these trends occurred in the predicted direction. However, the effect was quite small for long vowels in the ShSC syllable condition; a numerical increase in errors occurred for only two of the four long vowels. The overall increase in errors on short vowels in the LoSC syllables condition was more substantial; three of the four vowels showed a numerical increase in errors over the SC syllables condition. However, two of the long vowels, /e/ and /o/, also showed more errors in the LoSC syllables condition, relative to the SC syllables. Thus it might be that part of the increase in errors in this condition was due to factors other than the neutralization of durational information for vowel length.

One possible reason for the increase in errors on LoSC syllables is that the two components of the LoSC syllables were so spread in time that the integrity of the syllable as a single unit may have been jeopardized. Recall that the silent interval used in all these syllables was even longer than the longest silent interval in the original SC syllables. Thus the average change in temporal extent from the original was more extreme in the LoSC syllables condition than it was in the ShSC syllables condition. This might account, at least in part, for the asymmetry of perceptual results.

The relatively accurate identification of vowels in all three SC syllable conditions is a dramatic result when one considers traditional accounts of vowel perception. Neither the "primary" cue to vowel identity—the targets—nor the "secondary" cue of relative duration (in terms of elapsed time) was present in the ShSC and LoSC syllables, and yet vowel perception remained quite accurate. This finding supports the contention that the rapidly changing acoustic patterns at the beginning and end of a CVC syllable provide important information for vowel identity, independent of their (usually correlated) role of providing temporal information about vocalic duration or elapsed time between consonant gestures.

In order to assess the relative contribution of temporal information for vowel identity when transitional information is not present, or is attenuated, performance on the V centers and F centers conditions was compared. Tukey tests indicated that there were significantly more vowel identification errors in the F centers condition than in the V centers condition. (The latter was not significantly different from the controls.) Relative duration differences between short and long vowels were actually enhanced in the V centers condition because of the way in which these components were defined. (Recall that a larger proportion of the syllable was taken as the centers for long vowels than for short vowels.) The results suggest that perceivers utilized this enhanced relative duration information to disambiguate spectrally similar vowels.

Acoustical analysis indicated that there was significant movement of formants within the V centers. This was especially noticeable in the case of the /e/ and /o/, and reflects the fact that these vowels were diphthongized in the dialect of the speaker in this study. Thus formant movement provided another dynamic source of information for vowel identity in the V centers stimuli. In the F centers, formant movement was minimal, leaving only information about relatively static spectral targets. In the case of the /e/ and /o/, the F centers encompassed the primary target, but adequate information about diphthongal movement was probably not available within the 57-ms portion.

An inspection of the errors on the short, mid, and long vowels in these two conditions, shown in Table II, indicates that the major source of increased errors on F centers was confusion between spectrally similar short–long vowel pairs. As expected, the long vowels were misidentified as their short counterparts; error rates on /e/ and /o/ were especially high.

In general, the pattern of perceptual results reported here offers strong support for the view that vowels in CVC syllables are specified by dynamic spectral and temporal acoustic parameters. Of the three kinds of information under investigation, we found that both temporal parameters specifying intrinsic vowel length and dynamic spectral information carried in the transitional components of the acoustic signal contributed significantly to the identification of the vowels. When initial and final transitional components were both present, vowel identification was relatively accurate even when elapsed time differences were neutralized. On the other hand, vocalic duration differences appeared to be quite important for accurate perception of vowels when transitional information was not available. Static spectral targets, present in the middle of the syllable, provided relatively impoverished cues to vowel identity, although identification accuracy was still well above chance (see Assmann et al., 1982, for a similar pattern of results with phonetically trained listeners). We can conclude that information for the vowel as a gesture is spread throughout the changing acoustic pattern of the syllable. Portions of the acoustic pattern characterized by relatively rapid spectral change at the beginning and end of the syllable, taken together, appear to provide especially good information about the intended vowels.

II. MULTIPLE-SPEAKER EXPERIMENT

In the above experiment, the original corpus consisted of CVC syllables produced by a single speaker. Although some variability was introduced by a speaking-rate change, the acoustic patterns specifying the vowels did not reflect other sources of variability discussed in the Introduction. In order to provide a more stringent test of the claim that dynamic information specifies vowel identity and to extend the generality of the findings of the first experiment, we replicated the study, using a corpus which included syllables produced by four different speakers, two men and two women.

A. Method

1. Stimulus materials

The 20 tokens used in experiment I were also included in this study. In addition, two repetitions of each of the ten vowels spoken in /b/–/b/ syllables were produced by each of three additional speakers. The speakers were instructed to recite the syllables briskly; the second repetition was spoken more rapidly than the first. The second male speaker was a long-time resident of Minnesota who originally came from St. Louis, Missouri. One of the female speakers was a native of metropolitan Minnesota. The other was originally from Northern California and had resided in Minnesota for seven years at the time of recording. The dialect of all but the last speaker was similar to that spoken by the majority of subjects serving as listeners. The dialect of the second female was somewhat different and has been characterized by trained phoneticians as a variant of Southern Midland.

The 60 new syllables were filtered, digitized, and divided into initial, center, and final components, using the same procedures as described in experiment I. Average total duration of syllables for the four speakers varied from 167 ms for the original male speaker to 196 ms for one of the female speakers; the range in durations of individual tokens was from 114 to 251 ms. Center components ranged from 57 to 163 ms, with an average of 104 ms. Initial components were from 17- to 37-ms long, with an average duration of 27 ms. Final components were from 31 to 62 ms in duration with an average of 46 ms.

Seven modified syllable conditions and a control condition were constructed in the same way as for experiment I. SC syllables included initial and final components in their original temporal relationship. All 80 ShSC syllables had a silent interval of 57 ms; all 80 LoSC syllables contained a 163-ms silent interval. F centers were all about 57 ms in length and contained from six to eight pitch periods for the male tokens and from nine to 13 pitch periods for the female tokens.

Eight separate listening tests were constructed by randomly arranging the 80 appropriate syllables, converting digital waveforms to analog signals, filtering, and recording them on audio tape with a 4-s interstimulus interval and an 8-s interval between blocks of ten stimuli.

TABLE II. Identification errors (in percent) on short, mid, and long vowels in variable centers and fixed centers conditions: single-speaker experiment.

Condition	Vowels			
	Short /ɪ, ɛ, ʌ, ʊ/	Mid /i, u/	Long /e, æ, ɑ, o/	Overall vowels
Variable centers	10%	4%	9%	8%
Fixed centers	12%	3%	39%	21%

2. Procedure

Subjects were tested using the same procedures as described above. Task and response form familiarization was accomplished using control stimuli spoken by a single male speaker, after which subjects heard 20 tokens of the modified condition in which they were to be tested, including some tokens produced by each of the four speakers. As in experiment I, all eight groups of subjects were tested on control syllables after completing the experimental condition and performance on this test was used to discard subjects with error rates exceeding 20%.

3. Subjects

A total of 158 subjects were tested; data from six subjects were discarded because of high errors on control syllables on the second test (one in each of six conditions). Thus 19 subjects remained in each of the eight listening conditions. Subjects were native English speaking volunteers from introductory psychology classes, almost all of whom were from the Upper Midwest. They reported no hearing losses, and no expertise in phonetics.

B. Results and discussion

Overall results of perceptual tests for the eight stimulus conditions are presented in Fig. 4. Errors averaged over all 80 tokens in each test are given as percentages of opportunities. As in experiment I, there were marked differences in identification accuracy across the eight conditions. An analysis of variance showed that mean differences between groups were highly significant, $F(7,144) = 172.39, p < 0.001$.

As the figure shows, errors in the control condition were extremely low (5%) despite the presence of considerable acoustic variability contributed by speaker and speaking rate differences. All four speakers' tokens were accurately perceived even though the syllables were randomly arranged and no information about the identity of the speaker was available prior to each test syllable. Identification of the first male speaker's tokens was as accurate in this study as in experiment I. These results corroborate earlier findings (Verbrugge et al., 1976; Strange et al., 1979; Gottfried and Strange, 1980; see also Macchi, 1980; Diehl et al., 1981) and support the claim that vowels can be unambiguously specified within CVC syllables despite speaker-contributed acoustic variations.

Tukey tests of honestly significant differences ($p = 0.05$) indicated that error rates for all seven modified conditions were significantly greater than in the control condition. However, some modified syllable conditions yielded fewer errors than others. As in experiment I, vowels in SC syllables were identified relatively well, despite the fact that the vowel nuclei were not present in the signals. Subjects made an average of 11 errors in 80 trials (14%). These errors were not equally distributed across vowel types or speakers. Tokens of the second female speaker, whose dialect varied most from that of the majority of listeners, were misidentified more often (27%) than those of the other three speakers (10%). Vowels which contributed most to the error rate for the former were the vowels, /ɛ,æ,ɑ,ʌ,ʊ/. Thus while listeners were able to identify vowels of a different dialect with equal accuracy when the unmodified CVC syllables were presented (6% errors), they appeared to have more difficulty in identifying these variants when the vowel nuclei were removed.

Error rates for the initial and final conditions were far greater than for all other conditions, and not significantly different from each other. Again, this shows that the intended vowels very often could not be identified on the basis of information contained within either of these components presented alone. The relatively accurate identification of the SC syllables was dependent on information specified over both components as an integrated stimulus.

A comparison of the SC, ShSC, and LoSC syllable conditions showed a pattern of results similar to that found in experiment I. Tukey tests indicated that, while the ShSC syllables were not identified with significantly less accuracy than the SC syllables, the LoSC syllables yielded a significantly higher error rate ($p = 0.05$). Again, this shows an asymmetry in the perceptual consequences of neutralizing elapsed time information for vowel length.

Table III shows the pattern of errors on intrinsically short, mid, and long vowels in these three SC syllables conditions. As expected, errors on long vowels in the ShSC condition and short vowels in the LoSC condition increased relative to the original SC syllables. However, as in experiment I, the effect was minimal for the ShSC syllables. All four short vowels in the LoSC condition were misidentified considerably more often relative to the original SC syllables. But again, as in experiment I, errors also increased for some mid and long vowels, suggesting that factors other than neutralization of elapsed time information were affecting the perceptual results. Again, these findings support the conclusion that dynamic information about vowel gestures, specified

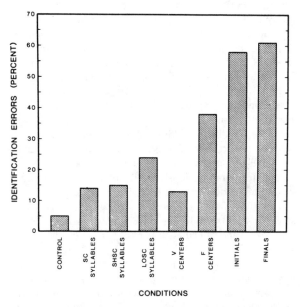

FIG. 4. Average identification errors (expressed as percentages of opportunities) for each stimulus condition in the multiple-speaker experiment.

TABLE III. Identification errors (in percent) on short, mid, and long vowels in silent-center syllables, shortened silent-center syllables, and lengthened silent-center syllables conditions: multiple-speaker experiment. Data in parentheses give error rates, excluding tokens by the one female speaker whose dialect was different from the listeners'.

| | Vowels | | | |
Condition	Short /ɪ, ɛ, ʌ, ʊ/	Mid /i, u/	Long /e, æ, ɑ, o/	Overall vowels
SC syllables	23 (16)%	3 (4)%	11 (6)%	14%
ShSC syllables	19 (18)%	5 (5)%	16 (10)%	15%
LoSC syllables	42 (39)%	8 (9)%	15 (12)%	24%

over the transitional portions of the syllable (taken as an integral unit), contributes to the accurate identification of vowels even when temporal parameters which usually accompany intrinsic vowel length are neutralized.

The V and F centers conditions were compared as in experiment I to assess the relative efficacy of vocalic duration and target information for vowel identification. The V centers were identified quite accurately overall, whereas vowels in the F centers condition were misidentified significantly more often. The increase in errors occurred for all ten vowel types and ranged from an increase of 6% to 63%. Table IV presents the error rates for intrinsically short, mid, and long vowels. As expected, the errors for the long vowels were especially great in the F centers condition. However, errors on short and mid vowels were also greater than in the V centers condition. This was probably due to the increased variability of vowel targets contributed by speaker and speech rate differences. However, duration information was apparently less affected by differences in speakers and speaking rate. The relatively accurate identification of V centers suggests that this temporal source of information was useful in the disambiguation of vowels despite the variation in absolute duration contributed by differences in speaking rate within and across subjects. (Again, see Assmann et al., 1982, for similar findings with a multiple-speaker corpus.)

It is interesting to note that performance on tokens contributed by the female speaker whose dialect differed was, in general, not different from that on the other speakers' productions in either the V centers or F centers conditions. That is, her vowel nuclei were identified as well (or as poorly) as those of other speakers. It appears then, that the dialect variation present in this corpus changed the nature of the dy-

TABLE IV. Identification errors (in percent) on short, mid, and long vowels in variable centers and fixed centers conditions: multiple-speaker experiment. Data in parentheses give error rates, excluding tokens by the one female speaker whose dialect was different from the listeners'.

| | Vowels | | | |
Condition	Short /ɪ, ɛ, ʌ, ʊ/	Mid /i, u/	Long /e, æ, ɑ, o/	Overall vowels
Variable centers	13 (13)%	3 (4)%	17 (18)%	13%
Fixed centers	29 (23)%	13 (15)%	60 (56)%	38%

namic information present in transitional components rather more than the static target information.

The general pattern of results found in this study replicated that obtained in experiment I with only minor differences. Vowels were identified relatively accurately in conditions which contained one or more sources of dynamic spectral or temporal information. Vowels in "vowel-less" syllables could be identified with relatively few errors, despite variations in the acoustic patterns contributed by speaker differences, speaking rate differences, and even dialect differences. This was true even when elapsed-time differences were neutralized, as in the ShSC syllables condition. Vowel nuclei were also identified quite accurately when initial and final transitions were deleted, but only when (enhanced) relative duration information was available. Identification of fixed duration vowel nuclei was relatively poor, with error rates for individual vowel types ranging from 11% to 68%. The rather large increase in errors from experiment I to experiment II for this condition (21% to 38%) can be attributed to the increase in ambiguity of static target information due to speaker and speaking rate differences.

III. GENERAL DISCUSSION

In these experiments, our goal was to explore three sources of information available in coarticulated CVC syllables which support the perception of vowels. We used a technique by which utterances produced by one or more speakers were modified electronically in order to delete or alter the acoustic pattern presented to perceivers. This paradigm differs from the one employed in our previous studies in which differences in the production of vowels in different syllabic conditions could have confounded the perceptual results. The procedure used here provides better control over the acoustic signals presented, while still using "natural" speech (as opposed to synthetic speech) in which the acoustic consequences of coarticulation are present. This is important if the goal is to discover what acoustic parameters normally carry information for vowel identity.

Three kinds of information for vowel identity were manipulated in these studies: (1) information provided in the vowel nuclei of the syllables, which corresponds most closely to the static spectral targets thought to be the primary differentiating cues for vowels, (2) information provided by durational differences (either vocalic duration or elapsed time from syllable onset to offset), considered a secondary cue for vowel identity in English, and (3) dynamic spectral information defined over the initial and final transitional portions of the syllables, taken together. We found that the presence of the third kind of information was sufficient to maintain accurate identification of the vowels, even when vowel nuclei were attenuated to silence. Further, this source of information appeared to be relatively independent of duration information. When differences in elapsed time between consonant gestures for intrinsically short, mid, and long vowels were neutralized, perceivers were still able to disambiguate the vowels most of the time on the basis of relational information defined over the initial and final transitions taken together.

What is the nature of this information provided in the rapidly changing patterns at the beginning and end of the syllables? We can tentatively rule out the hypothesis that the initial and final transitions specify formant trajectories, the asymptotes of which correspond to the static vowel targets (Lindblom and Studdert-Kennedy, 1967). Changing the time interval between initial and final components, as in the ShSC and LoSC syllables conditions, would also change the asymptotes specified by these two components. Yet vowel identity was not significantly disrupted by the ShSC modification. The LoSC modification did produce a significant increase in errors in experiment II. However, the pattern of errors suggested that the perceptual problem may have been due, at least in part, to the disruption of the integrity of the syllable as a unitary acoustic and articulatory event.[5]

Returning to the perspective presented in the Introduction, we may speculate that the acoustic patterns given in the initial and final parts of a syllable provide especially useful information about the characteristic gestures which differentiate the vowels. That is, if the articulatory movements (as well as the achieved vocal tract state) are essential defining characteristics of a vowel type, then the perceiver must obtain information from the acoustic pattern about those movements. The results reported here suggest that that information, defined relationally, is available in the portions of the acoustic pattern that correspond to the beginning and end of the vowel gesture.

An inspection of the acoustic patterns of syllables containing different vowels (Lehiste and Peterson, 1961) suggests some possible relational dynamic acoustic parameters that may be perceptually relevant. CVC syllables containing long vowels (sometimes referred to as tense vowels) have formant patterns that are nearly temporally symmetrical about the vocalic nucleus. That is, transitions into and out of the quasi-steady-state nucleus tend to be approximately equal in slope and duration (for a particular consonant). In addition, the proportions of the total syllable length taken up by initial and final transitions are approximately equal. In contrast, syllables containing short (lax) vowels are characterized by asymmetrical initial and final transitions. Transitions out of the vowel into the final consonant are more gradual than transitions into the vowel, and take up a relatively greater proportion of the total syllable length.[6] Lehiste and Peterson conclude the following: "Thus it appears that the characteristic difference between the long and short monophthongs may be described as a difference in the articulatory rate of change associated with the movement from target position to the following consonants. The traditional terminology "lax" and "tense" seems appropriate to label this difference. "Lax" vowels, then, are those vowels whose production involves a short target position and a slow relaxation of the hold; for "tense" vowels the target position is maintained for a longer time, and the (articulatory) movement away from the target position is relatively rapid. The relationship of the three stages to the total duration remain approximately constant, regardless of the fluctuation in duration produced by the following consonant" (1961, pp. 274–275).

In summary, we can say that vowels, as gestures, are differentiated by their timing with respect to adjacent seg-

ments and syllables, as well as by the positioning of the tongue during the relatively sustained vocalic portion of the syllable. The perceiver must identify the intended vowels on the basis of information in the acoustic pattern about the *timing* of the gesture as well as the vocal tract state attained. Dynamic spectral parameters such as those described above, as well as differences in vocalic duration and elapsed time from closure to closure are all correlated with (or determined by) articulatory timing constraints. As such, these acoustic parameters may serve as information for the perceiver about the identity of the vowels. The results of the present study indicate that perceivers can utilize these abstract acoustic parameters in identifying vowels even when static vowel targets are completely missing from the signal. To the extent that these relational parameters remain invariant over variations in speaker identity, speaking rate, and consonantal context, they may provide especially good information for vowel identity and account for the perceptual constancy evidenced by perceivers.

ACKNOWLEDGMENTS

We wish to express our thanks to Dr. Alvin Liberman and the staff of Haskins Laboratories for their continued support of our research (partially supported by NICHHD Contract 71-2420) and to our research staff at Minnesota (Thomas Edman, Lenief Heimstead, James Nead, Grant Miller, Christopher Jenkins, Elizabeth Balow, David Pollak, Karen Siegel) for their assistance in this project. We also express our appreciation to Robert Verbrugge, Terrance Nearey, and an anonymous reviewer for their critical comments on the manuscript. Portions of this research were reported at the 95th meeting of the Acoustical Society of America. This research was supported by grants to James J. Jenkins and Winifred Strange from the National Institute of Mental Health (MH-21153) and to the Center for Research in Human Learning from NICHHD (HD-0098) and NSF (BNS-75-03816). Winifred Strange and James J. Jenkins are now at the University of South Florida. Requests for reprints should be sent to Winifred Strange, Department of Communicology, University of South Florida, Tampa, FL 33620.

[1] Vowel length is not considered phonologically distinctive in English. However, phonetically, stressed English vowels vary redundantly in "intrinsic" vowel duration (sometimes referred to as tenseness), which is specified acoustically by systematic differences in the duration of vocalic nuclei (Peterson and Lehiste, 1960). Traditionally, these temporal parameters have been considered "secondary" cues for vowel identity in English. In our view, phonetic vowel length can be considered a control variable in the specification of timing parameters for coarticulated speech, and might thus have acoustic consequences throughout the syllable.

[2] Because of the variation in absolute durations of initial and final components, the total elapsed time of the ShSC syllables ranged from 113 to 126 ms. For LoSC syllables, elapsed times ranged from 219 to 233 ms. While syllables containing intrinsically short vowels were, on the average, slightly shorter than syllables containing long vowels, the ratios of even the shortest to longest syllables in ShSC and LoSC conditions (0.90 and 0.93, respectively) were far greater than in the SC syllables and control syllables (ratio = 0.56) and probably not perceptually relevant.

[3]We were concerned that, despite cutting at zero crossings, the sudden onsets and offsets of these stimuli might spuriously increase identification errors. Thus a second set of F centers stimuli were constructed in which the first and last pitch periods of each stimulus were attenuated by digital multiplication, thus shaping the amplitude contours of these stimuli. However, perceptual tests indicated a significant increase in errors on these shaped F centers, relative to the unshaped ones, especially for /e/ and /o/. Therefore the data reported below are those obtained on the unshaped F centers stimuli.

[4]Several studies have shown that the type of response forms used, and the compatibility of stimuli and responses, can have significant effects on vowel identification performance (Macchi, 1980; Diehl *et al.*, 1981; Assmann *et al.*, 1982). Pilot studies using both score sheets described here on the V centers and F centers conditions showed a small (4%–8%) but significant advantage in performance with the "eat, it,..." score sheets over the "beeb, bib,..." score sheets. No differences between score sheets were found for control stimuli; we did not redo the other modified syllables conditions. While the differences in performance attributable to score sheets in the V centers and F centers did not significantly affect the pattern of results described below, we report performance on V centers and F centers conditions using the better score sheets. Note that the major comparisons of interest are between groups who used the same score sheets.

[5]More research, including both acoustical analyses and perceptual studies, is needed before ruling out this hypothesis. However, the fact that stimuli which actually contained the asymptotic vowel nuclei were not well perceived argues quite strongly against the trajectory hypothesis in its simple form. In addition, Verbrugge and Rakerd (1980) presented SC syllables in which the initial and final portions were contributed by different speakers (a man and a woman, respectively). Vowel identification for these "hybrid" syllables was not significantly worse than identification of vowels of SC syllables in which both initial and final portions were contributed by the same speaker. This provides strong evidence against the formant trajectory hypothesis.

[6]Formant transition rate and duration varies as a function of the place of articulation of the consonant, especially for stops. The data reported by Lehiste and Peterson (1961) included many different consonants and their conclusions about proportionality are independent of variations due to consonant identity.

Assmann, P. F., Nearey, T. M., and Hogan, J. T. (**1982**). "Vowel identification: Orthographic, perceptual, and acoustic aspects," J. Acoust. Soc. Am. **71**, 975–989.

Diehl, R. L., McCusker, S. B., and Chapman, L. S. (**1981**). "Perceiving vowels in isolation and in consonantal context," J. Acoust. Soc. Am. **68**, 239–248.

Fowler, C. A. (**1980**). "Coarticulation and theories of extrinsic timing," J. Phonet. **8**, 113–133.

Gay, T. (**1978**). "Effect of speaking rate on vowel formant movements," J. Acoust. Soc. Am. **63**, 223–230.

Gerstman, L. J. (**1968**). "Classification of self-normalized vowels," IEEE Trans. Audio Electroacoust. **AU-16**, 78–80.

Gottfried, T. L., and Strange, W. (**1980**). "Identification of coarticulated vowels," J. Acoust. Soc. Am. **68**, 1626–1635.

Jenkins, J. J., Strange, W., and Edman, T. R. (in press). "Identification of vowels in vowel-less syllables," Percept. Psychophys.

Joos, M. A. (**1948**). "Acoustic phonetics," Lang. Suppl. **24**, 1–136.

Keppel, G. (**1973**). *Design and Analysis: A Researcher's Handbook* (Prentice-Hall, Englewood Cliffs, NJ).

Ladefoged, P., and Broadbent, D. E. (**1957**). "Information conveyed by vowels," J. Acoust. Soc. Am. **29**, 98–104.

Lehiste, I., and Peterson, G. E. (**1961**). "Transitions, glides, and diphthongs," J. Acoust. Soc. Am. **33**, 268–277.

Lieberman, P., Crelin, E., and Klatt, D. (**1972**). "Phonetic ability and the related anatomy of the newborn, adult human, Neanderthal man and the chimpanzee," Am. Anthropol. **74**, 287–307.

Lindblom, B. E. F. (**1963**). "Spectrographic study of vowel reduction," J. Acoust. Soc. Am. **35**, 1773–1781.

Lindblom, B. E. F., and Studdert-Kennedy, M. (**1967**). "On the role of formant transitions in vowel recognition," J. Acoust. Soc. Am. **42**, 830–843.

Macchi, M. J. (**1980**). "Identification of vowels spoken in isolation versus vowels spoken in consonantal context," J. Acoust. Soc. Am. **68**, 1636–1642.

Nearey, T. M. (**1977**). "Phonetic feature systems for vowels," PhD. thesis, University of Connecticut, 1977 (reproduced by Indiana University Linguistics Club, 1978).

Peterson, G. E., and Barney, H. L. (**1952**). "Control methods used in a study of vowels," J. Acoust. Soc. Am. **24**, 175–184.

Peterson, G. E., and Lehiste, I. (**1960**). "Duration of syllable nuclei in English," J. Acoust. Soc. Am. **30**, 693–703.

Shankweiler, D. P., Strange, W., and Verbrugge, R. R. (**1977**). "Speech and the problem of perceptual constancy," in *Perceiving, Acting and Knowing: Toward an Ecological Psychology*, edited by R. E. Shaw and J. Bransford (Erlbaum, Hillsdale, NJ), pp. 315–345.

Skinner, T. E. (**1977**). "Speaker invariant characterizations of vowels, liquids, and glides using relative formant frequencies," J. Acoust. Soc. Am. Suppl. 1 **62**, S5.

Stevens, K. N., and House, A. S. (**1963**). "Perturbation of vowel articulations by consonantal context: An acoustical study," J. Speech Hear. Res. **6**, 111–128.

Strange, W., Edman, T. R., and Jenkins, J. J. (**1979**). "Acoustic and phonological factors in vowel identification," J. Exp. Psychol.: Human Percept. Perform. **5**, 643–656.

Strange, W., Verbrugge, R. R., Shankweiler, D. P., and Edman, T. R. (**1976**). "Consonant environment specifies vowel identity," J. Acoust. Soc. Am. **60**, 213–224.

Verbrugge, R. R., and Rakerd, B. (**1980**). "Talker-independent information for vowel identity," J. Acoust. Soc. Am. Suppl. 1 **67**, S28.

Verbrugge, R. R., Strange, W., Shankweiler, D. P., and Edman, T. R. (**1976**). "What information enables a listener to map a talker's vowel space?," J. Acoust. Soc. Am. **60**, 198–212.

A perceptual model of vowel recognition based on the auditory representation of American English vowels

Ann K. Syrdal

AT&T Bell Laboratories, Room 6C-320, Naperville-Wheaton Road, Naperville, Illinois 60566

H. S. Gopal

Callier Center, University of Texas at Dallas, 1966 Inwood Road, Dallas, Texas 75235

(Received 11 February 1985; accepted for publication 17 December 1985)

A quantitative perceptual model of human vowel recognition based upon psychoacoustic and speech perception data is described. At an intermediate auditory stage of processing, the specific bark difference level of the model represents the pattern of peripheral auditory excitation as the distance in critical bands (barks) between neighboring formants and between the fundamental frequency ($F0$) and first formant ($F1$). At a higher, phonetic stage of processing, represented by the critical bark difference level of the model, the transformed vowels may be dichotomously classified based on whether the difference between formants in each dimension falls within or exceeds the critical distance of 3 bark for the spectral center of gravity effect [Chistovich *et al.*, Hear. Res. **1**, 185–195 (1979)]. Vowel transformations and classifications correspond well to several major phonetic dimensions and features by which vowels are perceived and traditionally classified. The $F1–F0$ dimension represents vowel height, and high vowels have $F1–F0$ differences within 3 bark. The $F3–F2$ dimension corresponds to vowel place of articulation, and front vowels have $F3–F2$ differences of less than 3 bark. As an inherent, speaker-independent normalization procedure, the model provides excellent vowel clustering while it greatly reduces between-speaker variability. It offers robust normalization through feature classification because gross binary categorization allows for considerable acoustic variability. There was generally less formant and bark difference variability for closely spaced formants than for widely spaced formants. These findings agree with independently observed perceptual results and support Stevens' quantal theory of vowel production and perceptual constraints on production predicted from the critical bark difference level of the model.

PACS numbers: 43.71.An, 43.71.Es, 43.70.Fq, 43.71.Cq

INTRODUCTION

Chiba and Kajiyama (1941) and Potter and Steinberg (1950) hypothesized that vowels are recognized on the basis of spatial patterns of excitation in the peripheral auditory system regardless of their specific location along the spatially coded frequency dimension. Such patterns would presumably remain relatively constant for a given vowel produced by different speakers. The pattern for one vowel category would also presumably be distinctive from the patterns associated with other categories of vowels, while retaining similarities reflecting common attributes among vowel subsets which optimally would relate to phonetically useful descriptions of vowel features.

The goals of this paper are (1) to construct a quantitative perceptual model of the representation of vowels based on auditory patterns, and (2) to evaluate it on acoustic analyses of natural utterances with respect to (a) its phonetic validity and its ability to normalize acoustic variability as a vowel recognition model, and (b) its perceptual constraints on production and its general implications for the efficiency of speech communication. The proposed model incorporates findings from speech perception and psychoacoustics research, described below.

A. The spectral center of gravity effect

Auditory averaging of two or more formants in a naturally spoken vowel may be simulated by a single formant in synthetic vowels. Delattre *et al.* (1952) first reported that it was easier to synthesize satisfactory one-formant back vowels (whose first and second natural formants are rather close in frequency) than one-formant front vowels (whose first and second natural formants are widely separated.) The best one-formant approximations of high back vowels /u/ and /o/ were close to their natural first formant frequencies, and for more open back vowels, such as /a/ and /ɔ/, the one-formant phonetic equivalent was intermediate in frequency between the natural $F1$ and $F2$. Two formants generally were found to be necessary for the synthesis of satisfactory front vowels. The perceptually most effective second formant of two-formant synthetic front vowels was found to be higher in frequency than the actual second formant of naturally spoken front vowels, whose second and third formants are relatively close in frequency. Delattre *et al.* hypothesized that the ear effectively averages two formants which are relatively close in frequency, and perceives from them a global quality roughly equivalent to that which would be produced by a single formant intermediate in frequency. Effects consistent with the above phenomenon are also evident in Fant's (1959) results from listeners' forced choice associations of sine wave tone bursts to a set of nine Swedish vowels.

The formant averaging effect was studied further by Carlson *et al.* (1970), who concluded that all vowels in the rich Swedish vowel system could be matched by two-formant synthetic approximations. Four-formant synthetic vowels were used as the standards to which subjects matched a two-formant synthetic vowel in which $F1$ was fixed at the same frequency as the standard, and the frequency of the effective second formant ($F2'$) could be adjusted by the subject. $F2'$ was near the natural second formant ($F2$) in back and mid vowels, and between $F2$ and the natural third formant ($F3$) in front vowels except /i/, for which it was in the region of $F3$ or higher. Carlson *et al.* (1975) quite accurately predicted $F2'$ in two-formant synthetic Swedish vowels on the basis of $F1$, $F2$, $F3$, and $F4$ of a standard, using either an empirical formula or an analog model of the cochlea.

Chistovich *et al.* (1979) and Chistovich and Lublinskaya (1979) reported a critical distance between formant frequencies within which the "spectral center of gravity" effect appeared to operate. The critical distance between formants could be represented as a constant in an auditory scale and was important in the perceived phonetic identity of Russian vowels. They found that if the first and second formants of a synthetic two-formant Russian vowel standard were within about 3 to 3.5 critical bands (bark) of each other, listeners required to match the standard to a single formant synthetic vowel choose a single formant frequency intermediate between $F1$ and $F2$. Within this critical distance, relative formant amplitudes of the standard influenced the frequency subjects chose for the intermediate matched formant. If the distance between the two formants of the standard exceeded the critical distance of 3 to 3.5 bark, listeners chose a single formant that matched one or the other of the two formants, but not an intermediate frequency. For stimuli in which the critical distance was exceeded, relative formant amplitudes of the standard did not affect the frequency of the matched single formant until amplitudes were so low that one or the other formant was inaudible. Chistovich and her colleagues have reported several types of experimental estimates of critical distance that agree quite closely with those obtained from the matching procedure. Results were similar whether stimuli were noise excited or buzz excited.

Chistovich *et al.* (1979), along with Carlson *et al.* (1975), have suggested a serial model of vowel spectrum shape processing, with peak extraction occurring at low levels of the auditory system during the first stage, and spatial integration over wide frequency intervals occurring at higher levels of the auditory system during the second stage. Thus integration within a range of 3 bark does not imply a lack of resolution of the formants within the critical distance. Perceptual experiments by Traunmüller (1982) with nonspeech stimuli suggest that integration of spectral peaks across the 3- to 3.5-bark critical distance is a nonperipheral process and may be specific to the perception of speech. His results support the findings of Delattre *et al.* (1952), who did not observe formant averaging in vowel-like stimuli which were outside the acoustic range of human vowel production.

The fact that Chistovich and her colleagues found the critical distance between first and second formants to be a constant in auditory units implies that the critical distance may remain the same over a wide range of frequencies and between other formants. The model proposed here incorporates formant distance measures between $F2$ and $F1$ and between $F3$ and $F2$, $F4$ and $F3$, and $F4$ and $F2$. It also has extended the concept to include the distance between $F1$ and the fundamental frequency ($F0$).

The $F1$–$F0$ distance dimension is included in the proposed auditory model despite the differences between $F0$ and formant frequencies. With reference to production, fundamental frequency corresponds to the frequency of vocal fold vibration (source), whereas formant frequencies correspond to the resonances of the vocal tract (filter). In acoustic terms, $F0$ corresponds to the frequency of the first harmonic and the distance between subsequent harmonics, while formant frequencies correspond to spectral peaks composed of several harmonics. Nevertheless, both first formant frequency and fundamental frequency vary systematically across vowels, such that high vowels have relatively lower $F1$ and higher $F0$ than do low vowels. The proposed model combines $F0$ and $F1$ indices of vowel height or openness into a single measure.

Furthermore, the fundamental frequency of a vowel has been shown to influence vowel perception. For example, Fant *et al.* (1974) have shown that the same formant structure can result in the perception of two different vowels, depending upon the frequency of the source. Traunmüller (1981) has specifically proposed the $F1$–$F0$ distance in bark to be critical to phonetic judgments related to vowel openness in a Bavarian dialect. It is interesting that, in Seneff's (1984, 1985) functional model of synchronous auditory processing, fundamental frequency and formant frequencies are extracted by the same temporal processor and are represented in the same way in the output spectrum. Thus $F0$ and formant peaks may be more similar to the human auditory system than they appear from a consideration of their production and acoustic differences.

B. Critical band (bark) scale

The transformation of physical frequency measures to an appropriate auditory scale is fundamental to the proposed model of vowel recognition. The scale probably most appropriate for the representation of the complex speech spectrum is the critical band scale. The critical band scale has been determined from a wide variety of psychoacoustical experiments, including loudness summation, narrow-band masking, two-tone masking, threshold of complex sounds, phase sensitivity, musical consonance, and discrimination of partials in a complex tone (Scharf, 1970). A current functional view of the auditory system is that it is composed of a series of internal bandpass filters whose bandwidths overlap (Plomp, 1975; Schroeder, 1975; Schroeder *et al.*, 1979). The bandwidth of each one of these internal filters corresponds to a critical band. Acoustic energy falling within the critical bandwidth of an internal filter is integrated. The critical band has physiological correlates: One critical band represents a relatively constant length of about 1.3 mm along the basilar membrane and about 1300 cochlear neurons. The critical band scale increases with frequency linearly up to about 500 Hz and approximately logarithmically thereafter. Zwicker (1961) proposed that an empirically defined critical band scale be adopted as a standard tonality scale. His proposed scale divides the human auditory range below 16 kHz into 24 critical band units or barks, named after Barkhausen, the creator of the unit of loudness level. Figure 1 is a plot of barks as a function of log frequency.

In Sec. I of this paper, formant measurements from spoken vowels are transformed to represent auditory patterns of excitation, according to the proposed model. Acoustic data collected by Peterson and Barney (1952) for ten American English vowels spoken by 32 men, 28 women, and 15 children form the data base studied. Evaluation of the proposed model focuses on phonetic feature classification. In Sec. II, characteristics necessary for an adequate normalization procedure as described by Disner (1980) are discussed: (1) whether vowels of the same category cluster together and are distinct from other vowels, and (2) the extent to which variability across speakers is reduced by the model's transformations. In addition, acoustic variability is analyzed and related to independent perceptual observations, to the proposed perceptual model, and to Stevens' quantal theory of speech production (1972). A general summary and conclusions are presented in Sec. III.

I. TRANSFORMATION AND CLASSIFICATION OF VOWELS PRODUCED BY MEN, WOMEN, AND CHILDREN

Transformations were performed on acoustic vowel data to model important aspects of the auditory processing of speech signals, including conversion of the frequency scale to the critical band scale, and representation of each vowel as a pattern of differences between frequency components. Classification of the resulting patterns was performed in each bark-difference dimension according to the criterion of a critical distance. The proposed model will be evaluated with respect to its usefulness in relating acoustic properties to phonetic features.

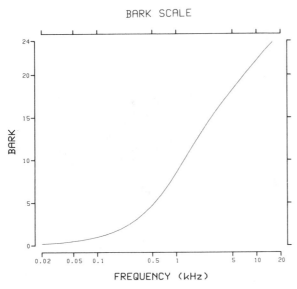

FIG. 1. Critical band (bark) as a function of frequency, using Zwicker and Terhardt's (1980) approximation.

A. Vowel transformation

1. Acoustic data

Spectrographic measurements by Peterson and Barney (1952) of ten American English vowels spoken by 32 men, 28 women, and 15 children provided the data base for study I. Vowels were produced in citation form in /hVd/ words: "heed, hid, head, had, heard, hod, hud, hawed, hood, and who'd." Measurements of $F0$, $F1$, $F2$, and $F3$ from each of two repetitions of each vowel by each speaker were transformed according to the algorithms to be described.

2. Transformation procedure for bark-difference representation

Two mathematical approximations to the empirically defined critical band scale were considered. The approximation suggested by Schroeder et al. (1979) was originally employed (Syrdal, 1982a,b), but it underestimated the width of critical bands at higher frequencies within the speech range. The approximation proposed by Zwicker and Terhardt (1980) was adopted because it corresponds more accurately to the empirically defined critical band scale. According to Zwicker and Terhardt, frequency in kHz and critical band value in bark are related according to the formula

$$B = 13 \arctan(0.76 f) + 3.5 \arctan(f/7.5)^2,$$

where B is the critical band value in bark, and f is the frequency in kHz. When the bark scale was modified to approximate Traunmüller's (1981) proposed low-frequency end correction, all frequencies below 150 Hz were raised to 150 Hz, and for frequencies between 150 and 200 Hz, the end-corrected frequency was defined as

$$f_c = f - 0.2(f - 150),$$

whereas for frequencies between 200 and 250 Hz,

$$f_c = f - 0.2(250 - f),$$

where f_c is the corrected frequency and f is the frequency in Hz.

Three bark-difference measures were calculated from the bark-transformed formant frequencies: $F0$ was subtracted from $F1$, $F1$ from $F2$, and $F2$ from $F3$. The bark-difference values define a three-dimensional auditory space in which each vowel is represented by a point.

3. Results

Each of two repetitions of each vowel spoken by each talker is plotted in Figs. 2–4. It should be noted that the scatter plots include those vowels measured by Peterson and Barney (1952) that were perceptually ambiguous to listeners. Figure 2, provided for reference, is a scatter plot of the untransformed vowels with $F1$ frequency represented on the abscissa and $F2$ in log frequency on the ordinate. Figure 3 represents end-corrected bark-difference dimensions $F1$–$F0$ on the abscissa and $F2$–$F1$ on the ordinate, while Fig. 4 represents end-corrected $F1$–$F0$ on the abscissa and $F3$–$F2$ on the ordinate.

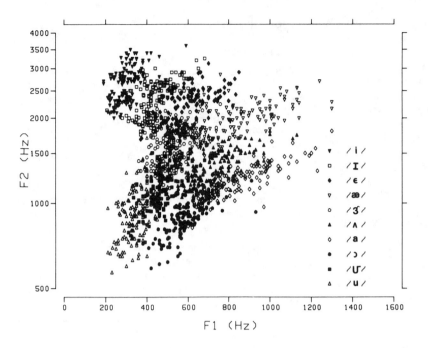

FIG. 2. Scatter plot of F_2 frequency versus F_1 frequency for both productions of ten American English vowels spoken by men, women, and children.

The three mean bark-difference values of each vowel category for each speaker group are listed in Table I. Bark differences less than the critical distance of 3 bark are italicized. Bark differences listed in parentheses were calculated from the end-corrected bark scale suggested by Traunmüller (1981). The end-corrected scale resulted in more similarity among speaker groups in F_1-F_0 measures of high vowels (primarily by reducing men's F_1-F_0 values), but slightly greater differences among speakers for low levels.

Table II lists the proportion and number (in parentheses) of tokens from each vowel category which fell within or exceeded a 3-bark critical distance in F_1-F_0, F_2-F_1, and F_3-F_2 bark-difference dimensions. In addition, the proportion and total number of tokens from each vowel type which were correctly classified in all three dimensions are listed. Classification of a token was assumed correct if it agreed with the majority of classifications for that vowel category, with the exception of /ɜ/ and /ɔ/ in the F_1-F_0 dimension. Since /ɜ/ and /ɔ/ straddled the 3-bark boundary in the F_1-F_0 dimension and were not readily classifiable in that dimension, they were not included in the tally of correct classifications. Bark-difference values from the end-correct-

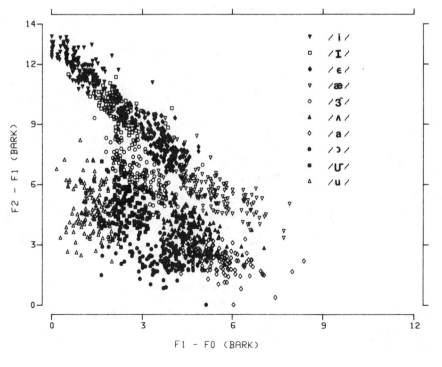

FIG. 3. Scatter plot in F_1-F_0 and F_2-F_1 bark-difference dimensions of both individual utterances of ten American English vowels spoken by men, women, and children.

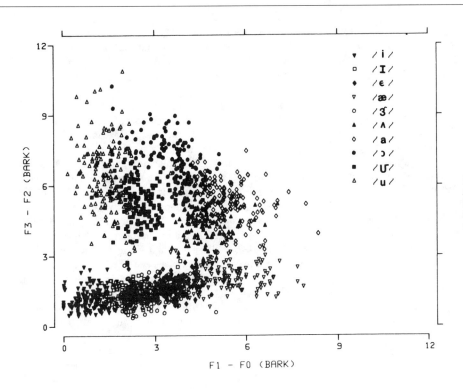

FIG. 4. Scatter plot in $F1-F0$ and $F3-F2$ bark-difference dimensions of both individual utterances of ten American English vowels spoken by men, women, and children.

TABLE I. Bark-difference means for ten American English vowels [Peterson and Barney (1952) data base]. [Numbers in parentheses are based on end-corrected bark values as suggested by Traunmüller (1981).]

Vowels	Speakers	$F1-F0$		$F2-F1$	$F3-F2$
	M	1.3	(1.2)	11.3	1.5
/i/	W	0.8	(0.8)	12.1	1.0
	C	0.8		12.4	0.9
	M	2.5	(2.3)	9.3	1.6
/ɪ/	W	1.9	(2.0)	10.2	1.3
	C	2.4		10.0	1.5
	M	3.7	(3.5)	7.6	1.8
/ɛ/	W	3.5	(3.6)	8.4	1.5
	C	3.8		8.4	1.8
	M	4.9	(4.6)	6.0	2.1
/æ/	W	5.5	(5.6)	5.7	2.0
	C	6.1		5.5	2.1
	M	3.4	(3.2)	5.9	1.5
/ɝ/	W	2.6	(2.7)	7.0	1.2
	C	2.7		7.1	1.2
	M	4.6	(4.4)	3.8	4.5
/ʌ/	W	4.6	(4.7)	3.9	4.3
	C	4.9		4.1	4.5
	M	5.3	(5.1)	2.5	5.2
/a/	W	5.5	(5.6)	2.3	5.3
	C	6.1		1.9	5.2
	M	4.1	(3.9)	2.1	6.8
/ɔ/	W	3.3	(3.4)	2.5	7.1
	C	3.7		2.7	7.1
	M	2.9	(2.7)	4.4	5.2
/ʊ/	W	2.2	(2.2)	5.0	5.5
	C	2.6		5.5	5.4
	M	1.6	(1.4)	4.6	6.2
/u/	W	1.3	(1.4)	4.5	6.7
	C	1.4		5.4	6.4

TABLE II. Proportion and number (in parentheses) of vowel tokens within or exceeding a 3-bark critical distance in $F1-F0$, $F2-F1$, and $F3-F2$ dimensions [Peterson and Barney (1952) data base]. The classification was made on end-corrected bark values.

Intended vowel	$F1-F0$		$F2-F1$		$F3-F2$		Total correct
	< 3 bark	⩾ 3 bark	< 3 bark	⩾ 3 bark	< 3 bark	⩾ 3 bark	
/i/	0.9933	0.0067	0.0000	1.000	1.000	0.0000	0.9933
	(149)	(1)	(0)	(150)	(150)	(0)	(149)
/ɪ/	0.9533	0.0467	0.0000	1.000	1.000	0.0000	0.9533
	(143)	(7)	(0)	(150)	(150)	(0)	(143)
/ɛ/	0.1200	0.8800	0.0000	1.000	1.000	0.0000	0.8800
	(18)	(132)	(0)	(150)	(150)	(0)	(132)
/æ/	0.0000	1.000	0.0000	1.000	0.9467	0.0533	0.9467
	(0)	(150)	(0)	(150)	(142)	(8)	(142)
/ɝ/	0.5200[a]	0.4800[a]	0.0000	1.000	0.9933	0.0067	0.9933
	(78)	(72)	(0)	(150)	(149)	(1)	(149)
/ʌ/	0.0000	1.000	0.0867	0.9133	0.0200	0.9800	0.8933
	(0)	(150)	(13)	(137)	(3)	(147)	(134)
/a/	0.0000	1.000	0.8867	0.1133	0.0000	1.000	0.8867
	(0)	(150)	(133)	(17)	(0)	(150)	(133)
/ɔ/	0.1944[a]	0.8056[a]	0.8542	0.1468	0.0000	1.000	0.8542
	(28)	(116)	(123)	(21)	(0)	(144)	(123)
/ʊ/	0.8467	0.1533	0.0067	0.9933	0.0000	1.000	0.8400
	(127)	(23)	(1)	(149)	(0)	(150)	(126)
/u/	0.9867	0.0133	0.0333	0.9667	0.0000	1.000	0.9533
	(148)	(2)	(5)	(145)	(0)	(150)	(143)

[a] These listings were not included in the tally of tokens correctly classified into features.

ed bark scale were used in the classification shown in Table II. Without end correction, classifications were identical except for /ɪ/, /ɜ/, /ɔ/, and /ʊ/, for which 141, 73, 25, and 116 tokens, respectively, had $F1–F0$ values within 3 bark, and for 126 /ɔ/ tokens which had $F2–F1$ values within 3 bark.

The proposed perceptual model of vowel recognition consists of two levels. The transformation of fundamental and formant frequencies to the bark-difference dimensions constitutes an intermediate stage in auditory processing represented by the specific bark difference level of the model. Subsequently, vowels are classified into two categories in each bark-difference dimension according to whether or not they exceed a 3-bark critical distance. The application of the 3-bark criterion to the bark-difference dimensions constitutes a higher, phonetic stage of processing represented by the critical bark difference level of the model.

B. Phonetic feature classification

1. Bark-difference dimensions

Inspection of Tables I and II and of Figs. 3 and 4 indicates several features of interest with respect to bark-difference dimensions for the ten American English vowels represented. The $F1–F0$ dimension corresponds well to a dimension of vowel height (or openness). High vowels /i,ɪ,u,ʊ/ have $F1–F0$ values less than the critical distance of 3 bark, whereas mid and low vowels predominantly have $F1–F0$ values greater than the critical distance. The $F1–F0$ distance is greater with increasingly more open vowels, thus representing a continuum of openness as well as providing a basis for binary classification. The vowel /ɜ/ is not distinctively classified in this dimension; its mean $F1–F0$ value for men exceeds 3 bark, but mean values for women and children are within the critical distance. As seen in the scatter plots and Table II, the vowel /ɔ/ also straddles the critical distance, but the majority of utterances for all speakers have $F1–F0$ values that exceed 3 bark.

Figure 3 illustrates the $F2–F1$ bark-difference dimension plotted along the ordinate. Only the two vowels /a/ and /ɔ/ fall almost entirely within the 3-bark critical distance. The lower $F1$ and $F2$ frequencies of /ɔ/ distinguish it from /a/. Eight vowels have $F2–F1$ means which exceed 3 bark, ranging from 4–12 bark.

Although Fant (1983) related the $F2–F1$ dimension to the front–back distinction in Swedish vowels, American English vowels are clearly not separated into front and back categories along this dimension. Fant reported that all Swedish back vowels have $F2–F1$ distances within 3 bark. However, while two American English back vowels fall within the $F2–F1$ critical distance, three other back vowels, /ʌ,ʊ,u/, clearly exceed it. The $F2–F1$ dimension does not represent the continuum of vowel place of articulation well either, since some American English front and back vowels, such as /æ/ and /u/, have $F2–F1$ values that overlap substantially. Thus the $F2–F1$ dimension cannot be said to relate universally to front–back vowel distinctions.

For American English, front and back vowels are clearly distinguished along the $F3–F2$ bark-difference dimension.

As seen from Tables I and II, front vowels /i,ɪ,ɛ,æ,ɜ/ have $F3–F2$ values less than 3 bark, and back vowels /ʌ,a,ɔ,ʊ,u/ have $F3–F2$ differences which exceeded the critical distance. There are only 12 of 1494 tokens which cross the boundary between these two categories, as indicated in Table II.

In the Swedish vowel data reported by Fant (1983), the $F3–F2$ bark-difference dimension would also separate front from back vowels, with one possible exception. The pre-r allophone /œ:/ of the rounded front vowel /ø:/ has a mean $F3–F2$ distance of 4.5 bark, placing it among the back vowels (similar to /ʌ/) according to the American English classification system proposed in this paper. However, it has been classified variously as a rounded mid vowel (Fant, 1971), as a rounded front vowel (Fant, 1983), and among the Swedish back vowels (Liljencrants and Lindblom, 1972). In all other cases, Swedish front vowels had $F3–F2$ values less than 3 bark, and Swedish back vowels exceeded 3 bark in $F3–F2$ distances. Analyses of the scatter of many tokens of Swedish vowels produced by men, women, and children speakers would be useful in further comparing vowel classification systems and differences between Swedish and American English vowels.

The differences in bark between $F4$ and $F3$ and between $F4$ and $F2$ in American English vowels were described by Syrdal (1982a, 1984, 1985) using other data bases which included $F4$ measures. For all American English vowels except /ɜ/, $F4–F3$ bark-differences are within 3 bark. /ɜ/ has a mean $F4–F3$ value of 4.5 bark for both women and men speakers, and a mean of 4.0 bark for children. Also, $F4–F2$ differences exceed 3 bark for all American English vowels except /i/, for which the mean $F4–F2$ values are 2.6, 2.5, and 2.0 bark for men, women, and children, respectively.

Table III summarizes the classification of the ten American English vowels studied by Peterson and Barney (1952) according to the 3-bark critical distance criterion applied in five bark-difference dimensions. A + indicates that the vowel characteristically falls within 3 bark in a bark-difference dimension, and a − indicates that the vowel characteristically exceeds 3 bark in the dimension. A blank entry in the table indicates that the vowel is not distinctively classified in a particular dimension.

The scatter plot shown in Fig. 4 bears a striking resemblance to the traditional vowel quadrilateral, which is

TABLE III. Vowel classification based on critical distance features in five bark-difference dimensions.

Vowels	$F1–F0$ < 3 bark	$F2–F1$ < 3 bark	$F3–F2$ < 3 bark	$F4–F2$ < 3 bark	$F4–F3$ < 3 bark
/i/	+	−	+	+	+
/ɪ/	+	−	+	−	+
/ɛ/	−	−	+	−	+
/æ/	−	−	+	−	+
/ɜ/		−	+	−	−
/ʌ/	−	−	−	−	+
/a/	−	+	−	+	+
/ɔ/		+	−	−	+
/ʊ/	+	−	−	−	+
/u/	+	−	−	−	+

loosely based on articulatory dimensions. The two primary parameters of vowel quality, height and place of articulation, are represented by the two bark-difference dimensions $F1-F0$ and $F3-F2$, respectively. At the specific bark difference level of the model, the representation of each vowel as a point along bark-difference dimensions mirrors an intermediate stage of auditory processing. A higher, phonetic stage of processing is represented in the critical bark difference level of the model, in which each dimension is divided into two categories according to whether bark-difference values are within or exceed the perceptually defined critical distance of 3 bark. The resulting binary classification of vowels correlates well with phonetic distinctions of high–low and front–back features. Thus the proposed model of the auditory representation of vowels provides a perceptually based, quantitative definition of the primary phonetic features used to describe vowel quality.

2. Comparison between bark-difference and perceptual classifications

The classification matrix of vowel tokens by critical distance, shown in Table II, is not significantly different from a comparable classification of perceptual data which Peterson and Barney (1952) obtained from a group of listeners. Table IV lists the proportion and number (in parentheses) of tokens of each vowel type classified by listeners into the same vowel groupings used in Table II. For example, the first entry in Table IV indicates that there were 10 272 perceptual judgments of /i/ tokens (99.92%) which were classified as any of the four high vowels /i,ɪ,ʊ,u/, and 8 (0.08%) classified as any of the four mid or low vowels /ɛ,æ,ʌ,a/. This

entry compares directly to the 149 of 150 /i/ tokens (99.33%) whose $F1-F0$ bark differences were less than 3 bark (a feature shared with /ɪ/, /ʊ/, and /u/), as shown in Table II. Similarly, 93.20% of the presentations of /ɪ/ tokens were classified as any of the four high vowels by listeners, as compared to 95.33% of the /ɪ/ tokens which had $F1-F0$ values less than 3 bark.

To pursue this correspondence more rigorously, we performed two-tailed t tests for matched pairs to compare the proportion of correct classifications by vowel for critical distance criteria (Table II) to the corresponding perceptual classifications by listeners (Table IV). The two classifications do not differ significantly in any of the three feature groupings, even at a liberal 90% level of significance. Presence or absence of end correction in the bark scales makes no difference to this result. The impression of similarity of results between Tables II and IV is, therefore, statistically confirmed.

Also included in Table IV are a tally of perceptual classifications into short and long vowel categories (a temporal dimension not captured by bark-difference classifications), and the total proportion of correctly classified presentations in each vowel category.

II. VOWEL NORMALIZATION AND ACOUSTIC VARIABILITY

Vowel normalization attempts to capture an invariant description of a vowel, and is generally considered as a means of reducing the extreme acoustic variability between speakers, but even within-speaker variability presents a problem to vowel recognition.

TABLE IV. Proportion and number of tokens classified by listeners into feature groupings. (Numbers do not include high–low classification of /ɝ/ or /ɔ/ tokens.)

Intended vowel	High–Non H		Compact–Non C		Front–Back		Short–Long		Total correct
	iɪʊu	ɛæʌa	aɔ	iɪɛæɝʌʊu	iɪɛæɝ	ʌaɔʊu	ɪɛʌ	iæɝaɔu	
/i/	0.9992 (10272)	0.0008 (8)	0.0003 (3)	0.9997 (10277)	0.9997 (10277)	0.0003 (3)	0.0010 (10)	0.9990 (10270)	0.9987 (10267)
/ɪ/	0.9320 (9555)	0.0680 (697)	0.0002 (2)	0.9998 (10277)	0.9998 (10277)	0.0002 (2)	0.9965 (10243)	0.0035 (36)	0.9290 (9549)
/ɛ/	0.0251 (257)	0.9749 (9966)	0.0004 (4)	0.9996 (10273)	0.9994 (10271)	0.0006 (6)	0.9023 (9273)	0.0977 (1004)	0.8771 (9014)
/æ/	0.0001 (1)	0.9999 (10236)	0.0004 (4)	0.9996 (10274)	0.9982 (10259)	0.0018 (19)	0.0307 (316)	0.9693 (9961)	0.9651 (9919)
/ɝ/	0.0000 (0)	1.000 (33)	0.0005 (5)	0.9995 (10274)	0.9993 (10272)	0.0007 (7)	0.0024 (25)	0.9976 (10254)	0.9965 (10243)
/ʌ/	0.0103 (104)	0.9897 (10025)	0.0694 (667)	0.9306 (9610)	0.0030 (31)	0.9970 (10246)	0.9323 (9581)	0.0677 (696)	0.9221 (9476)
/a/	0.0076 (70)	0.9924 (9183)	0.9685 (9949)	0.0315 (324)	0.0026 (27)	0.9974 (10246)	0.0290 (298)	0.9710 (9975)	0.8699 (8936)
/ɔ/	0.1040 (76)	0.8960 (655)	0.9849 (10124)	0.0151 (155)	0.0017 (17)	0.9983 (10262)	0.0130 (134)	0.9870 (10145)	0.9275 (9534)
/ʊ/	0.9815 (10020)	0.0185 (189)	0.0065 (67)	0.9935 (10212)	0.0020 (21)	0.9980 (10258)	0.9822 (10096)	0.0178 (183)	0.9655 (9924)
/u/	0.9997 (10274)	0.0003 (3)	0.0002 (2)	0.9998 (10277)	0.0003 (3)	0.9997 (10274)	0.0077 (79)	0.9923 (10200)	0.9919 (10196)

A. Normalization

Speaker normalization using an auditory approach has been proposed recently by Miller *et al.* (1980), Syrdal (1982a, 1984, 1985), and Bladon *et al.* (1984a,b). Normalization using the Miller *et al.* log-ratio approach was discussed and evaluated in Syrdal (1985); results were significantly poorer than the bark-difference approach, although the underlying rationale of the two approaches is similar in some respects. The bark scale is a more accurate representation of the spatial coding of frequency by the auditory system than is the log scale, however, and the bark-difference algorithm bears a closer resemblance to probable auditory processing than does the Miller *et al.* (1980) algorithm in which the logarithms of the ratios of the physical frequency values are computed.

The Bladon *et al.* (1984a,b) approach differs from the formant-based bark-difference and log-ratio normalizations in that the entire vowel spectrum is represented on a bark versus sone (loudness) plot assumed to represent its peripheral auditory pattern, and normalization is achieved by sliding the entire peripheral auditory spectrum of a vowel sample along the bark axis and matching it to a standard. Thus many features such as spectral tilt, formant amplitude, and formant bandwidth contribute to the normalization of vowels via template matching as proposed by Bladon *et al.* (1984a,b). While research to date indicates that such spectral features are relatively unimportant to listeners' perception of phonetic similarity (as distinct from psychoacoustic similarity), and that formant frequencies are the primary determinants of phonetic judgments (Klatt, 1979, 1982a, b; Carlson and Granström, 1979; Chistovich, 1985; Assman *et al.*, 1982), further experimentation is needed on the questions of phonetic similarity and psychoacoustic similarity. In addition, the sliding template approach of Bladon *et al.* should be evaluated as a normalization procedure. Unlike the bark-difference approach, neither the Miller *et al.* log-ratio normalization nor the Bladon *et al.* (1984a, b) sliding spectral template normalization has provided a system for classifying vowels into phonetic features.

We evaluate vowel normalization at two levels of the bark-difference model. At the specific bark difference level, the exact bark-difference values along each dimension are employed. The specific bark difference level of the model is similar to the Miller *et al.* (1980) log-ratio normalization and less closely related to the Bladon *et al.* (1984a, b) sliding auditory spectrum normalization because the latter is not formant based. In contrast, the critical bark difference level of the model applies a 3-bark critical distance to categorize vowels into binary features along each bark-difference dimension. We view both specific bark difference and critical bark difference levels as stages of normal vowel perception in humans. The specific bark difference level represents the results of an intermediate auditory analysis, and the critical bark difference level represents the results of a higher, phonetic analysis resulting in a phonetic feature matrix. An auditory spectral template model such as that of Bladon *et al.* represents a preliminary stage of auditory processing lower than the specific bark difference level, before formant extraction. The question is: At which level of processing does normalization occur?

1. Method

A series of linear discriminant analyses (Tatsuoka, 1970) was performed on the Peterson and Barney (1952) vowel data. Linear discriminant analysis performs a classification function that assigns each sample token to a group according to which estimated *a posteriori* probability of group membership is the greatest. Linear discriminant analyses classify statistically into specified groups on the basis of numeric variables along one or several continuous dimensions. Thus discriminant analysis evaluates normalization at the specific bark difference level of the model; that is, the binary distinctions related to critical distance in the critical bark difference level play no part in the statistical process involved in discriminant analysis. Instead, each token is essentially represented in terms of its normalized distance from the mean of each vowel group along each variable dimension, and ultimately in a composite distance measure (Mahalanobis D^2) from each group mean, from which *a posteriori* probabilities are calculated. Results are presented from both the R (resubstitution) method of classification and the U (jackknifed) method of classification. In the R method, each sample token is classified into a group according to the algorithm computed from all the data. The R method classification matrix and percent correct classification serve as useful indices of resolution of a specific data set into groups. In the U method of classification, each token is classified into a group according to the algorithm computed from all the data except the token being classified; the jackknifed method is a more unbiased estimate of what classification rate would result from forming the statistical algorithms on one data set and using it to classify another sample from the same population.

The extent to which formant-based normalization procedures reduce acoustic variability while clustering together vowels of the same category, distinct from other vowels, may be evaluated statistically through a series of linear discriminant analyses (Syrdal, 1984, 1985). Separate statistical classifications of either vowel category or speaker category yield separate indices of vowel clustering and between-speaker variability.

2. Vowel classification

From the linear discriminant analysis for ten vowel categories, we obtain a matrix which shows how the vowel tokens were classified. Table V lists the R method vowel classification matrix for $F0$, $F1$, $F2$, and $F3$ data in hertz from all subjects. Table VI lists the R classification matrix for the same utterances expressed at the specific bark difference level as bark-difference values $F1–F0$, $F2–F1$, and $F3–F2$.

Vowel classification based on discriminant analysis of bark differences was significantly more accurate than classification based on the unnormalized hertz data when differences between classifications by the two procedures were tested for significance at the 95% level by two-tailed t tests

TABLE V. Classification matrix for ten vowels in hertz.

Group	Percent correct	Number of tokens classified into group									
		/i/	/ɪ/	/ɛ/	/æ/	/ɜ/	/ʌ/	/a/	/ɔ/	/ʊ/	/u/
/i/	89.3	134	16	0	0	0	0	0	0	0	0
/ɪ/	80.7	13	121	6	0	0	0	0	0	0	0
/ɛ/	81.3	0	27	122	1	0	0	0	0	0	0
/æ/	85.3	0	1	19	128	0	1	1	0	0	0
/ɜ/	96.7	0	1	3	1	145	0	0	0	0	0
/ʌ/	82.7	0	0	0	0	0	124	19	7	0	0
/a/	77.3	0	0	0	0	0	26	116	7	1	0
/ɔ/	75.0	0	0	0	0	0	10	8	108	4	14
/ʊ/	75.3	0	0	0	0	0	3	0	5	113	29
/u/	78.7	0	0	0	0	1	0	0	2	29	118
Total	82.3	147	166	160	130	146	164	144	129	147	161
Jackknifed total	81.8										

for matched pairs ($df = 9$). However, both classifications were significantly poorer than listeners' vowel classifications reported by Peterson and Barney (1952) and listed in Table IV. It should be noted, however, that listeners had the advantage of more complete acoustic data, including temporal as well as spectral information. Thus statistical treatment of vowel tokens represented at the specific bark difference level as points along continuous bark-difference dimensions results in quite accurate, though not optimal, phonemic classification.

Vowel classifications from linear discriminant analyses based on bark-transformed $F0$, $F1$, $F2$, and $F3$ were equivalent to those from bark-difference data, indicating that translation from hertz to the bark scale itself improves accuracy significantly, and that no information relevant to phonemic identity was lost in representing tokens in three bark-difference dimensions rather than in four bark dimensions.

Binary feature classification of vowels performed at the critical bark difference level according to the criterion of critical distance, while shown in the preceding section to be very accurate in grouping vowels into traditional feature classes, cannot perform vowel classification without the additional consideration of the temporal distinction between

long and short vowels. Recent preliminary findings (Gopal and Syrdal, 1984; Syrdal and Steele, 1985) indicate that while specific bark-difference values for a vowel may vary significantly within speakers across speaking rates and segmental and prosodic contexts, the binary critical distance classifications appear to be very robust. Because of the extreme acoustic variability of speech, robust context- and rate-independent normalization may best be achieved through phonetic feature classification. In this view, the transformation from acoustic to bark-difference values at the specific bark difference level reduces variability between speakers, and the further transformation from bark-difference values to phonetic features at the critical bark difference level normalizes within-speaker variability related to contexts and rate. Additional research is needed to test normalization via feature extraction at the critical bark difference level of analysis.

3. Speaker classification

A second set of linear discriminant analyses involving the classification of speakers into groups of men, women, or children illuminates the properties of these scales from an-

TABLE VI. Classification matrix for ten vowels in bark differences.

Group	Percent correct	Number of tokens classified into group									
		/i/	/ɪ/	/ɛ/	/æ/	/ɜ/	/ʌ/	/a/	/ɔ/	/ʊ/	/u/
/i/	95.3	143	7	0	0	0	0	0	0	0	0
/ɪ/	84.0	10	126	14	0	0	0	0	0	0	0
/ɛ/	86.7	0	20	130	0	0	0	0	0	0	0
/æ/	86.7	0	0	20	130	0	0	0	0	0	0
/ɜ/	94.0	0	2	6	1	141	0	0	0	0	0
/ʌ/	88.7	0	0	0	0	0	133	14	3	0	0
/a/	88.7	0	0	0	0	0	10	133	6	1	0
/ɔ/	79.9	0	0	0	0	0	3	11	115	4	11
/u/	77.3	0	0	0	0	0	4	0	3	116	27
/u/	77.3	0	0	0	0	0	0	0	3	31	116
Total	85.9	153	155	170	131	141	150	158	130	152	154
Jackknifed total	85.7										

other point of view. It was found that the specific bark difference representation reduced between-speaker variability significantly relative to hertz and bark representations of the data. Speaker groups were classified by discriminant analysis with 89.6% accuracy from the hertz data, 88.0% accuracy from the bark data, but only 41.7% accuracy from the bark-difference data, only slightly above 33% chance level (Syrdal, 1984, 1985). Reduction in the accuracy of classifying the three speaker groups reflects a substantial reduction in between-speaker variability through normalization. The bark-difference normalization was most satisfactory in this regard, since it greatly reduced between-speaker variability, but yet preserved some differences between speaker groups which may reflect linguistically valid dialectical differences such as those reported by Labov (1972) and Goldstein (1980) and discussed by Bladon *et al.* (1984a,b).

4. Discussion

As Disner (1980) pointed out, scatter reduction is not the only achievement by which vowel normalization procedures should be evaluated. In addition, linguistically important phonetic detail should be preserved by a normalization whose output agrees with independent auditory evaluations of vowel quality. This would allow different languages and dialects to be compared with another. Similarly, it is essential for studies of speech development or for the evaluation of speech produced by special populations to be able to compare speech samples from different speakers, such as children and adults or normal and impaired speakers, in a phonetically meaningful way. In evaluating several normalization schemes, Disner concluded that since speaker-dependent measures used to anchor vowels eliminate linguistically relevant phonetic differences among languages, these procedures had poor linguistic validity. A significant advantage of the bark-difference procedure is that it preserves this linguistic information and even provides perceptually based dimensions and vowel categories that correspond well to traditional phonetic features, while it also substantially reduces between-speaker variability. The quantitative definition of features at the critical bark difference level may also provide a robust method of normalization for contextual and rate-related variability through feature extraction.

A second advantage of the bark-difference representation of vowels, as well as of the log-ratio normalizations proposed by Miller *et al.* (1980), is that it is an inherent or speaker-independent normalization procedure. Only the acoustic parameters present in an individual segment are used in the normalization. In contrast, speaker-dependent normalizations require a sampling of vowels from the same speaker. Since human listeners are generally capable of accurately identifying vowels produced by speakers they have never heard before, a model of the auditory perception of vowels should perform an inherent normalization. This is not to preclude the possibility of eventually incorporating speaker-dependent variables into a perceptual model; the evidence suggests that familiarity with the speech of an individual speaker improves vowel recognition slightly (Verbrugge *et al.*, 1976; Assmann *et al.*, 1982).

B. Formant and bark-difference variability among vowels

Normalization is a necessary component of a model of vowel recognition because of the considerable acoustic variability between different speakers and even within the same speaker. The variability of vowel formant structure is itself an important topic of study which has often been neglected. We compare vowels in their formant variability and in their variability in bark-difference dimensions, both between and within speakers. Implications of different levels in the model of vowel recognition on formant and bark-difference variability are discussed from the perspective of their possible perceptual constraints on vowel production. The implicit predictions about acoustic variability made by the critical bark difference level, the specific bark difference level, and an auditory spectral template level such as described by Bladon *et al.* (1984a,b) are compared. Results of the analysis of variability are related also to Stevens' (1972) quantal theory of speech production, which has seldom been studied empirically.

The definition of acoustic-phonetic features at the critical bark difference level by a perceptually determined critical distance between formants may provide perceptual constraints on speakers' productions which would influence bark-difference variability in naturally spoken vowels. Considering the binary nature of classifications based on a critical distance boundary, proximal formants may vary only within a 3-bark range from one another, but more distant formants have a much wider range over which to vary. Widely spaced formants in the Peterson and Barney (1952) data vary over a 6-bark range in the $F1–F0$ dimension, an 8-bark range in $F3–F2$, and an 11-bark range in $F2–F1$.

The specific bark difference level treats all specific bark-difference values equally. It therefore imposes no perceptual constraints on vowel production.

Bark difference levels of the model contrast with perceptual constraints on production predicted at an auditory spectral template level. According to the latter, the auditory pattern of a sample vowel spectrum is compared to a template of each vowel category and the closest match determines vowel recognition. Formant spacing is very influential in the template match, as well as spectral tilt, formant amplitude, and bandwidth. Template matching incorporating this detail contrasts with vowel feature classification at the critical bark-difference level based on two gross categories in each bark-difference dimension, i.e., less than or greater than 3-bark spacing. At the auditory spectral template level, closely spaced formants merge into a single integrated peak centered on their spectral center of gravity, particularly if a 3-bark integration is applied to the auditory spectrum. Variability in relatively isolated formants affects auditory spectral template matching much more than the variability of formants within 3 bark of one another. Therefore, for optimal vowel recognition at the auditory spectral template level, there is more lee-way for formant variability in closely spaced, integrated formants than in more widely separated, nonintegrated formants. This prediction is the opposite of that predicted by the critical bark difference level of the model and by Stevens' quantal theory.

Stevens (1972) proposed that the relationship between speech articulation and the resulting acoustic signal is quantal in nature. According to the quantal theory, the places of articulation actually used by human languages are constrained to those general places in the vocal tract where variations in the place or shape of the constriction will have minimal effects on the acoustic output. In this way, human speech affords the maximum possible imprecision in articulation and thus conveys acoustic information in a highly efficient manner. Stevens described quantal effects related to two aspects of vowel production, the degree of vocal tract constriction and the place of articulation of vowels. Mid and low vowels permit an unimpeded flow of air through the vocal tract, and $F1$ is sufficiently high that there is essentially no interaction between supraglottal resonances and vocal cord vibrations. For high vowels, such as /i/ and /u/, however, the constriction is sufficiently narrow that $F1$ drops low enough in frequency to interact with vocal cord vibration, which must then be adjusted in order to be maintained. Vowels also fall into discrete categories with respect to several features relating to place of articulation. Resonances affiliated with the back and front cavities (such as $F1$ and $F2$ of /a/, and $F2$ and $F3$ of /i/, respectively) may be close together in frequency. Only when the two cavities differ substantially in length does the central energy concentration formed by the two closely spaced formants separate into two well-defined spectral peaks. In each case, there is a broad region of the vocal tract for which the resulting acoustic spectrum maintains its characteristic energy concentration formed by two closely spaced formants.

Pisoni (1980) studied the variability of vowel formant frequencies produced by two adult male talkers and related his results to Stevens' quantal theory. Pisoni predicted, according to quantal theory, that formant frequencies of vowels /i/, /a/, and /u/ would have lower standard deviations than other vowels because these point vowels were produced at places in the vocal tract where small articulatory perturbations produce minimal acoustic changes. The results, however, provided little support for this hypothesis. The variability of $F1$, $F2$, and $F3$ (expressed in hertz) formed no clear pattern over the eight different vowels studied, and differed between speakers as well.

In the analyses presented below, predictions made by different levels of the vowel recognition model and by quantal theory are examined using the bark and bark-difference representations of vowels. Analyses were performed in which within-vowel variability of individual formants observed in the Peterson and Barney (1952) and Pisoni (1980) data bases was expressed in hertz and in bark. Variability of each vowel in each of the three bark-difference dimensions was also studied. One hypothesis tested is that formant variability is smaller for vowels in which the formant is proximal to another formant or $F0$ than for vowels in which it is widely separated. That is, it is expected that the formant standard deviation of a vowel is proportional to the smaller of the two distances in bark between the formant and its higher and lower neighboring formants in the vowel (including the $F1$–$F0$ difference in the case of $F1$ variability). This hypothesis relates to Stevens' descriptions of the quantal nature of

speech in terms of the acoustic stability produced by articulatory configurations in which formants are close to one another in frequency. The auditory spectral template level implies the opposite predictions about formant variability for within-speaker data.

A second hypothesis tested is that bark-difference standard deviations are smaller for vowels with closely spaced formants than for vowels whose formants exceed the critical distance. This hypothesis relates to the conflicting predictions of the critical bark difference and auditory spectral template levels of the model concerning perceptual constraints on vowel productions, and to Stevens' quantal theory because of its concern for patterns of variability across vowels in the auditory representation of the acoustic spectral pattern. In addition, while a comparison of the standard deviations in hertz erroneously treats a given frequency range equivalently whether it occurs at low or at high frequencies, the transformation to the bark scale provides for perceptual equivalence across the frequency range.

1. Method

In between-speaker analyses, $F1$, $F2$, $F3$, and $F1$–$F0$, $F2$–$F1$, and $F3$–$F2$ bark-difference measures from all utterances of each of the ten vowels spoken by all speakers studied by Peterson and Barney (1952) were treated as a group and their variances were compared between vowels. Between-speaker variability, however, could be influenced by dialectical heterogeneity in the Peterson and Barney data. Thus general conclusions about formant variability should not be based solely on between-speaker data.

Other analyses were restricted to within-speaker variability, for which dialectical heterogeneity between speakers is irrelevant. For the bark-transformed Peterson and Barney data, differences in $F1$, $F2$, $F3$, $F1$–$F0$, $F2$–$F1$, and $F3$–$F2$ between the first and the second productions of each vowel by each speaker were analyzed. Means and standard deviations of the differences between each speaker's first and second productions were calculated for the ten vowels across all 75 speakers for each of the six within-speaker measures listed above. Also reanalyzed were $F1$, $F2$, and $F3$ means and standard deviations reported by Pisoni (1980) from each of two speakers of eight vowels.

Bark values tested were not end corrected so as to avoid biasing the results in the direction of the critical bark difference level's predictions and those from quantal theory, since end correction reduced $F1$–$F0$ bark difference variability for high vowels and increased it for low vowels. Also F tests for equal variances between Peterson and Barney vowels were computed from ratios of variances of each of the four formants (expressed in bark) and of each of the three bark-difference dimensions, $F1$–$F0$, $F2$–$F1$, and $F3$–$F2$. In all F tests, significance was established at $p < 0.05$, with $df = 149,149$ for between-speaker data, and $df = 74,74$ for within-speaker data. Correlations were also performed to ascertain the relationships between formant means and their standard deviations and between standard deviations and associated bark differences. The significance of correlations was established by the t statistic at $p < 0.05$, with $df = 8$ for the Peterson and Barney (1952) data, and $df = 14$ for the

Pisoni (1980) data. Table VII lists between-speaker standard deviations of each format (in hertz and in bark) and of each bark-difference dimension for ten vowels. Comparisons across vowels of formant variability expressed in hertz are essentially meaningless with regard to the hypotheses tested because standard deviations of formants in hertz are highly positively correlated with mean formant frequencies. The correlation between means and standard deviations is 0.923 for $F1$, 0.952 for $F2$, and 0.537 for $F3$. Significant positive correlations between the standard deviations and means of $F1$ ($r = 0.693$) and of $F2$ ($r = 0.583$) within speakers were also found in the Pisoni data (for $F3$, $r = 0.408$). Computation of standard deviations from bark transformed data avoids the limitation of the hertz analysis because critical band units approximate equal perceptual intervals (Scharf, 1970). Consequently, all further analyses were performed on data transformed to the bark scale. To illustrate the difference made by this transformation, the $F2$ standard deviations listed in Table VII are 376 Hz for /i/ and 222 Hz for /u/, but in the bark scale the /i/ standard deviation of 0.84 bark is actually smaller than the /u/ standard deviation of 1.38 bark.

2. Formant variability

Quantal theory predicts low $F1$ variability in high vowels because of $F1$ proximity to $F0$, and low $F1$ variability also in low vowels /a/ and /ɔ/ because of $F1$ proximity to $F2$. Predictions from quantal theory were realized in the results, although the variances of /a/ and /ɔ/ were higher than expected. For between-speaker Peterson and Barney data, relatively high vowels /i/, /ʊ/ and /ɜ/ had significantly lower variances than other vowels, while low vowels /a/ and /æ/ had significantly higher variances than other vowels. Within-speaker results were generally similar, with significantly lower variances for /i/, /ʌ/, /ʊ/, /u/, and /ɜ/ than for /a/ and /ɔ/. A series of correlations were performed to test the significance of the relationship between standard deviations and the proximity of $F1$ to $F0$ or to $F2$ as measured by bark differences. Between-speaker $F1$ standard deviations were significantly correlated ($r = 0.731$) with the smaller of the two associated bark differences for each vowel, $F1-F0$ or $F2-F1$. In a similar analysis using within-speaker Peterson and Barney $F1$ standard deviations, however, the correlation

of -0.018 was nonsignificant. Since $F0$ measures were not reported by Pisoni (1980), mean $F1-F0$ bark differences were estimated from Pisoni's $F1$ means for each subject and from men's mean $F0$ values for each vowel reported by Peterson and Barney (1952). The correlation of 0.496 between $F1$ standard deviations and the smaller of $F1-F0$ or $F2-F1$ bark differences was significant. Thus a majority of the analyses indicate that $F1$ variability tends to be significantly lower for high vowels, as predicted by quantal theory.

Quantal theory predicts low $F2$ variability in front vowels, especially /i/, /ɜ/, and /ɪ/, because of the proximity of $F2$ to $F3$, and low $F2$ variability also for /a/ and /ɔ/ because of $F2$ proximity to $F1$. Between-speaker $F2$ variances for /u/ and /ʊ/ were significantly larger than for other vowels, and /ɜ/ variance was also significantly larger than those of the two least variable vowels, /i/ and /a/. In within-speaker Peterson and Barney $F2$ data, all front vowels were significantly less variable than /u/, /ɔ/, and /ʊ/, the most variable vowels. The correlation of 0.747 obtained for between-speakers $F2$ standard deviations and the smaller bark differences, $F2-F1$ or $F3-F2$, was significant, as was the correlation of 0.694 for within-speaker $F2$ data. A significant correlation of 0.445 was also observed in similar analyses of the within-speaker Pisoni data. Thus there is consistent evidence that both between-and within-speaker $F2$ variability is lower for vowels in which $F2$ is proximal to either $F1$ or $F3$, as predicted from quantal theory.

Because $F3$ in all vowels is proximal to either $F2$ or $F4$ or both, quantal theory predicts generally low $F3$ variability. The lowest $F3$ variability might be expected for /i/, in addition to relatively low $F3$ variability for all front vowels (except /ɜ/), because of the proximity of $F3$ to both $F2$ and $F4$. Between-speaker $F3$ variance for /i/ was significantly smaller than all other vowels, while $F3$ variances of /u/ and /ʊ/ were significantly larger than those of most other vowels. For Peterson and Barney within-speaker $F3$ data, /i/, /ɪ/, and /ɛ/ were the least variable vowels, while /a/ and /ɜ/ were the most variable. Since $F4$ was not measured by Peterson and Barney (1952), the $F3$ correlation procedure was modified. A correlation was performed on $F3$ standard deviations and the smaller of the two bark-difference measures, $F3-F2$ from the Peterson and Barney data, and $F4-F3$ measures for the same ten vowels in another large American

TABLE VII. Standard deviations of formants and bark-difference values for ten American English vowels (Peterson and Barney data).

| Vowels | Hertz | | | Bark | | | Bark difference | | |
	$F1$	$F2$	$F3$	$F1$	$F2$	$F3$	$F1-F0$	$F2-F1$	$F3-F2$
/i/	60	376	379	0.56	0.84	0.63	0.55	0.72	0.45
/ɪ/	75	339	426	0.66	0.90	0.80	0.52	0.76	0.38
/ɛ/	97	336	441	0.80	0.96	0.86	0.55	0.85	0.42
/æ/	172	290	413	1.21	0.92	0.83	0.85	1.01	0.52
/ɜ/	73	239	289	0.62	0.99	0.93	0.65	0.96	0.47
/ʌ/	114	191	411	0.85	0.95	0.86	0.53	0.71	0.73
/a/	147	158	378	1.02	0.85	0.79	0.68	0.61	0.81
/ɔ/	96	142	417	0.78	0.96	0.87	0.79	0.65	1.00
/ʊ/	71	196	457	0.62	1.11	0.99	0.59	0.85	0.87
/u/	76	222	454	0.69	1.38	1.00	0.56	1.14	1.40

English data base from 50 men, 50 women, and 50 children (Syrdal, 1985). For between-speaker data, the correlation of 0.696 was significant, but for within-speaker data, the correlation of 0.307 was not. Since $F4$ measures were not reported by Pisoni (1980), $F4$–$F3$ bark differences for the purposes of correlation were estimated from $F3$ standard deviations for each speaker and from men's mean $F4$ values for each vowel reported by Syrdal (1985). There was a nonsignificant correlation of −0.166 between $F3$ standard deviations and the smaller bark difference, $F3$–$F2$ or $F4$–$F3$. Thus $F3$ standard deviations correlated with bark differences only for between-speaker data, although the analyses should be repeated for data which includes $F4$ measures before general conclusions are drawn.

3. Bark-difference variability

Variances of each of the bark-difference dimensions are compared among vowels for the Peterson and Barney between- and within-speaker data sets. The Pisoni data could not be used in these analyses because the variability of bark-difference measured could not be calculated from it.

Within- and between-speaker variability in the $F1$–$F0$ bark-difference dimension was moderately positively correlated with $F1$–$F0$. In the $F1$–$F0$ bark-difference dimension, high vowels /i,ɪ,u,ʊ/ and mid vowels /ɛ,ʌ/ were all significantly less variable between speakers than low vowels /ɔ,a,æ/. The between-speaker $F1$–$F0$ standard deviations were significantly correlated ($r = 0.572$) with the $F1$–$F0$ bark-difference means. Considering within-speaker variability, /a/ was significantly more variable than all vowels, and /ɔ/, more variable than /i/, /ʌ/, /u/, and /ʊ/, the least variable vowels. The within-speaker $F1$–$F0$ standard deviations were marginally correlated with the $F1$–$F0$ means ($r = 0.515, p < 0.10$).

Standard deviations of the eight vowels whose $F2$–$F1$ distances exceed 3 bark were generally negatively correlated with $F2$–$F1$ means, but results are inconsistent concerning the variability of vowels whose first and second formants are closely spaced. In the $F2$–$F1$ bark-difference dimension, the between-speaker variances of vowels /a/ and /ɔ/ were significantly lower than other vowels, and /u/, /æ/, and /ɝ/ were significantly higher. However, $F2$–$F1$ between-speaker standard deviations and bark-difference means were not significantly correlated ($r = 0.099$) probably because there was a moderate negative correlation of −0.46 for the eight vowels which exceed 3 bark in $F2$–$F1$ distance. Results were reversed for within-speaker variances, with /i/ and /ɪ/ the least variable vowels, and /a/ and /ɔ/, the most variable. Indeed, the within-speaker $F2$–$F1$ standard deviations were significantly negatively correlated with $F2$–$F1$ means ($r = −0.876$). The critical bark difference level makes no clear predictions about variability among vowels with widely spaced $F1$ and $F2$, but the results observed for these eight vowels in the $F2$–$F1$ dimension agree with auditory spectral template predictions.

Between-speaker variances in the $F3$–$F2$ bark-difference dimension were significantly smaller for all five front vowels /i,ɪ,ɛ,æ,ɝ/ than all five back vowels /ʌ,a,ɔ,ʊ,u/. The correlations between $F3$–$F2$ standard deviations and bark-difference means were highly significant for both between-speaker data, ($r = 0.910$) and for within-speaker data ($r = 0.885$). Thus there is strong, consistent evidence that both within- and between-speaker variability in the $F3$–$F2$ bark-difference dimension is significantly lower for front than for back vowels, as predicted by the critical bark difference level of the model and by quantal theory.

4. Discussion

It is unlikely that inaccuracies in spectrographic measurements of the center frequencies of proximal formants produced the significantly smaller standard deviations of bark differences less than 3 bark, because the differences in variability observed between small and large bark differences were too large to be explained by measurement errors alone. Peterson and Barney (1952) made careful checks of their measurements for accuracy and precision, and it is unlikely that large measurement errors were committed. It is possible, however, that a systematic error could have contributed somewhat to the general effect, although whether inaccuracy would result in smaller rather than larger standard deviations is not clear.

Significant differences in measures of variability were observed among vowels. Generally, formant and bark-difference standard deviations were positively correlated with associated bark-difference values. While the causes of these effects cannot be determined from this study, results are consistent with hypotheses about perceptual constraints on production generated by the critical bark difference level of the perceptual vowel recognition model and with quantal theory, which implies that there are general regions in the vocal tract, i.e., those which yield closely spaced formants, at which articulatory imprecision will have minimal acoustic and perceptual effects.

The results of analyses of variability in naturally spoken vowels are also consistent with perceptual studies of formant variability. Traunmüller (1981) has shown that variation in the auditory distance between widely separated formants, such as $F1$ and $F2$ of synthetic front vowels, is perceptually acceptable over a much wider range than that of closely spaced formants, such as $F1$ and $F2$ of /a/. The relatively lower perceptual tolerance for variability in the differences between proximal formants supports the critical bark difference hypothesis that feature categories are defined by a critical distance which provides perceptual constraints on speakers' productions; that is, proximal formants may only vary within a 3-bark range from one another, but more distant formants have a much wider range over which to vary while still maintaining a distance greater than 3 bark. The need for gross binary categories in bark-difference dimensions may be further emphasized when the within-speaker variability related to segmental and prosodic contexts and speaking rate is considered (Gopal and Syrdal, 1984; Syrdal and Steele, 1985). Thus perceptual constraints related specifically to vowel classification by critical distance may help to explain the differences in variability observed with naturally spoken vowels.

The constraints on vowel production hypothesized by the critical bark difference model and Stevens' quantal theory are alternative explanations for the patterns of variability observed, but they also may be viewed as complementary in function; that is, from articulatory and acoustic considerations, the quantal theory predicts minimal acoustic variability for closely spaced formants. From consideration of the perceptual constraints predicted by the critical bark difference level of the vowel recognition model, greater variability is perceptually tolerated for widely spaced formants than for those within 3 bark of one another. Thus, from this viewpoint, articulatory, acoustic, and perceptual constraints are coordinated to achieve maximal efficiency in speech communication.

III. SUMMARY AND CONCLUSIONS

A quantitative perceptual model of vowel recognition was proposed based on the spatial pattern of auditory excitation produced by American English vowels. In the earlier stages of processing, represented by the specific bark difference level of the model, vowels are represented by the auditory distance between formants and between the fundamental frequency and first formant. Fundamental and formant frequencies are transformed to a critical band (bark) scale, and the simple Euclidean distance between them represents auditory distance. At the higher, phonetic stages of processing, represented by the critical bark difference level, a critical distance of 3 bark for the auditory averaging of two or more formants is used to classify vowels into binary categories along each bark-difference dimension.

Bark-difference transformations were performed on individual productions of ten American English vowels spoken by 32 men, 28 women, and 15 children studied by Peterson and Barney (1952). The $F1$–$F0$ dimension represents a continuum of high to low vowels, in which high vowels have $F1$–$F0$ differences less than 3 bark, and mid and low vowels have $F1$–$F0$ differences greater than the critical distance. The $F3$–$F2$ dimension represents the front–back vowel distinction; front vowels have $F3$–$F2$ differences of less than 3 bark, while $F3$–$F2$ values of back vowels exceed the critical distance. Since the bark-difference dimensions and binary critical distance classifications of vowels correspond closely to traditional phonetic descriptions of vowel quality and feature classifications, the proposed bark difference model provides a perceptually defined quantitative link between some acoustic characteristics of vowels and their phonetic qualities.

A series of linear discriminant analyses were performed on various forms of the Peterson and Barney (1952) vowel data. Vowel classification matrices produced from bark and specific bark difference transformations of the data were significantly more accurate than similar classifications of the same data represented in hertz. Furthermore, the specific bark difference transformation greatly reduced the wide acoustic differences between vowels spoken by different talkers. Thus the model serves as an inherent, speaker-independent normalization which preserves linguistic validity. Ultimately, a feature classification of vowels based on critical distance boundaries in bark-difference dimensions applied at the critical bark difference level and on temporal

characteristics, may provide a more robust means of normalization and vowel recognition.

Finally, hypotheses generated from perceptual constraints imposed by the critical bark difference level of the model and from Stevens' (1972) quantal theory of speech production were generally supported by analyses of the variability in bark-transformed formant frequencies and along bark-difference dimensions of Peterson and Barney (1952) and Pisoni (1980) vowel data. There was significantly less variability in formants which were closely spaced than in formants which were more distant from one another. Analyses of variability among vowels in bark-difference dimensions indicated that $F3$–$F2$ variability was significantly lower for front than for back vowels, and $F1$–$F0$ variability was significantly lower for high vowels. Results also agree with the perceptual findings of Traunmüller (1981), who found that more variability in formant separations is tolerated by listeners for widely separated than for closely spaced formants. Articulatory and acoustic constraints on speakers' productions described by quantal theory and perceptual constraints predicted from feature classification by critical distance at the critical bark difference level may act in a complementary fashion to achieve efficiency in speech communication.

In conclusion, the proposed bark difference model of vowel perception by humans offers a powerful, comprehensive solution to two major problems of vowel recognition: the inherent speaker-independent normalization of acoustic variability and a perceptually based quantitatively defined link between acoustic and phonetic features.

ACKNOWLEDGMENTS

The authors wish to thank Dr. Gunnar Fant, Dr. Kenneth Stevens, Dr. Bruno Repp, and two anonymous reviewers for helpful comments and suggestions, and Dr. Dennis Klatt and Dr. Richard Schwartz for providing the Peterson and Barney vowel data. Support through a NINCDS Research Career Development Award (CMS 5 KO5 NS00548) to the first author, and through an Organized Research Proposal from the University of Texas at Dallas is gratefully acknowledged. The research described was performed at the University of Texas at Dallas, the Research Laboratory of Electronics, Massachusetts Institute of Technology, and the Department of Speech Communication and Music Acoustics, Royal Institute of Technology, Stockholm. This paper incorporates data some of which have been reported earlier by Syrdal (1982a, 1984, 1985).

Assmann, P. F., Nearey, T. M., and Hogan, J. T. (**1982**). "Vowel identification: Orthographic, perceptual, and acoustic aspects," J. Acoust. Soc. Am. **71**, 975–989.

Bladon, R. A. W., Henton, C. G., and Pickering, J. B. (**1984a**). "Outline of an auditory theory of speaker normalization," in *Proceedings of the Tenth International Congress of Phonetic Sciences, Utrecht, Netherlands*, edited by A. Cohen and M. P. R. Van den Broecke (Foris, Dordrecht).

Bladon, R. A. W., Henton, C. G., and Pickering, J. B. (**1984b**). "Towards an auditory theory of speaker normalization," Lang. Commun. **4**, 59–69.

Carlson, R., Fant, G., and Granström, B. (**1975**). "Two-formant models, pitch and vowel perception," in *Auditory Analysis and Perception of Speech*, edited by G. Fant and M. A. A. Tatham (Academic, London), pp. 55–82.

Carlson, R., Granström, B., and Fant, G. (**1970**). "Some studies concerning perception of isolated vowels," Speech Transmission Laboratory: Q. Prof. Stat. Rep. **2–3**, 19–35.

Carlson, R., and Granström, B. (**1979**). "Model predictions of vowel dissimilarity," Speech Transmission Laboratory: Q. Prog. Stat. Rep. **3–4**, 84–104.

Chiba, Ts., and Kajiyama, M. (**1941**). *The Vowel: Its Nature and Structure* (Tokyo-Kaiseikan, Tokyo).

Chistovich, L. A. (**1985**). "Central auditory processing of peripheral vowel spectra," J. Acoust. Soc. Am. **77**, 789–805.

Chistovich, L. A., and Lublinskaya, V. V. (**1979**). "The 'center of gravity' effect in vowel spectra and critical distance between the formants: Psychoacoustical study of the perception of vowel-like stimuli," Hear. Res. **1**, 185–195.

Chistovich, L. A., Sheikin, R. L., and Lublinskaja, V. V. (**1979**). " 'Centres of gravity' and spectral peaks as the determinants of vowel quality," in *Frontiers of Speech Communication Research*, edited by B. Lindblom and S. Ohman (Academic, London), pp. 143–157.

Delattre, P. C., Liberman, A. M., Cooper, F. S., and Gerstman, L. J. (**1952**). "An experimental study of the acoustic determinants of vowel colour: Observations on one- and two-formant vowels synthesized from spectrographic patterns," Word **8**, 195–210.

Disner, S. F. (**1980**). "Evaluation of vowel normalization procedures," J. Acoust. Soc. Am. **67**, 253–261.

Fant, G. (**1959**). "Acoustic description and classification of phonetic units," Ericsson Tech. **1**, reprinted in *Speech Sounds and Features*, edited by G. Fant (MIT, Cambridge, MA, 1973), pp. 32–83.

Fant, G. (**1971**). "Notes on the Swedish vowel system," in *Applications of Linguistics, Selected Papers of the Second International Congress of Applied Linguistics, Cambridge, 1969*, edited by G. E. Perren and J. L. M. Trim (Cambridge U. P., London); also in *Speech Sounds and Features*, edited by G. Fant (MIT, Cambridge, MA, 1973), pp. 171–191.

Fant, G. (**1983**). "Feature analysis of Swedish vowels—a revisit," Speech Transmission Laboratory: Q. Prog. Stat. Rep. **2–3**, 1–19.

Fant, G., Carlson, R., and Granström, B. (**1974**). "The [e]–[ϕ] ambiguity," Proc. Speech Commun. Semin., Stockholm **3**, 117–121.

Goldstein, U. (**1980**). "An articulatory model for the vocal tracts of growing children," Sc. D. thesis, MIT, Cambridge, MA.

Gopal, H. S., and Syrdal, A. K. (**1984**) "Some effects of speaking rate on spectral and temporal characteristics of American English vowels," J. Acoust. Soc. Am. Suppl. 1 **76**, S17.

Klatt, D. H. (**1979**). "Perceptual comparisons among a set of vowels similar to /æ/: Some differences between psychophysical distance and phonetic distance," J. Acoust. Soc. Am. Suppl. 1 **66**, S86.

Klatt, D. H. (**1982a**). "Prediction of perceived phonetic distance from critical-band spectra: A first step," Proc. IEEE Int. Conf. Speech, Acoust. Signal Process., 1278–1281.

Klatt, D. H. (**1982b**). "Speech processing strategies based on auditory models," in *The Representation of Speech in the Peripheral Auditory System*, edited by R. Carlson and B. Granstrom (Elsevier, Amsterdam), pp. 181–196.

Labov, W. (**1972**). *Sociolinguistic Patterns* (Blackwell, Oxford).

Liljencrants, J., and Lindblom, B. (**1972**). "Numerical simulation of vowel quality systems: The role of perceptual contrast," Language **48**, 839–862.

Miller, J. D., Engebretson, A. M., and Vemula, N. R. (**1980**). "Vowel nor-

malization: Differences between vowels spoken by children, women, and men," J. Acoust. Soc. Am. Suppl. 1 **68**, S33.

Peterson, G. E., and Barney, H. (**1952**). "Control methods used in a study of the vowels," J. Acoust. Soc. Am. **24**, 175–184.

Pisoni, D. B. (**1980**). "Variability of vowel formant frequencies and the quantal theory of speech: A first report," Phonetica **37**, 285–305.

Plomp, R. (**1975**). "Auditory analysis and timbre perception," in *Auditory Analysis and Perception of Speech*, edited by G. Fant and M. A. A. Tatham (Academic, London), pp. 7–22.

Potter, R. K., and Steinberg, J. C. (**1950**). "Toward the specification of speech," J. Acoust. Soc. Am. **22**, 807–820.

Scharf, B. (**1970**). "Critical bands," in *Foundations of Modern Auditory Theory*, edited by J. V. Tobias (Academic, New York), Vol. 1, pp. 157–200.

Schroeder, M. R. (**1975**). "Models of hearing," Proc. IEEE **63**, 1332–1350.

Schroeder, M. R., Atal, B. S., and Hall, J. L. (**1979**). "Objective measure of certain speech signal degradations based on masking properties of human auditory perception," in *Frontiers of Speech Communication Research*, edited by B. Lindblom and S. Ohman (Academic, London), pp. 217–229.

Seneff, S. (**1984**). "Pitch and spectral estimation of speech based on auditory synchrony model," in *Speech Communication Group Working Papers* (Research Laboratory of Electronics, MIT, Cambridge, MA), Vol. IV, pp. 43–56.

Seneff, S. (**1985**). "Pitch and spectral analysis of speech based on an auditory synchrony model," Ph.D. thesis, M.I.T. (unpublished).

Stevens, K. N. (**1972**). "The quantal nature of speech: Evidence from articulatory-acoustic data," in *Human Communication: A Unified View*, edited by P. B. Denes and E. E. David, Jr. (McGraw-Hill, New York), pp. 51–66.

Syrdal, A. K. (**1982a**). "Frequency analyses of American English vowels," J. Acoust. Soc. Am. Suppl. 1 **71**, S105–S106.

Syrdal, A. K. (**1982b**). "Frequency analyses of syllable initial and final liquids spoken by American English talkers," J. Acoust. Soc. Am. Suppl. 1 **71**, S105.

Syrdal, A. K. (**1984**). "Aspects of an auditory representation of American English vowels," in *Speech Communication Group Working Papers, Vol. IV*, May 1984 (Research Laboratory of Electronics, MIT, Cambridge, MA), pp. 27–41.

Syrdal, A. K. (**1985**). "Aspects of a model of the auditory representation of American English vowels," Speech Commun. **4**, 121–135.

Syrdal, A. K., and Steele, S. A. (**1985**). "Vowel *F* 1 as a function of speaker fundamental frequency," J. Acoust. Soc. Am. Suppl. 1 **78**, S56.

Tatsuoka, M. (**1970**). *Selected Topics in Advanced Statistics: An Elementary Approach Pt. 6: Discriminant Analysis* (Institute for Personality and Ability Testing, Champaign, IL).

Traunmüller, H. (**1981**). "Perceptual dimension of openness in vowels," J. Acoust. Soc. Am. **69**, 1465–1475.

Traunmüller, H. (**1982**). "Perception of timbre: Evidence for spectral resolution bandwidth different from critical band?" in *The Representation of Speech in the Peripheral Auditory System*, edited by R. Carlson and B. Granstrom (Elsevier, New York), pp. 103–108.

Verbrugge, R. R., Strange, W., Shankweiler, D. P., and Edman, T. R. (**1976**). "What information enables a listener to map a talker's vowel space?" J. Acoust. Soc. Am. **60**, 198–212.

Zwicker, E. (**1961**). "Subdivision of the audible frequency range into critical bands (Frequenzgruppen)," J. Acoust. Soc. Am. **33**, 248.

Zwicker, E., and Terhardt, E. (**1980**). "Analytical expressions for critical-band rate and critical bandwidth as a function of frequency," J. Acoust. Soc. Am. **68**, 1523–1525.

PROSODY AND SPEECH INTELLIGIBILITY

Paper 31. C. A. Fowler (1983), Converging sources of evidence on spoken and perceived rhythms of speech: Cyclic production of vowels in monosyllabic stress feet. *Journal of Experimental Psychology: General* **112**, 386–412.

Paper 32. N. R. French and J. C. Steinberg (1947), Factors governing the intelligibility of speech sounds. *Journal of the Acoustical Society of America* **19**, 90–119.

Paper 33. I. Lehiste (1977), Isochrony reconsidered. *Journal of Phonetics* **5**, 253–263.

Paper 34. G. A. Miller and P. E. Nicely (1955), An analysis of perceptual confusions among some English consonants. *Journal of the Acoustical Society of America* **27**, 338–352.

Paper 35. G. A. Miller, G. A. Heise, and W. Lichten (1951), The intelligibility of speech as a function of the context of the test materials. *Journal of Experimental Psychology* **41**, 329–335.

Paper 36. J. M. Pickett and I. Pollack (1963), Intelligibility of excerpts from fluent speech: Effects of rate of utterance and duration of excerpt. *Language and Speech* **6**, 151–164.

Paper 37. R. Plomp (1978), Auditory handicap of hearing impairment and the limited benefit of hearing aids. *Journal of the Acoustical Society of America* **63**, 533–549.

Two sets of papers are included in this section. One set is concerned with the prosodic structure of language, in particular, with the perceived timing of utterances. A central theme in research on timing has been the extent to which the rhythmic structure of language is isochronous (with given units spanning equal temporal intervals), and the underlying basis of the isochrony. In her summary paper, Lehiste (1977) reviews the literature on isochrony—including many of her own studies—and concludes that the tendency toward isochrony in English is largely a perceptual phenomenon, with timing in speech production playing a relatively minor role. In contrast, Fowler (1983) uses linguistic phenomena and experimental data on the temporal/spectral microstructure of syllables to argue that perceived timing is not "imposed" by the listener, but reflects timing in speech production. In particular, she suggests that consonants and vowels are coproduced in an independent, though overlapping fashion, with timing in production based on the sequencing of vowels and timing in perception based on the listener's sensitivity to the acoustic information that specifies this sequencing.

The second set of papers focuses on the topic of the intelligibility of speech, an issue that has received considerable attention in the speech communication literature. Over the years, efforts have been made both to determine the factors that govern speech intelligibility and to develop methods for its reliable and valid assessment. The intelligibility papers in this section touch on both of these matters. One now classic paper, by Miller and Nicely (1955), investigates perceptual confusions among different classes of English consonants in different types of noise and filtering conditions, and presents an analysis in terms of information transmission for individual linguistic features. Another classic paper is by French and Steinberg (1947). It is here that the widely investigated "articulation index" is introduced—a computational as opposed to subjective method of assessing speech intelligibility for communication systems. The topic of hearing loss is the focus of the paper by Plomp (1978). He considers how hearing loss alters the intelligibility of speech in both quiet and noise, explaining the effects of loss in terms of the relative contributions of attenuation and distortion.

Finally, two papers discuss the role of context in the intelligibility of speech. Miller, Heise, and Lichten (1951) demonstrate that as the context of the test material is altered such that the number of response alternatives decreases, intelligibility increases. Of particular interest is their finding that words are identified more accurately in a sentence context than when presented in isolation. In a related study, Pickett and Pollack (1963) use a gating paradigm, wherein increasingly long excerpts of speech are presented to listeners, to show how the intelligibility of a target word increases as the number of words in its contextual frame increases. These two papers provided early and influential demonstrations of sentence-level context effects in the perception of speech.

Journal of Experimental Psychology: General
1983, Vol. 112, No. 3, 386–412

Converging Sources of Evidence on Spoken and Perceived Rhythms of Speech: Cyclic Production of Vowels in Monosyllabic Stress Feet

Carol A. Fowler
Dartmouth College and Haskins Laboratories, New Haven, Connecticut

SUMMARY

The article reviews the literature from psychology, phonetics, and phonology bearing on production and perception of syllable timing in speech. A review of the psychological and phonetics literature suggests that production of vowels and consonants are interleaved in syllable sequences in such a way that vowel production is continuous or nearly so. Based on that literature, a hypothesis is developed concerning the perception of syllable timing assuming that vowel production is continuous.

The hypothesis is that perceived syllable timing corresponds to the timed sequencing of the vowels as produced and not to the timing either of vowel onsets as conventionally measured or of syllable-initial consonants. Three experiments support the hypothesis. One shows that information present during the portion of an acoustic signal in which a syllable-initial consonant predominates is used by listeners to identify the vowel. Compatibly, this information for the vowel contributes to the vowel's perceived duration. Finally, a measure of the perceived timing of a syllable correlates significantly with the time required to identify syllable-medial vowels but not with time to identify the syllable-initial consonants.

Further support for the proposed mode of vowel–consonant production and perception is derived from the literature on phonology. Language-specific phonological conventions can be identified that may reflect exaggerations and conventionalizations of the articulatory tendency for vowels to be produced continuously in speech.

To their speaker/hearers, both naive (Donovan & Darwin, 1979; Lehiste, 1972) and expert (Abercrombie, 1964; Classe, 1939; Pike, 1945), languages sound rhythmical. The term *rhythm* as applied to speech refers generally to an ordered recurrence of strong and weak elements. In this general sense, languages clearly are rhythmical: Consonants and vowels approximately alternate, and, in stress languages such as English, so do stressed and unstressed syllables. However, attempts to validate the intuition that speech is rhythmical have focused on recurrence defined temporally—in particular, on the question of whether the regular recurrence of certain spoken units is isochronous.

Three classes of rhythm have been proposed for languages; stress timing (English, Swedish), syllable timing (Spanish, Italian, French), and mora timing (Japanese). In rhythmical utterances a unit of speech—the stress foot, the syllable, or the mora—is said to be regulated temporally, so that onset–onset intervals between units are approximately isochronous.[1] In a stress-timed language, for example, intervals between onsets of stressed syllables are said to approach isochrony, even though some intervals may be monosyllabic and others di- or trisyllabic (e.g., Abercrombie, 1964; Catford, 1977; Classe, 1939; Pike, 1945).

The bases for linguists' and other listeners' impressions of isochronous rhythms in speech are unknown. However, with the possible ex-

---

[1] A foot is a unit of metrical structure in speech consisting of a strong syllable and one or more weak syllables. In English, the weak syllables of a foot always follow the strong syllable. A mora is a "light" syllable (i.e., a short vowel optionally preceded by a consonant), or it is part of a "heavy" syllable. A heavy syllable consists of a syllable-initial consonant, if any, a long vowel or a short vowel, and a postvocalic consonant; it is two morae in length.

386

ception of mora timing in Japanese (e.g., Han, 1962; Dalby & Port, Note 1), it is known that the basis is not acoustic isochrony, or, in stress-timed languages, even near-isochrony, of the intervals that have been proposed as relevant. English is probably the most studied language in this regard, and many researchers have reported large departures from measured acoustic isochrony of stress feet in spontaneous (Lea, Note 2; Shen & Peterson, Note 3) and more constrained (Classe, 1939; Lehiste, 1972) utterances.

It is unlikely, then, that any units of naturally produced speech are *realized* isochronously. In view of that, the interesting questions to ask now are where the impression of rhythmicity comes from, whether recurrence of any of the units of speech that do recur is perceptually significant, whether it is linguistically significant, and whether it is articulatorily significant. Evidence bearing on these questions is derived from research reported in the psychological literature and the linguistics literature on phonetics and phonology. This article and one following (Fowler, Note 4) are intended to bring together these research lines and thereby to assess the state of our understanding of spoken and perceived rhythms of speech.

The two articles in the series differ in scope. This article considers only monosyllabic utterances in which all syllables are stressed (e.g., from Bolinger, 1965: "Pa made John tell who fired those guns"). The reason for this narrow focus is that fairly extensive but disparate lines of research—in psychology relating to perception, in phonetics concerning articulation, and in phonology concerning structure in sound sequences—converge to suggest a coherent perspective on rhythmic speech production and on perception of rhythmic speech in an idealized stress-timed language where feet are monosyllabic. Less extensive lines of research provide a less coherent picture of production and perception of speech where unaccented syllables are produced. This latter literature is the subject of the second article.

In this article, discussion is limited also in a second way. Initially, I consider ways in which talkers comply with *instructions* to produce stress(syllable)-timed speech and the ways in which listeners assess those productions. Before it is possible to draw realistic conclusions concerning rhythms that may or may not underlie production of spoken languages, and before we can ascertain whether the impression of rhythm is realistic or illusory, it is imperative that we learn how to recognize rhythm in speech when it occurs.

I first review the literature concerning production and perception of sequences of monosyllabic stress feet. The literature under review suggests two conclusions, one concerning the production of vowels in fluent speech and one concerning their perception. These proposals are tested in a series of three experiments.

In the second part of the article, I introduce evidence from the linguistics literature on phonology that may converge with the experimental evidence reviewed or presented in the first part. In the second part, I attempt to introduce and defend three basic ideas. One is the general idea that direct investigation of linguistic structure can provide a useful source of converging evidence with that provided by experimental investigations of language use. The second is the more specific idea that some phonological rules can be identified as exaggerations and conventionalizations of articulatory dispositions, and as such, can provide converging evidence for the identity of dispositions. Third, I attempt to identify several instances of phonological rules that are "natural" (i.e., reflect articulatory dispositions) if the manner of vowel production proposed in the first part of the article is in fact an articulatory disposition.

In the final part of the article, conclusions are drawn from the array of findings reviewed and presented in the first two parts.

This research was supported by National Science Foundation Grant BNS 8111470 and by National Institute of Child Health and Human Development Grant HD 16591-01 to Haskins Laboratories. I thank Alan Bell and Gary Dell for their comments on drafts of this article.

Experiment 1 was carried out in collaboration with Louis Tassinary and has been summarized in Fowler and Tassinary (1981).

Requests for reprints should be sent to Carol A. Fowler, Department of Psychology, Dartmouth College, Hanover, New Hampshire 03755.

Monosyllabic Stress Feet

The Perceptual Evidence and Some Articulatory Correlates

Several years ago, Morton, Marcus, and Frankish (1976; Marcus, 1981) reported a systematic discrepancy between the measured timing of a sequence of digits and its perceived timing. In particular, they found that sequences of digits with acoustically isochronous onset–onset intervals sound unevenly timed to listeners. Given an opportunity to adjust the intervals between digits until the timing sounds isochronous, listeners introduce systematic departures from measured acoustic isochrony. This finding is almost complementary to one reported by Lehiste (1972) and others (Donovan & Darwin, 1979) on listeners' perceptions of sentential rhythms. This literature (reviewed by Fowler, Note 4) reports that listeners may *fail* to detect departures from measured isochrony in spoken sentences. Although this latter collection of studies is interpreted as revealing listener insensitivity to foot durations, the findings by Morton et al. (1976) cannot have that interpretation. Indeed, taken together, the two sets of findings suggest that listeners' impressions of speech timing are not based on the same intervals measured by investigators. This was the interpretation offered by Morton et al. of their own findings.

An investigation of talkers' productions of isochronous sequences suggests one important difference between measured and perceived rhythmic intervals. In particular, the latter but not the former sometimes can be identified with rhythmic articulatory intervals (Fowler, 1979; Fowler & Tassinary, 1981). Asked to produce isochronous sequences of monosyllables, talkers produce sequences with just the measured departures from isochrony that listeners require in order to hear the sequences as evenly timed (Fowler, 1979).

This research indicates that talkers' and listeners' notions of rhythmicity in speech agree but differ from those of experimenters. Such a pattern of agreement and disagreement invites two interpretations. One is that talkers and listeners are subject to an illusion that experimenters, working on visible rather than audible displays of speech, evade. Another is that talkers produce rhythmic speech on request in these studies and listeners recognize it as such. For their part, experimenters fail to detect the rhythmicity because their experimental measurements somehow fail to reflect the natural structure of the spoken sequences. The latter is the more conservative of the two views because it ascribes no special processes or behaviors to listeners and talkers. The talker is assumed simply to follow instructions, and the listener, to detect the natural structure of the acoustic signal provided by the talker. In addition, this interpretation appears a realistic one in view of the well-known difficulties involved in the measurement of speech because it is coarticulated.

From the perspective of this second interpretation, assessments of the rhythmic structure of naturally produced speech sequences will be inaccurate until experimenters discover what counts as rhythmicity for talkers and listeners. This best can be determined, to begin with perhaps, by studies in which talkers are asked to produce sequences with specified timing and in which their performances are examined.

In the study by Fowler (1979), talkers produced sequences consisting of a pair of rhyming consonant–vowel–consonant (CVC) syllables in alternation (e.g., /bad sad bad . . ./). In these sequences, talkers produced long intervals between measured acoustic onsets of syllables when the first syllable in the interval began with a long-duration prevocalic segment. Indeed the departures from measured isochrony of successive intervals could be predicted very closely from differences in the measured durations of the syllable-initial consonants. Figure 1 displays the relationship found in Fowler's (1979) article. The onset–onset time differences in these productions ranged from a minimum of about 35 msec for sequences such as /mad nad . . ./, in which initial consonants were similar in manner class, to a maximum of about 200 msec when consonants differed in manner and in other features (e.g., /bad sad . . ./).

Although measured vowel onsets tend to be aligned more evenly than onsets of acoustic energy for the initial consonants of the syllables, intervals between vowel onsets are not isochronous either; instead they show departures from isochrony complementary to those of syllable onsets.

Articulation may be isochronous in these productions, however. When monosyllables in a sequence are rhyming CVCs, measures of intervals between onsets of muscle activity involved in segment production have revealed isochrony both of initial consonant and of vowel-related muscle activity. This is found even in sequences showing substantial departures from measured acoustic isochrony (Tuller & Fowler, Note 5). For example, in a sequence /bak fak bak . . ./, electromyographic (EMG) activity of the orbicularis oris muscle involved in lip closure was found to be isochronous; this implies that lip closures for /b/ and /f/ also were isochronous in these utterances. Necessarily, however, acoustic intervals from stop release for /b/ to onset of frication for /f/ were shorter than the opposite intervals from frication to release. This departure from isochrony of acoustic-energy onsets follows from the timing relation between the consonant articulations and their acoustic correlates. Consonants are produced in three broad phases: a closing phase, a closure interval, and a release phase. During the closure interval for the stop consonant /b/, the lips are shut, and in

stressed, syllable-initial position, the interval is silent. The stop burst occurs on release of the closure in the final phase of consonant production. In contrast to the stop consonant /b/, the fricative /f/ has a noisy closure interval. During closure, the lower lip approximates the upper teeth but does not seal off the oral cavity to the passage of air. Air passing through the narrow constriction produces frication. Consequently, a talker who aligns closure phases of syllable-initial stops and fricatives will produce syllables with systematically anisochronous onsets of acoustic energy.

These studies suggest, then, that talkers comply with instructions to produce isochronous monosyllables by producing isochronous *articulations*. Intervals between onsets of acoustic energy for successive monosyllables, then, are anisochronous because different manner classes of consonants have nonsilent acoustic consequences at different times after articulatory onset. Talkers do not attempt to compensate for this anisochrony of acoustic-energy onsets. For their part, in these experiments, listeners only hear isochrony when articulation is isochronous. They hear uneven timing when acoustic-energy onsets of different manner classes of consonants are aligned. I conclude, therefore, that in these experiments

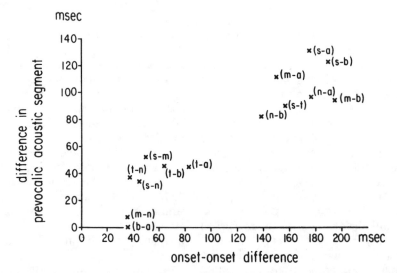

Figure 1. Differences in duration of prevocalic acoustic energy in syllables produced in alternation (Fowler, 1979) plotted as a function of syllable onset–onset asynchrony. (Data is from a single talker instructed to produce the syllables evenly stressed and timed. Paired letters on the figure refer to syllable-initial segments. For example, [s–a] refers to utterance /sad ad . . ./.)

listeners' perceptions of the rhythmic structure of speech are based on their extraction of acoustic information specifying articulatory timing (cf. Liberman, Cooper, Shankweiler, & Studdert-Kennedy, 1967). This conclusion is compatible with that based on other evidence (e.g., Fitch, Halwes, Erickson, & Liberman, 1980; Lehiste, 1970). For example, listeners' judgments of the relative loudness of two vowels correspond more closely to the articulatory effort required to produce them than to their relative intensities (Lehiste, 1970).

The conclusion that perceived timing is produced timing does not tell the whole story, however. The experiment by Tuller and Fowler (1980) found isochrony of both consonant- and vowel-related muscle activity. A later experiment (Fowler & Tassinary, 1981) showed that initial consonants are not always articulated at isochronous intervals in sequences that talkers intend to be isochronous. Figure 2 displays measurements of a set of syllables produced in time to a metronome by three talkers (see Rapp, Note 6, for similar data on Swedish talkers, and Allen, 1972a, 1972b, for analogous data on English ob-

tained using a different procedure). The location of the metronome pulse in the CVCs is indicated by the vertical line at zero in the figure. Points generally to the left of the metronome pulse indicate the onset of acoustic energy of the syllable. Points generally just to the right of the pulse indicate the measured vowel onset, and points farther to the right indicate measured vowel offset. By showing the alignment of rhyming syllables with the metronome pulse, the figure also reveals how syllables are aligned in relation to one another. The figure shows the effect reported by Morton et al. (1976) and studied further by Fowler (1979) and by Tuller and Fowler (1980). Acoustic-energy onsets for fricatives are early relative to those for voiced stops. Of interest here is another finding, however. Acoustic-energy onsets of intervals beginning with consonant clusters are early relative to others. A talker producing the sequence /sad strad sad . . ./ in time with the metronome does not produce isochronous acoustic onset–onset times—as he or she would if /s/ production were initiated at temporally equidistant intervals. Consequently, whatever the

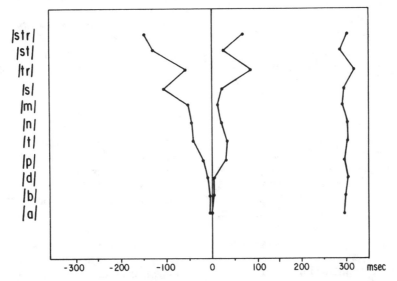

Figure 2. Measures of syllables produced by talkers in time with a metronome. (The vertical line at zero represents the metronome pulse. Different syllables are plotted top to bottom in the figure. The points generally to the left of the line represent the onset of acoustic energy for each syllable relative to the metronome pulse. Points generally just to the right of the pulse represent the measured vowel onset, that is, the onset of voiced oral formants for the vowel. Points to the far right represent measured vowel offset—the beginning of closure for final /d/. From "Natural Measurement Criteria for Speech: The Anisochrony Illusion" by C. A. Fowler and L. Tassinary, in J. Long and A. Baddeley (Eds.), *Attention and Performance, IX.* Hillsdale, N.J.: Erlbaum, 1981. Copyright 1981 by Erlbaum. Reprinted by permission.)

talker may have been producing rhythmically in these utterances, it was not initial-consonant production.

The alignments are not related to the amplitude contours of the syllables (Morton et al., 1976; Tuller & Fowler, Note 5) or, apparently, to their fundamental frequency contours (Rapp, Note 6).

In this study, the only acoustic measure temporally equidistant from the metronome pulse and consequently isochronous in these productions was the measured vowel offset. This finding perhaps can be rationalized by examining two separate research lines that investigate the temporal and articulatory microstructure of syllables: studies of phonetic shortening and of coarticulation.

The Temporal and Articulatory Microstructure of Syllables

Figure 2 reveals a pattern of vowel shortening in the context of various syllable-initial consonants. This pattern of shortening has been reported by other investigators for other languages (e.g., Lindblom, Lyberg, & Holmgren, 1981). In Figure 2, the measured duration of the vowel shortens as that of the prevocalic consonant or consonants increases in duration. Figure 3a replots the shortening effects in Figure 2 beside others (3b) reflecting effects of syllable *final* consonants on vowel duration.[2] These data resemble those reported by Lindblom et al. on speakers of Swedish and show that a vowel's measured duration also shortens as syllable-final consonants are added to the syllable.

Two interpretations of the shortening effects suggest themselves. According to one, talkers attempt to maintain a constant syllable duration in production (e.g., Shaffer, 1982). This might be a manifestation of a syllable- or stress-timing tendency. If for whatever reason talkers *are* trying to maintain a constant syllable duration, however, they are unsuccessful, as Figure 2 reveals. An examination of the articulatory evidence suggests a different interpretation.

In syllables, the production of consonants and vowels is context sensitive, usually in an assimilative way. The context sensitivity, called *coarticulation,* occurs very generally in syllables (e.g., MacNeilage & DeClerk, 1969).

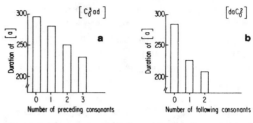

Figure 3. Measured vowel shortening in the context of preceding (a) and following (b) consonants in English.

For example, closure for a /b/ followed or preceded by the close vowel /i/ is achieved with a more closed jaw than that for /b/ followed or preceded by the open vowel /a/ (Sussman, MacNeilage, & Hanson, 1973). Similarly, the place of articulation of /k/ is fronted in the context of a front vowel as compared with a back vowel (e.g., Perkell, 1969).

Coarticulation has various explanations in the literature. One explanation, first proposed by Öhman (1966), appears to account for the vowel-shortening effects just described as well as for the context sensitivity of segment production. Öhman proposed that syllable-initial and -final consonants are superimposed on a vowel's leading and trailing edges. Moreover, in a VCV disyllable, vowel-to-vowel gestures of the tongue body are produced somewhat separately from articulatory gestures for the consonant. Öhman's evidence for his rather counterintuitive view of disyllable production was meager, but it has been substantiated by several subsequent studies. His evidence was derived from acoustic measures of implosive and explosive formant transitions in VCV disyllables produced by a Swedish talker. In Öhman's data, implosive transitions, representing the closing phases of voiced stop production, were affected by both vowels in the disyllable. So were the explosive transitions following consonant release. This seemed to indicate diphthongal production of the two vowels in the disyllables *during* production of the consonant.

---

[2] The data in Figure 3b were collected from a single talker (myself) who produced CVC syllables in a carrier phrase.

Compatible articulatory data have been provided by several investigators. Carney and Moll (1971) provided cinefluorographic tracings of tongue movements during production of $C_1V_1C_2V_2$ disyllables in which the second consonant is a fricative. They find movement of the tongue body from V_1 to V_2 during production of C_2. Similarly, Kent and Moll (1972) found indistinguishable trajectories and velocities of the tongue moving from /i/ to /a/ in "he monitored" and "he honored," even though in one, but not the other, utterance, the two vowels are separated by a bilabial consonant. Compatible findings are reported by several other investigators (Barry & Kuenzel, 1975; Butcher & Weiher, 1976; Perkell, 1969). This set of findings establishes the vowel as the articulatory foundation of a syllable, in the sense that it is produced throughout the syllable's articulatory extent, and suggests that in VCVs, (stressed) vocalic gestures are realized in relation to production of other (stressed) vowels, even if a consonant intervenes. In addition, this view of vowel and consonant production may explain the measured shortening effects that consonants exert on vowels.

Figure 4 illustrates the relationship between coarticulation and shortening implied by these studies. The figure's horizontal dimension represents time, and its vertical dimension, an abstract attribute: prominence. Prominence refers at once to the extent to which vocal tract activity is given over to the production of a particular segment and the extent to which the character of the acoustic signal reflects articulatory gestures associated with the segment. During the closure phase of a consonant, for example, the character

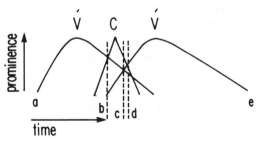

Figure 4. Schematic representation of vowel and consonant production. (The horizontal axis represents time, and the vertical axis, an abstract dimension: prominence.)

of the acoustic signal is largely determined by the consonant's manner and place of closure; the signal is noisy if the segment is a fricative, silent if it is a stop, and so on. Even though a coproduced vowel can influence the signal during consonant closure, giving rise to the context sensitivity of the signal for the consonant, the voiced formant structure most characteristic of vowels is absent during consonant closure. This is indicated in the figure by giving the vowel a lesser degree of prominence than the consonant during consonantal closure.

Measuring conventions locate segment boundaries approximately where ordinal changes take place in the prominence of two segments. Thus, boundaries delimit acoustic intervals during which an individual phonetic segment is the most prominent one in the signal. (Moreover, ambiguities arise concerning where a boundary should be located—e.g., between a voiceless stop and a vowel, see Lisker, 1972—when it is not obvious over a certain extent of the signal which of two segments is predominant.) In the VCV depicted in Figure 4, vowels would be given boundaries at *a* and *b* and at *d* and *e,* while the consonant would extend from *b* to *d.* If the consonant were deleted and a VV were produced, the first vowel's measured extent would be from *a* to *c,* and the second vowel's from *c* to *e.* Because of these conventions, even if the vowels in the VCV and the VV had identical articulatory extents, both would be measured to shorten in the VCV as compared with the VV. A first-approximation hypothesis, however, in view of the bidirectional coarticulation and shortening effects, would be that vowels do not change their produced durations in consonantal contexts. Rather, the consonants overlap them more or less. Although this most conservative hypothesis almost certainly will have to undergo revision, it is the simplest one to explain both coarticulation and shortening in syllables.

Now let us consider syllables produced in sequence. Öhman proposed that in VCVs, transconsonantal vowels are produced as continuous diphthongal gestures, to a first approximation, unperturbed by a medial consonant (see also Kent & Moll, 1972). Extrapolation of this view to longer speech sequences (at least to longer sequences of stressed syllables) suggests that vowels are produced cyclically—that is, continuously, one after the other—and constitute a somewhat separate articulatory stream from gestures involved in consonant production.[3]

This hypothesis gives rise to the question of how consonants might be timed relative to the vowel stream. Some research by Tuller, Kelso, and Harris (1982) suggests part of an answer. Across utterances of the form pV_1CV_2p, produced at various rates with different stress patterns and two different medial consonants, Tuller et al. found an invariant linear relationship between duration of a vocalic cycle (i.e., the interval between the onset of muscle activity for V_1 and that for V_2) and the time lag between onsets of activity for V_1 and C. That is, timing of consonant production relative to vowel production was invariant over substantial changes in the duration of a vocalic cycle. The evidence suggests a strategy of initiating production of a consonant at an invariant phase in the production of a vowel's cycle. (Evidence of vowel shortening as consonants are added to a cluster implies, however, that the critical phase in production of a vowel at which consonant production is initiated would be different for the single consonants studied by Tuller et al. than for clusters.) As Tuller et al. pointed out, preservation of relative timing of muscle activity or gestures over changes in rate and amplitude of movement is commonly observed across a variety of activities, for example, handwriting (Viviani & Terzuolo, 1980; Wing, 1978; Hollerbach, Note 7), locomotion (Grillner, 1975), and respiration (Grillner, 1977).

Spoken and Perceived Syllabic Isochrony Reconsidered

The temporal structure of the syllable as just outlined may help to rationalize the behaviors of talkers and listeners in the experiments by Morton et al. (1976), Fowler (1979), and Fowler and Tassinary (1981) summarized earlier. By interpretation, the measured shortening of a vowel estimates how much it has been overlaid by surrounding consonants.[4] Estimates of the effective overlapping of a vowel by a consonant can be obtained by examination of Figure 2. In the figure, the metronome pulse is temporally equidistant from the measured vowel offset across the syllables. Moreover, in /ad/, with no initial consonant, the metronome pulse nearly coincides with the measured vowel onset. In other syllables, then, vowel shortening is the same as the interval from the metronome pulse to measured vowel onset. This interval estimates the interval of effective CV overlap in these syllables. By hypothesis, based on the EMG evidence provided by Tuller and Fowler (1980), talkers initiate vowels at temporally equidistant intervals under instructions to produce isochronous sequences of syllables. For their part, listeners appear to hear vowel timing; moreover, their judgments evidently are based on the articulatory timing of vowels, not on the timing of their periods of prominence in the acoustic signal as reflected by usual ways of identifying their onsets.

For listeners to hear produced rather than measured vowel timing, they must segment the speech stream in an unexpected way. They must do so in such a way that the summed duration of the segmented consonants and vowels exceeds the duration of the spoken syllable from which they have been segmented. The duration of the vowel must be its measured duration plus the extent of its effective overlap by the consonant.

Experiments 1 and 2 are designed to ask

---

[3] Further evidence in support of the view that vowel and consonant production is separate is available in the literature on speech errors. Anticipation errors, perseverations, exchanges, and substitutions never involve interaction *between* consonants and vowels. Instead, vowels intrude on other vowels, and consonants on consonants.

[4] This may be an oversimplification in two senses. First, vowels shorten for some reasons that have nothing to do with coarticulation, for example, when speech rate increases. Therefore, whereas coarticulation implies shortening, the reverse need not be true. Second, stressed vowels coarticulate with consonants *and* with unstressed vowels that precede or follow them (e.g., Fowler, 1981a, 1981b; and see Experiment 2). To coarticulate with an unstressed vowel, stressed-vowel production necessarily extends throughout (and beyond) production of a medial consonant at least in utterances where an unstressed vowel precedes the stressed vowel. But the vowel's measured shortening is less than the full extent of its overlap by other segments (again, at least in utterances including unstressed vowels). Possibly, the *effective* duration of a stressed vowel for a listener does not include the entire period of time during which it influences the acoustic signal.

394   CAROL A. FOWLER

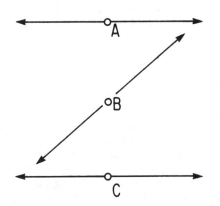

Figure 5. A display used by Johansson (1950) to study perceptual vector analysis. (Lights A and C move horizontally back and forth in phase; light B moves diagonally.)

whether such a segmentation occurs in perception. First, however, we ask, in an abstract way, *how* such a segmentation might occur.

In the literature on perception, investigators are familiar with an analogous segmentation in which separate contributions to complex events are perceptually distinguished. Figure 5 displays an example from Johansson's (1950) research (see also Johansson, 1974). The figure represents a visual display in which three moving lights are shown to subjects. The top and bottom lights, A and C, move horizontally in phase, while a third light, B, moves in a diagonal trajectory. Viewers do not report seeing two lights moving horizontally and one diagonally. Instead they report horizontal movement of an apparent rod extending from A to C, with B moving vertically along the rod.

Based on this and similar evidence, Johansson concluded that viewers perform a "perceptual vector" analysis in which movements common to a set of points serve as a perceptual frame relative to which residual motions are perceived. In the figure, all points include vectors of horizontal motion. Horizontal motion extracted from points A and C exhausts the description of their movements, but extracted from B leaves a residual, vertical motion vector.

Perceptual vector analysis is a realistic perceptual behavior. Ordinarily when components of a visual scene move together, they belong to the same event; consequently, the common movements are appropriately as-

cribed to coherent movement of a common frame. Imagine, for example, watching a child on a merry-go-round. If the child is seated on a horse that moves up and down relative to the surface on which it is mounted, then the child on the horse in fact moves in a complex, cycloid motion. The complex motion combines the rotation of the merry-go-round with the up and down movement of the horse relative to the floor of the merry-go-round. Observers do not see the complex movement, however. Instead, and appropriately, they see rotational movement of the merry-go-round as a whole, and an up-and-down motion of the child and the horse relative to the rotational movement. That is, they extract rotational movement, which is common to the merry-go-round and its components. This exhausts the movement of the merry-go-round's fixed structure, but, extracted from the motion of the horses, it leaves a vertical motion vector.

When we ask whether a listener can detect a vowel's produced extent despite coarticulatory overlap of part of it by a consonant, we are asking whether listeners can do the speech-perception equivalent of a perceptual vector analysis. We have seen that the vowel serves as the articulatory foundation of the syllable; for clarity in making the analogy to the visual examples, we call the vowel the *frame*. It is produced during syllable-initial and -final consonants as well as during its own interval of prominence in the signal. Therefore, acoustic reflections of the vowel's component tongue body and jaw movements provide the analogue to the vectors of common movement. These reflections exhaust the contributions to the acoustic signal during the time that the vowel is the most prominent segment in the syllable, but not during consonant production. During consonant production, two kinds of articulatory gesture contribute to the acoustic signal: the relatively slow gestures of the tongue body and jaw associated with the vocalic frame, and the relatively fast gestures of the articulators (possibly including the tongue body and jaw) associated with the consonant. If a perceptual vector analysis is possible, the gestures common to the vocalic frame may be "factored" from those specific to the consonantal portion, leaving, on the one hand, perception of the whole vocalic frame and, on the other hand, as residual, a relatively context-free version of the consonant.

This proposed analysis, like its visual counterpart, would be a realistic one for perceivers, because it recovers the natural structure of speech events.

Experiments 1 and 2 were designed to test two predictions derived from the hypothesis that listeners perform a perceptual vector analysis on syllables and, hence, may attend to articulatory timing of vowels in the experiments outlined at the beginning of the first part of this article. One prediction is that the effective duration of a vowel for a listener is its measured duration plus its effective overlap by a syllable-initial consonant. The second prediction is that information for vowel identity is available to listeners during the production of an overlaid segment. Experiment 1 tests the first prediction, and Experiment 2, the second. Experiment 3 is designed to assess the relation between vowel perception and the perceived timing of syllables in experiments such as that by Morton et al. (1976).

Experiment 1

To ask whether listeners are sensitive to the temporal microstructure of syllables and in particular to the relationship of overlap between syllable-initial consonants and postconsonantal vowels, we used a technique developed by Raphael (1972). Raphael has shown that a syllable-final stop or fricative can be synthesized that is identified as voiced after a long-duration vowel and as voiceless after a short-duration vowel. This is compatible with the fact that, particularly in English, voiced syllable-final consonants are preceded by longer vowels than are voiceless consonants. By generating a set of stimuli with a range of vowel durations before the final consonant and by asking subjects to label the final consonant as voiced or voiceless, Raphael was able to identify a voicing boundary within the continuum of vowel durations. The boundary is defined as the vowel duration at which subjects label the syllable equally often as /d/ or /t/, that is, the 50% crossover point. In later studies, Raphael, Dorman, and Liberman (Note 8) and Raphael and Dorman (1980) showed that the

crossover point is shifted toward the /t/ (short vowel) end of the continuum by a syllable-initial consonant. That is, the final consonant is heard more frequently as /d/ when a consonant precedes the vowel than when the vowel is syllable-initial. This may indicate that the vowel is heard as being longer when preceded by a consonant than when it is syllable-initial. For syllable-initial /d/, all or most of the transitions, which in these stimuli were necessary in order to specify the initial /d/, were also heard to belong to the vowel. This interpretation is consistent with the facts of production; the direction and extent of second formant (F2) transitions appropriate for /d/ are conditioned by the following vowel because the two segments are coarticulated during the release of the consonant.

In the study by Raphael et al. (Note 8), an initial /r/ also shifted the /t/–/d/ boundary substantially, whereas steady-state frication characteristic of /s/ shifted it only slightly. This latter outcome was replicated by Raphael and Dorman (1980) with natural speech. These experiments made it clear that the perceived voicing of a final stop can be affected by vowel length. In the following experiment, I attempt to extend these findings to some of the syllables depicted in Figure 2. If adding initial consonants to a vowel increases the vowel's effective duration, then, following Raphael et al. (Note 8), we should observe a change in the voicing boundary of syllables beginning with /a/, /b/, /m/, and /s/. Furthermore, we predict a greater effective lengthening of the vowel by consonants that according to Figure 2 shorten the vowel substantially (e.g., /s/) than by those that shorten it very little (e.g., /b/).[5]

---

[5] This prediction may appear contradictory to the findings of Raphael et al. who found limited effects of /s/ on apparent vowel duration and substantial effects of /d/. The difference in prediction and outcome is derived from a difference in measurement criteria for the vowel. In experiments by Raphael et al., voiced formant transitions following release of /d/ were identified as belonging to the consonant and not to the vowel; hence, when the addition of transitions affected the voicing judgments, the influence was identified as one of the consonant on the effective duration of the vowel. In our measurements, however, voiced formant transitions are included in the measurement of vowel duration. Therefore, the predicted *additional* effect of a voiced stop such as /d/ or /b/ on voicing judgments is small.

396   CAROL A. FOWLER

Method

Subjects. Subjects were 63 introductory psychology students at Dartmouth College.

Stimuli and materials. We selected the syllables /ad/, /bad/, /mad/, and /sad/ spoken by two of the talkers who provided the data for the experiment reported by Fowler and Tassinary (1981; and who were two of the three talkers who provided that data shown in Figure 2).[6] These syllables had shown a range of vowel shortening that spanned 20 msec collapsed over the two talkers. The order of measured vowel durations decreased in the series: /ad/, /bad/, /mad/, and /sad/.

For each talker, a single token of each of the four syllables was selected from the nonmetronome condition of the experiment reported by Fowler and Tassinary. These syllables were digitized and edited using the pulse-code modulation system at Haskins Laboratories.

The final portion of the syllable /ad/ was spliced from the rest (50 msec for talker 1 and 85 for talker 2). The portion excluded any voicing during the closure for the /d/ and any release of the /d/ to facilitate a shift in identification from /d/ to /t/. This final section of the syllable /ad/ replaced the final portion of the other three syllables to ensure that the final consonant of the four syllables was equivalently /d/- or /t/-like. Finally, the vowels in each syllable were made equal in duration (within a pitch pulse) by deleting pitch pulses from the steady-state portions of syllables with longer vowel durations. The original vowel durations of the four syllables averaged 225 msec for talker 1 and 236 for talker 2. From each of these syllables, a 10-step continuum was constructed by successively deleting one pitch pulse taken for talker 1 and two for talker 2 (a female), insofar as possible from the relatively steady-state portion of the vowel. This gave continua with a range of approximately 75 msec for talker 1 and 90 msec for talker 2.

For each talker, four test orders were constructed, one for each continuum (syllable). Each test order began with 20 trials in which the two end points of the continuum were repeated 10 times each in alternation. These served to familiarize the listeners with the most /d/- and /t/-like sounds they would hear. The introductory series of 20 trials was followed by 100 trials in which the 10 stimuli were presented 10 times each in random order. This pattern, 20 trials in which the end point stimuli were repeated in alternation and 100 randomized trials, was repeated twice more for a total of 60 introductory trials and 300 test trials. The first third of the test served as practice; the data to be reported are from the last set of 200 test trials. There were 2 sec between trials with a longer delay of 4 sec following every 10th trial.

Design. Subjects were nested within the four levels of the independent variable, syllable (/ad/, /bad/, /mad/, and /sad/), and the two levels of the variable talker. With a single exception, eight subjects were assigned to each cell in the design. Only seven subjects were run for the syllable /bad/ produced by the first talker. We expected a shift in the /d/-/t/ boundary toward the short-vowel (/t/) end of the continuum progressively in the sequence /ad/, /bad/, /mad/, and /sad/.

Procedure. Subjects listened to the test orders over earphones in groups of one to four in a sound-treated room. They were instructed to listen to the initial 20 sounds of alternating /d/- and /t/-final syllables on each third of the test, writing *d* or *t* as appropriate on their answer sheet as they followed along. On the next 100 trials in each third of the test, they were instructed to write *d* or *t* depending on which final consonant they heard, choosing only between the responses *d* and *t*.

Results and Discussion

The prediction that the voicing boundary would shift toward /t/ progressively in the series /ad/, /bad/, /mad/, and /sad/ was assessed by comparing the four syllables on the measure of number of *d* responses to each stimulus in the continuum. Figure 6 displays the results of this procedure collapsed over talkers 1 and 2. The ogival curves for the four syllables cross over the 50% point in just the predicted order. Interpolating from the figure, the boundaries for /ad/, /bad/, /mad/, and /sad/ are 5.36, 5.70, 5.90, and 6.39.

In an analysis, the average number of *d* responses given to the four syllables was compared for stimuli near the voicing boundaries, that is, stimuli 5, 6, and 7. Collapsed over talker and stimulus number (5–7), because neither variable interacted with syllable, the average number of *d* responses out of 20 to the four syllables was 7.4, 8.7, 9.1, and 11.4. This increase reflects the increasing resistance to labeling the final consonant as *t* throughout the series. The increase was significant according to a trend test in which the mean for each syllable was weighted according to its measured vowel shortening in the syllables displayed in Figure 2. In the analysis, both subject and talker were treated as random factors, $F(1, 3) = 18.86$, $p = .02$.

In this analysis, listeners' judgments of syllables produced by talker 1 showed just the predicted increase, whereas their judgments of talker 2 showed a reversal of /bad/ and /mad/. This reversal in fact occurred on just one of the three crossover stimuli.

The outcome of this analysis, though certainly not striking, is compatible with the hypothesis that the duration of the vowel as perceived by listeners increases with increases in the vowel's measured overlap by the consonant (its measured shortening). Nonethe-

---

[6] We attempted to create continua using syllables of the third talker in the metronome study. However, we were not successful in creating continua of syllables that listeners could label consistently.

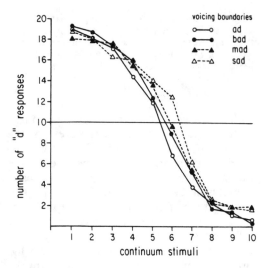

Figure 6. Number of /d/ responses to four different vowel-duration continua.

less, whereas the range of shortening was about 20 msec in the experiment by Fowler and Tassinary (1981), the difference in perceived vowel duration as assessed by the present experiment was only about 10 msec.

Experiment 2

Experiment 1 has an alternative interpretation to the one that we have proposed. Possibly, listeners are familiar with different durations of vowels following /b/, /m/, and /s/; consequently, they expect relatively shorter vowels following /s/ than /m/ and following /m/ than /b/. If so, the results of Experiment 1 document those expectations but do not reveal a tendency to hear a vowel during that part of the acoustic signal in which vowels and consonants coarticulate but consonants predominate in the signal.

Experiment 2 was designed to provide evidence converging with Experiment 1 that perceivers extract vowel information during production of segments that coarticulate with it. If they do, then time to identify a vowel, timed from the vowel's *measured* acoustic onset, should be shorter, the more extensive its effective overlap with preceding segments. After estimating overlap by vowel shortening, then, time to identify /a/ should be shorter in /sa/ than in /ma/ and shorter in /ma/ than in /ba/. Experiment 2 was designed to test that prediction.

Method

Subjects. Subjects were 14 undergraduates at Dartmouth College.

Stimuli. Stimuli were naturally produced VCV disyllables in which the first vowel was unstressed schwa, the consonant was /b/, /m/, /s/, or /p/, and the second vowel was /a/ or /i/. A disyllable with /p/ replaced the syllable /ad/ in Experiment 1. As Figure 2 shows, vowel shortening after /p/ is greater than that following /s/. Therefore, predicted time to identify a vowel is expected to decrease in the series əbV, əmV, əsV, əpV.[7]

Three tokens of each disyllable were produced, giving 24 different stimuli in all. The stimuli were randomized into five 48-trial blocks with the constraint that in each block each token occurred twice. Stimuli were recorded on audiotape with 2 sec between trials and 10 sec between blocks.

Table 1 provides durational measures of the stimuli. Measures of schwa duration were taken from the onset of periodicity in the signal to closure for the consonant. For the consonants, the onset of the closure interval to the onset of voicing for the vowel was measured. Stressed vowels were measured from the earliest evidence of voicing following release of the consonant to signal offset. As others have found (see also Figure 3), the durations of consonants and stressed vowels were negatively correlated ($r = -.76$).

Table 2 provides measures of F2 during the initial schwa of each disyllable. (Measures were obtained by the method of linear prediction.) Measures were taken during the four 20-msec time frames preceding closure for the consonant. The table shows that F2 for schwa is lower when the forthcoming stressed vowel is /a/ than when it is /i/. This is compatible with the substantially higher F2 for the high vowel /i/ than for the low vowel /a/ and indicates that anticipatory coarticulation of the stressed

---

[7] This prediction requires clarification. The observation that vowel shortening in /pV/ is greater than in other syllables is true if vowel onset is defined as the onset of voicing following release of a syllable-final consonant. If the onset were located instead at the onset of the formant transitions following release of the /p/—an equally defensible location because the transitions provide vowel information as well as being sufficient to specify the /p/ to a listener—the rank ordering would change. However, it is not necessary for the aims of the present experiments to defend either of these measuring points as superior. Indeed, according to the present arguments, any measuring point is indefensible that purports to divide an acoustic signal into nonoverlapping phonetic segments. The aims of the experiments can be met if a reference point is selected and used consistently in assessing syllable-timed productions (Figure 2), judgments of vowel duration (Experiment 1), vowel and consonant classifications (Experiments 2 and 3), and syllable-timing judgments (Experiment 3). If syllables are aligned similarly around the selected reference point for syllable-timed productions and judgments as for assessments of vowel durations and for vowel classifications, but not for consonant classifications, then the conclusion is warranted that syllable timing is related to vowel sequencing more than to consonant sequencing.

398   CAROL A. FOWLER

Table 1

Durational Measures (in msec) of the Disyllables Used in Experiments 2 and 3, Averaged Over the Three Tokens of Each Type

Disyllable	/ə/	C	V
əba	61	128	434
əbi	61	123	465
əma	43	144	402
əmi	56	123	390
əsa	45	189	387
əsi	51	195	337
əpa	42	206	370
əpi	40	218	371

vowel precedes closure for the consonant (see also Fowler, 1981a, 1981b).

Figure 7 displays this more clearly by plotting the difference between F2 for /ə/ preceding /i/ and /a/ separately for each disyllable pair during the last four 20-msec intervals preceding consonant closure. This evidence of coarticulation is compatible with Öhman's findings and other evidence cited earlier.

Until the final frame, disyllables including /b/ and /m/ appear to be more differentiated than those containing /s/ and /p/. If listeners use average frequency of the second formant of schwa over these time frames as a source of information about the forthcoming vowel, they will not show the rank ordering of response times we have predicted. However, the predicted ordering is reflected in the rate of change in the plotted difference score over the last three frames where the change is monotonic; /b/ shows the lowest rate of change, and /p/ the highest. If this measure reflects information about ongoing adjustments in vocal tract shape for the forthcoming vowel to which listeners are sensitive, then Figure 7 may offer acoustic support for the predicted ordering of response times.

Design. The major independent variable was consonant identity; a second was vowel identity. All subjects participated at all levels of the independent variables.

Table 2

Measures of F2 of Schwa During the Four 20-msec Frames Preceding Consonant Closure Averaged Over the Three Tokens of Each Type

Disyllable	Frame number before closure			
	4	3	2	1
əba	1,464	1,406	1,334	1,304
əbi	1,676	1,641	1,628	1,619
əma	1,469	1,470	1,403	1,314
əmi	1,755	1,687	1,640	1,670
əsa	1,689	1,698	1,693	1,702
əsi	1,794	1,791	1,853	1,921
əpa	1,451	1,415	1,373	1,328
əpi	1,517	1,426	1,517	1,683

Note. F2 = Second formant.

The dependent variable was time to classify the vowel, timed from the vowel's measured onset. Based on the findings of Fowler and Tassinary (1981) displayed in Figure 2, I expected reaction time to classify a vowel as /i/ or /a/, measured from the acoustic onset of the vowel's period of prominence, to decrease in the series əbV, əmV, əsV, əpV because the measured vowel durations decrease in the series. I had confidence that this rank ordering of vowel durations is stable because the same rank ordering was reported by House and Fairbanks (1953) for vowels in symmetrical bVb, mVm, sVs, and pVp contexts. Having previously examined only stimuli in which the stressed vowel was /a/, I had no reason to expect a difference in reaction time to /i/ or /a/ nor any interaction between the variables, consonant and vowel identity.

Procedure. Subjects were tested individually. They listened to the test sequence over earphones, classifying the stressed vowel on each trial as /i/ or /a/ by making a button-press response. For half the subjects, /i/ corresponded to the left-hand button and for the other half, /a/ corresponded to the left-hand button. Responses and reaction times were collected by microcomputer. Times were measured from the acoustically defined vowel onset by placing a click on the second channel of the audiotape, 100 msec prior to measured vowel onset on the first channel. In the experiment, these clicks caused a millisecond clock to be read; the clock was read again on receipt of the subject's button-press response, and the difference in the times minus 100 msec was the subject's reaction time.

Subjects were instructed to make their responses as quickly as possible but to minimize errors.

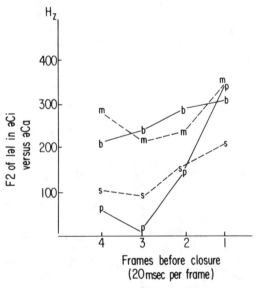

Figure 7. Anticipatory coarticulation of stressed /i/ and /a/ in the disyllables of Experiments 2 and 3. (Second formant [F2] of initial schwa in əCa subtracted from F2 of schwa in əCi is plotted for each of the four disyllable pairs and for four 20-msec frames preceding closure of the consonant.)

Results

Results are reported for the final four blocks of the experiment, the first block serving as practice. Subjects were quite accurate, averaging 95% correct overall.

Average reaction times to the disyllables əbV, əmV, əsV, and əpV were 483, 468, 463, and 424 msec, respectively. The effect of consonant identity is significant, $F(3, 39) = 33.7$, $p < .001$. More important, however, the decrease in reaction time in the series occurred as predicted. Based on the measured shortening in Figure 2 (averaged over three talkers—those whose productions provided stimuli for Experiment 1 and one other), the predicted differences in reaction time in the series is 14 msec for əbV versus əmV, 8 msec for əmV versus əsV, and 8 msec for əsV versus əpV. The first two predicted differences fit the observed differences fairly well; however, the obtained difference between əsV and əpV is 39 msec rather than the predicted 8 msec. A planned comparison weighting reaction times according to the predicted differences is highly significant, $F(1, 39) = 81.10, p < .0001$.

The main effect of vowel identity is nonsignificant in the analysis, $F(1, 13) = 1.65$, $p = .22$, but the interaction between consonant and vowel identity is significant, $F(3, 39) = 9.55$, $p < .001$. One reason for the interaction is that the ordinal relation of əmV and əsV is as predicted when the vowel is /i/ (465 vs. 441 msec) but is reversed when the vowel is /a/ (472 vs. 484 msec). In addition, when the vowel is /i/, reaction times to əsV and əpV are the same (441 msec) but differ when the vowel is /a/ (406 vs. 484). I had no reason to predict a difference in rank ordering of reaction times based on vowel identity, because in earlier studies the vowel was invariably /a/. Whereas articulatory support for this interaction or other reasons for it will have to be investigated, the reasons for the interaction will not be pursued here. However, a similar interaction will be sought in listeners' assessments of the timing of the syllable sequences in the next experiment.

Discussion

This experiment provides evidence that vowels are detected during intervals when the vowels coarticulate with prevocalic segments (including initial consonant and the preceding schwa). Experiment 2 shows that the time to identify a vowel, timed relative to measured vowel onset, is correlated with the vowel's measured shortening. Based on the coarticulation evidence cited earlier (and represented schematically in Figure 4), we interpret the relative shortening as an index of relative overlap by the prevocalic consonant (and, perhaps, by the unstressed schwa; see also Fowler, 1981a, 1981b). Therefore we interpret the decrease in vowel classification time with shortening as evidence that listeners use information for the vowel in the prevocalic segments *as* information for vowel identity.

These results converge with those of Experiment 1. That experiment found that the measured duration of a vowel at which judgments of voicing of a syllable-final consonant shift from voiced to voiceless decreases progressively in the series /ad/, /bad/, /mad/, and /sad/. One interpretation of this outcome is that listeners are sensitive to the shortening effects of consonants and vowels displayed in Figure 3a, but another interpretation is promoted by the results of Experiment 2—that the effective duration of a vowel for a listener is the vowel's measured duration plus the overlap of part of its perceived extent by a syllable-initial consonant.

Previous experiments in this series (Fowler, 1979; Fowler & Tassinary, 1981) have used the vowel /a/ exclusively. Experiment 2 introduced the vowel /i/ and obtained an interaction between initial consonant and vowel in vowel-classification times. In Experiment 3, assessments are made of the relative rhythmic alignment of the syllables used in Experiment 2. If perception of vocalic timing underlies the perception of speech rhythms as I propose, then the interaction found in Experiment 2 should be reflected also in listeners' rhythmic alignments of these disyllables. Experiment 3 tests this prediction.

Experiment 3

In this experiment, I relate listeners' vowel-classification times, obtained in Experiment 2, to listeners' perceptions of rhythmicity, which I propose have their bases in perception of cyclic vowel production. In addition I also assess the relation of listeners' consonant classifications to their perception of rhythm. According to the view of perception being developed here, consonant classifications are not related to the perceived timing of syllables.

Method

Subjects. Subjects were 30 Dartmouth undergraduates. Fifteen participated in the tapping task, and 15 in the consonant-classification task.

Stimulus materials. The experiment used the audiotape devised for the vowel-classification task of Experiment 2.

Procedure. In Experiment 2, subjects were asked to classify the stressed vowel on each trial as /i/ or /a/. In the present experiment, one group of subjects was asked to tap a key in time with the successive disyllables, tapping once for each disyllable at a point corresponding to the syllable's "beat." This technique, like the metronome technique used by Rapp (Note 6) and by Fowler and Tassinary (1981), enables discovery of the perceived temporal alignment of different syllables (see Figure 2).

A second group of subjects was asked to classify the consonants on each trial as /b/, /m/, /p/, or /s/, making a button-press response as quickly as possible. Assignment of phoneme labels to buttons was varied over subjects.

Design. As in Experiment 2, independent variables are consonant identity (/b/, /m/, /p/, /s/) and stressed-vowel identity (/i/, /a/). The dependent measure is response time, measured initially as relative to measured vowel onset and next as relative to measured stressed-syllable onset. I expected vowel-classification times obtained in Experiment 2 to correlate with tap times in the present experiment. This would suggest a close relation between information necessary to identify a vowel and perceived relative timing of the disyllables. No such relation was predicted between consonant-classification times and tapping times.

Results

When tapping times are measured relative to vowel onset, the effect of consonant is highly significant, $F(3, 42) = 297.78$, $p < .0001$. Tap times follow vowel onset by 207, 187, 137, and 125 msec for the disyllables əbV, əmV, əsV, and əpV, respectively. This is exactly the rank ordering of disyllables obtained in Experiment 2, although responses to əsV are closer in reaction time to əpV in the present experiment and to əmV in Experiment 2.

As in Experiment 2, the effect of vowel identity is nonsignificant, $F(1, 14) = 2.16$, $p = .16$, but the interaction is significant, $F(3,$ 42$) = 20.63$, $p < .001$. In Experiment 2, there were two reasons for the interaction. First, the rank ordering of times to əmV and əsV was as predicted (based on measured shortening in Figure 2) when the vowel was /i/ but reversed when the vowel was /a/. Next, there was no difference in reaction time to əsi and əpi, but a large difference between əsa and əpa. In the present experiment, the predicted rank ordering of əmV and əsV was obtained for both vowels. However, as in Experiment 2, there was essentially no difference in tapping times to əsi and əpi (123 vs. 121 msec), but the predicted direction of difference appeared between əsa and əpa.

Table 3 provides mean response times in the tapping and consonant-classification tasks, respectively, with response times now measured relative to onset of acoustic energy for the consonant (i.e., release for /b/ and /p/). Table 3 provides comparable times for the vowel classifications of Experiment 2. As predicted, vowel and tap times pattern similarly. The correlation between them, computed over the eight disyllables, is .95. Consonant times also pattern similarly to tap times ($r = .79$). Moreover, the patterns of vowel and consonant times are correlated ($r = .73$). All of these correlations are significant. However, the significant relationship between tap times and consonant response times is due to shared variance between vowel and consonant times. When that variance is partialed out, the correlation between tap times and consonant times falls to .46, a nonsignificant value. In contrast, when variance shared by consonant- and vowel-identification times is partialed from the tap–vowel correlation, the partial correlation remains significant ($r = .90$). In a multiple regression analysis, only the vowel times contribute significantly to predictions of tap response times. This suggests that perceived timing of stressed syllables is a function only (or primarily) of perceived information pertaining to vowel identity as predicted and is not significantly a function of perceived consonant identity.

Discussion of Experiments 1–3

I have attempted to establish a relationship, on the one hand, between the temporal and articulatory structures of spoken sylla-

Table 3
Measures of Response Time (in msec) in Experiments 2 and 3

Disyllable	Tap			Consonant			Vowel		
	RT(AE)	RT(C)	SD	RT(AE)	RT(C)	SD	RT(AE)	RT(C)	SD
əba	328	205	45	728	605	83	618	495	74
əbi	338	218	46	757	637	82	600	480	79
əma	—	328	55	—	670	83	—	616	72
əmi	—	313	54	—	668	83	—	588	77
əsa	—	339	59	—	683	59	—	673	73
əsi	—	320	54	—	673	73	—	638	94
əpa	335	233	58	762	660	127	612	510	83
əpi	339	246	49	703	610	99	660	567	76

Note. RT(AE) = response timed from onset of acoustic energy for the consonant; RT(C) = response timed from onset of closure for /b/ and /p/.

bles and, on the other hand, between both of these systematic properties of produced speech and the perceived timing of syllables in productions that talkers intend to be rhythmical. I have proposed that measured vowel shortening in the context of surrounding consonants is an index of coarticulatory overlap of the vowel by consonants. This proposal is supported by the coarticulation literature, which shows that vowels are coproduced with consonants (Barry & Kuenzel, 1975; Butcher & Weiher, 1976; Carney & Moll, 1971; Öhman, 1966) and provides evidence for vowel-to-vowel gestures of the tongue body occurring concurrently with medial consonant production. Based on an elaboration of Öham's proposal suggesting that vowels are produced continuously in sequences of stressed vowels, I hypothesized that the perceived timing of syllables is based on the perceived timing of vowels.

The research presented here supports this view, showing that both the perceived duration of a vowel (Experiment 1) and the time necessary to identify a vowel (Experiment 2) are affected by the identity of the syllable-initial consonant. In particular, Experiment 1 showed that the more extensive the shortening effect of a consonant on a vowel (and hence, by hypothesis, the more the consonant overlaps the vowel), the more the consonant helps resist shifts in perceived voicing of the syllable-final consonant, which occur as the vowel's measured duration decreases. Experiment 2 found that the more extensive the shortening effect of a consonant on a vowel,

the shorter the subjects' response time to classify the vowel as /i/ or /a/, timed from the vowel's measured onset.

Experiment 3 established a relation between perception of the stressed vowel in a sequence of disyllables and the perceived timing of the sequence. Vowel-classification times and tap times were highly correlated.

Some problems with the present view of vowel production as continuous have been raised in a recent article by Shaffer (1982). Shaffer pointed out that with changes in rate of production, vowels change in duration more than consonants. But if vowels and consonants were produced coordinately but separately as proposed here, either of two different outcomes would be expected. Just one segment type might be affected by rate change without any effect on the other; alternatively, being coordinate, consonants and vowels might change proportionately. Neither outcome corresponds to what is observed.

There is a way in which separate, but coordinate, segment types could change disproportionately, however. There is nonlinearity in the articulatory system in the form of an upper limit on segment shortening due to rate changes. If at slow rates of talking, consonants are closer to this limit than are vowels, then they would shorten less with an increase with rate than do vowels. Consonant gestures *are* faster than vocalic gestures at slow or conversational rates of talking. In a recent study, Tuller, Harris, and Kelso (in press) reported a shorter duration of muscle activity supporting consonant than of vowel production at a slow rate of talking. At a fast rate, duration of activity for the consonant and vowel is more similar, that for the consonant having decreased by 13% and that for the vowel by 23%.

Shaffer (1982) also argued that the present proposal

fails to account for the coarticulation of consonants and for coarticulation across syllable boundaries; it does not consider the timing of postvocalic consonants or show why syllable duration is affected by the size of the consonant clusters. (p. 121)

The present view *does* fail to account for the coarticulation of consonants, but only because it does not yet address consonant production except in relation to vowel production. Consonants are considered primarily as they may affect perceived rhythm or, more often, as they mask evidence of vowel production used by listeners to guide rhythm judgments. However, I do not detect anything in principle that will prevent incorporation of information about relative timing of consonants into a theory of vowel production as separate from consonant production. The timing of postvocalic consonants *relative* to the vowel and the coarticulation of consonants with vowels across syllable boundaries are addressed.

As for increases in syllable duration with increases in consonant cluster size, the theory can offer two possible hypotheses. Segments have compression limits (e.g., Klatt, 1976). In particular, the constraint that consonants be initiated at a particular phase in the production of vowels (Tuller et al., 1982) may prevent excessive overlap of the vowel by consonants in a cluster. If so, then production of a large cluster may force a discontinuity in vowel production with the consequence that initial consonants in a prevocalic cluster may not coarticulate with the following vowel but may with a preceding vowel; similarly, final consonants in a postvocalic cluster may not coarticulate with the preceding vowel but may with the subsequent one. However, in view of the findings that stressed vowels coarticulate over long extents when unstressed vowels follow (Bell-Berti & Harris, 1979; Fowler, 1981a, 1981b), a different outcome is also possible. Consonant clusters may force an *increase* in the duration of a vowel cycle to preserve continuity of the vowel stream.

Further research will have to distinguish these possibilities and to distinguish them from others that might be proposed.

Contributions From Phonetics and Phonology

In this part of the article, I develop the three ideas outlined in the introduction. First is the general idea that investigation of language structure, which proceeds largely independently from studies of language use, can provide a useful source of evidence converging (or failing to converge) with results of experimental studies. The second, more specific, idea is that some phonological rules are "natural" in the specific sense that they reflect exaggerations and conventionalizations of articulatory dispositions. Insofar as they can be identified as such, they offer a source of evidence concerning the nature and identity of some dispositions. Third, I provide examples that I suggest are exaggerations and conventionalizations of the articulatory tendency to produce vowels in a continuous, cyclic fashion.

Phonological descriptions of languages characterize systematic properties in the phonological forms of lexical items. That is, the descriptions factor systematic (general) phonological properties common to lexical items, expressed as general rules, from properties idiosyncratic to individual items. This factoring reveals a number of characteristics of the lexicons of languages that are relevant to psychological interests. Spoken-language systems exist only as they are used by speaker/hearers; moreover, they are evolutionary acquisitions of speaker/hearers. In view of these facts, systematic phonological properties provide clues to the nature of the speaker/hearers themselves (see also Chomsky, 1980, who, however, focuses on their revealed cognitive nature rather than on their perceptual and articulatory natures as I will emphasize here).

Some of these clues appear to be more fundamental or significant than others. They are systematic properties that are popular across languages. For example, many languages devoice final obstruents. In German, the noun *Bund* is pronounced /bunt/ in the nominative, but /bund/ in the genitive *Bundes*. In Polish, *snow* is /s'n'ek/ in the nominative but

/s'n'ega/ in the genitive. In Russian, the nominative of *leg* is /noga/, but the genitive plural is /nok/. (The German example is from Comrie, 1980, and the Polish and Russian examples, from Kenstowicz & Kisseberth, 1979.) That this phonological rule is somehow natural to language users is suggested by the fact that children learning language also have a tendency to devoice final consonants. This occurs even in English where it is inappropriate (Oller, Wieman, Doyle, & Ross, 1976).

Systematic phonological properties that are popular across languages may be popular for a reason. Indeed, there may be many reasons why a particular kind of systematic property is favored by languages, but of interest here is the possibility that many properties are natural in resembling articulatory dispositions. Word-final devoicing may be an example.

If some phonological regularities do resemble articulatory dispositions, then phonological investigation can serve a useful function for psychological investigation of speech production. Articulation is difficult to study with respect to issues of psychological (as opposed, say, to physiological) interest, not simply because the articulators are difficult to access, but also because direct study of articulation tends to provide more detail than current psychological perspectives on speech motor-control can organize and explain. Identification of popular systematic properties of the phonologies of languages can contribute to direct study of articulation in two ways. First, it can suggest the kinds of articulatory regularities that have served as resources for the evolution of phonologies. These suggestions can help to focus the search for regularities or organizing principles in articulation. Next it can serve as converging evidence for hypothetical organizing principles, such as that of cyclic vowel production, that may have emerged, perhaps, dimly, from articulatory or perceptual investigations of speech. That is the use to which phonological evidence will be put here.

Systematic and Idiosyncratic Properties of Language

Not all systematic properties of lexical items are factored out in phonological rule systems. Two kinds of systematic properties of lexical items can be identified that I will call *conventional* and *necessary*. Conventional systematic properties are expressed by general rule, whereas necessary ones are not. Conventional systematic properties are specific to individual languages; they are conventions, which are used to convey linguistic information. An example is the formation of the plural in English. The plural is formed by adding (morphological) *s* to a word. The pronunciation of the *s* is conditioned in a ruleful way by properties of the phonological segment adjacent to which the *s* is appended. If the segment is unvoiced and is neither a fricative nor an affricate, the plural is realized as /s/. If the segment is voiced and neither a fricative nor an affricate, the plural is /z/. Otherwise, the realization is /ɨz/. This conditioning is systematic—it can be expressed as a rule—but it is a convention. An alveolar fricative after a voiced segment need not be voiced (witness *dance*, phonemically /dæns/). And other languages have other plural formation rules.

Other systematic properties of language are "necessary"; that is, they are essentially universal and (to a first and close approximation) could not be other than they are. An example is the f_0 contour on a vowel following a voiced or voiceless stop. Following release of a voiced stop, the fundamental frequency of the voice is low and gradually rises over a period of more than 100 msec (e.g., Hombert, Ohala, & Ewan, 1979; Ohala, 1978). After a voiceless stop, f_0 is high and gradually falls. The reasons for this patterning are not fully understood, but it is generally agreed that the f_0 contour is a necessary consequence of the aerodynamic and articulatory adjustments made to maintain or resist voicing during stop closure (Ohala, 1978). The f_0 contour following a stop is a systematic property of a word but is not a convention and is not expressed as a phonological rule in the phonologies of languages.

In the subsequent sections, I focus on both necessary and conventional phonological properties. Necessary systematic properties are direct sources of evidence about articulatory constraints on production. For this reason, they are very useful to study. However, I focus primarily on a second aspect of necessary properties—they may serve as a source of new linguistic conventions as languages change. Thus it is important to look at the evolution of conventions to gain insight into necessary systematic properties.

Leakages From Articulation Into the Phonologies of Languages

Ohala (1974, 1981) has argued that exaggerated versions of necessary systematic properties of languages occasionally enter the language as conventions due, in his view, to systematic misperceptions by listeners. For example, Ohala suggested (1974, 1981) that tone languages such as Punjabi may have evolved from atonal languages with voicing distinctions among stop consonants.

This evidence is derived from comparisons of related languages, one of which is a tone language and the others of which are not. Punjabi, for example, is a tone language related to Hindi and other languages that are not. In Punjabi, the distinction between aspirated voiced consonants and unaspirated unvoiced consonants, present in Hindi, is absent. Words starting with an aspirated voiced consonant in Hindi have a low tone on the vowel in Punjabi. In the history of Punjabi, apparently, the distinction between voiced aspirated and unvoiced unaspirated consonants was lost, leaving behind a tonal distinction between words formerly differing in voicing of the initial consonant.

Ohala ascribed this sound change to consistent misperceptions by listeners. Hearing the f_0 contours produced by voiced and voiceless consonants on following vowels, language learners may have interpreted the contours mistakenly as systematic conventions. Consequently, when these listeners produced voiced or voiceless stop-initial syllables, they intentionally produced a tone on the following vowel. Being exaggerated, the contours were more salient than the unintentionally produced contours that necessarily accompany stop voicing or voicelessness. As numbers of language learners made the error (uncorrected for unexplained reasons[8]), syllables differing in voicing of the initial consonant were marked in two ways—one by the voicing distinction itself and the other by the tonal pattern on the vowel. In some languages,

the tonal contours replaced the voicing difference as the critical difference between certain syllables. These languages became tone languages. Ohala (1981) offered many other examples in which conventions apparently entered languages as exaggerations of necessary systematic properties of speech (see also Wright's, Note 10, analysis along similar lines of the [continuing] vowel shift in English).

If the examples are real, they imply that some systematic conventions that are popular among unrelated languages may reflect exaggerations of necessary regularities in speech production and, hence, in fact may provide clues to the identity of some of these regularities. Review of the phonological literature reveals several systematic properties suggestive of the mode of vowel production proposed here to underlie (in part) the impression of rhythmicity of speech. As we have characterized (stressed) vowel production, it has two central aspects. Vowels' leading and trailing edges are overlaid by consonants, and vowels are produced as a cyclic stream somewhat separate from the production of consonants. Reflections of both of these aspects can be found in the phonologies of languages. I know of no conventions that contradict the proposed mode of vowel production.

Language Conventions Suggestive of Continuous Vowel Production

Vowel Shortening and Lengthening

A number of languages have adopted conventions whereby consonant and vowel length serve a distinctive function in the language (i.e., a long vowel, V:, or long consonant, C:,

---

[8] Louis Goldstein (Note 9) has suggested a reason for this. Locke's (e.g., 1979) research on the so-called "fis" phenomenon in children reveals that immediately after producing a word, children are more aware of what they meant to say than of what they in fact uttered. Locke's research focuses on children whose speech does not seem to distinguish pairs of sounds (e.g., /w/–/l/ or /r/–/w/) that are distinct in adult language. After having produced something like /weyk/ meaning "rake," they will deny having said "wake." But if their production is recorded and replayed to them 1 day later, they are no better than other listeners in distinguishing their *wake*s from their *rake*s.

is considered a different vowel or consonant from its short counterpart). In some of these languages, rules ensure that consonant and vowel length are complementary. These rules may constitute exaggerations and conventionalizations of the shortening effects of consonants on vowels depicted in Figure 3.

For example, Swedish distinguishes long and short versions of vowels and consonants phonologically. In Swedish, constraints on syllable structure prevent long postvocalic consonants and long vowels from co-occurring in a syllable, and they prevent short vowels and (only) short postvocalic consonants from co-occurring in stressed syllables (Elert, 1964, cited in Lindblom & Rapp, Note 11). Allowed stressed syllable structures are (C)V:(C) and (C)VC:(C). (Parentheses indicate that segments are optional.) This reciprocal relationship between vowel and consonant length at the phonological level of description of the language is *not* the same as the (phonetic) shortening depicted in Figure 3. Lindblom et al. (1981) showed that Swedish *long* vowels are shortened by intra- or transsyllabic consonants, just as English vowels are. But the phonetic shortening of the long vowels does not transform them into phonologically short vowels. (Thus, although V: in V:C is shorter than V: in isolation, both are phonologically long vowels.) In Swedish, then, a reciprocal relation exists between consonants and vowels at two levels—at a phonetic level where it also occurs generally across languages, and at a phonological level where it is a convention special to Swedish.

Yawelmani, a native American language once spoken in California, like Swedish, distinguishes phonologically long and short vowels. Also like Swedish, Yawelmani maintains a reciprocal relation between vowel length and, in this case, the *number* of following consonants. In Yawelmani, a phonologically long vowel in a stem is made short if a suffix is added to the stem causing the stem vowel to be followed by more than one consonant. According to Kenstowicz and Kisseberth (1979):

Examination of a variety of other languages reveals that alternations in [phonological] vowel length typically revolve around differences in the consonant–vowel structure of words, with long vowels preferred in "open syllables" (__CV) and short vowels preferred in "closed syllables" (__CC). (p. 83)

This is just what we would expect if languages tend to conventionalize by exaggeration, properties of production that already are necessarily systematic in language. By virtue of the coproduction of vowels and consonants in syllables, vowels are overlaid by consonants, leading to their measured shortening. In many languages, vowel length is made phonologically distinctive and, in some of these languages (Swedish, Yawelmani, and others), rules conventionalize the reciprocal relation between vowel duration and consonant duration.

Historical Sound Change

Some historical sound changes reflect a similar reciprocal relation between vowel length and the vowel's consonantal context. These changes are called *compensatory lengthening* (e.g., Ingria, 1980) and occur when a consonant is lost in a word or set of words and a vowel in the vicinity of the consonant—formerly phonologically short—becomes long. This occurred both in Latin and Greek. Both languages lost /s/ in certain contexts. In Latin, /sisdo:/ became /si:do:/, for example, and in Greek, /ekrinsa/ became /ekri:na/ (Ingria, 1980). Phonetically, loss of a consonant should "uncover" part of a vowel's produced extent, giving it a longer measured duration. The historical change appears analogous except that the lengthening of the vowel is phonological. (However, see deChene & Anderson, 1979, for a skeptical look at the historical phenomenon of compensatory lengthening.)

Vowel Infixing[9] and Vowel Harmony

Languages reveal two other conventional structures suggestive of the basic organization of consonants and vowels that I have suggested. In contrast to the conventions just described, which reflect (so we suppose) the overlap of consonants and vowels in production, the following conventions may reflect the separateness of the vowel "stream" from the production of consonants. In particular,

---

[9] I am grateful to Judy Kegl for pointing out the relevance of McCarthy's analysis to my proposal that vowel production is continuous.

they are conventions in which phonetically nonadjacent vowels are treated in some respects as if they were adjacent (and hence a separable stream from the consonants).

In Arabic (McCarthy, 1981), derivationally related words may share a triconsonantal root: For example, words in which *ktb* occurs all have to do with the concept *to write*. Examples of words are /katab/, /ktaabab/, /kutib/, and /uktab/. McCarthy did an analysis of these word systems in which separate vocalic and consonantal tiers are proposed to underlie word generation.

To generate a particular verb form in Arabic, three choices are made. The choice of the triconsonantal root determines the word family. The choice of a "prosodic template" selects the derivational form of the verb. Finally, selection of a vocalic infix determines the voice and aspect of the verb.

The prosodic template is a word schema that specifies the numbers and orderings of the consonants and vowels in the word (e.g., CVVCVC). Some templates have more vowel slots than vowels in the infix and more consonant slots than consonants in the root. In general, consonants in the root are assigned left-to-right to the C slots, and vowels in the infix, left-to-right to the V slots of the template. If there are unfilled C or V slots, the right-most consonant or vowel is "spread" to the unfilled slots of the appropriate type. So, for example, /ktb/ and the infix /a/ (perfective, active), inserted into the template CVCVC, give /katab/ (*write*); inserted into CCVCVC, give /ktabab/.

McCarthy has captured this system's structure using a so-called "autosegmental" analysis (Goldsmith, 1976). An autosegmental approach differs from the usual segmental/suprasegmental approach in allowing several segmental tiers to underlie the expression of an utterance. Traditionally, one or two are allowed: one for phonological segments and, perhaps, another for tonal contours and other aspects of prosody. However, according to Goldsmith, utterances cannot be sliced vertically (perpendicular to the time axis) in such a way that the utterance is partitioned into coherent units. Instead, different features of the utterances start and stop at their own individually appropriate intervals and to a degree independently of the startings and stop-

pings of other features. In an autosegmental formulation, properties regulated separately are assigned to different tiers of a structure representing the utterance. The different tiers are related by simple rules of association.

In McCarthy's analysis, vowels and consonants are assigned to separate tiers. So, for example, /katab/ is represented by the structure in Figure 8a, and /ktabab/ by that in Figure 8b. In this kind of formulation, the "spreading" to unfilled consonant or vowel slots now can literally be a spreading. For /a/, there are no relevant segments (see discussion below of the Relevancy Condition) intervening between two V slots.

This autosegmental structure, proposed by McCarthy, obviously is compatible with the articulatory dynamics proposed to underlie syllable production. It differs from the structure, however, in being a convention of Semitic languages, not a necessary property of syllable production. Nonetheless, its existence suggests that of an underlying necessary property of production not unlike the one proposed in the first part of this article.

Another, more frequent, language convention possibly reflecting the same articulatory structure is *vowel harmony*, that is, a tendency for certain vowels to assimilate to other vowels in their neighborhood. Vowel harmony occurs in many languages including Turkish, Hungarian, Yawelmani, and Igbo. In Turkish, for example, properties of a suffix vowel are assimilated in backness and rounding to the stem vowel to which it is attached. Rules of vowel harmony operate over any number of intervening consonants. Thus, vowel harmony, like vowel infixing, is captured naturally in an autosegmental analysis in which vowels and consonants occupy separate tiers.

Vowel harmony may be an instance of a class of rules tending to conform with a constraint on phonological rules known as the *Relevancy Condition* (Jensen, 1974; Jensen & Stong-Jensen, 1979).[10] The constraint specifies the conditions under which phonological rules can refer to influences of segments on nonadjacent segments ("action at a distance").

---

[10] I thank Alan Bell for directing me to the work of Jensen and Stong-Jensen.

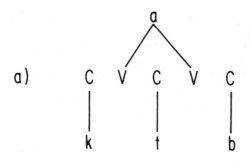

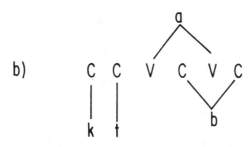

Figure 8. Vowel infixing in Arabic from McCarthy (1981).

Phonological rules may be characterized as having the following abstract form:

focus → structural change/determinant,

irrelevant segments, ___.

For example, a rule of vowel harmony in Yawelmani can be written as follows:

$$\begin{bmatrix} + \text{syll} \\ \alpha \text{ high} \end{bmatrix} \rightarrow$$

$$\begin{bmatrix} + \text{round} \\ + \text{back} \\ - \text{low} \end{bmatrix} / \begin{bmatrix} + \text{syll} \\ + \text{round} \\ \alpha \text{ high} \end{bmatrix} C_o \text{ ___}.$$

In words, a vowel (focus) is realized as rounded, back, and nonlow (structural change) following a rounded vowel matching it in height (determinant) and by any number of intervening consonants (irrelevant segments). According to the Relevancy Condition, any features shared by the focus and the determinant (here, any vowel) define a class of *relevant segments*. The complement of that

class, the irrelevant segments, serves as the "distance" over which a phonological segment can exert its effect. The influence cannot skip over relevant segments. Hence in the Yawelmani harmony rule, the irrelevant segments skipped over are all and exclusively consonants.

Conceivably, the relevancy conditions of a language may be useful in defining its autosegmental tiers. The relevant segments defined by a rule may define segments that share a tier, and irrelevant segments define a different tier or tiers. If so, it is interesting that in the examples of rules conforming to the constraint provided by Jensen and Stong-Jensen (1979), relevant segments are either consonants only or vowels only, never both.

Conclusions

Talkers

When talkers produce sequences of stressed vowels and consonants, production of the two segment types overlaps. This is shown by coarticulatory evidence, by evidence of measured shortening of vowels in consonantal contexts, and, by inference, by the existence of phonological rules in some languages that ensure a complementary relation between consonant and vowel length.

In addition, evidence suggests a degree of separateness of vowel from consonant production, which in fact allows the overlap just described. Evidence for the separation of vowel from consonant production is threefold. Coarticulation suggests it, the patterning of speech errors suggests it, and so, inferentially, does the existence of phonological rules, in which an autosegmental analysis distinguishes a vocalic from a consonantal tier.

When talkers intend to produce a rhythmic sequence of stressed monosyllables, evidence suggests they produce evenly timed vowels. Timing of syllable-initial consonants depends on the ways in which consonants or clusters are produced relative to vowels. A relaxed cyclicity in production of stressed vowels in natural speech may explain in part the impression of temporal rhythm in stress- and syllable-timed languages.

As to *why* talkers might produce speech in this way, only tentative answers may be given.

408   CAROL A. FOWLER

Liberman and Studdert-Kennedy (1978) suggested that speech is coarticulated ("encoded") for the listener's sake. Speech has to be produced at a rapid rate to enable retention of sufficient speech for syntactic analysis. But at the required rate, were speech a sequence of discrete sounds, listeners would be unable to recover the segments or their order (see, e.g., Warren, 1976). Coarticulation allows a large number of relatively long sounds to occupy the same interval as a much smaller number of shorter, but temporally discrete, segments. We have shown here that listeners make use of information for a vowel during the portion of the signal dominated by consonant information. This is entailed by the proposal of Liberman and Studdert-Kennedy that coarticulation *facilitates* the perceptibility of serially ordered speech sequences (see also, Shankweiler, Strange, & Verbrugge, 1977).

A second reason for separate vowel and consonant production may have to do with production rather than perception. Elsewhere (Fowler, 1977; Fowler, Rubin, Remez, & Turvey, 1980) I have proposed that talkers may exploit the fact that vowels constitute a natural articulatory class. All vowels, in contrast to consonants, are produced as relatively slow changes in the global shape of the vocal tract effected largely by movements of the tongue body and jaw.

Each particular vowel itself is a *class* of tongue body and jaw positions that yield approximately the same global vocal tract shape. This is shown by perturbation studies where, for example, talkers produce vowels clenching a bite block between the teeth so that the jaw is fixed. In these studies, the acoustic properties of the vowels are near normal (e.g., Fowler & Turvey, 1980; Lindblom, Lubker, & Gay, 1979), suggesting that tongue movement has compensated for the inability of the jaw to move. It is shown, too, by studies of coarticulation where positioning of the jaw in CV and VC syllables is affected jointly by the identity of the consonant and vowel (Sussman et al., 1973). These observations are displayed schematically in Figure 9. In the figure, each vowel is represented as a curve in a jaw–tongue coordinate space. This is meant to show the capacity that a speaker has to achieve any given vowel by a class of

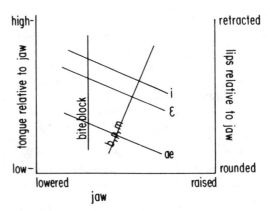

Figure 9. Schematic representation of constraints on the jaw and tongue during production of vowels /i/, /ɛ/ and /æ/ and on the jaw and lips during bilabial consonant production. (A vowel is produced by a range of negatively correlated jaw and tongue positionings that yield the same tongue–palate approximation. Similarly, a bilabial stop is realized by a variety of negatively correlated jaw and lip positionings that achieve bilabial closure; e.g., Folkins & Abbs, 1975.)

jaw positionings and tongue positionings relative to the jaw. Due to this capacity, when a bite block prevents jaw movement, or when a consonant perturbs it, all is not lost; an acceptable version of the vowel is achieved by adjusting the tongue to the special constraints on jaw position.[11]

Vowels differ one from the other largely (but not entirely) in terms of the tongue body's positioning (front/back, high/low) relative to the palate. The idea that vowels constitute a natural articulatory class is indicated in Figure 9 by showing /i/, /ɛ/, and /æ/ as if the functions for each vowel relating jaw position to the position of the tongue relative to the jaw were parallel. By hypothesis, producing a vowel, any vowel, involves organizing the musculature of the jaw and tongue body so that the two structures work in a compensatory fashion. Producing a *particular* vowel may be modeled as choosing a parameter value for the jaw–tongue relationship that ensures an "equilibrium position" for the jaw–tongue system appropriate to the selected vowel.

---

[11] In Figure 9, I have drawn the curves for each vowel as if they were straight lines and the lines for different vowels as if they were parallel. There is no reason to suppose that either constraint is accurate. The lines are meant to serve as schematic representations.

This proposal is analogous to Bizzi's (1978) hypothesis that pointing to positions by monkeys is achieved when the monkey establishes appropriate levels of activation of agonist and antagonist muscles in the arm. Appropriate activation levels create an equilibrium position of the arm (i.e., the position of the arm when the opposing muscle forces balance) at the target position.

What would such a system buy a talker? First, establishing a compensatory relationship between jaw and tongue may constitute an example of a general way in which movement systems responsible for reproducing positions (as opposed to movements) tend to be organized. The organizations have the advantage of "equifinality," that is, of enabling achievement of the goal position in a variety of ways without requiring reorganization (see, e.g., Keele, 1981; Kelso & Holt, 1980). This makes vowel production context sensitive.

Second, the aspects of vowel organization that hypothetically are shared among vowels may buy the talker an increment in efficiency in facilitating cyclic vowel production. Cyclic activities such as locomotion and respiration (see Grillner, 1977) are efficient in terms of the motor organizations they require. In locomotion, muscle systems are organized to generate a step. Once so organized, the same muscle systems will produce an indefinite number of subsequent steps without requiring any change in organization. Cyclic vowel production may provide another example of this kind of motor organization. If it is possible for a talker to coordinate his or her tongue and jaw in a compensatory fashion but also in a way that is *general* to the class of vowels, then once established, the organization can serve the production of vowels throughout an utterance, individual vowels being produced by cyclic reparameterizations of the tongue–jaw system.

Of course, this proposal currently begs a number of critical questions: Most important, how might the muscles of the jaw and tongue be coordinated in a compensatory fashion? Second, is the notion of a difference in values of *parameters* of an invariant organization of muscles a realistic way to describe the different jaw–tongue relations characteristic of different vowels?

However, if vowel production *were* cyclic, it would help to rationalize the linguist's and naive listener's judgments of rhythm in speech. Indeed, this is my tentative proposal, based on studies of monosyllabic stress feet and subject to revision when I turn to more natural productions in a subsequent article (Fowler, Note 4).

Listeners

The most important conclusion to be drawn about listeners' perceptions of rhythmic speech is that they mirror the natural structure of the spoken utterance. Listeners hear speech sequences largely as talkers produce them and essentially as talkers intend them to be heard.

Doing so involves hearing through coarticulatory overlap of segments, and I have shown at least one circumstance in which listeners appear to do just that (Experiment 2). I have proposed that their hearing through coarticulation is analogous to their perceptual segmentation of visually complex events and involves something like a perceptual vector analysis of the acoustic speech stream.

By interpretation, listeners hear isochronous speech when talkers produce it by attending to acoustic information specifying timing of (stressed) vowel production. In the isochronous sequences of stressed monosyllables, talkers produce vowels cyclically, and listeners attend to the timing of vowels.

Measurement

As I have argued elsewhere (Fowler & Tassinary, 1981), conventional measurements of phonological segments and measures of acoustic segments do not always reflect the psychological structure of the spoken or perceived utterance. This is not because (or only because) listeners "interpret" the acoustic message, whereas measurements are "objective" assessments. Rather, there are other possible objective segmentations of a signal than conventional ones, and the listener's perspective on the signal may constitute an alternative objective segmentation. In particular, conventions for measurement in which phonological segments are demarcated as if they were temporally discrete do not reflect the possibly equally objective perspectives that respect coarticulatory overlap. The judgments of listeners may in the future guide decisions concerning natural measurement criteria for speech.

Sources of Evidence

Products of linguistic analysis offer a reservoir of evidence, largely untapped by psychologists, that can converge with evidence obtained from experimental investigation. Although the procedures of phonological analysis are nonexperimental, the products of the analysis, systematic phonological properties of languages, *are* behavioral regularities because they reflect language use. As such, they are relevant to psychological theories of language use including theories of speech production and perception.

Here we have used evidence from phonological analysis of language to buttress proposals that the talker's overlap of vowels and consonants is perceptually real and that separate, perhaps cyclic, vowel production is sufficiently real for language users that it gives rise to analogous phonological phenomena.

Reference Notes

1. Dalby, J., & Port, R. Temporal structure of Japanese: Segment, mora and word. In *Research in phonetics* (Report 2). Bloomington: Indiana University, Department of Linguistics, 1981.
2. Lea, W. *Prosodic aids to speech recognition: IV. A general strategy for prosodically-guided speech understanding* (Report No. PX10791). Arlington, Va.: Advanced Research Projects Agency, 1974.
3. Shen, Y., & Peterson, G. Isochronism in English. In *Studies in linguistics, Occasional Papers* (Vol. 9). Buffalo, N.Y.: University of Buffalo, 1962.
4. Fowler, C. A. *Converging sources of evidence on spoken and perceived rhythms of speech: II. Polysllabic sequences.* Manuscript in preparation, 1983.
5. Tuller, B., & Fowler, C. A. *The contribution of amplitude to the perception of isochrony* (SR-65). New Haven, Conn.: Haskins Laboratories, 1981.
6. Rapp, K. A study of syllable timing. In *Speech transmission laboratory: Quarterly progress report* (Vol. 1). Stockholm, Sweden: University of Stockholm, 1971.
7. Hollerbach, J. M. *An oscillation theory of handwriting.* Cambridge, Mass.: Massachusetts Institute of Technology, Artificial Intelligence Laboratory, 1980.
8. Raphael, L., Dorman, M., & Liberman, A. *The perception of vowel duration in VC and CVC syllables* (SR-42/43). New Haven, Conn.: Haskins Laboratories, 1975.

9. Goldstein, L. Personal communication, 1982.
10. Wright, J. The behavior of nasalized vowels in the perceptual vowel space. In *Report of the phonology laboratory, Berkeley* (Vol. 5). Berkeley: University of California, 1980.
11. Lindblom, B., & Rapp, K. Some temporal regularities of spoken Swedish. In *Papers in linguistics from the University of Stockholm* (Vol. 21). Stockholm, Sweden: University of Stockholm, 1973.

References

Abercrombie, D. Syllable quantity and enclitics in English. In D. Abercrombie, D. B. Fry, P. A. D. MacCarthy, N. C. Scott, & J. L. M. Trim (Eds.), *In honour of Daniel Jones.* London: Longman, 1964.

Allen, G. The location of rhythmic stress beats in English: An experimental study. Part I. *Language and Speech,* 1972, *15,* 72–100. (a)

Allen, G. The location of rhythmic stress beats in English: An experimental study. Part II. *Language and Speech,* 1972, *15,* 170–195. (b)

Barry, W., & Kuenzel, H. Coarticulatory airflow characteristics of intervocalic voiceless plosives. *Journal of Phonetics,* 1975, *3,* 263–282.

Bell-Berti, F., & Harris, K. Anticipatory coarticulation: Some implications from a study of lip rounding. *Journal of the Acoustical Society of America,* 1979, *65,* 1268–1270.

Bizzi, E. Processes controlling arm movements in monkeys. *Science,* 1978, *201,* 1235–1237.

Bolinger, D. Pitch accent and sentence rhythm. In I. Abe & T. Kanekiyo (Eds.), *Forms of English: Accent, morpheme, order.* Cambridge, Mass.: Harvard University Press, 1965.

Butcher, A., & Weiher, E. An electropalatographic investigation of coarticulation in VCV sequences. *Journal of Phonetics,* 1976, *4,* 59–74.

Carney, P., & Moll, K. A cineflourographic investigation of fricative consonant–vowel coarticulation. *Phonetica,* 1971, *23,* 193–202.

Catford, J. *Fundamental problems in phonetics.* Bloomington: Indiana University Press, 1977.

Chomsky, N. On cognitive structures and their development: A reply to Piaget. In M. Piattelli-Palmarini (Ed.), *Language and learning.* Cambridge, Mass.: Harvard University Press, 1980.

Classe, A. *The rhythm of English prose.* Oxford: Blackwell, 1939.

Comrie, B. Phonology: A critical review. In B. Butterworth (Ed.), *Language production, I.* London: Academic Press, 1980.

deChene B., & Anderson, S. Compensatory lengthening. *Language,* 1979, *55,* 505–535.

Donovan, A., & Darwin, C. The perceived rhythm of speech. *Proceedings of the Ninth International Congress of Phonetic Sciences,* 1979, *2,* 268–274.

Fitch, H., Halwes, T., Erickson, D., & Liberman, A. Perceptual equivalence of two acoustic cues for stop-consonant manner. *Perception & Psychophysics,* 1980, *27,* 343–350.

Folkins, J., & Abbs, J. Lip and jaw motor control during speech: Responses to resistive loading of the jaw. *Jour-*

nal of Speech and Hearing Research, 1975, *18,* 207–220.

Fowler, C. Timing control in speech production. Bloomington: Indiana University Linguistics Club, 1977.

Fowler, C. A. "Perceptual centers" in speech production and perception. *Perception & Psychophysics,* 1979, *25,* 375–388.

Fowler, C. A. Perception and production of coarticulation among stressed and unstressed vowels. *Journal of Speech and Hearing Research,* 1981, *46,* 127–139. (a)

Fowler, C. A. A relationship between coarticulation and compensatory shortening. *Phonetica,* 1981, *38,* 35–50. (b)

Fowler, C. A., Rubin, P., Remez, R., & Turvey, M. Implications for speech production of a general theory of action. In B. Butterworth (Ed.), *Language production, I.* London: Academic Press, 1980.

Fowler, C. A., & Tassinary, L. Natural measurement criteria for speech: The anisochrony illusion. In J. Long & A. Baddeley (Eds.), *Attention and performance, IX.* Hillsdale, N.J.: Erlbaum, 1981.

Fowler, C. A., & Turvey, M. T. Immediate compensation in bite-block speech. *Phonetica,* 1980, *37,* 306–326.

Goldsmith, J. *Autosegmental phonology.* Bloomington: Indiana University Linguistics Club, 1976.

Grillner, S. Locomotion in vertebrates. *Physiological Reviews,* 1975, *55,* 247–304.

Grillner, S. On the neural control of movement—A comparison of different basic rhythmic behaviors. In G. S. Stent (Ed.), *Function and formation of neural systems.* Berlin: Dahlem, 1977.

Han, M. The feature of duration in Japanese. *Study of Sounds,* 1962, *10,* 65–75.

Hombert, J.-M., Ohala, & Ewan, W. Phonetic explanation for the development of tones. *Language,* 1979, *55,* 37–58.

House, A., & Fairbanks, G. The influence of consonant environment upon the secondary acoustical characteristics of vowels. *Journal of the Acoustical Society of America,* 1953, *25,* 105–113.

Ingria, R. Compensatory lengthening as a metrical phenomenon. *Linguistic Inquiry,* 1980, *11,* 465–495.

Jensen, J. A constraint on variables in phonology. *Language,* 1974, *50,* 675–686.

Jensen, J., & Stong-Jensen, M. The Relevancy Condition and variables in phonology. *Linguistic Analysis,* 1979, *5,* 125–160.

Johansson, G. *Configurations in event perception.* Uppsala, Sweden: Almqvist and Wiksell, 1950.

Johansson, G. Projective transformations as determining visual space perception. In R. MacLeod & H. Pick (Eds.), *Perception: Essays in honor of James J. Gibson.* Ithaca, N.Y.: Cornell University Press, 1974.

Keele, S. Behavioral analysis of movement. In V. Brooks (Ed.), *Handbook of physiology: Motor control.* Washington: American Physiological Society, 1981.

Kelso, J. A. S., & Holt, K. Evidence for a mass-spring model of human neuromuscular control. In C. Nadeau, W. Halliwell, K. Newell, & G. Roberts (Eds.), *Psychology of motor behavior and sport.* Champaign, Ill.: Human Kinetics, 1980.

Kenstowicz, M. J., & Kisseberth, C. W. *Generative phonology: Description and theory.* New York: Academic Press, 1979.

Kent, R., & Moll, K. Tongue body articulation during vowel and diphthong gestures. *Folia phoniatrica,* 1972, *24,* 278–300.

Klatt, D. Linguistic uses of segmental duration in English: Acoustic and perceptual evidence. *Journal of the Acoustical Society of America,* 1976, *59,* 1208–1221.

Lehiste, I. *Suprasegmentals.* Cambridge, Mass.: MIT Press, 1970.

Lehiste, I. Rhythmic units and syntactic units in production and perception. *Journal of the Acoustical Society of America,* 1972, *54,* 1228–1234.

Liberman, A., Cooper, F., Shankweiler, D., & Studdert-Kennedy, M. Perception of the speech code. *Psychological Review,* 1967, *74,* 431–461.

Liberman, A., & Studdert-Kennedy, M. Phonetic perception. In H. Leibowitz & H.-L. Teuber (Eds.), *Handbook of sensory physiology, Vol. VIII: Perception.* Berlin, West Germany: Springer-Verlag, 1978.

Lindblom, B., Lubker, J., & Gay, T. Formant frequencies of some fixed-mandible vowels and a model of speech-motor programming by predictive simulation. *Journal of Phonetics,* 1979, *7,* 147–161.

Lindblom, B., Lyberg, B., & Holmgren, K. *Durational patterns of Swedish phonology: Do they reflect short-term memory processes?* Bloomington: Indiana University Linguistics Club, 1981.

Lisker, L. On time and timing in speech. In T. Sebeok (Ed.), *Current trends in linguistics, 12.* The Hague: Mouton, 1972.

Locke, J. The child's processing of phonology. In W. A. Collins (Ed.), *Minnesota Symposium on Child Psychology* (Vol. 17). Hillsdale, N.J.: Erlbaum, 1979.

MacNeilage, P., & DeClerk, J. On the motor control of coarticulation in CVC monosyllables. *Journal of the Acoustical Society of America,* 1969, *45,* 1217–1233.

Marcus, S. Acoustic determinants of perceptual center (P-center) location. *Perception & Psychophysics,* 1981, *30,* 247–256.

McCarthy, J. A. A prosodic theory of nonconcatenative morphology. *Linguistic Inquiry,* 1981, *12,* 373–418.

Morton, J., Marcus, S., & Frankish, C. Perceptual centers (P-centers). *Psychological Review,* 1976, *83,* 405–408.

Ohala, J. Experimental historical phonology. In J. Anderson & C. Jones (Eds.), *Historical linguistics, II: Theory and description in phonology.* Amsterdam: North-Holland, 1974.

Ohala, J. The production of tone. In V. Fromkin (Ed.), *Tone: A linguistic survey.* New York: Academic Press, 1978.

Ohala, J. The listener as a source of sound change. In M. F. Miller (Ed.), *Papers from the parasession on language behavior.* Chicago: Chicago Linguistic Association, 1981.

Öhman, S. Coarticulation in VCV utterances: Spectrographic measurements. *Journal of the Acoustical Society of America,* 1966, *39,* 151–168.

Oller, D. K., Wieman, L. A., Doyle, W. J., & Ross, C. Infant babbling and speech. *Journal of Child Language,* 1976, *3,* 1–11.

Perkell, J. *Physiology of speech production: Results and implications of a quantitative cineradiographic study.* Cambridge, Mass.: MIT Press, 1969.

Pike, K. *Intonation of American English.* Ann Arbor: University of Michigan Press, 1945.

Raphael, L. Preceding vowel duration as a cue to the

412   CAROL A. FOWLER

perception of the voicing characteristic of word-final consonants in American English. *Journal of the Acoustical Society of America,* 1972, *51,* 1296–1303.

Raphael, L., & Dorman, M. The contribution of CV transition duration to the perception of final-consonant voicing in natural speech. *Journal of the Acoustical Society of America,* 1980, *67,* S51.

Shaffer, L. H. Rhythm and timing in skill. *Psychological Review,* 1982, *89,* 109–122.

Shankweiler, D., Strange, W., & Verbrugge, R. Speech and the problem of perceptual constancy. In R. Shaw & J. Bransford (Eds.), *Perceiving acting and knowing: Toward an ecological psychology.* Hillsdale, N.J.: Erlbaum, 1977.

Sussman, H., MacNeilage, P., & Hanson, R. Labial and mandibular dynamics during the production of bilabial consonants: Preliminary observations. *Journal of Speech and Hearing Research,* 1973, *16,* 397–420.

Tuller, B., & Fowler, C. A. Some articulatory correlates of perceptual isochrony. *Perception & Psychophysics,* 1980, *27,* 277–283.

Tuller, B., Harris, K., & Kelso, J. A. S. Stress and rate: Differential transformations of articulation. *Journal of the Acoustical Society of America,* in press.

Tuller, B., Kelso, J. A. S., & Harris, K. Interarticular phasing as an index of temporal regularity in speech. *Journal of Experimental Psychology: Human Performance and Perception,* 1982, *8,* 460–472.

Viviani, P., & Terzuolo, B. Space-time invariance in learned motor skills. In G. Stelmach & J. Requin (Eds.), *Tutorials in motor behavior.* Amsterdam: North-Holland, 1980.

Warren, R. Auditory sequence and classification. In N. Lass (Ed.), *Contemporary issues in experimental phonetics.* New York: Academic Press, 1976.

Wing, A. Response timing in handwriting. In G. Stelmach (Ed.), *Information processing in motor control and learning.* New York: Academic Press, 1978.

Received June 25, 1982
Revision received October 19, 1982 ■

90 N. R. FRENCH AND J. C. STEINBERG

THE JOURNAL OF THE ACOUSTICAL SOCIETY OF AMERICA VOLUME 19, NUMBER 1 JANUARY, 1947

Factors Governing the Intelligibility of Speech Sounds

N. R. French and J. C. Steinberg
Bell Telephone Laboratories, New York, New York
(Received November 22, 1946)

The characteristics of speech, hearing, and noise are discussed in relation to the recognition of speech sounds by the ear. It is shown that the intelligibility of these sounds is related to a quantity called articulation index which can be computed from the intensities of speech and unwanted sounds received by the ear, both as a function of frequency. Relationships developed for this purpose are presented. Results calculated from these relations are compared with the results of tests of the subjective effects on intelligibility of varying the intensity of the received speech, altering its normal intensity-frequency relations and adding noise.

1. INTRODUCTION

THIS paper discusses the factors which govern the intelligibility of speech sounds and presents relationships for expressing quantitatively, in terms of the fundamental characteristics of speech and hearing, the capability of the ear in recognizing these sounds. The relationships are based on studies of speech and hearing which have been carried on at Bell Telephone Laboratories over a number of years. The results of these studies have in large measure already been published. The formulation of the results into relationships for expressing speech intelli-

gibility, which has also been in progress for a number of years, has not been previously published. The purpose of this paper is to bring the relationships and basic data together into one report.

Speech consists of a succession of sounds varying rapidly from instant to instant in intensity and frequency. Assuming that the various components are received by the ear in their initial order and spacing in time, the success of the listener in recognizing and interpreting these sounds depends upon their intensity in his ear and the intensity of unwanted sounds that may be present, both as a function of frequency. The relationships presented here deal with intelligibility as a function of these intensities. Relationships having the same objective were formulated about 25 years ago by H. Fletcher. While the present relationships are based largely on data not then available, their development has employed to a considerable extent the concepts of the earlier formulation.

Before proceeding with the subject matter of the paper a word concerning applications of the material may be in order. Material of this type has, of course, been of considerable service for many years in the Bell System. It has, for example, helped to guide the direction of development work on transmission instrumentalities and has aided the preparation of the quantitative transmission data used in engineering the telephone plant.[1] Other factors, however, in addition to those discussed here, often need to be considered in appraising the transmission performance of a speech communication system. For example, echoes, phase distortion, and reverberation may affect intelligibility.[2,3] The naturalness of the received speech may need consideration as a separate item. This is also true of loudness because speech may be too loud for comfort or so faint that the effort of concentrating on the sounds is excessively annoying, even though the sounds are intelligible.

In addition, there is usually the question whether some of the data used in applying the computational methods or, for that matter, in testing the transmission performance of speech communication systems in the laboratory, are truly representative of the conditions of actual use. In either case the value of the results depends upon the degree to which these conditions and the reactions of the users to them can be specified. This information is often difficult to obtain. It is desirable, therefore, in applying the results of computational methods or laboratory tests, to check any modifications of speech communication systems by testing them under actual service conditions and determining their effect on overall performance as judged by the users. The

reasons for such a procedure are indicated briefly below and in more detail in a paper by W. H. Martin.[4]

The intensity of the speech received by the ear at each frequency depends on the intensity of the original speech sounds, the position of the mouth of the talker with respect to the microphone, the efficiency at each frequency of the latter in converting to electrical form the speech sounds which reach it, the transmission characteristics of the circuit intervening between the microphone and receiver, the efficiency of the latter in reconverting the speech waves to acoustical form and finally the coupling between the receiver and the ear. It is important to note that those items which are under the control of the user are subject to large variations. For example, there are large natural differences between the intensities of the same sounds spoken by different people or by the same people at different times. In addition, a person tends to adjust the output of his voice in part by the loudness with which he hears his own speech and the incoming speech, both being functions of the response characteristics of the communication system employed. Speech intensities also depend on the intensity of unwanted sounds, such as ambient noise in which the speaker may be immersed. These same factors also partly control the speaker's position with respect to the microphone and the way in which the listener holds the receiver to his ear.

Unwanted sounds in the ear have a masking effect on speech and constitute another major variable. They may arise from electrical disturbances originating within or without the communication system or from ambient noise. The latter may reach the ear by several paths: (1) by leakage between the receiver cap and the ear, or directly when loud speakers are used; (2) by being picked up by the microphone at the listening location and transmitted to the local receiver by sidetone; and (3) by transmission from the distant microphone.

Summarizing, it can be seen that the speech and noise received by a listener are the net result of a large number of factors of which several different types can be discerned: (1) the basic characteristics of speech and hearing, (2) the

[1] F. W. McKown and J. W. Emling, Bell Sys. Tech. J. 12, 331 (1933).
[2] V. O. Knudsen, J. Acous. Soc. Am. 1, 56 (1929).
[3] J. C. Steinberg, J. Acous. Soc. Am. 1, 121 (1929).

[4] W. H. Martin, Bell Sys. Tech. J. 10, 116 (1931).

92   N. R. FRENCH AND J. C. STEINBERG

electrical and acoustical characteristics of the instruments and circuits intervening between talker and listener, (3) the conditions under which communication takes place, and (4) the behavior of the talker and listener as modified by the characteristics of the communication system and by the conditions under which it is used.

By expressing the intelligibility relationships in terms of the intensities of speech and noise in the ear of the listener, the complicating factors discussed in the previous paragraphs do not appear explicitly in the relations. They appear only when the speech and noise intensities in the listener's ear are required in order to apply the relationships to the solution of a particular problem. There is also the question of the effect of variations in the acuity of hearing of the listeners. The relationships presented here apply specifically to young men and women who have good hearing but in general, as discussed later, their field of application is broader than this.

There are a set of consistent and well-defined concepts which underlie the intelligibility relationships. As these may be lost sight of in the details of formulation given in the succeeding pages, they are summarized briefly in the next section.

2. BASIC CONCEPTS

The intelligibility of the received speech sounds is related to a quantity which has been called the articulation index and designated A. It is a quantity such that increments ΔA carried by increments Δf of the speech frequency range may be added together to obtain the total A. The maximum possible value of A is assigned a value of unity; the minimum value is zero.

Any increment Δf of the speech frequency range may at best carry a maximum value of ΔA designated as ΔA_m. When conditions are not optimum for hearing speech in the increment Δf, this increment contributes only a fractional amount W of its maximum, or $\Delta A = W \cdot \Delta A_m$. For convenience in making computations, the frequency range may be divided into twenty bands whose frequency limits are so chosen that the ΔA_m of each band is 0.05, i.e., one-twentieth of the articulation index of the full band under optimum conditions. The general procedure for computing articulation index involves the de-

termination of a value of W for each of the twenty bands, the addition of these twenty values of W and the division of this sum by twenty.

The particular value of W for any one band of speech depends upon a quantity E called the effective sensation level of the band in the ear of the listener, which is simply the sensation level of the band minus the total masking. The sensation level of a speech band is the attenuation needed to reduce the band to the threshold of hearing in the absence of noise and is determined from the intensities of the speech components within the band at the ear of the listener and the acuity of hearing. The total masking is the shift in threshold due to the presence of noise and is the resultant of three kinds of masking: (a) residual masking due to components of preceding speech sounds within the band, (b) interband masking due to speech components in adjacent bands, and (c) masking from extraneous noise components. The factor W is equal to the fraction of $\frac{1}{8}$th second time intervals in which the speech intensity in the particular band is of sufficient intensity to be heard. Stated differently, it is the fraction of these intervals in which the speech intensity in a band exceeds the intensity which corresponds to an effective sensation level of 0 db.

In this paper the relationship between ΔA_m and Δf is obtained empirically from the results of articulation tests on appropriate high pass and low pass filter systems. However, Mr. R. H. Galt has shown, in an unpublished memorandum, that this relationship can be derived from data on the differential pitch sensitivity of the ear. This suggests that the articulation index has a more fundamental significance than might be indicated by its empirical derivation.[5]

Although the response characteristics of a telephone system and its component parts do not enter explicitly into the articulation relationships, they are required in applications of the latter to particular problems. To serve the desired purpose the basic speech, noise, and hearing data and the over-all response of the telephone system must be so specified that they can be combined to obtain intensities received in the listener's ear. The type of response needed is obviously not one based

---

[5] W. A. Munson, J. Acous. Soc. Am. 17, 103A (1945).

alone on physical measurements of microphone, circuit, and receiver apart from voice and ear. It should include the effects of using real voices and ears. The methods of expressing response characteristics and the characteristics of speech and hearing which underlie the articulation index relationships, are essentially interdependent. Consequently, these subjects are discussed in the following two sections prior to the derivation and detailed discussion of the articulation index relations.

The following are the principal symbols used in this paper. A number of the symbols represent intensity levels; these are in db above 10^{-16} watt/cm².

A articulation index,

ΔA increment of articulation index carried by an increment Δf of the speech frequency range,

ΔA_m maximum possible value of ΔA,

W fractional part of ΔA_m obtained when listening conditions are not optimum,

S syllable articulation,

R over-all orthotelephonic response,

β intensity level of a single frequency tone,

β_0 threshold intensity level of a single frequency tone,

K $10 \log_{10} \Delta f_c$,

Δf_c width of critical bands of the ear in cycles,

X $(\beta_0 - K)$,

B the long average intensity per cycle level of the noise received from all sources,

B_f component of B produced in a particular frequency region by speech in the same region,

B_n component of B produced in a particular frequency region by speech in other frequency regions,

B_E component of B from all sources other than speech,

Z level above threshold of a critical band of noise, i.e., effective level,

M masking, i.e., shift of threshold caused by noise,

m $(M-Z)$ for values of Z greater than 50 db,

B_s' the long average intensity per cycle level of an idealized spectrum of speech at one meter from the lips (Fig. 2),

B_s the long average intensity per cycle level of the speech received over a communication system,

V the actual speech level, for any talker, at two inches from the lips, as measured with a sound level meter with 40-db weighting,

H level of a critical band of speech above its threshold level in the absence of noise, i.e., band sensation level,

E the effective sensation level of a band of speech, and

p difference in db between the intensity in a critical band exceeded by 1 percent of ⅛th second intervals of received speech and the long average intensity in the same band.

3. CHARACTERISTICS OF SPEECH AND HEARING

3.1 The Spectrum of Speech

Figure 1 shows the results of several sets of measurements of the intensity of speech as a function of frequency. Curve A represents the average spectrum of four men and four women members of the testing crew used in carrying out the last extensive program of fundamental articulation tests. The spectrum is at a point two inches directly in front of the lips and is expressed in terms of the long time average intensity per cycle, in db relative to 10^{-16} watt/cm². Curves B and C are the spectra given for six men and five women in Fig. 10 of a paper by Dunn and White.[6] In the present paper the latter spectra have been shifted to change from 30 cm, the point of measurement, to the 2-inch position at which curve A applies. In order to provide a better basis for comparing shapes, the curve for the women has been shifted upward an additional 3 db because their total power was that much less than the men's.

It will be observed that there is an appreciable difference between the shapes of the Dunn and White spectra and the spectrum of the articulation testing crew. Because of the long interval (several years) between the two sets of measurements, it has been impracticable to determine whether the differences are real or result from one or more of the numerous differences in the testing arrangements and procedures. In view of this and the substantial differences which may exist between the spectra of individual voices, the smoothed and somewhat arbitrary compromise

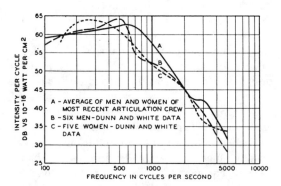

Fig. 1. Comparison of speech spectra at two inches from lips.

[6] H. K. Dunn and S. D. White, J. Acous. Soc. Am. 11, 278 (1940).

94   N. R. FRENCH AND J. C. STEINBERG

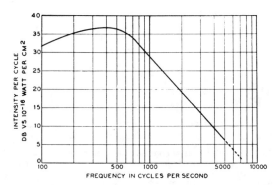

FIG. 2. Idealized long average speech spectrum at one meter from lips in a sound field free from reflections.

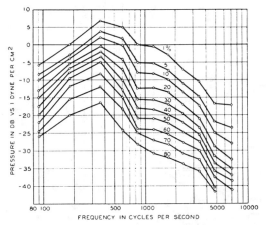

FIG. 3. R.m.s. pressure, during one-eighth second intervals, of speech at 30 cm from lips. Dunn and White composite data for six men (reference 6). Each curve shows the pressure exceeded in the indicated percentage of intervals.

spectrum of Fig. 2 has been adopted for use in this paper. For reasons which will appear later, this spectrum is given at a distance of one meter from the lips. The intensity of this spectrum, integrated over the entire frequency range, amounts to 65 db relative to 10^{-16} watt/cm². The corresponding figure at 2 inches from the lips, which is a more accurate point of measurement, is 90 db. If the speech level of a speaker having this idealized spectrum were measured by a sound level meter,[7] using flat weighting, with the microphone at 2 inches from the lips, the observed level would be about 3 db higher than the integrated value or around 93 db. This difference would occur because readings of rapidly varying material tend to be taken on the frequent peaks. With 40 db weighting the observed level should be close to the integrated level or 90 db.

3.2 Level Distribution of Speech

The spectra of speech which have just been discussed represent the average intensity over an appreciable period of time. From moment to moment the intensity of speech fluctuates rapidly above and below this average curve giving rise, at any frequency, to a level distribution of speech as a function of time. This distribution is one of the factors affecting the intelligibility of speech and consequently enters into the relationships presented later. In Fig. 3, taken largely from Fig. 3 of the previously mentioned paper[6] by Dunn and White, are shown the results of level distribution measurements made on a number of male voices.

7 "ASA—American Standard—Sound Level Meters for Measurement of Noise and Other Sounds" (Z24.3—1944) July 28, 1944.

The same paper shows a similar set of data for women's voices. These charts show the distribution of $\frac{1}{8}$ second intervals (roughly the duration of a syllable) with respect to the r.m.s. pressure measured during these intervals in the frequency bands indicated along the abscissa. The differences between levels which are exceeded by 1 percent and 50 percent of the intervals in the bands are shown in Table I for both the men and women talkers. It can be inferred from this table that the range over which the speech intensity fluctuates and the relative occurrence of intervals of different intensities are roughly the same for all bands and for both men and women. Taking all the bands to be alike in these respects results in certain simplifications of the relationships which are presented.

To determine the actual form of the speech level distribution, the data taken with male voices and the 1000–1400 cycle band have been used.

TABLE I. Difference in db between r.m.s. pressures of speech exceeded in 1 percent and in 50 percent of one-eighth second intervals.

Frequency band	Men's voices	Women's voices
250– 500	12 db	15 db
500– 700	18	18
700–1000	21	21
1000–1400	20	21
1400–2000	19	21
2000–2800	18	20
2800–4000	18	20

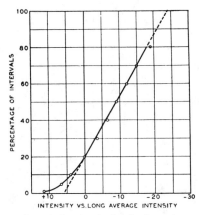

FIG. 4. Cumulative level distribution of average intensity of speech in one-eighth second intervals in db *versus* long average intensity. 1000–1400 cycle band of men's voices.

The first step was to compute the long average intensity by integrating over all of the $\frac{1}{8}$ second intervals in this band. Then the level difference between this long average intensity and the average intensity which was exceeded in 1 percent of the intervals was determined. The value of 1 percent was then plotted against this level difference to determine the point at the lower left corner of Fig. 4. The other points in the figure were obtained by the same process, using the levels exceeded in 5 percent, 10 percent, etc., of the intervals. It will be seen from the resulting curve that 1 percent of the intervals have average intensities 12 db or more above the long average intensity. It will be noted further that over the range between the 20 percent and the 80 percent points of Fig. 4, the distribution can be closely represented by a straight line. Although no accurate data are available to show the shape of the curve above the 80 percent point, it will be

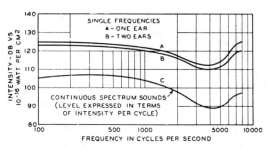

FIG. 6. 120-db loudness contours for open air borne sounds.

advantageous for reasons discussed later to assume that the distribution continues as a straight line up to 100 percent as shown by the dotted line.

If the same procedure is followed for the other bands and for women's voices it will be found that the resulting curves are similar to the curve of Fig. 4, although they tend to be somewhat steeper in slope. On the other hand it would be desirable for the purpose of this paper to measure the level distribution with bands approximating the critical band widths of the ear (Section 3.4), which are narrower bands than those used in the above measurements. This would cause some reduction in the slope of the curves. Figure 4 appears to be a reasonable compromise between these two offsetting factors. In the development of simple relationships it will be convenient and reasonably accurate to use the single curve of this figure as applying to all frequency regions.

3.3 Zero and 120 db Loudness Contours

Curves *A* and *B* of Fig. 5 show the thresholds of audibility for single frequency tones when listening with one and two ears. These curves apply to the most acute ears and indicate about the absolute minimum of sound that can be heard. The two ear curve is identical with the zero loudness contour of the "American Standard for Noise Measurement."[8] The one ear curve is the two ear curve increased by the curve of Fig. 9. In communicating by speech many of the sounds, both wanted and unwanted, tend to approach the continuous spectrum type instead of being discrete frequencies. Under these conditions the application of the single frequency threshold

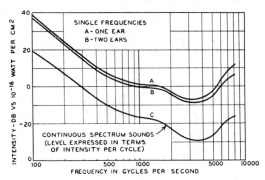

FIG. 5. Zero loudness contours for open air borne sounds.

[8] "ASA—American Standard for Noise Measurement" (Z24.2—1942) J. Acous. Soc. Am. **13**, 102 (1942).

96   N. R. FRENCH AND J. C. STEINBERG

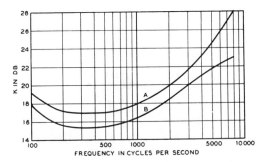

Fig. 7. Critical band widths (*K*) of ear. In db, $K = 10 \log_{10} W_c$, where W_c is the width of a critical band in cycles. Curves *A* and *B* are, respectively, for one- and two-ear listening.

curves requires the specification of a band width over which the intensity of the continuous spectrum sound is integrated. This is discussed later. For the present it is sufficient to note that curve *C* of Fig. 5 may be considered as a threshold curve for sound of the continuous spectrum type, when its level is expressed in terms of the intensity per cycle.

Curve *B* of Fig. 6 shows the two ear 120-db loudness contour for single frequency tones taken from the same source as curve *B* of Fig. 5. Curve *A* of Fig. 6 for one ear listening was obtained by adding to curve *B* of the same figure the curve of Fig. 9. The significance of the 120-db loudness contours lies in the fact that more intense sounds lying in the region above these curves are apt to annoy the listener, produce a sensation of feeling or, if of sufficiently high level, produce an actual sensation of pain. Curve *C* applies to sounds of the continuous spectrum type. This figure is of interest primarily in situations where there is extremely intense noise at the receiving position and higher than normal levels of received speech are required for the attainment of adequate intelligibility.

When there are no unwanted sounds in the ear the practical limits within which the wanted sounds should lie are bounded by the region just above the 120-db loudness contour and the threshold of audibility. These curves apply to the case where the sound waves arrive from a source at some distance from the observer who faces the source in a place free of reverberation. The intensities are measured with the observer out of the sound field, but at the position he takes in listening. Thus they do not represent the in-

tensities which actually exist in the ear except over the lower part of the frequency range. To use these curves in applications in which the listening is done with head receivers, it is necessary to express the output of the receiver in terms of the intensity of open airborne sounds which produce the same sensation as the sounds from the receiver.

3.4 Masking

In most problems involving speech reception, unwanted sounds are present in the ear of the listener and reduce the sensitivity of the ear to other sounds. This reduction in sensitivity is known as masking and at any frequency the amount of the masking *M* is equal to the difference between the levels β and β_0 of a single frequency tone which are just audible in the presence of the noise and in the total absence of noise, or

$$M = \beta - \beta_0. \qquad (1)$$

The plot of *M* as a function of frequency is known as the masking spectrum of the noise. In general, interfering noises in the ear of a listener are of the continuous spectrum type, such as room noise. The masking relations provide a means for computing the masking caused by noise of this type when its spectrum affecting the ear is known. The amount of masking which is given by these relations is the threshold shift which would be observed by a highly idealized group of individuals whose thresholds β_0 in the absence of noise are given by the curves of Fig. 5. Actually, the threshold varies greatly among individuals depending upon such factors as fatigue, health, and age, the chosen curves representing about the absolute minimum of sound that can be heard by the most acute ears. The formula will thus, in general, compute a masking figure which is somewhat larger than would be observed by a random crew of observers. This, however, will usually be of no practical importance because computed levels of wanted sounds, above the same threshold, will be too large by the same amount. The margin of the wanted sounds above the unwanted ones is largely independent of the absolute threshold of the observer provided the noise is above the actual threshold. Observed tone levels which can just be heard in the presence of appreciable amounts of noise should be in good agreement with computed tone levels obtained by adding computed maskings to the idealized threshold curve, regardless, within fairly large limits, of the absolute thresholds of the observers.

Tests have shown that the masking effect on single frequency tones of noises having continuous spectra, which do not change in intensity too rapidly with frequency, is dependent only upon the level difference in db between (1) the intensity of the noise integrated over a narrow frequency band whose frequency limits are somewhat below and above the frequency of the masked tone, and (2) the single frequency threshold intensity in the absence of noise. These narrow bands are known as critical bands[9] of the ear and the above level difference at any frequency is referred to as the effective level of the noise at that frequency. The width of the critical bands is a function of frequency, varying from about 30 cycles at low frequencies to several hundred cycles at high frequencies.

The level difference in db between the noise intensity integrated over a critical band and the single frequency threshold (β_0) is given by

$$Z = (B+K) - \beta_0 = B - (\beta_0 - K), \quad (2)$$

where

Z = level above threshold of a critical band of noise, i.e., effective level,

B = the long average intensity per cycle level of the noise received from all sources, expressed in db above 10^{-16} watt/cm^2,

$K = 10 \log_{10} \Delta f_c$, where Δf_c is the critical band width in cycles.

The values of K for one and two ear listening, as derived from masking tests, are shown by Fig. 7. The above expression for effective level is equivalent to referring the noise B to a new threshold which is K db lower than the single frequency threshold. Thus, instead of always being obliged to add a quantity K to the noise spectrum, it will be more convenient, where the noise spectrum is expressed in terms of the intensity per cycle, to subtract from B a new threshold X where

$$X = \beta_0 - K \quad (3)$$

and then

$$Z = B - X. \quad (4)$$

[9] H. Fletcher and W. A. Munson, J. Acous. Soc. Am. 9, 1 (1937).

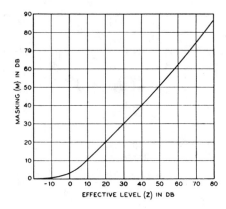

FIG. 8. Relation between the effective level of noise in any frequency region and the resulting masking in the same region.

The value of X is shown by the bottom curve of Fig. 5. It may be noted that the differences between the one- and two-ear single frequency threshold curves in Fig. 5 are identical with the differences between the one- and two-ear K's of Fig. 7. As a result, a single value of X applies to both one- and two-ear listening.

When the value of the effective level Z is known, the amount of masking M that is produced can be read from the curve* of Fig. 8. As a matter of interest, it will be noted that the masking and the effective levels are equal over the range of 20 to 50 db masking. Within this range a tone can just be heard through a steady noise when the intensity of the former is equal to the intensity of the noise integrated over the critical band in the region of the tone. However, as the effective level in a band increases above 50 db the resulting masking increases at a somewhat faster rate. The tests which gave this result used noises covering a broad frequency range as they generally do in communication problems. This upturn in the masking curve under such conditions has a bearing on some practical problems. For example, consider a case where the only important noise affecting a listener is transmitted along with a signal and the absolute level of reproduction can be varied. Under these conditions, where the signal-to-noise ratio remains constant, the signal may not be heard as well at an intense level of reproduction as at some lower

* The values of K and M vs. Z of the present report differ slightly from those given in reference 9 as a result of additional experimental data.

98   N. R. FRENCH AND J. C. STEINBERG

level. The effect of noise at low levels is also worthy of note. Figure 8 shows that some masking is produced by noise even though it is below the threshold of audibility (Z less than zero db). This is exactly the effect which would be obtained if the threshold in the absence of noise were itself determined by a residual noise, which combines on a power basis with other noises which may be present. The form of the masking curve over its entire range is given by

$$M = (B(+)X) - X + m, \tag{5}$$

where $(+)$ represents power addition of the quantities B and X, and m is the amount, in db, that the masking exceeds the effective level of the noise. Values of m for effective levels greater than 50 db are given in Table II; for values of Z less than 50 db, m is zero.

At this point it may be of interest to indicate the reasons why the differences between the one- and two-ear thresholds and the one- and two-ear K's are taken to be alike. Figure 9(A) shows observed differences in the acuity of hearing of the best ear and the average of both ears, taken from Fig. 20 of a paper[10] by Fletcher and Munson. The effect of one- $vs.$ two-ear listening on K was determined by adjusting the levels of single frequency tones until they could just be heard in the presence of a noise of the continuous spectrum type. This was done alternately with one- and two-ear listening, while maintaining the same noise level for both conditions. These tests showed that higher tone levels relative to the noise levels were required when listening with one ear as compared to two. These differences, which will be shown to represent the differences in K for the two conditions are indicated by Fig. 9(B). It will be seen that a single curve represents these masking data and also the audibility data of Fig. 9(A). That the

differences in tone levels for one- and two-ear listening represent the differences in their K's can be shown by noting that the level of a tone which can just be heard in the presence of noise is, from Eq. (1), given by

$$\beta = M + \beta_0.$$

From Eq. (2) the effective level of the noise is

$$Z = B + K - \beta_0.$$

Also, for the levels used in the above tests, the masking M is numerically equal to the effective level of the noise; thus Z in the second equation can be substituted for M of the first equation, which can then be written

$$\beta = B + K. \tag{6}$$

In this equation B is the intensity level per cycle of the noise and β the intensity level of the tone which can just be heard. It follows that, if the tone level β is greater with one ear listening than with two, the value of K must increase by the same amount since B was constant for the two conditions.

4. RESPONSE CHARACTERISTICS

An over-all response which has been called "orthotelephonic[11] response" is used for applying the information of the preceding section to the derivation of the intensity of speech received over a communication system. This response may be thought of as a usage response, in that it includes the effects on the received speech of distance and coupling between the microphone and the speaker's mouth and the coupling of the receiver to the ear. By definition a telephone system has an orthotelephonic response of zero db at all frequencies when it can be replaced by a one-meter air path, between talker and listener, without changing the loudness of the received speech at any frequency. The speaker and listener face each other in an otherwise unobstructed sound field. Listening to the sound over the air path is done with either one or two ears, depending upon whether one or both ears are used with the communication system.

A telephone system having the above characteristics is designated as an orthotelephonic system. It is convenient to specify the output of such

TABLE II. Values of m to the nearest db.

Z in db	m in db	Z in db	m in db
54–60	1	78–80	6
61–65	2	81–83	7
66–70	3	84–86	8
71–74	4	87–89	9
75–77	5	90–91	10

[10] H. Fletcher and W. A. Munson, J. Acous. Soc. Am. **5**, 82 (1933).

[11] A. H. Inglis, Bell Sys. Tech. J. **17**, 358 (1938).

a system, at any frequency, in terms of the intensity, at the same frequency, of the speech received over the air system, but measured before insertion of the listener's head into the sound field. As a result, the speech received over an orthotelephonic system is identical to that received over the air system in loudness and intensity when the talker speaks at the same level in both cases. Specifying the intensity of the received speech in this manner is in conformity with the manner of expressing the zero and 120-db loudness contours discussed in the previous section.

If a telephone system, which is not an orthotelephonic system, has an orthotelephonic response of R db at any frequency, this means that the speech received over an orthotelephonic system, at the same frequency, must be raised R db in intensity to be as loud as that heard over the telephone system in question. Thus the intensity level of speech received over a telephone system at any frequency is the sum of the intensity level of speech at one meter from the lips and the orthotelephonic response of the system.

In general, a person will talk at a different level than that corresponding to the idealized spectrum of Fig. 2. Correction for this can be made by raising the spectrum by an amount $V-90$, where

V = the actual speech level, for any talker, at two inches from the lips in db $vs.$ 10^{-16} watt/cm², as measured with a sound level meter using 40 db weighting,

90 = the corresponding level for the idealized speech spectrum of Fig. 2 when shifted to the two inch point.

The above information can be combined into the following equation for computing the intensity levels of received speech:

$$B_s = B_s' + (V-90) + R, \qquad (7)$$

where

B_s = the long average intensity per cycle level of the speech received over a communication system, expressed in db $vs.$ 10^{-16} watt/cm²,

B_s' = the long average intensity per cycle level of an idealized spectrum of speech (Fig. 2) at one meter from the lips in a place free of reverberation, expressed in db $vs.$ 10^{-16} watt/cm².

The intensity level of the received speech B_s is, of course, in terms of the free field intensity which produces, in the uncovered ear of an observer placed in the sound field, the same sensation ob-

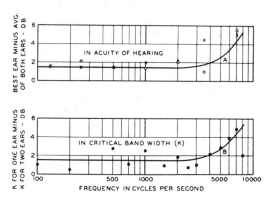

Fig. 9. Differences between one-ear and two-ear listening.

tained with speech delivered by a telephone receiver. It is equally important to note that the intensity level of received noise B, discussed previously, is also expressed in the same terms.

In concluding this section it may be in order to bring out some of the practical aspects of the problem of obtaining the orthotelephonic response of a telephone system. The over-all response is not usually measured as a whole in accordance with the above description but is derived from separate measurements of the response of microphone, electrical circuit, and receiver. The circuit responses are derived from purely physical measurements using single frequency tones. The real ear responses of receivers are also determined with single frequency tones by balancing the tone heard in the receiver against a comparison tone of the same frequency transmitted over a one-meter air path. The intensity of the output of the receiver is specified, exactly as described above, in terms of the intensity of the comparison tone, measured in the free sound field. The input to the receiver is measured in any suitable terms which will combine properly with the measurements of circuit response up to the receiver. Receiver measurements made in this way are usually accompanied by purely objective measurements, using mechanical couplers for example, from which conversion factors are obtained which do away with the need for further real ear measurements on other receivers of the same type.

The real voice response of a linear microphone can be obtained from two sets of measurements. In one, a person speaks into the microphone, taking whatever position with respect to it that

100   N. R. FRENCH AND J. C. STEINBERG

is regarded as typical, while measurements are made of the output of the microphone in narrow frequency bands throughout the entire frequency range. In the other, a similar analysis is made of the speech intensity near the lips of the speaker, usually at two inches, the microphone having been removed from the sound field. These latter speech intensities, or these intensities reduced to one meter from the lips, are taken as the input to the microphone. Supplementing these measurements by objective response measurements using, for example, single frequency tones and an artificial voice, provides conversion factors which enable real voice responses of other microphones of the same type to be derived from purely objective measurements. These conversion factors allow for the interaction effects and distance losses between the artificial source and microphone relative to these effects between a real voice and the microphone. The application of this method without modification, to non-linear microphones, can give results which may be somewhat in error due to modulation products, generated by the microphone when complex waves of speech are impressed upon it. This may be avoided by a more complicated procedure beyond the scope of this paper to describe. It is also beyond the scope of the paper to go into details concerning the responses needed for determining the levels of noise in the ear. It should be sufficient to point out that the basic noise data and the response of each separate path by which noise can enter the ear should be so coordinated and expressed that they can be combined to give the noise intensity in the ear in the same terms as the received speech.

5. ARTICULATION INDEX

5.1 General

A distinguishing characteristic of speech is movement. Conversation at the rate of 200 words per minute, corresponding to about four syllables and ten speech sounds per second, is not unusual. During the brief period that a sound lasts, the intensity builds up rapidly, remains comparatively constant for a while, then decays rapidly. The various sounds differ from each other in their build-up and decay characteristics, in length, in total intensity, and in the distribution of the intensity with frequency. With the vowel sounds the intensity is carried largely by the harmonics of the fundamental frequency of the voice and tends to be concentrated in one or more distinct frequency regions, each sound having its own characteristic regions of prominence. The consonant sounds, as a group, have components of higher frequency and lower intensity than the vowel sounds. In addition, the intensity tends to be scattered continuously over the frequency region characteristic of each sound. Thus when the elementary sounds are combined in sequence to form syllables, words, and phrases, there is a continuous succession of rapid variations in intensity, not only in particular frequency regions but also along the frequency scale. The interpretation of speech received by the ear depends upon the perception and recognition of these constantly shifting patterns.

The importance of the different regions of intensity and frequency to the recognition process was determined, in the investigation described here, by articulation tests, using a test circuit into which electrical networks and different amounts of attenuation were introduced to alter the intensity-frequency distribution and level of the called material prior to its reception by the listeners. The material consisted of meaningless monosyllables of the consonant-vowel-consonant type. The results were expressed as the percentage of syllables of which all three component sounds were perceived correctly. This percentage is designated as the syllable articulation, or simply the articulation, of the condition tested. The sounds used in these syllables include those commonly used in conversation.[12] A detailed description of this method, including the reasons for its choice, is given in other papers.[13, 14]

Syllable articulation, in common with all other known subjective measures of intelligibility such as word or sentence intelligibility, has certain limitations which impair its usefulness as a basic index. First, the value obtained from tests is not independent of the skill and experience of the testers. This difficulty can be partially overcome by calibrating a crew and correcting the results

---

[12] N. R. French, C. W. Carter, Jr., and W. Koenig, Jr., Bell Sys. Tech. J. **9**, 290 (1930).
[13] H. Fletcher and J. C. Steinberg, Bell Sys. Tech. J. **8**, 806 (1929).
[14] T. G. Castner and C. W. Carter, Jr., Bell Sys. Tech. J. **12**, 347 (1933).

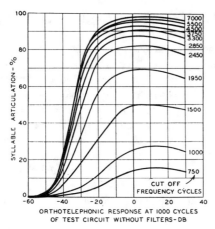

FIG. 10. Smoothed results of 1928–1929 articulation tests on low pass filters having the indicated cut-off frequencies.

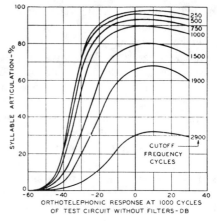

FIG. 11. Smoothed results of 1928–1929 articulation tests on high pass filters having the indicated cut-off frequencies.

by methods described elsewhere.[13] Of more importance is the fact that syllable articulation, in common with other subjective measures, is not an additive measure of the importance of the contributions made by the speech components in the different frequency regions. Stated differently, the articulation observed with a given frequency band of speech is not equal to the sum of the articulations observed when the given band is subdivided into narrower bands which are then individually tested. For the purpose of establishing relations between the intelligence carrying capacity of the components of speech and their frequency and intensity, a more fundamental index free of the above defects is needed. Such an index, called "articulation index," can be derived from the results of articulation tests. The magnitude of this index is taken to vary between zero and unity, the former applying when the received speech is completely unintelligible, the latter to the condition of best intelligibility.

The articulation index is based on the concept that any narrow band of speech frequencies of a given intensity carries a contribution to the total index which is independent* of the other bands with which it is associated and that the total contribution of all bands is the sum of the contributions of the separate bands. Letting ΔA represent the articulation index of any narrow

band of speech frequencies and n the number of narrow bands into which the total band is subdivided for computational purposes, the articulation index A of the total band reaching the listener is

$$A = \sum_1^n \Delta A. \qquad (8)$$

The value of ΔA, which is carried by any narrow frequency band, varies all the way from zero to a maximum value ΔA_m as the absolute levels of speech and noise in the ear are independently varied over wide ranges. Letting W represent the fractional part of ΔA_m which is contributed by a band with a particular combination of speech and noise, the value of articulation index for that band is given by

$$\Delta A = W \cdot \Delta A_m. \qquad (9)$$

Hence,

$$A = \sum_1^n W \cdot \Delta A_m. \qquad (10)$$

The establishment of relations for computing A thus involves two main steps: (1) the determination of the increments of frequency which give equal values of ΔA_m throughout the frequency range and (2) the determination of relationships between W and the levels of speech and noise in the ear.

The desired relations are derived below from the results of articulation tests on a broad-band transmission system into which high pass and low pass filters were inserted. The system included distortionless attenuators and amplifiers for varying the absolute level of the received speech.

---

* Not absolutely true; the contribution of a band may be modified somewhat by masking produced by intense speech in neighboring bands.

102   N. R. FRENCH AND J. C. STEINBERG

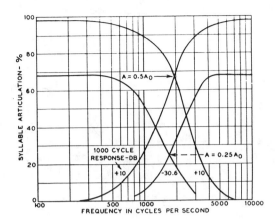

FIG. 12. Syllable articulation *versus* cut-off frequency of high pass and low pass filters at two different settings of test circuit. A_0 is articulation index of test circuit at its optimum setting.

The orthotelephonic response of the system with particular settings of attenuators and amplifiers is shown by curve A of Fig. 28. The departures of this response from flatness largely reflect usage factors and the method adopted for specifying the receiver output, which were discussed earlier in the paper. For example an imperfect seal between a receiver and the ear provides a shunting leakage path to the outside air and causes the drop in response noted at low frequencies.

The results of a few articulation tests with the frequency band limited by filters appear in a previous paper[3] by one of the writers. The smoothed results of more comprehensive tests, which provide the basis for the following relations, are given by Figs. 10 and 11. The former applies to low pass and the latter to high pass filters. The results are composite data taken with men's and women's voices. The ordinate of the curves represents the percentage of syllables which were recorded correctly. The abscissa is the orthotelephonic response at 1000 cycles of the test circuit before insertion of the filters. The filters introduced a negligible loss within their passed bands and also caused practically complete suppression of the speech components beyond their cut-off frequencies. Thus the abscissa of Figs. 10 and 11, in combination with the response Curve A of Fig. 28 and the cut-off frequency of the filters, permits the determination of the response, at all frequencies, of the test condition corresponding to any value of articulation shown on these figures.

During each articulation test electrical measurements were made of the total speech output of the microphone. Computations were also made to determine what the output of the microphone would be with a talker having the speech spectrum of Fig. 2. By comparing these results it is estimated that this particular articulation testing crew talked at an acoustic level 4 db higher than that to which Fig. 2 applies.

5.2 Relation between ΔA_m and Frequency

Referring now to the curves of Figs. 10 and 11, it will be noted that articulation rises rapidly as the circuit response is varied to raise the level of the received speech and reaches a maximum value at about the same setting of the system with each of the filters. The 1000-cycle orthotelephonic response of the system at this generally optimum setting is +10 db. The articulation values indicated for the different filters at this setting, plotted against the filter cut-off frequencies, are shown by the top pair of curves of Fig. 12. Now letting S_1 represent the indicated value of syllable articulation when the frequency range below a certain cut-off frequency is transmitted and S_2 the syllable articulation when the range above the same cut-off frequency is transmitted, it will be noted that the sum of S_1 and S_2 is generally greater than the articulation S_3 observed when both bands are transmitted together. In other words, the articulation of 27 percent for a 1000-cycle low pass filter, when added to 89 percent for the complementary high pass filter, does not yield the value of 98 percent which was observed for the full band. It follows, therefore, that syllable articulation is not an additive index. This is also true for observed values of letter articulation, word articulation and sentence intelligibility. However, the curves of Figs. 10 and 11 offer a means of deriving an additive index from the articulation test data, as described below.

Since the full-band system which was used may not be an optimum system for articulation, the articulation index of the speech received over it, which is presumably close to but not necessarily equal to unity at the optimum level, is here designated A_0. For this value of articulation index the syllable articulation is that observed for the full-band at a setting of +10 db, or $S = 98$ percent. It will be noted also from Fig. 12 that the high pass and low pass filter curves for this +10-db condition intersect at about 1900 cycles; this means that for this particular system half of the articulation index carried by the full-band of received speech is below and half above this frequency. At the point of intersection the observed value of S was 68 percent and consequently a syllable articulation of 68 percent for this particular testing group corresponds to an articulation index of $0.5A_0$.

If the top curve of Fig. 10 is now referred to, this curve applying to a 7000-cycle low pass filter and also to the unrestricted band, it will be noted that, by increasing the attenuation of the system, the S of the full band can be reduced to 68 percent which, as previously noted, corresponds to an articulation index of $0.5A_0$. The 1000-cycle response of the system at which this occurs is -30.6 db. If the syllable articulation obtained with the different filters at this setting of the system is now plotted against the cut-off frequency of the filters, another pair of intersecting curves will be obtained as shown in the lower part of Fig. 12. The articulation index of each of the two complementary bands, below and above the frequency of intersection (1700 cycles), consequently has by definition an articulation index of $0.25A_0$ and the corresponding value of S is 25 percent. This procedure may be followed further

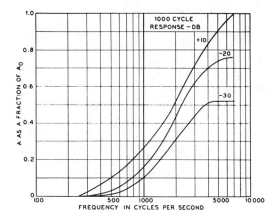

FIG. 14. Relation between articulation index and cut-off frequency at three different settings of the test circuit. Articulation index is expressed as a fraction of the articulation index (A_0) of test circuit at its optimum setting.

to find that a syllable articulation of 8 percent corresponds to an articulation index of $0.125A_0$.

Knowing from the above that a syllable articulation of 25 percent corresponds to an articulation index of $0.25A_0$ reference is again made to the +10 db curves of Fig. 12. It will be seen that a low pass filter (about 950 cycles) yielding an articulation index of $0.25A_0$ has as its complement a high pass filter having a syllable articulation of 90 percent. Since the contributions of these two complementary filters must add to A_0 it follows that $S = 90$ percent corresponds to an articulation index of $0.75A_0$. By following these procedures a sufficient number of points may be found to determine satisfactorily the curve shown in Fig. 13. This curve shows the relationship between syllable articulation and articulation index expressed as a fraction of the articulation index A_0 of the full-band of the speech received at its optimum level over the system which was tested.

Having obtained the relationship shown in Fig. 13, it is now possible to construct a set of curves showing, for each of several levels of the full-band of speech, the cumulative total of articulation index, expressed as a fraction of A_0, as the upper end of the passed band is increased in frequency. This is accomplished by reading from Fig. 10 the syllable articulation values obtained with all the filters at each of several fixed settings of the full band system, converting these values of S into fractional values of A_0 by means of the curve of Fig. 13 and plotting the

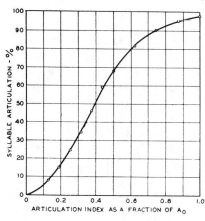

FIG. 13. Relation between syllable articulation and articulation index. The latter is expressed as a fraction of the articulation index (A_0) of the test circuit at its optimum setting.

104   N. R. FRENCH AND J. C. STEINBERG

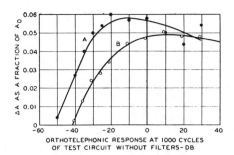

FIG. 15. Fractional values of A_0, the articulation index of the test circuit at its optimum setting, carried by individual bands. Curve A—band from 1300 to 1520 cycles. Curve B—band from 490 to 620 cycles.

results against the cut-off frequency of the filters. The results of this operation are shown in Fig. 14.

The next step is to separate the frequency range into a large number of bands (20 were used) having equal fractional values of A_0. The +10-db curve of Fig. 14 is used for this purpose since this is the optimum setting of this system with the full band. Having established by this method the frequency limits of bands of equal importance (.05A_0) *in the system tested*, the contribution of these bands at other levels can be read from a complete family of curves like those of Fig. 14. The resulting values are then plotted against the orthotelephonic response of the system at 1000 cycles* to obtain, for each of the twenty bands, curves of the type illustrated by Fig. 15. These curves show that the increment ΔA, carried by a band, first increases as the gain of the system is increased, then reaches a maximum value after which it drops off slowly as the gain is further increased. If the system tested had been an optimum system, the maximum contribution of each of the twenty bands should be .05, since the frequency limits of the bands were selected on the basis of a 5 percent contribution by each band at the optimum setting of the system. Also the maximum contribution of each band should occur at the same setting of the system. Inspection of the curves of Fig. 15 shows that neither of these expectations is precisely fulfilled, thus indicating that the testing system fell somewhat short of being an optimum system. Actually, a summation of the maximum values of ΔA_0 of the twenty curves gives a value about 3

* Any other parameter which reflects changes in received level, such as the response of the system within each of the 20 bands, could be used equally well.

percent above unity. If a value of unity is assigned to the articulation index of the speech received over an optimum system, this means that the speech received over the system tested had an articulation index of 0.97, or $A_0 = 0.97$. With this information the curve of Fig. 13, showing the relation of syllable articulation to articulation index as a fraction of A_0, can be converted to a relation between syllable articulation and absolute values of articulation index by multiplying the abscissa by 0.97. The resulting curve is shown on Fig. 23. Although this curve may be lacking in general interest the detailed description of how it was obtained is of general interest since the same method could be used by others who might start with a system having different response characteristics from that used in the tests which have been described.

We are now in a position to draw up a cumulative curve of the absolute value of articulation index *versus* frequency when all bands are simultaneously at their optimum settings. The maximum value of articulation index which can be contributed by each of the twenty bands discussed above is obtained by multiplying the maximum value of each of the twenty curves, like those of Fig. 15, by 0.97. The resulting value for the band of lowest frequency, plotted against the upper frequency limit for this band, provides one point on the desired curve. By adding successive bands, one at a time, the final relation, shown by the curve of Fig. 16 is obtained. It differs only slightly from the top curve of Fig. 14 which

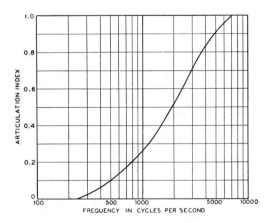

FIG. 16. Articulation index *versus* cut-off frequency. All bands are at their optimum levels. Curve is based on about equal numbers of men's and women's voices.

applied when the system used was tested at its optimum setting. In fact, the differences between the two curves are so small that it is open to question whether the data are sufficiently precise to justify the above operation in this case. It is believed, however, that the operation will be of interest in the event of additional basic studies of this nature which, caused by the particular characteristics of the circuits which may be employed, may require greater corrections.

The derivative or slope of the curve of Fig. 16 at any frequency shows the importance of that frequency with respect to its maximum possible contribution to articulation index. At any frequency the product of the slope of this curve and the factor W, discussed in the next section, represents the contribution of this frequency to the total articulation index. In general, the levels of speech and noise in the ear, and hence W, will vary sufficiently slowly with frequency to permit the use of a single value of W over a considerable frequency range. For the general run of computations twenty values of W at suitably selected frequencies should be adequate. For this purpose, it is convenient to divide the frequency range into twenty parts or computation bands such that the maximum possible contribution of each band is equal to that of the others and to determine W at the mid-frequency of each band. The limits of the twenty bands chosen in this way are obtained by reading from the continuous curve of Fig. 16 the frequencies corresponding to all the articulation indices which are multiples of .05. These band limits are given in Table III.

The importance curve of Fig. 16 is based on composite data taken with about equal numbers

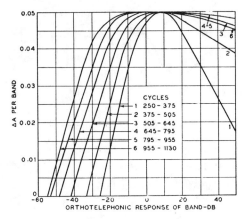

FIG. 17. Effect of level variations on articulation index carried by narrow bands. Band limits are so chosen that the articulation index of each band is 0.05 at its optimum level.

of men and women talkers. Men's voices are about an octave lower in pitch than women's and the latter tend to be somewhat richer in high frequency sounds. As a result it is probable that separate importance curves for men's and women's voices would approximate the curve of Fig. 16 in shape but be shifted somewhat toward lower and higher frequencies, respectively.

5.3 Variation of ΔA with Level

Having obtained the frequency limits of the twenty bands which individually contribute 0.05 to articulation index when each band is making its maximum possible contribution, the next step is the determination of the contribution of each band under other than optimum conditions. This includes the specification of the conditions in usable terms. The starting point is the twenty curves illustrated by the two curves of Fig. 15. The ordinates of these curves are first multiplied by 0.97 to convert to absolute values of articulation index, as discussed previously. They are then used to draw up additional curves of cumulative articulation index *vs.* frequency, similar to the curve of Fig. 16 but for levels 10, 20, 30, etc., db below the optimum level of each band, or above the reasonably well-defined settings at which the contribution of the individual bands drops to zero. After smoothing these curves, one for each relative level, they are divided into bands having the frequency limits of Table III. The contribution of each of these bands at each level is then obtained from the new set of curves (not shown)

TABLE III. Frequency bands making equal (5 percent) contributions to articulation index when all bands are at their optimum levels. Composite data for men's and women's voices.

Band	Frequency limits cycles	Band	Frequency limits cycles
1	250–375	11	1930–2140
2	375–505	12	2140–2355
3	505–645	13	2355–2600
4	645–795	14	2600–2900
5	795–955	15	2900–3255
6	955–1130	16	3255–3680
7	1130–1315	17	3680–4200
8	1315–1515	18	4200–4860
9	1515–1720	19	4860–5720
10	1720–1930	20	5720–7000

106   N. R. FRENCH AND J. C. STEINBERG

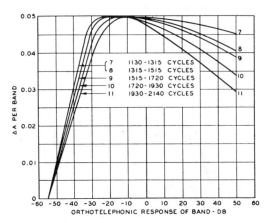

FIG. 18. Effect of level variations on articulation index carried by narrow bands. Band limits are so chosen that the articulation index of each band is 0.05 at its optimum level.

and plotted to obtain the twenty curves of Figs. 17–20, inclusive. These show the effect of level changes on the articulation index carried by each of the twenty equally important bands. The abscissa of each curve is the orthotelephonic response of the transmission system at the mid-frequency of the particular band. The specification of the response of each band in this way was accomplished by shifting the abscissa of the curves illustrated by Fig. 15 by the amount that the orthotelephonic response at the band frequencies exceeds the orthotelephonic response at 1000 cycles, Curve A of Fig. 28 providing the necessary data.

The absolute placement of the curves applies only to the particular acoustic talking level used in the basic articulation tests. However, the curves can obviously be specified on an absolute basis, if desired, in terms of the absolute intensity of the received speech, by adding to the abscissa the intensity, in each band, of the crew's speech at one meter. Such a group of curves could be used for computational purposes. A different procedure is followed, however, to obtain a solution which will not only more readily handle problems involving noise but also more clearly bring out the nature of the relationships.

The fraction of the maximum possible contribution which a band makes when it is not at an optimum level is designated by W. Curves of W against level would consequently be identical in shape to the curves of Figs. 17–20. It will be noted that these curves are essentially straight

lines except in the region where the articulation index is approaching a maximum and that the slopes of the straight line portions are approximately alike and equal to about 3 db for a change of 10 percent in W. This is the same slope that was derived earlier for the level distribution of speech in narrow bands (Fig. 4).

When speech, which is constantly fluctuating in intensity, is reproduced at a sufficiently low level only the occasional portions of highest intensity will be heard, but if the level of reproduction is raised sufficiently even the portions of lowest intensity will become audible. Thus the similarity in slope of the straight line portions of the W curves and the speech distribution curve suggests that W is equal to the fraction of the intervals of speech in a band that can be heard. It will be noted, of course, that the shapes of the W and speech curves are different in the region where W is approaching zero. Actually the W curves in this region cannot be determined accurately and probably do taper off in much the same manner as the speech level distribution (low portion of curve of Fig. 4).

As regards the upper part of the curves of Figs. 17–20 it will be seen that their shapes in this region do not agree with the speech level distribution of Fig. 4. As pointed out previously the latter was extrapolated in the 80–100 percent region and consequently may be in error. For reasons which will be pointed out later, it appears advantageous to assume that the straight line of

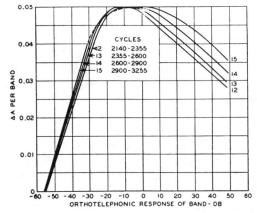

FIG. 19. Effect of level variations on articulation index carried by narrow bands. Band limits are so chosen that the articulation index of each band is 0.05 at its optimum level.

Fig. 4 represents the true speech level distribution up to 100 percent (i.e., down to the lowest level intervals) and to offer a different explanation for the bending over of the ΔA curves, and hence of W, as the level of maximum contribution is approached. This is taken up later as the explanation to be given involves a consideration of the effects of noise.

If W is equal to the fraction of the time intervals that speech in a critical band can be heard, it should be possible to derive W from the characteristics of speech and hearing and to use Figs. 17–20 for testing the method. The first step in this process is the definition of a new term H, where

H = the level of a critical band of speech above its threshold level in the absence of noise. This is termed the band sensation level.

The band sensation level of speech is given by

$$H = B_S + p + K - \beta_0 = B_S + p - X. \qquad (11)$$

The terms B_S, K, β_0, and X have been defined previously. The term p is the difference in db between the intensity in a critical band exceeded by 1 percent of $\frac{1}{8}$th second intervals of received speech and the long average intensity in the same band.

Tests have shown that speech does not become inaudible until its long average intensity per cycle is reduced to about 30 db below the single frequency threshold β_0. This results from two causes which bring about the introduction of the p and K terms in the above equation. Since speech is far from constant in intensity its threshold level in any frequency region is determined by the most intense sounds in that region. As pointed out previously, the intensity of these sounds integrated over $\frac{1}{8}$th second time intervals and over frequency bands which approximate the critical bands in width, is about 12 db above the long average intensity within the same bands; hence $p = 12$ db. Actually this difference varies somewhat from band to band and in the direction of smaller values at low frequencies. In the interests of simplicity it is here considered to be independent of frequency.

The need for the K term, which is of the order of 20 db, has already been pointed out in connection with the discussion of masking of continu-

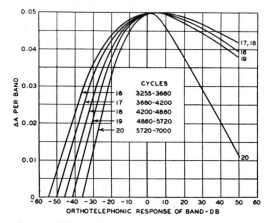

FIG. 20. Effect of level variations on articulation index carried by narrow bands. Band limits are so chosen that the articulation index of each band is 0.05 at its optimum level.

ous spectra sounds. While speech is not rigorously of this type, the spacing of its single frequency components, which are constantly varying up and down the frequency scale, corresponds roughly to the width of the critical bands over which the intensity has to be integrated to obtain a true measure of the sensation which is produced. Therefore, without much loss of accuracy, the same values of K and hence X, which have been determined for sounds having continuous spectra can be applied to speech.

Now referring back to Figs. 4 and 17–20 it will be appreciated that there are certain consequences that can be tested if the hypothesis is correct that W is equal to the proportion of the intervals of speech in a band which can be heard. These are

(1) The computed sensation levels of the speech received in the 20 bands should be substantially alike when these bands all have the same value of W.

(2) The computed sensation level in each band for the zero point of the twenty ΔA curves, which are drawn down to the zero point as straight lines, should be 6 db. This results from the shape of the speech level distribution (Fig. 4) and the choice of the 1 percent highest intervals for expressing the sensation level of the speech in a band.

The sensation level corresponding to $W = 0$ is desired for each of the twenty frequency bands of Figs. 17–20. Although these bands are wider than the critical bands their sensation levels are nevertheless given correctly by Eq. (11). This equation involves B_S which in turn is given by

TABLE IV. Computation of the sensation level (H) of the received speech at which $W=0$ in the 1928–1929 articulation tests. For the particular crew, $H=Bs'+16+R-X$.

Band	Bs' (db)	R (db)	X (db)	H (db)
1	36.5	−26	−1.5	28
2	36.6	−33.5	−8.0	27
3	35.7	−42	−11.6	21
4	33.4	−48.5	−14.1	15
5	30.7	−53.5	−15.7	9
6	28.3	−55	−16.7	6
7	26.0	−55	−17.5	5
8	24.0	−55	−18.3	3
9	22.1	−55	−19.4	2
10	20.4	−55	−21.0	2
11	18.9	−55	−23.3	3
12	17.5	−55.5	−25.2	3
13	16.1	−56	−26.6	3
14	14.6	−56	−27.8	2
15	13.0	−56	−28.5	2
16	11.3	−55.5	−28.9	1
17	9.5	−50.5	−28.8	4
18	7.5	−46	−27.8	5
19	5.1	−41.5	−25.1	5
20	2.5	−36	−19.7	2

TABLE V. Values of W for values of E between 0 and +12 db.

E in db	W	E in db	W
1.0–2.2	.01	8.4–8.7	.11
2.3–3.1	.02	8.8–9.1	.12
3.2–3.9	.03	9.2–9.5	.13
4.0–4.6	.04	9.6–9.9	.14
4.7–5.3	.05	10.0–10.3	.15
5.4–6.0	.06	10.4–10.7	.16
6.1–6.6	.07	10.8–11.1	.17
6.7–7.2	.08	11.2–11.5	.18
7.3–7.8	.09	11.6–11.8	.19
7.9–8.3	.10	11.9–12.1	.20

Eq. (7). Combining Eqs. (7) and (11) we obtain

$$H=Bs'+(V-90)+p+R-X.$$

The term $(V-90)$ represents the acoustic talking level of the particular articulation test crew relative to the talking level corresponding to the idealized spectrum of Fig. 2; hence $(V-90)$ is +4 db as mentioned previously. Also p is +12 db as discussed above. Combining these numerical values, the values of H for this particular crew are given by:

$$H=Bs'+16+R-X.$$

This equation has been applied to the computation of H for each of the twenty bands whose frequency limits are given on Figs. 17–20. The values of Bs' and X, at the mid-frequencies of the bands, were taken from Fig. 2 and curve C of Fig. 5. The values of the orthotelephonic response R of the circuit were read from the abscissa of Figs. 17–20 at the points of zero contribution of the twenty bands. The results of the computations are given in the last column of Table IV. For bands 5 to 20, inclusive, the computed levels are all within a range of 8 db and the average level for these bands is within $2\frac{1}{2}$ db of the required value of 6 db. In view of the many sources of error, involving the measurement of the acoustic level of the talkers, the real voice and ear calibrations of microphone and receivers and

possible differences in the manner in which the latter were talked into and held to the ear in the calibrating and articulation tests, the results for bands 5–20 are considered to be in reasonable agreement with the requirements which are being tested.

The levels computed for bands 1 to 5, inclusive, are too high. However, they are qualitatively in agreement with what would be expected if there had been a low level of room noise in the listening booth during the tests, resulting in masking of the speech. Since room noise usually falls off rapidly with increasing frequency and the shielding effect of receivers held against the ear increases with frequency, extraneous low level noise would have its greatest masking effect in the lowest bands, and negligible effects above 1000 cycles or so. One of several possible sources of noise is the movements of the four observers who were in the booth at the same time. Another uncertainty at the lower frequencies lies in the manner in which the receiver is held to the ear. The above computation of absolute levels in the ear involves the real ear response of the receiver, and consequently the tacit assumption that the coupling between receivers and ears in the articulation tests was the same as in the subjective determinations of the receiver response. Here again any differences which may exist between the responses in the two cases are likely to be greatest at low frequencies. In view of these various effects it is believed that the computed absolute levels are sufficiently close to those required by the above hypothesis of the significance of the W factor, to justify it as a working basis in the formulation of a method for computing the articulation index of received speech.

5.4 Derivation of W—Noisy Conditions

It is apparent that values of W over the range from 0 to about 0.7 can be determined closely, for speech reproduced over linear systems and listened to under quiet conditions, by computing the fractional part of the speech distribution of Fig. 4 which is above threshold. When more than about 70 percent of the speech distribution is above threshold in the absence of noise, an additional factor is included to account for the rounded portion of the ΔA curves of Figs. 17–20, covering values of W in the range from about 0.7 to unity. This part of the curves can be arrived at on the basis of a fatigue effect which may be considered as self-masking. On this basis the hearing of the relatively infrequent low level sounds in a band is considered to be impaired through a temporary loss of sensitivity owing to the preceding sounds of higher level in the same band. This loss of sensitivity will be treated as equivalent to the effect of noise. It is necessary, therefore, to develop relations for noisy conditions before the development for quiet condition can be completed.

If there were no such loss of sensitivity and no other source of masking, and if the speech level distribution is taken to be a straight line, the value of W for any speech band would be given by the fraction of the speech intervals which have sensation levels above 6 db, or

$$W = (H-6)/30 \qquad (12)$$

for sensation levels between 6 and 36 db. To provide a basis for accounting for the gradual tapering off of the twenty ΔA curves as $W=1$ is approached, and also for evaluating the effects of noise generally, this equation will be rewritten as follows:

$$W = (E-6)/30, \qquad (13)$$

where E is a new term called the effective sensation level of a band of speech, given by the following equation:

$$E = H - M, \qquad (14)$$

where M is the masking resulting from all sources of interference, including the masking of speech on itself. By application of Eq. (11) this becomes

$$E = (B_S + p - X) - M. \qquad (15)$$

This can be written in the following more convenient form for computations by replacing M by its equivalent from Eq. (5), or

$$E = B_S + p - m - (B(+)X). \qquad (16)$$

To obtain W, this expression is substituted in Eq. (13), and

$$W = 1/30[B_S + p - 6 - m - (B(+)X)]. \qquad (17)$$

This is the equation ordinarily used for computing W. Actually it is an approximation for values of W less than 0.2 (effective sensation levels less than 12 db). In cases where reception is poor and the effective sensation levels of the

TABLE VI. Values of β_0, X, K, and B_S' at selected frequencies. Values of K are in db; other quantities are in db vs. 10^{-16} watt/cm^2.

Bands for which ΔA_{max} =0.05	Band center cycles	One ear β_0	One ear K	Two ears β_0	Two ears K	X	$B_{S'}$
1	310	15.5	17.0	14.0	15.5	− 1.5	36.5
2	440	9.0	17.0	7.5	15.5	− 8.0	36.6
3	575	5.5	17.1	4.0	15.6	−11.6	35.7
4	720	3.3	17.4	1.8	15.9	−14.1	33.4
5	875	2.0	17.7	0.5	16.2	−15.7	30.7
6	1040	1.4	18.1	−0.1	16.6	−16.7	28.3
7	1225	.9	18.4	−0.6	16.9	−17.5	26.0
8	1415	.5	18.8	−1.0	17.3	−18.3	24.0
9	1615	− .2	19.2	−1.7	17.7	−19.4	22.1
10	1825	−1.4	19.6	−2.9	18.1	−21.0	20.4
11	2035	−3.3	20.0	−4.8	18.5	−23.3	18.9
12	2250	−4.8	20.4	−6.3	18.9	−25.2	17.5
13	2475	−5.9	20.7	−7.4	19.2	−26.6	16.1
14	2750	−6.6	21.2	−8.2	19.6	−27.8	14.6
15	3080	−6.9	21.6	−8.5	20.0	−28.5	13.0
16	3470	−6.7	22.2	−8.6	20.3	−28.9	11.3
17	3940	−5.9	22.9	−8.0	20.8	−28.8	9.5
18	4530	−4.1	23.7	−6.5	21.3	−27.8	7.5
19	5300	−0.3	24.8	−3.3	21.8	−25.1	5.1
20	6350	+6.5	26.2	+2.6	22.3	−19.7	2.5

TABLE VII. Values of $(B(+)X) - X$ as a function of $B - X$.

$B-X$ (db)	$(B(+)X)-X$ (db)
−9	0.5
8	0.6
7	0.8
6	1.0
5	1.2
4	1.5
3	1.8
2	2.1
−1	2.5
0	3.0
+1	3.5
2	4.1
3	4.8
4	5.5
5	6.2
6	7.0
7	7.8
8	8.6
+9	9.5

110   N. R. FRENCH AND J. C. STEINBERG

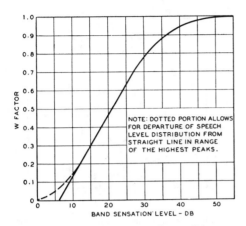

FIG. 21. The W factor for quiet conditions.

speech in a number of computation bands are less than 12 db, computations can be improved in accuracy by using Eq. (16) and Table V for these particular bands to allow for the departure of the most intense part of the speech level distribution from a straight line (Fig. 4). Values of m are given in Table II for values of Z above 50 db; at lower levels m is zero. Values of B_s', from which B_s is derived, and of X are given by Table VI. Values of $(B(+)X)$ relative to X are given by Table VII as a function of $(B-X)$. Outside the range for which values are given, $(B(+)X)$ equals either B or X, depending upon which is the larger.

In the above equations B represents the level above 10^{-16} watt/cm² of the combined intensity per cycle of all the various noises reaching the ear at any particular frequency. In addition to the usual sources of noise, B includes the noise equivalent in its effect to the self-masking of a band of speech on itself and also the noise equivalent in its effect to the masking of one speech band on another. These are all combined on a power basis and the sum then expressed in db. Self-masking and interband masking are further considered in the following sections.

5.5 Derivation of W—Quiet Conditions

It is now possible to consider self-masking and its effects on the form of the ΔA curves. Referring back to Eq. (13) it will be seen that if W is not to exceed unity the effective sensation level must not exceed 36 db. This is accomplished by taking the equivalent noise of self-masking as 24 db

below B_s, where B_s is the long average intensity per cycle level of speech. This equivalent noise, designated by B_f, is

$$B_f = B_s - 24. \qquad (18)$$

Substituting this value of B_f for B in Eq. (17) it follows that, for quiet conditions,

$$W = 1/30[B_s + p - 6 - m \\ - ((B_s - 24)(+)X)]. \qquad (19)$$

The relationship between W, as computed by this equation, and the sensation level of a speech band, as computed by Eq. (11), is shown by the continuous curve of Fig. 21. This curve applies to the case where there is no noise and no non-linear elements are between the voice and the ear to change the form of the time variation of speech received in a band from that of the original speech. If this curve is compared with the twenty curves of Figs. 17–20, it will be seen that it is a reasonable representation of their shapes over the entire range below their maximum values. It may be worth noting here that the self-masking factor, which produces the tapering effect as W approaches unity under quiet conditions, will also produce the same sort of an effect when other noises are present, and when the speech is raised to a level considerably above the noise level.

Figure 21 indicates that the maximum contribution of a band of speech under quiet conditions, except for the equivalent noise of self-masking B_f, is reached at a band sensation level of 50 db. At this speech level the effective level Z of the noise having an intensity per cycle level of B_f is only 14 db since B_f is 24 db below B_s and the sensation level of a speech band is determined by the levels of speech $p = 12$ db above B_s. The value of m in Eq. (19) is consequently zero over the range of the curve of Fig. 21.

Referring now to Fig. 8, it will be noted that masking does not start to increase faster than the effective level of noise until the latter exceeds 50 db. Consequently, when self-masking is the only source of masking, the value of m in Eq. (19) does not change from zero until the sensation level of speech in a band rises above 86 db. It follows that W for quiet conditions, as given by the above equations, has a value of unity for band sensation levels of speech ranging between 50 and 86 db. Thus the relations do not account for the reduction of A at high speech levels as shown on Figs. 17–20. Overloading in the ear, resulting in the generation of intermodulation products, which could act as noise, is a possible explanation of this reduction. If the noise equivalents of these products could be determined their effects could be allowed for, presumably, in the same manner as other noises. It is possible that the downward droop of the curves of Figs. 17–20 above the optimum levels is excessive. Because of the small variation of the measured values of articulation with level above the optimum level with the various filters, the derivation of the variation of the contributions of the individual bands with level in this region is not at all precise.

The unimportance of m, as discussed above, applies specifically to quiet conditions. In problems involving high levels of extraneous noise the inclusion of m in the above equations may have a considerable effect on W.

5.6 Interband Masking of Speech

Articulation tests have shown that at high received levels the articulation tends to decrease as the level is increased. The effect is most evident in systems that contain pronounced peaks or frequency regions that are partially suppressed. The effect is believed to be caused in part by speech in one frequency region masking the speech sounds in other frequency regions. One rather elaborate method for allowing for this

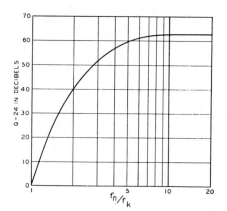

FIG. 22. Function used in determining the masking of speech by speech in lower bands.

effect has been developed but is too lengthy to describe here and also too laborious in applications involving many computations. This method involves, for example, the determination of the effect of each band of speech on each of the other bands. These effects are functions of the levels in each of the bands. In the computational method described here a simpler but presumably less accurate procedure has been followed. One simplification is to consider the effect of a speech band on only those bands which are of higher frequency. As in the case of self-masking, it will be convenient to consider the interband masking as equivalent to the masking produced by a noise B_n in the speech band being masked. The estimated intensity level of this equivalent noise B_{nk}

TABLE VIII. Q, i.e., the number of db that the noise produced in any band, by speech in any lower band, is below the long average intensity of the speech in the lower band.

Producing band	2	3	4	5	6	7	8	9	10	11	12	13	14	15	16	17	18	19	20
1	49	62	70	75	78	81	83	85	85	85	86	86	87	87	87	87	87	87	87
2		44	56	64	70	74	78	80	82	83	84	85	85	86	86	87	87	87	87
3			42	52	61	67	71	75	78	79	81	83	84	85	85	86	86	87	87
4				40	50	57	64	68	71	75	78	79	81	82	83	84	85	86	87
5					38	49	56	62	66	70	72	75	78	79	81	83	85	85	86
6						36	46	54	59	64	67	70	72	75	77	80	82	84	85
7							35	45	51	56	61	65	69	72	75	77	79	81	84
8								35	43	50	55	59	64	67	71	74	77	80	83
9									35	42	47	52	57	63	67	71	74	78	81
10										34	41	47	52	57	63	67	71	76	79
11											33	40	46	52	57	63	68	72	77
12												33	40	47	54	60	65	71	75
13													34	41	50	55	61	67	72
14														34	42	49	56	64	70
15															35	43	51	59	65
16																35	45	54	61
17																	35	46	56
18																		36	49
19																			39

produced in band n by speech in band k is given by:

$$B_{nk} = B_{sk} - Q, \qquad (20)$$

where

B_{sk} = the intensity level of speech in band k which is doing the masking,

f_k = the mid-frequency of band k, and

f_n = the mid-frequency of the band n in which speech is being masked.

The quantity Q, derived empirically, is given on Fig. 22 as a function of (f_n/f_k). Values of Q for the particular frequency bands of Table III are given in Table VIII. To simplify the computations Q is here taken to be independent of the absolute level of B_{sk}.

Assuming the equivalent noises from the various bands to combine on a power basis, the total equivalent noise in band n produced by speech from all lower bands is given by

$$B_n = B_{n1}(+)B_{n2}(+)\cdots(+)B_{n,\,n-1}. \qquad (21)$$

In cases where very high levels of speech are necessary to ride over excessive levels of noise, and the response of the communication system contains sharp peaks or dips, interband masking may be appreciably larger than these formulas indicate.

5.7 Summary of Relationships—Linear Systems

If the speech frequency range is subdivided, for computational purposes, into twenty bands having the frequency limits of Table III, the value of ΔA_m for each band is 0.05 and the articulation index of the received speech by Eq. (10) is

$$A = 0.05(W_1 + W_2 + \cdots W_{20}). \qquad (10a)$$

The subscripts refer to the individual bands of Table III. The value of W in any particular computation band is determined by the following relation in which the quantities that vary with frequency are usually specified at the mid-frequencies of the bands

$$W = 1/30[B_S + p - 6 - m - (B(+)X)]. \qquad (17)$$

The symbol $(+)$, between two terms expressed in db, indicates that they are to be combined on a power basis and then reconverted to db. This is the basic equation for determining W except

for non-linear systems, discussed in Section 5.8, or in cases where reception is poor and the effective sensation level (Eq. (16)) of the speech in a number of the computation bands is less than 12 db. In this event Eq. (16) should be used for these particular bands and the values of W read from Table V.

The quantity B_S is the level, in db vs. 10^{-16} watt/cm², of the long average intensity per cycle of the received speech, the intensity being expressed as a free field intensity in the manner described in Section 4. B is a similar quantity but applies to the total noise per cycle received from all sources. The value of p is ordinarily taken as 12 db at all frequencies. X is a function of frequency only; its values are given in Table VI. Values of $(B(+)X)$ relative to X are given in Table VII as a function of $B-X$. The term m can be omitted unless extraneous noise of high level is present; values of m as a function of the effective level Z of the noise B are given in Table II, where

$$Z = B - X. \qquad (4)$$

The value of B_S in Eq. (17) is given by

$$B_S = B_S' + (V - 90) + R, \qquad (7)$$

where B_S' is the intensity level, at the appropriate frequency, of the idealized speech spectrum of Fig. 2, values of which are tabulated in Table VI. The symbol V represents the actual speech level of any particular talkers, at two inches from the lips, as determined by a sound level measurement using 40-db weighting. R is the orthotelephonic response of the communication system at the appropriate frequency.

The value of B in Eqs. (4) and (17) is given by a new equation

$$B = B_E(+)B_J(+)B_n, \qquad (22)$$

where B represents the intensity per cycle level of the total noise from all sources except that produced by the received speech, and

$$B_J = B_S - 24 \qquad (18)$$

and

$$B_n = B_{n1}(+)B_{n2}(+)\cdots B_{n,\,n-1}, \qquad (21)$$

where n is the number of the particular band in which the noise is being determined and the subscripts 1, 2, etc., refer to the bands, one to

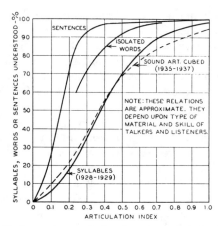

FIG. 23. Approximate relations between articulation index and subjective measures of intelligibility.

$(n-1)$, from which the noise arises because of the speech in these bands. The values of B_{n1}, B_{n2}, etc., relative to the levels B_S of speech in bands $1, 2 \cdots (n-1)$, can be read from Table VIII.

In applying these relations it should be noted that the equivalent noises B_f and B_n vary with the level of the received speech B_S. B_n can usually be omitted entirely unless the response of the communication system falls off rapidly with increasing frequency or has sharp peaks and valleys.

5.8 Non-Linear Relation between Original and Received Speech

The above derivation of the W factor applies to cases where the intensity of the received speech in any band is proportional to the initial speech. It is now necessary to consider whether the same relations which specify the W factor in such cases will hold for cases where the speech is transmitted through systems containing a non-linear element, such as a carbon transmitter. Tests have shown that for a given value of received talking volume the articulation obtained with a carbon transmitter may be somewhat less than that obtained with a linear transmitter which has the same shape of frequency response characteristic. Attempts have been made to explain this effect by considering as noise the resulting inter-modulation products of speech. While there probably is such an effect, the reduction in articulation can also be accounted for by self-masking in conjunction with the effect

of the non-linear device in altering the level distribution of the speech sounds. In some cases the output of a carbon transmitter changes r db for each db change in input, where r is nearly constant over a considerable range of levels and is usually greater than unity. It follows that the level distribution of the output of such a transmitter in a speech band would cover a range which is broader by the factor r than that of the original speech. Consequently on the basis of the self-masking theory, a greater fraction of the lower level intervals of speech would be masked by speech of higher levels in the band, thus reducing the maximum possible value of W.

The effect of such an expanding action where the output-input characteristic on a db basis is approximately linear, but with a slope different from unity, can consequently be computed from the relations which have already been given, by considering the basic speech level distribution to be r times as broad as that shown in Fig. 4 and then proceeding with the computations exactly as if the instrument were a linear one. The relationship between effective sensation level and the W factor has already been given, as follows:

$$W = (E-6)/30. \qquad (13)$$

In this equation the number 30 represents the range between the maximum and minimum levels of speech in a band, assuming a straight line

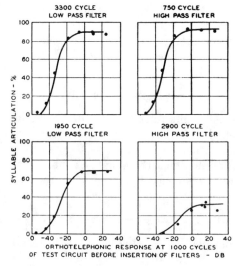

FIG. 24. Comparison of observed and computed results for 1928–1929 articulation tests. Points show observed data.

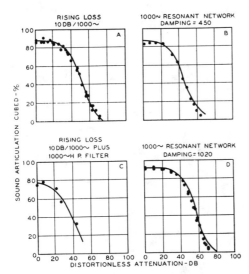

FIG. 25. Comparison of observed and computed results for 1935–1936 articulation tests. Points show observed data.

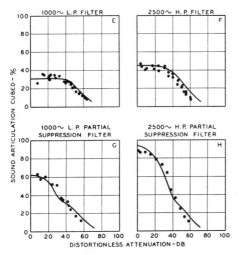

FIG. 26. Comparison of observed and computed results for 1935–1936 articulation tests. Points show observed data.

relationship between percentage of intervals and levels over the entire range. Consequently with an expanding type device the range is 30r and Eq. (13) can be rewritten as follows:

$$W = (E-6)/30r. \qquad (23)$$

The values of the effective sensation levels are computed by Eq. (16) as before. This equation contains a peak factor p, representing the level difference between the intensity exceeded by 1 percent of $\frac{1}{8}$th second intervals of speech and the long average intensity of all intervals, which may be changed in value by the expanding action from the 12-db figure which applies to the ordinary distribution of speech levels. This can be easily computed for any value of r, but for values of r between 1 and 1.2 the values of p are practically constant at 12 db.

In cases of compression, large ratios of expansion or expansion that varies with level, it is necessary to calculate the level distribution of the received speech sounds from the characteristics of the non-linear device and the level distribution of speech shown in Fig. 4. The lower curved portion of this distribution, rather than the straight line approximation, should be used in cases of compression. Then W can be computed by determining the fraction of sounds in the modified distribution that are audible. It can be seen that, in general, this procedure will be laborious and cannot be expressed in a convenient mathematical form.

At the present time this treatment of non-linearity should be regarded primarily as an hypothesis. It has, however, been successful in explaining qualitatively the results obtained with a few systems containing non-linear elements, but other complicating factors are also involved. For example, in computations involving non-linear elements the conception of response is not as clear as it is in the case of linear elements and the shape of the response characteristic that is obtained may vary widely, depending upon the type of measurement that is made. Considerable caution must, therefore, be used in interpreting the results of computations of the articulation index of speech, received over systems containing non-linear elements.

5.9 The Effect of Hearing Loss

The term β_0 used in the above relations is an idealized threshold for single frequency tones and is close to the minimum of sound that can be heard by people having the most acute ears. The hearing of most people will be some 10–15 db less acute than this.[15,16] In practical problems

---

[15] J. C. Steinberg and M. B. Gardner, J. Acous. Soc. Am. 11, 270 (1940).
[16] J. C. Steinberg, H. C. Montgomery, and M. B. Gardner, J. Acous. Soc. Am. 12, 291 (1940).

there is usually sufficient noise to cause a threshold shift of more than 10–15 db by masking. Under these conditions calculations should be valid even though they are based on the acute β_0. In general, computations employing β_0 should be valid, except perhaps in the region where W normally is approaching unity, for all individuals having hearing losses somewhat less than the masking caused by noise, up to masking values of 40–50 db. For quiet conditions it is necessary to replace the idealized β_0 by the actual threshold values of the individuals under consideration. This procedure should give reasonably valid results for hearing losses up to 40–50 db from the idealized threshold. For greater hearing losses, the validity of the methods becomes questionable because of modulation and other effects.

6. RELATION OF ARTICULATION INDEX TO SUBJECTIVE MEASURES

While the computational method which has been described was derived from syllable articulation tests, it is possible to interpret the resulting index in terms of subjective measures which use words or sentences. For this purpose it is only necessary, with a particular testing crew, to make subjective tests of the desired character under a variety of conditions where all the required data on the circuits, the speech spectrum, etc., are sufficiently well known to permit computing the articulation index of the received speech. These computed indices plotted against the measured word or sentence intelligibility will thus provide an empirical relationship for interpreting the results of other computations. Approximate relations of this character are given by Fig. 23. Taking, as a starting point, the curve of this figure which shows the relation, derived previously, between articulation index and syllable articulation, the other curves were obtained by using published relations[13] between syllable articulation and word and sentence intelligibility.

Although these relations apply only to specific testing crews and types of material, several features are worth noting. For instance, if speech is impaired sufficiently to lower its articulation index to one-half, sentence intelligibility may still remain high. For comparing transmission systems which have articulation indices in the range of 0.5 to unity, sentence intelligibility tests, afford-

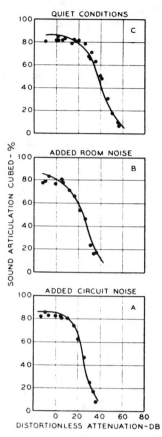

FIG. 27. Comparison of observed and computed results for 1936–1937 articulation tests. Points show observed data.

ing only a small range of errors, are consequently impracticable. Articulation tests are more useful for this purpose. Sentence tests are useful, however, for comparing conditions which provide poor reception. For articulation indices in the range of zero to 0.3, sentence intelligibility is a sensitive measure, varying from zero to about 90 percent. Another point—although sentence intelligibility may fall by only a small amount when the articulation index is reduced to only half its maximum value, it is apparent, by referring to the curve for syllables, that a listener fails under this condition to recognize correctly a substantial portion of the sounds which are received. The high sentence intelligibility in this case must be attributed to the listener's ability to utilize context and to guess the unintelligible sounds, owing to the restricted number of sound

116 N. R. FRENCH AND J. C. STEINBERG

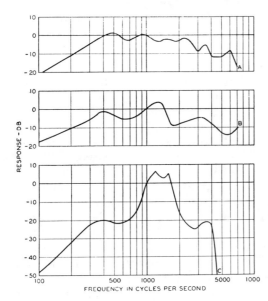

FIG. 28. Orthotelephonic response of test circuits before insertion of networks—expressed in db relative to *OT* response at 1000 cycles. Curve *A* applies to 1928–1929 articulation tests, curve *B* to 1935–1936 tests and curve *C* to 1936–1937 tests.

combinations which form actual words. This requires some effort. It seems probable that the relatively flat portion of the sentence curve is accompanied by an appreciable change of effort.

7. APPLICATIONS—ILLUSTRATIVE EXAMPLES

Although the development of the relationships which have been discussed appears rather complex, they are comparatively simple in application. For certain types of problems, at least, the solutions are practically self-evident once the fundamental data are available, as will appear from an illustrative example.

Let it be assumed that speech is being received in the presence of noise of the continuous spectrum type, and that the response of the communication system is such, that there is a constant difference in db at all frequencies between the average intensity of the speech per cycle and the average intensity of the noise per cycle, both in the ear. Let it be assumed that this difference is 0 db, i.e., that the noise and speech spectra are identical at all frequencies and that there is no limitation on band width. Under these conditions, unless both the speech and noise have large variations in their absolute levels from one

frequency band to another, the controlling source of interference will be the noise. In other words, masking of speech on itself, either in the same band or on adjacent bands will be negligible relative to the noise. From Eq. (17)

$$W = 1/30(B_S + p - 6 - m - (B(+)X)).$$

In the example under discussion, $B = B_S$ and, if the level of the noise is well above threshold, B is so large with respect to X that $(B(+)X)$ is equal to B and hence to B_S. Also, unless the noise is very intense, m is zero. Then letting $p = 12$ db, the equation reduces to

$$W = 6/30 = 0.2.$$

In other words, each of the twenty bands makes one-fifth of its maximum possible contribution to articulation index, and thus the articulation index of the received speech is 0.2. According to Fig. 23 this corresponds to a sentence intelligibility of about 70 percent.

Now let it be supposed that the band width is restricted to the frequencies below 1900 cycles which, according to Table III, eliminates ten of the twenty bands. The articulation index is consequently cut from 0.2 to 0.1 and sentence intelligibility to about 25 percent.

It is now natural to ask how much the remaining passed band would have to be raised in level, with respect to the noise, to restore the intelligibility to its original amount, namely 70 percent. To do this the articulation index of the limited band has to be restored to its original amount, namely 0.2. Since only half the bands are now contributing, the contribution of each band must consequently be doubled, or W for each of the ten lower bands must be raised from 0.2 to 0.4. Substituting $W = 0.4$ in Eq. (17) the corresponding value of $B_S - B$ is found to be +6 db. Thus the speech has to be raised by 6 db as compared to the original condition to restore the intelligibility to 70 percent.

Although a great deal can be learned by analyzing problems in the above manner this is not always possible without some loss of accuracy. With intense noise the term m in Eq. (17) should be evaluated. Also the equivalent noise of self-masking B_f should be included in the total noise B whenever the effective sensation level E of the speech in a band is greater than about 25 db.

8. COMPARISON OF COMPUTED AND OBSERVED ARTICULATIONS

Articulation index computations have been made, covering the test circuits which provided the basic data for the formulation, and also a wide variety of additional circuits for which articulation test data were available. Comparisons of the observed and computed results are given by Figs. 24–27. These figures, representing only a small part of similar comparisons, were selected because they cover a rather wide range of types of distortion and are representative of the kind of agreement between observation and calculation that is generally obtained. These figures cover tests made with three circuits having, before insertion of the networks to be tested, the response characteristics shown in Fig. 28. Curve A applies to Fig. 24, curve B to Figs. 25 and 26, and curve C to Fig. 27.

In the tests of Fig. 24 the observed quantity was syllable articulation, shown by the points. The data were obtained during 1928–1929 and are part of the fundamental data on which the present formulation is based. The curves represent computed values of articulation index translated into syllable articulation by means of the previously derived relationship (Fig. 23) between these quantities for the 1928–1929 crew.

The data of Figs. 25–27 were obtained during 1935–1937 with a different testing crew. The same type of syllables used in the 1928–1929 tests were employed, but the automatic equipment used by the observers for recording and totaling the results gave the results in terms of sound articulation, i.e., the percentage of the called sounds that were correctly understood. Each point on Figs. 25–27 is the cube of the observed sound articulation, which is approximately equivalent to syllable articulation. The curves of these figures represent computed values of articulation index translated into sound articulation cubed by means of the relationship between these quantities shown on Fig. 23. This relationship was established by determining with the 1935–1937 crew the maximum sound articulation (as a function of received level) of each of a number of sharp cut-off filters, and plotting the

cube of the maximum sound articulation of each filter against its known value of articulation index at optimum volume, as derived from the 1928–1929 tests.

The computations leading to the curves of Figs. 24–27 were carried out in accordance with the procedures summarized in Section 5.7. The data needed are the over-all response characteristics of the test circuits, the acoustic speech level of the callers and the spectrum, in the observer's ears, of any interfering noise that may have been present. The over-all response of the circuits of the Fig. 24 tests may be obtained, at any value of abscissa, by adding the abscissa value to curve A of Fig. 28 and assuming an infinite loss beyond the filter cut-off frequency. The response corresponding to any value of the abscissas of Figs. 25 and 26 may be obtained by subtracting the abscissa value from curve B of Fig. 28, adding a constant value of 39 db and subtracting the insertion loss of the appropriate network of Fig. 29. For Fig. 27 the response is obtained by subtracting the abscissa value from curve C of Fig. 28 and adding a constant value of 21.5 db.

Measurements of the speech output of the microphone were made during the tests. The speech output of the microphone was also computed by adding the acoustic speech spectrum of Fig. 2 to the response of the microphone and integrating the resulting spectrum. The amount

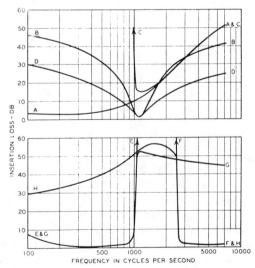

FIG. 29. Insertion loss of networks used in 1935–1936 tests.

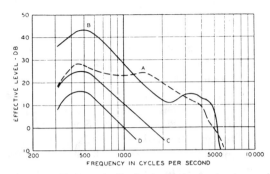

FIG. 30. Estimated effective level of noise in observer's ears during articulation tests. Curve A—added circuit noise (several 1936–1937 tests). Curve B—added room noise (several 1936–1937 tests). Curve C—assumed residual noise during 1936–1937 tests. Curve D—assumed residual noise during 1935–1936 and 1928–1929 tests.

that a measured value exceeds a computed value represents the amount that the acoustic speech level (V) at two inches from the lips for the tests exceeds 90 db. It was determined in this way that the average value of V for the tests of Fig. 24 was 94 db and 92.5 db for the tests of Figs. 25–27. The values of V for the individual test conditions were generally within ±1 db of these average values.

Preliminary computations of an articulation index of the three basic circuits *without added networks*, yielded at low levels of received speech, somewhat higher values than the test results, indicating that the effective sensation levels (E) of the received speech during the tests were somewhat lower than the computed levels. Such a disagreement was to be expected in view of the discrepancies shown in Table IV, since they indicate that the effective sensation levels of the low frequency bands were considerably lower in the tests than the calculated values would predict. The reasons for the discrepancies are not definitely known. They could arise from one or more of the following factors:

(a) A low level residual noise, such as might be produced by the movements of the several observers in the test booths, might have been present during articulation tests. Owing to the leakage characteristic of a receiver held to the ear, such a noise would be expected to produce its principal masking in the low frequency bands.

(b) The observers might have held their earphones less tightly to their ears during articulation tests than the earphones were held in the real ear calibrating tests of receiver response. The principal effects of such a variation would be to decrease the receiver response in the low frequency bands.

(c) In calculating the effects of interband masking, the masking effects of a given band on bands of lower frequency were neglected. These effects may not be negligible and the lower bands might be masked to some extent by adjacent higher frequency bands.

(d) In calculating the thresholds of the speech bands, the method assumes that, irrespective of the frequency of the band, the threshold is determined by the 1 percent points of the speech intensity distributions. These are taken to be 12 db above the long average intensity for all bands. There is some evidence that the peak factors for the low frequency bands are less than 12 db.

(e) The 1928–29 derived ΔA curves (Figs. 17–20) were drawn to zero articulation contribution (W=0) as straight lines. It has been assumed that the effective band sensation level at this zero point is 6 db for all bands. It may be that this factor should be larger for the low frequency bands which would be in the direction to reduce the discrepancies in Table IV.

The effects of all of these factors if known and taken into account, would tend to result in the calculation of lower effective sensation levels for the low frequency bands and hence smaller values of W, than is now done with the present method. The procedure that has been used was to take residual noise as the entire cause of the discrepancy, assume this noise to have the same shaped spectrum as room noise, modify it by the response of the leakage path between receiver and ear and then make computations for different absolute levels of the noise until the best agreement was obtained between the computed and observed articulations *at low levels* on the basic circuits *before* insertion of any of the distorting networks. Having derived in this manner estimates of an assumed residual noise, these same estimates were then used in all the remaining computations. Curve D of Fig. 30 shows the effective levels (Z) of the residual noise used in the computations of Figs. 24–26. Curve C of Fig. 30 applies to Fig. 27.

The tests of the two lower curves of Fig. 27 were made with noise added deliberately. Curve B of Fig. 30 shows the effective levels (Z) of the room noise introduced into the booth for the tests of the center curve of Fig. 27. The values of (Z) were obtained by subtracting X from the intensity levels (B) of this noise in the ear. The intensity levels were obtained by combining the measured spectrum of the noise in the booth with the measured shielding effect of the receiver on the ear. Curve A of Fig. 30 shows the effective levels of the added noise used in the tests of the lower curve of Fig. 27. This noise was introduced electrically into the receiver. The intensity levels in the ear, used in computing the effective levels, were obtained by combining the electrical spectrum of the noise with the real ear response of the receiver.

Certain broad conclusions can be reached from the comparisons of computed and observed results afforded by Figs. 24–27: (1) the computational method appears to define reasonably well the steep parts of the articulation *vs.* received speech level curves and (2) the calculated results at high received levels tend to be too large. The latter tendency may result in part from omission of intermodulation products produced in the ear at high speech levels as discussed in Section 5.5. Also, it may result in part from the assumption of equivalent noises of self and interband masking as fixed numbers of decibels below the speech levels, independent of absolute level, and the omission, in the interband masking functions, of masking on speech by speech at higher frequencies.

Although the assumption of a residual noise in the observing booth improves the agreement between computed and observed articulation at low speech levels by reducing the effective sensation levels of the speech in the lower frequency bands, it should be noted that the procedure is arbitrary and does not indicate that residual noise of this magnitude was actually present during the tests. It simply indicates that for the range of transmission conditions for which tests and calculations have been made, the effects of the discrepancies in the low frequency bands may be lumped into an effect produced by the assumed residual noise.

Although the present computational procedure has given reasonably good agreement between calculated and observed results for a wide variety of systems and hence throws light on the factors which govern the intelligibility of speech sounds, it is hoped that future work will improve the approximations and also throw additional light on the empirical procedures that have been used.

9. ACKNOWLEDGMENTS

The work reported here has drawn on the contributions of a number of people. First should be mentioned the names of H. Fletcher, W. H. Martin, and E. C. Wente, who not only were responsible for the broad content of the work but contributed significantly to the fundamental studies and their application to problems in telephone engineering and design. In the formulation of the relationships, the major portion of the work was carried out by A. B. Anderson, P. V. Dimock, J. W. Emling, R. H. Galt, W. Koenig, Jr., and W. A. Munson. The basic speech, hearing, and articulation data, which enter into the relationships, involved these same people and others to whom reference has been made throughout the text.

Journal of Phonetics (1977) **5**, 253–263

Isochrony reconsidered

Ilse Lehiste

Department of Linguistics, Ohio State University, Columbus, Ohio 43210, *U.S.A.*

Received 13*th August* 1976

Abstract: Two points are made in this paper. The first is that isochrony—the rhythmic organization of speech into more or less equal intervals—is primarily a perceptual phenomenon. Although isochrony is based on production, perception seems to play a decisive role. The second point is that there exists a way in which isochrony is integrated into the grammar of English at the syntactic level. Since the listener expects isochrony (interstress intervals to be of approximately equal size), it is possible to manipulate the duration of the interstress intervals for linguistic purposes. In English, lengthening of interstress intervals is frequently used to signal the presence of a syntactic boundary.

Isochrony in production

The term "isochrony" refers to the phenomenon that in a stress-timed language, such as English, stressed syllables follow each other at approximately equal time intervals (Pike, 1945). While the notion has been under discussion for quite a long time, the first instrumental investigation seems to have been that of Classe (1939). Classe failed to find absolute isochrony, but nevertheless did not dismiss isochrony out of hand; he argued that it constitutes the basis of the rhythmic system of English, "although, frequently, it only remains as an underlying tendency of which some other factor at times almost completely obliterates the effects" (p. 90). Not having found perfect isochrony in objective measurements, he held open the possibility that isochrony might be a subjective phenomenon: "In speech, long groups, provided other circumstances are not too unfavorable, will tend to be made subjectively isochronous by the reader or listener because of his speech habits" (p. 133).

Classe's formulation is rather careful: he claims neither perfect isochrony in production nor in perception, just a tendency to speak in rhythmic units that are perceived as isochronous. Several other linguists have studied isochrony, primarily from the point of view of production (Shen & Peterson, 1962; O'Connor, 1965, 1968; Bolinger, 1965; Uldall, 1971, 1972; Lea, 1974). Shen & Peterson measured first the distance between two primary stresses. According to their system, only one primary stress occurs per sentence; the terminal juncture separating the two sentences was included in the stretch of speech between the two primary stresses. The materials recorded consisted of written prose; the length of the sentences was not controlled in any way. There were three readers, each of them reading different material. The time spans between primary stresses ranged from 410 to 1820 ms for the first speaker, from 380 to 2500 ms for the second speaker, and from 550 to 3610 ms for the third speaker, with no obvious clustering around some average value. Time intervals were also measured in stretches of speech that did not contain a terminal. The time intervals between what Shen & Peterson designated primary and

254   *I. Lehiste*

secondary stresses ranged (for all readers combined) from 40 to 810 ms; between secondary and primary stresses, from 190 to 990 ms, and between two secondary stresses from 190 to 880 ms. On the basis of these measurements, Shen & Peterson rejected the notion of isochrony.

Bolinger (1965) had six speakers record two rather lengthy sentences, identified the accents, and measured the intervals between the accents. His results gave little support to the idea of isochronous rhythm in production. Of the 53 intervals, 13 had approximately twice the length of the shortest interval. The lengths of the intervals appeared to be determined by syllable structure, nearness to initial or final position, and relative semantic importance, besides the number of syllables. Bolinger concluded that such factors seem to have a good deal more influence than rhythm has in determining the length of accentual groups.

O'Connor (1965) recorded a limerick with as strict a rhythm as possible, and accompanied the speech with a click, produced by hand, at each stress. There were 15 stress groups with an average duration (measured from click to click) of 518 ms. The duration difference between the shortest and longest stress group (488 and 566 ms) was 88 ms. O'Connor concluded that physical isochrony was clearly not present even under these very favorable conditions. In 1968, O'Connor studied a set of seven utterances, each containing three monosyllabic feet. The first and third foot remained constant, the second varied in segmental length from three to nine segments. Four speakers read the sentences once each, and a fifth speaker read the entire set 10 times. Duration measurements showed that the variable foot had a clear tendency to greater duration as segmental length increased. There was no evidence that the duration of the frame items adjusted itself to compensate for the changes in the variable foot. On the basis of these results, O'Connor expressed continued doubt as to the existence of isochrony in production.

Uldall (1971, 1972) analyzed a reading by David Abercrombie of "The North Wind and the Sun". The reading, which lasted for 45 s, was later divided into rhythmic feet by Abercrombie. There were 56 metric feet, ranging in duration from 260 to 870 ms. In spite of the large differences between the extremes, Uldall acknowledged a tendency to isochronism for this speaker in the moderately slow "news reading" style employed by him. More than half (57%) of the filled feet (i.e. feet not containing any pauses) fell between 385 and 520 ms. The average duration of all filled feet was 520 ms; the average duration of all monosyllabic feet was 440 ms, all disyllabic feet 510 ms, and all trisyllabic feet 540 ms. The four-syllable feet, of which the text contained six, had an average duration of 760 ms and thus differed considerably from the average.

One of the more detailed recent instrumental studies of isochrony in production is that by Lea (1974). Using eight talkers reading 31 sentences, six talkers reading the Rainbow script (a standard text used in speech experiments) and two talkers reading a monosyllabic script, Lea tested several hypotheses concerning isochrony. The first of these corresponds to the standard notion that stressed syllables follow each other at regular intervals. This presupposes that the number of unstressed syllables between two stresses has little or no effect on the interstress time intervals. Pike (1945) had described isochrony as the drawing out of unstressed syllables when there are few of them in an interstress interval and the jamming together of unstressed syllables as their number increases between two stresses. Lea's results show that interstress intervals are indeed substantially affected by the number of intervening unstressed syllables; the average time intervals appeared to increase almost linearly with the number of intervening syllables. The original definition of isochrony was therefore rejected.

Lea hypothesized that his results might be interpreted as a manifestation of an alternating stress and unstress pattern: "as one inserts more and more unstressed syllables between two stresses, he tends to make one of the intervening syllables more like a stressed syllable, to re-establish something like the ideal alternation pattern" (p. 41). This suggests that whenever three or four syllables intervene between stresses, one of them will acquire some characteristics of a stressed syllable. This was indeed the case for most of the interstress intervals with three or four intervening syllables in Lea's materials: of 38 such instances, 21 included a syllable which was perceived as stressed by one of his listeners, and of the 17 remaining cases, 10 had syllables that were declared stressed by Lea's stressed syllable location algorithm.

Histograms published by Lea (p. 35) of the number of occurrences of various sizes of interstress intervals show both a fairly large amount of clustering around certain mean values and a large amount of variability. For example, the average interstress interval for eight speakers producing 31 sentences was 532 ms, with a standard deviation of 230 ms. For one of the speakers, the mean was 480 ms, the standard deviation 198 ms. For another speaker, the mean for the Rainbow script was 470 ms, the standard deviation 131 ms, and for the Monosyllabic script, 502 and 184 ms. The regularities thus are quite apparent, even though absolute isochrony could not be found.

All of these studies have shown that interstress intervals vary in duration to a greater or lesser degree. Most investigators have therefore either rejected the claim that English is a language characterized by isochrony, or have attempted to reinterpret the experimental findings to take into account the fact that perfect isochrony cannot be found in production. An example is provided by Halliday (1967), who claims that isochrony is phonological. This makes it possible for him to overlook phonetic differences in the realization of phonologically isochronous units. In Halliday's system, the phonological units are, in descending order, the tone group, foot, syllable and phoneme. It is the foot that is characterized by phonological isochronicity, which Halliday describes as follows: "There is a tendency for salient syllables to occur at roughly regular intervals of time whatever the number of weak syllables, including zero, in between" (p. 12). Rees (1975, pp. 22–3) proposes the tone group as the domain of isochrony (in Halliday's system, the tone group is the basic phonological unit of intonation). A sentence may consist of more than one tone group; the possibility remains open that two or more consecutive tone groups might have their salient syllables fall at regular intervals, and that thus isochronicity might appear to embrace the whole sentence, but according to Rees, such instances are rare.

Constraints on production

In deciding whether English is indeed a language characterized by isochrony, it is necessary to establish the constraints on production and perception that might influence isochrony. Two questions that need to be settled are (a) what are the limits of the ability of a speaker to produce regular rhythms, and (b) what are the limits within which a listener perceives regular rhythm. The constraints on production will be discussed first.

Allen has explored the control of speech timing in a series of studies (Allen, 1972, 1973, 1975). In his most recent paper, he summarizes several previous studies of the temporal variability of speech, and reports that the variability of production of speech segments matches the variability of other rhythmic activities such as finger-tapping. Short speech segments have variabilities of about 10%, longer stretches of speech about 4%, while the overall range for standard errors for motor rhythms is about 3–11% of the length of the time intervals being produced.

The variability in interstress interval duration reported by, e.g., Shen & Peterson and by Lea, was considerably larger than 10%. However, the materials used in their studies were quite heterogeneous, and some of the differences they found may have been due to the different type and length of the sentences. I would like to quote Classe (1939) again at this point: isochrony exists, but only under favorable circumstances, namely, "the groups concerned must not contain very different numbers of syllables; the phonetic structure of the component syllables must not differ too widely; the grammatical connexion between the groups and the grammatical structure of these groups must be similar" (p. 85). To test Classe's theory under conditions outlined by Classe, I conducted several studies in which I analyzed relatively more homogeneous material (Lehiste, 1973a, 1975a).

To summarize these studies very briefly, I constructed 17 sentences, each consisting of four metric feet. The sentences were designed to contain monosyllabic feet and various types of disyllabic feet in each of the four positions within the utterance. The feet were established according to criteria set up by Abercrombie (1964, 1965). Two speakers read the randomized sequence of 17 sentences 10 times each. The set of 1360 metric feet was analyzed acoustically, and measurements were made of the duration of the various metric feet. The results indicated that there were some aspects of the data that spoke for the presence of isochrony, and other aspects that spoke against it. The same foot types—like monosyllabic metric feet or disyllabic long–short feet—had remarkably similar durations, especially in positions 2 and 3 (the sentences consisted of four metric feet). But there were clear differences between the average durations of different foot types in the same position. To take a concrete example, the average durations of disyllabic long-short metric feet in productions by the first speaker in positions 1 and 2 differed by only 10 ms; the average durations of monosyllabic metric feet and disyllabic long–short metric feet in the second position, produced by the second speaker, differed by 133 ms. Other differences ranged between these extreme values. Clearly there exist differences in the size of the interstress intervals in production. However, some of the differences look so small that it seems reasonable to assume they would be below the perceptual threshold, which for metric foot durations in the range of 300–500 ms would be about 10% of the duration of the metric foot. If the differences are indeed below the perceptual threshold, they are perceptually irrelevant and from the point of view of perception, the rhythm of the sentences must be considered isochronous.

Limits of perception

Just noticeable differences in duration have been established in a series of earlier investigations (*cf.* Lehiste 1970, for a review). In comparing the differences which emerged in my studies with previously established thresholds for duration, I wondered whether these thresholds were directly applicable to my data, since the published just noticeable differences had been established on the basis of comparing two stimuli, and I was concerned with sequences of four intervals. Therefore I ran a few additional experiments.

I reproduced the temporal patterns of the four-measure sentences as non-speech stimuli (Lehiste 1973a). The durations of the measures were replicated as noise-filled intervals separated by clicks. The stimuli were produced on a Glace-Holmes speech synthesizer. Thirty listeners judged both the actual sentences and the sequences of filled intervals, deciding in each case which of the four units was longest or shortest. In the case of spoken sentences, listeners had considerable difficulty in identifying the measures which were actually the longest or shortest. With nonspeech materials, the corresponding intervals were identified with much greater success. I reasoned that if listeners cannot identify the actually longest or shortest measures in spoken English sentences, the measures must seem to them to have equal duration; if you cannot tell them apart, they must be alike. Isochrony would then be a perceptual phenomenon. The fact that listeners did better with nonspeech materials suggests that the phenomenon is language-bound: isochrony would then characterize spoken language, in this case English, rather than being a general feature of the perception of rhythm. At least if there is a gradient, it is slanted in favor of perception of spoken language.

The just noticeable differences for duration reported in the literature had been established by using nonspeech stimuli, like pure tones or white noise. Since listeners did better with nonspeech stimuli and did not do as well when they listened to speech, one might assume that the just noticeable differences for spoken language are actually larger than the just noticeable differences for duration that have been reported in psychophysical literature. Just noticeable differences established for nonspeech can then be considered the baseline against which the perceptibility of durational differences in speech may be measured. I ran an experiment to establish such a baseline for sequences of four intervals (Lehiste, 1975*b*).

I chose three basic reference durations: 300, 400 and 500 ms. These durations corresponded to the range observed in actual productions of metric feet in my four-measure sentences. For each reference duration, the length of each of the four intervals, one at a time, was decreased and increased in nine 10-ms steps. Three of the four intervals were always of the same duration; one of the four was either shorter or longer. The sequences were again produced using a Glace-Holmes speech synthesizer, randomized and presented to 30 listeners, who were asked to identify first the longest intervals, and on a second presentation, were asked to identify the shortest intervals. To control for response bias, tokens of sequences consisting of equal intervals were also included in the test. In the cases when all intervals had the same duration, the listeners tended to hear the first interval as longer than the others; furthermore, the number of "longest" judgments increased with the reference duration. The increase of "longest" judgments in the first interval seems to have taken place at the expense of the fourth interval, which the listeners tended to underestimate. Making "shortest" judgments, the fourth interval was more frequently judged "shortest", even though all intervals had objectively equal duration. The first interval, too, received a relatively large number of "shortest" judgments.

The judgments listeners made when one interval was actually changed were then compared with the judgments they had made when all intervals were equal. The results showed that to get significant agreement among listeners that a given interval was "longest", an increment was needed that ranged from 30 to more than 100 ms. Differences smaller than 30 ms were never reliably identified. The decrement needed for significant "shortest" judgments ranged also from 30 to 100 ms. There were differences according to reference duration and according to position within the sequence. The greatest changes were required in the duration of the first interval before the difference was perceived. The listeners seemed to be most sensitive to changes that occurred in the third position.

If my assumption is correct and the difficulty in identifying actually longer or shorter intervals may be interpreted to mean that in such cases the intervals must sound alike in duration (if you cannot tell that one of them is different, they must be perceptually the same), then quite large differences in duration are not really perceptible. Most of the differences that I had observed in the production of four-measure sentences were actually smaller than the differences that emerged as the limits of perception in this particular study. There is then very good reason to believe that the differences found in productions of sentences would be even less likely to be perceptible, since my results had shown that listeners perform less accurately when they are judging durational differences within real speech.

There is independent evidence that listeners do better with nonspeech materials than with speech. Fujisaki, Nakamura & Imoto (1973) have shown that accuracy in the perception of duration in word context is inferior to accuracy of discrimination when the same signal is presented in isolation at a nonspeech stimulus. They used noise that was heard as a sibilant in a speech context, and simply as nonspeech noise outside of speech context, but it was the identical signal.

The just noticeable differences in my sequences of four noise-filled intervals ranged from 30 to more than 100 ms. I claim that in listening to speech, the hearer cannot perform any better and is likely to perform somewhat worse, so that the just noticeable differences for speech would be somewhat larger. Differences in the duration of interstress intervals found in several production experiments are of this order of magnitude. For example, Uldall (1971) found that the average duration of monosyllabic feet was 440 ms, disyllabic feet 510 ms, and trisyllabic feet 540 ms. O'Connor (1965) reported a durational difference between the longest and shortest stress group (488 and 566 ms respectively in his materials) of 88 ms. I believe it quite likely that such differences are simply not perceived. Thus sentences that are not produced with absolutely isochronous intervals between stresses may still be perceived as if the interstress intervals were identical.

Imposing structure on perceived sequences

It is, furthermore, quite likely that the listener imposes a rhythmic structure on sequences of interstress intervals in spite of the fact that their durational differences are above the perceptual threshold. This seems to be a fairly general phenomenon. It is well known that when we hear a sequence of short sounds (pulses or clicks), separated from each other by time intervals that are no smaller than about 0·1 s and no longer than 3 s, we will impose some rhythmic structure on the sequence. Allen (1975) has reviewed the literature dealing with the phenomenon. Two related aspects of the problem can be identified. One of them involves imposing a rhythmic structure on a sequence of identical pulses, so that one of the pulses sounds subjectively stronger. The other involves underestimation of the duration of long time intervals and overestimation of short intervals, as a result of which we may hear sequences of only approximately equal time intervals as more equal than they really are. Allen notes that listeners have a general tendency to adjust their perception of time interval durations towards some central, or average, duration; this, in addition to the tendency to impose a rhythm on any sequence of intervals, contributes to the perception of regular rhythm in languages with stress accent.

Suggestions have in fact been made by several researchers in recent publications that listeners may partially compensate for existing durational constraints and perceive speech as being more rhythmic than it really is. Barnwell (1971) attempted to develop an algorithm for segment durations and isolated a number of durational constraints in English which counteract an observed tendency to make words approximately the same size. He concluded that all words cannot be forced into the same size, but only moved in the proper direction, and conjectured that this may have some importance in the perception of rhythm in English. I would like to quote his insightful conjecture in full (Barnwell, 1971, p. 88):

> "The implication is that speech attempts to be very rhythmic, but fails
> because of durational constraints. Hence it may be that what is heard as

> rhythmic may be really the interpretation of changes in duration in the direction of true rhythm. Hence, just as the perception of pitch is not necessarily directly related to F_0, so the perception of rhythm may not be directly related to true time intervals in speech."

Several perceptual studies by Huggins (1972*a*, *b*) can be interpreted as supporting the idea that isochrony is a perceptual phenomenon. Huggins studied the effects of durational changes in segments on the perceived "normality" of sentences. He found that there was a small negative correlation between changes involving two adjacent segments when the change to the second segment was in the direction towards re-establishing isochrony (restoring the onset time of the next stressed vowel to its former distance from the onset of the preceding stressed vowel).

Some data pointing towards the same conclusion were presented by Coleman in an as yet unpublished dissertation written at the University of Washington (Coleman, 1974). The dissertation constitutes a study of acoustic and perceptual attributes of isochrony in spoken English. Coleman investigated isochrony within sentences with controlled phonetic and grammatical context. Ten speakers read 16 real and 16 nonsense word samples placed in a carrier sentence. Each word contained two interstress intervals, and each interval contained one stressed syllable and from zero to three unstressed syllables. Forty listeners made perceptual judgments comparing the duration of the first and second interstress interval in each sentence. The interstress interval increased significantly as syllables were added; but the listeners tended to hear the interstress intervals as more isochronous than they really were.

Manipulation of durational constraints to achieve isochrony

I believe to have shown that there exists a tendency to hear spoken English as possessing a certain degree of isochronicity. First of all, many actual differences in the duration of interstress intervals may be below the perceptual threshold. Second, listeners tend to impose a rhythmic structure on stretches of sounds and thus subjectively to perceive isochrony even in sequences where the durational differences should be above the perceptual threshold. There is nevertheless some evidence that speakers also have a tendency to aim at isochrony in production. This emerges from the way in which they treat durational constraints in production.

If speakers do indeed aim at isochrony in production, they have to make certain adjustments in the duration of speech sounds and their sequences. For this purpose, various well-known constraints on duration in production must be modified in the direction toward isochrony; such constraints that have not been modified must be compensated for in perception to arrive at perceived isochrony. There is some evidence for both processes, in spite of the counter-evidence presented earlier (O'Connor 1968; Lea 1974).

The factors that constrain the duration of segments have been described by Lehiste (1970) and recently reviewed in detail by Klatt (1976). I shall therefore limit myself to a few examples. It is generally known that in English, the duration of vowels depends on the nature of the postvocalic consonant; the duration of consonants is affected by their membership in clusters. Besides segmental and suprasegmental factors, the duration of segments is influenced by their position within a word. Lehiste (1960) showed that word-initial consonants are characterized by greater length. Non-final segments in words of more than one syllable are shorter, the farther away they are from the end of the word: their duration appears to depend on the number of syllables that remain to be produced.

260   *I. Lehiste*

Word-final segments, on the other hand, tend to be lengthened (Lehiste, 1972; Nooteboom, 1972; Lindblom & Rapp, 1973; Oller, 1973).

The influence of the position of the word within a sentence on the duration of segments (and syllables) has been known for some time. Fónagy & Magdics (1960) showed that a syllable at the end of an utterance is longer. Gaitenby (1965) demonstrated that words immediately preceding a pause receive extra length. Klatt (1975) found segment lengthening at phrase boundaries. Lea & Kloker (1975) showed that lengthening affects several syllables before the end of a sentence.

Several of the listed factors seem to be relatable to isochrony through the intermediate stage of preserving the durations of words resp. adjusting the durations of different words so that their durations approach a common average. The shortening of consonants in clusters seems to be directed towards achieving this purpose. Another example of a similar phenomenon would be the observation that the addition of resonants either before or after the vowel in a monosyllabic word beginning and ending in an obstruent does not increase the duration of the time span between the obstruents (Lehiste, 1975c). The reduction in duration of monosyllabic stems when various suffixes are added is a manifestation of the same tendency (Lehiste, 1972): in each case, the duration of the word as a whole is changed less than it would have been if new segments had been added without adjustment in the duration of the segments already present.

The tendency to keep word length constant may be more general, since it is also found in languages for which isochrony has not been claimed. Rapp (1971), working with Swedish materials, found evidence for compensation between consonant and vowel durations within a word. In her study, consonants and consonant clusters varied in duration between 100 and 225 ms, while the total length of words varied between 625 and 670 ms. Since the latter variation was smaller, one can infer that a compensation has taken place in the other segments. The compensation showed up as a slightly negative correlation between intervocalic consonants and the other segments of the word.

In addition to examples of compensation in perception presented above (Barnwell, 1971; Huggins, 1972a, b; Coleman, 1974), I would like to refer again to the results of my study concerning the perception of the duration of sequences of four intervals (Lehiste, 1975b). As was mentioned above, the duration of the fourth interval was regularly underestimated: when all intervals had objectively equal durations, the fourth was most frequently judged "shortest". It seems that listeners expect the last interval (corresponding to the last word before a pause) to be longer than the other intervals, and if the extra length is not present, the listeners hear the interval as shorter than what they would normally expect.

Integration of isochrony into English syntax

Having now established that there exists a tendency toward isochrony in production as well as in perception, I would like to review the steps that have led me to the conclusion that isochrony is integrated into the syntax of English in at least one quite specific way.

My studies of the relationship between speech timing and syntax started with an exploration of the strategies speakers use for disambiguating syntactically ambiguous sentences. In a paper published in 1973 (Lehiste, 1973b), I reported the results of an investigation involving 15 ambiguous sentences, produced by four speakers, and listened to by 30 listeners. Some examples might be the following: *The hostess greeted the girl with a smile* (either the hostess smiled or the girl smiled); *The old men and women stayed at home* (either the men were old, or both the men and women were old), etc. The speakers first read the list of sentences; then the ambiguities were pointed out to them, and I asked which of the possible meanings they had had in mind. The speakers then produced each sentence again, this time making a conscious effort to produce first one and then the other meaning. I thus had three versions of each sentence—a spontaneous production of one meaning, and an intentionally disambiguated version for each of the two meanings. Listeners were given the two possible meanings and asked which of the two the speaker had had in mind. Some of the sentences received very high scores, while others were not successfully disambiguated. Of special interest are the cases in which the spontaneous version received a random score, and the consciously disambiguated versions were correctly identified. This made it possible to analyze the means that the speakers had used to achieve disambiguation. In every case, successful disambiguation was achieved when the speakers had increased the interstress interval that contained the relevant boundary. For example, the production of the sentence "The old men and women stayed at home" by speaker LS received 100% correct identification for both meanings. When the meaning was "*the old* (*men and women*)" (*men and women* containing no boundary), the duration of the sequence *men and women* was 690 ms; when the meaning was "(*the old men*) *and women*" (the sequence *men and women* containing a boundary), the duration of the same sequence of words was 1225 ms. The speakers would use several ways to achieve the same aim, namely lengthening of the interstress interval: the most straightforward, of course, was the insertion of a pause, but equally successful were other means like lengthening one or more segmental sounds preceding the boundary.

Similar results were obtained by O'Malley, Kloker & Dara-Abrams (1973) in a study of parentheses in spoken algebraic expressions. They found that the speakers used "junctures" to indicate the presence of parentheses. The "junctures", which the authors define as "an abstract linguistic unit that is postulated to account for the ability of a native listener to locate certain kinds of boundaries in a spoken utterance on the basis of direct acoustic cues and/or his knowledge and expectations about the lexical, syntactic, and semantic constraints of English", were associated with pitch changes, vowel elongation, and pauses. Their strongest perceptual correlate was silence: there was an almost perfect correlation between measured silence and perceived juncture. Mathematically experienced and mathematically naïve listeners (four and six subjects respectively) were equally successful in recovering the parentheses. The authors suggest that the acoustic cues used by the speakers to indicate syntactic structure in this restricted domain of discourse may have a more general applicability.

O'Malley, Kloker & Dara-Abrams located their boundary signals at given points in a linear sequence, without relating them to the general rhythmic structure of the utterances. Pauses were the primary cue, accompanied by segmental lengthening and by pitch changes. In a more recent study, Lehiste, Olive & Streeter (1976) showed that increase in the interstress interval is a sufficient boundary signal, even in the absence of intonation and specific segmental lengthening. We processed ten of the sentences used in Lehiste, 1973 (those that had been successfully disambiguated) through an analysis-resynthesis program, changed fundamental frequency to monotone, and manipulated systematically the duration of interstress intervals. A listening test, similar to the one used in Lehiste, 1973*b*, was given to 30 subjects. Disambiguation was achieved when the relevant interval reached a certain duration, the actual value of which depended on the particular sentence. I would like to emphasize here that we did not insert any pauses; neither did we introduce pre-pausal lengthening. The interstress interval was increased by increasing the duration of each sampling period by the same factor; the durational relationships of the segments to

262   *I. Lehiste*

each other remained the same. Thus the disambiguation was produced solely by increasing the interstress interval, and the results of our study show that this is indeed a sufficient cue for signalling the presence of a boundary.

The important conclusion to be drawn here is the following. Increase of an interstress interval can be used to signal the presence of a syntactic boundary precisely because this increase constitutes a deviation from the expected pattern. The listener expects isochrony— expects the stresses to follow each other at approximately equal intervals. A deviation from the pattern—an increase in the interstress interval large enough to be perceived— could not signal the presence of the boundary unless the pattern exists in the first place. In principle, of course, a deviation from the pattern could be used to signal anything. In English, it appears to be part of the knowledge of both speakers and hearers that an increase in the interstress interval signals the presence of a syntactic boundary. It is in this sense that isochrony is integrated into the grammar of English at the syntactic level.

This paper summarizes much of my research concerning isochrony and the relationship between syntax and speech timing. The research has been supported in part by the National Science Foundation Grant No. GS-31494. A preliminary version of the paper was presented on 28 December 1975, at the Modern Language Association meeting in San Francisco. The paper was written while the author was in residence at the Center for Advanced Study in the Behavioral Sciences as a National Endowment of Humanities fellow; the findings and conclusions presented in the paper do not necessarily represent the view of the Endowment.

References

Abercrombie, D. (1964). Syllable quantity and enclitics in English. In *In Honour of Daniel Jones* (Abercrombie, D., Fry, D. B., MacCarthy, P. A. D., Scott, N. C. & Trim, J. L. M., Eds). Pp. 216–22. London: Longmans.

Abercrombie, D. (1965). A phonetician's view of verse structure. In *Studies in Phonetics and Linguistics*. Pp. 16–25. London: Oxford University Press.

Allen, George D. (1972). The location of rhythmic stress beats in English: an experimental study II. *Language and Speech* **15**, 179–95.

Allen, George D. (1973). Segmental timing control in speech production. *Journal of Phonetics* **1**, 219–37.

Allen, George D. (1975). Speech rhythm: its relation to performance universals and articulatory timing. *Journal of Phonetics* **3**, 75–86.

Barnwell, T. P. (1971). An algorithm for segment durations in reading machine context. *Technical Report 479*. Cambridge, Mass.: M.I.T. Research Laboratory of Electronics.

Bolinger, D. L. (1965). Pitch accent and sentence rhythm. In *Forms of English: Accent, Morpheme, Order*. P. 163 *ff*. Cambridge, Mass.: Harvard University Press.

Classe, André. (1939). *The Rhythm of English Prose*. Oxford: Blackwell.

Coleman, Colette L. (1974). A study of acoustical and perceptual attributes of isochrony in spoken English. Ph.D. Dissertation, University of Washington.

Fónagy, I. & Magdics, K. (1960). Speed of utterance in phrases of different lengths. *Language and Speech* **4**, 179–92.

Fujisaki, H., Nakamura, K. & Imoto, T. (1973). Auditory perception of duration of speech and non-speech stimuli. *Research Institute of Logopedics and Phoniatrics, Annual Bulletin No. 7*. Pp. 45–64. University of Tokyo.

Gaitenby, J. (1965). The elastic word. *Haskins Laboratories Status Report on Speech Research*, SR-2, 3.1–3.12.

Halliday, M. A. K. (1967). *Intonation and Grammar in British English*. The Hague: Mouton.

Huggins, A. W. F. (1972*a*). Just noticeable differences for segment duration in natural speech. *Journal of the Acoustical Society of America* **51**, 1270–78.

Huggins, A. W. F. (1972*b*). On the perception of temporal phenomena in speech. *Journal of the Acoustical Society of America* **51**, 1279–90.

Klatt, Dennis H. (1975). Vowel lengthening is syntactically determined in a connected discourse. *Journal of Phonetics* **3**, 129–40.

Klatt, D. H. (1976). Linguistic uses of segmental duration in English: acoustic and perceptual evidence. *Journal of the Acoustical Society of America* **59**, 1208–21.

Lea, W. A. (1974). Prosodic aids to speech recognition: IV. A general strategy for prosodically-guided speech understanding. *Univac Report No. PX10791*. St. Paul, Minn.: Sperry Univac, DSD.

Lea, W. A. & Kloker, D. R. (1975). Prosodic aids to speech recognition: VI. Timing cues to linguistic structure and improved computer programs for prosodic analysis. *Univac Report No. PX11239*. St. Paul, Minn.: Sperry Univac, DSD.

Lehiste, Ilse (1960). An acoustic–phonetic study of internal open juncture. *Phonetica* **5** (Supplement), 1–54.

Lehiste, Ilse (1970). *Suprasegmentals*. Cambridge, Mass.: M.I.T. Press.

Lehiste, Ilse (1972). The timing of utterances and linguistic boundaries. *Journal of the Acoustical Society of America* **51**, 2018–24.

Lehiste, Ilse (1973a). Rhythmic units and syntactic units in production and perception. *Journal of the Acoustical Society of America* **54**, 1228–34.

Lehiste, Ilse (1973b). Phonetic disambiguation of syntactic ambiguity. *Glossa* **7**, 107–22.

Lehiste, Ilse (1975a). The role of temporal factors in the establishment of linguistic units and boundaries. In *Phonologica* 1972 (Dressler, Wolfgang U. & Mares, F. V., Eds). Pp. 115–22. München-Salzburg: Wilhelm Fink Verlag.

Lehiste, Ilse (1975b). The perception of duration within sequences of four intervals. Paper presented at the 8th International Congress of Phonetic Sciences, Leeds, Aug. 21.

Lehiste, Ilse (1975c). The syllable nucleus as a unit of timing. *Proceedings of the Eleventh International Congress of Linguists*. Bologna-Florence, 1972. (Heilman, Luigi, Ed.). Pp. 929–32. Societa editrice il Mulino Bologna.

Lehiste, Ilse, Olive, J. P. and Streeter, L. A. (1976). The role of duration in disambiguating syntactically ambiguous sentences. *Journal of the Acoustical Society of America* **60**, 1199–1202.

Lindblom, B. & Rapp, K. (1973). Some temporal regularities of spoken Swedish. *Papers from the Institute of Linguistics, University of Stockholm*, Publication **21**.

Nooteboom, S. G. (1972). *Production and Perception of Vowel Duration. A Study of Durational Properties of Vowels in Dutch*. Utrecht.

O'Connor, J. D. (1965). The perception of time intervals. *Progress Report 2*, Phonetics Laboratory, University College, London, 11–15.

O'Connor, J. D. (1968). The duration of the foot in relation to the number of component sound-segments. Phonetics Laboratory, University College, London. *Progress Report 3*, 1–6.

Oller, D. K. (1973). The duration of speech segments: the effect of position in utterance and word length. *Journal of the Acoustical Society of America* **54**, 1235–47.

O'Malley, M. H., Kloker, D. R. & Dara-Abrams, B. (1973). Recovering parentheses from spoken algebraic expressions. *IEEE Transactions on Audio and Electro-acoustics AU-21*, 217–20.

Pike, K. L. (1945). *The Intonation of American English*, Ann Arbor, Mich.: University of Michigan Press.

Rapp, K. (1971). A study of syllable timing. *STL-QPSR* **1**, 14–19.

Rees, Martin. (1975). The domain of isochrony. Edinburgh University, Department of Linguistics. *Work in Progress* **8**, 14–28.

Shen, Yao, & Peterson, G. G. (1962). Isochronism in English. University of Buffalo, Studies in Linguistics, *Occasional Papers* **9**, 1–36.

Uldall, E. T. (1971). Isochronous stresses in R.P. In *Form and Substance: Phonetic and Linguistic Papers Presented to Eli Fischer-Jørgensen*, (Hammerich, L. L. Jakobson, Roman & Zwirner, Eberhard, Eds). Pp. 205–10. Copenhagen: Akademisk Forlag.

Uldall, E. T. (1972). Relative durations of syllables in two-syllable rhythmic feet in R.P. in connected speech. Edinburgh University Department of Linguistics. *Work in Progress* **5**, 110–111.

THE JOURNAL OF THE ACOUSTICAL SOCIETY OF AMERICA   VOLUME 27, NUMBER 2   MARCH, 1955

An Analysis of Perceptual Confusions Among Some English Consonants

GEORGE A. MILLER AND PATRICIA E. NICELY

Lincoln Laboratory, Massachusetts Institute of Technology, Cambridge, Massachusetts

(Received December 1, 1954)

Sixteen English consonants were spoken over voice communication systems with frequency distortion and with random masking noise. The listeners were forced to guess at every sound and a count was made of all the different errors that resulted when one sound was confused with another. With noise or low-pass filtering the confusions fall into consistent patterns, but with high-pass filtering the errors are scattered quite randomly. An articulatory analysis of these 16 consonants provides a system of five articulatory features or "dimensions" that serve to characterize and distinguish the different phonemes: voicing, nasality, affrication, duration, and place of articulation. The data indicate that voicing and nasality are little affected and that place is severely affected by low-pass and noisy systems. The indications are that the perception of any one of these five features is relatively independent of the perception of the others, so that it is as if five separate, simple channels were involved rather than a single complex channel.

THE over-all effects of noise and of frequency distortion upon the average intelligibility of human speech are by now rather well understood. One limitation of the existing studies, however, is that results are given almost exclusively in terms of the articulation score, the percentage of the spoken words that the listener hears correctly. By implication, therefore, all of the listener's errors are treated as equivalent and no knowledge of the perceptual confusions is available. The fact is, however, that mistakes are often far from random. A closer look at the problem suggests that we might learn something about speech perception and might even improve communication if we knew what kinds of errors occur and how to avoid the most frequent ones. Such was the reasoning that led to the present study.

Perhaps the major reason that confusion data are not already available is the cost of collecting them. Every phoneme must have a chance to be confused with every other phoneme and that large number of potential confusions must be tested repeatedly until statistically reliable estimates of all the probabilities are obtained. Such data are obtained from testing programs far more extensive than would be required to evaluate some specific system.

In order to reduce the magnitude of the problem to more manageable size, we decided to study a smaller set of phonemes and to explore the potential value of such data within that smaller universe. Since the consonants are notoriously confusable and are quite important for intelligibility, we decided to begin with a comparison of 16 consonants: $|p|$, $|t|$, $|k|$, $|f|$, $|\theta|$, $|s|$, $|\int|$, $|b|$, $|d|$, $|g|$, $|v|$, $|\eth|$, $|z|$, $|\mathfrak{z}|$, $|m|$, and $|n|$. These 16 make up almost three quarters of the consonants we utter in normal speech and about 40 percent of all phonemes, vowels included. It was our suspicion that when errors begin to occur in articulation tests, the culprits would usually be found among this set of 16 phonemes. A further reason for being interested in consonants is that the information-bearing aspects of these sounds are less well understood than is the case for vowels; we hoped to pick up some clues as to what the important features of these phonemes might be.

The major portion of the work to be reported here was done with the aforementioned 16 consonants. However, a number of other, even smaller, experiments were conducted with subsets of those 16. In general, the results of the smaller studies agree with and support the conclusions of the larger study. These results will be introduced into the discussion where appropriate, but the major emphasis will be placed on the 16-consonant data.

EXPERIMENTAL PROCEDURES

Five female subjects served as talkers and listening crew; when one talked, the other four listened. Since the tests lasted several months, some of the original crew members departed and were replaced; care was taken to train new members adequately before their data were used. The subjects were, with one Canadian exception, citizens of the United States. None had defects of speech or hearing and all were able to pronounce the 16 nonsense syllables without any noticeable dialect. Since rhythm, intonation, and vowel differences were not involved, we have assumed that regional differences in speech habits were not a significant source of variability in the data.

The 16 consonants were spoken initially before the vowel |a| (father). The list of 200 nonsense syllables spoken by the talker was prepared in advance so that the probability of each syllable was 1 in 16 and so that their order was quite random within the list and from one list to the next. The syllables were spoken at an average rate of one every 2.1 seconds and the listeners were forced to respond—to guess, if necessary—for every syllable. When the speech was near the threshold of hearing, the listeners were kept in synchrony with the talker by a tone that was turned on at fixed intervals. Otherwise, a 2.1-second pause was inserted after every block of five syllables. With four listeners, there were 800 syllable-response events per talker for which confusions could be studied. Pooling the five talkers gives us 4000 observations at each condition tested.

At the completion of each test of 200 syllables, the talker went from the control room back to the test room and the crew proceeded to tabulate their responses. Each listener had a table showing what syllable was spoken and what syllable she had written in response; each cell of the table represented one of the $16 \times 16 = 256$ possible syllable-response pairs, and the number entered in that cell was the frequency with which that syllable-response pair occurred. We shall refer to such tables as "confusion matrices."

A headrest on the talker's chair insured that the distance to the WE-633A microphone was constant at 15 inches. The speech 15 inches from the talker's lips was about 60 db re 0.0002 dyne/cm². The speech voltage was amplified, then filtered (if frequency distortion was to be used), then mixed with noise, then amplified again and presented to the listeners by PDR-8 earphones. In all tests the noise voltage was fixed at −32 db below one volt across the earphones and the signal-to-noise ratio was varied by changing the gain in the speech channel. A separate amplifier was used to drive a monitoring VU-meter with the output of the microphone. The gain to the VU-meter was fixed so that the talker could maintain her speech level at a constant value. The talkers did succeed rather well in keeping a constant level; several hundred sample readings of peak deflections gave an average of +0.18 VU with a standard deviation of 1.04. However, it should be noted that with this system, the signal-to-noise ratios are set by the peak deflection of the VU needle and that peak occurs during the vowel. The consonants, which are consistently weaker than the vowel, were actually presented at much less favorable signal-to-noise ratios than such a vowel-to-noise ratio would seem to indicate. It was, therefore, especially important to keep the same speech level for all tests since otherwise the vowel-to-consonant ratio might have changed significantly and the data would not be comparable.

The frequency response of the system was essentially that of the earphones, which are reasonably uniform between 200 and 6500 cps. A low-pass filter at 7000 cps in the random noise generator insured that noise voltages could be converted directly to sound pressure levels according to the earphone calibration. A Krohn-Hite 310-A variable band-pass filter was used to introduce frequency distortion into the speech channel; the skirts dropped off at a rate of 24 db per octave and the cutoff frequency was taken as the frequency 3 db below the peak in the pass band.

RESULTS

The results of these tests are confusion matrices. Since these matrices represent a considerable investment and since other workers may wish to apply summary statistics differing from those which we have chosen, the complete confusion matrices are presented in Tables I–XVII. Data for all listeners and all talkers have been pooled so that 4000 observations are summarized in each matrix; on the average, each syllable was judged 250 times under every test condition.

Tables I–VI summarize the data obtained when the speech-to-noise ratio was −18, −12, −6, 0, +6, and +12 db and the band width was 200–6500 cps. Tables VII–XII summarize the data when the high-pass cutoff was fixed at 200 cps and the low-pass cutoff was 300, 400, 600, 1200, 2500, and 5000 cps with a speech-to-noise ratio corresponding to +12 db for unfiltered speech. Tables XII–XVII summarize the data when the low-pass cutoff was fixed at 5000 cps and the high-pass cutoff was 200, 1000, 2000, 2500, 3000, and 4500 cps with a speech-to-noise ratio that would have been +12 db if the speech had not been filtered.

In these tables the syllables that were spoken are indicated by the consonants listed vertically in the first column on the left. The syllables that were written by the listener are indicated horizontally across the top of the table. The number in each cell is the frequency that each stimulus-response pair was observed. The number of correct responses can be obtained by totalling the frequencies along the main diagonal. Row sums would give the frequencies that each syllable was written by the listeners.

340   G. A. MILLER AND P. E. NICELY

A GENERALIZATION OF THE ARTICULATION SCORE

The standard articulation score is obtained from Tables I–XVII by summing the frequencies along the main diagonal and dividing the total by n, the number of observations. Although this score is useful, it tells us nothing about the distribution of errors among the off-diagonal cells. If we wanted to reconstruct an adequate picture of the confusion matrix, we would need other scores to supplement the usual articulation score.

In order to generalize the articulation score, we can combine stimuli (and their corresponding responses) into groups in such a way that confusions within groups are more likely than confusions between groups. Combining stimuli creates a smaller confusion matrix that shows the confusions between groups, and the sum along the diagonal gives a new articulation score for this new, smaller matrix. The new score will be greater than the original score, since all the responses that were originally correct remain so and in addition all the confusions within each group are now considered to be "correct" in the new score. If the original score, A, is supplemented with such an additional score, A', we would reconstruct the data matrix by spreading the fraction A along the main diagonal. Then $A' - A$ would go off the diagonal but within groups, and $1 - A'$ would be distributed off the diagonal between groups. This general strategy can be repeated quite simply if the several groupings used form a monotonic increasing sequence of sets: $A \leq A' \leq A''$, etc.

A simple example will illustrate this technique. A test was conducted at $S/N = -12$ db over a 200–6500-cps channel using six stop consonants in front of the vowel $|a|$. The confusion matrix for 2000 observations

TABLE I. Confusion matrix for $S/N = -18$ db and frequency response of 200–6500 cps.

	p	t	k	f	θ	s	ʃ	b	d	g	v	ð	z	ʒ	m	n
p	14	27	22	23	25	22	14	15	16	7	17	11	12	11	16	12
t	16	26	21	15	15	18	14	7	10	6	17	9	13	11	9	13
k	20	22	24	15	14	29	12	4	11	9	12	10	16	11	17	14
f	27	22	27	23	13	12	10	19	20	14	16	16	15	3	13	18
θ	17	18	18	13	15	21	12	14	20	14	23	6	14	9	12	14
s	18	17	23	11	18	21	17	11	24	15	15	16	11	13	17	5
ʃ	16	20	27	17	13	37	14	10	21	7	20	18	9	8	16	15
b	12	11	24	15	19	15	12	24	20	19	24	12	15	11	18	17
d	16	24	18	13	15	15	14	22	25	21	25	17	18	13	15	25
g	11	20	29	9	18	18	15	26	30	14	18	14	16	20	24	22
v	9	17	18	11	7	12	9	25	14	13	15	15	19	11	12	17
ð	16	11	10	7	6	14	10	20	17	18	15	7	17	12	18	18
z	18	18	15	9	13	19	7	22	14	9	21	12	23	10	22	12
ʒ	8	16	17	14	12	15	7	22	18	8	15	11	15	11	18	13
m	19	24	15	14	14	14	8	14	15	12	13	8	11	6	25	28
n	11	18	20	6	9	18	9	14	14	13	9	8	10	12	33	32

TABLE II. Confusion matrix for $S/N = -12$ db and frequency response 200–6500 cps.

	p	t	k	f	θ	s	ʃ	b	d	g	v	ð	z	ʒ	m	n
p	51	53	65	22	19	6	11	2		2	3	3	1	5	8	5
t	64	57	74	20	24	22	14	2	3	1	1	2	1	1	5	1
k	50	42	62	22	18	16	11	4	1	1	1	2			4	2
f	31	22	28	85	34	15	11	3	5		8	8	3		3	
θ	26	22	25	63	45	27	12	6	9	3	11	9	3	2	7	2
s	16	15	16	33	24	53	48	3	5	6	3	1	6	2		1
ʃ	23	32	20	14	27	25	115	1	4	5	3		6	3	4	2
b	4	2	2	18	7	7	1	60	18	18	44	25	14	6	20	10
d	3		1	4	7	4	11	18	48	35	16	24	26	14	9	12
g	3	1	1	1	4	5	7	20	38	29	16	29	29	38	10	9
v		1	1	12	5	4	5	37	20	23	71	16	14	4	14	9
ð		1	4	17	2	3	2	53	31	25	50	33	23	5	13	6
z	6	1	2	2	6	14	8	23	29	27	24	19	40	26	3	6
ʒ	3	2	2	1		6	7	7	30	23	9	7	39	77	5	14
m		1			1	1		11	3	6	8	11		1	109	60
n	1			1		1		2	2	6	7	1	1	9	84	145

TABLE III. Confusion matrix for $S/N = -6$ db and frequency response of 200–6500 cps.

	p	t	k	f	θ	s	ʃ	b	d	g	v	ð	z	ʒ	m	n
p	80	43	64	17	14	6	2	1	1			1	1		2	
t	71	84	55	5	9	3	8	1					1	2	2	3
k	66	76	107	12	8	9	4					1			1	
f	18	12	9	175	48	11	1	7	2	1	2	2				
θ	19	17	16	104	64	32	7	5	4	5	6	4	5			
s	8	5	4	23	39	107	45	4	2	3	1	1	3	2		1
ʃ	1	6	3	4	6	29	195		3							1
b	1			5	4	4		136	10	9	47	16	6	1	5	4
d							8	5	80	45	11	20	20	26	1	
g					2			3	63	66	3	19	37	56		3
v				2		2		48	5	5	145	45	12		4	
ð					6			31	6	17	86	58	21	5	6	4
z					1	1	1	7	20	27	16	28	94	44		1
ʒ								1	26	18	3	8	45	129		2
m	1							4			4	1	3		177	46
n					4			1	5	2		7	1	6	47	163

TABLE IV. Confusion matrix for $S/N = 0$ db and frequency response of 200–6500 cps.

	p	t	k	f	θ	s	ʃ	b	d	g	v	ð	z	ʒ	m	n
p	150	38	88	7	13											
t	30	193	28	1												
k	86	45	138	4	1		1									1
f	4	3	5	199	46	4		1				1			1	
θ	11	6	4	85	114	10					2					
s		2	1	5	38	170	10			2						
ʃ		3	3			3	267									
b				7	4			235	4		34	27	1			
d									189	48		4	8	11		
g									74	161		4	8	25		
v				3	1			19		2	177	29	4	1		
ð								7		10	64	105	18			
z									17	23	4	22	132	26		
ʒ									2	3	1	1	9	191		1
m								1							201	6
n												3		1	8	240

TABLE V. Confusion matrix for $S/N = +6$ db and frequency response of 200–6500 cps.

	p	t	k	f	θ	s	ʃ	b	d	g	v	ð	z	ʒ	m	n
p	162	10	55	5	3							1				
t	8	270	14													
k	38	6	171	1												
f	5	1	2	207	57			3			1					
θ	5	1	2	71	142	3					2	2				
s			1	1	7	232	2			1						
ʃ						1	239									
b				1	2			214			31	12				
d									206	14		9	1	2		
g								11	64	194		4	2	1		
v				1	1			14		2	205	39	5			1
ð								2		4	55	179	22	2		
z									3	10	2	20	198	3		
ʒ									3	4			2	215		
m															217	3
n								1							2	285

342

G. A. MILLER AND P. E. NICELY

TABLE VI. Confusion matrix for $S/N = +12$ db and frequency response of 200–6500 cps.

	p	t	k	f	θ	s	ʃ	b	d	g	v	ð	z	ʒ	m	n
p	240		41	2	1											
t	1	252	1	1						1						
k	18	3	219													
f				225	24			5			2					
θ	9		1	69	185			3				1				
s						232										
ʃ							236									
b					1			242			24	12	1			
d									213	22			1			
g					1				33	203		3				
v								6			171	30			1	
ð					1			1		3	22	208	4			1
z									2	4	1	7	238			
ʒ														244		
m												1			274	1
n																252

TABLE VII. Confusion matrix for $S/N = +12$ db and frequency response of 200–300 cps.

	p	t	k	f	θ	s	ʃ	b	d	g	v	ð	z	ʒ	m	n
p	47	61	68	15	11	17	9	3	3	1		1	2	2	3	1
t	59	63	64	19	15	14	13	3	4	1		5	2	2	2	2
k	37	47	56	10	13	15	10	1	2	1		2		1		1
f	21	29	21	38	37	47	19	2	2	1		2	2	3	3	1
θ	13	23	25	23	39	54	39	2	2	1		5	1		4	5
s	16	25	10	29	52	65	34	1	4	2	4	5	1	1	1	2
ʃ	15	33	23	18	28	70	41	1	1			7	3	1	1	2
b		1	1	8	8	5	3	98	28	17	38	19	9	2	8	7
d	1		1	11	7	12	5	70	84	33	12	10	24	9	1	
g	4	1	2	7	5	13	8	56	74	33	13	15	21	13	6	1
v		2	1	1	2	1	1	44	34	18	77	34	36	14	2	1
ð	1				3		1	22	16	19	45	46	45	23	11	8
z	2	3	2	2	4	3	2	15	15	20	46	35	64	21	2	
ʒ	1	1		1	2		1	11	15	24	54	42	70	39	2	5
m			1	1	2	2		1	3	3	4	5	1	4	161	60
n	1	3	2	1	1	1	2	1	3	2	2	4	2	2	133	108

TABLE VIII. Confusion matrix for $S/N = +12$ db and frequency response of 200–400 cps.

	p	t	k	f	θ	s	ʃ	b	d	g	v	ð	z	ʒ	m	n
p	72	68	90	20	15	4	1	2	4	1		1				2
t	73	72	74	20	8	6	3	1	2	2		2		1		
k	63	74	127	9	7	5	2			1		1	1	1		1
f	7	7	10	63	69	41	8	3	1	1	1	3		1	1	
θ	5	8	11	60	85	45	14	2	4	2	6	5	1			
s	1	6	5	19	49	125	60	5	2	1	2	9	4			
ʃ	2	6	8	8	22	69	89	2	4	1		3	5	1		
b		1	1	19	14	5		134	20	13	14	11	4	1	2	1
d			2		1	6	4	19	120	23	2	3	11	3	1	2
g			2	1		5	1	11	116	59	8	7	11	4	1	2
v		1	1	1	1	2		25	4	8	111	55	18	2	2	2
ð		1	1	6	5	1		43	16	15	75	66	23	11	1	4
z	2		2	1	5	5	2	21	20	17	18	33	91	25	1	1
ʒ					4		2	1	27	29	11	16	83	78	1	
m								12	3		1				219	57
n					1	1		12	3	1	1	2			99	120

PERCEPTUAL CONFUSIONS AMONG CONSONANTS

TABLE IX. Confusion matrix for $S/N = +12$ db and frequency response of 200–600 cps.

	p	t	k	f	θ	s	ʃ	b	d	g	v	ð	z	ʒ	m	n
p	115	43	70	10	3	2						1				
t	69	63	71	4	4							1				
k	59	49	134	4	1					1						
f	2	3	2	126	89	11	1	2			1	8	1		1	1
θ	2	1	1	103	97	35	7	2	1		5	1				1
s	3	3		34	88	93	26	4	1			7		1		
ʃ	3	6	12	7	31	98	87	1	2	1	2	1	1			
b			1	10	5	1		201	13		13	4				
d		1		1	1	6	1	29	169	39	3	3	6	5		
g				1		7		12	99	97		4	8	11		1
v				5	2			14	1	2	141	57	9	4	1	
ð								10	6	10	109	90	31	7	1	
z						1	2	3	15	30	17	42	116	22		
ʒ			1				1		10	21	8	17	110	116		
m						1						1			215	39
n				1											119	120

TABLE X. Confusion matrix for $S/N = +12$ db and frequency response of 200–1200 cps.

	p	t	k	f	θ	s	ʃ	b	d	g	v	ð	z	ʒ	m	n
p	165	46	31	3	1			1				1				
t	91	83	68	4	1	2		1				2				
k	48	55	147	2	3						1					
f	16	4	3	146	60	3	2	11			1	2				
θ	4	3		109	76	17	2	12	1			2	1	1		
s	2	1	1	43	83	83	11	3		1	1	7				
ʃ	1	6	2	12	41	86	90		6	4		4				
b				14	5			223	4		5	1				
d	1				1	3	4	4	173	37		2	1	2		
g	1					1			102	107	1	2	7	7		
v	2	2		2	1			23	1	2	163	62	14	3	1	
ð		1				3	2	27	6	32	87	107	36	7		
z	1							4	12	48	10	15	114	39		1
ʒ							1		3	35	1	16	60	134	2	
m	1											1			229	9
n															5	247

TABLE XI. Confusion matrix for $S/N = +12$ db and frequency response of 200–2500 cps.

	p	t	k	f	θ	s	ʃ	b	d	g	v	ð	z	ʒ	m	n
p	215	29	26	5	1											
t	74	91	47													
k	15	16	201													
f	6		1	186	31	2		3				7				
θ	1	5	1	93	81	25	1	1		2	2	4				
s	1	3	1	31	78	142	9	1		1		5				
ʃ		1	1			23	210			1						
b				11	6	1		206	4		11	1				
d							1	1	217	30			1	6		
g				2		1	1	1	54	169		1		3		
v				1	2	1		36		1	178	39	9	1	1	
ð				3	6	2		14		17	58	146	45	1		
z						2			17	40	7	24	122	20		
ʒ				1			5		5	9		11	11	265		
m															242	18
n															2	242

344

G. A. MILLER AND P. E. NICELY

TABLE XII. Confusion matrix for $S/N = +12$ db and frequency response of 200–5000 cps.

	p	t	k	f	θ	s	ʃ	b	d	g	v	ð	z	ʒ	m	n
p	228	7	7	1			1									
t		236	8													
k	26	5	213													
f	6	1	1	194	35			3			1	3				
θ		2	2	96	146	2		2	1	4	1	8				
s		2		1	31	204	1	1	9	4			7			
ʃ						1	243									
b				13	12			207	2	3	19	8				
d									240	9				3		
g								1	41	199			2	1		
v				3	3			20		2	182	47	2			1
ð					7			10	3	22	49	170	19			
z					1			3	8	24	2	22	145	3		
ʒ							1	2					13	264		
m															213	11
n																248

TABLE XIII. Confusion matrix for $S/N = +12$ db and frequency response of 1000–5000 cps.

	p	t	k	f	θ	s	ʃ	b	d	g	v	ð	z	ʒ	m	n
p	179	9	44	6	3					2	1					
t		272	3					1			2					1
k	15	1	227					1	1		2					1
f	12	1	7	162	28	3	1	34	2	1	6	19	1		4	
θ	8	2	7	39	125	13	2	6	2	1	4	19	3		1	
s				3	28	200		2	1	1	4	6	9	1		1
ʃ							221							2		
b	2			9	10	1		130		6	74	24			16	
d		2					1		195	35	6	2	2	8		5
g				2					48	151		3	4	5		11
v	1			28	8			48	1	3	145	33	3		17	1
ð	1			1	14			8	11	12	31	116	26	5	21	6
z			1		2	24	2	1	19	7	3	31	163	4	2	1
ʒ				1			20		2	2				207		
m	3		2	5	4	1		10			6				224	1
n			1	1	1			1	8	4	2	1	1	1		207

TABLE XIV. Confusion matrix for $S/N = +12$ db and frequency response of 2000–5000 cps.

	p	t	k	f	θ	s	ʃ	b	d	g	v	ð	z	ʒ	m	n
p	94	32	26	15	6	3	1	10	4	4	13	12	1	5	3	3
t	7	223	3	3	1		3		7	1	1	1		5	1	
k	24	25	126	4	7	4	2	3	6	15	1	3	1	2	7	2
f	38	7	19	72	24	5	2	24	3	12	28	11	4	3	12	4
θ	22	7	11	20	63	27		19	8	13	22	26	16		12	10
s	2	9	1	5	23	148			4	3	3	4	44	6		8
ʃ	1	1					208	1					1	28		
b	15	5	5	37	12	2		72	7	8	40	30	4		40	7
d	2	6	7		2			4	192	19	4	6	3	2	2	23
g	2	1	3	1	8	4	1	8	44	122	10	6	6	1	3	20
v	17	1	12	13	7		1	39	5	14	42	23	2	4	32	12
ð	5		6	9	20	5		17	16	19	17	64	20	1	36	25
z	3	2	2	5	8	44		5	22	7	1	13	99	5	7	9
ʒ							37			4				199	4	
m	10	4	3	8	7		1	9	5	10	10	16	2		113	26
n	2		2		3	2		1	20	11	3	7	6	3	4	192

PERCEPTUAL CONFUSIONS AMONG CONSONANTS   345

TABLE XV. Confusion matrix for $S/N = +12$ db and frequency response of 2500–5000 cps.

	p	t	k	f	θ	s	ʃ	b	d	g	v	ð	z	ʒ	m	n
p	69	30	37	26	16	4	4	21	9	18	13	12	9	3	7	10
t	4	164	9	2	2	2		1	4	4	1	2	2		3	
k	20	35	76	9	11	5	6	3	5	25	5	3	15	11	7	4
f	27	8	7	24	28	7	8	15	8	14	34	14	6	2	11	11
θ	15	19	7	20	49	10	8	12	16	16	13	20	10	5	16	16
s	6	8	2	1	19	160	4		16	10	8	11	27	2	7	11
ʃ	1	1	2	1	5	1	204	1				1	2	44		1
b	23	4	10	13	17		2	48	17	17	34	28	10	1	28	12
d	1	7	6	5	4	2	1	1	128	16	8	6	5	13	5	16
g	6	3	16	5	6	5	2	17	39	85	11	13	6	7	6	13
v	22	6	6	26	18	3	3	33	12	9	32	28	7	2	18	7
ð	21	11	9	16	28	4	2	35	14	22	20	44	10	2	24	22
z	4	5	1	2	9	60	5	1	27	21		12	86	6	2	3
ʒ	2	4	2			3	49	1	7	1	2	1	5	167		
m	18	3	7	11	16	8	2	13	16	12	16	21	3	1	68	37
n	8	4	12	7	9	2		10	22	17	13	8	5	4	16	119

TABLE XVI. Confusion matrix for $S/N = +12$ db and frequency response of 3000–5000 cps.

	p	t	k	f	θ	s	ʃ	b	d	g	v	ð	z	ʒ	m	n
p	31	15	15	15	14	11	6	19	11	8	15	15	5	9	12	19
t	11	184	16	6	5	5	5	8	9	3	4	2	5	3	6	4
k	15	35	50	7	16	7	2	14	14	24	7	9	8	9	8	7
f	19	12	12	15	19	8	2	25	16	25	15	12	6	2	17	11
θ	15	14	13	13	30	15	3	15	24	12	14	17	10	3	14	20
s	4	4	8	11	8	140	4	7	8	6	6	11	35	7	2	7
ʃ		6	2	3	1	4	177	1	2	2	1	6	1	23	7	
b	17	13	11	25	23	8	1	27	13	19	25	13	5	6	17	13
d	14	23	15	11	11	4	3	15	63	25	14	10	13	6	19	14
g	14	15	17	17	12	8	1	23	39	45	14	10	13	7	17	16
v	19	19	22	18	20	8	10	35	18	16	19	21	7		28	16
ð	19	13	12	12	24	8	6	22	24	15	24	21	10	5	33	16
z	9	21	9	7	17	59	6	6	11	13	10	15	41	4	10	14
ʒ	4	6	1	5	1	11	51	3	3	7	1	10	9	128	7	5
m	16	7	14	11	19	5	4	31	16	17	17	10	10	6	58	19
n	16	7	12	6	16	7	6	14	29	16	13	22	7	4	19	58

TABLE XVII. Confusion matrix for $S/N = +12$ db and frequency response of 4500–5000 cps.

	p	t	k	f	θ	s	ʃ	b	d	g	v	ð	z	ʒ	m	n
p	26	21	23	16	24	20	4	15	16	14	20	9	10	9	16	9
t	10	141	12	3	4	4	3	5	11	5	7	11	4	5	8	3
k	16	34	25	14	11	13	8	20	20	8	18	13	20	10	12	22
f	9	9	22	18	18	6	6	18	17	9	17	19	9	3	27	13
θ	16	21	25	5	20	10	2	29	23	24	27	28	11	5	16	10
s	8	5	15	7	11	138	7	6	4	11	13	7	34	5	6	7
ʃ	3	3	7	1	1	12	190	1	4	2	2	4	6	26	6	4
b	12	8	23	11	18	13	9	26	14	18	21	14	11	6	16	16
d	24	26	28	16	19	8	4	19	18	19	13	11	6	3	16	14
g	12	16	17	14	21	11	10	12	17	21	18	19	7	10	22	13
v	21	11	17	15	24	12	8	19	15	14	33	23	6	3	23	16
ð	18	19	15	16	20	7	5	24	16	16	22	28	9	11	24	10
z	8	12	8	8	7	64	5	12	10	9	12	17	51	11	6	8
ʒ	5	18	10	8	9	11	57	5	4	5	9	11	15	85	9	7
m	8	13	20	13	15	14	7	18	8	16	16	17	12	2	15	18
n	20	15	15	18	15	7	6	19	20	12	17	15	12	4	21	16

TABLE XVIII. Confusion matrix at $S/N = -12$ db with a 200–6500-cps channel.

	p	t	k	b	d	g	Sum
p	117	58	115	14	10	2	316
t	74	101	103	8	4	6	296
k	105	109	153	5	8	4	384
b	13	9	10	217	45	26	320
d	3	4	5	47	200	117	376
g	3	11	8	45	147	94	308
							2000

is given in Table XVIII. There are 882 entries on the main diagonal, so $A = 0.441$. If we group the consonants $|pk|$, $|t|$, $|b|$, and $|dg|$, there are 1366 correct responses, so $A' = 0.683$. If we again group $|ptk|$ and $|bdg|$, there are 1873 correct responses, so $A'' = 0.9365$. Now if we wish to reconstruct the matrix from these three articulation scores, we would first divide the 882 correct responses equally among the six diagonal cells, which gives 147 observations per cell. When we add the four cells for $|pk|$ and $|dg|$ to the diagonal cells, the count increases from 882 to 1366, so the additional 484 observations must be divided equally among the four additional cells, which gives 121 per cell for $|pk|$ and $|dg|$ confusions. When we add the eight remaining cells for the $|ptk|$ and $|bdg|$ groups, the count increases from 1366 to 1873, so the additional 507 observations must be divided evenly among those eight cells, which gives 63.4 per cell. The remaining 127 observations are then divided equally among the 18 cells remaining in the lower left and upper right quadrants, which gives 7.1 per cell. In this way the generalized, three-valued articulation score gives a reasonably clear picture of the distribution of errors.

The procedure just described can lead to serious errors if the stimulus frequencies are quite disparate. For example, if one stimulus is presented much more often than any other, it will contribute more to the total number of correct responses and then the equipartition of correct responses among the diagonal cells will be in error. In such cases the original data matrix should first be corrected to the frequencies that would presumably have been obtained if the stimuli had been equally frequent. This correction is made by multiplying the entries in each row by n/kn_i, where n_i is the frequency of occurrence of the ith stimulus ($i = 1, 2, \cdots, k$) in a sample of n observations. Then the "articulation scores corrected for stimulus frequencies" are calculated for the revised matrix. To reconstruct the data matrix, the corrected frequencies should be partitioned as before and then each row multiplied by kn_i/n in order to remove the correction and regain the original stimulus frequencies. Whenever an experimenter employs some unusual (nonuniform) distribution of stimulus frequencies, this fact should be stated explicitly in order to avoid misinterpretations of the articulation scores so obtained.

Some such generalization of the articulation score seems essential in order to preserve the data on clustering of errors. In our own analysis of the data, however, we have preferred a somewhat more elaborate statistical analysis. We have presented this simpler technique for the reader who feels that the information measures we have employed are too abstract or do not permit a simple reconstruction of the original matrix. Having pointed out this simpler technique, however, we shall make little use of it in the following discussion.

LINGUISTIC FEATURES

For many years linguists and phoneticians have classified phonemes according to features of the articulation process used to generate the sounds. These features of speech production are reflected in certain acoustic characteristics which are presumably discriminated by the listener. When we begin to look for reasonable ways to group the stimuli in order to summarize the pattern of confusions, it is natural to turn first to these articulatory features for guidance. In order to describe the 16 consonants used in this study we adopted the following set of features as a basis for classification.

(1) *Voicing.* In articulatory terms, the vocal cords do not vibrate when the consonants $|ptkfθsʃ|$ are produced, and they do vibrate for $|bdgvðzʒmn|$. Acoustically, this means that the voiceless consonants are aperiodic or noisy in character, whereas a periodic or line-spectrum component is superimposed on the noise for voiced consonants. In addition, in English the voiceless consonants seem to be more intense and the voiceless stops have considerable aspiration, a sort of breathy noise between the release of pressure and the beginning of the following vowels, and may be somewhat briefer than the voiced stops. Thus the articulatory difference is reflected in a variety of acoustic differences.

(2) *Nasality.* To articulate $|m|$ and $|n|$ the lips are closed and the pressure is released through the nose by lowering the soft palate at the back of the mouth. The nasal resonance introduced in this way provides an acoustic difference. In addition, $|mn|$ seem slightly longer in duration than their stop or fricative counterparts and somewhat more intense. Also, the two nasals are the only consonants in this study lacking the aperiodic component of noisiness.

(3) *Affrication.* If the articulators close completely, the consonant may be a stop or a nasal, but if they are brought close together and air is forced between them, the result is a kind of turbulence or friction noise that distinguishes $|fθsʃvðzʒ|$ from $|ptkbdgmn|$. The acoustic turbulence is in contrast to the silence followed by a pop that characterizes the stops and to the periodic, almost vowel-like resonance of the nasals.

(4) *Duration.* This is the name we have arbitrarily adopted to designate the difference between $|sʃzʒ|$ and the other 12 consonants. These four consonants are

long, intense, high-frequency noises, but in our opinion it is their extra duration that is most effective in setting them apart.

(5) *Place of Articulation.* This feature has to do with where in the mouth the major constriction of the vocal passage occurs. Usually three positions, front, middle, and back, are distinguished, so that we have grouped $|pbfvm|$ as front, $|td\theta s\eth zn|$ as middle, and $|kg\int\textrm{3}|$ as back consonants. Although these three positions are easy to recognize in the production of these sounds, the acoustic consequences of differences in place are most complex. Of the various accounts of the positional feature that have been given, the work done by the Haskins Laboratory[1,2] seems to provide the best basis for an interpretation of our data. For the voiced stops $|bdg|$ the most important acoustic clue to position seems to be in the initial portion of the second formant

TABLE XIX. Classification of consonants used to analyze confusions.

Consonant	Voicing	Nasality	Affrication	Duration	Place
p	0	0	0	0	0
t	0	0	0	0	1
k	0	0	0	0	2
f	0	0	1	0	0
θ	0	0	1	0	1
s	0	0	1	1	1
$\int$	0	0	1	1	2
b	1	0	0	0	0
d	1	0	0	0	1
g	1	0	0	0	2
v	1	0	1	0	0
$\eth$	1	0	1	0	1
z	1	0	1	1	1
$\textrm{3}$	1	0	1	1	2
m	1	1	0	0	0
n	1	1	0	0	1

of the vowel $|a|$ that follows; if this formant frequency rises initially, it is a $|b|$, but if it falls it is $|d|$ or $|g|$. Since the vowel formant is relatively audible, the front $|b|$ is easily distinguished from the middle $|d|$ and the back $|g|$. The latter two positions are much harder to distinguish and probably cannot be differentiated until their aperiodic, noisy components become sufficiently audible so that high-frequency noise can be assigned to middle $|d|$ and low-frequency noise to back $|g|$. For the voiceless stops $|ptk|$, however, the story is different because the transitional portion of the second formant occurs during the period of aspiration, before vocalization has begun, and is correspondingly much harder to hear. The plosive part of the voiceless stops is relatively intense, however, so that the high-fre-

[1] Liberman, Delattre, and Cooper, Am. J. Psychol. **65**, 497–516 (1952).
[2] Liberman, Delattre, Cooper, and Gerstman, Psychol. Monographs **68**, No. 8, 1–13 (1954).

quency noise of middle $|t|$ distinguishes it from the low-frequency noise of front $|p|$ and back $|k|$. The distinction between $|p|$ and $|k|$ is slightly harder to hear because it seems to depend upon hearing the aspirated transition into the second vowel resonance. What acoustic representation there is for place of articulation of the fricative sounds is even more obscure. Probably the middle $|sz|$ are distinguished from the back $|\int\textrm{3}|$ on the basis of the high-frequency energy in $|sz|$. The distinction between front $|fv|$ and middle $|\theta\eth|$, however is uncertainly attributable to slight differences in the transition to the following vowel. The distinctions between $|f|$ and $|\theta|$ and between $|v|$ and $|\eth|$ are among the most difficult for listeners to hear and it seems likely that in most natural situations the differentiation depends more on verbal context and on visual observation of the talker's lips than it does on the acoustic difference. In any event, when we summarily assign these consonants into three classes on the basis of "articulatory position," we are thereby concealing a host of difficult problems. The positional feature is by all odds the most superficial and unsatisfactory of the five features we have employed.

In Table XIX a digital notation is used to summarize the classification of these 16 consonants on the basis of these five features. From Table XIX it is easy to see in what ways any two of the consonants differ.

Now if we apply the groupings given in Table XIX to the data matrices in Tables I–XVII, we can obtain a set of articulation scores, one score for each feature. For example, we can group the voiceless consonants together *versus* the voiced consonants and so estimate the probability that the voicing feature will be perceived correctly—the articulation score for voicing. The necessary summations for each feature for every table have been made and are given in Table XX.

A COVARIANCE MEASURE OF INTELLIGIBILITY

The recent development of a mathematical theory of communication has made considerable use of a measure

TABLE XX. Frequencies of correct responses in Tables I–XVII.

Condition	S/N	Band	All	Voice	Nasal	Frict	Durat	Place
1	−18	200–6500	313	2286	3200	2032	2600	1439
2	−12	200–6500	1080	3586	2610	3095	3095	1842
3	−6	200–6500	1860	3877	3921	3202	3429	2386
4	0	200–6500	2862	3977	3992	3706	3780	3099
5	6	200–6500	3336	3985	3998	3861	3910	3472
6	12	200–6500	3634	3985	3997	3916	3980	3691
7	12	200–300	1059	3725	3864	2922	2905	1717
8	12	200–400	1631	3801	3939	3402	3388	2088
9	12	200–600	1980	3903	3991	3696	3475	2341
10	12	200–1200	2287	3891	3994	3641	3526	2616
11	12	200–2500	2913	3927	3999	3778	3673	3224
12	12	200–5000	3332	3920	3999	3811	3853	3522
13	12	1000–5000	2924	3735	3861	3566	3801	3476
14	12	2000–5000	2029	3208	3573	3087	3689	2992
15	12	2500–5000	1523	2857	3472	2871	3552	2587
16	12	3000–5000	1087	2527	3283	2601	3390	2227
17	12	4500–5000	851	2283	3267	2463	3260	1927
Random guessing			250	2031	3125	2000	2500	1406

of covariance between input and output. This measure has been defined in terms of the mean logarithmic probability (MLP). If the input variable is x, which can assume the discrete values $i=1,2,\cdots,k$ with probability p_i, then the measure of the input is

$$\mathrm{MLP}(x)=E(-\log p_i)=-\sum_i p_i \log p_i.$$

If the logarithm is taken to the base 2, then the measure can be called the number of binary decisions needed on the average to specify the input, or the number of bits of information per stimulus. A similar expression holds for the output variable y, which can assume the values $j=1,2,\cdots,m$. Similarly, the number of decisions needed to specify the particular stimulus-response pair is $\mathrm{MLP}(xy)$, where p_{ij} is the probability of the joint occurrence of input i and output j. A measure of covariance of input with output is given by

$$T(x;y)=\mathrm{MLP}(x)+\mathrm{MLP}(y)-\mathrm{MLP}(xy)$$

$$=-\sum_{i,j} p_{ij}\log\frac{p_i p_j}{p_{ij}}.$$

$T(x;y)$ is often referred to as the transmission from x to y in bits per stimulus. The relative transmission is given by

$$T_{\mathrm{rel}}(x;y)=T(x;y)/H(x).$$

Since $H(x)\geq T(x;y)\geq 0$, the ratio varies from 0 to 1; if the transmission is poor and the response is not closely correlated to the stimulus, then $T_{\mathrm{rel}}(x;y)$ will be near zero, but if the response can be predicted with considerable accuracy from the stimulus, then $T_{\mathrm{rel}}(x;y)$ will be near unity.

In practice the true probabilities are not known and must be estimated from the relative frequencies

obtained in a finite sample taken during the experiment. The maximum likelihood estimate of $T(x;y)$ is obtained by using n_i/n, n_j/n, and n_{ij}/n in place of p_i, p_j, and p_{ij}, respectively, where n_i is the frequency of stimulus i, n_j is the frequency of response j, and n_{ij} is the frequency of the joint occurrence of stimulus i and response j in a sample of n observations. In Tables I–XVII the cell entries are the n_{ij}, row sums give n_i, column sums give n_j, and n is 4000. Like most maximum likelihood estimates, this estimate will be biased to overestimate $T(x;y)$ for small samples; in the present case, however, the sample is large enough that the bias can safely be ignored.

The covariance measure of intelligibility can be applied to the several linguistic features separately in just the same way that the articulation score for each feature was obtained for Table XX. For example, we can construct a fourfold confusion matrix by grouping the voiceless sounds together as one stimulus and the voiced sounds as the other and then tabulating the frequency of voiceless responses to voiceless stimuli, of voiced responses to voiceless stimuli, of voiceless responses to voiced stimuli, and of voiced responses to voiced stimuli. For this 2 by 2 confusion matrix we can calculate the covariance of response with stimulus in the same way as described above and so measure the transmission of information about voicing. Similar measures can be calculated for nasality, affrication, duration, and position.

This breakdown of the confusion matrix into five smaller matrices and the measurement of transmission for each one of these five separately is equivalent to considering that we are actually testing five different communication channels simultaneously.[3] Of course, the five channels will probably not be independent. Some interaction or "cross talk" is to be expected, in the sense that knowing one feature may make some other feature easier to hear. However, the impressive thing to us was that this cross talk was so small and that the features were perceived almost independently of one another.

At first thought one might expect that if all five channels were independent, then the sum of the information transmitted by the separate channels should equal approximately the transmission calculated for all five taken together in the whole 16 by 16 matrix. This first thought would be true except for one fact; the inputs to the five channels are not independent and, therefore, even if the channels themselves are independent, the amounts transmitted through each channel will be related.

In Table XXI the average amounts of information in bits per stimulus that the listeners received are presented for the composite channel and for the five subchannels individually for all 17 conditions of masking and filtering. The last row in the table gives the amounts

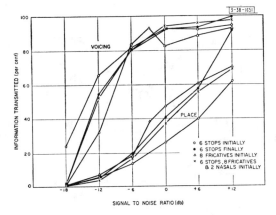

Fig. 1. The relative information transmitted about voicing (top four curves) and place (bottom four curves) is plotted as a function of signal-to-noise ratio in decibels. The four curves for each feature were obtained from four independent experiments using different test vocabularies. Voicing information is transmitted at signal-to-noise levels 18 db below those needed for place information.

[3] W. J. McGill, Psychometrika **19**, 97–116 (1954).

TABLE XXI. Amounts of information transmitted in bits per stimulus in Tables I–XVII for composite channel and for each feature separately.

Con-dition	S/N	Band	All	Voice	Nasal	Frict	Durat	Place
1	−18	200–6500	0.061	0.021	0.008	0.000	0.001	0.001
2	−12	200–6500	0.959	0.516	0.264	0.069	0.087	0.058
3	−6	200–6500	1.834	0.797	0.397	0.279	0.249	0.249
4	0	200–6500	2.797	0.944	0.495	0.620	0.483	0.578
5	6	200–6500	3.226	0.951	0.543	0.782	0.636	0.856
6	12	200–6500	3.546	0.956	0.555	0.853	0.751	1.090
7	12	200–300	1.155	0.623	0.371	0.159	0.042	0.025
8	12	200–400	1.686	0.709	0.457	0.393	0.218	0.125
9	12	200–600	2.159	0.821	0.520	0.614	0.272	0.231
10	12	200–1200	2.379	0.805	0.523	0.583	0.281	0.359
11	12	200–2500	2.828	0.852	0.544	0.702	0.419	0.721
12	12	200–5000	3.185	0.847	0.521	0.730	0.581	0.936
13	12	1000–5000	2.643	0.638	0.350	0.506	0.520	0.872
14	12	2000–5000	1.582	0.273	0.160	0.229	0.426	0.499
15	12	2500–5000	1.053	0.130	0.083	0.143	0.348	0.296
16	12	3000–5000	0.624	0.048	0.023	0.067	0.235	0.143
17	12	4500–5000	0.455	0.014	0.002	0.045	0.193	0.068
Maximum possible			4.000	0.989	0.544	1.000	0.811	1.546

that would be transmitted if no mistakes at all occurred (on the assumption that all 16 syllables occurred equally often). The degree of redundancy in the input is indicated by the fact that the sum of the transmissions for the five channels is 4.890 bits, whereas the composite channel can transmit only 4 bits. This difference means that some of the input information is going through more than one channel. However, for the conditions and phonemes tested, the sum for the five channels can be used to give a rough approximation for the composite channel if the sum is corrected by the factor 4/4.89. If all of the features were transmitted equally well, this correction factor would be exact, but in most cases it is only an approximation.

The fact that the measures for the separate channels can be summed in a simple manner to give an approximate value for the total transmission is of considerable practical significance. This perceptual independence of the several features implies that all we need to know about a system is how well it transmits the necessary clues for each feature; measurements for the individual features can be made much more quickly and easily than can a measurement for the composite channel, and the correction factor for the input redundancy depends entirely on the input vocabulary and not upon an experimental test.

In the following we shall discuss the relative transmission measures. The relative measure is computed from Table XXI by dividing each entry in that table by the maximum value given at the bottom of each column. The advantage of the relative measure is that it permits an easy comparison of one channel with another. Differences in transmission due simply to the fact that the input to one channel was greater than the input to another channel are removed when we examine the relative efficiency of the two channels. We ask simply, what fraction of its input did each channel transmit? The ratio of transmitted to input information provides us with a normalized measure of stimulus-response covariation.

DISCUSSION

In Fig. 1 the normalized covariance measure—relative transmission in percent—is plotted as a function of the signal-to-noise ratio for two linguistic features, voicing and place of articulation, for the data presented in Tables I–VI. In Fig. 2 a similar plot is shown for the features of nasality, affrication, and duration. In addition to the data in Tables I–VI, the results of three smaller studies are also plotted on the same graph. In one of these smaller studies only the six stop consonants $|p|$, $|t|$, $|k|$, $|b|$, $|d|$, and $|g|$, were used initially before the vowel $|a|$. In a second study these same six stop consonants occurred finally after the phonemes $|ta|$. And in the third study only the eight fricative consonants $|f|$, $|\theta|$, $|s|$, $|\int|$, $|v|$, $|\delta|$, $|z|$, and $|\mathfrak{z}|$ were used initially before the vowel $|a|$. Both voicing and place of articulation are involved in these three smaller test vocabularies, so the relative transmission for these two features can be compared in Fig. 1 with the results obtained from the complete set of 16 consonants. Duration was also tested with fricative sounds and this function is added in Fig. 2. The comparisons show a gratifying degree of agreement from one study to the next.

The glaringly obvious statement that must be made about Figs. 1 and 2 is that voicing and nasality are much less affected by a random masking noise than are the other features. Affrication and duration, which are so similar that a single function could represent them both, are somewhat superior to place but far inferior to voicing and nasality. Voicing and nasality are discriminable at signal-to-noise ratios as poor as −12 db whereas the place of articulation is hard to distinguish at ratios less than 6 db, a difference of some 18 db in efficiency.

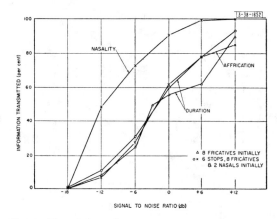

FIG. 2. The relative information transmitted about nasality, affrication, and duration is plotted as a function of signal-to-noise ratio in decibels. The two curves for duration were obtained from independent experiments using different test vocabularies. Nasality and voicing are equally discriminable.

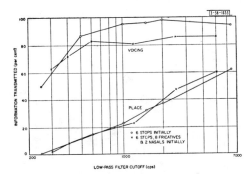

FIG. 3. The relative information transmitted about voicing and place is plotted as a function of the cutoff frequency of the low-pass filter. The two curves for each feature were obtained from independent experiments. The relation between voicing and place is the same for low-pass filtering as for masking with random noise (see Fig. 1).

In Figs. 3 and 4 similar functions are drawn for the results given in Tables VII–XII for low-pass filters. An additional small study with just the six stop consonants is also represented in Fig. 3. Figure 3 looks much like Fig. 1; voicing is greatly superior to place of articulation. Figure 4 is similar to Fig. 2, except that the results for affrication and duration are now somewhat different. These comparisons show that there is a considerable correspondence between masking by random noise and filtering by low-pass filters. This correspondence seems reasonable if we think of the high-frequency components of speech as relatively weak and therefore most susceptible to masking by the uniform spectrum of the noise. That is to say, the uniform noise spectrum should mask high frequencies more than low, so it is in effect a kind of low-pass system.

Whereas low-pass filtering and noise have much the same effect on speech perception, high-pass filtering presents a totally different picture. In Fig. 5 the relative transmissions calculated from Tables XII–XVII are plotted for all five features as a function of the filter cutoff frequency. With a minor exception for duration, all features deteriorate in about the same way as the low frequencies are removed. Duration holds up some-

what better, probably because $|s|$, $|\int|$, $|z|$, and $|3|$ are characterized in part by considerable high-frequency energy. This homogeneity reflects a fact that can be seen from visual inspection of Tables XIII–XVII; the errors do not cluster or fall into obvious patterns in the confusion matrix, but seem to distribute almost randomly over the matrix. When an error occurs with high-pass filtering, there is little chance of predicting what the error will be. Thus we find an important difference between high- and low-pass filtering; low-pass filters affect the several linguistic features differentially, leaving the phonemes audible but similar in predictable ways, whereas high-pass filters remove most of the acoustic power in the consonants, leaving them inaudible and, consequently, producing quite random confusions. Of course, this difference must be tempered by the fact that a random noise was used along with the filters, so that the noise acted "with" the low-pass filter to eliminate high frequencies but "against" the high-pass filter in such a way as to produce a narrow band-pass system. However, casual observations made since these tests were completed convince us that the difference cannot be explained entirely in this way and that, even without noise, audibility is the problem for high-pass systems and confusibility is the problem for low-pass systems.

An important application of data on filtered speech has been to divide the frequency scale into segments making equal contributions to intelligibility. The high-pass and low-pass functions are plotted on the same graph and the frequency at which the two functions cross is said to divide the frequency scale into two equivalent parts; the frequencies above the crossover are exactly as important as the frequencies below the crossover frequency. We have observed this traditional method of analysis in Fig. 6 where the solid functions are the articulation scores and they are seen to cross at about 1550 cps. This frequency is somewhat lower than one would expect for female talkers, but the test vocabulary used here may not permit valid comparisons with other research.

We would like to argue that the meaning of these crossover points is apt to be a bit tricky. In the first place, the point depends crucially upon the test materials, in the sense that we can obtain very different crossover points for the different linguistic features: 450 cps for nasality, 500 cps for voicing, 750 cps for affrication, 1900 cps for place of articulation, and 2200 cps for duration. What crossover point we get depends on how we load the test vocabulary with these different features. In the second place, high- and low-pass filters do different things to speech perception, as we pointed out previously. If we plot the relative amount of information transmitted, instead of the articulation score, we obtain the dashed functions shown in Fig. 6. The crossover point for the information measure is about 1250 cps, a good 300 cps lower than for the articulation score.

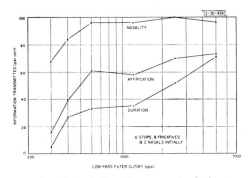

FIG. 4. The relative information transmitted about nasality, affrication, and duration is plotted as a function of the cutoff frequency of the low-pass filter. Nasality is somewhat more discriminable than voicing.

By the same argument as before, there is as much information above 1250 cps as there is below. Why do these two measures give different divisions of the frequency scale? The answer lies in the fact that low-pass errors are more predictable and so carry some information, whereas high-pass errors are more random and contain no hint about what the true message might have been. Relative to the articulation scores, therefore, the high-pass information is smaller and the low-pass information is greater; the relative shifts move the crossover point downward in frequency. Which of these two crossover points is the more meaningful? Here the answer depends upon what use is to be made of the voice communication system. If isolated words, numerals, station call letters, etc. are the only messages, then a miss is as good as a mile; there is no redundancy in the message to enable the listener to correct an error, so the percentage of messages correctly received is what we want to know. On the other hand, if connected discourse in all its notorious redundancy is sent over the system, a listener can detect perceptual errors on the basis of context and can correct them more easily if they are consistent and predictable; then the transmission measure is what we want to know. However, if we arrive at a position where we must weight the frequency scale one way for isolated words and another way for conversational speech, the beautiful simplicity that makes the traditional crossover argument so attractive seems spurious. Our own intuitions would lead us to search for a different line of attack on the problem.

It may be possible to evaluate voice communication systems more adequately if we explore the implications of the multiple-channel argument used to analyze our data. It is not obvious that things will be any simpler if we must replace a single complicated channel with a dozen simpler channels in our theoretical model of speech perception. However, transmission of the separate features may be easier to relate to the system parameters. Even if a completely automatic computational procedure cannot be developed along multiple-channel lines, a short series of relatively simple articulation tests may suffice to determine the necessary parameters. In any event, the development and standardization of tests for the individual features would seem to have considerable value for the diagnosis both of inefficient equipments and of hard-of-hearing people.

One advantage of a multichannel approach to speech perception is that the message, as well as the equipment, is included in the analysis. Given any specific vocabulary of speech signals, we can calculate the relative importance of each feature for distinguishing the alternative signals and so derive a weighting factor for each channel. If the messages are coded properly into those channels or features that the system handles well, considerable advantage may be gained. For ex-

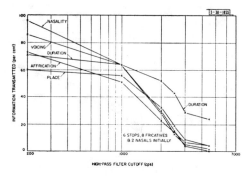

FIG. 5. The relative information transmitted about all five features is plotted as a function of the cutoff frequency of the high-pass filter. The effect of eliminating the low frequencies is the same on all features except duration.

ample, a low-pass system would perform best for speech signals that were distinguishable on the basis of voicing and nasality.

A set of rules for developing an optimally distinguishable vocabulary for a given communication system would be rather complex and involved. There is, however, a very simple procedure for testing any given vocabulary. If the relative efficiencies of the system for the several features are known, we may know that some features will not be transmitted and cannot be used to distinguish two signals. Any two phonemes that differ only with respect to such missing features can be regarded as equivalent stimuli for the listener. Now suppose that we take any one of such a set of equivalent stimuli and use it wherever any of the set occurs; for example, if $|p|$, $|t|$, and $|k|$ are indistinguishable, we might use $|t|$ for all three. When all the speech signals are rewritten with $|t|$ wherever $|p|$, $|t|$, or $|k|$ occurred before and similar substitutions are made for all other sets of equivalent stimuli, the rewritten signals will approximate what the listener will hear. If we now alphabetize the rewritten signals, we will probably find some that are identical. These are the signals that will be confused and we can then take steps to eliminate such confusions.

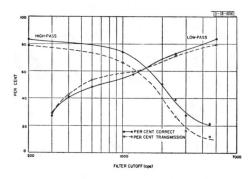

FIG. 6. Both the articulation score and relative information transmitted are plotted as a function of the frequency cutoff for both high-pass and low-pass filters. The crossover points are different for the two measures.

For example, if we look at Figs. 3 and 4 to see what happens when frequencies above 1000 cps are filtered out of the speech, we find that the features of place and duration are effectively absent and that voicing, nasality, and affrication are doing all the work. In other words, the filter has effectively deleted the last two columns in Table XIX. With those two columns gone there are really just five distinguishable phonemes left: $|ptk|$, $|f\theta s\int|$, $|bdg|$, $|v\delta z_3|$, and $|mn|$. Replace these by, say, $|t|$, $|s|$, $|d|$, $|z|$, and $|n|$, respectively. Now when we rewrite the vocabulary of speech signals with just these five consonants instead of the original 16, we will discover which signals are transformed into indistinguishable forms by the filter. Insofar as possible, no two signals should be the same in their rewritten versions. The basic idea behind this procedure is that redundancy in the input signals will be most effective in reducing errors if we insure that frequent confusions do not transform one permissable signal into another permissable signal.

We have explored the validity of this substitution scheme for just those conditions described in the preceding example. Sentences and longer texts were rewritten with the indicated substitution of five for 16 phonemes. Such rewritten passages are appropriately called "elliptic" English, the ellipsis referring to the omission of two features, place and duration. With a little practice it was possible to speak the elliptic passages at normal rates and with normal intonation. Over a high quality communication system the elliptic speech was intelligible but sounded a little as though the talker had a marked dialect or speech defect. Then the low-pass filters were introduced. When all the frequencies above 1000 cps were removed (the conditions for which the substitutions were designed), the ellipsis could no longer be detected. Elliptic speech sounded just the same as normal speech under these conditions of distortion. A similar result was obtained with a masking noise at signal-to-noise ratios of about 0 db. The illusion is quite compelling and this demonstration that we could duplicate the effects of noise or distortion by deleting certain features of the speech increased our confidence in a multichannel model of speech perception.

An interesting sidelight on elliptic speech is provided by the art of ventriloquism. A ventriloquist talks without moving his lips. The consonants $|p|$, $|f|$, $|b|$, $|v|$, $|m|$, and $|w|$ are normally produced with lip movements and so pose a problem. A variety of solutions are possible; these sounds are avoided or omitted or produced out of the side of the mouth, or made in alternative ways (especially $|f|$ and $|v|$). In most of the older books on ventriloquism, however, a system of substitutions is proposed; $|k|$ for $|p|$, $|g|$ for $|b|$, and $|n|$ for $|m|$ are common suggestions. These substitutions should be especially satisfactory for the "voice in a box" trick, where the high frequencies should be attenuated in passing through the walls of the box and the confusion of sounds would be expected to occur naturally.

The place of articulation, which was hardest to hear correctly in our tests, is the easiest of the features to see on a talker's lips. The other features are hard to see but easy to hear. Lip reading, therefore, is a valuable skill for listeners who are partially deafened because it provides just the information that the noise or deafness removes.

Erratum: An Analysis of Perceptual Confusions Among Some English Consonants

[J. Acoust. Soc. Am. 27, 339 (1955)]

GEORGE A. MILLER AND PATRICIA E. NICELY

Lincoln Laboratory, Massachusetts Institute of Technology, Cambridge, Massachusetts

THE authors wish to call attention to the following error which was introduced during the typing of the manuscript. The last sentence on page 339 should read, "Row sums would give the frequencies that each syllable was spoken by the talkers. Column sums would give the frequencies that each syllable was written by the listeners."

THE INTELLIGIBILITY OF SPEECH AS A FUNCTION OF THE CONTEXT OF THE TEST MATERIALS [1]

BY GEORGE A. MILLER, GEORGE A. HEISE, AND WILLIAM LICHTEN

Harvard University

For many years communication engineers have used a psychophysical method called the "articulation test" (2, 3). An announcer reads lists of syllables, words, or sentences to a group of listeners who report what they hear. The articulation score is the percentage of discrete test units reported correctly by the listeners. This method gives a quantitative evaluation of the performance of a speech communication system.

There are three classes of variables involved in an articulation test: the *personnel*, talkers and listeners; the *test materials*, syllables, words, sentences, or continuous discourse; and the communication *equipment*, rooms, microphones, amplifiers, radios, earphones, etc. The present paper is directed toward the second of these three classes of variables, the test materials. The central concern can be stated as follows: Why is a stimulus configuration, a word, heard correctly in one context and incorrectly in another?

Three kinds of contexts are explored: (a) context supplied by the knowledge that the test item is one of a small vocabulary of items, (b) context supplied by the items that precede or follow a given item in a word or sentence, and (c) context supplied by the knowledge that the item is a repetition of the immediately preceding item. All three kinds of context enable the listener to limit the range of alternatives from which he selects his response. A word selected from a small vocabulary must be one of the few words agreed upon in advance. A word in a sentence must be one of the relatively few words that make a reasonable continuation of the sentence according to grammatical rules agreed upon in advance. A repeated word must be one of the few words similar to the word just heard. Not anything can happen, and the listener can set himself to make the required discrimination. Context, in the sense the word assumes here, is the S's knowledge of the conditions of stimulation. The experimental problem is to vary the nature and amount of this contextual knowledge in order to study its influence upon perceptual accuracy.

EQUIPMENT AND PROCEDURE

The apparatus consisted of components from military communication equipment used during the recent war. The output voltage of a carbon microphone was amplified and delivered to the listener's dynamic earphones. The talker monitored his speaking level with a volume indicator (VU meter) that responded to the voltage generated at the output of the amplifier. A random noise voltage, with a spectrum that was relatively uniform from 100 to 7,000 cps, was introduced at the listener's earphones. The signal-to-noise ratio (S/N) was varied by holding the average voice level constant and changing the level of the noise. The S/N was measured by a vacuum tube voltmeter across the terminals of the earphones, and the measurements reported in

[1] This research was carried out under Contract N5ori-76 between Harvard University and the Office of Naval Research, U.S. Navy (Project NR147-201, Report PNR-74). Reproduction for any purpose of the U.S. Government is permitted.

329

Journal of Experimental Psychology 41, 329–335 (1951).

the following pages represent the ratio in decibels of the average peak deflection of the meter for the words (in the absence of noise) to the level of the noise in the 7,000-cycle band. A S/N of zero db means, therefore, that the electrical measurements indicated the two voltages, speech and noise, were equal in magnitude. Since the earphones transduce frequencies only up to about 4,500 cps, however, the acoustic level of the noise was about 2 db lower than these electrical measurements indicate. The over-all acoustic level of the voice at the listener's ears was approximately 90 db re .0002 dyne/cm².

The speech channel was not a high quality system. Only the speech frequencies between 200 and 3,000 cps were passed along to the listener.²

Only two Ss were used throughout the experiments. Both had normal auditory acuity, and both were familiar with the design and theory of the experiments. The Ss were located in different rooms, connected only by the communication channel described above, and they alternated as talker and listener. Some particular S/N was set up in the channel, and the talker proceeded to read a list of test items. These items were pronounced after a carrier sentence, "You will write. . . ." During this carrier sentence the talker adjusted his voice level to give the proper deflection of the monitoring VU meter, and then the test item was delivered with the same degree of effort. This procedure preserves the inherent variability of English words—the word "peep" has much less acoustic energy than the word "raw" when both words are pronounced with equal emphasis by a normal talker. By monitoring the carrier sentence rather than the test item, the relative intensities of the speech sounds are preserved in a natural fashion. The listener then recorded the item on a test blank, and these test sheets were later graded and the scores converted to percentages.

IMPORTANCE OF TEST MATERIALS

The kind of speech materials used to test communication systems is an important variable determining the results of the tests.   Figure 1 illustrates

² For the convenience of those who may wish to apply one of the several schemes for predicting articulation scores, the frequency response of the system may be obtained by ordering Document 3250 from American Documentation Institute, 1719 N Street, N. W., Washington 6, D.C., remitting $1.00 for microfilm (images 1 in. high on standard 35 mm. motion picture film) or $1.00 for photocopies (6 × 8 in.) readable without optical aid.

how much difference the test materials can make. These three functions were obtained for the communication channel and the personnel described above.   The test materials used for these three functions were the following.

(a) The *digits* were pronounced *zero, wun, too, thuh-ree, four, f-i-i-v, six, seven, ate, niner*. (b) The *sentences* were those constructed at the Psycho-Acoustic Laboratory (1). A sentence consists of five major words connected by auxiliary "of's," "the's," etc. The score shown in Fig. 2 represents the percentage of these major words heard correctly. (c) The *nonsense syllables* used were also those published by Egan (1). To standardize the pronounciation and recording of the nonsense syllables, an abbreviated phonetic symbolism was used.

The values of S/N necessary for 50 per cent correct responses are approximately −14 db for digits, −4 db for the individual words in a sentence, and +3 db for nonsense syllables. At a S/N where practically no nonsense syllables were recorded correctly, nearly all the digits were correctly communicated. Differences of this magnitude require explanation. What differences among these spoken stimuli make some easy to hear and others quite difficult? A list of perceptual aspects—rhythm, accent, grouping, meaning, or phonetic composition—can be suggested.

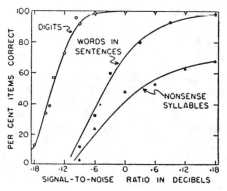

FIG. 1. Relative intelligibility of different test materials

Our experiments indicate, however, that these various characteristics of the stimulus that *did* occur are less important than the characteristics of the stimuli that *could* have occurred but didn't. The most important variable producing the differences is the range of possible alternatives from which a test item is selected. A listener's expectation (or, more precisely, his freedom of choice) is determined by the context in which the particular phonetic pattern occurs. When digits are used, the listener can respond correctly with a marginal impression of the relatively intense vowel sound alone, because all the digits, with the exception of *five* and *nine*, have different vowels. Since the alternatives are thus limited, the digit is interpreted correctly, although the same acoustic stimulus is quite ambiguous when the alternatives are not so limited. With nonsense syllables, however, this limitation of possibilities is far less helpful; the listener feels that anything can happen. To record the nonsense syllable correctly, a listener must perceive each phoneme correctly, and the perception of one phoneme in a syllable does not give a clue to the other phonemes in the same syllable. Not only must the listener hear the vowels correctly, but the less intense consonant sounds must also be distinguished.

SIZE OF TEST VOCABULARY

An articulation test is a rather unusual combination of the familiar psychophysical procedures. The experiment requires the listener to select, not one out of two or three, but one out of several thousand alternative responses. Thus the number of alternatives involved becomes an interesting variable.

Suppose we try to adapt spoken stimuli as closely as possible to the traditional method of constant stimuli. To this end we might use a single speech sound or a single syllable as the stimulus, present this speech unit at various intensities, and ask *S* to report whether or not he heard each presentation. This procedure determines a threshold of audibility for the particular speech unit. The practical value of this isolated datum is negligible. The experiment must be repeated for all the forty or fifty different speech sounds or the thousands of different syllables of English. And then we know only about audibility, not intelligibility.

Consider this distinction between audible speech and intelligible speech. It is intuitively clear that the words *audible* and *intelligible* are not synonyms, and listeners give reliably higher thresholds when asked to make continuous discourse "just understandable" instead of "just audible" (2). The crux of the difference is that intelligibility involves a complex discrimination and identification, whereas audibility is simply a discrimination of presence or absence.

It seems reasonable, therefore, to call a speech unit intelligible when *it is possible for an average listener with normal hearing to distinguish it from a set of alternative units.* By a speech unit is meant any combination of vocal noises—phonemes, syllables, words, phrases, sentences. The act of distinguishing can take various forms—repeating the unit, writing it down, pointing to it, behaving in accordance with its content, etc. The critical part of this definition concerns the set of alternative speech units from which the particular unit is selected. This part of the definition reduces intelligibility to discriminability, and avoids the questions of semantic rules and meaning. Discriminability is a function of the number of alternatives and the similarities among them. The word "loot" is easily discriminated if all the alternatives are trisyllabic, but difficult to distinguish, other things being equal, in a set of alternatives that includes "boot," "loop," "jute," "lewd," "mute," "loose," etc.

An articulation test is analogous to a test of visual acuity where the percentage of correct judgments of a fixed set of test figures is plotted as a function of the level of illumination. A differential judgment is required under various favorable and unfavorable conditions. In such an experiment we determine the most unfavorable conditions under which the discrimination can be made, rather than the most unfavorable conditions under which the presence of the stimuli can be detected. These are clearly different thresholds and correspond to what we have called the thresholds of intelligibility and of audibility.

A difficult discrimination quickly becomes impossible as the conditions are made unfavorable, whereas an easy and obvious difference remains noticeable almost as long as the stimuli can be detected. The discrimination of a difference of 3 cycles in frequency, for example, is fairly accurate under favorable conditions—at 1,000 cps and 100 db. If the intensity is progressively reduced, however, such a small difference becomes imperceptible. For a simpler discrimination, say 30 cycles difference in frequency, the listener can respond accurately at all intensities down to 5 or 10 db above the threshold of audibility.

The situation is manageable so long as we have some index of the difficulty of the discrimination. Thus, in the tonal example, the difficulty can be gauged by the size of the difference in frequency. With the articulation test, however, such an index is not available. We could utilize known differences in the spectra of the sounds to construct an index of the distance between speech sounds, but this index is not yet available. For the present we must approach the problem in a simpler way.

Imagine a many-dimensional space with a separate coordinate for each one of the different frequencies involved in human speech sounds. Along each coordinate plot the relative amplitude of the component at that frequency. In this hyperspace each unique speech sound is represented by a single point. Each point in the hyperspace represents a single acoustic spectrum. The group of similar sounds comprising a phoneme is represented by a cluster of points in the hyperspace. If a language utilized only two different phonemes, the hyperspace could be split into two parts, one for each phoneme. The distance between the two phonemes could be made as large as the vocal mechanism permits, and discrimination would be relatively easy. But suppose the number of different phonemes in the language is increased from two to ten. With ten different phonemes the hyperspace must be divided into at least ten subspaces, and the average distance between phonemes must be smaller with ten phonemes than it is with two. The discriminations involved must be correspondingly more precise. If the number of alternative phonemes is increased to a thousand, then the listener is required to make even more precise discriminations.

In other words, the ease with which a discrimination of speech sounds can be made is limited according to the number of different speech sounds that must be discriminated. From this line of reasoning it follows that the number of alternatives can be used to gauge the difficulty of discrimination. This argument has been developed by Shannon (5) to give a measure of the amount of information in a message. The interesting aspect of this index of difficulty, or of amount of information, is that it does not depend upon the characteristics of the particular item,

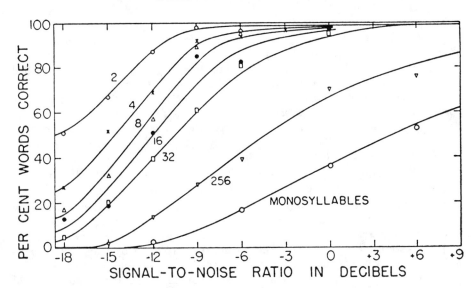

FIG. 2. Intelligibility of monosyllables as a function of the size of the text vocabulary. (Data are not corrected for effects of chance.)

but upon the range of items that *could* occur.

The range of alternatives was used as the experimental variable in the following way. The listener was informed that each test word would be one of the items from a given restricted vocabulary. The size of the test vocabulary was alternatively 2, 4, 8, 16, 32, or 256 words. The talker always spoke one of the words from the prearranged list.

The words used in the restricted vocabularies were chosen at random from the list of phonetically balanced monosyllables published by Egan (2). For the two-alternative vocabulary, different pairs of words were chosen and typed on the listener's answer sheet. The talker read one of the pair, and the listener checked the item he heard. A similar procedure was used for the four- and eight-word vocabularies. For the 16-, 32-, and 256-word vocabularies the listeners had a list of all the words before them, and studied this list until they made their choice. The choice was recorded and a signal given to the talker to proceed to the next item. The Ss studied carefully the particular list used in any test and arranged the words according to the vowel sounds before the tests began.

The results are summarized in Table I and in Fig. 2. Included with the data for restricted vocabularies are data for words from the original list of 1,000 monosyllables, obtained

with no list of choices available to the listener. When these data are corrected for chance, the two-word vocabulary gives a threshold (50 per cent of the words correct) at −14 db, the 256-word vocabulary gives a threshold at −4 db, and the unrestricted list of

TABLE I

PER CENT WORDS CORRECT IN ARTICULATION TESTS WITH VOCABULARIES OF VARIOUS SIZES

S/N in db	Size of Vocabulary							
	2	4	8	Digits	16	32	256	Mono-syllables
−21	49							
−18	51	27	17	13	13	5		
−15	67	52	32	38	19	20	2	
−12	87	69	57	73	51	39	14	3
− 9	98	92	89	92	85	61	28	
− 6		94	95	99	82	81	39	17
− 3		96						
0				100	97	95	70	37
+ 6				100			76	53
+12				100			90	70
+18								82

334   G. A. MILLER, G. A. HEISE, AND W. LICHTEN

monosyllables gives a threshold at +4 db. With the same test words the threshold is changed 18 db by varying the number of alternatives. This result supports the argument that it is not so much the particular item as the context in which the item occurs that determines its intelligibility.

CONTEXT OF THE SENTENCE

A word is harder to understand if it is heard in isolation than if it is heard in a sentence. This fact is illustrated by Fig. 3. Sentences containing five key words were read, and the listener's responses were scored as the percentage of these key words that were heard correctly. These data are shown by the filled circles in Figs. 1 and 3. For comparison, the key words were extracted from the sentences, scrambled, and read in isolation. The scores obtained under these conditions are shown by the open circles of Fig. 3. The removal of sentential context changes the threshold 6 db.

The effect of the sentence is comparable to the effect of a restricted vocabulary, although the degree of restriction is harder to estimate. When the talker begins a sentence, "Apples grow on ———," the range of possible

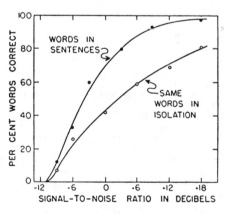

FIG. 3. Effect of sentence context on the intelligibility of words

continuations is sharply restricted. This restriction makes the discrimination easier and lowers the threshold of intelligibility. A detailed statistical discussion of the restrictions imposed by English sentence structure is given by Shannon (5), and is used in a simple recall experiment by Miller and Self-ridge (4).

EFFECTS OF REPETITION

When an error occurs in vocal communication, the listener can ask for a repetition of the message. The repeated message is then heard in the context provided by the original message. If the original message enabled the listener to narrow the range of alternatives, his perception of the repeated message should be more accurate. A series of tests were run with various kinds of test materials to evaluate the importance of the context of repetition. These tests were run with automatic repetition of every item and, also, with repetitions only when the listener thought he had not received the test item correctly.

The improvement in the articulation scores obtained with automatic and with requested repetitions was found to be about the same. A slight but insignificant difference was found in favor of the requested repetition, and if we add to this the savings in time achieved by omitting the unnecessary repetitions, the requested repetition is clearly superior.

The advantage gained by repetition is small for all types of test materials. In Fig. 4 data are given for the effects of repeating automatically the monosyllabic words. The difference in threshold between one presentation and three successive presentations is only 2.5 db. Similar data for words heard in sentences show a shift of 2 db, and for digits, 1.5 db.

These results indicate that the improvement that can be achieved by the simple repetition of a message is

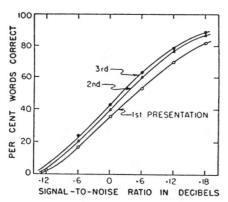

Fig. 4. Effects of repetition of test words on the articulation score

slight. The repeated message contains approximately the same information, and the same omissions, that the original message contained. If the listener thinks he heard the word correctly, he persists in his original response, whether it is right or wrong. If he thinks he heard the word incorrectly, he does not use this presumably incorrect impression to narrow the range of possibilities when the item recurs. In any case, no strong factor is at work to improve the accuracy on repeated presentations, and so we obtain only the slight improvement indicated in Fig. 4.

The results indicate that far more improvement in communication is possible by standardizing procedures and vocabulary than by merely repeating all messages one to two times.

In general, therefore, the results are in qualitative agreement with the mathematical theory of communication presented by Shannon (5). A precise quantitative comparison of the data with the theory cannot be made in the absence of trustworthy information about the distributions of errors. Seemingly reasonable assumptions about the error distributions give results consistent with theoretical predictions, but a more thorough study would be rewarding. For a given sig-nal-to-noise ratio the listener receives a given amount of information per second (according to Shannon's definition), and articulation scores can be predicted for different types of test materials on the basis of the average amount of information needed to receive each type of test item correctly.

Summary

Articulation tests showed the effects of limiting the number of alternative test items upon the threshold of intelligibility for speech in noise. The number of alternative test items was limited by providing three kinds of context: (a) restricting the size of the test vocabulary, (b) using the words in sentences, and (c) repeating the test words. Differences among test materials with respect to their intelligibility are due principally to the fact that some materials require more information than others for their correct perception. The relative amount of information necessary for a given type of item is a function of the range of alternative possibilities. As the range of alternatives increases, the amount of information necessary per item also increases, and so the noise level must be decreased to permit more accurate discrimination.

(Manuscript received April 24, 1950)

References

1. Egan, J. P. *Articulation testing methods, II.* OSRD Report No. 3802, February, 1942. (Available through Office of Technical Services, U.S. Department of Commerce, Washington, D.C., as PB 22848.)
2. Egan, J. P. Articulation testing methods. *Laryngoscope*, 1948, **58**, 955–991.
3. Fletcher, H., and Steinberg, J. C. Articulation testing methods. *Bell Syst. Tech. J.*, 1929, **8**, 806–854.
4. Miller, G. A., and Selfridge, J. Verbal context and the recall of meaningful material. *Amer. J. Psychol.*, 1950, **63**, 176–185.
5. Shannon, C. E. A mathematical theory of communication. *Bell Syst. Tech. J.*, 1948, **27**, 379–423, 623–656.

151

INTELLIGIBILITY OF EXCERPTS FROM FLUENT SPEECH:
EFFECTS OF RATE OF UTTERANCE AND
DURATION OF EXCERPT*

J. M. PICKETT**   and   IRWIN POLLACK***
*Air Force Cambridge Research Laboratories and Air Force Electronic Systems
Division, Bedford, Mass.*

The purpose was to study factors in the intelligibility of words removed from fluent speech. The talker recorded a short text at three rates of continuous utterance : very fast, normal, and very slow. Then samples representing one or more text words were removed by gating. The same text words were removed at each rate of utterance. The samples were presented to listeners in intelligibility tests. Four talkers were tested, each with a different text from which 24 to 28 samples were removed at each rate. Short samples were less intelligible than long samples. On the average, fast and slow samples were equal in intelligibility when equated in duration. This is interpreted to indicate a balanced trade-off between slow, precise articulation of a small amount of text and rapid, slurred articulation of a large amount of text in the same time interval. Slow utterance was slightly more intelligible in noise. Finally, the samples were vocoded and then reconstructed synthetically on both a stretched time base and the normal time base. The stretch-vocoded fast samples were slightly longer in duration than the normal-vocoded slow samples representing the same words. However, the stretch-vocoded samples were lower in intelligibility.

Speech communication is normally a rather fluent, sequential activity. However, for purposes of standardization and control, investigations of speech intelligibility have tended to concentrate upon words spoken in isolation or within well-defined carrier sentences. Isolated words spoken in such contexts are not entirely representative of fluent utterances. For example, Shearme and Holmes (1962) have shown that the vowel formants of fluent speech are located at more neutral positions than the formants of the same vowels spoken in isolated " carrier " words. Effects of the rate of fluent speech on vowel formant frequencies have been studied recently by Miller, Pierce, and Mathews (1962), and by Lindblom (1963).

One approach to the study of normal speech is to test the perception of words spoken at different rates. For words spoken in isolation, Black (1955) found that short, staccato words were less intelligible than normal words and prolonged words. Stowe and Hampton (1961) studied the intelligibility of messages assembled from isolated pre-recorded words and pre-recorded syllables. Slow rates of utterance in

* This is joint research of the Speech Research Branch, Data Sciences Laboratory, A. F. Cambridge Research Laboratories, under Project 5628, Communication Processes, and of the Decision Sciences Laboratory, A. F. Electronic Systems Division, under Project 7682, Man Computer Information Processing. This report is identified by the Electronic Systems Division as ESD-TDR-36-361 ; further reproduction of it is authorized for purposes of the U.S. Government.

** Now at Research Division, Melpar, Inc., Falls Church, Virginia.

*** Now at Mental Health Research Institute, University of Michigan, Ann Arbor, Michigan.

Language and Speech, Vol. 6, 151–164 (1963).   © 1963, Kingston Press Service.

For a fixed duration of utterance, however, a trade-off relation may be available. Slow rates of utterance permit more careful articulation than rapid rates. On the other hand, higher rates of utterance squeeze more words within a given period and thus provide more context, which can help a listener to resolve uncertainties in the original recording yielded higher intelligibility in the assembled messages than faster rates.

the details of articulation.

Computers have recently been programmed to identify words when they are spoken in isolation and when the vocabulary is not too large (David and Selfridge, 1962). Ultimately, we shall want our computers to perceive fluent speech. The use of surrounding context has been proposed as a way to resolve ambiguities in machine perception of speech (Fry and Denes, 1958; Peterson, 1961). We felt that initial studies of how much fluent context aids the human speech receiver might be useful in planning for context in computer programmes.

In the present set of experiments we try to assess the role of fluent context in the intelligibility of speech excerpts taken from continuous utterance at various rates of speaking.

PROCEDURE

Four short paragraphs were selected to record for speech material. The paragraphs were :

" Going back in time we come first to the ice age when a large part of the world was covered with ice and some animals looked quite like they do today ". (Talker HP)

" From earliest times men have used canals to irrigate their farm lands and to drain swampy or flooded districts and to transport goods from one place to another within a country." (Talker JMP)

" We need water most when the weather is hot : it comes out of the pores of our skin making us cooler but then we are thirsty and need to take a drink."

(Talker WWD)
" On a little island off the rocky Maine coast, John's father was a lighthouse-keeper. Although most of the family was overweight, John's mother was a light house-keeper. John's mother taught school all day but, because servants were expensive, she was also a light housekeeper. On this rocky island where John's father was a lighthouse-keeper, his mother who was so small that everyone said that she was a light housekeeper, had to, despite the lack of electrical appliances, be a light housekeeper to a family of ten." (Talker PL)

The underlined sections in the paragraphs are those from which excerpts were later removed for testing. No words were underlined in the written texts provided for the talkers. A given paragraph was recorded by one talker at three rates of utterance : deliberately slow, normal, and deliberately fast. Four experienced male talkers were used. They rehearsed the types of utterance under coaching by one of the experimenters. Particular attention was given to making the slow utterance fluent and continuous with as few silences as possible.

Excerpts of one or more words were excised from fluent sections containing no silent periods other than those of normal stop consonants. The same set of excised samples was made for each of the three rates of utterance of a talker. The excerpts were prepared with an editing system consisting of a playback head which repeatedly scanned a two-second section of the original tape recording and a variable electronic gate which was synchronized to open at a given location on each scan.[1] The sychronization was controlled by a reference pulse which occurred at the beginning of each scan. The reference pulse triggered two variable intervals, one of which opened the gate, and one of which closed the gate. Each proposed excerpt was scanned repeatedly while the first author adjusted the beginning and end of the gate, listening to the excerpt over a high quality audio system. The gate was finally adjusted so that the experimenter could hear none of the last sound in the preceding word and none of the first sound of the succeeding word. The resulting sample was recorded.

The samples from a scanned section were made in an ascending serial procedure. After the initial word of a section was first gated and recorded, the duration of the gate was increased to include the succeeding word ; the next sample was made by adding, the third word, etc., until a section of 3 to 7 words, of about 1.5 to 2.0 sec. in duration was obtained. The duration of each excerpt was measured by an electronic counter operating upon a 1,000 cps. timing signal passed by the gate. The rise-time and fall-time of the gate was 1 msec. Clicks occurred only infrequently and they were easily eliminated by a small change in gate duration (1 to 5 msec.).

The average syllable rate during the longest samples of each section was calculated for each talker at each rate of utterance. The rate was calculated on the basis of the number of syllables specified in the text and the total duration of the sample. The resulting range of talkers' rates was 3.0 to 4.0 syllables per second (syl./sec.) for slow utterance, 4.4 to 5.5 syl./sec. for normal utterance, and 6.2 to 7.7 syl./sec. for fast utterance.

For the listening tests, excerpts were played back in an ascending temporal sequence. The samples from one talker were played back in a single test where the order of the samples proceeded from short to long samples and from fast to slow utterance. A given sample spoken at a fast rate occurred before a slower version of the same text. Otherwise, the samples were roughly arranged in order of increasing duration except that successive samples of the same text were avoided. This resulted in a quasi-

---

[1] *This system was designed by Caldwell P. Smith, Chief, Digital Speech Compression Branch, Data Sciences Laboratory. The authors are very grateful to him and to the Branch Technician, James Eng, who set up and checked the system.*

random sampling of the original text over any portion of the tests. The object of these manipulations of the test order was to strike a compromise between a test where the listener received each sample with no outside context and a more practical test where a body of analyzed data could be gathered on the same set of words. With the procedure used, outside context is low initially for the short samples, but increases as the test proceeds to the long samples, which provide their own context anyway.

The listeners were instructed before a test that the samples were taken from the fluent speech of a male talker, that initially the samples were very short, that each sample represented one or more words, and that sometimes the talker spoke very rapidly while at other times he spoke slowly and distinctly. After hearing a sample, the listener wrote the word or words which he thought the talker had intended. Then the next sample was played, the listener wrote his response, and so on, until all the samples of a talker had been played. Each test required about 45 minutes. Listeners were tested in groups of three to six. There were fifteen different listeners ; they were college students who were paid for their services. None of the listeners knew the texts spoken by the talkers.

All recording, copying, and playback equipment was of high quality with smooth frequency response.[2] The particular combinations of recording and playback equipments used in the experiment resulted in an over-all response-frequency characteristic that increased at an average rate of 2 db./octave between 100 and 4,000 cps. and fell 5 db. between 4,000 and 7,000 cps. The overall speech-to-noise ratio was approximately 34 db. In the listening tests, matched binaural earphones (Grason-Stadler Telephonics) were used.

The test responses were scored word by word against the text. To be scored as correct, the response word was required to match the text word and be in the same relative word-position. Errors of spelling were ignored when it appeared that they were phonetically "correct". Errors of insertion, and errors of words added to the text after the positions of the text words, were also ignored ; these occurred on 3% of the responses. This method of scoring allowed us to count any correct words following any extra or omitted word. Omissions were scored incorrect. The percentage of correct response words was calculated for each sample.

EFFECTS OF SAMPLE DURATION AND RATE OF UTTERANCE

We first sought to determine if the intelligibility of words of excised samples was strongly influenced by the word-position within the sample. By our procedures, the

---

[2] *The microphone was a Bruel and Kjaer 4133 condenser microphone located in an anechoic room ; the first recorder was an Ampex 354. The excerpts were recorded on an Ampex 350, played back on an Ampex 351, and recorded on the tracks of a Teleprompter Spot-Tape from which they were played back for final assembly of a test tape recorded on the Ampex 351. Test tapes were played back on the Ampex 351 through a high-quality laboratory amplifier to Telephonics TDH-39 headsets.*

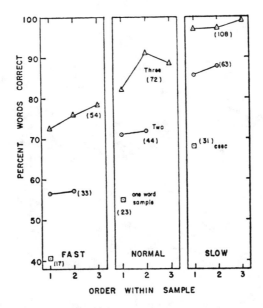

Fig. 1. Word intelligibility within short speech samples excised from fluent speech which was uttered at fast, normal, and slow rates. At each rate the results are given according to the position, represented on the abscissa, of the test word within the sample. The shape of the points is coded according to the number of words in the sample. At a given word position the test words were the same, irrespective of rate or number of words in sample. Average sample durations are given in parentheses (csec = 0.01 sec.). It will be noted that position within sample has only small effects on intelligibility relative to the effects of rate and/or duration and number of words in sample.

same set of words occurred at a given position in the samples, irrespective of the length of sample or of the rate of utterance. Fig. 1 examines the intelligibility of the first three word-positions at each of three rates of utterance. The number of words in the sample is coded by the shape of the points and word-position is plotted along the abscissa. For example, the points above 1 on the abscissa represent the intelligibility of the first words of 1-word samples (squares), the first words of 2-word samples (circles), and the first words of 3-word samples (triangles). The numbers in parentheses give the mean duration in csec. of the samples. Fig. 1 suggests :

(1) Within any utterance, represented in the aggregate by connected points, word intelligibility is only slightly determined by the position of the word within the sample. Therefore, the results of subsequent figures are given by the mean word intelligibility, averaged over all the words of the sample.

(2) For the same words at the same word-position, represented by the points within a given column, word intelligibility increases with the number of words in the sample and/or with the duration of the sample.

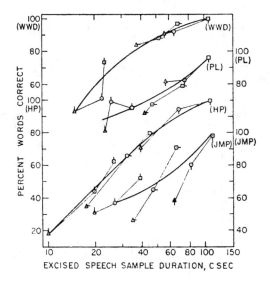

Fig. 2. Average word intelligibility of speech samples excised from the utterance of four talkers, WWD, PL, HP, and JMP. The ordinate gives the intelligibility, displaced to separate the talkers. The abscissa gives the average duration of the speech samples formed in sets of one-word, two-word, and three-word samples at each rate of utterance. The number of words is coded by a clock-hand on each point; 12 o'clock = one-word, 3 o'clock = two-word, and 6 o'clock = three-word. The shape of the points represents the rate of utterance; triangles = fast rate, circles = normal rate, and squares = slow rate. For a given talker the test words were the same at each rate of utterance and points representing the same set of words are connected by thin lines. Duration of sample and/or rate of utterance have a strong influence on intelligibility and they appear to be interchangeable except for talker JMP.

(3)   For excerpts of equivalent duration, indicated by equal parenthetic numbers in the different sections, intelligibility is approximately constant and independent of the rate of utterance.

The average results for individual talkers are shown in Fig. 2 as a function of average sample duration. In this figure it is clear that sample duration has large effects on intelligibility and that the trend is similar for all talkers. In addition it appears that the effect of a change in sample duration is roughly the same whether the change is due to a change in rate of utterance or to a change in the number of words in the sample. The results of three of the four talkers are consistent with this rule; talker JMP is the exception.

Fig. 3 presents a closer examination of effects of the rate of utterance on short and long, one-word and two-word, samples. The one-word samples of each talker under fast utterance were arranged in order of duration. Then a set of eight short words was obtained by taking the two shortest words of each of the talkers. This

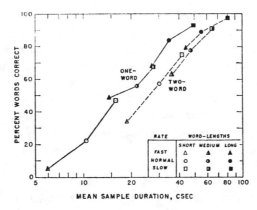

Fig. 3. Summary of effect of sample duration on intelligibility. The one- and two-word samples from fast utterance were divided into short, medium, and long sets (sets differing in word-length); each talker was represented equally within a set. The same word-sets were also formed from normal and slow utterance. The average intelligibility and average sample duration of each set is plotted by a point coded according to the legend-box. The average effect of increasing sample duration is the same whether the increase is due to a slower rate of utterance of the same words or due to taking longer words at a given rate of utterance.

set of words was : *or, a, and, the, we, are, who, and.* A set of medium-length words was formed by taking the two next longer words of each talker ; this set was : *to, when, to, we, and, off, another, most.* A set of long words was formed by taking the two longest words of each talker ; the words were : *it, like, back, making, times, because, irrigate, despite.* The open symbols of Fig. 3 show the results for the set of short words under fast, normal, and slow rates of utterance ; the half-filled symbols are for the set of medium-length words, and the solid symbols are for the set of long words. By this procedure, we examine short and long words under slow, medium, and fast rates of utterance.

The main point to be seen in Fig. 3 is that the average effect of increasing sample duration on intelligibility is the same whether the samples are lengthened by choosing words that are intrinsically longer, or whether the samples are lengthened by retarding the rate of utterance of the same set of words. We interpret this to indicate that, for a given average duration of sample, there is an intelligibility trade-off between rapid, approximate articulation of a large number of speech sounds and slow, precise articulation of a smaller number of speech sounds.

A similar analysis was made for the two-word samples. The set of short two-word samples was : *when a, to the, and to, who was, and to, off the, to take, we need.* The set of medium-length two-word samples was : *and some, we come, the weather, most of, or flooded, another within, a family, are thirsty.* The set of long two-word samples was : *back in, like they, it comes, making us, times men, despite the, irrigate their, because servants.* The set of long two-word samples was actually formed by adding the following word to each word of the long one-word set. It turned out that six of these samples were actually the two longest two-word samples from each of three talkers. As in the one-word analysis, the sets of short, medium, and long two-word samples contained the same text words at all three rates of utterance.

For the two-word samples of Fig. 3, just as for the one-word samples, the average effect on intelligibility of increasing sample duration is the same whether the increase is obtained by retarding the rate of utterance of the same words or by taking longer words at the same rate of utterance.

The two-word samples appear to have lower intelligibility than the one-word samples of the same duration. However, it is easy to show the aiding effects of context on the two-word results. Assume that the two-word samples were made up of two unrelated one-word samples. Then a reasonable two-word curve would be the present one-word curve shifted to twice the one-word sample durations. But the actual two-word results are well above these hypothetical two-word results. We would predict this difference for two reasons. First, each word of an actual two-word sample provides a contextual aid to identification of the other word (Stowe, Harris, and Hampton, 1963) ; second, in the test procedure, two-word samples were heard after previous presentation of shorter one-word samples from the same talker. Nevertheless, one-word samples are more intelligible than two-word samples of equal duration. That is to say that, if two words are to occur in the time for one long word, they must be short, relatively unrelated words, whereas the long single word may be of two syllables that are highly redundant, as may be seen by comparing the words of the short two-word set with the words of the long one-word set. Also there was a slight procedural bias which favoured one-word intelligibility because responses of only one word occurred to 15.6% of the two-word samples but two-word responses rarely occurred for one-word samples.

In characterizing the relation between intelligibility and sample duration, using the data of Fig. 3, we need to keep in mind the artifacts and biases due to our methods. In the initial part of each test, context was very low and, in addition, false auditory cues due to the gating rate would have a high weight. Thus our measured intelligibility of the early, short samples tends to be biased toward low intelligibility relative to the long, later samples. On the other hand, the intelligibility of the long samples is higher than would be expected without the preceding context of the test. Thus, although it appears in Fig. 3 that intelligibility is a rather linear function of the logarithm of the average sample duration, the removal of the biases would tend to make the function more sigmoid.

In regard to the amount of fluent speech, isolated from its context, that is necessary before a listener can approach perfect identification of the words, we can make the conservative estimate that a sample of at least 80 csec. is required. We may also state that this amount of time is relatively independent of the rate of utterance. If the rate of utterance is high, individual speech sounds might be poorly articulated or omitted, but a larger number of syllables or words will occur in a given time. If the rate of utterance is low, articulation may be more precise but fewer words can occur

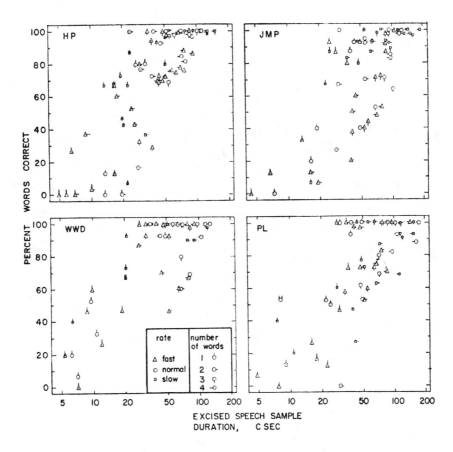

Fig. 4. Intelligibility of excised speech samples. Intelligibility is plotted on the ordinate vs. duration of the sample on the abscissa. Each point represents responses of 15 listeners. Each graph is for one of the talkers. At a given sample duration there is a wide range of intelligibility.

in the given time. This trade-off effect is less subject to the test contextual bias mentioned above because samples of approximately equal duration occurred in the same portion of a test and thus were subject to equal effects of preceding test context.

The effect of sample duration is demonstrated in Fig. 4 for individual excised samples for each of the talkers. Fig. 4 suggests :

(1) There is extremely large variability in scores for different excised samples of nearly equal duration. For example, for excised samples of about 30 csec. of Talker PL, intelligibility scores ranged from zero to 100%.

(2) In general, intelligibility improves with the duration of the utterance and is relatively independent of the rate of speaking for a fixed duration of utterance.

160   *Intelligibility of Excerpts from Fluent Speech*

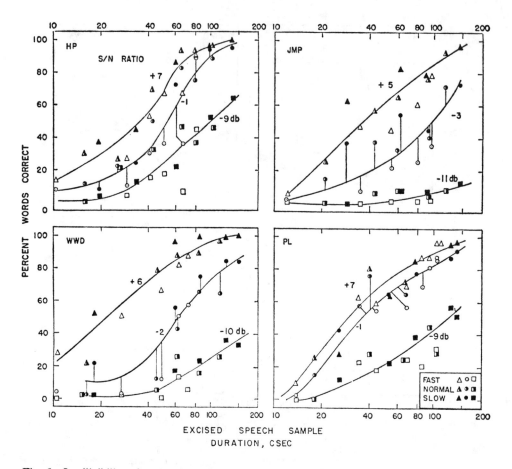

Fig. 5. Intelligibility of excised speech samples heard in noise.

INTELLIGIBILITY OF SAMPLES IN NOISE

Tests of the excised samples were also performed with a white noise background, using new listening crews. The aim was to determine whether fast speech would be more sensitive to noise interference than slow speech. The noise was at a constant level of about 85 db. in the listeners' headsets and the speech samples were heard mixed with the noise at various speech-to-noise ratios (S/N ratios). The S/N ratios were based on the means of the speech levels of the longest samples as read on a VU meter. A new crew of 3 to 6 listeners was used at each S/N ratio.

The intelligibility of the samples heard in noise is shown in Fig. 5 according to average sample duration. Sets of samples having increasing average duration were formed by taking the five shortest samples, the next five shortest samples, and so on, for each talker and at each rate. Each point in the figure gives the intelligibility of a set of five samples plotted at their average duration and is the result of two tests where the S/N ratios were 2 db. above and 2 db. below the mean S/N ratio shown on the graphs. A separate graph is plotted for each talker. The shapes of the points correspond to low, medium, and high S/N ratios ; the points are filled according to the rate of utterance. It will be noted that fast utterance (unfilled symbols) tends to be lower in intelligibility than slow utterance (filled symbols) at all S/N ratios. However, these differences are small relative to the large effects of sample duration and S/N ratios.

TIME-STRETCHING VIA DIGITAL SPECTRAL PATTERNS

Up to this point in the discussion we have assumed that the main factor which causes intelligibility to rise with increasing sample duration is the increasing acoustic and verbal context. However, there is a possibility that the sheer shortness of the short samples is a factor in itself, i.e. that there is some point in the perceptual process where a short stimulus cannot be effectively processed. If this were true we might assume that if acoustic segments of a short word could be stretched to cover a longer period of time, then the stretched word would be more intelligible.

A digital analyzing and processing system was made available to us for stretching the speech samples without altering their frequency spectrum. The system was the Air Force Cambridge Research Laboratories' Digital Voice Data Processor, designed by Caldwell P. Smith. The system, in brief, consists of an 18-channel spectrum analyzer with digital channel outputs, a magnetic drum for storing the digitized spectral patterns, and a speech synthesizer which can be operated from the digital patterns as an input. When the patterns are stored on the drum they may be played back to the synthesizer on an expanded time scale by iterating each pattern a number of times before proceeding to the next pattern.[3]

The procedure was to process all of our original samples and store them on the drum. Then the samples were synthesized in two ways : first, on their normal time base and, second, on a doubled time base obtained by iterating once each pattern

---

[3] *The spectrum analyzing channels ranged from 100 to 5,000 cps. The sampling rate of each channel output for the digitizing process was 50 samples per second and each sample was quantized into eight logarithmically spaced levels normalized relative to the average channel output. The maximum information rate of spectral analysis was 18 channels × 50 samples per sec. × 3 amplitude bits = 2,700 bits/sec. In addition, the fundamental pitch of each voiced sample is detected, digitized in 64 levels, and stored with the spectral pattern. Voiced-unvoiced source and amplitude information required 200 bits/sec. The total information rate, then, was 200 plus 2,700 spectral bits plus 300 pitch bits, or 3,200 bits/sec. The information rate of normal speech is estimated to be more than 50,000 bits/sec, so we may expect the processed samples from speech to be less intelligible than the original samples.*

input to the synthesizer. Finally, the intelligibility of both the normal synthesized samples and the doubled synthesized samples was measured. The intelligibility tests were divided into six tests of about 100 samples per test and each test was presented to a different group of listeners. Each test consisted of four parts ; each part presented all the synthesized samples from one of the four texts for one of the talkers at one rate of utterance. Each of the four parts presented a different talker. Thus, no text was repeated in a test. Within a test, alternate parts were normal synthesized and double synthesized in a counterbalanced order. The samples were not arranged in the order of the main experiment but were taken in the order originally used in removing the samples from the recorded utterances. At a given position, a single word was removed and re-recorded, then that word plus the following word was recorded, these two words plus the third word were recorded, and so on until 3 to 7 words had been removed and recorded from each of the sampling sections indicated above in the texts. The sections were taken in the order of the text. This was the order of samples used in the tests with synthesized speech. Each set of samples from a given section of the text was thus presented in an expanding order, the last sample of the set being the entire section. This test procedure should be contrasted with the presentation in the main experiment which was quasi-random.

TABLE 1

Number of Words in Excerpt	Rate of Utterance	Mean Duration	PER CENT INTELLIGIBILITY	
			Normal Synthesis	Doubled Synthesis
	Fast	16.9 csec.	15.4%	13.2%
One	Normal	23.4 ,,	25.4%	17.4%
	Slow	30.9 ,,	39.8%	27.6%
	Fast	33.0 ,,	18.9%	16.3%
Two	Normal	44.3 ,,	31.0%	25.2%
	Slow	63.1 ,,	50.3%	36.4%
	Fast	54.0 ,,	24.0%	16.7%
Three	Normal	72.4 ,,	41.0%	32.4%
	Slow	108.1 ,,	59.0%	42.1%
	Fast	77.2 ,,	27.8%	19.6%
Four	Normal	101.8 ,,	45.5%	36.4%
	Slow	149.0 ,,	74.8%	44.8%

Intelligibility of synthesized versions of the excerpts processed by a digital vocoder. Each excerpt was synthesized in two ways, normal synthesis on the original time base, and doubled synthesis on a double time base. Mean durations of sets of excerpts are given for the normal time base. Each entry of per cent intelligibility is the per cent words correct in responses of 6 listeners to each word of 5 to 7 excerpts. Stretching to double duration resulted in lower intelligibility.

The listeners were informed of the conditions of sampling and processing of the speech signals. They responded to each sample by recording the word or words they thought had been intended by the talker. For each sample the listeners knew the number of text words represented. Their responses were scored for per cent words heard correctly as described earlier.

The results with the synthesized samples are shown in Table 1. The doubled versions of a given set of samples were always lower in intelligibility than the normal synthesized samples.

The fast-utterance doubled samples are slightly (5%) longer in duration than the original slow-utterance samples but they are much lower in intelligibility. Thus, we would conclude that the primary effect of sample duration in our main experiment is due to contextual and articulatory factors.

SUMMARY AND CONCLUSION

The intelligibility of one or more words removed from fluent speech was studied at various rates of utterance. As the duration of the speech sample increased its intelligibility increased. Nearly perfect intelligibility was obtained with an average sample duration of 80 csec.

The rate of utterance did not produce large effects on intelligibility when the effect of sample duration was taken into account. Thus it appeared that, for a given duration of sample, any slurring of articulation that occurs in fast utterance is compensated by covering more context, while a slow utterance may cover less context but be articulated more clearly.

When the samples were heard in noise, the fast utterance was slightly less intelligible than slow utterance of the same duration.

Control tests were performed with synthetic speech against the possibility that the duration effect is due to duration *per se* rather than to the variation in context. The fast samples were stretched in duration by a factor of two, using a speech analyzer-synthesizer system. The system used digital storage and playback arrangements that allowed the playback to be stretched in time without shifting the speech frequencies. Tests of the synthetic versions of the samples showed that intelligibility of the fast stretched samples was lower than that of the slow unstretched samples (also synthesized from the input of original samples). Thus it appeared that the effect of sample duration in increasing intelligibility is due to the amount of speech context included in the sample.

164   *Intelligibility of Excerpts from Fluent Speech*

REFERENCES

BLACK, J. W. (1955). Some Effects of Changing Time Patterns and Articulation upon Intelligibility and Word Reception. JPR 40, USN School of Aviation Medicine, Pensacola, 31 Jan. 1955.

DAVID, E. E., JR. and SELFRIDGE, O. G. (1962). Eyes and ears for computers. *Proc. I.R.E.*, 50, 1093.

FRY, D. B. and DENES, P. (1958). The solution of some fundamental problems in mechanical speech recognition. *Language and Speech*, 1, 35.

LINDBLOM, B. On Vowel Reduction. Report 29, Speech Transmission Laboratory, Royal Institute of Technology, Stockholm, Sweden, May 15, 1963.

MILLER, J., PIERCE, J. R. and MATHEWS, M. (1962). Study of articulator dynamics, *J. acoust. Soc. Am.*, 34, 1978 (Abstract).

PETERSON, G (1961). Automatic speech recognition procedures. *Language and Speech*, 4, 200.

SHEARME, J. N. and HOLMES, J. N. (1962). An experimental study of the classification of sounds in continuous speech according to their distribution in the Formant 1 - Formant 2 plane. *Proc. 4th Internat. Cong. of Phonetic Sciences* (The Hague), 232.

STOWE, A. N. and HAMPTON, D. B. (1961). Speech synthesis with prerecorded syllables and words, *J. acoust. Soc. Am.*, 33, 810.

STOWE, A. N. HARRIS, W. P. and HAMPTON, D. B. (1963). Signal and context components of word-recognition behaviour, *J. acoust. Soc. Am.*, 35, 639.

Auditory handicap of hearing impairment and the limited benefit of hearing aids

Reinier Plomp

Institute for Perception TNO, Soesterberg, The Netherlands, and Faculty of Medicine, Free University, Amsterdam, The Netherlands
(Received 29 April 1977; revised 31 August 1977)

The aim of this article is to promote a better understanding of hearing impairment as a communicative handicap, primarily in noisy environments, and to explain by means of a quantitative model the essentially limited applicability of hearing aids. After data on the prevalence of hearing impairment and of auditory handicap have been reviewed, it is explained that every hearing loss for speech can be interpreted as the sum of a loss class A (attenuation), characterized by a reduction of the levels of both speech signal and noise, and a loss D (distortion), comparable with a decrease in speech-to-noise ratio. On the average, the hearing loss of class D (hearing loss in noise) appears to be about one-third (in decibels) of the total hearing loss (A+D, hearing loss in quiet). A hearing aid can compensate for class-A hearing losses, giving difficulties primarily in quiet, but not for class-D hearing losses, giving difficulties primarily in noise. The latter class represents the first stage of auditory handicap, beginning at an average hearing loss of about 24 dB.

PACS numbers: 43.66.Sr, 43.70.Dn, 43.66.Ts

INTRODUCTION

Our insights into why hearing-impaired people appear to be so seriously handicapped in everyday listening situations seem to be very scanty. This lack of knowledge particularly manifests itself in the uncritical way in which hearing aids are assumed to be of benefit. Since most conductive defects in the transmission chain up to the cochlea can nowadays be successfully rehabilitated by means of surgery, the great majority of the remaining inoperable cases are sensorineural hearing impairments. Although it is generally recognized that electronic amplification cannot compensate satisfactorily for these losses, it is remarkable how much hearing-aid prescribers expect from careful selection and fitting followed by good training. On the other hand, many hearing impaired appear to be rather disappointed about their hearing aids.

In view of these diverging opinions on the merits and benefits of hearing aids, it seems worthwhile to present a critical review on the various aspects of sensorineural hearing impairment as far as speech reception, both in quiet and against a background of interfering sounds, is concerned. Although many references are given, no attempt at completeness has been made. The aim of this article is to promote a better understanding of hearing impairment as a communicative handicap and to explain the essentially limited applicability of the hearing aid.

I. PREVALENCE OF HEARING IMPAIRMENT AND OF AUDITORY HANDICAP

The importance of the problem under study does not only depend upon the degree to which subjects with sensorineural hearing losses are handicapped, but also upon the percentage of population involved. We start with the latter question.

It may seem obvious that one should investigate the occurrence of auditory handicap by means of inquiries including a sufficiently large sample of population. The results of several studies along this line are available. As early as 1935–1936 the United States Health Service conducted a nationwide investigation into the state of health including impaired hearing (Beasley, 1940). More than 700 000 households were visited and data on 2. 5 million people were collected. Any type of hearing impairment was classified as belonging to one of the following five groups (literal quotations):

(1) *Partial deafness, stage* 1: The individual has difficulty in understanding speech in church, at the theater, or in group conversation, but can hear speech at close range without any artificial assistance.

(2) *Partial deafness, stage* 2: The individual has difficulty hearing direct conversation at close range, but can hear satisfactorily over the telephone or can hear loudly spoken speech.

(3) *Partial deafness, stage* 3: The individual has difficulty hearing over the telephone at ordinary intensities, but can hear amplified speech by means of hearing aids, trumpets, or other means of amplification.

(4) *Total deafness for speech*: The individual cannot hear speech under any circumstances, but acquired the hearing defect after learning to speak language by ordinary means.

(5) *Deaf mute*: The individual was born deaf or acquired severe deafness sufficiently early in life to prevent him from learning speech through the usual means.

Similar inquiries, but on a much smaller scale, were carried out in 1947 in Great Britain (Wilkins, 1950) and in 1950–1951 in Denmark (Bentzen and Jelnes, 1955). Whereas in these investigations the classification just quoted was adopted, this was not the case in more recent inquiries by the United States National Health Survey in 1962–63 and 1971 (NCHS, 1967, 1975a).

Although it is usually overlooked, data obtained from

interviews are of only limited value. Evidence will be presented below showing that such data underestimate the percentage of population actually handicapped. In evaluating the degree to which a person is handicapped, one cannot avoid taking the age of the subject into account.

Experimental evidence indicating that age affects the evaluation of one's own hearing status has been published by Merluzzi and Hinchcliffe (1973). In a study on auditory thresholds of a random sample of a rural population, each subject was asked the question: "Is your hearing normal, or not as good as it used to be?" Both for the subjects who answered "yes" and for those who answered "no," the frequency distributions of hearing levels were determined. It appeared that the intersection of the two distribution curves rose substantially as a function of age. Accepting for this intersection the average hearing loss at 500, 1000, and 2000 Hz (AHL) as a representative single measure of hearing status, this average was found to shift from 5 dB for the 30-yr age group to 28 dB for the 70-yr age group. Apparently subjects cannot avoid evaluating their hearing status with reference to their age, in a more or less comparative manner.

We may assume that the data from the inquiries referred to above have also been influenced by this behavior. This can be verified by comparing the age dependence of the percentage of subjectively handicapped people with the age dependence of the percentage of subjects with AHL exceeding various critical values. This comparison can be performed rather easily because both percentage curves can be satisfactorily approximated by

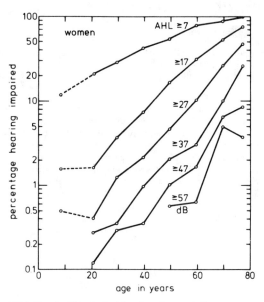

FIG. 2. As Fig. 1, but for female population.

means of exponential curves characterized by the number of years required for doubling the percentage of auditory handicapped, or of AHL beyond some critical value. Although the absolute levels of the handicap curves differ substantially for the various inquiries, the exponent appears to be rather invariant, corresponding to a doubling of the percentage of handicapped every 13–14 yr. As will be shown below, the doubling time for AHL values that are not too low is less than 10 yr. This difference is so large that data obtained from inquiries should not be used for investigating how the percentage of the population handicapped by hearing impairment depends upon age. This percentage has to be derived from audiometric surveys.

Such an audiometric survey, based on 6672 adults from 18 to 79 years of age, was carried out in 1959–1962 by the U. S. National Health Survey (NCHS, 1965), complemented with a similar investigation for children from 6 to 11 years of age in 1963–1965 (NCHS, 1970). [The most recent investigation for youths from 12 to 17 years of age (NCHS, 1975b) does not give the percentage distribution of AHL.] Since, on the average, the AHL for the better ear appears to be a good predictor of the hearing loss for speech (see Sec. IV) this AHL will be considered here.

Figures 1 and 2 represent, as a function of age, the percentage of subjects with AHL exceeding certain values for men and women, respectively. Plotted along a logarithmic percentage scale, most data points agree quite well with straight lines indicating that the percentage increases exponentially with age. The only substantial deviations are the higher AHL values for men below 50. We may assume that hearing loss due to exposure to high-level noise is the disturbing factor. Excluding these cases by considering only the data points above 1%, linear regression lines for the average data of men and women were computed resulting in the lines

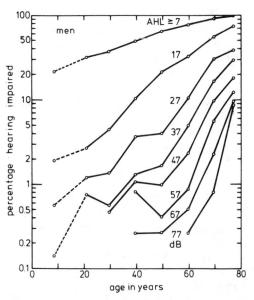

FIG. 1. Percentage of male population with average hearing loss at 500, 1000, and 2000 Hz in the better ear (AHL) equal to or larger than 7, 17, ..., 77 dB, respectively, as a function of age. In this and all further diagrams hearing losses are given in dB ISO. (Data adapted from NCHS, 1965, Table 11 and NCHS, 1970, Table 26.)

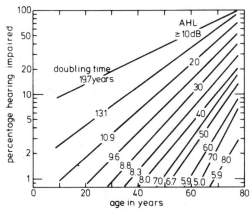

FIG. 3. Average percentage of men and women with AHL ≥ 10, 15, ,.,, 80 dB, respectively, as a function of age. The lines are regression lines based on average data points from Figs. 1 and 2. The slopes of these lines are expressed in the number of years for doubling the percentage.

of Fig. 3. The slopes of the lines are expressed in the number of years in which percentage is doubled.

These diagrams indicate how hearing losses as a measure of auditory handicap increase with age, but they do not reveal which curve should be considered to represent the lower limit of auditory handicap in everyday listening situations. To arrive at this, we have to "calibrate" the lines of Fig. 3 with the aid of the results of the inquiries mentioned earlier. Accepting the responses of the 20-yr age groups as representing the most reliable estimate of the percentage of auditory handicapped, Table I was obtained. The percentage includes all degrees of partial deafness except monaural hearing impairment and is the average for men and women. The last column gives the corresponding AHL, read from Fig. 3. With the exception of the earliest investigation, the dB-values do not differ very much, and we may conclude that young people begin to have hearing difficulties when their AHL is equal to about 24 dB.

Accepting an AHL of 24 dB as the lower limit of auditory handicap, we see from Fig. 3 that at the age of 65 no less than about 24% of the population is handicapped. This value is considerably higher than the 10% we would have concluded directly from inquiries. (Recall that inquiries yield a doubling time of 13.5 yr which means that in the 45-yr period from 20 to 65 the percentage increases from 1% to 10%.)

TABLE I. Percentage of subjectively auditory handicapped among the 20-yr age groups in five enquiries.

	% handicapped of 20-yr group	Corresponding AHL (in dB)
US 1935–36	0.35	≥ 32
UK 1947	1.0	≥ 24
Denmark 1950–51	~1.5	≥ 21
US 1962–63	~0.8	≥ 25
US 1971	~1.3	≥ 22

Up to now we have included all degrees of auditory handicap, corresponding to stage 1 of Beasley's classification quoted above. It appears to be much more difficult to find out what percentage of population has difficulties in accordance with stage 2 and higher stages. The U. S. National Health Surveys in 1962–1963 and 1971 adopted a different classification in which the distinction between hearing difficulties in noise (including reverberation; stage 1) and in quiet (stage 2 and higher) was not maintained. However, there is ample evidence (e. g., Quist-Hanssen, 1967) that this is a meaningful distinction and that stage 2 corresponds to a substantially greater AHL than stage 1. From the data available we may accept as a rough estimate that, on the average, subjects begin to have difficulties in direct one-to-one conversation at close range with AHL ~ 35 dB for the better ear. If stage 3 may be interpreted as defining those people who are really hard of hearing and have difficulties in understanding loud speech without a hearing aid, this stage corresponds to AHL ≥ ~ 55 dB. Subjects may be considered to be totally deaf (stage 4) for AHL ≥ ~ 90 dB (Erber, 1974).

Figures 1 and 2 give the percentage of hearing impaired as a function of age, but do not reveal what percentage of total population is handicapped. This can be determined by applying the percentage data of Figs. 1 and 2 on the age distribution of population. On the basis of estimates for the U. S. for 1 July, 1975, the curve of Fig. 4 was calculated. From the data points for men and women separately we see that above 40 dB AHL the percentage for men is slightly, but consistently higher than for women. For 20 dB < AHL < 50 dB the slope of the curve corresponds rather well with a halving of the percentage per 10 dB increase of AHL.

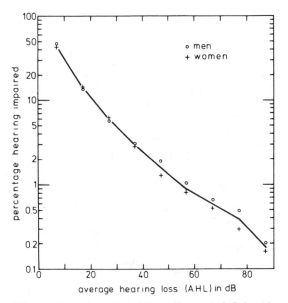

FIG. 4. Percentage of population, all ages included, with AHL ≥ abscissa indicating that 30% has an AHL equal to or larger than 10 dB, etc. The solid line holds for the total population of the United States, the symbols for males and females separately.

TABLE II. Estimates of the hearing loss, averaged over 500, 1000, and 2000 Hz in the better ear, for four successive stages of auditory handicap, and the percentage of the population involved.

Stage	Difficulties in understanding speech	AHL in the better ear (in dB)	Percentage of population
1	In noisy environments	≥ 24	7.5%
2	In close-range conversation in quiet	≥ 35	3.4
3	Loud speech without hearing aid	≥ 55	1.0
4	Totally deaf	≥ 90	0.2

Combining the AHL corresponding to the different stages of auditory handicap with the data reproduced in Fig. 4, we arrive at Table II which gives the corresponding percentages of population for the various stages of partial deafness.

Figure 5 illustrates, on the basis of the lines of Fig. 3 and the population estimates, how the cumulative percentage of auditory handicapped increases with age. We see that, even for an AHL as low as 20 dB, the age of more than half of the handicapped is over 65 yr. It is clear from this diagram that presbycusis is the main cause of hearing difficulties.

It should be noticed that, owing to the strongly improved possibilities of rehabilitating conductive deafness by operation, the large majority of hearing impairments nowadays is sensorineural. Recent figures on the origin of the hearing impairment of patients applying for a hearing aid reveal that only about 20% of the cases are considered as conductive losses, more than 50% as sensorineural losses, with the rest as cases of mixed origin (Chüden, 1969; Brooks, 1972; Carstairs, 1973; Ewertsen, 1974; Pedersen et al., 1974). The specific problems of sensorineural hearing impairment will be discussed in the next sections. It will also be shown that the given relation between AHL and subjective handicap is only significant as an average but cannot be applied satisfactorily on an individual level. Two subjects with the same threshold in quiet may differ widely in the extent to which they are handicapped (Ewertsen and Birk Nielsen, 1973; Birk Nielsen and Ewertsen, 1974).

II. EFFECT OF HEARING IMPAIRMENT ON THE SPEECH-RECEPTION THRESHOLD (SRT)

Section I showed how many people are to be considered to be hearing impaired. This section discusses the implications for speech understanding. As we are interested here in auditory handicap in everyday situations, not only will speech presented in quiet be considered, but also speech presented against a background of interfering noise. Although no statistics seem to be available, it might not be exaggerating to assume that 50% of speech communication takes place in ambient noise with a sound-pressure level (SPL) of 50 dB A or higher. In many cases the disturbing sounds are from

traffic or industrial plants, from domestic equipment or music, but perhaps in most cases the human voice is the source of interference. This may be from a single competing speaker in the same room or reproduced by a radio or TV set, or from several speakers in a restaurant or other place where different conversations take place at the same time, with extreme situations at lively parties and in the foyers of concert halls and theaters. The following discussion considers only human voices as the interfering sound, so that the spectrum of the noise can be treated as identical to the spectrum of the speech one is listening to.

As a measure of our capacity to understand speech in quiet or in noise we use the *speech-reception threshold* (SRT) defined as the sound-pressure level of speech at which 50% of the speech material (words or sentences) is correctly understood. The difference between the SRT of an individual or group and the SRT of young normal-hearing subjects in the same situation is the loss of hearing for speech or *speech-hearing loss* (SHL). As will be shown in Sec. IV, the AHL is generally a good approximation of SHL in quiet.

It is a well-known fact, verified experimentally by Hawkins and Stevens (1950), that SRT is governed by the speech-to-noise ratio. The data points of Hawkins and Stevens agree excellently with

$$\text{SRT} = 10 \log \left[10^{L_0/10} + 10^{(L_n - \Delta L_{SN})/10} \right] , \qquad (1)$$

where L_0 is SRT in quiet, L_n is sound-pressure level of the noise, and ΔL_{SN} is the number of decibels that SRT in noise is below L_n (ΔL_{SN} = speech-to-noise ratio at threshold, with opposite sign); all levels in dB A. By

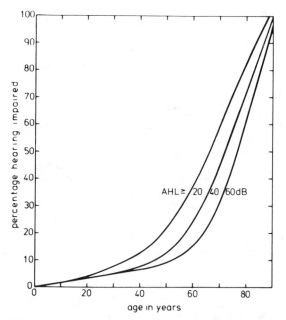

FIG. 5. Cumulative age distribution of the categories with AHL ≥ 20, 40, and 60 dB, respectively, indicating that the ages up to and including 50 contain only 21% of all subjects with AHL ≥ 20 dB, the ages up to and including 70 contain 59%, etc. The curves are based on the lines of Fig. 3.

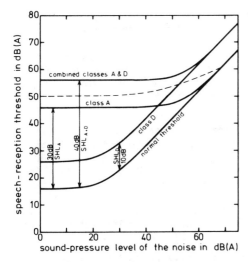

FIG. 6. Speech-reception threshold for sentences in a typical everyday listening situation as a function of noise level. The lower solid curve holds for normal hearing, the other ones for hearing losses for speech as indicated. The dashed curve represents the average sound-pressure level of conversational speech at a distance of 1 m. The listening situation in this figure, on which Figs, 7, 10, and 14–19 are based, is that the listener is situated in a diffuse noise field (average speech-spectrum noise) with the speech signal reproduced by a loudspeaker in front of his head at a distance of 1 m, with reverberation time of the room 0.4 s.

writing $L_0 = L_i - \Delta L_{SN}$ it is clear that SRT can be interpreted as determined by the sum of an internal noise, with level L_i, in the ear and the external noise L_n. The lower curve in Fig. 6 represents SRT in dB A for a listening situation highly representative of everyday situations

$$SRT = 10 \log \left[10^{1.6} + 10^{(L_n - 8)/10} \right] \qquad (2)$$

This curve holds for sentences as speech material and the listener situated in a diffuse noise field with the speech signal reproduced by a loudspeaker in front of his head at a distance of 1 m, room volume 65 m³, reverberation time 0.4 s (unpublished data by the author). We see that in this case $L_0 \sim 16$ dB A and $\Delta L_{SN} \sim 8$ dB. (Throughout this paper SPL of speech is the long-term average intensity of connected discourse, measured by computing the root-mean-square value of a great many samples with the aid of a computer.) We shall regard this situation as a standard in the further calculations.

The dashed curve represents the SPL speech may have. In face-to-face conversation in quiet over a distance of 1 m the SPL at that distance is about 50 dB A (Gardner, 1971). People increase their voice level automatically when interfering noise is present (cf. review by Lane and Tranel, 1971). Above 35 dB A the curve is drawn in accordance with measurements by van Heusden et al. (1978), approximated by the function

$$SPL = 10 \log \left(10^5 + 10^{0.05 L_n + 2.6} \right) \qquad (3)$$

We see that the average speech level in quiet at a distance of 1 m is about 34 dB above SRT. This value

agrees with the AHL at which difficulties in understanding speech in direct conversation in quiet begin (Table II).

For a better description of the effect of hearing impairment on speech intelligibility we may interpret any hearing loss as a combination of two parts belonging to two extreme classes: The effect of the impairment can be compared with either (1) *attenuation* of all sounds entering the ear or (2) *distortion* of these sounds. As will be shown below, this formalistic distinction should not be confused with the traditional anatomically oriented distinction between conductive and sensorineural hearing losses. Let us consider the two classes of hearing impairment in more detail.

(1) *Hearing loss of class* A, *comparable with attenuation* (SHL_A). This is the simplest way in which hearing may deteriorate, manifesting itself in a threshold shift in quiet of A dB which can be fully compensated for by an equal increase in level of the sounds entering the ear. In this case Eq. (2) becomes

$$SRT_A = 10 \log \left[10^{(A+16)/10} + 10^{(L_n - 8)/10} \right]. \qquad (4)$$

In quiet, $SHL_A = SRT_A - 16 = A$ dB, but in noise $SHL_A = 0$ dB, because the hearing loss of class A does not affect the speech-to-noise ratio required for understanding speech. As an illustration, in Fig. 6 the threshold curve for $SHL_A = 30$ dB in quiet is drawn.

(2) *Hearing loss of class* D, *comparable with distortion* (SHL_D). A quite different class of hearing losses manifests itself when a subject declares: "I can *hear* what people say, but I can't *understand* them" (Olsen and Tillman, 1968). In this case the speech signal appears to be subjected to a distortion process in the ear rather than to attenuation. This distortion may have its origin, for example, in a deterioration of the ear's frequency selectivity, in a severe loss of hearing over a limited frequency range, etc. (For a general review of origins see Stephens, 1976.) It will affect speech intelligibility in quiet as well as against a background of noise. As long as the effect on intelligibility is not too large, it can be compensated for by improving the speech-to-noise ratio. Assuming as a first-order approximation that the required improvement in speech-to-noise ratio is independent of level, we may suppose that distortion results in a rise of the speech-reception threshold, *both* in quiet and in noise, of D dB, transforming Eq. (2) into

$$SRT_D = 10 \log \left[10^{(D+16)/10} + 10^{(L_n + D - 8)/10} \right]. \qquad (5)$$

In Fig. 6 the curve for $SHL_D = 10$ dB is drawn.

By comparing the two curves labeled as class A and class D with the dashed curve, the very different nature of the corresponding handicaps is apparent. The curve for $SHL_A = 30$ dB represents a considerable loss at low noise levels, whereas above about 55 dB A hearing is almost normal. On the other hand, the curve for $SHL_D = 10$ dB represents a minor hearing loss at low noise levels, but may result in a substantial handicap above 55 dB A because speech level is much sooner below threshold than for $SHL_D = 0$ dB. The two extreme kinds

538   Reinier Plomp: Auditory handicap and benefit of hearing aids   538

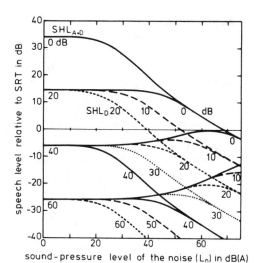

FIG. 7. Speech level relative to speech-reception threshold for sentences as a function of noise level (listening situation as in Fig. 6). The parameters are hearing loss for speech in quiet (SHL_{A+D}) and hearing loss for speech in noise (SHL_D).

of hearing losses manifest themselves primarily in opposite situations: class A at low and class D at high noise levels.

Most actual hearing losses are a combination of the classes A and D, given by

$$SRT_{A+D} = 10 \log \left[10^{(A+D+16)/10} + 10^{(L_n + D - 8)/10} \right] , \quad (6)$$

in which $A + D = SHL_{A+D} =$ loss of hearing for speech in quiet, and $D = SHL_D =$ loss of hearing for speech in noise, both in decibels. Equation (6) is illustrated by the curve labeled correspondingly in Fig. 6. In this example the total hearing loss of 40 dB in quiet is the sum of 30 dB SHL_A and 10 dB SHL_D.

The different effects of SHL_A and SHL_D on speech intelligibility as a function of noise level is explained more extensively in Fig. 7. As speech intelligibility is governed by the speech level relative to threshold, the curves represent $SPL - SRT_{A+D}$, found by subtracting Eq. (6) from Eq. (3). In Fig. 7 hearing loss in quiet, $SHL_{A+D} = A + D$, is 0, 20, 40, or 60 dB, and hearing loss in noise, $SHL_D = D$, is varied from 0 to SHL_{A+D} in steps of 10 dB. Since for sentences the increase in the intelligibility score is about 7% per decibel of increase in speech-to-noise ratio (unpublished data by the author; cf. Brinkmann, 1974), we may conclude that speech is fully intelligible for ordinate values greater than 7 dB (for large hearing losses of class D a score of 100% may need a substantially larger ordinate value).

The diagram shows that, for $SHL_D = 0$ dB, speech intelligibility in quiet may be greatly reduced, whereas speech intelligibility at high noise levels is almost normal, as was verified by Carhart and Tillman (1970) for subjects with conductive hearing losses. For $SHL_A \sim 40$ dB speech intelligibility in noise is even slightly better than in quiet. The observation that hard-of-hearing people may hear better in noise is known as Paracusis Willisii, named after the British scientist who described

it as early as 1672. (See, e.g., Lanos, 1952; Dudok de Wit and van Dishoeck, 1964.) The most fantastic theories were developed to explain the enigmatic character of paracusis, observed by many partially deaf people after the introduction of the railways with their noisy carriages in the 19th century. Apparently it is simply due to the automatic increase in voice level at high noise levels.

Although corresponding cases are usually not so well recognized clinically, the other extreme possibility, $SHL_A = 0$ and $SHL_D \neq 0$, also occurs in practice. Figure 7 shows that even an SHL_D of 10–20 dB results in a considerable decrease of the highest noise level at which speech level is still above threshold. We may assume that many of the traditionally puzzling cases of patients described as having hearing difficulties but with a rather normal audiogram (in quiet!) belong to this class.

It is very important to realize that an SHL_D of 10 dB, numerically very small compared with the SHL_{A+D} usually found clinically, represents a considerable handicap in everyday listening situations. This can be easily demonstrated even for the favorable case of only one competing talker. Suppose that both speakers are at the same distance from the listener, so that the speech-to-noise ratio is zero. It has been found experimentally (Plomp, 1976) that for a typical situation (reverberation time 0.4 s, both speakers at a distance of 0.7–1.0 m, the wanted talker straight in front, the competing talker at random azimuth) the S/N ratio required for just understanding connected discourse is − 8 dB, so that normal-hearing subjects have a margin of only 8 dB. This implies that a subject with an SHL_D of 10 dB will not be able to follow what is said (additional information from lip-reading being left out of consideration). The margin diminishes gradually when more and more interfering talkers are present, and appears to be almost zero at cocktail parties and acoustically similar social gatherings (Plomp, 1977).

III. DATA ON SHL IN NOISE AS A FUNCTION OF SHL IN QUIET

After having explained that in principle, any hearing loss for speech may be interpreted as a combination of two classes labeled as attenuation and distortion, we have to consider the relationship between the two classes in practice. It would be ideal if data were available on how the SRT of hard-of-hearing people changes as a function of the SPL of interfering noise. In that case we would be able to verify whether the assumption underlying the curves of Figs. 6 and 7 that class-D hearing loss manifests itself in a parallel, vertical shift of the curve is correct or not. However, such extensive data have not been published and we have to be content with the average results of experiments in which SHL in noise is measured at only a single noise level, together with SHL in quiet. Assuming that the 45° slope of the curves for $SHL_D \neq 0$ in Fig. 6 is justified as a first-order approximation, the two data points are sufficient to characterize the hearing status for speech reception at any noise level.

A search through the literature for investigations in

TABLE III. Main conditions of five investigations with group data on hearing loss in quiet and in noise.

Author(s)	Diagnosis	Number of subjects	Age	Speech material	Interfering sound	Presentation	SHL_{A+D} (quiet) (in dB)	SHL_D (noise) (in dB)
Lindeman (1967)	Noise trauma †presbycusis	161	30–39	Monosyllabic words	Av. speech spectrum ~ 70 dB A	Loudspeakers binaural	~ 10	2.3
		153	40–49				~ 15	3.7
		182	50–59				~ 20	6.3
		99	≥ 60				~ 25	8.0
Carhart and Tillman (1970)	Sensorineural losses	12		Monosyllabic words	Sentences ~ 80 dB A	Loudspeakers monaural	37	~ 11
Kell et al. (1971)	Presbycusis	11	< 55	Monosyllabic words	Low-frequency noise (~ voice babble) 60 dB A	In quite: headphones; in noise: loudspeakers binaural	5	0
		31	55–64				7	0
		42	65–74				12	2
		12	≥ 75				22	9
	Noise trauma + presbycusis	10	< 55				16	5
		33	55–64				26	8
		42	65–74				35	12
		11	≥ 75				32	14
Jokinen (1973)	Presbycusis	20	30–39	Disyllabic words	White noise 65 dB A	Headphone monaural	1.5	1.8
		20	40–49				3.3	2.7
		20	50–59				9.5	4.0
		20	60–69				18.2	3.7
		20	≥ 70				26.6	6.0
Fröhlich (1976)	Noise trauma	20	av. 35	Sentences	Airplane cockpit noise 80 dB A	Loudspeakers	2.3	3.9
		20	38				3.6	4.7
		20	41				5.3	5.3
		11	42				11.6	5.9

which both SHL_{A+D} and SHL_D for groups were measured, yielded publications by Lindeman (1967), Carhart and Tillman (1970), Kell et al. (1971), Jokinen (1973), and Fröhlich (1976). There are several more articles dealing with SRT in noise which, because they do not include data on SRT in quiet or for other reasons, are not suitable as a basis for determining SHL_D as a function of SHL_{A+D} (e.g., Simonton and Hedgecock, 1953; Palva, 1955; Niemeyer, 1967; Dirks and Wilson, 1969; Groen, 1969; Acton, 1970; Cooper and Cutts, 1971; Keith and Talis, 1972; Aniansson, 1973, 1974; Kuzniarz, 1973; Schultz-Coulon, 1973, 1974; Olson et al., 1975; for SRT in noise in central deafness see, e.g., Morales-Garcia and Poole, 1972). As far as could be checked, these investigations do not disagree essentially with the results presented in the first five articles referred to.

Table III gives a summary of the main conditions and values of SHL in quiet and in noise, derived from the data reported in these papers. We see that the conditions vary considerably. Nevertheless the data points, plotted in Fig. 8, can be approximated reasonably well by a straight regression line. The data do not justify

a distinction between the behavior with hearing losses due to noise trauma, presbycusis, or other origins. It appears that, on the average, SHL in noise increases gradually with SHL in quiet. As a rule of thumb we may

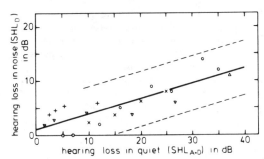

FIG. 8. Average hearing loss for speech in noise as a function of hearing loss for speech in quiet for various groups of hearing impaired, see Table III. The regression line is given by $y = 0.99 + 0.28x$. The dashed lines represent a rough estimate of the standard deviation of interindividual differences. × Lindeman, 1967; △ Carhart and Tillman, 1970; ○ Kell et al., 1971; ▽ Jokinen, 1973; + Fröhlich, 1976.

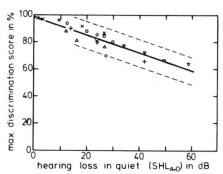

FIG. 9. Average maximum discrimination score as a function of hearing loss for speech in quiet for various groups of hearing impaired. Apart from Jokinen (1973) who used disyllabic words, all authors applied CID No. W-22 lists of one-syllabic PB-words for measuring MDS. The regression line is given by $y = 98.72 - 0.67x$. The dashed lines represent a rough estimate of the standard deviation of interindividual differences. Δ Goetzinger et al., 1961; ○ Young and Gibbons, 1962; ▽ Harbert et al., 1966; + Punch and McConnell, 1969; and × Jokinen, 1973.

conclude that for every 3-dB increase of SHL_{A+D}, SHL_D increases by 1 dB. Without going into detail now, the diagram demonstrates that an SHL in quiet of 24 dB, found as the limit of auditory handicap, appears to be accompanied by an SHL in noise of, on the average, about 8 dB. As we saw above, the latter loss has to be considered as a substantial auditory handicap in many everyday situations. It is just about equal to the margin for normal-hearing people in a typical listening situation with one competing talker.

The individual data on SHL_D vs SHL_{A+D} are not available, hence we are not able to mark accurately the degree to which the SHL_D for the individual may deviate from the line in Fig. 8. Standard deviations for various age groups reported by Jokinen (1973) suggest that the standard deviation of SHL_D may be 5-6 dB, but it is probable that this estimate largely reflects measuring accuracy rather than interindividual differences of SRT in noise.

Indirect evidence indicating that the interindividual differences in SHL_D are, indeed, rather large is provided by experiments in which the maximum discrimination score in quiet (MDS) has been measured as a function of SHL in quiet. Subjects who are not able to identify isolated words correctly, presented at the most comfortable level, have a discrimination loss. As this discrimination loss cannot be explained by attenuation, we may assume that it is due to some kind of distortion in the hearing process, and that it is highly correlated with SHL in noise. This appears to hold for group averages but, for lack of data, cannot be checked for individuals.

MDS has been often measured as a function of SHL in quiet; summarized in Fig. 9 are some of the results, published by Young and Gibbons (1962), Goetzinger et al. (1961), Harbert et al. (1966), Punch and McConnell (1969), and Jokinen (1973). Apart from the first-mentioned study, which is based on patients with sensori-

neural hearing losses, all data concern presbycusis (patients with Menière's disease reveal lower MDS values, see Hood and Poole, 1971, but are excluded here because they represent a very small percentage of all cases). The diagram shows that even for hearing losses of 60 dB the PB-word score exceeds 50%, corresponding to a score of more than 80% for sentences; this means that for such a relatively large loss our definition of SRT (50% score) makes sense, but that complete understanding cannot be reached by increasing speech level. The data points represent group averages, and the authors also report estimates of the interindividual spread. Only Harbert et al. (1966) include a scatter diagram of their data for 50 subjects and from this diagram it can be derived that the standard deviation of MDS relative to the regression line is about 10%. This spread (dashed lines in Fig. 9) agrees well with estimates from the other data. Jokinen's (1973) data indicate that 10% in MDS corresponds to about 5 dB in SHL_D, which value is in accordance with the estimate given above. Although this derivation is rather indirect, its result may be accepted as a rough estimate (dashed lines in Fig. 8). (A third, still more indirect, derivation is 10% spread in MDS corresponds in Fig. 9 to 15 dB in SHL_{A+D}, which corresponds in Fig. 8 to 5 dB in SHL_D.) It demonstrates that individual data can differ considerably from the mean so that we have to be careful in applying the average results.

It should be mentioned that both in Fig. 8 and Fig. 9 data points based on presbycusis agree well with data points based on studies of other sensorineural hearing impairments. This strongly suggests that, at least at ages up to 70-75, presbycusis may be considered to be primarily due to deterioration in the auditory pathway rather than to mental impairment as some authors seem to believe (e.g., Bergman, 1971). Our conclusion is supported by the results of studies by Kasden (1970) and Schon (1970).

Having arrived at the average relationship between SHL_D and SHL_{A+D}, we are now able to specify the curves of Fig. 7. The curves in Fig. 10 represent speech level above threshold for sentences [Eq. (6) minus Eq. (3)] as a function of noise level for $SHL_{A+D} = 0, 10, 20, \ldots,$ 80 dB, respectively, with values of SHL_D taken from the solid line of Fig. 8. As SHL_D for $SHL_{A+D} > 40$ dB has to be extrapolated because of lack of data, position of the curves should be considered to be more and more uncertain as SHL_{A+D} increases from 40 to 80 dB. The diagram demonstrates nicely that, up to $SHL_{A+D} \sim 35$ dB, hearing difficulties occur primarily at higher noise levels.

IV. PREDICTIVE SIGNIFICANCE OF THE TONE AUDIOGRAM FOR SHL

In Sec. I, AHL (the average hearing loss for 500, 1000, and 2000 Hz) was accepted as a measure for characterizing auditory handicap. It may be worthwhile to pay some attention to the reliability of this or other relationships between thresholds for tones and for speech. Many serious attempts have been made to predict SHL from the tone audiogram and we have to know

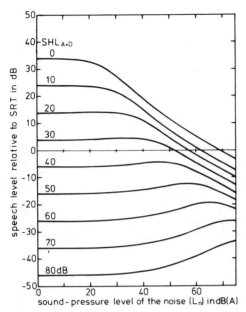

FIG. 10. Speech level relative to speech-reception threshold for sentences as a function of noise level, with hearing loss for speech in quiet (SHL$_{A+D}$) as the parameter (listening situation as in Fig. 6). The curves hold for a relationship between SHL$_D$ and SHL$_{A+D}$ in accordance with the regression line of Fig. 8.

in what respects prediction succeeds and in what respects it fails.

Shortly after the modern, electronic, audiometer was introduced in the twenties, Fletcher (1929) concluded from experiments that the average hearing loss at 500, 1000, and 2000 Hz agrees rather well with the hearing loss for spoken digits. Many investigators have repeated his experiments for various groups of patients (for a review see Noble, 1973), of which only one of the most recent studies will be considered. Gjaevenes (1969) found for a group of 300 subjects (100 conductive hearing losses, 100 hearing losses of cochlear origin, and 100 presbycusis, each subgroup consisting of 50 males and 50 females) that the standard deviation of the difference between measured SHL in quiet for phonetically balanced monosyllabic Norwegian words and predicted SHL (=AHL according to Fletcher) was about 7.9 dB. This deviation could be reduced to 6.4 dB by computing and using the optimal weighting factors for the hearing losses at 500, 1000, 2000, and 3000 Hz instead of the factors 0.33, 0.33, 0.33, and 0, respectively, in the simple AHL formula. These standard deviations are typical of values found by other investigators. They tell us that for 5% of subjects the SHL in quiet will be at least about 13 dB greater than predicted from AHL (about 10.5 dB for optimal weighting factors). This may be regarded as a reasonably good prediction compared with the accuracy usually accepted in clinical audiometry.

Although no data on the accuracy of predicting SHL in noise from the tone audiogram are available, we may

conclude from investigations on the correlation of MDS in quiet with tone audiograms (also reviewed by Noble, 1973) that no reliable prediction is possible. Group averages may correlate rather well, as we have seen in Fig. 9 for MDS as a function of SHL in quiet, but this does not hold for individual data.

These results are understandable in terms of the two classes, A and D, of speech-hearing loss introduced above. We may assume that SHL$_A$, because it is an attenuation, correlates perfectly with AHL or other appropriate measures derived from the tone audiogram. However, this does not hold necessarily for SHL$_D$ because the hearing threshold for pure tones may not include kinds of nonlinear distortion that are active in speech discrimination. Since, on the average, SHL$_{A+D}$ is about three times as large as SHL$_D$ (Fig. 8), SHL in quiet is dominated by SHL$_A$ so that we may expect a reasonably good predictability of SHL in quiet from the audiogram. This improving effect of SHL$_A$ is absent in SHL in noise, resulting in lower predictability. Moreover, the same number of decibels weighs much more in speech-to-noise ratio than in absolute threshold. An accuracy corresponding to a band of ±10.5–13 dB covering 90% of individual data may be acceptable for SHL in quiet, but is certainly not so for SHL in noise.

V. USE AND SATISFACTORINESS OF HEARING AIDS

The previous sections dealt with the prevalence of hearing impairment and its effect on the threshold of speech reception both in quiet and in noise. In this and the next sections we pay attention to the degree to which speech understanding can be improved by hearing aids. We first consider how well these prostheses are received and evaluated by their users.

Some recent publications give data on the age distribution of applicants for new hearing aids. Brooks (1972) reported on 200 patients, Carstairs (1973) on 301, and Ewertsen (1974) on 947 patients. Their cumulative percentage data are plotted in Fig. 11. There are only minor differences between these three sources. The curve agrees rather well with the cumulative distribution curve for people with an AHL of 40 dB and more (Fig. 5), suggesting that this loss is a rough estimate of the borderline between users and nonusers of hearing aids.

Ewertsen (1974) also presented data on the distribution of hearing aids as a function of hearing loss for speech in quiet and the percentage of subjects who always use their aids. These data are reproduced in Figs. 12 and 13, respectively. The first diagram shows that about one-third of 992 patients had an SHL for the better ear of less than 40 dB. The percentage of subjects always using their hearing aids appeared to be almost independent of age.

Several authors published general figures about the use of hearing aids by their owners (Gillissen, 1970b; Brooks, 1972; Green and Byrne, 1972; Carstairs, 1973; Kapteyn, 1973, 1977; Ewertsen, 1974). Since they did not apply the same categories, their results are diffi-

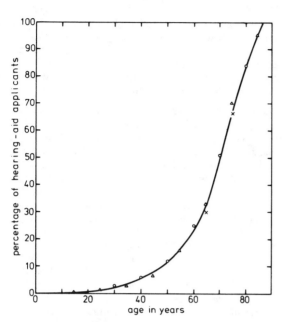

FIG. 11. Cumulative age distribution of applicants for new hearing aids according to three investigations. The curve has been fitted by eye and should be compared with the curves in Fig. 5. oBrooks, 1972; ×Carstairs, 1973; and △Ewertsen, 1974.

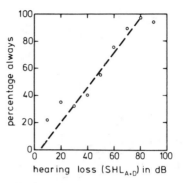

FIG. 13. Percentage of hearing-aid users always wearing their aid as a function of hearing loss for speech in quiet. For calculating the regression line, each data point was provided with a weighting factor equal to the number out of all 922 patients with corresponding SHL_{A+D}. (Data adapted from Ewertsen, 1974.)

cult to compare. On the basis of the responses of the hearing impaired themselves it seems that 60%–90% use their aid always or frequently, 5%–30% occasionally, and 5%–10% never. All investigators agree that subjects with conductive losses use their hearing aids more frequently than subjects with sensorineural hearing losses (including presbycusis).

The use of hearing aids by hard-of-hearing people reflects their satisfaction with the aid. From von Arentsschild and Fröber (1972), Pedersen et al. (1974), and the authors referred to above it can be concluded that less than 20% of users is highly satisfied, whereas 10%–20% is strongly dissatisfied, indicating that the majority of the hearing impaired does not consider their hearing aid as an ideal device for hearing-loss compensation. One author (Gillissen, 1970a) even considers dissatisfied users to be the main reason why many aged people with severe presbycusis do not apply for a hearing aid.

It is clear that subjects are most satisfied with their hearing aid when they are talking to one other person in quiet, whereas group conversation is the worst condition (Green and Byrne, 1972; Carstairs, 1973). Gillissen (1970b) found that, roughly, a hearing aid is satisfactory with one other person in the room, moderately satisfactory with two or three other people, and unsatisfactory with many people in the same room. From all publications it is abundantly clear that the overwhelming number of complaints about the aid is in respect to background noise (Carstairs, 1973).

VI. IMPROVEMENT OF SPEECH INTELLIGIBILITY BY HEARING AIDS

In this section we determine the degree to which the impaired speech-reception threshold SRT_{A+D} represented by Eq. (6), is improved by hearing aids. As the quantification attempted in this article has to be regarded as a first-order approximation with the aim of explaining the communicative difficulties of the hearing impaired, the hearing aid will also be simplified. We need the following three quantities to characterize the hearing aid: (1) the acoustic gain G equal to the increase of SPL at the ear caused by the hearing aid, (2) the increase S in the threshold for speech against a background of noise due to technical imperfections of the aid (nonideal frequency response, nonlinearities, etc.), and (3) the equivalent input noise level L_e representing the internal noise. This approach presupposes that both ears are provided with hearing aids so that we have no losses due to head shadow or to absence of binaural masking level difference (cf. Tillman et al., 1973 and Nabelek and Pickett, 1974b, who showed that the latter effect seems to contribute only a few dB; see also Frederiksen et al., 1974). Furthermore, our model does not include any effect of recruitment in the ear and amplitude limiting in the amplifier, nor the in-

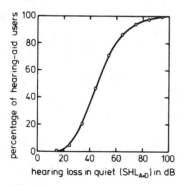

FIG. 12. Cumulative distribution of hearing loss for speech in quiet for 922 hearing-aid users. The curve has been fitted by eye. (Data adapted from Ewertsen, 1974.)

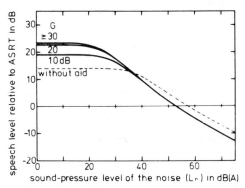

FIG. 14. Speech level relative to speech-reception threshold for sentences without hearing aid (dashed curve) and with hearing aid included (solid curves) for subjects with hearing loss for speech in quiet (SHL$_{A+D}$) of 20 dB as a function of noise level. Parameter is the acoustic gain G. Fixed conditions: increase in the masked threshold due to hearing-aid distortion: 3 dB; equivalent input noise level: 25 dBA; relationship between SHL$_D$ and SHL$_{A+D}$ in accordance with the regression line of Fig. 8; listening situation as in Fig. 6.

fluence of varying the frequency response of the aid (group averages of intelligibility scores are rather independent of frequency response, see Knight, 1967).

It is easy to account for the three hearing-aid parameters in the equation for SRT given by Eq. (6): (1) The gain of G dB means that the apparent hearing loss of class A with the aid included is A-G dB rather than A dB, (2) the distortion term, S must be added to the distortion term, D of the ear, and (3) the internal noise, interpreted as a noise level of L_e dB A at the aid's microphone, should be added to the external noise level resulting in a total noise level of

$$L'_n = 10 \log \left[10^{L_n/10} + 10^{L_e/10} \right] \qquad (7)$$

instead of L_n dB A. With these additions the threshold for speech with the hearing aid included, the *aided speech-reception threshold* ASRT$_{A+D}$ changes from Eq. (6) into

$$\text{ASRT}_{A+D} = 10 \log \left[10^{(A-G+D+16)/10} + 10^{(L'_n+D+S-8)/10} \right] \qquad (8)$$

with L'_n according to Eq. (7). In Figs. 14–17 the speech level relative to threshold, obtained by subtracting Eq.

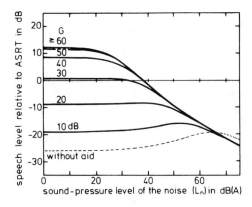

FIG. 16. Similar to Fig. 14, but for SHL$_{A+D}$ = 60 dB.

(8) from Eq. (3), is plotted as a function of L_n for SHL$_{A+D}$ = A + D = 20, 40, 60, and 80 dB, respectively, with the acoustic gain G as the parameter. The value of D was read from the straight line in Fig. 8 (whether it was permissible to extrapolate SHL$_{A+D}$ to 80 dB cannot be verified). Since no reliable estimate of the distortion term S for typical hearing aids is available, S = 3 dB was adopted as a rough approximation (much higher values of S were found by Tillman *et al.*, 1970, corrected by more recent investigations by Nabelek and Pickett, 1974a and Nielsen, 1976). For the equivalent input noise level, L_e a typical value of 25 dB A was taken.

Figures 14–17 demonstrate the possibilities and limitations of hearing aids. The convergence of the curves at high noise levels in all four diagrams illustrates that the hearing aid is of no benefit in noise. The noise level at which the aided speech-reception threshold is reached for large values of G diminishes gradually from 52.5 dB A for SHL$_{A+D}$ = 20 dB to 31 dB A for SHL$_{A+D}$ = 80 dB. As 35–45 dB A is generally accepted as characterizing quiet environments, it is clear why hard-of-hearing subjects, though wearing hearing aids, are unable to understand speech in many everyday listening situations.

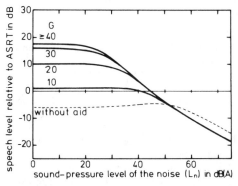

FIG. 15. Similar to Fig. 14, but for SHL$_{A+D}$ = 40 dB.

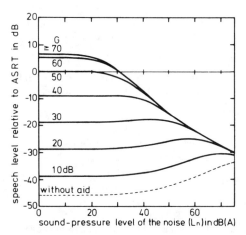

FIG. 17. Similar to Fig. 14, but for SHL$_{A+D}$ = 80 dB.

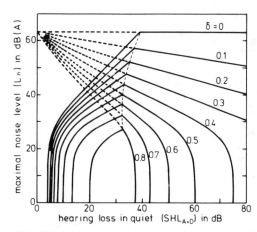

FIG. 18. Maximum noise levels at which hearing aids are of benefit at conversational speech levels as a function of hearing loss for speech in quiet, with $\delta = \mathrm{SHL_D}/\mathrm{SHL_{A+D}}$ as the parameter. The curves with positive slopes correspond to noise levels (see Fig. 14) at which the curves for $G = \infty$ intersect the curves without hearing aid. The curves with the negative slopes correspond to the noise levels in Figs. 14–17 at which speech level is at threshold. Further conditions as given in Figs. 6 and 14.

At low noise levels hearing aids are only beneficial as long as the ordinate value *with* hearing aid is larger than it is *without*. Figure 14 shows that for $\mathrm{SHL_{A+D}} = 20$ dB this holds for noise levels below 37 dB A. Although this critical level is very sensitive to variations of S, the gain from reducing S is so marginal (less than 3 dB) that the value given can be maintained as a practical limit. In the other diagrams the critical level is reached for negative sensation levels so that it has only theoretical value. In those cases the noise level at which threshold is reached, discussed in the previous paragraph, determines the usefulness of the hearing aid. As the limit of L_n up to which hearing aids are beneficial is an important characteristic of the aid, it may be useful to show how it depends upon the combination of class A and class D hearing impairments.

For small values of $\mathrm{SHL_{A+D}}$ the critical L_n for which speech level above SRT without hearing aid is equal to speech level above ASRT with hearing aid follows from the requirement that Eq. (6) is equal to Eq. (8):

$$10^{(A+D+16)/10} + 10^{(L_n+D-8)/10} = 10^{(A-G+D+16)/10} + 10^{(L'_n+D+S-8)/10} \ .$$

Assuming a high value of G (Figs. 14–17 show that this holds for $G = \mathrm{SHL_{A+D}}$), we may ignore the third term and we get

$$A = 10 \log\left[10^{(L'_n+S)/10} - 10^{L_n/10}\right] - 24, \tag{9}$$

indicating that the critical L_n depends exclusively upon $\mathrm{SHL_A}$, not on $\mathrm{SHL_D}$, and with $\delta = D/(A+D)$:

$$A+D = \frac{10 \log\left[10^{(L'_n+S)/10} - 10^{L_n/10}\right] - 24}{1 - \delta} \ . \tag{10}$$

With $L_e = 25$ dB A and $S = 3$ dB, the curves with positive slopes in Fig. 18 represent this relationship between the hearing loss in quiet, $A + D$ and noise level, L_n above

which the hearing aid does not improve speech-to-noise ratio, with δ as the parameter.

As was said above, at higher noise levels we require that loud speech is not below threshold, implying that now the critical L_n, again for $G \to \infty$, is given by

$$10^5 + 10^{0.05 L_n + 2.6} = 10^{(L'_n + D + S - 8)/10} \ ,$$

$$D = 10 \log\left[10^5 + 10^{0.05 L_n + 2.6}\right] - L'_n - S + 8 \ , \tag{11}$$

indicating that in this case the critical L_n depends exclusively upon $\mathrm{SHL_D}$, not on $\mathrm{SHL_A}$, and with $\delta = D/(A+D)$:

$$A+D = \frac{10 \log\left[10^5 + 10^{0.05 L_n + 2.6}\right] - L'_n - S + 8}{\delta} \ . \tag{12}$$

This relationship is represented in Fig. 18 by the partly dashed curves with negative slopes.

The curves in this diagram demonstrate the large effect of δ, the ratio between hearing loss in noise and hearing loss in quiet, on the auditory handicap. If we may assume that, in accordance with the dashed curves of Fig. 8, for a moderate $\mathrm{SHL_{A+D}} = 30$ dB, δ spreads in practice from 0.6 to nearly zero (90% of cases within this range), the maximum level of ambient noise in which a hearing aid is beneficial varies among subjects from 35 to 54 dB A, whereas the maximum noise level for understanding average conversational speech varies from 38 to 63 dB A, respectively. The curves for $\delta = 0.3$ represent the average condition illustrated in Figs. 14–17. The noise levels at which both classes of curves intersect are of particular interest. They define, as a function of δ, the highest noise level, irrespective of $\mathrm{SHL_{A+D}}$, up to which hearing aids are advantageous. For $\delta = 0.3$, the average case, this level is only 48 dB A. It should be realized that these figures, as is the case with all figures presented earlier, only hold for ambient noise with the spectral composition of speech.

Finally we discuss the effect of varying the acoustic gain. In Figs. 14–17 the asymptotic speech levels in quiet relative to ASRT are determined by the internal noise of the hearing aid. The maximum level cannot exceed the level for $L_n = 25$ dB A by more than 3 dB because of the constant L_e of that value. Although the ordinate value diminishes gradually for increasing $\mathrm{SHL_{A+D}}$, it still exceeds speech-reception threshold in very quiet surroundings for $\mathrm{SHL_{A+D}} = 80$ dB if adequate amplification is given.

It is important to realize that, due to the internal noise of the aid, it does not make sense to fully compensate for the hearing loss in quiet by amplification. The curves in Figs. 14–17 show that speech level relative to internal-noise level is not substantially improved by, for example, increasing the gain from 50 to 60 dB for $\mathrm{SHL_{A+D}} = 60$ dB. Accepting an ordinate value of 3 dB below the asymptotically maximum level for $G \to \infty$ as a good compromise between improving speech-to-noise ratio and the annoyance caused by the much higher speech level required for obtaining it, we can calculate the gain, G_p, to be preferred. From Eq. (8) it follows that G_p is given by

545   Reinier Plomp: Auditory handicap and benefit of hearing aids   545

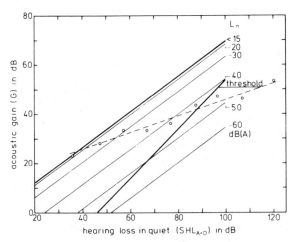

FIG. 19. Preferred acoustic gain of hearing aids as a function of hearing loss for speech in quiet. The parallel curves have been calculated with noise level as the parameter. The steeper solid line represents aided speech-reception threshold for loud speech in quiet. Further conditions as given in Figs. 6 and 14. The data points are average actual gain settings from Martin (1973) and Martin *et al.* (1976). The regression line is given by $y = 12.59 + 0.33x$.

$$10^{(L'_n + D + S - 8 + 3)/10} = 10^{(A \cdot G_p + D + S + 16)/10} + 10^{(L'_n + D + S - 8)/10} \quad ,$$

$$L'_n - 8 + 10 \log(10^{3/10} - 1) = A - G_p + 16 \quad .$$

As $10 \log(10^{3/10} - 1) \sim 0$ dB, we obtain the simple formula for the preferred acoustic gain

$$G_p = A - L'_n + 24 \quad . \tag{13}$$

We see that G_p is determined exclusively by the class-A component of hearing loss, the one which can be compensated for. In quiet $L'_n = L_e = 25$ dB A for a typical hearing aid, giving

$$G_p \sim A \quad . \tag{14}$$

This means that the maximum useful gain is about equal to hearing loss for speech in quiet, $\text{SHL}_{A+D} = A + D$, minus hearing loss for speech in noise, $\text{SHL}_D = D$.

The upper heavy line in Fig. 19 represents G_p in quiet and the thin lines give G_p in noise of 20, 30, 40, 50, and 60 dB A according to Eqs. (13) and (7). The lower heavy line gives the minimum gain required for loud speech of 65 dB A to reach speech-reception threshold, equal to

$$G_m = A + D + S + 16 - 65 \quad , \tag{15}$$

with $S = 3$ dB:

$$G_m = A + D - 46 \quad . \tag{16}$$

All curves are based on the relation between D and A + D given by the (extrapolated) straight line in Fig. 8. If this derivation is valid, we should expect that average gain adjustments by hard-of-hearing people are within the heavy lines.

Data on preferred gain adjustments in practive were published by Martin (1973) and Martin *et al.* (1976) for a total of 241 subjects covering a wide range of hearing

losses (similar data were reported by Brooks, 1973). Assuming that AHL from the former investigation and the hearing loss at 1000 Hz from the latter may both be accepted as good estimates of SHL in quiet, these data can be compared with the curves of Fig. 19. The circles represent average preferred gain settings per decade of hearing loss, the dashed line is the regression line based on the 241 individual points. Considering that even in quiet environments the noise level is 25–30 dBA, implying that subjects will adjust their gain to that condition, we may conclude that the agreement between the theoretical lines and the average data points is quite good for SHL_{A+D} below 60 dB. For greater losses the gain settings deviate more and more from the predicted values. For $\text{SHL}_{A+D} > \sim 90$ dB the settings are even lower than required for understanding loud speech, illustrating that the benefit from the hearing aid is quite doubtful in that range, as is known from experience (Erber, 1974). For these very large hearing losses the only cues are the temporal amplitude variations acoustically and/or mechanically (vibrations) detected.

An obvious explanation of the finding that the dashed line reflecting actual gain settings is considerably flatter than the predicted values is the increasing effect of annoyance, e.g., due to recruitment, of high gain settings for greater hearing losses. However, we should not exclude the possibility that the discrepancy is, at least partly, due to an overly optimistic extrapolation of the factor $\delta = D/(A + D)$ from Fig. 8. An increase of the slope of the line in this diagram means that the parallel lines in Fig. 19 become flatter resulting in a better agreement with the data points. More data will be required to decide upon the relative significance of these two causes.

VII. DISCUSSION

The previous section showed that hearing aids may be quite beneficial in many situations but of almost no use in other situations. We have discussed the different roles of the two classes of hearing loss as well as the maximally permissible level of interfering speech noise for obtaining satisfactory results. Let us now briefly consider the more general question of the minimum hearing loss for which a hearing aid should be recommended and, directly related to that question, what percentage of the population may be considered to need a hearing aid.

Assuming that difficulties in understanding speech define the main auditory handicap of the hearing impaired, the minimum hearing loss necessitating a hearing aid can be estimated from the graphs given in the previous section. We confine ourselves primarily to the average case for which the relation between hearing loss of class A and class D is represented by the line in Fig. 8. The factor $\delta = D/(A + D)$ for any subject may deviate considerably from this line implying that, without modifications, the conclusions are not generally applicable to individual cases.

It is clear from Fig. 14 that a hearing aid is not of much use with a hearing loss in quiet of 20 dB. Only in very quiet situations with noise levels below about 37 dB *A* we may expect some benefit, but even without a prosthesis speech intelligibility is still rather good in such quiet surroundings. For a hearing loss of 40 dB, however, the situation is rather different. The hearing aid is useful up to a noise level of about 45 dB *A* (Fig. 15). Without a hearing aid speech level will be about 6 dB below threshold. It seems justified to conclude that, generally, hearing aids are of benefit for hearing losses greater than or equal to ~35 dB. For losses greater than or equal to ~50 dB, amplification is required even for loud speech. For SHL_{A+D} increasing up to 80 dB, the maximally permissible noise level diminishes gradually to 31 dB *A*.

The conclusion that hearing aids are of minor importance for hearing losses below 35 dB reflects practical experience rather well. Figure 11 indicates that according to Ewertsen (1974) only 20% of the hearing aids in Denmark are supplied to patients with hearing losses below 35 dB and less than 40% of these patients seem to use their aid all the time (Fig. 12).

Several authors argue that hearing aids may be useful even for people with slight hearing losses. Though considering patients with minimal or high-frequency sensorineural hearing losses to be difficult hearing-aid candidates, Ross (1969) believes that these patients have often been fitted successfully with hearing aids. As a typical example, Ewertsen (1972) mentions a patient, with a slight symmetrical hearing loss due to presbycusis, who comes to the clinic because he cannot follow group conversation although he is still capable of talking with one person sitting near to him. According to Ewertsen, such patients are given binaural hearing glasses attached to open ear moulds. However, I cannot see how hearing aids may be beneficial to this group with, apparently, relatively large hearing losses of class D. This was admitted by Nielsen (1976) on the basis of intelligibility scores in noise. We may assume that many of the 20% of patients with hearing losses below 35 dB in Fig. 11 belonged to that group.

Assuming an SHL in quiet of 35 dB to be the minimal hearing loss for applying hearing aids, we may conclude from Fig. 4 that about 3.4% of the population belongs to the category for which wearing a hearing aid may be beneficial. This percentage is considerably higher than figures on hearing aids supplied might suggest. Even in Denmark with its free distribution, less than about 2% of the population seems to apply for a hearing aid (Ewertsen, 1972). From a comparison presented by Bentzen and Courtois (1973) we may conclude that the corresponding percentage for the U.S. does not exceed 1%. This illustrates that many hard-of-hearing persons, for one reason or another, do not believe that a hearing prosthesis is of benefit to them.

As a final question let us consider briefly how the auditory handicap of the hearing impaired, with or without hearing aids, can be lessened. From the previous sections it follows that this can be reached only by improving the speech-to-noise ratio. Apart from the obvious gain from raising voice level, possible ways are as follows:

(1) *Reduction of noise levels.* As the attention in this article is focused on speech as the interfering noise we only consider this condition. Usually reduction of the level of competing speech can only be achieved by attenuating it on its way to the listener by means of sound-insulating walls or panels, or by sound-absorbing surfaces. It should be realized that currently fashionable environments such as open-plan schools and offices in which (human) noise is used as a background for privacy run counter to the requirements of the hearing impaired who need a more quiet environment the greater the hearing loss is. Competing speech produced in the same room cannot be abated very effectively (cf. Plomp, 1977). However, a modest improvement of some dB appears to be already highly effective: Combining the rule of thumb that the percentage of hearing impaired is halved for every 10 dB more of SHL_{A+D} (Fig. 4) and the one that for every 4-dB decrease in noise level 10 dB more of SHL_{A+D} is allowed for comparable hearing difficulties (slope of curve for $\delta=0.3-0.4$ in Fig. 18), we may conclude that a 4-5 dB improvement of speech-to-noise ratio halves the percentage of auditory handicapped of any degree (~15% per dB).

(2) *Reduction of reverberation.* In situations in which a substantial part of the speech energy from the speaker reaches the listener indirectly by reverberation, a reduction of the usually too large reverberation time is beneficial. This can be achieved either acoustically by sound-absorbing surfaces or electroacoustically by loudspeaker columns radiating the sound more directionally to the listener.

(3) *Use of visual speech perception (lipreading).* In recent years much attention has been given to the significance of visual perception of speech by hearing-impaired subjects. (For a review see Birk Nielsen and Kampp, 1974.) From various studies (Lindeman and van Leeuwen, 1970; Ludvigsen, 1974; Hasselrot, 1974; Binnie, 1974) it can be concluded that lipreading may improve SRT maximally by 5-8 dB.

(4) *Separate microphone near to the speaker.* The most effective way of improving the speech-to-noise ratio for the hearing-aid wearer is by bringing the microphone near to the mouth of the speaker. Although it may be applicable in a few situations (for example, one-to-one conversation at home), this possibility must for obvious reasons be excluded as a general solution.

(5) *Application of directional microphones.* Since about 1970 more and more hearing aids with microphones with a directional sensitivity have come onto the market, primarily for improving the signal-to-noise ratio. In this respect the quality of a directional microphone is defined by its sensitivity to a sound arriving straight from the front relative to the sensitivity averaged over all directions, the so-called front-random ratio. Theoretically this value is 5-6 dB for cardiod microphones. Although comparative data on intelligibility scores obtained with hearing aids provided with directional microphones versus omnidirectional microphones have been published (e.g., Birk Nielsen, 1973; Lentz, 1974; Sung *et al.*, 1975), no results on the improvement of SRT in a diffuse noise field, representing

the front-random ratio, seem to be available. Preliminary measurements by the author (unpublished data) strongly suggest that the front-random ratio for the miniature directional microphones fitted in hearing aids is considerably smaller than predicted from theory and may be only 1–2 dB.

(6) *Individual fitting of hearing-aid frequency responses.* Although group averages of intellibigility scores are rather independent of the aid's frequency response (Knight, 1967), it appears that careful matching of the frequency response to the individual subject's hearing can result in a significant improvement of speech intelligibility (Pascoe, 1975). It seems unlikely, however, that by such a procedure the threshold for speech in noise can be improved by more than a few decibels.

(7) *Compensation of the ear's distortion.* Undoubtedly the best way to improve intelligibility would be to neutralize the ear's hearing loss of class D by some kind of processing of the speech signal in the hearing aid. The compensation for loudness recruitment in the pathological ear by means of amplitude compression is an attempt in this direction. A recent review of this was given by Rintelmann (1972) who reported that a modest, but significant, improvement of the discrimination score in quiet has been observed. However, Blegvad (1974) found that out of 42 patients 29 preferred linear amplification because of a smaller tendency to pick up background noises, which suggests that amplitude compression does not improve SRT in noise. More sophisticated signal-processing techniques tried out by Villchur (1973) may eventually lead to better results if the underlying presumption that recruitment is the (main) cause of degraded speech perception is correct.

VIII. CONCLUSIONS

The main results arrived at in the previous sections can be summarized as follows:

(1) Inquiries appear to give an overly optimistic, and therefore unreliable, picture of the auditory handicap of elderly people compared with tone audiograms (average hearing loss for 500, 1000, and 2000 Hz in the better ear, AHL).

(2) Adopting the percentage of young adults complaining of hearing difficulties, being equal to 1%, as a base, we can conclude that people are auditory handicapped for AHL $\geq$ 24 dB. For 24 dB $\leq$ AHL < 35 dB the hearing impaired mainly have difficulties in understanding speech in noisy environments; for AHL $\geq$ 35 dB close-range conversation in quiet is also impeded.

(3) Irrespective of the degree of auditory handicap considered, the percentage of the population involved increases approximately exponentially with age. For subjects with AHL $\geq$ 24 dB the percentage is doubled every 10 years resulting in 24% of auditory handicapped at the age of 65.

(4) The percentage of the total population with AHL exceeding some critical value is approximately halved

for every 10-dB increase of AHL. The percentage is 7.5% for AHL $\geq$ 24 dB and 3.4% for AHL $\geq$ 35 dB.

(5) More than 50% of all auditory handicapped are older than 67.

(6) Every hearing loss for speech (SHL) can be interpreted as the sum of $SHL_{A(ttenuation)}$, characterized by a reduction of the levels of *both* speech signal and noise, and $SHL_{D(istortion)}$, comparable with a reduction of speech level *relative* to noise. Up to SHL_{A+D} (=hearing loss in quiet)~40 dB, SHL_D (=hearing loss in noise) is, on the average, about one-third of SHL_{A+D}. SHL_A manifests itself primarily in hearing difficulties in quiet, SHL_D in hearing difficulties in noisy environments.

(7) The SHL_D of 8 dB occurring for AHL = SHL_{A+D} = 24 dB is numerically equal to the number of decibels by which connected discourse can be attenuated before normal-hearing subjects become unable to understand speech in a typical everyday listening situation with one competing talker. This means that hearing difficulties appear to begin where this margin is nullified by hearing losses.

(8) The fact that the hearing aid does not compensate for SHL_D, but only for SHL_A, should be considered to be the main reason why so many hard of hearing are dissatisfied with their hearing aid.

(9) It can be proved that, irrespective of SHL_{A+D}, hearing aids are of no benefit to the average hearing-impaired person listening to conversational speech at ambient-noise levels (average-speech spectrum) exceeding about 50 dBA.

(10) Assuming that $SHL_D \sim \frac{1}{3} SHL_{A+D}$ (Conclusion 6) also holds for $SHL_{A+D} > 40$ dB, it follows that the maximum useful acoustic gain of the hearing aid is equal to ~$SHL_A = \frac{2}{3} SHL_{A+D}$. Probably due to recruitment, etc., the average acoustic-gain settings in practice are increasingly lower for $SHL_{A+D} > 60$ dB.

(11) Only for $SHL_{A+D} \geq 35$ dB are hearing aids generally recommended. This means that about 3.4% of the population (Conclusion 4) may benefit by wearing a hearing aid.

(12) Every 4–5 dB of noise reduction halves the percentage of auditory handicapped of any degree (~15% per dB).

Acton, W. I. (1970). "Speech Intelligibility in a Background Noise and Noise-Induced Hearing Loss," Ergonomics 13, 546–554.

Aniansson, G. (1973). "Binaural Discrimination of 'Everyday' Speech," Acta Oto-Laryngol. 75, 334–336.

Aniansson, G. (1974). "Methods for Assessing High Frequency Hearing Loss in Everyday Listening Situations," Acta Oto-Laryngol. Suppl. No. 320.

Arentsschild, O. von, and Fröber, B. (1972). "Comparative Measurements of the Effect of a Directional Microphone in the Hearing Aid," Z. Hörgeräte-Akustik 11, 204–229.

Beasley, W. C. (1940). "Characteristics and Distribution of Impaired Hearing in the Population of the United States," J. Acoust. Soc. Am. 12, 114–121.

Bentzen, O., and Courtois, J. (1973). "Statistical Analysis

of the Problem for the Deaf and Hard of Hearing in the World of 1970," Scand. Audiol. 2, 17–26.

Bentzen, O., and Jelnes, K. (1955). "Incidence of Impaired Hearing in Denmark," Acta Oto-Laryngol. 45, 189–197.

Bergman, M. (1971). "Hearing and Aging," Audiol. 10, 164–171.

Binnie, C. A. (1974). "Auditory-Visual Intelligibility of Various Speech Materials Presented in Three Noise Backgrounds," Scand. Audiol. Suppl. 4, 255–280.

Birk Nielsen, H. (1973). "A Comparison between Hearing Aids with Directional Microphone and Hearing Aids with Conventional Microphone," Scand. Audiol. 2, 173–176.

Birk Nielsen, H., and Ewertsen, H. W. (1974). "Effect of Hearing Aid Treatment," Scand. Audiol. 3, 35–38.

Birk Nielsen, H., and Kampp, E. (Eds.) (1974). "Visual and Audio-Visual Perception of Speech," Scand. Audiol. Suppl. 4.

Blegvad, B. (1974). "Clinical Evaluation of Behind-the-Ear Hearing Aids with Compression Amplification," Scand. Audiol. 3, 57–60.

Brinkmann, K. (1974). "Speech Audiometry in a Free Sound Field and with Earphones," 8th Int. Congr. Acoust. Contributed Papers 1, 216.

Brooks, D. N. (1972). "The Use and Disuse of Medresco-Hearing Aids," Sound 6, 80–85.

Brooks, D. (1973). "Gain Requirements of Hearing Aid Users," Scand. Audiol. 2, 199–205.

Carhart, R., and Tillman, T. W. (1970). "Interaction of Competing Speech Signals with Hearing Losses," Arch. Otolaryngol. 91, 273–279.

Carstairs, V. (1973). "Utilisation of Hearing Aids Issued by the National Health Service," Br. J. Audiol. 7, 72–76.

Chüden, H. (1969). "Hörgeräteeigenschaften bei den verschiedenn Schwerhörigkeitstypen," HNO 17, 279–281.

Cooper, J. C., Jr., and Cutts, B. P. (1971). "Speech Discrimination in Noise," J. Speech Hear. Res. 14, 332–337.

Dirks, D. D., and Wilson, R. A. (1969). "Binaural Hearing of Speech for Aided and Unaided Conditions," J. Speech Hear. Res. 12, 650–664.

Dudok de Wit, C. A., and van Dishoeck, H. A. E. (1964). "Paracusis Willisii," Int. Audiol. 3, 43–53.

Erber, N. P. (1974). "Pure-Tone Thresholds and Word-Recognition Abilities of Hearing-Impaired Children," J. Speech Hear. Res. 17, 194–202.

Ewertsen, H. W. (1972). "Hearing Aid Distribution in Denmark," Scand. Audiol. 1, 77–79.

Ewertsen, H. W. (1974). "Use of Hearing Aids (Always, Often, Rarely, Never)," Scand. Audiol. 3, 173–176.

Ewertsen, H. W., and Birk Nielsen, H. (1973). "Social Hearing Handicap Index: Social Handicap in Relation to Hearing Impairment," Audiol. 12, 180–187.

Fletcher, H. (1929). Speech and Hearing (van Nostrand, New York).

Frederiksen, E., Blegvad, B., and Røjskjaer, C. (1974). "Binaural Hearing Aid Treatment of Presbycusis Patients Aged 70 to 80 Years," Scand. Audiol. 3, 83–86.

Fröhlich, G. (1976). "Die Auswirkungen von Hörverlusten im Tonaudiogramm auf das Satzverständnis von Flugzeugführern in Ruhe und im Fluglärm," Wehrmed. Monatsschr. 20, 65–69.

Gardner, M. B. (1971). "Factors Affecting Individual and Group Levels in Verbal Communication," J. Audio Eng. Soc. 19, 560–569.

Gillissen, J. P. A. (1970a). "Het Hoorapparaat bij Bejaarden," Tijdschr. Soc. Geneeskd. 48, 73–74.

Gillissen, J. P. A. (1970b). "Een Onderzoek naar het Gebruik van Hoorapparaten in Amsterdam," Ned. Tijdschr. Geneeskd. 114, 185–187.

Gjaevenes, K. (1969). "Estimating Speech Reception Threshold from Pure Tone Hearing Loss," J. Aud. Res. 9, 139–144.

Goetzinger, C. P., Proud, G. O., Dirks, D., and Embrey,

J. (1961). "A Study of Hearing in Advanced Age," Arch. Oto-Laryngol. 73, 662–674.

Green, A. C., and Byrne, D. J. (1972). "The Pensioner Hearing Aid Scheme. A Survey in South Australia," Med. J. Aust. 2, 1113–1116.

Groen, J. J. (1969). "Social Hearing Handicap; its Measurement by Speech-Audiometry in Noise," Int. Audiol. 8, 182–183.

Harbert, F., Young, I. M., and Menduke, H. (1966). "Audiologic Findings in Presbycusis," J. Aud. Res. 6, 297–312.

Hasselrot, M. (1974). "Exploration of an Audiovisual Test Procedure with Background Noise for Patients with Noise-Induced Hearing Loss Using Hearing Aids," Scand. Audiol. Suppl. 4, 165–181.

Hawkins, J. E., Jr., and Stevens, S. S. (1950). "The Masking of Pure Tones and of Speech by White Noise," J. Acoust. Soc. Am. 22, 6–13.

Heusden, E. van, Plomp, R., and Pols, L. C. W. (1978). "Effect of Ambient Noise on the Vocal Output and the Preferred Listening Level of Conversational Speech," Appl. Acoust. (in press).

Hood, J. D., and Poole, J. P. (1971). "Speech Audiometry in Conductive and Sensorineural Hearing Loss," Sound 5, 30–38.

Jokinen, K. (1973). "Presbyacusis. VI. Masking of Speech," Acta Oto-Laryngol. 76, 426–430.

Kapteyn, T. S. (1973). "Het Hoortoestel als Revalidatiemiddel voor Slechthorendheid," Tijdschr. Soc. Geneeske. 51, 102–106.

Kapteyn, T. S. (1977). "Satisfaction with Fitted Hearing Aids," Scand. Audiol. (in press).

Kasden, S. D. (1970). "Speech Discrimination in Two Age Groups Matched for Hearing Loss," J. Aud. Res. 10, 210–212.

Keith, R. W., and Talis, H. P. (1972). "The Effects of White Noise on PB Scores of Normal and Hearing-Impaired Listeners," Audiol. 11, 177–186.

Kell, R. L., Pearson, J. C. G., Acton, W. I., and Taylor, W. (1971). "Social Effects of Hearing Loss Due to Weaving Noise," in Occupational Hearing Loss, edited by D. W. Robinson (Academic, London), pp. 179–191.

Knight, J. J. (1967). "Redetermination of Optimum Characteristics for a Hearing Aid with Insert Telephone," Int. Audiol. 6, 322–326.

Kuźniarz, J. J. (1973). "Hearing Loss and Speech Intelligibility in Noise," in Proceedings of the International Congress on Noise as a Public Health Problem, Dubrovnik, 1973 (U. S. Environmental Protection Agency, Washington, DC), pp. 57–71.

Lane, H., and Tranel, B. (1971). "The Lombard Sign and the Role of Hearing in Speech," J. Speech Hear. Res. 14, 677–709.

Lanos, P. (1952). "La Mesure de la Paracousie de Willis en Audiométrie Vocale; Réflexions sur son Mécanisme et sa Valeur Clinique," Annales Oto-Laryngol. 69, 590–660.

Lentz, W. E. (1974). "A Summary of Research Using Directional and Omnidirectional Hearing Aids," Z. Hörgeräte-Akustik 13, 42–65.

Lindeman, H. E. (1967). "Bepaling van de Validiteit van het Gehoor met Behulp van een Bedrijfsspraakaudiometer," Tijdschr. Soc. Geneeskd. 45, 814–837.

Lindeman, H. E., and van Leeuwen, P. (1970). "Invloed van Spraakafzien op Uitkomst Bedrijfsspraakaudiogram," Tijdschr. Soc. Geneeskd. 48, 279–283.

Ludvigsen, C. (1974). "Construction and Evaluation of an Audio-Visual Test (the Helen Test)," Scand. Audiol. Suppl. 4, 67–75.

Martin, M. C. (1973). "Hearing Aid Gain Requirements in Sensori Neural Hearing Loss," Br. J. Audiol. 7, 21–24.

Martin, M. C., Grover, B. C., Worrall, J. J., and Williams, V. (1976). "The Effectiveness of Hearing Aids in a School Population," Br. J. Audiol. 10, 33–40.

Merluzzi, F., and Hinchcliffe, R. (1973). "Threshold of Subjective Auditory Handicap," Audiol. 12, 65–69.

Morales-Garcia, C., and Poole, J. P. (1972). "Masked Speech Audiometry in Central Deafness," Acta Oto-Laryngol. 74, 307–316.

Nabelek, A. K., and Pickett, J. M. (1974a). "Reception of Consonants in a Classroom as Affected by Monaural and Binaural Listening, Noise, Reverberation, and Hearing Aids," J. Acoust. Soc. Am. 56, 628–639.

Nabelek, A. K., and Pickett, J. M. (1974b). "Monaural and Binaural Speech Perception through Hearing Aids under Noise and Reverberation with Normal and Hearing-Impaired Listeners," J. Speech Hear. Res. 17, 724–739.

NCHS (1965). "Hearing Levels of Adults by Age and Sex, United States 1960–62," Nat. Cent. Health Statist., Vital and Health Statist., PHS Pub. No. 1000-Series 11-No. 11, Public Health Service, Washington, DC.

NCHS (1967). "Characteristics of Persons with Impaired Hearing, United States July 1962–June 1963," Nat. Cent. Health. Statist. Vital and Health Statist., PHS Pub. Series 10—No. 35, Public Health Service, Washington, DC.

NCHS (1970). "Hearing Levels of Children by Age and Sex, United States," Nat. Cent. Health Statist., Vital and Health Statist., PHS Pub. No. 1000-Series 11-No. 102, Public Health Service, Washington, DC.

NCHS (1975a). "Prevalence of Selected Impairments, United States 1971," Nat. Cent. Health Statist., Vital and Health Statist., PHS Publ. Series 10-No. 99, DHEW Publ. No. (HRA)75-1526, Rockville, MD.

NCHS (1975b). "Hearing Levels of Youths 12–17 years, United States 1966–70," Nat. Cent. Health. Statist., Vital and Health Statist., PHS Publ. Series 11-No. 145, DHEW Publ. No. (HRA)75-1627, Rockville, MD.

Nielsen, T. E. (1976). "Hearing Aid Characteristics and Fitting Techniques for Improving Speech Intelligibility in Noise," Br. J. Audiol. 10, 1–7.

Niemeyer, W. (1967). "Speech Discrimination in Noise-Induced Deafness," Int. Audiol. 6, 42–47.

Noble, W. G. (1973). "Pure-Tone Acuity, Speech-Hearing Ability and Deafness in Acoustic Trauma," Audiol. 12, 291–315.

Olsen, W. O., Noffsinger, D., and Kurdziel, S. (1975). "Speech Discrimination in Quiet and in White Noise by Patients with Peripheral and Central Lesions," Acta Oto-Laryngol. 80, 375–382.

Olsen, W. O., and Tillman, T. W. (1968). "Hearing Aids and Sensorineural Hearing Loss," Ann. Otol. Rhinol. Laryngol. 77, 717–726.

Palva, T. (1955). "Studies of Hearing for Pure Tones and Speech in Noise," Acta Oto-Laryngol. 45, 231–243.

Pascoe, D. P. (1975). "Frequency Responses of Hearing Aids and Their Effects on the Speech Perception of Hearing-Impaired Subjects," Ann. Otol. Rhinol. Laryngol. 84, Suppl. 23.

Pedersen, B., Frankner, B., and Terkildsen, K. (1974).

"A Prospective Study of Adult Danish Hearing-Aid Users," Scand. Audiol. 3, 107–111.

Plomp, R. (1976). "Binaural and Monaural Speech Intelligibility of Connected Discourse in Reverberation as a Function of Azimuth of a Single Competing Sound Source (Speech or Noise)," Acustica 34, 200–211.

Plomp, R. (1977). "Acoustical Aspects of Cocktail Parties," Acustica 38, 186–191.

Punch, J. L., and McConnell, F. (1969). "The Speech Discrimination Function of Elderly Adults," J. Aud. Res. 9, 159–166.

Quist-Hanssen, S. (1967). "Subjective Appraisal and Objective Assessment of the Hearing of Speech amongst a Group of Adults with Impaired Hearing," Acta Oto-Laryngol. Suppl. 224, 177–185.

Rintelmann, W. F. (1972). "Effects of Amplitude Compression upon Speech Perception: A Review of Research," Scand Audiol. 1, 127–134.

Ross, M. (1969). "Changing Concepts in Hearing Aid Candidacy," Eye Ear Nose Throat Mon. 48, 147–153.

Schon, T. D. (1970). "The Effects on Speech Intelligibility of Time-Compression and -Expansion on Normal-Hearing, Hard of Hearing, and Aged Males," J. Aud. Res. 10, 263–268.

Schultz-Coulon, H. J. (1973). "Über die Bedeutung des Umweltgeräusches für den Hochtonschwerhörigen," HNO 21, 26–32.

Schultz-Coulon, H. J. (1974). "Sprachaudiometrie mit Sätzen und Geräusch," Laryngol. Rhinol. Otol. Grenzgebiete 53, 734–749.

Simonton, K. M., and Hedgecock, L. D. (1953). "A Laboratory Assessment of Hearing Acuity for Voice Signals against a Background of Noise," Ann. Otol. Rhinol. Laryngol. 62, 735–747.

Stephens, S. D. G. (1976). "The Input for a Damaged Cochlea-A Brief Review," Br. J. Audiol. 10, 97–101.

Sung, G. S., Sung, R. J., and Angelelli, R. M. (1975). "Directional Microphone in Hearing Aids. Effects on Speech Discrimination in Noise," Arch. Otolaryngol. 101, 316–319.

Tillman, T. W., Carhart, R., and Nicholls, S. (1973). "Release from Multiple Maskers in Elderly Persons," J. Speech Hear. Res. 16, 152–160.

Tillman, T. W., Carhart, R., and Olsen, W. O. (1970). "Hearing Aid Efficiency in a Competing Speech Situation," J. Speech Hear. Res. 13, 789–811.

Villchur, E. (1973). "Signal Processing to Improve Speech Intelligibility in Perceptive Deafness," J. Acoust. Soc. Am. 53, 1646–1657.

Wilkins, L. T. (1950). "The Prevalence of Deafness in England, Scotland and Wales," Acta Oto Laryngol. Suppl. 90, 97–115.

Young, M. A., and Gibbons, E. W. (1962). "Speech Discrimination Scores and Threshold Measurements in a Non-Normal Hearing Population," J. Aud. Res. 2, 21–33.

Note correction: Equation (8) should read

$$\text{ASRT}_{A+D} = 10 \log[10^{(A-G+D+S+16)/10} + 10^{(Ln+D+S-8)/10}]$$

DEVELOPMENTAL ISSUES

Paper 38. P. D. Eimas, E. R. Siqueland, P. Jusczyk, and J. Vigorito (1971), Speech perception in infants. *Science* 171, 303–306.

Paper 39. P. K. Kuhl (1979), Speech perception in early infancy: Perceptual constancy for spectrally dissimilar vowel categories. *Journal of the Acoustical Society of America* 66, 1668–1679.

Paper 40. J. Mehler, P. Jusczyk, G. Lambertz, N. Halsted, J. Bertoncini, and C. Amiel-Tison (1988), A precursor of language acquisition in young infants. *Cognition* 29, 143–178.

Paper 41. J. F. Werker and R. C. Tees (1984), Cross-language speech perception: Evidence for perceptual reorganization during the first year of life. *Infant Behavior and Development* 7, 49–63.

Over the past two decades there has been substantial research on the ontogeny of speech perception. This research is not only important in its own right, or as part of an account of language acquisition, but has played a role in theory construction in adult speech perception [see Liberman and Mattingly (1985) and Stevens and Blumstein (1978) in the section on Theoretical Perspectives].

One of the most striking findings from the developmental research is that young, prearticulate infants possess highly sophisticated abilities to perceive speech. In their seminal paper, Eimas, Siqueland, Jusczyk, and Vigorito (1971) demonstrated that infants not only distinguish between stimuli varying in linguistically relevant acoustic properties—a striking ability in its own right—but that they do so in terms of categories that resemble (and presumably provide the basis for) adult phonetic categories. The basic phenomenon, that infants readily discriminate stimuli varying along an acoustic continuum if they belong to different categories but not if they belong to the same category, has since been replicated many times. Kuhl (1979) provides evidence for yet another type of categorization by young infants, in this case the tendency to treat stimuli from a given phonetic category equivalently, even though the stimuli were synthesized to represent different talkers and were highly discriminable. This finding suggests that infants have the means to accomplish talker normalization at a very young age (see the section on Perception of Vocalic Distinctions).

The above findings provide strong evidence that young infants process speech in terms of linguistically relevant categories. Such categorization arguably plays a fundamental role in the infant's emerging abilities to imitate speech and ultimately to acquire a phonology and a lexicon. Not surprising, given current controversies regarding adult speech perception (see the section on Theoretical Perspectives), the nature of the mechanism underlying the infant's categorization abilities, for example, whether they are part of an innate, specialized processing system for speech or lie in the functioning of the auditory system itself, remains unresolved.

Because languages of the world differ in their phonetic structures, and adults process speech in terms of the categories used in their respective language, it must be the case that the early linguistically relevant categorizations of infants (which appear to be universal) are modified as a particular language is acquired. Werker and Tees (1984) provide compelling evidence that at least for some phonetic contrasts, such modification occurs somewhere between 6 and 12 months of life—interestingly, during the same time period as infants begin to attach meaning (though perhaps not the adult meaning) to spoken words. But although the influence of listening to a particular language on speech-sound categorization may not be seen until the end of the first year of life, its influence on other aspects of perception can be seen much earlier. Mehler, Jusczyk, Lambertz, Halsted, Bertoncini, and Amiel-Tison (1988) report the intriguing finding that infants as young as four days of age can distinguish utterances in their native language (i.e., the language of their parents) from those in another language, although they cannot distinguish utterances in two unfamiliar languages. The papers in this section thus provide evidence that the ontogeny of speech perception involves both strong biological constraints and very early learning.

Reprinted from
22 January 1971, Volume 171, pp. 303-306

SCIENCE

Speech Perception in Infants

Abstract. *Discrimination of synthetic speech sounds was studied in 1- and 4-month-old infants. The speech sounds varied along an acoustic dimension previously shown to cue phonemic distinctions among the voiced and voiceless stop consonants in adults. Discriminability was measured by an increase in conditioned response rate to a second speech sound after habituation to the first speech sound. Recovery from habituation was greater for a given acoustic difference when the two stimuli were from different adult phonemic categories than when they were from the same category. The discontinuity in discrimination at the region of the adult phonemic boundary was taken as evidence for categorical perception.*

In this study of speech perception, it was found that 1- and 4-month-old infants were able to discriminate the acoustic cue underlying the adult phonemic distinction between the voiced and voiceless stop consonants /b/ and /p/. Moreover, and more important, there was a tendency in these subjects toward categorical perception: discrimination of the same physical difference was reliably better across the adult phonemic boundary than within the adult phonemic category.

Earlier research using synthetic speech sounds with adult subjects uncovered a sufficient cue for the perceived distinction in English between the voiced and voiceless forms of the stop consonants, /b-p/, /d-t/, and /g-k/, occurring in absolute initial position (1). The cue, which is illustrated in the spectrograms displayed in Fig. 1, is the onset of the first formant relative to the second and third formants. It is possible to construct a series of stimuli that vary continuously in the relative onset time of the first formant, and to investigate listeners' ability to identify and discriminate these sound patterns. An

investigation of this nature (2) revealed that the perception of this cue was very nearly categorical in the sense that listeners could discriminate continuous variations in the relative onset of the first formant very little better than they could identify the sound patterns absolutely. That is, listeners could readily discriminate between the voiced and voiceless stop consonants, just as they would differentially label them, but they were virtually unable to hear intraphonemic differences, despite the fact that the acoustic variation was the same in both conditions. The most measurable indication of this categorical perception was the occurrence of a high peak of discriminability at the boundary between the voiced and voiceless stops, and a nearly chance level of discriminability among stimuli that represented acoustic variations of the same phoneme. Such categorical perception is not found with nonspeech sounds that vary continuously along physical continua such as frequency or intensity. Typically, listeners are able to discriminate many more stimuli than they are able to identify absolutely, and the dis-

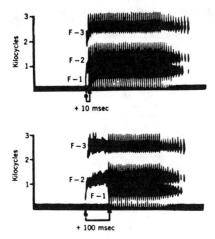

Fig. 1. Spectrograms of synthetic speech showing two conditions of voice onset time (VOT): slight voicing lag in the upper figure and long voicing lag in the lower figure. The symbols *F-1*, *F-2*, and *F-3* represent the first three formants, that is, the relatively intense bands of energy in the speech spectrum. [Courtesy of L. Lisker and A. S. Abramson]

criminability functions do not normally show the same high peaks and low troughs found in the case of the voicing distinction (3). The strong and unusual tendency for the stop consonants to be perceived in a categorical manner has been assumed to be the result of

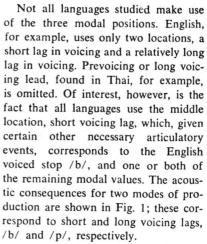

the special processing to which sounds of speech are subjected and thus to be characteristic of perception in the speech or linguistic mode (4).

Because the voicing dimension in the stop consonants is universal, or very nearly so, it may be thought to be reasonably close to the biological basis of speech and hence of special interest to students of language development. Though the distinctions made along the voicing dimension are not phonetically the same in all languages, it has been found in the cross-language research of Lisker and Abramson (5) that the usages are not arbitrary, but rather very much constrained. In studies of the production of the voicing distinction in 11 diverse languages, these investigators found that, with only minor exceptions, the various tokens fell at three values along a single continuum. The continuum, called voice onset time (VOT), is defined as the time between the release burst and the onset of laryngeal pulsing or voicing. Had the location of the phonetic distinctions been arbitrary, then different languages might well have divided the VOT continuum in many different ways, constrained only by the necessity to space the different modal values of VOT sufficiently far apart as to avoid confusion.

Not all languages studied make use of the three modal positions. English, for example, uses only two locations, a short lag in voicing and a relatively long lag in voicing. Prevoicing or long voicing lead, found in Thai, for example, is omitted. Of interest, however, is the fact that all languages use the middle location, short voicing lag, which, given certain other necessary articulatory events, corresponds to the English voiced stop /b/, and one or both of the remaining modal values. The acoustic consequences for two modes of production are shown in Fig. 1; these correspond to short and long voicing lags, /b/ and /p/, respectively.

Given the strong evidence for universal—and presumably biologically determined—modes of production for the voicing distinction, we should suppose that there might exist complementary processes of perception (6). Hence, if we are to find evidence marking the beginnings of speech perception in a linguistic mode, it would appear reasonable to initiate our search with investigations of speech sounds differing along the voicing continuum. What was done experimentally, in essence, was to compare the discriminability of two synthetic speech sounds separated by a fixed difference in VOT under two conditions: in the first condition the two stimuli to be discriminated lay on opposite sides of the adult phonemic boundary, whereas in the second condition the two stimuli were from the same phonemic category.

The experimental methodology was a modification of the reinforcement procedure developed by Siqueland (7). After obtaining a baseline rate of high-amplitude, nonnutritive sucking for each infant, the presentation and intensity of an auditory stimulus was made contingent upon the infant's rate of high-amplitude sucking. The nipple on which the child sucked was connected to a positive pressure transducer that provided polygraphic recordings of all responses and a digital record of criterional high-amplitude sucking responses. Criterional responses activated a power supply that increased the intensity of the auditory feedback. A sucking rate of two responses per second maintained the stimulus at maximum intensity, about 75 db (13 db over the background intensity of 62 db).

The presentation of an auditory stimulus in this manner typically results in an increase in the rate of sucking com-

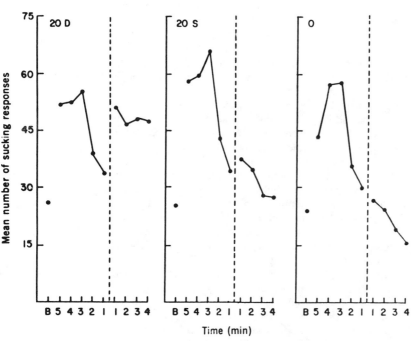

Fig. 2. Mean number of sucking responses for the 4-month-old infants, as a function of time and experimental condition. The dashed line indicates the occurrence of the stimulus shift, or in the case of the control group the time at which the shift would have occurred. The letter *B* stands for the baseline rate. Time is measured with reference to the moment of stimulus shift and indicates the 5 minutes prior to and the 4 minutes after shift.

pared with the baseline rate. With continued presentation of the initial stimulus, a decrement in the response rate occurs, presumably as a consequence of the lessening of the reinforcing properties of the initial stimulus. When it was apparent that attenuation of the reinforcing properties of the initial stimulus had occurred, as indicated by a decrement in the conditioned sucking rate of at least 20 percent for two consecutive minutes compared with the immediately preceding minute, a second auditory stimulus was presented without interruption and again contingent upon sucking. The second stimulus was maintained for 4 minutes after which the experiment was terminated. Control subjects were treated in a similar manner, except that after the initial decrease in response rate, that is, after habituation, no change was made in the auditory stimulus. Either an increase in response rate associated with a change in stimulation or a decrease of smaller magnitude than that shown by the control subjects is taken as inferential evidence that the infants perceived the two stimuli as different.

The stimuli were synthetic speech sounds prepared by means of a parallel resonance synthesizer at the Haskins Laboratories by Lisker and Abramson. There were three variations of the bilabial voiced stop /b/ and three variations of its voiceless counterpart /p/. The variations between all stimuli were in VOT, which for the English stops /b/ and /p/ can be realized acoustically by varying the onset of the first formant relative to the second and third formants and by having the second and third formants excited by a noise source during the interval when the first formant is not present. Identification functions from adult listeners (8) have indicated that when the onset of the first formant leads or follows the onset of the second and third formants by less than 25 msec perception is almost invariably /b/. When voicing follows the release burst by more than 25 msec the perception is /p/. Actually the sounds are perceived as /ba/ or /pa/, since the patterns contain three steady-state formants appropriate for a vowel of the type /a/. The six stimuli had VOT values of −20, 0, +20, +40, +60, and +80 msec. The negative sign indicates that voicing occurs before the release burst. The subjects were 1- and 4-month-old infants, and within each age level half of the subjects were males and half were females.

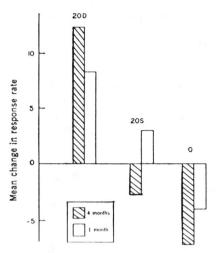

Fig. 3. The mean change in response rate as a function of experimental treatments, shown separately for the 1- and 4-month-old infants. (See text for details.)

The main experiment was begun after several preliminary studies established that both age groups were responsive to synthetic speech sounds as measured by a reliable increase in the rate of sucking with the response-contingent presentation of the first stimulus ($P < .01$). Furthermore, these studies showed that stimuli separated by differences in VOT of 100, 60, and 20 msec were discriminable when the stimuli were from different adult phonemic categories; that is, there was reliable recovery of the rate of sucking with a change in stimulation after habituation ($P < .05$). The finding that a VOT difference of 20 msec was discriminable permitted within-phonemic-category discriminations of VOT with relatively realistic variations of both phonemes.

In the main experiment, there were three variations in VOT differences at each of two age levels. In the first condition, 20D, the difference in VOT between the two stimuli to be discriminated was 20 msec and the two stimuli were from different adult phonemic categories. The two stimuli used in condition 20D had VOT values of +20 and +40 msec. In the second condition, 20S, the VOT difference was again 20 msec, but now the two stimuli were from the same phonemic category. In this condition the stimuli had VOT values of −20 and 0 msec or +60 and +80 msec. The third condition, 0, was a control condition in which each subject was randomly assigned one of the six stimuli and treated in the same manner as the experimental subjects, except that after habituation no change in

stimulation was made. The control group served to counter any argument that the increment in response rate associated with a change in stimulation was artifactual in that the infants tended to respond in a cyclical manner. Eight infants from each age level were randomly assigned to conditions 20D and 20S, and ten infants from each age level were assigned to the control condition.

Figure 2 shows the minute-by-minute response rates for the 4-month-old subjects for each of the training conditions separately. The results for the younger infants show very nearly the identical overall pattern of results seen with the older infants. In all conditions at both age levels, there were reliable conditioning effects: the response rate in the third minute prior to shift was significantly greater than the baseline rate of responding ($P < .01$). As was expected from the nature of the procedure, there were also reliable habituation effects for all subjects. The mean response rate for the final 2 minutes prior to shift was significantly lower than the response rate for the third minute before shift ($P < .01$). As is apparent from inspection of Fig. 1, the recovery data for the 4-month-old infants were differentiated by the nature of the shift. When the mean response rate during the 2 minutes after shift was compared with the response rate for the 2 minutes prior to shift, condition 20D showed a significant increment ($P < .05$), whereas condition 20S showed a nonsignificant decrement in responding ($P > .05$). In the control condition, there was a fairly substantial decrement in responding during the first 2 minutes of what corresponded to the shift period in the experimental conditions. However, the effect failed to reach the .05 level of significance, but there was a reliable decrement when the mean response rate for the entire 4 minutes after shift was compared with the initial 2 minutes of habituation ($P < .02$). The shift data for the younger infants were quite similar. The only appreciable difference was that in condition 20S there was a nonsignificant increment in the response rate during the first 2 minutes of shift.

In Fig. 3 the recovery data are summarized for both age groups. The mean change in response rate (that is, the mean response rate for the initial 2 minutes of shift minus the mean response rate during the final 2 minutes before shift) is displayed as a function of experimental treatments and age. Analyses of these data revealed that the magnitude of recovery for the 20D condition was reliably greater than that for the 20S condition ($P < .01$). In addition, the 20D condition showed a greater rate of responding than did the control condition ($P < .01$), while the difference between the 20S and control conditions failed to attain the .05 level of significance.

In summary, the results strongly indicate that infants as young as 1 month of age are not only responsive to speech sounds and able to make fine discriminations but are also perceiving speech sounds along the voicing continuum in a manner approximating categorical perception, the manner in which adults perceive these same sounds. Another way of stating this effect is that infants are able to sort acoustic variations of adult phonemes into categories with relatively limited exposure to speech, as well as with virtually no experience in producing these same sounds and certainly with little, if any, differential reinforcement for this form of behavior. The implication of these findings is that the means by which the categorical perception of speech, that is, perception in a linguistic mode, is accomplished may well be part of the biological makeup of the organism and, moreover, that these means must be operative at an unexpectedly early age.

PETER D. EIMAS
EINAR R. SIQUELAND
PETER JUSCZYK
JAMES VIGORITO

*Department of Psychology,
Brown University,
Providence, Rhode Island 02912*

References and Notes

1. A. M. Liberman. P. C. Delattre, F. S. Cooper, *Language and Speech* 1, 153 (1958); A. M. Liberman, F. Ingemann, L. Lisker, P. C. Delattre, F. S. Cooper, *J. Acoust. Soc. Amer.* 31, 1490 (1959). It should be emphasized that the cues underlying the voicing distinction as discussed in the present report apply only to sound segments in absolute initial position.
2. A. M. Liberman, K. S. Harris, H. S. Hoffman, H. Lane, *J. Exp. Psychol.* 61, 370 (1961).
3. P. D. Eimas, *Language and Speech* 6, 206 (1963); G. A. Miller, *Psychol. Rev.* 63, 81 (1956); R. S. Woodworth and H. Schlosberg, *Experimental Psychology* (Holt, New York, 1954).
4. A. M. Liberman, F. S. Cooper, D. P. Shankweiler, M. Studdert-Kennedy, *Psychol. Rev.* 74, 431 (1967); M. Studdert-Kennedy, A. M. Liberman, K. S. Harris, F. S. Cooper, *ibid.* 77, 234 (1970); M. Studdert-Kennedy and D. Shankweiler, *J. Acoust. Soc. Amer.*, in press.
5. L. Lisker and A. S. Abramson, *Word* 20, 384 (1964).
6. P. Lieberman, *Linguistic Inquiry* 1, 307 (1970).
7. E. R. Siqueland, address presented before the 29th International Congress of Psychology, London, England (August 1969); ——— and C. A. DeLucia, *Science* 165, 1144 (1969).
8. L. Lisker and A. S. Abramson, *Proc. Int. Congr. Phonet. Sci. 6th* (1970), p. 563.
9. Supported by grants HD 03386 and HD 04146 from the National Institute of Child Health and Human Development. P.J. and J.V. were supported by the NSF Undergraduate Participation Program (GY 5872). We thank Dr. F. S. Cooper for generously making available the facilities of the Haskins Laboratories. We also thank Drs. A. M. Liberman, I. G. Mattingly, A. S. Abramson, and L. Lisker for their critical comments. Portions of this study were presented before the Eastern Psychological Association, Atlantic City (April 1970).

14 September 1970

Speech perception in early infancy: Perceptual constancy for spectrally dissimilar vowel categories

Patricia K. Kuhl

Department of Speech and Hearing Sciences and Child Development and Mental Retardation Center, University of Washington, Seattle, Washington 98195
(Received 14 December 1978; accepted for publication 14 August 1979)

While numerous studies on infant perception demonstrate the infant's ability to discriminate individual speech-sound pairs, very few demonstrate the infant's ability to recognize the similarity among phonetic units when they occur in different phonetic contexts, in different positions in a syllable, or when they are spoken by different talkers. In two studies, six-month-old infants demonstrated the ability to distinguish two spectrally dissimilar vowel categories (/a/ and /i/) in which the vowel tokens were generated to simulate tokens produced by a male, a female, and a child talker. In experiment I, the infants were initially trained to discriminate the /a/ and /i/ tokens produced by the computer-simulated male voice. They were then gradually exposed to a number of novel tokens in a progressive transfer-of-learning task. In experiment II, the infants were initially trained to discriminate the same vowel contrast, but were then immediately tested with all of the tokens in both vowel categories. In both experiments the infants demonstrated rapid transfer of learning from the traning tokens produced by the male talker to the tokens produced by female and child talkers. Both experiments provide strong evidence that the six-month-old infant recognizes acoustic categories that conform to the vowel categories perceived by adult speakers of English.

PACS numbers: 43.70.Dn, 43.70.Ve

INTRODUCTION

A classic problem in the fields of visual and auditory perception is the identification of the criterial stimulus information that underlies an adult listener's perception of "constancy" for visual and auditory events. Object perception, for example, depends upon the detection of certain relations that remain constant despite the fact that the object, or the perceiver, move about in space (see Epstein, 1977a; 1977b, for general discussion). Similarly, we presume that the perception of the phonetic units of speech involves the detection of acoustic information that remains constant over changes in the phonetic target's context, its position in an utterance, and the talker who utters it (see Shankweiler, Strange, and Verbrugge, 1977, for discussion related to vowel perception). The problem in both fields has been the precise specification of the criterial cues that a perceiver uses in assigning stimuli to categories. The literature on speech perception, for example, attests to the context dependency of the acoustic cues to speech sounds (Liberman *et al.*, 1967), and while more recent work has emphasized abstract characterizations of the acoustic cues with the aim of specifying context independent stimulus features (Stevens and Blumstein, 1978; Blumstein and Stevens, 1977), the criterial acoustic information that is utilized by the auditory system to classify phonetic units remain largely unspecified.

One component to the study of perceptual constancy for visual events has been the rather extensive investigation of its development in human infants (Bower, 1975; 1966). This work was motivated by early theorists (Piaget, 1954) who hypothesized that the infant gradually learned to preserve the constancy of an object by associating the changes in retinal image with a constant shape or size. Later experiments on shape and size constancy with young infants (Bower, 1966) did not support this hypothesis, but the precise role that learning might play in the perception of visual constancies is still being debated.

In contrast to the extensive developmental visual literature, investigations of the perception of speech by human infants have not been directed toward questions regarding the human infant's perception of speech-sound constancies and their possible developmental sequences. The data we do have on the perception of speech by young human infants has examined the infant's ability to discriminate a single speech sound representing one phonetic category from a single speech sound representing a second phonetic category. These data, representing some 30 published studies and a decade of research [see Kuhl, 1979; Eilers (in press); Morse, 1978; Eimas, 1977, for recent reviews], strongly suggest that at least by four months of age, human infants possess sufficient auditory acuity to discriminate among many, if not all, of the sounds of human speech.

However extensive the list of studies on speech-sound perception by infants, we have little information concerning the infant's perception of phonetic similarity for units which appear in different phonetic contexts, different positions in a syllable, or are spoken by different talkers. Fodor, Garrett, and Brill (1975) examined the acquisition of a head-turn response for visual reinforcement in 14 to 18-week-old infants under two stimulus conditions. In both conditions, three syllables were randomly presented (/pi/, /ka/, /pu/) but only two of the three were reinforced. In one condition, the stimuli being reinforced were phonetically related (/pi/ and /pu/); in the other condition, the stimuli being reinforced were not phonetically related (/pi/ and /ka/). The authors hypothesized that if infants tend to hear the similarity between two syllables that share the initial consonant in spite of the differences in the acoustic cues for that consonant and in spite of the irrelevant differences between the two syllables, like their vowels, then their tendencies to learn the association ought to differ in the two conditions. Their hypothesis was supported; the proportion of head turns when phonetically similar sounds were reinforced was significantly greater than the proportion of head turns when phonetically dissimilar sounds were reinforced.

These data demonstrated that infants grouped syllables that shared the initial consonant more readily than they grouped syllables that did not share the initial consonant, but the data also demonstrated that neither task was accomplished very accurately. Two factors may have made the task inordinately difficult. First, observations in our own laboratory demonstrate that until $5\frac{1}{2}$ months of age, a large percentage of infants do not make volitional head-turn responses for a visual reinforcer with ease. At $5\frac{1}{2}$ months, or older, infants make head-turn responses easily and it is our impression that over 90% of the infants are conditionable for contrasts that are relatively easy, like /a/ vs /i/. Secondly, the task involved a two-response differentiation. That is, a head turn either to the right or to the left, dependent upon which of two loudspeakers presented the reinforced stimulus, was required. Tasks which require two-response differentiation for auditory stimuli have been shown to be inordinately difficult for young infants (see Papoušek, 1967a; 1967b, for examples) and for nonhuman animals [see Burdick (in press) for review].

Kuhl and Miller (1975) took a preliminary step toward testing perceptual constancy for vowel categories by infants. Vowel categories were considered ideal for beginning investigations on category formation for speech sounds, since there has been considerable debate concerning the critical acoustic cues which define vowel identity across talkers (see Shankweiler, Strange, and Verbrugge, 1977, and Fant, 1973, for review and discussion). Kuhl and Miller (1975) (described in Kuhl, 1976) asked whether 4–16-week-old infants could detect a change in a target dimension if an irrelevant dimension was randomly varied throughout the experiment, serving as a kind of "distracting" stimulus. The high-amplitude-sucking paradigm was employed. A change in the "target" dimension occurred at the "shift point" while an "irrelevant" dimension was randomly varied throughout both the pre- and post-shift periods.

In one condition, the target dimension was a phonemic change in the vowel and the irrelevant dimension was the pitch contour of the vowel; in a second condition, the target dimension was the pitch contour of the vowel and the irrelevant dimension was the vowel color. The stimuli were two /a/'s and two /i/'s synthesized such that one /a/ and one /i/ had identical monotone pitch contours and one /a/ and one /i/ had identical rise–fall pitch contours. Discrimination of vowel color and pitch contour "targets" were tested *with* and *without* irrelevant variation in the second dimension. The data demonstrated that infants detect a vowel change regardless of the distraction posed by a random change in the pitch contour of a vowel. In contrast, infants detected a change in the pitch contour of a vowel when all other dimensions were held constant, but failed to re-

spond to a pitch-contour change when the vowel color was randomly changed. In addition, infants responded for a significantly longer period of time before habituating during the pre-shift period of the experiment when vowel color was randomly varied. This research demonstrated the infant's ability to tolerate some degree of distraction and still make the discrimination but it did not demonstrate the infant's ability to recognize the phonetic similarity among vowel tokens whose critical acoustic dimensions varied.

In order to extend these results to a situation in which the infant had to contend with variation in both the critical and noncritical dimensions of the signals, these experiments combined the use of a head-turn technique for visual reinforcement with a classic transfer-of-learning experimental format. Infants were initially trained to discriminate two single tokens, one from each of two vowel categories, and then novel exemplars from the two vowel categories were systematically introduced. The exemplars were synthesized to cover a range of different vocal tracts, simulating productions by a male, a female, and a child talker. In experiment I, the novel tokens from two vowel categories (/a/ and /i/) were gradually introduced in a progressive transfer-of-learning experiment; in experiment II, the same vowel stimuli were used, this time with changes in the procedure which eliminated the gradual introduction of the novel tokens and allowed a specification of the degree of generalization to each of the novel tokens.

I. EXPERIMENT I

A. Method

1. Subjects

Four infants, aged $5\frac{1}{2}$–$6\frac{1}{2}$ months of age, served as subjects for the experiment. One additional infant cried when the visual reinforcer was presented and was dropped from the experiment. Subjects were obtained by mail solicitation to the parents of newborns in the Seattle area. Parents were questioned about familial histories of hearing loss and treatment for ear infections so that we could screen out infants who might be "at risk" for hearing loss. The infants were full term and were presumed, by their parents, to be developing normally. The subjects were paid at a rate of $5.00 per visit.

2. Stimuli

The stimuli were synthesized at Central Institute for the Deaf in St. Louis on a terminal analog serial synthesizer. Two tokens of the vowel /a/ and the vowel /i/, one with a rise–fall pitch contour and one with a rising pitch contour, were synthesized to simulated each of three "talkers," a male, a female, and a child. Table I lists the center frequencies and bandwidths of the first three formants for /a/ and /i/ for each talker. These center frequencies were taken from Peterson and Barney's (1952) averages of the center-frequency measurements of naturally produced /a/ and /i/ in an /h-d/ context. The bandwidths were taken from Dunn (1963). The upper formants (in Table II) were obtained by taking Rabiner's (1968) estimates of the center fre-

TABLE I. Center frequencies and bandwidths of the first three formants of the /a/ and /i/ vowels for male, female, and child talkers.

		Male	Female	Child
/i/	F_3	3010 (111.5)	3310 (130.7)	3730 (165.4)
	F_2	2290 (77.4)	2790 (98.9)	3200 (123.0)
	F_1	270 (52.6)	310 (79.5)	370 (71.6)
/a/	F_3	2440 (83.2)	2810 (99.9)	3170 (121.0)
	F_2	1090 (48.4)	1220 (53.9)	1370 (55.5)
	F_1	730 (45.2)	850 (53.4)	1030 (52.9)

TABLE III. Pitch contour specifications for the rising and falling pitch-contour stimuli for the /a/ and /i/ vowels. The falling stimuli were synthesized in a piece-wise linear fashion, changing from the first value to the second in the first 100 ms, remaining there for 40 ms, and then falling to the third value in the remaining 360 ms. The rising stimuli were linear over their entire 500-ms duration.

	Male	Female	Child
Fall	112 → 132 → 92	189 → 223 → 155	224 → 264 → 184
Rise	112 → 132	189 → 223	224 → 264

quencies for the upper formants of a male talker and modifying them using Fant's (1973) correction factors for the shorter vocal tract lengths of female (0.87) and child (0.70) talkers. The stimuli were synthesized at a 20-kHz sampling rate and formants over 10 kHz were eliminated to avoid aliasing problems. All stimuli were 500 ms in duration.

Table III lists the pitch-contour specifications. The rise–fall contours were synthesized in a piecewise linear fashion, changing from the first value to the second value in the first 100 ms, remaining there for 40 ms, and then falling to the third value in the remaining 360 ms. The rising-pitch contours were linear over their entire course.

The /a/ and /i/ stimuli were originally synthesized with equal overall RMS sound pressures. As one would expect, the /i/ tokens were perceived to be louder than the /a/ tokens by adult listeners under these conditions. Therefore, two adult listeners adjusted the intensity of the /i/ tokens until they were perceived to be as loud as the /a/ tokens. For both listeners this involved a 3-dB decrease in intensity. The tokens were then resynthesized, adjusting the overall intensities of all /i/ tokens to achieve a 3-dB decrease.[1] The resulting stimuli were judged to be good exemplars of either the vowel /a/ or /i/ when they were presented in an open set of vowels. In a forced-choice task, the tokens were readily attributed to either a male, female, or child talker. The tokens were readily identified as having either a rising or falling intonation contour.

The synthesized tokens were stored digitally on a disk pack (Control Data, model 846-2-16) of the Random-Access Programmable Recorder of Complex Sounds (RAP), a self-contained digital recorder (Spenner et al., 1974). Stimulus tapes for the experiment

TABLE II. Center frequencies and bandwidths of the upper poles (F_4–F_{10}) for male, female, and child talkers (in kHz).

	Male	Female	Child
F_4	3.5 (0.175)	4.03 (0.225)	5.01 (0.35)
F_5	4.5 (0.281)	5.18 (0.380)	6.44 (67.5)
F_6	5.5 (0.458)	6.33 (0.640)	7.87 (1.5)
F_7	6.5 (0.722)	7.48 (1.25)	9.3 (4.25)
F_8	7.5 (1.25)	8.63 (2.40)	...
F_9	8.5 (2.125)	9.78 (7.0)	...
F_{10}	9.5 (4.75)	...	...

were made on a two-channel tape recorder (Sony model #4204). The /a/ and /i/ vowels were recorded synchronously on two separate channels of the tape with stimulus onsets spaced 2 s apart. During the recording process, the signals were again adjusted at the input to the tape recorder to achieve a perceived loudness balance on the two channels of the tape recorder. The tape recorder's meter readings that achieved this perceived balance were noted. These loudness-balance techniques prior to and during the recording process made daily calibration quite easy. Both channels were adjusted to the meter readings established during the recording process. At this setting, the /a/ stimulus produced a 68-dB (A scale) reading on a sound level meter (Bruel and Kjaer, model #2203) when it was placed in the approximate position of the infant's head. The /i/ channel was then finally checked to ensure that it was perceived to be equally loud; small adjustments were made if necessary.

3. The experimental suite

The experimental/control suite is shown in Fig. 1. The infant was held by a parent so that he or she faced an assistant. The assistant maintained the infant's attention at midline or directly in front of the assistant by manipulating a variety of silent toys. A loudspeaker (Electrovoice, SP12) was located at a 90° angle to the

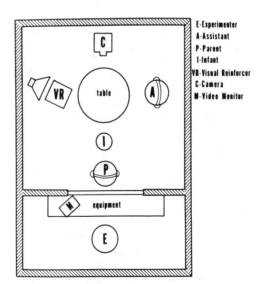

FIG. 1. The experimental/control suite.

assistant; the visual reinforcer was placed directly in front of the loudspeaker. The visual reinforcer consisted of a commercially available animated toy animal (a monkey clapping cymbals, a bear pounding a drum, or a dog wagging its tail) that was housed in a dark Plexiglas box so that the animal could not be seen until lights mounted inside the box were illuminated. The Plexiglas box and the loudspeaker were mounted on stands so that both were at eye level for the infant. The camera, placed on the back wall of the room, fed a TV monitor located in the control room.

The experimenter was housed in an adjoining control room. The control room contained a two-channel tape recorder (Teac, model #2300 SD) and a logic device. The two channels of the tape recorder fed the two-channel logic device which had a single output. The control room also contained a TV monitor for observation of the infant and a cassette tape player so that music could be fed to two sets of earphones in the experimental room which were worn by the assistant and the parent. The music could be interrupted by an audio intercom which allowed the experimenter to communicate with the assistant.

The logic device contained a probability generator, set to 0.5 probability, which determined whether a given observation interval would be a change or a control trial. Since other work in the laboratory suggested that long strings of change or control trials greatly increased the probability that the infant would produce an error, the experimenter was instructed to override the probability generator for one trail after three consecutive change trials or control trials occurred. The logic device also included a "start" button, a "vote" button, a timer for the trial duration, a timer for the reinforcer duration, and an "override" switch which activated the toy animal without other contingencies. The logic device automatically recorded the head-turn judgements made by the experimenter and the assistant, scored the trial, activated and timed the visual reinforcer, recorded the latency of the infant's response and printed all of the data for each trial on line.

4. Procedure

a. General procedure. The technique employs a head turn for visual reinforcement and was originally designed by Wilson, Moore, and Thompson (1976) to obtain auditory thresholds for infants as young as $5\frac{1}{2}$ months of age. Eilers, Wilson, and Moore (1977) adapted the technique to study speech-sound discrimination in 6–8 and 12–14-month-old infants. In the Eilers, Wilson, and Moore (1977) study, infants were trained to make a head turn whenever a speech sound, repeated once every second as a "background" stimulus, was changed to "comparison" speech sound. A head turn which occurred during the presentation of the comparison stimulus was rewarded with the presentation of a visual stimulus, a toy bear tapping a drum, or monkey clapping cymbals. In the current adaption of the technique a similar strategy was taken with the addition of certain controls for bias on the part of the parents, the assistant and the experimenter, and a format appropriate for testing category formation.

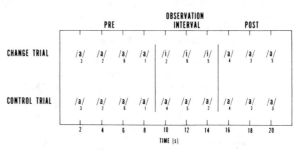

FIG. 2. Stimulus presentation format which occurred prior to, during, and after observation intervals for change trials and control trials. As shown, a random presentation of the tokens from the "background" category (shown here as the vowel /a/ with the six subscripts indicating the six different vowels presented during the final stage of experiment I) occurred at all times other than during the observation interval of a "change" trial, when a random presentation of stimuli from the "comparison" category (shown here as the vowel /i/) occurred. Head turns were judged during the 6-s observation intervals of both change and control trials. See text for additional details.

Throughout the experiment, two kinds of trials, "change" trials and "control" trials, were run. During the 6-s observation interval on a change trial, the random presentation of stimuli from the background category was interrupted while a random presentation of stimuli from the comparison category occurred (see Fig. 2 for illustration). During the 6-s observation interval of a control trial, stimuli from the background category were continuously presented.

The experimenter initiated an observation interval when the infant was in a "ready" state; that is, attending to the toys held by the assistant and not crying, fussing, or babbling. During both change and control trials, the experimenter and the assistant judged whether a head turn occurred and had "vote" buttons with which to record their affirmative decisions. The assistant was cued that an observation interval was occurring by a vibrating pin which was located on the hand-held vote button. The pin vibrated for the duration of the observation interval.

If both the experimenter and the assistant judged that the infant had turned her/his head during the 6-s observation interval on a change trial, the visual reinforcer was automatically activated by the logic device for a 3-s period. If neither (or only one of them) judged that a head turn had occurred, the visual reinforcer was not activated and an error was scored. During a control trial if neither the experimenter nor the assistant judged that a head turn had occurred, the trial was scored as correct. If both (or either) judged that a head turn had occurred, an error was scored.

To control for potential bias, both the parent and the assistant wore headphones and listened to music; therefore, neither could inadvertently cue the infant that a stimulus change occurred. The assistant did not know whether a given observation interval was a change or a control trial, so that neither the criterion for judging a head turn, nor a subtle change in the way in

TABLE IV. The stimulus ensembles for the background and comparison categories for all five stages of the experiment. The talker and pitch-contour values for each stimulus are given in parentheses.

| | Experimental stages | |
	Background	Comparison
Conditioning	/a/ (Male, fall)	/i/ (Male, fall)
Initial training	/a/ (Male, fall)	/i/ (Male, fall)
Pitch variation	/a/ (Male, fall)	/i/ (Male, fall)
	/a/ (Male, rise)	/i/ (Male, rise)
Talker variation	/a/ (Male, fall)	/i/ (Male, fall)
	/a/ (Female, fall)	/i/ (Female, fall)
Talker × pitch variation	/a/ (Male, fall)	/i/ (Male, fall)
	/a/ (Male, rise)	/i/ (Male, rise)
	/a/ (Female, fall)	/i/ (Female, fall)
	/a/ (Female, rise)	/i/ (Female, rise)
Entire ensemble	/a/ (Male, fall)	/i/ (Male, fall)
	/a/ (Male, rise)	/i/ (Male, rise)
	/a/ (Female, fall)	/i/ (Female, fall)
	/a/ (Female, rise)	/i/ (Female, rise)
	/a/ (Child, fall)	/i/ (Child, fall)
	/a/ (Child, rise)	/i/ (Child, rise)

which the toys were manipulated, could differentially occur during the two kinds of trials. The experimenter did not know ahead of time whether a change or control trial was to occur, but did, of course, hear the stimuli during the trial. Since the votes of both the assistant and the experimenter were automatically recorded for both change and control trials (an element not provided in earlier studies) any systematic bias on the part of the experimenter could be observed.

b. Experimental stages. The experiment progressed in six stages. The stimulus ensembles for both the background and the comparison categories are listed in Table IV for all six stages of the experiment. The vowel category specified as the background was appropriately counterbalanced across subjects. In both the conditioning and initial-training stages of the experiment, each of the two categories was represented by a single token, matched in every detail except for the critical cues which differentiate the two categories.

During the conditioning stage, only change trials occurred. The change from the background stimulus to the comparison stimulus was paired with the presentation of the visual reinforcer. Since activating the visual reinforcer resulted in both a prominent visual and auditory event, infants readily turned away from the assistant to look at it. Eventually, the infant anticipated the presentation of the visual reinforcer when the speech sound was changed from the background to the comparison stimulus. After three consecutive anticipatory head turns occurred during appropriate stimulus-change intervals, the initial-training stage was begun. The infant remained in the initial-training stage, and in all subsequent stages, until the performance criterion, nine out of ten consecutive trials correct, was met.

In stage three (pitch variation), the pitch contour of the vowels in both categories was randomly varied between a rising and a falling pitch contour. The pitch-contour variation stage was included because it pro-

vided the infant with a cognitive set regarding the rules of the "game." That is, the pitch variation encouraged the infant to ignore the acoustically prominant differences among the background (and the comparison) stimuli, while attending to a dimension along which the stimuli in each category were similar, vowel color. Successful completion of the pitch-contour stage served as proof that the infant was capable of the task, so that a failure to generalize along the talker dimension could be separated from a more general cognitive difficulty with the task.

In stage four (talker variation), the "talker" producing the vowels was randomly varied between the male voice and the female voice. In stage five, both talkers produced the vowels with a randomly changing pitch contour. In the final stage, the child's tokens, also with pitch-contour variations, were added to the ensemble bringing the total number of tokens in each category to six (3 talkers × 2 pitch contours).

Typically, 25 trials were run each day in a 20-min session. However, sessions were always terminated when an infant began to fuss or not attend to the assistant's toys; if, on the other hand, an infant was alert, the session was extended. Infants were tested on consecutive days whenever that was possible.

B. Results

The number of conditioning trials and the number of trials that were run before the criterion was met for each of the five stages of the experiment are shown in Table V for each of the four infants. The testing session in which the criterion was met is shown in parentheses.

The data demonstrate that fairly rapid acquistion of the head-turning response occurred; all four of the infants produced three consecutive anticipatory head-turn responses within the first 13 trials during the first session. Two of the four infants went on to meet the criterion (nine out of ten consecutive correct responses)

TABLE V. Trials to criterion for each condition of the experiment for each subject. The session in which the criterion was met is listed in parentheses.

Condition	S_1	S_2	S_3	S_4	$\overline{X}$
Conditioning	12(1)	13(1)	5(1)	9(1)	9.75
Initial training	23(2)	14(1)	32(2)	13(1)	20.5
Pitch variation	11(2)	11(2)	10(2)	15(1)	11.75
Talker variation	10(3)	10(2)	10(2)	14(2)	11.0
Talker × pitch variation	10(4)	29(3)	10(3)	18(2)	16.75
Entire ensemble	10(4)	29(4)	22(4)	19(3)	20.0
Total trials to complete	76	106	89	88	89.75
Total days to complete	4	4	4	3	3.75

for passing the initial-training stage of the experiment on the first day of testing; the other two infants passed initial training on the second day of testing.

It took three to four sessions to complete the experiment, and the total number of trials to completion ranged from 76 to 106. The criterion (nine out of ten consecutive correct) mandates a minimum of 50 trials to complete the experiment.

The mean latencies of response for correct head-turn responses for each condition were as follows: Conditioning, 2.5 s; initial training, 2.6 s; pitch variation, 2.2 s; talker variation, 2.3 s; talker × pitch variation, 2.1 s; and entire ensemble, 2.2 s. The agreement between the experimenter and the assistant on head-turn judgements for both change trials and control trials was 98.3%.

II. DISCUSSION

To the extent that these data on human infants demonstrate rapid transfer-of-learning to the novel tokens of the two vowel categories, and to the extent that one can rule out alternative hypotheses, one can accept the data as providing a strong suggestion that the infant recognizes some criterial attribute which serves as a "sorting rule" for these stimuli.

The most efficient sorting rule for these stimuli (and the most natural one for adult listeners) involves recognizing some criterial attribute which predicts the membership of the vowel categories /a/ and /i/. Recognizing and attending to the variable which predicts vowel color serves to perceptually minimize the differences for stimuli within each of the vowel categories, while also serving to maximize the differences between the two categories.

Before examining this hypothesis further, however, let us rule out two alternate accounts of the infant's performance, ones which would not require the infant to recognize the membership of either of the vowel categories. First, rather than recognize the similarity among the /a/ (or the /i/) tokens, the infant might simply produce a head-turn response when the training token was presented. However, the latency-of-response data collected in this and other related experiments suggest that this is not the case. Average latencies of response suggest, first, that the infants begin making

their head-turn responses just after the first stimulus is presented [see Kuhl (in press) for further examples and discussion of latency data in experiments of this kind]. Since each of the six stimuli has an equal chance of occurring first during the observation interval, the latency data would support the notion that each of the six stimuli evoke the head-turn response, rather than just the training token. Second, the latency data suggest that the average latency of response does not increase as the experiment progresses, which one would expect to happen if the infants were waiting to hear the training token.

Another alternate account of the infant's behavior is that the infants simply memorized all of the tokens in one or both of the categories. The rapid transfer of learning does not support such a hypothesis from the standpoint that one would expect that the number of trials to criterion would have to increase as the number of tokens in the stimulus ensemble increases if infants were attempting to memorize the stimulus set. The data, however, demonstrate that no systematic increase in the number of trials to criterion occurs. A second line of evidence, discussed elsewhere in detail [see Kuhl (in press)], suggests that infants are not capable of memorizing the stimuli in one or both of the two categories; experiments in which we have compared performance for categories defined by phonetic identity versus categories that are defined by the random assignment of the same stimuli to two groups demonstrate that infants fail to succeed in the "random category" experiments.

While infants do not appear to be capable of memorizing the two sets of stimuli, the strategies they adopt in attempting to solve the experimental problem are revealing. For example, in one random-category experiment, the stimuli varied along three dimensions, the consonant, the vowel, and the sex of the talker. Neither of the two random categories could be organized along a single dimension (hence the term "random"). After infants were trained to distinguish two exemplars, one from each category, they tended to select a prominent dimension upon which the two stimuli differed, like the sex of the talker, and generalize to other stimuli in which that dimension was present. This, of course, was not a successful strategy, but it demonstrated the infant's tendency to attend to some criterial dimension to "see if it worked."

Similarly, in this experiment, infants behave as though they are attending to a criterial attribute that they discover by listening to the stimuli. For example, at the beginning of a new condition, particularly the first one in which random variation in the tokens occurs (pitch variation), the infants tend to orient toward the reinforcer at the beginning of the random presentation of stimuli from the background category, prior to the first trial. As soon as the infant ceases to orient toward the reinforcer and attends to the assistant's toys (approximately 10–15 s), testing begins. Watching the infant leads one to suspect that during this short period of exposure the infant attempts a perceptual grouping of the stimuli in the background category. The data suggest that this must be fairly easy for these vowel stimuli since, when testing begins, many infants perform without error. It is also pertinent to note that as the experiment progresses, this tendency to orient toward the reinforcer at the beginning of a new condition gradually decreases, even though the number of novel stimuli being presented is increasing. This again suggests that the infant has adopted a strategy of selectively listening for the criterial attribute.

The explanation we prefer, then, is that the infant demonstrates a proclivity to try to discover a criterial attribute which separates the two categories. The infant, in effect, displays a tendency to be a "natural sorter," and is attracted to a dimension which makes a set of multidimensional auditory stimuli fit into easily recognized perceptual groupings. While this tendency to search for constancy among auditory stimuli may reflect a more general cognitive strategy favoring the organization of perceptual categories, its particular relevance to speech perception and to auditory–vocal learning has not been overlooked [Kuhl, (in press); Lieberman (in press); Studdert-Kennedy, 1976].

This explanation would be further supported if the infant did equally well at the task when the intermediate stages of the experiment were eliminated. In addition, in experiment I the infant was always presented with three tokens during the observation interval, so that any one of the three could be responsible for the infant's head turn. As previously stated, however, latencies of response suggested that the head turn was produced after the first sound, supporting the idea that each token in the category evoked the response. Modification of the stimulus-presentation format such that only a single stimulus was presented on each trial would further clarify the extent to which the infant recognized each member of the category. Experiment II was designed to establish these two points.

A. Method

1. Subjects

Eight new infants, $5\frac{1}{2}$–$6\frac{1}{2}$ months of age, served as subjects in the experiment. An additional two infants did not pass the training phase of the experiment within 90 trials and were dropped from the study. Subjects were obtained in the exact same manner as that described in experiment I.

2. Stimuli

The /a/ and /i/ stimuli were exactly the same as those described for experiment I.

3. Procedure

Subjects were tested using the head-turn technique in the exact same manner as that previously described. In this experiment, however, the infant was tested in only three stages rather than in six. The first and second, the conditioning and initial-training stages, were run exactly as they had been in the previous experiment. That is, infants were required to meeting the conditioning criterion (three consecutive correct responses) and the initial-training criterion (nine out of ten consecutive responses correct) in the discrimination of two

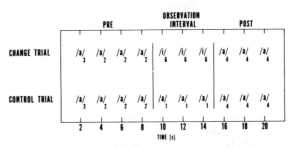

FIG. 2. Stimulus presentation format which occurred prior to, during, and after observation intervals for change and control trials in experiment II. The format was similar to that used in experiment I, with the exception that each stimulus token in the random sequence was repeated three times. The observation intervals of both change and control trials were synchronized to begin when the first sound in the triplet was presented and end after the last sound in the triplet was presented, thus insuring that the infant's response during the observation interval could be attributed to a specific stimulus token.

single tokens of /a/ and /i/ in order to progress to the third (transfer-of-learning) stage of this experiment. In this third stage, all six of the tokens in each of the two vowel categories were randomly presented, as in the final stage of experiment I. However, unlike the final stage of experiment I, each token was repeated three times before the next stimulus in the random sequence was presented (Fig. 3 illustrates). In this way, only a single stimulus was presented during a particular change or control observation interval.

In this experiment, limits were imposed on the number of trials the infant was tested in all stages of the experiment. If the infant did not pass the conditioning criterion within 40 trials, the subject was dismissed from the study (they were also scheduled for audiometric assessment). Similarly, if the infant did not pass the initial-training criterion in the first 90 trials the subject was dropped from the study. These limits were imposed to ensure that the infant would reach the transfer-of-learning phase of the experiment before becoming satiated on the visual reinforcer. All infants who passed the first two stages were subsequently given 90 trials (three test sessions) in the transfer-of-learning phase of the experiment, regardless of their performance. Ninety trials were considered adequate to sample each of the stimuli in the two vowel categories.

B. Results

1. Training phase

The number of trials to criterion in the conditioning and initial-training stages of the experiment are listed in the top of Table VI for all eight subjects. The mean number of trials run before infants passed the conditioning criterion (11.6) is very close to the mean number required in experiment I (9.75). The same is true for the initial-training stage; the mean number of trials run before infants passed the criterion in this experiment (25.75) is close to that required in experiment I (20.50).

TABLE VI. The number of trials to criterion during the training phase of the experiment for each subject (top); the percent head turns on change and control trials and the overall percent-correct scores, for each subject in the transfer-of-learning phase of the experiment (bottom).

| | Training phase | | | | | | | | |
	S_1	S_2	S_3	S_4	S_5	S_6	S_7	S_8	$\overline{X}$
Conditioning	5	18	6	4	5	24	5	25	11.5
Initial training	15	17	14	75	22	10	40	10	25.4
	Transfer-of-learning								
Percent headturns on change trials	100.0	95.3	98.0	64.7	100.0	83.0	82.9	23.0	80.9
Percent headturns on control trials	34.0	27.7	20.5	23.7	23.3	11.6	26.5	12.0	22.4
Overall percent correct	83.0	83.8	88.8	70.5	88.4	85.7	78.2	55.5	79.2

2. Transfer-of-learning

a. *Overall performance.* The data obtained in the transfer-of-learning phase of the experiment are summarized in the bottom of Table VI for all eight subjects. The percentage of head turns which occurred during all change trials (hits), as well as the percentage of head turns which occurred during all control trials (false alarms) is shown for each subject. The overall percent-correct score (% hits + correct rejections ÷2) is also shown for all subjects. Note that in calculating the overall percent-correct score, the infant's performance on both change trials and control trials is considered. For all subjects except one (subject #8) overall percent-correct scores are well above 70% correct. This subject's data are excluded from further analyses since he did not respond consistently to any of the stimuli, including the training token, during the transfer-of-learning phase of the experiment. A correlated t-test comparing the number of head-turn responses which occurred during change and control trials is highly significant ($t = 7.2$; $p < 0.005$).

b. *First-trial data.* The data obtained on the first presentation of each of the novel tokens from the comparison category (that is, change-trial data) and from the first presentation of each of the novel tokens from the background category (that is, control-trial data)

for the seven subjects are listed in Table VII.

The first-trial data for novel tokens from the comparison category show that for two of the five novel tokens (the female, falling-pitch token and the child, falling-pitch token) performance was perfect. That is, on seven out of seven trials, infants produced the head-turn response to the novel token on the first presentation. The other three novel tokens were identified correctly in five out of seven trials. Notice that the trend was toward slightly better performance on the token for each "talker" which preserved the value of the pitch dimension (falling pitch contour) that had been represented by the training token (male, falling pitch).

Similarly, the first-trial data for novel tokens from the background category (that is, control-trial data) also demonstrate the infant's tendency to behave correctly by almost totally refraining from making the head-turn response. The total number of correct responses for each token, the number of correct head-turn responses (hits) on change trials plus the number of control trials in which head-turn responses did not occur (correct rejections) is listed at the bottom of Table VII. In no case was the total number correct less than 11 out of 14 trials; the binomial expansion tables (Hayes, 1973) indicate that these outcomes are statistically significant ($p < 0.05$).

TABLE VII. The first-trial data are shown as the number of head-turn responses for novel tokens representing the comparison category (that is, presented on change trials) and the number of head-turn responses for novel tokens representing the background category (that is, presented on control trials) which occurred during the first presentation of the stimulus to each of the seven subjects. The male-fall token was presented during the training phase of the experiment. The total number of correct responses for each token type, obtained by adding the number of head-turn responses obtained for change trials (hits) and the number of trials during which the infant refrained from turning on control trials (correct rejections), is shown at the bottom of the table.

Token type	Male, fall	Male, rise	Female, fall	Female, rise	Child, fall	Child, rise
Change trials	7/7	5/7	7/7	5/7	7/7	6/7
Control trials	0/7	1/7	1/7	1/7	2/7	2/7
Total correct	14/14[c]	11/14[a]	13/14[c]	11/14[a]	12/14[b]	11/14[a]

[a] $P < 0.05$.
[b] $P < 0.01$.
[c] $P < 0.001$.

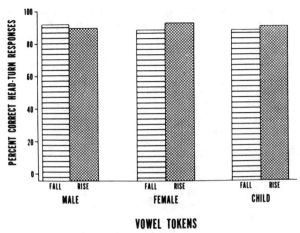

FIG. 4. Group data representing the percentage of head-turn responses which occurred during all change trials for each of the six stimuli presented during the transfer-of-learning phase of experiment II. While not shown, head-turn responses during control trials did not exceed 25% for any single token.

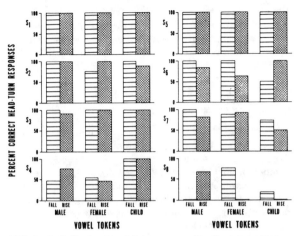

FIG. 5. Individual-subject data representing the percentage of head-turn responses which occurred during all change trials for each of the six stimuli presented during the transfer-of-learning phase of experiment II; S_8's data were eliminated from group analyses.

As previously discussed, the first presentation of stimuli from the background category occurs as soon as the transfer-of-learning phase begins. The infant, therefore, has a limited (10–20 s) exposure to the random presentation of these novel tokens in the background category before the first trial occurs. Since the first-trial data demonstrate almost perfect performance on both change trials and control trials, it would appear that the infant isolates and attends to a criterial attribute of these stimuli very rapidly.

c. Total-trial data. The distribution of head-turn responses for each of the six stimuli obtained for all change trials during the transfer-of-learning phase is shown in Fig. 4. The percentage of correct head-turn responses for novel stimuli from the comparison category (change trials) varies from 93.5% correct on the female's rising-pitch token to 88.8% correct on the child's falling-pitch token. While not shown on the graph, head-turn responses to novel tokens from the background category (control trials) were always below 25%. A two-way repeated-measures analysis of variance comparing the number of head-turn responses obtained for each type of token occurring in both types of trials (change and control) revealed a highly significant ($p < 0.005$) main effect for the type of trial (change versus control) but no significant effect for the type of token

and no significant interactions.

The distribution of head-turn responses for individual subjects for each of the six stimuli presented during change trials is shown in Fig. 5. Note that for some subjects performance is perfect (S_1 and S_5) or near perfect (S_2 and S_3) for all tokens in the category. For other subjects, notably S_8, whose data has not been considered in group analyses, the introduction of the great variety of tokens in the transfer-of-learning phase appeared to confuse the infant, and very few correct head-turn responses were produced, even for the previously learned training token (male, falling pitch). A single infant (S_7) performed well on the training token while failing to do as well on the novel tokens, and then only the child's tokens were poorly identified.

Analysis of the average latencies of response (see Table VIII) reveals that during the training phase of the experiment the average latency on correct change trials (hits) was 2.4 s. Since the stimuli are spaced at 2-s intervals, this would again suggest that the infant begins making the head-turn response before the onset of the second stimulus during the observation interval. The average latency of response for all change trials during the transfer-of-learning phase was very similar, 2.3 s. The average latency of response to the training token (male, falling pitch) was similar (2.3 s) to that obtained

TABLE VIII. The mean latency of response for each subject on correct change trials (hits) during initial training, during the transfer-of-learning phase, and on the training token (male, fall) during the transfer-of-learning phase of the experiment.

	S_1	S_2	S_3	S_4	S_5	S_6	S_7	S_8	$\overline{X}$
Hits/ Initial training	2.2	2.5	2.8	2.4	2.2	2.8	2.4	1.6	2.4
Hits/ Transfer phase	1.8	2.5	1.8	3.2	1.4	2.4	2.6	2.4	2.3
Hits/ Transfer phase training token	1.5	3.1	1.8	3.3	1.5	1.9	2.3	2.6	2.3

for all change tokens during the transfer-of-learning phase. Analysis of variance on the latency data revealed no significant differences among the tokens. The agreement between the experimenter and the assistant on head-turn judgements for both change trials and control trials was 98.9%.

III. DISCUSSION

These data strongly support the conclusion suggested by experiment I; that is, the infants convincingly demonstrated the tendency to respond correctly to a number of novel tokens of /a/ and /i/ after training on a single exemplar from each of the categories. In addition, the findings extend the results of experiment I by demonstrating that generalization to tokens produced by different talkers occurred in the absence of specific training, since the first-trial data demonstrated excellent performance for all of the tokens in the category. There was a trend toward slightly better performance on falling-pitch tokens which preserved the value of the pitch-contour dimension which the infant was exposed to during training.

It is important to note that the infant's tendency to recognize the similarity among vowel tokens produced by different talkers is of considerable importance to the development of speech production. It would be difficult, if not impossible, to learn to produce speech if the infant adopted the strategy of trying to imitate the absolute formant frequencies produced by adult speakers. The data from this study would suggest that an alternate strategy is available to the infant. If the infant recognizes the similarity among tokens produced by a male, a female, and a child, then it seems likely that the infant recognizes the perceptual similarity between certain sounds produced by his/her own vocal tract and those produced by the caretaker. If so, then the infant might attempt to achieve this perceptual match rather than to reproduce the absolute formant frequencies produced by adult speakers.

Speculation as to the exact nature of the sorting role used by the infants to complete the task is difficult, since we cannot, as yet, identify the exact nature of the auditory information used by adult listeners in the recognition of vowel categories (see Shankweiler, Strange, and Verbrugge, 1977, for review). But whatever the acoustic cues responsible, it is likely that the mammalian auditory system extracts them quite naturally since it has been demonstrated that both the dog (Baru, 1975) and the chinchilla (Burdick and Miller, 1975) form categories based on the vowels /a/ and /i/. Both of these studies involved a large ensemble of tokens produced by different "talkers"; Burdick and Miller (1975) demonstrated transfer of learning from a training pair to the tokens produced by 48 talkers with random variation in intensity and pitch contour, as well as to synthetically produced vowels, while Baru (1975) demonstrated transfer among synthetic vowels with variations in fundamental frequency, formant frequencies, intensity, and duration. In the latter study, trained dogs performed the task equally well after bilateral ablation of the central auditory cortex.

The synthesized /a/ and /i/ vowels used in this experiment were identical with the exception of their formant structures. The formant frequencies are closely spaced (compact) for /a/ and widely spaced (diffuse) for the /i/. A simple characteristic such as this might serve, therefore, as a sorting role for the infant. It will be fairly important from a developmental standpoint to determine whether infants tend to form auditory categories based on fairly complex stimulus properties or whether they tend to utilize fairly simple and specific stimulus properties to form perceptual groupings.

This work on the formation of speech-sound categories by human infants complements the data stemming from another kind of investigation on the human infant's tendency to "cut up" the auditory world in ways which conform to an adult's perceptual categories. Just as the work on "categorical perception" of speech sounds by human infants (Eimas et al., 1971; Eimas, 1974; 1975) supports the notion that infants perceive a natural discontinuity for stimuli on an acoustic continuum precisely at the place where the languages of the world divide the continuum into two distinct phonetic categories, these data suggest that the infant may have a natural tendency to group certain stimuli together based on a criterial attribute that remains constant despite the fact that other aspects of the stimulus undergo change.

One goal in ensuing research will be to determine whether the infant's tendencies to form perceptual groupings for auditory stimuli are distinct from the perceptual groupings preferred by nonhuman listeners or whether both the infant's and animal's tendencies to form auditory categories are similar. As it now stands, we have far more data on an animal's ability to form auditory categories that are based on a phonetic distinction than we do on the human infant (see Kuhl, 1978, for review).

Future research will be required, then, to determine whether the human infant has a general tendency to form auditory categories for groups of sounds that are defined as phonetic categories by adult listeners. Research in our own laboratory using other vowel categories (e.g., /a/ versus /ɔ/) tends to support the notion that by 6 months of age infants recognize auditory categories that conform to vowel categories perceived by adult speakers of English (Kuhl, 1977). In addition, research in our laboratory demonstrates that 6-month-old infants are capable of sorting these same vowel sounds on the basis of another dimension, pitch contour. That is, infants trained to produce a head-turn response for a rising-pitch vowel token and to refrain from producing the response to a falling-pitch vowel token easily generalize to other exemplars of rising-pitch and falling-pitch tokens (Kuhl and Hillenbrand, 1979). Comparisons between performance when the set of stimuli are sorted on the basis of vowel color versus when the same stimuli are sorted on the basis of pitch contour would be valuable if obtained both for infants being raised in a linguistic environment in which pitch contour is not phonemically relevant, as well as for infants being raised in a linguistic environment in which pitch contour is phonemically relevant. While it is likely that both populations would be capable of utilizing either vowel color or pitch contour as a sorting rule, it is possible that experiments would reveal increasing salience for dimensions that are phonemically relevant in the infant's linguistic environment. Experiments like these are providing valuable information about the processing of species-specific auditory signals in non-human primates (Zoloth *et al.*, 1979).

ACKNOWLEDGMENTS

This research was supported by a contract from the National Institute of Health, Education and Welfare (NICHD N01-HD-3-2793). The author also wishes to acknowledge the support provided by Central Institute for the Deaf (NS 03856 and RR 00396) and particularly A. Maynard Engebretson who synthesized the stimuli and assisted in the preparation of the stimulus tapes for this experiment. The author also is indebted to Kyum-Ha Lee of the Child Development and Mental Retardation Center for the development of the logic device used to run the experiment. The author thanks James Hillenbrand for assisting in the experiment.

[1]While 6-month-old infants demonstrate audiometric thresholds that are within 10 dB of normal adult thresholds using an operant head-turn procedure similar to that employed in this study (Wilson, Moore, and Thompson, 1976), there are presently no data on difference limens for intensity, the growth of loudness, nor data which would provide equal-loudness contours for infant listeners. It would appear, then, that the best strategy for removing the intensity cue would be to (1) test discrimination under both condition, that is, when the vowels are loudness balanced by adults and when the vowels have equal RMS pressures, or (2) randomize intensity. Regarding the first, Kuhl and Miller (1975) demonstrated that 1-4 infants discriminated these same computer-simulated male /a/ and /i/ tokens under both conditions. Regarding the second point, in the final stages of this experiment when the tokens of /a/ and /i/ vary with regard to talker and pitch contour, the tokens are perceived to have randomly jittered intensities, primarily because tokens with rising contours are perceived to be louder than those with falling contours. This random jitter makes it unlikely that intensity provided the critical cue for infant listeners.

Baru, A. V. (1975). "Discrimination of synthesized vowels [a] and [i] with varying parameters in dog," in *Auditory Analysis and the Perception of speech*, edited by G. Fant and M. A. Tatham (Academic, London).

Blumstein, S. E., and Stevens, K. N. (1977). "Acoustic invariance for place of articulation in stops and nasals across syllabic contexts," J. Acoust. Soc. Am. 62, S26(A).

Bower, T. G. R. (1966). "Slant perception and shape constancy in infants," Science 151, 832-834.

Bower, T. G. R. (1975). "Infant perception," in *Infant Perception: From Sensation to Cognition* (Vol. 1), edited by L. B. Cohen and P. Salapetek (Academic, New York), pp. 48-59.

Burdick, C. K. (in press). "The effect of behavioral paradigm on auditory discrimination learning: I: A literature review," J. Aud. Res.

Burdick, C. K. (in press). "The effect of behavioral paradigm on auditory discrimination learning: II: Auditory discrimination learning by the Chinchilla: Comparison of go/no-go and two-choice procedure," J. Aud. Res.

Burdick, C. K., and Miller, J. D. (1975). "Speech perception by the chinchilla: Discrimination of the sustained /a/ and /i/," J. Acoust. Soc. Am. 58, 415-427.

Dunn, H. K. (1963). "Acoustic characteristics of vowels," in *Engineering Summer Conference on Automatic Recognition* (University of Michigan, Ann Arbor, 8-19 July 1963), I, D1-D5.

Eilers, R. E. (in press). "The complex nature of infant speech perception," in *Child Phonology: Data and Theory*, edited by G. Yeni-Komshian, J. Kavanaugh, and C. Ferguson (Academic, New York).

Eilers, R. E., Wilson, W. R., and Moore, J. M. (1977). "Developmental changes in speech discrimination in infants," J. Speech Hear. Res. 20, 766-780.

Eimas, P. D. (1974). "Auditory and linguistic processing of cues for place of articulation by infants," Percept. Psychophys. 16, 513-521.

Eimas, P. D. (1975). "Auditory and phonetic coding of the cues for speech: Discrimination of the [r-1] distinction by young infants," Percept. Psychophys. 18, 341-347.

Eimas, P. D. (1977). "Developmental aspects of speech perception," in *Handbook of Sensory Physiology and Perception*, edited by R. Held, H. Leibowitz, and H. L. Tenber (Springer-Verlag, New York), pp. 357-374.

Eimas, P. D., Siqueland, E. R., Jusczyk, P., and Vigorito, J. (1971). "Speech perception in infants," Science 171, 303-306.

Epstein, W. (1977a). "Historical introduction to constancies," in *Stability and Constancy in Visual Perception*, edited by W. Epstein (Wiley-Interscience, New York), pp. 1-22.

Epstein, W. (1977b). "Observations concerning contemporary analysis of perceptual constancies," in *Stability and Constancy in Visual Perception*, edited by W. Epstein (Wiley-Interscience, New York), pp. 437-447.

Fant, G. (1973). *Speech Sounds and Features* (MIT, Cambridge, MS).

Fodor, J. A., Garrett, M. F., and Brill, S. L. (1975). "Pi ka pu; The perception of speech sounds by pre-linguistic infants," Percept. Psychophys. 18, 74-78.

Hayes, W. L. (1973). *Statistics for the Social Sciences* (Rinehart and Winston, New York), 2nd ed.

Kuhl, P. K. (1976). "Speech perception in early infancy: The acquisition of speech sound categories," in *Hearing and Davis: Essays Honoring Hallowell Davis*, edited by S. K. Hirsh, D. H. Eldredge, I. J. Hirsh, and S. K. Silverman (Washington U.P., St. Louis, MO), pp. 265-280.

Kuhl, P. K. (1977). "Speech perception in early infancy: Perceptual constancy for the vowel categories (a) and (ɔ)," J. Acoust. Soc. Am. 61, S39(A).

Kuhl, P. K. (1978). "Predispositions for the perception of speech-sound categories: A species-specific phenomenon?" in *Communicative and Cognitive Abilities—Early Behavioral Assessment*, edited by F. D. Minifie and L. L. Lloyd (University Park, Baltimore), pp. 229-255.

Kuhl, P. K. (1979). "The perception of speech in early infancy," in *Speech and Language: Advances in Basic Research and Practice*, edited by N. J. Lass (Academic, New York), Vol. 1, pp. 1-47.

Kuhl, P. K. (in press). "Perceptual constancy for speech-sound categories in early infancy," in *Child Phonology: Perception and Production*, edited by G. Yeni-Komshian, J. Kavanaugh, and C. Ferguson (Academic, New York).

Kuhl, P. K., and Hillenbrand, J. (1979). "Speech perception by young infants: Perceptual constancy for categories based on pitch contour," paper presented to the Society for Research in Child Development, San Francisco, March 1979.

Kuhl, P. K., and Miller, J. D. (1975). "Speech perception in early infancy: Discrimination of speech-sound categories," J. Acoust. Soc. Am. 58, S56(A).

Liberman, A. M., Cooper, F. S., Shankweiler, D. P., and Studdert-Kennedy, M. (1967). "Perception of the speech code," Psych. Rev. 74, 431-461.

Lieberman, P. (in press). "On the development of vowel production in young children," in *Child Phonology: Perception and Production*, edited by G. Yeni-Komshian, J. Kavanaugh, and C. Ferguson (Academic, New York).

Morse, P. A. (1978). "Infant speech perception: origins, processes and alpha centauri," in *Communicative and Cognitive Abilities—Early Behavioral Assessment*, edited by F. D. Minifie and L. L. Lloyd (University Park, Baltimore).

Papousek, H. (1967a). "Experimental studies of appelitional behavior in human newborns and infants," in *Early Behavior: Comparative and Developmental Approaches*, edited by H. Stevenson and H. Hess (Wiley, New York).

Papousek, H. (1967b). "Conditioning during early postnatal development," in *Behavior in Infancy and Early Childhood*, edited by A. Brackbill and A. Thompson (Free Press, New York).

Peterson, G. E., and Barney, H. L. (1952). "Control methods used in a study of the vowels," J. Acoust. Soc Am. 24, 175–184.

Piaget, J. (1954). *The Construction of Reality in the Child* (Basic Books, New York).

Rabiner, L. R. (1968). "Digital-formant synthesizer for speech synthesis studies," J. Acoust. Soc. Am. 24, 175–184.

Shankweiler, D., Strange, W., and Verbrugge, R. (1977).

"Speech and the problem of perceptual constancy," in *Perceiving, Acting and Knowing: Toward an Ecological Psychology*, edited by R. Shaw and J. Bransford (Lawrence Erlbaum Associates, New Jersey), pp. 315–346.

Spenner, B. F., Engebretson, M. A., Miller, J. D., and Cox, J. R. (1974). "Random-access programmable recorder of complex sounds (RAP): A digital instrument for auditory research," J. Acoust. Soc. Am. 55, 427.

Stevens, K. N., and Blumstein, S. E. (1978). "Invariant cues for place of articulation in stop consonants," J. Acoust. Soc. Am. 64, 1358–1368.

Studdert-Kennedy, M. (1976). "Speech perception," in *Contemporary Issues in Experimental Phonetics*, edited by N. J. Lass (Academic, New York).

Wilson, W. R., Moore, J. M., and Thompson, G. (1976). "Auditory thresholds of infants utilizing Visual Reinforcement Audiometry (VRA)," paper presented at the American Speech and Hearing Association Convention, Houston, Texas, November 1976.

Zoloth, S. R., Peterson, M. R., Beecher, M. D., Green, S., Marler, P., Moody, D. B., and Stebbins, W. (1979). "Species-specific perceptual processing of vocal sounds by monkeys," Science 204, 870–872.

Cognition, 29 (1988) 143–178

2

A precursor of language acquisition in young infants*

JACQUES MEHLER,
PETER JUSCZYK,
GHISLAINE LAMBERTZ

CNRS & EHESS, Paris

NILOFAR HALSTED

University of Oregon

JOSIANE BERTONCINI

CNRS & EHESS, Paris

CLAUDINE AMIEL-TISON

Clinique Universitaire Baudelocque

Abstract

Four-day-old French and 2-month-old American infants distinguish utterances in their native languages from those of another language. In contrast, neither group gave evidence of distinguishing utterances from two foreign languages. A series of control experiments confirmed that the ability to distinguish utterances from two different languages appears to depend upon some familiarity with at least one of the two languages. Finally, two experiments with low-pass filtered versions of the samples replicated the main findings of discrimination of the native language utterances. These latter results suggest that the basis for classifying utterances from the native language may be provided by prosodic cues.

*This research was supported by grants from P.R.C./I.N.S.E.R.M. (Brain and mental health), A.T.P., C.N.R.S./C.N.E.T. (83 7B d 28 00790 9245) and N.I.C.H.H.D. (15795). We would like to thank N. Sanchez, R. Bijeljac-Babic, A. Rehak, S. McAdams, S. Dehaene, J.L. Aucouturier, M. Zerbib, E. Bylund, L. Kennedy, and A.M. Jusczyk for their assistance with this project. We also extend our gratitude to Dick Aslin, Peter Eimas and Deborah Kemler Nelson for comments that they made on previous versions of this manuscript. Reprint requests should be sent to Jacques Mehler, Laboratoire de Sciences Cognitives et Psycholinguistique, CNRS & EHESS, 54 Bd. Raspail, 75006 Paris, France.

Editor's note: The editorial review process for this manuscript was handled by John Morton.

The remarkable capacities of young infants for perceiving speech are well-documented (e.g., see Aslin, Pisoni, & Jusczyk, 1983; Kuhl, 1987 for recent reviews). For example, infants discriminate a wide variety of phonetic contrasts soon after birth (Bertoncini, Bijeljac-Babic, Blumstein, & Mehler, 1987; Eimas, Siqueland, Jusczyk, & Vigorito, 1971), and they are also able to cope with variations resulting from changes in intonation contours or talkers' voices (Kuhl, 1985). These speech perception capacities seem to have obvious relevance to the acquisition of language by providing the infants with a framework for organizing the linguistic input into categories. Such a perceptual framework serves to limit the space of possible hypotheses that the learner can entertain concerning the structure of the language being acquired (Chomsky, 1968; Morgan, 1986; Osherson, Stob, & Weinstein, 1984; Pinker, 1984; Wexler & Culicover, 1980).

A critical task for the infant acquiring language is to distinguish speech from the manifold array of noises that are present in the acoustic environment. Indeed, the infant will have to segregate sounds emitted from trucks, bells, machines, animals, and so forth from the class of sounds emitted by the human vocal tract. Even if such a classification were to be easily achieved by the infant, an additional problem must be solved. Namely, the infant must find some way to cope successfully with the variation that occurs in the speech signal as a result of changes in speaking rate, accents, talkers' voices, and so forth and yet do so in a way so as never to treat utterances from two different languages as belonging to the same language. The ability to segregate utterances issuing from different languages is critical from the point of view of language acquisition. Learning a language requires mastery of the regularities that hold among its utterances. If utterances from several different languages are classified as belonging to the same language, then inappropriate generalizations may be drawn about the regularities that hold within the native language. At present, little is known about the ability of infants to detect the common identity of utterances issuing from the same language. Are the means to separate utterances in one language from another in place soon after birth or is a long period of familiarization with a particular language necessary?

To explore this issue, we have been conducting an extensive series of studies with 4-day-old French and 2-month-old American infants. The present paper provides a first report of our investigations. It relates our basic findings and presents some indication that they hold across different language backgrounds and test procedures.

Experiment 1

One indication that infants are able to group together utterances belonging to the same language would be if they could distinguish utterances in one language from those of another. However, it is not sufficient to show that infants discriminate a specific utterance in one language from one in another language because there is a myriad of differences (acoustic, phonetic, prosodic, etc.) that could support such a discrimination. Thus, even two different sentences from the same language could be discriminated on these bases. Consequently, what is required is that the infant be attentive to some identity that holds among utterances in a particular language despite any acoustic, phonetic or prosodic differences that exist among them. In other words, the infant must be able to classify together utterances from the same language on some basis that serves to differentiate them from utterances in other languages. For this reason, we decided to expose infants to a variety of utterances from one language and see whether they could detect a change to a variety of utterances in a second language.

A potential confounding factor in this type of study is that the infants might respond on some other basis than the change in languages. This could arise if different talkers were used to produce the utterances in the two languages, because previous studies have shown that infants are sensitive to changes in talkers (e.g., DeCasper & Fifer, 1980; Mehler, Bertoncini, Barriere, & Jassik-Gerschenfeld, 1978). One way of circumventing this potential confound is to have the same talker produce the utterances in the two languages. For this purpose we recruited a fluent bilingual speaker who spoke both languages without foreign accent (as judged by native speakers of the two languages) and at about the same rate. The talker who met these criteria was a French–Russian bilingual. We recorded speech samples from her in each of the two languages and presented these to 4-day-old French infants to see if they gave evidence of distinguishing French from Russian utterances.

Method

Subjects

The subjects were forty 4-day-old full-term infants from French monolingual families. The criteria for selection were that the infants weigh at least 2700 g, have a gestational age of 38 weeks or more, have an Apgar score of 10 five minutes after birth and have no known hearing deficit. The infants had an average weight of 3300 g (range: 2700 to 4070 g). In order to obtain 40 subjects, it was necessary to test 64. Infants were excluded for crying (4 Ss), failing to suck for three consecutive samples (16 Ss), and for failing to habituate within 30 trials (4 Ss).

146   *J. Mehler et al.*

Stimuli

A fluent French–Russian bilingual speaker tape recorded an oral account of some events in her life, once in French and once in Russian. The monologues in the two languages covered the same series of events. The speaker was not aware of what the speech samples were to be used for. From the tapes, 15 different samples with durations from 13 to 22 s were selected for each language. The samples from the two languages were matched as closely as possible for their overall durations and amplitudes. The overall mean durations for the French and Russian samples were 17.2 and 17.5 s respectively. Samples of speech were chosen to provide the infants with good indications of the prosodic characteristics of sentences in the two languages. For this reason, we were careful to select only samples that contained complete sentences. Thus, although the samples often contained several sentences, they always began and ended at a sentence boundary. For each language, a test sequence was prepared by randomly ordering the utterances and interspersing a 5-s silent interval between successive samples. This same sequence of samples was then recorded twice in a row to produce the test tape for the language.

Apparatus

All testing took place inside a specially equipped sound attenuated testing chamber at the Maternité Baudelocque (Hospital Cochin) in Paris. A sterilized blind nipple mounted on an adjustable mechanical arm and connected to a pressure transducer was used to record the infants sucking responses. The pressure transducer was in turn connected to a series of electronic circuits and devices (specially designed by CEMI in Lyon) that were used to monitor and record sucking during the presentation of the speech sounds. Two Tandberg TD 20A tape recorders, a Scott 417A stereo amplifier and a Braun L 620 loudspeaker were used to provide the auditory output. An Apple computer was programmed to record and store the sucking rate to each sample and signaled the change from the first to the second phase of the test period.

Procedure

Ten infants were assigned randomly to each of four test conditions. Two of these were no language change control conditions: one consisted exclusively of Russian (Group RR) and the other of French (Group FF) samples. The other two groups were experimental groups. For one of these groups (FR), the infants heard French samples during the first phase of the test period, followed by Russian samples in the second phase. For the other group (RF), the Russian samples occurred first, followed by the French samples in the second phase. The stimulus samples were presented at an average sound level of 70 ± 2 dB SPL (approximately 15 dB above the background noise created by the ventilation system).

During testing infants were placed in a bassinet in a semi-reclining position facing a loudspeaker in the sound-attenuated chamber. After the pacifier was inserted in the infant's mouth, the threshold level of the suck counter linked to the pressure transducer was adjusted to yield sucking rates of between 25 and 35 sucks a minute. The adjustment to the threshold level was made in an effort to reduce the intersubject variability in sucking rates because of the large individual differences that exist in the amplitudes at which infants suck. A one-minute baseline period followed during which time sucking was recorded in the absence of any auditory stimulation. Up to this point, the procedure was identical to that of the HAS procedure (e.g., see Jusczyk, 1985b). During the two-phased test period that followed, each sample was presented in its entirety regardless of the infant's sucking behavior. Thus, unlike the typical HAS procedure, there was no contingency between sucking and the presentation of the speech samples.[1] Rather, the sucking method used here indexed the level of arousal exhibited by the infants during a period of stimulus presentation (e.g., see Bronshtein & Petrova, 1967). However, momentary fluctuations often occur in sucking rates. Given the short durations of our test trials (i.e., 13–22 s, equivalent to the durations of the samples), the variability introduced by these fluctuations is apt to be aggravated over such short time spans. For this reason, sucking rates (sucks/min) were averaged over three consecutive samples. Habituation to the samples from the first language was measured on the basis of a decline in sucking rate. Because we wanted to give the infants ample exposure to samples in a particular language, the criterion for declination was not calculated until after the sixth samples occurred. From this point on, samples from the same language were presented until the sucking rate for a three-sample period declined by 33% from the maximum rate attained during a preceding non-overlapping three-sample period. Then the experimental groups heard samples from the other language, whereas the control groups continued to receive samples from the original language. This second phase lasted for nine samples.

---

[1]The problem with using a contingent sucking procedure like HAS is that the very contingency that it imposes upon sucking and sound presentation makes it impossible to ensure that infants will receive only completed sentences. Thus, using HAS in the present circumstances would often result in utterances that began somewhere in midstream and ended at a place other than a sentence boundary. In other words the prosodic flow would be extremely unnatural.

148   *J. Mehler et al.*

Results and discussion

The average sucking rates for the four groups did not differ during the baseline period ($F(3,36) < 1.00$). Next, the data for the test period were examined. Some interesting asymmetries were noted in the way in which the infants responded, suggesting that the native language may have a special status for them. Thus, during the first phase (Figure 1), sucking rates were significantly higher for infants listening to French (groups FF and FR) than to Russian (groups RR and RF) as verified by an ANOVA on the last nine samples of this phase ($F(1,38) = 7.47$, $p = .009$). Also, during the second phase of the experiment, only the RF group (Figure 2) displayed a significant increase in sucking relative to its RR control ($F(1,18) = 8.16$, $p = .01$). By contrast, the FR group did not differ significantly from its FF control ($F(1,18) < 1.00$).

One interpretation of these asymmetries is that 4-day-old infants not only discriminate the two languages, but also that they prefer to listen to French. The suggestion of a preference comes from the fact that, in the first phase, infants displayed greater arousal to the French than to the Russian samples (i.e., they sucked at significantly higher rates for French). Moreover, in the

Figure 1.   *Displays the change in sucking rate for the last three blocks of three consecutive samples during the first phase of Experiment 1 for the infants who heard French (F) and the infants who heard Russian (R). The bars above and below each point indicate the standard error of the mean.*

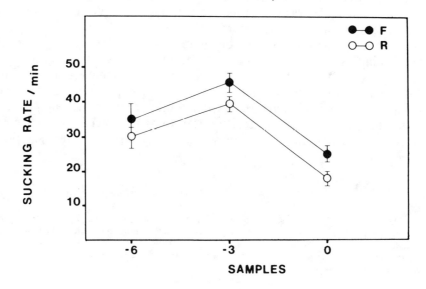

Figure 2.   *The top panel displays the sucking rates of the infants who heard Russian during the first phase of Experiment 1. Group RF heard French during the second phase while group RR heard Russian. The comparable data for subjects who heard French during the first phase are shown in the bottom panel. Group FR heard Russian during the second phase while group FF continued to hear French. The bars above and below each point indicate the standard error of the mean.*

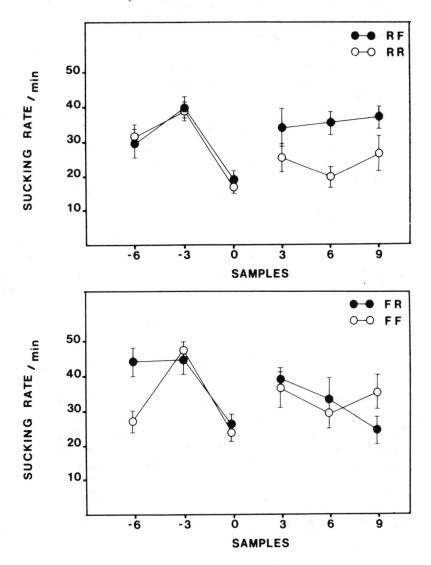

150   *J. Mehler et al.*

second phase, which began after they met the habituation criterion, the two experimental groups did not react to the language change in the same way. In the case of the RF group, the postshift stimulus is not only novel but from the preferred language, hence, sucking increases. However, for the FR group, the novelty effect for the change in language is offset by the fact that it is a change away from the preferred language.

Other explanations of the asymmetry are possible, but not very plausible to us. One possibility is that the noncontingent procedure was simply not sensitive enough to detect evidence of discrimination in infants going from French to Russian. However, this line of argument provides no account of the asymmetry itself, nor of the significant difference in sucking during the first phase of the experiment between those infants listening to French and those listening to Russian. A second possibility—that the discrimination results were simply a chance finding—cannot be ruled out definitively at this point (however, see Experiment 7).

Why do French infants have significantly higher response rates to French than to Russian samples? Is it because French is already familiar to them or is there some intrinsic property of the utterances themselves that would be attractive to infants of any culture, French or otherwise? For example, is there some characteristic property of French rhythm, prosody or phonological structure that is inherently attractive? An analysis of the samples indicated that the Russian utterances were spoken at a rate of 245 ($\pm$ 30) syllables per minute compared to 270 ($\pm$ 32) per minute in French.[2] Could a rhythmic difference of this sort have been responsible for the higher sucking rates to French samples? If so, then infants of any culture or language background should display the same sort of elevated responding in the presence of French samples. To explore this possibility, we conducted the following experiment.

Experiment 2

Every year in Paris there is a considerable number of infants born to foreign families—ones for whom the primary language spoken in the home is something other than French. Testing this group of subjects is one means of approaching the question of whether infants whose parents are not French speakers would also show greater arousal to French than to Russian samples.

---

[2]This estimate assumes that even syllables which begin with long consonant clusters are to be counted as a single syllable. Halle (personal communication) notes that there are some grounds for counting syllables with long clusters as two syllables. If so, then the Russian rate should be increased from the estimate here, bringing it more closely in line with the French rate.

Method

Subjects

The subjects were twenty-four 4-day-old infants. The infants had an average weight of 3486 g (range: 3079 to 3892 g). Although these infants were born in Paris at the same maternity hospital, the primary language spoken at home was not French, but one of a diverse array of languages including Arabic, Portuguese, Spanish, Chinese, Indonesian, German, Polish, Italian and three African languages (Faong, Senegal, Togo). The infants were selected according to the same criteria as described in Experiment 1. In order to obtain the necessary number of subjects, 35 infants were tested. Infants were excluded for crying (2 Ss), failing to suck for three consecutive samples (8 Ss), and failing to habituate within 30 trials (1 S).

Stimuli

Same as described in Experiment 1.

Apparatus

Same as described in Experiment 1.

Procedure

Six infants were randomly assigned to each of four test conditions: French–French (FF), French–Russian (FR), Russian–Russian (RR) and Russian–French (RF). In all other details, the procedure followed was the same as described for Experiment 1.

Results and discussion

Once again there was no evidence of significant differences among the groups for the baseline period ($F(3,20) = 1.38$, $p > .30$). However, in contrast to the previous experiment, the sucking rates registered during the test period provided no evidence that foreign infants discriminated the French and Russian samples. Thus, during the second phase, neither the FR group ($F(1,10) < 1.00$) nor the RF group ($F(1,10) < 1.00$) differed from its respective control group.

However, the most convincing evidence that foreign infants did not respond to the French samples as did the French infants comes from a consideration of the first phase data (Figure 3). The foreign infants listening to French sucked at rates comparable to French infants listening to Russian, rather than French infants listening to French. This observation is strongly confirmed by an ANOVA of a two (background: French vs. foreign) by two

152   *J. Mehler et al.*

Figure 3.   *Displays sucking rates for the last three blocks of three consecutive samples during the first phase of Experiment 2 for infants from foreign speaking homes listening to Russian (R*) and to French (F*). For purposes of comparison, the data are also presented for the French infants in Experiment 1 who listened to the French (F) and the Russian (R) samples.*

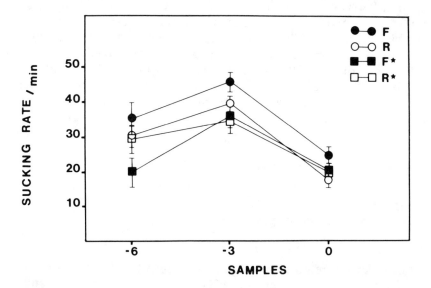

(language: French vs. Russian) design performed on the combined data of Experiments 1 and 2. This analysis revealed a significant interaction ($F(1,60) = 5.86$, $p < .02$) directly attributable to the higher sucking rates manifested by French infants to French samples.

The data from the foreign infants indicate that it is not something intrinsic to the French and Russian samples that permit them to be discriminated. Rather, it appears infants must have some familiarity with a language in order to discriminate it from another. Moreover, the degree of familiarity required seems to be more than the occasional contact that foreign infants have with the French language. Nevertheless, the first two experiments only involved a comparison between French and Russian. It is difficult to know just how far one can generalize from this case to other languages. For this reason, we decided to investigate whether French infants might display some capacity to discriminate utterances from two different foreign languages. Not only would this extend our study to a new pair of languages, but it would provide a check on the results of the present experiment. Thus, one implication of the present results is that French newborns might not distinguish two foreign languages if some familiarity with at least one of the languages is necessary.

Experiment 3

In order to examine the ability of French infants to distinguish between utterances in two foreign languages, we recruited a new bilingual speaker who spoke Italian and American English fluently. As with our previous talker, this woman spoke the two languages without foreign accent and at about the same rate. She chose to orally recount several fairy tales in both languages while being tape recorded in a sound-insulated room. She had no prior knowledge of the nature of the experiment that we were planning. The test samples prepared from these recordings were then presented to a group of 4-day-old French infants to see whether they gave evidence of distinguishing the two languages.

Method

Subjects

The subjects were thirty-six 4-day-old infants from monolingual French homes. The infants had an average weight of 3332 g (range: 2948 to 3716 g). The infants were chosen according to the same birthweight and gestational criteria as in Experiment 1. In order to obtain the necessary number of subjects, 60 infants were tested. Infants were excluded for crying (8 Ss), failing to suck for three consecutive samples (15 Ss) and failing to habituate within 30 trials (1 S).

Stimuli

The stimuli were prepared in exactly the same way as for our French–Russian materials. Our bilingual speaker was tape recorded telling the same story in both English and Italian. From these tapes, 15 samples from each language were chosen. The mean overall durations of the samples were 15.0 and 15.1 s for the English and Italian respectively (the overall range was from 13 to 22 s). Once again, all samples began and ended at sentence boundaries. Test sequences for each language were prepared by randomly ordering the samples, interspersing a 5-s pause between samples, and recording the sequence twice in succession.

Apparatus
Same as in the previous experiments.

Procedure

Ten infants were assigned randomly to each of two experimental groups, English–Italian (EI) and Italian–English (IE). Eight subjects were randomly assigned to each control group, English–English (EE) and Italian–Italian (II). In all other respects, the procedure was the same as followed in the previous experiments.

Results and discussion

A check of baseline level responding revealed no significant differences among the four groups ($F(3,32) < 1.00$). The data were inspected for signs that one of the languages resulted in higher levels of sucking during the first phase of the experiment. No significant asymmetries in responding to the two languages were observed during the phase ($F(1,34) < 1.00$). Moreover, during the second phase (Figure 4), neither the IE nor the EI groups differed significantly from their respective control groups (IE vs. II, $F(1,16) = 1,11$; EI vs. EE, $F(1,16) = 1.45$). Hence, French 4-day-olds gave no evidence of discriminating English from Italian utterances.

Given the previous findings, one interpretation of the present results is that the ability to discriminate utterances from two languages depends upon some familiarity with at least one of the languages. However, some alternative explanations are also possible. For example, the fact that there was no evidence of discrimination in the present case need not be the result of a lack of familiarity with the two languages. Instead, perhaps the French infants failed because Italian and English utterances are somehow less discriminable than French and Russian ones. If this were the case, then we might expect that even infants who were familiar with one of the languages might have difficulty in discriminating English and Italian utterances.

Experiment 4

Was the failure of the French infants to distinguish English and Italian utterances a consequence of their lack of familiarity with the two languages or are these languages simply less discriminable? To explore these possibilities, as well as to examine the generalizability of our findings to other cultures and to different age groups, we decided to test American infants on both the French–Russian and the Italian–English contrasts. The first part of our investigation focused on the Italian–English contrasts. If it is the case that some familiarity with one of the languages is a prerequisite for discriminating it from another language, then American infants should have the necessary

Figure 4.   *The top panel displays the sucking rates of the infants who heard Italian during the first phase of Experiment 3. Group IE heard English during the second phase while group II heard Italian. The comparable data for subjects who heard English during the first phase are shown in the bottom panel. Group EI heard Italian during the second phase while group EE continued to hear English.*

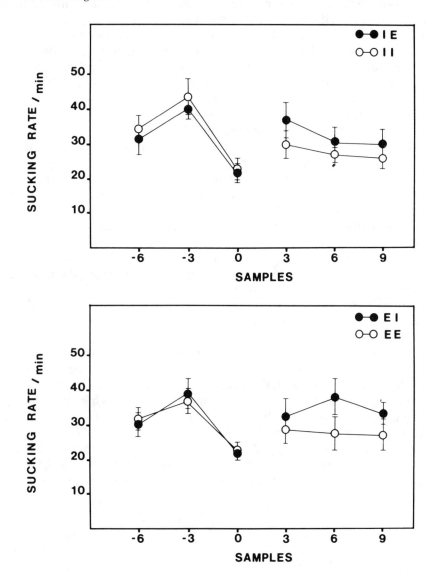

experience to discriminate the two languages. Alternatively, if the Italian–English contrast is simply more difficult than the French–Russian contrast, then they may be less able to distinguish the former as compared to the latter contrast.

Because facilities for testing 4-day-old American infants were not available to us at the time of testing, we decided to conduct our investigation with 2-month olds. This difference in age between American and French infants may appear to be a drawback. However, it provided us with an opportunity to detect possible developmental changes that might occur in older infants as a result of additional experience listening to a particular language. Developmental studies of speech perception in this age range have been relatively rare. The available data do suggest little in the way of perceptual changes during the first few months of life (but see Werker & Tees, 1984 for evidence of such changes between 8 and 12 months of age). Thus, Eimas et al. (1971) found no evidence of a difference in the way in which 1- and 4-month-olds responded to changes in voicing cues. Similarly, the report by Bertoncini et al. (1987) that newborns discriminate contrasts in place of articulation fits well with what has been observed for infants 3-months-old and older (e.g., Eimas, 1974; Morse, 1972). The one exception to this pattern comes from a paradigm that goes beyond the simple discrimination of two syllables and taps the capacity of infants to represent different syllables (Bertoncini, Bijeljac-Babic, Jusczyk, Kennedy, & Mehler, 1988). These researchers found some indication that 2-month-olds had finer grained representations of consonantal differences than did 4-day-olds. Given that the discrimination of two languages also requires infants to go beyond a simple discrimination of two syllables, the exploration of potential developmental differences seems worthwhile.

Although the HAS procedure works well with 2-month-olds (e.g., Jusczyk, 1985b), pilot work in our laboratory suggested that the sucking arousal method that we used with the 4-day-olds was not well-suited to testing infants at this age.[3] This led us to adopt a measure of "looking while listening" as an index of the infant's ability to distinguish the utterances in the two languages. The change in methods provided us with an additional opportunity to examine the generalizability of our results. To the extent that the same patterns of results obtain despite the different methods, we have powerful converging evidence that infants can discriminate one language from another.

---

[3]The problem is that because of the noncontingency between sucking behavior and the production of the sounds, there are great individual differences with respect to the 2-month-old infant's persistence in sucking during the course of the experiment. The individual differences with respect to willingness to suck tend to be reduced for a contingent procedure like HAS, but as we noted above (Footnote 1) this procedure does not allow for an uninterrupted presentation of the samples. For this reason, we chose the looking while listening method.

Method

Subjects

The subjects were 40 infants from monolingual English-speaking families. The infants averaged 10.7 weeks in age (range: 7.9 to 12.2 weeks). In order to obtain the necessary number of subjects, 110 were tested. Infants were excluded for crying (49 Ss), failing to habituate within 24 trials (13 Ss), sleeping (5 Ss) and failing to look at the display for two successive trials during the first phase (3 Ss).

Stimuli

The same Italian–English recordings were used as in Experiment 3. Only two slight modifications were made in preparing the stimulus tapes. First, for each language, we recorded a randomly ordered sequence of 12 stimulus samples (as opposed to all 15) twice in a row to prepare the stimulus sequence for the first phase of the experiment. The remaining three samples were held out for use as test stimuli. Only these three stimuli were recorded for use during the second phase of the experiment. This allowed us to present infants in the control groups with novel utterances from the same language that they had been listening to during the first phase of the experiment. The second change was a slight prolongation of the intertrial interval (ITI) to 7 s (as opposed to the 5 s used previously). The longer ITI seemed preferable given the change to a looking while listening procedure.

Apparatus

All testing took place inside a small sound-insulated room. Situated inside this room were an infant chair, a JBL(4301B) loudspeaker and an opaque projection screen. The opaque screen was situated just above the loudspeaker and included a small slit through which an experimenter in an adjacent room could view the infant. The equipment in the adjacent room included a stereo-amplifier, two tape recorders, a Kodak slide projector and a response box which was linked to a LSI 11/73 computer. The response box was used to record looking times which were stored on the computer. The computer was programmed with an algorithm to calculate the habituation criterion, and determined when testing advanced to the second phase.

Procedure

Infants were seated in the chair facing the projection screen. Parents were seated behind and out of view of the infant. The parents wore headphones and listened to recorded music during the test period. Two experimenters were situated in the adjacent room. One of them, the observer, looked through a small slit and pressed buttons on a response box to indicate the start and finish of each trial and when the infant was fixating on the picture projected on the screen. The observer was wearing headphones and listening to recorded music. In addition, she had no knowledge of the test condition to which the infant had been assigned. Thus, she was a blind (or, more accurately, deaf) observer. The second experimenter was responsible for assigning the infant to the appropriate test condition, operating the slide projector and tape recorders and for changing the stimulus set once the habituation criterion had been achieved. For some infants, a second observer was also used in order to provide a reliability check on judgments of fixation. The interobserver reliability scores were on the order of 90% agreement.

For all test trials, the sequence of events was the same. A slide of a woman was projected on the screen and remained on throughout the trial. The same slide was used for every trial; it never varied. At the end of a trial, the slide was extinguished and remained off for 7 s, at which time the next trial began. The onset and offset of the slide coincided with the auditory presentation of one of the speech samples. The observer was alerted to the start and termination of a trial by the switching on and off of the slide projector. She pressed different buttons to indicate when the infant was and was not looking at the slide during the trial. The computer calculated the percentage of the time for a given sample that the infant fixated on the slide.

During the first phase of the experiment, infants heard different samples from only one of the two languages (20 heard English and 20 heard Italian). The samples were presented at intensity levels comparable to those used for the French infants (i.e., 70 ± 2 dB SPL). The first phase lasted until the fixation time for a block of three consecutive trials declined by 50% from the longest time recorded for an earlier block of three consecutive trials. Then the second experimenter stopped the first tape recorder and started the second one. The second phase of testing began and lasted for three trials. During this second phase, half of the subjects (10 from each language group) heard three samples from the other language, whereas the remaining subjects served as controls and heard three new samples from the same language as before. Thus, as in Experiment 3, there were four test conditions: English–Italian (EI), English–English (EE), Italian–English (IE) and Italian–Italian (II).

Results and discussion

The data were examined to determine whether the groups differed in their fixation times during their initial exposure to the two languages, i.e., during phase one. A one-way ANOVA indicated no significant differences across

Figure 5.   *Displays the mean percentage increase in looking for the postshift period for the experimental (change language) and control (same language) groups in Experiment 4. Note that the groups are designated according to which language (Italian or English) was presented during the first phase of the experiment.*

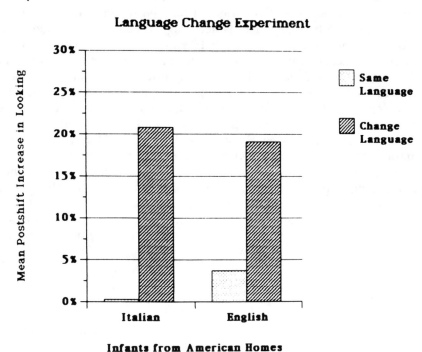

Language Change Experiment

Infants from American Homes

conditions in the time to habituate $(F(3,36) = 1.17)$. Thus, there was no indication that the two languages differed in their initial impact upon looking times. Moreover, the control and experimental groups did not differ during the first phase of the experiment.

Discrimination of the utterances from the two languages was indexed using difference scores obtained by subtracting the average fixation time for the last three first-phase trials from that of the first three second-phase trials. The scores for each experimental group were compared to that of the appropriate control group (i.e., EI vs. EE and IE vs. II). In both instances (see Figure 5), the experimental group manifested significantly longer fixation times than the controls $(t(18) = 2.61, p < .01$ for IE vs. II and $t(18) = 2.11, p < .025$ for EI vs. EE).

Thus, 2-month-old American infants are able to discriminate English from Italian utterances. Because the same stimulus materials were used here as in Experiment 3, the failure of the French infants to distinguish the utterances from the two languages must be attributed to something other than the discriminability of the utterances themselves. A number of possibilities suggest themselves. First, as noted earlier, it may be the case that some familiarity with one of the two languages is necessary to be able to distinguish them. In this sense, the present results accord well with those of Experiment 1. In both cases, infants tested on a contrast between their native language and another language gave evidence of distinguishing utterances from the two languages. However, other explanations are also possible. For example, the infants in the present study were considerably older than the 4-day-olds in Experiment 3. Hence, it could be argued that the Italian–English discrimination is still a more difficult one than the French–Russian one, and that the greater maturity of the older infants brings with it some enhanced ability to detect such a difficult contrast. In other words, that as in the Bertoncini et al. (1988) study, we have uncovered additional evidence for developmental changes in speech processing during the first 2 months of life. A further possibility is that the looking while listening task is a more sensitive measure of discrimination than the sucking task used with younger infants. To explore these alternatives, we decided to conduct the following experiment.

Experiment 5

The notion that it was the greater sensitivity of the task or greater maturity of the 2-month-olds and *not* their familiarity with one of the languages that enabled them to discriminate English and Italian implies that these infants should also be able to distinguish the French and Russian utterances. In contrast, if familiarity with one of the two languages is necessary, then one would expect that American infants unfamiliar with either French or Russian should not be able to discriminate utterances from these two languages. For this reason, we decided to test a group of 2-month-olds on their ability to distinguish the French and Russian samples used in Experiments 1 and 2.

Method

Subjects

The subjects were 40 infants from monolingual English-speaking homes. All parents of prospective subjects were questioned to determine whether the infants had any occasion to listen to either Russian or French speakers. Only those infants without such prior exposure were tested. The infants averaged 10.1 weeks in age (range 7.8 to 12.1 weeks). In order to obtain the necessary number of subjects, 115 infants were tested. Infants were excluded for crying (55 Ss), failing to habituate within 24 trials (12 Ss), sleeping (4 Ss), and failing to look for two consecutive trials during phase one (4 Ss).

Stimuli

The same Russian and French materials employed in Experiments 1 and 2 were used here. The only difference was that the test tapes were prepared in the fashion described in Experiment 4. That is, for each language, a randomly ordered sequence of 12 samples was recorded twice in a row for use in the first phase of the experiment. The remaining three utterances from the language were recorded separately for use in the second phase. Thus, once again new utterances from either the familiar or novel language were always presented during the second phase.

Apparatus

The same apparatus was used as in Experiment 4.

Procedure

Ten infants were assigned randomly to each of four test conditions: French–Russian (FR), French–French (FF), Russian–French (RF) and Russian–Russian (RR). In all other respects, the procedure followed was identical to that in Experiment 4.

Results and discussion

Once again during the first phase of the experiment there was no evidence of significant differences in fixation times that resulted from listening to French versus listening to Russian ($t(38) = 0.35$). Nor were there any indications of differences between experimental and control groups in fixation times for the first phase.

Discrimination performance was analyzed using the difference scores obtained by subtracting the average fixation time for the last three trials of the first phase from that of the first three trials of the second phase (see Figure 6). In contrast to the previous experiment, neither experimental group differed significantly from its control in fixation time during the second phase of the experiment ($t(18) = 0.21$ for FR vs. FF and $t(18) = 1.28$ for RF vs. RR). Moreover, as with the English and Italian samples in the previous experiment, there was no evidence of significant asymmetries in responding to the French and Russian samples during the second phase. Hence, there

162   *J. Mehler et al.*

Figure 6.   *Displays the mean percentage increase in looking for the postshift period for the experimental (change language) and control (same language) groups in Experiment 5. Note that the groups are designated according to which language (Russian or French) was presented during the first phase of the experiment.*

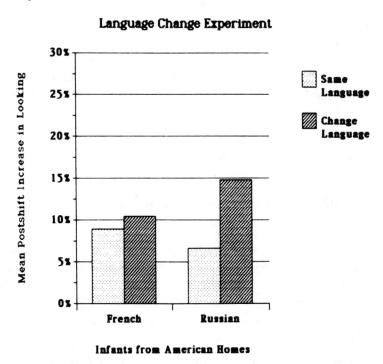

was no indication that American infants discriminated the French and Russian utterances.

The present results appear to undercut the suggestion that the American infants' ability to distinguish the Italian and English samples was the result of either task or age factors. Were it simply a question of the kind of task used or the greater maturity of the 2-month-olds that permitted them to distinguish the English and Italian samples, then it is hard to understand why they did not discriminate the French and Russian samples given the ability of 4-day-old French infants to do so. Instead, the fact that the same overall pattern of results obtains for 2-month-old American infants tested with a different procedure provides converging evidence for the tentative conclusion that we drew regarding the results of the first three experiments. Namely, some familiarity with one of the languages is apparently necessary in order to distinguish it from another language.

Having shown that the young infant's ability to discriminate the native language from a foreign language generalizes to another culture and another language pair, it is necessary to discover the means by which this is accomplished. Thus, we can begin to ask about the information that the infant uses to make this distinction. The following three experiments address the issue of what sort of information is sufficient to allow the infant to distinguish the native language from another language.

Experiment 6

There are many ways in which languages differ with respect to their sound structure. For example, they may include different phonetic segments. They also may differ in their prosodic characteristics such as their rhythms or stress patterns. Because such differences are manifested directly in the acoustic stream of speech, one may question whether the source for the discriminative ability that we have noted is based upon some gross acoustic characteristics rather than on some coherent linguistic organization of the utterances. For example, in the present case, perhaps our talkers employed different pitch registers for each of the languages. More generally, we might ask if the infant could simply be responding to the appearance of certain spectral characteristics (e.g., such as the proportion of aperiodic to periodic noise) when discriminating the native language from another one. If so, then any permutation of the original input strings may suffice to allow the infant to distinguish ones derived from the native language from those of another language. Alternatively, it may be necessary that the acoustic cues preserve the essential patterning of spectral changes characteristic of utterances in the language in order for discrimination to occur.

One means of examining this issue is to present infants with the same overall variations in spectral energy that occurred in our speech samples, but to do so in a way inconsistent with the spectral changes associated with lawful utterances in the language. Playing the original stimuli backwards is one way of doing this. Manipulating the stimuli in this manner preserves their absolute spectral characteristics while distorting the direction of changes in a way inconsistent with the linguistic organization of the languages. To the extent that infants still discriminate the utterances derived from the native language from those of another language, it would indicate that some attention to gross variations in spectral energy are sufficient for this purpose. It seemed most reasonable to examine this issue with 4-day-olds because, by 2 months, one might expect that the exposure that infants have had to sentences in the native language may well have led them to develop expectations about the direction of spectral changes that occur in the language. Hence, any tendency to rely on overall spectral features seems most apt to show itself in the younger age group.

Method

Subjects

The subjects were thirty-two 4-day-old infants from monolingual French homes. The infants had an average weight of 3370 g (range: 2830 to 4060 g). The same birthweight and gestational criteria as in Experiment 1 were used in selecting subjects. In order to obtain the necessary number of subjects, 64 infants were tested. Infants were excluded for crying (9 Ss), failing to suck for three consecutive samples (21 Ss), failing to habituate within 30 trials (1 S) and equipment failure (1 S).

Stimuli

The same stimulus samples employed in Experiment 1 were used in the present study. The stimulus tapes were re-recorded backwards for use in the present experiment. In all other respects, the stimuli were identical to the original ones.

Apparatus

Same as described for Experiment 1.

Procedure

Eight infants were assigned randomly to each of two experimental groups—backwards French–Russian (bFR) and backwards Russian–French (bRF) – and to each of two control groups—backwards French–French (bFF) and backwards Russian–Russian (bRR). In all other aspects, the procedure was identical to the one used in Experiment 1.

Results and discussion

A check of baseline level responding revealed no significant differences among the four groups. The data were inspected for signs that one of the two languages resulted in higher levels of sucking during the initial phase of the experiment. Unlike Experiment 1 wherein French samples produced significantly higher sucking rates, no significant differences ($F(1,30) < 1.00$) were observed in sucking rates during the first phase for the backwards French

Figure 7.   *The top panel displays the results of the infants who heard the backwards Russian samples during the first phase of Experiment 6. Group bRF heard French during the second phase while group bRR continued to hear Russian. The comparable data for those infants who heard the backwards French samples during the first phase are shown in the bottom panel. Group bFR heard Russian during the second phase while Group bFF continued to hear French.*

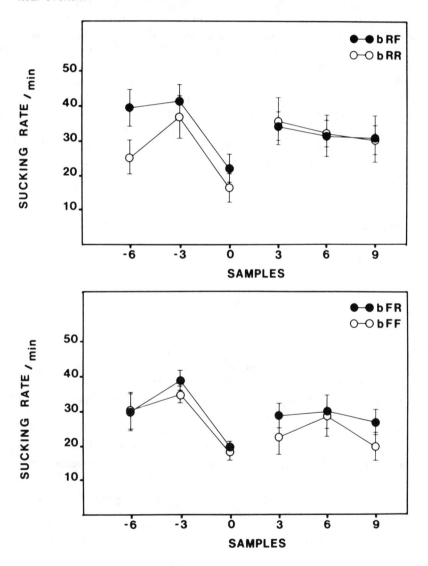

versus the backwards Russian samples. Similarly, during the second phase of the experiment (see Figure 7), neither the bFR nor the bRF groups differed significantly from their respective control groups (bFR vs. bFF, $F(1,14) < 1.00$; bRF vs. bRR, $F(1,14) < 1.00$). Hence, the French 4-day-old infants gave no evidence of discriminating the backwards French and Russian samples.

The present results suggest that French 4-day-olds are basing their discrimination of French and Russian samples on something other than the simple presence of certain spectral features in the different language samples (e.g., more aperiodic noise in the Russian samples due to the greater number of fricatives present). Similarly, it is unlikely that some other global factor such as the ratio or distribution of pauses to speech provide the basis for discrimination of the different language samples. Nor could possible changes in pitch register associated with each language serve as a basis for discriminating the two languages since the same range of pitches was available in the backwards samples. Thus, it appears necessary that the patterning of the spectral changes be consistent with ones found in the native language in order for discrimination to occur.

Experiment 7

Given the suggestion that the cues for discriminating the native language from another may be closely tied to the particular patterns of spectral changes associated with utterances in the language, we can attempt to specify more precisely the type of information that the infant uses. There are a number of possibilities. With respect to their sound structures, languages differ in which sounds they include (i.e., their phonetic structure), the way these sounds can be ordered in utterances (i.e., phonotactic structure), and in their prosodic characteristics (e.g., rhythm, intonation and stress patterning). Potentially, any of these characteristics might serve to distinguish one language from another. However, there are some reasons for favoring the role of prosodic cues. First, the results of the preceding experiment suggest that it is not simply the presence of particular types of sounds in the input that is important (i.e., the existence of particular phonetic segments), but of some patterning consistent with the language structure (such as the phonotactic or prosodic features). Second, given that infants as young as 4 days old are able to discriminate the native language from another, it is not unlikely that prenatal exposure plays a role in the process. Certainly, recent studies appear to indicate that some speech information passes through the uterus to the fetus (e.g., DeCasper & Spence, 1986; Querleu & Renard, 1981; Vince, Armitage,

Baldwin, Toner, & Moore, 1981). However, any speech information that does get to the fetus is greatly attenuated with respect to its intensity and frequency range (best estimates are that only information below about 800 Hz gets through). This means that much of the information necessary for distinguishing among phonetic segments is not available prenatally. However, some information regarding prosodic characteristics such as rhythm, stress and intonation may be preserved in the impoverished signal. Thus, the potential exists for prenatal exposure to the characteristic prosodic patterning of the native language. Consequently, we decided to investigate whether there is sufficient information in the prosodic characteristics of utterances to allow infants to discriminate the native language from a foreign one. To test this possibility, we created low-pass filtered versions of our original French and Russian samples and presented them to a new group of 4-day-old infants.

Method

Subjects

The subjects were thirty-two 4-day-old infants from monolingual French homes. The infants had an average weight of 3386 g (range: 3036 to 3766 g). The infants were selected according to the same birthweight and gestational criteria as in Experiment 1. In order to obtain the necessary number of subjects, 64 infants were tested. Infants were excluded for crying (6 Ss), failing to suck for three consecutive samples (20 Ss), sleeping (4 Ss), and equipment failure (2 Ss).

Stimuli

The same French and Russian samples used for Experiment 1 were low-pass filtered at 400 Hz for use in the present experiment. Stimulus tapes were prepared from the low-pass filtered versions of the samples. Because the filtering process reduces the overall amplitude of the signal, adjustments were made in the volume controls so that the stimuli could be played at the same loudness levels as in previous experiments (i.e., 72 ± 2 dB SPL). In all other respects, the stimuli were the same as those in Experiment 1.

Apparatus

Same as that used in Experiment 1.

Procedure

Eight infants were assigned randomly to each of two experimental groups—filtered French–Russian (fFR) and filtered Russian–French (fRF)—and to each of two control groups – filtered French–French (fFF) and filtered

168   *J. Mehler et al.*

Figure 8.   *The top panel displays the results of the infants who heard the low-pass filtered versions of the Russian samples during the first phase of Experiment 7. Group fRF heard French during the second phase while Group fRR continued to hear Russian. The comparable data for those infants who heard the filtered French samples during the first phase are shown in the bottom panel. Group fFR heard French during the second phase while Group fFF continued to hear French.*

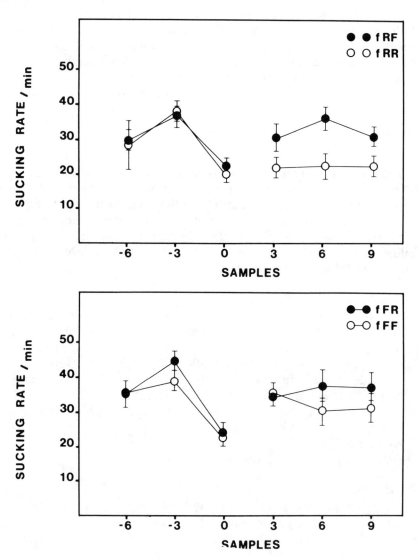

Russian–Russian (fRR). In all other respects, the procedure was identical to that used in Experiment 1.

Results and discussion

There was no evidence of significant differences among the four groups in their baseline rates of sucking ($F(3,28) < 1.00$). The data for the first phase were then inspected for evidence that significantly higher sucking rates were associated with filtered versions of the native language, French, as opposed to the foreign language, Russian. In contrast to the findings of Experiment 1, the difference between French and Russian, although in the same direction, was not statistically significant ($F(1,30) = 2.10$, $p = 0.146$). However, the data from the second phase of the experiment (see Figure 8) did fully replicate those of Experiment 1. Namely, there was a significant increase in sucking for the fRF group relative to the RR control ($F(1,14) = 6.50$, $p < .02$), but no significant difference between the fRR group and the fFF control ($F(1,14) = 1.10$ $p > .30$). Thus, infants gave some evidence of discriminating the low-pass filtered versions of the utterances from the two languages.

Several comments about the data are in order. First, the data confirm the pattern of discrimination noted for the 4-day-olds in Experiment 1. Thus, the infants showed significant increases in sucking for changes from the foreign language to the native language, but not for changes in the opposite direction. Thus, this tendency survived even the drastic reduction of available speech information brought about by low-pass filtering the signal at 400 Hz. In contrast, the significantly elevated rates of sucking for the native language strings that we observed in the first phase of Experiment 1 was not reproduced. It is difficult to say whether the filtering is responsible for this or whether it is simply a consequence of random variation. Thus, it is possible that the filtering renders the speech uninteresting for the newborns, or perhaps it contains only some of the cues which they attend to in unfiltered speech samples. In order to gain a fuller understanding of the role of prosodic cues, we decided to test an additional group of American 2-month-olds on filtered versions of the Italian and English utterances.

Experiment 8

Methods

Subjects

The subjects were 48 infants from monolingual English-speaking families. The infants averaged 11.4 weeks in age (range: 9.3 to 12.1 weeks). In order to obtain the necessary number of subjects, 136 were tested. Infants were excluded for crying (63 Ss), failing to habituate within 24 trials (14 Ss), sleeping (4 Ss), and failing to look at the display for two successive trials during the first phase (7 Ss).

Stimuli

The same English and Italian samples employed in Experiment 4 were used to prepare the stimuli for the present experiment. Test tapes were prepared using a Krohn-Hite filter to low-pass filter the utterances at 400 Hz. The output levels on the playback equipment were adjusted to compensate for the loss of intensity caused by the filtering process. The stimuli were played to the subjects at loudness levels comparable to Experiment 4 (i.e., 70 ± 2 dB SPL). In all other aspects, the stimuli were comparable to those in Experiment 4.

Apparatus

Same as described in Experiment 4.

Procedure

Twelve infants were assigned randomly to each of four test conditions: filtered English–Italian (fEI), filtered English–English (fEE), filtered Italian–English (fIE) and filtered Italian–Italian (fII). In all other respects, the procedure was identical to that followed in Experiment 4.

Results and discussion

The data during the first phase of the experiment were analyzed to determine whether there were any indications that the infants fixated longer while listening to the filtered samples from one language as opposed to the other. As was true for the unfiltered samples used in Experiment 4, there was no evidence of significant differences in fixation times while listening to the filtered English versus the filtered Italian samples ($t(22) = 1.25$, $p > .50$). Nor were there any indications of significant differences between experimental and control groups in fixation times for the first phase.

Discrimination performance was analyzed using the difference scores obtained by subtracting the average fixation time for the last three first-phase trials from that of the first three second-phase trials (see Figure 9). As in Experiment 4, both the fIE and the fEI groups displayed significantly longer fixation rates than their respective control groups during the second phase of the experiment (fIE vs. fII, $t(22) = 2.52$, $p < .01$; fEI vs. fEE, $t(22) = 4.15$, $p < .001$). Thus, the present results with the low-pass filtered samples com-

Figure 9.   *Displays the mean percentage increase in looking for the postshift period for the experimental (change language) and control (same language) groups in Experiment 8. Note that the groups are designated according to which low-pass filtered language (English or Italian) was presented during the first phase of the Experiment.*

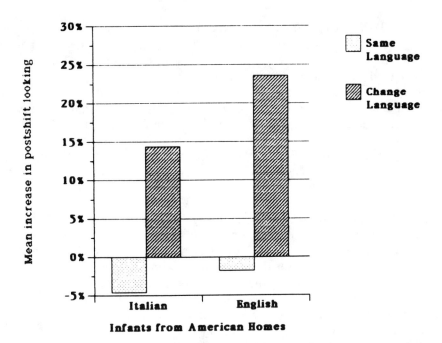

pletely replicate those obtained with the unfiltered versions in Experiment 4. Hence, the low-pass filtered versions of the utterances contain enough information to allow American infants to distinguish the English and Italian samples.

Taken together, the results of these last two experiments suggest that prosodic cues may be important in allowing the infant to identify utterances as belonging to the native language. Thus, even when most information about other types of cues is stripped away, the remaining prosodic cues are sufficient for distinguishing utterances from the native language. This is not to say that the infant might not be able to successfully discriminate the utterances on some other basis as well if the prosodic distinctions were neutralized in some way. Only further testing will be able to tell us whether the prosodic cues are absolutely necessary. In the meantime, the present findings demonstrate that prosodic factors must be given serious consideration in accounting for the way in which infants are able to identify utterances as belonging to their native language.

General discussion

Overall, these experiments show that infants, as young as 4-days-old, are able to discriminate utterances in their native language from those in an unfamiliar one. In contrast, when both languages were unfamiliar to them, the infants displayed no capacity to distinguish the utterances in one language from those in another. Moreover, the failure to distinguish the two unfamiliar languages is not simply due to their being less discriminable than the other contrast. This point is made forcefully by the fact that each type of language contrast was successfully discriminated by infants for whom one of the languages was familiar. Finally, the results of Experiments 7 and 8 with low-pass filtered speech samples suggest that there is enough information in the prosody to allow infants to distinguish the native languages strings from those of a foreign language.

One of the striking aspects of the present study is the fact that the overall pattern of findings holds across two different cultures, with infants of two different ages and under different test procedures. We recognize that questions can be raised about the wisdom of varying all these factors in the same study. However, what we find most striking about the data reported here is the fact that, despite the differences in age and in procedure, the same basic pattern emerges. Namely, a contrast involving a familiar language is detected, whereas one involving two unfamiliar languages is not. In this sense, the two different procedures can be said to provide converging evidence that the phenomenon reported is indeed a real one. Thus, the infant has an aptitude to classify together utterances from the language to which he or she is exposed (i.e., the native language). The only indication of any sort of developmental trend is that the older infants do not show a preference for the familiar language. This may arise for a number of reasons, including the methods used and the possibility that, at two months, the response to novelty may simply outweigh any preference for the native language.

As we noted earlier, the present study is only the first step towards understanding how the infant is able to classify utterances as belonging to the same language. Many aspects remain to be investigated before we can have a clear understanding of this process. For example, what is the source of the information that allows the infant to discriminate native language strings from foreign ones? The present study demonstrates that there is sufficient information in speech that is low-pass filtered at 400 Hz to discriminate the utterances. As noted earlier, attenuating the signal in this fashion, leaves the prosody intact while stripping away most of the distinctive phonetic information. Therefore, the results demonstrate that infants have the capacity to discriminate the utterances on the basis of their prosodic organization. The suggestion that attention to prosody may be important to discriminating the utterances fits well with other observations made regarding infant speech perception. For example, Fernald and Kuhl (1987) have shown that prosodic factors are an important determinant in the preference that older infants display for motherese over adult-directed speech. Similarly, it has been shown that certain discrimination results (e.g., recognition of the mother's voice from that of a stranger) cannot be obtained under conditions where the natural flow of prosodic is disrupted (Mehler et al., 1978).

However, we are *not* presently in a position to say that infants rely solely, or even principally, on prosodic information to distinguish intact native language utterances from foreign ones. It may very well be the case that a manipulation that neutralized prosodic differences, while leaving the phonetic structure intact, would also allow infants to distinguish utterances belonging to their native language. In other words, it may be the case that infants are also able to use phonetic differences as a basis for discriminating native language utterances from foreign ones. Certainly, the whole history of research on speech perception capacities demonstrates that young infants are remarkably sensitive to fine distinctions between phonetic segments, even those that exist in languages other than their native one (e.g., Aslin, Pisoni, Hennessey, & Perey, 1981; Lasky, Syrdal-Lasky, & Klein, 1975; Streeter, 1976; Werker & Tees, 1984). Thus, the present study shows only that the infants are capable of using prosodic differences for discriminating the languages. It does not rule out other possible sources for this capacity. Additional work is necessary to determine which, if any, other factors are reasonable bases for the discrimination ability noted here.

Moreover, even if the question regarding the importance of prosodic factors were to be resolved, a number of important questions would still remain concerning the precise nature of the information that the infant uses. For example, if attention to prosodic structure is the chief basis for the discriminative ability, then which aspect of prosody is critical? Is it the intonation contour, the stress pattern or something else? A closely related issue concerns the extent to which the ability observed here is tied to the native language. The present study only looked at four different languages, all of which are Indo-European. Would use of a wider set of languages produce the same type of results? It seems difficult to believe that the capacity to discriminate utter-

174   *J. Mehler et al.*

ances from two different languages is so specifically linked to the native language. Hence, one might speculate that there are other languages that share in the same properties that infants use for discriminating the native language utterances from foreign language utterance.

Let us consider one such possibility. An often noted distinction in the prosodic organization of languages is the one between stress-timed and syllable-timed languages. Stress-timed languages are ones wherein the time between accented syllables is said to be approximately constant. In contrast, in syllable-timed languages, each syllable is presumed to have about the same duration. Consequently, if the infant were classifying utterances on such a basis one would expect that discrimination between a syllable-timed and a stress-timed language should be relatively easy compared to one, say, between two syllable-timed languages. In fact, the present pattern of results suggests that the important parameter is something other than one distinguishing stress-timed and syllable-timed languages. Russian and English are both considered to be stress-timed (e.g., see Cruttenden, 1986), whereas French and Italian are both syllable-timed languages.[4] This means that the same type of distinction was posed in each of our language pairings. Hence, if the stress-timed versus syllable-timed distinction were a sufficient basis for classifying the utterances, then both the French and American infants should have been able to distinguish both pairings. In fact, each group only distinguished the one involving the native language.

Although the present results appear to preclude a grouping of utterances based on a factor such as stress- versus syllable-timing, they do not rule out other such means of grouping languages into families based on their structural features. The notion that there are certain important parameters that distinguish groups of languages, and that language acquisition proceeds by setting certain parameters according to the input being received is not a new one (e.g., Chomsky, 1981). It is a proposal that merits serious consideration in the study of language acquisition and the paradigms employed in the present study may provide a means of gathering empirical data on it.

Similarly, a number of questions can be raised concerning the type of familiarization that is necessary with a language in order for it to be discriminable from another. The present study suggests that a long period of postnatal

---

[4]We note that there is considerable disagreement in linguistic circles over the validity of the stress-timed/syllable-timed distinction. Moreover, assumption that Russian is a stress-timed language is not universally accepted. Thus, it is sometimes claimed that Russian is more properly classified as a syllable-timed language. If this is the case, then the present study had one pairing involving two syllable-timed languages (i.e., French and Russian) and another involving a stress-timed (English) versus a syllable-timed language (Italian). However, recall that the French infants did not distinguish the English from the Italian utterances. Therefore, the main point—that the syllable-timed versus stress-timed distinction cannot explain our results—still stands.

experience is not necessary, as witnessed by the performance of 4-day-old French infants. However, it does not answer the question of whether any postnatal experience is required or whether the limited type of information available to infants prenatally (e.g., Querleu & Renard, 1981; Vince et al., 1981; Spence & DeCasper, 1987) is sufficient for this purpose. One way to examine this issue would be to test infants during the first day of life as a means of reducing the amount of postnatal exposure that they have to language. Research of this type is currently under way in our laboratory. In any case, whether the critical exposure to the native language occurs prenatally during the last few months of gestation or postnatally during the first few days of life, it is clearly something other than a learned behavior in traditional terms. Prenatally or within the first few days of life, there is little that could be construed as selective reinforcement or feedback for classifying utterances as belonging to the native language. Indeed, to say that our subjects have "learned" to classify utterances in this way does not bring us any closer to understanding the underlying mechanisms. Clearly, a great deal of biological prewiring must be in place to account for the precocity with which the infant groups together utterances from the native language. Indeed, the speed and facility with which infants detect characteristic features of the native language suggest an innately guided learning process (Gould & Marler, 1987). Thus, many other species appear to be genetically programmed to attend to specific cues in specific behavioral contexts. The well-known abilities of many bird species to fixate on certain physical characteristics in identifying members of their own species is a good example of this process. An even more pertinent parallel may be found in the song-learning behavior of swamp sparrows. Marler and Peters (1977) have shown that, although song input is necessary for song sparrows to learn the species-typical song, these birds are highly selective with respect to the kind of input that they will accept. In the realm of human behaviors, the highly specialized nature of linguistic processes and their predominant role in communication would seem to target them as likely candidates for innately guided learning processes. Indeed, the early competences which infants display in perceiving speech sound differences (e.g., Aslin et al., 1983; Kuhl, 1987) suggest a strong genetic component.

Attention to the early age at which infants discriminate native language utterances should not cause us to overlook possible developmental changes. As noted earlier, there is little evidence of developmental changes in basic speech perception processes over the first few months of life. In fact, the picture most often presented is one in which the young infant is portrayed as able to discriminate phonetic differences that could potentially occur in any language, and develops by focusing on only those contrasts that are relevant to the native language (e.g., Jusczyk, 1985a; Mehler, 1985). Evidence in support of this position comes from recent work demonstrating that at 6 months of age infants from English-speaking homes are able to distinguish foreign language contrasts, but by 12 months of age they do not (Werker & Tees, 1984). One suggestion as to what is happening is that as infants begin to acquire a vocabulary for recognizing words, they attend only to those differences relevant to distinguishing among words in the native language (Jusczyk, 1985a). In effect, the non-native language contrasts come to be ignored because they play no role in word distinctions in the native language.

How do the present results fit with what we know about the development of speech perception? The only suggestion of a developmental change in the present study was that there was an asymmetry in the discrimination results of the newborns (i.e., changes to the native language produced higher sucking rates, whereas changes to the foreign language did not) that did not occur for the 2-month-olds. Other than this, the main findings for the two age groups were the same despite the changes in procedure. We interpreted the difference in the two groups as attributable to the newborn's preference for the native language. However, to verify this, it would be wise to collect more data with a group of Russian infants at this age. Presumably, they, too, should show a preference, but this time for Russian over French. Similarly, if by 2 months of age, novelty effects offset the preference for the native language, then one would expect that not only would French and Russian infants display no preference for the native language strings, but neither would Italian infants.

Other than this, there were no apparent developmental differences in the ability to distinguish utterances from two languages.[5] Thus, neither age group discriminated contrasts between two foreign languages. However, this is not to say that there are no changes in this ability with increasing age and linguistic experience. In particular, if the ability to discriminate languages is not tied so specifically to the native language, but rather to a family of languages, then one would expect that the infant might become attuned to the differences among the various languages within the family. Evidence from the cross-linguistic studies (i.e., Werker & Tees, 1984) as well as some recent work looking at speech segmentation in long utterances (e.g., Hirsh-Pasek, Kemler Nelson, Jusczyk, Cassidy, Druss, & Kennedy, 1987; Jusczyk, Hirsh-Pasek, Kemler Nelson, Kennedy, Woodward, & Piwoz, submitted) suggests that a basic reorganization of speech perception processes may occur in the latter half of the first year of life.

---

[5]There is some suggestion that this ability may be stable at least through the first 5 months of life. Thus, Bahrick and Pickens (in press) found that 5-month-olds from the Miami area were able to discriminate Spanish from English passages.

In conclusion, although many details remain to be investigated, the present series of experiments demonstrates that infants as young as 4 days old are capable of distinguishing utterances from their native language from those of another language. This ability appears to be another indication of the way in which the infant comes biologically prepared to acquire language.

References

Aslin, R.N., Pisoni, D.B., Hennessy, B.L., & Perey, A.J. (1981). Discrimination of voice onset time by human infants: New findings and implications for the effect of early experience. *Child Development, 52*, 1135–1145.

Aslin, R.N., Pisoni, D.B., & Jusczyk, P.W. (1983). Auditory development and speech perception in infancy. In M. Haith & J. Campos (Eds.), *Carmichael's handbook of child psychology: Infancy and developmental psychology* (pp. 573–687). New York: Wiley.

Bahrick, L.E., & Pickens, J.N. (in press). Classification of bimodal English and Spanish passages by infants. *Infant Behavior and Development, 11.*

Bertoncini, J., Bijeljac-Babic, R., Blumstein, S.E., & Mehler, J. (1987). Discrimination in neonates of very short CV's. *Journal of the Acoustical Society of America, 82*, 31–37.

Bertoncini, J., Bijeljac-Babic, R., Jusczyk, P.W., Kennedy, L.J., & Mehler, J. (1988). An investigation of young infants' perceptual representations of speech sounds. *Journal of Experimental Psychology: General, 117*, 21–33.

Bronshtein, A.I., & Petrova, E.P. (1967). An investigation of the auditory analyzer in neonates and young infants. In Y. Brackbill & G.C. Thompson (Eds.), *Behavior in infancy and early childhood*. New York: Free Press.

Chomsky, N. (1968). *Language and mind*. New York: Harcourt, Brace & Jovanovich.

Chomsky, N. (1981). *Lectures on government and binding*. Dordrecht: Foris Publications.

Cruttenden, A. (1986). *Intonation*. Cambridge: Cambridge University Press.

DeCasper, A.J., & Fifer, W.P. (1980). Of human bonding: Newborns prefer their mothers' voices. *Science, 208*, 1174–1176.

DeCasper, A.J., & Spence, M.J. (1986). Prenatal maternal speech influences newborns' perception of speech sounds. *Infant Behavior and Development, 9*, 133–150.

Eimas, P.D. (1974). Auditory and linguistic processing of cues for place of articulation in infants. *Perception & Psychophysics, 16*, 513–521.

Eimas, P.D., Siqueland, E.R., Jusczyk, P.W., & Vigorito, J. (1971). Speech perception in infants. *Science, 209*, 1140–1141.

Fernald, A., & Kuhl, P.K. (1987). Acoustic determinants of infant preference for motherese speech. *Infant Behavior and Development, 10*, 279–293.

Gould, J.L., & Marler, P. (1987). Learning by instinct. *Scientific American, 256*, 62–73.

Hirsh-Pasek, K., Kemler Nelson, D., Jusczyk, P.W., Cassidy, K., Druss, B., & Kennedy, L. (1987). Clauses are perceptual units for young infants. *Cognition, 26*, 269–286.

Jusczyk, P.W. (1985a). On characterizing the development of speech perception. In J. Mehler & R. Fox (Eds.), *Neonate cognition: Beyond the blooming, buzzing confusion* (pp. 199–229). Hillsdale, N.J.: Erlbaum.

Jusczyk, P.W. (1985b). The high amplitude sucking procedure as a methodological tool in speech perception research. In G. Gottlieb & N.A. Krasnegor (Eds.), *Measurement of audition and vision in the first year of postnatal life: A methodological overview* (pp. 195–222). Norwood, N.J.: Albex.

178   *J. Mehler et al.*

Jusczyk, P.W., Hirsh-Pasek, K., Kemler Nelson, D.G., Kennedy, L.J., Woodward, A., & Piwoz, J. (submitted). Perception of acoustic correlates to major phrasal units by young infants.

Kuhl, P.K. (1985). Categorization of speech by infants. In J. Mehler & R. Fox (Eds.), *Neonate cognition: Beyond the buzzing, blooming confusion.* (pp. 231–262). Hillsdale, NJ: Erlbaum.

Kuhl, P.K. (1987). Perception of speech and sound in early infancy. In P. Salapatek & L. Cohen (Eds.), *Handbook of infant perception, vol. 2.* (pp. 275–382). New York: Academic Press.

Lasky, R., Syrdal-Lasky, A., & Klein, R. (1975). VOT discrimination by four- to six-and-a-half-month-old infants from Spanish environments. *Journal of Experimental Child Psychology, 20,* 215–225.

Marler, P., & Peters, S. (1977). Selective vocal learning in a sparrow. *Science, 198,* 519–521.

Mehler, J. (1985). Language related dispositions in early infancy. In J. Mehler & R. Fox (Eds.), *Neonate cognition: Beyond the blooming, buzzing confusion.* (pp. 7–28). Hillsdale, NJ: Erlbaum.

Mehler, J., Bertoncini, J., Barriere, M., & Jassik-Gerschenfeld, D. (1978). Infant perception of mother's voice. *Perception, 7,* 491–497.

Morgan, J.L. (1986). *From simple input to complex grammar.* Cambridge, MA: MIT Press.

Morse, P.A. (1972). The discrimination of speech stimuli in early infancy. *Journal of Experimental Child Psychology, 14,* 477–492.

Osherson, D., Stob, M., & Weinstein, S. (1984). Learning theory and natural language. *Cognition, 17,* 1–28.

Pinker, S. (1984). *Language learnability and language acquisition.* Cambridge, MA: Harvard University Press.

Querleu, D., & Renard, K. (1981). Les perceptions auditives du fetus humain. *Médicine et Higiene, 39,* 2102–2110.

Spence, M.J., & DeCasper, A.J. (1987). Prenatal experience with low-frequency maternal-voice sounds influence neonatal perception of maternal voice samples. *Infant Behavior and Development, 10,* 133–142.

Streeter, L.A. (1976). Language perception in 2-month-old infants shows effects of both innate mechanisms and experience. *Nature, 259,* 39–41.

Vince, M.A., Armitage, S.E., Baldwin, B.A., Toner, J., & Moore, B.C.J. (1981). The sound environment of fetal sheep. *Behaviour, 81,* 296–315.

Werker, J.F., & Tees, R.C. (1984). Cross-language speech perception: Evidence for perceptual reorganization during the first year of life. *Infant Behavior and Development, 7,* 49–63.

Wexler, K., & Culicover, P. (1980). *Formal principles of language acquisition.* Cambridge, MA: MIT Press.

Resume

Deux groupes de bébés de communautés linguistiques différentes ont été testés sur leurs capacités à discriminer des séquences de discours spontané prononcées par un locuteur bilingue en deux langues différentes. Des nouveau-nés de quatre jours, français, sont capables de discriminer des séquences en français de séquences similaires en russe. Des nourrissons américains de deux mois ont manifesté un comportement similaire en présence de séquences en anglais et en italien. Cependant aucun groupe d'enfants ne montre de réponse de discrimination pour des séquences extraites de deux langues étrangères (français, russe pour les enfants américains; anglais, italien pour les nouveau-nés français). Ceci est également le cas pour des nouveau-nés étrangers nés en France, en présence d'énoncés en français et en russe. Ainsi pour discriminer des énoncés de deux langues différentes, une certaine familiarité avec l'une d'entre elles semble nécessaire. Enfin les nouveau-nés et les nourrissons ont également montré des réactions de discrimination pour des versions filtrées des énoncés. Ces derniers résultats suggèrent que les enfants pourraient classer les énoncés comme appartenant à leur langue maternelle sur la base d'indices prosodiques.

INFANT BEHAVIOR AND DEVELOPMENT 7, 49–63 (1984)

Cross-Language Speech Perception: Evidence for Perceptual Reorganization During the First Year of Life*

JANET F. WERKER AND RICHARD C. TEES

University of British Columbia

Previous work in which we compared English infants, English adults, and Hindi adults on their ability to discriminate two pairs of Hindi (non-English) speech contrasts has indicated that infants discriminate speech sounds according to phonetic category without prior specific language experience (Werker, Gilbert, Humphrey, & Tees, 1981), whereas adults and children as young as age 4 (Werker & Tees, in press), may lose this ability as a function of age and or linguistic experience. The present work was designed to (a) determine the generalizability of such a decline by comparing adult English, adult Salish, and English infant subjects on their perception of a new non-English (Salish) speech contrast, and (b) delineate the time course of the developmental decline in this ability. The results of these experiments replicate our original findings by showing that infants can discriminate nonnative speech contrasts without relevant experience, and that there is a decline in this ability during ontogeny. Furthermore, data from both cross-sectional and longitudinal studies shows that this decline occurs within the first year of life, and that it is a function of specific language experience.

infants   speech perception   cross-language   decline

While a large (but finite) number of sound segments occur in the languages of the world, only a subset is used phonemically (to differentiate meaning) in any particular language. Several researchers have predicted that human infants are born with the ability to discriminate the universal set of phonetic contrasts regardless of language experience, and that this ability declines as a function of specific linguistic experience (Eimas, 1978; Morse, 1978; Werker et al., 1981). Alternatively, it has been proposed that experience listening to a language may be necessary to facilitate the perception of the phonetic distinctions used in that language (Eilers, Gavin, & Wilson, 1979). Most relevant data support the first of these predictions, suggesting that rather than having to learn to differentiate phonetic features, young infants seem to respond to speech sounds according to the categories that could serve as the basis for adult phonemic

* This work was jointly supported by grants to Richard C. Tees from the Social Sciences and Humanities Research Council (410-81-0796), the National Research Council (PA0179) of Canada, and the National Institute of Mental Health (1R03NH35829), and by NICHD Grant HD12420 to Haskins Laboratories. We thank the infants and mothers who made this study possible. We also thank Kathy Searcy, Sue Tees, and Carole Bawden for their assistance. Special thanks to Al Liberman for making us welcome at Haskins Laboratories. Requests for reprints should be sent to Janet F. Werker, Department of Psychology, Dalhousie University, Halifax, Nova Scotia, B3H 4J1, or to Richard C. Tees, Department of Psychology, University of British Columbia, Vancouver, BC, V6T 1Y7, Canada.

categories (for a review, see Jusczyk, 1980). Specifically, evidence shows young infants can discriminate speech sounds according to phonetic category, even if those phonetic distinctions are not used in their native language. This has been shown in the case of stop consonants differing in voice onset time (VOT) (Aslin, Pisoni, Hennessy, & Perey, 1981; Syrdal-Lasky, & Klein, 1975; Streeter, 1976); sibilants (Trehub, 1976); vowels (Trehub, 1976), and in the case of liquids (Eilers, Oller, & Gavin, 1978). The one possible exception is the lead boundary in VOT. Although this non-English boundary has been shown to be discriminable to young English-learning infants (Aslin et al., 1981), there is evidence to suggest that it may be more difficult to discriminate without experience than other phonetic distinctions (Eilers et al., 1979).

In contrast to the evidence pointing to the infant's high level of competence, research with adults has shown that they may easily perceive only those sound differences which are used phonemically in their native language and, in many cases, may no longer be able to identify or discriminate sound distinctions used in nonnative language. This has been shown to be the case in nonnative speech contrasts involving differences in VOT (Lisker & Abramson, 1970; Singh & Black, 1966) and in place and manner of articulation (Goto, 1971; McKain, Best, & Strange, 1980; Miyawaki, Strange, Verbrugge, Liberman, Jenkins, & Fujimura, 1975; Tees & Werker, 1982; Trehub, 1976). If, as suggested, infant speech perception is characterized by a high degree of initial ability and adult speech perception is more restricted, it becomes of interest to ask how and when speech perception becomes modified (i.e., limited) to more precisely match only those sound units which are used phonemically in the learner's native language.

In our previous work (Werker et al., 1981), we compared English adults, English infants, and Hindi adults on their ability to discriminate two pairs of Hindi speech contrasts that are not used in English. One of the Hindi contrasts was the dental voiceless aspirated versus the voiced aspirated voicing distinction /tʰa/-/dʰa/ and the other, the voiceless, unaspirated retroflex versus dental place of articulation distinction /ṭa/-/ta/. The results showed that infants aged 6–8 months can discriminate these sounds as well as Hindi adults, but that English adults cannot, particularly in the case of the place of articulation contrast. Furthermore, English children at ages 12, 8, and 4 were as poor as the English adults in terms of their discriminative performance (Werker & Tees, 1983), showing the decline to be evident in children as young as 4 years of age. The present research was designed to examine the generality of these earlier results, and to identify the developmental time period within which the decline in nonnative speech perception might occur.

EXPERIMENT 1

The first study attempted to determine whether the results obtained in this earlier work were representative of developmental changes in cross-language speech perception. To test this, an experiment similar to that reported by Werker and colleagues (1981) was designed using a different non-English

(Thompson) place-of-articulation distinction. The Thompson language is an Interior Salish (Native Indian) language spoken in south central British Columbia. The consonantal system of this language has two contrasting series of back stops, including plain and glottalized versions of rounded and unrounded sounds. These are variously called velars (*k*'s) and uvulars (*q*'s) or pre- and postvelar sounds (Mayes, 1979). In English, there is no distinction between back consonants, in that only velar stops carry phonemic significance. The Thompson pair chosen contrasts glottalized velar and glottalized uvular sounds, /k̓i/-/q̓i/. English infants, English adults, and Thompson adults were compared on their ability to discriminate the non-English, Thompson contrast, /k̓i/-/q̓i/.

Method

Subjects. Twelve full-term infants (8 girls, 4 boys) ranging in age from 6 months, 4 days, to 7 months, 29 days, with an average age of 6 months, 29 days, were recruited by advertising in local newspapers. Infants were requested to participate on days when they had no evidence of colds or ear infections. Care was taken to ensure that each infant was comfortable in the experimental room before testing began.

Ten English-speaking adults (6 males, 4 females), aged 22–35, were recruited from the University of British Columbia campus. As it is difficult to find adults with no second language training, notes were made on formal and informal training. No English adults had exposure to a second language containing the contrast being studied.

Five native Thompson-speaking adults (3 females, 2 males) ranging in age from 30 to 65 were tested on their discrimination of the Thompson tokens.

Stimuli. Multiple natural exemplars of each sound were used in the discrimination task, so that subjects would have to ignore within category acoustic variability and differentiate the sounds according to phonetic category, much as is done in natural language processing. Care was taken to ensure that the exemplars from the two categories were equated for intensity, fundamental frequency, duration, and intonation contour. The English contrast used was the place of articulation distinction, /ba/-/da/, in which bilabial and alveolar voiced stop consonants are differentiated. Four exemplars of /ba/ and four exemplars of /da/ were used. The Thompson (non-English) contrast /k̓i/-/q̓i/ involved two glottalized voiceless stop consonants where the uvular versus velar place of articulation distinction is the critical difference. These sounds are produced by obstructing the air flow by raising the back of the tongue either against the velum (velar) or behind the velum (uvular). Back consonants are characteristic of North American Indian languages. English listeners typically label both velar and uvular stops as velar, since uvular consonants are not typically used in English.

In recording native Indians who are not accustomed to reading their language, it was necessary to record whole words, and then ask the speaker to repeat the first consonant-vowel (CV) sound. It was then possible to perform acoustic analyses of words and CV repetitions to ensure that the CV syllables contained the same consonant sounds as the words. The vowels in Interior Salish languages vary (somewhat in free variation and in a somewhat systematic fashion) between speakers and between consonants (Thompson & Kinkade, in press). In over 100 recordings of k and q words and sounds from three different speakers, we were unable to find exemplars wherein a similar enough vowel followed multiple CV only repetitions of k and q.

In the CV repetitions from the words $kixm$ (to fry an egg) and $qixm$ (to make one see), however, there was one exemplar (or token) of $/ki/$ and one token of $/qi/$ in one speaker's recording in which the vowels sounded nearly identical to one another and appeared similar in a wave form analysis. Since there is a discontinuity in the wave form of glottalized stops, (a 0 amplitude segment in the wave form) it was easy to use the $/i/$ periodic segment from a single $/ki/$ and the $/i/$ periodic portion from a single $/qi/$ to splice on to additional exemplars of the ejective portion taken from other k and of q repetitions. This was done to yield three tokens of $/ki/$ with a single $/i/$ segment and three different ejective portions, and three tokens of $/qi/$ with a single $/i/$ segment and three different ejective portions.

Classical spectrographic analysis has been shown to provide little information as to the acoustic differences between velar and uvular sounds (Mayes, 1979). In our spectrographic analysis, the only apparent differences between typical spectograms from $/ki/$ and $/qi/$ were in the third formant transition, and possibly in the amplitude and duration of the burst. F_3 is flat for $/qi/$ at around 2300 kHz, whereas it rises for $/ki/$ from 2400 kHz to approximately 2900 kHz. The amplitude and duration of the $/q/$ burst are greater than in the $/k/$ burst. Representative spectrograms are shown in Fig. 1. The average duration for each token was 400 ms with a 1500-ms silent interval between tokens. Final tapes were prepared and set up with the use of the PDP-224 computer at Haskins Laboratories in New Haven, CN. All tapes were played on a Revox A-77 tape recorder at approximately 65 db SPL in a tracoustics sound-attenuated test chamber. The entire operation was controlled by a logic system (Werker et al., 1981).

Procedure. Infants were tested in a "head turn" (HT) paradigm (sometimes referred to as "visually reinforced infant speech discrimination" paradigm) in which the infants were conditioned to turn their heads away from an experimental assistant and toward a loud speaker within a specified time interval (4 1/2 s) when there is a change in the speech sound category. Correct head-turns are reinforced with the presentation, and illumination, of an electrically activated toy animal inside a smoked plexiglass box while incorrect head-turns (i.e., false positives) are not reinforced. Three exemplars of $/ki/$ were set up in random order on Track 1 of a two-track tape, and 3 exemplars of $/qi/$ were set up and aligned on Track 2. When changes from Track 1 to Track 2 occurred during the testing, the subject's task was to indicate when there was a change

GLOTTALIZED VELAR /k̓i/

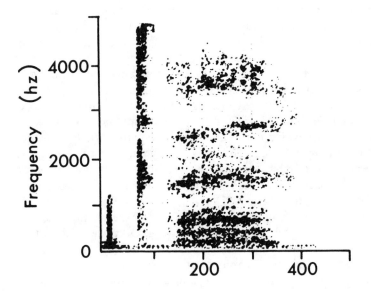

GLOTTALIZED UVULAR /q̓i/

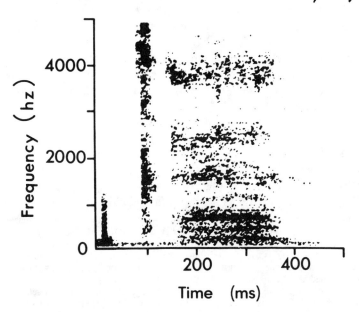

Figure 1. Spectograms of typical exemplars of the Thompson glottalized velar/uvular contrast (/k̓i/-/q̓i/).

53

in the phonetic category from /ǩi/ to /q̇i/. In this sense, it could be argued that the HT procedure functioned as a categorizing discrimination task since multiple exemplars were used. However, exemplars from a single category were much more similar than those typically used in categorizing tasks (cf Kuhl, 1979).

In the experimental setup the infant sat on its parents' lap facing an experimental assistant (E2) across the table in a sound-attenuated chamber. The speaker and the visual reinforcer were located at a 110°-angle, 90 cm to the left of the parent/infant. Both the parent and E2 wore headphones through which music was played so they would not be able to influence the infant's behavior. The E2 kept the infant looking in his/her direction by manipulating small toys. Another Experimenter (E1) sat outside the chamber observing the infant through a one-way observation window and monitored the logic system console (for details, see Werker et al., 1981).

In the conditioning phase of this procedure, the experimenter activated the toy animal immediately following a sound change. Once the infant formed the association between the sound change and activation of the toy animal (usually within 2 to 10 trials), the infant, upon hearing the sound change, turned its head to see the toy animal perform, and activation of the reinforcer became contingent on an appropriate head turn.

When conditioning was successful (i.e., three correct anticipatory head turns in a row) presentation of stimuli and activation of the visual reinforcer became controlled by a logic system. Every time the infant turned its head, E2 pressed a button on the floor. All button presses were recorded on a Grason-Stadler event recorder. If the button press occurred within 4 1/2 s of the stimuli changing from one phoneme (i.e., *ba*) to another (i.e., *da*), the visual reinforcer was activated by the logic system. A record of each was recorded. The operation of the logic system also yielded a record of each time an infant did not turn his/her head during a change trial (i.e., misses) and each incorrect head turn (i.e., false positives).

A variate of this paradigm was used with adult English subjects where a button press rather than a head-turn was the required behavioral response (see Werker & Tees, 1983).

The criterion for successful discrimination was 8 out of 10 correct responses to *change* trials with no more than two errors (i.e., two misses or two false positives).[1] The criterion for deciding an infant could not discriminate a

---

[1] Typically, in the HT procedure, head-turns are only counted during demarcated observation intervals (e.g., Aslin et al., 1981; Kuhl, 1979; Werker et al., 1981). In this series of experiments, we modified the procedure and controlled for bias by random manipulation of the timing between experimental trials. To do this, we had to bring each infant under tight experimental control during conditioning. For example, if an infant was inclined to make frequent false positive head-turns, we extinguished that response proclivity by lengthening the interval between sound changes. Following conditioning, experimental trials occurred according to a random schedule (every 4 to 15 trials) when the infant was continuously oriented toward the experimental assistant. Since the timing of experimental trials varied, control trials were not used. Every head-turn during this period was counted, yielding an overall probability of $< .01$ for achieving an 8 out of 10 correct response to change trials.

contrast had two phases. First, the infant had to successfully discriminate /ba/-/da/ directly before and after failing to reach criterion on a nonnative contrast. This was done to ensure that the failure of the infant was due to an inability to readily perceive the sound difference, and was not due to nonspecific factors such as boredom, dirty diapers, etc. Two infants (1 male, 1 female) were eliminated from further analysis because they failed this phase. Second, the infant was given 25 change trials on the nonnative contrast in their unsuccessful attempt to reach criterion. Adults were also given 25 change trials in which to reach criterion.

Results and Discussion

The portion of subjects that either reached or did not reach the 8 out of 10 criterion on the Thompson contrast is illustrated in Fig. 2. All 5 of the adult Thompson speakers reached criterion, whereas only 3 out of 10 adult English speakers did so. Of the English infants tested, 8 out of 10 reached criterion.

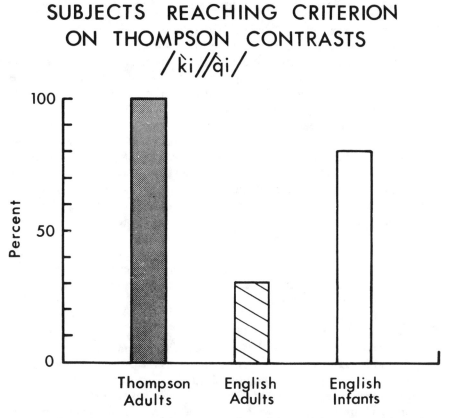

Figure 2. Proportion of Thompson-speaking adults, English-speaking adults, and infants from English-speaking homes reaching criterion on the Thompson glottalized velar/uvular contrast (/k̓i/-/q̓i/).

An analysis of proportions based on a chi-square analogue of the Scheffe theorem (Marascuilo, 1966) was applied to these data. This yielded a significant overall chi-square ($p < .05$; $\chi^2 = 8.94$). Multiple comparisons between the different groups were performed to determine which groups differed. The results showed that performance of the Adult-English speakers was significantly worse than performance of either the Adult-Thompson or the Infant-English groups. The difference between the English infants and the Thompson adults was not significant.

These results were similar to those obtained in our earlier work (Werker et al., 1981). They showed that a decline in cross-language speech perception is evident between infancy and adulthood. That is, young infants discriminate the place of articulation contrasts according to linguistic category without specific linguistic experience, whereas adult speech perceptual ability is more limited, reflecting discrimination of only those contrasts which are phonemic in the listener's native language.

EXPERIMENT 2

The second experiment was designed to establish the developmental time period in which the decline in speech discriminative ability occurred. In this endeavor, subjects were tested on both the Thompson /k̓i/-/q̓i/ contrast, as well as on one of the Hindi contrasts (/ʈa/-/ta/) employed in our earlier research (Werker et al., 1981). Two contrasts were used to increase our confidence in the generality of any results we might obtain.

Since we had already ascertained that by age 4, children appear to discriminate nonnative contrasts as poorly as adults (Werker & Tees, 1983), we decided to examine perception in children between the ages of 8 months and 4 years. After testing about 15 children of various ages, it became apparent that important changes were occurring during the first year of life. At that time, we narrowed our investigation to study cross-language perception in infants between 6 and 12 months of age. In addition to testing English infants, there was an attempt to test infants being raised in homes in which either Hindi or Thompson was primarily spoken. This was done to determine whether the observed decline was a result of specific language experience, or whether it could be explained by a general developmental decline in the ability to make difficult perceptual distinctions.

Method

Subjects. In this study, data were collected from infants aged 8–10 months and 10–12 months, and were compared to the earlier data we had collected on infants aged 6- to 8-months-old under identical testing conditions, either in a previous study (Werker et al., 1981) in the case of the Hindi contrast or from Experiment 1 of the present study in the case of the Thompson contrast. One group of 8- to 10-month-old children (7 females and 5 males, ranging in age from 8 months, 3 days, to 9 months, 10 days, with an average age of

8 months, 20 days) was tested on the Hindi contrast. A second group of 9 females and 5 males (ranging in age from 8 months to 9 months, 12 days, with an average age of 8 months, 18 days) was tested on the Salish contrast. (An additional 3 infants were dropped from further analysis for failing to reach criterion on /ba/-/da/). One 10- to 12-month-old group (5 females and 5 males, ranging in age from 10 months, 2 days, to 11 months, 15 days, with an average age of 10 months, 20 days) was tested on the Hindi contrast. A second group of 5 males and 5 females (ranging in age from 10 months, 2 days, to 12 months, 4 days, with an average of 10 months, 29 days) was tested on the Salish contrast. (Data from 12 infants aged 10 to 12 months had to be discarded because they failed to reach criterion on the /ba/-/da/ contrast). All subjects were recruited from advertisements in the local newspapers.

Stimuli and Procedures. All infants were tested on the English labial/alveolar contrast /ba/-/da/. The two non-English contrasts used were the Thompson glottalized velar/uvular contrast /k̓i/-/q̓i/ (as described in Experiment 1) and the Hindi unvoiced, unaspirated retroflex/dental contrast /ṭa/-/ta/. The Hindi language distinguishes four places of articulation in contrast to the three used in English. Dental stops are produced by obstructing the air flow by placing the tongue behind the front teeth. Retroflex stops are produced by curling the tongue back, and placing the top posterior to the alveolar ridge. The retroflex and dental Hindi stop consonants would both be typically categorized as alveolar, [t], stops by an English listener.

Four exemplars of each sound were recorded by a native speaker. Final exemplars were chosen so that variations in duration, fundamental frequency, and intonation contour were randomized both within and between phonetic categories. The average duration of a stimulus exemplar was 500 ms, with a 1500-ms interstimulus interval.

Acoustic analyses showed the main cues differentiating these naturally produced speech sounds to be in amplitude of the burst, and in the slope of the second and third formant transitions (see Fig. 3); for a full description of those stimuli, see Werker et al. (1981). Infants were tested in the HT procedure, as described in Experiment 1. Requirements for concluding an infant could or could not reach criterion on a contrast were identical to those of Experiment 1.

Results and Discussion

The number of subjects that either reached or did not reach criterion on the two contrasts is shown in Table 1. As can be seen, most of the infants aged 6 to 8 months reached criterion on both contrasts, whereas by 10 to 12 months of age, few infants reached criterion on either. An analysis of proportions was performed on this data for each of the two contrasts. The overall χ^2 was significant ($p < .05$) for both contrasts ($\chi^2 = 21.67$ for /k̓i/-/q̓i/; $\chi^2 = 24.59$ for /ṭa/-/ta/). Planned multiple comparisons showed the significant differences to be between the 6- to 8-month and the 10- to 12-month groups ($p < .001$), and between the 8- to 10- and the 10- to 12-month groups ($p < .05$). This suggests

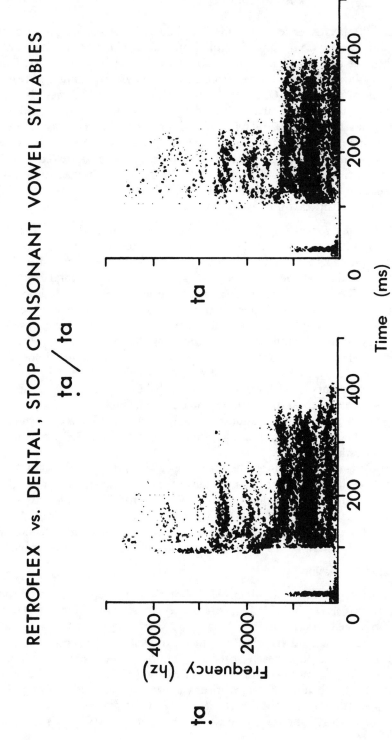

Figure 3. Spectrograms of typical exemplars of the Hindi retroflex/dental contrast, /ʈa/-/t̪a/.

58

TABLE 1
Infant Discrimination Performance on Two Non-English Speech Contrasts

Reached Criterion	(1) 6–8 months	(2) 8–10 months	(3) 10–12 months
	The Retroflex/Dental Contrast /ta/-/ta/		
Yes	11	8	2
No	1	4	8
	The Velar/Uvular contrast /ki/-/qi/		
Yes	8	8	1
No	2	6	9

that the 10- to 12-month-olds performed significantly less well than the two groups of younger infants on both contrasts.

The number of trials to criterion was compared across contrasts and across ages for those infants who could discriminate the sounds. It was assumed that if the decline in the ability to discriminate nonnative contrasts according to phonetic category occurred gradually between 6 and 12 months of age, this gradual change would be evident in an increase in the number of trials required to reach criterion. However a 3×3 repeated measures analysis of variance showed there to be no significant differences between age groups, $F = 1.57$, $p < .05$, or between sound contrasts $F = 2.78$, $p < .05$, making it difficult to argue that there was a gradual increase across age in the number of trials required to reach criterion.

To make sure that the decline around 10–12 months of age was not simply a function of a general performance decline for difficult perceptual tasks at this age, a few same-aged babies being raised in homes in which Hindi or Thompson are primarily spoken were also tested. To date, we have only been able to find 5 infants (3 Hindi and 2 Thompson) between 11 and 12 months who meet this criterion, and only 3 of these infants who would condition in the HT procedure (i.e., reach criterion on the *ba/da* contrast). This drop-out rate is similar to that found in the same-aged English infants. All three of these infants reached discrimination criterion on their native contrast within 10 change trials.

These findings show the decline in the ability to discriminate nonnative phonetic contrasts occurs within the first year of life. That is, most of the English infants tested could discriminate both non-English contrasts at 6 to 8 months of age. By 8 to 10 months a smaller percentage could discriminate the contrasts, and by 10 to 12 months the infants were performing as poorly as the young children and adults in Experiments 1 and 2. However, infants being raised to speak Hindi or Thompson sounds could still discriminate the relevant contrasts at 11 to 12 months of age. The results provide strong support for the supposition that specific linguistic experience is necessary to maintain phonetic discrimination ability. Without such experience, there is a loss in this ability by 10 to 12 months of age.

EXPERIMENT 3

The two-part criterion employed in Experiment 2 (i.e., reaching criterion within 25 change trials and passing /ba/-/da/ before and after failing a non-English contrast) for concluding that an infant could or could not discriminate a nonnative contrast resulted in an unequal drop-out rate which may have biased the results obtained for infants in the 10- to 12–month range. (Completion rate was only 60% in the 10- to 12–month group compared to 85% in the 6–8,- and 8–10 month group. Older infants prefer to try to "visit" the toy animal, rather than simply turn their head to see it.) To control for this possible confound and to examine within subject developmental change, we decided to attempt to replicate Experiment 2 using a longitudinal design.

Subjects

Six subjects, 3 males and 3 females, were tested successively at three ages. Subjects were chosen who were particularly cooperative in the procedure at 6 to 8 months of age, in the hope that these same subjects would be relatively more cooperative at 10 to 12 months of age. During Time 1 (6 to 8 months), infants ranged in age from 6 months, 22 days, to 7 months, 29 days, with an average age of 7 months, 15 days. At Time 2 (8 to 10 months), the infants ranged in age from 8 months, 22 days, to 9 months, 25 days, with an average of 9 months, 2 days. At Time 3 (10 to 12 months), the infants ranged in age from 10 months, 2 days to 11 months, 11 days, with an average of 10 months, 22 days.

Stimuli and Procedure

Infants were tested on the Hindi contrast /ṭa/-/ta/, the Salish contrast /k̓i/-/q̓i/, and the English contrast /ba/-/da/. In addition, the HT procedure was used.

Results and Discussion

The results from this longitudinal study replicate those from the cross-sectional study. In this experiment, all 6 subjects reached criterion on both non-English contrasts when they were 6 to 8 months of age. When the subjects reached 8 to 10 months, all 6 reached criterion on the Hindi contrast, and only 3 reached criterion on the Thompson contrast. By 10 to 12 months of age, none of the 6 infants reached criterion on either contrast even though they could reach it on the English /ba/-/da/ both before and after failing the Thompson sound.

In examining the data, it can be seen that the results from the longitudinal study closely match those from the cross-sectional study (see Fig. 4). The pattern of change across infancy is precisely mirrored for the Thompson contrast. The time course of the change was somewhat different in the case of the Hindi contrast, with an apparent abrupt decline in discriminability occurring when subjects reached 10 to 12 months of age.

CROSS-LANGUAGE SPEECH PERCEPTION   61

INFANT SUBJECTS REACHING CRITERION ON HINDI AND SALISH CONTRASTS

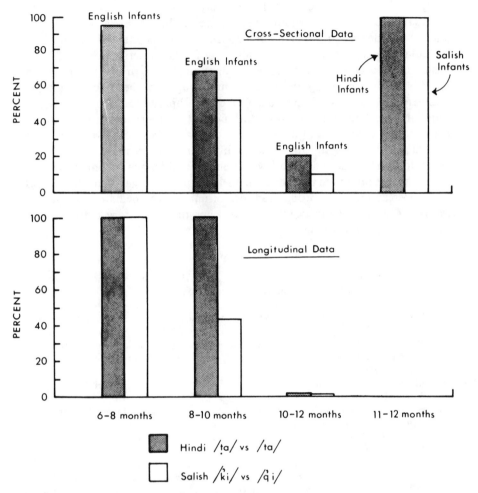

Figure 4. Proportion of infant subjects from three ages and various backgrounds reaching criterion on Hindi and Thompson (Salish) contrasts.

GENERAL DISCUSSION

In summary, these experiments provide strong support for the claim that young infants can discriminate many of the phonetic distinctions used across natural languages without relevant experience, and that there is a decline in this ability as a function of specific language experience. Furthermore, these experiments provide data showing that this decline may be evident by the end of the first year of life.

It is easy to understand how an innate ability to perceive speech sounds according to phonetic categories would ease the process of language learning, and the eventual identification of meaningful units by predisposing the infant to segment sounds according to functionally useful categories. In addition, highly refined infant discriminative abilities followed by a selective loss (and/or broadening) of category boundaries could facilitate the learning of particular languages and dialects by allowing for the selective tuning of initial sensitivities in accordance with a specific phonology. It is probably no accident that this decline, or tuning, occurs at about the age that the child is beginning to understand and possibly produce sounds appropriate to his/her native language. It could be expected that this perceptual reorganization is closely related to the acquisition of phonological contrasts. In future work we are interested in investigating the relationship between cross-language speech perception performance and both vocal output and language comprehension. Finally, we are interested in ascertaining whether the changes identified in both speech perception and production performance are mediated by general changes in cognitive functioning, or whether they are more a function of specific perceptual learning.

REFERENCES

Aslin, R. N., Pisoni, D. B., Hennessy, B. L., & Perey, A. V. (1981). Discrimination of voice onset time by human infants: New findings and implications for the effect of early experience. *Child Development, 52,* 1135–1145.

Eilers, R. E., Gavin, W., & Wilson, W. R. (1979). Linguistic experience and phonemic perception in infancy: A cross-linguistic study. *Child Development, 50,* 14–18.

Eilers, R. E., Oller, D. K., & Gavin, W. J. (1978). *A cross-linguistic study of infant speech perception.* Paper presented at the Southeastern Conference on Human Development. Atlanta, Georgia, 1978.

Eimas, P. D. (1978). Developmental aspects of speech perception. In R. Held, H. W. Leibowitz, & H. L. Teuber (Eds.), *Handbook of sensory physiology,* (Vol. 8). Berlin: Springer-Verlag.

Goto, H. (1971). Auditory perception by normal Japanese adults of the sounds "L" and "R." *Neuropsychologia, 9,* 317–323.

Jusczyk, P. W. (1980, June). *Auditory versus phonetic coding of speech signals during infancy.* Paper presented at the C.N.R.S. Conference, Paris.

Kuhl, P. K. (1979). Speech perception in early infancy: Perceptual constancy for spectrally dissimilar vowel categories. *Journal of the Acoustical Society of America, 66,* 1668–1679.

Lasky, R. E., Syrdal-Lasky, A., & Klein, R. E. (1975). VOT discrimination by four and six and a half month old infants from Spanish environments. *Journal of Experimental Child Psychology, 20,* 215–225.

Lisker, L., & Abramson, A. S. (1970). The voicing dimensions: Some experiments in comparative phonetics. In *Proceedings of the Sixth International Congress of Phonetic Sciences.* Prague: Academia.

MacKain, K. W., Best, C. T., & Strange, W. (1980). Native language effects on the perception of liquids. *Journal of the Acoustical Society of America, 27.*

Marascuilo, L. A. (1966). Large-scale multiple comparisons. *Psychological Bulletin, 69,* 280–290.

Mayes, S. V. (1979). An acoustic analysis of Thompson velar /k/ and uvular /q/. *University of Hawaii, Working Papers in Linguistics, 11,* 11–22.

Miyawaki, K., Strange, W., Verbrugge, R. R., Liberman, A. M., Jenkins, J. J., & Fujimura, O. (1975). An effect of linguistic experience: The discrimination of (r) and (l) by native speakers of Japanese and English. *Perception and Psychophysics, 18,* 331–340.

Morse, P. A. (1978). Infant speech perception: Origins, processes and *alpha centauri*. In F. D. Minifie & L. L. Lloyd (Eds.), *Communicative and cognitive abilities—Early behavioral assessment*. Baltimore, MD: University Park Press.

Singh, S., & Black, J. W. (1966). Study of twenty-six intervocal consonants as spoken and recognized by four language groups. *Journal of the Acoustical Society of America, 39*, 371–387.

Streeter, L. A. (1976). Language perception of two-month-old infants shows effects of both innate mechanisms and experience. *Nature, 259*, 39–41.

Tees, R. C., & Werker, J. F. (1982, June). *Perceptual flexibility: Recording of the ability to discriminate nonnative speech sound*. Paper presented at the meeting of the Canadian Psychological Association, Montreal, Canada.

Thompson, L. C., & Kinkade, M. D. (in press). Linguistic relations and distributions. In W. Sturtevant (Eds.), *Handbook of North American Indians. Vol. 8, The northwest coast*.

Trehub, S. (1976). The discrimination of foreign speech contrasts by infants and adults. *Child Development, 47*, 466–472.

Werker, J. F., Gilbert, J. H. V., Humphrey, K., & Tees, R. C. (1981). Developmental aspects of cross-language speech perception. *Child Development, 52*, 349–355.

Werker, J. F., & Tees, R. C. (1983). Developmental changes across childhood in the perception of nonnative speech sounds. *Canadian Journal of Psychology, 37*, 278–286.

20 October 1982; Revised 11 January 1983 ■

Papers in Speech Communication: Speech Perception

INDEX (Keyed to Paper Numbers)

TABLE OF CONTENTS AND INDEX
FOR EACH OF THE COMPANION VOLUMES IN THIS
THREE-VOLUME SERIES

Papers in Speech Communication: Speech Production

TABLE OF CONTENTS

VOCAL TRACT AND ACOUSTIC RELATIONSHIPS

ACOUSTIC CHARACTERISTICS OF SPEECH

ARTICULATORY MOVEMENTS

SPEECH SYNTHESIS

Papers in Speech Communication: Speech Production

INDEX (Keyed to Paper Numbers)

Papers in Speech Communication: Speech Processing

TABLE OF CONTENTS

AUTOMATIC SPEECH RECOGNITION

AUTOMATIC SPEAKER RECOGNITION

Papers in Speech Communication: Speech Processing

INDEX (Keyed to Paper Numbers)